HOLOCAUST LITERATURE

EDITORIAL BOARD

HOLOCAUST LITERATURE

AN ENCYCLOPEDIA OF WRITERS AND THEIR WORK

Volume I
Agosín to Lentin

S. Lillian Kremer
Editor

Routledge
New York London

Editorial Staff
Project Editor: Laura Smid
Production Editor: Jeanne Shu
Production Manager: Anthony Mancini, Jr.
Production Director: Dennis Teston
Director of Development Reference: Kate Aker
Publishing Director: Sylvia Miller

Published in 2003 by
Routledge
29 West 35 Street
New York, NY 10001-2299
www.routledge.ny.com

Published in Great Britain by
Routledge
11 New Fetter Lane
London EC4P 4EE
www.routledge.uk.com

Routledge is an imprint of Taylor & Francis Books, Inc.

10 9 8 7 6 5 4 3 2 1

Printed on acid-free, 250-year-life paper

Manufactured in the United States of America

Acknowledgements on page 1451.

Library of Congress Cataloging-in-Publication Data
Holocaust literature : an encyclopedia of writers and their work / S. Lillian Kremer, editor.
v. cm.
Contents: Vol. 1. A-L—vol. 2. M-Z.
ISBN 0-415-92985-7 (set : alk. paper)—ISBN 0-415-92983-0 (vol. 1 : alk. paper)—
ISBN 0-415-92984-9 (vol. 2 : alk. paper)
1. Holocaust, Jewish (1939–1945), in literature—Encyclopedias. 2. Holocaust, Jewish
(1939–1945)—Bio-bibliography. I. Kremer, S. Lillian, 1939-

PN56.H55 H66 2002
809'.93358—dc21

2002023694

CONTENTS

Acknowledgments

I gratefully acknowledge a National Endowment for the Humanities Fellowship that allowed me to pursue this project free of teaching obligations for a year and the generous financial support of Kansas State University throughout the project. I am indebted to Margaret Burton for her remarkable dedication and expertise as a researcher and editorial and administrative assistant. I am also grateful to the Librarians of Kansas State University who have been helpful throughout the project. Much credit is due to the contributors from several continents who shared their knowledge and concern for Holocaust literature. My greatest debt of gratitude remains for my husband, Eugene Kremer, who helped me at every stage of the project and sustains with with wise counsel and loving encouragement.

—S. L. K.

Dedication

In memory of the six million Jews who perished in the *Shoah* and in celebration of those who survived and their descendants dedicated to furthering their legacy. And for Lucas Joseph and Benjamin Josef.

LIST OF ARTICLES

LIST OF ARTICLES

LIST OF ARTICLES

LIST OF ARTICLES

LIST OF ARTICLES

LIST OF ARTICLES

LIST OF ARTICLES

LIST OF ARTICLES

Major Nazi Camps, 1943–1944

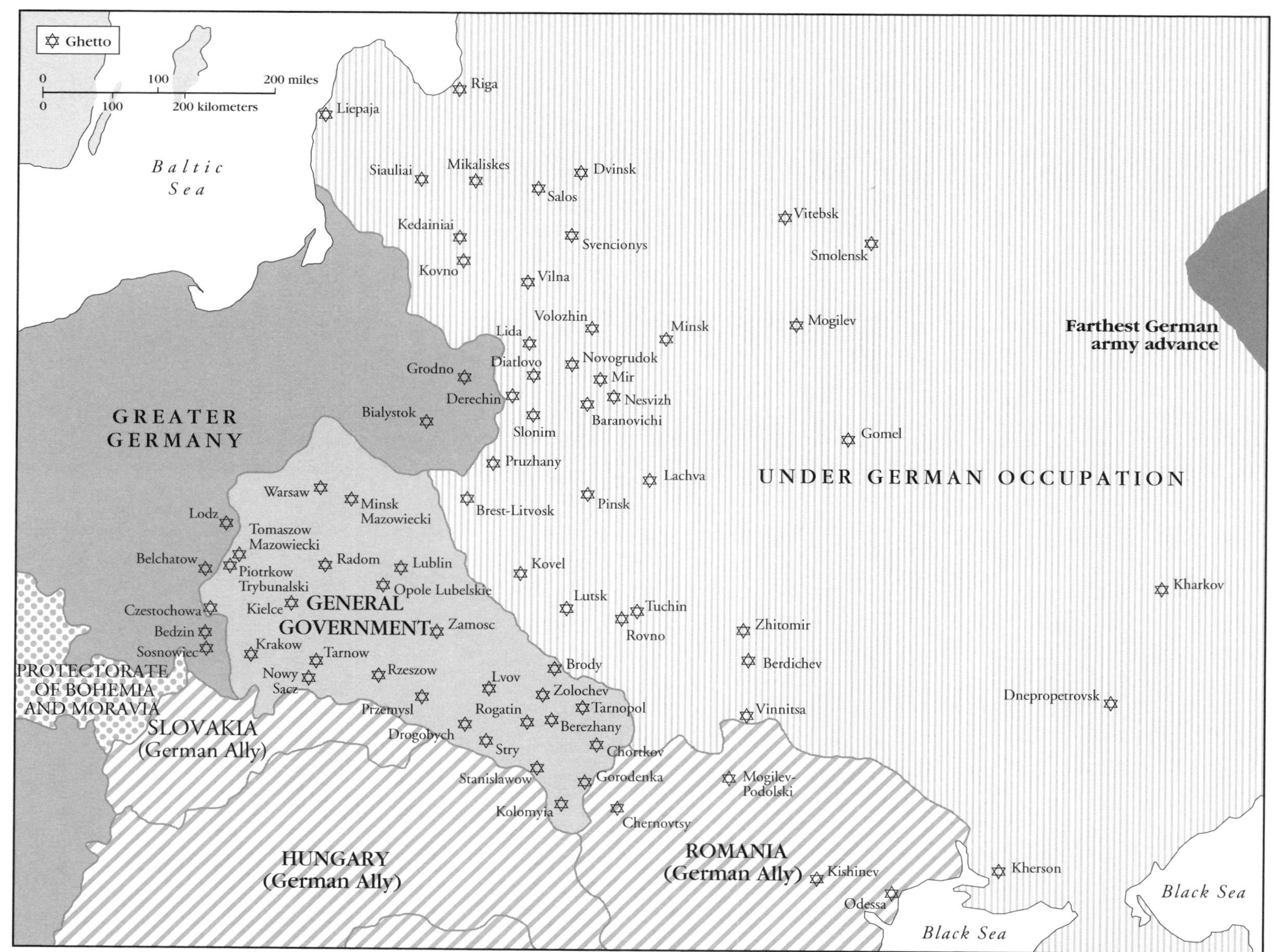

Selected Ghettos in Occupied Eastern Europe, 1941–1942

PREFACE

Since the close of World War II the Holocaust (*Shoah* in Hebrew) has been an essential touchstone in critical thinking about the human condition. Interdisciplinary inquiry and debate on the literary representation of the Holocaust increasingly engage scholars, theorists, and creative writers. The ever burgeoning number of books, films, academic conferences, public commemorative events, museums and monuments, as well as university courses and state-mandated public education programs testify to the significance of the *Shoah* in our time and for the future.

Holocaust Literature fills the pressing need for a reference source providing access to a broad, comparative perspective of diverse national Holocaust literatures and genres. The books present critical analyses and assessments of literary representation of the Holocaust and its consequences. The alphabetically arranged bio-critical essays of 1800 to 8000 words cover the writing of over 300 memoirists, poets, novelists, dramatists, and a small number of influential religious and secular philosophers and theorists. Collectively, they constitute a literary history of traditional and experimental texts and theories of Holocaust remembrance, representation, and reflection and extend the Holocaust canon with fresh insights on familiar writers, introduction of less well-known non-English texts, and examination of the works of emerging second and third generation writers. American, Canadian, Latin American, British, French, German, Dutch, Russian, Polish, Czech, Hungarian, Italian, Greek, Hebrew, Yiddish, Australian, Algerian, and Tunisian writers are represented.

The broad range of authors and works permits coverage of the full historic experience of the Holocaust from the onslaught of early Nazi discriminatory legislation through the mechanisms of Aryanization of conquered property, establishment of ghettos, labor, concentration, and death camps of the Nazi universe. In addition to charting the terrain of the Nazi universe, these writers map the legacy and impact of the *Shoah* ranging from survivor syndrome and survivor mission of the witnessing and contemporary generations to second and third generation authors writing about the psychological, philosophical, and political reverberations of the Holocaust.

Holocaust Literature is designed to inform and facilitate research by students, scholars, and the general public. The "Introduction" offers an overview of critical and theoretical Holocaust inquiry and cultural indices apparent in many *Shoah* literatures. Among the theoretical issues treated are the problematics of Holocaust literary transmission, construction and reconstruction of survivor memory, postmemory of children of survivors, trauma theory, positionality, and gender specificity and reference to influential Holocaust literary critics and theorists including Theodor Adorno, Maurice Blanchot, Saul Friedländer, Geoffrey Hartman, Dominick La Capra, Berel Lang, Sara Horowitz, Lawrence Langer, Alvin Rosenfeld, Sidra DeKoven Ezrahi, Marianne Hirsch, and James Young. Two bibliographies follow the "Introduction," an extensive critical/theoretical bibliography and another focused on language groups. Each author entry succinctly identifies the Holocaust history or interest of the author, discusses major titles, themes, and stylistic representations. The subject essays demonstrate the authors' contribution to understanding the historic event and comment on the specific cultural contexts of the writing, Holocaust or post-Holocaust sensibility, and the critical reception of the author's work and are followed by full primary and selected critical bibliographies.

Among the distinctive features of this work is an apparatus consisting of a comprehensive index, a glossary of terms, ghetto and camp maps, and a series of appendices (ghettos, camps, historic figures and key events, Holocaust literary themes, genres, language distribution, authors' birthplace and language of composition). Each appendix includes an alphabetical list of authors within the established category. Hence, a reader interested in a specific national literature may turn to that appendix, another interested in a specific ghetto or camp or historic event or person will find a list of authors who treat those subjects, those who want to trace a specific theme such as survivor syndrome will be able to consult the theme appendix, and those who want to pursue Holocaust memoir, poetry, fiction, or drama will turn to the genre appendix.

More than 120 distinguished scholars from over sixty universities in North and South America, Europe,

Israel, and Australia, interpret the writing from formalist, psychoanalytic, feminist, and poststructuralist critical perspectives. The participation of critics from diverse faculties, critical positions, and disciplines of literature, history, political science, sociology, psychology, and philosophy ensures that *Holocaust Literature* is a comprehensive scholarly work providing new information and clarifying existing perspectives, an up-to-date, intellectually lively, indispensable resource for the humanities and social science communities.

Holocaust Literature invites readers to ponder the myriad ways of confronting Holocaust evidence and memory and the role of testimonial and creative literature in representing memory of a novum in human history.

INTRODUCTION

S. LILLIAN KREMER

The Holocaust (*Shoah* in Hebrew and *Hurban* in Yiddish) encompasses the period between 1933 and 1945 when the Nazi forces of Germany and their accomplices murdered more than six million European Jews in an attempt to eradicate the Jewish presence in the world. The Jews of Europe were stripped of their possessions, disenfranchised, isolated in sealed ghettos where they were starved, exposed to disease, and impressed as slave labor. This process ensured the slow death of hundreds of thousands. Survivors were either deported to labor and concentration camps where existence was even more brutal or murdered directly in mass executions carried out by special killing units or in specially designed extermination camps.

The *Shoah* engenders profound questions about the political, social, cultural, and theological constructs of western civilization. Victims, survivors, bystanders, and others born after the Holocaust, but moved by its enormous legacy, have responded to these questions. A generation ago, Alvin Rosenfeld wrote "Holocaust literature must be counted among the most compelling literatures of our day. . . . if we were to deny centrality to Holocaust literature, we would be falsifying not only the literary history of our time but a large part of its moral history as well" (*A Double Dying,* p. 4). That evaluation is even more compelling at the beginning of the twenty-first-century than when it was published in 1980.

The Nazi Holocaust and its aftermath have created cultural and intellectual contexts profoundly impacting individual and collective consciousness and generating a significant body of literature that has itself undergone important paradigm shifts. *Shoah* literature is a literature of witness and mourning, a literature mediating trauma and its implications for postwar thought. *Holocaust Literature* examines texts in all literary genres, the response of writers who were there and writers who had the good fortune "not to be there"; writers of widely differing cultural and national backgrounds; and writers of diverse aesthetic philosophies. Among those who were not there are members of the contemporaneous generation who responded when they absorbed the news in the years immediately following the *Shoah*; those who wrote in response to postwar *Shoah* evocations such as the 1961 Eichmann trial and the controversy surrounding Hannah Arendt's report of the trial, the German Auschwitz trial, the ominous Nazi annihilation rhetoric associated with the 1967 Arab-Israeli Six-Day War, the 1968 international students' revolts, and relaxation of the ban on Holocaust information with the demise of Soviet control of eastern Europe. Perhaps the most compelling writing by those who were not there is the recent work of second- and third-generation authors, the children and grandchildren of Holocaust survivors.

As scholars from many disciplines approach Holocaust subject matter, contentious debates ensue regarding historiography and literary representation, philosophic, theological, political, and psychological implications of the *Shoah.* Theorists debate whether to discuss the event as a unique historic experience or as part of historic continuity, the (im)possibility of and the need to address the *Shoah* in forms other than documentary, the legitimacy of fusing history and art, and the propriety and "limits of representation". Creative writers and theoreticians alike engage the problem of communicating the incommunicable, the predicament of representing experience that has no historic or imagined analogue.

Because Holocaust literary theory is closely related to the historic, it is useful to ground our literary discussion in the historians' theoretical considerations. Noted Holocaust historian, Saul Friedländer presents a lucid account of the range and shifting perceptions of the Nazi period from the immediate postwar era through the mid-1980s and the significant break that occurred in 1986. In "Historical Writing and the Memory of the Holocaust," he traces two divergent movements and their subpaths with the attendant implications for each determining the interpretations of perpetrators, bystanders, and victims. Until the mid-1980s, Friedländer explains, both liberal and structuralist approaches were "essentially linear, ideologically determined representation of Nazi policies." Despite differences, each still

> focused on the responsibility of the perpetrators as a German group within a system, the roots of which were to be found within German society; and both identified the bystanders within that same society, with only nuanced divergences about degrees of conformism, passivity, tacit acceptance, . . . [until] the mid-1980s, some kind of implicit moral stand suffused the representation of this past, clearly considering the problem of responsibility from the viewpoint of the victims (p. 71).

Friedländer assesses the revisionist viewpoint as a "symmetric vision of the past" consisting of an "equation of crimes"—and therefore of responsibilities—between atrocities committed by the Nazis and the Allies, particularly the Soviets. In this view the Bolsheviks become the original perpetrators, the initiators of the policies of total annihilation of populations and the Nazis mere emulators. Within this narrative the crimes of the Nazis are relativized and the Nazis themselves become the victims (pp. 72–73). It is this latter position that the Frankfurt philosopher Jürgen Habermas denounced in 1986 as "apologetic," initiating the famous "historians' controversy." It is at this point that Ernst Nolte and Andreas Hillgruber weighed in and annunciated the equivalency argument, but with the additional perception of the Wehrmacht as the heroic defenders of Germany from the savage Bolsheviks in the last year of the war and the bystanders now presented not as facilitators of Nazism, but innocent victims of the savage Soviets. The doubling of the perpetrator group extends in this reading to the doubling of the victim group; the German bystanders equated with that other group of victims, the Jews. This leads to positioning the Nazi epoch as any other in history, no longer fit for exercises in "ever-recurring memory" but relegated to distant history; no longer to be perceived as a unique, singular event in the course of human history (pp. 73–76). These debates, as we shall soon see, have analogues in literary discussions.

The historians' debate led Friedländer to invite a group of scholars from diverse disciplines to examine the subject that has since been published under the title *Probing the Limits of Representation: Nazism and the Final Solution.* As the title indicates, the essays focused on the problematics of *Shoah* representation and representational adequacy in historiography and literary narrative. The essays inquire whether it is beyond our capability to describe and understand the *Shoah,* whether the application of aesthetic formulations is appropriate to the subject, whether objective truth is possible, or as postmodernists would have it, interpretation is inevitable. If narrative is dependent upon language and language is itself suspect, how should the Holocaust text be written and read? Hayden White described history as narrative "emplotment" and therefore subject to interpretation. Because it is impossible to separate a "concept" of history from the way history is told, White therefore locates the meaning of historical narrative in the relationship of narrator, audience, and the social context of the narrative. Yet, he concedes that in the case of the Holocaust some interpretations of the Nazi period are to be excluded because of their incompatibility with the historical facts.

Close to Hayden White's position, Dominick LaCapra addresses the indeterminacy surrounding historical significance of an event and the transferential impact of the Holocaust, to argue for a new rhetorical mode. LaCapra writes:

> The Holocaust presents the historian with transference in the most traumatic form conceivable—but in a form that will vary with the difference in subject position of the analyst. Whether the historian or analyst is a survivor, a relative of survivors, a former Nazi, a former collaborator, a relative of former Nazis or collaborators, a younger Jew or German distanced from immediate contact with survival, participation, or collaboration, or a relative "outsider" to these problems will make a difference even in the meaning of statements that may be formally identical ("Representing the Holocaust: Reflections on the Historians' Debate", p. 110).

During the last two decades, Geoffrey Hartman has been a salient voice among critics interested in the implications of the Holocaust and its aftermath and matters of representation. In the final essay of *The Longest Shadow,* he reflects on the abundance of historic knowledge and testimony to insist on its ethical use and raise questions about limits of representation: "questions less about whether the extreme event can be represented than whether truth is served by our refusal to set limits to representation" (p. 151).

Tzvetan Todorov also takes up the issue of memory's constructs and transference asserting that memory "cannot reconstruct the totality of the past. . . . It can only reconstruct a selection of those elements we consider worth remembering . . ." (p. 257). He distinguishes between forms and uses to which reminiscence is put, either to a literal reading or a paradigmatic interpretation. The literal is a deterministic approach controlling who can be linked to the memory and continuity between a people's past and present. Or the event can be used as a "model by which to understand new situations . . . it becomes an exemplary, or paradigmatic, memory, one that teaches us certain lessons. The associations it evokes for us are analogical . . . and the task . . . becomes to determine whether the analogies are justified" (p. 258).

Geoffrey Hartman, who has written on many aspects of the implications of the Holocaust for the post-*Shoah* period and has been instrumental in creating the Yale University oral testimony archives, distinguishes generational memory as "The eyewitness generation express[ing] a return of memory despite trauma [and] the 'second' generation express[ing] the trauma of memory turning in the void, and . . . all the more sensitive, therefore, to whatever tries to fill the gap" (*Holocaust Remembrance,* p. 18).

Historic memory itself, and its formation, significance, and dissemination within a culture in the form of collective memory, have become important subjects for both historians and literary critics. Individual memory and traumatic memory are the focused study of psychologists and creative writers. Theologian and novelist Arthur Cohen gives eloquent voice to the religious commitment of witness literature by invoking the liturgical injunction to remember Jewish history:

> The Passover Haggadah commands that every Jew consider himself as though he has gone forth in exodus from Egypt. . . . I was really, even if not literally, present at Sinai. . . . The fact that history could not prevision and entail my presence is irrelevant. No less is it the case that the death camps account my presence really, even if not literally: hence my obligation to bear witness as though I were a witness (*The Tremendum,* p. 23).

Philosopher Berel Lang shares Arthur Cohen's view of progress beyond collective listening to each Jew's obligation to narrate and regard oneself present at the Exodus and Sinai as the appropriate analogue for "the presence of all Jews . . . fixed within the events of the Nazi genocide" (*Act and Idea in the Nazi Genocide,* p. xiii).

As the critical debate shifted from the legitimacy of Holocaust writing to aspects of representation of the unrepresentable, many scholars turned to examination of memory itself. James Young, who understands both traditional Judaic concepts of remembrance and postmodern thinking about memory, points to some crucial distinctions: "memory of historical events and the narratives delivering this memory have always been central to Jewish faith, tradition, and identity" whereas "postmodern responses devote themselves primarily to the dilemmas of representation, their difficulty and their irresolvability" ("Jewish Memory in a Postmodern Age," p. 213). "Jewish memory in a postmodern age generates disparate, occasionally competing meanings for the same historical events." Of the diarists writing in the ghettos, Young observes

> In addition to time and place, the diarists' very language, traditions, and world view played crucial roles in the making of their literary witness. . . . each victim 'saw'—i.e. understood *and* witnessed—his predicament differently, depending on his own historical past, religious paradigms, and ideological explanations, (*Writing and Rewriting the Holocaust,* p. 26).

"Rather than a singular master narrative of memory—that which has traditionally been recited as liturgy—there are now many forms of memory, each owing a debt to the particular Jewish community doing the memory-work" (p. 214). Young rejects the idea that a single interpretive mode could convey the meaning of the Holocaust and instead argues for a Bakhtinian dialogical interplay between artists and audience to determine the shape of memory, and defends the right of each community to its memory construct.

Controversy about the legitimacy of Holocaust creative literature arose with the publication of early postwar texts. Theodor Adorno, a Jewish refugee from Nazi Germany who returned to the Federal Republic after World War II to found the Frankfurt School of critical theory, had immense influence on writers and critics. After reading Paul Celan's haunting "Todesfugue," Adorno feared that the aesthetic quality of the poem would call attention to itself and deflect attention from its *Shoah* subject. He provocatively declared 'to write poetry after Auschwitz is barbaric." (*Noten zur Literatur*). Ever since Adorno's famous injunction (often misquoted as "no poetry after Auschwitz") the propriety of depicting the Holocaust in creative literature has been compellingly debated. The critical discussion centers on two elements, literary silence or representation of the concentrationary universe and the notion of a sharp divide between pre- and post-*Shoah* thinking and aesthetics. Adorno's virtually unquoted reconsideration and refinement of his position deserves recognition equal to that accorded his original prohibition. Moved by Paul Celan's poetry, Adorno recognized that "Perennial suffering has as much right to expression as a tortured man has to scream; hence it may have been wrong to say that after Auschwitz you could no longer write poems" (*Negative Dialectics,* p. 362). He acknowledged that "the abundance of real suffering tolerates no forgetting . . . this suffering demands the continued existence of art [even as] . . . it prohibits it. . . . It is now virtually in art alone that suffering can still find its own voice, consolation, without immediately being betrayed by it" (*Aesthetics and Politics,* p. 188).

Literary and cultural critic, George Steiner, whose family had the good fortune to escape from Austria, is credited with promulgating Adorno's aesthetic position in his own thinking about the Nazi legacy and its impact on language. In his critical writing and fiction, Steiner interrogates language in the context of its cultural underpinnings as a source of truth and a source of destruction. Although he is impressively prolific, Steiner's writing focuses on a coherent core of central concerns: theories of language; the role of literary culture in the modern world, particularly in relation to moral values; Jewish identity and historic experience, most conspicuously in relation to the Holocaust, which he identifies as a focal point of the modern imagination. Steiner places the knowledge of the death camps at the center of modern thought and asserts "that Jews everywhere [those physically present and absent] have been maimed by the European catastrophe" ("A Kind of Survivor," *Language and Silence,* pp. 143–144). In the essays of *Language and Silence,* Steiner ponders the disruption of Western culture that continues to challenge the moral purpose of literature; hence, the collection's subtitle: *Essays on Language, Literature, and the Inhuman.* His investigations into the relationship between the *Shoah* and language led to his conclusion that language is vulnerable to corruption; that the German language was contaminated by service to Nazism that "found in the language precisely what it needed to give voice to its savagery" (*Language and Silence,* p. 99). "Use a language," Steiner insists, "to conceive, organize, and justify Belsen, use it to make specifications for gas ovens; use it to dehumanize man during twelve years of calculated bestiality. Something will happen to it" ("The Hollow Miracle," in *Language and Silence,* p. 124). Although language is besmirched, it also must be the site of memory. That the architects of this disaster came from a literate and cultured people is particularly painful.

One of the consequences of the *Shoah* for Steiner

> is to have transported . . . into Judaism, both religious and secular, the hermeneutic dilemma. The problem as to whether there is a human form of language adequate to the conceptualization and understanding of Auschwitz, as to whether the limits of language do not fall short of the limits of the *Shoah* experience, is now ineradicably installed in Jewish existence ("The Long Life of Metaphor, *Language and Silence,*" p. 155)

Influenced by Adorno's early dictum, the prevailing view of many writers and critics was that language was unable to convey the Nazi world and that it is, perhaps, immoral to attempt to write about the *Shoah* imaginatively. Some believe that only eyewitness accounts of the events are valid. Hannah Arendt, who wrote brilliantly on the nature of totalitarianism, believed the horror of life in the concentration camps could never be fully embraced by the imagination "for the very reason that it stands outside of life and death" (*Origins of Totalitarianism,* p. 142). In the years immediately following the *Shoah,* with but few exceptions, professional writers remained largely silent about "l'univers concentrationnaire." Elie Wiesel asserted that literature of the Holocaust is impossible, and claimed that Auschwitz negates any form of literature, "A novel about Auschwitz is not a novel, or else it is not about Auschwitz. The very attempt to write such a novel is a blasphemy" (quoted in Alvin Rosenfeld's *A Double Dying,* p. 14). Charlotte Delbo, one of the most admired writers of the Holocaust genre, expressed concern that lack of previous experience of an event comparable to the *Shoah* could render language and memory unreliable. And Primo Levi, the supreme chronicler in the view of many of the most respected critics, informs readers of *Survival in Auschuwitz,* of his recognition shortly after his arrival that "our language lacks words to express this offense, the demolition of man" (p. 26). He elaborated the concept of the insufficiency of language in the context of his masterpiece, demonstrating how ordinary linguistic constructs and connotations fail to convey Auschwitz experience:

> Just as our hunger is not that feeling of missing a meal, so our way of being cold has need of a new word. We say 'hunger' we say 'tiredness', 'fear', 'pain', we say 'winter' and they are different things. They are free words, created and used by free men who lived in comfort and suffering in their own homes. If the Lagers had lasted longer, a new harsh language would have been born; and only this language could express what it means to toil the whole day in the wind, with the temperature below freezing, wearing only a shirt, underpants, cloth jacket and trousers, and in one's body nothing but weakness hunger and knowledge of the end drawing nearer (p. 123).

Yet Levi, Wiesel, Delbo, and Steiner clearly believe it is important to confront the *Shoah* and its legacy so that people might begin to understand the basest tendencies that generated such unprecedented brutality.

Two Americans, Lawrence Langer and Alvin Rosenfeld, are among the critics whose work has influenced a generation of Holocaust literary scholarship. In *The Holocaust and the Literary Imagination* (1975), the first book-length study of such work to appear in English, Lawrence Langer countered proscriptions against writing Holocaust literature, asserting that "the fundamental task of the critic is not to ask whether it should or can be done, since it already has been, but to evaluate how it has been done, judge its effectiveness, and analyze its implications for literature and society" (p. 22). The Holocaust was beyond normal human experience and its representation required a new artistic style, a new language. "The difficulty," as A. Alverez suggests, "is to find language for this world without values, with its meticulously controlled lunacy and bureaucracy of suffering'' (''The Literature of the Holocaust,'' p. 67). In *A Double Dying: Reflections on Holocaust Literature,* Alvin Rosenfeld defines Holocaust literature as an attempt ''to express a new order of consciousness, a recognizable shift in being. The human imagination after Auschwitz is simply not the same as it was before'' (p. 13). Perhaps for this reason, he concludes that Holocaust literature does not lend itself to the conventional critical methods. After Auschwitz, he contends, ''we know things that before could not even be imagined.'' Therefore, traditional critical approaches—Freudian, Marxist, formalist, structuralist, linguistic—will not work for Holocaust literature (p. 19). Langer argues that literature provides the only adequate means of making the inconceivable ''imaginatively available,'' that ''the challenge to the literary imagination is to find a way of making this fundamental truth accessible to the mind and emotions of the reader'' (p. xii). In his discussion of what he calls ''the literature of atrocity,'' Langer argues that works of the imagination can in fact ''establish an order of reality . . . in which the unimaginable becomes imaginatively acceptable'' (p. 43), and that the most effective artistic strategy for imaginatively entering the world of Holocaust atrocity is through reality's ''disfiguration, the conscious and deliberate alienation of the reader's sensibilities from the world of the usual and the familiar, with an accompanying infiltration into the work of the grotesque, the senseless, and the unimaginable'' (p. 3). Twenty years after this statement issued in *The Holocaust and the Literary Imagination,* Langer decries what he still observes as a tendency to sweeten the material, to ''speak of the survivor instead of the victim and of martyrdom instead of murder, . . . or evoke the redemptive rather than the grievous power of memory, . . . an arsenal of words that urges us to build verbal fences between the atrocities of the camps and ghettos and what we are mentally willing—or able—to face.'' He cautions against a redemptive discourse, urging readers to adopt a ''discourse of ruin'' rather than a ''discourse of consolation'' that merely serves to protect the uninitiated from confronting Holocaust reality (*Admitting the Holocaust,* p. 6). Because the *Shoah*'s victims were so brutalized and dehumanized, the Holocaust so extreme that it threatens our sense of civilization and morality, Langer regards redemptive and consoling language as escapist. Rosenfeld contends that ''there are no metaphors for Auschwitz. Just as Auschwitz is not a metaphor for anything else. . . Because the flames were real flames, the ashes only ashes, the smoke always and only smoke'' (p. 27). Although Rosenfeld notes that ''Holocaust literature relies for its expression on the received languages and the established literary forms,'' he explains, ''It does so, however, in a profoundly revisionary way . . . turning earlier literary models against themselves and, in the process, overturning the reigning conceptions of man and his world'' (p. 31). Holocaust texts, in Rosenfeld's view, are ''refutation and repudiation, a denial not only of an antecedent literary assertion but also of its implicit promises and explicit affirmations'' (p. 31).

Fidelity to the historic experience is, for many readers, an essential component of Holocaust writing. Although he defends imaginative exploration of the Holocaust, Langer also insists,

> When the Holocaust is the theme, history imposes limitations on the supposed flexibility of artistic license. We are confronted by the perplexing challenge of the reversal of normal creative procedure: instead of Holocaust fictions liberating the facts and expanding the range of their implications, Holocaust facts enclose the fictions, drawing the reader into an ever narrower area of association, where history and art stand guard over their respective territories, wary of abuses that either may commit upon the other (*Admitting the Holocaust,* pp. 75–76).

For Alvin Rosenfeld, any writing purporting to be Holocaust literature that does not accurately reflect the historic event is of little value because it distorts reality.

Historic verity is also a significant consideration in the judgment of Berel Lang and Leon Yudkin. Lang favors historical writing and appears to dismiss imaginative writing. He argues: ''It seems obvious to me that anything written now about the Nazi genocide against the Jews that is not primarily documentary, that does not uncover new information about the history of that singular event, requires special justification'' (p. xi). Lang shares the concerns critics of imaginative *Shoah* literature have about its artifice, the introduction of genre experimentation, metaphor, literary tropes, interpretation and reconstruction, or imposition of a literary structure. Nonetheless, he is in favor of ''a moral discourse'' such as that exemplified in Jewish *midrashic* tradition and the Passover Haggadah, that facilitates the notion of presence and engagement in the narrative, participation in the collective memory. Israeli critic Leon Yudkin agrees, ''what interests us in regard to Holocaust literature is appropriate usage of the event. . . . the various ways in which writers can shape the material, while remaining true to history, and thoughtful regarding its transmission'' (p. 29). The moral obligation to transmit historic memory is central to the thinking of these critics.

Another early important voice in Holocaust literary criticism is the Israeli, Sidra DeKoven Ezrahi, whose book *By Words Alone* examines the manner in which writers transmit Holocaust experience. She categorizes prose fiction from documentary realism to surrealism. The scope of her work is impressive, extending the range from the canonical Western and secular writers to the literary and philosophical traditions that shape Hebrew Holocaust literature. After tracing the ''legacy of Lamentations'' in Yiddish and Hebrew writing, she demonstrates the same religious patterns at work in European and American literatures. Her interest is in mapping the ways in which writers convey, not the Holocaust itself, but ''the acquisition of that event by the creative mind'' (p. 48). Among the approaches she examines are ''concentrationary realism,'' the response rooted in biblical and lamentation traditions, the covenantal context, and ''mythologized'' treatments of the Holocaust.

James Young, who has commented on many aspects of Holocaust commemoration, including literature, and museum and memorial design, addressed the problem of novelists who share the fear that Adorno raised in his initial aesthetic admonition, ''the essential rhetoricity of their literary medium inadvertently confer[ing] a certain fictionality onto events themselves'' (''Holocaust Documentary Fiction: The Novelist as Eyewitness,'' p. 200). But Young does not consider metaphor a necessary displacement of the real. He reminds his readers that survivors and victims used figurative language in diaries, memoirs, and testimonies that were part of the available cultural conventions. In *Writing and Rewriting the Holocaust,* Young acknowledges the objection some writers and critics have to metaphor because it cannot directly transmit facts and may even falsify facts and thereby mislead readers, but concludes that ''Rather than seeing metaphors as threatening to the facts of the Holocaust, we must recognize that they are our only access to the facts, which cannot exist apart from the figures delivering them to us. Indeed, to leave Auschwitz outside of metaphor would be to leave it outside of language altogether'' (p. 91).

Early attitudes shaped by a reverential approach to the tragedy of the *Shoah* manifested the concern that language was insufficient to convey Holocaust reality. The postmodernist assessment of the unspeakable is grounded in conviction that the word is compromised and that representation is impossible. While Saul Friedländer and Berel Lang warned that facticity was crucial to Holocaust narrative, postmodernist theorists proclaim that language by its very nature cannot represent facts.

Illustrative of the French postmodern theorists who examine the annihilation of European Jewry in philosophic-linguistic terms rather than in its historic and ethical terms, Jean-François Lyotard contends that events upset preexisting reference so that we lack certainty about the relative interpretive contexts for any given event. The writer's task, therefore, is not to represent Auschwitz but to testify to its unrepresentability, to the limits of representation, to acknowledge in the act of memorialization that it is impossible to capture the past as it really was. Although he notes in *Le Differend* that for the European ''the Jew'' constitutes an incomprehensible alterity that has consistently been repressed or forgotten, Lyotard has been criticized for using ''the jews'' allegorically to articulate his theories of writing, alterity, and the unrepresentable, erasing Jewish particularity and history while urging sensitivity to language, identity, and the relationship of history and memory. Ann Parry concludes that Lyotard

> sees 'Auschwitz' as a symbol of [reason's] failure, so that the *Shoah* takes on the status of an originary repressed . . . that . . . cannot be represented. . . . The paradox is, therefore, that the *Shoah* . . . is ever present, but forgotten. . . . Conceived in this way 'Auschwitz' becomes the immemorial, that which cannot be remembered, which cannot be represented to consciousness (pp. 419–420).

Maurice Blanchot recognizes the Holocaust as a definitive event that puts in question the very possibility of literature and language, yet offers a definition of what it is to be a Jew and arrives at negative connotations, which he renders positively, all the while retaining a negative cast. Elizabeth Bellamy demonstrates how the more Maurice Blanchot, who calls for ''disaster notation'' (*écriture du désastre*) when writing about the Holocaust, ''critiques the antisemitic need to impute a 'being negative' to the Jew, deplores antisemitism's negative ontology of the Jew, the more his discourse threatens to replicate the very impulse he is rightly reviling.'' Thus, she observes, as do others, that even while having renounced his earlier antisemitic views, Blanchot depicts the Jew as ''the exigency of strangeness,'' ''the exigency of uprooting,'' a subjectivity of ''uneasiness and affliction,'' and ''the affirmation of a nomadic truth,'' descriptions that Bellamy discerns ''have the unintended effect of constituting a repetition compulsion to rehearse and perpetuate the same antisemitic stereotypes that Sartre claimed inevitably transformed the Jew into the 'Other' for French antisemitism'' (*Affective Genealogies,* pp. 29–30). Blanchot's depiction of the Holocaust as history's ''excess'' has since inaugurated a philosophical discourse that evokes 'Auschwitz' (virtually always cast in quotation marks) as less a real historical event than a metaphor for the 'unthought' in the transition from modernism to postmodernism'' (p. 31). Bellamy shares the position of readers who characterize Blanchot's work as ''symptomatic of how within French postmodernism, real Jews have tended to be transformed into tropes or signifiers for the decentered, destabilized postmodern subject in a theoretical system that persists in defining (or 'fetishizing') them from without'' (p. 31).

Scholars working on trauma theory, such as Shoshana Felman, Dori Laub, and Cathy Caruth, center their writing more directly and specifically on Holocaust reality than postmodernists whose interest lies in the ''unrepresentability'' of the Holocaust. LaCapra posits that

> The *Shoah* calls for a response that does not deny its traumatic nature or cover it over through a 'fetishistic' or redemptive narrative that makes believe it did not occur or compensates too readily for it. . . . what is necessary is a discourse of trauma that itself undergoes—and indicates that one undergoes a process of at least muted trauma insofar as one has tried to understand events and empathize with victims (*Representing the Holocaust,* pp. 220–221).

In the late 1960s and the beginning of the 1970s analysts such as Henry Krystal and Judith Kestenberg pointed to a connection between the experience of Holocaust survivors and emotional disturbances in their children. Traumatic symptoms were found in the second generation that were characteristic of the parents' own Holocaust experience, suggesting a transgenerational transference of the survivors' syndrome. The late 1970s and 1980s brought a new paradigm of Holocaust writing to the fore, that of Holocaust survivors' children, the ''children of Job,'' as Alan Berger calls them, or ''memorial candles'' as Israeli psychologist Dina Wardi identifies them. They inhabit a traumatic world of their parents' memories that is distinguished by a phenomenon Marianne Hirsch aptly calls ''postmemory'' and describes as ''distinguished from [survivor] memory by generational distance and from history by deep personal connection.'' She theorizes

> Postmemory is a powerful and very particular form of memory precisely because its connection to its object or source is mediated not through recollection but through an imaginative investment and creation. . . .Postmemory characterizes the experience of those who grow up dominated by narratives that preceded their birth whose own belated stories are evacuated by the stories of the previous generation shaped by traumatic events that can be neither understood nor recreated (p. 22).

Others whose parents did not speak of the exile from home or their Holocaust experiences, who ''did not have access to the repressed stories that shaped them'' speak of ''absent memory.'' Some second-generation writers experience a void in their identity because of their parents' Holocaust silence or alienation from Judaism as a means of protecting themselves and their children from further persecution. For others, Holocaust postmemory leads to a positive connection to Jewish identity, a link between past and present. While some reiterate their parents' protest against God for lack of intervention, for many, as Alan and Naomi Berger explain in *Second Generation Voices,* the Holocaust background is a source of mission to repair the self (*tikkun atzmi*) and to repair the world (*tikkun olam*), to bear witness and live in such a way as to heal Holocaust rupture. Hirsch discerns that the second-generation memory ''brings with it its own narrative genres and aesthetic shapes and thus it permits us to return . . . to the aesthetics of postmemory—the . . . capacity to signal absence and loss, and at the same time to make present, rebuild, reconnect, bring back to life'' (p. 243).

Equally crucial to understanding the new paradigm of second-generation Holocaust writing has been Alain Finkielkraut's study of Jewish identity of the post-Holocaust generation in its relationship to the *Shoah.* He identifies a new character type, ''the imaginary Jew,'' who lives after the Holocaust yet tries to identify with the destroyed civilization, a nostalgic quest. These writers born after the Holocaust ''for whom it is an absent memory,'' like David Grossman and Henri Raczymow, reconstitute the past from their parents' stories from research rather than from direct knowledge.

Holocaust gender scholarship and literary criticism of women's Holocaust writing have grown impressively during the last dozen years as women assume a more prominent role in Holocaust studies and literary scholarship. Joan Ringelheim is among the pioneers of women's Holocaust history. She argues that when we fail to recognize that men and women suffer oppression differently, we ''lose the lives of women for a second time'' (p. 147). She is a forceful voice for recognition that

> traditional attitudes and responses toward women, as well as gender-defined conditions, made women especially vulnerable to abuse of their sexuality and of their maternal responsibility—to rape, murder of themselves and their children, the necessity of killing their own or other women's babies, forced abortion, and other forms of sexual exploitation—in the ghettos, in resistance groups, in hiding and passing, and in the camps (p. 743).

Literary critics who have isolated gender-based Holocaust experience in women's Holocaust writing, Marlene Heinemann, Myrna Goldenberg, Sara Horowitz, Ellen Fine, Pascale Bos, Tobe Levin, and S. Lillian Kremer, have extended the scope of canonical Holocaust literary criticism.

Holocaust Literature includes articles on every genre of Holocaust writing, from testimony in diary and memoir to poetry, drama, fiction, fantasy, and blended genres. Diaries, memoirs, and autobiography motivated by the moral imperative to bear witness constituted a poignant literature documenting the daily struggle for survival, the ongoing psychological struggle of living with *Shoah* experience and memory, personal experiences of loss and degradation, survivor syndrome, and survivor mission. Imaginative writers, too, have sought to enter that universe and understand what it meant to exist in its corrosive sphere, of what its legacy means for the post-*Shoah* world.

German Writing

As the Nazi atrocities were revealed and the Nuremberg Trials were underway, denial and rationalizations prevailed among the German public. Rather than the enormous suffering Germany inflicted on others, its own pain and the need to rebuild consumed the nation. National Socialism was a subject of postwar non-Jewish German literature, but the genocide of European Jewry was not; memory of the Holocaust was repressed. ''Overcoming the past'' was the aim of the dominant German authors of the period, known as ''Group 47,'' whose purpose was the revival of German literature after the Third Reich. All victims of National Socialism were seen to be equal; the Jews were no different from other victims; they were not the primary population designated for annihilation. Ernestine Schlant explains that the pervasive Holocaust silence of German literature ''rested on unstated shared thinking, established unconscious bonds of complicity and relied on code words for communication'' (*The Language of Silence,* p. 25).

Holocaust silence and repression ended with the 1961 Eichmann Trail and the 1963 through 1965 Auschwitz Trial in Frankfurt. These events stimulated discussion of the annihilation of European Jewry and inspired several dramas touching on or emphasizing German culpability, including Rolf Hochhuth's controversial play *The Deputy* and Peter Weiss's *The Investigation.* Jews are seen as victims, but their Jewishness, the reason for their persecution, was not thematized. Among non-Jewish writers, only Alfred Andersch gives resonance to Jewish issues in three of the four novels he published. Illustrative is *Efraim,* which has as its narrator a German-Jewish naturalized English journalist who returns to Germany and recalls the fate of his parents killed in Theresienstadt and Auschwitz, a character who thus perceives of his Jewish identity as directly related to the Holocaust.

Jewish German authors expressed their anguish about the brutality of the Nazi regime and its distortion of German culture while still living in Germany in hiding, in exile, or even in the ghettos and camps. As a privileged Jew married to an Aryan, Victor Klemperer continued to live in Germany and clandestinely chronicled the daily humiliation that anti-Jewish legislation imposed on those spared deportation but deprived of sufficient food, expelled from their homes and professions, and demeaned by countless civic restrictions. Despite restricted access to non-German news sources, it is clear that in March 1942, Klemperer was aware of Auschwitz as a concentration camp, belying the myth of German ignorance of the camps. Before her deportation and murder, Gertrud Kolmar wrote about silencing victims and the poet's mission to give them voice. Reflecting her roots in Jewish history, she addresses the suffering of prisoners in the camps, their tortured bodies and minds. Among the early postwar writers and intellectuals who continued to write in German are Paul Celan from France, Nelly Sachs from Sweden, and Erich Fried from England, as well as Austrians Jean Améry in Belgium, Ruth Klüger from the United States, Ilse Aichinger from the Federal Republic, and, until he turned to English prose, Jakov Lind from England. Nelly Sachs, whose escape to Sweden spared her the concentration camp universe, nevertheless identified with the victims. She wrote passionate poetry of witness, mourning, and remembrance, introducing themes of persecution, exile, death, and the fragile condition of survivors, poems whose recurring imagery consists of flames, smoke, and ash. The author of perhaps the best-known Holocaust poem, ''Todesfuge,'' Paul Celan continued to write in German, but in a style that reflected the impact of the Holocaust and the tension of considering German his language as well as that of the murderers, a language that was tainted and needed to be renewed.

In addition to public discussion sparked by airing of the American television series *Holocaust,* which contributed to Jewish and non-Jewish Holocaust examination and public discussion, events such as the Fassbinder scandal, the Bitburg controversy, the historians' debate, and the proposal to establish a memorial for all the dead of World War II, engendered new critical consciousness among Jews living in postwar Germany who, in fear of antisemitic reprisals, had, until these eruptions, maintained a low profile. Younger German Jewish writers began to treat the Holocaust and Jewish experience directly, drawing their materials from family stories, and inventing characters and situations that convey post-*Shoah* German Jewish survivor and second-generation identity issues. They delineate not only the manner in which Germany has marked Jewish lives, but also the way in which Jews perceive themselves and Jewish history. Edgar Hilsenrath details Nazi dehumanization of victims struggling for survival in a hellish Ukrainian ghetto, the perspective of the SS perpetrator, and postwar Jewish marginality and identity concerns. Insisting on the importance of the *Shoah* as a central theme of contemporary literature, Maxim Biller examines the manner of Holocaust remembrance and critiques Holocaust representation and the German endeavor to come to terms with the past. He interrogates myths and legends of the relationships of non-Jewish and Jewish Germans as well as those of young German Jews and Holocaust survivors. Rather than examining the Holocaust itself, Barbara Honigmann explores its pervasive presence in her postwar life and the struggle of post-Holocaust Jews to construct Jewish identities in near-Jewless societies. She celebrates Jewish identity constructed not only of Holocaust memory, but also of the fullness of Jewish life and texts. The *Shoah* identity commands an important presence in the writing of young German Jews for, as Sander Gilman and Jack Zipes observe, these writers have taken on topics that "elucidate Jewish views to the German public and undermine German antisemitism and stereotyping" (p. xxv).

Austrian Writing

After the *Anschluss* (Germany's March 1938 annexation of Austria) and the *Kristallnacht* pogrom of 9 and 10 November 1938, the Viennese Jewish community was effectively destroyed. The *Shoah* later succeeded in virtually annihilating Austria's Jewish population. While east European Holocaust survivors settled in postwar Austria, few Austrian Jews who survived the *Shoah* or exile returned to their homeland. Unlike Germany, which has had to face its past, postwar Austria denied its blatant collaboration in the Nazi genocide. Austria claimed to have been the first victim of Nazi aggression rather than Germany's eager accomplice in the *Anschluss,* an attitude reflected in postwar literature by non-Jewish Austrians.

Austrian Holocaust literature is primarily the work of Jews living abroad and the children of Holocaust survivors. In her 1946 essay "Aufruf zum Mifstrauen" ("A Summons to Mistrust"), Ilse Aichinger, who grew up in Vienna under the Nazis, called "for introspection and self-criticism on the part of all those who survived the war and the Nazi dictatorship and strongly suggest[ed] that the time to conduct business as usual has not yet come, if it ever will" (quoted by Lorenz, p. xix). In *Herod's Children,* she describes the devastating effects of Nazi racial politics and the public support the Nazis enjoyed. *At the Mind's Limits,* a canonical Holocaust work of documentary and literary value, is Jean Améry's (born Hans Maier) disclosure of his painful understanding of himself as an outsider in the eyes of his Austrian countrymen, testimony on torture he endured at the hands of the SS, warning of the implications of the concentration camp experience for modern European societies, and acknowledgement of a self-determined postwar Jewish identity. The works of other exiles, Jakov Lind, Elias Canetti, Manes Sperber, and Ruth Klüger, are also important exemplars of writing that Dagmar Lorenz classifies as an "alternative discourse" to prevailing postwar Austrian resistance to confront its Holocaust history. Jakov Lind survived the Holocaust when he was sent on a children's transport to Holland and by posing as a Gentile in Holland and, later, in Germany. He recounted these "adventures" in the autobiographical, *Counting My Steps.* His *Soul on Wood* is better known for its dark humor, reflective, according to Lawrence Langer, of Lind's "efforts to invent a bleak, comic style for such unruly material" (*Art from the Ashes,* p. 405). Lind wrote critically and irreverently about such sensitive issues as the Nazi "euthanasia" program, exposed the callousness of the perpetrators, and satirized the post-*Shoah* discourse of coming to terms with the past. American émigré Ruth Klüger's autobiography *weiter leben,* told from the point of view of a survivor and a literary and cultural critic, maps her childhood memories of Viennese antisemitism, her understanding of herself as "Other," her recollections of Theresienstadt and Auschwitz, and the impact of the Holocaust on life after. Her critical writing also addresses Holocaust literature and the Holocaust in popular culture.

Dagmar Lorenz maintains that Austrian Jewish writers born toward the end of the war or after the war

> turned to the literary production of the pre-Nazi era, particularly to works and authors outlawed under Nazi rule, to establish an oppositional or at least alternative Austrian discourse distinct from the mainstream. . . . [in works that] record their insecurity, disorientation, mistrust, . . . as well as feelings of being marginalized and of belonging to a vulnerable minority (pp. xiv–xv, xviii).

This younger generation's understanding of the *Shoah* and their relationship to Austria stems from their reading of Paul Celan, Ilse Aichinger, Jean Améry, and Simon Wiesenthal as well as the narratives and the silence of their own relatives. Sensitive to the impact that the *Shoah* and the Nazi legacy had on them, postwar-generation Austrian authors of Jewish background "realized that among many non-Jews their age, knowingly or unknowingly, the attitudes of the Nazi generation, authoritarian patterns and proto-fascist gender, race, and class stereotypes were reproduced'' (p. xvii). They record these phenomena with an outside observer's detachment, as in Elfriede Jelinek's satiric novel *Wonderful, Wonderful Times* (Lorenz, p. xvii). Jelinek

> defines herself through the tradition of Jewish writing and, identif[ies] herself as the daughter of a Jewish victim of Nazi persecution, as an Austrian Jew. . . . She portrays the outlook of the lower middle class, the social stratum that had been Hitler's stronghold, as reflecting an unwillingness to confront Austria's collective guilt. (pp. xxii–xxiii)

Robert Schindel's novel Gebürtig (Born-Where) traces non-Jewish characters engaged in denial, repression, and occasionally, shame, and Jewish characters who often identify themselves as victims reflecting their deep association with the generation of Nazi victims. His characters are obsessed with the past, which is central to their present and to their self-definition. As an important member of an emerging group of Viennese Jewish writers, Schindel's literary focus on Holocaust survivors and their children, and on questions of Jewish identity and assimilation, are clear indicators that the Holocaust will continue to engage Austrian writers of Jewish origin.

Lorenz contends that

> The works of the post-*Shoah* generation [of Jewish writers] reveal fundamentally different attitudes toward the past and Austria than those of non-Jewish writers, regardless of their specific political outlook, and they differ from the writing of the previous generations. . . . A pervasive sense of exclusion and self-exclusion permeates the works of the children and grandchildren of exiles and Holocaust survivors because of their foremost internal reference point, the *Shoah*. . . . they are outspoken about it: they name the death camps, reveal the details of the persecution, and do not shrink from discussing what the previous generation conveyed to them through their words and actions. They connect the memory of the Holocaust and Jewish exile to that of a larger Ashkenazic and Austrian Jewish culture. . . of former generations (p. xxvii).

In his reading of postwar Austrian and German writers, Michael André Bernstein detects ''backshadowing,'' which he characterizes as looking back from a postwar perspective on the life of Austro-German Jewry and taking a tone of ''patronizing incredulity.'' Further, he finds

> a curious symmetry in the way backshadowing has structured the configuration of prewar European Jewry. Both Jewish and gentile Austrian writers portray the Jewish community as a single homogeneous entity. . .[an] incarnation of a universal Jewishness whose inevitable destruction the audience ought to mourn and even feel a certain uncomfortable guilt about, (pp. 24–25).

Most notable about Jews in Gentile Austrian writing, however, Bernstein admits, is their absence. On the rare occasions when they are present, Bernstein argues, ''the backshadowing of the genocide makes them in some fundamental way unrepresentable in their specificity and particularity'' (p. 25).

Italian Writing

In 1938 Italy instituted racial laws depriving Italian Jews of the assimilated life they had enjoyed in Italian society. However, there was a vast difference between the commitment to antisemitism in Germany and in Italy. Enforcement of the Italian racial laws was slow and somewhat lax. Compared to most German-occupied countries, the plight of the Italian Jews was less severe and, most significantly, they were not ghettoized. By January 1943, Germany became impatient with Italy's failure to deport its Jews. In September, an order that all Jews were to be deported was issued. By December, Italian law branded the Jews ''enemy foreigners'' and ordered their transfer to concentration camps. In March 1944 deportation to to Auschwitz began.

Italian Holocaust literature is not extensive. Most World War II writing is in the neo-realist style and heavily centered on the Italian resistance. Even Italian Jewish writers have in the main, refrained from direct representation of the Holocaust. Representative is Natalia Ginsburg's brief two sentence mention of German Jewish refugees in Turin and equally brief treatment of the racial laws in *Family Sayings.*

Direct focus on women's Holocaust experience appears in *There Is a Place on Earth,* Giuliana Tedeschi's witness to her existence in Auschwitz. Her writing is sensitive to the gendered experience of women, especially those with children. Fellow inmate Liana Millu also dwells, in *Smoke over Birkenau,* on the biologically-based and gender-based suffering of women she observed who concealed a pregnancy, were assigned to the camp brothel and coped with gender-based coping strategies. Unlike Tedeschi, who concludes her story with liberation, Millu includes a woman's postliberation psychological readaptation to freedom.

Better known than the writing of the women, is that of Georgio Bassani, principally his Ferrara cycle, charting the isolation of the Jews under Fascist law. *The Garden of the Finzi-Continis,* his best-known novel, deals explicitly with the racial laws of 1938, the delusion of the Jews who refuse to interpret their peril and their efforts to carry on ''normal lives'' despite their isolated circumstances. The novel concludes internment in anticipation of deportation to Germany. Like the Israeli Aharon Appelfeld and the Yiddish writer I. B. Singer, Bassani refrains from depicting the world of the camps to focus on before and after.

Although Italy cannot boast as many writers of Holocaust literature as other European countries, if it had only one and that one were Primo Levi, Italy could count itself as having the most profound and critically acclaimed Holocaust writer. The extraordinary power of *If This Is a Man* (also issued as *Survival in Auschwitz*) clearly places it as a canonical Holocaust text. This account of the transformation from resister to concentration camp inmate, the analytical examination of various types of prisoners, and their accommodation and resistance to the Nazi universe offers extraordinary testimony on what Auschwitz meant and how it transformed its victims. Levi's writing style, allusions to Dante and Homer, scientific precision, elegantly moral tone combined with dry wit, and elegantly structured text, combine with the Holocaust subject matter to achieve a multileveled sociological and psychological work raised to the level of art, placing his work on par with that of Paul Celan. In a forty-year career, Levi returned to the Holocaust subject repeatedly in essays, poetry, and fiction. *If Not Now, When* is the Italian's immersion in Yiddish culture, the chronicle of a Jewish partisan band traveling across eastern Europe that is a microcosm of Jewish nationalist, religious, and Marxist orthodoxy, engaged in a survival struggle and dedicated to inflicting pain on the Germans before building a new life in Palestine. In *The Drowned and the Saved,* Levi returns to Auschwitz to demonstrate the fallacious new relativism propounded by German historians Ernst Nolte and Andreas Hillgruber, resistance to ''normalization'' of the Holocaust, and to support the view of the Holocaust as unique, and to discuss its legacy and contemporary significance. He interprets the moral and historical implications of the *Shoah* based not only on his own experience, but on extensive Holocaust scholarship. Once again he assesses the victims and victimizers, but in this work devotes more attention to the perpetrators and insists on their individual responsibility.

Eastern Block Countries

Holocaust silence is particularly evident in the literatures of the former Soviet block countries where the particularity of Jewish fate in the Holocaust was suppressed and the national calamity under Nazi control was privileged. Nevertheless, a modest body of Holocaust literature exists in the works of Russian, Czech, and Hungarian writers. Illustrative is the career of the Russian Jew, Vasilii Grossman, whose work as a journalist covering the Soviet struggle gave him opportunity to observe many situations individual citizens could not see. Stalinist censorship obstructed his efforts to tell the true and complete story of Jewish suffering and heroism during the *Shoah. Life and Fate,* completed in 1960, but not published in Russia until 1990, is a huge realistic novel that reveals not only the Nazi atrocities but the Stalinist violence as well. It is in this work that the Holocaust theme as Grossman knew it is developed including such hitherto silenced data as Ukrainian complicity in the murder of Jews and the details Grossman learned when he entered Treblinka that he had originally wanted to report in the aborted *Black Book* (finally published in 1980).

In addition to the realistic documentary writing of Czech Arnost Lustig, who charts the struggles of Jews to maintain life, dignity, and identity in a universe designed to destroy them, others like Jiří Weil and Ladislav Fuks turn to surrealism to map the absurdist context of life under Nazi occupation. In a prolific body of Holocaust short fiction and novels, Lustig presents a huge cast of characters facing the rawness of hunger and other forms of deprivation, yet consumed as much by moral dilemmas engendered by the Nazi quagmire as they are by their physical hardships. Weil's *Life with a Star* locates the absurd in historical reality, and the consciousness of his narrator in a world mirroring the contradictory German pronouncements meant to deceive the populations of the occupied territories of Bohemia and Moravia. In *Mendelssohn on the Roof,* Weil blends magical realism and intimations of the golem of Prague legend of Jewish folklore with references to Reinhard Heydrich, the ranking German officer of the ''Protectorate,'' to convey the sense of power he wielded over his victims.

Hungarian Imre Kertész, a survivor of the concentration camps, focuses on postwar recovery of life to highlight the caesura that was signified by the Holocaust and the need for new beginning. His aim is to write in a new atonal language that marks the discontinuity with pre-Holocaust sensibility. In *Fateless,* he conveys the typical experience of a youngster uprooted from Budapest, life under the yellow star, ghettoization, deportation, survival struggle and adaptation in Auschwitz, and postwar survival marred by memories of the camp. Poet János Pilinszky, who served with the Axis forces as a laborer and witnessed the work of the Nazis, features the Holocaust as a central motif. Bystander and perpetrator share responsibility for the world he delineates in documentary detail and figurative language to suggest the degradation of the malnourished camp prisoner performing excruciating labor.

Polish Writing

Among the Slavic literatures, Polish Holocaust literature is the most prolific. This is understandable given that Poland was the main site of the "Final Solution" and because Jews played a more significant role in postwar Polish writing than in other eastern European literatures.

From their confinement in the ghettos or while in hiding in Aryan sectors, Jewish poets and diarists wrote of the plight of their people in conventional Polish and Yiddish literary modes. Diarists and historians Emanuel Ringelblum, Chaim Kaplan, and Adam Czerniakow documented ghetto conditions. Władysław Szlengel wrote of the suffering of the ordinary people, the liquidation of the Warsaw ghetto, the procession of Janusz Korczak and the children of his orphanage to the ghetto deportation site, and the Warsaw Ghetto Uprising. From the Aryan side of Warsaw, Czesław Miłosz recorded "volleys from behind the ghetto wall / . . . muffled by a lively melody" from a carousel as Poles went about their ordinary pleasures in "Campo di Fiori." In the middle and late 1940s Adolf Rudnicki, Kazimierz Brandys, and Artur Sandauer added their voices to chronicling the catastrophe. Zofia Nałwska was, according to poet Henryk Grynberg, "the first to realize the need for new literary means of expression when dealing with [the] Holocaust" (p. 118) in work distinguished by her recognition of the genocide "not as a cataclysm but as a concrete, organized, systematic action . . ." (p. 119).

Postwar Polish literature is marked by Soviet political domination. From late 1948 until 1956, Polish Holocaust publications were limited to a narrowly defined version of socialist realism. Henryk Grynberg characterizes the period as one in which

> a writer had to create the impression that the Polish poor classes helped the Jews under the Nazi occupation, themselves seeking no material compensation, whereas the middle class made denunciations to the Gestapo, although the earlier Polish literature proved that in reality the situation was often reversed. Also, Jews had to be presented in a prescribed fashion: the brave and sacrificing were to be Jewish proletarians, particularly leftist-oriented, whereas affluent Jews were viewed as selfish and cowardly, (p. 127).

The communist underground and partisan forces also were to be credited with helping Jews, when, in fact, their leaders were often antisemitic (p. 128). This situation led to the abandonment of the Holocaust as subject until the political thaw of the mid-1950s with the death of Stalin and the reinvigoration of literature including new Holocaust stories by Adolf Rudnicki and Stanisław Wygodzki.

Madeline Levine identifies two distinct patterns of Holocaust and Occupation Polish literature of the immediate postwar period and ensuing decades: "a Polish Polish literature and a Jewish Polish literature" (p. 190). She then subdivides these classifications further as the "literature of the Poles in exile and the literature of the diaspora of Polish Jewry" (p. 190). For the most part, the Holocaust fate of Polish Jewry is conspicuously absent or relegated to the background in writing by non-Jewish Poles whose writing is primarily concerned with the Nazi Occupation rather than the *Shoah* and its aftermath in a virtually *Judenrein* Poland. The Polish writers who deal directly with the Holocaust "tend to do it within the context of measuring and judging the morality of the Polish response" (p. 196). Tadeusz Borowski provided readers a brilliant glimpse of life and dehumanization under extremity with *This Way for the Gas, Ladies and Gentlemen* in stories that have become classics. Written in the form of a camp inmate's first-person narrative, Borowski's stories pose as testimony, in Barbara Foley's words "a pseudo-documentary in the mimetic mode" about his internment in Auschwitz. However, this is a work of fiction, signaled by the author's ironic tone and deprecating attitude toward the narrator who is presented as a victim turned victimizer, assigned to work in a unit that collects the vast Auschwitz cache of plundered victim property, driven by the dehumanizing camp process to welcome the arrival of incoming prisoners for their parcels of food, which can be scavenged.

Polish-Jewish relations are a dominant theme of Polish Holocaust writing. Jerzy Ficowski's *Reading of the Ashes* confesses that repentance will never be final in the haunted land. Czesław Miłosz and Jerzy Andrzejewski also acknowledge Jewish isolation from Polish society. Jewish writers trapped in Poland and in the ghettos, like Władysław Szlengel, understood that the severed bonds would not be mended, while exile Julian Tuwim evinces rage against Polish antisemites, love of Polish culture and language, as well as a fervent hope that the catastrophe will lead to a strengthened bond between Poles and Jews. Among the most important Holocaust chronicles and memories have been the works of writers who experienced the Holocaust in the ghettos and camps on Polish soil, among them Emanuel Ringelblum's *Notes from the Warsaw Ghetto,* the Warsaw diaries of Adam Czerniakow and Chaim

Kaplan, as well as Marek Edelman's account of the Warsaw Ghetto Uprising.

The sixties and early seventies witnessed the publication of work by the younger generation of Polish Jewish writers who were children during the Holocaust—Henryk Grynberg, Hanna Krall, and Bogdan Wojdowski. Among the dominant themes of representative postwar Jewish Polish writers Bogdan Wojdowski, Adolf Rudnicki, Henryk Grynberg, and American émigré Elżbieta Ettinger are the struggle to survive in the ghettos and the concentration camps, the tensions between ordinary and privileged Jews, terror of living under false papers in Aryan zones, betrayal of Jews to the Nazis, resistance, postwar Holocaust trauma, and the theological implications of the Holocaust.

Dutch Writing

Occupied by Nazi Germany for five years, the Dutch suffered enormous hardships. There were fatalities in the ranks of underground resistance fighters, civilians were sent to forced labor in Germany, and the nation experienced the "hungerwinter" of 1944 and 1945. Beginning in 1940, Dutch Jews were systematically identified and isolated in the Westerbork and Vught transit camps where life was extremely difficult, especially once deportations for "labor camps in the east" were initiated. During 1942 and 1943, virtually all Dutch Jews who were not in hiding or had not fled Holland were deported to Bergen-Belsen, Theresienstadt, and the killing camps, primarily to Auschwitz-Birkenau and Sobibor. After liberation the survivors found that their gentile countrymen were, in the main, disinterested in their experience, preferring instead to speak of their own hardships under Nazi occupation.

Jolanda Vanderwal Taylor traces the "waves" of interest and distance for the Dutch who refer to "the war" rather than the factually correct "occupation." She reads the important shift in terminology from "occupation" to "war" as "creat[ing] and sustain[ing] the early image of an occupied populace as combatants rather than citizens, and of communal behavior during the occupation as a protracted . . . conflict" (p. 9). She attributes the relative paucity of postwar literary works to the physical need for rebuilding and the psychological tension between the desire "to forget and on another level the intermittent and inconsistent need to remember" (p. 4).

In the late 1960s, when Holland experienced the generation gap affecting other European nations, which demythologized the older generation, students criticized the "establishment," unmasked the resistance myth, exposed the lie of a widespread heroic response to Nazism by the older generation, and began to pay more attention to the Dutch Holocaust experience. With publications such as Jack Presser's *Ondergang* (Ashes in the Wind) mapping the abandonment and betrayal of Dutch Jewry despite its integration in Dutch society, the Dutch began to confront the past more objectively than they had hitherto. Historians Dick van Galen Last and Rolf Wolfswinkel observe that since the 1970s, World War II literature and film have been welcomed in Holland, with resistance and collaboration the most popular subjects in general literature and the Holocaust a major theme for Jewish writers who treat survivor syndrome and second-generation trauma. These historians note a shift in Dutch response of the 1980s and 1990s characterized by a new eagerness to understand and a corresponding "inability to represent the unrepresentable" (p. 150).

Dutch Holocaust literature treats subjects ranging from collaboration in the Final Solution to resistance and aid to the Jewish population. It documents conditions of Jews in hiding and those incarcerated in the transit camps awaiting deportation to the killing centers, records the paradoxical role of the Jewish Council prior to completion of the deportations, and describes the survival struggle within the concentrationary universe. Among the victims who wrote of their ordeal while it was occurring are diarists like Anne Frank, who recorded her experience in hiding with her family; Etty Hillesum and Philip Mechanicus, who were determined to let the outside world know about Westerbork transit camp, powerfully describing the physical conditions, the functions associated with camp administration, and the psychological terror of deportation. Upon his return from Bergen-Belsen, Abel Herzberg analyzed the behavior of inmates in reaction to the harsh camp conditions. Many years after liberation, Gerhard Durlacher recorded his experiences in occupied Holland, Theresienstadt, and Auschwitz. Marga Minco, one of Holland's most acclaimed writers, addressed her wartime experience through the perspective of a fifteen-year-old narrator charting the incremental development of isolation and oppression in a narrative style blending directness and constraint in *Het bittere kruid* (*Bitter Herbs*).

Beyond the Nazi world, Dutch writing confronts the return of survivors to Holland and the impact of the *Shoah* on the next generation. Liberation did not bring psychological release from the concentrationary universe. Instead, the literature conveys the plight of survivors living in silence and shame as recognition dawns of the comparative magnitude of Dutch Jewish losses: two of three European Jews were murdered in the *Shoah,* but three of four Dutch Jews, the highest percentage on the continent, perished, and Dutch Nazi collaborators facilitated that lethal persecution.

In the 1980s the exclusivity of survivor and resistance writing gave way to inclusion of works by other constituencies such as the child survivors and children of the victims in which the issue of inherited memory and its impact on the lives of children of victims, bystanders, and perpetrators is a central theme. Paralleling the shift from history (experience of the period) to memory and its implications for the survivor, Taylor finds "an interesting and useful dynamic posed by representing 'remembered' time, which coincides with the childhood of the texts' central characters" (p. 9). Arnon Grunberg, the postwar child of survivors, has published autobiographical fiction that evidences profound stress of a child growing up with parents suffering from survivor syndrome: one parent who constantly speaks of *Shoah* pain and is emotionally needy and another who maintains a code of silence and emotional distance. Judith Herzberg, daughter of Holocaust chronicler Abel Herzberg, initially intended to leave the subject to her father. Following her work on a film about German Jewish artist Charlotte Salomon, Herzberg decided to write about the continuing impact of the Holocaust past on the present. The emergence of wartime trauma among characters who have refrained from breaking silence on the subject, the tensions within a survivor family and those between Jews and Dutch non-Jews became her subjects. Her autobiographical writing illuminates the pain of a child hidden apart from her parents, the experience of living under false identity and the emotional complications of family reunion. Andreas Burnier, who also survived the war hidden separately from her parents, adds another dimension to postwar writing of family reunion marred by the hidden child's Holocaust-wrought contempt for Judaism since she internalized the religiously based anti-semitism of her Christian protectors. From the vantage point of one who has returned to Judaism, Burnier recounts recurrent traumatic experiences of displacement and betrayal, and the emotionally wrenching need to remain silent while listening to the antisemitic utterances of her rescuers. Pascale Bos credits Burnier with presenting an entirely original view to the Netherlands of the late 1960s of Dutch citizens, who contrary to the popular myth of widespread rescue, were indifferent to the fate of the Jews or betrayed them if this proved to be advantageous.

French Writing

French national memory of the Holocaust has been complicated by its wartime complicity in Germany's genocide and a postwar desire to "create a positive identity on the ruins of a murderous history" (Wiedmer, p. 4). During years of evasion and falsification it was asserted that rather than the Vichy collaborator, the Gaullist figure of the resistance fighter was representative of France under the German occupation. The student revolts of 1968 and Marcel Ophuls's film *Le Chagrin et la pitié* (The Sorrow and the Pity) challenged this revisionist presentation and precipitated a reappraisal. Serge and Beate Klarsfeld's investigations into France's role during *les années noires,* "the black years" of the Vichy government, have led, since 1995, to official acknowledgement of France's voluntary role in the implementation of the Nazi genocide of Jews.

Elaine Marks observes, "Jews writing in French 'after Auschwitz' may be divided roughly into two groups: those who write about 'Auschwitz,' and those who write about how to write about 'Auschwitz' " (p. 36). She defines the approach of the first group, writers such as Elie Wiesel and André Schwarz-Bart, as writing within a tradition that "does not necessarily put into question the relation between the text and the *hors texte* . . ." and that includes two generations of Jewish intellectuals who, like Emmanuel Lévinas, "engaged in preserving the remains of Eastern European Jewish culture through the revival of Jewish studies" (p. 36), "attempt to memorialize and to mourn through familiar narrative strategies" (p. 38). The second group, including Hélène Jabès Cixous, Jacques Derrida, Serge Doubrovsky, Edmond Jabes, Alain Finkielkraut, Sarah Kofman, Claude Lanzman, Patrick Modiano, Georges Perec, and Robert Antelme, manifest "dissatisfaction with the mimetic principles that sustain the fictional and historical narratives of the first group" (p. 36). Influenced by the philosophy of Martin Heidegger and Maurice Blanchot and by deconstruction, poststructuralism, and psychoanalysis, these writers transform "the historical-social-ethical question of the extermination of the Jews into a philosophical-poeticallinguistic question of presence and absence" (p. 36). What is essential for them is to write about writing about "Auschwitz," avoiding representation.

Of the witness generation, writers from differing religious and political backgrounds, Charlotte Delbo, Pierre Gascar, Anna Langfus, Fania Fenelon, Elie Wiesel, and David Rousset write testimonial works on the concentrationary universe, and in some cases engage the difficulties faced by survivors in postwar France. Their writings, based on direct experience, map the geography and character of the concentrationary universe, including the political organization of the camps. Bearing witness to French acquiescence to German atrocities, many of these writers address the nature and problematics of memory.

In *Le Juif Imaginaire* (*The Imaginary Jew*), Alain Finkielkraut analyzes and codifies the phenomenon that young Jews of his generation experienced: being close to the impact of the Holocaust, identifying with its victims, but separated from it in time. "We are the children of 'l'après-génocide,' born too close to the event to be detached from it, almost its victims, inheritors of its suffering, yet excluded from its reality" (p. 13). For French second-generation writers Henri Raczymow, Georges Perec, Serge Doubrovsky, and Patrick Modiano, confronting the Holocaust is a means for coming to terms with their Jewish origins and identity in postwar Europe. Raczymow treats the problematics of Holocaust writing and, as his Jewish identity grows increasingly important, enters the *shtetl* of Eastern Europe imaginatively to relate Jewish legends and to record the overwhelming sense of absence wrought by the Holocaust and by second-generation guilt. In his intentionally fragmentary autobiography of childhood memories, Perec, who lived through the Holocaust without experiencing it directly, includes a chapter on attending an exhibition on concentration camps. At the time of his death, he was working on a book including the story of Holocaust betrayal and collaboration. Doubrovsky maps his childhood experience of hiding, and acknowledges the relationship between autobiography and fiction, the relationship of his wartime experience to his theory of autofiction—prose reflecting historic rupture. Modiano interrogates the Vichy collaboration, the tension between resistance and collaboration, and French responsibility for Jewish deportations, thereby exposing the twenty-five-year revisionist myth of France united in resistance against Nazism. Ellen Fine characterizes the plight and vision of this generation as

> suffer[ing] doubly from the predicament of how to live with Auschwitz after Auschwitz. On the one hand, along with survivors they have inherited a collective memory, and are pained by its unhealed wounds. On the other hand, unlike the survivors who carry their deeply personal memories within, they feel shut out from this impenetrable universe that ultimately they cannot share. The feeling of exclusion evokes a sense of alienation, incomprehension and guilt, that can be called *the guilt of non-participation*. . .they project themselves back into the era imaginatively and metaphorically (p. 124).

Yiddish Writing

Before the Holocaust, Yiddish, the European language without a country, was the daily language of millions of Jews from many nations. As members of the primary target population of the Nazi regime, Yiddish authors were among the first chroniclers of the *Shoah* sounding the alarm before the Jews' isolation from their countrymen, from the partisan units in the forests, from the ghettos and camps, and—for the fortunate few—from exile, and then from a post-Holocaust perspective. Using Scriptural archetypes from the Book of Lamentations to modern satire, irony, and parody, their writing charted every phase of the catastrophe. Writing in the ghettos implied faith that the nations of the world would come to the rescue of European Jewry and that there would continue to be a significant postwar audience to be addressed in Yiddish. Survivor writing harbors no such illusions, for this remnant lived to understand that the nations of the world were either indifferent to or complicit in the slaughter of the Jews that led to the near demise of Yiddish as well.

Yiddish literature, like Hebrew literature, is distinguished by its emphasis on the theological and religious implications of the *Shoah.* Their poets are, in Alvin Rosenfeld's words, "strong contenders with God" (*A Double Dying,* p. 114), rebuking the self-concealing Deity, expressing the strain on the faithful who anticipated divine intervention in the contemporary tragedy that far surpassed the ancient Egyptian model recounted in the biblical exodus. The mood and mode of Yiddish authors' response to the *Shoah* are exemplified in Kadya Molodowsky's deeply personal response in the form of bitterly ironic lamentation poetry; in Abraham Sutzkever's accounts of wartime experiences of the Vilna ghetto and the Vilna partisans, his invocation of Akedah (the binding of Isaac) to call God to account, and in his memorial verse honoring the partisans of Vilna and all the dead; and in Yitzhak Katzenelson's references to the prophets of exile and Job to explore the implications of the ghetto, and his *midrashic* response to the *Shoah* in which he locates God in an abandoned boxcar emptied of its Jewish cargo. From within the whirlwind, Simkha Bumir Shayevitch described the deportations from the Lodz ghetto evoking the *lekh-lekho* command to Abraham: "Go forth from your native land," and Rachel Auerbach maps ghetto cultural life and struggle for survival from the perspective of the guilt-ridden survivor in hiding in the Aryan sector of Warsaw and in her postwar writing. Among the small group of writers continuing to write in Yiddish from the lands of their immigration, I. B. Singer recreates and mourns the fallen world of east European Jewry and charts survivors' anguish; Jacob Glatstein and Chaim Grade passionately and philosophically denounce the culture that spawned and sustained the Holocaust. Irena Klepfisz, a child survivor, laments the lost people and lost language, and Chava Rosenfarb poignantly recollects the lost Yiddish world and poets.

In describing Yiddish writers' response to the catastrophe in *Against the Apocalypse,* David Roskies argues that they had ''basically two approaches to draw upon from the fund of ancient and modern sources; one that imploded history, and the other that made the Holocaust the center of apocalypse'' (p. 226). Writers steeped in Jewish history had a surfeit of events to draw upon from the centuries-long history of persecution suffered by European Jews. Nazi requirement that Jews wear distinguishing markings on their clothing, defilement of Torah scrolls, burning of Jewish books and synagogues, public humiliation of rabbis, establishment of Jewish ghettos, expropriation of Jewish property, as well as mass expulsions and murder, had long precedent in European Christian conduct toward Jewry. Consequently, Yiddish writers often locate the modern genocide on a continuum by invoking historic, religiously based antisemitic persecutions as referents and correspondents to the *Shoah.* They invoke the paradigms of destruction and desecration (the destruction of The Temple, the Inquisition, persecutions in the time of Akiva, the Chmielnicki and Petlurian Massacres, villains like Pharaoh and Haman) as imprecise evocations of Holocaust loss. Countercommentary, parody, and inversion of sacred texts are techniques that Yiddish writers incorporate to emphasize the subversion of God's principles in the historic context. This irreverent use of the sacred text by Yiddish and Hebrew writers ''imitate[s] the sacrilege, [disrupts] the received order of the text in the same way as the enemy, . . .disrupted the order of the world'' (Roskies, p. 20). David Roskies distinguishes between those who use parody constructively and destructively, effectively arguing that this is a highly mediated and ritualized form of expressing anger. ''By making the text seem. . .corrupt, the individual sufferer expands its meaning, allowing subsequent sufferers to enter the breach'' (p. 20) [and] ''inverting Scripture can be seen as a means of keeping faith'' (p. 19). While the ''sacred parodists'' of pre-*Shoah* catastrophes accepted the covenantal archetypes of sin and retribution, modern writers, according to Roskies, use parody ''to unmask the artificiality of the accepted conventions and to argue for radical change'' (p. 69).

Hebrew Writing

The destruction of European Jewry and the redemption of the remnant through establishment of Israel are central to the collective Israeli consciousness. Although Israeli literature has been profoundly preoccupied with questions of national origin and identity, it is surprising to many that the Holocaust has, until the latter decades of the twentieth-century, not been a major theme of most Israeli writers. Unlike some critics who argue that there has been Holocaust ''silence'' in Israeli writing in the decades immediately following the *Shoah,* Dan Laor asserts that ''Israeli literature has always been obsessed with the Holocaust.'' He cites poet Nathan Alterman's 1942 poem ''Mikol ha-Amim'' (''From All Peoples'') in protest of the Jewish people being chosen for annihilation, and the early witness literature of several survivor-émigrés, Abba Kovner, Ka. Tzetnik (Yehiel Dinur), and Aharon Appelfeld. To that list, one could add Uri Zvi Greenberg, who escaped from Poland two weeks after the war started in 1939 and wrote both in Yiddish and Hebrew within the lamentation mode and antithetical countercommentary. Greenberg's pre-Holocaust poetry was prophetic in its anticipation of mass murder resulting in the destruction of European Jewry. His post-Holocaust poetry contextualizes the *Shoah* within the long history of antisemitic persecutions, condemns the Christian church for its history of teaching contempt for Judaism, denounces God's failure to intervene, and laments the six million. Among the first to publish Holocaust poetry in Hebrew, his *Rehovot ha-Nahar* (*Streets of the River*) is both a chronicle of personal loss and a masterpiece in the lamentation tradition. Incorporating narrative, dramatic, and lyric poetry, the poem charts a summary of Jewish history as a river of blood, and mourns the poet's family and the European Jewish community. The poem, addressing longing for renewal in Israel, and revenge and redemption themes, has been characterized by Alan Mintz as ''the single most important work on the Holocaust in Hebrew literature'' (p. 165).

Abba Kovner, former resistance leader of the Vilna ghetto partisans and an officer in the new Israeli army, wrote long narrative poems ''addressing the wide scope of Jewish collective experience'' (Laor, p. 119) and evoking partisan resistance efforts in the Lithuanian forests, ghettoization, partisan rejection of the diaspora passivity and presaging the *sabra* spirit as well as poetry in the lamentation mode. His long poem, *Ha Mafteah Zalal* (The Key Sank), published in 1950, was ''the first attempt in Hebrew poetry to present an epic of a ghetto in the Nazi period'' (Laor, p. 120). Because Kovner followed his Holocaust poems with work on the rebirth of modern Israel, Laor associates him with ''the common Zionist notion of the linkage between Diaspora destruction and 'redemption' in modern Jewish history'' (p. 121).

Aharon Appelfeld, the best known outside Israel of the early postwar writers, avoids direct treatment of

Holocaust horror, but his writing is imbued with a singular poetic style that has won both Israeli and international critical acclaim. Appelfeld's novels are noted for their absence of ghettos, camps, forced labor, mass murder, and all that is conventionally associated with Holocaust writing, yet is regarded as the epitome of Holocaust literature. Like the world of I. B. Singer's Holocaust fiction, Appelfeld's portrayals of Jews limn them as deceived by the prewar lures of assimilation at the brink of destruction or traumatized in the postwar world of survivors, "filter(s) through which Appelfeld faces the issue of Jewish destiny in the twentieth-century" (Laor, p. 127).

Dan Pagis spent four years of his childhood in a German concentration camp, migrated to Palestine following liberation, and began what was to become an exemplary scholarly and literary career. After avoiding the subject of the Holocaust in his writing for many years, the sight, during a family visit in New York in 1967, of some objects retrieved from his grandfather's home, forced him to begin writing about the Holocaust. It became a major element of his lyric poetry offering new perspectives on the meaning of the Holocaust in a style very different from Kovner's public voice or Ka. Tzetnik's literature of atrocity. Pagis's poetry is more closely associated with the approach of Appelfeld, his compatriot from Bukovina, although it differs in its direct evocation of the Holocaust universe.

There are many explanations for the limited early Israeli literary response to the demise of European Jewry. Self- and externally imposed silence affected many survivors, as did shame especially among young *sabras* (native-born Israelis) who were dismayed by what they perceived as the passivity of diaspora Jews. During the early period of the state, many survivors maintained a protective code of silence born of survivor guilt, conviction that the ghettos and camps were incomprehensible to those who did not actually inhabit the Nazi universe, and deference to Israeli sensibilities and counsel encouraging individual healing and a collective redemptive effort. Israeli critic Gilead Morahg perceives the combination of Zionist ideology and Holocaust sanctity merging into "a dominant national metanarrative that precluded the possibility of an imaginative engagement with the experience of the Holocaust and was a major cause of the long literary silence on the subject" (Morahg, p. 151). The 1961 Eichmann Trial in Jerusalem was a catalyst that changed the Holocaust consciousness of Israelis, directing attention to survivors and their stories.

The current generation of Israeli writers, more sensitive than the *yishuv* (pre-state) community to the pain of the survivor generation and the harm caused by the effort to suppress their histories, subverts the discourse of denial and silence. These writers acknowledge a vital connection to the survivor generation and recognize that Israel's rescue and rehabilitation mode silenced and marginalized survivors. Morahg attributes the emergence of the Holocaust theme in recent Israeli literature to a

> general cultural reorientation towards the Holocaust that seems to have begun in the late 1970s, and is also evident in many areas of Israeli popular culture, political discourse, educational policy, and academic research. . . . part of an increasingly intense national quest for a viable post-Zionist identity, and of the multifaceted public debate over the manner in which this identity should relate contemporary Israelis to their historical Jewish roots (p. 143).

The issue is no longer whether to remember the Holocaust, but rather which lessons are to be learned from it. While Israel's political establishment includes the Holocaust in its ideological agenda to forge a unified national identity, Morahg asserts that Israel's writers "are at the forefront of a countereffort to explore the continuing impact of the Holocaust on the individual psyche and determine its relevance to a personal sense of Israeli identity" (p. 144). The work of younger writers like David Grossman, Shulamith Hareven, Itamar Levy, Nava Semel, Savyon Liebrecht, Rivka Miriam, Tanya Hadar, and Michal Govrin reveals that they have found that Israeli identity is poignantly linked to the European Jewish calamity. Their texts employ contrasting approaches to shatter the barriers of silence and explore the impact of the Holocaust on contemporary Israeli lives and society. Some, including Govrin, Liebrecht, and Semel, depict the social and psychological impact of the Holocaust on the personal lives and family relationships of the survivors and their children and thus, by extension, on Israeli society. Hadar and Miriam express "the magic and charm of the lost Jewish world and their identification with it" (Yaoz, "The Heritage of Trauma," p. 1645). These second-generation Holocaust writers who have not experienced the *Shoah* directly, regard it as an integral part of their consciousness, indirectly experienced through their parents' traumatic memories and silences. They trace the ways in which the story is received and passed on, the ways European history has shaped their identities (p. 1645). David Grossman (who is not a child of survivors) and Itamar Levy extend and transcend narrative boundaries to explore the implications of the Holocaust and possibilities of healing. In highly experimental narrative modes veering toward the fantastic, they acknowledge "the impossibility of an authentic representation of the concentrationary experience," an experience which nevertheless "continues to be powerfully present in the lives of Jews, including those who were not even born at the time'' (Morahg, p. 163). David Grossman's examination of the consequences for Israeli society of repressing Holocaust trauma in *See Under: Love,* which has received international acclaim for its intricate structure, innovative technique, and extraordinary magical realistic prose style, is a marked departure thematically from Israeli redemptive Holocaust writing. Citing the major differences between the first and second generations, Hanna Yaoz observes the tendency of the survivor generation to write of the ''living dead,'' feeling ''marked and tainted,'' motifs of illness and war in a blended rhetoric of code words from biblical archetypes and those from planet Auschwitz. The second generation write about the ''heritage of trauma,'' the ''attraction-repulsion'' response to their parents' experiences reaching its climax in their confrontation with the question of Jewish and Israeli identity and impacting their choice of language, including the introduction and merging of Yiddish and Ladino (the vernacular language of the Jews from Greece and Salonika) with Hebrew in a blend of past and present (Yaoz, 1645–1646).

British Writing

The tolerance for Jews in British society had largely been won at the expense of overt manifestation of their Jewish identity. Realization of the precariousness of their position led British and Commonwealth Jewish citizens to strenuously forego petition of their governments to adopt generous refugee immigration policies, to vigorously attack the rail lines leading to the concentration camps, or to take any other action that might be perceived as promoting sectarian ''Jewish'' interests during World War II. Hence, while British Jews actively supported the Allied position, fear of an antisemitic backlash relegated intervention in the Holocaust to a secondary wartime goal.

Not surprisingly, prior to the coming of age of writers who had found refuge in England as part of the *kindertransports,* the Holocaust had been conspicuously absent from Anglo-Jewish writing. To avoid being perceived as ''too Jewish'' and consequently insufficiently British, most Anglo-Jewish authors avoided reference to Jewishness. Illustrative is Bryan Cheyette's observation that Anita Brookner's saga of 1930s German Jewish émigrés to Britain is an instance of ''overt silence.'' He contends, ''what is left unsaid in *Latecomers* becomes the subject of the novel'' (p. xli). In a similar vein, David Brauner observes that because Jewish authors have been reticent to write Holocaust literature, they have more often left the subject to non-Jews Thomas Keneally, D. M. Thomas, and Martin Amis, whose controversial works do not focus directly on Jewish experience. Amis and Thomas are engaged in postmodernist experimentation with perception and form, as in *Time's Arrow* representing the Holocaust in reverse chronology from the point of view of a Nazi doctor and *White Hotel*'s Freudian focus and problematic borrowings from Anatoli Kuznetsov's novel *Babi Yar* transmogrified for the novel's erotic final scene. *Schindler's List* is focused more directly on the Holocaust, but on an atypical large-scale Nazi rescue of Jews by a Nazi Party member.

Rare examples of Anglo-Jewish treatment of the Holocaust appear in British drama and fiction. The Holocaust is an allusive element in several Harold Pinter works, an important component of his directorial work such as that for Robert Shaw's *Man in the Glass Booth,* and is more visible in his examination of the Nazi genocide in *Ashes to Ashes* where he presents Holocaust memory and invests his character with Holocaust sensibility, albeit without Holocaust experience. British acceptance of Jewish children from Nazi-controlled Europe prior to September 1939 constituted a major rescue effort and looms large in Anglo-Jewish consciousness. Furthermore, it is the sort of consoling or triumphal Holocaust story that has more appeal for the British public than does the fate Jewry suffered in Nazi Europe. Diane Samuels's 1995 memory play *The Kindertransports,* set in contemporary London, interweaves scenes from wartime Germany and England to convey a young Jewish girl's experience of survival and assimilation. Elaine Feinstein turned to Jewish identity and European history as fictional subjects in the late 1970s. *The Children of the Rose* conveys Holocaust sensibilities and knowledge of hidden children who escaped the ghetto and camp environments, and children born in the postwar era who encounter a history that is largely repressed in mainline British culture.

Rejecting Holocaust silence that characterized most Anglo-Jewish writing, and Holocaust subservience to other themes of non-Jewish British writing, émigré Jewish writers have been more faithful to Jewish themes and experience. Cheyette conjectures that foreign-born Jewish writers thrive better in England because they ''do not have to transcend an Englishness [they learned from childhood] . . . because they do not need to engage with the cultural fixity of the past in Britain'' and because they have ''a skeptical and detached relationship both to the past and to national cultures in general'' (p. xliii). George Steiner, born in Paris to Viennese parents, emigrated and educated in the United States, with long periods of residence and academic appointments in Europe and England, has made the Holocaust a dominant theme of his discursive and creative writing. Michael Hamburger, born in Germany, translator of Nelly Sachs and Paul Celan, may have been moved as other Jews raised and educated in England were to examine their Jewish identities as a result of the Eichmann trial and Hannah Arendt's report of it. His poem on Eichmann, "In a Cold Season," is "one of several that recorded the delayed breakthrough" (Sicher, *Beyond Marginality,* p. 158). Karen Gershon's books address the Holocaust and its legacy including survivor guilt and the moral imperative of bearing witness in poetry and prose. *A Lesser Child* chronicles the impact of Nazism on an assimilated German Jewish child. *Bread of Exile,* her fictionalized autobiography, delineates loneliness of the refugee child made unwelcome by commentary on her foreignness in a land where German-Jewish refugees from Nazi Germany were interned as possible German enemy aliens, and "the agony of the lack of memory which drives the poet back to Germany to reclaim loss" (Sicher, 1992, p. 152). *We Came as Children* is a collective autobiography of the child refugees from Nazi Germany. Lotte Kramer, a *kindertransport* refugee, writes poetry that includes vignettes of life in Nazi Germany, meditations on the lives lost in Europe, and English safety juxtaposed with European peril, in poetry rich in Holocaust allusions. Ronit Lentin, an Israeli-born Irish writer who confronts her mother's Holocaust history in a fictionalized autobiography, treats second-generation Holocaust angst in addition to survivor syndrome, themes that are dominant in recent Israeli literature. The second-generation perspective of a child born after the war, but deeply scarred by her survivor-parents' narratives, is the subject of Anne Karpf's *The War after: Living with the Holocaust.* Karpf's book is of import not only for its delineation of the survivor's stories and their impact on her life, but for her forthright political analysis of British response to the plight of European Jewry and Anglo-Jewry's reticence to confront the Holocaust.

Canadian Writing

Among the Commonwealth nations, Canadian Holocaust literature is the most prolific, perhaps because of its physical distance from Britain's relative disinterest, its proximity to America's obsession with the Holocaust, and because of its own fairly large immigrant Jewish population. In addition to Canadian writing in Yiddish, there is an ample body of Holocaust literature in English. Among the most interesting stylistically is the poetry of A. M. Klein. "The Hitleriad" is a historically based mock-heroic satire attacking Hitler and his henchmen. "The Second Scroll," cast as a Holocaust survivor's retrospective, is constructed as five chapters named for the five books of the Bible. It blends poetry, fiction, and essay to bracket the Holocaust between eastern European pogroms and the creation of the State of Israel. The absurdity of the Nazi universe is the subject of Leonard Cohen's surrealistic novel that incorporates black humor to make the horror of the Holocaust and the role of its legacy in the contemporary culture accessible. Henry Kriesel features themes of the impotence of North American Jews to rescue European Jewry and the impossibility of postwar return to Europe. One of Canada's best-known authors outside the provinces, Mordecai Richler, populates several novels with Germans, Jews, and Canadians who must confront Holocaust specificity and antisemitism in their midst, and an evermore-pessimistic post-Holocaust world. In *St. Urbain's Horseman,* Richler turns to fantasy and magical realism to put the Nazi past on trial and attack British antisemitism, twin subjects that he returns to in the satiric mode in *Joshua Then and Now.* Toronto poet and novelist Anne Michaels foregrounds themes of memory, language, Holocaust survival, and mediation in the highly acclaimed *Fugitive Pieces,* which probes the psychological circumstances of growing up in the shadow of the Holocaust and the continuing effects of Holocaust trauma.

American Writing

By 1978 the Holocaust had become so firmly established in American consciousness that President Jimmy Carter established a presidential commission to oversee the creation of the United States Holocaust Memorial Museum. In the same year, NBC aired the miniseries *Holocaust,* reportedly watched by 120 million people. Commenting on the transformation resulting from these defining events, noted Holocaust scholar Raul Hilberg described a surge in academic study of the Holocaust, a marked increase in books published, conferences developed and courses established in numerous academic disciplines. On the popular culture front, Hollywood abandoned its shameful wartime policy of Holocaust silence based on the prospect of an antisemitic backlash, and began to produce such films that achieved commercial success. In contrast to their earlier silence, Holocaust survivors became more visible and vocal with the development of post-1970s civic commemorative activities and oral history projects dedicated to preserving *Shoah* testimony. The year 1993 witnessed the opening of the

United States Holocaust Memorial Museum in Washington and the screening of Spielberg's *Schindler's List.* The museum established an attendance record for a national museum and the film elicited passionate critical and lay responses attesting to the prominence of the Holocaust in American culture. American embrace of the Holocaust has been a cause of concern among some observers including Alvin Rosenfeld, who asks whether one can remain true to the historic event while tailoring its representation to contemporary social and political agendas. Writing that the *Shoah* has a ''privileged status in the pantheon of genocides,'' Phillip Lopate posits a class and racial bias in Holocaust studies because the victims are white, perceived as middle-class and individualized, rather than Third World dark-skinned masses (p. 58).

American writers are among the cultural leaders who have grappled with Holocaust inclusion and representation. Long before the current debate on the ''Americanization'' of the Holocaust, Norma Rosen addressed the issue in her 1974 essay, ''The Holocaust and the American Jewish Novelist.'' She questioned how ''the virtues of fiction—indirection, irony, ambivalence—[can] be used to make art out of this unspeakable occurrence'' (*Accidents of Influence,* p. 9). Thirteen years and several Holocaust works later, she argued that the paradox for novelists working in this sphere lies ''in the tension between writing and not writing about it. If the writer treats the subject, the risk is that it may be falsified, trivialized. Even a 'successful' treatment of the subject risks an aestheticizing or a false ordering of it, since whatever is expressed in art conveys the impression that it, too, is subject to the laws of composition. Yet not to write means omitting the central event of the twentieth-century'' (*Accidents of Influence,* p. 49).

Not even among Jewish American authors who were gaining their long awaited place in American letters, did the Holocaust appear as a subject of significant literary interest during the first two postwar decades. In 1966 Robert Alter lamented: ''With all the restless probing into the implications of the Holocaust that continues to go on in Jewish intellectual forums . . . it gives one pause to note how rarely American Jewish fiction has attempted to come to terms . . . with the European catastrophe'' (''Confronting the Holocaust,'' p. 67). Yet, three years later, Lothar Kahn observed ''No Jewish writer . . . has written a book without the memory of Auschwitz propelling him to issue warnings, implied or specific against the Holocaust'' (p. 3). The beginnings of widespread Jewish American collective and literary Holocaust reflection were fuelled by the 1961 Jerusalem trial of Adolf Eichmann, the intellectual debate aroused by Hannah Arendt's analysis of the trial and the 1967 Arab-Israeli Six Day War, during which Arabs evoked Nazi annihilation rhetoric.

American Holocaust literature is a tapestry of three primary threads: memoir and autobiographical fiction by survivor-writers, and compelling work by descendents of survivors. The survivor writers Elżbieta Ettinger and Ilona Karmel write autobiographical fictions of their experiences of hiding and running in Aryan sectors of Poland, of living in the ghettos and labor and concentration camps, and in Ettinger's case, of working in the Jewish resistance. Autobiographical fiction by adults who were child survivors often focus on the tensions of loss of parents and dependence on other adults for their survival. Louis Begley's young orphan and his aunt dissemble their way through encounters with Gestapo and Polish predators. Hana Demetz recounts the peculiar existence of a *Mischlinge,* the child of mixed German-Jewish parentage. Irena Klepfisz laments the loss of her father, a fighter in the Warsaw Ghetto Uprising, and celebrates her mother's resilience and courage. Lore Segal conveys the loneliness of a children's transport survivor who lives in other people's houses in a foreign culture and is burdened by responsibility for her parents' survival.

Although American-born writers generally devote less attention to direct representation and dramatization of the Nazi universe than do Europeans and Israelis who endured the terror, some approach the Holocaust directly, setting their works in ghettos and camps and modeling their characters on recognizable historic figures or having characters refer to them by name. The Lodz, Vilna, and Warsaw ghettos, and Kaiserwald and Auschwitz, are represented in the fictional and poetic worlds of Leslie Epstein, Richard Elman, Susan Fromberg Schaeffer, Marge Piercy, John Hersey, Cynthia Ozick, and William Styron. Charles Reznikoff's long epic poem, *Holocaust,* is based on actual trial testimony. Most Americans, including Jacqueline Osherow, Alicia Ostriker, Adrienne Rich, Irving Feldman, Jerome Rothenberg, Alan Shapiro, Gerald Stern, Ruth Whitman, Louis Zukofsky, and novelist Melvin Bukiet approach the Holocaust indirectly through representation of prewar and postwar real and imagined Jewish life. These writers allow readers to anticipate the coming catastrophe from the vantage point of their hindsight in opposition to the fictional characters' innocence. Others, like I. B. Singer, Wallant, Bellow, and Ozick present a postwar perspective focusing on the psychology of survivor trauma as played out in voluntary and involuntary memory and nightmare evoking Holocaust degradation. Their characters suffer from a condition the psychiatric literature classifies as ''survivor syndrome,'' comprising guilt for outliving families and friends, recurrent nightmares and traumatic memories of Holocaust indignities, betrayals and torture, postwar identity and religious crises and failure to resume prewar lives and interests. Alternately, several authors explore survivor mission as part of a restorative and regenerative process of rebuilding Judaism and the Jewish community in America and Israel. Central to the concerns of the religious are the preservation and transmission of the Jewish past, emergence of a vibrant American Judaism, and textual preservation. Arthur Cohen's and Chaim Potok's survivors build centers of Jewish learning in America, and Cynthia Ozick's and Hugh Nissenson's transmit Yiddish cultural and textual heritage and retain the Holocaust in the historic record by opposing forces that would diminish or deny its significance. In their fiction preservation and transmission of the Jewish sacred legacy is essential to witness testimony; the protagonists respond to the Holocaust tragedy by revitalizing their Jewish identities and commitments. Alan Berger interprets these writers' use of "biblical, messianic, and mystical themes [as] their attempt to maintain a covenantal perspective on the catastrophe" (p. 15).

Avoiding any suggestion that Israel's birth was an acceptable outcome of the Holocaust, American writers eschew linking the *Shoah* and the establishment of the Jewish state. They do, however, articulate the abundant parallels they perceive between contemporary Israeli survival surrounded by hostile neighbors and Nazi Germany's menace to European Jewry. Bellow, Roth, Singer, and Elman set portions of their Holocaust narratives in Israel and introduce Israeli Holocaust survivors who compare Arab annihilation rhetoric and belligerence to the Nazi antecedent.

More than any other event in modern Jewish history, the Holocaust taxes the Jew's faith in a just and merciful God, provoking questions about the nature of God and the covenant between God and the people. Holocaust-era writers worked in the tradition of theological protest dating from the biblical histories of Job, Abraham, Moses, and Jeremiah. They question and rebuke the passive God, articulating the gamut of theological and philosophical responses as varied as those of Richard Rubenstein, Emil Fackenheim, Eliezer Berkovits, and Irving Greenberg, and differ widely in their conclusions ranging from outright rejection of God to reaffirmation of faith in God and Judaism.

As in European and Israeli literatures, second-and third-generation *Shoah* writing is a new paradigm in American literature introducing a young generation of authors including Art Spiegelman, Thane Rosenbaum, Melvin Bukiet, Rebecca Goldstein, Allegra Goodman, Helen Epstein, Joseph Skibell, and Harvey Grossinger. Their themes are inherited memory and trauma, the problematics of growing up with Holocaust silence and narrative as an intrusive presence in the lives of their characters. The dynamics of post-trauma response and representation, and post-Holocaust Jewish identity formation enter these works as the authors engage in the kind of "working through" that Dominick LaCapra identifies in *Representing the Holocaust,* as crucial to mourning and "acquiring some perspective" on traumatic experience (p. 200) by "mak[ing] even more specific what was lost and to feel, again, the anguish of losing" (p. 215).

Foregoing narrative experimentation on the European scale, Americans more often write realistic Holocaust texts and use traditional Western forms to highlight the connections between Holocaust brutality and the civilization that spawned and sustained persecution of the Jews. Illustrative of this method is Leslie Epstein's introduction of Greek, medieval, and Shakespearean models and allusion to render his themes of the Lodz ghetto's *Judenrat* corruption and Nazi radical evil, and to connect the Holocaust and its antecedents in European culture. The Judaically literate Ozick and Cohen introduce Hebrew *midrashic* legend, Potok employs lamentation liturgy biblical allusions, and Hasidic implications of restoration, as well as covenant theology to place the Holocaust in the historic context and continuum of Jewish martyrdom. Jewish Americans also share the lamentation tone, as well as parodic countercommentary commonly found in the writing of Jewish European and Israeli writers to dramatize Holocaust-wrought rupture. Addressing the position of his own generation, which was contemporaneous with the witnessing generation, Arthur Cohen identified them as "the generation that bears the scar without the wound, sustaining memory without direct experience. It is this generation that has the obligation, self-imposed and self-accepted . . . to wrest instruction from the historical" (p. 2).

Latin-American Writing

Traditionally underrepresented in discussions of Holocaust literature, which tends to be Euro-U.S.-Israeli-centric, Latin American writers have been given short shrift. A body of Latin American Holocaust literature is being brought to the attention of readers outside the region by scholars such as Ilan Stavans, Marjorie Agosin, Edna Aizenberg, Joseph Abraham Levi, and Nelson H. Vieira. Argentina's great writer, Jorge Luis Borges, confronted Nazism directly in "Deutsches Requiem." He has dealt with issues now fashionable in Holocaust studies—the limits of representation and the psychology of victims and perpetrators. Edna Aizenberg claims, ''Much before Lyotard, ... Borges inscribed the double movement [of the necessity and the impossibility of representing the disaster] in his prose'' (Aizenberg, p. 258–259).

Ilan Stavans explains the low literary profile of Jews in Latin American countries as stemming from ''fear of antisemitism and fear of being stigmatized as a minority, which still runs high.'' Contributing to survivor discomfort is the ironic circumstance of living in close proximity to their former Nazi persecutors who also found refuge in Latin America. Stavans optimistically notes a ''refreshing new sense of self-consciousness about the Nazi period in Latin America and the role of Jews in Hispanic society.'' However, Stavans adds a cautionary word indicating that Latin Jewish writers' treatment of the Holocaust is not as well known in the region as it is in North America. Brazilian writers Carlos Heitor Cony, Roberto Drummond, and Moacyr Scliar introduce Holocaust subjects and images into their works, intimately linking them to the harsh sociopolitical realities of Brazil during the authoritarian dictatorship of 1964 through 1984. Comparison of Hitler's Germany of the 1930s and Brazil of the 1960s and 1970s is a dominant theme. Illustrative is Scliar's *The World War in Bom Fim,* a narrative about a young Jewish boy chronicling life and customs of his Brazilian *bairro* ghetto upbringing, his fear of local Germans and spectral Nazis, and his fantasies of his alter ego defeating the Nazis. Drummond, too, focuses on the Nazi mentality, and his Auschwitz and Buchenwald survivor is obsessed with capturing Mengele.

One of the most prolific Latin Jewish writers, the poet Marjorie Agosín, the child of German Jewish immigrants to Chile, writes about Jewish experience in Latin America, her own identity as a Latin American Jewish woman, and her engagement with the Holocaust through the memory of many members of her family who perished in the Nazi camps and others who survived. Anne Frank occupies a place of privilege in Agosín's writing. The poet has an ongoing correspondence with Anne in *Dear Anne Frank,* treating both the specifics of the Holocaust and other persecutions, including parallels to the suffering of women living under Latin American fascist regimes.

One of the defining events of the twentieth-century, the Holocaust has changed the way we think of humanity and has become pivotal in our understanding of our times and the human condition. All disciplines and the arts are engaged in contending with this extraordinary event in human history. Of those fields, literature has been among the most persistent and salient in shaping the Holocaust as a collective memory.

Bibliography

Critical Sources

Abramson, Glenda. ''The Plays of the Holocaust.'' In *Modern Hebrew Drama.* New York: St. Martin's Press, 1979, 116–140.

Abrahamson, Irving, ed. *Against Silence: The Voice and Vision of Elie Wiesel.* New York: Holocaust Library, 1985.

Adorno, Theodor W. *Aesthetics and Politics.* Translated and edited by Ronald Taylor. London: New Left Books, 1977.

———. *Negative Dialectics.* Translated by E. B. Ashton. New York: Seabury Press, 1973.

———. ''Engagement.'' *Noten Zur Literatur.* Vol. 3. Frankfurt: Suhrkamp, 1963.

Alexander, Edward. ''The Holocaust in Jewish Novels.'' *Jewish Book Annual* 35, no. 5738 (1977–1978): 25–32.

———. *The Resonance of Dust: Essays on Holocaust Literature and Jewish Fate.* Columbus: The Ohio State University Press, 1979.

Alter, Robert. ''Confronting the Holocaust.'' *Commentary* 41 (March 1966): 67. In *After the Tradition.* New York: E. P. Dutton and Co., 1969, 163–180.

———. *Defenses of the Imagination: Jewish Writers and Modern Historical Crisis.* Philadelphia: The Jewish Publication Society of America, 1977.

———. ''Deformations of the Holocaust.'' *Commentary* (February 1981): 48–54.

Alvarez, A. ''The Literature of the Holocaust.'' *Commentary* 38 (November 1964): 65–69.

———. ''The Literature of the Holocaust.'' In *Beyond All This Fiddle.* London: Penguin Press, 1968, 22–33.

Améry, Jean. *At the Mind's Limits.* Translated by Sidney Rosenfeld and Stella P. Rosenfeld. New York: Schocken Books, 1986.

———. *Radical Humanism: Selected Essays.* Translated and edited by Sidney Rosenfeld and Stella P. Rosenfeld. Bloomington: Indiana University Press, 1984.

Appelfeld, Aharon. ''After the Holocaust.'' In *Writing and the Holocaust.* Edited by Berel Lang. New York: Holmes and Meier, 1988, 83–92.

Arendt, Hannah. *Eichmann in Jerusalem: A Report on the Banality of Evil.* Rev. ed. New York: Penguin, 1965.

———. *The Jew as Pariah: Jewish Identity and Politics in the Modern Age.* Edited by Ron Feldman. New York: Grove Press, 1978.

———. *The Origins of Totalitarianism.* New York: Harcourt, Brace, and World, 1951.

Auerbach, Erich. *Mimesis: The Representation of Reality in Western Literature.* Translated by Willard Trask. Princeton: Princeton University Press, 1953.

Bartov, Omer. *Murder in Our Midst: The Holocaust, Industrial Killing, and Representation.* New York: Oxford University Press, 1996.

Bauman, Zygmunt. *Modernity and the Holocaust.* Ithaca: Cornell University Press, 1991.

Bellamy, Elizabeth J. *Affective Genealogies: Psychoanalysis, Postmodernism, and the ''Jewish Question'' after Auschwitz.* Lincoln: University of Nebraska Press, 1997.

Benjamin, Walter. *Illuminations.* Translated by Harry Zohn. New York: Schocken Books, 1969.

———. *Gesammelte Schriften.* Vol. 1.2. Frankfurt: Suhrkamp, 1974.

Berenbaum, Michael. *The World Must Know: The History of the Holocaust as Told in the United States Holocaust Memorial Museum.* Boston: Little, Brown and Company, 1993.

Berger, Alan L. *Children of Job: American Second-Generation Witnesses to the Holocaust.* Albany: State University of New York Press, 1997.

———. *Crisis and Covenant: The Holocaust in American Jewish Fiction.* Albany: State University of New York Press, 1985.

Berger, James. "Trauma and Literary Theory." *Contemporary Literature* 38 (1997): 569–582.

Berkovits, Eliezer. *Faith after Auschwitz.* New York: Ktav, 1973.

Bernstein, Michael André. *Foregone Conclusions: Against Apocalyptic History.* Berkeley: University of California Press, 1994.

———. "Homage to the Extreme: The *Shoah* and the Rhetoric of Catastrophe." *Times Literary Supplement,* 6 March 1998, 6–8.

Bilik, Dorothy Seidman. *Immigrant-Survivors: Post-Holocaust Consciousness in Recent Jewish American Fiction.* Middletown, Conn.: Wesleyan University Press, 1981.

Blanchot, Maurice. *The Space of Literature.* Translated by Ann Smock. Lincoln: University of Nebraska Press, 1982.

———. *The Writing of the Disaster.* Translated by Ann Smock. Lincoln: University of Nebraska Press, 1986.

Bosmajian, Hamida. *Metaphors of Evil: Contemporary German Literature and the Shadow of Nazism.* Iowa City: University of Iowa Press, 1979.

Boyarin, Daniel, and Jonathan Boyarin. "Diaspora: Generation and the Ground of Jewish Identity." *Critical Inquiry* 19, no. 4 (summer 1993): 693–725.

———, eds. *Jews and Other Differences: The New Jewish Cultural Studies.* Minneapolis: University of Minnesota Press, 1997.

Boyarin, Jonathan. *Storm from Paradise: The Politics of Jewish Memory.* Minneapolis: University of Minnesota Press, 1992.

Boyers, Robert. *Atrocity and Amnesia.* New York: Oxford University Press, 1985.

Braham, Randolf, ed. *Reflections of the Holocaust in Art and Literature.* New York: Social Science Monographs, Boulder and Csengeri Institute for Holocaust Studies of the Graduate School and University Center of the City of New York, 1990.

Brinkley, R., and S. Joura. "Tracing *Shoah.*" *Publications of the Modern Language Association* (1996): 108–127.

Caruth, Cathy, ed. *Trauma: Explorations in Memory.* Baltimore, Md.: Johns Hopkins University Press, 1995.

———. *Unclaimed Experience: Trauma, Narrative, and History.* Baltimore, Md.: Johns Hopkins University Press, 1996.

Cheyette, Bryan, and Laura Marcus. *Modern, Culture, and "the Jew".* Stanford, Calif.: Stanford University Press, 1998.

Cohen, Arthur A. *The Tremendum: A Theological Interpretation of the Holocaust.* New York: Continuum, 1993.

Des Pres, Terrence. *The Survivor: An Anatomy of Life in the Death Camp.* New York: Oxford University Press, 1976.

———. "Terror and the Sublime." *Human Rights Quarterly* 5 (1983): 135–146.

Diner, Dan, ed. *Zivilisationsbruch: Denken nach Auschwitz.* Frankfurt: Fischer, 1988.

Ezrahi, Sidra DeKoven. *By Words Alone: The Holocaust in Literature.* Chicago: University of Chicago Press, 1980.

Fackenheim, Emil. *From Bergen-Belsen to Jerusalem: Contemporary Implications of the Holocaust.* Jerusalem: World Jewish Congress, 1975.

———. *God's Presence in History.* New York: Harper and Row, 1970.

———. *To Mend the World: Foundations of Post-Holocaust Jewish Thought.* New York: Schocken Books, 1982.

Felman, Shoshana, and Dori Laub. *Testimony: Crises of Witnessing in Literature, Psychoanalysis, and History.* New York: Routledge, 1992.

Fine, Ellen S. "Literature as Resistance: Survival in the Camps." *Holocaust and Genocide Studies* 1, no. 1 (1986): 79–89.

———."The Surviving Voice: Literature of the Holocaust." In *Perspectives on the Holocaust.* Edited by Randolph L. Braham. Boston: Kluwer-Nijhoff Publishing, 1983, 105–117.

Finkielkraut, Alain. *The Imaginary Jew.* Translated by Kevin O'Neill and David Suchoff. Lincoln: University of Nebraska Press, 1994.

Flanzbaum, Hilene, ed. *The Americanization of the Holocaust.* Baltimore, Md.: The Johns Hopkins University Press, 1999.

Foley, Barbara. "Fact, Fiction, Fascism: Testimony and Mimesis in Holocaust Narratives." *Comparative Literature* 34, no. 4 (1982): pp. 330–360.

Frankl, Viktor E. *Man's Search for Meaning.* Translated by Ilse Lasch. Rev. ed. Boston: Beacon Press, 1962.

Fridman, Lea Wernick. *Words and Witness: Narrative and Aesthetic Strategies in the Representation of the Holocaust.* Albany: State University of New York Press, 2000.

Friedlander, Henry. *The Origins of Nazi Genocide: From Euthanasia to the Final Solution.* Chapel Hill: University of North Carolina Press, 1995.

Friedländer, Saul. "The 'Final Solution': On the Unease in Historical Interpretation." In *Lessons and Legacies: The Meaning of the Holocaust in a Changing World.* Edited by Peter Hayes. Evanston, Ill.: Northwestern University Press, 1991, pp. 23–35.

———. "Historical Writing and the Memory of the Holocaust." In *Writing and the Holocaust.* Edited by Berel Lang. New York: Holmes & Meier, 1988, pp. 66–77.

———. *Memory, History, and the Extermination of the Jews of Europe.* Bloomington: Indiana University Press, 1993.

———, ed. and author of Introduction. *Probing the Limits of Representation: Nazism and the "Final Solution."* Cambridge: Harvard University Press, 1992.

———. *Reflections of Nazism: An Essay on Kitsch and Death.* Translated by Thomas Weyr. Bloomington and Indianapolis: Indiana University Press, 1993.

Friedman, Saul S. *Holocaust Literature: A Handbook of Critical, Historical, and Literary Writings.* Westport, Conn.: Greenwood Press, 1993.

Garver, Zev, and Bruce Zuckerman. "Why Do We Call the Holocaust 'The Holocaust'? An Inquiry into the Psychology of Labels." *Modern Judaism* 9, no. 2 (1989): 197–211.

Gilman, Sander. *Jewish Self-Hatred: Anti-Semitism and the Hidden Language of the Jews.* Baltimore, Md.: Johns Hopkins University Press, 1986.

Goldenberg, Myrna. "Different Horrors, Same Hell: Women Remembering the Holocaust." In *Thinking the Unthinkable: Meanings of the Holocaust.* Edited by Roger S. Gottlieb. New York: Paulist Press, 1990, pp. 150–166.

Gottlieb, Roger S. *Thinking the Unthinkable: Meanings of the Holocaust.* New York: Paulist Press, 1990.

Haas, Peter J. *Morality after Auschwitz: The Radical Challenge of the Nazi Ethic.* Philadelphia, Pa.: Fortress, 1988.

Habermas, Jürgen. *The Philosophical Discourse of Modernity.* Translated by Frederick Lawrence. Cambridge: Massachusetts Institute of Technology Press, 1987.

Halperin, Irving. *Messengers from the Dead: Literature of the Holocaust.* Philadelphia, Pa.: Westminster Press, 1970.

———. "Spiritual Resistance in Holocaust Literature." *Yad Vashem Studies* 7 (1968): 75–82.

Hartman, Geoffrey. ed. *Bitburg in Moral and Political Perspective.* Bloomington: Indiana University Press, 1986.

———. "The Book of Destruction." In *Probing the Limits of Representation: Nazism and the "Final Solution."* Edited by Saul Friedländer. Cambridge: Harvard University Press, 1992.

———, ed. *Holocaust Remembrance: The Shapes of Remembrance.* Cambridge: Blackwell, 1994.

———. "Introduction: Darkness Visible." In *Holocaust Remembrance: The Shapes of Remembrance.* Edited by Geoffrey Hartman. Cambridge: Blackwell, 1994.

———. *The Longest Shadow: In the Aftermath of the Holocaust.* Bloomington: Indiana University Press, 1996.

———. "On Traumatic Knowledge and Literary Studies." *New Literary History* 26 (1995): 537–563.

Hayes, Peter, ed. *Lessons and Legacies: The Meaning of the Holocaust in a Changing World.* Evanston, Ill.: Northwestern University Press, 1991.

———. ed. *Lessons and Legacies: Memory, Memorialization, and Denial.* Evanston, Ill.: Northwestern University Press, vol. III, 1999.

Heinemann, Marlene. *Gender and Destiny: Women Writers and the Holocaust.* Westport, Conn.: Greenwood Press, 1981.

Hirsch, David. *The Deconstruction of Literature: Criticism after Auschwitz.* Hanover, R.I.: Brown University Press, 1991.

Hirsch, Marianne. *Family Frames: Photography, Narrative, and Postmemory.* Cambridge: Harvard University Press, 1997.

———. "Family Pictures: *Maus* and Post-Memory." *Discourse* 15, no. 2 (1992–93): 3–29.

Horowitz, Sara R. "Auto/Biography and Fiction after Auschwitz: Probing the Boundaries of Second-Generation Aesthetics." In *Breaking Crystal: Writing and Memory after Auschwitz.* Edited by Efraim Sicher. Urbana and Chicago: University of Illinois Press, 1998, pp. 276–294.

———. "Gender, Genocide, and Jewish Memory." *Prooftexts* 20, nos. 1–2 (winter/spring 2000): 158–189.

———. "Rethinking Holocaust Testimony: The Making and Unmaking of the Witness." *Cardozo Studies in Law and Literature* 4, no. 1 (spring/summer 1992): 45–68.

———. *Voicing the Void: Muteness and Memory in Holocaust Fiction.* Albany: State University of New York Press, 1997.

Howe, Irving. "Auschwitz and High Mandarin." In *The Critical Point: On Literature and Culture.* New York: Horizon, 1973.

———. "Writing and the Holocaust." In *Writing and the Holocaust.* Edited by Berel Lang. New York: Holmes and Meier, 1988, pp. 175–199.

Huyssen, Andreas. "Monument and Memory in a Postmodern Age." *Yale Journal of Criticism* 6, no. 2 (1993): 249–261.

———. "The Politics of Identification." *New German Critique* 19 (1981): 117–136.

———. *Twilight Memories: Marking Time in a Culture of Amnesia.* New York: Routledge, 1995.

Isser, Edward R. *Stages of Annihilation: Theatrical Representations of the Holocaust.* Teaneck, N.J.: Fairleigh Dickinson University Press, 1997.

Jabès, Edmond. *Le livre des questions.* Paris: Gallimard. "L'imaginaire." 1963–1965.

Katz, Steven T. *The Holocaust in Historical Context.* Vol. 1. New York: Oxford University Press, 1994.

———. *Post-Holocaust Dialogues: Critical Studies in Modern Jewish Thought.* New York: New York University Press, 1983.

Klein, Dennis B. "History versus Fiction." *Dimensions: A Journal of Holocaust Studies* 8, no. 1 (1994): 2.

Köppen, Manuel, ed. *Kunst und Literatur nach Auschwitz.* Berlin: Erich Schmidt Verlag, 1993.

Kremer, S. Lillian. *Witness through the Imagination: Jewish American Holocaust Literature.* Detroit, Mich.: Wayne State University Press, 1989.

———. *Women's Holocaust Writing.* Lincoln: University of Nebraska Press, 1999.

Krystal, Henry. "Integration and Self-Healing in Post-Traumatic States: A Ten-Year Retrospective." In *Psychoanalysis, Culture, and Trauma.* Edited by Cathy Caruth. Special Issue *American Imago* 48 (spring 1991): 93–118.

———, ed. *Massive Psychic Trauma.* New York: International Universities Press, 1968.

LaCapra, Dominick. *History and Criticism.* Ithaca, N.Y.: Cornell University Press, 1985.

———. *History and Memory after Auschwitz.* Ithaca: Cornell University Press, 1998.

———. "Lanzmann's *Shoah:* 'Here There Is No Why.'" *Critical Inquiry* 23 (winter 1997): 231–269.

———. *Representing the Holocaust: History, Theory, Trauma.* Ithaca, N.Y.: Cornell University Press, 1994.

———. "Representing the Holocaust: Reflections on the Historians' Debate." In *Probing the Limits of Representation: Nazism and the "Final Solution."* Edited by Saul Friedländer. Cambridge: Harvard University Press, 1992, pp. 108–127.

Landsberg, Alison. "America, the Holocaust, and the Mass Culture of Memory: Toward a Radical Politics of Empathy." *New German Critique* 71 (spring–summer 1997): 63–86.

Lang, Berel. *Act and Idea in the Nazi Genocide.* Chicago: University of Chicago Press, 1990.

———. "The Representation of Limits." In *Probing the Limits of Representation: Nazism and the "Final Solution."* Edited by Saul Friedländer. Cambridge: Harvard University Press, 1992, pp. 300–317.

———, ed. *Writing and the Holocaust.* New York: Holmes and Meier, 1988.

Langer, Lawrence L. *Admitting the Holocaust.* New York: Oxford University Press, 1995.

———. *The Age of Atrocity: Death in Modern Literature.* Boston: Beacon, 1978.

———. *The Holocaust and the Literary Imagination.* New Haven: Yale University Press, 1975.

———. *Holocaust Testimonies: The Ruins of Memory.* New Haven: Yale University Press, 1991.

———. *Versions of Survival: The Holocaust and the Human Spirit.* Albany: State University of New York Press, 1982.

Lanzmann, Claude. "Holocauste, la représsentation impossible." *Le Monde* (3 March 1994): "Arts et Spectacles," I, VII.

———. "The Obscenity of Understanding: An Evening with Claude Lanzmann." In *Trauma: Explorations in Memory.* Edited by Cathy Caruth. Baltimore, Md.: Johns Hopkins University Press, 1995, 200–220.

Laub, Dori, and Nannette C. Auerhahn, eds. "Knowing and Not Knowing the Holocaust." *Psychoanalytic Inquiry* 5, no. 1 (1985).

———, and Nanette C. Auerhahn. ''Failed Empathy—a Central Theme in the Survivor's Holocaust Experience.'' *Psychoanalytic Psychology* 6, no. 4 (1989): 377–400.

———. ''Truth and Testimony.'' In *Psychoanalysis, Culture and Trauma.* Edited by Cathy Caruth. Special issue of *American Imago* 48, no. 1 (spring 1991): 75–91.

Leak, Andrew N, and George Paizis, eds. *The Holocaust and the Text: Speaking the Unspeakable.* Houndmills, Basingstoke, Hampshire: New York: Macmillan, St. Martin's Press, 2000.

Levinas, Emmanuel. *Totalité et infini.* Amsterdam: Martinus Nijhoff, 1971.

Lewis, Stephen. *Art out of Agony: The Holocaust Theme in Literature, Sculpture and Film.* Montreal: CBC Enterprises, 1984.

Linenthal, Edward T. ''The Boundaries of Memory: The United States Holocaust Memorial Museum.'' *American Quarterly* 46, no. 3 (1994): 406–433.

Lipstadt, Deborah. *Denying the Holocaust.* New York: Free Press, 1993.

Lyotard, Jean-François. ''Discussions, or Phrasing 'after Auschwitz.' '' translated by Georges Van Den Abbeele. In *Auschwitz and after: Race, Culture, and ''the Jewish Question'' in France.* Edited by Lawrence Kritzman, New York: Routledge, 1995, pp. 149–179.

———. *Heidegger and ''the jews.''* Translated by Andreas Michel and Mark Roberts. Minneapolis: University of Minnesota Press, 1990.

Marrus, Michael R. *The Holocaust in History.* New York: Penguin, 1987.

———. ''The Use and Misuse of the Holocaust.'' In *Lessons and Legacies: The Meaning of the Holocaust in a Changing World.* Edited by Peter Hayes. Evanston, Ill.: Northwestern University Press, 1991, pp. 106–119.

Mintz, Alan. *Hurban: Responses to Catastrophe in Hebrew Literature.* New York: Columbia University Press, 1984.

———. ''The Rhetoric of Lamentation and the Representation of Catastrophe.'' *Prooftexts* 2 (1982): 1–17.

Murdoch, Brian. ''Transformation of the Holocaust: Auschwitz in Modern Lyric Poetry.'' *Comparative Literature Studies* 6 (1974): 123–150.

Neher, André. *The Exile of the Word.* Translated by D. Maisel. Philadelphia, Pa.: Jewish Publication Society, 1981.

Novick, Peter. ''Holocaust Memory in America.'' In *The Art of Memory: Holocaust Memorials in History.* Edited by James E. Young. New York: Prestel, 1994, pp. 159–165.

Parmet, Harriet L. *The Terror of Our Days: Four American Poets Respond to the Holocaust.* Bethlehem, Pa.: Lehigh University Press, 2001.

Parry, Ann. ''Idioms for the Unrepresentable: Post-war Fiction and the *Shoah.*'' *Journal of European Studies* 27, no. 4: 417–432.

Patraka, Vivian M. ''Contemporary Drama, Fascism, and the Holocaust.'' *Theatre Journal* 39, no. 1 (March 1987): 65–77.

———. ''Situating History and Difference: The Performance of the Term *Holocaust* in Public Discourse.'' In *Jews and Other Differences: The New Jewish Cultural Studies.* Edited by Daniel Boyarin and Jonathan Boyarin. Minneapolis: University of Minnesota Press, 1997, pp. 54–78.

Patterson, David. *Sun Turned to Darkness: Memory and Recovery in Holocaust Memoir.* Syracuse, N.Y.: Syracuse University Press, 1998.

Peli, Pinhas H. ''In Search of Religious Language for the Holocaust.'' *Conservative Judaism* 32 (1979): 3–24.

Pinsker, Sanford. ''Fictionalizing the Holocaust.'' *Judaism* 29 (1980): 489–496.

Rawson, C. J. ''Cannibalism and Fiction: Reflections on Narrative Forms and 'Extreme Situations.' '' *Genre* 10 (1977): 677–711.

Ringelheim, Joan. ''Thoughts about Women and the Holocaust.'' In *Thinking the Unthinkable: Meanings of the Holocaust.* Edited by Roger S. Gottlieb. New York: Paulist Press, 1990, pp. 141–149.

———. ''The Unethical and the Unspeakable: Women and the Holocaust.'' *Simon Wiesenthal Center Annual* I (1984): 69–87.

———. ''Women and the Holocaust.'' *Signs* 10, no. 4 (1985): 741–761.

Rosen, Norma. ''The Holocaust and the American-Jewish Novelist.'' *Midstream* 20, no. 8 (October 1974): 54–62.

Rosen, Robert S. ''The Holocaust in Theatre and Film.'' *Modern Jewish Studies Annual II* (1978): 84–88.

Rosenberg, Alan, and Gerald E. Myers, eds. *Echoes from the Holocaust: Philosophical Reflections on a Dark Time.* Philadelphia, Pa.: Temple University Press, 1988.

Rosenberg, David. *Testimony: Contemporary Writers Make the Holocaust Personal.* New York: Random House, 1989.

Rosenfeld, Alvin H. ''Another Revisionism: Popular Culture and the Changing Image of the Holocaust.'' In *Bitburg in Moral and Political Perspective.* Edited by Geoffrey Hartman. Bloomington: Indiana University Press, 1986, pp. 90–102.

———. *A Double Dying: Reflections on Holocaust Literature.* Bloomington: Indiana University Press, 1980.

———. ''The Holocaust in American Popular Culture.'' *Midstream* 29, no. 6 (1983): 53–59.

———. *Imagining Hitler.* Bloomington: Indiana University Press, 1985.

———. ''Popularization and Memory: The Case of Anne Frank.'' In *Lessons and Legacies: The Meaning of the Holocaust in a Changing World.* Edited by Peter Hayes. Evanston, Ill.: Northwestern University Press, 1991, pp. 243–278.

Roskies, David G. *Against the Apocalypse: Responses to Catastrophe in Modern Jewish Culture.* Cambridge: Harvard University Press, 1984.

———. ''The Holocaust According to the Literary Critics.'' *Prooftexts* 1 (1981): 209–213.

———. *The Literature of Destruction: Jewish Responses to Catastrophe.* Philadelphia, Pa.: The Jewish Publication Society, 1988.

Rothberg, Michael. *Traumatic Realism: The Demands of Holocaust Representation.* Minneapolis: University of Minnesota Press, 2000.

Rubenstein, Richard. *After Auschwitz: Radical Theology and Contemporary Judaism.* New York: Bobbs-Merrill, 1966.

Samuels, Maurice Anthony. ''Representing the Holocaust: Art Spiegelman's *Maus* and the Postmodern Challenge.'' *Manuscript,* 1990.

Santner, Eric. ''History beyond the Pleasure Principle: Some Thoughts on the Representation of Trauma.'' In *Probing the Limits of Representation: Nazism and the ''Final Solution.''* Edited by Saul Friedländer. Cambridge: Harvard University Press, 1992, 143–154.

———. *Stranded Objects: Mourning, Memory, and Film in Postwar Germany.* Ithaca, N. Y.: Cornell University Press, 1990.

Schumacher, Claude. *Staging the Holocaust: The Shoah in Drama and Performance.* Cambridge: Cambridge University Press, 1998.

Schwarz, Daniel R. *Imagining the Holocaust.* New York: St. Martin's Press, 1999.
Shatzky, Joel. "Creating an Aesthetic for Holocaust Literature." *Studies in American Jewish Literature* 10, no. 1 (1994): 104–114.
Shaviro, Steven. "Complicity and Forgetting." *Modern Language Notes* 105 (1990): 819–832.
Sicher, Efraim, ed. *Breaking the Crystal: Writing and Memory after Auschwitz.* Urbana and Chicago: University of Illinois Press, 1998.
———. "The Holocaust in the Postmodernist Era." In *Breaking Crystal: Writing and Memory after Auschwitz.* Urbana and Chicago: University of Illinois Press, 1998, pp. 297–328.
Skloot, Robert. *The Darkness We Carry: The Drama of the Holocaust.* Madison: University of Wisconsin Press, 1988.
Stavans, Ilan. "The Impact of the Holocaust in Latin America." *The Chronicle of Higher Education* XLVII, no. 37 (25 May 2001): B7–B10.
Steiner, George. *In Bluebeard's Castle.* New York: Atheneum, 1971.
———. *Language and Silence: Essays on Language, Literature, and the Inhuman.* New York: Atheneum, 1967.
———. "The Long Life of Metaphor: An Approach to the '*Shoah.*' " In *Writing and the Holocaust.* Edited by Berel Lang. New York: Holmes and Meier, 1988, pp. 154–71.
Stern, David. "Imagining the Holocaust." *Commentary* (July 1976): 45–51.
Syrkin, Marie. "The Literature of the Holocaust." *Midstream* (May 1964): 3–20.
Tal, Kali. *Worlds of Hurt: Reading the Literatures of Trauma.* New York: Cambridge University Press, 1996.
Todorov, Tzvetan. *Face à l'extrême.* Paris: Seuil, 1991.
———. *Facing the Extreme: Moral Life in the Concentration Camps.* New York: Henry Holt, 1996.
Van Alphen, Ernst. *Caught by History: Holocaust Effects in Contemporary Art, Literature, and Theory.* Stanford, Calif.: Stanford University Press, 1997.
Vice, Sue. *Holocaust Fictions.* New York: Routledge, 2000.
Vidal-Naquet, Pierre. *Assassins of Memory: Essays in the Denial of the Holocaust.* Translated by Jeffrey Mehlman. New York: Columbia University Press, 1992.
Wiesel, Elie. "Art and Culture after the Holocaust." In *Auschwitz: Beginning of a New Era?* Edited by Eva Fleischner. New York: KTAV, 1977.
White, Hayden. *The Content of Form: Narrative Discourse and Historical Representation.* Baltimore, Md.: Johns Hopkins University Press, 1987.
———. "Historical Emplotment and the Problem of Truth." In *Probing the Limits of Representation: Nazism and the "Final Solution."* Edited by Saul Friedländer. Cambridge: Harvard University Press, 1992, pp. 37–53.
———. "The Value of Narrativity in the Representation of Reality." In *On Narrative.* Edited by W. J. T. Mitchell. Chicago: University of Chicago Press, 1981, pp. 1–23.
Yerushalmi, Yosef Hayim. *Zakhor: Jewish History and Jewish Memory.* Seattle: University of Washington Press, 1982.
Young, James E, ed. *The Art of Memory: Holocaust Memorials in History.* New York: Prestel, 1994.
———. "The Arts of Jewish Memory in a Postmodern Age." In *Modernity, Culture and 'the Jew'.* Edited by Bryan Cheyette and Laura Marcus. Stanford, Calif.: Stanford University Press, 1998, 211–225.
———. "Holocaust Documentary Fiction: The Novelist as Eyewitness." In *Writing and the Holocaust.* Edited by Berel Lang. New York: Holmes and Meier, 1988.
———. *The Texture of Memory: Holocaust Memorials and Meaning.* New Haven: Yale University Press, 1993.
———. *Writing and Rewriting the Holocaust: Narrative and the Consequence of Interpretation.* Bloomington: Indiana University Press, 1988.
Yudkin, Leon I. "Narrative Perspectives in Holocaust Literature." In *Hebrew Literature in the Wake of the Holocaust.* London: Associated University Presses, 1993, 13–32.

National and Language Group Bibliographies

American Bibliography

Alter, Robert. "Confronting the Holocaust: Three Israeli Novels." *Commentary* 41 (March 1966).
Berger, Alan. *Crisis and Covenant: The Holocaust in American Jewish Fiction.* Albany: State University of New York Press, 1985.
Budick, Emily Miller. "Acknowledging the Holocaust in Contemporary American Fiction and Criticism." In *Breaking Crystal: Writing and Memory after Auschwitz.* Edited by Efraim Sicher. Chicago: University of Illinois Press, 1998, pp. 160–169.
Kremer, S. Lillian. *Witness through the Imagination: Jewish American Holocaust Literature.* Detroit, Mich.: Wayne State University Press, 1989.
———. *Women's Holocaust Writing.* Lincoln: University of Nebraska Press, 1999.

Austrian Bibliography

Bernstein, Michael André. "Unrepresentable Identities: The Jew in Post-war European Literature." In *Thinking about the Holocaust: After Half a Century.* Edited by Alvin H. Rosenfeld, Bloomington: Indiana University Press, 1997.
Lorenz, Dagmar, ed. *Contemporary Jewish Writing in Austria: An Anthology.* Lincoln: University of Nebraska Press, 1999.

British and Commonwealth Bibliography

Bermant, Chaim *Troubled Eden: An Anatomy of British Jewry.* London: Vallentine Mitchell, 1969.
Brauner, David. *Post-War Jewish Fiction: Ambivalence, Self-Explanation and Transatlantic Connections.* Basingstoke, Hampshire: Palgrave, 2001.
Cheyette, Bryan. *Contemporary Jewish Writing in Britain and Ireland: An Anthology.* Lincoln: University of Nebraska Press, 1998.
Greenstein, Michael. *Third Solitudes: Tradition and Discontinuity in Canadian-Jewish Literature.* Kingston, Ont. McGill-Queen's University Press, 1989.
Hart, Alexander. Writing and the Diaspora: A Bibliography and Critical Commentary on Post-*Shoah* English Language Jewish Fiction in Australia, South Africa and Canada." Ph.D. Diss. University of British Columbia, December 1996.
Sicher, Efraim. *Beyond Marginality: Anglo-Jewish Literature after the Holocaust.* Albany: State University of New York Press, 1985.
———. "Writing after: Literary and Moral Reflections of the Holocaust." *Holocaust Studies Annual* (1991): 147–168.

Dutch Bibliography

Galen Last, Dick van, and Rolf Wolfswinkel. *Anne Frank and after: Dutch Holocaust Literature in Historical Perspective.* Amsterdam: Amsterdam University Press, 1996.

Schogt, Henry. ''Motives and Impediments in Describing War Memories: The Tragedy of the Jews.'' *Canadian Journal of Netherlandic Studies* 11, no. 1 (spring 1990): 3–7.

Taylor, Joyce Vanderwal. *A Family Occupation: Children of the War and the Memory of World War II in Dutch Literature of the 1980s.* Amsterdam: Amsterdam University Press, 1997.

French Bibliography

Astro, Alan, ed. *Discourses of Jewish Identity in Twentieth-Century France.* Special Issue of *Yale French Studies* 85 (1994).

Fine, Ellen S. ''The Absent Memory: The Act of Writing in French Holocaust Literature.'' In *Writing and the Holocaust.* Edited by Berel Lang. New York: Holmes & Meirer, 1988, pp. 41–57.

———. ''New Kinds of Witnesses: French Post-Holocaust Writers.'' *Holocaust Studies Annual: Literature, the Arts and the Holocaust* III (1987): 121–136.

———. ''The Search for Identity: Post-Holocaust French Literature.'' In *Remembering for the Future.* New York: Pergamon, 1989.

Haft, Cynthia. *The Theme of Nazi Concentration Camps in French Literature.* The Hague: Mouton, 1973.

Kritzman, Lawrence D., ed. *Auschwitz and after: Race, Culture, and 'the Jewish Question' in France.* New York: Routledge, 1995.

Marks, Elaine. ''*Cendres juives:* Jews Writing in French 'after Auschwitz.' '' In *Auschwitz and after: Race, Culture, and 'the Jewish Question' in France.* Edited by Lawrence D. Kritzman. New York: Routledge, 1995, pp. 35–46.

Marrus, Michael R., and Robert O. Paxton. *Vichy France and the Jews.* New York: Basic Books, 1981.

Wiedmer, Caroline. *The Claims of Memory: Representations of the Holocaust in Contemporary Germany and France.* Ithaca, N.Y.: Cornell University Press, 1999.

German Bibliography

Bier, Jean-Paul. ''Paradigms and Dilemmas in the Literary Awareness of West Germany, with Regard to the Persecution and Murder of the Jews.'' In *Comprehending the Holocaust Historical and Literary Research.* Edited by Asher Cohen, Joav Gelber, and Charlotte Ward. New York: Peter Lang, 1988.

Cernyak-Spatz, Susan E. *German Holocaust Literature.* New York: Peter Lang, 1985.

Gilman, Sander L., and Jack Zipes. *Yale Companion to Jewish Writing and Thought in German Culture: 1096–1996.* New Haven: Yale University Press, 1997.

Jaspers, Karl. *The Question of German Guilt.* Translated by E. B. Ashton. New York: Dial Press, 1947.

Klüger, Ruth. ''Gibt es ein 'Judenproblem' in der deutsche Nachkriegsliteratur?'' In *Katastrophen. Uber deutsche Literatur.* Gottingen: 1994, 9–38. First published in English under the title: ''A 'Jewish Problem' in German Postwar Fiction.'' *Modern Judaism* 5 (1985): 215–233.

Mason, Ann. ''Nazism and Postwar German Literary Style.'' *Contemporary Literature* 17 (1976): 63–83.

Schlant, Ernestine. *The Language of Silence: West German Literature and the Holocaust,* New York: Routledge, 1999.

Hebrew Bibliography

Ezrahi, Sidra DeKoven. ''Revisioning the Past: The Changing Legacy of the Holocaust in Hebrew Literature.'' *Salmagundi* 68–69 (fall/winter 1985): 245–270.

Feldman, Yael. ''Whose Story Is It, Anyway? Ideology and Psychology in the Representation of the *Shoah* in Israeli Literature.'' In *Probing the Limits of Representation: Nazism and the ''Final Solution.''* Edited by Saul Friedländer. Cambridge: Harvard University Press, 1992, pp. 223–239.

Kohn, Murray J. *The Voice of My Blood Cries Out: The Holocaust as Reflected in Hebrew Poetry.* New York: Shengold Publishers, 1979.

Laor, Dan. ''The Legacy of the Survivors: Holocaust Literature in Israel.'' In *Lessons and Legacies II: Teaching the Holocaust in a Changing World.* Edited by Donald G. Schilling. Evanston, Ill.: Northwestern University Press, 1998, 118–130.

Mintz, Alan. *Hurban: Responses to Catastrophe in Hebrew Literature.* New York: Columbia University Press, 1984.

Morahg, Gilead. ''Breaking Silence: Israel's Fantastic Fiction of the Holocaust.'' In *The Boom in Israeli Fiction.* Edited by Alan Mintz. Hanover, N. H.: University Press of New England, 1997, 49–83.

Ramras-Rauch, Gila. Introduction to *Facing the Holocaust: Selected Israeli Fiction.* Edited by Gila Ramras-Rauch and Joseph Michman-Melkman. Philadelphia: Jewish Publication Society, 1985.

Sicher, Efraim, ed. *Breaking Crystal: Writing and Memory after Auschwitz.* Chicago: University of Illinois Press, 1998.

Yaoz, Hanna. *The Holocaust in Modern Hebrew Poetry.* Tel Aviv: Eked, 1984.

———. ''The Heritage of Trauma—Hebrew Poetry on the Holocaust.'' In *Remembering for the Future: The Impact of the Holocaust on the Contemporary World.* Vol. 2. Oxford: Pergamon Press, 1988, 1643–1647.

———. ''Inherited Fear: Second-Generation Poets and Novelists in Israel.'' Merican Bibliography.

Yudkin, Leon I., ed. *Hebrew Literature in the Wake of the Holocaust.* Teaneck, N.J.: Fairleigh Dickinson University Press, 1993.

Polish Bibliography

Adamczyk-Garbowska, Monika. ''A New Generation of Voices in Polish Holocaust Literature.'' *Prooftexts* 9, no. 3 (September 1989): 273–287.

Contemporary Jewish Writing in Poland. Edited by Antony Polonoky and Monika Adamczyk-Garbowska. Lincoln: University of Nebraska Press, 2001.

Grynberg, Henryk. ''The Holocaust in Polish Literature.'' *Notre Dame English Journal: A Journal of Religion in Literature* 11, no. 2 (April 1979): 115–140.

Levine, Madeline G. ''Polish Literature and the Holocaust.'' *Holocaust Studies Annual: Literature, the Arts, and the Holocaust* 3 (1985): 189–202.

Yiddish Bibliography

Aaron, Frieda W. *Bearing the Unbearable: Yiddish and Polish Poetry in the Ghettos and Concentration Camps.* Albany: State University of New York Press, 1990.

Rosenfeld, Alvin. *A Double Dying: Reflections on Holocaust Literature.* Bloomington: Indiana University Press, 1980.

Roskies, David. *Against the Apocalypse: Responses to Catastrophe in Modern Jewish Culture.* Cambridge: Harvard University Press, 1984.

MARJORIE AGOSÍN

(1955–)

DARRELL B. LOCKHART

MARJORIE AGOSÍN WAS born in Bethesda, Maryland, in 1955 to Chilean parents descended from Europeans who had immigrated to Chile in the early twentieth century. Shortly after her birth, the family moved back to Chile where Agosín spent her youth growing up in Santiago and southern Chile, a region also populated by German refugees, many of whom were Nazis. Agosín attended the Instituto Hebreo (Hebrew Institute) in Santiago, and became proficient in Hebrew in addition to her native Spanish. With the imminent military takeover and rise to power of dictator Augusto Pinochet in the early 1970s, Agosín's parents moved the family back to the United States, where she earned a Ph.D. from Indiana University with a dissertation on Chilean writer María Luisa Bombal (1910–1980). A professor at Wellesley College for over twenty years, Agosín has established a considerable reputation as an academic and creative writer. Her books have garnered numerous awards and won her the praise of many writers, including fellow Chilean exile Isabel Allende. As a political activist who has struggled on behalf of human rights with a special emphasis on women's experience in Latin America, Agosín is an untiring advocate for the Mothers of the Plaza de Mayo in Argentina and the Chilean *arpilleristas*, documenting the often heroic struggle of women against political oppression in the two southern Cone nations under neofascist military governments.

As an author, Agosín began as a poet and concentrates her creative efforts mainly in that genre. Her poems comprise a vast geography of topics and subjects, but in general they reveal a sensibility toward emotion and passion as essential to the human experience, as a means of survival, and ultimately as sources of empowerment. Most recently, Agosín has begun to address the topic of the Jewish experience in Latin America and specifically how that experience has been lived by women. She is the editor of several anthologies of criticism and literature dealing with Latin American Jewish women writers. Agosín's self-identification as a Jewish Latin American woman has been a constant in her work beginning with the collection of poems *Conchalí* (1980), named for the Jewish cemetery in Santiago. In subsequent volumes of poetry she has written poignantly on her relationship to such specifically Jewish-centered themes as the Holocaust, Israel, and Anne Frank. In her volume of short stories, *La felicidad* (Happiness, 1991), she writes more openly and extensively on the Jewish experience in her native Chile. Three of her most recent books—*A Cross and a Star: Memoirs of a Jewish Girl in Chile* (1995), *Always from Somewhere Else: A Memoir of My Chilean Jewish Father* (1998), and *The Alphabet in My Hands: A Writing Life* (1999)—represent the author's attempt to preserve family history and memory. The trilogy, written as memoirs, can be read as pseudonovels combining history, autobiography, anecdote, and visual archive (all contain photographs of Agosín and her family) in a style that is eloquent, intimate, and informative. Marjorie Agosín's contributions to Latin American literature are irrefutably valuable. Her inexhaustible effort to promote women's writing and her particularly feminist articulation of the issues that affect Latin American women in general have made her a prominent figure and earned her a reputation in both academic and nonacademic circles. Her own literature, moreover, constitutes a unique talent in women's writing expressed through her lyrical, feminist, and always engaging voice.

The Holocaust as Influence

Agosín's relation to Holocaust issues is readily apparent in her personal life and in her writing. Many members of her family perished in concentration camps while others managed to escape and find their way to

Chile. The stories in Agosín's trilogy are populated with relatives and survivors who bear tattooed numbers on their arms and bring to Chile memories of Treblinka and Auschwitz. She does not attempt to represent their experience of the *Shoah*; rather, she speaks of these survivors as almost ghostlike figures that, as a young girl, she is not capable of fully understanding. For example, the narrator in *A Cross and a Star* (University of New Mexico Press) states,

> My girlfriend's mother has a tattoo on her arm that is tinted and sometimes can be confused with a faded meadow. She doesn't exert the slightest effort to hide it, and the curious ask her when she had it done, if it was an act of will, of fellowship. She looks at them satisfied with their blessed ignorance. They are for the most part peasants from the farmlands who have never left Chilean territory and for whom the word *Jew* sounds as strange as words like *Treblinka* or *boutique* (pp. 26–27, emphasis in original).

Agosín was indelibly marked by this influence from her youth and it has given her a unique perspective on human suffering that carries over to her concern for all oppressed peoples. In *Always from Somewhere Else* (The Feminist Press) Agosín describes visiting Auschwitz as an adult in 1995. She observes

> There are no flowers or brides in the Auschwitz fields. The voices of the dead children are carried by the winds. Behind the voices there can be heard the steps of guards. They say that this is the most sterile desert on the planet: Auschwitz. Even the name fills me with a perverse tremor. But we are here, and we do not turn away when we pass by the haunted barracks and the empty crematoria, all the places filled with bats and the ashes of dead women and hair that resembles sleepwalking algae (p. 233).

One of the recurring figures in her literature is her great-grandmother Helena Broder. In her most recent volume of poetry, *The Angel of Memory* (Wings Press, 2001), Agosín makes her forebear the central axis of the text as she reconstructs the past from the memory of her great-grandmother, the eponymous angel of memory.

The volume is prefaced by a narrative tracing Broder's memory and history from prewar Vienna to her decision to emigrate to Chile in 1939, and reflecting on the effects of the Holocaust, those who perished, and how it changed everything permanently. These issues are addressed in poems that are painfully intimate in their lyric description of lives absurdly lost, such as "Unpredictable Northern Train" (pp. 37–43), which portrays in chilling detail the emotional detachment of a train conductor whose job it is to deliver Jews to Auschwitz, and "Helena Broder Sobs over Terezin" (pp. 79–81), an ode to the children who died in that concentration camp. The memory of those who perished is always present in the Jewish community of Chile, as is evidenced in the poem "Passover in Chile" (pp. 127–131), in which the poet writes "We name the stars / and repeat the name of those camps / where we also died: / Bergen Belsen, Dachau, Treblinka, / Auschwitz" (p. 129).

Larger Themes

Agosín's texts addressing the anguish of the Holocaust are merely part of a larger program of writing that describes human suffering of all kinds. Her poem "Auschwitz" (*Toward the Splendid City*, Bilingual Press, 1994, p. 86) is an eloquent evocation of the horror suffered there.

> II
> And we were not crying,
> we were not singing:
> we were praying
> with the age-old doubts
> of a people naked
> and heroic in damnation,
> and there we were
> in the gas
> chambers
> in the loneliness
> of petrified, silent
> nights
> and someone stretched out their arms
> into the dark florescence of fear itself (p. 86).

And yet this poem, this experience, is only part of a larger human tragedy, an aspect of which is gendered suffering. In "Naked Girls in the Forests of Barbed Wire" (*An Absence of Shadows*, White Pine Press, 1998, pp. 183–185), Agosín speaks directly of young girls who suffered pain, humiliation, and death in Dachau, Treblinka, and Baden-Baden, drawing a parallel between their suffering and that of the women living during Latin American fascist regimes. In a blurring of eroticism and the relationship between power and pornography, the poetic voice speaks directly to the Nazi guard, both as a lover/protector and a tyrant/torturer. Here Agosín quite eloquently describes the difficult circumstances of gendered objectification suffered by women in concentration camps.

> Streaming into the illusory warmth of the room they come, drift among the sunflowers and the woolen covers, hover over the sheets blessed with sea breezes, invade through the walls, besiege the immense space, erupt through the volcano of tree trunks, the naked Jewish girls from the thick forests of Dachau, Treblinka, Baden-Baden, de-

fenseless Jewish girls coming through the smoky fog. Defenseless before a forest of Aryan serpents slithering over breasts, buttocks. The body of one Jewish girl distilled from the forests of barbed wire (pp. 183–185).

Dear Anne Frank

In Agosín's poetry and narrative, Anne Frank occupies a place of privilege. Agosín does not merely write about Frank; rather, she has sustained a dialogue with her for years, which culminates in her bilingual poetry collection *Dear Anne Frank* (Brandeis University Press, 1994). As with other volumes, *Dear Anne Frank* brings together diverse experiences:

> My dialogue with Anne Frank also raises questions that have to do with the dictatorships of Latin America's extremist right, and particularly that of my native country Chile. . . . The victims of the Holocaust perished in the blue gas chambers, exterminated, deformed beyond recognition. The victims of military dictatorships just disappeared like transfigured, nocturnal ghosts (pp. 9–10).

Agosín transforms Anne Frank into a symbol of memory and the importance of preserving individual and collective memory from generation to generation.

> It began with the banning of your bicycles,
> banning you from going out after eight at night,
> restricting you to only buying goods in certain shops
> for Jews,
> to only walking down certain avenues
> with a gold star between your open, blossoming
> arms (p. 17).

Agosín seeks not to portray Frank as martyr, heroine, or victim, but to discover the girl behind the famous image, addressing her directly and asking her personal questions; she would like Anne Frank to serve as a synecdoche for all those, especially women, who suffer injustices. *Dear Anne Frank* alerts the reader to social injustice, human affliction, and the beauty of the human spirit. This is not to say that the poet glosses over the specifically Jewish experience of the Holocaust, as is clear in the following quote:

> Would it have been possible to take in the Jews,
> the squalid gypsies?
> Was it possible to whisper in their blackened ears
> that even in Amsterdam torn asunder
> someone loved them,
> would rescue them from the chill of death?
> Wasn't it possible to take in all the sick
> who were waiting for misfortune's trains?
> Was it possible to approach with an open heart
> the destitute Jewish children?
> Was it possible to be human?
> Though, yes, it was possible
> to accuse,
> to denounce,
> to banish,
> to terrorize the sick, the crippled,
> to destroy shops,
> smashing windows, fire-bombing.
> It was possible
> to force them to undress,
> with the prophecy of a Star tattooed
> on their breasts (p. 23).

While Agosín acknowledges the strictly Jewish experience, her writings present a broader understanding of the many persecutions that have plagued us. As a response to such agonizing suffering in the world, she seeks to understand what can be learned from it, how to alleviate it, and how to prevent it in the future. Agosín's work is truly unique not only in Latin American literature, but as a presence in English translation as well. She has been an important force in presenting to an English-speaking public the realities of the Latin American Jewish diaspora, a world that often goes unnoticed due to its decentered status within Luso- and Hispano-Catholic societies.

Like many Jewish authors of Latin America, Agosín is just now beginning to receive belated critical attention. Many critics have focused on the author's human rights issues, her poetic style, or the autobiographical elements in her works. Consequently, there is yet little critical appraisal of her writing as it pertains to specifically Jewish topics, and even less with regard to the presence of the Holocaust in her work. Given Agosín's increasing presence and renown, one foresees that this imbalance will soon be corrected.

Bibliography

Primary Sources

Conchalí (*Conchalí Cemetery*). 1980.
Zones of Pain / Las zonas del dolor. 1988.
La felicidad (*Happiness*). 1991, 1993.
Las alfareras (*The Women Potters*). 1994.
Sagrada memoria: reminiscencias de una niña judía en Chile (*A Cross and a Star: Memoirs of a Jewish Girl in Chile*). 1994.
Toward the Splendid City. 1994.
A Cross and a Star: Memoirs of a Jewish Girl in Chile. 1995.
An Absence of Shadows. 1998.
Always from Somewhere Else: A Memoir of My Chilean Jewish Father. 1998.
Dear Anne Frank: Poems. 1998.
El gesto de la ausencia (*The Gesture of Absence*). Compilation of texts from *Las alfareras* and *Sagrada memoria*. 1999.
The Alphabet in My Hands: A Writing Life. 2000.
The Angel of Memory / El angel de la memoria. 2001.

Secondary Sources

Hall, Nancy Abraham. Introduction to *The Alphabet in My Hands: A Writing Life*, by Marjorie Agosín. New Brunswick, N.J.: Rutgers University Press, 2000.

Horan, Elizabeth Rosa. "Agosín, Marjorie." *Jewish Writers of Latin America: A Dictionary*. New York: Garland, 1997, pp. 7–13.

———. Introduction to *Always from Somewhere Else: A Memoir of My Chilean Jewish Father*, by Marjorie Agosín. Translated by Celeste Kostopulos Cooperman. New York: The Feminist Press at the City University of New York, 1998.

Kostopulos-Cooperman, Celeste. Introduction to *A Cross and a Star: Memoirs of a Jewish Girl in Chile*, by Marjorie Agosín. Albuquerque: University of New Mexico Press, 1995.

Lockhart, Darrell B. "Lo judío en la obra de Marjorie Agosín." In *Memorial de una escritura: un acercamiento a la obra de Marjorie Agosín*. Edited by Emma Sepúlveda. Santiago: Cuarto Propio, forthcoming 2002.

ILSE AICHINGER

(1921–)

DAGMAR C. G. LORENZ

ILSE AICHINGER, ONE of the most prominent Austrian post-*Shoah* authors, and her sister Helga were born to the teacher Leopold Aichinger and his wife Bertha (née Kremer), a physician, on 1 November 1921 in Vienna; a third sister died at birth. Aichinger's mother came from a background of assimilated Jews and converts, and although she raised her daughters Catholic she was classified as Jewish according to the 1938 Nuremberg racial laws. She was divorced, and thus exempt from deportation to a concentration camp because she was the sole caregiver of a "half-Aryan" minor. Helga Aichinger escaped to England in 1939, but Ilse stayed in Vienna posing as a young girl to protect her mother. In 1939 she graduated from high school and was consigned to forced labor. She participated in antifascist activities and began writing her novel *Die größere Hoffnung* (1948, *Herod's Children*, 1963). Ilse Aichinger and her mother survived at the periphery of Nazi-dominated Austria, but her grandmother was deported. These traumatic experiences are central to Aichinger's work. Her narrative "Das vierte Tor" (1945, The Fourth Gate) was the first literary text in Austria to thematize the concentration camps. Since she wrote about the Holocaust from the point of view of the victims, Aichinger met with immediate criticism. Her works were held in extremely high regard by a select readership, but they were never popular.

Life after World War II

Soon after the liberation Aichinger visited England and was impressed with the liberal atmosphere of the island nation. In 1947 she enrolled in the University of Vienna Medical School, but writing remained her real interest. A protegée of Hans Weigel, a leading intellectual in postwar Vienna who had returned from his Swiss exile to help rebuild Austrian culture, and the journalists Zeno von Liebl and Elisabeth Löcker, Aichinger launched a successful literary career. The publishing house Bermann-Fischer published *Die größere Hoffnung*, and Aichinger worked as an editor for the Frankfurt publishing house S. Fischer. In 1949 she became the assistant to Inge Scholl, the sister of the executed student resistance fighters Hans and Sophie Scholl, who was instrumental in establishing the Volkshochschule für Gestaltung (Academy for Arts and Design) in Ulm. In 1951, together with the poet and Holocaust survivor Paul Celan, Aichinger made her debut at the gathering of important postwar writers known as the Group 47, where she read her now famous short story "Der Gefesselte" (1951, The Bound Man). As Jews, Aichinger and Celan had been excluded from Nazi culture and their language differed markedly from that of German mainstream writers, most of whom were "denazified" veterans. Aichinger did not join other German writers in calling for a fresh start at point zero. Rather, she positioned herself alongside Jewish and oppositional gentile authors whose legacy the Nazis had distorted or erased. She considered the end of the war not a defeat but an opportunity for the legitimate German language to reemerge.

In 1953 Aichinger married the writer Günter Eich, whose literary career dated back to the interwar years. The couple eventually took up residence in Groß-Gmain close to the German/Austrian border and traveled extensively. They had two children, Mirjam and Clemens. A few years after Günter Eich's death in 1972 Aichinger moved to Frankfurt and later to Vienna, where she lives today. Clemens Eich, who became an acclaimed avant-garde author, died in Vienna in 1998.

Aichinger's literary prizes include the Advancement Prize of the Austrian Federal Ministry for Instruction and Culture and the Prize of the Group 47, the Advancement Prize of the Austrian Federal Ministry for Instruction and Culture (1952), the Immermann-Prize of the City of Düsseldorf (1955), the Literary Award of the City of Bremen (1957), the Literature Prize of the Bavarian Academy of Fine Arts (1961), the Anton Wildgans Prize of Austrian Industry (1968), the Nelly Sachs Prize (1971), the City of Vienna Prize (1971), the Appreciation Prize of the Federal Ministry for Instruction (1974), the Georg Trakl Prize, the Roswitha von Gandersheim Medal and the Austrian State Prize (1979), the Petrarca Prize (1982), the Franz Kafka Prize (1983), the Marie-Luise Kaschnitz Prize (1984), the Europalia-Literary Prize of the EG, the Weilheim Prize (1987), the Great Literary Prize of the Bavarian Academy of Arts (1991), and the Great Austrian State Prize for Literature (1995). She joined the Academy of the Arts in West Berlin in 1956, the PEN-Center of the Federal Republic of Germany in 1957, and, in 1977, the German Academy of Language and Poetry.

Literary Responses to *Shoah* and Post-*Shoah* Trauma: Fiction, Plays, Poetry, and Prose

Aichinger's sensual, finely-chiseled language calls to mind German classical and romantic literature, the Bible, myths, legends, and fairy tales. History and memory are key elements in her work. Through her use of imagery and allusions to previous works of literature she associates the Nazi era with other periods of persecution and situates her generation's experience within a seemingly endless history of suffering and oppression. Her encompassing sense of reality embraces the material world, imagination, poetry, and dreams. King David, the local Viennese hero Augustin, Thomas Edison, and Joan of Arc seem as immediate in her work as the contemporary characters or the ghostlike apparitions of Holocaust victims and perpetrators.

Aichinger's earliest works address the uncertainty experienced under a totalitarian regime. *Die größere Hoffnung* reveals that daily survival under National Socialism necessitated transcending bourgeois ethics and trusting one's own intuitive potential. Her protagonist, Ellen, the daughter of a Jewish mother and a Nazi father, must face the chaos alone. She learns lessons from each new adventure and identifies ever more closely with her Jewish friends. Following the Talmudic precept that it is better to be persecuted than to persecute, she opts to wear the Yellow Star, thus abandoning her privileged status as a "half Aryan." Ellen's fate ties together the novel's loosely connected episodes, all of which reveal through their unexpected turns and epiphanies the horrors of life under National Socialism and the courage of Ellen and her close friends. The novel also depicts the despair of other individuals such as Ellen's grandmother, who commits suicide to avoid deportation, and the separation of family members (Ellen's mother has fled the country). Ellen's loyalty to the victims is a recurring motif in Aichinger's work, for example, in the poem "Widmung" (1961, "Dedication"), "Dreizehn Jahre" (1955, Thirteen Years), and the narrative "Rahel's Kleider" (1975, Rachel's Clothes). Ellen does not resign herself to the role of a victim, but uses her inner strength to resist Nazi ideology by designing a counter-language all her own. With a young person's resilience she meets dangerous situations with resolve—adults often panic or give up the fight. Ellen understands that the denigration of Jewish symbols like the Star of David reflects the depraved state of the Nazi mentality, whereas this practice demoralizes her grandmother and precipitates her suicide. Sensing the deep-seated insecurity of her Nazi father, Ellen even goes so far as to pity the Nazis who, she feels, act out of fear. Until her romantic encounter with an Allied officer, Ellen maintains her autonomy. Only when she subordinates her mission to his does she become vulnerable. Risking her life to do his bidding, she is killed by an exploding shell on the eve of the armistice.

When the Second Republic of Austria was established, the Cold War was well under way. In the 1950s Aichinger took part in a protest against nuclear arms proliferation, but her literary texts became increasingly reserved and cryptic. The poems "Ortsanfang" and "Ortsende" (Corporation Limit) reveal her mistrust toward the presumably rehabilitated Nazi countries, their orderly communities, nicely kept gardens, and the serene countryside. "Seegasse" (Lake Street) evokes the site of a destroyed Viennese Jewish cemetery and suggests parallels between the African American experience and the Jews of Europe, intimating that all is not well with the would-be liberators.

Cognizant of the centuries-old plight of the Jews in Europe, Aichinger explores how members of a minority group may preserve their integrity in times of adversity. Like Ellen in *Die größere Hoffnung*, the protagonist in "Ambros" (Ambros) resists peer pressure. His rejection of the dogma of resurrection calls to mind Jews staunchly upholding their faith and satirizes Christian ideas. Ambros dismisses the latter as unrealistic—he has never seen anyone return from the grave. As a nonviolent man, he senses extreme aggression among the new sectarians (the members of the new cult). Such criticism of doctrine appears in Aichinger's other works as well. "Wiegenfest" (Baptism) parodies the conditioning of an infant exposed to two different-colored cones, ensuring that future perceptions will be formed according to this simplistic binary pattern. "Einunddreißig" (Thirty-One), "In und Grimm" (Out and Raged) and "Jüngste Nacht" (Doomsnight) are overtly blasphemous.

The revelations of the Nazi atrocities and the bombing of Japan produced an apocalyptic mood that was reflected in the Existentialist movement of the late 1940s and early 1950s. The influence of this movement on Aichinger is apparent from her skeptical, even nihilistic, worldview. In "Rede unter dem Galgen" (1949, Speech Under the Gallows) she configures mercy as an anticlimactic experience for a man who is prepared to be executed. The pardoned delinquent could be a Jew or a Nazi. In a pompous monologue reminiscent of Nietzsche's *Zarathustra*, he defies those who condemned him, but the sudden reprieve leaves him disoriented—having to rejoin the human race comes as a shock to him. As in this narrative, Aichinger frequently associates the inability to live a normal life with the male gender, self-discipline, and common sense, and humility with the female gender, suggesting that freedom affects men and women differently. This theme of gender and freedom is found in "Der Gefesselte" (1953, The Bound Man), in which a woman who sets a bound man free realizes, to her shock, that the shackles are a part of the man's identity, which he seeks to reclaim through violence.

In many narratives, including "Zweifel an Balkonen" (1973–1974, Doubts About Balconies), Aichinger exposes the latent ethnocentrism and aggression fostered by patriarchal structures. Private property, even the seemingly innocuous balconies in a rural setting, is associated with claims of territory and status. The narrative "Liebhaber der Westsäulen" (1970, Lovers of the Western Columns) suggests that fascism prevails in the contemporary world after all—whoever does not embrace the tastes and values of the majority, "the merry ones,'" becomes the target of resentment and oppression. The narrator directs disparaging comments at the United States and the USSR, at the youth and body cult formerly propagated by Nazi society and later by the victor nations in which youth and physical fitness were glorified. The Nazis' ambitions are also linked with those of the postwar leaders by an allusion to freeway construction, a reference to the monumental autobahn project conceptualized and undertaken by the Nazis and expanded in the postwar German and Austrian republics.

Concerned that Nazism was but an overture to future disasters, Aichinger viewed the liberation in 1945 with caution. The essay "Aufruf zum Mißtrauen" (1946, Call for Distrust) warned against complacency at a time when internalized fascist paradigms continued to shape the public sphere. In her introduction to *Der Gefesselte* Aichinger notes that poets of her generation were succinct to the point of silence. In her own case, the rejection of Holocaust literature in postwar Germany and Austria was undoubtedly a factor in the increasing abstractness and the periods of silence between her publications. Aichinger addresses the problems of silence and communication in some of her works. The protagonist of "Rahel's Kleider," for example, refuses to communicate for fear of being misunderstood or misinterpreted and explores ways to use language to hide a truth too painful to articulate: the memory of the Holocaust and the tragic certainty about the fate of loved ones.

Rather than interacting with the German readership she distrusted, Aichinger engaged increasingly in a dialogue with the dead. The radio plays of the 1950s and 1960s express her disillusionment with the new materialism in a country seemingly oblivious of its narrow escape from annihilation. To Aichinger, the voices of the dead are more real than her contemporaries and articulate the repressed anguish of the survivors. Other works, notably the prose vignettes "Plätze und Straßen" (1954, Places and Streets) offset the commercial idyllic portrayal of Vienna by naming scenes of atrocities: the depopulated former Jewish quarter, the bombed-out "Philippshof," the burnt-out Gonzagagasse; they parody the bureaucratic language, which subtly exonerates the responsible parties. "Gare maritime" (1972–1973), a play set in a concentration camp-like environment, explores strategies for emotional survival using the example of two puppets of varying shape and substance. Reversing Nazi terminology, according to which Jews were nonhuman, Aichinger's nonhumans embody courage and unselfishness, whereas the "humans" display insensitivity and gratuitous brutality. When the puppets are broken to pieces because they are no longer considered useful, they consider it progress. Similar to the poem "Neuer Bund" (New Covenant), the play suggests that in a society of oppressors the best option is to be considered garbage.

Aichinger's autobiographical texts reveal the close connection between the author's life and her writing. The title of *Kleist, Moos, Fasane* (1987, Kleist, Moss, Pheasants) alludes to three streets in Vienna's third district. The point of departure for the narratives in the volume is the kitchen of the narrator's grandmother, a simple setting epitomizing the Austrian-Jewish symbiosis. The sense of security associated with this environment is irretrievably lost for the narrator as she is coming of age and the pressure of anti-Jewish legislation causes an irreparable rift between past and present. "Vor der langen Zeit" (1964, Before the Long Time) focuses on the events of 1938, the year of the annexation of Austria and the nationwide persecution of Jews during the "Kristallnacht" pogrom. In this novel, Aichinger juxtaposes the narrator's subjective experience with the violence of historical events. Just when the history of assimilation comes to an end and Austria's Jewish society is brutally destroyed, the youthful narrator enjoys life to the fullest. Likewise, for a young girl in "Der 1. September 1939" (1 September 1939), nothing is more important on the day of the German attack on Poland than the most recent movies and her piano and English lessons. Rather than condemning such selfish pleasures, Aichinger emphasizes how necessary play, education, and fun were for survival. "Hilfstelle" (Support Station), written with greater detachment, addresses the issue of forgetting. The narrator finds it hard to believe that there ever was a war or that Jews were deported to concentration camps and killed. However, traces of destruction in the cityscape cause her to remember both the horrors and the support that enabled her to survive. Aichinger emphasizes the importance of a spiritual outlook in order to escape despondency. "Nach der weißen Rose" (After the White Rose) is devoted to yet another source of hope: the anti-Nazi flyers disseminated by the Scholl siblings, a hope that came to fruition through her friendship with Inge Scholl. Aichinger's work reveals the lingering presence of the *Shoah* in the language and culture of contemporary Germany and Austria, and the still unresolved crises of identity and belonging in the post-*Shoah* world.

Bibliography

Primary Sources

"Aufruf zum Mißtrauen" (A Summons to Mistrust). 1946.

Die größere Hoffnung (*Herod's Children*) 1948.

Rede unter dem Galgen (Speech Under the Gallows). 1952.

Der Gefesselte (*The Bound Man and Other Stories*). 1953.

Zu keiner Stunde (*Never at Any Time*). 1957.

"*Knöpfe*" (Buttons) 1961.

Wo ich wohne: Erzählungen, Gedichte, Dialoge (Where I Live: Narratives, Poems, Dialogues). 1963.

Eliza, Eliza: Erzählungen (Eliza, Eliza: Narratives). 1965.

Ilse Aichinger: Selected Short Stories and Dialogues, edited by James C. Allridge. 1969.

Auckland. Hörspiel (Auckland. Radio Play). 1969.

Nachricht vom Tag: Erzählungen (News of the Day: Narratives). 1970.

"Wien 1945" (Vienna 1945). 1970.

Dialoge, Erzählungen, Gedichte (Dialogues, Narratives, Poems). 1971.

Schlechte Wörter (Bad Words). 1976.

Verschenkter Rat: Gedichte (Free Advice. Poems). 1978.

Meine Sprache und ich: Erzählungen (My Language and I). 1978.

Spiegelgeschichte: Erzählungen und Dialoge (Life Story in Retrospect). 1979.

Knöpfe: Hörspiel (Buttons. Radio Play). 1980.

"Sich nicht anpassen lassen" (Refusing to Become Adjusted). 1980.

"Die unmüden Schläfer: Szene aus einem Schauspiel" (The Untired Sleepers. Scene from a Drama). 1980.

(Co-Author) *Die Weisse Rose* (The White Rose). 1982.

"Die Zumutung des Atmens: Zu Franz Kafka" (The Imposition of Breathing: About Franz Kafka). 1983.

Ilse Aichinger: Selected Poetry and Prose, edited by Allen H. Chappel. 1983.

(Co-Author with Vinke Hermann) *Das kurze Leben der Sophie Scholl* (*The Short Life of Sophie Scholl*). 1984.

Kleist, Moos, Fasane: Erinnerungen, Notate, Reden (Kleist, Moss, Pheasant: Memoirs, Notes, Addresses). 1987.

Aufzeichnungen: 1950–1985 (Notes from 1950 to 1985). 1987.

UXB: Poems and Translations, tran. Patricia Dobler. 1991.

(Co-Author with Gert Jonke) *Das Verhalten auf sinkenden Schiffen: Reden zum Erich-Fried-Preis* (How to Behave on Sinking Ships: Speeches of Recipients of the Erich-Fried Prize). 1997.

(Co-Author) *Dem Dichter des Lesens: Gedichte für Paul Hoffmann von Ilse Aichinger bis Zhang Zao* (To the Poet of Reading: Poems for Paul Hoffmann from Ilse Aichinger to Zhang Zao). 1997.

Film und Verhängnis. Blitzlichter auf ein Leben (Film and Fate. Flash Lights on a Life). 2001.

Kurzschlüsse: Wien (Short Circuits: Vienna) 2001.

Secondary Sources

Bartsch, Kurt, and Gerhard Melzer, ed. *Ilse Aichinger*. Graz: Droschl, 1993.

Fried, Erich. "Über Gedichte Ilse Aichingers," *Neue Rundschau* 91 (1981): 25–38.

Hetzer, Tanja. *Kinder Blick auf die Shoah: Formen der Erinnerung bei Ilse Aichinger, Hubert Fichte und Danilo Kiš*. Würzburg: Königshausen & Neumann, 1999.

Kersten, Kurt. *Ein Kinderroman aus der Nazizeit: Ilse Aichinger "Die größere Hoffnung."* Berlin: Aufbau, O.J.

Langer, Lawrence. *The Holocaust and the Literary Imagination*. New Haven: Yale University Press, 1975.

Lorenz, Dagmar C. G. *Ilse Aichinger*. Königstein: Athenäum, 1981.

———. "Alien Homeland: The Second Republic from the Perspective of Austrian Women Authors Aichinger, Bachmann, Haushofer, and Frischmuth." In *Barbara Frischmuth in Contemporary Context*. Edited by Renate Posthofen. Riverside: Ariadne, 1999, pp. 21–37.

———. "Ilse Aichinger (1921–)." In *Women Writers in German-Speaking Countries: A Bio-Bibliographical Critical Sourcebook*. Edited by Elke P. Frederiksen and Elizabeth Ametsbichler. Westport: Greenwood, 1998, pp. 1–11.

———. "Ilse Aichinger (1921–). 'A Summons to Mistrust'; 'Rahel's Clothes'; 'My Father.' " In *Contemporary Jewish Writing in Austria. An Anthology*. Lincoln: University of Nebraska Press, 1999, pp. 159–166.

Moser, Samuel, ed. *Ilse Aichinger. Materialien zu Leben und Werk*. Frankfurt: Fischer, 1990.

———. *Ilse Aichinger: Leben und Werk*. Frankfurt am Main: Fischer, 1995.

Müller, Heidy Margrit, ed. *Verschwiegenes Wortspiel. Kommentare zu en Werken Ilse Aichingers*. Bielefeld: Aisthesis Verlag, 1999.

Pickar, Gertrud Bauer. "Kalte Grotesken. Walser, Aichinger, and Dürrenmatt and the Kafkan Legacy." In *Crossings — Kreuzungen. Festschrift für Helmut Kreuzer*. Columbia: Camden House, 1990, pp. 115–143.

Purdie, Catherine. *"Wenn ihr nicht werdet wie die Kinder": The Significance of the Child in the World-View of Ilse Aichinger*. Frankfurt am Main: P. Lang, 1998.

Reichensperger, Richard. *Die Bergung der Opfer in der Sprache: über Ilse Aichinger, Leben und Werk*. Frankfurt am Main: Fischer, 1991.

Reiter, Andrea. "Ilse Aichinger: The Poetics of Silence." In *Contemporary German Writers, Their Aesthetics and Their Language*. Edited by Arthur Williams, Stuart Parkes, Julian Preece. Bern: Peter Lang, 1996, pp. 209–221.

———. *Narrating the Holocaust*. London: Continuum, 2000.

Thums, Barbara. "Den Ankünften nicht glauben wahr sind die Abschiede." In *Mythos, Gedächtnis und Mystik in der Prosa Ilse Aichingers*. Freiburg: Rombach, 2000.

Weigel, Hans. "Es begann mit Ilse Aichinger." *Protokolle* 1 (1966): 3–8.

Gini Alhadeff

(1951–)

DIANE MATZA

GINI ALHADEFF was born in 1951 in Alexandria, Egypt, to Nora Pinto and Carlo Alhadeff. Raised in Khartoum, Tokyo, and Florence, Italy, she was educated in Harrow, England, and at the Pratt Institute in Brooklyn, New York. Currently Alhadeff divides her time between New York City and Chianti, Italy. In her professional life she has been a translator, journalist, and founder of the literary magazines *Normal* and *XXIst Century*. This eclectic history shapes her writing.

Critical Response to *The Sun at Midday*

As an essayist, Alhadeff has written dozens of articles on topics ranging from design to travel. It is her first book, a family memoir, *The Sun at Midday* (1997), that justifies her inclusion in this work devoted to literary representation of the Holocaust. Baptized a Catholic and unaware of her Jewish heritage until she was twenty, Alhadeff details the recovery of her family's history. Her uncle Nissim's incarceration at Auschwitz is part of this incredible story. Through it, and through her own musings on life and identity, Alhadeff tackles the legacy of the Holocaust with probity and poignance.

Most critics give only a nod to the one long chapter that is Uncle Nissim's first-person account of the Holocaust and to its effect on his niece. Penelope Lively, for example, writing in *The New York Times Book Review*, notes with sensitivity Alhadeff's interest in the big abstract issues—Jewish identity and the Holocaust—but goes on to discuss the book primarily as a fascinating memoir. Another reviewer, Samir Raafat, writing in the *Cairo Times*, offers a more mixed response. As entertainment, the memoir receives high praise. As history, the book is compelling, but Raafat finds the sections on Egypt marred by errors of fact, such as Alhadeff's contention that women could not attend university in Egypt in the 1930s. Perhaps annoyance with Alhadeff's failure to check her relatives' stories provokes Raafat's sharp criticism of the Nissim section, for example, his assertion that amid the "thousands" of extant volumes of Holocaust documents, the Nissim episodes are merely "parochial." Raafat seems unaware that few Sephardic Holocaust stories have been told. Thus, he ignores Alhadeff's most significant contributions to Holocaust literature: the interplay between her uncle's story and her deft exploration of personal identity, and the role Nissim's position as a Sephardic physician played in determining his Holocaust experience.

Content and Style of *The Sun at Midday*

The Sun at Midday, exquisitely written and contemplative, narrates Alhadeff's peripatetic family's long sojourn across the Mediterranean. Bound by a shared identity as Sephardim, the Alhadeffs, Pintos, and Tilches find themselves expelled from Spain, buffeted by history's caprice, centuries of wars, racial politics, and economic upheaval. By no means mere victims of serendipitous events, they nonetheless too often find themselves confronting a world that equates identity and destiny. Their distinctive Sephardic survival lies in the adaptive arts, at which they are masters, though by no means is their escape from the world's deviousness always assured. In this profoundly moral tale that resonates with dislocations, Alhadeff places at the very center of her book her uncle Nissim's Holocaust experience. She finds lessons everywhere—in history, in the details of everyday life, in the individual struggle for hope—and weaves them into a nonlinear but vigorously articulated narrative that rejects any ready-made identity. *The Sun at Midday* is a post-Holocaust meditation on the nature of one's freedom to be anything or anyone one wants to be.

In this memoir, which links the freedom to create the self with a freer, looser narrative structure, Alhadeff repeatedly doubles back to ideas she has mentioned in earlier chapters, showing how these ideas become modified over time. In less skilled hands Alhadeff's frequent shifts among locales, time periods, and individual voices might seem jarring and fragmentary. The memoir interweaves Alhadeff's own story with the stories of her ancestors—tales of an immutable tension between self-creation and the obligations of family, history, and ideology. Yet the quirky narrative achieves a dazzling thematic unity. At its heart lies the truth of Sephardic life, the inevitable fluctuation between prominence and abasement, welcome and rejection.

Alhadeff takes the reader from Sicily to Andalusia to the Ottoman Empire of Sultan Mehmet II, who welcomes the exiled Jews. Here "the first remembered ancestor, Hadji Bohour, known as H. B., was born in Rhodes in 1783 and died in Jerusalem in 1880" (*The Sun at Midday*, New York: Pantheon Books, 1997, p. 77). We meet briefly the Alhadeffs whose business at one time controlled "90 percent of the economy of Rhodes, the export of cotton, sesame, and figs" (p. 82) but was decimated by the fascist racial laws promulgated in 1938. Most of the Alhadeffs moved to the cosmopolitan Jewish community of Alexandria, where they remained until Nasser's nationalist policies forced their ouster in 1956.

For much of this history, they remained Jews, but if the world of the Sephardim prior to 1943 had been quixotic, it was then shaken apart by a colossal randomness. The Holocaust injected a finality into the already hazardous world of Jewish identity.

The Sun at Midday describes how, during World War II, zones of occupation determined life and death for Jews. When the Germans entered Salonika, in northern Greece, they met no resistance from the population, which was unaware of Nazi intentions; 97 percent of Salonika's Jews perished in the camps and crematoria. In Athens, however, the Italian occupiers ignored the racial laws; many Jews survived in hiding after the Germans arrived, aided by their Greek compatriots. The Alhadeffs' fortunes are part of this story. In Rhodes, a Greek island off the coast of Turkey, where the Alhadeffs were living, Italian protection served the Jews until Germans overran the island and in one day deported nearly all the Jewish inhabitants.

Alhadeff's memoir recounts how, through a mix of self-assertion and formidable luck, Jacques Alhadeff—Carlo and Nissim's eldest brother—acquires a Turkish passport and escapes the roundup that destroys the Rhodian Jewish community. When the Germans realize their mistake, it is too late. No second deportation boat ever docks in Rhodes. However, in Rome, Nissim quickly falls prey to the Nazis' intensified manhunt, instituted after General Badoglio signs an armistice with the Allies. Amazingly, some Sephardim escape entrapment altogether. Among them is Gini Alhadeff's mother. Living in Alexandria, under British occupation, she avoids listening to the news so as to preserve the illusion that the war does not exist at all. The conflation of luck and survival punctuates the narrative. Years after the war has ended the power of fortune still resonates. As Alhadeff's cousin Pierre, the elegant Sephardic convert to the priesthood, announces: "Still, we are here . . . with our coffee, and wine, and *here*—we are very lucky, if you think what happened to millions of people" (p. 47).

What is the aftermath of the war for the Alhadeffs? One response is that of Carlo, Gini's father. He defiantly converts his family to Christianity as protection from Jewry's subjection to antisemitic violence, although in truth he merely trades one house of worship he does not attend for another. Although such a conversion is clearly ironic to readers attuned to the antisemitic history of the church, Carlo acts expediently; analysis of church doctrine plays no role in his decision. Unlike her father, Gini Alhadeff chooses not to deny the past but to recover it. She becomes passionately engaged with her Sephardic history, though her primary strategy is to offer impressions rather than probe for explanations. This may explain her silence on the issue of Christian antisemitism and its role in Nazi behavior, despite the fact that the Holocaust haunts the memoir, shaping Gini Alhadeff's reflections on identity and her narrative choices.

Alhadeff on Identity

Alhadeff issues a resounding challenge to anyone's authority but her own to say who she is. When she discovers her own Jewish history, she enters a synagogue to test whether she might feel a mystical connection to Judaism. She experiences none, but this is oddly fitting for a baptized Catholic whose only deeply rooted connection to Christianity appears to be the recollection of a few hymns. Theology itself, Christian or Jewish, has made little impression on her, a fact that undoubtedly contributes to her idiosyncratic view of religion: it is "merely a question of aesthetics—music and architecture—on one hand, and method on the other" (p. 12). Even heritage and culture have a tenuous hold on her: "What does our past—his [her father's] and mine—have to do with our present? Why should I care about a little island in the Aegean from which he was after all cast off? Why should I have the disadvantages of attachment and roots when I and he have not had their advantages" (p. 13)? Resolutely, she disclaims any single allegiance: "I want no family, no religion, no country, no self I have to answer to, please, conform to, die for" (p. 14). At the same time, however, she has glanced into the mirror, seen she is a Jew, and become committed to exploring her Jewish history.

Paradoxically, the lessons of history make Alhadeff insist on a profound personal freedom to define the self, which she repeats again and again in the memoir's first hundred pages. To be a Jew, then, is to accept contradiction. Alhadeff makes her Jewishness public by writing this memoir, but her most fervent statements of belief highlight a universalist consciousness. Note how firmly Alhadeff argues that any but the truly protean self is dangerous: take any "sense of being different, and of being superior," she says,

> though by a fraction only, add the matter of territory and you have a bloody war. What need is there to witness the killing? Every ritual, religious service, baptism, initiation, in the sweetest of peace times, is a killing, by the saying of what a person is, and isn't, a refutation of what others are, and aren't—the point where violence begins (p. 52).

History's challenge to an idealized autonomous self appears again as Alhadeff ends her discussion of her father's religious conversion. Here, she asserts with a flourish, "As for race, [her father] knew as well as anyone that there is no converting either to or from it" (p. 101).

Nissim's Story

Because few Sephardic memoirs of the Holocaust have been published, Alhadeff's choice not to mediate this story but to allow her uncle to speak for himself is a brilliant move. At once, she valorizes Nissim's individuality and implicitly refutes the Nazi power to dehumanize its victims.

In 1943 Nissim Alhadeff is living in Rome, where he has just completed his medical training. When the Nazi trap tightens, he has some early success in finding shelter. However, his hostility to religious ritual leads him to abandon the safe haven of the Vatican for a more perilous hiding place, and he is caught.

Nissim's fate during the Holocaust is clearly linked to his idiosyncratic identity as an unobservant Sephardic Jew, a physician, a speaker of many languages, a man with memories of the love and discipline of his past. When he works in the mines at Iavishovitz, his medical assistance to a civilian worker buys him some limited protection. Months later, toward the end of the war, on the long death march that takes him through Buchenwald and Dachau, he rouses himself from a deepening lethargy to devise a plausible lie about a medical errand; thus, he manages to secure a sleeping place for himself and a friend and saves his own life: "Still, we are here . . . we are very lucky" (p. 47).

Though many Sephardim experienced a disorienting isolation from their fellow Jews in the camps because they did not speak Yiddish, Nissim does not seem to have been affected in this way. He speaks of knowing several other Sephardic Jews, and his knowledge of French and a little German dramatically alters his fate. At the end of the war, his French friends use Nissim's oddly non-Jewish-sounding patronymic to get him transferred to the far less perilous Russian section of the camp. Again, his life is saved.

There is a remarkable lack of sentimentality in Nissim's chronicles of the grueling details of day-to-day reality. These are set against glimpses of the camp inmates' proud and sensitive interiors—Nissim's own struggles with his conscience, Enriquez's attempts at humor, another Salonikan's "desperate courage"—each one a stunning example of deeply rooted humanity. Here is the evidence that the Nazis did not fully erase their victims' sense of who they were before the Holocaust.

Nissim is a master storyteller. He enriches his tale with many personal recollections. One is his quiet act of defiance when he first enters Auschwitz. Afraid, even panicked, he nonetheless blunts his pen and cracks his watchcase just before he adds them to the camp collection boxes. As descriptive as such incidents are of Nissim's singular spirit, his story is about much more than one man's agonizing experience. Nissim is a keen observer of other inmates, the camp hierarchy, and the structure and organization of the camps. Though he is never in Monowitz or Birkenau, he meets prisoners from these camps and reports their testimony. In the section on Iavoshovitz, Nissim shows that in this small labor camp twenty minutes from Auschwitz, inmates worked grueling hours in the mines, but death was not the only release for men too weak to continue. Nissim tells the story of a Salonikan Jew who devised an amazing survival strategy. He "put one finger on the railway track and waited for the little wagon loaded with stones to run over it," convinced the overseer he had had an accident, and spent thirty days in the infirmary. Much later, when the Americans liberate the camp, Nissim again shows he possesses the consciousness of a witness. He tours the inside of the crematoria to understand the details of operation. It is as if he is already aware that his personal testimony will have a public forum.

Nissim's tale ends with the arrival of the Americans. His explication of the meaning of this event—"A new star rose, bringing hope, perhaps peace and well-being to this old world racked by insane passions" (p. 147)—matches the cautious optimism that is also the hallmark of his niece's sensibility. Combining personal reflection, rich historical detail about a group whose Holocaust experience remains little examined, and thoughtful examination of the most troubling moral questions of our time, *The Sun at Midday* is a very worthy addition to the literature of the Holocaust.

Bibliography

Primary Sources

"Art by Fiat." *Vogue*, June 1985.
"Teaching an Old Castle New Tricks." *Vogue*, June 1985.
"Style and Seduction." *The New York Times Magazine*, 25 August 1985.
"The Designer and the Readymade." *I.D.*, May 1993.
"Pamela Dennis: A Young Talent Keeps It Simple in New Jersey." *Architectural Digest*, October 1994.
"Under the Volcanoes." *The New York Times Magazine*, 14 August 1994.
"Hudson River Anthology: Playing with Periods and Historical Allusions." *Architectural Digest*, July 1994.
"In Milan with Donatella Versace." *Architectural Digest*, January 1994.
"Jules Fisher: The Lighting Designer's New York Spot." *Architectural Digest*, November 1995.
"Versace's Home Style." *Architectural Digest*, February 1995.
The Sun at Midday. 1997.
"Apulia, The Far Side of Italy." *Travel and Leisure*, July 1996.
"Corfu, Island of White Light." *Travel and Leisure*, July 1997.
"House of Kieselstein-cord: A Manhattan Residence and Private Showroom for the Style Innovator." *Architectural Digest*, July 1998.
"New York Geometries: Pilar Crespi Infuses Her East Side Apartment with Color and Pattern." *Architectural Digest*, March 1998.
"Robert Couturier." *Architectural Digest*, September 2000.
"Benetton in South America: The Argentine Estancias of the Italian Fashion Giant." *Architectural Digest*, May 2000.
"Palazzo Perfecto." *Elle USA*, 2001.

Secondary Sources

Angel, Rabbi Marc. *The Jews of Rhodes: The History of a Sephardic Community*. New York: Sepher-Hermon Press and Union of Sephardic Congregations, 1980.
Gaon, Solomon, and Mitchell Serels. *Sephardim and the Holocaust*. New York: J. E. Safra Institute of Sephardic Studies, Yeshiva University, 1987.
Hizkia, Franco M. *The Jewish Martyrs of Rhodes and Cos*. New York: Harper Collins, 1994.
Levy, Jack Isaac. *Jewish Rhodes, A Lost Culture*. Berkeley, Calif.: Judah L. Magnes Museum, 1989.
Levy, Rebecca Amato. *I Remember Rhodes*. New York: Sepher-Hermon Press for Sephardic House at Congregation Shearith Israel, 1987.
Roth, Cecil. "Last Days of Jewish Salonica: What Happened to a 450 Year Old Civilization." *Commentary* 10, no. 1 (July 1950): 49–55.
Stavroulakis, Nicholas. *Salonika, Jews and Dervishes*. Athens: Talos Press, 1993.

Reviews of *The Sun at Midday*

Kakutani, Michiko. "*The Sun at Midday*: Colorful Family Made For Memoirs." *New York Times*, March 7, 1997. http://www.stolaf.edu/people/leming/soc265rel/news/Mar 7.html#A2067.html.
Lively, Penelope. "A Citizen of the World," *New York Times*, April 13, 1997. http://www.nytimes.com/books/97/04/13/reviews/990413.13livelyt.html.
Raafat, Samir. " 'The Sun at Midday': Another Memoir of a Jewish Family from Alexandria," *Cairo Times*, April 18, 1997. http://www.egy.com/judaica/97–04–18.shtml.

Gila Almagor

(1939–)

NAOMI B. SOKOLOFF

An acclaimed Israeli writer, Gila Almagor is the author of two bestselling works of fiction that deal with Holocaust survivors in Israel. *Hakayits shel Aviya* (*The Summer of Aviya*, 1985) and *'Ets hadomim tafus* (*Under the Domim Tree*, 1992) contributed significantly to a transformation of Israeli attitudes toward the Holocaust that took place in the 1980s and 1990s. During those years an intense new attention to the second generation emerged in literature and film, popular song, documentaries, and school curricula. This interest was accompanied by a new empathy for survivors and a new degree of identification with their experiences. *The Summer of Aviya*, which focuses on a little girl whose mother is a survivor, helped pioneer this phenomenon as it gained prominence in several cultural arenas. It appeared first as a novel geared to young readers and then as a one-act play, performed by Almagor, that was attended by both adults and children. A film version that achieved international fame appeared in 1989. In it Almagor stars as the mother, and she also provides voice-over narration to convey the words of the daughter who, as a grown-up, recounts the story of her childhood. Crossing genre boundaries, this work also crossed generational boundaries and reached audiences of many ages. *Under the Domim Tree* further explores the experience of Holocaust survivors in Israel. It focuses on young refugees from Hitler's Europe as they build a new life for themselves in a youth village. This novel, too, became a highly successful film, which was released in 1994.

Almagor's work helped foster a reorientation in Israeli thinking about the Holocaust. This shift in awareness, which entailed greater identification with the Jewish past and with a history of persecution and victimization, marked a striking change from earlier eras when Israelis defined themselves in opposition to Diaspora Jews. In the formative years of the 1940s and 1950s, intent on nation building, the young state of Israel set about constructing a new proud, militarily strong society, and Israelis conceived of themselves as a new breed who would be unlike the victimized Jews of the past. The Diaspora Jew, in this worldview, was associated with shameful passivity and weakness, in contrast to the ideal of valiant toughness embodied in the so-called new Hebrews or sabras. Israeli literature and films of this era often depicted refugees through the lens of the sabra; the new arrivals were viewed as unfortunates in need of rescue, new names, new homes, and new training so that they might become pioneers and soldiers in the Israeli mold. Over time this distance and sense of opposition between sabras and survivors lessened. In the 1980s a burst of new literary and other cultural activity focused on the Holocaust and showed a new receptivity to the survivor's own stories, told from their perspectives or in sympathy with their experiences.

The Summer of Aviya

The Summer of Aviya takes place in 1953. Aviya, the protagonist, is nine turning ten, and she has been living at an agricultural boarding school. Her mother, Henya, suffers bouts of mental illness, but when she is well enough to leave the psychiatric hospital she brings Aviya home for a summer. In the following months the little girl oscillates between joy and heartbreak as she tries to forge a relationship with her emotionally fragile mother. Though loving, Henya has been traumatized by her experiences during the Holocaust and is by turns anxious, overprotective, and neglectful. Seeing her suffering, Aviya takes on responsibility for her in a painful inversion of parent-child roles. Aviya is also eager to learn more about the family secrets. She is especially curious about her father, whom she never met because he died before her birth. She knows that her name is a memorial to him (it means "her father"), and she hungers to understand her special bond with him.

In addition to this psychological portrait of the second generation, a portrait that bears similarities to second-generation accounts from across national boundaries, Almagor paints a picture of the particular Israeli social milieu in which Aviya lives. The sabras in the town view survivors with contempt and refer to her mother as "that crazy partisan." Other children torment and exclude Aviya. Vulnerable to their taunts, the little girl yearns to embrace an alternative, more glorious and heroic version of her family history. She cherishes the story her aunt has told her: that her mother was a legendary figure of the resistance in Poland and was known there for both her bravery and her beauty. When some newcomers to town, themselves refugees, reinforce this image, Aviya intertwines the little information she has with her dream of learning about her father. Building up her hopes and her desire to make her family whole again, she imagines that one of the new neighbors is in fact her father, separated by war from her mother and unable to reveal his identity because he now has a new family. As this fantasy crumbles and the mother's health deteriorates, Aviya returns to the boarding school. The summer has provided a brief reprieve from her usual routine, during this time she has gained respect for her mother, and she has forged a deeper sense of connection to the past, but she has also suffered dashed hopes and made a painful reckoning with the realities of loss, illness, and death.

Under the Domim Tree

Following Aviya into adolescence, *Under the Domim Tree* ostensibly offers a sequel to *The Summer of Aviya*. This novel, too, is conceived as Aviya's memoirs and explores her troubled relationship with her parents. However, significant inconsistencies separate the first story from the second. One is a temporal discrepancy. Though Aviya is some years older and is now in high school, the year is still 1953. Furthermore, her mother is not a Holocaust survivor in *Under the Domim Tree*. This novel, then, is less a sequel than a re-imagining of the Aviya character and her relationships with her family and with Holocaust survivors. In this tale Aviya lives in a youth village, her mother remains hospitalized, and Aviya yearns for her father. She seeks information about where he is buried, and when she finally discovers his grave in Haifa, she not only finds solace in locating the site, but establishes a compelling sense of communion with him by visiting there.

Aviya's classmates at the youth village share with her a hunger for parental love and a need to clearly understand their connections with the past. Many of them are survivors and war orphans. The novel is set during an era of great public furor over reparations from Germany, and the resulting debates give occasion for the youngsters to delve into their memories of the Holocaust. As Aviya's discovery of her father's grave unfolds, so does the story of a girl named Yola, who discovers that her father, amazingly, has not died but has survived the war and is living in Poland. This wondrous turn of events rivets the attention of all the young people, who are eager to participate in her happiness and want to believe that they, too, could experience such a miracle. When Yola's father dies, tragically, before she can visit him, all of the children are heartbroken. Yet another variation on the theme of orphanhood is the story of Mira, who has run away from cruel and abusive adoptive parents. They are survivors who claimed her, after the war, as their daughter. She insists they are not her real parents and resists their demand for renewed custody of her. Ultimately, in a dramatic courtroom scene, she recovers memories of a long-forgotten past and so wins her freedom. Remembering the color of her mother's eyes, Mira then also recalls her true family name and the other members of her family; she reclaims her authentic roots, and in doing so she persuades the judge to let her return to the youth village with her friends. Like her classmates, Mira struggles to establish her sense of who she is and her right to be herself. Recognizing and holding onto her past is key to her success. All the youngsters accept one another in this quest, and even the most bereft find a new home together. The ones most haunted by their past are two boys who spent the war wandering in the forests. At night they run wild and howl like wolves; by day they adjust to their new environment. Banding together and refusing to be separated, they serve as substitute family for one another and are welcomed into the community.

Under the Domim Tree is a celebration of Youth Aliyah, the Zionist efforts to save Jewish children from Hitler and to absorb them into Israeli life. Often such children were placed in youth villages, agricultural schools, and kibbutzim. Earlier Hebrew literature that dealt with this theme emphasized the goal of redeeming young people and bringing them from death to rebirth by transforming them into Israelis according to the sabra ideal. Almagor introduces a vital new element to this familiar tale of Zionist rescue as she emphasizes the experiences, memories, and perceptions of survivors. Respecting the integrity of their past even as it celebrates their ability to support one another, *Under the Domim Tree* affirms their individuality. The significance of the title is that the tree on the hill is a place to find solitude within communal life. This is where the youngsters go for contemplation, to be alone with private feelings, and to cry. Here is hallowed ground for personal memory. Such sentiments are ordinarily kept under control in the group, but they are cast, by the author, as something to be treasured. Delving into dimensions of survivor experience once overlooked in Israeli literature and film, the touching stories of *Under the Domim Tree* present a more nuanced picture of Israel in its early days.

The relationship of this artistic material to Almagor's own life is a complicated one. *The Summer of Aviya* was promoted as autobiographical fiction. In fact, though, Almagor was not a child of survivors. She did grow up with a mother who suffered mental illness, and her father died before she was born. In addition she had firsthand experience living in a youth village, and she has written warmly and appreciatively about that institution in the introduction to the English translation of *Under the Domim Tree*. In *The Summer of Aviya*, Almagor thus grafted autobiographical elements onto a story of the second generation. Some critics saw that choice as an attempt to gain sympathy. This critical response provides an interesting measure of how much attitudes changed in Israel since the period portrayed in the fiction. In the 1950s, Aviya finds it shameful and isolating to have a mother who is a survivor. Yet, in the 1980s Almagor's adoption of the Holocaust survivor into her plot is seen as a bid for popularity. It is certain that, as Almagor overlays the collective experience onto her own, she creatively mines her personal feelings of orphanhood, loss, and exclusion to explore the experience of the second generation with great sensitivity. *Under the Domim Tree* then presents an artistic reconfiguration of this material that not only extends the sympathetic treatment of survivors but also offers tribute to the child from a troubled family who, through personal tragedy, also suffers a great sense of loss and displacement.

Almagor was born in Israel in 1939 and found her calling in theater at an early age. She joined the company of Habima National Theater at seventeen, later performed with the Kameri Theater, and then spent several years studying acting in New York. She has appeared in over fifty films and is the recipient of numerous awards, including an Israeli Oscar for Lifetime Achievement in Israeli Cinema and a range of international prizes. Her books have become required reading in Israeli secondary schools and have been translated into many languages, including Danish, Dutch, French, German, Hindi, Italian, Russian, and Spanish, as well as English. *Under the Domim Tree* won a National Jewish Book Award in the United States after it appeared in translation in 1995.

Bibliography

Primary Sources

Hakayits shel Aviya (*The Summer of Aviya*). 1985.
'Ets hadomim tafus (*Under the Domim Tree*). 1992.

Secondary Sources

Avisar, Ilan. "Personal Fears and National Nightmares: The Holocaust Complex in Israeli Cinema." In *Breaking Crystal: Writing and Memory after Auschwitz*. Edited by Ephraim Sicher. Urbana: University of Illinois Press, 1998, pp. 137–159.

Geertz, Nurit. "The Others in Israeli Cinema of the 1940s and 1950s: Holocaust Survivors, Women, and Arabs." In *Israeli and Palestinian Identities in History and Literature*. Edited by Kamal Abdel-Malek and David C. Jacobson. New York: St. Martin's Press, 1999, pp. 35–62.

Sokoloff, Naomi. "Voices of Children in Literature: Fiction by David Grossman and Gila Almagor." In *Multiple Lenses, Multiple Images: Perspectives on the Child Across Time, Space and Disciplines*. Edited by Hillel Goelman, Sheila Marshall, and Sally Ross. Forthcoming.

JENNY ALONI

(1917–1993)

HARTMUT STEINECKE

JENNY ROSENBAUM WAS born in Paderborn, Germany, on 7 September 1917, the daughter of Henriette and Moritz Rosenbaum. Turning to Zionism as early as 1933, she prepared herself in 1935 and 1936 for emigration to Palestine in a Hachshara camp of Youth Aliya Gut Winkel, near Berlin. Out of concern for her parents, she remained for several more years in Berlin and completed her studies in the last authorized Jewish high school at the beginning of 1939.

At the end of 1939 she left Germany with a group of children in her charge. Palestine was no land of exile for her, but her homeland, "Eretz Israel." In 1942 she broke off her studies at the Hebrew University in Jerusalem, joined the Auxiliary Troop Service (ATS) of the British army in Palestine, and worked in hospitals, mainly in Sarafand. During the war she heard on occasion of the mass murders of the Jews in Europe. Only after the war did she find out that many members of her family had died, among them her parents and her sister, in Theresienstadt and Auschwitz. In 1948 she married Ezra Aloni (Erich Eichengruen). The couple lived in Jerusalem and in Ganei Yehuda, near Tel Aviv, where Jenny died on 9 September 1993.

From her early youth onward Jenny Rosenbaum wrote poems, stories, and plays, and in the 1940s and 1950s she published a few texts in German and Hebrew. In 1960 and 1961 her first story and novel appeared in Germany. The majority of Aloni's literary compositions are set in her new home, Israel. Many of her works mirror the course of the country from the time of the mandate, the founding, the growth, and the problems of the State of Israel.

Accounts to a Later Generation

After a short time in Palestine, Aloni also took on the self-imposed literary task of giving "an account to a later generation" of what she had seen and experienced in Germany, telling of her experiences as a Jewess in a series of works, predominantly stories. She describes a crime in her home town in 1932, which the Nazis labeled as a Jewish ritual murder, and the consequent poisoning of human relationships (Brown Parcels). She writes about the ways in which a Jewish schoolgirl was excluded by former classmates and friends shortly after the Nazi takeover in 1933 (The Torch Parade, The Synagogue and the Cathedral) and about the pogrom night (the *Kristallnacht*) in Berlin and Paderborn in November 1938. A look into the diaries (to be published in 2002) that Jenny Rosenbaum Aloni wrote from 1935 on shows the intensive processing of her own experiences. On the day before the pogrom of 1938 she notes with foresight: "Will there be a tomorrow, and if so, how will it look? . . . In order to experience what history means, one has to be a Jew." The story "Crystal and Alsation" shows the change of an idyllic picture of a November day to a sinister and threatening atmosphere. After the night when "the synagogues were burning" ("Kristall und Schäferhurd," Collected Works [*CW*] vol. 6, Paderborn, Schöningh, 1995, p. 202) the narrator walks through the familiar streets, watches the plundering of a Jewish shop, sees the passive attitude of police and passersby, and hears the slogans full of hatred. Looks and gestures are the firm signs of exclusion, followed by verbal and overt attacks, the enthusiastic participation and the indifferent or embarrassed "looking on" or "looking away"—all these moments are captured in her writing. "They were not the same streets anymore. And not the same people. Now they were only painted scenes in a play and legions of enraptured eyes in the estranged faces of puppets. I walked and walked" (p. 207). In a few paragraphs the narrative sketches the road from calmness and peacefulness to estrangement and alienation, and, with this as a backdrop, then goes on to describe the destruction of the family house and the deportation of father and uncle to Buchenwald. At the same time—in a merging of documentary, fact, and cleverly chosen symbols—her writing marks a break with previous existence and the prediction of the loss of the country where she was born and where she grew up and of the extermination camps of the Holocaust.

In a series of other stories, she mirrors her actual visits in postwar Germany, meetings with survivors from concentration camps, but predominantly with perpetrators and followers of the Nazi regime. Here she finds concealment, suppression, excuses, but never an admission of guilt. She herself, however, enters a state of self-accusation, "that I should have survived, where others died, were shot, beaten to death, gassed, starved. . . . Millions of others, only not I. . . . Why I of all people?" (*CW* vol. 9, p. 41)

Aloni seldom writes realistically, naming places and objects directly. Sometimes the versions of her manuscripts show how she takes back concrete description and either naively de-familiarizes it or leaves it out altogether. In 1947, as part of an Israeli delegation, she visited southern Germany and Dachau in order to help displaced persons, particularly children, emigrate to Israel. From this visit came the short story manuscript "Visit in Dachau," which in the published version is titled "Visit 1947." The layout of a camp is described in pictures of a chamber and ovens; the reader understands the reality that these are death chambers. Such literary techniques have their basis in the conviction that giving names to things cannot explain what happened in the Holocaust, and that literature, if it dares to touch this subject, must make the reader part of the responsibility and trust him or her to fill in the empty spaces.

Holocaust as Nightmare and Trauma

In one of her most impressive short stories, "Two Inscriptions," Aloni shows two worlds colliding with each other. The principle of duality shows itself in the construction of the whole and in sentences without links between subjects and predicates or without verbs: "Christian convent, Jewish orphanage" (*Zwei Inschriften*, *CW* vol. 6, p. 249). Even the inscriptions on both buildings in the story are the same—"Love thy neighbor as thyself"—but they are written in German and Hebrew. Only gradually we learn as we read the story of the deportation of Jewish children, which is watched by the concealed occupants of the nearby convent without any reaction on their part.

The story is characteristic of the manner in which Jenny Aloni deals with the Holocaust itself. Very seldom does she depict aspects of the Holocaust directly, as she does in the fate of a Jewish woman and her mentally retarded daughter in a concentration camp (The Glass Bell), or in a story caused by the trial in Israel against Adolf Eichmann, the Nazi responsible for carrying out the extermination of European Jews (The Meeting). Yet the Holocaust is present in many of her stories and novels as story and personal experience, as nightmare and trauma, because the experiences of deportation, selection, life in the camps, and murder are part of the lives of many people in the Israel of the 1950s and 1960s. However, as a result of the political reality in Israel of those years, most of the survivors concealed their memories, because they were reproached for their political naivite, passivity, or even collaboration. Therefore the fates of Holocaust victims are often related in fragments or in dreamlike sequences. The "contemporary witnesses" who were embarrassed by the hidden concentration camp numbers on their arms usually begin to speak only when they are naively and stubbornly questioned by a young person. This is the way in which the Holocaust is developed, in a long, tormenting dialogue, in the novel *Der Wartesaal* (The Waiting Room, 1969) that relates "the truth about this number, which cannot be described and not imagined, only experienced" (*CW* vol. 5, p. 92). When the first horror pictures emerge, the concepts of the "unutterable" and "indescribable" are picked out once more as the central theme and the dialogue is broken off because "nobody believes it. It is more comfortable to deny it." Nevertheless, the blue numbers remain as "indestructable symbols" (p. 92).

While Aloni wrote in a more traditional style until the mid-1960s, the dominant factor in her later works is the conciseness, the direct confrontation of irreconcilable differences, the alienated abstraction, which force the reader to think. By these means, she finds her own way and stands apart from the dominant German and Israeli Holocaust discourses of her time.

A Voice of the Young German-Speaking Literature of Israel

In the 1960s Jenny Aloni became known as a distinctive voice of the young German-speaking literature of Israel but was then mostly forgotten. The publication of her *Collected Works* in 1990–1997 led to her rediscovery. She received literatary prizes and shortly before her death was designated as the "most important literary personality writing in German in Israel" (Schardt). Since the completion of her collected works she is also becoming better known internationally.

Bibliography

Primary Sources

Gedichte (poems). 1956.

Zypressen zerbrechen nicht. Roman (Cypresses Do Not Break: Novel). 1961.

Jenseits der Wüste. Erzählungen (The Other Side of the Desert: Stories). 1963.

Der blühende Busch. Roman (The Blossoming Bush: Novel). 1964.

Die silbernen Vögel. Erzählungen (The Silver Birds: Stories). 1967.

Der Wartesaal (The Waiting Room). 1969.

In den schmalen Stunden der Nacht. Gedichte (In the Thin Hours of the Night: Poems). 1980.

Die braunen Pakete (The Brown Parcels). 1983.

Selected Shorter Works

Ausgewählte Werke 1939–1986 (Selected Works). Edited by Friedrich Kienecker und Hartmut Steinecke, 1987.

"Ich möchte auf Dauer in keinem anderen Land leben." Ein israelisches Lesebuch 1939–1993 ("I do not want to live in the long run in a different country." An Israeli Reader 1939–1993). Edited by Hartmut Steinecke, 2000, 155–163.

". . . man müßte einer späteren Generation Bericht geben." Ein literarisches Lesebuch zur deutsch-jüdischen Geschichte (". . . One should give an Account to a later Generation." A Literary Reader to German-Jewish History). Edited by Hartmut Steinecke, 1995, 131–165.

Gesammelte Werke (Collected Works [CW]). Edited by Friedrich Kienecker und Hartmut Steinecke, 10 vols., 1990–1997.

Secondary Sources

Pazi, Margarita. "Jenny Aloni, eine deutschschreibende, israelische Autorin." In *Ausgewählte Werke*, pp. 162–173.

Schardt, Michael M. "Späte Ehre: die Schriftstellerin Jenny Aloni. Literaturpreise und eine Werkausgabe." *Neue Zürcher Zeitung*, 9 July 1993.

Steinecke, Hartmut. "Jenny Aloni." *KLG. Kritisches Lexikon zur deutschsprachigen Gegenwartsliteratur*. Edited by Heinz Ludwig Arnold. München: edition text + kritik, 55. Nachlieferung März 1997.

———. "1990. Jenny Aloni's *Das Brachland* is published as volume 1 of her *Gesammelte Werke in Einzelausgaben*." *Yale Companion to Jewish Writing and Thought in German Culture 1096–1996*. Edited by Sander L. Gilman and Jack Zipes. New Haven, Conn.: Yale University Press, 1997, pp. 820–826.

———. "Jenny Aloni. Ich muß mir diese Zeit von der Seele schreiben." *H. S.: Gewandelte Wirklichkeit—verändertes Schreiben? Zur neuesten deutschen Literatur: Gespräche, Werke, Porträts.* Oldenburg, Germany: Igel 1999, S. 155–171.

———, ed. *"Warum immer Vergangenheit?" Leben und Werk Jenny Alonis (1917–1993).* Münster, Germany: Ardey, 1999.

Interviews

Interview by Cornelia Gottschalk and Klaus Müller-Salget. In *Gessamelte Werke* 10, 135–148.

Interview by Hartmut Steinecke. In *Gessamelte Werke* 10, 149–157.

Jean Améry
(1912–1978)

D. G. MYERS

Jean Améry was a Jewish victim of the Nazis whose entire career was devoted to exploring and resisting the notions of *Jew* and *victim*. Although he rejected the advances of those who wished him to become a professional survivor, he equally scorned those who might deny that his Auschwitz number was "a basic formula of Jewish existence" or that the Holocaust is "the existential reference point for all Jews." An autobiographical and philosophical essayist whose texts are notoriously intransigent—hard to categorize, even harder to cherish—Améry wrote only one slim volume on the Holocaust. *At the Mind's Limits* (1980) is one of the central texts, however, on Jewish victimhood.

Life

Améry was born Hans Maier in Vienna on 31 October 1912. As a boy he made his home in his parents' native Hohenems, a small resort city in the state of Vorarlberg, in the alpine provinces of western Austria. The family had been settled there since the seventeenth century. His great-grandfather, a Vorarlberg innkeeper and butcher, "spoke fluent Hebrew," according to Améry. By the time of Améry's birth, however, the Hebrew fluency had disappeared; the family was estranged from its Jewish origins, assimilated and intermarried. Améry's father was more Austrian than Jewish. "The picture of him did not show me a bearded sage," Améry said, "but rather a Tyrolean Imperial Rifleman in the First World War." The father died in battle, in 1916, when his son was too young to remember him. Améry's mother, who supported her only child and herself by keeping an inn, was Roman Catholic. "Several times a day she invoked Jesus, Mary, and Joseph," he says, "which sounded in our native dialect like 'Jessamarandjosef.' "

Améry was educated in philosophy and literature in Vienna. He was studying there when the Nazis came to power in Germany in 1933. At once he immersed himself in the canonical writings of antisemitism and National Socialism; thus began, he said, "an entirely impossible *éducation sentimentale* for a young Jew. . . ." Coupled with the political situation in Austria, this reading deeply complicated Améry's thinking about being Jewish. "I wanted by all means to be an anti-Nazi, that most certainly," he explains, "but of my own accord; I was not yet ready to take Jewish destiny upon myself. . . . I really found myself in a confusing state of mind: I was an Austrian who had been raised as a Christian, and yet I was not one." For the first time Améry began to understand himself as an outsider to the culture in which he lived. The decisive event was the promulgation, in 1935, of the Nuremberg Laws. Améry soon came to know the text of the laws by heart. "The overwhelming majority not only of the German people but also of my own Austrian people," he realized, "had excluded me from their community." But it did not follow that there was a place for him in the organized Jewish community. Orthodox Judaism was "another, thoroughly alien world." It was rather Christianity that drew him, because to be a Christian "means *participation* in our culture" (his emphasis). Judaism left Améry bored; "the synagogue was the Other." Over time, however, he became increasingly convinced that his intellect and "spiritual constitution" were Jewish—"not in the sense of upbringing or milieu," he says, "which in my case were as un-Jewish as possible, but by birth." This essentialist conviction, which he did not flinch at being described as racist, influenced his self-understanding for the rest of his life.

After the *Anschluss* (German invasion of Austria) in March 1938, Améry fled first to France and then, upon its defeat by the Germans in May 1941, to Belgium. There he joined the Resistance, although he later acknowledged that this was merely the last unconscious attempt to evade his Jewish identity. "The Jews were hunted, cornered, arrested, deported *because they were Jews*," he writes, underlining every word, "and only because of that. Looking back, it appears to me that I didn't want to be detained by the enemy as a Jew but rather as a resistance member." In due course—in July 1943—he was arrested by the Gestapo for spreading anti-Nazi propaganda among the German occupation forces in Belgium. Améry believed he knew what was in store for him. He was widely read in the already substantial literature of the concentration camps. Whatever happened to him, he believed, would have merely to be "incorporated into the relevant literature, as it were." But nothing could prepare him for the experience of torture. Imprisoned in Fort Breendonk, Améry was interrogated by the SS for several days. His hands were shackled behind him, and he was suspended by his wrists from a hook in the ceiling ("there was a crackling and splintering in my shoulders that my body has not forgotten until this hour. . . . I fell into a void and now hung by my dislocated arms, which had been torn high from behind and were now twisted over my head"). Then he was beaten with a horsewhip. Although he told the Gestapo nothing useful, it was not because of heroic opposition. He confessed everything—he even invented political crimes—but he knew only the aliases of his comrades in the Resistance and had no real information to divulge. Once they realized he was useless to them—once they realized he was a Jew and not just a political prisoner—the Gestapo shipped him off to Auschwitz.

Auschwitz and Beyond

Améry endured a year in Auschwitz III, the Buna-Monowitz labor camp. Lacking a manual skill, he was assigned to a labor detail at the I-G Farben site, digging dirt, laying cables, lugging sacks of cement and iron crossbeams. He survived—somehow. Unlike his fellow Auschwitz inmate Viktor E. Frankl (author of *Fein Psychologerlebt des Konzentrationslager*) Améry refused to derive theory from his survival. Many years later he agreed that the "religiously or politically committed" (Orthodox Jews, orthodox Marxists) had a better chance of surviving, or at least of dying with more dignity. They were able to look beyond the basic reality of Auschwitz. For them the horrors were weakened by being reinterpreted as a renewal of creation when evil was released into the world, or as natural political martyrdom. They had, in other words, a *mode of transcendence* that was anchored to a reality that the Nazis could not reach, because it existed in faith. "[W]hoever is, in the broadest sense, a believing person, whether his belief be metaphysical or bound to concrete reality, transcends himself," Améry says. "He is not the captive of his individuality; rather he is part of a spiritual continuity that is interrupted nowhere, not even in Auschwitz." Améry was, however, an unbeliever from first to last. He had nothing but himself to fall back upon. He was an intellectual. But confronted by a reality that could not be interpreted as anything other than horror, he found that intellect had lost its fundamental quality of transcendence. There was no other reality to which a mere intellectual could appeal. The claim of Auschwitz was total.

Améry was evacuated first to Buchenwald and then to Bergen-Belsen ahead of the advancing Red Army, and it was at Belsen that he was liberated in April 1945. Returning to Brussels, he passed the rest of his life outside the cultural mainstream. When he began to write for the German-language press of Alemannic Switzerland, he chose a "French-sounding pen name," a translation of Hans into French and an anagram for a common variant of his surname. The pseudonym signified his rejection of German culture, his identification with the French; yet Améry continued to write in German. Even so, he refused to travel to Germany for two decades after the war. Only in 1964, at the urging of the German poet Helmut Heissenbüttel, who worked for the South German Broadcasting Corporation, did Améry finally break his silence in Germany, delivering a radio address on the intellectual in Auschwitz. It became the opening essay in *Jenseits von Schuld und Sühne* (Beyond Guilt and Atonement), his first and only Auschwitz book, which followed in 1966. Translated by Sidney and Stella P. Rosenfeld as *At the Mind's Limits*, the book was published in English in 1980.

Journalist

By 1966 Améry had published five collections of journalism: *Karrieren und Köpfe* (Careers and Heads: Portraits of Famous Contemporaries, 1955), *Teenager-Stars* (Teenager Stars: The Idols of Our Time, 1960), *Im Banne des Jazz* (Under the Spell of Jazz, 1961), *Geburt der Gegenwart* (*Preface to the Future: Culture in a Consumer Society*, 1961), and a study of Gerhart Hauptmann, "the eternal German" (1963). He estimated that he had published some 15,000 pages before he undertook *At the Mind's Limits*. Only then did his literary career—his "entry into German literature," as he preferred to say—really begin. The Auschwitz book changed everything; he was fifty-four and at last had found the literary identity he had been seeking since adolescence. Although the book did not make him very much money, at least it made him famous. Suddenly he was in demand; he was invited to contribute essays, to deliver radio talks, to join conferences and symposia. "I have the suspicion," he said later, "that I merely struck a chord that began to vibrate just at a time when it was still fashionable to occupy oneself with the fate of the Nazi victims, and that [by the late seventies], when my friends on the Left are representing Israel as a universal plague and everyone's sympathies are focused on the Palestinian resistance fighters, I couldn't tempt a soul with this book."

At the Mind's Limits released him from "the drudgery of writing articles." Améry could afford at last to take his time and to worry a subject—to write the things that were weighing upon him. The public, however, wanted to hear nothing else from him except more about victimhood. Améry was resistant. His new-found status was a "market phenomenon, hostile to the intellect"; and as such, it was a threat to him. He never again wrote at any length about Auschwitz. His next book, *Über das Altern* (*On Aging*, 1994) was published three years later—in 1969. Two years after that came *Unmeisterliche Wanderjahre* (Lean Journeyman Years, 1971). This chronological account of Améry's intellectual development left a gaping hole at its center. It said nothing whatever about the years of the Holocaust. (It has never been translated into English.) Améry describes these "slim volumes" as an "autobiographical trilogy," but they are not autobiography in any conventional sense. They omit "everything private and anecdotal." Améry does not tell stories about himself, but accepts his own pressing concerns as occasions for reflection and, to permit him his own emphasis, he "*subjectively* explore[s]" rather than objectively records his experience. He starts from the concrete event, but does not become lost in it. His later books are, in the words he used to describe *At the Mind's Limits*, "personal confession refracted through meditation." He found his literary voice at last, in his fifties, and his "personal and intellectual life . . . became a contemplative essay." Two novels followed: *Lefeu oder der Abbruch* (Lefeu, or the Demolition, 1974) and *Charles Bovary, Landarzt* (Charles Bovary, Country Doctor, 1978). His philosophical inquiry on suicide, *Hand an Sich Legen*, was published in 1976. Two years later, on 17 October 1978, Améry took his own life in Salzburg and was buried in the Zentralfriedhof in Vienna.

At the Mind's Limits

At the Mind's Limits is neither a systematic nor a chronological treatment of Améry's experience in the Holocaust. The hundred-page book consists of five essays, arranged in the order of their composition. They are held together not by careful organization but by a common theme, which Améry describes as "the subjective state of the victim." The title essay explores the fate of the mind in Auschwitz. "Torture" reaches back to narrate what Améry had undergone at Fort Breendonk. "How Much Home Does a Person Need?" takes a further step back to detail the psychic experience of the refugee. "Resentments" moves forward to take up the interior life of the victim after the Holocaust. "On the Necessity and Impossibility of Being a Jew" offers Améry's conclusions on Jewish identity after a lifetime of being forced to confront the question.

Améry's principal contribution to understanding the Holocaust is his concept of *losing trust in the world.* Perhaps better than any other Holocaust writer, Améry shows that the liberal pillars upon which Western civilization rests are not dug very deep; they are merely taken for granted. Political freedom and human dignity are measured by what is possible and humanly acceptable; they are temporary and hastily constructed social arrangements that disappear at the first blow aimed at a prisoner. "[W]e can live," Améry says, "only if we grant our fellow man life, ease his suffering, bridle the desire of our ego to expand." In the material security of our daily lives, we are unaware just how much we trust others to grant us life, and if not to ease our suffering at least not to cause it. But the victim of torture, the survivor of Auschwitz, has lost that trust forever. "Whoever was tortured, stays tortured," Améry concludes. He is indelibly burned with the knowledge that trust in the world—the trust that no one will lay hands on you—is astonishingly fragile, and can be lost at any moment. He knows something that they do not teach you in schools: that the Other can be absolute, and can exercise this absolute power by inflicting suffering.

For Améry, then, the Holocaust is central to human self-understanding because it represents not an accidental function of the Nazi regime, but its essence. Améry would have liked to "introduce certain Auschwitz books into the upper classes of secondary school as compulsory reading," because these books would introduce students to an idea that is indispensable to any humanistic curriculum in a post-Holocaust era—the idea of the victim, the "dead man on leave." If dignity is the right to live granted by society, then the Third Reich demonstrates how easily the grant can be revoked. Améry is not particularly interested in the perpetrators of the Holocaust. "The crimes of National Socialism had no moral quality for the doer," Améry explains. "The monster, who is not chained by his conscience to his deed, sees it from his viewpoint only as an objectification of his will, not as a moral event." Améry's literary ambition in *At the Mind's Limits* was to speak from the viewpoint of the victim, for whom National Socialism had a moral quality. He seeks to understand suffering from the inside rather than extorting pity and special consideration for victims.

Améry thus stands as a challenge to the increasingly common view, of which the historian Peter Novick is merely one representative, that the Holocaust encourages contemporary Jews to adopt a "victim identity based on the Holocaust," a "fashionable victimhood" that is exploitative and phony (see *The Holocaust in American Life*, pp. 190–202). While Améry certainly agrees that the existence of the Jews has been forever determined by the Holocaust, *At the Mind's Limits* does not celebrate victimization. Instead, the book engages in a fundamental redefinition of victimhood. To be a victim is no longer to be the *object* of other people's designs. In the sort of post-Holocaust thinking practiced by Améry, the Jewish victim makes himself the *subject* of his own history.

"Whoever attempts to be a Jew in my way and under the conditions imposed upon me," Améry says, "whoever hopes, by clarifying his own Holocaust-determined existence, to draw together and shape within himself the reality of the so-called Jewish Question, is wholly void of naïveté." *Wholly void of naiveté* because such a Jew is no longer lulled by "[d]eclarations of human rights, democratic constitutions, the free world and the free press." He no longer dwells in the illusion that human identity is something optional, like a Christmas gift that can be exchanged. He has learned that his identity—his personhood—is a *necessity*. "I . . . am precisely what I am not," Améry says, "because I did not exist until I became it, above all else: a Jew." "I became a person," Améry explains, "not by subjectively appealing to my abstract humanity but by discovering myself within the given social reality as a rebelling Jew and by realizing myself as one." Note the emphasis on *rebelling*: he is a Jew who grasps but also rebels against the social declaration that to be a Jew is to be sentenced to death. Another name for this sentence was *Auschwitz*. Thus Améry's "phenomenological description of the existence of the victim," as he calls it in the preface to the first edition, is the exact opposite of the exploitation of victimhood. If the Jews now see their existence as having been determined by the Holocaust it is not that they have not adopted a "fashionable victimhood," but rather that they have become the necessary subject of their own drama. "Without the feeling of belonging to the threatened," Améry says, "I would be a self-surrendering fugitive from reality."

Although not halakhically a Jew, Améry insists nevertheless that being Jewish is a necessity for him. It is also an impossibility precisely because he is not halakhically Jewish; not, that is, a Jew as a member of a community. "With Jews as Jews I share practically nothing," he writes: "no language, no cultural tradition, no childhood memories." Perhaps then a "catastrophe Jew" rather than a halakhic Jew, or a "non-non-Jew": lacking faith in the God of Israel, lacking Yiddish or Hebrew, lacking the Jewish tradition, he is a Jew because he learned under the Nazis that he is not permitted to be anything else. To be a Jew and a victim—to be a Jewish victim—is to live without "positive determinants." Unlike most men and women, Améry was willing to live this way, because he was willing to see his thought through to the end.

According to Améry, the Holocaust assumed importance only later—a generation after the liberation of the camps—because the Jewish victims of the Nazis "were forced to relinquish" any sense of victory in the defeat of Germany. The rehabilitation of the nation that had been the Third Reich outstripped the rehabilitation of its victims. By the sixties, when he began at last to speak publicly on the camps, the world reaction to Germany and Israel made the discrepancy even more evident to Améry. While Germany had been rejoined to Europe, normalized and eventually to be reunited, Israel remained a pariah nation. The Holocaust was a wound that had not been healed.

Améry occupied an "uncomfortable position between all of the parties," which suited his personality but made him difficult to rely upon. Readers on the Left were disgusted by his criticism of their side (he broke with the New Left over its support for terrorism and its sneering condemnation of Israel) while readers on the Right quite naturally understood him to be a subversive figure. Not that this disturbed Améry overmuch. To be a good writer, he believed, one must become independent of "all external signs of success." Starting with *At the Mind's Limits*, all of his books venture into the "closed world" of suffering. Améry declines to offer "cheap consolation" or to find a redemptive message in suffering. His approach instead is unsparing, relentlessly bleak; "disconsoling," to use his word. And indeed it's difficult to know why anyone at all reads them—except perhaps to face the truth.

Bibliography

Primary Sources

Karrieren und Köpfe: Bildnisse Berühmter Zeitgenossen (Careers and Heads: Portraits of Celebrities). 1955.

Teenager-Stars: Idole Unserer Zeit (Teenager Stars: Idols of Our Time). 1960.

Im Banne Des Jazz: Bildnisse Grosser Jazz-Musiker (Under the Spell of Jazz: Portraits of Great Jazz Musicians). 1961.

Geburt der Gegenwart: Gestalten und Gestaltungen der Westlicen Zivilisation Seit Kriegsende (Preface to the Future: Culture in a Consumer Society). 1961, 1964.

Gerhart Hauptmann: Der Ewige Deutsche (Gerhart Hauptmann: The Eternal German). 1963.

Jenseits Von Schuld Und Sühne: Bewältigungsversuche Eines Überwältigen (*At the Mind's Limits: Contemplations by a Survivor of Auschwitz and Its Realities*). 1966, 1984.

Über das Altern: Revolte Und Resignation (*On Aging: Revolt and Resignation*). 1968, 1994.

Unmeisterliche Wanderjahre (Lean Journeymen Years). 1971.

Lefeu Oder Der Abbruch (Lefeu, or the Demolition). 1974.

Hand an Sich Legen (*On Suicide: A Discourse on Voluntary Death*). 1976, 1999.

Charles Bovary, Landarzt (Charles Bovary, Country Doctor). 1978.

Bücher Aus Der Jugend Unseres Jahrhunderts (Books from Our Century's Youth). 1981.

Radical Humanism: Selected Essays. 1984.

Der Integrale Humanismus: Zwischen Philosophie Und Literatur. Aufsätze Und Kritiken Eines Lesers, 1966–1978 (The Integral Humanism: Between Philosophy and Literature, Essays and Reviews 1966–1978). 1985.

Jean Amery, der Grenzganger: Gesprach mit Ingo Hermann in der Reihe "Zeugen des Jahrhunderts" (Jean Amery, the Border-crosser: Interview with Ingo Hermann in the series "Witnesses of the Century"). 1992.

Cinema: Arbeiten Zum Film (Cinema: Works on Film). 1994.

Secondary Sources

Cinanni, Maria Teresa. *Testimoni di voci sommerse: l'esperienza del nazismo in alcuni scrittori ebrei europei: Joseph Roth, Primo Levi, Jean Améry, Miklos Radnoti*. Cosenza: Periferia, 1997.

Coquio, Catherine. "La Fin a l'infini: Le Temoignage inacheve de Jean Amery." *Op. Cit.: Revue de Litteratures Francaise et Comparee* 12 (1999): 197–215.

Fiero, Petra. "The Body in Pain: Jean Amery's Reflections on Torture." *Publications of the Missouri Philological Association* 18 (1993): 26–32.

Goodheart, Eugene. "The Passion of Reason: Reflections on Primo Levi and Jean Améry." *Dissent* 41 (1994): 518–527.

Heidelberger-Leonard, Irene. *Über Jean Amery*. Heidelberg: Winter, 1990.

Lorenz-Lindemann, Karin. "Wieviel Heimat braucht der Mensch? Aspects of Jewish Self-Determination in the Works of Jean Amery and Primo Levi." In *The Jewish Self-Portrait in European and American Literature*. Edited by Hans-Jurgen Schrader, Elliott M. Simon, and Charlotte Wardi. Tubingen: Niemeyer, 1996, pp. 223–230.

Mavridis, Thomas. " 'Wer der Folter erlag, kann nicht mehr heimisch werden in der Welt': Vom verlorenen Weltvertrauen Jean Amerys." *Fussnoten zur Literatur* 38 (1996): 70–79.

Neiman, Susan. "Jean Améry Takes His Life." In *Yale Companion to Jewish Writing and Thought in German Culture, 1096–1996*. Edited by Sander L. Gilman and Jack Zipes. New Haven: Yale University Press, 1997, pp. 775–784.

Schneider, Gerd K. "Die Verwandlung oder der Altersprozess als Entfremdung bei Jean Amery." *Modern Austrian Literature* 28 (1995): 111–125.

Sebald, W. G. "Mit den Augen des Nachtvogels: Über Jean Améry." *Etudes Germaniques* 43 (1988): 313–327.

Steiner, Stephan. *Jean Amery (Hans Maier): mit einem biographischen Bildessay und einer Bibliographie*. Basel: Strömfeld/Nexus, 1996.

Stone, Dan. "Homes Without Heimats? Jean Amery at the Limits." *Angelaki* 2 (1995): 91–100.

Tagliacozzo, Franca. "Memoria e catarsi: Didattica della storia dopo Auschwitz." *Rassegna Mensile di Israel* 63 (1997): 107–120.

YEHUDAH AMICHAI

(1924–2000)

HANOCH GUY

YEHUDAH AMICHAI WAS born in 1924 in Wurtzburg, Germany, to Jewish orthodox parents. He was educated in religious schools, where he learned Hebrew. In 1936 his family relocated, first living in Petach Tikvah, Israel, and then in Jerusalem. During World War II, Amichai volunteered for the Jewish Brigade of the British army and served for four years in the Middle East. In the late 1940s, a time when the British authorities had forbidden the acquisition of arms by the Jewish community and set a strict quota for Jewish immigrants, he smuggled arms and illegal newcomers into the land of Israel. After his discharge from the British army he was certified as a teacher and taught for fifteen years. While Amichai does not bear the scars of the Holocaust, he nevertheless knows of the experience of displacement, exile, and reconstituted identity as mapped by departure from the Diaspora for life in Israel, signified by changing his original surname of Pfeuffer to Amichai, meaning "My people lives." The poet served in the Israeli army during the 1948 war of independence and encountered bitter fighting against the Egyptian army in southern Israel. He also fought in the Sinai campaign. In 1949 he studied literature and the Bible at the Hebrew University of Jerusalem. Amichai published his first poetry book in 1955 and has since published 12 volumes of poetry, a collection of one-act plays, short stories, and a novel. He died in 2000.

Overview

According to Glenda Abramson, Amichai began to read modern English poetry in the late 1940s and was particularly influenced by W. H. Auden. This influence appears to have affected Amichai's departure from ornate Hebrew poetry in favor of contemporary Hebrew, including the colloquial (Abramson, 1989, p. 13). Following the publication of his first collection in 1955, Amichai's poems became the battlefield between the old guard and the new among Israeli poets. He commented that his split fate willed him to be planted in two generations. Surprising and abundant imagery drawn from traditional Hebrew sources as well as colloquial Israeli Hebrew irritated critics but delighted his readers. He became the most popular poet in Israel. Eulogizing him, the author Meir Shalev said that "He allowed every day Hebrew to walk in the palaces of poetry" and the speaker of the Israeli Knesset called him: "The foundation stone of Israeliness." Yehudah Amichai is the most widely translated Israeli poet, having been translated into twenty-nine languages. The main themes in Amichai's poetry are love, war, and Jerusalem. The *Shoah* is a minor theme and sometimes appears in conjunction with the main themes. Altogether there are twenty-seven poems that specifically mention the *Shoah* or people who died in it. Out of the twenty-seven, seventeen are from his last book, *Open Closed Open* (1998), which indicates an increased interest in the subject. Amichai received numerous literary awards including the Shlonsky award (1957), the Brenner award (1969), the Bialik award (1976), the State of Israel award for literature (1982), and the Agnon award (1986). He was elected as an honorary foreign member of the American Academy of Arts and Sciences in 1987.

How Do You Preserve Memory?

Although Amichai was not born in Israel but immigrated there at the age of twelve, he shares the attitude of his Israeli-born contemporaries who de-emphasized the Holocaust and tried to suppress its memory. This generation concentrated their energies on fighting for and building the State of Israel. Their suppression also stemmed from guilt and disappointment—believing they did not do enough to save Jews—and from the inability to cope with the horrors (Abramson, 1989, pp. 148–149). This suppression contrasts the Jewish injunction to remember the commandments and the freedom from slavery. "The verb Zakhor [remember] appears in its various declensions in the Bible no less than one hundred and sixty nine times" (Yerushalmi, p. 5). Throughout Jewish history the injunction to remember has shifted from different traumatic events, the culmination of which is the *Shoah*. *Zakhor* became the imperative word that compelled Jews to commemorate the Holocaust.

Amichai explores the remembrance and forgetfulness of his generation in *Open Closed Open*. In one poem he writes: "We keep forgetting where we came from. Our Jewish names, / From the Diaspora unmask us, evoke memories . . ." (Abramson, *Yehudah Amichai: A Life of Poetry*, p. 193). Amichai refers to the name-changing custom of immigrants to Israel, marked by the donning of Hebrew names. In another poem he acknowledges that his generation also remembered:

> Now, two generations of forgetting have passed
> and the first generation of remembrance has come. Woe to us that we have
> already come to remember
> because memories are the hard shell over an empty heart (*Open Closed Open* Harcourt, 2000, p. 63).

The tension between forgetting and remembering is evident in a poem about Israel's independence day in Amichai's book *Hazman* (Time, 1977): "Let us not talk about the famous six millions. / We will talk about the eleven millions that remained" (*Hazman*, Schocken Books, 1977, p. 43 [translation by Hanoch Guy]). It seems that the state of Israel is the antithesis of the *Shoah*. The tensions remain as the poet ponders:

> And who will remember? And what do you use to preserve memory? . . .
> The best way to preserve memory is to conserve it inside forgetting
> so not even a single act of remembering will seep in
> and disturb memory's eternal rest (*Open Closed Open*, p. 171).

Memory was disturbed when the poet visited his hometown in Germany. He discovered an abandoned cemetery and a ritual bath in ruins. The pool's vapors turned into witnesses of the deaths of women who bathed after the cycle of purity. A man showed him a new, empty synagogue, telling him: "Nor should you forget the red memorial candle; the eternal burning candle" (*Open Closed Open*, p. 124). The poet changes the traditional white memorial candle into a bloody one, a constant reminder of the perennial Jewish conflagration (*Open Closed Open*, p. 124). Other memories were evoked by pictures on a wall in the city of Petach Tikvah—an opening for hope—but the poem transmits the opposite message:

> Pictures of dead Jews on the wall of a room in Petah Tikva
> like stars that died eons ago
> Whose light has only just reached us (*Great Tranquility*, Harper & Row, 1983, p. 49).

Death, Life, and Love in a Forest

Trees and forests serve Amichai as symbols of life and death. They serve also as the triple symbol for the Jewish people, the *Shoah*, and the state of Israel. The *Shoah* is a distant event that is only remembered through a marker in the forest, in a poem from *Great Tranquility* (1983). Here, Amichai remarks with irony that: "Everybody here is busy with the craft of remembering . . . . And the forest that was planted remembers a distant *Shoah* on a marble slab" (*Shalvah gedolah, she-elot uteshuvot*, Schocken Books, 1980, p. 21 [translation by Hanoch Guy]).

Sometimes one remembers and at other times forgets. Both are "saving lands":

> The world is full of forgetfulness and remembrance
> like sea and land. Sometimes the memory
> is the solid existing land
> and sometimes the memory is the sea that covers everything (*Patuah sagur patuah*, Schocken Books, 1998, p. 112 [translation by Hanoch Guy]).

Jewish history of persecution and pogroms is often remembered as a burning forest. Amichai shifts the forest imagery to serve as a metaphor for Jews who are:

> an eternal forest preserve . . .,
> and even the dead
> Cannot lie down. They stand upright, leaning on the living,
> and you cannot tell them apart. Just that fire
> Burns the dead faster (Abramson, *A Life of Poetry*, p. 462).

Burned trees are also mentioned in a poem about seeking roots in a Warsaw cemetery. Instead of the people searching for roots, the roots are splitting the earth, overturning tombstones, and looking for names and dates as well as burned victims. This may be an allusion to Deuteronomy 20:19: "You must not cut them down. Trees of the field are human beings." However, the forest also customarily appears as a major metaphor for the national revival of the State of

Israel: "Because the destruction of trees often accompanied military defeat and exile, the growth of new trees has long been a symbol of messianic redemption. For Zionists, planting trees has become a symbol of the rebirth of the land" (Frankel and Teusch, p. 182). A Zionist Federation poster reinforced the importance of this arboreal imagery with its slogan, "Branches of our people are chopped down and fall off, but the tree is alive and well" (Zerubavel, p. 60).

Representative of the forest as a symbol of the rebirth is the couple who engages in passionate love making in the memorial forest in Israel—contrasting the *Shoah*'s destruction. Another couple celebrates life while mindful of the slaughtered Jews:

> The two of us stayed alive and in love
> in the memory of the burnt forest and in memory of the burnt ones that the forest
> remembered (*Open Closed Open*, p. 85).

The smoke and fire that accompanied the Israelites in the desert and became symbols of the *Shoah* were in Amichai's blood despite his not being a survivor nor leaving Egypt:

> I wasn't one of the six millions who died in the *Shoah*,
> I wasn't even among the survivors . . .
> though I still have . . . within me, pillars of fire and pillars of smoke that guide me.
> (*Open Closed Open*, p. 7).

The final poem in Amichai's last book, *Open Closed Open*, offers Jewish history as seen through a broken tombstone, broken tablets, rusty crucifixion nails, broken housewares, and images associated with the *Shoah*:

> Eyeglasses shoes prostheses false teeth
> empty cans of lethal poison. All these broken pieces
> fill the Jewish time bomb until the end of days (*Open Closed Open*, p. 173).

All these form a touchstone "more whole than wholeness," indicating the poet's acceptance of Jewish history.

The poet is painfully aware of his good fortune in escaping the fate of European Jewry and living in Jerusalem—the distilled essence of Judaism and the *Shoah*'s antithesis. Being alive, however, obligated him to the previous generations. Amichai was aware that if his parents had not immigrated to Israel in 1936 he would have met his beloved "in 1944/on the ramp in Auschwitz" (*Open Closed Open*, p. 356).

Amichai further explored the *Shoah* in two poems of *Open Closed Open*, in which he saw himself as a detached observer standing behind a barrier and watching Jewish history. The use of the major *Shoah* symbol—a train and its boxcars—enhances the empty feeling of the poem.

> I take it all in: Carloads of passengers and history, carloads packed full of war, carloads teeming with human beings
> for extermination, windows with faces of parting
> men and women (*Patuah sagur patuah*, p. 356 [translation by Hanoch Guy]).

The poem ends with the poet standing by the barrier that has been knocked down forever. He seems to feel alienated from God and Jewish history. Bitterness toward God is expressed in the poem "I Guard the Children": "I'm an old father keeping watch in the place of the great God/Who struts around forever in his eternal youth." This God is oblivious to what is happening in concentration camps, where fathers did not beat their sons, mothers did not quarrel with their daughters, and there were no rebellious sons in transport wagons. Amichai eulogized the victims' innocence and purity (*The Selected Poetry of Yehudah Amichai*, Harper & Row, 1986, p. 165).

Old Survivors and Little Ruth

Amichai connected to the *Shoah* through Jews who left Germany before the *Shoah*, those who perished, and survivors. Of an Israeli who was a famous dancer in Germany, he writes: "If he would have continued to dance in Germany and did not come to Jerusalem he would/have danced to his death in the camps" (*Patuah sagur patuah*, p. 132 [translation by Hanoch Guy]). One of the deepest connections Amichai felt toward the *Shoah* can be found in poems about his childhood friend Ruth, whom the poet often returned to in hidden memories and dreams. He felt her loss deeply and wished for her return:

> She's a stand-in for Otherness.
> Otherness is death, death is Otherness.
> Will you come back to me like the dead sometimes
> Come back to the living, as if they were born again? (*Open Closed Open*, p. 131).

The poet sees Ruth getting up after she was killed by smashed glass. He cries in order to forget and suffers. Instead of the prayer for the dead "Yizkor" (remember) he wanted to recite the prayer to forget, "Yishkah":

> little and dead Ruth
> gets up from bed
> covered with glass shards
> Half is her dream and half mine . . .
> Sobbing
> I recited the prayer of forgetfulness (*Patuah sagur patuah*, p. 139 [translation by Hanoch Guy]).

Ruth returns to him and he mourns her premature death by reciting "Kaddish," the prayer for the dead, changing the exaltation of God to the exaltation of Ruth: "Ruth Ruth, your name is great./May it be magnified and sanctified, your name" (*Patuah sagur patuah, p. 139 [translation by Hanoch Guy]).*

The poet reacts to the Theodor Adorno statement that there could be no poetry after Auschwitz by writing a poem refuting Adorno's statement and implying the futility in dealing with the *Shoah* through theology. This poem is perhaps the most direct wrestling Amichai has with the *Shoah*, indicting God while sanctifying the victims. Unlike the white smoke that billows from the Vatican when a new pope is chosen, the black smoke exhaled from the crematoria indicated that God had not yet chosen his people. Amichai wrote further that numbers on the forearms of the inmates were the telephone numbers of God, who did not respond to anyone's "calls," and who may have been absent from the event altogether:

> After Auschwitz there is no theology:
> The Jews who died in the *Shoah*
> Have now come to be like their God
> Who has no likeness and has no body (*Open Closed Open*, p. 47–48).

The Deaths of Amichai's Father

The story "The Deaths of My Father," included in Amichai's only short story collection *In This Terrible Wind* (1961), deals with crucial experiences and decisions in the life of the poet's father. As a soldier in World War I his father fought in Emperor Wilhelm's army and was invited by his comrades to a party on the eve of Hitler's ascension to power. Realizing that his comrades were either supporting Hitler or keeping silent about his actions, he refused the invitation. The event marked one of his deaths because, although he was very well liked by his comrades, he could not consider them his friends anymore. "They came to arrest him for throwing the Nazi pin that I found into the garbage. The black uniforms broke the door down, and the boots marched in" (*Modern Hebrew Stories*, Bantam, 1967, p. 151). This was the poet's first personal encounter with the Nazis; the second occurred when sentries were stationed before his father's store to keep people from shopping there because Jews owned it. His father died again then. The third death occurred when the family left Germany in 1935 to emigrate to Palestine. Amichai empathizes with his father because the country he had fought for turned against him. His father's decision to leave Germany, his friends, and the landscape that he loved tore him apart. Yet although he experienced a major loss when leaving, he never went back.

Bells and Trains

Amichai's visit to Wurtzburg at the age of thirty-five led to his radio play, *Bells and Trains* (1962), which was the seed for his later novel, *Not of This Time, Not of This Place* (1968). The play was received favorably by critics who praised the interesting combination of the *Shoah* and the universal issue of old age. One critic found in the play elements of the work of the French writer Jean Cocteau, while another negated the possibility of a poetic play (Tzvik, 1988). The plot of the play revolves around Hans, returning to his birth town of Ziegenburg to arrange reparations for his father. He also comes to remember his childhood and the places where atrocities occurred. He goes to an old-age home and meets survivors of the *Shoah* he used to know as a child. In Amichai's attempt to connect with the *Shoah* through Hans, he discovers that the German government maintains the home about which he has written. The old Jews at the home make references to German people and places that remind them of deportations and death. They comment that almost everybody was involved. An old woman adds sarcastically that only those who did not commit evil atoned for it. It seems that Amichai's attempt to go back and remember was an encounter with ghosts.

Not of This Time, Not of This Place

Gershon Shaked claims that Amichai's short stories were a preparatory exercise for his novel, *Not of This Time, Not of This Place*. Shaked further observes that the author meant to write the story of the war of independence generation and not the story of the individual protagonist, Joel (Shaked in Tzvik, p. 191). The novel is constructed in two interwoven plots, a third-person narrative set in Jerusalem, where the protagonist is engaged in an extra-marital affair, and a first-person narrative set in Weinburg, where Joel, the archaeologist, somewhat aimless after the war of independence, travels to confront the Nazi murderers of his childhood companion, Ruth. A wide array of characters populate the book, ranging from German Jews living in Jerusalem and a group of aging survivors living in an old-age home in Weinburg. The personal tug-of-war between Eros in Jerusalem and Thanatos in Weinberg propels the Israeli to find some new meaning upon which to anchor his life. Encounters with the past prove to be more symbolic than historic and the protagonist's vengeance mission dissipates. However, memory of the dark years of the Holocaust do not dissipate, but remain a painful undercurrent suggested by a scene in which an unmarked mine from another war explodes.

Amichai's experimental literary techniques, subplots, and numerous characters drew sharp criticism and were deemed deficient by several critics. Kurtzweil described the novel as a supermarket of literary techniques (Abramson, 1989, p. 150). Even Robert Alter, who deems it "the first important novel by an Israeli dealing with the Holocaust," considers the structure of the novel a "brilliant but not fully worked out invention . . . provid[ing] a kind of diagrammatic illustration of the difficulties Israeli writers have in trying to imagine this ultimate catastrophe and how one can live with the knowledge of it" (Alter, p. 68).

Bibliography

Primary Sources

Akhshav uveyamim ha-aherim. (*Now and in Other Days*). 1955.
Baginah hatiburit. (*In the Public Park*). 1959.
Baruakh hanora hazot (*In This Terrible Wind*). 1961.
Bells and Trains. 1962.
Shirim. (*Poems*). 1967.
"Mitot avi" (The Deaths of My Father). In *Modern Hebrew Stories*, edited by Ezra Spicehandler. New York: Bantam, 1967.
Akhshav bara'ash. (*Now in the Noise*). 1968.
Pa'amonim verakovot. 1968.
Not of This Time, Not of This Place. 1968.
Mi yitneni malon. (*Who Will Give Me Lodging*). 1971.
Baruah hanora-ah hazot. (*In This Terrible Wind*). 1973.
Me-ahorei kol zeh mistater osher gadol. (*Behind This Hides a Great Happiness*). 1974.
Lo me'akhshav, lo mikan. 1975.
Velo 'al menat lizkor. (*And Not in Order to Remember*). 1975.
Hazman. (*Time*). 1977.
Shalvah gedolah, she-elot uteshuvot. 1980.
She'at hahesed. (*The Hour of Grace*). 1981.
Great Tranquility: Questions and Answers. 1983.
Me-adam atah ve'el adam atah tashuv. (*From You Are and To a Man You Will Return*). 1985.
Travels. 1986.
Gam ha-egrof haya pa'am yad petuhah v'etzbaut. 1989.
Even a Fist Was Once an Open Palm with Fingers. 1991.
Patuah sagur patuah. 1998.
Open Closed Open. 2000.

English Collections

Amen. Translated by Yehudah Amichai and Ted Hughes. New York and London: Oxford University Press, 1978.
Open Eyed Land. Translated by Linda Zisquit. Photographs by Frank Wieler. Tel-Aviv: Schocken, 1992.
Poems. Translated by Assia Gutmann. New York: Harper & Row, 1969.
Selected Poems. Translated by Assia Gutmann. London: Cape Gollard, 1968.
Selected Poems. Translated by Assia Gutmann and Harold Schimmel. Harmondsworth: Penguin Books, 1971.
Selected Poems. Translated by Chana Bloch and Stephen Mitchell. London: Penguin Books, 1988.
The Selected Poetry of Yehudah Amichai. Translated by Chana Bloch and Stephen Mitchell. New York: Harper & Row, 1986.
Songs of Jerusalem and Myself. Translated by Harold Schimmel. New York: Harper & Row, 1973.
Yehudah Amichai: A Life of Poetry. Translated by Benjamin and Barbara Harshav. New York: Harper & Row, 1994.

Secondary Sources—English

Abramson, Glenda. *The Experienced Soul*. Boulder: Westview Press, 1997.
———. *The Writing of Yehudah Amichai*. Albany: State University of New York Press, 1989.
Alter, Robert. "Confronting the Holocaust: Three Israeli Novels." *Commentary* (March 1966): 67–73.
———. "Poetry in Israel." *Commentary* (December 1965).
———. "Vistas of Annihilation." *Commentary* (January 1985).
Anderson, Elliott, ed. *Contemporary Israeli Literature*. Philadelphia: The Jewish Publication Society of America, 1977.
Arad, Miriam. "Amichai's Poetry Begins to Mellow." *The Jerusalem Post Weekly*, May 12, 1969.
———. "Yehudah Amichai Looks Back." *Jerusalem Post*, May 10, 1963.
———. "Poems Better Forgotten." *Jerusalem Post*, February 1, 1972.
———. "Expiation in Love and Hate." *Jerusalem Post*, July 12, 1963.
Bargad, Warren, and Stanley F. Chyet, trans. *Israeli Poetry*. Bloomington: Indiana University Press, 1986.
Birman, Abraham, ed. *An Anthology of Modern Hebrew Poetry*. London: Abelard-Schuman, 1968.
Burnshaw, Stanley, T. Carmi, and Ezra Spicehandler, eds. *The Modern Hebrew Poem Itself*. Cambridge: Harvard University Press, 1989.
Carmi, T., ed. *The Penguin Book of Hebrew Verse*. New York: The Viking Press, 1981.
Cohen, Joseph. *Voices of Israel: Essays on and Interviews with Yehuda Amichai, A. B. Yehoshua, T. Carmi, Aharon Appelfeld, and Amos Oz*. Albany: State University of New York Press, 1990.
Fenton, James. "*Time* by Yehudah Amichai." *London Review of Books*, December 6, 1979.
Frank, Bernhard, trans. *Modern Hebrew Poetry*. Iowa City: University of Iowa Press, 1980.
Frankel, Ellen, and Betsy Platkin Teusch. *The Encyclopedia of Jewish Symbols*. Northvale: Jason Aronson, Inc. 1992.
Intrater, Roseline. "Yehudah Amichai and the Interrelatedness of All Things." *Jewish Quarterly* 32, no. 2 (autumn 1985): 119.
Mindlin, Meir. "Major Poetic Event." *Jerusalem Post*, May 9, 1958.
———. "A Brave New Voice." *Jewish Affairs* (South Africa) November 1957, 43–44.
Mintz, Ruth Finer, ed., trans. *Modern Hebrew Poetry*. Berkeley: University of California Press, 1966.
The New Oxford Bible. Oxford: Oxford University Press, 1991.
Nimrod, Noah. "A Hebrew Poet Abroad." *Jewish Chronicle* (London) August 21, 1959.

Rorty, Robert. "A Tale of Two Cities." *Midstream* (November 1968): 73–77.

Sachs, Arieh. "The Poetry of Yehudah Amichai." *Zionist Record and Jewish Chronicle* (South Africa) September 14, 1966.

Wigoder, Geoffrey. "Israel." *Jewish Chronicle* (London) March 2, 1964.

Yerushalmi, Yosef Haim. *Zakhor*. Seattle: University of Washington Press, 1982.

Young, Vernon. "It Makes You Wonder: *Time*: Poems by Yehudah Amichai." *New York Review of Books*, November 22, 1979.

Zerubavel, Yael. "The Forest as a National Icon: Literature, Politics, and the Archeology of Memory." *Israel Studies* 1, no. 1 (spring 1996): 60.

Secondary Sources—Hebrew

Arpaly, Boaz. *The Flowers and the Jar*. Tel Aviv: Hakibbutz Hameuchad, 1986.

Gold-Sharf, Nili. *Not as a Cypress*. Tel Aviv: Schocken Books, 1994.

Tzvik, Yehudit. *Yehudah Amichai: A Selection of Critical Essays on His Writings*. Tel Aviv: Hakibbutz Hameuchad, 1988.

ANDA AMIR-PINKERFELD

(1902–1981)

WENDY ZIERLER

ANDA AMIR-PINKERFELD was born in Rzesza in Western Galicia on 26 June 1902 to an assimilated Polish Jewish family. Her father, Julian Pinkerfeld, a former captain in the Polish army, was an architect who designed train stations for the Austro-Hungarian government. Anda began writing poetry in Polish at a very young age. Her first poem, written when she was seven years old, was a patriotic prayer for the liberation of her country. Her first volume of Polish poetry (*Pie'sni Zycia*, Song of Life, 1921) was published when she was only eighteen years of age. An ardent Zionist, Anda immigrated to Palestine in 1920, but due to illness, was compelled to return to Europe, where she studied microbiology at the universities of Leipzig and Lvov. In 1924 she immigrated to Palestine once again, this time with her husband, the agronomist A. Krampner-Amir. Around this time, influenced by the poet Uri Zvi Greenberg, Anda abandoned her native Polish and began to write Hebrew poetry, publishing her first Hebrew collection, *Yamim Povevim* (Whispering Days), in 1929. After World War II, Anda was sent by the Jewish Agency to work in the displaced persons camps in Germany. She later worked in the archives of the Ministry of Defense, chronicling the lives of those who were lost in the 1948 War of Independence. Best known in Israel as a children's writer, Amir-Pinkerfeld also wrote prolifically for adults, receiving the prestigious Haim Greenberg prize in 1971.

Amir-Pinkerfeld's early Hebrew poetry consisted mainly of love poems and imaginative reworkings of the stories of biblical women, written in free verse form without set meter or rhyme. The outbreak of World War II, however, precipitated a major transformation in Amir-Pinkerfeld's poetry, both in terms of form and subject matter. As one critic encapsulates, "Anda ceased writing about herself and began to write about those who perished in the gas chambers and the crematoria; at the same time, her poetry took on a new form, shifting from the lyric to the epic form" (Harim, pp. 4–5, 7). In assuming this epic voice, Amir-Pinkerfeld stood apart from other contemporary Hebrew women poets such as Rachel Bluwstein (1890–1931) and Esther Raab (1894–1981), who confined their writing largely to the lyric genre. In her willingness to tackle the subject of the Holocaust, Amir-Pinkerfeld was anomalous not only among female but also among male Israeli writers. As novelist A. B. Yehoshua writes,

> [t]he literature of the War of Independence generation approached the subject of the Holocaust with the wariness of scrutinizing an unfamiliar reptile. This caution was prompted by an overwhelming lack of comprehension, a sense of shame and guilt. Nothing could have been further from the experience of the War of Independence than that of the Holocaust (Mintz, p. 157).

According to Hebrew literary historian Alan Mintz, this sense of incomprehension and shame prevented the creation of any significant works of Holocaust literature in Hebrew before the early 1960s, with the exception of the poetry of Uri Zvi Greenberg, whose epic Holocaust work, *Rehovot hanahar* (Streets of the River), appeared in 1951. In making this observation about the late development of Israeli Holocaust literature, however, Mintz completely omits the achievements of Amir-Pinkerfeld herself, who from as early as 1943 was writing and publishing important Holocaust-related poetry.

Holocaust Poetry

Anda Amir-Pinkerfeld's first Holocaust works were short poems, written in response to newspaper reports of the Nazi atrocities. In the poem "Hatzilu!" (Save

Us), published in May 1943, Amir-Pinkerfeld gives voice to the unheeded plea by the leaders of the Warsaw ghetto Uprising for outside help. The poem offers a harsh critique of those Jewish communities of the world, including her own in Palestine, for failing to answer this call:

> And with this cry: Save us! Let's gladden our hearts
> With naïve legendary delusions,
> And last smiles:
> Perhaps, perhaps you'll come,
> You'll come and save us,
> You who breathe with ease
> In the wide spaces of the world (*Gadish*, Tel Aviv: Divir, 1949, p. 378, translation by Wendy Zierler).

"*Hatzilu!*" is a free verse poem. In general, however, Amir-Pinkerfeld composed her Holocaust poems with consistent rhyme and meter, as if to impose literary order on the chaos and ineffability of the subject matter and to imbue the poems with a traditional, even liturgical weight. In "*K'fafot lvanot*" (White Gloves), she uses the folk form of the ballad to expand upon a newspaper account of a Nazi commander presiding over a mass execution of Jews wearing "a white fur coat, a white hat, and white gloves" (*Gadish*, p. 383). The ballad begins with an ostensibly joyous description of a snowfall, with its thousands of jumping, dancing snowflakes. Against this festive background, the "white commander" rises like a "Northern God" (*Gadish*, p. 384). The consistent rhymed iambic tetrameter form heightens the seeming cheerfulness of the poem, which is abruptly and ironically undercut when the commander orders the Jews assembled in the snowy forest to strip off their clothes and dig their own graves before their execution by firing squad. While hundreds of men, women, and children are being murdered, the commander sees a young virgin whom he attempts to set aside for his own sexual pleasure. After the killing is finished, the commander looks around again for the young virgin and calls out to her, promising to "cover her breasts with his white fur and cover her hands with his white gloves" (*Gadish*, p. 398). The poem veers in the direction of the gothic as the morally soiled commander, ironically dressed in white, searches for the virgin, calling out for her among the piles of Jewish corpses. In keeping with the supernatural elements of the ballad genre, the ghost of the dead virgin rises like a cloud from her bloody grave and orders the commander to strip off his fur, uniform, and shoes, and to bow down, naked and debased, before the corpses of the dead Jews. She then orders the commander to spread his white fur out upon the mass grave and maintain an eternal watch over the dead, an order that he (quite implausibly) obeys unto death. In the spring, a group of young girls and boys go out to the forest and find a pair of white gloves on the hands of the commander's skeleton. To be sure, the storyline of "*K'fafot lvanot*" is utterly fantastic, reflecting a desire on the part of the poet to reimagine history and mitigate the horror by incorporating some aspect of divine or supernatural retribution and redemption.

Likewise with the poem "*Ze'evim haililu*" (Howling Wolves, 1944), which is based on a newspaper account of Nazis taking Jewish children out to the fields on a cold day and pouring water on them in order to freeze them to death. The poem closes surreally with a group of peasant women howling and bowing down before the ice statues of dead Jewish children and then clasping them to their bosoms with a pledge of eternal revenge (*Gadish*, pp. 396–401).

Amir-Pinkerfeld's poetic yearning for divine retribution is expressed perhaps most dramatically in her poem "*Milyon na'alayim*" (A Million Shoes, 1945), in which she focuses on a heap of shoes, once belonging to the exterminated Jews of Maidanek. Over the course of the poem, the shoes of the dead magically come alive to kick, beat, and kill the murderous Nazi guards. At their rebellious "head," is a pair of blue velvet slippers, handmade by a mother for her baby girl, representing the poet's moral outrage at the murder of young children, as well as her belief in the important role played by girls and women in stories of heroic rebellion.

Woman Victim, Woman Warrior

The notion of female bravery in the face of unspeakable tragedy is best represented in Amir-Pinkerfeld's most extended Holocaust work, her epic verse-novel, *Ahat* (One, 1952), based on the diary of a young woman named Rachel Seltzer, who survived the horrors of the Holocaust and immigrated to Palestine, only to join the Palmach (the military precursor to the Israeli Defense Force) and die tragically during the 1948 War of Independence. *Ahat* remains an important milestone in the history of Israeli Holocaust literature insofar as it is the first work that attempts to use the broad sweep of the epic form to depict what critic Dan Pines describes as the "*shoah* [destruction] and *gevurah* [bravery] of Israel in our generation" (Pines, p. 54). Written in rhymed hexameter, the story of *Ahat* unfolds over some two hundred pages, depicting the Holocaust experiences of the family of Samuel the tax collector, focusing in particular on Samuel's scientist daughter,

Ada, and his granddaughter Rachel. Soon after the war breaks out, the once wealthy and respected Samuel is jailed and beaten to death, while Ada and Rachel are deported to a ghetto. When the Nazis come to arrest Ada because of her prewar scientific work for the Polish government, Ada orders Rachel to flee and make her way to Palestine. A good deal of this first section of the poem is given over to an account of Rachel's experiences as a child fugitive, hiding out in alleys and on rooftops, furtively boarding and jumping off trains, eking out her existence in a state of constant fear. One of the most powerful passages in the work is Amir-Pinkerfeld's description of a Nazi commander's brutal murder of a four-year-old Jewish boy hiding on a rooftop near Rachel:

> The commander draws near, attempting to push him out with his bayonet,
> Then thinks again, bending over himself to pull him out by his curly
> Soot-covered head; rolling with laughter: "Little darky, little darky!"
> Picking him up like a yelping dog, turning him to and fro,
> He shoots and laughs all at once [*k'ahat*], and throws him into the jaws of night (*Ahat,* Tel Aviv: Dvir, 1952, p. 28, translation by Wendy Zierler).

For the commander, the boy is a "darky" and a dog, a lower life form to be hunted for sport. The perverse conjunction [*k'ahat*] in this passage of laughter and murder is crucial as it represents the indulgence in killing for its own sake. In contrast, Amir-Pinkerfeld's *Ahat* argues for a similarly oxymoronic albeit recuperative linkage, whereby one element heals or redeems the other: *shoah* and *gevurah*, suffering and bravery, Holocaust and Zionist salvation. This linkage is implied throughout the account of Rachel's experiences, in which stories of Holocaust horror alternate with accounts of bravery, self-sacrifice, and Zionist determination, culminating with Rachel's arrival in Palestine aboard an illegal immigrant vessel called *Tikvah* (hope) and her enlistment in the Palmach.

Miraculously her mother, Ada, survives the death camps and also makes her way to Palestine. An emotional reunion ensues during which Ada offers Rachel an account of the atrocities of the camps (*Ahat*, pp. 145–150), including her own guilt-ridden experience of working as a scientist for the Nazis, analyzing the blood of dead Jewish children. Ada initially resents her daughter's dangerous involvement in the Palmach. When Rachel is killed in the line of duty, Ada is devastated. Eventually, however, she comes to view the establishment of the state as a form of restitution for the death of her beloved Rachel.

Ahat has a kind of encyclopedic sweep, attempting to encapsulate a whole range of representative Holocaust and War of Independence experiences. It is important to note, however, the greater weight placed in the poem on the War of Independence narrative. Of the two hundred plus pages in this verse novel, some fifty pages depict events that take place in Europe either before or during World War II. The remaining pages focus on the drama of the burgeoning, embattled Israeli state, again underscoring Amir-Pinkerfeld's desire to inscribe the Holocaust within a redemptive Zionist narrative.

Critical Reception

Anda Amir-Pinkerfeld's Holocaust poetry has been given relatively scant attention by historians of Holocaust literature, although at the time of publication, her *Ahat* garnered considerable critical praise. While Dov Vardi in the *Jerusalem Post* took issue with what he considered the passivity of the main character, Rachel, as well as some of Amir-Pinkerfeld's hackneyed Holocaust descriptions, Shlomo Tenai lauded the realism of the work and called attention to its importance both as a response to the Holocaust and an attempt at the epic form (Tenai, pp. 59–60). Dan Pines offered similar praise; punning on the expression "there are those who acquire their peace in the world [to come] *b'Ahat* [with one good deed]," Pines concluded that Amir-Pinkerfeld had earned her place in the [literary] world with her *Ahat* (Pines, p. 55). For contemporary readers, the redemptive nationalism and militarism of *Ahat* might seem facile, even disturbing. Nevertheless, the literary-historical significance of *Ahat* as well as her earlier Holocaust poetry endures, evidence of the poetic bravery of a poet who dared to confront the horror when so many others could not.

Bibliography

Primary Sources

Pie'sni Zycia (Song of Life). 1921.
Yamim Devevim (Whispering Days). 1929.
Yuval: Shirim. 1931.
Geisha Lian Tang Shavan (Liang Tang the Geisha Sang). 1935.
Gittit. 1937.
Dudaim (Mandrakes). 1947.
Gadish: Shirim (Grain Heaps). 1949.
Ahat: Poema. 1952.
Kokhavim ba-deli: Shirim li-yeladim (Stars in a Bucket). 1957.
Tehiyot: Shirim. 1967.
U-u'khol zot. 1980.

Secondary Sources

"Anda Amir." *Encyclopedia Judaica.* Volume 2. Jerusalem: Keter, 1971, 848–849.

Harim, Alexander. "Dmuyot asher pagashti: Anda Pinkerfeld." *Hador* 20, no. 11, 1953.

Kressel, Getzel. "Amir, Anda." *Leksikon ha-sifrut ha-ivrit bad-orot ha-ahronim.* Vol. II. Merhaviah: Sifriyat Poalim, 1967, 560–561.

Mintz, Alan. *Hurban: Responses to Catastrophe in Hebrew Literature.* New York: Columbia University Press, 1984.

Pines, Dan. "Ahat." In *Anda: Kovets ma'amarim.* Edited by Zahava Beilin. Tel Aviv: D. Ben-Nun, 1977, 54–55.

Tenai, Shlomo. "Poema ne-emanah lametsiut." In *Anda: Kovets ma'amarim.* Edited by Zahava Beilin. Tel Aviv: D. Ben-Nun, 1977, 59–60.

Vardi, Dov. "Pitfalls of Epic Poetry." *The Jerusalem Post,* March 6, 1953.

MARTIN AMIS

(1949–)

SUE VICE

THE BRITISH WRITER Martin Amis was born on 25 August 1949 to Hilly Badwell and Kingsley Amis in Oxford, where his father—later to become a Booker Prize–winning novelist—was studying. After his parents divorced Amis spent his youth in the places where his father taught: Swansea, South Wales; Princeton, New Jersey; Cambridge, England; and Majorca. From the age of thirteen, Amis attended many different tutorial colleges, attaining only moderate success until he passed the entrance examination at Oxford University in 1968. After graduating with top honors in English, Amis worked as an editor for a variety of newspapers and periodicals, including the *Times Literary Supplement*, the *New Statesman*, and the *Observer*. Since 1980, he has worked full time as a writer, authoring many novels as well as collections of short stories, nonfiction works, and journalistic essays published in Britain and the United States.

In 1984 Amis married Antonia Phillips, with whom he had two sons. The couple divorced in 1996 and Amis then married Isabel Fonseca, with whom he had a daughter.

In Britain, Amis is something of a celebrity author, with his work and lavish lifestyle both admired and deplored in equal measure. Amis's novels take place in contemporary settings; are often peopled with upwardly mobile, materialistic, and amoral characters; and are narrated in a slick and ironic manner. His autobiography, *Experience*, was published in 2000 to widespread acclaim.

Very little of Amis's background or early work suggests that he might focus on the Holocaust as the subject for a novel. Yet there are some hints at this possibility. For example, he has always identified with non-British concerns such as American culture and with writers such as Vladimir Nabokov and Saul Bellow, whom he claims have had the most influence on him.

In the 1980s, Amis became concerned about the possibility of "planetary extinction," and comments on the alarming idea that the title of his essays about the United States, *The Moronic Inferno and Other Visits to America* (1986), could become literal (p. xi). His volume of short stories, *Einstein's Monsters*, is about the threat and aftermath of nuclear war. A moral approach has always characterized Amis's novels, with the narrative stance of his work representing, but not endorsing, "the decline of the West."

Time's Arrow

Amis's only Holocaust novel, *Time's Arrow*, or *The Memory of the Offence* (1991), was published to a mixture of acclaim and outrage. On the one hand, it was shortlisted for the prestigious Booker Prize; on the other hand, critics accused Amis of trying cynically to acquire moral seriousness by appropriating a subject to which he had no right. However, it cannot be denied that *Time's Arrow* is an innovative and striking novel, both stylistically and structurally. The story is narrated backward and features a split main character: although the narrator resides in the body of the protagonist, the narrator and the protagonist are separate from each other. Beginning with the death of the protagonist, the naturalized American doctor Tod Friendly, né Odilo Unverdorben, and ending with his birth, the story unfolds in ironic contrast to the usual biographical study. Likewise, details about events of American postwar history, as well as everyday actions such as eating, hailing cabs, and conversations between men and women are told in reverse. All events are meticulously and comically rewound. With more sinister effect, the narrator describes how medical professionals work backward: instead of healing, doctors destroy. When the text rewinds to the wartime period, the reader gains a sense of why time is reversed and what the terrible secret is that plagues Odilo Unverdorben: he was a Nazi doctor at Auschwitz and this trauma has pushed time out of joint. In *Time's Arrow*, it is only at Auschwitz that destruction creates and murder heals. The Nazis may have claimed that they were cleansing and healing their nation through genocide; however, this novel reminds readers that this could only have been true in an impossible, mirror-imaged world.

Backward and divided narration is an ingenious metaphor in *Time's Arrow* for the violence done by the Nazis to medicine, morality, and history itself. In an afterword to the book, Amis credits the sources he drew upon in writing his novel. These range from Primo Levi and Kurt Vonnegut to Robert Jay Lifton's monumental study of Nazi medicine, *The Nazi Doctors: Medical Killing and the Psychology of Genocide.* Amis's detractors have pointed out that he admits in his own afterword that the idea of writing a man's life backward preceded that of making the Holocaust the setting for such a life, as if the event were simply a convenient and shocking peg on which to hang a clever, formalistic trick. But in an interview Amis said of reading Lifton's study, "It's the most extraordinary donnée I've ever had as a writer. It all fell into place at once. A doctor at Auschwitz was the absolute example of the inverted world . . . German doctors went, almost overnight, from healing to killing" (Lawson, p. 43).

Rather than amorally appropriating the Holocaust to fit a preconceived design, it seems that Amis felt that backward narration would most fittingly represent its enormity. In *The Nazi Doctors*, Lifton presents two arguments that Amis has followed extremely faithfully. First, Lifton puts forward his notion of the "healing-killing paradox" (Lifton, p. 350): in a moral turnaround, murder was seen as a "therapeutic imperative" by the Nazis (Lifton, pp. 361–362). In an ironic reversal, doctors supervised the whole mechanism of genocide at Auschwitz, from ramp selections to gassings. Amis has economically transformed Lifton's finding into novelistic form: only if events are narrated backward at Auschwitz does killing look like healing. It takes such fantastical deformation of narrative logic to represent what the Nazis did. The second of Lifton's findings, which Amis has novelized, is the notion of "doubling." In order to function at all in the Auschwitz world, all perpetrators—and particularly the doctors whom Lifton studied—had to undergo an internal splitting to deal with untenable activities. The "everyday" self of doctors in the death camps was maintained separately from the murderous self. This appears to account for the fact that the first-person narrator of *Time's Arrow* is divided from his own body: the narrator is the soul, or conscience, of the doctor but there is little contact between them. However, in contrast to Lifton's argument, it is at Auschwitz that Unverdorben (as he is then) is most significantly a unified subject:

> I, Odilo Unverdorben, arrived at Auschwitz Central somewhat precipitately and by motorbike. . . . Was there a secret passenger on the back seat of the bike, or in some imaginary sidecar? No. I was one. I was also in full uniform. (Harmondsworth: Penguin 1992, p. 124).

Either "doubling" in Lifton's sense and in Amis's novel mean quite opposite things or, more troublingly, the soul-narrator is being disingenuous in claiming not to know what Odilo's dark secret is until he reaches it. The narrator's amnesia amounts to the specious defence of "just obeying orders," and both the narrator and Odilo were equally involved in genocide, as their unity in Auschwitz shows.

Critical Conclusions

Some criticisms can be fairly levelled at *Time's Arrow* as a Holocaust novel. For instance, the material that concerns the Holocaust itself is only briefly—and rather chaotically—narrated. It could be argued that the conceit of backward narration actually works better with the postwar material, which is described in a blackly comic way with an eye for absurd detail, than with the depiction of mass death. In the prewar period, the repopulating of Europe with its murdered millions is not represented, and this seems to be a missed opportunity. Instead, Odilo Unverdorben's activities in the *Einsatzgruppen* and the euthanasia program are related backward; the Nuremberg Laws are subject to the same treatment; by the time readers reach 1933, Odilo's life is relatively innocent. Amis's focus on a perpetrator rather than on the victims of the Holocaust can be seen in two ways: as an honest admission of the limits of his powers of identification, or as an easy way out of fully imagining the Holocaust. Finally, readers might question whether a satire on the Holocaust world is really necessary; after all, the reality of it was bad enough. The answer to this might be that by a supreme irony the facts and images of the Holocaust have become commonplace and that people now suffer from "image-fatigue" in relation to it. By making readers work hard to unravel what is happening and giving them practice in this way of reading early on in the lighter parts of *Time's Arrow*, Amis forces readers to confront anew the atrocities with which they are already familiar.

Bibliography

Primary Sources

The Rachel Papers. 1974.
Dead Babies. 1976.

Success. 1978
Other People: A Mystery Story. 1981.
Invasion of the Space Invaders. 1982.
Money: A Suicide Note. 1984.
The Moronic Inferno and Other Visits to America. 1986.
Einstein's Monsters. 1987.
London Fields. 1989.
Time's Arrow, or *The Nature of the Offence*. 1991.
Visiting Mrs. Nabokov and Other Excursions. 1993.
The Information. 1995.
Night Train. 1997.
Heavy Water and Other Stories. 1998.
Experience. 2000.
The War Against Cliché. 2001.

Secondary Sources

Bernstein, Michael André. *Foregone Conclusions: Against Apocalyptic History*. Berkeley and London: University of California Press, 1994.

Diedrick, James. *Understanding Martin Amis*. Columbia, S.C.: University of South Carolina Press, 1995.

Easterbrook, Neil. " 'I know That It is to do with Trash and Shit": Narrative Reversal in Martin Amis's *Time's Arrow*'." . *Conference of College Teachers in English Studies* 55 (1995): 52–61.

Kermode, Frank. "In reverse." *London Review of Books* (12 September 1991): 11.

Lifton, Robert Jay. *The Nazi Doctors: Medical Killing and the Psychology of Genocide*. New York: Basic Books, 1986.

Slater, Maya. "Problems When Time Moves Backwards: Martin Amis's *Time's Arrow*." *English* 42, no. 173 (summer 1993): 141–152.

Tredell, Nicholas, ed. *The Fiction of Martin Amis*. London: Icon Books, 2000.

Updike, John. "Nobody Gets Away With Everything." *New Yorker* (May 25 1992): 86.

Vice, Sue. *Holocaust Fiction*. London and New York: Routledge, 2000.

Interviews

Lawson, Mark. "The Amis Babies." *Independent Magazine* (7 September 1991): 43.

ALFRED ANDERSCH

(1914–1980)

WULF KOEPKE

ALFRED ANDERSCH WAS born in Munich, 4 February 1914. This predated, by only a few months, the outbreak of World War I, the shattering experience for a whole generation and for Andersch's father in particular. Andersch's father, Alfred A. Andersch, an antiquarian bookseller, served in the German army with distinction and rose to the rank of captain, but came home after the defeat with an amputated leg, traumatized, and unable to cope with the changing times. He joined extreme right-wing groups such as the Thule-Gesellschaft and neglected his business as an independent real estate broker and insurance agent. When he died in 1930, he left his widow and three sons in abject poverty.

Career and Politics

Alfred, the second son, rebelled against the bourgeois and nationalistic milieu to which his father belonged. In 1928 he was relegated from the gymnasium whose principal and teacher of classical Greek was none other than the father of Heinrich Himmler, the future leader of the SS and Gestapo. Alfred became an apprentice in a right-wing bookstore. In 1931 he began his activities in the youth organization of the Kommunistiche Partei Deutschlands (The Communist Party of Germany) and, as a leader of a communist organization, suffered torture by the Sturmabteilung (The Nazi Storm Troopers) in 1933 and incarceration in the concentration camp of Dachau. He was released after two months due to the efforts of his mother, and then incarcerated again, to be released once more, but under constant surveillance. Forced to be extremely cautious and also disappointed by the Komintern policies and the tactics of the illegal KPD after 1933, Andersch withdrew from politics and began to write.

The trauma of the separation from the KPD must have been deep, as the figure of the disenchanted idealistic young communist stands out in his entire narrative work. He survived first as an employee in the Nazi publishing house of Lehmann. In 1935 he married Angelika Albert, who was half Jewish. He moved to Hamburg and worked writing advertisements for his brother-in-law's photo paper factory. Andersch and Angelika were divorced after his return from the United States. He married the painter Gisela Groneuer in 1950 and they had three children.

In 1939 Andersch was drafted into military service, but he deserted his unit on 6 June 1944 on the Italian front, crossing over to the American side. He spent a year as a prisoner of war in the United States, where he worked as a coeditor of the prison camp newspaper, *Der Ruf*, between April and August 1945; when he returned to Munich he cofounded, with Hans-Werner Richter, the political-literary journal of the same name (September 1946). Andersch and Richter were dismissed as editors by the American Military Government, who had the authority to control and censor books and other publications, in 1947 due to their stand against Cold War politics. This led to the founding of the literary "Gruppe 47," whose annual meetings had a decisive influence on literary life in Germany for the next two decades. Andersch, however, soon withdrew from the group. He opposed both sides in the Cold War, and was especially against rearmament in the Federal Republic of Germany. He remained an influential editor of literary radio programs and journals until he withdrew in 1958 to Berzona in the Ticino in Switzerland, where he lived until his death on 21 February 1980.

Andersch was an exception among the early postwar writers in that he was given to programmatic statements. He left an important body of essays in addition to novels, stories, radio plays, travelogues, and poems (mostly political). His early brochure *Deutsche Li-*

teratur in der Entscheidung (1948, German Literature in the Hour of Decision) was seen as a programmatic pronouncement of the new generation of German post-war writers. Andersch adopted the dichotomy of "outer" and "inner" emigration, and after a short panorama of major authors and works of both, he offered his prescription for a future German literature. He envisioned a realistic literature of social engagement and criticism, though not without surrealist elements. He pointed as examples to the works of Erich Kästner, Bertolt Brecht, Elisabeth Langgässer, and Georges Bernanos, but above all to Jean-Paul Sartre and his existentialism.

Andersch wrote a considerable number of stories and radio plays, but became more widely known through his larger narrative works. His autobiographical "docu-novel" (*bericht*), *Die Kirschen der Freiheit* (1952, The Cherries of Freedom), recounts his youth, centering on his decision to desert the German army in 1944. His best-known novel, *Sansibar oder Der letzte Grund* (1957, Sansibar or the Last Reason, *Flight to Afar*), portrays a group of people faced with existential dangers and decisions during the Nazi years. *Die Rote* (1960, *The Red-Head*) places the aftermath of World War II, and the ongoing struggle between Nazis and antifascists, in the context of Italian politics in contemporary Venice. In *Efraim* (1967, *Efraim's Book*), also a "*bericht*" work, a British journalist and former German Jew tries in vain to come to grips with his past and the Holocaust. *Winterspelt* (1974, A Town in Eifeln), Andersch's longest novel, narrates the attempt of a German major, in October 1944, to surrender his battalion to the Americans, which might have prevented the senseless slaughter of the Battle of the Bulge. Finally, in *Der Vater eines Mörders* (1980, The Father of a Murderer), Andersch recounts the perversion of humanism in the German classrooms, drawing on the memory of his expulsion from the gymnasium by his rektor, the classicist Himmler, father of Heinrich Himmler, the leader of the SS.

Sansibar

Alfred Andersch's dominant themes are the aftermath of the Holocaust and of World War II, the survival of fascist mentality, and the need for a free socialist society, a "third way," between or beyond the ideologies of East and West in the Cold War. The urgent call for existential freedom through independent decisions is the main theme in *Sansibar*. Here, in 1937, a group of people is gathered in the small coastal town of Rerik, located in Mecklenburg on the Baltic Sea between Wismar and Rostock, opposite the coast of Denmark (the novel says Sweden), to undertake the dangerous voyage to freedom. The group is comprised of Judith Levin, whose mother committed suicide in order to free Judith for the difficult decision to leave Germany to escape the persecution of the Jews; Gregor, the young disenchanted communist who comes on orders from the party to reorganize their group in Rerik; and Helander, the Lutheran minister committed to saving his church's statue of the "Lesender Klosterschüler" (reading disciple of a monastery school), an archaic wooden sculpture representing the stillness of the spirit in contrast to the hectic anxiety and flight of the people. The statue, declared "degenerate art" because of its humane earthiness and genuine religiosity, is unmistakably the work of the sculptor and writer Ernst Barlach (1870–1938). A crucial figure of *Sansibar* is Knudsen, the fisherman who is to take the party to freedom. He is a communist and feels a moral duty to resist, but he is preoccupied with worry about his mentally ill wife, who is in danger of becoming a victim to the Nazis' "euthanasia" program. Finally, there is Knudsen's helper, "der Junge" (the boy), who wants to get away like Huckleberry Finn from the confines of his small town, and who dreams of the freedom of the wide world.

In the end, the daring exploit succeeds, but with an unexpected outcome. Knudsen saves Judith and the statue, but the Junge renounces the chance to get away and returns with Knudsen, to avoid incriminating him; Knudsen returns to stay with his wife. Gregor is given the chance to flee to Sweden, but he decides to stay in Germany and start a new life of resistance independent of the party. Helander the minister, seeing that he is to be arrested by the Gestapo, shoots and kills the first of the agents, and is then killed by the others.

During the course of the action, less than a day, the statue takes on a new meaning for each of the participants. Its preservation is an act of resisting the destruction of the aesthetic, moral, and religious values by the "others"—an ironic contrast with the real history where the art world of the democracies stole and squandered the treasures of the museums and private collections the German Jews were forced to give up.

The sequence of decisions to reach inner freedom and to claim moral responsibility in *Sansibar* makes it clear that resistance to evil took many forms, but was possible and needed everywhere. Andersch undercuts wholesale categories and condemnations, but insists on the crucial role of the individual decision. In political terms, he provides representatives of the full array of forces opposing the Nazis—the socialists and communists, the church, the Jews—but he insists on the crucial role of the common people like the fisherman and their spontaneous humanity. The allegorical and generalizing elements lift the story out of the anecdotal, but lessen the direct impact, as the political and moral dimensions are dissolved into the spiritual sphere and the allegories become somewhat ambiguous and arbitrary. Still, no other book of the postwar period emphasizes the moral duty of the Germans to save the Jews and to save German cultural values and freedom with such clarity and points to independent socialism as the path to a better future.

Die Rote

Although *Sansibar* is saturated with symbols, and religious as well as political meaning, *Die Rote*, with its inner monologue technique, is a rather straightforward action story and, on its surface, belongs to the genre of crime novels. It is the final chase of a Nazi murderer and torturer with a thrilling ending, but it is also the story of a woman seeking a way out of a dead-end existence and a novel about how to live in the present and remain true to pre-1945 ideals. In 1960 Andersch still hoped for the chance of a modest new beginning symbolized by the union of Franziska and her (yet unborn) child with Fabio Crepaz, the Italian resistance fighter, leading eventually to a transformation of society. In a second version (1972) with a radically different ending, ambivalence and some resignation take over. It is true that the Nazi demon dies, but neither of the other two male protagonists seems to be able to start a new life; only Franziska is determined to do so. The wounds from Nazi torture and the disappointment of the antifascist partisan over the developments after 1945 reach too deep to allow for new involvements in 1960. In its optimistic 1960 version, *Die Rote* became Andersch's great international commercial success, translated into thirteen languages, and made into a movie.

Efraim

Efraim, which Andersch started to write at the beginning of the Auschwitz trials in 1963, portrays a middle-aged weary journalist, a Jewish protagonist and narrator, not living up to his former brilliance but feeling a need to take stock of his life in the form of a very autobiographical novel. Having sworn not to return to his past home in Berlin, he does so nevertheless, and is faced with memories of his murdered family, and especially Esther, the neighbor and girlfriend of his youth who was also the daughter of Keir, his present chief editor, and whose Jewish mother perished in Auschwitz. She walked out of her house and disappeared, either to her death or to hide in a convent. Born in Berlin in 1920 and having had the good fortune to flee the Nazi regime for England in 1937, Efraim is resigned to his survivor guilt feelings as he remembers his father, killed in Theresienstadt, and mother, killed in Auschwitz, and it is doubtful that the book he is writing will bring the hoped-for relief. While Efraim seems to survive, being a real survivor in a double sense, he is still close to the suicide syndrome of other survivors. Situated "in the problematics of post-Holocaust Jewish existence" (Schlant, p. 170), his visit in Germany confronts him with postwar guilt feelings of Germans who live in houses formerly owned by Jews, and the dilemma of the idealistic communist caught between East and West in the figure of his Marxist German girlfriend.

The novel ends with an utter skepticism about potential post-Holocaust healing or improvement of society. With the unresolved mystery of Esther's disappearance and Efraim's separation from his estranged wife, his German Marxist girlfriend, and his friend and editor Keir, Efraim renounces all judgmental pronouncements on the Holocaust and people's attitudes and actions and retires into total isolation in Rome. This unsatisfactory ending can only be seen as a provocation for the reader. Ruth Klüger Angress, who argues that the novel "exemplifies serious and superficially conscientious German efforts to come to terms with what the previous generation inflicted on their Jewish fellow citizens" (pp. 219–220), faults the novel for its presentation of all the Germans as concerned with the Nazi past "in an appealing, soul-searching and intense way" and comments on the absence of former Nazis or sympathizers (p. 220). In her analysis of the novel, Ernestine Schlant counterpoints the juxtaposition of Esther, who functions as "the central character, but as absence and silence" (Schlant, p. 173) with the novel's documentary voice in the form of witness testimony at the concurrent Auschwitz and Treblinka trials, which address the brutal murder of the "anonymous many" children and thereby speak "with an authority and authenticity that are beyond Efraim's experience" (Schlant, p. 174).

Winterspelt

Winterspelt takes place in October 1944 in a small town in the Eifel, shortly before the Battle of the Bulge.

The story does not deal with the Holocaust, but with German resistance and its internal problems. Its different representatives are all decent human beings, but face unsolvable moral and practical dilemmas. Major Dinklage's decision to go ahead with his plan to surrender his unit is made with the complete awareness that after the failure of the conspiracy of 20 July, it is really too little and too late. Still, he cannot bear the moral responsibility for senseless deaths of soldiers and civilians anymore. The failure of his plan, even before it has been initiated, raises the additional question of whether it would not be much better to preserve one's life for the reconstruction of the country after the end of the war that is clearly in sight. *Winterspelt*, like *Efraim*, shows that the Holocaust looms in the background of all moral questions concerning the period of 1933 through 1945, even if the issue at hand is not directly related. The existentialist background is discernable in the decisions to act irrespective of the chances for success, and thus to gain freedom; spiritual values motivating selfless actions are symbolized by the Paul Klee painting saved by a protagonist. *Winterspelt* reverts to the genre of the "*bericht*," the report, used by Andersch for his *Kirschen der Freiheit*.

Conclusion

Alfred Andersch's narrative work deals primarily with the permanent damage done by the Holocaust period to survivors of all kinds and persuasions. Equally, it portrays people who had the hope and felt the responsibility to contribute to a new and better world after 1945, and who found out that nothing had changed and nothing was likely to change. The fading away of hope for a better world is the saddest aspect of his work. It remains surprising that Andersch, who wanted his contemporaries to remember the past in order not to repeat it, and who knew firsthand what a concentration camp was like, never wrote about this experience, except a few glimpses in *Die Kirschen der Freiheit*.

While Andersch's novels, with the exception of *Die Rote*, were acclaimed by the critics, it is hard to say that they made an impact. He remained largely an outsider. *Sansibar*, with its more indirect and symbolic description of the Third Reich, as well as its religious connotations, was often used for discussions about the period, especially in schools. However, *Sansibar* leaves room for generalizations and concurrent interpretations and, therefore, for ways to evade the hard questions. It is similar in this respect to Max Frisch's *Andorra*, and even to Paul Celan's "Todesfuge," a major reason for their popularity, to Paul Celan's dismay.

Andersch remained committed to a world of peace, to his struggle against the ruling ideologies, and to the preservation of the freedoms guaranteed by the Grundgesetz, the constitution of the Federal Republic. He opposed discrimination, commercialization, and, generally, the exploitation associated with the capitalist system. It is ironic that his preferred narrative genres, the action novel and the "docu-novel" he called "*bericht*," are clearly of American origin. Indeed, during his year in America (1944–1945), American literature made a deep impact on him. Andersch belongs to the group of German writers who remind their audience that the terrifying past is still present among us. He also expresses the resignation of the postwar generation that had started a new life after 1945 only to find out that society was not going to change.

Bibliography

Primary Sources

Deutsche Literatur in der Entscheidung (German Literature at the Crossroads). 1948.
Die Kirschen der Freiheit (The Cherries of Freedom). 1952.
Sansibar oder Der letzte Grund (*Flight to Afar*). 1957.
Geister und Leute Zehn Geschichten. (*The Night of the Giraffe and Other Stories*). 1958.
Die Rote (*The Redhead*). 1960.
Ein Liebhaber des Halbschattens (A Lover of a Little Shade). 1963.
Fahrerflucht. Hörspiele (A Runaway Driver. Radio Plays). 1965.
Die Blindheit des Kunstwerks und andere Aufsätze (The Blindness of the Work of Art and Other Essays). 1965.
Aus einem römischen Winter. Reisebilder (From a Roman Writer. Travel Impressions). 1966.
Efraim (*Efraim's Book*). 1967.
Mein Verschwinden in Providence (My Disappearance in Providence). 1971.
Norden, Süden, rechts und links. Von Reisen und Büchern 1951–1971 (North South Left and Right. About Traveling and Books). 1972.
Winterspelt (A Town in the Eifel). 1974.
Empört euch der himmel ist blau. Gedichte und Nachdichtungen (Get Angry the Sky Is Blue. Poems and Translated Poems). 1977.
Der Vater eines Mörders. Eine Schulgeschichte (The Father of a Murderer. A School Story). 1980.
Flucht in Etrurien (Escape in Etruria). 1981.
Studienausgabe in 15 Bänden (Collected Works, Edition in 15 Volumes). 1979.

Letters

Arno Schmidt: Der Briefwechsel mit Alfred Andersch. 1985.
Winfried Stephan, ed. *Einmal wirklich leben. Ein Tagebuch in Briefen an Hedwig Andersch, 1943–1975*. 1986.

Secondary Sources

Angress, Ruth Klüger. "A 'Jewish Problem' in German Postwar Fiction." *Modern Judaism* 5 (1985): 215–233.

Arnold, Heinz Ludwig, ed. *Alfred Andersch*. Munich: text + kritik, 1979.

Jendricke, Bernhard. *Alfred Andersch. Mit Selbstzeugnissen und Bilddokumenten*. Reinbek: Rowohlt, 1988.

Littler, Margaret. *Alfred Andersch (1914–1980) and the Reception of French Thought in the Federal Republic of Germany*. Lewiston, N.Y.: Mellen Press, 1991.

Schlant, Ernestine. *The Language of Silence*. New York: Routledge, 1999.

Schütz, Erhard. *Alfred Andersch*. Munich: C. H. Beck, 1980.

Stephan, Reinhard. *Alfred Andersch. Eine Biographie*. Zurich: Diogenes, 1990.

Wehdeking, Volker. *Alfred Andersch*. Stuttgart: Metzler, 1983. (Sammlung Metzler No. 207)

Wehdeking, Volker, ed. *Zu Alfred Andersch*. Stuttgart: Klett, 1983.

Winkler, Michael. "Alfred Andersch." In *Dictionary of Literary Biography*, vol. 69. Detroit, MI: Bruccoli, Clark and Layman, 1988, 3–10.

JERZY ANDRZEJEWSKI

(1909–1983)

MONIKA ADAMCZYK-GARBOWSKA

THE WRITING OF Jerzy Andrzejewski can be seen as a prose equivalent to that of Czesław Miłosz, as his novella *Wielki tydzień* (*Holy Week*, 1943) was written more or less at the same time as Miłosz's "Campo di Fiori" and "A Poor Christian Looks at the Ghetto" after the failure of the Warsaw Ghetto Uprising. Both works shared a similar fate of neglect as they were hardly available in Communist Poland.

Andrzejewski was born in Warsaw, the son of a delicatessen owner. From 1927–1937 he studied Polish language and literature at Warsaw University. Before World War II, Andrzejewski was a declared Roman Catholic writer who made his debut as a novelist with *Ład serca* (Inner Peace), a story about a Catholic priest, while in postwar years he became a supporter and member of the Communist Party and an author of prose written according to Communist principles of social realism, finally joining the dissident movement from the mid-1950s on. His best known novel is *Popiół i diament* (1948, *Ashes and Diamonds*).

Wielki tydzień

Holy Week takes place during the Warsaw Ghetto Uprising, but the action of the story is set beyond the ghetto walls because most of the characters are observers from the "Aryan" side. The Jewish tragedy is seen by Andrzejewski, as in most Polish Gentile literature on the Holocaust, as a reflection and trial for Christian conscience and behavior. The narrator leaves no doubt that in general, Jews can expect very little support from the Christian population:

> Like all greater events in Warsaw, this too, when viewed from the outside, had something of the spectacle to it. Varsovians are fond of fighting and just as fond of watching fights.
>
> A swarm of young boys and nicely dressed girls with waved hair came running from the nearby streets of the Old Town. The more curious thrust as far as they could into Nowiniarska Street from where they had the widest view of the walls of the ghetto. In general, there was hardly anyone who felt sorry for the Jews. The people were glad that the hated Germans were having new troubles. From the point of view of the average man in the street, the very fact that they were forced to fight against a handful of isolated Jews made the victorious occupiers look foolish (as quoted in Segel, p. 341).

The novella is very well constructed. By setting it in a house with a number of apartments where the protagonist Jan Malecki and his wife, Anna, hide Irena Lilien, an attractive Jewish woman from a prosperous assimilated family, Andrzejewski has a chance to present a variety of attitudes. The building is inhabited by all kinds of people: uneducated and refined, courageous and terrified, compassionate and indifferent. The Maleckis represent the Polish intelligentsia, but the building houses representatives of all social strata, from the working class to nobility. This closed environment is occasionally extended by some additional settings—for example, the office where Malecki works and where his colleagues express opinions ranging from the openly antisemitic to those condemning antisemitism.

The symbolic meaning of the story is strengthened by the fact that the action takes place at the time when Christians get ready to celebrate the resurrection of Christ. The climax is reached on Good Friday when Irena is expelled from her shelter by a primitive couple (the husband, frustrated in his failed attempt to seduce Irena, and his suspicious and jealous wife) soon after they have attended the solemn mass commemorating the crucifixion of Christ.

Critical Reaction

The novella has given rise to some conflicting opinions and controversies. Madeline G. Levine, for example, perceived the "moral outrage" of the story as highly "ambiguous." Praising Andrzejewski for showing the varied Christian responses to the Holocaust, she criticizes him for some one-sidedness in presenting the sole Jewish heroine. Also by identifying the author's voice with that of the most positive gentile character in the novella, Anna Malecka, Levine is confused by the words reflecting the latter's inner monologue in which she perceives the Jewish tragedy as "the most painful test of Christian conscience," for Christians more than any other people "should be moved by the cruel fate of that most unhappy of nations, the tribe that having once rejected the truth drags behind it the burden of betrayal amidst the unbelievable sufferings, humiliations and wrongs" (Levine, "The Ambiguity," p. 394).

These words certainly sound outrageous for today's reader. One must remember, however, that this was the typical way of thinking at that time (still persisting among some Polish Christians), far removed from the present Jewish-Christian dialogue of intellectuals, belatedly enlightened by the bitter historical lesson. It is difficult to say to what extent Andrzejewski identifies with his female character, but in order to make her plausible he had to make Anna express such thoughts, which are comparable to the words of writer Zofia Kossak-Szczucka, a devoted Catholic and one of the founders of Żegota, the Council for Aid for Jews, who deserved great credit for saving Jews in occupied Poland. During the war she made an appeal to save Jews and condemned the Nazi crimes, but at the same time underlined the fact that this did not change her feelings toward Jews, whom she considered an alien element, hostile to Polish interests.

In addition to timing of publication and suppression under Communism, another element that Andrzejewski's novella and Miłosz's "Poor Christian" have in common is the perception of the Holocaust as a curse and stigma for Poland. While in Miłosz's poems the guardian mole stands for both the conscience and the voice of accusation, the novella ends with a curse expressed by abandoned Irena Lilien: " 'The lot of you can croak like dogs!' she cried out vindictively. 'I hope you're burned the same as us! Shot to death, murdered' " (as quoted in Segel, p. 362). Irena is left no other choice but to return to the burning ghetto, a return described by the narrator in an apocalyptic mode as the "distant sound of heavy cannon fire [can] be heard in the distance and a bloody moon burn[s] above amid the black clouds" (as quoted in Segel, p. 362).

Although one can agree with some of Levine's points, one must acknowledge that Andrzejewski was certainly very critical of Polish antisemitism and he did not really attempt to defend it in any way. This is confirmed in his article "Zagadnienie polskiego antysemityzmu" (The Issue of Polish Anti-Semitism) published in the weekly *Odrodzenie*, no. 28, on 14 July 1946. The problem with Irena as a fictional creation is not so much that she might be treated as a stereotype of a beautiful arrogant Jewess from the upper middle class, but that she constitutes the only fully developed Jewish character in the novella.

According to Artur Sandauer, the published version of Andrzejewski's novella differs from the original one in which the narrator was more strongly identified with the main protagonist, Jan Malecki, who expresses mixed feelings about Jews. In the published version the same protagonist is treated with some irony and is juxtaposed with his wife and younger brother who are much nobler characters. Those changes might have been caused by the writer's changed political stance as well as his conviction that the modified version would be more acceptable to the postwar Communist authorities among whom were a number of people of Jewish descent. It is known from various reports that when Andrzejewski read his novella at clandestine meetings of writers and other intellectuals in June 1943, it was not well received. Reportedly, most of them felt suspicious of the fact that so soon after the terrible tragedy of the ghetto, Andrzejewski tried to transpose such an unprecedented reality into a neat literary form. After the war there were also attempts at reading the novella in a biographical context as a projection of Andrzejewski's frustrated prewar relationship with Wanda Wertenstein, a Jewish woman from an assimilated family, who survived the war and made her name as a film critic. She herself claimed that Andrzejewski's portrayal of Irena might have been the writer's revenge for unreciprocated love.

The novella was adapted for the screen by Andrzej Wajda, the leading Polish film director, in a 1995 film called *Wielki tydzień*. Wajda also filmed *Popiot i diament*, an adaptation of Andrzejewski's novel *Ashes and Diamonds*, in 1958. In that novel, a number of critics have pointed out, despite the fact that the action takes place right after the war, the plight of Jews is not even hinted at. This omission may have been caused by Andrzejewski's sensitivity to political suppression of the truth about the Holocaust in Communist-bloc countries or his predominant concern with the mainstream Polish perception of World War II.

Bibliography

Primary Sources

Drogi nieuniknione (Unavoidable Ways). 1936.
Ład serca (Inner Peace). 1938.
Apel (The Roll-Call). 1942.

Noc. Opowiadania (Night. Stories). 1945.
"Zagadnienie polskiego antysemityzmu" (The Issue of Polish Anti-Semitism), *Odrodzenie*, 14 July 1946, no. 28.
Popiół i diament 1948. (*Ashes and Diamonds*). 1980.
Aby pokój zwyciężył! (May Peace Win!). 1950.
O człowieku radzieckim (About the Soviet Man). 1951.
Ludzie i zdarzenia (People and Events), vols. 1–2. 1951–1952.
Partia i twórczość pisarza (The Party and the Writer's Work). 1952.
Wojna skuteczna, czyli Opis bitew i potyczek z Zadufkami (A Succesful War or a Description of Battles and Skirmishes with the Cock-Sure). 1953.
Książka dla Marcina (A Book for Marcin). 1954.
Złoty lis (Golden Fox). 1955.
Ciemności kryją ziemię (Darkness Covers the Earth). 1956. English edition *The Inquisitors*, 1960.
Święto Winkelrida (The Winkelrid Feast). 1946.
Niby gaj. (The Mock Wood). 1959.
Bramy raju (*Gates of Paradise*). 1960. English edition, 1963.
Idzie skacząc po górach (*He Cometh Leaping upon the Mountains*). 1963. English edition, 1965.
Apelacja (*The Appeal*). 1968. English edition, 1971.
Prometeusz; widowisko (Prometheus; a play). 1973.
A teraz na ciebie zagłada... (And Now You Will Be Destroyed ...). 1976.
Już prawie nic (Almost Nothing Now). 1979.
Nowe opowiadania (New Stories). 1980.
Miazga (Pulp). 1981.
Nikt (Nobody). 1983.
Z dnia na dzień: dziennik literacki. (From Day to Day: A Literary Diary). 1988.

Secondary Sources

Detka, Janusz. *Przemiany poetyki w prozié Jerzego Andrzejewskiego*. Kielce: WSP, 1995.
Levine, Madeline G. "The Ambiguity of Moral Outrage in Jerzy Andrzejewski's *Wielki Tydzień*." *The Polish Review* 4 (1987): 385–400.
———. "Polish Literature and the Holocaust." *Holocaust Studies Annual* 3 (1985): 189–202.
Sandauer, Artur. *O sytuacji pisarza polskiego pochodzenia żydowskiego w XX wieku*. Warszawa: Czytelnik, 1982.
Segel, Harold B. *Stranger in Our Midst: Images of the Jew in Polish Literature*. Ithaca and London: Cornell University Press, 1996.

Robert Antelme

(1917–1990)

COLIN DAVIS

IN 1985 THE GONCOURT Prize–winning French novelist Marguerite Duras published *La Douleur* (Suffering, published in English as *The War: A Memoir*), a collection of stories set during and immediately after the German occupation of France. The title story recounts the anguish of a woman as she waits for news of her husband, Robert L., who has been deported to Germany. Eventually she hears that he has been discovered in Dachau; he is rescued, brought to Paris, and nursed back to health. After his recovery, his wife tells him that she is leaving him in order to have a child with a mutual friend.

The story (purportedly based on a real journal) was immediately read as having a strong autobiographical element, referring to Duras's own experience of waiting for her deported husband, Robert Antelme, whom she left for their friend Dionys Mascolo shortly after the war. *La Douleur* also had the effect of renewing interest in Antelme's only published book, *L'Espèce humaine* (The Human Species, 1947), one of the earliest and most important French testimonies of the German concentration camps.

Antelme was born in Sartène in Southern Corsica on 5 January 1917 and lived first in Corsica and then in mainland France. He took his baccalauréat in Bayonne and moved to Paris in 1936 and began to study law. In 1943 he joined a resistance group headed by the future French president François Mitterrand. Arrested by the Gestapo in 1944, he was deported to Buchenwald and then to Gandersheim, one of its subcamps. After the evacuation of Gandersheim, he was moved to Dachau where he remained until its liberation. Although the camp was in quarantine because of an outbreak of typhoid, Antelme was rescued by Mitterrand's Resistance group. Back in France, he wrote *L'Espèce humaine*, an account of his experiences in the camps first published in 1947 by Editions de la Cité universelle, and reissued by Gallimard in 1957. After the war he worked in publishing and became involved in politics, initially as a member of the Communist Party, from which he was expelled in 1950. He died on 26 October 1990.

Duras's story encouraged critics to explore the connections or differences between Antelme's text and that of his former wife on issues such as memory, testimony, and ethics. But it is a mistake to see Antelme only in relation to Duras. The importance of his text is attested to by the attention it has received from major intellectuals and writers such as Maurice Blanchot, Georges Perec, and Sarah Kofman. Written within months of the war, *L'Espèce humaine* is a traumatized yet thoughtful account of life and death in the camps; it depicts experiences with sometimes brutal directness, and attempts to probe those experiences so that the significance of the camps emerges amidst the apparent senselessness of it all.

The Sense of Experience

L'Espèce humaine is divided into three parts of unequal length. The first and longest part, "Gandersheim," begins with the narrator already in Buchenwald; it describes his transfer to Gandersheim and the conditions of life there: the constant search for scraps of food, the need to keep warm and to avoid strenuous, life-threatening work, the relations between the different groups of prisoners and between the prisoners and the SS. The second section, "La Route" (The Journey), describes the evacuation of Gandersheim, alluding to the execution of prisoners unfit to travel and charting the increasingly brutal summary murder of prisoners as they trek through war-torn Germany. The final section, "La Fin" (The End), describes the eventual arrival in Dachau and the final liberation of the camp. The book ends in a moment of regained solidarity and freedom as the narrator talks in the dark with an unseen, unknown Russian prisoner:

> Nothing exists any more other than the man whom I can't see. My hand has settled on his shoulder.
> In a low voice:
> —*Wir sind frei* [We are free]
> He gets up. He tries to see me. He shakes my hand.
> —Yes. (Antelme, *L'Espèce humaine*. Paris: Gallimard, 1957, p. 306; all translations by Colin Davis).

The book begins after the narrator's arrival in Buchenwald and it ends before his return to France. It contains no narrative of life before or after the war, no account of Antelme's Resistance activities, or of his arrest and deportation, and it says nothing about his return to France. The past survives only as fragments of memory, and a future outside the camps cannot be envisaged. The experience of the camps thus appears as the sole reality that eclipses all else. The much-quoted opening paragraph of the preface describes the dilemma of the returning prisoner who is still caught within the experience he has escaped, torn between the need to recount and the difficulty of making himself intelligible to others:

> Two years ago, during the first days which followed our return, we were all, I think, prey to a real delirium. We wanted to speak, finally to be heard. We were told that our physical appearance was eloquent on its own. But we were just back, we were bringing with us our memory, our still vivid experience, and we felt a frenetic desire to tell it as it was. And yet from the very first days, it seemed to us to be impossible to bridge the distance which we discovered between the language at our disposal and that experience which, in the majority of cases, was still carrying on in our bodies. How could we resign ourselves to not attempting to explain how we had got to that point? We were still back there. And yet it was impossible. Hardly did we begin to recount than we began to suffocate. To ourselves, what we had to say began then to appear to us to be *unimaginable* (p. 9).

These lines constitute an eloquent summary of the survivor's dilemma in terms echoed in numerous subsequent testimonies by survivors of the camps and of the Holocaust. They also explain the near-total absence of reference to a life outside the camps within *L'Espèce humaine*. In a crucial sense, the returning survivor has not returned, the past is still not past. The survivor's own experience is unimaginable even to himself, it is not available to him, not identifiable as his own. The present tense, which is adopted in much of the text, suggests that the narrator is still imprisoned within the camps, in part because their horror still remains to be encountered; his ability to take possession of his own experience has been torn away from him. So, the experience of the camps lies in the future at least as much as in the past because that experience has not yet been appropriated and assimilated as belonging to the narrating subject. What is at stake here is whether or not the unimaginable experience of the camps can finally be narrated, assumed, understood, and consigned to the past.

The survivor's dilemma described in the preface is echoed at the very end of the text. After the liberation of Dachau by the Americans, a soldier describes what he sees as "Frightful, yes, frightful!" (p. 301; in English in the text). The response is pitifully inadequate and associated with a failure or unwillingness to enter into a world that exceeds the soldier's frames of reference. The survivors attempt to tell of their experiences, but the more they say, the less they convey: "First of all the soldier listens, then the men are unstoppable: they recount, they recount, and soon the soldier isn't listening any more" (p. 301). At the moment of their liberation, the prisoners understand that they cannot grasp their own experience or transmit it to their listener. So at the very point when they are set free, they are also condemned to remain within the camp because it has alienated them from their own past and robbed them of their ability to communicate with others. Throughout the text, the narrator endeavors to resist the fate that dissolves his own identity and separates him from others, and to assume and make intelligible an experience that seems inconceivable.

A crucial step in such an assumption of experience is to isolate the trace of individual identity that even the camps could not obliterate. From the opening sentence of the first section ("I went to take a piss," p. 15), Antelme refers incessantly to eating, urination, and defecation in a language that refuses euphemism. These functions, however basic, demonstrate that some remnant of the individual has survived, even if he is reduced to being little more than the subject of his own hunger and pain. For this reason, the body and its functions occupy a central place in the book. Throughout the text, the first person subject pronoun, "I", is used sparingly but defiantly because the narrator's ability to say "I" represents a triumph, however minimal and fragile, over the attempt to deny his humanity and subjectivity. The whole text can be read as the narrator's endeavor to gather together the fragments of memory and experience through which the self may be retrieved. The self, like the text that registers and reflects its broken remains, may have neither unity nor coherence; but the very fact that the text is written, that the narrator can continue to say "I," asserts a survival of sorts. *L'Espèce humaine* recounts the subject's persistence in the face of what it can neither assimilate nor escape, and its determination to confront and to survive a trauma that threatens to destroy it.

L'Espèce humaine is, then, the story of the survivor's attempt to remain the subject of his own experience. On the basis of this preservation of some trace of subjectivity, it seeks also to find a broader perspective that might make sense of the trauma of the camps. At the beginning of the text, the narrator and his group have only recently arrived in Buchenwald. They are described as innocents abroad, novices who have not yet learned the ways of the camp. In this respect they parallel the text's readers, to whom the camps must appear terrifyingly alien, or perhaps just unintelligible as Dachau seemed to the American soldier. Much of the rest of the text can be read as an apprenticeship in intelligibility, as the narrator searches for the emergence of meaning in the apparent senselessness of experience. The camps, it transpires, are not as alien as they first appear; they are, after all, available to interpretation and intelligible within frameworks that exist outside them. When the narrator is sweeping the floor in an office in Gandersheim, he observes that a German woman working there is surprisingly intimidated by him. He plays upon the combination of antagonism, hostility, and fear that he perceives in her. Shortly afterward, he returns to the office and is sent away, and a moment later a German civilian tells him to "Clear off." The narrator sees something within these incidents that surpasses and explains them:

> But it was the very movement of scorn—the wound of the world—such as it reigns everywhere in human relations, more or less disguised. Such as it reigns still in the world from which we have been removed. But here it was more distinct. We provided scornful humanity with the means to unveil itself completely (p. 56).

The crucial step here is to establish a connection between the camps and the world outside them. The narrator suggests that, all appearances to the contrary, the camps are not an exception to the rule of normal society; rather they reveal, in its purest form, a truth about human relations in general. The anecdote that gives rise to this insight is raised to a higher level as it becomes the occasion where an aspect of the meaning of the camps can be grasped. Experience, after all, begins to make sense.

A New Humanism?

In influential readings by Blanchot and Kofman, Antelme's text has been described in terms of the relation or non-relation between self and other. Blanchot argues that the destitution of the prisoners strips them of their humanity, leaving only a residue of otherness which is thereby revealed as the paradoxical and ineradicable core of human identity. Using a similar vocabulary, Kofman describes the ethical attitude that results from this as "a new 'humanism' " (Kofman, p. 82): the old figures of Man have been irrevocably shattered, the self is torn open and exposed to the other, forced to confront its imbrication with alterity. Antelme's "new humanism" has little in common with the confident identification of Man as the proud, self-assured center and creator of his own values. It can be argued, however, that the reduction of the self to pure otherness, the eradication of all traces of identity, is perceived throughout *L'Espèce humaine* as a threat to be resisted at all costs rather than as an ethical opportunity to be embraced. The effort of the text consists in preserving the "I" as subject of its own experience; by recognizing pain, hunger, and the body's most basic functions as one's own, at least some remnant of identity is retained. On the basis of this, the subject can begin to make sense of its tribulations, and some form of community can be reestablished. At the end of the text, the "I" of the opening sentence has been reintegrated with the plural "we": "—*Wir sind frei* (We are free)" (p. 306). And this possibility, indeed ultimately the inevitability that all people share a common humanity, is announced from the beginning in the book's title, *L'Espèce humaine*. The SS endeavored to dehumanize their victims, to gouge out an unbridgeable ontological gulf between themselves and their enemies. The guiding faith of *L'Espèce humaine* is that this can never be done. The human species is single and indivisible. The error of the Nazis was to base their politics on difference and to justify their crimes as acts against creatures of a lesser species. Antelme concedes that in the camps difference reigned, but he also insists that differences of race, class, nationality, or condition mask an underlying unity. His demand is not for an experience of alterity but for an ethics and a politics that recognize the indivisibility of the human species:

> [We] are obliged to say that there is only one human species. That everything which masks this unity in the world, everything that puts beings in the situation of being exploited or enslaved and thereby would imply the existence of varieties of species, is false and mad; and that here we have the proof of the matter, the most irrefutable proof, since the worst victim cannot do other than remark that, at its worst, the executioner's power cannot be other than one of man's powers: the power of murder. He can kill a man, but he can't change him into something else (p. 230).

Central to Antelme's analysis of the camps is that they do not entail the revelation of something new, which might bring in its wake a philosophical, theological, or aesthetic crisis. Rather, as for David Rousset in

L'Univers concentrationnaire (The Concentrationary Universe, 1946), the camps bring to light a possibility within society, and specifically within capitalism. Gandersheim is presented as a highly stratified class system, with its aristocracy (the SS), its proletarians (the French political prisoners), and numerous gradations in between (the Lagerältester, the Kapos, those working in the kitchens, the interpreters, and so on). The situation of the prisoners is described as "the extreme experience of the condition of the proletarian" (p. 101). Thus, the struggle to survive is viewed through the lens of class conflict. The constant search for food and the need to sustain the individual body can be understood as a demand to preserve the highest human values. Eating potato peel turns out to be part of the fight for "the liberation of humanity as a whole" (p. 101). Tracking the emergence of meaning in the most extreme and the most senseless experiences, *L'Espèce humaine* recounts the survival of the individual subject and its inscription in a political and moral context that makes sense of its private torment.

For all its distressing rawness, its first-hand knowledge of the human capability for brutality, and its awareness of the inadequacy of testimony to encapsulate and convey the reality of the camps, *L'Espèce humaine* recounts a victory of sorts. The very fact that the text is written at all attests to Antelme's survival as author and subject of his own text. The "I" has not been obliterated, the human species is still intact, even the camps are explicable as an extreme manifestation of the evils of capitalism. Already in this early testimony, we can see a web of meaning beginning to form over the trauma of experience. Indeed, it is the characteristic move of the text to trace the emergent signs of meaning in the apparent senselessness of reality. For other writers, less confident of their political convictions, more radically undermined in their sense of self and their faiths, the prospect of overcoming trauma would remain far in the distance. Testimony would be deferred or interminable; closure could not be achieved so rapidly, or perhaps ever. *L'Espèce humaine* suggests, however, that while the camps may remain for the moment the survivor's sole reality, it may ultimately or even soon be possible to escape from them once and for all. In the forty-three years that remained to him after the publication of *L'Espèce humaine*, Robert Antelme never wrote another book.

Bibliography

Primary Sources

L'Espèce humaine (The Human Species). 1947.

Textes inédits, Sur "L'Espèce humaine," Essais et témoignages (Unpublished Essays, On "The Human Species," essays and testimonies). 1996.

Secondary Sources

Blanchot, Maurice. "L'Espèce humaine." In *L'Entretien infini*. Paris: Gallimard, 1969, 191–200.

Chaouat, Bruno. " 'La Mort ne recèle pas tant de mystère': Robert Antelme's Defaced Humanism." *L 'Esprit créateur* 40, no. 1 (2000): 88–99.

———. "Ce que chier veut dire (Les *ultima excreta* de Robert Antelme)." *Revue des sciences humaines* 261 (2001): 147–162.

Crowley, Martin. " 'Il n'y a qu'une espèce humaine': Between Duras and Antelme." In *The Holocaust and the Text: Speaking the Unspeakable*. Edited by Andrew Leak and George Paizis Basingstoke. Macmillan, 2000, 174–192.

———. "Remaining Humain: Robert Antelme's *L'Espèce humaine*." *French Studies* (forthcoming).

Davis, Colin. "Duras, Antelme and the Ethics of Writing." *Comparative Literature Studies* 34, no. 2 (1997): 170–183.

Duras, Marguerite. *La Douleur*. Paris: P.O.L., 1985.

Gorrara, Claire. "Bearing Witness in Robert Antelme's *L'Espèce humaine* and Marguerite Duras's *La Douleur*." *Women in French Studies* 5 (1997): 243–251.

Kofman, Sarah. *Paroles suffoquées*. Paris: Galilée, 1987.

Mascolo, Dionys. *Autour d'un effort de mémoire*. Paris: Maurice Nadeau, 1987.

Perec, Georges. "Robert Antelme ou la vérité de la littérature" (1963). In *L.G. Une aventure des années soixante*. Paris: Seuil, 1992.

AHARON APPELFELD

(1932–)

GILA RAMRAS-RAUCH

AHARON APPELFELD WAS born in Jadova, Bukovina, on 16 February 1932. His parents Bunia (née Sternberg) and Michael Appelfeld resided permanently in Czernowitz, the capital of Bukovina (in what is today regarded as Romania). Both sets of Appelfeld's grandparents were Hasidic Jews. His first language in his semi-assimilated Jewish home was German.

In the summer of 1941 Appelfeld went to visit his maternal grandmother in the town of Drogobych, where his father, who sold machinery for mills, owned property. One day, as his parents and grandmother were sitting in the garden, a shot rang out; the Germans, accompanied by Romanian collaborators, had begun the terrorization and subsequent destruction of the Jews of Bukovina. Appelfeld's mother and grandmother were killed in the garden; his father managed to escape to a nearby cornfield, where Aharon, then known as Irwin, joined him. After a period of hiding, Appelfeld and his father managed to reach the Ukraine in the winter. In Mogilev Podolski, men and women were separated, with the men taken to labor camps. Both Appelfeld and his father were interned in a labor camp in Luchinetz in the Ukraine, but were separated later that year, not seeing each other again until they were reunited in Israel after the end of World War II.

Left alone, Appelfeld began to roam the countryside. He wandered from village to village, from town to town. He lived on the village outskirts, alongside a marginal population of prostitutes and horse thieves. Appelfeld became a servant, seldom staying in any one place for too great a period of time.

In 1944 the Russian army entered the Ukrainian villages and the young Appelfeld joined the soldiers as a kitchen aide. He stayed with the mobile army for a year. As the unit advanced toward Bukovina and Romania, Appelfeld and eight other boys decided to escape to Yugoslavia and from there proceeded to the shores of Italy. Eventually, after a short stay in a monastery, the boys met a soldier from the British Army's Jewish Brigade, who informed them of the availability of passage to Palestine.

In 1946 Appelfeld reached Palestine aboard the ship *Haganah.* Toward the end of that year, Appelfeld and other boys were taken to an experimental agricultural school in Jerusalem. He was conscripted into the Israeli army in 1950 and served for two years. In the early 1950s he began his studies at the Hebrew University in Jerusalem, where he met a group of Jewish intellectuals from Germany and Central Europe, including Martin Buber, Max Brod, Gershom Scholem, and Dov Sadan. For Appelfeld, studying under Scholem and Buber was his primary schooling. Appelfeld was at once influenced by numerous sources: Hebrew, Yiddish, Bible, kabbalah—all contributing to the shaping of his perception, style, and point of view. Appelfeld has lived in or near Jerusalem ever since his arrival in Israel. After a number of years teaching at Ben Gurion University of the Negev he was appointed professor emeritus of literature in 2000.

As a young man, Appelfeld was preoccupied with a search for language and the process of reindividuation. He was grappling with a new country and a new language. During his first years in Israel he went through a reconstruction of self in which acquiring the Hebrew language was his greatest challenge. The task of fashioning a world in Hebrew is difficult enough for native-born modern Hebrew writers, because Hebrew is a language of various canonic sources and is forever at play, with temptations abounding to connect to a great font of imagery and allusion. Appelfeld, challenged even further as a nonnative speaker, nonetheless resisted the temptation to enrich his language with canonic allusions. A master stylist, Appelfeld instead aspired—and continues to aspire—to clarity of expression and to the singularity of an image, a note, a word. He opts for metaphoric language and uses subtle, impressionistic techniques. Like Elias Canetti and Elie

Wiesel, Appelfeld writes in a language other than that of his birthplace, transcending his roots, and working shards of history into his prose.

In his search for a language and an idiom, he has relinquished the strictly descriptive mode, avoiding a mimetic treatment of past events. Appelfeld's fiction involves two seemingly incompatible spheres. While he belongs historically to the tradition of Central European Jewish writers, he also belongs to the postmodern generation of post–World War II Israeli fiction writers. His earlier narratives can be read as fundamentally postmodern in nature. The atomistic, decentralized, irresolvable nature of the narrative exposes a protagonist detached from any definite social framework, cultural matrix, or historical continuity. Like other modern and postmodern characters (such as those of Franz Kafka or Samuel Beckett), his are non-accumulative in nature; they are fragmented and often caught in a remote moment, which in turn serves to symbolize their entire existence. This style may at times create an enigmatic character, one difficult for the reader to parse and understand.

Appelfeld writes highly sensitive tales about individuals in the pre- and post-Holocaust worlds. His characters are affected by the Holocaust in a fundamental way. However, they are formed not so much in its fires, but rather in times before and after the conflagration itself. Often these are disjointed human beings, depleted and mute, roaming through Appelfeld's fantastic narratives in a state of silent quest. In his earlier fiction, particularly his first short story collections (most of which have unfortunately not been translated into English) such as *Be-Komat Ha-Karka* (On the Ground Floor, 1968) and *Adanei Ha-Nahar* (The Foundation of the River, 1971), Appelfeld often suspends the historical framework of the Holocaust. We are brought to the penultimate station in the lives of the characters, knowing full well the end that awaits them. (See *Badenheim 1939* [1980], *To the Land of the* Reeds [1986], *Age of Wonders* [1981].)

Appelfeld's fiction is a profound and moving testimony to the Holocaust; yet it also demonstrates the limitations of finding expression for it in the literary realm. It is the relationship—and indeed often the tension—between autobiographical experience and fiction that lies at the heart of Appelfeld's work. Appelfeld erases raw memory and writes unrealistic tales. The relationship between the expressed and the suppressed is therefore essential in his work. Even his most detailed and "realistic" novels of the 1990s and early 2000s are nonetheless highly stylized, touching upon personal experiences but not elaborating on them.

Appelfeld's fiction raises basic questions: How is a modern reader to come to terms with his unique form of narrative? Can the literature of the Holocaust retreat into the fantastic? In the face of the inherent difficulties of expression when confronting such extreme horror, authors of Holocaust literature make use of the fantastic, transcending the flow of the narrative and inserting a different reality within it, thereby suspending realistic time and placing within it another, nonreferential reality. In some of Appelfeld's fiction—for example, *Badenheim 1939* (1980) and *The Healer* (1990)—the fantastic is a quality of the individual, a consequence of a wounded psyche. During the Holocaust, the impossible and inconceivable became reality. For Appelfeld's characters—as for actual Holocaust victims and survivors—the impossible and the inconceivable are all too real, yet unable to be explained by the laws and within the constraints of the familiar world. The effect of this conflict is shattering. It is precisely this impossible world that is internalized in Appelfeld's characters.

With the suspension of normally unfolding time, space gains a central importance. The encapsulation of a solipsistic individual within an airless bubble enhances the depiction of outwardly and inwardly passive individuals. In *Katerina* (1989), *Unto the Soul* (1994), and *For Every Sin* (1989) Appelfeld's characters finally emerge more actively from their total insularity, beginning at last to broach the realities of an outside world, realities some had long borne under the weight of their own impossibility.

In Appelfeld's world, Europe after the Holocaust is a Jewish wasteland: there are few Jewish survivors, and those who have survived are constantly on the move. These dynamics, however, produce no essential change in the lives of the characters. It is as though Appelfeld's Jews have moved and yet continue to stand in the same spot on the map; that is, they continue to be the strangers, the "others," the hovering shadows of an extinct reality. For Appelfeld's characters, post-Holocaust Europe is an archeological site, the largest Jewish cemetery in history.

The Shape of His Career

On the whole, Appelfeld's fiction develops along two courses. The first considers the actions of assimilated Jewish society before the war, including the excessive cultivation and intellectualism that brings it to the point of atrophy; the second focuses on the experience of the survivors, with their suppressed memories as well as their fundamental need to be on the move, to be in a state of constant motion. Jadova, Czernowitz, and Jerusalem are departure points for many of Appelfeld's literary excursions. They appear in a variety of guises, at Badenheim and other places.

Appelfeld's work may be divided into three distinct periods. In the 1960s his intent was modest—to exorcise the haunting ghosts of the past. He published surreal short stories with strong elements of the fantastic. This body of work consists of five short story collections, some of which were translated into English. The second period, the 1970s and 1980s, is dominated by his novels of deportation. During the third period, from the 1990s to the early 2000s, a more realistic strain enters Appelfeld's narratives. By the 1980s, when Appelfeld won, among numerous other literary awards, the prestigious Israel Prize, he had declared his desire to reconstruct a hundred years of Jewish suffering and isolation.

Together, his works of fiction amount to an extended saga, a Jewish map of disrupted lives. Throughout this development, Appelfeld has chosen a personal, ahistorical route. In the absence of "pure" memory, he reconstructs a map of charted and uncharted Jewish "terrain." His map of Europe is a Jewish map whose boundaries are not clearly defined because it is thematic rather than truly representative.

Ultimately, Appelfeld must be seen as a unique modernistic writer. His highly stylized fiction summons the Holocaust, not through direct depiction, but rather through metaphorical associations. Appelfeld's stories, novellas, and novels create a singular fictional universe for his characters—at once drawn from the horrors of the external world, yet simultaneously enmeshed in the personal and the isolated.

The Early Short Fiction

Consistently, the geographical terrain inhabited by Appelfeld's early characters is a forest. Some are ultimately incapable of leaving their forest, even after movement and escape, even after arriving in Israel. His first collection, *Ashan* (Smoke, 1962), includes some mature stories that are at once realistic and impressionistic. In none of the stories is an attempt made to reach the totality of experience. The stories vary in the extent and intensity of their disclosure of the past.

Of the few reliable elements in the incomplete worlds of these narratives, the change of seasons often functions as an indicator. The constancy of nature is the basis for both the presence and absence of familiarity, carrying a variety of meanings. It is a time marker in a world where civilization has betrayed human beings—loss of the ability to predict, and the subsequent destruction of the capacity to conjure up a feasible future, is a basic trauma felt by many survivors.

The natural world serves as a hiding place, with the flight to the fields or the forests providing temporary relief. Appelfeld's early characters, some oblique, some unexpressive, seem to listen to voices that speak to them and them alone. Their limited verbal and emotional vocabulary gives them a unique quality. They are moored in an inner world that reacts only selectively to the outside world. Even in their new home, Israel, they continue their survivalist existence. They make no apparent attempt to adjust themselves to the new reality or to answer its implicit expectations.

Appelfeld is not interested at this stage in intellectualizing his characters or in lending them an inner or articulated voice. His stories are peopled with merchants, peddlers, cabdrivers, and butchers, who expose us to the everyday reality of cooking, knitting, stomach ailments, and excessive smoking—the humdrum lives of the survivors in Israel. The emotional distance traveled by some of Appelfeld's early protagonists is illustrated by how small a part their interactions with other Israelis play. The survivors all share a secret language, one that needs no articulation. These characters struggle to interact with an external world, to express their trauma, their loss, their sorrow. The characters in *Ashan* (Smoke), for example, are often afflicted by mysterious physical or mental ailments.

In his second collection, *Ba-Gai Ha-Poreh* (*In the Wilderness*, 1963), Appelfeld addresses Christian imagery. The images of the monastery and the convent, which appear to some extent in his first collection, feature centrally in this second narrative collection about the adjustment of young refugees to life in Israel. One of Appelfeld's early stories from this collection, "Kitty," combines his plastic, almost sensory, depiction of the rapport between the psyche and the surrounding world in a masterly fashion. The intricate pictorial descriptions, the detailed and impressionistic depiction of mood and atmosphere, and the diminution of dialogue all contribute to the highly stylized quality of the story.

The story centers on an eleven-year-old girl who finds herself in a French convent toward the end of the war, devoid of language, identity, and memory. She emerges from her insulated, autistic state through a series of revelations, discovering life through her senses. What happened to Kitty and her family in the Holocaust is left unrevealed. We see her trauma but know little of its root cause.

> She was expected to read slowly and to memorize the sentences. She felt how the words hit the stone and returned to her, chilled. They called her name, which rus-

tled within her as the starched linen dresses which made her shudder. . . . Sometimes she felt the full impact of the air gripping the back of her neck, stifling the syllables in her mouth. But at other times the flow increased, the good words remained within her, like a warm secret which planted itself slowly, spreading its roots (Translated by Tirza Zandbank in *Modern Hebrew Stories*, Ezra Spicehandler, ed. New York: Bantam Books, Dual Language Edition, 1971, pp. 220–222).

The synesthetic "conversion" lifts her from an elemental, preverbal creature into a person who relates to the world through her body. As she grows she becomes open to touch, sound, and sight. Paradoxically, while opening up she continues to weave her unique, enclosed, solipsistic self. With the onset of puberty she acquires language and begins to ask questions. The silence of the convent has protected her like a womb; yet it bursts open with the encroaching reality of the approaching Germans. In the meantime she discovers her Jewishness, and with it both antisemitism and greed. Through all of this, she maintains her world of fantasy and epiphany. As the war draws to a close, a German shoots her. The protagonist here is typical of Appelfeld's early characters: at once within the world and removed from it, defined ultimately by a past that is fragmentary at best, and a future inseparable from horror.

Appelfeld is especially attuned to the fate of young girls. In Kitty we encounter a young woman whose internalized trauma, undetailed in the story, is connected with Christian symbolism. Kitty feels that in her rebirth she is the daughter of God, whose tormented body on the cross she observes. Like other Appelfeld characters, she senses a mysterious flow of movement, which points to another reality embedded in the visual signs of the world. And yet, outside the world of imagination, the protracted silence of the convent functions as her salvation.

Kitty's transition from innocence to experience comes with the posing of questions, whether of puberty or war, all portending penetration. German soldiers, their half-naked bodies suggesting sensuality and sexuality, have entered Kitty's existence, surrounding the convent. Peppi, a vulgar local cleaning woman who does not hide her sexual encounters with the Germans, exposes Kitty to a world unexplored by her tutor, the nun Maria. When Peppi tries to lure Kitty into stealing the convent's golden candelabra, Kitty's refusal to go along with her scheme unleashes a barrage of antisemitic slurs. Peppi calls her "a dirty Jewess" and threatens to expose her to the Nazis. As a result, Kitty is confined to the cellar. Yet in her descent there is also an element of ascent: through spiritual resignation and calm she weaves a new relationship with the things that surround her. Two voices are at war within her. One, filled with a sense of divine grace, leads her to think that she is one of God's chosen children and as such must suffer until his light shines upon her. The other voice repeatedly asks her whether she is a "dirty Jewess." Despite the questioning, she awaits her fate in an attitude of spiritual resignation. The story concludes with a spiritual, indeed almost hagiographic, element, combined with the irreversible reality of the Holocaust.

The movement from the short story to the novel marks Appelfeld's transition into a deeper psychological study of character and an attempt at his own historicization of Jewish existence in the modern era. Complexity of character, the emergence of a clear protagonist, and a wider gallery of personae signal a deepening and broadening of narrative scope.

For most of Appelfeld's characters, Israel brings little change into their lives. Bartfuss, the protagonist of *The Immortal Bartfuss* (1988), guards against sentimentality and emotional reactions. Living in the port of Jaffa, he is estranged from his Balzacian wife and two grown daughters. The bare room in which he lives reflects his barren existence—his self-reliance, austerity, frugality, and stark financial and emotional independence. Many of Appelfeld's male characters feel a great connection with their lives in the forests of Europe or on the shores of Italy after liberation. There, in a morally and socially vacuous no-man's-land, survivors could tell themselves they were in a transitional state. In Israel, Bartfuss continues his life of shady illegal financial dealing but limits himself to fifteen minutes a day devoted to business. The rest of the time he is free.

Bartfuss's sense of dignity never leaves him. *The Immortal Bartfuss* is a study of a man who, in Appelfeld's words, has "swallowed the Holocaust whole." In essence Bartfuss is a trapeze artist for whom existence on the edge of danger provides a true sense of freedom. In Israel he becomes a creature of habit and hates himself for it. Bartfuss is a three-dimensional character, self-aware and introspective.

The underlying question is whether Bartfuss, who was once a sensitive young man longing for death, a daredevil moved by Dostoevsky, changes after years of humiliating experiences. Bartfuss poses questions: "What have we Holocaust survivors done? Has our great experience changed us at all?" Bartfuss is a modern epic protagonist in search of spirituality. He is a modern, post-Holocaust man who exists in his psychological lair.

Novels of Deportation

Appelfeld employs several basic motifs and archetypes. Two of the most prominent that apply to the assimilated Jew in his fiction are those of self-denial and self-deceit as modes of existence. In this second period, Appelfeld's fascination with the Jewish intelligentsia continues. His fiction portrays the attitude of the Germans and Austrians toward the Jews as an alien element, demons from another world who have penetrated their culture and contaminated it. In *Badenheim 1939* (which first appeared in Hebrew in 1975 with the grimly ironic title "Badenheim Resort Town"), two themes inform the slowly unfolding plot: the forthcoming spring cultural festival and the presence of the Sanitation Department inspectors, who are there to begin the transformation of the town into a concentration camp. The resort town faces a slow and irreversible invasion. The festival, like mythical spring rites, revives the visitors, whose need for the yearly pilgrimage is acute. Appelfeld shows us this penultimate phase in the lives of his characters in a tale where the beginning (the ostensibly innocent appearance of two inspectors) portends the end (the transition of the town into a camp).

Badenheim 1939 has no central protagonist other than Dr. Pappenheim, who emerges from the forest like a Hasidic miracle worker to preside over the festival as its impresario. His annual task is to bring to the town the best talent in the performing arts. Like Sisyphus, he never achieves his goal, coming closest during preparations for the very last festival in Badenheim. The bitter irony that pervades the novel borders on the grotesque and the tragic, resembling the caricature sketches of George E. Grosz. In the novel's highly stylized manner, Badenheim emerges as a microcosm of the assimilated existence of Central European Jews on the eve of World War II.

As the novel unfolds, a sense of doom besets the characters, as their lack of a way out becomes more and more apparent. We are left with artists and vacationers, the Jewish inhabitants of Badenheim, on the eve of the *Anschluss* between Germany and Austria. The preparations for the festival correspond to the preparations for the deportation. Remote, alien Poland begins to seem a pastoral place to many of the assimilated vacationers, who appear to be enthralled by powers beyond their control. Like marionettes they go through the motions, presenting in a most civilized manner the stylized horror story of the twentieth century.

Appelfeld does not try to come to terms openly with the cause of assimilation. However, through careful signs and symbols he depicts its detrimental effects, among them the psychological dislocation it has produced in his characters. What was the source of the breach in the Jewish psyche in the twentieth century? What was the cause of the tragic excess? Was it the attempt to erase stereotypical Jewish traits? A deep guilt over leaving the fold? Self-hate and/or self-denial? A quest for the unattainable? Appelfeld poses questions concerning the entire last century of modern Jewish history in Europe.

Superimposing a structure of common sense and causality on the Appelfeldian universe does not enlighten the reader. In parallel with the world of Kafka, Appelfeld's fiction in many cases creates an enclosed verbal universe that answers only to its own inner laws. In *Badenheim 1939* the message of doom is transmitted on two levels: through the actions of the Sanitation Department and through Rilke's "Sonnets to Orpheus" and "Duino Elegies," recited by twin readers from Vienna. These two represent the motif of duality, portraying the double life of the visitors to Badenheim as vacationers on the one hand and, on the other, human beings with fractured psyches who are intoxicated by the sickness in their voices.

A barrier is placed at the entrance to the town, and the movement of the vacationers is limited. The cold horror of the narrative lies in its slow pace and the quiet process of the telling of the tale. The strength of *Badenheim 1939* lies in its power to portray the macabre in a subtle way, not with garish colors and harsh sounds. Muffled utterances, everyday small talk, and bizarre behavior, seemingly within the boundaries of order, paint the picture. And yet the novel challenges the claims of order, culture, and civilization. Appelfeld shuns the melodramatic, remaining a student of such Central European Jewish writers as Jakob Wassermann, Arthur Schnitzler, and Franz Kafka as well as Thomas Mann in *The Magic Mountain*. The tone of the narrative is stoic despite the underlying madness in mankind. The infrastructure of the novel functions through irony: The characters remain in the singular and ultimately limited domain of the apparent, whereas the reader is capable of combining the two disparate realities, knowing full well that the trains out of Badenheim carry the vacationers to their doom.

The sense of exile from the familiar and the known is a central theme in Appelfeld's fiction of this period. A perfect example of this is *Tor Ha-Plaot* (1978; *The Age of Wonders*, 1981) a highly sensitive first-person narrative related by a young storyteller who observes a new reality slowly encroaching upon his family. Like *Badenheim 1939*, the novel ends with deportation. Also permeating the events is the atmosphere of prewar Europe, foreshadowing the fate of one Jewish family. The obsessive theme in this story of an assimilated Jewish family is the deep sense of life being beyond one's control. In *Badenheim 1939* the movement comes as the circumference of the town slowly diminishes, creeping toward the center of town, the hotel.

The process of confinement renders movement impossible until the moment of deportation. *The Age of Wonders*, on the other hand, describes constant movement, by train and on foot. The movement is part of the undoing of the family and its last attempt at denial of the Holocaust and antisemitism. The mother is a prophetess of doom while the father, a successful novelist, shuttles back and forth between Prague and Vienna. His volatile and exhibitionist nature is pitted against the mother's isolation and silence. The family members—father, mother, and son—are constantly on the move. Starting out in first-class train cars, they are soon relegated to freight cars and slow milk trains. The train is a major image in Holocaust literature and a central element in this novel, as in other Appelfeld narratives.

In *The Age of Wonders* the movement of the characters constantly plays up the uncertainty they feel and the certain doom we know awaits them. The impending Holocaust is always present in the details and the map of these movements, underlying, indeed becoming, the inner map of the Jewish psyche. The most striking movements are those of conversion/inversion. Theresa, the narrator's spiritual and graceful aunt, converts to Christianity in her quest for solace, silence, and escape. The ill (Theresa) returns to St. Peters Sanatorium:

> Theresa was now brisk, polite, and hospitable, like a woman returning to her own and familiar furnishings: to me it seemed that she would soon remove her holiday clothes and don a nun's habit (*The Age of Wonders*, Boston: David R. Godinz Publisher, 1981, p. 102).

On the other hand, the half-Jewish sculptor Stark, raised as a Christian, embraces Judaism despite his gentile appearance and bearing. He wishes to be circumcised.

> The son of a Jewish mother, Stark was at this time tortured by cruel perplexities. . . . For the past year he had been wandering from one rabbi to another and one rabbinical court to the next. The rabbis did not welcome him. His robust, Aryan looks only made them suspicious. In the end one of the rabbis said to him, "Why take this trouble on yourself at a time like this?" They put him off on all kinds of pretexts, but their unwillingness only fuelled his obscure passion to return to the crucible of his origins, the origins of the mother he adored; it was her faith, or rather the faith of her forefathers, that he wanted to embrace (p. 102).

The father in *The Age of Wonders* personifies the attempts at self-negation of his Jewish identity. His fiction is praised for bringing new beauty to Austrian literature, a beauty tainted by malaise. Yet his attempts to enter and imitate intellectual society fail as his fiction is ultimately attacked. The broken spirit of Jewish intellectualism expresses once again the sense of looming catastrophe. In the first half of the novel the roads eventually lead to deportation. At the end of the first part of the novel, all Jews face the same fate: They are brought to a common point, a leveling, for both those who have denied their Judaism and those who have affirmed it. A reverse movement appears in the second half of the novel, which takes place years later: The protagonist, a child in the first half of the novel, now emerges as an adult returning to his birthplace. Details that were unknown to the reader in the first half of the novel are explicitly stated here. The technique of the third-person narrator, who takes over in the novel's latter half, creates a certain distance between the reader and the protagonist.

Appelfeld's unpublished play *Locked In* is an elaboration on and an extension of the last scene in the first half of *The Age of Wonders*. The play, which takes place in the sanctuary of a synagogue in a small Austrian town in 1939, hovers thematically between Kafka's "Before the Law" and Jean-Paul Sartre's *No Exit*. A year after the *Anschluss*, some of the characters still deny the signs of impending disaster. Thrown or forced into a situation about which they have no prior knowledge, they expose their truths and their lies through the new conditions imposed upon them. Ultimately, the presence of others serves to reveal, in some cases, the depths of the characters' self-deceit, while the reader or viewer provides the historical framework for the characters' fate. Against this background, everything uttered in the play gains a profoundly tragic dimension, accenting human frailty.

The theme of return, a basic motif in Appelfeld's fiction, gains depth and dimension in his fiction after the 1970s. In pre-Holocaust narratives, people return home only to be deported. Appelfeld's novels of deportation center on the penultimate stage in the lives of his characters. The *Anschluss* is looming heavily; yet Toni, the romantic protagonist of *To the Land of the Cattails*, goes back to Bukovina to ask her parents' forgiveness for abandoning them and running away with a gentile man. Toni, typical of Appelfeld's characters who are frozen in time while constantly moving in space, is traveling with her adolescent son Rudi in 1938. All signs foretelling disaster are disregarded. The penultimate point in the ceaseless movement of Toni and Rudi will be deportation. In narratives depicting the survivors, the return can have a variety of destinations: Israel, home, or (usually) nowhere—what might be termed "sites of forgetfulness."

Unifying the themes in Appelfeld's early and late narratives is the motif of the return to one's roots in a search for meaning. In the novel *The Healer* four members of a family leave Vienna and travel to the Carpathian Mountains in the hope of curing their ailing daughter, Helga. They seek the help of a *zaddik*, a Hasidic holy man. Illness and malaise also seem to infect the other members of the family: the father, Felix; the son, Karl; even the mother, Henrietta, all of whom suffer the malaise of alienation from their roots.

The *zaddik* suggests drawing close to the holy letters and contemplating them as a road to redemption. He instructs Henrietta to teach Helga the Hebrew characters, telling her that reading the prayer book will be the beginning of her cure. Meanwhile, Helga is in the process of seeking a voice. Voices burst from her lips; strange sounds are strangled in her throat. Those wild sounds seek a tongue. Language itself is a central protagonist in this novel. The holy man tells the sick Helga:

> The Holy letters bring us closer to our home—like a person returning to his home village after years. The smell of the trees and the grass drives foreign parts away from him. We have a great many foreign parts within us, do we not? But we, thank God, have a home. We can return home. . . . When darkness falls, we simply enter our home (*The Healer*, New York: Grove Weidenfeld, 1990, pp. 135–136).

The Healer ultimately points to an attempt to find healing from within. The family's pilgrimage is in the tradition of the Hasidic custom of seeking the help of a *rebbe* or a *zaddik*. The young woman here, like Kitty, represents the inner crisis of identity of the Jew disconnected from roots or home.

Healing is a motif that continues to appear in Appelfeld's fiction of this period, with many characters aspiring to find a cure for their malaise. Along with the motifs of return and healing is the motif of movement that informs most of Appelfeld's work. *The Healer* combines these three motifs and evokes Appelfeld's earlier stories in which mystical, kabbalistic themes were prominent.

From a structural vantage point, Appelfeld's novels of the 1970s and 1980s are longer and more complex than his earlier works. More important, however, the early Appelfeld, the Appelfeld of singular, solipsistic individuals, expands to the realm of the complex family, capturing the conflict and isolation among family members, which is ultimately indistinguishable from his most central theme: the conflict and isolation in the identity of European Jewry in the face of destruction.

Work of the 1990s and Early 2000

Appelfeld's novels of this period are true to their author's declared intention: "To write about the last hundred years of Jewish solitude." Appelfeld uses basic archetypes but creates new settings for them. He collects personal snapshots of autobiography and, like a meticulous goldsmith, places shards of memory into a fictional setting. The technique of fictional autobiography has no boundaries. Appelfeld can move characters through time while remaining faithful to the various places his characters have inhabited: Austria, Galicia, Bukovina, and the Ukraine. Many of the characters portrayed embody a repeated motif, continual failure to achieve their potential and their aspirations.

A new dimension appears in the novels of this period: revenge and hatred erupt, as a means of escape for the perpetual "other" who is physically or psychologically abused, particularly in the Holocaust. Further, the Jewish convoy becomes a sign of the wandering tribe. Appelfeld's narrative skill achieves an epic breadth that enables him to re-create an overarching Jewish narrative of the twentieth century in Central Europe and beyond.

Forever fascinated by the terminally intellectual Jew of Europe, in the early 2000s Appelfeld began to expand on the figure of the wandering Jew. As noted, Europe after the Holocaust is a Jewish wasteland in Appelfeld's world: there are few Jewish survivors, and they are always on the move. The dynamic, however, does not bring about change in Appelfeld's characters. It is a repeated pattern that has left the historical domain and entered the metahistorical. In his later novels Appelfeld's characters remain in Europe and do not look for new opportunities. An almost sick fascination draws them to return to their hometowns in Europe. This theme appears in both *For Every Sin* (1989) and *Mesilot Ha-Shahar* (1991; *The Iron Tracks*, 1998). The refusal or inability to change is enhanced by the unique nature of those who belong to the tribe of the survivors. Conversion is an additional theme in Appelfeld's later novels. In *The Retreat* (1984), one of the characters talking about his two sons explains his remedy for sparing them from antisemitic persecution:

> But I had them converted when they were still young, while I had little control over them. . . . So that they wouldn't come and blame their father for bequeathing them a malignant disease. Their father did what had to be done. Now let them carry on (*The Retreat*, New York: E. P. Dutton, Inc., 1984, p. 116).

The glorification of the Jew as an intellectual and a miracle worker persists in a different combination in Appelfeld's tales. In *The Iron Tracks,* a modern picaresque tale set in the 1980s, the narrator Irwin Zigelbaum recounts his forty years of wandering in the European countryside, continually moving in trains from south to north and back again. Trains make him a free man; they enable him to live unattached. After forty years of wandering, he has developed his favorite spots, his places and people. Haunted by memories of the death of his parents, he nevertheless visits all the stations in his and his parent's lives.

Not unlike Appelfeld's character Bartfuss from *The Immortal Bartfuss*, Zigelbaum has swallowed the Holocaust whole. He maintains a yearly cycle, like the reading of the Torah in weekly portions, visiting twenty-two stations, one for each letter in the Hebrew alphabet. He returns compulsively to a forlorn train station where, during the war, after three days in a sealed car, the people inside were deserted by the Germans.

The life of the narrator is a loose compilation of the post-Holocaust experience of Appelfeld's characters. Further, there is additional emphasis here on the death of the narrator's father as well as the death of father figures in general. The protagonist's father and mother are ardent Communists. The mother takes part in the assassination of a high official and later becomes a recluse. The father works with the local Ruthenian peasants, indoctrinating them, and takes the young Irwin (Appelfeld's childhood name) with him on missions for the party, choosing not to send the boy to school. The mother, silent and pining, tries to instill in the child a love of learning. Tragically, the family is united in the camp, where the parents are shot to death by a German officer. The novel marks a departure from earlier Appelfeld narratives: until the 1990s, Appelfeld's stories, characters, and plots were situated geographically away from the war and the concentration camps. For the first time, a direct depiction of the Holocaust appears; the freight trains and the camp experience enter the story.

> Thus we arrived at Nachtigal's camp. It was a small, brutal labor camp, where people died from cold and hard work. . . . I worked, loading coal like a trained laborer. Father, too, worked at this, without falling behind.
>
> One morning Nachtigal shot him [father] because he came late to the lineup (*The Iron Tracks,* New York: Schocken Books, 1998, p. 144).

Personal quest appears both as a subtext and as the surface text in the novel. The information that Nachtigal, the German officer who killed the narrator's parents, is about to return to his hometown, Weinberg, allows the protagonist to fulfill his task: to kill Nachtigal. The belated act of revenge is, however, not accompanied by a sense of mission. Nachtigal is by now a toothless old man, mourning the death of his wife. The act of killing has more to do with finality and closure.

Appelfeld tends to erase or suppress his autobiographical story and create imagined autobiographies that combine fact and fiction, often using female characters. This approach allows for more than one autobiography, and indeed autobiographical traces are to be found throughout his works. There is a certain parallelism between Appelfeld's own literary persona and the depiction of his female characters. Women in his novels of deportation frequently aspire to a perfection that eventually produces tragedy. Often they are artists, mostly musicians, whose total dedication to art brings about their emotional demise. Helga in *The Healer* is just one example. The quest for excessive culture, as portrayed in the festival in the imagined town of Badenheim, points to a certain sickness of the acculturated and assimilated Jews, namely, that of being severed from their own roots and yet not achieving the European ideal. Excessive cultivation and intellectualism collapse into atrophy.

The young women depicted in Appelfeld's fiction may be characterized by a sense of estrangement and distance, of being perennially trapped in their own worlds. Some of the young women, like Kitty or Helga, refuse to grow up. They are afraid of change, of puberty, of the transition into womanhood. Somehow, directly or indirectly, many of his female characters depict a sense of uprootedness and sickness.

Another permanent motif in Appelfeld's work is that of the mother-son relationship. This motif appears in *The Age of Wonders*, *The Retreat* (1984), *To the Land of the Reeds*, *Ritzpat Esh* (Tongue of Fire, 1988), *For Every Sin*, and other works. This symbiotic relationship recurs in Appelfeld's narratives depicting life both before and after the war. Often, as in *Badenheim 1939*, Appelfeld creates an insular world, with its own fictional space and its own ground rules. The mother-son axis is multifaceted in Appelfeld's fiction; yet its precise nature varies from text to text: Christianity in *For Every Sin*, Judaism in *To the Land of the Reeds*. On a number of occasions the mother-son relationship has an Oedipal component. In many of the novels, an absent or rejected father plays no meaningful role in the life of the son. As a method of compensation, the son adopts the mother's world and pledges allegiance to it. The mother, often depicted as weak, dependent, and impractical, makes the son the "man" in her life. In *The Age of Wonders* the family triangle is still intact and the father has importance, yet the closeness is between the son and the mother, who becomes the pivotal character in the family.

Appelfeld, a prolific writer, has not directly addressed his childhood transition from Bukovina to Jerusalem. His short novel *Tzili: Sipur Haim* (1983; *Tzili: The Story of a Life*, 1983) comes as close to a fictional autobiography as anything he has written. However, even here there is a distance, in that Appelfeld's protagonist is not a young boy but rather a young girl. For Appelfeld in this book, as elsewhere, "pure memory" does not exist. The story of Tzili is the story of a young girl in Bukovina whose family leaves her to take care of the house for one evening. That night soldiers enter the town and destroy it. Tzili survives, separated from her family, by hiding in the yard among sackcloth. Much as Appelfeld did, Tzili encounters lowlife characters in her efforts to survive: both the fictional character and her author worked for prostitutes. Appelfeld reconstructs remnants of memory and tries to expand the scope of his fiction beyond personal remembrance to create a gallery of characters neither directly nor indirectly reflecting himself.

Appelfeld's personal and aesthetic credo is most clearly expressed in his slim volume of talks, essays, observations, and memoirs, *Masot Be-Guf Rishon* (First Person Essays, 1979). His book of essays and a conversation with Philip Roth appeared in English in *Beyond Despair* (1994). In both books Appelfeld tries to come to terms with his life, his art, and the state of the artist as a survivor. He pays his respects to people who helped him expand his intellectual spheres, people who ushered him into the domain of Hebrew, Yiddish, and world literature. His reflections on the post-Holocaust period, especially on the shores of Italy, are closely connected to his aesthetic meditation on artistic expression in the light of the Holocaust.

For Appelfeld, art, not history or theology, is the key to the particularization of experience. The key to Appelfeld's aesthetic sense is that as a creative artist he searches for a way beyond both the general and the particular. Both are unsatisfactory: the first degrades the personal experience, while the latter leaves it in the domain of the autobiographical. It is the personal vision itself, not the rehashed personal account, that allows the particular and the universal to dwell in one text. His answer is to place the individual in the selective domain of fictional narrative. This technique applies to Appelfeld's *Sippur Haim* (A Life Story, 1999), where he writes about his early years and the death of his mother, his existence as a young child wandering over the plains of Bukovina, and his very painful adaptation to life in Israel. He talks about the loneliness of the refugee, about his time at the Hebrew University in Jerusalem, and about the effect of these events on his self-acceptance. It was at this point, in the late 1950s, that Appelfeld rid himself of his ambition to be an Israeli writer and instead focused on his identity as a Jewish writer, born out of the experience of European Jewry: an immigrant, a refugee, a man who carries within him the child of war.

In Appelfeld's narratives of the late 1990s the child emerges as protagonist. Again the family is fractured on the eve of war and its fate is tragic, as in *Col Asher Ahavti* (All That I Have Loved, 1999). The first-person narrator in this novel, a nine-year-old child, is torn between his quarreling parents. Discord, silence, and tension accompany the child's reality. Again the connection between mother and child is strong and painful. Obsession takes over the life of the parents and the child. However, through the young boy Appelfeld introduces us to places that were seminal in his own childhood: Czernowitz, the city of his youth, and Stroznitz, his grandparents' village.

Appelfeld's later work—both fiction and nonfiction—is marked by the continuation of various themes combined with the development of numerous new ones: revenge and rage, description of camps, and an attempt to depict events more realistically. Appelfeld's five collections of short stories published in the 1960s and 1970s attracted critics and readers. In Israel's early days of statehood, with the country still reeling from the tremendous impact of the Holocaust, literature was mostly autobiographical and based in personal reality. Appelfeld's terse and often laconic style was a new experience for readers, and in this respect Appelfeld was one of the first to show that it is possible to write fiction addressing the Holocaust and its survivors without the specific limitations of the autobiographical form. This is particularly the case when one places the writing in the context of the day in which it was written—prior to the Eichmann trial, which brought the Holocaust palpably into the awareness of the Israeli—and world—public.

As early as 1971, Gershon Shaked, in his book *A New Wave in Hebrew Fiction*, points to the themes of terror and escape as major themes in Appelfeld's fiction. Shaked sees it as a return to a topic prevalent in Jewish fiction of the nineteenth century. Shaked refers to Appelfeld's style as "stylized terror," pointing correctly to the fact that terror does not become melodramatic in Appelfeld's early fiction. The power of the landscape to become an almost poetic interpretation of the dire reality adds another dimension to Appelfeld's fiction.

Appelfeld's style, his language, his efforts not to attempt a reconstruction of reality, all contribute to the voice he developed in Holocaust literature. In his book *Hurban*, Alan Mintz observes that "Appelfeld's stories succeeded in creating the aura of a credible fictional world" (New York: Columbia University Press, 1984, p. 204). Sidra D. Ezrahi notes correctly:

> There is the quality of primal struggle in Appelfeld's prose, a chiseling and shaping of language by a writer who encounters Hebrew unencumbered by layers of classical association (*By Words Alone*, Chicago: Chicago University Press, 1982, p. 366).

Despite the seemingly "realistic" depiction of the Holocaust in Appelfeld's later fiction, he continues to depict a hermetic internal universe using symbols such as the convoy and the process of wandering. He is more explicit about the names of places in Bukovina, where he was born, and the village of his grandparents. This change clearly contributes to a more realistic perception of time and place. At the same time his personal experiences, for example, meeting his father in later years in Israel, are but fragments woven into his verbal fabric.

Summary

The fact that Appelfeld is not a purely realistic writer, that he creates highly fictional works, which at the same time relate to historical and personal occurrences, opens his texts to more than one reading. The combination of autobiographical elements and fictional situations is evident in many of his narratives. Yet although there is an element of conscious concealment in the Appelfeldian story, it evokes the unconscious revelation of matters through a process at once fictional, symbolic, and rhetorical. We are made aware of a voice behind the fictional characters, the presence of a persona whose sensitivity and sensibility, preference and judgment, moral stance and taste, organize the final text presented to us.

Again and again in Holocaust literature, life appears as an unreal game in which the old rules no longer hold. And yet there is the fact that literature itself is to be accounted for. Amid the ruins of reason and meaning, literature has been the most profound attempt in our time to find meaning for what is otherwise absurd, reason in what is otherwise inexplicable. Appelfeld is foremost in the ranks of those who have used literature to this end.

Bibliography

Primary Sources

Ashan (Smoke). 1962. Stories.
Ba-Gai Ha-Poreh (In the Fertile Valley). 1963. Stories.
Kfor Al Ha-Aretz (Frost on the Land). 1965. Stories.
Be-Komat Ha-Karka (On the Ground Floor). 1968. Stories.
Adanei Ha-Nahar (The Foundation of the River). 1971. Stories.
Ha-Or Ve-Ha-Kutonet (The Skin and the Gown). 1971. Novel.
Ke-Ishon Ha-Ayin (As an Apple of His Eye). 1973. Novella.
Ke-Meah Edim (A Hundred Witnesses). 1975. Selected Stories.
Shanim Ve-Shaot (Years and Hours). 1975. Novellas.
Badenheim Ir Nofesh (*Badenheim 1939*). 1975. Novel.
Tor Ha-Plaot (*The Age of Wonders*). 1978. Novel.
Masot Be-Guf Rishon (First Person Essays). 1979.
Makot Ha-Or (Searing Light). 1980. Novel.
Ha-Kutonet Ve-Ha-Pasim (The Shirt and the Stripes). 1983. Novella.
Tzili: Sipur Haim (*Tzili: The Story of a Life*). 1983. Novel.
Be-Et U-Be-Ona Ahat (At One and the Same Time). 1985. Novel.
Be-'Et Uve-'Onah Ahat. 1985.
Ritzpat Esh (Tongue of Fire). 1988.
Katerina (*Katerina*). 1989. Novel.
Mesilot Ha-Shahar (The Railway). 1991. Novel.
Laish (Laish). 1994.
Timion (*Lost*). 1995.
Ad She-Ya'ale Amud Ha-Shahar (Until the Dawn's Light). 1995.
Michreh Ha-Kerah (The Ice Mine). 1997.
Col Asher Ahavti (All That I Have Loved). 1999.
Sipur Haim (The Story of a Life). 1999.

Books Published in English

In the Wilderness. 1965.
Badenhaim 1939. 1980.
The Age of Wonders. 1981.
Tzili: The Story of a Life. 1983.
The Retreat. 1984.
To the Land of the Reeds (also published as *To the Land of the Cattails*). 1986.
The Immortal Bartfuss. 1988.
For Every Sin. 1989.
The Healer. 1990.
Katerina. 1992.
Beyond Despair: Three Essays and a Conversation with Philip Roth. 1994.
Unto the Soul. 1994.
The Iron Tracks. 1998.
Lost (also published as *The Conversation*). 1998.

Secondary Sources

Aschkenasy, Nehama. *Eve's Journey: Feminine Images in Hebraic Literature and Tradition*. Philadelphia: University of Pennsylvania Press, 1986.
Chertok, Haim. *We Are All Close: Conversations with Israeli Writers*. New York: Fordham University Press, 1989.
Cohen, Joseph. *Voices of Israel*. Albany: State University of New York Press, 1990.
Ezrahi, Sidra Dekoven. *By Words Alone: The Holocaust in Literature*. Chicago: University of Chicago Press, 1980.
Lang, Berel. *Act and Idea in the Nazi Genocide*. Chicago: University of Chicago Press, 1990.
Langer, Lawrence. *The Holocaust and the Literary Imagination*. New Haven: Yale University Press, 1975.
McCagg, William O., Jr. *A History of the Habsburg Jews, 1670–1918*. Bloomington: Indiana University Press, 1989.
Mintz, Alan. *Hurban: Responses to Catastrophe in Hebrew Literature*. New York: Columbia University Press, 1986.
Miron, Dan. *Pinkas Patuach*. Tel Aviv: Sifriat Poalim, 1979.
Ramras-Rauch, Gila. *Aharon Appelfeld: The Holocaust and Beyond*. Bloomington: Indiana University Press, 1994.
Ramras-Rauch, Gila, and Joseph Michman-Melkmen, eds. *Facing the Holocaust: Selected Israeli Fiction*. Philadelphia: Jewish Publication Society, 1985.
Rattok, Lily. *A Precarious House: The Narrative House of A. Appelfeld*. Tel Aviv: Hekker Press, 1989.

Rosenfeld, Alvin H. *A Double Dying: Reflections on Holocaust Literature*. Bloomington: Indiana University Press, 1980.

Schwartz, Yigal. *Aharon Appelfeld: From Individual Lament to Tribal Eternity*. Hanover, Mass. and London: Brandeis University Press, 2001.

Shaked, Gershon. *Gal Hadash Ba'siporet Ha'ivrit*. Tel Aviv: Sifriat Poalim, 1971.

———. *Modern Hebrew Fiction*. Bloomington: Indiana University Press, 2000.

Yerushalmi, Yosef Hayim. *Zachor: Jewish History and Jewish Memory*. Seattle: University of Washington Press, 1982.

Young, James E. *Writing and Rewriting the Holocaust: Narrative and the Consequences of Interpretation*. Bloomington: Indiana University Press, 1988.

LISA APPIGNANESI

(1946–)

DAVID BRAUNER

LISA APPIGNANESI WAS born Elsbieta Borensztejn, the daughter of Hena and Aaron Borensztejn, in Poland on 4 January 1946. After her birth, the family moved briefly to Paris, France, before emigrating to Canada in 1951. Appignanesi studied English Literature at McGill University in Montreal, where she was awarded a B.A. in 1966 and an M.A. in 1967. After completing her Ph.D. in Comparative Literature at the University of Sussex in England in 1970, Appignanesi spent a year in New York as a staff writer for the Centre for Social Research before returning to England to take up lecturing posts in European Studies at the University of Essex and at the United Kingdom branch of New England College. During the 1980s she worked for the Institute of Contemporary Arts in London, first as director of Talks, Seminars, and Publications and then as deputy director. Since 1990 she has devoted most of her time to her writing, publishing seven works of fiction and two works of nonfiction, but has also continued to work occasionally as a freelance journalist, broadcaster, and television producer. Although her marriage to Richard Appignanesi (himself an author, best known for his contributions to a number of volumes in the *For Beginners* series introducing the work of famous writers and thinkers to students) ended many years ago, she has retained her married name. Lisa Appignanesi lives in London with her two children.

Work

Lisa Appignanesi's oeuvre is not easy to categorize: she is the author of romantic novels populated by priapic men and promiscuous women, but also of feminist academic studies of Sigmund Freud, Simone de Beauvoir, and the fiction of Henry James, Marcel Proust, and Robert Musil; she has edited collections of learned essays on subjects as diverse as post-modernism, French theory, Eastern European politics, the ethics of genetic research, and the Salman Rushdie affair, as well as writing a history of cabaret. Like the hero of her first novel, a "polymath [. . . who] dreamt of somehow being able to unite the disparity of fields which interested him" (*Memory and Desire*, London: Harper Collins, 1991, p. 72), she seems intent on pursuing several different careers concurrently.

The events of the Holocaust form part of the backdrop of Appignanesi's first novel, *Memory and Desire* (1991), in which the protagonist, Jacob Jardine, spends the war working for the resistance in France. Although Jardine is the son of a Jewish doctor born into a "wealthy Jewish banking family" (p. 56) and a Catholic mother (and hence, according to orthodox Jewish law, not Jewish at all), and himself marries a Polish Catholic, he spends much of the war working to save "refugees from Hitler's Nazi state which was bent on the elimination of a people he counted amongst his own" (pp. 137–138). After the war, he "spent all his time working with [camp] survivors . . . as if he had disappeared inside them" (p. 215) and his daughter, Katherine, becomes a sort of surrogate daughter to Thomas Sachs, a German-Jewish immigrant to America whose entire family was killed by the Nazis. In her fourth novel, *The Things We Do for Love* (1997), one of the key figures, Simone Lalande Debray, is a Jew whose mother dies as a result of the "unassuageable guilt . . . of having been left alive" while the rest of her family perished in Auschwitz (*The Things We Do for Love*, p. 198) and her most recent novel, *Paris Requiem* (2001), deals with antisemitism in turn-of-the-century France. Her most significant contribution to Holocaust literature, however (and the work for which she is best known), is *Losing the Dead* (1999).

Subtitled "A Family Memoir," *Losing the Dead* is also part novelistic reconstruction of her family's war years, part history of Polish-Jewish relations, part philosophical meditation on the elusive, allusive nature of memory. As one might expect from a Freudian novelist, Appignanesi is both adept at constructing a compelling narrative from the raw materials of her own and her parents' memories, and profoundly skeptical about the relationship of this story to objective history. To quote from my own book, *Post-War Jewish Fiction: Ambivalence, Self-Explanation, Transatlantic Connections* (2001), which features the only published critical analysis of Appignanesi's work to date, "it is the process of self-explanation itself, rather than its results, which becomes both the subject and the medium of the book" (Brauner, p. 34). To put it another way, *Losing the Dead*, in common with many recent works by the children of Holocaust survivors (Art Spiegelman's *Maus* books being perhaps the great prototypes of the genre), is as much about what Appignanesi calls "transgenerational haunting" (*Losing the Dead*, London: Vintage, p. 8)—the difficulties of negotiating between the pain of the survivors and that of their children, and the ethical and aesthetic problems of writing about the Holocaust—as it is about the Holocaust itself.

Unlike most memoirs by Holocaust survivors, or their children, *Losing the Dead* does not deal with life in the death camps: Appignanesi's parents were among the small number of Polish Jews who managed to survive the war outside the camps through a mixture of audacity, serendipity, and charity, while recognizing that Hitler's rise to power in the 1930s coincided with an upsurge of antisemitism and that many Poles were only too happy to collude in, and to opportunistically profit from, the Nazi's genocidal project. She also notes that "The fact that the Nazis found it necessary to impose the death penalty [for helping Jews] in Poland and in no other occupied country suggests . . . that the Poles were rather more prone than other nations to helping the Jews" (p. 155). In telling their story, she attempts to correct the "tendency . . . to merge all wartime experience into the one overwhelming experience of the killing camps," to challenge the "blanket use of the term [Holocaust] to cover the entirety of the horrific experience of the Jews in the war" (p. 60). Her parents' war stories, she notes, were "both more particular and more diverse" than the popular images of "heaped skeletal bodies and emaciated prisoners in striped pyjamas" allow for. Moreover, this monolithic version of the fate of European Jewry effectively silences her parents: once the "collectively sanctioned narrative of an iconic Holocaust had achieved coherence . . . their own storytelling began to fizzle out" (p. 60). In this sense, Appignanesi's book is, among other things, a way of restoring these individual voices that have been drowned in the clamorous memorialization of the Holocaust, a means of accommodating these personal stories in the larger historical framework, of re-inscribing "the jagged marks of individual memory which often won't fit neatly into the grand historical narrative" (p. 60) in the canon of Holocaust literature.

As a child, the author was told (or overheard), countless war stories, "stories of heroism, of Herculean feats or Odyssean wiliness," stories of survival that "had not yet acquired the political freight of the word Holocaust" (p. 21). As an adult, she becomes acutely aware that those narratives reflect both the extraordinary heightened reality of an era when, as Jacob Jardine puts it, "daily heroisms and daily atrocities, strained the bounds of peacetime belief" (*Memory and Desire*, p. 200) and, at the same time, the mythologizing tendency engendered by the exigencies of war. The overwhelming fact of the mass killing of Jews—the Holocaust itself—is curiously absent from these stories, in which "pain . . . was metamorphosed into triumph" (p. 21). In part, this may be attributed to repression, a reluctance to articulate the full horror: "The worst . . . was left to silence" (p. 21)—but it also represents a genuine sense of exultation at the simple fact of survival. Again, contrary to the conventional wisdom about survivor guilt, Appignanesi writes, "I don't think anyone [among her parents' circle of survivor friends] felt guilty about having made it through" (p. 21). Instead, there is pride in their own resourcefulness.

In *Memory and Desire*, Jardine marvels at the "rich spontaneous fictions people concocted to get themselves out of a tight spot," concluding that "The paranoias of occupation had given birth to countless novelists" (p. 186). Appignanesi's mother, Hena, is an example. For Hena, whose mental deterioration provides the spur for Appignanesi's excavation of her own past, "being blonde was an easy path into assimilation" and, during the war, "a means of survival" (p. 49). Emboldened by her impeccably Aryan looks, she not only ensures her own survival, but intervenes with both Polish and German authorities on several occasions (cleverly exploiting her sexuality) to rescue her (more conventionally Jewish-looking, and therefore more vulnerable) mother and husband. In common with many other survivors, the wartime experiences of Appignanesi's parents leave a legacy of self-hatred, an "internalized Nazi ideology" (p. 57) in which "Jewishness . . . carried a shameful taint" (p. 35). Even before the war, Hena had taken a certain (self-hating) satisfaction in being (mis)taken for a shiksa (female Gentile); after the war she revels in the "blonde power" (p. 57) that she believes renders her invulnerable and infallible. Appignanesi's father, Aaron, in contrast, can never shake off his fear and suspicion of all authority. Consequently, neither are able or willing to relinquish their double lives: they remain deeply ambivalent about their Jewishness, acknowledging it in certain situations, denying it in others. What was in wartime a survival strategy, a pragmatic duplicity, becomes a pathological compulsion, a deception so ingrained that as an adolescent, Appignanesi cannot be certain even of basic facts, such as her name and place of birth. On the one hand, then, the Holocaust exerts a grip so tenacious that neither Appignanesi's parents nor she herself can ever entirely break free of it, while on the other, its traces are almost too faint to decipher. The book is full of observations on the unreliability and unruliness of memory (exacerbated in her mother's case by the onset of dementia), and when Appignanesi travels to Poland she finds physical evidence of her family history equally elusive. Old homes have been demolished, documents lost, gravestone inscriptions effaced.

At the end of *Memory and Desire*, the Freudian analyst Jacob Jardine reflects on a life spent mediating between "the twin pivots of memory and forgetting," the paradoxical project of "Making memories forgettable" (p. 433), and it is Appignanesi's willingness to wrestle with, if not resolve, this paradox that makes *Losing the Dead* much more than simply a "modish search for roots" (p. 74). Only when she has made every attempt to retrieve the memory of her family history, to resurrect the ghosts of her dead relatives, can she truly forget them; only "by remembering them [can she] lose them properly" (p. 8).

Bibliography

Primary Sources

Fiction

Memory and Desire. 1991.
Dreams of Innocence. 1994.
A Good Woman. 1996.
The Things We Do for Love. 1997.
The Dead of Winter. 1999.
Sanctuary. 2000.

Fiction under Pseudonym of Jessica Ayre

Not to be Trusted. 1982.
One-Man Woman. 1982.
Hard to Handle. 1983.
New Discovery. 1984.

Nonfiction

Femininity and the Creative Imagination: A Study of James, Proust and Musil. 1973.
Dialogue of the Generations. 1974.
Cabaret: The First Hundred Years. 1975.
Simone de Beauvoir. 1988.
Freud's Women (with John Forrester). 1992.
Losing the Dead. 1999.

Edited Volumes

Desire. 1984.
Culture and the State. 1984.
Ideas from France. 1985.
Postmodernism. 1986.
Science and Beyond (edited with Steven Rose). 1986.
Identity. 1987.
Black Film-British Cinema. 1988.
Novostroika. 1989.
Brand New York. 1989.
Dismantling Truth: Reality in the Post-modern World (with Hilary Lawson). 1989.
The Rushdie File (with Sara Maitland). 1989.

Translations

Belotti, Elena Gianini. *Little Girls: Social Conditioning and Its Effects on the Stereotyped Role of Women During Infancy*. London: Writers' and Readers' Publishing Co-Op, 1975.
Bielski, Nella. *Oranges for the Son of Alexander Levy*. London: Writers' and Readers' Publishing Co-Op, 1982.
Appignanesi has also translated a number of children's books into English (from French, Italian, and German).

Secondary Source

Brauner, David. *Post-War Jewish Fiction: Ambivalence, Self-Explanation and Transatlantic Connections*. Harmondsworth: Palgrave, 2001.

ALICIA APPLEMAN-JURMAN

(1930–)

TOBE LEVIN

UNDER RUSSIAN OCCUPATION of Poland from 1939–1941, Alicia Appleman-Jurman lost her brother Moshe, killed in prison. Then, once the Nazis arrived, her father, who "registered" with five hundred other leading Buczacz citizens, was shot by a firing squad. Next, her brother Bunio became the tenth man in a Borki Wielki work camp execution—reprisal for an escapee. Zachary, her beloved eldest brother, organized resistance. The Nazis hanged him. Alicia, only eleven, defied authority to retrieve his body—a Holocaust Antigone. Left alive only to face numerous *Aktionen* (brutal rounding up of Jews either for immediate murder or transportation to camps) and to be transported to the Kopechince ghetto were Alicia, her little brother Herzl, and her mother. Later, a friend would denounce Herzl, and a bullet intended for Alicia would murder her mother. As sole survivor of her family, Appleman-Jurman devoted her life to Holocaust education, fulfilling her mother's wish as recorded in her book *Alicia: My Story* (1988)—"Alicia, you must live" (New York: Bantam, 1988, p. 179)—to tell. Appleman-Jurman's memoir won the 1989 Christopher Award for affirming the "high values of the human spirit" (David, p. 5); the Literary Guild made the book a featured alternate. Translations have appeared in Sweden, Denmark, Finland, France, Italy, Holland, and Switzerland. Compared to Anne Frank, Appleman-Jurman's narrator, who was between nine and fifteen in the setting of the memoir, speaks in a girl's voice—straightforward, humble, and courageous.

On 9 May 1930, Alicia Appleman-Jurman was born in Rosulna, Poland, to Frieda Kurtz and Sigmund Jurman, a rabbi's son and decorated Austrian World War I veteran who sold textiles. They moved to Buczacz, now in the Ukraine but then in southeastern Poland. Its 18,000 Jews, one-third of the population, "were . . . well-integrated into the community" (p. 1) with a few Poles. The majority of Ukrainians were eager to serve Hitler, who promised them independence. Antisemitism, always a fact of life, soon fueled the collaboration that Alicia documents. Having escaped a final action in which the ghetto was made altogether free of Jews, she and her mother survived by hiding in the wheat fields by day, in ravines by night, and in the home of a righteous Gentile through the bitter winter of 1943. In return for bread and sour milk, Alicia labored alongside the farmers, at times passing as Ukrainian and at other times as a Pole. She was proficient in both of these languages as well as in Hebrew. Although many villagers knew her identity, they hired this conscientious worker and, after the harvest, gave her alms when she begged.

Following liberation, Appleman-Jurman's actions continue to reveal qualities that helped her endure: leadership and empathy. Although only fifteen, she found weeping Jewish orphans wandering the Lvov streets—her "first real contact with . . . what had happened in German concentration camps" (p. 268). Supported by Jewish Soviet soldiers, she opened an orphanage but not before being repulsed by an enraged Polish municipal official of whom she'd requested funding: " 'You Jews survived?' he cried. 'You cursed Jews survived?' " (p. 271). Aware of unabated antisemitism in the "big Jewish cemetery" (p. 290), which Europe had become, Alicia resolved to get to Palestine and joined the Brecha, who smuggled Jews out of Eastern Europe. She worked with them until pneumonia forced her retirement. "Promoted" to the status of DP (Displaced Person), she was cared for in Badgastein's UNRRA (United Nations Relief and Rehabilitation Administration) hotel, transferred to schools in Belgium, and finally shipped to Israel, the Promised Land. She spent another eight months in a Cypriot detention camp before gaining access to an agricultural school near Tel Aviv. Later, with her American husband, Gabriel, Appleman-Jurman settled in the United States, where Daniel, Ronit, and Zachary were born. She now resides in South Bay, California.

Survival: Luck and Guilt

The "feeling . . . shared by most survivors" breaks out in Appleman-Jurman postwar nightmares. This feeling is guilt. "Any one of [her] brothers" (p. 231) would have been more deserving. Appleman-Jurman believes, like most survivors, that she owed her escape sometimes to pluck, but more often to fortune. First, captured while visiting a neighbor and placed on an early transport, she was slim enough to pass through the debarred cattle car window. Admonished to live, she hurtled herself out and landed beside the track. It is uncertain precisely how she made it home, as her next memory was of waking, after a feverish delirium. She then knew, however, that the Nazis lie: "Where could they be taking women and children? Certainly not to a work camp" (p. 24).

A second reprieve, even more spectacular, was her rescue from a pile of corpses. Ukrainian police had come for her mother, but the tall, twelve-year-old Appleman-Jurman took her mother's place. Her ribs having been cracked in Chortkov prison, she was deprived of drink for days before imbibing typhus-contaminated water. Unconscious, she failed to respond to the daily kicking intended to identify the dead and was hauled away for burial. Perceiving warmth in her still body, Mr. Gold of the *Judenrat* (the Nazi-appointed council of Jews assigned to ensure compliance with Nazi orders concerning the ghetto, deportation, and other related matters) smuggled her out of the prison cemetery and, with his wife, nursed her back to life.

Appleman-Jurman also twice survived a firing squad. Protecting a neighbor's infant, she was found outside the bunker during a liquidation. Marching to an open grave and aware of the impending shooting, she "experience[d] that familiar feeling of hate [that] acted in a strange way . . . actually clear[ing] [her] brain. [She] felt like a spectator [not] personally involved" (Appleman-Jurman, p. 94). She was thus better prepared for the sudden appearance of Jewish armed resistance: her friend Milek, shooting, yelled, "Alicia, run!" (Appleman-Jurman, p. 95). Later, when she was captured after her mother's execution, she stayed near the end of the line, so that when her turn came to approach the ditch, she could more easily bolt to the river and dive under a hollow log whose mouth faced away from the shore, thereby eluding the dogs.

Collaborators and Perpetrators

Parading to death, Alicia writes of "people along . . . the streets . . . cursing us and . . . throwing stones" (p. 94). Here, treachery meets the Jews at every turn. For instance, in the marketplace, Alicia recognizes the Gurali accent of Solotvina farmers. These farmers, from her mother's village, tell her what happened there and tell her about the fate of her maternal grandparents: pointed out by "those Ukrainian bastards" (p. 35), the Kurtzs, her mother's family, were victims of the *Einsatzgruppen* (the mobile killing squads), the maternal grandfather was buried alive, the others were shot. Perhaps to atone, the Solotivian farmer couple offered to take Alicia home with them. "After all, you hardly look like a Jew" (p. 36), they suggested. The phrase exploded in her brain: "*Look like a Jew, look like a Jew* . . . Had my father and Bunio looked like Jews, with their blond hair and blue eyes? Would the Germans have known they were Jews if they hadn't been betrayed by . . . our own neighbors?" (p. 36). Again in Buczacz, she and her mother were betrayed by the concierge. Were it not for such local aid, the Germans [could] never have so efficiently destroyed Jewish lives (David, p. 4).

Righteousness

Despite all, several Gentiles did help: Manka, whose family blessed Alicia with days of "normality"—meals, warmth, acceptance, on condition only that she spaced her visits. Maria, a Polish gentile farm woman, housed both mother and daughter in her barn until they were threatened with exposure. Alicia's school friend Slavka tried to stand by her: she provided a jacket and shoes. But Alicia owes most to an epileptic Polish nobleman already housing several women and children when she and her mother arrived. He also accepted three more people whom Alicia rescued from imminent capture when, in the field, she overheard a threat. Resisting, Wujciu (uncle) reminded her, "I could be killed if you were found in my house. . . . I could die for this!" (p. 135).

Heroism

His fears were well founded. The shout "Open up, you damned Jews!" violated the evening peace. While the others hid, Alicia faced the intruders alone. Through Wujciu's door stomped the Banderovcy, Ukrainian "patriots," who aided the Nazis in persecuting Jews, with Pietro among then, Slavka's co-worker in the fields. "What are you doing here with the Jews?" he asked, amazed (p. 160). Declaring proudly that she is a

Jew, she used two appeals, warning that "commit[ing] such a crime against innocent women and children" (p. 160) would stain their consciences as they grew older. She ensures regret by cursing them, swearing "in the name of my God and [theirs to] haunt [them] from [her] grave" (p. 150). It works.

But the most dramatic act of heroism earned Appelman-Jurman a Russian medal, which reads, *Za advahu*—for bravery—(p. 207), awarded by the Kalpak partisans. She rescued them while crawling along a train station ledge in her own attempt to escape a (voluntary) work transport of Ukrainian youth to Germany. Through the windowpane she spotted the wounded; opening the window from the outside, she extended her arm, allowing them to pull themselves up and escape.

Appleman-Jurman's importance to Holocaust literature lies in the narrative voice of the young, resourceful victim, "representative of over one million people who did not die in camps, but were murdered at open graves, in their homes or on the streets or [who] died as partisans fighting the Germans and their collaborators. Alicia tells of . . . heroic children in the ghettos . . . [whose] bravery and sacrifices serv[e] as shining examples for the youth of today" (David, p. 6). Appleman-Jurman spares no details: she starves, she has lice, she is surrounded by antisemites avid for Jewish homes. After the war, Jews attempting to reclaim Polish property risked murder, leaving Alicia to conclude that "there was no future for the Jews in Poland, or, for that matter, anywhere else in Europe" (p. 291). In the United States, she educates students about the Holocaust to this very day, reminding students that "six million people died of a disease called indifference." Alicia hopes to teach "tolerance and peace" (Matschal).

Bibliography

Primary Source

Alicia: My Story. 1988.

Secondary Sources

Matschal, Melissa. "Holocaust Survivor Brings Her Story to Middle School." *The Campbell Reporter.* http://www.metroactive.com/papers/campbell.reporter/03.21 .01/author–0112.html (3 December 2001).

David, G. "Alicia Appleman-Jurman: Survival and Heroism of a Young Girl During the Holocaust." http://www.datasync.com/~davidg59/alicia.html (21 June 2001).

HANNAH ARENDT

(1906–1975)

JENNIFER RING

Biography

HANNAH ARENDT WAS born in Konigsberg, Prussia, in 1906, the only child of Paul and Martha Cohn Arendt. Her parents were well-educated, progressive-minded Jews, who doted on their daughter's early secular education, but did not neglect an education in Judaism. Before her father died when she was seven, she was tutored by the local reform rabbi several times a week, for several years. At eighteen she began her university studies in philosophy with Martin Heidegger at Marburg, became personally involved with him, and decided to transfer to Heidelberg, completing her degree with the psychoanalytically trained philosopher, Karl Jaspers. Her doctoral dissertation was on the subject of love in the philosophy of Augustine.

As the Nazis came to power in Germany, Arendt became involved in a Zionist group led by Kurt Blumenfeld. Blumenfeld and Arendt were sharply critical of assimilation, and sought to build a Jewish community in Zion that was cooperative with its non-Jewish neighbors, but where assimilation would not be "the price of citizenship." Arendt's work for Blumenfeld ultimately led to the first stage of her flight from the Nazis. In 1933 the research she was doing for Blumenfeld's organization in the Prussian State Library on nongovernmental antisemitism in Germany caused her arrest and the search of her apartment. She regarded her release as a lucky warning and a very close call, and immediately left Germany with her husband and mother.

She lived in Paris, working for organizations that helped Jewish refugees emigrate to Palestine and supplied legal aid to anti-fascists. In May 1940, Arendt and her husband, Heinrich Blucher, were ordered to report to separate internment camps in France. Officially defined as "enemy aliens," Arendt sarcastically described herself as one of the "new kinds of human beings" who are "put into concentration camps by their foes and into internment camps by their friends" (Young-Bruehl, p. 152). She was held, along with over six thousand other women and children, at Gurs. The period was one of the lowest of her life. In her essay "We Refugees" (*Menorah Journal*, January 1943) she commented:

> At the camp of Gurs . . . where I had the opportunity of spending some time, I heard only once about suicide, and that was the suggestion of a collective action, apparently a kind of protest in order to vex the French. When some of us remarked that we had been shipped there *"pour crever"* [to be done in] in any case, the general mood turned suddenly into a violent courage of life (p. 59).

After Arendt had been in Gurs for several weeks, France fell and all communications broke down. In the resulting chaos Arendt obtained liberation papers and left the camp. She was one of the fortunate ones: she and her husband had arranged a place to meet in the French countryside, in a house rented by friends, which she reached by walking and hitchhiking. The presence of mind to leave in the midst of the chaos saved her life. Arendt and her husband escaped to New York later that year by bicycling to Marseilles, once again having good luck in obtaining exit visas, and using their wits to complete the escape. Blucher was identified as a communist and summoned to the front desk of the hotel where police would have arrested him, had he not casually walked out while his wife created a loud distraction, shouting at the hotel clerk that her husband had been arrested and that the clerk was responsible for his fate! Arendt and Blucher had arranged to meet at a café and completed their escape to Lisbon and finally New York.

Once in the United States, Arendt found work for herself with Jewish youth organizations. Although she was a European scholar who had worked under the supervision of the two most highly esteemed philosophers in Germany, American academia was no more open to women than were European universities, and Jewish male scholars were just beginning to make inroads in the United States. In New York she wrote for *Aufbau*, a German language newspaper, in which she advocated a Jewish army to fight against Hitler, and a Jewish homeland in Palestine that would negotiate peace with its Arab neighbors. The failure of her Jewish political hopes convinced her that her talents were better utilized in writing than in political activism, and she took a job as an editor at Schocken Books.

She became disillusioned with intellectuals per se during her last years in Europe. She witnessed her beloved mentor, Martin Heidegger, fall under the sway of Nazi antisemitism and realized that thinking philosophically was no guarantee of being able to act responsibly in the world. She referred to intellectuals' inability to act as a "deformacion professionelle," a sort of occupational hazard of scholarly life. She wrote that Hitler's rise to power was not as surprising to German Jews as the cooperation of people whom they had regarded as their friends, and concluded that the intellectual community was more likely to find a rationale for cooperating with the Nazis than ordinary people.

Nonetheless, Arendt's inability to renounce Martin Heidegger publicly is probably the single most tenacious grievance raised by Jews who believe she had trouble with her own Jewish identity. Heidegger, one of the preeminent philosophers of the twentieth century, never renounced his involvement with the Nazi party, and Arendt never publicly disavowed her teacher. Privately, in letters to Jaspers after the war, she was unsparing about Heidegger's utter moral failure. In July 1946 she wrote, "Regarding the Heidegger note, your assumption about the Husserl letter is completely correct. . . . It always seemed to me that at the moment Heidegger was obliged to put his name to this document, he should have resigned. However foolish he may have been, he was capable of that." In September 1949 she was even more damning:

> What you call impurity I would call lack of character—but in the sense that he literally has none. . . . This living in Todnauberg, grumbling about civilization and writing *sein* with a "y," is really a kind of mouse hole he has crawled back into because he rightly assumes the only people he'll have to see there are the pilgrims who come full of admiration for him. Nobody is likely to climb 1,200 meters to make a scene (Arendt and Jaspers *Correspondence*, Letters 42 and 93, pp. 47–48, 93).

Still, the fact that she said nothing publicly critical of Heidegger, agreed to meet with him in Europe in 1949, and wrote a tribute two decades later titled "Martin Heidegger at Eighty" (in *Heidegger and Modern Philosophy*, Yale University Press, 1978), in which she still attempted to explain his murderous political behavior, is deeply troubling. It may be that her youthful involvement with Heidegger when he was a widely revered teacher was more than she could overcome, or it may reflect a more general inability to distance herself from European scholarly canon. In her 1944 essay "The Jew as Pariah: A Hidden Tradition" she was clear about her disdain for arrivistes and parvenus in political and social life, and portrayed "the Conscious Pariah" as the most admirable stance for the marginalized peoples of any society. One proudly claims one's status as a pariah, which permits action from that excluded standpoint. This, she believed, was the most potent place for a Jew to stand mid-twentieth century.

> In contrast to his unemancipated brethren who accept their pariah status automatically and unconsciously, the emancipated Jew must awake to an awareness of his position and, conscious of it, become a rebel against it—the champion of an oppressed people. His fight for freedom is part and parcel of that which all the down-trodden of Europe must needs wage to achieve national and social liberation (*Jew as Pariah,* p. 76).

However, when it came to embracing her own marginalized position as a Jewish intellectual woman, Arendt suffered from a failure of nerve, defending the centrality of Western European (male) scholarship. She was a brilliant critic of Western philosophy, but was fundamentally accepting of the rules of the establishment. In this sense, *she* was an intellectual parvenu and consciously a political pariah at the same time. This may enable us to understand the contradictions and weakness in her attitude toward Heidegger.

Although Arendt vowed to have nothing to do with professional scholars, she began a massive project, which developed out of her involvement in Jewish politics, but also marked the first moment since her exile when she could do any scholarly research. The result was publication of a three-volume work that has become a classic and path-breaking work on twentieth-century political history. When *The Origins of Totalitarianism* was published in 1951, Arendt was catapulted to American-style celebrity, appearing on the covers of *Time* magazine and *Newsweek* during the same week. She wrote to Jaspers in Germany that she was now an American "Cover Girl." Arendt received offers from the most prestigious universities in the United States, and accepted part-time positions at various times at The Princeton Center for Advanced Study, the University of Chicago, the University of California at Berkeley, the Stanford Center for Advanced Study in the Behavioral and Social Sciences, and the New School for Social Research in New York City. In spite of her newly won international reputation, Arendt remained independent from organized intellectual life and avoided a full-time position at any university. This was partly because she was an intellectual maverick, who by her own description "somehow just didn't fit." She insisted on her independence from organized academic life, and safeguarded her time to write and to visit old friends in Europe on an annual basis. She died in New York in 1975, a page of what was to have been her final manuscript still in her typewriter.

Writings on Political Evil

Arendt was a profoundly independent and provocative thinker who appealed to an educated lay audience as well as to professional scholars. She was as likely to infuriate as to inspire readers from both milieus. Her impact on post-Holocaust thought has been enormous because of her prescience and breadth of outlook. She has been at the center of several political and intellectual storms, and the impact of her work is probably best understood when viewed in the context of two works, published a dozen years apart: *The Origins of Totalitarianism* (1951) and *Eichmann in Jerusalem: A Report on the Banality of Evil* (1963).

In *The Origins of Totalitarianism*, Arendt offered a historically based theory about the origins of antisemitism and imperialism in order to understand what could have permitted the rise to power of Hitler and Nazism. She regarded Nazi genocide as an ominous new development in world history, referring to it as she was writing in the mid-1940s as "race imperialism," the culmination of antisemitism, imperialism, and racism. As she continued her research, the concept evolved to include Stalinist terrorism, and her work grew to include analysis of the common elements of right- and left-wing extremism. The phrase Arendt coined to describe the political system she regarded as unprecedented in world history was *totalitarianism.*

The use of terror in the totally controlled environment of concentration camps provided Arendt with the element that she believed linked Nazism with Stalinism, and permitted both to be described as totalitarian regimes. Arendt thus focused on two concepts that have proven eerily prescient for global politics at the turn of the millennium: totalitarianism and terrorism. Terrorism and concentration camps permit totalitarianism to control all aspects of human existence, with an irrational basis never before seen in the world. Totalitarianism was a system beyond politics, morality, and rationality. She characterized its underpinning as "radical evil," unprecedented and with no basis for comprehension in any philosophical system in history.

The amassing of human beings into concentration camps divested them of individuality, uniqueness, hence their very humanness. The use of terror, of previously unimaginable cruelty, torture, pain, not for any of the conventional "motives," but for the sheer ability to control the world, *totally*, was used on the inhabitants of concentration camps in an attempt to disorient them to the point of making their humanity as inaccessible as possible.

In Arendt's political lexicon, "public space," "private space," and "individual uniqueness" are necessary for human freedom, which she described as the capacity for action. To *act* is to begin something new in the world, which is defined in terms of its public space (*polis*), as contrasted with the household (*oikos*), or private space. She developed these concepts in *The Human Condition* (1958), an exploration of "anti-totalitarian" society: a democracy, modeled on the ancient Athenian democracy, with all its strengths and weaknesses. To be truly human, one must be free to act politically, to speak publicly among equals. Other aspects of the human condition are work, or the making of objects for the world, and labor, which is necessary to human existence but not to a distinctly human life. Labor is characterized by repetitive motions and the absence of a final product. More like behavior than action, it does not distinguish human from animal life. Her categorization of labor as less human than work or skilled artisanry set Marxists against Arendt and earned her a reputation for conservatism and elitism—at least until the late 1960s when the student left discovered her.

Three years after she published *The Human Condition* and a decade after *The Origins of Totalitarianism* made her famous, Arendt asked the *New Yorker* magazine for permission to cover the Jerusalem trial of accused Nazi war criminal, Adolph Eichmann, who had been captured by the Israelis. She had escaped the worst ravages of the Holocaust by her political alertness and her willingness to act. Now, she said, she wanted an opportunity to "look the devil in the face" by traveling to Jerusalem to witness the trial for his part in the murder of hundreds of thousands of Jews. What she found was not what she expected. Instead of the face of radical evil, she saw, she believed, a man who simply lacked the capacity to think. Mindless evil, rather than extreme, diabolical, racist, genocidal intent, is what Eichmann seemed to personify. She referred to Eichmann in her journalistic account, first published in a five-part *New Yorker* article, and the next year as a book, as "banal." The subtitle of her book, *A Report on the Banality of Evil*, set off a firestorm of criticism and turned many prominent Jewish intellectuals and leaders against her. She was accused of being a "self-hating Jew" who betrayed the Jewish community with her suggestion that the Holocaust could not be understood in terms of polarized concepts of good and evil. In fact, she gave the world a concept that is now commonly accepted: bureaucratic murder and administrative indifference as aspects of both war and "peace."

Controversial Reception of Her Work

Two elements of her argument deeply offended many Jews. First was her claim that Eichmann was not a monster, harbored no extreme antisemitic views, but was nonetheless capable of sending hundreds of thousands of Jews to their deaths. The thoughtless, almost passive desire to please his superiors, to perform well on the job, is what accounted for the destruction of innocent life. In arguing that enormous evil can be committed thoughtlessly, Arendt implied that all might be vulnerable to this type of failure.

A second dimension of her argument that aroused anger was Arendt's contention that the Jewish leadership's desire to keep their community together led them to negotiate with the Nazis and contributed to the slaughter of Jews.

> True it was that the Jewish people as a whole had not been organized, that they had possessed no territory, no government, and no army, that, in the hour of their greatest need, they had no government-in-exile, no caches of weapons, no youth with military training. But the whole truth was that if the Jewish people had really been unorganized and leaderless there would have been chaos and plenty of misery, but the total number of victims would hardly have been between five and six million (*Eichmann in Jerusalem*, New York: Penguin, 1963, p. 125).

The irony is that while her stance was widely criticized as "blaming the victims" and betraying her own people, the more conservative Jews in the newly formed State of Israel were arguing with Ben Gurion and the moderates over the same issue, accusing any suspected *Judenrate* of treason for having negotiated with Nazis. There were incidents of mob violence against European Jewish immigrants in Israel who were believed to have been members of the *Judenrate*. The highly politicized trial of Hungarian refugee Rudolf Kastner over his attempts to save European Jews polarized Israeli Jews in 1954.

In the United States the controversy over Eichmann centered on a series of articles and reviews in the *Partisan Review* in 1963, additional articles in *Commentary*, *The New Republic*, and *Dissent*, and forums and meetings in New York. Vicious personal attacks were written by Lionel Abel and Norman Podhoretz, who accused Arendt of "blaming the victims" and of appropriating and distorting the data in Raul Hilberg's *The Destruction of the European Jews*, which had been published the previous year and received with respect. Arendt was defended in print by Dwight MacDonald, who referred to Abel as "solemnly foolish," and by Mary McCarthy, who attempted to untangle Abel's "logic" in accusing Arendt of both stealing Hilberg's highly respected data and also somehow being inaccurate ("The Hue and Cry," p. 94). She concluded that his argument was "a maze. It is like arguing with a hydra (pp. 87, 88)."

More responsible criticisms were raised by Gershom Scholem and Marie Syrkin. In his well-known letter of 23 June 1963, Scholem chastised Arendt for emphasing Jewish weakness against the Nazis, of writing in a "heartless, frequently almost sneering and malicious tone, and of lacking *Ahavath Israel*, "Love of the Jewish People."

> A discussion such as is attempted in your book would seem to me to require—you will forgive my mode of expression—the most old-fashioned, the most circumspect, the most exacting treatment possible. . . . To speak of all this, however, in so wholly inappropriate a tone—to the benefit of those Germans in condemning whom your book rises to greater eloquence than in mourning the fate of your own people—this is not the way to approach the scene of that tragedy (Feldman, p. 241).

Scholem believed Arendt should have written from a more self-consciously Jewish perspective. His criticism was echoed, ironically, by American sociologist Daniel Bell, who had made his scholarly reputation as an "objective" social scientist, but who now called upon Arendt to take a more "tribal" perspective: "The agony of Miss Arendt's book is precisely that she takes her stand so unyieldingly on the side of disinterested justice, and that she judges both Nazi and Jew. But abstract justice, as the Talmudic wisdom knew, is sometimes too 'strong' a yardstick to judge the world" (Bell, p. 428). Dwight MacDonald responded to Daniel Bell on Arendt's behalf, "A yardstick is not a yardstick if it is more or less than three feet long, and justice is not justice unless it is universalistic. I am old-fashioned enough . . . to still find these favored, special, exceptional categories of race or nation morally suspect and intellectually confusing" (MacDonald, p. 269). MacDonald also regretted "the violence of the Jewish attacks on Miss Arendt's book."

Arendt answered Scholem in a respectful but wounded letter, insisting that he had missed the irony in her language, and that she did not think in terms of collectivities and therefore neither "loved" the Jews, nor "believed" in them as an entity. "I merely belong to them as a matter of course beyond dispute or argument." She also insisted to Scholem in what amounted to a prescient attack on "political correctness" that he was upset because her views were not conventional and did not adhere to a party line (pp. 240–251).

Marie Syrkin raised troubling questions about what she considered to be Arendt's selective use of the data in Hilberg's book in a less contradictory, better-balanced manner than Lionel Abel. She accused Arendt of possessing an "ability to disregard whatever does not suit her thesis" and of "willfully ignoring" inconvenient data. For example, with regard to Arendt's argument that the Jews would have been better served if the *Judenrate* had not participated in the process of organizing and "selecting" Jews for surrender to the Nazis in order to "save the remnant," Syrkin wrote, "What does Miss Arendt suggest as an alternative to 'selection'? Should the Palestinians merely have announced: 'Run pell-mell to the ships and let the fastest board!'?" (Syrkin, p. 9). This is a real question, but one with no single obvious answer. Postwar Israel also found itself in agonizing conflict about how the European Jews should have behaved, when in fact, there was little that could have been done by either European or Israeli Jews without relying on assistance from the Allied forces.

In fact, Hilberg's data and conclusions are very similar to Arendt's, and the fact that his work was not attacked with anything close to the vehemence Arendt experienced raises questions with regard to the reasons her work so enraged her Jewish critics. Her tone, which was indeed caustic, was certainly an issue. So was the fact that Arendt refused to think in terms of oversimplified categories of good and evil. Instead, her argument that great evil could be committed with a "banal" or administrative mindset introduced troubling ambiguities that implicated all of us. Of the American Jewish intellectuals who were critical of *Eichmann in Jerusalem*, only Alfred Kazin recognized that the tone of the attack on Arendt resembled that of a lynch party, and attributed it at least in part to guilt on the part of New York Jewish intellectuals. As early as 1944 he referred to "our silent complicity in the massacre of the Jews." He was referring to their embarrassment at appearing "too Jewish" in their attitude toward Hitler (Ring, 1997, p. 100).

Israeli Jews were also struggling to come to terms with the fact that they had been unable to help the Jews caught in the Holocaust, unable to amass any defense against Hitler, and had sought refuge from their impotence by distancing themselves emotionally from the victims. They had, during the war years, regarded European Jews as assimilationists, insufficiently identified with Zionism and Judaism, weak and effeminate compared to the rugged Zionist pioneers in Israel. After the war, they had to come to terms with those unpleasant responses to the victims and refugees of the Holocaust, many of whom now sought to emigrate to Israel. Once again, Arendt's refusal to generalize Jews and Nazis into simplified categories of good and evil caused discomfort, as did the implication that the Israelis, particularly Prime Minister David Ben Gurion's party, might be exploiting the Eichmann trial and the Holocaust for political reasons. Arendt would have preferred an international tribunal to treat his crimes against the Jews as crimes against humanity. Ben Gurion himself influenced the decision not to translate Arendt's book into Hebrew for release in Israel.

Arendt supported the death penalty for Eichmann in the conclusion of her report, although she believed that the deeds he carried out were beyond punishment. Her explanation was that he had, by his acts, removed himself from human existence:

> In politics obedience and support are the same. And just as you supported and carried out a policy of not wanting to share the earth with the Jewish people and the people of a number of other nations . . . we find that no one, that is no member of the human race, can be expected to want to share the earth with you. This is the reason, and the only reason you must hang (*Eichmann*, p. 279).

Arendt's Impact

Hannah Arendt was one of the first to articulate the concept of institutional war crimes against humanity, forcing us to think about passive acquiescence in, for example, genocide in parts of the world that seem remote, corporate crimes against the environment, internationally sanctioned global capitalist exploitation of the poor, and indulgence in oversimplified categories that foreclose thinking about seemingly unresolvable conflicts involving race and religion. Totalitarianism has evolved into the threat of world terrorism, but still can be understood with her emphasis on the individual responsibility to think. Arendt devoted her scholarly life to attempting to awaken the world to the dangers that permitted totalitarian genocide to arise in Germany and to preventing its recurrence ever again. Her unflinching eye and willingness to articulate the most unpleasant political and ethical truths have made her both revered and the subject of brutal criticism. Her controversial legacy is the result of her original and penetrating brilliance.

Bibliography

Primary Sources

Books

Der Liebesbegriff bei Augustin (Concept of Neighborly Love in the Philosophy of Augustine). 1929.

Sechs Essays. 1943.

The Origins of Totalitarianism. 1951, 1968.

The Human Condition. 1954, 1958.

Karl Jaspers: Reden Zure Verleihung des Frienpreises des Deutschen Buchlhandels (Karl Jaspers as Citizen of the World). 1958.

Eichmann in Jerusalem: A Report on the Banality of Evil. 1961, 1963.

On Revolution. 1962.

Between Past and Future: Eight Exercises in Political Thought. 1968.

Men in Dark Times. 1968.

Crises of the Republic. 1972.

Rahel Varnhagen: The Life of a Jewish Woman. 1974.

The Jew as Pariah.: Jewish Identity and Politics in the Modern Age. Edited and introduced by Ron Feldman. 1978.

The Life of the Mind: One/Thinking, Two/Willing. 1978.

Articles

"A Believer in European Unity." *Review of Politics* 4/2 (April 1942): 245–247. (A review of P. R. Sweet, *Friedrich von Gentz: Defender of the Old Order.*)

"From the Dreyfus Affair to France Today." *Jewish Social Studies* 4 (July 1942): 195–240. (Reprinted in *Essays on Anti-Semitism*, Conference on Jewish Relations, 1946 and used in *The Origins of Totalitarianism*, Part 1.)

"We Refugees." *Menorah Journal* 31 (January 1943): 69–77.

"Concerning Minorities." *Contemporary Jewish Record* 7, no. 4 (August 1944): 353–368. (Used in *The Origins of Totalitarianism*, Part 2.)

"Our Foreign Language Groups." *Chicago Jewish Forum* 3, no. 1 (fall 1944): 23–34.

"Organized Guilt and Universal Responsibility." *Jewish Frontier*, January 1945, 19–23. (Reprinted in Roger Smith, ed., *Guilt: Man and Society*, New York: Doubleday Anchor, 1971.)

"Approaches to the 'German Problem.' " *Partisan Review* 12, no. 1 (winter 1945): 93–106.

"Nightmare and Flight." *Partisan Review* 12, no. 2 (spring 1945): 259–260. (A review of Denis de Rougemont, *The Devil's Share.*)

"The Assets of Personality." *Contemporary Jewish Record* 8, no. 2 (April 1945): 214–216. (A review of Meyer W. Weisgal, ed., *Chaim Weismann.*)

"The Stateless People." *Contemporary Jewish Record* 8, no. 2 (April 1945): 137–153. (Used in *The Origins of Totalitarianism*, Part 2.)

"The Seeds of a Fascist International." *Jewish Frontier*, June 1945, 12–16.

"Zionism Reconsidered." *Menorah Journal* 33 (August 1945): 162–196. (Translated into German for *Die Verborgene Tradition* and reprinted in M. Selzer, ed., *Zionism Reconsidered*, New York: Macmillan Co., 1970, 213–249.)

"Parties, Movements and Classes." *Partisan Review* 121, no. 4 (fall 1945): 504–512. (Used in *The Origins of Totalitarianism*, Part 2.)

"Imperialism, Nationalism, Chauvinism." *Review of Polities* 7/4 (October 1945): 441–463. (Used in *The Origins of Totalitarianism*, Part 2.)

"What Is Existenz Philosophy?" *Partisan Review* 18, no. 1 (winter 1946): 55–56.

"Privileged Jews." *Jewish Social Studies* 8, no. 1 (January 1946): 3–30. (Reprinted in Duker and Ben-Horiii, *Emancipation and Counteremancipation*, New York: Ktav Publishing House, 1947).

"Imperialism: Road to Suicide." *Commentary* I (February 1946): 27–35.

"The Streets of Berlin." *Nation*, 23 March 1946, 350–351. (A review of Robert Gilbert, *Meine Reime Deine Reime.*)

"The Jewish State: 50 Years After, Where Have Herzl's Politics Led?" *Commentary* I (May 1946): 1–8.

"The Image of Hell." *Commentary* 2, no. 3 (September 1946): 291–295. (A review of *The Black Book: The Nazi Crime against the Jewish People*. Compiled by the World Jewish Congress et al. and Max Weinreich. *Hitler's Professors.*)

"The Ivory Tower of Common Sense." *Nation*, 19 October 1946, 447–449. (A review of John Dewey, *Problems of Men.*)

"Tentative List of Jewish Cultural Treasures in Axis-Occupied Countries." *Supplement to Jewish Social Studies* 8, no. 1 (1946). (This was prepared by the Research Staff of the Commission on European Jewish Cultural Reconstruction headed by Arendt.)

"Tentative List of Jewish Educational Institutions in Axis-Occupied Countries." *Supplement to Jewish Social Studies* 8, no. 3 (1946). (This was prepared by the Research Staff of the Commission on European Jewish Cultural Reconstruction headed by Arendt.)

"The Hole of Oblivion." *Jewish Frontier*, July 1947, 23–26. (A review of *The Dark Side of the Moon.*)

"Creating a Cultural Atmosphere." *Commentary* 4 (November 1947): 424–426.

"Jewish History, Revised." *Jewish Frontier*, March 1948, 34–38. (A review of Gershom Scholem, *Major Trends in Jewish Mysticism.*)

"To Save the Jewish Homeland: There Is Still Time." *Commentary* 5 (May 1948): 398–406.

"The Concentration Camps." *Partisan Review* 15, no. 7 (July 1948): 743–763. (Anthologized in *Partisan Reader*, 1945–1953, and used in *The Origins of Totalitarianism*, Part 2.)

"About Collaboration." *Jewish Frontier*, October 1948, 55–56.

"The Mission of Bernadotte." *New Leader* 31 (23 October 1948): 808, 819.

"Totalitarian Terror." *Review of Politics I* 1/1 (January 1949): 112–115. (A review of David 1, Dallin and Boris 1.)

"Single Track to Zion." *Saturday Review of Literature* 32 (5 February 1949): 22–23. (A review of Chaim Weizmann, *Trial and Error: The Autobiography of Chaim Weizmann.*)

" 'The Rights of Man': What Are They?" *Modem Review* 3, no. 1 (summer 1949): 24–37. (Used in *The Origins of Totalitarianism*, Part 2.)

"The Aftermath of Nazi Rule, Report from Germany." *Commentary* 10 (October 1950): 342–353. (Anthologized in *The Commentary Reader.*)

"Mob and the Elite." *Partisan Review* 17 (November 1950): 808–819. (Used in *The Origins of Totalitarianism*, Part 3.)

"Religion and the Intellectuals, A Symposium." *Partisan Review* 17 (February 1950): 113–116.

"Social Science Techniques and the Study of Concentration Camps." *Jewish Social Studies* 12, no. 1 (1950): 49–64.

"The Imperialist Character." *Review of Politics* 12, no. 3 (July 1950): 303–320. (Used in *The Origins of Totalitarianism*, Part 2.)

"Me Road to the Dreyfus Affair." *Commentary I* I (February 1951): 201–203. (A review of Robert F. Byrnes, *Anti-Semitism in Modem France*.)

"Totalitarian Movement." *Twentieth Century* 149 (May 1951): 368–389. (Used in *The Origins of Totalitarianism*, Part 3.)

"Bei Hitler Zu Tisch." *Der Monat* 4 (October 1951): 85–90.

"The History of the Great Crime." *Commentary* 13 (March 1952): 300–304. (A review of Léon Poliakov. *Bréviare de la Haine: Le IIIe Reich et Les Juifs*.)

"Magnes, The Conscience of the Jewish People." *Jewish Newsletter* 8, no. 25 (24 November 1952): 2.

"Rejoinder to Eric Voegelin's Review of *The Origins of Totalitarianism*." *Review of Politics* 15 (January 1953): 7"5.

"The Ex-Communists." *Commonweal* 57, no. 24 (20 March 1953): 595–599. (Reprinted in *Washington Post*, 31 July 1953.)

"Ideology and Terror: A Novel Form of Government." *Review of Politics* 15, no. 3 (July 1953): 303–327. (Included in the 1958 edition of *The Origins of Totalitarianism*. A German version appeared in *Offener Horizont: Festschrift fiir Karl Jaspers*. Munich: Piper, 1953.)

"Understanding and Politics." *Partisan Review* 20, no. 4 (July–August 1953): 377–392.

"Understanding Communism." *Partisan Review* 20, no. 5 (September–October 1953): 580–583. (A review of Waldemar Gurian, *Bolshevism*.)

"Religion and Politics." *Confluence* 2, no. 3 (September 1953): 105–126. (Cf. Arendt's reply to criticism of this article in *Confluence*, pp. 118–120.)

"Tradition and the Modern Age." *Partisan Review* 22 (January 1954): 53–75. (Drawn from a series of lectures delivered at Princeton as the Christian Gauss Seminars in Criticism, 1953, and used in *Between Past and Future*.)

"Europe and the Atom Bomb." *Commonweal* 60, no. 24 (17 September 1954): 578–580.

"Europe and America: Dream and Nightmare." *Commonweal* 60, no. 23 (10 September 1954): 551–554.

"Europe and America: The Threat of Conformism." *Commonweal* 60, no. 25 (24 September 1954): 607–610.

"History and Immortality." *Partisan Review* 24, no. 1 (winter 1957): 11–53.

"Jaspers as Citizen of the World." In *The Philosophy of Karl Jaspers*. Edited by P. A. Schilpp. La Salle, Ill.: Open Court Publishing Co., 1957, pp. 539–550. (Reprinted in *Men in Dark Times*, 1968.)

"Authority in the Twentieth Century." Review of Politics 18, no. 4 (October 1956) 403–417.

"Totalitarian Imperialism: Reflections on the Hungarian Revolution." *Journal of Politics* 20, no. 1 (February 1958): 5–43. (Reprinted in *Cross Currents* 8, no. 2 [spring 1958]: 102–128, and added to the 1958 edition of *The Origins of Totalitarianism*.)

"The Crisis in Education." *Partisan Review* 25, no. 4 (fall 1958): 493–513. (Reprinted in *Between Past and Future*, 1968.)

"Totalitarianism." *Meridian* 2, no. 2 (fall 1958): 1. (Arendt's reflections on *The Origins of Totalitarianism* at the time of its second edition.)

"The Modern Concept of History." *Review of Politics* 20, no. 4 (October 1958): 570–590. (Reprinted in *Between Past and Future*, 1968.)

"What Was Authority?" In *Authority*. Edited by C. Friedrich Cambridge: Harvard University Press, 1959. (Reprinted in *Between Past and Future*, 1968.)

"Reflections on Little Rock." *Dissent* 6, no. 1 (winter 1959): 45–56. (Included in the same issue are criticisms of Arendt by David Spitz and Melvin Tumin. In *Dissent* 6, no. 2 [spring 1959]: 179–181, Arendt replied to her critics. The article was reprinted in *Public Life: A Journal of Politics* 4, no. 3–4 [May–June 1973] 92–97.)

"A Reporter at Large: Eichmann in Jerusalem." *New Yorker*, 16 February 1963, 40–113; 23 February 1963, 40–111; 2 March 1963, 40–91; 9 March 1963, 48–131; 16 March 1963, 58–134. (A revision of this five-part article was published as *Eichmann in Jerusalem: A Report on the Banality of Evil*.)

"The Formidable Dr. Robinson: A Reply to the Jewish Establishment." *New York Review of Books*, 20 January 1966, 26–30. (Arendt's response to letters about this article appeared in the 17 March 1966 issue.)

Introduction to *Auschwitz*, by Bernd Naumann. New York: Frederick A. Praeger, 1966. (Reprinted in Falk, Kolko, and Lifton, eds., *Crimes of War*, New York: Random House, 1971.)

"The Negatives of Positive Thinking: A Measured Look at the Personality, Politics and Influence of Konrad Adenauer." *Book Week*, *Washington Post*, 5 June 1966, 1–2. (A review of Konrad Adenauer, *Memoirs 1945–1953*. Translated by Beate Ruhm von Oppen.)

Preface to *The Future of Germany* by Karl Jaspers. Chicago: University of Chicago Press, 1967.

"Thinking and Moral Considerations: A Lecture." *Social Research* 38, no. 3 (autumn 1971).

"Martin Heidegger at Eighty." *New York Review of Books* 17, no. 6 (21 October 1971): 50–54. (Originally in German, *Merkur* 10 [1969]: 893–902. Translated by Albert Hofstadter. Reprinted in English in Michael Murray, ed., *Heidegger and Modern Philosophy*. New Haven: Yale University Press, 1978.)

Secondary Sources

Abel, Lionel. "New York City: A Remembrance." *Dissent* 8, no. 3 (summer 1961).

———. "The Aesthetics of Evil: Hannah Arendt on Eichmann and the Jews." *Partisan Review* 30, no. 1 (spring 1963).

Alvarez, A. "It Did Not Happen Everywhere." *New Statesman* 11 (October 1963): 488, 489.

Arendt, Hannah, and Karl Jaspers. *Correspondence*. Edited by Lotte Kohler and Hans Saner, translated by Robert Kimber and Rita Kimber, New York: HardCourt, 1991.

Barnouw, Dagmar. *Visible Spaces: Hannah Arendt and the German-Jewish Experience*. Baltimore, Mary.: Johns Hopkins University Press, 1990.

Bauer, Yehuda. *Jews for Sale: Nazi-Jewish Negotiations, 1933–1945*. New Haven, Conn.: Yale University Press, 1994.

Bazon, Jeanette M. "Hannah Arendt: Personal Reflections." *Response* 30, no. 1 (1980).

Beatty, Joseph. "Thinking and Moral Considerations: Socrates and Arendt's Eichmann." *Journal of Value Inquiry* 10, no. 1 (1976).

Beiner, Ronald, ed. *Hannah Arendt's Lectures on Kant's Political Philosophy*. Chicago: University of Chicago Press, 1982.

Bell, Daniel. "The Alphabet of Justice: Reflections on *Eichmann in Jerusalem*." *Partisan Review* 30, no. 3 (fall 1963).

Benhabib, Seyla. "Feminist Theory and Hannah Arendt's Concept of Public Space." *History of the Human Sciences* 6, no. 2 (1993).

Bermann, Aaron. *Nazism, the Jews and American Zionism, 1933–1948*. Detroit, Mich.: Wayne State University Press, 1990.

Bernstein, Richard. *Hanna Arendt and the Jewish Question*. Cambridge, Mass.: MIT Press, 1996.

Bloom, Alexander. *The New York Intellectuals and Their World*. New York: Oxford University Press, 1986.

Boehm, Eric H., ed. *We Survived*. Santa Barbara, Calif.: Clio, 1966.

Bradshaw, Leah. *Acting and Thinking: The Political Thought of Hannah Arendt*. Toronto: University of Toronto Press, 1989.

Breines, Paul. *Tough Jews: Political Fantasies and the Moral Dilemma of American Jewry*. New York: Basic, 1990.

Brightman, Carol. *Writing Dangerously: Mary McCarthy and Her World*. New York: Clarkson Potter, 1992.

Brightman, Carol, ed. *Between Friends: The Correspondence of Hannah Arendt and Mary McCarthy, 1949–1975*. New York: Harcourt Brace Jovanovich, 1995.

Canovan, Margaret. *The Political Thought of Hannah Arendt*. New York: Harcourt Brace Jovanovich, 1974.

———. "Friendship, Truth, and Politics: Hannah Arendt and Toleration." In *Justifying Toleration: Conceptual and Historical Perspectives*. Edited by Susan Mendes. Cambridge: Cambridge University Press, 1988.

———. "Socrates of Heidegger: Hannah Arendt's on Philosophy and Politics." *Social Research* 51, no. 1 (spring 1990).

———. *Hannah Arendt: A Reinterpretation of Her Political Thought*. Cambridge: Cambridge University Press, 1992.

Cooney, Terry. *The Rise of the New York Intellectuals: Partisan Review and Its Circle*. Madison: University of Wisconsin Press, 1986.

Cutting-Gray, Joanne. "Hannah Arendt, Feminism, and the Politics of Alterity: What Will We Lose if We Win?" *Hypatia* 8, no. 1 (winter 1993).

Dietz, Mary G. "Feminist Receptions of Hannah Arendt." In *Feminist Interpretations of Hannah Arendt*. Edited by Bonnie Honig. University Park: Pennsylvania State University Press, 1995.

Disch, Lisa J. *Hannah Arendt and the Limits of Philosophy*. Ithaca, N.Y.: Cornell University Press, 1994.

Ettinger Elzbieta. *Hanna Arendt, Martin Heideger*. New Haven, Conn.: Yale University Press, 1995.

Fackenheim, Emil L. *Encounters between Judaism and Modern Philosophy: A Preface to Future Jewish Thought*. New York: Basic, 1973.

Feldman, Ron, ed. and intro. *The Jew as Pariah*: Jewish Identity and Politics *in the Modern Age*. New York: Grove Press, 1978.

Gillian, Rose. "Love and the State: Varnhagen, Luxemburg and Arendt." In *Broken Middle: Out of Our Ancient Society*. Oxford: Blackwell, 1992.

Gilman, Sander. *Jewish Self-Hatred*. Baltimore, Mary.: John Hopkins University Press, 1986.

Hausner, Gideon. *Justice in Jerusalem*. New York: Schocken, 1974.

Helibut, Anthony. *Exiled in Paradise*. New York: Viking, 1983.

Hertz, Deborah. "Hannah Arendt's Rahel Varnhagen." In *German Women in the Nineteenth Century: A Social History*. Edited by John C. Fout. New York: Holmes and Meier, 1984.

Hilberg, Raul. *The Destruction of the European Jews*. Chicago: Quadrangle Books, 1967.

———. *Documents of Destruction: Germany and Jewry*. Chicago: Quadrangle Books, 1971.

Hill, Melvin A. *Hannah Arendt: The Recovery of the Public World*. New York: St. Martin, 1979.

Hinchman, Lewis P., and Sandra K. Hinchman, eds. *Hannah Arendt: Critical Essays*. Albany: State University of New York Press, 1994.

Honig, Bonnie, ed. *Feminist Interpretations of Hannah Arendt*. University Park: Pennsylvania State University Press, 1995.

Howe, Irving. "*The New Yorker* and Hannah Arendt." *Commentary* 36, no. 4 (1963).

———. "More on Eichmann." *Partisan Review* 31, no. 2 (spring 1964).

———. "Mid-Century Turning Point: An Intellectual Memoir." *Mainstream* (June–July 1975).

———. *World of Our Fathers*. New York: Harcourt Brace Jovanovich, 1976.

Hyman, Paula. *Gender and Assimilation in Modern Jewish History: The Roles and Representation of Women*. Seattle: University of Washington Press, 1995.

Isaac, Jeffrey C. "Oasis in the Desert: Hannah Arendt on Democratic Politics." *American Political Science Review* 88, no. 1 (March 1994).

Jacoby, Russell. *The Last Intellectuals: American Culture in the Age of Academe*. New York: Basic, 1987.

Jay, Martin, and Leon Botstein. "Hannah Arendt: Opposing Views." *Partisan Review* 95, no. 3 (summer 1978).

Jonas, Hans. "Hannah Arendt 1906–1975." *Social Research* 43, no. 2 (1976).

Kaplan, Gisella T., and Clive S. Kessler, eds. *Hannah Arendt: Thinking, Judging and Freedom*. Sydney: Allen and Unwin, 1989.

Kateb, George. "Hannah Arendt: Alienation and America," *Raritan* 3, no. 1 (1983).

———. *Hannah Arendt, Politics, Conscience, Evil*. Totowa, N.J.: Rowman and Allenhead, 1984.

Kazin, Alfred. "In Every Voice, in Every Ban." *New Republic* 110, no. 2 (10 January 1944).

Klawiter, Maren. "Using Arendt and Heidegger to Consider Feminist Thinking on Women and Reproductive/Infertility Technologies." *Hypatia* 5, no. 3 (fall 1990).

Kohn, Jerome. *Hannah Arendt: Essays in Understanding, 1930–1954*. New York: Harcourt Brace, 1994.

Lang, Berel. "Hannah Arendt and the Politics of Evil." *Judaism* 37, no. 3 (1988).

MacDonald, Dwight. "More on Eichmann." *Partisan Review* 31, no. 2 (spring 1964).

McCarthy, Mary. "The Hue and Cry." *Partisan Review* 31, no. 1 (winter 1964).

———. "Saying Good-bye to Hannah." *New York Review of Books* 22, no. 21–22 (22 January 1976).

Minnich, Elizabeth Kamarck. "Hannah Arendt: Thinking As We Are." In *Teachers and Artists Write about Their Work on Women*. Edited by Carol Ascher, Louise DeSalvo, and Sara Ruddick. Boston: Beacon, 1984.

Mosse, George L. *German Jews beyond Judaism*. Bloomington: Indiana University Press, 1985.

Phillips, William. "More on Eichmann," *Partisan Review* vol. 30, no. 1 (Winter 1964).

———. "How Partisan Review Began." *Commentary* 49, no. 4 (December 1976).

Podhoretz, Norman. "Hannah Arendt on Eichmann: A Study in the Perversity of Brilliance." *Commentary* 36, no. 3 (September 1963).

Porat, Dina. *The Blue and Yellow Stars of David: The Zionist Leadership in Palestine and the Holocaust, 1939–1945.* Cambridge: Harvard University Press, 1990.

Ring, Jennifer. "On Needing Both Marx and Arendt: Alienation and the Flight from Inwardness." *Political Theory* 17, no. 3 (August 1989).

———. "The Pariah as Hero: Hannah Arendt's Political Actor." *Political Theory* 19, no. 3 (August 1991).

———. *The Political Consequences of Thinking: Gender and Judaism in the Work of Hannah Arendt.* Albany: State University of New York Press, 1998.

Robinson, Jacob. *And the Crooked Shall Be Made Straight.* Philadelphia: Jewish Publication Society, 1965.

Segev, Tom. *The Seventh Million: The Israelis and the Holocaust.* Translated by Haim Watzman. New York: Hill and Wang, 1993.

Shklar, Judith N. "Hannah Arendt as Pariah." *Partisan Review* 50, no. 1 (winter 1983).

Syrkin, Marie. "Miss Arendt Surveys the Holocaust." *Jewish Frontier*, May 1963.

Trunk, Isaac. *Judenrat: The Jewish Councils in Eastern Europe under Nazi Occupation.* New York: Macmillan, 1972.

Wald, Alan. *The New York Intellectuals: The Rise and Decline of the Anti-Stalinist Left from the 1930s to the 1980s.* Chapel Hill: University of North Carolina Press, 1987.

Yahil, Leni. *The Holocaust: The Fate of European Jewry.* New York: Oxford University Press, 1990.

Young-Bruehl, Elisabeth. *Hannah Arendt: For Love of the World.* New Haven, Conn.: Yale University Press, 1982.

Carol Ascher

(1941–)

VICTORIA AARONS

CAROL ASCHER'S *The Flood* (1987) is a coming-of-age novel narrated by the precocious and compelling voice of Eva Hoffman, the nine-year-old daughter of Holocaust survivors, who comes to realize her identity as a Jew in large part through the lens of American racism. Ascher's novel takes place in Topeka, Kansas, during the uneasy, even sinister summer of 1951 and is set against the backdrop of the famous *Brown v. the Topeka Board of Education* decision abolishing segregated schools. This important part of the history of American race relations becomes, for Ascher, the point of departure for examining American antisemitism. *The Flood*, significantly, is written entirely from a child's perspective, a child who is forced to come to terms with the institutionalized racism at this particular time in America's history and to understand as well the history of Europe in the 1930s and 1940s, specifically to face the Holocaust, which haunts her parents' lives and, in large part, defines her own. The Holocaust is ultimately the moral backdrop against which the novel's events are portrayed, for it contrasts human evil with the menace of the natural world, in this case the flood of the summer of 1951, the rising waters of which threatened to inundate the town and left homeless refugees in its wake. The flood, which refers both to the real natural disaster that devastated Kansas in 1951 and to the Judaic reading of the biblical flood, serves as the opening frame for Ascher's searing treatment of antisemitism and American racism.

A Novel of America

The Flood is a novel about the lives of Holocaust refugees in America and about the ways in which their pasts influence their American-born children. *The Flood*, however, is less a novel of the Holocaust and far more a novel of America, of the failure of American tolerance and liberality as experienced by David and Leah Hoffman, secular, intellectual, cultured Austrian Jews and refugees of the Holocaust. *The Flood* places David and Leah Hoffman in the city of Topeka, Kansas, where David Hoffman, a psychoanalyst, is on the staff of the Menninger Clinic. David is a skeptic, something of a cynic, a Jew for whom the notion of God is nothing but a convenient myth and whose faith in open-minded human progress is meager because "people's memories fade" (*The Flood*, Willimantic, Connecticut: Curbstone Press, 1996, p. 28). While his wife, Leah, is more inclined to acknowledge the possibility for reparation or healing, *tikkun olam*, and hesitatingly, belatedly supposes she "should take [her daughters] to a synagogue" in order to maintain their Jewish identity, both adult Hoffmanns insist on the secular life and view themselves as assimilated Jews (p. 96). There are few Jews in Topeka, which here dramatizes the sense of disenfranchisement and disconnection of post-Auschwitz Jewish identity. When the Hoffmans associate with others outside the family, it is with the few other Jewish refugees in Topeka, fellow survivors, cultured European Jews with whom they feel most comfortable. Their daughters, Eva and her younger sister, Sarah, remain throughout the novel caught between both worlds, the world of American culture and opportunity, as viewed suspiciously here in the form of television (which the girls watch only at a neighbor's home) and evangelism. For the novel's narrator, especially, issues of identity, of Jewish identity, continually surface, a return of the immigrant's dilemma about assimilation, but here seen through the eyes of an American-born daughter of secular parents. The central question for this narrator is not whether one can remain a Jew in America, but what it means to be a secular Jew in America and how this shapes one's identity as both Jewish and American. The narrator's growing awareness and rejection of racism is the means by which she comes to understand antisemitism and the specter of the Holocaust that falls forever upon her family, the other survivors who gather in her home to play music, and, ultimately, upon herself.

Eva's confrontation with racism—in her friend's church, in the schools, and in her own neighborhood—is linked inexorably and disturbingly for this young child with antisemitism, a response all the more confusing for her because of her lack of religious training and identification. In fact, instead of the icons of her own ancestry, the walls of the Hoffman home prominently display a "large picture of a Negro man" that hangs as if in reproach or censure, "contemplating the odd little gathering of foreigners" (pp. 33, 68). The recognition of suffering, of the mutuality and shared conditions of suffering, defines Judaism in *The Flood*. Jewish identity, for Ascher and for her narrator, who is just becoming aware of the deep currents of racism that surround her and threaten to engulf her, is defined here not in religious terms, but rather as the shared recognition of suffering and the struggle to combat prejudice and injustice. Alan Berger defines this perspective, characteristic not only of those second-generation writers of the Holocaust, but of many American-Jewish writers (Grace Paley, for example), as "Jewish Universalism," an awareness of the suffering of all peoples in response to Jewish suffering in particular, a position that often results in political activism, the desire to help prevent prejudice, oppression, and injustice (Berger, p. 4). In Ascher's novel, racism and antisemitism become the measure of suffering and the response to suffering here becomes the measure of humanity.

The Defining Twins

Both racism and antisemitism are viewed in Ascher's novel as the defining twins of America in the 1950s, the one the flip side of the other. Both racism and antisemitism are viewed against the shadowy and hovering backdrop of the Holocaust, the events of which are revealed haltingly by Leah, the narrator's mother, whose narrative accounts are generally prompted by the racism she unexpectedly encounters in her new homeland. In response to the hotly contested argument about desegregating the schools, she tells her daughter, who receives information about her parents' experiences during the Holocaust in bits and pieces: "You can't tell one group to go to another school, or forbid them from attending school altogether. That's what the Nazis did in Austria!" (p. 25). The narrator's mother displays little reluctance in relating her experiences with antisemitism in Europe, but such experiences are invariably a response to the racism she views in America. In Ascher's novel, the summer of 1951 brings with it more than the tense and divisive battle waged over segregated schools. For the Hoffman family and others in the surrounding areas, the flood that threatens to destroy their homes, their towns, and their livelihoods becomes the catalyst for reassessing the past and for recognizing the importance of community and a universal appeal to brotherhood, regardless of racial background, ethnicity, or faith. The flood, both literally and figuratively, becomes the great equalizer in its potential to destroy everyone, black or white, Christian or Jew.

In many ways *The Flood* might be seen as at least partially autobiographical. Carol Ascher, born in Cleveland, Ohio, and trained as an anthropologist at Vassar College, Barnard College, and Columbia University, is the daughter of European refugees. Her mother, Ellen (Ascher) Bergman, fled Berlin in 1937 for a refugee camp in England. There she met her future husband, Paul Bergman, a psychoanalyst born in Vienna. Ascher, who married a non-Jew, describes her upbringing as secular, without a religious education, but "not denying . . . being Jewish" ("Fragments of a German-Jewish Heritage," p. 381). Clearly conflicted about the structure and shape of her identity, Ascher describes herself as having been "rather ashamed of those who were conspicuously Jews" ("Fragments of a German-Jewish Heritage," p. 381). In later years, Ascher seems to have resolved this conflict between being a religious and secular Jew, the conflict of self-definition that plagues her preadolescent narrator, because in her adult life Ascher finds herself "deeply connected" to the "rich and complicated religious and cultural tradition" of Judaism ("Fragments," p. 383). The tension described by Ascher in her own background is the tension that follows the narrator of *The Flood* through the tumultuous summer of 1951, a tumult caused in part by the narrator's awakening awareness of racial inequality. Racial inequality is configured in the novel by the school desegregation issue, but the potential catastrophic consequences of intolerance are figured further by her fear of the flood that threatens literally to displace her. Ironically, her family takes in victims of the flood who turn out to be antisemitic as well as racist, and so the narrator's Jewish identity hangs over her through most of the novel like the sky that promises more rain, like "a long gray cloud hung like a heavy weapon before us," the defining fact of her existence that refuses to retreat (p. 31). It is very significant here that the novel's events are narrated by a young child, whose growing perspective of hatred and oppression makes such cruelty all the more searing because the reader sees such barbarity through the awakening eyes of one whose innocence is now replaced with outrage, distrust, vulnerability, and a developing sense of her own impotence. Thus, while the ever-present danger of the flood in Ascher's novel is a literal reminder of the inadequacy of human agency and control, it also functions more importantly as a metaphorical admonition that exposes human weaknesses, prejudices, and self-serving inattention.

The flood, whose relentless waters deluge Topeka in the summer of 1951, threatening the drinking water and all that the inhabitants own, also generates the theological argument that is, for all its secular claims, at the very heart of this novel. Curiously, the religious interpretation of the flood comes from the mouth of one of David Hoffman's psychiatric patients at the Menninger Clinic. For Lillian, the narrator's "favorite of the crazy ones," the rising waters in Topeka are a reenactment of the biblical flood, "Forty days and forty nights," God's punishment of humankind's "wickedness, filth and lies!" (pp. 14–15). "Crazy" Lillian's proclamation opens the debate between the secular disbeliever, David Hoffman, and his fellow refugee and colleague, Mordecai Stone, a religious Jew, who may not believe that the present flood is evidence of God's wrath, but who does believe in a God of the Covenant. For David Hoffman, the narrator's father, the world itself is proof enough that there is no God, and, given the suffering of the Jews and the continuation of racism and oppression in America, even were there a God, Dr. Hoffman "couldn't pray to the One who would allow such evil" (p. 168). His friend, however, argues that the presence of "human corruption and suffering," that may be the result of human weakness and evil, does not disprove the existence of God. In this "unanswerable" quarrel, Mordecai relates the story of his father, who, as he went into the gas chamber, prayed, "My God, your world is perfect!" (p. 168). Ascher implies that all questions of God ultimately return to the central question of how one can reconcile a belief in a Covenantal and beneficent God with the fact of the Holocaust. For Ascher the answer is, finally, pragmatic: How one can hope to live responsibly in the world after the Holocaust?

Bibliography

Primary Sources

The Flood. 1987.

"Fragments of a German-Jewish Heritage in Four 'Americans,' " in "The German-Jewish Legacy in America, 1938–1988, A Symposium," *American Jewish Archives* 40, no. 2 (1988): 371–383.

Secondary Sources

Berger, Alan L. *Children of Job: American Second-Generation Witnesses to the Holocaust*. New York: State University of New York Press, 1997.

Hoffman, Roy. "*The Flood*, by Carol Ascher." *New York Times Book Review* (July 26, 1987): 17.

Steinberg, Sybil. "*The Flood*, by Carol Ascher." *Publishers Weekly* (March 6, 1987): 101.

Liliane Atlan

(1932–)

ELLEN SCHIFF

Since publishing two volumes of poetry in the 1960s under the pseudonym Galil, Liliane Atlan has been a bold and prolific innovator. On her way to becoming a major figure in contemporary French theater, she has experimented with prose poems and narratives she calls "books to speak, to live." She has adapted musical forms to prose works, written plays for radio broadcast and videocassette, and given drama soaring new dimensions in time and space. Unfettered by dramatic convention or the verbal limits of language, Atlan is taking her place with iconoclasts like Antonin Artaud, Samuel Beckett, and Jean Genet.

Life

I am coming back from a land where I have never gone: (Robert Desnos as quoted by Atlan, *Les Mers rouges,* Paris: L'Harmattan, 1998, p. 32).

Atlan was born Liliane Cohen in Montpellier in 1932 to Marguerite and Elie Cohen, emigrants from Salonika. Her father was an accomplished businessman, who parlayed a single textile shop into a network of seventy stores, including Paris's famous Grande Maison de Blanc. However, for Elie Cohen, money had only one use: to alleviate human suffering, which he could not tolerate. Legendary for his extraordinary generosity, he exhausted his fortune helping others.

As children of cautious and well-connected parents, Liliane and her sisters were sent to safety in Auvergne and Lyon in 1939. Because they rarely went out, they improvised plays to amuse themselves. Thus Liliane discovered the power of the theater; she was soon to find her subject. By the time the sisters were reunited with their parents in 1945, they knew that their mother's entire family had been killed. Searching unsuccessfully for other deported relatives, her parents took in survivors. Their horror-ridden appearance and stupefying stories haunted Liliane, as did newsreels of the camps. She was stricken with survivor guilt and the difficulty of living in so fractured and corrupted a world. This enduring psychic state, which she terms "le mal de terre" ("earthsickness"), informs all her work. She explains that she was "obsessed by the *Shoah*, as if I were myself returning from the camps" (quoted in Anissimov, p. 19).

Liliane's malaise intensified. When her father learned of Bernard Kuhl, a nineteen-year-old who was starving himself to death in despair at being the only member of his family to survive Auschwitz, he persuaded Kuhl to accept help and ultimately adopted him. Liliane became her adopted brother's confidante. Years later when she recounted his terrible stories in *Les Passants* (The Passers-By, 1998) she says simply, "[he] needed to talk, [I] needed to listen to him" (*Petites Bibles pour mauvais temps*, Paris: L'Harmattan, 2001, p. 28).

The abundance of *Shoah* details that she internalized curbed Liliane's appetite for life and she eventually refused to eat. During her last year of *lycée*, she spent several months hospitalized for anorexia. She would later dramatize herself at this juncture as a character named No. Recovering, she earned her baccalaureate degree and enrolled at the Sorbonne for an advanced degree in philosophy. Repelled by the values and texts of the civilizations that had given rise to the Holocaust, she turned to the newly founded Gilbert Bloch d'Orsay School where young Jewish adults studied the Bible, Talmud, the Zohar, and Hebrew metaphysics, seeking ways to understand their post-Auschwitz life.

At d'Orsay, Liliane met Henri Atlan, a scientist and physician. They married in 1952 and had a daughter, Mireille, and a son, Michael. Ultimately the marriage dissolved. Atlan earned her Diplôme d'Etudes Supérieures de Philosophie in 1953. Her thesis, directed by the eminent philosopher Gaston Bachelard, was titled "The Arbitrary and the Fantastic Since Nietzsche" (Knapp, *Liliane Atlan*, p. 10).

Family life, five years of teaching literature, and travels in Russia, Algeria, and California did not distract Atlan from her preoccupation with Holocaust-inspired questions. Although she eventually abandoned Jewish ritual—though not Jewish texts or her Jewish identity—her studies at d'Orsay left unanswered the questions about evil and the relevance of love, God, and the tenets of Judaism that underlie all her subsequent work. Despite her early delight in creating theater, she did not immediately seize on drama as the most appropriate genre in which to express moral and metaphysical concerns. Reading Frederico Garcia Lorca, Eugene O'Neill, Artaud, Eugene Ionesco, and Beckett changed her mind. After a false start, she produced a masterwork. *Monsieur Fugue ou Le Mal de terre* (*Mister Fugue or Earth Sick*, 1967) debuted in Paris to great acclaim; it was remounted by the Théâtre National Populaire the following year. The play has been translated into German, Hebrew, Yiddish, Japanese, Italian, and English; it has been performed internationally as well.

Expanding the Theater

In 1967 she confessed—not entirely mischievously, nor entirely erroneously—that she saw herself as "the messiah of the French theatre" because she had found a way to enlarge the theater enough to put humanity itself on stage ("La Première Fois" *Bref 110*, November 1967, p. 9). Like Armand Gatti in the preface to his Holocaust play *Les Chroniques d'une Planète provisoire* (Chronicles of a Temporary Planet), Atlan saw that the death of humanism in the camps had laid bare the relativity of human concerns. She felt "the latent fear that the planet might explode [and] the exaltation of traveling through the galaxy" ("La Première Fois," p. 9). Atlan envisioned the theater taking on the proportions of the universe. With her next play, *Les Messies ou Le Mal de terre*, (*The Messiahs or Earth Sick*, 1969), Atlan began to develop what is now aptly termed "cosmic theater." The four spheres in *Messies* (the Messiahs, the author and her cortege, corpses on a raft, and the earth and the galaxies) would ideally be staged in a planetarium. Hardly more modest in concept is *La Petite Voiture de flammes et de voix* (The Little Chariot of Flames and Voices, 1971), whose protagonists travel through the seven heavens, which the *Merkabah* mystics believed were traversed by the soul on its ascent or descent to the throne of God (Knapp, "Cosmic Theatre," pp. 227–228).

In a literal sense, many of Atlan's plays have gone out in time and space in radio broadcasts over France Culture, with which Atlan has had a long collaboration. Her limitless vision reached its fullest realization to date in the first production of *Un Opéra pour Terezin* (An Opera for Terezin, 1989), a work modeled on the Passover Seder. On 22 July 1989, from sunset until dawn, audiovisually connected participants worldwide celebrated the rite of the opera in several languages, simultaneously broadcast on radio. Atlan names this totally original dramaturgy "une recontre en étoile" ("a star-shaped meeting").

Broad Range of Work

Her cosmic vision notwithstanding, Atlan's activities have also been very much earthbound. In 1972, recognizing her need to work with others, she turned to collective creation. Two months of successful improvisation with children at the Jerusalem Museum yielded themes she then used in collaboration with Palestinian and Israeli actors. The result was *Les Musiciens, les émigrants* (The Musicians, the Emigrants, 1976), a dark, antiracist play. Atlan insists that in writing about similarities between Palestine and Israel, she did not write a political play. "It was," she admits, "a very aggressive play, very cruel in the sense that it was not pro-Palestine and it was not pro-Israel, but . . . meant to express . . . the wish to recuperate, to salvage our humanity" (Betsko and Koenig, p. 27). Israel holds great importance for Atlan, not just because her children now live there. In both *Musiciens* and *Les Mers rouges* (1998), Atlan appreciatively treats the historic interrelations of Jews and Arabs and their conflicting claims on the Holy Land.

Perhaps Atlan's most earthbound activity was her participation with a team of historians and scholars in writing the textbook, *Les Juifs dans l'histoire de 1933 à nos jours* (The Jews in History from 1933 to Our Day, 1984). Intended for students in their last year at *lycée* (equivalent to junior college level in the United States), the text is a model of clarity in presenting facts, chronology, photographs, documents, as well as historical analyses of this crucial era in Jewish history.

Atlan's creativity and experimentation with form and language continue undiminished. The last decade has seen the appearance of volumes of poetry including *Bonheur mais sur quel ton le dire* (Happiness, But in What Tone to Express It, 2000) and *Peuples d'argiles, forêts d'étoiles* (Nations of Clay, Forests of Stars, 2000) and several plays including *Leçons de bonheur* (Lessons in Happiness, 1982) and *Je m'appelle Non*

(My Name Is No, 1998). Of the last, Bettina Knapp has noted that it "ushers in a new brand of theatre based on a technique which Atlan herself defines as a 'passion de peindre par la parole' " ("passion to paint with words"; Knapp, *Je m'appelle Non,* p. 155). Here, for example, as in the vast *Petites Bibles pour mauvais temps* (Little Bibles for Bad Times, 2001), which incorporates and continues three earlier works, Atlan employs concepts and characters with aphoristic names like "I Will Create Myself" (based on Bernard Kuhl) and "God Does His Work Badly, I Am Replacing Him, But I Shall Accomplish It" (the altruistic Elie Cohen). The names contribute humor and leavening to the frequently troubling autobiographical account. They allow creative distance from the text for Atlan, who in mid-text changes her own name from "No" to "I Was Not Born for Myself."

Music, both vocal and instrumental, is an essential element of Atlan's oeuvre. All her works, whether or not they are intended for theatrical production, are meant to be recited. *Les Musiciens, les émigrants, Le Rêve des animaux rongeurs* (The Dream of the Rodents, 1985) and *Je m'appelle Non* are constructed of forms borrowed from oratorios, fugues, hymns, and canticles. In *Musiciens*, Atlan writes, "I want to find the elementary and indelible melody buried under all our stories" (p. 63). Musical structure is the basis of *Concert brisé* (Shattered Concert). A gamut of vocal interactions—unison, overlapping, interweaving, reiterations—becomes the artistic mechanism, in plays as well as her poetry, for probing the meaning of love and for searching for redemption from guilt and earth sickness.

If the transcendence of culpability and the aspiration to create a more perfect order are possible, the means to those ends lies in language. Writing is, for Atlan, the only way to metamorphose the life we cannot change. Words have awesome power: "After the war," she writes in a monologic prose poem, "she often imagined that she had been deported and thrown live into the flames which did not burn her, thanks to the poems she invented" (*Le Rêve des animaux rongeurs*, Paris: L'Ether Vague, p. 27). "The imagination," she told the actors rehearsing *Mister Fugue*, "is the human function that makes man reach out to divinity" ("J'espère que vous tiendrez," p. 7).

Critical Reception

Liliane Atlan's work has attracted wide critical attention. Her most prolific American critic and good friend is the distinguished scholar Bettina Knapp. In France, an entire issue of *Les Nouveaux Cahiers* was devoted to her work. Leonard A. Rosmarin, a Canadian scholar, is currently writing a critical book on Atlan's oeuvre. Her achievements have earned prestigious awards: *Mister Fugue* won the Israeli Habimah prize and the Morderai Anielewicz Prize in 1972; *Les Passants* (The Passers-By) was awarded the Wizo prize in 1989. Atlan was given the Radio Société des Auteurs et Compositeurs dramatiques and the Prix Mémoire de la *Shoah* awards in June 1999. She is a member of France's Comité d'Honneur. In 1992 she won the Prix Villa Medicis Hors les Murs grant, enabling her to travel to research *Les Mers rouges*.

Holocaust-Inspired Works

There have been the Iron Age, the Bronze Age, etc. Ours will go down in history as the Gas Age (*Petites Bibles pour mauvais temps,* p. 228).

"Auschwitz détermine tout" ("Auschwitz determines everything"), says a character in *Concert brisé*, a statement that announces the motive and the overarching subject of Liliane Atlan's work. From her initial guilt and revulsion at gratuitious and incomprehensible bestiality through the search for authentic postgenocide French-Jewish identity, Atlan rarely emerges from the shadow of the *Shoah.* Of her large body of Holocaust-inspired works, the following three exemplify her extended and explicit treatment of the subject and, at the same time, illustrate the range of her creativity.

Mister Fugue or Earth Sick (1967), Atlan's best known play, was inspired by her fascination with the deeds of Janusz Korczak. He was the Warsaw physician who chose to accompany the children in his orphanage to Auschwitz, "telling them stories to the end," Atlan writes in an epigraph. Those unrecovered stories also intrigue Atlan. Her eponym mirrors Korczak's acts rather than his persona. This chilling work opens in a ruined ghetto where soldiers are flushing survivors out of the sewers. Four wretched children emerge, clutching a doll that represents a dead playmate. One of the soldiers, his pockets stuffed with bread, is ordered to lie down and play dead. The children cannot resist the bait; captured, they are loaded onto the back of a truck bound for the Valley of Bones. Suddenly, the soldier who trapped the children decides to share their fate. He has always been ill at ease with life; unsavory military duties have only deepened his earth sickness. He becomes a willing, if often melancholy, participant in the stories and the game of life the children play out on the back of the truck. They call him Mister Fugue ("runaway").

The running time of the play circumscribes the life left to them. All that remains of the little victims' childhood is their enormous capacity to imagine: they play at "life." Matter-of-factly and with terrible accuracy, they reconstruct their dreadful past, stitching it seamlessly to a totally imaginary future full of the adventures, rites of passage, and aging that might have been, but that they know are as unreliable as the parents who had to abandon them. Their fantasies frequently move them to knowing, mirthless laughter. Atlan clearly shares Paul Klée's respect for what the painter called the "painful wisdom in the hobgoblin laughter of children." They mock the schools they once attended, the fear and cowardice of their elders during roundups, and the useless morality they had been taught (" 'Don't steal . . .' Don't steal, you don't stay alive," *Plays of the Holocaust*, edited by Elinor Fuchs, New York: Theatre Communications Group, 1987, p. 76).

Their black humor extends to their Judaism. They are merciless in teasing Iona, who continues to pray. They parody prayers: "Blessed art Thou, Lord of the World, who made Yossele Morgenstern and Raissa Dollfuss meet in a sewer . . . [and] who did not give them time to grow rotten from being too old" (p. 92). As Judith Morganroth Schneider points out, this sacred parody, along with sneering references to defenseless golems and a useless Messiah's rope that is supposed to signal God for help, illustrate some of the Jewish responses to catastrophe that David Roskies details in *Against the Apocalypse* (Schneider, p. 276).

So completely do the characters enter into their fabrications that although the periodic brutalities of the sadistic lieutenant leave them battered, they persevere in their dedication to the "realities" they create. What makes this unsentimental play so moving and nearly unbearable is the lucidity of the children and Fugue about their fate. They arrive at the Valley of Bones "detached" and "very old." Fugue too perishes, his singular but futile avuncular sacrifice having served, exactly like Korczak's, only to emphasize the corruption of human values in the Holocaust universe.

Les Mers rouges (The Red Seas, 1998) is one of Atlan's "books to live, to read." The text is presented as a script with five voices that speak for various other characters. The work is ambitious in scope as well as format. It is the fruit of Atlan's Villa Medicis grant, which allowed her to travel to Greece, Italy, Spain, and Israel for research on the history of the Chorale of Jewish Survivors of Auschwitz. The chorale was founded by Vidal Angel, a grocer in Israel, who literally sang his way out of the gas chamber.

In both the opening section and the conclusion, Atlan underscores the historic bond between Arabs and Jews. In Madrid, her narrator, Louna Sola, immerses herself joyously in "love songs . . . sung for centuries by Arabs and Jews, even after the Expulsion" (Paris: Harmattan, 1998, p. 16). She is not interested in recovering the sixteenth century, but rather in "inventing our age, that of the future" (p. 19). Her resolve is strengthened by the antisemitism she experiences during Holy Week in Madrid. Louna goes to Israel where she meets Angel and Moshe Gour, director of the Institute of the Music of Extermination. She sees a video of the chorale singing in Ladino and telling their stories. The chorale functioned for only two years; it sang "so our dead would be heard" (p. 58). Deeply impressed by the survivors' resilience, Louna resolves to write their stories, "to make them eternal" (p. 58).

These stories form the second and third sections of *Les Mers rouges*. They are survivor tales, gruesome, gripping, and often poignant. There are miracles in the camp: a mute is so overcome with the joyful Simchat Torah celebration held under the very noses of the Nazis that he sings for the only time in his life. There is unexpected praise for the Jewish *Sonderkommandos* whose foul deeds were counterbalanced by their daring to blow the shofar and pray on Rosh Hashanah and to help other Jews when they could. The third section focuses more narrowly on the descendants of Sephardic Jews and the music they kept alive, even—or especially—in the direst circumstances. The stories, like the defilements and surgeries inflicted on women in the camps, are unsparing and cruel. The first implication of Atlan's title appears in the account of a forced march where prisoners, given three minutes to slake their thirst in a stream, drank the blood of those who took too long to drink.

In the fourth section, set in Israel, the survivors have established second families, but they are very much aware of themselves as last survivors of Salonican Jews murdered at Auschwitz. "They sing their love songs," writes Atlan, "with exceptional fervor; it's the only way they have of making understood what they cannot say" (p. 191). The children of these survivors are now engaged in another war. As they drive tanks, destroy property, and enter refugee camps, they understand that the Arab tragedy is a consequence of their own (p. 192). The powerful final scene begins like a simultaneous celebration of a mass, recitation of the Koran, and Torah reading. Then Atlan throws open the question of the preeminence in the Holy Land claimed by all three groups. "One God of love in whose name three people who are brothers have for centuries made torrents and torrents of blood flow. What is this God who tolerates being honored by so many murders?" she asks (p. 195). Golden Age music of an unspecified religion accompanies the closing questions: "Who will open these Red seas which threaten to swallow the universe? Who, if not us?" (p. 197).

Un Opéra pour Terezin (An Opera for Terezin, 1989) is the supreme example of Atlan's cosmic vision. This enormous work borrows the form of a Seder; it too is a ritual meant to be celebrated worldwide, on the same date, in many languages. The major difference is that the participants can see and talk to one another from one end of the globe to another, as if space was not separating them (*Opéra*, Paris: L'Avant-Scène Théâtre, April 1997, p. 119).

Atlan's specifications are precise: each group of participants, who should gather around a table, must include at least four children (the wise, the wicked, the simple, and the one who does not know how to ask). Although there are many elements of spectacle, "the essential thing remains the telling of the story. . . . The main aim is not beauty but exactness" (p. 150). The musicians, who participate throughout, must play all the selections, which include Beethoven, Dvorak, and the Verdi "Requiem," on accordion and piano, as they were played at Theresienstadt. There are also traditional Seder melodies, popular tunes, and songs sung in the camp. The opera is dedicated to the camp musicians, forced by deportations to reconstitute their ranks continually, who kept creating almost to their death. Music, writes Atlan, was the spine of Theresienstadt.

Like much of Atlan's work, the opera is divided into four sections. Each precedes the drinking of one of the cups of wine and is called an overture. The order within each overture is formally specified. In the first, the celebrants play out with simple props, the humiliations, deceptions, and betrayals that led to deportation. One of the most striking rituals is the enactment of a human-drawn hearse, bringing to life Biedrich Fritta's well-known drawing, *The Only Means of Transport*.

In the second overture, the table on which the meal is served becomes Terezin. The central event is the thoroughgoing preparation for the Red Cross visit. (In 1943 the Germans refurbished Theresienstadt in an elaborate sham to convince Danish Red Cross inspectors that prisoners were living under model conditions.) A former inmate, deported to Auschwitz, escapes and makes his way back to plead, "get weapons and fight." The musicians, aware of an uncommon opportunity, realize that their only chance to make the visitors see through the Nazi façade lies with the Verdi "Requiem." As the delegation passes, the chorus performs the *Libera Me* as a fervent personal appeal. With sinking hearts, they see that their message has not been understood.

The third section incorporates horrifying testimonies and staggering statistics. The particularly powerful ritual of documents involves projections of evidence of the enormously rich cultural life of the camp: poems, pictures, and pages from *Vedem*, a magazine produced by The Republic of Abandoned Children. Children play a major role in this part because Atlan assigns them the task of choosing the documents. This section also contains the less well-known history of the Terezin Family Camp at Birkenau, founded for the same reason as Theresienstadt. Because the Red Cross commission was satisfied with its visit to the latter, the Family Camp lost its raison d'être and was liquidated (p. 99). There is a heart-stopping moment in which all the participants, everywhere, recite in unison in their own languages, "Each year, with all of our voices, we will allow the truth to cry out" (p. 89). In the ritual of the crayon, participants enumerate a lengthy list of Terezin artists until the wall is covered with living names and the recitation becomes "an incantation of resistance sung by every child everywhere" (p. 104). Atlan specifies that each year, different extracts from testimonies deposited at the Oral History Department at Jerusalem University of Jerusalem be read responsively. Of course there is music, tributes to the Terezim composers, Josef Bor, Karel Berman, Rafael Schachter, Victor Uillman, and Gideon Klein, and conductor Karl Ancerl.

The final overture is dominated by a display of art from the camp painters (Fritta, Otto Ungar, Leo Haas, and Malvina Shalkova). The celebrants comment on each drawing or perform an interpretive depiction. Intertwined is an enumeration of the ten plagues: sand, vermin, typhus, flies, the killers, hunger ("the most difficult to forget"), theft, corruption (corrected to "people, but sometimes they performed miracles"), fear, and mass murder. The opera ends with its performers singing until daybreak "the songs they love."

During the recitation of testimonies in the third overture, a character identified only as "the Frenchwoman" tells a story. It is not difficult to tell whose story it is:

> I went back to Terezin at the beginning of autumn, near the Jewish New Year. In the cemetery, the caretaker showed me a little cardboard box containing the ashes of an unknown prisoner, the only one that had not been thrown into the Ohre. It was the hour when the shofar was blown in the synagogues. I swore to tell the untellable story of these people who had disappeared into smoke, to do it so that each year they would be heard (p. 108).

Translations from the French by Ellen Schiff.

Bibliography

Primary Sources

Articles

"J'espère que vous tiendrez bien le coup dans cet enfer: Letter aux enfants de Fugue" (I Hope That You Will Hold Out In That Hell: Letter to Fugue's children). 1967.

"La Première Fois que j'ai fait du théâtre" (The First Time I Made Theater). 1967.

(Atlan, et al.) *Les Juifs dans l'histoire*: *De 1933 à nos jours* (The Jews in History: From 1933 to Our Day). 1984.

"Books to Say, to Live"

Le Rêve des animaux rongeurs (The Dream of the Rodents). 1985.

Corridor Paradise Concert brisé (Paradise Corridor Shattered Concert). 1998.

Les Passants (The Passers-By). 1998. Republished in *Petites Bibles pour mauvais temps* (Little Bibles for Bad Times). 2001.

Petites Bibles pour mauvais temps (Little Bibles for Bad Times). 2001. Includes *Les Passants, Concert brisé, Tuer la morte*, and *Petites Bibles pour mauvais temps.*

Drama

Monsieur Fugue ou Le Mal de Terre (Mister Fugue or Earth Sick). 1967.

Les Messies ou le Mal de Terre (The Messiahs or Earth Sick). 1969.

La Petite Voiture de flammes et de voix (The Little Chariot of Flames and Voices). 1971.

Les Musiciens, les Emigrants: *Une Pièce de théâtre enfouie sous une autre* (The Musicians, the Emigrants: One Play Buried Under Another). 1976.

Leçons de bonheur (Lessons in Happiness). 1982.

Un Opéra pour Terezin (An Opera for Terezin). 1989.

Je m'appelle Non (My Name Is No). 1998.

Les Mers rouges: *Un Conte à plusieurs voix* (The Red Seas: A Story for Several Voices). 1998.

Poetry

Lapsus. 1971.

L'Amour élémentaire (Elementary Love). 1979.

Quelques pages arrachées au Grand Livre des Rêves (Some Pages Snatched from the Great Book of Dreams). 1999.

Bonheur mais sur quel ton le dire (Happiness But In What Tone to Express It). 2000.

Peuples d'argile, forêts d'étoiles (Nations of Clay, Forests of Stars). 2000.

Secondary Sources

Anissimov, Myriam. "Portrait," *Les Nouveaux Cahiers* 121 (summer 1995): 17–22.

Betsko, Kathleen, and Rachel Koenig. "Liliane Atlan." In *Interviews with Contemporary Women Playwrights*. New York: Beech Tree Books, 1987.

Gaudet, Jeannette. *Writing Otherwise: Atlan, Duras, Giraudoux, Redonnet and Wittig*. Amsterdam: Rodopi, 1999.

Knapp, Bettina. "Cosmic Theatre: The Little Chariot of Flames and Voices." *Modern Drama* 17, no. 2 (1974): 225–234.

———. "Liliane Atlan." In *Off-Stage Voices*: *Interviews with Modern French Dramatists*. Edited by Alba Amoia. Troy, N.Y.: Whitson Publishing Co., 1975.

———. "Liliane Atlan's *The Messiahs* as Cosmic Theatre." *Comparative Drama* 9, no. 3 (fall 1975): 248–263.

———. "Collective Creation from Paris to Jerusalem: An Interview with Liliane Atlan," *Theatre* 13, no. 1 (fall–winter 1981–1982): 43–50.

———. Introduction. *Liliane Atlan Theatre Pieces*: *An Anthology*. Greenwood, Fla.: Penkevill, 1985.

———. *Liliane Atlan*. Amsterdam: Rodolphi, 1988.

———. "L'Eclatement de genres." *Les Nouveaux Cahiers* 121 (summer 1995): 28–35.

———. "Je m'appelle Non." *French Review* 73, no. 1 (October 1999): 155–156.

———. "Petites Bibles pour mauvais temps." *World Literature Today* 75, no. 1 (winter 2000): 135.

Moraly, Yehuda. "Liliane Atlan's *Un Opéra pour Terezin*." In *Staging the Holocaust*. Edited by Claude Schumacher. Cambridge: Cambridge University Press, 1998.

Oore, Irene. "*Les Passants* de Liliane Atlan." *LittéRealité* 4, no. 2 (fall 1992): 27–37.

———. "Entre l'horreur et l'émerveillement: *Les Musiciens, les Emigrants*." *Les Nouveaux Cahiers* 121 (summer 1995): 37–40.

Rosmarin, Leonard A. "Les Livres de musique de Liliane Atlan." *Les Nouveaux Cahiers* 121 (summer 1995): 23–27.

Schneider, Judith Morganroth. "Liliane Atlan: Jewish Difference in Postmodern French Writing." *Symposium* 43 (1989–1990): 274–283.

RACHEL AUERBACH
(1903–1976)

SAMUEL KASSOW

A YIDDISH WRITER IN prewar Poland, Auerbach was one of only two survivors of the circle that helped Emanuel Ringelblum in the *Oneg Shabes*, the secret archive of the Warsaw ghetto. Conscious of her responsibility to continue Ringelblum's legacy and to document the destruction of Polish Jewry, Auerbach helped organize the search that located the first cache of the archive in September 1946, and until her death in 1976 was one of the most eloquent memoirists of the Holocaust. Unfortunately, with the exception of "Yizkor," her 1943 essay commemorating Warsaw Jewry, little of her work has been translated into English. "Yizkor," however, contains many themes present throughout her Holocaust writing: the importance of the culture that was destroyed; the humanity and the specific identity of the victims; the responsibility of the survivor to remember; and ultimately, the difficulty of finding the right words to convey the enormity of the loss.

Just before she wrote "Yizkor," Auerbach—living in Warsaw on Aryan papers—watched a Polish woman mourn openly for her son who had just been shot, and realized that, unlike the Polish mother, she had to suppress her own grief. To mourn the murdered Jews of Warsaw carried the risk of instant betrayal. A short time later, Auerbach, who often wrote in Polish, wrote "Yizkor" in Yiddish. She poured out her soul as she tried to describe the murder of Warsaw Jewry: the toddlers, the children she remembered from the ghetto schools, the tough Jewish workers, the hardened women shopkeepers, young scouts, courting couples, intellectuals—all gone. Auerbach offered no explanations for the calamity. As David Roskies has pointed out, this secular writer could only repeat the Hebrew words of the traditional Jewish prayer for the dead: Yizkor.

As she groped for images to convey the sheer magnitude of the catastrophe in "Yizkor," she used the example of a flood.

> I saw a flood once in the mountains. Wooden huts, torn from their foundations were carried above the raging waters. One could see lighted lamps in them, men, women and children in cradles tied to ceiling beams. Other huts were empty inside but one could see a tangle of arms waving from the roof, like branches blowing in the wind waving desperately toward heaven, toward the riverbanks for help. At a distance one could see mouths gaping, but one could not hear the cries because the roar of the waters drowned out everything.
>
> And that's how the Jewish masses flowed to their destruction at the time of the deportations. Sinking as helplessly into the deluge of destruction.
>
> And if for even one of the days of my life I should forget how I saw you then, my people, desperate and confused, delivered over to extinction, may all knowledge of me be forgotten and my name be cursed like that of those traitors who are unworthy to share your pain (Translated by Leonard Wolf in *The Literature of Destruction*, edited by David Roskies, Philadelphia: Jewish Publication Society, 1988, pp. 459–460).

By using the imagery of a flood—a natural disaster—she anticipated future questions posed by those who were not there. What had happened to the millions of Polish Jews? Why had they let themselves be fooled? Those tough, bright resourceful Jews—why didn't they resist? The Holocaust was not a metahistorical event, but its enormity was too horrible and too unprecedented to allow for glib theories and facile questions that might compromise the memory of the Jewish masses she cherished so deeply.

In another essay of 1943 or 1944 in *Bi'khutsot Varsha* (In the Courtyards of Warsaw) (1954) Auerbach warned that she would only record facts and avoid any temptation to interpret and explain. Such restraint, she admitted, was difficult, but the alternative was to tread on dangerous ground. "The mass murder, the murder of millions of Jews by the Germans," she wrote, "is a fact that speaks for itself. It is very dangerous to add to this subject interpretations or analyses. [*Misukan mi'od lihabia kan hirhurim o perushim kolshehem*]" (p. 7). She quickly realized that such limitation was impossible—even for her.

Life

Born in 1903 in the small Podolian village of Lanowitz, Auerbach retained a deep interest in rural Jewish life and Jewish folklore, and a lifelong dedication to the Yiddish language. In the mid-1920s Auerbach entered Lwow University, where she studied philosophy and psychology. There she befriended the young poet Dvora Fogel, who persuaded her to write in Yiddish. Discovering the great literary talents of Fogel's friend, Bruno Schulz, in his letters to Fogel, Auerbach sent excerpts to the Polish writer Zofia Nałkowska, who had them published as *Sklepy Cynamonowe* (Cinnamon Stores), Schulz's first book.

Auerbach joined a small group of writers and journalists who wanted to develop secular Yiddish culture in Galicia, a region where the Jewish intelligentsia were predominantly Polish-speaking. In 1927 she began to write for the Lwow Yiddish journal *Morgn* and became an editor of *Tsushtayer*, a journal that promoted Yiddish culture in Galicia and soon attracted Galician Yiddish writers such as the young poet Rachel Korn.

In 1933 Auerbach moved to Warsaw, where she published literary and theater criticism in the Polish language Jewish daily *Nasz Przegląd* as well as in Yiddish journals such as *Literarishe Bleter*. She also published articles on psychology and supported herself by copyediting. As a companion of the famous Yiddish poet Itzik Manger, Auerbach preserved his manuscripts, hiding them in the Ringelblum archive after Manger was forced to leave Poland in 1938.

Shortly after Germany attacked Poland in 1939, Auerbach was preparing to leave for Lwow when she received an unexpected summons from Dr. Emanuel Ringelbum to help with the work of the *Aleynhilf* (Jewish Self Help), the large network of Jewish relief organizations in Warsaw that became a major base of the Warsaw Jewish intelligentsia. He asked Auerbach to run a soup kitchen for homeless refugees and told her "not everyone has the right to run away" (*Varshever Tsvoes*, Tel Aviv: Farlag Yisrael Bukh, p. 63).

Auerbach later recalled that this meeting with Ringelblum had a decisive impact on her future. Until July 1942 she directed the large soup kitchen, a complex operation that fed several thousand starving people from different social classes daily, at Leszno 40. Management of the soup kitchen demanded patience, tact, organizational skills, and quite often no small measure of callousness; public figures in the ghetto, including Ringelblum, often asked Auerbach to help save starving writers and intellectuals by giving them extra food. She also participated in the work of the IKOR, the Yiddish cultural organization in the Warsaw ghetto, which frequently used the kitchen as a locale for public lectures. At Ringelblum's request, she began to write for the *Oneg Shabes* archive. Auerbach wrote an essay (later revised and published after the war) about the Leszno soup kitchen, describing its significance as a microcosm of ghetto life and including compelling vignettes of some of the regular patrons: a German Jewish refugee, a band of young orphans, a large refugee family from the provinces who fought hard to hold on to their dignity. She described her staff with all their human foibles and inbred folk humor. Undermining the hopes of those who believed that the extensive network of soup kitchens made a significant difference in saving lives, Auerbach concluded that they were only of marginal value, a supplemental source of calories that might save lives only when there were other sources of income and food. Ringelblum agreed and recorded these conclusions in his diary of the Warsaw ghetto.

As part of her work for the *Oneg Shabes*, Auerbach kept a diary through 1941 and 1942. In the fall of 1942 Ringelblum asked her to take down the testimony of Abraham Krzepicki, who had escaped from Treblinka. Auerbach turned the Krzepicki interviews into the most detailed account that had yet been provided of the death camp. Krzepicki later perished in the Warsaw Ghetto Uprising and his testimony was recovered with the second part of the Ringelblum archive in 1950.

In March 1943 Auerbach escaped to the Aryan side of Warsaw. Through Adolph and Basia Berman, she quickly established contact with the Jewish underground on the Aryan side and with *Zegota*, the Polish council to help Jews. Auerbach joined a network of couriers that funneled money and other support to hidden Jews. At the same time she continued to write for the underground archive that the Bermans had organized after the destruction of the Warsaw ghetto.

During 1943 and 1944, Auerbach wrote some of her most important essays of the Holocaust. She buried them in 1944 and recovered them after the war. These writings, along with her earlier *Oneg Shabes* essays, formed the basis of the following books published in Israel: *Bi'khutsot Varsha* (In the Courtyards of Warsaw) (1954), *Varshever Tsvoes* (Warsaw Testaments) (1974), and *Baym Letstn Veg* (On the Last Road), which appeared in 1977, a year after her death. These essays and memoirs are especially valuable because they contain important information on members of the

Jewish cultural elite who were killed: writers, historians, composers, singers, and actors. This was her prewar milieu and she felt a special obligation to record how it perished. She also recorded the quiet heroism of Poles who helped rescue Jews.

Responding to the principle of *Yizkor* (Remembrance), Auerbach's life after the war was dedicated not only to writing her own memoirs, but also to gathering and preserving the diaries, memoirs, and testimonies from other survivors. To that purpose, Auerbach helped organize the Warsaw Jewish Historical Institute's collection of survivor diaries, memoirs, and testimonies, and published a book on Treblinka, based on a trip she took there with survivors. After her immigration to Israel in 1950, she helped organize a collection of survivor testimony and support for Yad Vashem, the Israeli Holocaust Archive and Museum. Protesting what she felt was an Israeli tendency to downplay the Holocaust, she also condemned what she feared was premature normalization of German–Jewish relations, refusing to allow her biography to appear in the *Leksikon fun der nayer Yidisher Literatur* because the project was partly financed with German reparations money.

Moved by concepts of memory and justice rooted in her Jewish heritage, Auerbach continued to write. She published a book on her emigration to Israel, *In Land Yisroel* (1964), as well as articles and book reviews. Of particular importance were many essays and reviews of literature that appeared in the *Goldene Keyt*.

Bibliography

Primary Sources

Oyf di Felder fun Treblinke (On the Fields of Treblinka). 1947.
Der Yidisher Oyfshtand (The Jewish Revolt). 1948.
Unzer Khezhbm mitn Daytchn Folk (Our Account with the German People). 1952.
Bi'khutsot Varsha (In the Courtyards of Warsaw). 1954.
Mered Geto Varsha (The Revolt of the Warsaw Ghetto). 1963.
In Land Yisroel (In the Land of Israel). 1964.
"Nisht oysgeshpunene fedem" (Unspun Threads). *Di Goldene Keyt* (The Golden Chain), no. 50 (1964): 131–143.
Varshever Tsvoes (Warsaw Testaments). 1974.
Baym Letstn Veg (On the Last Road). 1977.

Secondary Sources

Kahan, Berl. *Leksikon fun Yidish shraybers* (Lexicon of Yiddish Writers). New York: Raya Kahan, 1986, pp. 8–9, 537–538.
Kermish, Joseph. "Rokhl Oyrbakh-Di grinderin funm eydes-verk Yad Vashem" (Rachel Auerbach, the creator of the Yad Vashem personal histories program). *Baym Letstn Veg*. Tel Aviv: 1977, pp. 305–318.
Ravich, Melekh. *Mayn Leksikon* (My Lexicon). Vol. 2. Montreal: 1947, pp. 90–94; Vol. 3, Montreal: A Committee in Montreal 1958, pp. 44–46.
Roskies, David. *Against the Apocalypse: Responses to Catastrophe in Modern Jewish Culture*. Cambridge, London: Harvard University Press, 1984, pp. 199, 201, 202.
———. ed. *The Literature of Destruction: Jewish Responses to Catastrophe*. Philadelphia, New York, Jerusalem: Jewish Publication Society, 1989, pp. 459–464.
Sadan, Dov. "Rokhl Oyrbakh-Shtrikhn tsu ir geshtalt." *Baym Letstn Veg*. Tel Aviv: 1977, pp. 7–17.

JEROME BADANES

(1937–1995)

TRESA L. GRAUER

FOR JEROME BADANES, writing was a form of social responsibility, a means of fulfilling his obligation both as a human being and as a Jew to bear witness to events that informed the consciousness of the twentieth-century world. Whether writing street theater protesting American involvement in the Vietnam War or a film script and a novel depicting Jewish life before and after the Holocaust, Badanes used his work to express what he felt as a compulsion "to remember and to reimagine" those lives and experiences that would otherwise disappear. "Some say that only those people who experienced the Holocaust have the right to talk about it," Badanes explained in a *New York Times* interview. "But if that's the truth, there will be no one left . . ." (Pogrebin, p. 3). Concerned with the question of how one honors the memory of the dead without becoming either exploitative or subsumed in the memory, Badanes participates in the ongoing theoretical debates about what Saul Friedlander, a prominent Holocaust historian, calls the "limits" of Holocaust representation by actually incorporating them into his texts (Friedlander, *Probing the Limits of Representation: Nazism and the "Final Solution,"* Harvard University Press, 1992). For Badanes, the tensions between "truth" and aesthetics, between collective history and personal memory, between the need to bear witness to the past and the impossibility of doing so in figurative language, stand as the explicit subject of his work.

Background

Jerome Badanes was born on 21 February 1937 in Brooklyn, New York, to Leo and Rose Badanes. He received his B.A. in English in 1963 from the University of Michigan, where he won the Avery Hopwood Award for Poetry. During the 1960s he took a leading role in the civil rights and antiwar movements, founding and editing *CAW!*, the literary journal for Students for a Democratic Society. He also wrote antiwar street theater, and in 1969 was a cofounder of and scriptwriter for the national touring group Burning City Theater. Badanes' activism and idealism—coupled with his early memories of his parents' response to the news from Europe during World War II—lie at the heart of his work as the scriptwriter and interviewer for *Image Before My Eyes*, the 1981 award-winning documentary about prewar Jewish life in Poland. The voices of the people he interviewed for the film "began to haunt" him (Pogrebin, p. 3), he claimed, and inspired him to draw on the images, memories, and "voices he knew all his life" (Kinn) for his 1989 novel, *The Final Opus of Leon Solomon*. Though his Jewish identity did not have much resonance in his younger life ("I wanted to be an American," he explained), his later experiences compelled him to imagine the story of the Holocaust survivor and historian Leon Solomon. "You get wised up to leave your own roots," he told Robin Pogrebin, "and then you get wiser—you return" (Pogrebin, p. 3).

Although the body of Badanes's collected work is small, it has been widely acclaimed. His writing has been recognized through numerous awards and grants, including the Hopwood Award for Poetry, a New York State Council Grant for the Burning City Street Theater, a National Endowment of the Humanities grant for the screenplay and film of *Image Before My Eyes*, four fellowships at the Virginia Center for the Creative Arts, three Mellon Grants in fiction writing, a New York Foundation for the Arts Fiction Writers Grant, and the Edward Lewis Wallant Award for Best Jewish Novel of the Year for *The Final Opus of Leon Solomon*.

Though he wrote poetry, drama, and fiction continually through the 1970s, 1980s, and 1990s, Badanes also did a great deal of teaching. After serving as mentor and lecturer at Empire State College from 1976 through 1980 and at the State University of New York at Purchase from 1977 through 1980, he taught for many years at Vassar College, lecturing in English, religion, American culture, and urban studies. From 1986 until the time of his death, Badanes was a member of the creative writing faculty at Sarah Lawrence College, serving finally as the chairman of the graduate program in fiction writing. Jerome Badanes died suddenly of a heart attack in Bronxville, New York, on 18 May 1995 and was survived by his wife, the editor and writer Gail Kinn, and his daughter from a previous marriage, Shira.

Holocaust-Related Texts

As scriptwriter for the documentary *Image Before My Eyes* Badanes was able to depict the rich civilization of Eastern European Jewry between the two world wars, both through his text of the voice-over narration and through the sensitive interviews he conducted with émigrés remembering their younger days. The film, based largely on a 1977 photography exhibit at the YIVO Institute for Jewish Research, did more than merely record the still images; the photos were integrated with old home movies as well as with the memories, anecdotes, and even recollected songs of elderly interviewees. In the script that weaves together these diverse parts, Badanes shared director Josh Waletzky's desire to "destroy as many stereotypes as possible" (Insdorf, p. 1315). "Our hope," Waletsky explained, "is that after seeing *Image Before My Eyes*, no one will retain the idea that all the Jews in Eastern Europe were like characters in *Fiddler on the Roof*" (Insdorf, p. 1315). The film works to portray the vitality and variety within pre-Holocaust Jewish society, representing the poor and the affluent, the religious and secular, the bustling markets and the progressive schools, the differing ideologies of the Jewish political movements and the pleasure of summer camps. The filmmakers were especially concerned with countering the perception that Eastern European Jews were helpless and weak—"fiddling on roofs until they perished in the gas chambers," as one reviewer described it (Osnos). Instead, they chose to emphasize not only the energy and vibrancy of different factions of Jewish culture, but also the spirit of resistance particularly evident within the Jewish youth movements.

Badanes's desires to counter stories of passivity with examples of resistance, to depict the memories of individuals as well as the history of a people, to balance the need to commemorate the past with the necessity of living in the present, are reflected not only in his film script but in his masterful novel, *The Final Opus of Leon Solomon* (1989). The novel takes the form of the memoir of Leon Solomon, a Holocaust survivor and Jewish historian who has been caught stealing texts from the Judaica collection of the New York Public Library and surreptitiously selling them to Harvard, having come to the conclusion that "to be kept from death, documents must be handled by living hands" (Alfred A. Knopf, 1989, p.10). Conceiving of his historical project as a spy mission whereby he must always be "alert for any opportunity to make a lightning raid into . . . blackness to rescue a single image," Solomon is disgusted that he has been careless enough to be caught and, checking himself into a seedy New York City hotel room, prepares to end his life (p. 81). Over the course of three days he composes the memoir that constitutes the text of this novel.

Compelled to write but painfully aware of his inability to recover all that has been lost, Solomon simultaneously mourns and memorializes his life and his past. Memory has become for him both a moral imperative and that which consumes him, and the novel confronts the ongoing uneasiness over both the propriety and the necessity of Holocaust representation. Like many other contemporary Holocaust narratives, *The Final Opus of Leon Solomon* no longer spotlights the miracle of physical survival; rather, the principal question becomes how one can live with its emotional and epistemological consequences. Moreover, because he is not a survivor himself, the novel reflects Badanes's dilemma of writing as one removed from the experiences he feels compelled to confront. In the presence of revisionism and contemporary skepticism about the possibility of "truth," he carefully foregrounds the narrative apparatuses that order the reader's understanding of reality, self-consciously reflecting upon the text as *text*. His narrator is a survivor and historian who comes to understand that writing history is a fictional act that always involves interpretation. The realization that no chronicle is unmediated and that the boundaries between history and fiction are irrevocably blurred is devastating to Leon Solomon's sense of purpose as a historian. Where he once devoted his life to being the "archivist and savior" (p. 13) of Jewish lives lost to the Nazis, his "final opus" takes the form of a memoir that he uses to exorcise the demons of his own personal memories; only by writing his *own* Jewish life can he even provisionally reconcile individual memory and communal history.

Nevertheless, Badanes's self-consciousness about structure is tempered by the emotional urgency of his role in passing down stories to future generations, as well as his commitment to destroying stereotypes. Although Solomon has learned that "it is not possible to fully recover what is lost," he is intent on relaying the "actual bits and pieces of what is gone," and he justifies the content of his memoir by explaining that memory "selects out, just like the doctors in Auschwitz, sentencing some images of the past to the perpetual half-life of sentimentality and official versions, and dooming the remaining (and, I have learned, the more vital) images to immediate oblivion—almost" (p. 80). Fighting against the "perpetual half-life of sentimentality" as false to his understanding of history, Solomon evokes with poignancy not only the smells, sights, and sounds of his childhood in Vilna, but also the graphic details of his vengeful sexual fantasies. As his philosophy of historiography shifts from one of the recovery (or salvation) of the multitude of lost Jewish lives to one in which he attempts to interpret the events of his personal past, Solomon thereby works to redeem his own life as well. However painful his memories may be, acknowledging the specificity of his individual story is the only way that Solomon can feel himself part of a community of Jews. There is, he determines, no representative Holocaust story, but silence is not an acceptable alternative because it assumes the absence of an audience. Solomon's final opus is both a piece of communal history and a declaration of individuality—an assertion of resistance against the erasure of Jewish history and Jewish lives.

Badanes's juxtaposition of the good and the bad in his depiction of Solomon, his efforts to work "on the edges, pushing things almost too far" (Kinn), led to some critical disagreement about the book. While for many readers, Badanes's complex representation of "moral ambiguities sound[s] depths that few contemporary novels even aim for" (Milton, p. 3)—resulting in what one reviewer called "the most emotionally engaging, intellectually disturbing, and perversely erotic novel I have read in some time" (Horvath, p. 1)—others argued that "the constant braiding of Nazism and sex reduces both to exotic melodrama" (Gourevitch, p. 53). Other critics focus particularly on Badanes's loving images of prewar Poland, with some admiring his "reverence for the culture" (DiAntonio, p. 5H) and others accusing him of "pietistic nostalgia" (Dibdin, p. 17). It could be said that this range and diversity of critical responses point precisely to the success of Badanes's work and his larger concern with the paradoxes of attempting to represent what may be ultimately unrepresentable.

Bibliography

Primary Sources

Image Before My Eyes. 1981.
"The Man in the 12,000 Rooms." 1982.
The Final Opus of Leon Solomon. 1989.
"Change or Die." 1994.
Numerous poems and dramatic scripts in *ReCreation*, *Guerilla Theatre*, *Open Poetry*, *Hanging Loose*, *Michigan Quarterly Review*, *CAW!*, *Blood*, *Generation*, and *Landscapes*.

Secondary Sources

Anonymous. "Briefly Noted." *The New Yorker* (April 3, 1989): 115.
DiAntonio, Robert. "Archivist of the Holocaust." *St. Louis Post Everyday Magazine* (February 19, 1989): 5H.
Dibdin, Michael. "Book Review." *The Independent*, May 13, 1990, The Sunday Review, 17.
Grauer, Tresa. " 'Surprising the Darkness': History, Memory and Representation in Jerome Badanes' *The Final Opus of Leon Solomon*." *Studies in American Jewish Literature* 15 (1996): 78–89.
Gourevitch, Philip. "Death Kit." *Village Voice* (April 25, 1989): 53.
Greenwood, Douglas McCreary. "Meditations of a Survivor." *The Washington Post Book World* (May 4, 1989): B3.
Hinerfeld, Susan Slocum. "The Passions of a Survivor." *The Los Angeles Times Book Review* (March 5, 1989): 8.
Horvath, Brooke. "Untitled Review." *Review of Contemporary Fiction* 10, no. 1 (1990): 329–330.
Insdorf, Annette. "Rediscovering Polish Jewry." *The New York Times* (March 15, 1981): B15.
Kinn, Gail. Personal Correspondence. June 11, 2001.
Maslin, Janet. " 'Image Before My Eyes': Jewish Life in Pre-War Poland." *The New York Times* (March 19, 1981): C20.
Milton, Edith. "When Moral Life Is Impossible." *The New York Times Book Review* (February 12, 1989): 3.
Osnos, Peter. "World of My Father, 'Image Before My Eye', 'Images' of Poland From Days That are Past." *The Washington Post* (June 5, 1981): D1.
Pinsker, Sanford. "New Voices and the Contemporary Jewish Novel." *Jewish Book Annual* (1991): 6–20.
Pogrebin, Robin. "I Wanted to Be an American." *The New York Times Book Review* (February 12, 1989): 3.
Schwerner, Nancy. "Untitled." *The Antioch Review* 47 (summer 1989): 367.

JON ROBIN BAITZ

(1962–)

STEVEN DEDALUS BURCH

JON ROBIN BAITZ was born in Los Angeles in 1962, grew up, and was educated in the United States, Brazil, and South Africa. His father was an executive for Carnation Milk and was assigned to Brazil and South Africa during the 1960s and 1970s, providing Baitz with a firsthand look at the First World's postcolonial economic exploitation in developing countries on two continents, subjects that would become the basis for many of his most important plays, including *Three Hotels* and *A Fair Country*. Baitz's family returned to Los Angeles in 1978, and since then, he has worked as an actor, becoming a member of Naked Angels, an Off-Off Broadway theatre company in New York. Since his breakthrough with *The Substance of Fire* in 1990 he has produced a substantial body of work as a playwright. Baitz is a recipient of many awards, including one from the National Endowment for the Arts, Rockefeller and Revlon Fellowships, the Theatre Communications Group's Playwrights U.S.A. award, and a Humanitas award for *Three Hotels*. In addition, Baitz's *A Fair Country* was nominated for the 1996 Pulitzer Prize. In 1997, Baitz adapted *The Substance of Fire* to film. His recent play *Ten Unknowns* premiered in New York to critical acclaim in 2001.

The Substance of Fire, Baitz's only work that directly addresses the Holocaust, presents a "survivor," not from the camps but from the annihilation of his family as he remained hidden as a child during the war. The protagonist, Isaac Geldhart, lives in New York and runs a family publishing firm, a once prestigious company that is now being destroyed by Isaac's obsession with the *Shoah* and his attempt to understand his own infinitesimal part in it. Excluding his grown children from his business decisions, even though they are now partners through the shares of their dead mother, Isaac has embarked on publishing a series of costly books that explore the Nazi machine. This decision and his refusal to consider adding more commercially publishable books to the list, ensure a continuing and unsustainable financial loss to the firm.

More important, Isaac bans his children from his emotional life, building a wall of silence between his memories of the "wrecked world" and his new life as a successful survivor. This wall and its ultimate breaching become the focus of the struggle between the past and the present, and the destructive potential of memory in a generation that has been left with virtually nothing else. As old hostilities surface between Isaac and his offspring, one son, Martin, categorizes Isaac's "historical hardware" as obscene: "all that makes you is a very cautious academic pornographer, a sensationalist with Sulka ties. 'See the bodies pile up, watch the dead, see how bad everything is' " (*The Substance of Fire and Other Plays*, Theatre Communications Group, 1993, p. 80). Another son, Aaron, caustically refers to his father's sense of moral superiority, complaining to Isaac and his siblings that he, Aaron, doesn't have a "holocaust to pin on my chest" (p. 90), only his sense of family and continuity.

Edward Isser writes that the survivor drama is one of three subgenres of Holocaust drama and that the more recent survivor dramas such as *The Substance of Fire*, examine both the passage of time for the survivor and the "long-term legacy" of such distancing on both the protagonist and the protagonist's family (p. 24). Isaac's attempt to keep and honor his memory creates a profound rupture to his present-day family, and Baitz does not shy away from complicating Isaac's survivor's guilt by revealing Isaac's tendency to romanticize the survivors of the camps. In Baitz's screenplay adaptation, Isaac shares a park bench with Louis, a survivor-author Isaac is determined to publish, and watches as Louis feeds the pigeons. Glimpsing the tattooed number on Louis's arm, Isaac softly admits: "One gets covetous sometimes. Little badge of honor there." Then Isaac confesses that his family members had their tattoos as well (p. 77). Unlike Isaac's children or his business partners, Louis clearly hears Isaac's unspoken, anguished scream of guilt and gently offers to let the publisher join him in feeding the pigeons.

Significantly, both the play and the film adaptation suggest that Isaac can only be healed as an individual and as a father through his symbolic destruction of a totemic object, a souvenir postcard of Hitler's early attempts to be a watercolorist that Isaac fetishizes as a potential link into the puzzle of such monumental suffering: "He was not without a certain basic, rudimentary talent, was he not? You would certainly hope that he had been utterly devoid of talent. I mean, it would at least shed some tiny glimmer of light on the subsequent years, on all that came after" (pp. 103–104). However, such simplistic answers are not to be found, Baitz contends, even for those profoundly affected and disrupted.

It is the play's ending, in which Isaac reconciles with his son Martin as he burns his Hitler postcard, that, while not philosophically dishonest, disturbs some commentators. For instance, Alvin Goldfarb finds the play problematic as it "romanticizes" its survivor, suggesting a "universe in which there is always familial redemption" (p. 123). This brings to mind Lawrence Langer's admonition of American culture's inability to cope with unhappy and unresolved endings, an inability that speaks of a lack of artistic will and courage in dealing with this traumatic event (p. 215). Such traditional, commercial narrative tropes effectively reduce and contain the trauma, allowing the viewer a means of explaining such evil. It provides a structure that nullifies the horror by suggesting that one person's suffering can lead to greater understanding and betterment as a human being. Though Isaac's failure, through most of the play, to provide affection to his children is well and truthfully delineated as a scar that has not healed, Goldfarb's complaint nevertheless merits attention, especially as the play's commercial ending suggests an emotionally satisfying closure that problematizes the audience's response.

Most of Baitz's plays tangentially relate to the Holocaust as they concern such related issues as the loss of one's soul, one's identity, and one's connections to family and partners through the ethical compromises of a society that cannot see the consequences of such corruption. In several of Baitz's plays, this experience of loss and corruption becomes a means of dramatically charting the development, among American men and women, of a condition that may parallel that of a minor bureaucratic Nazi—a person adrift from any consideration either of an individual's ethical ties to humanity or of the consequences of such actions.

It is in his other works that Baitz incisively lays bare the foundations for the Holocaust by examining the frighteningly simple path toward becoming a perpetrator of genocide. *Three Hotels*, perhaps Baitz's most important play to date, presents a series of three interlocking monologues. Set in three different hotel rooms, in Morocco, in the Virgin Islands, and in Mexico, Baitz presents Kenneth Hoyle in the first and third room and his wife, Barbara, in the second. Kenneth, a former Peace Corps volunteer, is an executive for a corporation that markets powdered milk formula to impoverished families in the Third World. His job is the firing of executives who do not measure up to the corporation's standards and needs. In these three monologues, the audience witnesses the unraveling of a former idealist who has put his career ahead of his family and his sense of ethics.

With a stream of references in which he compares the powdered milk formula to Zyklon-B gas and to Kenneth's being the "Albert Speer of baby formula" (pp. 6, 9), Baitz targets his protagonist so that the audience cannot miss the trajectory of Kenneth's transformation into a Nazi, awaiting his orders. Further underscoring the loss of self is the revelation that Kenneth is a Jew who has denied his identity in order to climb the corporate ladder. At the play's end, after the death of his son, the loss of his job, and the estrangement of his wife, Kenneth sits alone in a Mexican hotel room on the Day of the Dead, painfully aware of what he has traded away, and softly sings a Yiddish lullaby.

The lack of a fixed ethical and familial compass also affects the characters of *A Fair Country* (1997). In the first scene, the protagonist, Patrice Burgess, arrives at an archaeological dig in the Mexican jungle, where she finds her estranged son Gil. A painful reunion ensues. They review their former lives together, including memories of deceased husband Harry and Patrice's older son Alec and the circumstances of their living in South Africa during the 1970s. Like the character of Kenneth in *Three Hotels*, Harry, a minor diplomat in South Africa, was once a believer in the dreams of his society, but he has gradually faced emotional and philosophical burnout. Tragedy strikes the family as it is revealed that Harry has betrayed both his ideals and his family in order to escape their imprisoning lives in Africa. In an interview with David Savran, Baitz describes Harry's decision as a "little sliver of rationalization and justification, first having to do with, 'I have to get my family out of this place. It's terrible.' But then comes the awful fact of his prospering in the short term from his decision" (p. 30). By quietly providing names of South African radical leaders who have been subsequently imprisoned and tortured by the Afrikaan police, Harry has received a coveted post at the Voice of America's office at The Hague.

Patrice also succumbs to a mentality that does not allow any escape from her own cultural prejudices, even as she tries desperately not to be a "boss" in a society where, as a white person, she cannot be anything else. Implicit in this characterization is the idea that any society that places an entire class or ethnic group as "bosses," solely on the basis of race and not by merit, is a society doomed to self-destruct as it attempts to destroy those it tries to control. Patrice actively chafes at her role even as she resents the servants for positioning her in that role. Savran writes that characters such as Patrice, Harry, and Kenneth "imagine themselves the stars of what is unmistakably a new global drama . . . a neocolonial order in which the corporations and representatives of Western governments have learned how to exert more subtle and insidious control over the Third World" (p. 26).

This loss of his characters' moral compass is the heart of Baitz's writing and the cause of his importance as a Holocaust writer of the late twentieth century. While Isaac from *The Substance of Fire* reveals the cost to him and his children because of his guilt at being a survivor, it is the compromises that Kenneth, Harry, and Patrice make that seal their fate. By losing their sense of morality, by allowing and not challenging immortality, each character begins to disintegrate from a victim to a bystander to a perpetrator. Tellingly, a 1995 production of *Three Hotels* in Berlin removed Kenneth's Jewishness and rationalized its cutting of any references to the Nazis by claiming that these moments "simply dredged up too many old demons to preserve the play's contemporary outlook" (Molner, p. 99). Baitz does not attempt to offer solutions. The world these characters inhabit is all too recognizable and too complex for such simplicities. But the small steps each character takes only lead, in the end, to self-destruction. Baitz's characters are all too recognizable among audiences that need his continual admonishment as they seek their own moral compasses.

Bibliography

Primary Sources

A Fair Country. 1997.
Mizlansky/Zilinsky or "Schmucks." 1998.
The Substance of Fire and Other Plays. 1993.
The Substance of Fire. 1996.
Three Hotels. 1994.

Interview

Savran, David. *The Playwright's Voice: American Dramatists on Memory, Writing and the Politics of Culture*. New York: Theatre Communications Group, 1999.

Plays

The Film Society. 1988.
The Substance of Fire. 1990.
Coq au Vin. 1991.
Four Monologues. 1991.
End of the Day. 1992.
Three Hotels. 1993.
It Changes Every Year. 1993.
Recipe for One. 1994.
A Fair Country. 1996.
Mizlansky/Zilinsky or "Schmucks." 1998.
Ten Unknowns. 2001.

Secondary Sources

Goldfarb, Alvin. "Inadequate Memories: The Survivor in Plays by Mann, Kesselman, Lebow, and Baitz." *Staging the Holocaust: The Shoah in Drama and Performance*. Edited by Claude Schumacher. Cambridge, Mass.: Cambridge University Press, 1998, pp. 111–129.

Isser, Edward R. *Stages of Annihilation: Theatrical Representation of the Holocaust*. Madison, N.J.: Fairleigh Dickinson University Press, 1997.

Langer, Lawrence L. "The Americanization of the Holocaust on Stage and Screen." In *From Hester Street to Hollywood*. Edited by Sarah Blacher Cohen. Bloomington, Ind.: Indiana University Press, 1983, pp. 213–230.

Molner, David. "*Three Hotels* in Germany Hits a Nerve." *Variety* 360, no. 11 (1995): 99.

MARK RAPHAEL BAKER

(1959–)

SIMONE GIGLIOTTI

"IT ALWAYS BEGINS in blackness, until the first light illuminates a hidden fragment of memory" (Sydney: Flamingo, 1997, pp. 1, 316). This sentence opens and closes the circuitous narrative of *The Fiftieth Gate*, by Melbourne-based author Mark Raphael Baker, who was born in 1959. Receiving his bachelor's degree from the University of Melbourne, and his doctorate from Oxford, Baker is not currently serving on any history faculty. However, he enjoys an honorary position as Senior Fellow of the Department of History at the University of Melbourne, where he has also acted as the Arnold Bloch Lecturer in modern Jewish history.

Published in 1997 to critical acclaim and the recipient of major Australian literary prizes, *The Fiftieth Gate* is the story of a son's attempt to understand his life through the Holocaust pasts of his survivor parents, Yossl Bekiermaszyn (b. 1927) and Genia Krochmal (b. 1934). Baker uses archival records from provincial Poland and Jerusalem to weave together the fragments of his father's incarceration in Auschwitz and Buchenwald and to recover his mother's lost childhood years in a dark cellar. *The Fiftieth Gate* presents a narrative that is a validation of personal memory by history's "appendage" of the public archive, and a paradoxical exposé of the archival document's struggle to reach those enduring memories of loss synonymous with Holocaust survival. The recognition of that paradox fuels the emotional and intellectual journeys of the book.

Light from Darkness

By and large, *The Fiftieth Gate* offers a Holocaust that is present and unresolved, in defiance of the closurelike attempts of many survivor narratives to offer homilies and hope wrested from trauma. The book's ostensibly redemptive theme is Baker's repeated insistence that "light" can emanate from the "darkness," and that his acts of investigation that transgress his parents' limits on telling their memories are necessary, in spite of the effects of those acts on his parents. While it is possible to read *The Fiftieth Gate* as three Holocaust stories—that of Baker and his parents—it is primarily Baker's quest for a meaningful post-Holocaust identity that initiates and concludes the memoir. While appearances by his parents and supporting family members populate the drama, Baker uses their memories to articulate for himself a Holocaust that cannot be contained by the archive. To find a voice in the void, Baker journeys to the lands of his family's memories in Eastern Europe as a traveler, inhabiting spaces of fear, terror, and flight, and speaking for losses and voices that were silenced long ago.

The journeys that propelled Baker to Europe ultimately began in the Melbourne of his youth and adulthood. He recalls going to costume parties dressed as Hitler and hoarding Nazi memorabilia in his room (p. 99). His profession as a scholar of Jewish history and the Holocaust provided an academic understanding of the topic but, in many ways, caused an estrangement from his parents, who inhabited a world that was inaccessible. Baker wanted to know why his mother suffered periodic depression. He also sought to unpack the ritual meanings of his father's "membership" in the Buchenwald Boys, a club open only to survivors. Central to his quest for understanding is a kind of guilt for having grown up as the son of excessively devoted parents who suffered stolen childhoods and adolescences. The need to make sense of this guilt compels Baker to imagine Holocaust scenes in suburban Melbourne:

> And there was the pain of displaced identification. I invented a biography for myself and elements of my parents' lives, characters more valorous than any protagonist found in fiction. As a child, I even gave myself a number, imagining myself as a ghetto fighter. . . . What was I

> doing? I now ask myself. Was it Australia I wished to escape, its suburban dross and culture of leisure? In the absence of a Holocaust, I was compelled to create my own. Trains, of which there was no shortage in Melbourne, were a favoured object of my mental manipulations. The rambling green trams moving toward the yawning jaws of Luna Park veiled a fate which terrorised my mind, while inside happy Australians flew over the seaside on Ferris wheels licking fairy-floss from their fingers (p. 99).

Baker's parents met in Australia and married in 1953, though before that their lives were tied to the rich linguistic and cultural milieu of Poland. Yossl was from Wierzbnik, a town southeast of Warsaw, while Genia was from Bołszowce, a town in the territories of eastern Poland that endured first Soviet then Nazi occupations in World War II, but is now a part of Ukraine. The task of recovering Baker's father's history proves less obstructed than recovering his mother's, but the book's structure reflects the difficulties posed by the resistance of Baker's parents to his invasion of their memories. The title "The Fiftieth Gate" is inspired by a belief in the Jewish mystical tradition that forty-nine gates separate good and evil, and it is through entering the final gate, the fiftieth, that a revelation is found: a validation of the self, an affirmation of identity, a tunnel of darkness in which light beckons. The book's unfolding chapters reflect the opening of the gates to reach the tunnel of his parents' darkness.

The fragmented biographies of Baker's parents emerge in their trip to Poland and Ukraine in 1995. The reader is not so much offered an orderly narrative of "this is my father's history" but vignettes of what his father remembers and what Baker can provide in terms of missing information when they return to Wierzbnik, Yossl's birthplace. The use of archival records to validate, if not provoke, memory was complicated and achieved unforeseen results in his father's case. Yossl was imprisoned in Starachowice, interned in Auschwitz from June 1944 to January 1945, and liberated in Buchenwald on 11 April 1945. Baker's grandfather, Leibush Bekiermaszyn, died in Buchenwald, and Baker is able to reconstruct from archival records in rural Poland his grandfather's movements in that camp. Baker found the school reports of Yossl's two sisters, Martale and Yenta, who were murdered by the Germans, and proceeds to read out their grades. The use of archival documents to provide "missing" histories is not simply empirical; it links Yossl's present memories to absent stories, and begins again his mourning for his murdered sisters. Baker found that the richest source of archival documents was in Radom in southeastern Poland, from where Starachowice-Wierzbnik was administered during the war. These archives inform the everyday history of the Bekiermaszyn family: their father's occupation during a particular year, the payment of taxes, school reports, and a birth certificate that ages Yossl Bekiermaszyn by two years.

Genia, Baker's mother, was the only child survivor among the people of Bołszowce. According to Baker, she relays her life through literary tragedies, though none is worse than hers. Baker's mother says to him: "If Tolstoy could tell my story, Anna Karenina would have thrown herself under the train much earlier in the book" (p. 98). His representation of her is the most moving and frustrating portrait in the book. She is a woman whose characteristics are difficult to reconcile: speaker of many languages, accomplished scholar, and a great theatrical performer, yet still today the little girl hiding in blackness. For years she had told Baker that she was, along with her parents, Leo and Rosa Krochmal, the only child to survive the deportations of 1,380 Jews to the death camp of Bełżec, a memory he was obsessed with validating in a fashion offered to his father. But here, the archival struggle proved intensely unsatisfying, and he is forced to rely, in spite of his sensibilities as a historian, on her word. This he cannot do:

> For months I had been searching for a sign of her former existence in Bołszowce. Not that either of us need confirmation. For my part, I did not doubt for a moment that she had once lived in this town, nor that she had experienced the events relayed in bits and pieces over the years. It was not facts that were held under suspicion, but her credibility as a survivor. Unlike my father, she could never show her children the scars on her arm; hers were invisible, numbered in the days and years of her stolen childhood (p. 133).

Nor could Genia locate her Holocaust experiences as easily as her husband's addresses of incarceration: Auschwitz and Buchenwald. The action in Bołszowce in October 1942 remains largely insignificant if historiography is a guide. There is no memory map for Baker's mother's addresses of Bursztyn, Bołszowce, and Rohatyn. In comparison to Baker's father's *Yizkor* (memorial book), which contains stories from friends and survivors around the world, the invisibility of records of Genia's incarceration causes Baker to ask: "Who will remember for my mother?" (p. 137).

What happens to Holocaust memories that cannot be validated and located "archivally," as in the case of Baker's mother? Baker the historian's quest for a "truth" to his mother's words prompts an outburst he can't forgive himself:

> It was an uncontrollable urge, this repeated questioning of her, this interrogation, as if I was David Irving and not her son pointing the video camera at her. And then, to my everlasting shame, I crossed the boundary: "Prove it,"

> I heard myself saying. "I don't believe this part. Prove it" (p. 190).

The representation of his parents' memories and their journeys to Poland and Israel to recover them leave the most lingering impressions of how the Holocaust is appropriated to construct the personal identities of the so-called second generation, although one should apply a certain caution to interpreting the meaning of the Holocaust as generationally distinct and contextualized by national preoccupations with remembrance.

Valid and Invalid Stories

The book's critical and popular success was seen to intensify the national preoccupation with remembrances of the Holocaust. It gave those remembrances a particularly Australian identity, and gave voice to the often unrepeatable and inexplicable experiences of survivors and the culture of received memories of their children. It brought clarity to the broader public's conflicting perceptions about valid and invalid Holocaust stories.

These conflicts were occasioned by the publication of Helen Demidenko's *The Hand That Signed the Paper* (1994), a controversial work about Ukraine and the Holocaust that was initially showered with praise and prizes but later denounced as a hoax and reissued in 1995 as "fiction." In circumstances similar to Binjamin Wilkomirski's *Fragments: Memories of a Childhood, 1939–1948* (1996), Demidenko was exposed as Helen Darville, the daughter of recent British immigrants, who falsified a Ukrainian identity in order to claim authorial license to write what was largely perceived as an antisemitic vision which denied that the Jews were the Nazis' primary victims.

In response to these anxious moments of national reflection about ethnicity and identity, *The Fiftieth Gate* was promoted as a irrefutably "valid" Holocaust story. It is clear that the literary processes involved in narrating the Holocaust memories of his parents are in fact Baker's testament to the problems of working through "displaced identification." His attempt to understand what displaced identification means involves a recognition both of the self and of one's responsibility to history and to contemporary crises of persecution, war, and mass suffering.

Australia provided homes to thousands of displaced persons and refugees after World War II, but their stories of suffering and struggle remained untold in the postwar years of social conservatism and economic boom, which was not dissimilar to the cultures of forgetting trauma in some Western European and North American countries. *The Fiftieth Gate* should be seen alongside other literary attempts not simply as responding to that absence or void of narration but also as contributing to a consciousness of killing and its moral and ethical implications that extend beyond the horror of the Holocaust. While in one sense *The Fiftieth Gate* promotes a Holocaust "consciousness," the territories of horror that are revisited and undoubtedly remain in his parents' minds force Baker to reckon with continued suffering, irrespective of racial, ethnic, and political specificities. *The Fiftieth Gate* is a text self-consciously aware of its implications as a story of living with humanity and inhumanity. Baker forces us to think about our responsibilities to the future in the context of a history of past genocidal crimes.

Certainly the critical reception of the work emphasized the innovative confluence of traditional historical methods and the novelistic genre. Baker's unfolding narrative of the ways archival records in Poland and Jerusalem contradicted or confirmed his parents' individual memories integrated an investigative writing style with elements of crime writing: mystery, the nature of evidence, continued evasion, and cover-ups. His vigilant pursuit of dual "truths"—those of "History" as recorded in archives and the repressed or forgotten memories of his parents—also presents the reader with an acutely contemporary story of the imperatives of reclaiming lost or buried narratives in the transition from first- to second-generation Holocaust memory.

The Fiftieth Gate was shortlisted for and received several prizes for nonfiction and continues to be discussed as a sophisticated and innovative contribution to the long-standing debate about the possibility of representing the Holocaust, though, unfortunately, the book remains unpublished outside Australia. *The Fiftieth Gate* effectively depicts a local identity to contrast the larger, general Australian narratives of Holocaust survival. Baker paints a specific portrait of the survivor community in Melbourne, offering at once an unflattering yet endearing portrait of men anchored by their survival, gathering together to dance annually at the Buchenwald Ball, comments on survivors (including his mother) who seek solace in the escapist world offered by the casino culture, and who also bathe in the resort and retirement city of Surfers Paradise in Queensland in northeastern Australia.

In terms of style, Baker inhabits multiple voices of the dead to bring them into our hearing. On the journey into the darkness, and through the fiftieth gate of the title, he appropriates celebrated poet Dan Pagis's poem "Written in Pencil in a Sealed Boxcar" to comment on the eternal silences of his paternal grandmother, Hinda, before imagining her journey to Treblinka with Martale and Yenta:

here in this carload
  i am Hinda
tell him that i (p. 261)

An issue unaddressed in the critical reception of the work is the enduring battle in the book between documentary evidence provided by the archive, referred to above as history's "appendage," and the credibility of memory. The book is one of the clearest examples of a tension in Holocaust studies at present: the cultural and performative work of personal memories in the "absence" of the archive. Though Baker is furnished with ample historical records in the case of his father, his frustration at the absence of equivalent records for his mother makes his telling of her story more strained, more difficult, and yet precisely more affecting because she rebukes his need for evidence of legitimate suffering so that she might be authentic and credible as a "survivor" in his eyes. In reply to her son's incessant questioning, Genia demands: "What do you mean, do I remember? Stop interrogating me. Stop testing me" (p. 194).

The Fiftieth Gate is a work of remembering and grieving that extends beyond the Holocaust in importance. Undeniably born from but unlimited by that event, the work marks a significant new departure in memoir writing. The need to make sense of, or explain, one's identity through parental pain, and to finally separate oneself from that pain, is to be liberated from the burden of overwhelming and obsessive desire for affirmation and self-validation. The author's ultimate recognition that both history and memory are interdependent constructs fighting for a voice animates the Baker family's journeys into darkness, and, in the end, light.

Bibliography

Primary Source

The Fiftieth Gate: A Journey Through Memory. 1997.

Secondary Sources

Manne, Robert. *The Culture of Forgetting: Helen Demidenko and the Holocaust.* Melbourne: Text Publishing, 1996.

McCooey, David. *Artful Histories: Modern Australian Autobiography.* Melbourne: Cambridge University Press, 1996.

PETER BARNES
(1931–)

CHARLES GRIMES

PETER BARNES'S CONTRIBUTION to Holocaust literature is the controversial play *Auschwitz* (premiered 1978, published 1981). Born in 1931 in London to a Jewish mother and an Anglican father who converted to Judaism to marry her, Barnes achieved acclaim with his play *The Ruling Class* (premiered 1968, published 1969), made into a 1972 film starring Peter O'Toole. More recently Barnes authored the TV miniseries *Merlin* and *Noah's Ark*. His playwriting features satire and grotesque comedy—in *The Ruling Class*, for example, he mocks the English aristocracy and religious hypocrisy. In *Auschwitz* Barnes investigates the role of comedy in responding to the tragedy of the Holocaust, while satirizing the Nazi German bureaucrats who enabled the mass killings. *Auschwitz*'s premiere at London's Royal Court Theatre provoked harsh responses. Critic Richard Allen Cave noted the "offensively crude" visualization of the gas chambers and lamented that the play "appear[ed] to be in very bad taste" (Cave, p. 255). Barnes recalls, "I felt waves of hate coming out of the audience" (Bly and Wager, p. 45). The playwright analyzed resistance to his play by claiming that British theatergoers want a "theatre of reassurance [and] affirmation," not "disturbance" (p. 45). The play has rarely been performed since this premiere, despite a smattering of positive reviews and subsequent praise from literary scholars.

Auschwitz

Auschwitz is the second act of a two-act play titled *Laughter!* The first half of *Laughter!* is *Tsar*, about Ivan the Terrible. Ivan tortures a courtier while taunting his own son that he is not sufficiently murderous to rule Russia. He glories in his country's eager submission to vicious misrule. Ultimately the Angel of Death collects Ivan, telling him that his atrocities will pale next to those of the future: "You made death too personal. . . . In the coming years they'll institutionalize it, take the passion out of killing, turn men into numbers and the slaughter'll be so vast no one mind'll grasp it, no heart will break 'cause of it" *(Laughter!* London: Heinemann Educational, 1978, p. 365). Having thus presaged the routinization of mass murder, Barnes's play then shifts setting from tsarist Russia to Nazi Germany.

Auschwitz portrays three employees of Branch C of the Wirtschafts-Verwaltungshauptamt, the Economic and Administrative Main Office of the SS. This office was in charge of coordinating camp slave labor and collecting booty from prisoners. The characters Viktor Cranach, Heinz Stroop, and Else Jost are bureaucratic drones who, although they coordinate the building of Auschwitz and other death camps, see their lives as apolitical and their tasks as value-neutral and administrative. Barnes manipulates us into temporary sympathy for these characters, whose jokes are at first unproblematically funny. "Coming to work this morning, I stopped to pull in my belt. Some idiot asked what I was doing. I said, 'Having breakfast' " (*Collected Plays*, London: Heinemann, 1981, p. 370). Cranach directs Else to retype a memo: "I know the first step's hard, but once you've tried it you'll enjoy using commas" (p. 370). Stroop, anxious he will be fired before he can retire, quips: "You can't please everyone, so I find it best to keep pleasing my superiors" (p. 373). These functionaries distance themselves from the reality in which they are involved, taking refuge in euphemisms and dry, technical jargon. They prefer "neutral language," which is "more concise and less emotive" than plain speech (p. 379). Their jobs are a logistical challenge requiring administrative expertise: "622.75 units per day're now being transported from all over Europe to Upper Silesia" (p. 373). They avoid any language that would indicate what their jobs are about.

In a bureaucratic turf war, Cranach, Stroop, and Jost are attacked by the rabid Nazi Hans Gottleb. Contrasted to Gottleb, the bureaucrats, able to joke at their own situation, appear safe and human. Gottleb prompts the bureaucrats to tell anti-Nazi jokes so that he can tape-record them and take Cranach's job. "What do you call someone who sticks his finger up the Führer's arse?!" asks Cranach: "A brain surgeon" (pp. 395–396). But Gottleb's tape recorder malfunctions, and so, enraged, he reveals to the civil servants what their memos have created. In a gruesome monologue, Gottleb recounts the atrocities at Auschwitz, using the name of the camp for the first time in the play. As he describes Jews converted into "fertilizer ash," guards using newborns as soccer balls, and other facts of Auschwitz (pp. 402–404), the back of the stage set opens and corpses (straw dummies) spill out. But even when Gottleb forces them to view the reality of their actions, the bureaucrats excuse their complicity in Nazi horror and rationalize their failure to oppose it: "This isn't the time to say 'no'. I've just taken out a second mortgage!"; "what can I do? I'm only one woman. How can I say 'no'?" (p. 406); "[Gottleb] was lying . . . he used *adjectives*" (p. 407).

The play argues that evil requires such banal formulas of self-preservation and that it is all too easy to evade reality through lack of imagination. As *Auschwitz* ends, Cranach and his cohorts oust Gottleb and seemingly eliminate from consciousness their participation in genocide. The scholar Vivian Patraka notes that the story of the play is "the [characters'] narrative of denial" (p. 100). Barnes finally likens these characters to his audience, indicting both for a predilection to apathy. Cranach concludes the play, asserting triumphantly that those who implemented the Final Solution are simply "ordinary people, people who liked people, people like . . . you, me, us" (p. 409). Here Barnes parallels the philosopher Hannah Arendt's evaluation of Adolf Eichmann, the SS official who helped to institute Nazi policies of expelling and exterminating Jews: "The trouble with Eichmann was precisely that so many were like him, and that . . . they were . . . terribly and terrifyingly normal" (p. 373). In generalizing from German functionaries to his audience, Barnes surely courted the feelings of outrage his play in fact provoked.

Barnes himself was evacuated from London during World War II; he used as the basis for *Auschwitz* not personal experience or his Jewish identity but disinterested scholarly research on the Third Reich (Fuchs, p. xvi; see also Dukore for a description of Barnes's working methods). As a result of this research, Barnes sets his play during 1942, when the German bureaucracy solved major organizational problems related to deportations and construction of the death camps. A major thrust of Barnes's research was how the Nazis manipulated language. The characters' bureaucratic terminology is taken from the historical record (Fuchs, p. xvi). This style of speech serves the purpose noted by Christopher Browning in his study of the Nazi gas van: this "euphemistic code language . . . hid reality from others and at least partially from themselves" (p. 67). The critic George Steiner also evokes how the Nazis debased German, using language as a cover "beneath which to conceal any amount of rawness and deception" (p. 97). "An immense outpouring of precise, serviceable words," as Steiner writes (p. 99) and Barnes dramatizes, was utilized to record inhuman actions in outwardly neutral terms.

Barnes introduces a political analysis of Nazi power, alluding for instance to the debate over the radical or conservative nature of National Socialism. Gottleb praises how Nazism's political innovations reinvigorated German society: "We flung the old order out of orbit . . . gave Germany social fluidity . . . there's always something happening in the Third Reich" (*Auschwitz*, p. 386). After Cranach points out Nazism's conservative appeal to the German middle-class desire for wealth, Stroop claims, "as Jews can be simultaneously scum and dregs, so National Socialism can simultaneously embody revolutionary and conservative principles" (p. 386). Barnes sees fascism as abetted by Germans' desire to be commanded: "The German people've always preferred strong government to self-government. . . . We're tormented by choice" (p. 376). The need to obey is connected to organized religion: in Catholicism, says Jost, "Obedience is regarded as a principle of righteous conduct. So I look on National Socialism as Catholicism with the Christianity left out" (p. 376). (Here Barnes adapts a joke told in Nazi Germany: "What is the difference between Christianity and National Socialism?" "In Christianity, one man died for everyone. In National Socialism, everyone has to die for one man" [Lipman, p. 91].) Throughout his work Barnes portrays "the psychology of submission" (Innes, p. 306) and moral indifference as universal human failings; he holds that apathy in the face of oppression characterizes all societies, past and present, not only Nazi Germany.

When Cranach notes "jokes carry penalties," he refers to Nazi regulations such as the year 1933's "law against treacherous attacks on the state and party and for the protection of the party uniform" (Lipman, pp. 33–34), which forbade jokes against the party, its leaders, and later the war effort, on the penalty of death. The play's jokes derive from history as much as Barnes's imagination. One 1943 German joke ran: "*Customer*: What kinds of dogs have you got for sale? *Salesman*: Pekinese, dwarf poodles, Yorkshire terriers. *Customer*: Stop, stop—haven't you got a dog big enough for a family of five?" (Hillenbrand, p. 184). Such opposition to the privations caused by the Nazi regime features in a new historical analysis of "resistance." Were such jokes subversive or simply a way to accommodate a reality no one wanted to change? In *Laughter in Hell*, Steve Lipman suggests that such jokes showed sincere anti-Nazi sentiment. Lipman also quotes the historian Richard Grunberger's claim that these jokes were for many Germans a way to evade confrontation with Nazi misrule (p. 10). The social historian Detlev Peukert suggests that "Diverse forms of criticism . . . were quite capable of existing side by side with partial recognition of the regime or at least with passive acceptance of authority" (p. 63). In historical fact, Hermann Göring, whom the characters jest at, allegedly propagated jokes against himself, aiming to humanize his image (Lipman, p. 40). Barnes gives his opinion on this debate in *Laughter!*'s prologue: "Laughter's the ally of tyrants. It softens our hatred. An excuse to change nothing, for nothing needs changing when it's all a joke" (p. 343).

In an epilogue, Barnes further engages humor in response to the Holocaust. Two camp inmates, Bimko and Bieberstein, perform a soft-shoe routine including one-liners such as "Bernie Litvinoff just died. Drunk a whole bottle of varnish. Awful sight, but a beautiful finish," and repartee such as "According to the latest statistics, one man dies in this camp every time I breathe." "Have you tried toothpaste?" (p. 410). As their awful act "dies," metaphorically, so do they, literally. There were, as Barnes has noted, theatrical performances within the ghettos and camps (see Goldfarb). By divorcing content (familiar jokes) from context (mass murder), Barnes induces audience discomfort. He has even linked humor to the fate of the Jews, offering a disturbing theory of how Jews have abetted antisemitism: "the Jews have a great reputation of being able to laugh . . . about their situation. I wonder if one of the reasons they have been persecuted (not the only reason of course) and haven't done anything about it is because of their ability to . . . laugh at the terrors that have afflicted them" (Bly and Wager, p. 46). Skloot writes, "The epilogue to *Auschwitz* achieves a maximum brutality because it is written as comedy . . . it drives home Barnes's passionate point . . . that in the face of atrocity, laughter is useless and immoral" (p. 67). The critic Bernard Dukore asked Barnes whether London audiences laughed at these jokes: "On the good nights, they didn't" (p. 47).

Conclusion

A character in *The Ruling Class* proclaims: "No God of love made this world. I've seen a girl of four's nails had been torn out by her father. I've seen the mountains of gold teeth and hair and the millions boiled down for soap" (London: Heinemann, 1969, p. 72). In later plays such as *Barnes' People II* (1984) and *The Spirit of Man; And More Barnes' People: Seven Monologues* (1990), Barnes deals with the dilemma of faith. He asks us to consider humanity's atrocities, the Holocaust among them, against the possibility of human morality. *Auschwitz* is often compared in this regard to C. P. Taylor's *Good*, which examines how Nazism seduced and corrupted even those with moral intelligence. According to Elinor Fuchs, Barnes wrote *Auschwitz* to denounce "the pernicious explanation that the Holocaust shows the operation of abstract evil" (p. xv); that is, Barnes regards evil as nonabstract, as executed always by real people on other actual people in specific social circumstances. Vivian Patraka also describes how Barnes links the normalcy of everyday life to the perpetuation of genocide: "Barnes, with his 'ordinary' office . . . dramatizes the fascist ideology implicit in the culture of the everyday, in the characters' relationship to a lived experience they perceive as expressing their private, apolitical selves" (p. 43). In *Auschwitz*, Barnes shows that banal, everyday motivations—wanting to keep your pension or not being courageous enough to speak truth to power—enable cruelty, illustrating that humans are damned creatures who can reconcile themselves to the personal knowledge and performance of ultimate evil.

Bibliography

Primary Sources

The Ruling Class. 1969.
Lulu. 1971.
The Frontiers of Farce. 1977.
Laughter! 1978.
Collected Plays. 1981.
Barnes' People II: Seven Duologues. 1984.
The Real Long John Silver and Other Plays (Barnes' People III). 1986.
Auschwitz. 1987.
Plays: One. 1989.
Revolutionary Witness and Nobody Here But Us Chickens. 1989.
The Spirit of Man; and More Barnes' People: Seven Monologues. 1990.
Tango at the End of Winter. 1991.
Plays: Two. 1993.

Secondary Sources

Arendt, Hannah. *Eichmann in Jerusalem*. In *The Portable Hannah Arendt*, edited by Peter Baehr. New York: Penguin Books, 2000.

Billington, Michael. "Laughter." Review of *Laughter! The Guardian* 25 Jan. 1978: p. 10.

Bly, Mark, and Doug Wager. "Theater of the Extreme: An Interview with Peter Barnes." *Theater*, 12 (spring 1981): 43–48.

Browning, Christopher R. *Fateful Months: Essays on the Emergence of the Final Solution*. New York: Holmes and Meier, 1991.

Cave, Ronald Allen. *New British Drama on the London Stage*. New York: St. Martin's Press, 1988.

Dukore, Bernard F. *Barnestorm: The Plays of Peter Barnes*. New York: Garland, 1995.

Fuchs, Elinor. Introduction. In *Plays of the Holocaust: An International Anthology*. New York: Theatre Communications Group, 1987, pp. xi–xxii.

Goldfarb, Alvin. "Theatrical Activities in Nazi Concentration Camps." *Performing Arts Journal* 1 (fall 1976): 3–11.

Hillenbrand, F. K. M. *Underground Humour in Nazi Germany 1933–1945*. London: Routledge, 1995.

Innes, Christopher. *Modern British Drama: 1980–1990*. Cambridge: Cambridge University Press, 1992, pp. 298–308.

Inverso, Marybeth. "*Der Straf-block*: Performance and Execution in Barnes, Griffiths, and Wertenbaker." *Modern Drama* 36 (September 1993): 420–430.

Lipman, Steve. *Laughter in Hell: The Use of Humor during the Holocaust*. Northvale, N.J.: Jason Aronson, 1991.

Patraka, Vivian M. *Spectacular Suffering: Theatre, Fascism, and the Holocaust*. Bloomington: Indiana University Press, 1999.

Peukert, Detlev. *Inside Nazi Germany*. New Haven: Yale University Press, 1987.

Steiner, George. *Language and Silence: Essays on Language, Literature, and the Inhuman*. New York: Atheneum, 1970.

http://www.peterbarnes.com.

HANOCH BARTOV

(1926–)

DVIR ABRAMOVICH

BARTOV WAS BORN on 13 August 1926, in Petach Tikva, Palestine (currently part of Israel), to Simkha and Miriam Bartov. He attended the Hebrew University of Jerusalem between 1946 and 1951, and married Yehudith Shimmer in 1946. Bartov served in the Jewish Brigade of the British Army from 1943 to 1946 and the Israel Defense Forces from 1947 to 1949. His time in the Jewish Brigade was instrumental in his writing of *The Brigade*, the work that is covered in this essay. Since the end of his military service he has worked as a high school teacher, a farmer, a news editor and U.S. correspondent, and a newspaper columnist. Bartov also served as a counselor and cultural officer at the Israeli Embassy in London between 1966 and 1968. He currently lives in Israel.

Hanoch Bartov's *The Brigade*, winner of the 1965 Shlonsky Award, asks how one should respond to the Holocaust and then adumbrates the attendant feelings that are associated with such a dilemma. It debates whether revenge is the appropriate reaction and whether it is even achievable. It is also about the relationship between the native-born Israelis and the European Jews who were the victims of genocide. At the center of the novel is the underlying motif of identity—is Israeli identity different from Jewish diasporic identity? As one commentator observed, "*The Brigade* is the first serious inquiry in Israeli literature into the emotions of shame and repulsion towards the survivors of the Holocaust" (Mintz, p. 245).

In the vein of other novels of this period, such as Yehuda Amichai's *Not of This Time, Not of This Place* (1963), the plot focuses on an adolescent who is plunged into war-torn Europe and confronts, for the first time, the slaughter of his people. Swirling in and out of the pages are questions of vengeance, morality, and the nature of relations between victim and perpetrator. Bartov, one of Israel's finest novelists, a playwright and journalist, and recipient of the 1988 President's Literature Award, like his protagonist Elisha, was born in Palestine in 1926 and joined the Jewish Brigades in 1943 at age seventeen.

The central hero of *The Brigade* is Elisha Kruk, and it is through his eyes that events are related. The nineteen-year-old Elisha enlists in the British army as a medic, supposedly to do battle with the Germans, whom he has learned to abhor, but also to flee the strictures of his father's home, which he perceives to be socially oppressive. We learn that his parents are Polish immigrants and that his father has immersed his son in the world of the Torah, an education Elisha wishes to escape. At one point, Elisha ruminates, "I was free of all obligations . . . Snap it, that damn last string tying you to your father's wretched world, to fear of sin, pure-mindedness, novelistic romance. Snap that string and float away like a balloon" (*Pitzei Bagrut*, Tel Aviv: Am Oved, 1965, p. 170). Principally, Elisha is a delicate, childish teenager trying to acquire recognition that he is indeed an adult, both from his beloved Noga as well as from his peers in the unit. The novel, essentially a *bildungsroman* (made explicit by the Hebrew title, which means *Wounds of Maturity*), shows how Elisha is forced to grow up and make ethical calls during his stay in post-*Shoah* Europe that ultimately lead him back to the traditions and mores that he imbibed at the Sabbath table of his father's house.

The story opens on the last day of World War II, just as news of the Nazi surrender reaches the Jewish brigade, stationed in Italy and waiting for orders to enter the front and rescue the survivors. Framing his tale within a closely knit group of soldiers of divergent backgrounds, Bartov is able to craft each character as a strict representation of an ideological posture, giving each a philosophical view about how to treat the defeated Germans whom they encounter. The mission of the brigade is to facilitate the transfer of the Jewish refugees from the displaced person camps to Palestine, so they can return to their homeland and join their brothers and sisters. Mostly young, the brigade consists of an extended roster of characters, including Kibbutz and settlement members, and students and former fighters of the various underground movements who have grown tired of their own organizations. Hearing reports of the atrocities in Europe, they have developed an intense hate for the Nazi butchers, leading to a deep desire to take immediate action against their enemies. Furthermore, they despise being relegated to the role of bystanders, especially because their own active defense of their land against the British and Arabs has marked them as different from their passive European counterparts, who, they think, accepted their fate with resignation. In a sense, the yearning for revenge can be read as a rebellion by the young men of the brigade against what they perceive as the habitual "Jewish fate" that was concretized *ne plus ultra* during the *Shoah*. As Sidra DeKoven Ezrahi maintains, the novel "reconstructs the brazen, self confident attitude of a generation of Israeli soldiers who regarded the victims with disdain mingled with a determination to avenge their death" (DeKoven Ezrahi, pp. 126–127).

Although they did not share in the suffering, their undertaking is to provide a response equivalent to the terrors committed by the Nazis. From the outset, we are reminded of the contingent's raison d'être:

> It wouldn't be much, only one Kishinev, in round numbers: one thousand houses burned down, five hundred killed, one hundred raped. What do you mean one hundred? I have to kill one by one by myself. In cold blood. And rape one woman. In cold blood . . . That's what we are here for (*Brigade*, pp. 46–47).

The issue here is that by retaliating against the Germans, even if it is after the fact, the Israeli warriors will differentiate themselves from the submissive European Jews with whom they resist any identification.

In the camp of those who hold that an eye for an eye is less important than saving the shattered Jews is the British colonel who alerts them to the difficult moral dilemma facing them, instructing them that they will have to exercise restraint against those who murdered morality. His plea falls on deaf ears. As they make their way to the Austrian-Italian border, with the slogan "The Jews are coming" splashed across their vehicles, they come across a column of trucks containing groups of German war prisoners. Undeterred by the previous appeal they hurl tins and tent pegs, hitting and injuring several (the sequence is laced with biblical overtones when the Palestinian Jews fling a cheap imitation figurine of Moses at the prisoners). As a result, the convoy is stopped by the English, who rebuke the Israelis for their reaction, making certain the line of trucks can pass safely. Later, while awaiting a train to take them to their permanent base, Elisha and his comrades decide to forcibly seize control of the station and in the process underscore their status as conquerors. When the manager, along with two other workers, tries to prevent the violent deed, one of the soldiers points his machine gun at him with the threat of emptying his bullets into the frightened administrator. Yet for all their bravado nothing happens. In the end, their nihilistic fantasies of destruction remain unfulfilled. They board the train that takes them back to their camp across the border, impotent in their inability to inflict damage on the Germans. In many respects, the failure of the gaggle of heroes to actualize their longing to fight the Germans (throughout the novel they fail to discharge a single shot, although stranded in Italy for close to two months) or to retaliate, stresses the author's depiction of the soldiers as onlookers standing apart from the action without affecting history.

The book's dramatic capstone occurs in a four-hour debate that erupts when the entire company is summoned to a roll call. It transpires that a German mother and a daughter have claimed that soldiers from the brigade broke into their house and tried to rape and kill them in addition to stealing money and other valuables. Bartov deftly draws us into this tense, emotionally charged sequence through the fiercely delineated opposing arguments made by various members of the brigade. Locked in intense conversation, all the disparate threads are knotted and thrust together in a battering ram fashion. Each is allowed his own pitch, his own moral rage in challenging and thwarting the other's thesis. Tamari, who insists the two accused men stand up and reveal themselves before having to undergo a humiliating parade before the two German women, rationally contends that no one has the right to pursue his own war, that they are here as emissaries sent for one purpose, to rescue the Jews. Giladi, in contradistinction, zealously promotes the value of revenge: "We don't believe in turning the other cheek, Tamari, and even if we did, we couldn't turn it because it no longer exists. They destroyed everything in their furnaces . . . Only one hand was saved, only one small fist. Us. Here. What should this clenched fist do Tamari, what do you suggest it to do?" (p. 116). He then expounds on the frustrating possibility that the dead will not be avenged: "The one small fist is still clenched, in a spasm. It will never open up, this fist. It will stay clenched, its fingernails piercing its own flesh, its blood frozen, the memory of vengeance never unleashed blackening it with gangrene" (p. 117).

According to Giladi, the only way to liberate oneself from the abhorrent terror of the Nazis is to reciprocate in a similar fashion. In his tirade, Giladi addresses the question of what will happen if Jews do not jettison their moral code and are not allowed to practice their own brand of justice, intoning to his captive audience that they pass on the hatred from one generation to the next. Advocating, "one day of wild revenge. Murder for its own sake. Rape for rape. Looting for looting. Innocent victims for innocent victims," he believes that only after such acts will they be able to rid themselves of "this canker, this rot, this nightmare of helplessness—only then, clean and at peace with ourselves can we take our place in human society once more. Then we can forget" (pp. 117–118). In the end, the two assailants own up and are replaced by two other soldiers in a degrading parade formation where the women fail to pick out their attackers after walking up and down the row of soldiers. Recollecting the event, the narrator says, "Many years have passed since then, but that day has stuck to me" (p. 128). Germane here is the ironic skewing of the situation in that the defeated Nazis are again, momentarily, the victors identifying and selecting Jews from a roll call.

A parallel theme operating in the book is the contact with the survivors and the reaction it stirs in the central protagonist. Notably, Bartov sheds light on the attitude of his principals toward their Diasporic counterparts by first grafting onto the page a meeting with the supposed antithesis of the victims. Nowhere is this better demonstrated than in the episode where Kruk and his fellow soldiers meet the representative of the greatly lauded partisan who has arrived at the railroad worker's building asking how he can reach headquarters to receive further instructions. Unsurprisingly, the paragon of wartime resistance and courage provokes a geyser of national pride fused with nationalism: "It seemed unbelievable—all of us squeezed into the room, surrounding the stranger . . . This stranger, who had come to us from out of the darkness, awesome in his appearance, was actually one of us, speaking our language, coming to us straight from the forest, directing his feet to this spot on the border as though to a star" (pp. 138–139). To wit, Zunenshtein wants to hug the stranger, whom he calls *haver* (friend) while another shoves bread into his hand.

Nonetheless, the real test comes when Kruk visits a refugee camp in the Italian Alps and confronts the remnant of the *Shoah*, in a chapter tellingly named "Growing Pains." Here the author piles shock after shock as the narrator-hero wanders through the landscape of human tragedy. Kruk is startled by the first man he sees—unshaven, bald, lips covered with rusty scales, dry skin, scraping his skin and gripping a bowl of soup. Astonished by the pitiful sight, he confides, "I was terror-stricken at the thought of his coming over to me and ashamed of that terror" (p. 146). Immediately afterward, he spots a woman, whom he describes as ugly with a swollen belly. Constrained by dismay, the young man cannot bear to look at the wretched appearance of the creature and is filled with a disgust that precludes him from approaching her. Later, in another shattering aside, he remarks, "I kept telling myself that these were the people we had spoken of for so many years—but I was so far removed from them that electric wire might have separated us" (p. 148).

In a revelatory moment, we learn that at home Elisha would leave in disgust every time his parents would speak about the family they lost, in effect disallowing any personal connection with the Jews "over there." Now, ashamed for feeling such instincts, he searches for any lost relative, praying that he can remember a single name. Sagaciously, Bartov hatches a subplot to push the matter a step further. Standing in front of the bulletin board listing the names of the communities of those persons in the camps, Elisha labors to dig up the names of the relatives he heard at home. As it happens, the young man meets one of his relatives, a twenty-three-year-old named Krochmal. Undoubtedly, the former Auschwitz inmate is delighted. He links arms with Kruk, who allows him the comfort of family, launching into a surprisingly affirmative declaration, "I felt a wonderful sense of satisfaction at being able to offer protection to this youth who was no longer an anonymous person" (p. 159). Be that as it may, what follows lingers in the mind far longer than the initial enthusiasm Kruk displays. When his relation discloses that he managed to survive by working in the crematorium, Kruk's sickening and vicious response burns a hole in the memory:

> More than anything else I was filled with revulsion at the thought of being connected with him. That feeling was more powerful than the terror and the nausea. If only I could get out of there quickly, not remember that jumpy puppet. Not look into his eyes. Not breathe the air around him. And he even said, "You wouldn't see me here today." Who wants to see you, goddamnit. Not me, that's for sure . . . didn't want to be there at all, not see, not hear, not remember . . . (p. 161).

Like a blast of wind, Elisha has swept into Krochmal's displaced and barren world, holding out hope for a tenuous nexus to a better future. But despite his relative's plea that he take a short letter (quickly written) to give his family or provide him with an address in Palestine so he can write to them directly, Elisha is resolute to snap any binding ties. Employing the excuse that he will miss the pickup and that his friends will not wait for him, Elisha runs away with the canard that he will return the next day. When the pitiful man extracts an assurance that Elisha will not forget him, we read, "It seemed that the shame engulfing me was visible even in the darkness" (p. 162). In doing so, in turning his back on the survivors, Kruk has violated the most fundamental and basic of commandments—that of remembering—hand in hand with abandoning his tenth duty, as sworn to, "Dedication, loyalty and love for the remnants of the sword and the camps" (p. 57).

To his credit, Bartov provides a seriously dark indictment of the Israeli's limitation of not identifying with the survivor in a direct and honest fashion, never letting any predictability seep into the well-observed scene. Altogether, Bartov invests Elisha with a savagely critical attitude toward the survivor that unabashedly illustrates how ill-equipped the outsiders were to absorb and understand such truths. Equally, this remoteness extends to and permeates the collective. Manifestly, this inescapable conclusion is strikingly exposed when the convoy of trucks crosses into Germany. As it passes a concentration camp, the gate is opened and a crowd of freed prisoners streams toward the soldiers, waving their hands, singing, and yelling *Shalom* and *Aretz.* Overwhelmed by the torrents of untamed emotions, the brigade throws candy and cigarette cartons to the mass of people standing by the side of the vehicles. Still, it is a cauterized response. Not once do the soldiers descend to touch or tangibly connect with their admirers, eschewing any act that would suggest that an unbridled, empathic bond has developed. Swiftly, the fleet moves on and the soldiers return to stretching on their gear as though "a sword had severed us from that scene. A strange silence blanketed the truck" (p. 217). Subsequently, Elisha confesses, "I wanted to flee. If I were able . . . I would look into getting my discharge as quickly as possible, do anything to escape that continent where I could not live either with our dead or with their living" (p. 233).

Elisha's maturity and acceptance of Jewish values is crystallized in a defiant act near the book's coda, when he rebuffs his friend Brodsky's cry for vengeance. On a night stop in the field near an Austrian town, the two men seeking a place to rest forcefully invade the home of a German SS officer, consisting only of the wife and daughter, alone after the father escaped. While in their room, Kruk wakes up to the sound of the daughter screaming from the kitchen. The narrator is unsettled by the smile ghosting around Brodsky's lips that reflects his own face. Although Brodsky implores him to go to bed because "They're our boys" (p. 229), Elisha loads his rifle and rushes downstairs to the aid of his prisoners. There he discovers a frightening sight: three soldiers from the Jewish brigade had undressed the daughter and pinned her down, ready to pounce and rape. Unwilling to allow the rape, he shoots towards the ceiling once. Stunned, the three men acquiesce to his demand and clear out. Before leaving, one of the culprits yells at him, "Kruk you're crazy. They're Nazis. The old whore's husband is an SS Man . . . No German ever stood with a rifle to protect a Jewish girl" (pp. 230–231).

Robert Alter persuasively opines that Elisha's high-principled prevention of the crime illustrates that he "has no choice but to go on with his old Jewish self, understanding now its terrible inadequacies, its confusions and cowardice—and, just possibly, its potential for moral sensitivity" (Alter, p. 179). In tandem, one can add that Kruk undergoes a maturing process both morally and politically at the moment he boldly protects the German woman. Having heard the polarized arguments articulated by Giladi and Tamari during the full throttle, bombastic marathon to expose the guilty, the conflicted young man reaches a clear-cut position that distances him from the nihilistic and crude worldview of Giladi and others. On the whole, the reassuring subtext of Kruk's final uplifting act of humanism is that only by exercising restraint in accordance with the discipline of religion can one achieve adulthood and integrity when drawn into an absurd universe such as post-Holocaust Europe. In fact, the novel's last sentence encapsulates this buried message, "And still I whisper over that memory, over that blood: *Thank God I did not destroy myself in Germany, thank God that was beyond me. I am what I am*" (p. 246).

Bibliography

Primary Sources

Ha-Hesbon Ve-Ha-Nefesh (The Reckoning and the Soul). 1953.
Arba Yisraelim Ve-Col America (Four Israelis and All America). 1961.
Lev Hachamim (The Heart of the Wise). 1962.
Pitzei Bagrut (*The Brigade*). 1965.
The Brigade. 1969.
Yisraelim Be-Hatzer Saint James (*Israelis at the Court of St. James*). 1969.
Shel Mi Ata Yeled (*Whose Little Boy Are You?*). 1970.
Ahot Rehoka (A Distant Sister). 1973.
Ha-Shuk Ha-Katan (The Little Market). 1973.
Shesh Knafaim Le-Ehad (*Everyone Had Six Wings*). 1973.
Ha-Badai (The Dissembler). 1975.
Dado 40 Shanim Ve Od 20 Yom (*Dado—48 Years and Another 20 Days*). 1978.
Yehudi Katan (Little Jew). 1981.
Be- emtza Haroman (In the Middle of It All). 1984.
Mazal Ayala (Mazal Ayala). 1988.
Yerid Be-Moskva (A Fair in Moscow). 1988.
Ze Ishel Medaber (This Is Ishel Speaking). 1990.

Mavet Be-Purim (Death on Purim). 1992.
Regel Ahat Ba-hutz (Halfway Out). 1994.
Ani Lo Ha Tzabar Ha-Mitologi (I Am Not the Mythological Sabra). 1995.
Lev Shafuch (*A Heart Poured Out*). 2001.

Secondary Sources

Alter, Robert. *After the Tradition: Essays on Modern Jewish Writing*. New York: Dutton, 1969.

DeKoven Ezrahi, Sidra. *By Words Alone: The Holocaust in Literature*. Chicago: University of Chicago Press, 1980.

"Hanoch Bartov." In *Contemporary Authors Online*. The Gale Group, 22 May 2001.

Mintz, Alan. *Hurban: Responses to Catastrophe in Hebrew Literature*. New York: Columbia University Press, 1984.

Ramras-Rauch, Gila, and Joseph Michman-Melkman, eds. *Facing the Holocaust: Selected Israeli Fiction*. New York: Jewish Publication Society, 1985.

Se Lavan, Yosef. *Hanoch Bartov*. Tel Aviv: Or-Am, 1978.

Giorgio Bassani

(1916–2000)

JUDITH KELLY

Giorgio Bassani was born in Bologna on 4 March 1916, the son of Dora Minerbi and Enrico Bassani. His family moved back to Ferrara—where the family had resided for several generations—during his early childhood. Bassani had two siblings, Paolo and Jenny. His father was a surgeon, as had been his grandfather, and the family was thus considered to be accepted socially within the professional classes of the city. Despite the daily evidence of the stranglehold that Fascism was gaining in Ferrara, as discussed in Paul Corner's *Fascism in Ferrara, 1915–1925* (Oxford University Press, 1975), the family remained apolitical. Consequently the introduction of the Racial Laws in 1938 was a profound shock to Bassani. He was forced to reevaluate the nature of certain friendships, and also to break off his engagement to a Catholic girl. He later married Valeria Sinigallia, a Ferrarese girl from a Jewish family, with whom he had two children.

In the manner of Primo Levi in Turin, Bassani was allowed to complete his studies at the University of Bologna because he had already started them before the ban upon the enrollment of Jewish students. He gained his arts degree in 1939 and became a teacher in a segregated Jewish school in Ferrara, where he went on to take part in the Resistance. Arrested for anti-Fascist activities in May 1943, he was imprisoned until 26 July. The fall of Mussolini's first Fascist government led to the release of political prisoners, but the establishment of Mussolini's second government at Salò, which was, in effect, a puppet regime of the Nazi occupying forces in the north of Italy, meant that Bassani was forced to go into hiding in Florence, where there were other family members including his parents and his sister, Jenny, whose studies had been curtailed following the imposition of the Fascist Racial Laws in 1938. Bassani moved to Rome just before the arrival of the liberating Allied forces. Meanwhile, his brother, Paolo, who had been attending university in Grenoble, and had been expelled from France upon Italy's declaration of war in 1940, had returned to Italy where he also took part in Resistance activities. At the end of the war the Bassani family discovered that relatives who had remained in Ferrara had been deported to Buchenwald in 1943.

Toward the end of his life Bassani suffered from heart problems, to which he succumbed on 13 April 2000. His death gave rise to family controversy about the disposition of the rediscovered private archive of his manuscripts, typescripts, and literary jottings. Bassani's two children, whom the author had nominated as the heirs to his literary memorabilia, are in legal dispute with Bassani's social companion of the final years of his life.

Literary Output

During the later months of World War II, Giorgio Bassani, under the pseudonym Giacomo Marchi, which he adopted to hide his Jewish identity, began writing the stories which were eventually to form part of his Ferrarese cycle. *Dentro le mura* (literally "Within the Walls") is the opening book of six that comprise *Il romanzo di Ferrara* (The Novel of Ferrara). The stories first appeared together in 1956 as *Cinque storie ferraresi* (*Five Stories of Ferrara*). In 1960 Bassani reissued the stories, plus two others and *Gli occhiali d'oro* (*The Gold-Rimmed Spectacles*), under the title *Le storie ferraresi* (Ferrarese Stories). In 1974 Bassani put all of the narrative writings together under the title *Il romanzo di Ferrara* (The Novel of Ferrara), regrouping some short stories with a thematic unity into the collection *Dentro le mura* (*Five Stories of Ferrara*). Two tales that he had included in 1960, "Il muro di cinta" (The Encircling Wall) and "In esilio" (In Exile), were revised and included in *L'odore del fieno* (1972, *The Smell of Hay*). However, between 1974 and 1980

Bassani continued to work on the revision of his published writings, and from 1980 onwards a new version of each of the narrative tales was published. This new version was thematically the same but stylistically enhanced, with changes to syntax, punctuation, and, occasionally, precise detail. Having completed the revision of his narrative writings, Bassani dedicated himself to writing poetry in his later years.

Upon publication, Bassani's writings were fiercely attacked by Italian literary critics who felt that fiction should deal with the political and social injustices of the Fascist period in a direct way, and that novels should explicitly denounce Fascism. However, the Italian reading public was tired of political rhetoric and Bassani's tales of individual humanity were quickly acclaimed.

The story that Bassani recounts in the Ferrarese cycle is that of the alienation and isolation of the Jews of Ferrara during the Fascist period, and their inability to escape the figurative walls of the ghetto behind which they were forced to retreat by the antisemitism of Fascist society. Bassani is not a writer of explicitly Holocaust fiction, nor did he experience Italian internment camps or Nazi concentration camps first-hand. However, the short stories and novels in his Ferrarese cycle were first published in the postwar period, then revised and republished from 1980, so the shadow of the deportations from the Italian Fascist internment camps to the Nazi extermination camps looms over the plot of the tales within the cycle.

Bassani explores human reality with enormous sympathy. Real or semifictionalized geographical locations within Ferrara, including the medieval city walls, create a vivid backdrop, and even imaginary locations come so alive for the reader that tourists arrive each year searching for the Finzi-Contini residence. Bassani's use of historical reality and the lyricism of his narrative style may explain why his tales of individual human plight have so caught the public imagination.

The themes introduced in the short stories that comprise *Dentro le mura* (*Five Stories of Ferrara*) are taken up and developed in subsequent tales in the Ferrarese cycle. The Italian title of the collection (literally "Within the Walls") denotes the encircling city walls that no longer protect those within, as in medieval times, but rather they now serve to isolate. The ghetto walls, which lay within the city walls, no longer exist physically but linger in the collective memory. In the opening story, "Lida Mantovani," a couple come together for a brief affair after which both remain socially excluded, the eponymous heroine because she bears an illegitimate child, and her lover because he is Jewish. The two spheres of incomprehension within which they each exist are echoed in "Una passeggiata prima di cena" (A Stroll Before Supper) in which the marriage of Elia Corcos and Gemma Brondi, a middle-class Jew and a Catholic peasant, respectively, is marked by resentment and distrust. Only the elderly Salomone Corcos can unite the separate cultures, but he is a representative of the golden age of Italian Jewry harking back to the united Italy of Garibaldi. Salomone's time is fading and his son, Elia, will be among those deported to the Nazi camps. The incomprehension that alienates one human being from another is vividly portrayed in "Una lapide in via Mazzini" (A Plaque in Via Mazzini), in which a concentration camp survivor is an uncomfortable reminder to the citizens of Ferrara of their complicity in the deportation of members of the Jewish community. Upon his return from the camps, Geo Josz quietly tries to fit back into society, but in a moment of truth he realizes that postwar Ferrara is simply trying to rebuild a society modeled on the old. There is no awareness of the consequences of past actions. After confronting the former Fascist who may have denounced his family, Josz's silence is broken and he recounts his experiences of Fossoli, deportation, and Mauthausen. He tells of his father's last words, his mother's final gesture, and his younger brother's death, but the citizens of Ferrara are bored by such tales, which they have already heard. Josz eventually disappears from the city after finding that all doors have closed against him. In "Gli ultimi anni di Clelia Trotti" (The Last Years of Clelia Trotti) both the eponymous protagonist and her young protegé, Bruno Lattes, are prisoners in the city. However, the difference between them is that Clelia Trotti has been put under house arrest by the Fascist authorities because of her socialist beliefs, and can therefore look forward to eventual release, whereas Bruno Lattes is a prisoner of the Racial Laws and the figurative walls of the ghetto are once again closing in. Pino Barilari in "Una notte del '43" (A Night in 1943) is a witness to the murder of eleven well-known members of the Ferrarese community by the Fascist militia, but he is unable to accuse anyone of the crime in a postwar court of law because to do so would be to admit his wife's infidelity. His silence is emblematic of the passive acceptance by many people of the imposition of Fascist policies, including the disgraceful Racial Laws.

In three of the novels that form part of the Ferrarese cycle, the story is recounted by a first-person narrator who, in each case, becomes gradually aware of his inner exile from society. In *Gli occhiali d'oro* (*The Gold-Rimmed Spectacles*), for which he was awarded the Strega prize for literature in 1958, the young Jewish student narrator describes the period of intolerance in Fascist Italy during the 1930s, observing the isolation of another social outcast, Dr. Fadigati, a physician whose homosexuality eventually leads to his suicide. However, even the nature of this final tragedy is denied because the Italian press was forbidden to report such incidents in case they reflected badly upon the policies of the Fascist regime. In *Il giardino dei Finzi-Contini* (*The Garden of the Finzi-Continis*) the Jewish narrator recalls, from a distance of several years, the period in which the Fascist Racial Laws placed restrictions upon the daily lives of Italian Jews, against which backdrop his relationship with the beautiful but elusive Micòl Finzi-Contini, the daughter of a wealthy Jewish family, developed unrequitedly. In *Dietro la porta* (*Behind the Door*) an earlier time in the life of the Jewish narrator-protagonist is portrayed: As a sensitive schoolboy he suffers the effects of racial intolerance, although as yet he is not fully conscious of why he is not accepted by his fellow pupils.

To the English-speaking public Bassani is possibly best known as the author of *Il giardino dei Finzi-Contini* (*The Garden of the Finzi-Continis*). The novel was made into a film (by Vittorio De Sica in 1970). Bassani was unhappy with the result because the cinematic version made explicit those aspects of the plot that are dealt with in a more subtle manner by the author. The novel is subdivided into four sections, together with a prologue and an epilogue, but the effect of the Fascist Racial Laws upon the Jewish community of Ferrara begins to become explicit only in the second section. The narrator and his Jewish friends are invited to use the tennis court at the home of the Finzi-Continis family after they are expelled from the local Fascist-run tennis club. The Finzi-Continis are later ordered to cease these tennis parties because they are viewed by the authorities as unacceptable at a time when all sports and leisure facilities were available only to card-carrying members of the Fascist Party. In an attempt to discuss the political situation with his son, the narrator's father enunciates the various restrictions imposed upon the Jewish community as a result of the anti-Jewish legislation of 1938: a ban upon mixed marriages and upon employing "Aryan" domestic help; exclusion from state schools and from the armed services; obituaries could no longer be published in the newspapers and Jewish names were excluded from the telephone directory. Yet despite this Draconian legislation, the narrator's father finds it difficult to believe that the situation has become dangerous. He represents the many Jews in Ferrara, some of whom had been members of the Fascist Party, who continued to cling to the hope that Mussolini would not be as vicious in his treatment of Italian Jews as Hitler had been in Germany. De Sica's film ends with scenes of the round-up of the Jews of Ferrara by the Fascists. In the novel this event, followed by their internment in Fossoli di Carpi and their deportation to Germany, is dealt with in just two sentences by the narrator as he recalls events he knows to have taken place, but to which he was not a witness.

The vivacious Micòl Finzi-Contini can be contrasted to Edgardo Limentani, the protagonist of Bassani's fourth novel, *L'airone* (1968, *The Heron*), which is the fifth volume in the Ferrarese cycle. For this novel Bassani was awarded the Campiello prize for literature in 1969; in the same year he was also awarded the Nelly Sachs prize for literary achievement. The plot concerns the activities and thoughts of Limentani on the final day of his life. He spends the day away from his family, hunting, and is oppressed by a feeling of disgust with all aspects of his life. Limentani, a Jew, has survived Fascist persecution but has been irrevocably damaged by it. Having married his gentile mistress, whom he does not love, in order to put his land in her name so that he could avoid the sequestration that would have taken place under the strictures of the Racial Laws, and having then fled to Switzerland, he has now returned to his family and his property. He judges himself and finds himself wanting; he has escaped death, but he does not feel himself to be alive anymore. During the hunting trip he identifies with the heron he has shot but not killed, and which he is unable to put out of its misery. In one of the most powerful scenes of the novel he sees the birds that fly overhead with a new intensity, noticing the minutiae of their "aliveness"; but by contrast, the heap of dead carcasses in his car trunk disgusts and embarrasses him. The year is 1947 and the imagery reflects the newsreel pictures of the piles of human corpses found in the Nazi concentration camps. Limentani's suicide is not described but is inevitable.

The short stories and novels that form Bassani's Ferrarese cycle do not progress in a chronological narrative order. Rather they move from the pre–World War II to the postwar period and back again. This temporal structure is linked by the theme of the merciless cycle of persecution, a cycle that will continue until citizens are willing to take responsibility for their own actions and to respect their fellow citizens, whatever their sexuality or faith. Bassani revised and re-organized the Ferrarese cycle with the express intention that the tales be read in sequence. *L'odore del fieno* (1972, *The Smell of Hay*), the final volume in the cycle, is a collection of several tales that range chronologically from the time before the deportation of the Jews, to the time the author spent in hiding during the final months of Fascism, to the period following the restoration of democratic government in Italy. It is best viewed as a collection of stories that tie up loose ends left dangling at the end of other tales within the cycle. Apparently autobiographical tales, such as "Ravenna" and "Les neiges d'antan," lend a historical validity to Bassani's writing because they remind the reader that the events described in his novels and short stories may be fictionalized, but they reflect the actual events that happened to real people during those years.

Bibliography

Primary sources

Una città di pianura (pseudonym Giacomo Marchi) (A City of the Plain). 1940.

Storie di poveri amanti e altri versi (Story of Poor Lovers and Other Verses). 1945.

Te lucis ante. 1947.

Cinque storie ferraresi (*Five Stories of Ferrara*). 1956.

Dentro le mura (*Five Stories of Ferrara*). 1956, or 1973.

Gli occhiali d'oro (*The Gold-Rimmed Spectacles*). 1958.

Le storie ferraresi (Ferrarese Stories). 1960.

Il giardino dei Finzi-Contini (*The Garden of the Finzi-Continis*). 1962.

L'alba ai vetri (Dawn on the Windows). 1963.

Dietro la porta (*Behind the Door*). 1964.

Le parole preparate e altri scritti di letteratura (Prepared Words and Other Writings About Literature). 1966.

L'airone (*The Heron*). 1968.

L'odore del fieno (*The Smell of Hay*). 1972.

Il romanzo di Ferrara (The Novel of Ferrara). 1974, 1980.

In gran segreto (In Great Confidence). 1978.

In rima e senza (In Rhyme and Without) (*Rolls Royce and Other Poems*). 1982.

Di là dal cuore (Beyond the Heart). 1984.

Relevant letters and other documents can be found in the Fondo Manoscritti (Manuscript Archive) which is housed at the University of Pavia.

Secondary Sources

Hughes, H. Stuart. *Prisoners of Hope: The Silver Age of the Italian Jews 1924–1974*. Cambridge, Mass., London: Harvard University Press, 1983.

Kelly, Judith. "The Trilogy of the Narrator-Protagonist: Anti-Semitism in the Novels of Bassani." *Tuttitalia*, no. 1 (June 1990): 33–38.

Moloney, Brian. "Tematica e tecnica nei romanzi di Giorgio Bassani." *Convivium*, no. 5 (1966): 484–495.

Oddo De Stefanis, Giusi. *Bassani entro il cercio delle sue mura*. Ravenna: Longo, 1981.

Radcliff-Umstead, Douglas. *The Exile into Eternity: A Study of the Narrative Writings of Giorgio Bassani*. London, Toronto: Associated University Presses, 1987.

Risari, Guia. *The Document Within the Walls: The Romance of Bassani*. Market Harborough, England: Troubador, 1999.

Varanini, Giorgio. *Bassani*. Florence: La Nuova Italia (Il castoro, 46), 1970.

JANINA BAUMAN

(1926–)

MONIKA ADAMCZYK-GARBOWSKA

JANINA BAUMAN WAS born in 1926 as Janina Lewinson in an assimilated Polish Jewish family. Her father and grandfather were doctors. Janina's father was killed as a Polish officer by the Soviets in the Katyn Massacre of 1940, about which the family learned much later (the truth about the massacre was revealed by the Germans in April 1943, but for many years the official version in the Communist bloc was that the Germans were responsible). After spending over two years in the Warsaw Ghetto, she hid on the "Aryan" side with her mother and younger sister, Zofia (Sophie), beginning in 1943. Helped by a Christian friend, they spent that time in a number of shelters, often compelled to bribe informers and policemen, German as well as Polish. After the war she studied political science and philosophy at Warsaw University, where she received her masters in 1959: she also worked for the Polish Film Company. In 1948 she married Zygmunt Bauman, who became a well-known sociologist. Together with their three daughters, the couple left Poland in 1968 due to the antisemitic campaign during which Zygmunt Bauman was accused of "revisionism" by the Communist Party. They spent a few years in Israel, and then settled in Leeds in Great Britain, where Zygmunt Bauman was awarded a university position.

Winter in the Morning

Janina Bauman made her debut with *Winter in the Morning* (1986), written in English but which has since been translated into many languages, adapted for the stage, and has appeared as an audio book. She dedicated the book to "those innumerable people who helped [her], [her] mother and [her] sister to survive the war" (London: Virago, 1986). The book combines three narrative perspectives: the author-narrator looking at the event from the distance of time, the protagonist of the fictionalized autobiographical story created by the author, and the narrator of the diary written by Bauman as a teenage girl during the war. She states that she tried "to be faithful not only to the facts but also to [her] own thoughts and feelings at the time" (p. vii).

Winter in the Morning is divided into two parts: The first covers the period from the establishment of the ghetto in the fall of 1940 until the mass deportations of summer 1942, while the second covers the period until 25 January 1943 when she escaped to the Aryan side. These different perspectives are seen in differing responses: for instance, when her family must leave their comfortable apartment, which is now outside the borders of the ghetto, and move to a place with no bathroom and toilet and with a kerosene lamp instead of central heating and electricity, the child sees their situation as an adventure: "All this was so unusual, so different from all other homes I had ever known that I could only wonder what other surprises life could bring" (p. 38). On the other hand, the adult perspective allows her to paint a detailed picture of the ghetto, focusing on different social groups and depicting both heroic and shameful acts, poverty, and luxury. She is often shocked by the behavior of people she has known in other circumstances; for instance her school friend Daniel whom she remembers as a boy pampered by his parents and "would burst into tears for the slightest reason" (p. 89) who has now become a policeman in the ghetto and deals brutally with the weak and elderly.

In some respects the book resembles a number of other Holocaust memoirs. For example, the author creates a contrast between an idealized childhood (recollections of a happy family life in a comfortable apartment, spending holidays in beautiful places) and what happened later. What distinguishes *Winter* from other similar books is that apart from juxtaposing the perspectives of a child and adult, she also includes fragments of historical or referential sources, such as *The New Encyclopaedia Britannica* or *Encyclopedia Judaica*. These objectifying fragments are merged with excerpts from the diary she kept as a young girl in the ghetto.

Reflecting upon her own book from the perspective of several years, Bauman tries to answer the hypothetical question that many a reader may ask regarding authenticity. In an unpublished manuscript, "Memory and Imagination: Truth in Autobiography," she explains:

> it is a true story of a young girl as she experienced it and as I, the author, remember it. It is not a historical document: it is this young girl's truth. And mine. If another eyewitness of the same events writes quite a different story—it may be true as well: it will be his truth (p. 8).

She further comments on the question of memory by recalling a letter she received from a reader, a survivor of the Warsaw ghetto, in which he listed a number of inaccuracies and omissions she had supposedly committed. It turned out, however, that he was twelve years her senior, which explains why he perceived and interpreted the same world differently.

Dream of Belonging

Her next book was *Dream of Belonging* (1988); the Polish version, published twelve years after the English language edition, bears the title *Nigolzie na ziemi* (*Nowhere on Earth*) and differs in a number of places as it was written with a different reader in mind. In this book Bauman describes her life after the war and sometimes makes references to her Holocaust experience. Her memories from that time become traumatic, especially at the height of the antisemitic campaign when the first secretary of the Communist Party, Władysław Gomulka, in his infamous speech at the Trade Unions Congress called Polish Jews "citizens of two fatherlands" (implying Poland and Israel) and compared them to the Fifth Column, that is, Nazi spies in the prewar Polish Republic. "We felt suddenly unable to breathe freely," she states (*Dream of Belonging*, London: Virago, 1988, p. 189). Later, even seemingly innocent political scenes bring back memories of the war. The scene from her office window on 8 March 1968 of students demonstrating and huge trucks bringing men in civilian clothes, sent by authorities to disperse the students, makes her think of the times when similar trucks, "full of armed Nazis, had rumbled along the streets of Warsaw hunting for victims." She is not alone in this association because the demonstrators also shout "Gestapo!" at the police (p. 170).

Powroty (Returns)

In her only novel so far, *Powroty* (1995, Returns), she describes the vicissitudes of Henryk Berg and his nephew Adam. Henryk lost all his relatives during the war and after the war married a Polish woman who won his heart with her devotion and constant support. They adopted Adam who survived the war protected by his parents' former servant and who turned out to be a difficult child. Through the eyes of Henryk, Bauman describes the postwar Warsaw Jewish quarter. Unlike other parts of the city showing signs of revival, in the Jewish section:

> there weren't half ruined houses, worn paths or other traces of human presence. Before him, all the way to the horizon, spread out a large area covered with a tarred shell of rubble, every now and then with ruts of former streets. . . . Faint hums from wires sticking out of the rubble and stirred by the wind seemed to increase the overwhelming silence. The echo answered with a sob when Henryk, defeated, finally surrendered to despair (*Powroty*, p. 12 [translation mine]).

This is an ominous depiction resembling the stories of Adolf Rudnicki or Czesław Miłosz's "A Poor Christian Looks at the Ghetto"; we know that completely different houses will be built in the place of the old ones and they will become inhabited by different people. The main part of the novel is devoted to the postwar experiences of Henryk and his relationship with Adam, who later leaves Poland in 1968 as a result of the antisemitic campaign, but who cannot find a place for himself anywhere. To some extent Adam seems to constitute Janina Bauman's alter ego as he is split between two countries: Poland and Britain. We learn that he does not want to return to Poland because he would have no place to go if, in the future, he found out that he was unwelcome there again. A similar sentiment was expressed by the writer in a survey on antisemitism conducted by the Cracow Catholic monthly *Znak* in 1996.

Bibliography

Primary Sources

Winter in the Morning: A Young Girl's Life in the Warsaw Ghetto and Beyond 1939–1945. 1986.

A Dream of Belonging. 1988.

"Memory and Imagination: Truth in Autobiography." Unpublished manuscript. 1993.

Nigolzie na ziemi (Nowhere on Earth). 2000.
Powroty (Returns). 1995.

Secondary Sources

Adamczyk-Garbowska, Monika. "Trudne powroty." *Akcent* 1 (1997): 131–133.

Bartoszewski, Władysław. "Review of *Winter in the Morning*." *Polin* 3 (1988): 425–429.

Bauman, Janina. *Znak* 4 (1996): 6–7. Zyć z antysemieyzmen.

Baumgarten, Murray. *Expectations and Endings: Observations on Holocaust Literature*. New York: Yeshiva University, 1989.

Lyons, Philip. "Teaching Children about the Holocaust through Literature." *The Use of English* 1 (1992): 39–47.

Zeidler-Janiszewska, Anna. "Adaptacja i dystans: O strategiach autobiograficznych Janiny Bauman." *Akcent* 1 (1995): 86–89.

Jurek Becker

(1937–1997)

ROBERT C. HOLUB

JUREK BECKER WAS THE foremost Jewish novelist and screenwriter in the German Democratic Republic (GDR). Although he did not identify himself with the Jewish community while he was living in East Germany, in many of his works he employed themes connected with the Holocaust and its survivors.

Biography

Owing to circumstances surrounding the Holocaust, Becker was unsure of the exact date of his birth, but after the war he adopted 30 September 1937 as his birthday. He was born into a large Jewish family in the Polish city of Łodz, which at the time was the second most populous city in the country; almost a third of its inhabitants were Jews. When Poland fell to National Socialist Germany in September of 1939, Łodz was renamed Litzmannstadt and became the site of the largest and longest enduring ghetto. Becker's family was forced to vacate their home and move with thousands of families into a ghetto surrounded by sixteen kilometers of barbed wire and reserved for the Jews of the city and the region. He escaped initial deportation when his father falsely identified his age as two years older than he really was and therefore qualified for labor. However, from 1939 until 1945, Becker was imprisoned either in the Łodz ghetto or in the concentration camps of Ravensbrück or Sachsenhausen. From his family, only Becker, his father, and a distant aunt, who escaped to America immediately after the German invasion, survived the Holocaust.

After the war Becker was reunited with his father, who decided to settle in East Berlin rather than in Poland because he reasoned that it was the German, not the Polish, antisemites who had lost the war. Becker was compelled to learn a new language, and most of his childhood memories faded along with his mother tongue. He was soon integrated into his new German and socialist surroundings. He became a member of the communist youth organization and in 1957 joined the Socialist Unity Party. In the same year, he began studying philosophy at Humboldt University but was expelled after three years because of political differences with the Party. In the early 1960s, Becker embarked on a career as a freelance writer, producing numerous scripts for the East German film industry.

First Novel

In 1967, Becker wrote *Jakob der Lügner* (*Jakob the Liar*) as a film script, but it was turned down because it did not conform to what the state deemed apposite with regard to the Holocaust. Becker recast the story as a novel, and upon its publication in 1969 it achieved enormous popularity in both Germanies. It was eventually filmed in 1974. After this literary breakthrough, Becker became one of the most celebrated novelists in Germany, noted in particular for his storytelling. Several of his works dealt with the Holocaust or its aftermath for survivors, but he also wrote novels, stories, and scripts in which the *Shoah* (Nazi genocide of the Jews) plays no role whatsoever. Because of his unusual background Becker remained an outsider: he did not identify with Judaism but did not regard himself as Polish or German either. And although he professed allegiances to East Germany and socialism, he became disillusioned with the GDR and lived in West Germany and traveled through Western Europe from 1979 until his death in 1997.

At the time of its publication, *Jakob der Lügner* represented a significant departure from the usual treatment of the Holocaust in the GDR. Narrated by a survivor, it relates the tale of Jakob Heym, who lives with his fellow Jews in a crowded Polish ghetto. Commanded to enter a guard-house, Jakob overhears a radio report concerning the advancing Soviet army. Miraculously he is allowed to leave unharmed. The next day, he attempts to save from certain death his friend Mischa, who is determined to steal potatoes, by telling him what he overheard, but Mischa believes him only when Jakob claims that he heard the news on his hidden radio. Thereafter, Jakob unwillingly and rapidly becomes the source of hope for the entire ghetto, and he is forced to fabricate daily reports about the military situation. There is black humor in the episodically related events, and, indeed, the entire structure of the novel, which plays off the stereotype of the Jew as a liar, is built on an unmistakable irony. The comic elements are further heightened by Becker's narrative technique, which relates even horrific occurrences, such as murder and deportation to death camps, in a straightforward fashion without pathos and contrived melodrama. Becker supplies two endings: in the first, Jakob dies trying to escape from the ghetto, and the Soviet army avenges his death, rescuing the remaining inhabitants. But the narrator states that this is not the actual ending, since in reality the ghetto was liquidated and everyone, including the hero, perished.

Becker's novel marks a turning point in the portrayal of the Holocaust in postwar German literature, in particular in the GDR. In the years immediately after the war, East Germany and West Germany had taken a similarly contrite stance toward the crimes of the National Socialist regime. But with the advent of the cold war, the physical and ideological separation of the two Germanies became firmly established. Since the GDR proclaimed itself anti-fascist because communists and socialists were the Nazis' first victims, it felt no compulsion to deal with vestiges of nazism. Under the anti-fascist mantra, the Jewish question was virtually nonexistent, and the Holocaust was neglected in most literary works for the first three decades of the GDR's existence. Inmates of concentration camps, such as in Bruno Apitz's novel *Nakt unter Wölfen* (*Naked among Wolves*), published in 1958, were heroes of resistance, but they were exclusively political prisoners or Eastern Europeans. Becker's novel goes against the grain of GDR injunctions for writers not only because it focuses on the Jewish Holocaust but more importantly because it refuses to indulge the reader in the clichéd poignancy of heroic struggle against National Socialism. Jakob and his fellow Jews perform small deeds of resistance, but the characters are not role models for class conflict and socialism. They are portrayed for the most part as ordinary, vulnerable people thrust into a horrible situation to which they are forced to accommodate. They are victims, but their plight is not romanticized, and they themselves are not particularly admirable. Jakob spreads hope throughout the ghetto with his lies, but this hope is ultimately dashed by the reality of deportations and death.

Subsequent Works

Becker's other writings on the Holocaust are marked with a similar ambivalence. In *Der Boxer* (The Boxer) Becker deals with the trauma of surviving the Holocaust. Aron Blank, who lost his wife and two children in the *Shoah*, attempts in the postwar years to establish a normal existence in East Berlin. On his identification papers, Aron changes his name to the more German Arno and dates his birthday six years earlier than it actually was in order to recover the six years lost in concentration camps. He finds a young boy who could be his remaining son Mark, and he adopts him and the nurse to whom Mark had become attached; the three then live together as an odd sort of family. Survivors Aron knows are unable to cope with life in postwar Germany, and as Mark grows older, the fragile existence Aron had built falls apart as well. Mark leaves for Israel, and his monthly letters cease at the beginning of the 1967 Arab–Israeli war.

Bronsteins Kinder (*Bronstein's Children*), Becker's final novel treating a Holocaust-related topic, explores the gulf between the survivor generation and their children. The narrator and main character, Hans Bronstein, born after the war to a survivor, prevents his father from implementing vigilante justice on a former concentration camp guard; as a postwar German, Hans does not feel bound up with the Holocaust and its aftermath. But the unfolding of events demonstrates that he cannot extricate himself from the legacy of German-Jewish history so easily. Ultimately Hans loses some of his certainty, admitting that he too may also be a victim of past German crimes against the Jews.

Summary

Becker's fictional works dealing with the Holocaust are in some sense part of his search for a Jewish identity. Having lived through the *Shoah* as a young child, he grew up in the society, and used the language, of the perpetrators. Trained during his formative years to downplay the Holocaust, he resembles Hans Bronstein, who only gradually and reluctantly acquires an understanding of his Jewish heritage. While Becker's novels may have helped him work through his own identity crisis, they remain crucial documents for a different and differentiated view of the Holocaust. Often praised for their originality, their humor, and their storytelling, they have also been accused of minimizing Jewish suffering. Jakob Heym of Becker's first novel, *Jakob der Lügner*, was based on a real figure whose story was related to Becker by his father. The unorthodox, humorous manner in which Becker fictionalizes this potentially heroic and tragic tale is apt to rankle those who believe that representations of the Holocaust must stick to the facts and avoid amusement at all costs. Becker's implicit challenge to the literature of the Holocaust is whether it can admit humor and still do justice to its topic.

Bibliography

Primary Sources

Jakob der Lügner (*Jacob the Liar*). 1969.
Irreführung der Behörden (Misleading the Authorities). 1973.
Der Boxer (The Boxer). 1976.
Schlaflose Tage (*Sleepless Days*). 1978.
Nach der ersten Zukunft (After the Initial Future). 1980.
Aller Welt Freund (A Friend to All the World). 1982.
Bronsteins Kinder (*Bronstein's Children*). 1986.
Erzählungen (Stories). 1986.
Warnung vor dem Schriftsteller. Drei Vorlesungen in Frankfurt (Warning against the Writer. Three Lectures in Frankfurt). 1990.
Die beliebteste Familiengeschichte und andere Erzählungen (My Favorite Family Story and Other Tales). 1992.
Amanda herzlos (Heartless Amanda). 1992.
Wir sind auch nur ein Volk 1–9 (We Are After All Just One People 1–9). 1994–1995.
Ende des Größenwahns (End of Megalomania). 1996.
Liebling Kreuzberg. Lieblings neues Glück (Darling Kreuzberg. Darling's New Happiness). 1997.
Liebling Kreuzberg. Der Verbieter (Darling Kreuzberg. The Prohibiter). 1997.

Secondary Sources

Arnold, Heinz Ludwig, ed. *Jurek Becker, edition text + kritik* 116 (1992).
Gilman, Sander. *How I Became a German: Jurek Becker's Life in Five Words.* Washington, D.C.: German Historical Institute, 1999.
Graf, Karin, and Ulrich Konietzny, eds. *Jurek Becker.* Munich: Judicium, 1991.
Heidelberger-Leonard, Irene, ed. *Jurek Becker.* Frankfurt: Suhrkamp, 1992.
Johnson, Susan M. *The Works of Jurek Becker: A Thematic Analysis.* New York: Peter Lang, 1988.
Jung, Thomas. *"Widerstandskämpfer oder Schriftsteller sein . . ." Jurek Becker—Schreiben zwischen Sozialismus und Judentum.* Frankfurt: Lang, 1998.
Riordan, Colin, ed. *Jurek Becker.* Cardiff: University of Wales Press, 1998.
Rock, David. *Jurek Becker: A Jew Who Became a German?* Oxford: Berg, 2000.
Wiese, Lothar. *Jurek Becker, Jakob der Lügner: Interpretation.* Munich: Oldenbourg Verlag, 1998.
Zimmermann, Werner. *Jurek Becker. Jakob der Lügner.* Munich: Mentor, 1995.

Interviews

"Answering Questions about *Jakob der Lügner.*" *Seminar* 19 (1983): 288–292.
Becker, Jurek. " 'Die wahre Aufregung . . .': Ein Gespräche mit Jurek Becker." *Dimension* 17 (1988): 8–29.
"Interview with Jurek Becker (Oberlin, May 1978)." *Dimension* 11 (1978): 407–416.
Schwarz, Wilhelm. "Jurek Becker (Interview 17.8.1977)." In *Protokolle: Gespräche mit Schriftstellern.* Frankfurt: Lang, 1990, pp. 113–130.
Volker Hage, ed. "Hinter dem Rücken des Vaters." In *Deutsche Literature 1986, Jahresüberblick.* Stuttgart: Reclam, 1987, pp. 331–342.

Louis Begley

(1933–)

SARA R. HOROWITZ

DESCRIBING THE RELATIONSHIP between the plot of his first novel, *Wartime Lies* (1991), and the details of his own early childhood, Louis Begley once explained, "To separate what is true from what is not would be like trying to unscramble an omelet" (quoted in Fein, p. C10). Indeed, the close resemblance of the circumstances of Begley's young life—living out the war as a Jewish boy posing as an Aryan child in Nazi-occupied Poland—to that of his similarly situated protagonist gives rise to readings of the novel as straightforward memory, and to frequent requests that he sort out wartime truth from wartime (or artistic) lies and separate memory from invention. Begley's ovular parry regarding the autobiographic boundaries of his work leaves unspoken—and thus, private—the coincidence and departures between fact and imagination. In addition, the author's comment suggests something about the complicated workings of autobiographical memory and narrative, particularly in relation to the shaping of identity—issues that all of Begley's novels grapple with.

Life

Born Ludwik Begleite in 1933, in the city of Stryj, Poland (now part of Ukraine), Begley was raised in a household of educated, affluent Polish Jews. His father, David, a physician, served in the Polish army, and was pressed into service in the Red Army and sent east in 1941. When the Germans occupied Poland, Begley's mother, Franciszka, sent her parents into hiding and concealed her own and her son's identities, surviving the Nazi genocide by pretending to be a Catholic mother and son. In September 1941, Germans and Ukrainian collaborators massacred one thousand Jews in Stryj, among them Begley's paternal grandparents. Begley and his mother traveled to Lvov, and then to Warsaw, where Franciszka kept the pair alive through daring and ingenuity. They changed identities several times, always retaining their own first names but altering their surname. After the war, the family was reunited. No physical remnants exist of their life prior to the war, except for a few family photographs belonging to an aunt who had come to the United States before the war.

Begley's family left Poland in 1946 and arrived in New York City in 1947 by way of Paris, where Begley and his father studied English briefly at a Berlitz language school. The family settled in Brooklyn, where Begley adapted to the life of an American boy, distancing himself from his European past. His father continued to practice medicine, specializing in cardiology, and his mother worked as his nurse. Begley graduated from Erasmus Hall, at the time a prestigious and selective public high school, earning a scholarship to attend Harvard University. As a student, he wrote several short stories, some of which were published in the *Harvard Advocate* and are regarded as preludes to the novel he would eventually compose many years later. By his third year at university he appears to have given up fiction writing. Begley was naturalized in 1953, a year before graduating from Harvard with a degree in English literature and high honors, alongside the writer John Updike. After serving in the United States Army, Begley married, and entered Harvard Law School. He obtained his law degree with honors in 1959, joining a prestigious New York law firm, Debevoise & Plimpton, immediately after graduation, where at the beginning of the twenty-first century he was a senior partner and headed its international practice group.

In the mid-1960s, Begley went to Paris for his law firm and began to establish a circle of European friends. In 1970, his first marriage ended in divorce; the couple had three children. In 1974, he married the French author Anka Muhlstein, whom he had met through her brother-in-law, the novelist François

Nourrissier. The couple settled in New York, where Muhlstein began a successful career in French letters, writing biographies and other historical books. Her works have earned her the History Prize of the French Academy, as well as the prestigious Prix Goncourt. A descendant, on her mother's side, of the financier Baron James de Rothschild, the founder of the French banking branch of the noted family, and the daughter of a Polish diplomat stationed in Paris, Muhlstein, like Begley, looked back on a European childhood marked by upheaval. Born in Paris in 1935, Muhlstein fled with her family to New York to escape the Nazi genocide, returning after the war. Like her husband, Muhlstein had children from a previous marriage; the couple raised five children.

In 1989, at the age of fifty-five, Begley requested a four-month sabbatical from his law firm, having worked there steadily since graduation from law school. While on leave in Europe, in three months' time, he completed the manuscript for his first novel, *Wartime Lies*. Published in 1991, the novel met with critical acclaim and garnered several important awards, including the PEN Hemingway Award, the Irish Times–Aer Lingus International Fiction Prize, and the Prix Médicis Etranger, as well as the American Academy of Letters prize for literature. *Wartime Lies* was followed by *The Man Who Was Late* (1993), *As Max Saw It* (1994), *About Schmidt* (1996), *Mistler's Exit* (1998), and *Schmidt Delivered* (2000). In 2000, Begley was awarded the medal of chevalier in the French Order of Arts and Letters.

Wartime Lies

Like all of Begley's fiction, *Wartime Lies* deals with secrets, lies, shame, and trauma, as well as the struggle to narrate a cohesive life story. In this first novel, the issues emerge through the story of Maciek, a fair-haired Jewish boy surviving the Nazi genocide with his beautiful and gutsy Aunt Tania under a series of aliases. Set in wartime Warsaw during the Nazi occupation of Poland, *Wartime Lies* portrays the war through a child's perspective. Framed by the reflections of an erudite middle-aged man who may be the adult Maciek, the novel follows Maciek's shifting identities. The implied relationship of the boy to this unnamed adult man who intermittently intrudes upon the child's wartime reflections points to the fragmented nature of identity and the complicated role of narrative in shaping the idea of self.

The title itself suggests some of the complexities of the issues that the author explores. On one level, "wartime lies" refer to the invented names and biographies necessary for the boy's and the aunt's survival. They also refer to the unmaking and remaking of the self—the internalization of the lies, the repeated erasure of life narratives and the assumption of new ones. While Tania and Maciek both conceal and masquerade their selves, Tania does so as an adult, while Maciek does so as a young child, one who has just begun the process of differentiating himself from his family, of carving out a sense of self. Before the Nazi invasion disrupts family life, Maciek recollects staging "tests of will" regarding food, bedtime, toilet habits, and other household events. Maciek describes this behavior as that of a "difficult, troubling child" (*Wartime Lies*, New York: Ballentine Books, 1992, p. 9), but it more aptly captures a phase in the normal developmental process. However, once thrust into a hostile world, Maciek finds himself utterly dependent upon Tania for concealment and survival. To keep their Jewish identity secret, Tania instructs him on how to speak, look, move, even which emotions to display and which sins to confess before taking Holy Communion. She drills him in German and rehearses him in a sequence of fabricated life histories. In the series of boarding-houses, cellars, and farms they inhabit, "One had to talk, one could not always talk about books, one had to be ready to talk about oneself. Which self? The issue was the limit of one's inventiveness and memory, because the lies had to be consistent—more consistent, according to Tania, than the truth" (p. 95). Young as he is, the boy understands the need to suppress the small and natural acts of boundary testing so vital to the construction of a sense of self. Thus, while Tania suffers from the lies and humiliations she must endure to survive, she knows who she is. In contrast, Maciek constructs a succession of false selves before attaining a coherent and independent sense of himself. In other words, the wartime lies take shape around an inner void.

Complicating this process further, Maciek also understands that however he may perceive himself, the society in which he exists—were his true identity known—would regard him in a singular, unidimensional way—as a Jew and thus, as prey. This flat definition of who he is emerges not from his will or his psyche or any act of self-assertion. Rather, it reflects an accident of birth, marked in his flesh as the sign of the circumcision. The need to conceal his true identity is concretized for Maciek in the need to conceal his body. While the boy internalizes some of the antisemitic values of the culture that has hunted him, his body remains marked as Jewish. Moreover, throughout the novel, Maciek experiences a profound sense of shame. The boy understands that both he and Tania must dedicate every act toward winning favor with the local population, who essentially hold life and death power over the pair. "Tania's speech and gestures . . . were never without purpose. That purpose was to conceal and please, to concentrate attention on what might gratify the listener and deflect it from us. I played the supporting role" (p. 154). Thus, Maciek and Tania do not merely tell wartime lies; they surrender the agency of voice in order to become, for others, desired objects. Maciek's performance, less polished than that of his aunt, frequently earns him the scorn of his interlocutors. They criticize what they see as his "weak character . . . my habit of insinuating flattery . . . always to be trying to make oneself liked" (p. 96); his "habit of smiling when there was nothing to smile about . . . because I was a little hypocrite" (p. 100). In addition, as a child, he feels shame at being Jewish, shame at partaking illicitly in church sacraments, shame at what the author has elsewhere referred to as "a talent for deception and for the quick lie" ("Who the Novelist Really Is," *New York Times Book Review*, 16 August 1993, p. 22), shame at his Jewish genitalia. The adult whose narrative opens the novel feels shame for the relatively easy circumstances of his survival—spared the ghetto, the camps, the aloneness that other victims of Nazi atrocity experience. If the child is the father of the man, this complicated feeling of shame, ambivalence, and emptiness takes shape around his developing sense of himself as a person.

The portrayal of Tania in the novel reverses the conventional image of women in war narratives, which depict heroic men rescuing passive women in distress. Tania uses her considerable skills—sharp powers of observation, a keen intelligence, wiliness, and courage—to keep the pair alive. Exhibiting a chameleon-like adaptability to play whatever role is necessary to deflect danger, Tania brings Maciek under the protectorship of her German lover, instructing the boy to show the man affection. She next poses as a widowed mother and child in a series of boardinghouses. Throughout the novel, she navigates a sequence of perilous situations that leave little time for reflection and deliberation but call for immediate action. For example, within the space of days, she reinvents herself several times to elude the genocidal net closing in on them. Herded into a massive group of Jews driven toward the railway station, she deliberately deflects attention from herself by edging into the center of the crowd, dirtying her face, and stooping over like an old woman as she walks. At night, when roving Germans and Ukrainians walk among the crowd raping and killing women, she orders Maciek to cover her up with a blanket and then lie atop her, as though on a bundle. The next day, at the railway station, she uses her precious supply of water to wash her face, applying some lipstick she acquires by bartering food. Assuming the posture and mannerisms of a German matron, she separates herself from the masses of Jews herded together and indignantly demands of a *Wehrmacht* captain that he place her in a proper compartment on the correct train.

Tania's masterly operation is not without an edge, however. In Maciek's eyes she assumes colossal proportions—a great protectress but also oppressive in the utter control she exerts over the boy. She scrutinizes his every word and gesture for telltale signs that would give away their Jewishness, and she pointedly corrects what she finds wanting. Maciek, in his total dependence on his aunt for survival, is not free to criticize her behavior, even to himself. As the narrative progresses, Maciek feels fathomless gratitude as well as increasing resentment toward his savior, a resentment that finds its way into small, sly rebellions against her regimen. His ambivalence toward his aunt is one illustration of the way in which Nazi atrocity intrudes even into one's intimate relationships, pulling them out of shape and recasting their tenor.

Tania's crucial role in Maciek's survival, and the psychological difficulties that her tight control and overweening closeness present to the boy, provide an opening on Maciek's inner struggle to make moral sense of a world that has lost its moral compass. The boy's moral confusion is evidenced in other ways, as well. He witnesses countless scenes of violent cruelty and indifference to human suffering. Over time, he begins to identify with the aggressor, awed by the life-and-death power of the Nazis and their collaborators. For example, when playing with his toy soldiers, Maciek designates one side—the victors in his games—as Germans. During the perpetual battle against bedbugs, the boy imagines himself a Nazi, rousting Jews from hiding and murdering them efficiently and en masse: "in this limited sphere, I could be a hunter and an aggressor, like SS units destroying partisans in the forest, or, very soon, rebellious Jews in the ghetto of Warsaw" (p. 84). Under religious instruction at the church, he learns that it is a sin to lie. Yet his presence at the church is in and of itself a lie that, were it to be unraveled, would reveal truth as a death sentence.

Begley's novel also points to an impoverishment of Jewishness and a diminished sense of the idea of a Jewish God in the wake of the Holocaust. As Tania drills into Maciek the Catholic rituals necessary to their masquerade, she has him hang on to one linguistic shard of Jewishness. She instructs him in "what every Jew must do when his death is near: cover his head, with only his hands if necessary, and say in a loud voice, *Shema Yisrael, Adonai elocheinu, Adonai echad*. Hear, O Israel, the Lord thy God, the Lord is one. That was a way for a Jew not to die alone, to join his death to all those that had come before and were still to come" (p. 71). Tania's rendition of the prayer, as recollected by the narrator, contains errors of transliteration and translation of this liturgical use of a biblical verse. The Hebrew word *eloheinu*, or "our God," has been mistransliterated, and also mistranslated as "thy God." This linguistic externalization—"our God" to "thy God"—underscores Maciek's separation and increasing alienation from Jews, from Judaism, from his Jewish self, and from the Jewish God. Only as a non-Jew may the boy live; he can only die into Jewishness. And, indeed, continued antisemitic violence after the war in Poland persuades Maciek's family not to reclaim their Jewish family name, and Maciek continues to participate in Catholic Church rituals.

The impossibility, for Maciek, of owning his own identity points to both the source of the boy's wartime trauma and its lasting effect, well into adulthood. Seemingly narrated in the first person by the child himself as events unfold, the narrative turns out to be only the most recent in an ongoing sequence of invented lives, this time by the adult who was once the child Maciek (but no longer goes by that name). This adult survivor displaces onto the figure of Maciek a reconstructed childhood, one he feels safe in narrating: "our man has no childhood that he can bear to remember; he has had to invent one" (p. 181). Like the child, the adult is a witness to wartime atrocity—and, similarly, only in the limited sense that he sees, he has seen, and he understands. But the man does not bear witness, does not speak what he knows. His profession is indeterminately described as one who teaches "how to compare one literature with another" or "a literary agent with a flair for dissident writing," the man "reads" or enables others to read "texts bearing witness against oppression and inhumanity" (p. 1). Yet, while retaining "the power to grasp meaning and to remember," he does not himself bring testimony, does not speak out of his own experience. Even the child's autobiographical narrative—seemingly that missing, belated personal testimony—turns out to be yet another kind of wartime "lie," attesting to the impossibility of narrative, a kind of silence that itself constitutes a kind of testimony.

The multiplying layers of fictionality indicate something of the complexities of Holocaust narrative. The disquieting play of Maciek's "real" story against the multiple invented lives he puts forth, and the adult narrator's admission that he has invented even this "real" story, makes it impossible to locate precisely within *Wartime Lies* an "actual" story against which to measure the myriad fabrications. This suggests that something of the actual experience of survival remains always outside narration, accessible only in the interplay between the unstated and the various versions of survival.

In addition to the events narrated, what contributes to the power of Begley's writing and moves it from the realm of historical documentation (albeit fictionalized) to art is the eloquence of language, the careful structuring of the book, and the dispassionate tone of the boy's narrative. It is both credibly childlike and incredibly chilling that Maciek witnesses events of increasing violence and cruelty and describes them with flat emotions. This understated tone sets the horror in full relief for the reader.

Beyond the specifics of a Jewish boy's experiences in eastern Europe during the Nazi genocide, *Wartime Lies* grapples with broad themes—history and memory; identity, trauma, and narrative; violence, shame, and anomie. In an essay on Franz Kafka, Begley locates the writer's uncanny sense of foresight in the coincidence of Kafka's personal wounds with "the wounds of the twentieth-century Western man and of twentieth-century Western society" ("Kafka," *Proceedings of the American Philosophical Society* 141[3] September 1997, p. 256). The same might be said of Begley's own writing. The issues introduced in *Wartime Lies* and explored further in Begley's later novels are not his concerns alone; they comprise the legacy of Western civilization after the Holocaust, after the shattering of faith in human goodness, cultural progress, divine benevolence, and other centers of human meaning. Begley's characterization of Kafka's master narrative could aptly describe the plot of *Wartime Lies*: "the insertion of man into a claustrophobic and totally cruel world, in which indifference and duplicity are the rule, and brutish sexual attraction and the equally brutish sexual act replace tenderness and love as the principal connection between man and woman" (p. 256). In Begley's analysis, Kafka's sensibilities gave him a prescient sense of the crisis that had yet to occur in Western culture, "a vision that turned out to match a reality he did not live long enough to experience" (p. 257), but one that Begley himself lived out. In the wake of that crisis, Begley's writing conveys a profound sense of loss, resonant with what the author discerns in Kafka's works: "loss of decent communication with one's fellow man, loss of the sense of one's own worth, loss of confidence in the proper functioning of institutions and in the rightness of laws, loss of contact with God. The result is the dehumanization of man" (p. 256). A sobering confrontation with the void marks all of Begley's works.

The Man Who Was Late and Subsequent Novels

Begley's second novel, *The Man Who Was Late*, is his only other volume connected with the Holocaust, although only at a distance and by omission. Its protagonist, Ben, survived the Nazi genocide as a Jewish child in Central Europe. One could see him as the adult that a child such as Maciek might become, brought by his parents to the United States shortly after World War II. Like the unnamed adult commentator in *Wartime Lies*, who "has no childhood he can bear to remember" (pp. 180–181) and "avoids dinner conversation about Poland in the Second World War even if his neighbor is beautiful, her eyes promise consolation" (p. 2), Ben never speaks of his childhood. Like that adult, Ben's surname is never revealed. A high-powered, self-made man, he distances himself from his parents, his past, his Jewishness.

By the book's beginning, Ben has committed suicide. His close friend Jack, who is also the executor of his estate, narrates Ben's life retrospectively. Jack goes through his friend's personal effects—letters, calendars, notes—and reflects upon recollected conversations, attempting to piece together a sense of who Ben was. In contrast to Ben, Jack is a WASP whose roots in the United States go back generations. The narrative—which traces Ben's unsatisfying sexual relations, his ongoing unhappiness, his interactions with a Nazi dentist and pimp in Rio—represents Jack's best attempt to understand his friend's traumatized existence. It may also reflect Jack's construction of a narrative that he can bear to contemplate.

Because Ben does not reflect upon his past or tell stories about his childhood, little can be gleaned of his childhood experience in Europe—and, indeed, that is not the focus of the novel. One can see in that omission a mark of the power of the past on Ben, even as he goes on to wild success as a corporate lawyer in New York. For this reason, Allan Hepburn has called *The Man Who Was Late* a "post-Holocaust novel that defies being one," noting that "silence about historical catastrophe . . . is a symptom of trauma" (p. 382). As Hepburn astutely notes in his analysis of the novel, belated witnessing is a central aspect of traumatic stress. "Lateness, as a symptom of neurosis, afflicts those who have shed their identities under the pressure of traumatic history and have invented alternative identities that have no reference to the past" (p. 380).

Although Begley's subsequent novels are not connected thematically with the Holocaust, they, too, treat issues such as traumatic memory, the construction of a self, and the place of narrative in shaping a life story, whether one's own or another's. The proximity of death—again, whether one's own or another's—heightens the sense of human mortality, focusing the narrative on questions of self-deception and lucidity, and the loss of and yearning for human values and human meaning. Often an outsider is juxtaposed with a successful American WASP who, through the encounter, comes to acknowledge something about the other's experience. In *As Max Saw It*, Max Hafter Strong, a professor of law at Harvard, observes over time the relationship between Charlie Swan and his gay lover, Toby. Toby is dying from an unspecified terminal illness, understood to be AIDS. The protagonist of *Mistler's Exit*, a successful head of an advertising agency with inherited wealth, learns he has terminal cancer. In retrospect, Thomas Mistler's life—characterized by greed, dishonesty, and lack of intimacy—feels hollow. Begley leaves open the possibility that Mistler's contemplation of that past may be just another of a series of self-deceiving lies. Two novels that share the same protagonist—*About Schmidt* and *Schmidt Delivered*—explore the world of the fabulously wealthy through the unfolding story of the recently widowed Alfred Schmidt, Esq. A retired New York lawyer with strong opinions (largely negative) about Jews, homosexuals, people of color, and other groups, Schmidt's prejudices are challenged by his daughter's choice of a Jewish husband and his own turning to a young Puerto Rican lover.

Critical Assessment

Begley's emergence as a mature writer, coupled with the power of his subject, immediately impressed reviewers, who responded to *Wartime Lies* both as a novel and as a key to the life of its author. Hal Espen termed the novel "one of the most dramatic self-excavations in contemporary literature" (p. 39). In her review of the novel, Janet Malcolm, a longtime friend of the author who knew nothing of his war experiences, reflects that after reading *Wartime Lies* she began "to know what he must have experienced, since a book like this could not have been written except out of first-hand knowledge of the history it chronicles" (p. 17).

Many interviews focused on discerning the autobiographical weave from the warp of invention—an effort Begley repeatedly resists satisfying. "Without exception," the author recollects,

> journalists who have interviewed me about *Wartime Lies* have assumed that it is autobiographical and have been particularly curious about what might have been added

> that is not true in the story of what they take to be my life. . . . My usual reply to questions about what is truth and what is invention has been that I am unwilling to separate incidents in my book that may be said to have happened to me or that I have witnessed from those I have imagined, because to do so would be like turning on the lights while a film is being shown [thereby spoiling the effect] ("Who the Novelist Really Is," p. 22).

The author also points to the unreliability of autobiographical memory, noting the differences between his own and his mother's recollection of shared wartime experiences. In addition, Begley wishes to preserve the prerogative of invention, the "magic force that operates when one writes" fiction, a genre different from documentation ("Who the Novelist Really Is," p. 22). One might also presume that Begley does not wish to get caught in the trap that Jerzy Kosinski, author of *The Painted Bird*, set for himself in claiming literal truth for what Begley, writing about that author, affirms as an "artistic truth" ("True Lies," review of *Jerzy Kosinski: A Biography* by James Park Sloane, *New York Times*, 21 April 1996).

While most critics and reviewers of the novel focus on the terrors that Maciek witnesses or endures, several focus on the complexities of the relationship between the boy and his aunt, and its pernicious effect on him. Malcolm sees in the utter control that Tania exerts over her young charge a microcosmic representation of the force and effect of fascism, "a kind of distorting mirror image of the Jew and the Nazi." By examining the dimensions of this relationship, the novel offers "a meditation on authoritarianism of great subtlety and originality" (p. 17). For Judith Grossman, the boy's ambivalent feelings toward his aunt reflect his inner conflict about the art of dissimulation in which she trained him. She observes, "The curse on Maciek's life is this essential bond of apprenticeship to a mistress he must love, admire and terribly resent; to save his own soul he must not succeed at the craft of lying—yet he cannot afford to fail, for that would mean death."

The effect of presenting the wartime reflections through the perspective of a child, and the interplay between child and adult, has also caught the attention of readers. Naomi Sokoloff analyzes the struggle for the emergence of an authentic child's voice, compromised both by Tania's tight control over what Maciek may say and the implied presence of the adult through whose memory Maciek is mediated. Sara R. Horowitz explores the suppression of Maciek's voice as both the source and the emblem of his traumatic experience, and she notes the continuity of a form of that muteness in the adult who has a special feel for "texts bearing witness against oppression and inhumanity" (*Wartime Lies*, p. 1) but does not speak of his own experiences. For Grossman, "the singular resonance of Maciek's story comes from its framing within the perspective of the man he later becomes, who after years of disclaiming his early history now confronts the inner wounds that have never healed."

The unnarrated years that intervene between the boy's and the man's narratives communicate the belatedness of traumatic memory, a theme that Hepburn locates at the heart of Begley's second novel. The presence of a second consciousness who reconstructs the life story of another—as Jack does for Ben in *The Man Who Was Late*, is another mark of trauma, which "requires a witness who can validate the story of violent occurrence by listening" (p. 381). Hepburn sees that novel as "inflected by the Holocaust" (p. 385) without actually taking the historical events as its subject matter. Like many other readers, Hepburn carries this sense of the trauma of the first two novels into his reading of subsequent ones, pointing to delay and belatedness as a component of all of Begley's fiction. Espen astutely notes that all of Begley's novels feature a somewhat "detached narrator to observe painful events from a certain remove" (p. 46), and explore questions of identity and survival. In a review of *Mistler's Exit*, Jack Miles sees self-deception, with a concomitant inner numbness, as the predominant concern of the corpus of Begley's fiction.

Begley's reflections on the controversy surrounding Jerzy Kosinski's novel *The Painted Bird* and the details of that writer's biography provide a strong articulation for the importance of the imagination in bearing witness: "Since the artistic truth [of the novel]—its portrayal of man's endless capacity for cruelty toward men in whom they do not recognize their brothers, which is the motive and theme of the Holocaust—is unimpeachable and entire, it turns out that [the author] did not bear false witness, after all, and need not have worried about his fabulations." *Wartime Lies* may be understood as a kind of "lie"—an invention, or a fiction, about childhood and loss of childhood during the war. Begley observes that he chose the form of a novel, rather than a memoir, to meditate on his wartime experiences, because "some doors one cannot open just by turning the doorknob; their opening must be conjured" ("Who the Novelist Really Is," p. 22). The novel illustrates the importance of imaginative literature in probing the human dimensions of history.

Bibliography

Primary Sources

Novels

Wartime Lies. 1991.
The Man Who Was Late. 1993.
As Max Saw It. 1994.
About Schmidt. 1996.
Mistler's Exit. 1998.

Schmidt Delivered. 2000.

Articles

"Who the Novelist Really Is." 1992.
"Time Is Everything." 1995.
"True Lies." 1996.
"Kafka: The Axe for the Frozen Sea Inside Us." 1997.

Secondary Sources

"Begley, Louis." In *Contemporary Authors*, vol. 140. Edited by Donna Olendorf. Detroit: Gale, 1993, pp. 27–28.

Espen, Hal. "The Lives of Louis Begley." (*New Yorker*, 30 May 1994): 38–46.

Fein, Esther B. "Inventing a Life, Then Living It: At the Office with Louis Begley." *New York Times*, 14 April 1993, pp. C1ff.

Grossman, Judith. "War and Memory." *New York Times Book Review*, 5 May 1991, p. 1. Review of *Wartime Lies*.

Hepburn, Allan. "Lost Time: Trauma and Belatedness in Louis Begley's *The Man Who Was Late*." *Contemporary Literature* 39 (fall 1998): 380–404.

Horowitz, Sara R. *Voicing the Void: Muteness and Memory in Holocaust Fiction*. Albany: State University of New York Press, 1997.

Malcolm, Janet. "A Matter of Life and Death." *New York Review of Books*, 13 June 1991, pp. 16–17. Review of *Wartime Lies*.

Miles, Jack. "Death in Venice." *New York Times Book Review*, 20 September 1998, p. 10. Review of *Mistler's Exit*.

Sokoloff, Naomi. "Childhood Lost: Children's Voices in Holocaust Literature." In *The Voice of the Child in Literature*. Edited by Elizabeth Goodenough, Mark A. Heberle, and Naomi Sokoloff. Detroit: Wayne State University Press, 1994, pp. 259–274.

SAUL BELLOW

(1915–)

S. LILLIAN KREMER

The Holocaust may even be seen as a deliberate lesson or project in philosophical redefinition: . . . "you believers in freedom, dignity, and enlightenment—you think you know what a human being is. . . . Look at our camps and crematoria and see if you can bring your hearts to care about these millions" (*To Jerusalem and Back*, New York: Avon Books, 1976, p. 78).

CELEBRATED AS ONE of the most important novelists of his generation, American Nobel Laureate Saul Bellow was born in Lachine, Canada, as Solomon Bellows in 1915 to Russian-Jewish immigrants, Abraham Bellows and Liza Gordon Bellows. He was raised in one of the poorest sections of Montreal in what he has described as, "The Jewish slums of Montreal . . . not too far removed from the ghettos of Poland and Russia" (*Great Jewish Short Stories*, New York: Dell, 1963, p. 13). Despite the seedy side of slum existence, Bellow has described his Montreal life as that of a highly verbal "medieval ghetto; . . . my childhood was in ancient times which was true of all orthodox Jews" (Bellow in interview with Nina Steers in *Conversations with Saul Bellow: Selected Interviews*, University of Mississippi Press 1994, p. 29). The languages of his childhood were Hebrew, Yiddish, French, and English. The family moved to Humboldt Park, an immigrant Chicago neighborhood, when Bellow was nine. He attended the University of Chicago and graduated from Northwestern University in 1937 with honors in sociology and anthropology. Although Bellow wished to study literature in graduate school, he was advised that antisemitism would thwart his career. For "as a Jew and the son of Russian Jews [he] would probably never have the right *feeling* for Anglo-Saxon traditions, for English words" (Steers Interview, p. 63). He accepted a scholarship to continue studies in anthropology at the University of Wisconsin, where his professor told him he wrote anthropology like a good novelist. By the end of the first semester, Bellow had dropped out of graduate school to become a writer.

Bellow has received many literary prizes, including awards from the National Institute of Arts and Letters and the Guggenheim and Ford Foundations, and honorary doctorates. He is the only American writer to win three National Book Awards (for *The Adventures of Augie March*, *Herzog*, and *Mr. Sammler's Planet*) and a Pulitzer Prize for *Humboldt's Gift*. He received the Croix de Chevalier des Arts et Lettres from France and was honored with the Nobel prize for literature in 1976. A distinguished body of work, hailed for its intellectual and stylistic brilliance and its treatment of cultural and social issues of consequence in an eclectic intellectually allusive manner combined with a comic gift has earned Bellow the accolades of critics, academics, and the book-buying public. Bellow has held numerous university appointments, most enduringly at the University of Chicago, where he served as member and chair of the Committee on Social Thought. Although his foremost impact has been as a novelist, Bellow has been an important commentator on the American cultural scene as a member of an elite group of intellectuals associated with the *Partisan Review*.

Intimations of the Holocaust: Antisemitism and the Road to the Gas Chamber

Bellow was at the forefront of American literary readiness to address antisemitism and the *Shoah* in fiction, including the concept of Jew as Christ-killer, in *The Adventures of Augie March* (1953); cultural and institutional antisemitism in *The Victim* (1947) and *Humboldt's Gift* (1975); economic and social antisemitism in "The Old System" (1967); and violent antisemitism in *Herzog* (1964), "Mosby's Memoirs" (1968), and *Mr. Sammler's Planet* (1970). The Holocaust is a subdued yet ever-present component, rarely at the dramatic center, but often surfacing in the thought and speech of characters haunted by its specter. *Dangling Man* (1944), published at the height of the Holocaust and set in the time of World War II, alludes to the European folkloric conception of the Jew as the incarnation of evil, but the Holocaust appears only metaphorically in the protagonist's dream of searching through a roomful of corpses, the result of a massacre. Historian Moses Herzog visits the Warsaw ghetto, finding "the stones still smelling of wartime murders" (*Herzog*, New York: Viking, 1964, p. 37). Humboldt Fleisher refuses an invitation to present a lecture series in Berlin, mindful that a year in Germany would be a constant reminder of "the destruction of the death camps, the earth soaked in blood, and the fumes of cremation still in the air of Europe" (*Humboldt's Gift*, New York: Viking, 1975, p. 156). It is, however, in *The Victim*, *Mr. Sammler's Planet*, and *The Bellarosa Connection* that Bellow turns to substantive Holocaust exploration and evocation.

The Victim, Bellow's most comprehensive exploration of antisemitism, was published two years after World War II. While critical discussion of the novel has rightly centered on the dynamics of the encounter between Jew and antisemite, it is also an early metaphoric evocation of the *Shoah*. Perhaps because Bellow was ahead of his time, perhaps because his treatment was on symbolic and allusive levels, perhaps because readers eager to get on with life after the war were unready to face Holocaust atrocities in literature, Holocaust imagery and allusion in *The Victim* have passed virtually unnoticed in literary criticism.

The major dilemma of *The Victim* centers on the issue of moral accountability for intended and unintended consequences of one's acts. Set against the backdrop of the Depression and World War II, the novel pits Asa Leventhal, a first-generation American Jew, and Kirby Allbee, a descendant of colonial Americans, against each other. Allbee, Asa's emotional double, attaches himself to the Jew in a parasitic relationship, charging that Asa has vindictively destroyed him to avenge derogatory remarks he made about Jews, and he demands compensation. Harboring antagonism toward Jews stemming from his feelings of membership in a class traditionally bred to rule and influence American society, which is being displaced by the descendants of non-English immigrants, Allbee sees himself as a pawn, "a victim of social determinism and social displacement" (Eisinger, p. 189).

Bellow invests Allbee's character with an amalgam of twentieth-century anti-Jewish arguments—economic displacement, cultural pollution, and racism—which had become dominant but had not eliminated historic religious antisemitism. Allbee repeatedly speaks of Jews as a people apart, referring to them as "You people" (*The Victim*, New York: New American Library, 1965, p. 133). In language and imagery corresponding to 1930s Nazi rhetoric, he denounces what he believes to be the inordinate Jewish presence in American civilization, paralleling not only the Nazi charge that Jews were gaining control of civic life, but their racist language positioning Jews as subhumans, referring to them as "the children of Caliban" (p. 133). He echoes the Nuremberg Laws of 1935 that restricted Jewish participation in German culture by insisting that Jews ought not interpret American music and literature when he publicly admonishes a Jew for singing an American spiritual and parallels the French antisemite of Jean Paul Sartre's *Anti-Semite and Jew* in his complaint that a Jewish scholar has had the audacity to publish a book on Emerson and Thoreau, certain that "people of such background simply couldn't understand" (p. 132). Distressed by Allbee's blatant antisemitic insistence that the Jew, no matter how assimilated to the host culture, can never fully appreciate non-Judaic Western philosophy and literature, Asa overtly links Allbee's racial and cultural antisemitism to the Nazi genocide.

Although Bellow includes a direct reference to the *Shoah* only once, his symbolic delineation of the period, rendered in images commonly associated with Nazi persecution together with Allbee's Nuremberg parallels, yield an absorbing holocaustic impression that augments the novel's thematic exploration of antisemitism. Bellow consistently foreshadows or follows antisemitic verbal assaults on Asa with a single or fused reference to the archetypal images of the Holocaust: the yellow badge of shame, the deportation trains, and asphyxiation by gas, which integrate realistic cityscape and metaphoric Holocaust landscape. Yellow images appear when Asa is oppressed by the antisemitic remarks and behavior of his employer, and by his Christian in-laws, whom he believes resent his marriage. Train imagery fused with yellow and gas images are central to his meditation about the de-Judaization of his nephew. Lethal gas, the final element in the novel's Holocaust imagery pattern, appears in debilitating exhaust fumes and in Allbee's aborted suicide/assassination attempt by gas.

A hallucinatory Kafkaesque dream, like those often found in Holocaust literature, suggests victim disorientation and dislocation, a disordered universe, and survival anxiety. While the dream suggests the psychological anxiety created by Allbee's intrusion into Asa's life, on a symbolic level it evokes scenes of Jews herded into cattle cars for transport to the death camps. Railroad station, flags, barriers, recoiling crowds pushed by guards, and sealed exits evoke the Jews of Europe trapped in the Nazi deportation net. Asa is pushed away from the train in a reminder that American Jews escaped the fate of European Jewry. The content, diction, and frenzied rhythms of the dream lend themselves to multiple interpretations including the association of antisemitism with the Holocaust as well as with American survivor guilt. The metaphoric implications of the novel's atmosphere, introduced in the first summer night meeting between Allbee and Leventhal, "a redness in the sky, like the flame in a vast baker's oven" (p. 28), establish the persecutor-victim relationship that is reconstituted in the dream and foreshadows Allbee's failed effort to simultaneously commit suicide and kill Asa.

Holocaust Witness and Representation

Mr. Sammler's Planet, Bellow's foremost Holocaust novel, follows a structural pattern similar to that of other survivor-centered American *Shoah* fiction, beginning and ending in the post-Holocaust period of survivorship and returning through memory and nightmare to the Holocaust universe. Although Bellow sets the novel in New York, it evokes the Holocaust through emergence of survivor traumatic memory of a mass killing and examination of present-day behavioral and emotional disorders springing from wartime brutality. Arthur Sammler, a Polish Jew who was brought up in an intellectually cultivated household, lived in London for some years before the war, serving as a correspondent for Polish journals. Upon his return to Poland, he and his wife were arrested, forced, along with many other Jews, to dig a mass grave, shot by an extermination squad, and left for dead. Sammler alone managed to emerge from the grave, with but one eye intact.

The mass grave is the novel's central Holocaust referent. In the first rendition of the scene, Bellow presents a brief synopsis of the massacre and Sammler's survival struggle:

> He and sixty or seventy others, all stripped and naked and having dug their own grave, were fired upon and fell in. Bodies upon his own body. Crushing. His dead wife nearby somewhere. Struggling out much later from the weight of the corpses, crawling out of the loose soil. Scraping on his belly. Hiding in a shed. Finding a rag to wear. Lying in the woods many days (*Mr. Sammler's Planet*, Greenwich, Conn.: Fawcett Publications, 1970, pp. 86–87).

A more complete account of the graveside experience, near the novel's midpoint, shifts from remembrance of physical detail to philosophic speculation and moral judgment underscoring a crucial distinction between accidental death and state-sponsored persecution of European Jewry. In addition, this second reflective distinction between an accidental fall to death in the Grand Canyon and toppling into a mass grave takes into account that, for the uninitiated, signifying practices take place in the realm of normalcy, a theory that Kali Tal has since articulated to explain how language ultimately fails to translate the traumatic experiences of the Holocaust for those who have not lived them (Tal, pp. 16–19). The novel's final chapter focuses on anticipatory terror as Bellow sketches the mass murder scene retrospectively and in greater sensory detail. "The hole deepened, the sand clay and stones of Poland, their birthplace, opened up . . . guns began to blast, and then came a different sound of soil" (p. 249). Bellow's prose is analogous to Charlotte Delbo's concept of "deep memory" based on sensory data as opposed to "external" or "intellectual" memory of the meditation and reflection that dominate the first and second graveside renditions. The retrospective approach also reconstructs the pattern of oral survivor testimony by avoiding strict chronology in a sequence that shifts from an overview of the traumatic event to self-conscious construction mediating philosophical/political consideration and concluding with heightened perception of the traumatic experience. In this manner, Bellow suggests permutations of Holocaust memory and how a survivor might recall the same event differently depending on the contemporary context and on the stimulus of the recollection.

In contrast to his evocation of the mass killings through incremental development of Sammler's memory of and increasingly complex reflection upon the event, Bellow evokes the ghetto and the excremental concentration camp environments in single extended scenes of the Lodz ghetto and Buchenwald camp. The words and phrases "deformed," "obsessed," "abnormality," "play acting," "dramatic individuality," theatrical posturing, and grotesque humor effectively map the bizarre tenure of Chaim Rumkowski, the Nazi-installed elder of the ghetto. Relying on historic records, Bellow presents Rumkowski as "a distasteful fun-figure" (p. 210) who rides through the ghetto in a dilapidated, but ornate, nineteenth-century gilded coach, wielding power of life and death over the ghetto population. The nightmarish quality of this episode evolves through extended juxtaposition of comic, absurd detail with realistic scenes of suffering and death, of parodic ceremony with a stark, graphic portrait of famine, the dead stacked on the sidewalk waiting for the corpse wagon, and the seizure of children for deportation to the death camps. Thus, despite limited use of realistic Holocaust representation, the passage addresses ghetto hardship and Nazi corruption. The excremental concentration camp universe is the subject of a secondary character's recollection of a Buchenwald inmate drowning in a latrine trench as German soldiers forbid fellow prisoners from rescuing him, an act calculated to generate self-disgust in the victims and contempt in the murderers who could then better cope with mass killings of "subhumans."

The Survivors

Like many American writers who treat the *Shoah*, Bellow focuses, in *Mr. Sammler's Planet*, on the consequences of survival. Death or distortion of the creative impulse; impairment of the capacity to love; and religious confusion mark survivors' continued trauma decades after their initial victimization. Sammler and his psychically scarred daughter were retrieved from a Displaced Persons Camp and brought to America where they were emotionally and financially supported by a relative. At the opening of the novel Sammler is a seventy-year-old introspective intellectual, living with a niece whose "family had been destroyed by the Nazis like his own" (p. 18). Despite having lived in New York for over twenty years, he still wonders if he belongs among the living and is convinced that he is marked forever and peculiarly distinguished from others who did not experience the *Shoah*. Even his current anxiety arising from an encounter with a petty thief manifests itself as a constriction at the base of the skull that suggests "The breath of wartime Poland passing over . . . damaged tissues" (p. 9). Because he is afflicted with survivor syndrome, when he escapes a pickpocket by descending into the subway, he relives his fall into a mass grave and his subsequent entombment in a mausoleum. With memory of fleeing from Polish partisans who betrayed the Jewish resistance fighters in an effort to purge postwar Poland of its Jewish remnant, past and present danger mesh in the post-Holocaust consciousness.

Sammler is surrounded by a community of survivors whose Holocaust-induced disorders are variations and reverberations of his own troubles and whose choral commentary corroborates and enhances Holocaust narrative and interpretation. Like Sammler, his son-in-law, Eisen, suffered for his Jewish identity during and after the catastrophe. The histories of both men are marred by non-Aryan, antisemitic persecution attesting to the complicity of non-Germans in the genocide. Each was assaulted by comrades-in-arms, by countrymen trying to rid Europe of the few Jews who survived the Holocaust. Sammler's escape from the massacre of Jewish partisans by Poles determined to "reconstruct a Jewless Poland" (p. 129) is paralleled in Eisen's deliverance from Russian soldiers who threw him—despite the wounds he suffered at Stalingrad—from a troop transport for no other reason but the discovery of his Jewish identity. Physically mutilated in war, Eisen remains a psychological cripple in peacetime. Just as Sammler refrains from writing about the subjects that interested him in prewar Europe, Eisen, a painter, foundry worker, and metal sculptor, suffers distortion of the creative impulse. His creative potential aborted, Eisen has himself become a grotesque, his work revealing psychological trauma.

In addition to physical deterioration and psychological stress, the impact of the *Shoah* is manifested in survivors' religious confusion and protest. Shula-Slawa, whose name reflects her identity conflict, suffers prolonged religious and cultural schizophrenia as a result of four childhood years spent in hiding from the Nazis in a Polish convent. Her character mirrors clinical psychological accounts of hidden children who were protected by Christian religious orders, and subsequently experienced confusion springing both from indoctrination by their protectors and the visible evidence that Jews were an endangered people and Christians were not.

That the Holocaust taxes the Jew's faith, provoking doubts about a just and merciful God, the covenant, and man, is axiomatic. Bruch, a Buchenwald survivor, ardently strives to reject God and Judaism. Although Bellow treats his "apostasy" ironically, he explores the significant implications of *Shoah*-inspired rejection of God and religion through this character's desperate disappointment in God's *Shoah* indifference. In the end, Bruch abandons neither God nor religion; he merely rebels against God and orthodox piety by adopting the liberal Reform interpretation of Judaism.

The religious theme is most profoundly explored in Sammler's spiritual transformation. A descendant of Orthodox Jews, Sammler was raised by assimilated parents and before the war took pride in being a free thinker. Yet, in his postwar analysis of his spiritual recovery, he mistakenly identifies the Holocaust as the catalyst for doubting God's purpose. Although the survivor indicts God for failure to uphold the covenant, and wants to reject God completely, the same involuntary, unwelcome persistence of belief found in the protagonists of Elie Wiesel and I. B. Singer prevails. Having attributed his capacity to kill an unarmed German soldier to his Holocaust era loss of faith, he marks his spiritual recovery to his postwar return to the ethics of Judaism, when he responds compassionately to a fallen Egyptian soldier during the Six Day War. Following this experience of empathy for an enemy of the Jews, he is convinced that he "was a man who had come back. He had rejoined life" (p. 264). Alan Berger describes the duality of Sammler's postwar spiritual condition as one that alternates "between a knowledge of divine indifference as manifested by the Holocaust and intimations of divine presence in everyday existence" (*Crisis and Covenant* p. 107).

Survivors are frequently placed in a judgmental role in American Holocaust literature and, despite his initial resistance, Sammler's relatives cast him in the judicial role because they respect his Holocaust experiences. Acceptance of that role and its attendant obligation to become socially engaged affect the victim's Holocaust regeneration. He now grapples with characteristic Bellovian ethical questions: "What is the true stature of a human being?" (p. 212); "Where is the desirable self that one might be?" (p. 214). When, near novel's end, Sammler fully accepts the role of moral authority that his family has sought to impose on him, he uses Holocaust experience as a moral touchstone. He rejects his social philosophy of the 1920s as charming but naïve, castigates the excess and romantic distortions of the 1960s, and affirms the values of God and soul. Sammler now seeks ethical wisdom and a reawakening of traditional values by which man can attain virtue: "Trying to live with a civil heart. With disinterested charity. With a sense of the mystic potency of humankind. With an inclination to believe in the archetypes of goodness" (pp. 125–126). Affirming the Judaic reverence for creation, Sammler argues that God's will demands morality and that human life demands an ethical code that sanctifies life and leads to holiness. His concluding prayer parallels Ecclesiastes and honors the covenantal bond between divinity and humanity. As a victim of radical evil, the one-eyed survivor speaks for remembrance of the evil philosophy that claimed the lives of millions, for spiritual illumination and social responsibility, and for reason, morality, and human dignity in the midst of chaos.

The apocalyptic experience of the Holocaust and its paralytic aftermath lead Sammler to reject Hannah Arendt's "banality of evil" thesis. He condemns the Nazi mentality in Judaic terms, stressing concepts such as the sacredness of life and individual moral responsibility:

> The idea of making the century's great crime look dull is not banal. . . . What better way to get the curse out of murder than to make it look ordinary, boring, or trite? With horrible political insight they found a way to disguise the thing . . . do you think the Nazis didn't know what murder was? Everybody . . . knows what murder is . . . The best and purest human beings, from the beginning of time, have understood that life is sacred. To defy that old understanding is not banality. There was a conspiracy against the sacredness of life. Banality is the adopted disguise of a very powerful will to abolish conscience (pp. 20–21).

Bellow's moral indignation finds voice in Sammler's resistance to Hannah Arendt's contention that Nazis of Adolf Eichmann's ilk were ordinary men, neither monsters nor pathological antisemites, but merely loyal Germans performing their duties. Moreover, he resents Arendt's conclusion that Nazi crimes emanated not from their own characters, but rather from their positions in a totalitarian state, insisting on the moral responsibility of the individual. Daniel Fuchs's analysis of an earlier manuscript version of the novel in which the protagonist was named Meyer Pawlyk, shows that the denunciation of Arendt's thesis was heightened in the final text via criticism of Arendt's intellectual method. Pawlyk charges that Arendt's "enemy is modern civilization itself. She is only using the Germans to attack the twentieth century—to denounce it in terms invented by Germans. Making use of a tragic history to promote the foolish ideas of Weimar intellectuals" (1984, p. 21). In an interview titled "Literature and Culture" published in *Salmagundi* five years after publication of the novel, Bellow elaborated his critique by challenging Arendt's exclusive political explanation for evil and refuting her vision of the citizen totally conditioned by historic circumstance, in what he perceives to be her relative neglect of human understanding of evil (pp. 16–17).

Holocaust Memory: Erasure or Perpetuation

In a parallel development with literary theory's increasing concern with the dynamics of traumatic memory, how it is perceived and represented, whether witness memory is reliable, and how memory is mediated, Bellow continues to explore the workings of individual and collective memory in his short narratives. In the Bellovian universe, rejection of memory is a sign of moral decay. Enlightened embrace of memory is a source of spiritual and moral growth. These dichotomies are nowhere more evident than in *The Bellarosa Connection* (1989) where the subject of memory is Holocaust retention and forgetfulness, and the focus shifts from survivor memory to suppression of Holocaust memory in postwar America. The pervasive irony of the novella is that its narrator, who "is denied the individuality of a defining name. . . . a fate which suggests that he stands for innumerable other Americans of his own and the next generations who fail to connect for lack of any substantial tie to the past" (Rosenthal, p. 91), recognizes at the end of a long career devoted to the mechanics of memory retention that he has been blind to the importance of personal and collective Jewish memory.

The lonely septuagenarian, founder of the Mnemosyne Institute, who trained executives, statesmen, and politicians in memory maintenance prefers, when the subject is the Holocaust, to "forget about remembering" (*The Bellarosa Connection*, New York: Penguin Books, 1989, p. 2). His tale is stimulated by his sudden, late realization that meaningful memory is essential for an individual's connection to humanity. The unsummoned memory dominating the text involves the narrator's reflection on the *Shoah* history of a distant cousin, Harry Fonstein, and his own response to the survivor. These reflections cause him to confront matters worthy of memory, the Nazi genocide, the Jewish-American response to survivors, and post-*Shoah* Jewish American identity.

The Bellarosa Connection juxtaposes two faces of contemporary Jewish-American response to group identification and historic memory. The survivor's American wife, Sorella Fonstein, argues for the significance of human connection through preservation of historic memory. Opposed to the manner in which the Fonsteins honor memory, the narrator and Fonstein's rescuer are exemplars of historic amnesia, which Bellow intimates characterized the reaction of many American Jews during the immediate postwar era. Beginning with his recollection of his father's interest in Fonstein, the narrator shifts to shards of childhood memory sketching Fonstein's wartime struggles and culminating in his escape from the Nazis with the aid of operatives of American show business impresario, Billy Rose. His dominant postwar memory of Fonstein is the survivor's unsuccessful efforts to express his gratitude directly to Rose, who repeatedly refuses any emotional involvement with the Jews he rescued. Illustrative of the narrator's youthful ignorance is his unuttered advice to abandon the effort to contact Billy Rose, to abandon Holocaust memory: "Forget it. Go American" (p. 29). This superficial attitude and thirty years of subsequent neglect refutes his claim that he "never lost sight of Fonstein's history, or of what it meant to be the survivor of such a destruction" (p. 48).

The narrator's new understanding about meaningful memory is the product of Sorella's tutoring. Sorella is "A spirited woman, at home with ideas" (p. 27) who sought to understand "the technics of annihilation, the large-scale industry aspect of it" (p. 28). Representative of the Jewish-American consciousness that feels a strong tie to European-Jewish history, she grasps the relevance of historic memory and argues that even though Americans "weren't threatened, we have a special duty to come to terms with [the Holocaust]" (p. 60). As Sorella's ambivalent student, the narrator vacillates between reluctance to engage the Holocaust and a morbid fascination with it. For him, "Hunting for causes was a horrible imposition added to the original 'selection,' gassing, cremation" (p. 29). In time, he is moved to recant his obdurate refusal to think "of the history and psychology of these abominations, death chambers and furnaces" (pp. 28–29), finally acknowledging that "you couldn't say no to Jewish history after what had happened in Nazi Germany. You had to listen" (p. 28). Newly troubled by his neglect of Fonstein and his professed disinterest in the Holocaust, the narrator has a nightmare of symbolic Holocaust import and commentary on his "lifelong mistake" (p. 87) of disengagement from the European Jew's pain. He finds himself in a pit—a hole suggestive of the mass graves dug by thousands of European Jews before they were summarily shot by the *Einsatzgruppen*. He is unable to extricate himself because his feet are entangled in ropes or roots.

Dream identification with and separation from the vulnerable refugee is solidified in the image of encumbered feet, for Fonstein wore an orthopedic boot, which would have meant an immediate death sentence had he been sent to Auschwitz. Identification with the victim is a staple of American guilt for failure to mount a significant rescue effort. Simultaneously, given the great good luck of living in a free society where they have imbibed the American dream, "a New World version of reality" of endless power and strength, American Jews regard themselves as different from submissive European Jews. Part American myth and part Hollywood fantasy, the narrator's vision of resistance to Nazism led him to think "You couldn't have locked a man like [Douglas Fairbanks] in a cattle car; he would have broken out" (p. 89). The problem with this acculturated perception is the American Jew's historic amnesia; he "was a Jew of an entirely different breed. . . . There was no way, therefore, in which [he] could grasp the real facts in the case of Fonstein. . . . You pay a price for being a child of the New World" (p. 89). Bellow thus seems to associate American privilege with willful neglect of *Shoah* history. A price some American Jews paid for the greater freedom and security than European Jews enjoyed was disengagement from Jewish identification and solidarity. Fear of an antisemitic backlash contributed to American Jewry's failure to mobilize government and public support for European Jewry.

Unlike the unrepentant Billy Rose, the narrator is responsive to Sorella's "illuminated particles of Jewish history" (p. 89). Her instruction and his revelation that he had long avoided "unbearable imaginations— . . . recognitions—of murder" (p. 90) culminate in self-rebuke, the first step toward spiritual repair (*tikkun*), followed by an effort to reestablish relations with the Fonsteins, to develop a meaningful relationship with those whose history is connected to his own.

Reflective of the narrator's moral transformation is his changed response to the Holocaust and his own Jewish identity. His pre-epiphanal tone was brusk, detached, even flippant, and on occasion, macabre. Later, he adopts a somber tone, and language more appropriate for Holocaust tragedy as he ponders Fonstein's probable fate in Auschwitz and concludes soberly with images that directly confront the radical evil of Nazism.

> Some Dr. Mengele would have pointed his swagger stick to the left, and Fonstein's boot might now have been on view in the camp's exhibition hall—they have a hill of cripple boots there, a hill of crutches and of back braces and one of human hair and one of eyeglasses (p. 4).

The metamorphosis from historic amnesiac to advocate for perpetuation of historic memory is realized in recognition of distinctions Sorella raises between European- and American-Jewish experience. Unlike the physical threat Nazism posed for Jewry, assimilation poses a threat to American Jewry's religious and cultural survival. Writing about Fonstein and Billy Rose helps the narrator redefine his post-Holocaust identity as an American Jew, to become the true son of his father, who appreciated the educational and humanizing purposes of historic memory, a father who "hoped it would straighten me out to hear what people had suffered in Europe, in the real world" (p. 5). The reverential tone and context that close the novel address the importance of relating to one's historic/cultural memory and situate memory in the sphere of religious obligation. In remembering the Jewish dead, and more significantly their history and values, Bellow's protagonists typically achieve or become candidates for communal connection and ethical sensitivity.

In a *Bostonia* interview reprinted in *Conversations with Saul Bellow*, Bellow speaks of the things that got away from him while writing *The Adventures of Augie March* and isolates the *Shoah*, claiming he "was very incompletely informed. . . . may even have been partly sealed off from it. . . . I understood what had happened. Somehow I couldn't tear myself away from my American life" (p. 276). He continues, "It was later when I myself went to Auschwitz in 1959 that the Holocaust landed its full weight on me" (p. 276). Speaking of the significance of great events that were not as central to his "formation" as the American experience was, Bellow muses "I didn't take hold of them as I now see I might have done. Not until *The Bellarosa Connection*" (p. 277).

Critical Reception

From his first novel, *Dangling Man*, which attracted the attention of prominent reviewers such as Edmond Wilson, Diana Trilling, Peter DeVries, and Delmore Schwartz, Bellow has earned the attention, accolades, and occasionally the political approbation of important scholars and critics as well as lay readers. Until recent leftist critics and feminists censured Bellow for his conservative cultural values, he long enjoyed ardent praise as a novelist of ideas, for his comedic voice, and stylistic mastery. He is recognized not only as one of America's best writers, but as an important figure in world literature who has published first-rate works of the imagination for nearly six decades. An American cultural icon, Saul Bellow is valued as a thinker and a storyteller, who is characterized by the Yale critic, Harold Bloom, as being "By general critical agreement . . . the strongest American novelist of his generation" (Bloom, *Saul Bellow: Modern Critical Views*, p. 1).

Bibliography

Primary Sources

Novels

Dangling Man. 1944.
The Victim. 1947.
The Adventures of Augie March. 1953.
Henderson the Rain King. 1959.
Herzog. 1964.
Seize the Day. 1968.
Mr. Sammler's Planet. 1970.
The Portable Saul Bellow. 1974.
Humboldt's Gift. 1975.
The Dean's December. 1982.
More Die of Heartbreak. 1987.
A Theft. 1989.
The Bellarosa Connection. 1989.
The Actual. 1997.
Ravelstein. 2000.

Nonfiction Books

To Jerusalem and Back: A Personal Account. 1976.
It All Adds Up: From the Dim Past to the Uncertain Future. 1994.

Collections

Mosby's Memoirs, and Other Stories. 1968.
The Portable Saul Bellow. 1974.
Him with His Foot in His Mouth, and Other Stories. 1984.
Something to Remember Me By: Three Tales. 1991.
Collected Stories. 2001.

Plays

The Wrecker. New World Writing 6 (1954).

Under the Weather. Three one-act comedies: *Orange Souffle,* published in *Esquire* (January 1965); *A Wen,* in *Esquire* (October 1965); and *Out from Under.*

The Last Analysis, a Play. First produced October 1, 1964; first printed under the title *Bummidge*; revision published 1965.

Selected Uncollected Short Stories

"Two Morning Monologues." *Partisan Review* 8 (May–June 1941): 230–236.

"The Mexican General." *Partisan Review* 9, no. 3 (1942): 178–194.

"Dora." *Harper's Bazaar* (November 1949): 118, 188–190, 198–199.

"The Trip to Galena." *Partisan Review* 17, no. 8 (1950): 779–794.

"Address by Gooley MacDowell to the Hasbeens Club of Chicago." *Hudson Review* 4 (summer 1951): 222–227.

"Burdens of a Lone Survivor." *Esquire* (December 1974): 176–185, 224, 226, 228, 230, 232.

Selected Essays, Articles, and Reviews

"Spanish Letter." *Partisan Review* 15, no. 2 (1948): 217–230.

"The Jewish Writer and the English Literary Tradition: A Symposium, Part II." *Commentary* (October 1949): 336–367. Bellow's contribution to a symposium by Jewish writers on the question "What can we do about Fagin?"

"How I Wrote Augie March's Story." *New York Times Book Review* (31 January 1954): 3, 17.

"The Writers and the Audience." *Perspectives USA* 9 (1954): 99–102.

"Isaac Rosenfeld." *Partisan Review* 23, no. 4 (1956): 565–567.

"A Talk with the Yellow Kid." *Reporter* (6 September 1956): 41–44.

"Distractions of a Fiction Writer." In *The Living Novel: A Symposium.* Edited by Granville Hicks. New York: MacMillan, 1957, pp. 1–20.

"The University as Villain." *Nation* (16 November 1957): 361–363.

"Deep Readers of the World, Beware!" *New York Times Book Review* (15 February 1959): 1, 34.

"The Sealed Treasure." *Times Literary Supplement* (1 July 1960): 414.

"Where Do We Go from Here: The Future of Fiction." *Michigan Quarterly Review* 1, no. 1 (1962): 27–33.

"Facts That Put Fancy to Flight." *New York Times Book Review* (11 February 1962): 1, 28.

"Literature." In *The Great Ideas Today.* Edited by Mortimer Adler and Robert M. Hutchins. Chicago: W. Benton, 1963, pp. 135–179.

"The Mass-Produced Insight." *Horizon* (January 1963): 111–113.

"The Writer as Moralist." *Atlantic* (March 1963): 58–62.

"Some Notes on Recent American Fiction." *Encounter* (November 1963): 22–29.

"My Man Bummidge." *New York Times* (27 September 1964): sec. 2: 1, 5.

"On Jewish Storytelling." *Jewish Heritage* 7, no. 3 (1964–1965): 5–9.

"The Thinking Man's Wasteland." *Saturday Review* (3 April 1965): 20. (Adapted from 9 March 1965 speech accepting National Book Award for *Herzog*.)

"Mind over Chatter." *New York Herald Tribune Book Week*(4 April 1965): 2. (Adapted from speech accepting National Book Award for *Herzog*.)

"Keynote Address before the Inaugural Session of the 34th Session of the International Congress of Poets, Playwrights, Essayists, and Editors, 13 June 1966." *Montreal Star* (25 June 1966): Special Insert, 2–3.

"Cloister Culture." *New York Times Book Review* (10 July 1966): 1.

"Skepticism and the Depth of Life." In *The Arts and the Public: Essays by Saul Bellow.* Edited by James E. Miller Jr. and Paul D. Herring. Chicago: University of Chicago Press 1967, pp. 13–30.

"Saul Bellow on America and American Jewish Writers." *Congress Bi-Weekly* Part 1 (23 October 1970): 8–11; Part 11 (4 December 1970): 13–16.

"Jewish Writers Are Somehow Different." *National Jewish Monthly* (March 1971): 50–51.

"Culture Now: Some Animadversions, Some Laughs." *Modern Occasions* 1 (1971): 162–178.

"Machines and Storybooks: Literature in the Age of Technology." *Harper's* (August 1974): 48–59.

"Man Underground." In *Ralph Ellison: A Collection of Critical Essays.* Edited by John Hersey. Englewood Cliffs, NJ: Prentice-Hall 1974, pp. 27–30.

"Starting out in Chicago." *American Scholar* 44, no. 1 (1974–1975): 71–77.

"Bellow on Himself and America." *Jerusalem Post Magazine* (3 July 1975): 11–12; 10 July 1975, 12.

"A World Too Much with Us." *Critical Inquiry* 2, no. 1 (1975): 1–9.

"The Nobel Lecture." *American Scholar* 46 (1977): 316–325.

"Americans Who Are Also Jews." *Jewish Digest* (April 1977): 8–10. Cited in *Index to Jewish Periodicals* (January–June 1977). Cleveland Heights, Ohio: Index to Jewish Periodicals.

"Recent American Fiction." *American Studies International* 15, no. 3 (1977): 7–18.

"A Writer from Chicago." In *The Tanner Lectures on Human Values* III, 1982. Edited by Sterling M. McMurrin. 1982, pp. 175–219.

"Intellectuals and Writers since the Thirties." *Partisan Review* 59, no. 4 (fall 1992): 531–558. Colloquium with William Phillips (moderator), Czesław Miłosz, Ralph Ellison, and Joseph Brodsky.

"Summations." In *Saul Bellow: A Mosaic.* Edited by L. H. Goldman, Gloria L. Cronin, and Ada Aharoni. Twentieth-Century American Jewish Writers 3. Gen ed. Daniel Walden. 1992, pp. 185–200.

"There is Simply Too Much to Think About." *Forbes* (September 14, 1992): 98–106.

"Summations." The Ben Belitt Lectures at Bennington College. In *The Ordering Mirror: Readers and Contexts.* Edited by Phillip Lopate and Elizabeth Coleman. New York: Fordham University Press, 1993, pp. 164–181.

"Writers, Intellectuals, Politics: Mainly Reminiscence." *National Interest* 31 (spring 1993): 124–134.

"Some Questions and Answers." In *Conversations with Saul Bellow: Selected Interviews.* Edited by Gloria L. Cronin and Ben Siegel. Jackson: University Press of Mississippi, 1994.

Translation

"Gimpel the Fool." Isaac Bashevis Singer. Translated by Saul Bellow. *Partisan Review* 20, no. 3 (1953): 300–313.

Selected Forewords and Introductions

Foreword to *Winter Notes on Summer Impressions* by Feodor M. Dostoevsky. New York: McGraw-Hill, 1955. Revised version of "The French as Dostoevsky Saw Them." *New Republic* (23 May 1955): 17–20.

Foreword to *An Age of Enormity: Life and Writing in the Forties and Fifties* by Isaac Rosenfeld. Edited by Theodore Solotaroff. 1962.
Introduction. *Great Jewish Short Stories*. Edited by Saul Bellow. 1963.
Foreword to *Recovery/Delusions, etc.* by John Berryman. 1974.
Foreword to *The Boundaries of Natural Science* by Rudolf Steiner. 1983.
Foreword to *The Closing of the American Mind* by Allan Bloom. 1987.
Foreword to *Preserving the Hunger: An Isaac Rosenfeld Reader*. Edited by Mark Schechner. 1988.

Selected Reviews

"Italian Fiction: Without Hope." Review of *The New Italian Writers: An Anthology from Botteghe Oscure*. Edited by Marguerite Caetani. *New Leader* (11 December 1950): 21–22.
"Dreiser and the Triumph of Art." Review of *Theodore Dreiser* by F. O. Matthiessen. *Commentary* (May 1951): 502–503. Reprinted in *The Stature of Theodore Dreiser: A Critical Survey of the Man and His Work*. Edited by Alfred Kazin and Charles Shapiro. Bloomington: Indiana University Press, 1955, pp. 146–148.
"Gide as Writer and Autobiographer." Review of *The Counterfeiters* with *Journal of the Counterfeiters* by Andre Gide. *New Leader* (4 June 1951): 24.
"Man Underground." Review of *Invisible Man* by Ralph Ellison. *Commentary* (June 1952): 608–611.
"Laughter in the Ghetto." Review of *The Adventures of Mottel and the Cantor's Son* by Sholom Aleichem. *Saturday Review* (30 May 1953): 15.
"Hemingway and the Image of Man." Review of *Ernest Hemingway* by Philip Young. *Partisan Review* 20, no. 3 (1953): 338–342.
"Rabbi's Boy in Edinburgh." Review of *Two Worlds* by David Daiches. *Saturday Review* (24 March 1956): 19.
"The Swamp of Prosperity." Review of *Goodbye, Columbus* by Philip Roth. *Commentary* (July 1959): 77–79.
"Beatrice Webb's America" Review of *Beatrice Webb's American Diary* (1898). Edited by David A. Shannon. *Nation* (7 September 1963): 116.

Work Edited by Bellow

Editor, with Keith Botsford and Jack Ludwig. *The Noble Savage*. Five volumes. Cleveland: World Publishing Company, 1960–1962.
Editor and author of Introduction to *Great Jewish Short Stories*. New York: Dell, 1963.

Collected Interviews

Cronin, Gloria L., and Ben Siegel, eds. *Conversations with Saul Bellow: Selected Interviews*. Jackson: University Press of Mississippi, 1994.

Selected Interviews

Bellow, Saul. "Interview with Myself." *New Review* 2, no. 18 (1975): 53–56.
Boyers, Robert T. "Literature and Culture: An Interview with Saul Bellow." *Salmagundi* 30 (summer 1975): 6–23.
Brans, Jo. "Common Needs, Common Preoccupations: An Interview with Saul Bellow." *Southwest Review* 62 (winter 1977): 1–19.
Gray, Rockwell, Harry White, and Gerald Nemanic. "Interview with Saul Bellow." *TriQuarterly* 60 (1985): 12–34.
"A Half Life: An Autobiography of Ideas." *Bostonia/1990* (November/December 1990): 37–47. Reprinted in *Conversations with Saul Bellow: Selected Interviews*. Edited by Gloria L. Cronin and Ben Siegel. Jackson: University Press of Mississippi, 1994, pp. 248–277.
Roudané, Matthew. "An Interview with Saul Bellow." *Contemporary Literature* 25, no. 3 (1984): 265–280.

Audio Cassette Tape

Saul Bellow on Art, Literature, and American Life. Danbury, Conn.: Grolier, 1982. Vital History Cassettes 3.

Secondary Sources

Selected Bibliographies

Cronin, Gloria L. "Saul Bellow Selected and Annotated Bibliography." *Saul Bellow Journal* 4, no. 1 (1985): 80–89. (Cronin and Blaine H. Hall have prepared Bellow bibliographies annually for the *SBJ*.)
Cronin, Gloria L., and Blaine H. Hall. *Saul Bellow: An Annotated Bibliography*, Second Edition. New York and London: Garland Publishing, Inc., 1987.
"Saul Bellow: Bibliographie." *Profils Americains* 9 (1997): 191–208.

Selected Biographies

Atlas, James. *Saul Bellow: A Biography*. New York: Random House, 2000.
Harris, Mark. *Saul Bellow: Drumlin Woodchuck*. Athens: University of Georgia Press, 1980.
Miller, Ruth. *Saul Bellow: A Biography of the Imagination*. New York: St. Martin's Press, 1991.

Selected Books and Monographs

Bischoff, Peter. *Saul Bellows Romane: Entfremdung Suche*. Abhandlungen Zur Kunst, Musik and Literaturwissenschaft 160. Bonn: Bouvier, 1975.
Bradbury, Malcolm. *Saul Bellow*. Contemporary Writers. London and New York: Methuen, 1982.
Braham, Jeanne. *A Sort of Columbus: The American Voyages of Saul Bellow's Fiction*. Athens: University of Georgia Press, 1984.
Clayton, John J. *Saul Bellow: In Defense of Man*. Bloomington: Indiana University Press, 1968, 1979.
Cohen, Sarah Blacher. *Saul Bellow's Enigmatic Laughter*. Urbana: University of Illinois Press, 1974.
Dommergues, Pierre. *Saul Bellow*. Paris: Grasset, 1967.
Dutton, Robert R. *Saul Bellow*. Twayne's United States Author Series 181. New York: Twayne, 1971, 1982.
Fuchs, Daniel. *Saul Bellow: Vision and Revision*. Durham: Duke University Press, 1984.
Goldman, Liela H. *Saul Bellow's Moral Vision: A Critical Study of the Jewish Experience*. New York: Irvington, 1983.
Kiernan, Robert F. *Saul Bellow*. Literature and Life. American Writers. New York: Continuum, 1989.
Lévy, Claude. *Les Romans de Saul Bellow: Tactiques Narratives et Strategies Oedipiennes*. Etudes Anglo-Américaines 5. Paris: Klincksieck, 1983.
Malin, Irving. *Saul Bellow's Fiction*. Crosscurrents/Modern Critiques. Carbondale: Southern Illinois University Press, 1969.
Newman, Judie. *Saul Bellow and History*. New York: St. Martin's; London: Macmillan, 1984.
Opdahl, Keith M. *The Novels of Saul Bellow: An Introduction*. University Park: Pennsylvania State University Press, 1967.
Pifer, Ellen. *Saul Bellow against the Grain*. Philadelphia: University of Pennsylvania Press, 1990.

Porter, M. Gilbert. *Whence the Power? The Artistry and Humility of Saul Bellow*. Columbia: University of Missouri Press, 1974.

Roderigues, Eusebio L. *Quest for the Human: An Exploration of Saul Bellow's Fiction*. Lewisburg, Penn.: Bucknell University Press, 1981.

Rovit, Earl. *Saul Bellow*. Minneapolis: University of Minnesota Press, 1967.

Scheer-Schaezler, Brigitte. *Saul Bellow*. Modern Literature Monographs. New York: Ungar, 1972.

Schraepen, Edmond, ed. *Saul Bellow and His Work*. Proceedings of a symposium held at the Free University of Brussels (V.U.B.), 10–11 December 1977. Brussels: Centrum voor Taal-en Literatuurwetenschap Vrije Universiteit Brussel, 1978.

Scott, Nathan A., Jr. *Three American Moralists: Mailer, Bellow, Trilling*. Notre Dame: University of Notre Dame Press, 1973.

Tanner, Tony. *Saul Bellow*. Writers and Critics. Edinburgh and London: Oliver and Boyd; New York: Barnes, 1965; New York: Chips, 1978.

Wilson, Jonathan. *On Bellow's Planet: Readings from the Dark Side*. Rutherford, N.J.: Dickinson University Press; London and Toronto: Associated University Presses, 1985.

Collected Essays

Bach, Gerhard, ed. *Saul Bellow at Seventy-Five: A Collection of Critical Essays*. With Jakob J. Kollhofer. Tübingen: Gunter Narr, 1991.

———, and Gloria L. Cronin, eds. *Small Planets: Saul Bellow and the Art of Short Fiction*. East Lansing: Michigan State University Press, 2000.

Bloom, Harold, ed. *Saul Bellow*. Modern Critical Views. New York: Chelsea, 1986.

Cronin, Gloria L., and L. H. Goldman, eds. *Saul Bellow in the 1980s: A Collection of Critical Essays*. East Lansing: Michigan State University Press, 1989.

Goldman, L. H., Gloria L. Cronin, and Ada Aharoni, eds. *Saul Bellow: A Mosaic*. Twentieth-Century American Jewish Writers 3. General editor Daniel Walden. New York: Peter Lang, 1992.

Hollahan, Eugene, ed. "*Philosophical Dimensions of Saul Bellow's Fiction*." *Studies in the Literary Imagination* 17 (fall 1984).

———, ed. *Saul Bellow and the Struggle at the Center*. New York: AMS, 1996.

Malin, Irving, ed. *Saul Bellow and the Critics*. New York: New York University Press, 1967.

Rovit, Earl. *Saul Bellow: A Collection of Critical Essays*. Twentieth-Century Views. Englewood Cliffs, N.J.: Prentice-Hall, 1975.

Trachtenberg, Stanley, ed. *Critical Essays on Saul Bellow*. Critical Essays on American Literature. Boston: G. K. Hall, 1979.

Special Journal Issues

American Studies International. February 1997.

Critique 3, no. 3 (1960). Special issue on Bellow and William Styron.

Critique 7, no. 3 (1965).

Delta [Paris] 19 (October 1984).

Journal of English Studies [India] 12, no. 1 (1980).

Modern Fiction Studies 25, no. 1 (1979).

Modern Jewish Studies Annual II (1978). Joint issue of *Studies in American Jewish Literature* (University Park, Penn.) 4, no. 2 and *Yiddish* 3, no. 3 (1978).

Notes on Modern American Literature 2, no. 4 (1978).

Profils Américains 9 (1997).

Salmagundi 30 (summer 1975).

Saul Bellow Journal 1, no. 2 (1982–). Published twice yearly since 1982.

Saul Bellow Journal 1, no. 1 (1981). Name changed from *Saul Bellow Newsletter* with vol. 1, no. 2 (1982).

Studies in American Jewish Literature 3, no. 1 (1977). Issue title: *Saul Bellow: The Vintage Years*.

Selected Essays, Articles, and Parts of Books

Aharoni, Ada. "*The Victim*: Freedom of Choice." *Saul Bellow Journal* 4, no. 1 (1985): 33–44.

Alexander, Edward. "Imagining the Holocaust: *Mr. Sammler's Planet* and Others." *Judaism: A Quarterly Journal of Jewish Life and Thought* 22 (1973): 288–300.

Alter, Robert. "Kafka's Father, Agnon's Mother, Bellow's Cousins." *Commentary* 81, no. 2 (February 1986): 46–52.

Baumbach, Jonathan. "The Double Vision: *The Victim* by Saul Bellow." In *The Landscape of Nightmare: Studies in the Contemporary American Novel*. New York: New York University Press, 1965, pp. 35–54.

Bayley, John. "By Way of Mr. Sammler." *Salmagundi* 30 (summer 1975): 24–33.

Berger, Alan L. *Crisis and Covenant: The Holocaust in American Jewish Fiction*. Albany: State University of New York Press, 1985, pp. 96–110.

———. "Holocaust Survivors and Children in *Anya* and *Mr. Sammler's Planet*." *Modern Language Studies* 16, no. 1 (winter 1986): 81–87.

———. "Remembering and Forgetting: The Holocaust and Jewish-American Culture in Saul Bellow's *The Bellarosa Connection*." In *Small Planets: Saul Bellow and the Art of Short Fiction*. Edited by Gerhard Bach and Gloria L. Cronin. East Lansing: Michigan State University Press, 2000, pp. 315–328.

Bilik, Dorothy Seidman. "Bellow's Worldly 'Tsadik.' " In *Immigrant Survivors: Post Holocaust Consciousness in Recent Jewish-American Literature*. New York: Wesleyan University Press, 1981, pp. 137–166.

Bolling, Douglass. "Intellectual and Aesthetic Dimensions of *Mr. Sammler's Planet*." *Journal of Narrative Technique* 4, no. 3 (1974): 188–203.

Bradbury, Malcolm. "Saul Bellow's *The Victim*." *Critical Quarterly* 5, no. 2 (1963): 119–128.

Bus, Heiner. "Saul Bellow: *Mr. Sammler's Planet*." In *Amerikanische Erzahlliterature 1950–1970*. Edited by Freider Bush and Renate Schmidt-von Bardeleben. Kridische Information 28. Munich: Fink, 1975, pp. 170–185.

Charlson, Joshua L. "Ethnicity, Power, and the Postmodern in Saul Bellow's *Mr. Sammler's Planet*." *The Centennial Review* 41, no. 3 (fall 1997): 529–536.

Chouard, Géraldine. "*Mr. Sammler's Planet*: Le funambule mélancolique." *Profils Américains* 5 (1997): 9, 69–87, 215–216.

Cronin, Gloria L. "Faith and Futurity: The Case for Survival in *Mr. Sammler's Planet*." *Literature and Belief* 3 (1982): 97–108.

Crownshaw, Richard. "Blacking Out Holocaust Memory in Saul Bellow's *The Victim*." *Saul Bellow Journal* 16, no. 2–17, no. 1–2 (summer–fall 2000; winter 2001): 215–252.

Cushman, Keith. "Mr. Bellow's *Sammler*: The Evolution of a Contemporary Text." *Studies in the Novel* 7, no. 3 (1975): 425–444.

Dittmar, Kurt. "The End of Enlightenment: Bellow's Universal View of the Holocaust in *Mr. Sammler's Planet*." In *Saul Bellow at Seventy-Five: A Collection of Critical Essays*. Edited by Gerhard Bach. Tübingen: Gunter Narr, 1991, pp. 63–80.

Eisinger, Chester E. "Saul Bellow: Love and Identity." *Accent* 18 (1988): 179–203.

Ertel, Rachel. "*Mr. Sammler's Planet*—Roman de memoire et d'Histoire." *Delta* 19 (October 1984): 155–169.

Fenster, Coral. "Ironies and Insights in *The Bellarosa Connection*." *Saul Bellow Journal* 9, no. 2 (1990): 20–28.

Fuchs, Daniel. "Literature and Politics: The Bellow/Grass Confrontation at the PEN Congress." In *Saul Bellow: A Mosaic*. Edited by L. H. Goldman, Gloria L. Cronin, and Ada Aharoni. Twentieth-Century American Jewish Writers 3. General editor Daniel Walden. New York: Peter Lang, 1992, pp. 49–58.

Galloway, David D. "*Mr. Sammler's Planet*: Bellow's Failure of Nerve." *Modern Fiction Studies* 19, no. 1 (1973): 17–28.

Gittleman, Sol. "*Mr. Sammler's Planet* Ten Years Later: Looking Back on Crises of 'Mishpocha.' " *Judaism* 30 (fall 1981): 480–483.

Glickman, Susan. "The World as Will and Idea: Comparative Study of *An American Dream* and *Mr. Sammler's Planet*." *Modern Fiction Studies* 28, no. 4 (1982–1983): 569–582.

Goldman, L. H. "The Holocaust in the Novels of Saul Bellow." *Modern Language Studies* 16, no. 1 (winter 1986): 71–80.

Gordon, Andrew. "The Return of the Repressed in *The Bellarosa Connection*." *Saul Bellow Journal* 16, no. 1 (winter 1999): 37–48.

Guttman, Allen. "Saul Bellow's *Mr. Sammler*." *Contemporary Literature* 14, no. 2 (1973): 157–166.

Hadari, Amnon. "Ha-professor Eino Me'uban; *Cohav Ha-lekhet Shel Mar Sammler* Me'et Saul Bellow." *Shedmot* 44 (1971): 102–113.

Harris, James Neil. "One Critical Approach to *Mr. Sammler's Planet*." *Twentieth-Century Literature* 18, no. 4 (1972): 235–250.

Hirsch, David H. "Jewish Identity and Jewish Suffering in Bellow, Malamud and Philip Roth." *Jewish Book Annual*. 29th ed. New York: Jewish Book Council, 1971, pp. 12–22.

Kremer, S. Lillian. "Acquiescence to Anti-Semitism in *The Victim*: An Alternate Reading to Bellow's Daniel Harkavy." *Saul Bellow Journal* 1, no. 2 (spring–summer 1982): 27–30.

———. "The Holocaust in *The Victim*." *Saul Bellow Journal* 2, no. 2 (spring–summer 1983): 15–23.

———. "The Holocaust in *Mr. Sammler's Planet*." *Saul Bellow Journal* 4, no. 1 (winter 1985): 19–32.

———. "Scars of Outrage: The Holocaust in *The Victim* and *Mr. Sammler's Planet*." In *Witness through the Imagination: Jewish American Holocaust Literature*. Detroit: Wayne State University Press, 1989, pp. 36–62.

———. "Memoir and History: Saul Bellow's Old Men Remembering in 'Mosby's Memoirs,' 'The Old System,' and *The Bellarosa Connection*." *Saul Bellow Journal* 12, no. 2 (spring–summer 1994): 44–58.

Kumar, P. Shiv. "Yahudim and Ostjude: Social Stratification in *Mr. Sammler's Planet*." *Literary Half-Yearly* 21, no. 2 (1980): 53–67.

Kuna, F. M. "The European Culture Game: Mr. Bellow's Planet." *English Studies* 53, no. 6 (1972): 531–544.

Le Pellet, Yves. "New York in Summer: Its Symbolic Function in *The Victim*." *Caliban* 8 (1971): 101–110.

Levy, Paule. " 'Black Holes' versus 'Connections': Conflicting Visions of the Holocaust in Bellow's *Mr. Sammler's Planet* and *The Bellarosa Connection*." In *Reclaiming Memory: American Representations of the Holocaust*. Edited by Pirjo Ahokas and Martine Chard-Hutchinson. Turku, Finland: University of Turku, 1997, pp. 131–148.

Lyons, Bonnie. "Seeing and Suffering in *The Pawnbroker* and *Mr. Sammler's Planet*." *Yiddish* 6, no. 4 (1987): 114–121.

Murai, Mami. "A Study of *The Victim* by Saul Bellow—Human Mortality and Chain of Life." *Kyushu American Literature* 23 (1982): 85–88.

Newman, Judie. "*Mr. Sammler's Planet*: Wells, Hitler, and the World State." *Dutch Quarterly Review of Anglo-American Letters* 13, no. 1 (1983): 55–71.

———. "Bellow's Ransom Tale: The Holocaust, *The Victim*, and *The Double*." *Saul Bellow Journal* 14, no. 1 (winter 1996): 3–18.

Nilsen, Helge N. "Anti-Semitism and Persecution Complex: A Comment on Saul Bellow's *The Victim*." *English Studies* 60, no. 2 (1979): 183–191.

Oz, Amos. "Mr. Sammler and Hannah Arendt's Banality." *Saul Bellow: A Mosaic*. Edited by L. H. Goldman, Gloria L. Cronin, and Ada Aharoni. Twentieth-Century American Jewish Writers 3. General editor Daniel Walden. New York: Peter Lang, 1992, pp. 21–26.

Pifer, Ellen. " 'Two Different Speeches': Mystery and Knowledge in *Mr. Sammler's Planet*." *Mosaic* 18, no. 2 (1985): 17–31.

Rosenthal, Regine. "Memory and the Holocaust: *Mr. Sammler's Planet* and *The Bellarosa Connection*." In *Saul Bellow at Seventy-Five: A Collection of Critical Essays*. Edited by Gerhard Bach. Tübingen: Gunter Narr, 1991, pp. 81–92.

Rozenberg-Zoltowska, Helene. "A propos du 'Roi Rumkowski': Note sur l'ecriture majoritaire de Bellow." *Caliban* 25 (1988): 111–117.

Sacks, June. "Questionings of a Survivor: A Reappraisal of the Role of Mr. Sammler." *Unisa English Studies: Journal of the Department of English* [Pretoria, South Africa] 26, no. 2 (September 1988): 21–26.

Safer, Elaine B. "Degrees of Comic Irony in *A Theft* and *The Bellarosa Connection*." *Saul Bellow Journal* 9, no. 2 (spring–summer 1990): 1–19.

Satlof, Marilyn R. "Disconnectedness in *The Bellarosa Connection*." In *Saul Bellow and the Struggle at the Center*. Edited by Eugene Hollahan. New York: AMS, 1996, pp. 177–188.

Schiff, Ellen. "American Authors and Ghetto Kings: Challenges and Perplexities." *America and the Holocaust*. Edited by Sanford Pinsker and Jack Fischel. Greenwood, Fla.: Penkevill, 1984, pp. 7–34.

Siegel, Ben. "Saul Bellow and Mr. Sammler: Absurd Seekers of High Qualities." In *Saul Bellow: A Collection of Critical Essays: Twentieth-Century Views*. Edited by Earl Rovit. Englewood Cliffs, N.J.: Prentice Hall, 1975, pp. 122–134.

Simon, Elliott M. "Saul Bellow and the Sacrament of Betrayal." *Yiddish* 11, no. 3–4 (1999): 135–158.

Sloss, Henry. "Europe's Last Gasp." *Shenandoah* 22, no. 1 (1970): 82–86.

Sugino, Kentaro. "Bellow's *The Victim*, or Nobody's World." *Saul Bellow Journal* 13, no. 2 (fall 1995): 49–62.

Tal, Kali. *Worlds of Hurt: Reading the Literatures of Trauma*. Cambridge: Cambridge University Press, 1996.

Weatherford, Kathleen Jeannette. "*The Bellarosa Connection* and the Hazards of Forgetfulness." *American Studies in Scandinavia* 24, no. 2 (1992): 65–82.

Wethington, Dirk. "Re/Establishing Boundaries in Bellow: Postmodernism and *Mr. Sammler's Planet*." *Saul Bellow Journal* 13, no. 2 (fall 1995): 3–18.

Wirth-Nesher, Hana, and Andrea Cohen Malamut. "Jewish and Human Survival on Bellow's Planet." *Modern Fiction Studies* 25, no. 1 (1979): 59–74.

STANISŁAW BENSKI

(1922–1988)

MONIKA ADAMCZYK-GARBOWSKA

STANISŁAW BENSKI, BORN IN Warsaw, spent most of World War II in the Soviet Union where he joined the communist Polish People's Army in 1943. He made his debut with stories published in, among others, the periodicals *Kultura* and *Tygodnik Zachodni*. He also worked for the Polish radio. Fragments from his diary were published in *Tygodnik Kulturalny*. His first collection of stories *Zwiadowcy* (1965, *Reconnoitering*) was published in 1965 by MON, the Ministry of Defense Publishers, and was well received as an example of combatant war fiction, a very popular genre in postwar Poland. The stories re-create his experience in the army from its establishment in the Soviet Union to the conquest of Berlin. Only one story, "Abram," deals indirectly with the Holocaust as it tells about a Jewish soldier who makes himself believe that after the war he will go back home to be greeted as a hero in his *shtetl*, miraculously left intact by the Nazi occupation. Jewish characters appear on a large scale much later in Benski's works, most of which were published in the 1980s after the relaxation of censorship on Jewish topics following the period of intense restriction from 1968 to 1977.

Characterization

Most of Benski's characters are survivors deeply affected by their experience of the Holocaust and World War II in general. Benski does not deal directly with the war years but writes from the perspective of those who managed to survive, presenting their experiences from scraps of their memories or accounts of others. This is the case with the two-part novella *Jeden dzień* (One Day, 1980), the novel *Ocaleni* (The Saved, 1986), and several collections of stories.

Both his novels and stories are very concise. Benski allows his characters to speak for themselves; plots are often constructed on the basis of dialogues between survivors, telephone conversations, or sometimes monologues. "Why do all those Jews [in Benski's works] constantly talk?" critic Jan Błoński asks rhetorically (p. 111) and answers that the main reason is that they are confused about who they really are. They could perhaps regain their identity if after the Holocaust they could find some fragments of their past, but this is not the case. The combined forces of Communist law suppressing religious, cultural, and economic freedom and the trauma caused by postwar pogroms (in The Saved there are a number of references to the pogrom in Cracow of August 1945) assure that no Jewish life in its prewar form can continue. Consequently, whatever chances of rebuilding the Polish Jewish community that seemed to exist right after the war are unrealized.

Often Benski's dialogues are based on paradox and contain elements of Yiddish humor (Yiddish vocabulary and syntax can be detected under the Polish-language surface). Such is the situation in the story "A Strange Country," taking place some time in the 1950s, which relates the visit of a man from Haiti who is looking for his twin brother. He accidentally encounters the narrator stepping out of a dark gateway and asks him about Gęsia Street, which was the location of the large Jewish cemetery before the war. The narrator gives an evasive response that "there hasn't been a Gęsia Street for some time" (Polonsky, p. 195), but the stranger does not give up and insists on asking about other streets of former Jewish Warsaw that he cannot locate. In the verbal encounter between the two men, the narrator-survivor and the visitor who heard about what happened in Warsaw during the war but could not believe it, we get glimpses of Holocaust imagery in the references to a girl sneaking out of the ghetto to the Aryan side in search of bread, the cattle cars waiting for the victims herded to the *Umschlag-*

platz, deportations, children going "into the furnace" (Polonsky, pp. 197–198). Eventually the visitor succeeds in finding his brother, but it turns out that the latter has turned Communist, works for the government, and does not want to admit that he has a brother from a "capitalist country." To be on the safe side he even wrote in his dossier that he did not have any relatives abroad so the brother from Haiti has to accept the fact that he does not "have a brother anymore" in this "strange country." Ironically the brother who survived the Nazis disappears from his sibling's life because of the "new order."

This feeling of both psychological and topographical estrangement, often related to the Communist regime's suppression of true and thorough knowledge about the Holocaust, appears in various forms. This estrangement not only concerns Warsaw, but other places. Most of Benski's characters live in Warsaw and the changes there were most drastic. The Jewish quarter was destroyed after the liquidation of the Warsaw ghetto in spring 1943 and what fragments remained were later annihilated after the uprising of August 1944. Even if the physical appearance of buildings survived the bombings and fires, their character is completely transformed because of the absence of their prewar inhabitants. In the *shtetls* emptied of Jews there is no quorum for Jewish prayer. In The Saved, Benski describes a *shtetl* that had eight thousand inhabitants before the war, seventy percent Jewish. Almost all of the Jews perished. No wonder the narrator feels as if he is exploring a moonscape:

> When I returned from the camp, our shtetl was completely empty. I looked at houses that didn't look like houses, at streets that didn't look like streets and I saw people who didn't look like people. And there was a skinny nanny-goat that didn't look like a nanny-goat, and a skinny nag that didn't look like a nag, and flowers that didn't look like flowers and a sky that wasn't a sky. I wandered around the non-streets, I hung around the non-market on which stood the non-church, non-town-hall and one single non-bench. In Grobelna Street there was a synagogue that wasn't there but it alone existed for me as did our one story house which wasn't there either (*The Saved*, Warsaw: Czytelnik, 1986 p. 6, translation by Monika Adamczyk-Garbowska).

The majority of Benski's characters are old or aging, usually without families, and living in institutions with other solitary individuals like themselves. The Holocaust is often seen from the perspective of survivors living in a Jewish rest home. Benski worked in a rest home and had a chance to listen to many life stories. The pensioners are uprooted and dwell more in imaginary than actual time. Sometimes they really have lost a sense of time. "Don't you happen to have a Jewish calendar?" one of them asks (*The Saved*, p. 41), explaining that he lost count of the months in the Jewish year 5699 when World War II broke out. The blind survivors are privileged because in their memories they preserve scenery untouched by the destruction, while others pretend to be blind so that they do not have to admit the changes they see around them. They are usually childless or orphaned and some of them imagine their fictitious children, like Julian in "List z Paryża" ("A Letter from Paris") who tells others that his son survived, became a famous doctor, and might even receive the Nobel prize.

Locales

In "Missing Pieces" a Jewish couple, residing in Warsaw after the war, are trying to fit in by inventing alternative life stories because their vicissitudes are so mild compared with other survivors. The narrator spent the entire war at his brother's home in New York City:

> Nobody in my family perished, nobody was gassed, nobody was shot in the forest or starved to death in the Ghetto. As a Warsaw Jew, I'm an exception, and to tell the truth, it's embarrassing (Polonsky, p. 200).

Because his wife spent the war in Uzbekistan and was also spared the worst, he decides that they need new vitae. However, when they try to imagine a new biography, the wife declares that there is no way they could have lived through such terrible things.

There are also Benski stories that take place in America or show the encounters of Jews who stayed in Poland with Jewish American visitors. Similar to works by Hanna Krall or Julian Stryjkowski is the ever-recurrent motif of the incompatibility of the experience of East European survivors with that of their relatives or friends who spent the war in the United States. This includes the dilemma of staying versus leaving the land that was desecrated by the Nazi crimes but is sacred in the memories of sages who lived there for generations. In the story "Prawnuczek cadyka" (The Miracle Rebbe's Grandson), religious American Jews encountering one of the pensioners in the Jewish rest home state that he is no longer Jewish because he abandoned Judaism. The pensioner responds to these accusations with the question, "And which of you has survived the ghetto?" For him Jewishness does not have to be synonymous with religious identification but with tragic Jewish history (*This Most Important Particle*, Warsaw: Czytelnik, 1982, p. 8).

Bibliography

Primary Sources

Zwiadowcy (Reconnoitering). 1965.
Tyle ognia wokoło (So Much Fire Around). 1979.
Jeden dzień (One Day). 1980.
Ta najważniejsza cząsteczka (This Most Important Particle). 1982.
Cesarski walc (Imperial Waltz). 1985.
Ocaleni (The Saved). 1986.
Strażnik świąt (The Guardian of Holidays). 1987.
Missing Pieces: Stories. 1990.

Secondary Sources

Błoński, Jan. "Autoportret żydowski." In *Biedni Polacy patrzą na getto*. Warszawa: Wydawnictwo Literackie, 1995, pp. 57–113.
Polonsky, Antony, and Monika Adamczyk-Garbowska. *Contemporary Jewish Writing in Poland: An Anthology*. Lincoln, Neb., and London: University of Nebraska Press, 2001.
Wróbel, Józef. *Tematy żydowskie w prozie polskiej 1939–1987*. Kraków: Universitas, 1991.

MARY BERG

(1924–)

SUSAN LEE PENTLIN

THE IMPACT OF Mary Berg on American knowledge of the Holocaust began on 19 April 1944. On that day, a crowd of thousands gathered at the Warsaw Synagogue in New York and marched to City Hall in commemoration of the first anniversary of the Warsaw Ghetto Uprising. Heading the marchers was the Wattenberg family, who had arrived in the United States as repatriates only four weeks earlier on a Swedish exchange ship. Mary had brought a diary of their experiences in the Warsaw ghetto in twelve small, spiral notebooks. With the help of S. L. Shneiderman (1906–1996), a Yiddish journalist who met her on arrival, she began immediately to rewrite the text of her notes, which she had kept in an abbreviated form. In the original, she obliquely referred to the Nazis throughout using "they" or other code words. She revised spellings and listed full names when she knew persons had perished or gave minor details to clarify what she had recorded.

In October and December of that year, Shneiderman published selected pages from the diary in English translation in *The Jewish Contemporary Record* and a Yiddish translation in *Der Morgn Zhurnal* (The Morning Journal), where Wattenberg's name was shortened to protect family members remaining in Europe. Her diary was among the first reports of the process used by the Germans to exterminate Jews in Poland with poisonous gas, although her knowledge of the death camps was not firsthand. She had learned about this in December 1942 from Dita W., a fellow Jewish inmate in Pawiak prison who had heard it directly from a camp official at Gestapo headquarters. In February 1945, L. B. Fischer published Berg's work in full as *Warsaw Ghetto: A Diary*. In a special edition of *Warsaw Ghetto: A Diary*, Joseph Thon, the president of the National Organization of Polish Jews, explained his urgency in making the diary known. He stated that the Germans had used gas and added: "It is therefore our duty to make known the horrible truth, to publicize documents and eyewitness accounts that reveal it beyond any doubt" (p. 5).

Life

Mary Berg was born in Lodz, in 1924, as Miriam Wattenberg. She and her younger sister, Anna (Ann), grew up in a prosperous home and attended the Polish Gymnasium on Piotrkowska Street. Her father, Stanley (Shya), was born in Pułtusk, Poland, and was an art and antiques dealer who belonged to an Orthodox synagogue. Her mother, Lena, an American citizen, had been born in New York, but had accompanied her Polish-born parents when they returned to Poland in 1914. Although this "American connection" probably did not play a large role in Mary's or her sister Anna's early years, that, of course, changed when the Germans invaded Poland. In the ghetto, the Wattenbergs were spared the worst of ghetto life, and ultimately survived because of family connections in America and Lena's citizenship.

The Diary

Berg's account of life in the Warsaw ghetto is the first detailed, eyewitness report published in English. The diary records Berg and her family's experiences in the ghetto from its establishment through the days of the Great Deportation in July 1942, when 300,000 Jews were marched to the *Umschlagplatz* for transport to Treblinka. She began writing in Lodz, in October 1939, giving a summary of her and her family's flight to Warsaw at the beginning of the German invasion. She made a few entries after the family returned to Lodz a few days later. However, in early November her father fled to Bialystok after being denounced by a neighbor and, in December, Berg and her sister returned to Warsaw where the family lived until the first major deportation from the ghetto began in July 1942.

She continued her entries after the family was interned in the Pawiak prison with other "foreigners" for eventual exchange with German citizens in America. Then, shortly before the first armed revolt in the ghetto on 18 January 1943, Berg and her family were sent to an internment camp in Vittel, France, where she continued to correspond with young friends who remained behind in Warsaw. She brought her account to its conclusion in March 1944 as the Wattenbergs sighted the skyscrapers of New York. It is important to note that her account not only ended, but it also appeared before the war in Europe was over, so neither she nor Shneiderman could know the full history of German crimes and of the "final solution." Nonetheless, the detail and accuracy of her diary are stunning and its authenticity is remarkable.

Berg lived a life of relative privilege in the ghetto as one of the "Golden Youth." Her family still had resources; they also had close connections with the *Judenrat*, and several friends and family members were members of the ghetto police. A young suitor's father was a member of the infamous underground organization of collaborationists in the ghetto known as the "13". Berg finished her education in a secret ghetto gymnasium and then won, with influence, a much sought-after place in the Graphic Arts School on Sienna Street run by the *Judenrat*. She performed theatrical reviews with a group of Lodz students known as the "Lodz Artistic Group" (LZT) and was active in the Youth Club of the House Committee in Sienna Street. She was recognized everywhere as the "American Girl" and felt a sense of protection from the American flag posted on their apartment door.

Berg also wrote from a unique perspective about ghetto life. Diary accounts of the ghettos are rare, especially those of young girls in Eastern Europe. Accounts of Warsaw by Chaim Kaplan, Emmanuel Ringelblum, Adam Czerniakow, and others are by men who had reached maturity and were considered successful members of the community. Young boys were expected either to care for their families or to go on forced labor. Berg was frustrated at her powerlessness and helplessness when Romek, her boyfriend, treated her like a child and consoled her by saying, "Little girl, it is good that you don't understand too much" (p. 92). She realized she did understand and could bear witness.

She was a sensitive young woman and her entries are a universal testimony of human suffering and a tribute to the human spirit. She could see beyond her privilege and describe with great compassion and simplicity the poverty, starvation, and fear she encountered in the standard community about her. In a May 1941 entry, she employed vivid prose and imagery to describe the hopelessness of life behind the ghetto walls:

> On the other side of the barbed wire spring holds full sway. From my window I can see young girls with bouquets of lilac walking on the "Aryan" part of the street. I can even smell the tender fragrance of the opened buds. But there is no sign of spring in the ghetto. Here the rays of the sun are swallowed up by the heavy gray pavement (p. 59).

She described how young people compensated by sitting at an outside garden cafe called "Bajka" or "Fairy tale" in Ogrowdowa Street and at a "beach" made of a few garden chairs (p. 61).

Filled with grief, she described the ghetto inhabitants and conditions. She wrote about "dreamers of bread" who sat outside of the food shops, "but their eyes no longer see the loaves that lie behind the glass, as though in some remote, inaccessible heaven" (p. 48). She felt anguish at the sight of starving children on the streets and reproached herself and others around her for their privilege. She expressed remorse over a hungry child in a refugee shelter she visited: "I was overcome by a feeling of utter shame. I had eaten that day, but I did not have a piece of bread for that child" (p. 69).

Looking about her in despair she rebuked the world, speaking perhaps as the "American girl": "Where are you, foreign correspondents? Why don't you come here and describe the sensational scenes of the ghetto? No doubt you don't want to spoil your appetite" (p. 87). From the Pawiak prison, she watched the deportations, and cried, "The whole ghetto is drowning in blood. . . . Why does no one come to our aid?" (p. 175). She wrote with bitterness about the fate she understood awaited the ghetto. Unlike other diarists of the ghetto, who had little hope they would survive, Berg had some hope as the daughter of an American. She was not writing a public account to be discovered after the ghetto was destroyed; she was keeping a private diary as a teenager, intended for herself and her friends, and perhaps as a memory to take with her of her friends and of the inhumanity she had seen. She often shared pages with her friends and they bought her diary notebooks for her birthday. She feared the impending separation from them and questioned, "Have I the right to save myself and leave my closest friends to their bitter fate?" (p. 162). Perhaps she changed her mind and agreed to publish the diary as a way to speak for them. As she explained in 1945, she wanted to "tell all who are still alive that I shall not forget them . . . those who were ground to ash, I shall always see them alive" (Elbaum, p. 24).

Critical Response

Warsaw Ghetto: A Diary was a best-seller in 1945 and Berg was interviewed by journalists and on the radio about her experiences. It became an alternate selection of the Book of the Month Club. The *Kirkus Review* recommended the diary and called it a "moving record of terrorism" (15 January 1945, p. 24) and the *Saturday Review* commented that it "bears the imprint of sincerity and authenticity" (3 March 1945, p. 35). In 1966, Marie Syrkin became one of the first literary critics to recognize its importance. In a study of key Holocaust diaries, she observed that "Mary Berg, less introspective and anguished than her elders, has a keen eye for detail. Perhaps because she is young, and healthy, biologically incapable of authentic despair, she has left extraordinarily vivid glimpses of life rather than the death of the ghetto" (Syrkin, p. 7). Since 1945 it has been published in seven languages. In 1986, *A Bouquet of Violets*, a play based on the diary, was performed in Warsaw. Recently, excerpts from the diary have appeared in documentary films, photo collections, histories, and anthologies of the ghetto diaries of children.

Bibliography

Primary Sources

"Pages from a Warsaw Diary." *Contemporary Jewish Record* 7 (October/December 1944): 497–510, 616–625.

Warsaw Ghetto: A Diary. 1945.

Dziennik z Getta Warszawskieg (Diary from the Warsaw Ghetto). 1983.

Secondary Sources

Bard, Mitchell G. *Forgotten Victims: The Abandonment of Americans in Hitler's Camps*. Boulder: Westview, 1994.

Berman, Adolf. "The Fate of the Children in the Warsaw Ghetto." In *The Catastrophe of European Jewry: Antecedents-History-Reflections: Selected Papers*. Edited by Yisrael Gutman and Livia Rothkirchen. New York: Ktav and Yad Vashem, n.d., 400–421.

Elbaum, Esther. "She Lived in the Warsaw Ghetto: An Interview with Mary Berg." *Hadassah Newsletter* (March–April 1945): 20–21.

Rosenthal, David. "The Unvanquished Sector of the Warsaw Ghetto: Its School System." *Jewish Frontier* 46, no. 4 (April 1979): 18–21.

Shulman, Abraham. *The Case of Hotel Polski*. New York: Holocaust Library, 1982.

Syrkin, Marie. "Diaries of the Holocaust." *Midstream* (May 1966): 3–20.

JOSEPH BERGER
(1945–)

EVA FOGELMAN

JOSEPH BERGER WAS born in Russia on 17 January 1945. His parents, Marcus and Rachel Berger, were both Holocaust survivors from Poland who fled east to Russia to escape the German invasion. Berger's mother fled Soviet-occupied Poland and spent most of the war in Lys'va in the Ural Mountains, where she met Marcus. Marcus was drafted into the Russian army after the Russians occupied eastern Poland. He fought in the infantry brigade and was then sent to work in a shoe factory. Joseph was born in 1945 and the Bergers succeeded in finding their way to a displaced persons camp near Berlin where a second son was born. The Bergers arrived in the United States on 3 March 1950; they settled on the Upper West Side of Manhattan and then moved to the Bronx.

Berger started his education at a Manhattan yeshiva (Jewish day school), and then attended Bronx High School of Science, the City College (B.A.) and Columbia University for a master's degree in journalism. Prior to starting a career in journalism, he taught English at a Bronx junior high school (1967 to 1971).

Before joining the *New York Times* in 1984, Mr. Berger worked as *Newsday*'s religion writer, where he was a three-time recipient of the Supple Award, the highest honor given by the Religion Newswriters Association. Berger also worked for the *New York Post*, covering such stories as the 1973 Yom Kippur War.

At the *New York Times*, Berger was a religion correspondent from 1985 to 1987, and national education correspondent from 1987 to 1990, a period when American school curricula were under attack as too European-focused. Between 1990 and 1993 (a contentious period) he covered New York City's schools and colleges, and was the recipient of the 1993 Education Writers Association award for exposing abuses in bilingual education. From 1993 until 1999 he was bureau chief of White Plains, New York, covering much of the state outside of New York City and Albany. Since September 1999 he has been a deputy education editor. Because of Berger's extensive Jewish knowledge, the *Times* often relies on him to write about Hasidim, Israel, and Jewish life in America. Berger is the author of *The Young Scientists* (1993), a study of the country's top science high school and its students; and a personal memoir, *Displaced Persons: Growing Up American after the Holocaust* (2001). He lives in Westchester with his wife Brenda, a clinical psychologist and psychoanalyst, and their daughter Annie.

Displaced Persons: Growing Up American after the Holocaust

Second generation voices have been heard in the literary sphere since 1965, when Menachem Rosensaft edited essays, short stories, and poems of the children born in the Bergen-Belsen displaced persons camp. A decade later, *Response: A Contemporary Jewish Review* devoted an issue to living after the Holocaust by sons and daughters of survivors who were then in their twenties. By the end of the 1970s, the openness of American society to confronting the effects of the destruction of European Jewry on children of survivors was crystalized in the seminal book of journalist Helen Epstein, *Children of the Holocaust: Conversations with Sons and Daughters of Survivors. Children of the Holocaust* helped catapult a heretofore invisible group to visibility and the second generation became a voice in American Jewish life.

At the beginning of the twenty-first century the publication of *Displaced Persons* is part of a burgeoning second-generation literary and artistic genre. This genre spans the gamut from fiction, poetry, autobiography, and biography of the survivor parent(s), to plays, films, music, visual art, and humor. Each creative endeavor of the second generation is a personal journey of mourning and self-exploration that often incorporates the theme of post-Auschwitz Jewish identity.

Joseph Berger's autobiography is interspersed with his mother's own written words and conversations about her experiences as a child in Poland, and her ordeals of survival after the German invasion. Her stories are replete with near-death encounters: she almost died serving a prison sentence of six months, and she nearly drowned when she had to push logs down a cold river. A Russian officer almost killed her when he asked her for half a loaf of bread. Like many other victims she miraculously survived typhus. Her direct testimony serves as an authentic rendition rather than one that is mediated. Berger's verbal and prolific mother is a stark contrast to his father's muteness. Berger feels that his father's "story will never be fleshed out. It will vanish like ashes and smoke" (*Displaced Persons*, Scribner, p. 340).

In Holocaust survivor families, the conversations (or the lack thereof) between the generations often differentiates them from nonsurvivor familial relations. Children of survivors never know when a parent will begin a conversation about the past, or if he or she will confront losses more directly. Thus, they often grapple with the degree to which to entice their parents to speak about the gory details of the past and about the people who were murdered.

Joseph Berger confronted such a dilemma. In 1981, when he attended the World Gathering of Holocaust Survivors with his parents in Jerusalem, he wanted them to enter information into the computer database that would enable them to search for missing relatives. He realized then, "I have forced her [his mother] to relive something painful" (p. 325). He adds, "For me, her search is a factoid of personal history. For her it is a brother she loved and never saw again" (p. 325). To Berger's surprise, his mother is relieved to have fulfilled her obligation. Berger became emotional when his silent father actually wrote a note looking for his six missing sisters. He was surprised to learn that his father was resourceful, and a risk-taker during the family's stay in a displaced-persons camp.

Berger does not whitewash the awkward incompatibility between his vivacious, upwardly mobile, educated mother and his painfully shy, quiet father—a man content with a factory job making shoes, and with mundane routines of daily life, such as polishing everyone's shoes on Sunday and enjoying a Sunday breakfast as a family. The reader feels that Marcus and Rachel's common goal of replacing losses equips them to transcend their individual differences. Joe Berger is spared being in a family that is marred by a "victim-oppressor" dynamic, or parents who cannot cope with daily life.

Unlike families whose response to the horrific losses destroyed any possibility of normalcy in parent-child relations or in the intimacy of spouses, the Berger family corresponds to the second generation probing biographies by literary critic Alan Berger ("Bearing Witness," 1998), who notices that most Holocaust survivor families "represent the triumph of hope over despair, while revealing a warm and healthy parent-child relationship" (p. 270). But he adds, "all of them have been touched by the Holocaust" (p. 270).

In *Displaced Persons*, Rachel's voice is replete with "hope over despair" (p. 270). Most blatant is the intergenerational dialogue between her and her son Joe. He asks her, "Ma, how do you explain that the survivors were able to go on after all they had been through?" She answers, "I know for me and my friends, the children probably helped us. Seeing you run around in the field outside the barracks with the other children of my friends gave me a kind of hope. You didn't know anything about what happened. You were just children exploring the world for the first time. You were another generation. There was something to look forward to. This gave me hope for the world, for myself" (p. 308).

Hope for the future cannot exist in a vacuum. It requires linkage to the life that was destroyed. What distinguishes Holocaust survivors as a group from other historically traumatized groups is how they embrace, reject, or deny their Jewish heritage. Illustrative of Alan Berger's observation that second generation texts show the contrast of orientations to the struggle with Jewish identity are the oppositional visions of Joseph Berger and Art Spiegelman. Unlike the author of *Maus*, who reads from the *Tibetan Book of the Dead* at his mother's funeral, an act some regard as an outward rejection of Jewish texts that are the core of Jewish ritual when observing life-cycle events, Joseph Berger is inspired to embrace Judaism when he observes his father's ability to keep his faith despite his anger with God for killing his parents and six sisters. Berger attends a liberal congregation but he stands next to his father at an Orthodox synogogue during Yom Kippur when all Jews ask, "Who shall live, and who shall die?"

Joseph Berger's Jewish identity is rooted in the Judaic covenant, whether he is attending a funeral of a survivor or his nephew's circumcision: "Triumph and pain are both worth tears, for so often they are indistinguishably mingled into each other." And he adds, "we are all part of that covenant and that covenant has survived through our tribe's history at some wrenching costs." Berger believes that newborns are "our continuation, our wistful stab at eternity. The covenant will go on as it has since Abraham" (pp. 336–337).

At times another identity, an occupational identity, is connected to growing up in the shadow of a historical trauma. Helping professionals of the second generation report feeling a heightened sense of empathy toward their survivor parents, which made it natural for them to choose their occupation. For others, a strong need to make a difference was the driving force. For Joseph Berger there is a link between writing and remembering his family history. He explains: "Reporting turned out to be no different from what I had been doing all my life—exploring, unearthing, inquiring, trying to figure out the boundaries and the rules and work within them" (p. 269). He adds, "I didn't realize it at the time but the detached attitude of my newly adopted vocation particularly suited me. I could be a comfortable part of this newspaper circle, yet elsewhere keep my habitual distance" (p. 269). Like others of the second generation, Berger learned to cope by distancing himself from overwhelming death imagery.

Joseph Berger attributes his interest in writing to being an immigrant. This universal theme of displaced persons finding refuge in America is one that most Americans can relate to personally or through a close contact. America is a country of displaced persons and their families.

Critical Reception

Berger's *Displaced Persons* has won critical acclaim. Elie Wiesel distinguished "this powerful and sweetly melancholic memoir," as a "brilliantly written . . . remarkable tribute not only to his parents but to an entire generation of Holocaust survivors who . . . succeeded in rebuilding their lives and dreams" (book flap). The narrative was described in the *New York Times* by novelist, essayist, and critic Jonathan Rosen as "a book that, built of small, remembered moments, manages to create an engaging portrait of a profoundly complex world" (p. E9). Mr. Rosen went on to say that "*Displaced Persons* is written with a high degree of self-awareness . . . parents and children take turns unmasking their inner identity to maintain a refugee family's hard-won harmony" (p. E9). Another reviewer in the *New York Times*, Thane Rosenbaum, a novelist, cultural essayist, and law professor praised "this important memoir" for "how unsparingly honest Berger is about the refugee condition." The account "is in part a conversation between mother and son, and includes several selections from the mother's memoir" (p. 28). Sandee Brawarsky, book critic of *Jewish Week*, described Rachel Berger as a fine storyteller whose excerpts are compelling.

Reviewers agree that there is something unique and moving about the Bergers adapting anew on Manhattan's Upper West Side and in the Bronx in the 1950s and 1960s as displaced refugees who succeed in restoring life. While much went unsaid, Rosenbaum is correct when he describes *Displaced Persons* as a "Holocaust-recovery" book.

Bibliography

Primary Sources

Displaced Persons: Growing Up American after the Holocaust. 2001.

The Young Scientists. 1993.

Secondary Sources

Berger, Alan L. *Children of Job: American Second-Generation Witnessess to the Holocaust.* Albany: State University of New York Press, 1997.

Berger, Alan L. "Bearing Witness: Theological Implications of Second Generation Literature." In *Breaking Crystal: Writing and Memory after Auschwitz.* Edited by Efraim Sicher. Urbana: University of Illinois Press, 1998, pp. 252–275.

Brawarsky, Sandee. "Refugee Status." Review of *Displaced Persons* by Joseph Berger. *Jewish Week*, 13 April 2001, 36.

Getlin, Josh. "Revealing the Struggles of Holocaust Survivors in U.S." Review of *Displaced Persons* by Joseph Berger. *Los Angeles Times*, 15 July 2001, A5.

Helman, Scott W. "*Displaced Persons* Is a Moving Survival Tale." Review of *Displaced Persons* by Joseph Berger. *The Boston Globe*, 3 May 2001, E2.

Rosen, Jonathan. "A Boy Dodges Shadows in a Sunny New Land." Review of *Displaced Persons* by Joseph Berger. *New York Times*, 18 April 2001, E9.

Rosenbaum, Thane. "The Shadow of the Holocaust: The Child of Polish Jews Who Survived the Nazis Recalls Life as a Refugee." Review of *Displaced Persons* by Joseph Berger. *New York Times Book Review*, 6 May 2001, 28.

Rosensaft, Menachem, ed. *Bergen-Belsen Youth Magazine.* New York: World Federation of Bergen-Belsen Associations, 1965.

Sicher, Efraim. *Breaking Crystal: Writing and Memory after Auschwitz.* Urbana and Chicago: Illinois University Press, 1998.

THOMAS BERNHARD

(1931–1989)

RUTH A. STARKMAN

THOMAS BERNHARD, THE prolific Austrian author of over seventy novels, plays, short stories, and verse, was born out of wedlock on 9 February 1931 in Heerland, Netherlands, to Austrian parents. Never having met his carpenter father, Alois Zuckerstätter, who died in 1943, Bernhard grew up in the Austria of the 1930s and 1940s, sometimes with his mother Herta Bernhard, her husband Emil Fabjan, and Bernhard's half-brother and sister, but largely under the aegis of his beloved grandfather, the little-known Austrian writer Johannes Freumbichler, and his long-time companion, Anna Bernhard. Freumbichler inspired in the young Bernhard a distrust for institutions, especially Catholicism and Austrian politics, and fostered instead a great devotion to art and culture. From 1949 to 1951 Bernhard spent two years in a sanatorium, because of a bad lung infection that had developed into tuberculosis. After working as a journalist for the Salzburg newspaper the *Demokratisches Volksblatt* from 1952 to 1955, Bernhard studied music and drama at the prestigious Salzburg Mozarteum from 1955 to 1957. He wrote poetry, short dramas, and prose before the success of his first novel, *Frost*, in 1963. From 1965 Bernhard lived and wrote at his small, rural estate in Ohlsdorf, Upper Austria. He died 12 February 1989 of complications of lung disease.

Controversy

A highly controversial writer even more than a decade after his death, Bernhard continues to elude categorization. His scathing attacks on Austria for its National Socialist past made him infamous among his countrymen and women and generated numerous public scandals. The most notorious scandal surrounded his last play, *Heldenplatz* (1988), a drama about the demise of an Austrian-Jewish family that returns to Austria in the 1950s only to find the country more antisemitic than before the *Anschluss*, the annexation of Austria to Nazi Germany in 1938. Commissioned in 1988 in honor of the one-hundredth anniversary of Austria's national theater, the Burgtheater, *Heldenplatz* also coincided with Austria's official efforts to commemorate the fiftieth anniversary of the *Anschluss*. Though the text was supposed to be kept secret prior to its premiere, the play's most injurious vilifications were leaked to the press. Text quoted out of context asserted that Austria was a sewer, that all Viennese were fascists and antisemites, that, among myriad personal attacks, "[t]he Bundespraesident [Waldheim] is a liar . . ." (*Heldenplatz. Eine Dokumentation*, p. 10). A near-public brawl ensued filling the pages of local and international newspapers for weeks on end. Many similar, smaller scandals brewed around other Bernhard texts that refer to Austria's Nazi past. Yet, for all his love of scandal and for his relentless tirade of insults on his fellow countrymen, Bernhard can hardly be called a committed political writer or one with a social conscience in the same manner as the generation of young German and Austrian writers who belonged to the student movement of the late 1960s and early 1970s. (Gerd Fuchs, "Selbstverstümmelung als Kunst," and the debate which ensued in the leftist magazine *konkret* 1971.)

For this reason, there are two prevailing receptions of Bernhard. His Austrian public at large sees him as a political gadfly eager for self-promotion who indulges in a kind of national *Nestbeschmützung* (dirtying of the nest), a writer who could not say enough bad things about his native land. His literary public, on the other hand, views Bernhard as a philosophical writer whose love-hate relationship with Austria plays a subordinate role to his formalist artistic project. The latter designation arises from the author's trademark musical style of cascading words and endless sentences and paragraphs as well as his highly internal themes:

aesthetic ruminations on art, the musicality of language, and tragicomic existential dilemmas. At once minimalist and modernist—a style that has Bernhard often compared to Samuel Beckett—and full of Austrian Baroque melancholy, Bernhard's writing also obsessively invokes the great thinkers of the European tradition such as Michel de Montaigne, Blaise Pascal, Immanuel Kant, Friedrich Nietzsche, Ludwig Wittgenstein, and especially Arthur Schopenhauer, though without ever engaging in a substantive philosophical debate. Such constant reference to philosophical thinkers proves inherently contradictory in Bernhard's work: where it enables the author to claim a cultural affinity outside of Austria, it also articulates a perpetually frustrated longing for a transcendent culture.

For Bernhard's protagonists, who often speak in first person and resemble himself, the search for transcendence usually leads to suffering and disappointment. His early most famous novels, *Frost* (1963), *Verstörung* (*Gargoyles*, 1967), *Das Kalkwerk* (*The Lime Works*, 1970), and *Korrektur* (*Correction*, 1975), present obsessive characters who must in some way or another confront the failure of their artistic, philosophical, and scientific projects. In these works, Austria is the setting, but the country's history exerts, if at all, an indirect influence on the action, functioning as a sort of submerged psychic landscape.

It is only after *Die Ursache. Eine Andeutung* (*An Indication of the Cause*, 1975), in which Bernhard relates his experiences growing up in Austria and attending a school run by the Nazis, that his prose addresses the National Socialist past directly and at length. Relating his sufferings as a young teenager at the hands of National Socialist and Catholic teachers, Bernhard asserts an unmistakable continuity between Austria's past and present. He describes how at the end of the war a crucifix replaced the picture of Hitler that had hung on the wall for twelve years. So blatantly seamless was this transition, according to Bernhard, that the school leadership did not bother to paint over the white rectangle on the wall where Hitler's portrait had been.

The Eve of Retirement and *The German Lunch Table*

The drama *Vor dem Ruhestand* (*The Eve of Retirement*, 1979) was the first theater piece on Nazism that Bernhard wrote for a longtime collaborator, the German director Claus Peymann. This play depicts a fictional former Nazi judge and his two sisters, who celebrate their yearly ritual of Himmler's birthday. The brother, Rudolf, and his one sister, Vera, also an old Nazi, reminisce about the past as they torture their socialist, crippled sister, Clara. A wickedly comic farce, *The Eve of Retirement* aims to rile public discussion about those whom Bernhard calls "Nazi fossils" (interview, *Der Spiegel*). Though Bernhard, typically cagey in interviews, tries to generalize the notion of the Nazi fossil, he also concedes that the piece refers to a particular judge in the German state of Baden-Württemberg, Hans Karl Filbinger. Filbinger was not only an example of Germany's many erstwhile Nazis who resumed power after the war, but he was notorious in 1979 for having defended death sentences he administered in the Nazi courts, declaring "what was then right, cannot be wrong now."

Rather than embarking on a concrete discussion of lingering Nazi elements in Germany and Austria's institutional infrastructures, *The Eve of Retirement* depicts the interior life of these "Nazi fossils," showing a private familial hell, full of psychic and physical torture, incest, and self-destruction. As Bernhard's Nazi character Rudolf propounds his Nazi ideas, nostalgic for days when he could more openly express his true beliefs, the play holds up a distorted mirror to the public. On the one hand, *The Eve of Retirement* shows characters whose fascist ideals cause them to say and do absurdly harmful things to each other; on the other, many of the Nazi statements are strikingly familiar comments one could hear on a contemporary German or Austrian street.

Bernhard elaborates on this idea of everyday Nazism in his series of short dramas *Der deutsche Mittagstisch* (*The German Lunch Table*), written between 1981 and 1988, which dramatizes the theme of the enduring presence of National Socialism in Germany and Austria among the entire population—from the highest elites to the most humble citizens. Bernhard's dark, violent, sometimes comic world in these theater pieces resembles that of his previous, less historically embedded fictional universes, only now the source of destruction is unambiguously linked to the National Socialist past.

Extinction and *Heldenplatz*

Bernhard's longest novel, *Auschlöschung* (*Extinction*, 1985) and his final play, *Heldenplatz*, continue his extended meditation of the sources of human destruction and their historic specificity in Austria. *Extinction*, considered by some as Bernhard's magnum opus, presents a first-person narrative of Franz-Josef Murau, the intellectual black sheep of a powerful Austrian land-owning family, who lives in Rome in self-imposed exile. Having sworn never to set foot in Austria again, he receives a telegram informing him of the death of his parents and brother in a car crash. Murau must go back to the family estate, Wolfsegg, and decide its fate. Written in two parts, *Extinction* rambles through Murau's memories of Wolfsegg as he stands at his window, in counterpoint to his return to Austria. Jumbled amid Murau's ruminations on music, art, philosophy, and the German language are stinging attacks on Austria's unacknowledged past. As the novel's protagonist prepares to visit the survivor Schermaier, he conceives of a book called *Extinction.* "It's my duty," Murau affirms when he decides to write about "the National Socialist criminals whose crimes are never mentioned today, having been hushed up for so many years" (*Extinction*, p. 230). Reflecting a bit further on the nature of a postwar Austrian society living in such denial of the past, Murau asserts, "this state is like my family, devoted to Nazi criminality"(p. 231).

Similar in its assertions about Austria, *Heldenplatz* begins with the suicide of the family patriarch, Professor Josef Schuster, who has killed himself because he could no longer stand contemporary Austria, which was "much worse than fifty years ago" (*Heldenplatz*, p. 11). While the dead professor's reflections on life and art in Austria are related through his family members and maids, his daughters' own contributions present two Jewish perspectives in contemporary Austria: One sees all Austrians as crypto-fascists, whereas the other is so desperate to assimilate she makes excuses for the Viennese who spit on her in the street. Meanwhile, the professor's brother, Robert, also a professor, assails every institution of government and culture in Vienna. All this storm and stress against their fellow Austrians, however, merely betray that their days in Vienna are numbered. For the Schuster family lives in an apartment overlooking the very public square where Hitler announced his annexation of Austria to crowds of cheering Austrians in 1938. Since the end of the war the Austrian public has disavowed these cheers, aided in its selective memory by an equally selective quote from the Moscow Declaration of 1943—saying that Austria was "the first free nation to fall victim to Hitlerite aggression." The phantom Austrian cheers now ring in the ears of Schuster's widow, returning with ever-greater ferocity until the final scene in which they become audible to the audience, rendering explicit for the characters as well as the public the unmistakable presence of Nazism in Austria.

While the reception of *Heldenplatz* and its intervention in the process of public memory in Austria remain without a doubt the play's most important aspects, thematically, it, like many other Bernhard narratives, is about the demise of an individual. In addition to all of its strategically placed attacks on Austria and Vienna, the play also tells the story of an "exactitude fanatic," who terrorizes his housekeeper for not properly folding his shirts, and for whom the imperfect world becomes too much to bear. As such, *Heldenplatz* presents itself both as a work about subjective crisis and as a public event, which records the battle for the soul of Austria in the wake of the Waldheim scandal and on the end of its year of remembrance.

Having written about the National Socialist past in Austria eschewing concrete, sociological, or historical detail in favor of ad hominem attack on his country, Thomas Bernhard presents himself as no sober, somber "Holocaust writer" in the sense of someone who adds to public understanding of the National Socialist destruction of European Jewry. Instead, his forte was hyperbolic provocation, as can be seen from such dramatic assertions as "Austria is nothing other than a stage upon which everything is rotten, murdered, and decayed . . ." and the like (*Heldenplatz. Eine Dokumentation*, p. 10). Public reaction often missed the essence of Bernhard's highly subjective narratives, but they nevertheless generated, and continue to generate, important discussions about Austrian antisemitism and the country's National Socialist past.

Bibliography

Primary Sources

Auf der Erde und in der Holle. Gedichte (On Earth and in Hell: Poems). 1957.

In Hora Mortis. 1958.

Unter dem Eisen des Mondes. Gedichte (Under the Iron Moon: Poems). 1958.

Die Rosen der Einöde. Fünf Saezte für Ballet, Stimmen und Orchester (The Roses of the Wasteland: Five Movements for Ballet, Voices and Orchestra). 1959.

Frost (Frost). 1963.

Amras. 1964.

Verstörung (*Gargoyles*). 1967.

Ungenach. Erzaehlung (Ungenach: A Narrative). 1968.

An der Baumgrenze. Erzaehlungen (At the Treeline: Stories). 1969.

Ereignisse (Incidents). 1969.

Watten. ein Nachlass (Watten: A Bequest). 1969.

Ein Fest für Boris (*A Party for Boris*). 1970.

Das Kalkwerk: Roman (*The Lime Works* [novel]). 1970.

Der Italiener (The Italian). 1971.

Gehen (Going). 1971.

Midland in Stilfs. Drei Erzaehlungen (Midland in Stilfs: Three Stories). 1971.

Der Ignorant und der Wahnsinnige (The Ignorant and the Crazy). 1972.

Der Kulterer. Eine Filmgeschichte (Der Kulterer: A Filmstory). 1974.

Die Jagdgesellschaft (The Hunting Party). 1974.

Die Macht der Gewohnheit (*The Force of Habit*). 1974.

Die Ursache. Eine Andeutung (*An Indication of the Cause*). 1975.
Korrektur. Roman (*Correction: A Novel*). 1975.
Der Präsident (*The President*). 1975.
Die Berühmten (The Famous Ones). 1976.
Der Keller. Eine Entziehung (*The Cellar: A Withdrawal*). 1976.
Der Wetterfleck. Erzaehlungen (The Weather-Spot: Stories). 1976.
Minetti. Ein Porträt des Künstlers als alter Mann (Minetti: Potrait of the Artist as an Old Man). 1977.
Der Atem. Eine Entscheidung (*The Breath: A Decision*). 1978.
Immanuel Kant (Immanuel Kant). 1978.
Ja (*Yes*). 1978.
Prosa (Prose). 1978.
Der Stimmenimitator (*The Voice Imitator*). 1978.
Vor dem Ruhestand. Eine Komödie von deutscher Seele (*The Eve of Retirement*). 1979.
Der Weltverbesserer (The World-Improver). 1979.
Die Billigesser (*The Cheap-Eaters*). 1980.
Am Ziel (At the Goal). 1981.
Die Kaelte. Eine Isolation (*The Cold: An Isolation*). 1981.
Ave Vergil. Gedichte (Ave Vergil: Poems). 1981.
Über allen Gipfeln ist Ruh. (A reference to a Goethe poem of the same name, commonly translated as Wanderer's/Wayfarer's Night Song II, or literally, Above All Peaks is Peace). 1981.
Beton (*Concrete*). 1982.
Ein Kind (*A Child*). 1982.
Wittgensteins Neffe. EineFreundschaft (*Wittgenstein's Nephew: A Friendship*). 1982.
Der Untergeher (*The Loser*). 1983.
Der Schein trügt (Appearances Are Deceiving). 1983.
Ritter, Dene, Voss. 1984.
Der Theatermacher (The Impressario). 1984.
Holzfaellen. Eine Erregung. (*Woodcutters*). 1984.
Alte Meister. Komodie (*Old Masters: A Comedy*). 1985.
Auslöschung. Ein Zerfall (*Extinction: A Novel*). 1986.
Einfach kompliziert (Simply Complicated). 1986.
Elisabeth II. Keine Komödie (Elizabeth II: No Comedy). 1987.
Der deutsche Mittagstisch. Dramolette. (*The German Lunch Table*). 1988.
Heldenplatz. 1988.
In der Hohe: Rettungsversuch, Unsinn (On the Mountain, Rescue Attempt, Nonsense). 1989.

Secondary Sources

Botond, Anneliese. *Über Thomas Bernhard.* Frankfurt am Main: Suhrkamp, 1970.
Dittmar, Jens, ed. *Thomas Bernhard: Werkgeschichte.* 2nd. ed. Frankfurt am Main: Suhrkamp, 1990.
Donnenberg, Josef. *Thomas Bernhard und Osterreich: Studien zu Werk und Wirkung 1970–1989.* Stuttgart: Hans-Dieter Heinz, 1997.
Dowden, Stephen D. *Understanding Thomas Bernhard.* Columbia: University of South Carolina Press, 1991.
Durhammer, Ilija, and Pia Janke, eds. *Der "Heimatdichter" Thomas Bernhard.* Vienna: Holzhausen, 1999.
Holler, Hans. *Kritik einer literarischen Form: Versuch über Thomas Bernhard.* Stuttgart: Akademischer Verlag Heinz, 1979.
Schmidt-Dengler, Wendelin. *Der Übertreibungskünstler: Studien zu Thomas Bernhard.* Second, expanded edition. Vienna: Sonderzahl, 1989.

Interviews, Archives, and Other Writings

Andre Mueller im Gespraech mit Thomas Bernhard. Weitra: Bibliothek der Provinz, 1992.
Aus dem Gerichtssaal: Thomas Bernhards Salzburg in den 50er Jahren. Edited by Jens Dittmar. Vienna: Edition S, 1992.
Thomas Bernhard. Eine Begegnung. Gespraeche mit Krista Fleischmann. Vienna: Edition S, 1991.
Thomas Bernhard, Karl Ignaz Hennetmair. Ein Briefwechsel 1965–1974, with commentary from Peter Bader in cooperation with Karl Ignaz Hennetmair. Weitra: Bibliothek der Provinz, 1994.
Von einer Katastrophe in die andere 13 Gesprache mit Thomas Bernhard. Edited by Sepp Dreissinger. Weitra: Bibliothek der Provinz, 1992.
Interview, *Der Spiegel* 26 (1980).
Lavant, Christine, ed. *Gedichte. Thomas Bernhard.* Frankfurt am Main: Suhrkamp, 1988.

Bruno Bettelheim
(1903–1990)

PAUL MARCUS

Bruno Bettelheim was born in Vienna to upper-middle-class assimilated Jewish parents, Pauline and Anton Bettelheim, on 28 August 1903. Though born when the Hapsburgs still ruled the Austro-Hungarian empire, Bettelheim grew up during the age of Freud. By age fourteen he was already voraciously reading in psychoanalysis, an angle of vision that was to inform his later writings on survivorship and the Holocaust. Bettelheim received his doctoral degree in philosophy and psychology from the University of Vienna in 1938. Soon after, he was incarcerated for approximately one year, as a Jewish political prisoner in two punishment-oriented concentration camps, Dachau and Buchenwald. Bettelheim was released in 1939 thanks to the intervention of Gov. Herbert Lehman of New York and Eleanor Roosevelt.

Life after the Holocaust

Bettelheim was married twice. His first marriage, to Gina Alstadt, ended in divorce. He married his second wife, Gertrude Weinfed, also from Vienna, prior to coming to the United States. She died in 1984 and Bettelheim was deeply saddened over her death. They had three children: Eric, Naomi, and Ruth.

After his liberation from the camps, Bettelheim eventually joined the faculty of the University of Chicago, where he taught until he retired in 1973. It was in 1944, on the grounds of the University of Chicago, that Bettelheim became the director of the Sonia Shankman Orthogenic School, which, under his direction, became a world renowned center for the treatment of disturbed children and adolescents, especially autistic children.

Unquestionably, like most survivors, Bettelheim was traumatized by his incarceration, which left its negative imprint on his personal life, his gruff interpersonal style, and, at times, his intellectual outlook, as shown by his insensitive and judgmental remarks about Anne Frank and Jewish group behavior during the Holocaust. However, Bettelheim's incarceration was also a source of tremendous creativity and moral insight. One of his first articles, "Individual and Mass Behavior in Extreme Situations," which was based on his experiences in Dachau and Buchenwald, received international attention and praise. As a traumatized survivor, Bettelheim's writing to some extent emanated from his need to "work through" his own camp experiences.

Bettelheim's incarceration was in part the basis for his new concept of treatment of severely troubled children and adolescents at the Orthogenic School, that is, milieu therapy. Milieu therapy includes using the entire staff, at all times, for therapeutic interactions that are part of the child's overall treatment, rather than restricting treatment to a few isolated hours with an individual therapist. According to Bettelheim's friend and colleague, Rudolf Ekstein, the Orthogenic School was a concentration camp in reverse. In a concentration camp, the inmates, the observers, and the persecutors could enter, but for the inmates there was no escape. At the Orthogenic School, the door was closed to outsiders such as curious intruders and parents, but it was always open to the children on the inside. Although this allowed the children to run away, most of the time they would return (Ekstein, 1991, p. 1080). Moreover, at the Orthogenic School the children ate from china plates and lived in a home that was attractive and comfortable by any standards for institutions. The children also had easy access to a cupboard that was always stocked with candies and snacks.

In 1990, at the age of 86, Bettelheim killed himself by asphyxiation while living in a retirement home. This event was shocking to the public, and in the popular press it was often interpreted as a sign of Bettelheim's personal weakness and mental illness; however, Bettelheim's suicide followed a series of personal setbacks that are, perhaps, more plausible explanations. His wife, Gertrude, died in 1984; he had suffered strokes, illnesses, and declining strength that prevented him from living a productive and meaningful intellectual life; he had strained relations with one of his three children; and he had sought treatment for a recent bout of depression. Bettelheim's decision to kill himself was entirely in sync with those core values that animated his notion of survivorship, such as his emphasis on personal autonomy and self-respect, especially in an extreme situation such as his experience in the concentration camp. It seems Bettelheim's horizon of meaning, his capacity for love and work, had dried up, and this may have led to his decision to commit suicide. In this context, Bettelheim's suicide is the ultimate affirmation of his belief that both inside and outside the concentration camp, personal autonomy and self-respect as manifested by one's capacity to create and live a meaningful life, are to be valued more than mere physical survival. It is not by chance that Bettelheim was always more interested in how concentration camp inmates "remained human" against all odds, than in how they physically survived. The latter, he thought, depended on the Nazis and was more a matter of luck than anything else.

Maintaining Autonomy in the Concentration Camp and the Mass Society

Bettelheim's provocative and controversial theory of behavior in the concentration camp is widely regarded as one of the most influential narratives to date on this topic. As Christian Fleck and Albert Müller have written, Bettelheim "undoubtedly numbers among the most important and influential analysts of the Nazi concentration camps." His work on the camps has "the status of a 'classic text' " (Fleck and Müller, pp. 28–29). However, before examining Bettelheim's extraordinary contribution to the understanding of the psychology of the camp inmates, readers need to put this work in the wider cultural perspective that was always his main focus.

Throughout his writings, Bettelheim has been concerned with how the mass society has a tendency to undermine people's struggle to maintain a sense of autonomy and integration. By the term *mass society*, Bettelheim means the highly organized, bureaucratized, technological society in which individuals' capacities to make decisions (that is, to be autonomous) about matters that are of deep concern to them are subverted, if not totally eliminated. Moreover, when individuals lose their ability to make decisions, their personal integration is also greatly diminished. Personal integration refers to the sense that the different parts of oneself are combined, organized, and working together as a complex whole. It is this potentially destructive tendency in mass society and its negative impact on autonomy and integration that Bettelheim tries to illuminate.

Bettelheim suggests that there is a fundamental progression between the depersonalizing effect of technological mass society (that is, impersonal bureaucracy, the trend-setting media, and intrusive surveillance); the total mass state, such as Nazi Germany; and, most importantly, the concentration camps. Bettelheim saw that if the dehumanizing tendency in mass society is not contained, it could evolve into a total mass state that is capable of using concentration camps to crush the individual's autonomy and integration. This development Bettelheim calls the "concentration camp society" (*Freud's Vienna and Other Essays*, New York: Knopf, 1990, p. 232). Bettelheim points out that the main purpose of the concentration camps reached far beyond their being a place where the SS took revenge on its enemies or made them slaves: "The concentration camp was the Gestapo's laboratory for subjecting free men, but especially the most ardent foes of the Nazi system, to the process of disintegration from their position as autonomous individuals" (*Surviving and Other Essays*, New York: Knopf, 1979, pp. 82–83). Thus, he thought concentration camps (as opposed to death camps, which were never his focus in his theory) should be studied by anyone concerned with comprehending what happens to a population when it is subject to the methods of the Nazi system of power.

For this reason Bettelheim says that if people understand what happens to the individual in the concentration camp, how autonomy and integration are destroyed, then they may acquire a better grasp of "both an oppressive mass society, and what it takes to remain autonomous in any mass society" (*The Informed Heart: Autonomy in a Mass Age*, Glencoe, IL: The Free Press, 1960, p. 107).

Critics of Bettelheim have frequently forgotten that for Bettelheim, the concentration camp was an extreme version of the dangers embedded in the modern mass society, the latter being what was always his main interest. That is, Bettelheim wanted to know what were the necessary inner developments, the higher personality integration as he called it, that individuals required as a counterpoint to progress, to the growing complexity of social and technological development.

Psychology of the Concentration Camp Inmate

In light of the Nazi aim of breaking the inmates' autonomy and integration, Bettelheim's (and by extension most other inmates') main goal in the concentration camp was "to survive in ways that would protect my physical and moral existence," that is, "retaining [my] humanity" (*The Informed Heart*, pp. 13, 156). Elsewhere, he explains that his main worry besides being killed was that after liberation he would not be the same person he was before he lost his freedom.

Bettelheim suggests that there was a dialectical tension, or two primary poles, that characterized surviving in the concentration camps. Inmates throughout their ordeal had to choose, in the morally ambiguous and shifting circumstances of the camps, the course they would follow. They could survive in a manner that generally reflected autonomy, integration, and humanity (as Jehovah's Witnesses, devout Jews and Christians, and, with qualifications, militant Marxists), or in a manner that did not reflect these qualities. The latter group gradually regressed, their pre-incarceration personalities progressively disintegrated, and they eventually identified with the Nazis and adopted a "survival at any price" attitude. These "old prisoners," says Bettelheim, had lost any orientation to the world outside the concentration camp. Bettelheim believed that inmates struggled within the two poles of this dialectical tension, and, furthermore, their attitudes continuously changed, depending on the circumstances in which they found themselves. Moreover, despite what his critics have alleged, Bettelheim never described these two poles as rigid categories; he was well aware that such a nomenclature of inmates was only meant to illustrate certain types of behaviors, and in reality most inmates had to function somewhere within the dialectical tension, what Primo Levi has called "the gray zone" (*The Drowned and the Saved*, New York: Summit, 1986, p. 58). As Bettelheim made quite clear many times, identification with the Nazis was neither inevitable nor a universal response of all inmates. As he wrote, "nearly all prisoners made common cause against the SS most of the time" (*Surviving and Other Essays*, p. 289); "all prisoners hated the Nazi regime, even if and when, without knowing it, they had taken some of its values for their own" (*The Informed Heart*, p. 202).

For those inmates who were more capable of maintaining their autonomy, integration, and humanity in the camps, a number of complex and interrelated modes of thought and action constituted their existence. Most important, Bettelheim emphasizes the critical function of passionately felt and flexibly applied consistent values and moral convictions and a strong, transcendent belief system. Bettelheim noted, as have Primo Levi, Jean Améry and Elie Wiesel, that "It is a well-known fact of the concentration camps that those who had a strong religious and moral conviction managed life there much better than the rest. . . . Deeply religious persons often helped others, and some voluntarily sacrificed themselves—many more of them than of the average prisoners" (*Surviving and Other Essays*, p. 296).

By virtue of their strongly held transcendent values and beliefs, autonomous inmates also tended to have a greater degree of freedom in choosing their attitudes toward their ordeals, such decision making being vital to maintaining a sense of agency, reducing degradation, and maintaining a semblance of their pre-incarceration personalities. These inmates also had a greater ability to maintain some areas of independent action and thought, as well as to develop meaningful relationships, relatively speaking, in the camps. In other words, for Bettelheim, autonomy, integration, and the inmates' humanity were both protected and expressed in the inmates' effort via their transcendent values and beliefs to sustain inner freedom while outwardly adapting.

Bettelheim's main purpose in studying the concentration camps was to understand what were the necessary psychological conditions to avoid personality disintegration and to remain human and how this could be applied to the mass society. Bettelheim summarizes his conclusion:

> But most of all, as I have intimated all along, autonomy, self-respect, inner integration, a rich inner life, and the ability to relate to others in meaningful ways were the psychological conditions which, more than any others, permitted one to survive in the camps as much a whole human being as overall conditions and chance would permit (*Surviving and Other Essays*, p. 109).

For Bettelheim, it was those inmates who lived not simply for life's sake but who had a religious or cultural ideal that transcended them, who were more likely to survive as autonomous persons in the camps.

The Critics

While Bettelheim's early work served as a point of departure for the expressions of fundamental positions pertaining to the nature of survivorship, and while his books attracted worldwide attention, Bettelheim was severely criticized by Holocaust scholars for a number of reasons. Many of these criticisms were overstated, unfair, or simply wrong, in part due to the fact that Bettelheim was disliked because he was frequently judgmental, unnecessarily provocative, abrasive, and, at times, historically inaccurate about very sensitive and complex subjects, such as the so-called Jewish passivity and cooperation with the Nazis, "ghetto thinking," and Anne Frank. Helen Fein (1980) has written a powerful, scholarly critique of Bettelheim's tendency toward near victim blaming, though there are important psychological insights embedded in Bettelheim's provocative analyses of these issues.

Bettelheim was also criticized for a number of other reasons. These include: (1) the implausibility of his concentration camp/mass society analogy (Des Pres, p. 190); (2) an account of survivorship that was distorted and demeaning, that is, his use of a reductionistic psychoanalytic framework and, in particular, his claim that some inmates regressed, became part of the anonymous mass without social base and organization, and identified with their Nazi captors (Des Pres, p. 185); (3) his lack of appreciation of political structures, social hierarchy and the duality of action in his camp narrative (Sofsky, pp. 96–163; Smith, pp. 94–97); (4) his overly individualistic focus and emphasis on self-assertion (Pfefferkorn, p. 676); and (5) for drawing general conclusions about inmate behavior that failed to respect the difference between an "extreme" situation, where the main Nazi goal was punishment and "reeducation" of inmates (in the concentration camps), and a "terminal" one, where the main goal was the extermination of inmates (in death camps) (Langer, p. 33).

Bettelheim's insightful description of the disintegration of dignity and personality in the concentration camps and its meaning for the modern dilemma of maintaining autonomy and integration in the mass society is an original and lasting contribution to the field of Holocaust studies. While Bettelheim was a brilliant, bold, and enormously gifted writer and social essayist on the camps, his work is perhaps best understood as the testimonial of a man who viewed himself, above all else, as a pained Jewish survivor. It is telling that although he did not observe Jewish religious practices, he asked that his family give him a religious burial. Even more uncanny and suggestive, 13 March, the day Bettelheim killed himself, was the same day as the Anschluss (annexation of Austria by Germany).

Bibliography

Primary Sources

"Individual and Mass Behavior in Extreme Situations." 1943.
The Informed Heart: Autonomy in a Mass Age. 1960.
Surviving and Other Essays. 1979.
Freud's Vienna and Other Essays. 1990.

Secondary Sources

Des Pres, Terrence. *The Survivor: An Anatomy of Life in the Death Camps*. New York: Pocket Books, 1977.

Ekstein, Rudolf. "Bruno Bettelheim (1903–1990)." *American Psychologist* (October 1991): 1080.

Fein, Helen. "Beyond the Heroic Ethic." *Culture and Society* (March/April 1980): 51–55.

Fleck, Christian, and Albert Müller. "Bruno Bettelheim and the Concentration Camps." *Journal of the History of the Behavioral Sciences* 33, no. 1 (Winter 1997): 1–37.

Langer, Lawrence L. *Versions of Survival. The Holocaust and the Human Spirit*. Albany: State University of New York, 1982.

Marcus, Paul. *Autonomy in the Extreme Situation. Bruno Bettelheim, the Nazi Concentration Camps and the Mass Society*. Westport, Conn.: Praeger, 1999.

Pfefferkorn, Eli. "The Case of Bruno Bettelheim and Lina Wertmuller's *Seven Beauties*." *Proceedings of the Fourth Yad Vashem International Historical Conference. Jerusalem, January 1980*. Jerusalem: Yad Vashem, 1984, 663–681.

Smith, Charles W. *A Critique of Sociological Reasoning*. Oxford, U.K.: Blackwell, 1979.

Sofsky, Wolfgang. *The Order of Terror: The Concentration Camp*. Princeton, N.J.: Princeton University Press, 1997.

ABRAHAM BIDERMAN

(1924–)

SIMONE GIGLIOTTI

PUBLISHED TO COMMEMORATE the author's fiftieth year of liberation from Bergen-Belsen, Abraham Biderman's *The World of My Past* is a searing portrait of Jewish responses to the Nazi occupation of Poland in World War II. Born in 1924 in Lodz, Poland, Biderman endured almost five years of ghettoization in Lodz (1940–1944) before his deportation to Auschwitz-Birkenau, followed by subsequent internment in the camps of Althammer and Dora, and liberation in Bergen-Belsen. After learning of the loss of his father, Shimon Dov, mother, Fradl, and brother, Lipek, in the Holocaust, Biderman and his cousin fled to Belgium disguised as American soldiers. It was there that Biderman met his future wife, Madeleine, with whom he emigrated to Australia in 1949.

The Holocaust memories that accompanied Biderman to Australia are the starting point from which to view *The World of My Past.* Although Biderman has been geographically removed from the European "world of my past" for almost fifty years, his formative years in Poland retain an indelible and energizing resonance that guides the narrative's unfolding. The themes of geography, landscape, and travel common in many Holocaust memoirs achieve a rare complexity in Biderman's depiction of ghetto life. Its distinctness lies in the use of images of "the everyday experience" during Nazi occupation to form a narrative of hope and perseverance, but ultimately powerlessness. Since Biderman spent most of his war years in the Lodz ghetto, that location serves as the principal site of experiences in the narrative.

Biderman writes of the daily existence of his family in the Lodz ghetto, the "choiceless choices" that confronted them and the Jewish *Sonderkommando*—the wartime labor force exploited by the Nazis. He paints a moving portrait of Lodz ghetto residents as a community-in-waiting for deportation. Biderman's most historically valuable comments concern the problematic figure of Chaim Rumkowksi, the chief "elder" or administrator of the Lodz *Judenrat.* The *Judenräte* (Jewish councils) were historically controversial bureaucratic organizations instituted to carry out the policies of the Nazi regime in the ghettos. The Nazis depended on the *Judenräte,* which were mainly composed of Jewish civilians, to carry out the daily administration of ghetto life, the provision of labor for industries, and the registration and collection of deportees for transports.

Biderman has much to say about Rumkowski, the rather tragic statesman of Lodz, who was sixty-two when chosen to head the *Judenrat.* Biderman portrays him not only as a loner, widowed and childless, whose prewar business ventures had ended in bankruptcy despite a wealth of contacts, but also as prosperous within the ghetto system: He remarried, adopted a young boy, and was a faithful servant of the Nazi plans for Lodz.

> Rumkowski meticulously executed all the orders given to him by the Germans. His philosophy was to collaborate with the Germans, believing that by doing so he would save more lives and reduce the bloodshed. He was convinced that by using the Jewish police to execute the German orders he would soften the blows that would inevitably come down upon the Jews (Biderman, Melbourne: AHB, 1995, p. 18).

He further paints Rumkowski's administration and its support of the Gestapo, the Jewish police, and Jewish *Sonderkommando* as an empire drunk an corruption, scandal, and self-interest. However, Biderman's portrayal of Rumkowski as a puppet figure, "Rumkowski was a classic case of a victim, a hostage, who inadvertently turned traitor" (p. 20), contradicts his earlier statement about the "collaborative" role of the *Judenrat.* Biderman's floating interpretation of Rumkowski's position implies that his actions as elder were fueled by dubious moral choices and egocentrism rather than compromised by the powerlessness of the institution itself to affect the ultimate fate of Jewish life in the ghetto. Biderman's assessment of Rumkowski's actions is an expression of the "gray zone" that such survivors as Primo Levi in *The Drowned and the Saved* have retrospectively applied to morally and ethically questionable behavior in the Holocaust.

Biderman also comments on the German administration of the ghetto, called the *Gettoverwaltung*, led by Hans Biebow, a "devout Nazi who had found a lucrative niche in the ghetto that gave him wealth and protected him from being drafted into the army" (p. 25). Biderman details the levels of decision-making and (often competing) jurisdictional power that flowed from regional to city to local levels, and eventually to the ghetto. The importance of the Lodz ghetto economy to the Reich meant that various departments, such as the Armament Ministry, headed by Albert Speer, could claim direct interest in administrative affairs. Additionally, the *Kripo*, or German criminal police, played, according to Biderman, "a most brutal role in the history of the Ghetto" (p. 26). The *Kripo* was boundless in its treatment and torture of ghetto inhabitants: Jews were beaten to death by German interrogators in the cellars of the *Kripo* headquarters, a former Catholic Church.

Stylistic Representation and Themes

The World of My Past can be analyzed not just in terms of content of ghetto life, but also in its narrative arrangement. In this respect, it reflects the interpretive need to impose order on one's past and to experiences sometimes described as inexplicable. Biderman's ghettoization in Lodz is recalled in year-by-year terms: "the Lodz Ghetto, 1940, the Lodz Ghetto, 1941. . . ." His need to inform the reader is revealed in his integration of postwar studies on mortality rates in the Lodz ghetto, his comments on the roots of the Holocaust, his "recollections of Polish antisemitism," and the indifference of the "free world" and Allies to the plight of the Jews. Although Biderman's inclusion of postwar sources and studies adds to the narrative's attempt to "*profess* historicity" (Lang, p. 20), the memoir should also be viewed as a contribution to the historiography of the "Holocaust effect" in postwar memoir literature.

The "Holocaust effect" refers to the ways that postwar experiences and knowledge have shaped memories, and consequently, dominate how Biderman narrates his prewar and wartime past as an experience of the everyday. In Biderman's memories, anti-Jewish discrimination and restrictions precede the Nazi invasion of Poland. The everyday world of life in Lodz is both public and private, and themes and representations in the memoir reveal an intense relationship between each. In the public world of prewar ghettoization, Biderman depicts the Polish ostracization of Jews as a violent, accepted, and advertised display. He recalls how Poles knifed Jews after Sunday mass (Biderman, p. 95), notes the strict quota for Jewish students at Polish universities (p. 96), and remembers the public slogans that inhibited Jewish livelihood: "Nie Kupoj U Zyda" ("Don't Buy from the Jew") (p. 96). To Biderman, the Nazi occupation of Poland and consequent physical ghettoization allowed for the expression of an inherent Polish antisemitism: There is distinct ambiguity in his narrative between Polish bystander and perpetrator. While a controversial attitude, it is by no means unique in survivor literature.

Biderman's continuing attachment to the world of his past from the refuge of Australia is expressed as mourning for the destroyed *shtetl* (Jewish village) life. Biderman recalls the nostalgia of Jewish and Christian multiculturalism by giving it an address: 13 Lagiewnicka Street, "a most colorful and exciting neighborhood, the embodiment of a Yiddish *shtetl* village" (p. 103). He recalls: "In my early childhood . . . 13 Lagiewnicka Street was a place where I was never called "Parszywy Zydie" ("diseased Jew") or told to go to Palestine. . . . The courtyard was always full of children playing games, singing, dancing, running happily without fear" (pp. 103–104).

Biderman's anchor to the past is also expressed in terms of weather. If memory can have a climate, Biderman's ghetto world is freezing: "Somehow, I always remember the ghetto in a perpetual winter, enveloped in ice and snow, with frost covering the inside of our home" (p. 106). Biderman's acclimatized memories affect his visions of the ghettoized body:

> January 1944 . . . Behind the barbed wires of the Ghetto, neither spring nor summer ever came. In my memory, an eternal winter lives on in a world of decay, filth, famine and death. The Ghetto people look as if they had been hewn from rock: their bloodless faces hard, silent and lifeless; only their eyes, deeply sunken into their foreheads, burned with a desire for life (p. 132).

On 31 August 1944 Biderman was deported from the Lodz Ghetto to Auschwitz-Birkenau, and subsequently to Althammer, Dora, and Bergen-Belsen. His time in Birkenau was relatively short, but it still allows Biderman to comment on the possibility of humanity in the camps: "When I remember Birkenau, it seems to me that those who somehow retained their human dignity and did not turn savage were in the majority" (p. 228). Biderman left Birkenau and arrived in Althammer in Upper Silesia after a three-hour journey. His entry into the camp is described in not dissimilar terms to other reports:

> Everything was wrapped in darkness. All I could see were SS men with their guns trained on the prisoner; Kapos and

> *Blockaeltesten* were everywhere. We were welcomed, as always, with a cacophony of barked orders backed up with truncheons and sticks (p. 246).

Biderman was forced to work on a building site during his brief incarceration in Althammer, and was evacuated in mid-January 1945 on a death march by foot and train to the Dora concentration camp, which took in, ahead of the advancing Russian army, parts of Czechoslovakia, Austria, and Germany. He arrived in Dora in early February 1945, after spending ten atrocious days in a cattle car that overflowed with corpses during the journey: "For two days, our wagon could not unload its accumulated corpses, and we had to lie on top of them. The stench, mixed with human waste and blood, was sickening" (p. 282).

While in Dora, Biderman discovered the secret construction of the Nazis' V1 and V2 rocket missiles. He was also surprised to find there a sports ground, a swimming pool, and a brothel, the last of which demonstrates the Nazis' sexual exploitation of women. The largely underexplored links between gender, sexuality, and survival in the Holocaust appear more complex than Biderman's reasoning of women's motivations for sexual interactions with Nazi officers: "For a little extra bread and soup, they accepted their fate and hoped it would save their lives" (p. 292). After Dora, Biderman was sent to Bergen-Belsen. His liberation by British forces in April 1945 compelled him to find his parents and brother, who, he discovered later, were no longer alive.

The underlying approach of Biderman to the reconstruction of his Holocaust past is the need to testify as postwar witness and historian. His pedagogic style departs from more conventional survivor memoirs through the incorporation of postwar historiographical and archival research into the text. This approach is oppositional: It is both potentially enriching and yet also evasive since it removes Biderman's subjectivity from the narrative, and consequently undermines its potentially visceral impact.

National Consciousness and Reception

In Australia, the response to *The World of My Past* marked a turning point for public confrontations with the Holocaust and its contemporary meaning. The book has received mainstream acceptance in the form of prizes for nonfiction and biography. This can be viewed cynically or positively in terms of national and community recognition of the multicultural foundations of Australian identities, particularly recognition of the visibility of European refugees and their traumas. In terms of critical analysis, the book has not received the scholarly attention and scrutiny it demands, although this is contingent on developing an active critical culture in which to receive the literature of Australian-Holocaust memory.

Importance to Holocaust Literature

The World of My Past impresses as a narrative that threads the genres of autobiography, history, and reportage. It is also full of the "Holocaust effects" often found in memoir literature: the difficulty in separating moralizing from moral commentary, the confusion of the accusatory with the objective narrative voice, the sometimes inexplicable response of individuals to public dehumanization, and the depiction of the enveloping net of the Nazi occupation. As a historiography of the everyday impact of Holocaust effects, its contribution is threefold. It is international in that it joins other literature of memory and reflects common themes in the representation of the Holocaust. It is national in that Biderman speaks from a country of refuge, multiculturalism, and a community of survivors of genocide. Most profoundly, *The World of My Past* is transnational in effect, as Biderman finally exorcises what is latent in the book, the distance between survival and postwar interpretive commentary about it as the space of silence:

> Perhaps nobody will ever fully understand the world of survivors, for we are people who have inhaled the smell of the burning flesh and bones of our mothers and fathers, our sisters and brothers, children and friends. That smell lives on in our subconscious forever. We were forged in the fires of hell, and welded with an eternal bond to Auschwitz, Treblinka and Belsen (p. 350).

Bibliography

Primary Source

The World of My Past. 1995.

Secondary Sources

Lang, Berel. "Holocaust Genres and the Turn to History." In *The Holocaust and the Text: Speaking the Unspeakable*. Edited by Andrew Leak and George Paizis. Houndmills: Macmillan, 2000, pp. 17–31.

Levi, Primo. *The Drowned and the Saved*. London: Abacus, 1987.

MAXIM BILLER
(1960–)

NORBERT OTTO EKE

MAXIM BILLER'S TEXTS follow the winding paths of the cultural inscription of the *Shoah* in the mentality and behavior of the postwar generations of Germans, Jews and non-Jews alike. Biller not only expressly refers to the continual importance of the *Shoah* in its effects on the complicated German Jewish relationship, but also calls for the *Shoah* to be regarded as a central theme of contemporary literature. The main flow of his writing is, however, less in the *Shoah* itself—which is narrated only as the echo of history, tales, myths, and legends—than in the Auschwitz trauma as *discourse configuration.*

The term "discourse configuration" aims at the specific intellectual attitudes toward the *Shoah* and the conventions of remembrance and mourning in Germany (Jewish and non-Jewish). Essential to discourse configuration is what Terrence Des Pres called a "sort of holocaust etiquette." It is criticism of representation, not representation itself, that forms the focus of Biller's texts that work through the enactment of memory in "shamefully-inhibited post-Holocaust Germany" (*Die Tempojare ["Tempo"-Years]*, München, 1991, p. 119). Focus for Biller means the criticism of the discourse of exoneration and coming to terms with a shamed philosemitism, on one hand, and the identifying agreement with the Jewish history of suffering as the focusing point of Jewish self-image, on the other hand.

Themes

Biller was born in Prague in 1960. When he was ten years old, he emigrated to Germany with his Russian Jewish parents, Raissa and Semjon, and his elder sister, Elena (Lappin). Germany was foreign to him because of the language, but here, as a Jew, he also developed a "sense of being the Other" for the first time, as he stated in his own words ("Brief Autobiography," *Neue Rundschau* 103, no. 4 [1990]: 49–51; 49). Using his keen sense of Otherness to recognize the inconsistencies and dismissal of the German Jewish culture of memory, Biller develops, in his essays and stories, a reply to the German Jewish discourse of coming to terms with the past. This reply is based on contradiction that mobilizes hate and uses anger to develop enlightenment. Aptly, Biller called the column he published regularly in the magazine *Tempo* during the 1980s "One Hundred Lines of Hate" (excerpts: *Die Tempojahre*). His column in *Tempo* gained Biller the reputation of being one of the sharpest polemicists on the German literary scene. Biller, a trained Germanist (University of Hamburg and University of Munich) and journalist (Journalist College in Munich), uses the contradiction-provoking power of critical development to open up chambers of memory that are blocked by stereotypes, clichés, taboos, and prejudices. Biller's provocations enable his German readers to conduct a real discussion with the German past and the problematic relationship between non-Jewish Germans and German Jews. Biller simultaneously polarizes and divides; he systematically violates the moral common sense ("Holocaust etiquette") that transfigures the victims.

Through his journalistic and literary works, Biller penetrates into the moral vacuum that the *Shoah* has left in the relationship between Germans and German Jews. He especially plays with the absurdity of this relationship in his early stories in *Wenn ich einmal reich und tot bin* (*When I Am Wealthy and Dead*) (1990) and the texts in his second collection of prose, *Land der Väter und Verräter* (*Land of Fathers and Traitors*) (1994). These stories clear the stereotypical separation of (German) perpetrator and (Jewish) victim, thus advancing beyond the exonerating myth of evil and its counterpart, the pure or sacred victim. Biller's texts disperse the set concepts and standardized perspectives of German Jews and non-Jews dealing with each other. The texts destroy the cozy philosemitism arising from the desire of many Germans to get rid of the past, forcing readers into a decision-making situation when they use clichés and stereotypes to talk about "ugly" Jews, about Jewish careerists and unscrupulous profiteers in postwar Germany.

In the story "When I Am Wealthy and Dead" (Wenn ich einmal reich und tot bin), Amichai Süssmann, who subsequently becomes a Zionist, is a model case of the careerist. He is described as having "immediately after the war gained control of the Frankfurt Station district by subjecting his organisation to the same rules he had previously learned in [the concentration camp] Treblinka" (*Wenn ich einmal reich und tot bin*, Köln, 1990, p. 59). The big-time builder Salomon Pucher in the story "Robots" (Roboter) is a model of the profiteer. He is reported to have initially "[gobbled] his way with relish through the fifties" as a dealer in hard liquor and a pimp until the 1960s, when he became one of the most respected men in Frankfurt: a sort of "court Jew" loved by the Germans "out of a sense of self-pity and fear of a Jewish Zyklon-B retaliation act" (pp. 59 and 203).

Biller's stories also subvert the usual memory semantics of German cultural life. The memory semantics, ritualized rites of mourning, tend to purify by removing all that is dubious or ugly; the result of this ideological purification is the sacred victim. The stories in the second prose collection, *Land of Fathers and Traitors*, speak of the involvement of the survivors and the postwar generation in guilt suppression, or tell of people who have established themselves within their own sufferings and those of others. Conspicuously, in *Land of Fathers and Traitors*, Biller has developed the central conflict of all his stories out of the relationship of young Jews to the survivors of the *Shoah*. In doing this he puts the collective myth of the victim to the test. He especially brings to the foreground the paralyzing and destructive effect of the myths and legends on the relationship between the generations: the hate of the young for the myth of death and survival and their own banishment in this myth. Thus the criticism of the unsolvable conflicts and tensions of the official Holocaust discourse becomes simultaneously the focus of a criticism of the identity constructs of Jews in the country of the perpetrator.

By questioning the stereotypes and clichés of the perpetrator / victim pattern in his texts, Biller confronts the symbolic representation of the existing "Holocaust etiquette." The texts disturb the ritual of emotional reliving and break with the simplified view of cleanly separated history, with its tragically heightened victim biographies and sentimentalizations that threaten to change horror into kitsch, while simultaneously allowing the reader self-satisfying consent. The desire to break the taboo is, however, secondary. It is less inspiring for his writing process than is this dynamic moment that, apart from the criticism of German philosemitism, is at the center of Biller's poetic writing strategy about German Jewish differences. Thus, Biller's texts turn the usual structures of discourse upside down, for example, by presenting images of Jewish figures both unable to live in Germany and unable to leave Germany. He then withdraws the construction of a Jewish identity through the victim role and and in the process redefines a Jewish/German identity not outside, but in spite of, the *Shoah*.

"Harlem Holocaust"

The story "Harlem Holocaust" in *When I Am Wealthy and Dead* translates this conflict with the ritualized coming-to-terms process into a multilayered narrative model that reveals the German Jewish guilt syndrome through a line of multiple projections in an especially sarcastic manner. The story reflects the complex relationship between Jews and non-Jews in the strange coexistence and conflict between two characters, both of whom have only indirect knowledge of the *Shoah* gained through the experiences of survivors. One character is a professor of linguistics and an author, Gerhard (Gary) Warszawski, an American Jew with German ancestry. The other, Efraim Rosenhain, is his German translator, who is also the first-person narrator (after much narrative confusion, he is replaced, at the end of the story, by an editorial first-person narrator). Warszawski strains the nerves of the sensitized German public, using his Jewishness as a basis for his career (which he is able to do only in Germany), and unifying all antisemitic stereotypes in his character: intellectual brilliance and arrogance, cynicism and unscrupulousness, uninhibited lust and (super) potency (not to mention physiognomic features). A "suffering German son of a perpetrator" (*Harlem Holocaust*, Köln, 1998, p. 12), he maneuvers through the depths of the German Jewish relationship. Linked together, the first name, Efraim, and family name, Rosenhain, make a German reader think the person is Jewish, although Efraim Rosenhain is not Jewish. Rosenhain is the son of a Nazi family that wants to get rid of the past guilt. This name suggests a desire for absolution without making atonement for the *Shoah* crime in a real sense. Equipped with the "overbearing Auschwitz bonus" (p. 52), Warszawski calculatingly plays up the rituals of coming to terms and reparation, while his German "voice," Rosenhain, outwardly succumbs with pleasure to the "greed for guilt and atonement" (p. 9). Thus, in a strange way, Warszawski's socialization as an author follows a double-layered meaning in the victim status: he turns his back on his upper-middle-class Jewish roots in his identification with African-American victims of racial discrimination and with the socially underprivileged, and simultaneously in his adolescent revolt against the politically impotent "nostalgic fuss" of the German Jewish emigrants living in New York (p. 15). When a cousin of his mother, a victim of the *Shoah*, comes to stay with the Warszawski family, Gerhard Warszawski shifts his identification of the victim from African Americans to the Jews. Thus, through the direct contact with a victim that he himself as Jew could have been, Gary Warszawski moves away from Harlem to the Holocaust, from the "Negro passion" (p. 36) to the suffering of the Jews, from the reality of American class and race discrimination to the physical fight for survival by his persecuted European fellow believers. Gary Warszawski, the privileged New Yorker son of an emigrant, is transformed into the *Jewish* author Gerhard Warszawski, who writes of experiences unknown to him in the "surfiction" (Biller uses the term "surfictions" to mean more like reality than dream) of his prose, and with great success in the German book market he works off his "survivor's self-hate" (p. 7).

As a "Dybbuk" (a ghost that adheres to the body of the living, p. 48), the successful Jewish author Warszawski is a figure projected by the spirit of the German sense of guilt, represented by the shamed son of a perpetrator, Efraim Rosenhain. Rosenhain attempts to publicly prove his "strength and goyish equality" (p. 53) by writing a *Shoah* story with the title "Warsaw's Inheritance" (Warschauers Vermächtnis). The attempt fails both aesthetically and morally. At the end of Biller's story, the relationship between Warszawski and Rosenhain is shown as a literary (fictitious) construction written by an author whose real name is Friedrich (not Efraim) Rosenhain, who suffered beginning at an early age from a "phantasmagoric system." Rosenhain himself, the bastard son out of (latent and manifest) antisemitic traits and a desire for apology (or absolution), has supposedly commited suicide. Antisemitic traits and a desire for apology (absolution) are presented as typical attitudes of Germans.

Biller offers the reader a distorted image of German guilt projection, including its antisemitic clichés, in the figure of the all-powerful Warszawski, who insists on the answer to the question of guilt in the figure of his shadow, Efraim Rosenhain. He lures the reader into the perspective of the paranoid narrator, only then to cut the ground of prejudice from under the reader's feet and to repeatedly question (positive and negative) attitudes. The "nasty" Jew, who projects himself in the form of the victim, becomes in turn the projection of a shamed philosemite, whose story is no more than an attempt at exorcism in a longing to be rid of the dead. Thus, "Harlem Holocaust" can be read in retrospect as a picture puzzle that includes clichés and projections and that keeps open the question of both German and Jewish cultural identity that embraces the guilt of both the perpetrator and the survivor.

The Daughter

In Biller's first novel, *The Daughter (Die Tochter)* (2000), the *Shoah* is only a vague reference to past guilt. Following from David Vogel's novel *A Marriage in Vienna* (*Eine Ehe in Wien*) (1929–1930), Biller deals with the experience of the Other (as a Jew in Germany) including all the problems associated with the German Jewish identity and a search for redemption that ends in the collapse of all efforts by philosophy, religion, and other disciplines to make sense of the world. At the center of the novel is an Israeli who has developed into a murderer in the Israeli intervention in Lebanon in 1982. He flees from those he has killed to Germany, which, with its "morbid philosemitism," seems to be the perfect "place to forget" (*"Tempo"-Years*, p. 116). In the perpetrator's "land of the dead" (*The Daughter*, p. 13), he slowly learns to forget his "minor" guilt, as the Germans have learned to forget their "major" guilt—only to reawaken from the temporary happiness of unconsciousness. *The Daughter* is a disturbing journey into the depths of a soul. The reader finds, hidden beneath sensation-demanding excitement and shocking sexual obsession, a confrontation with the life of Jews during the Diaspora.

Conclusion

Biller's criticism of the mythicization in the collective memory connects him with the works of other Jewish authors, such as Edgar Hilsenrath and George Tabori (the older generation) and Robert Schindel (the middle generation). Nevertheless, his ironic and distancing treatment of the *Shoah* and its results is not without its critics. Although Biller has received many awards for his writing (Tukan-Preis, 1994; Preis des Europäischen Feuilletons, 1996, OHO Stoessl-Preis, 1996; Theodor-Wolff-Journalistenpreis der deutschen Zeitungen, 1999), he has been accused of calculating obscenity in breaking the taboo of the sacred victim and of a self-complacent lust for success that has caused him to distort a sensitive topic. Biller himself understands his texts as a challenge to the general moral indifference of the German public that still exists in contemporary literature. Even if, as Biller said in a lecture given in the spring of 2000 called "About the Problems of Telling the Truth" ("Über die Schwierigkeiten beim Sagen der Wahrheit"), "the dead Jews are dragged from their graves, or rise from them themselves, and . . . we talk about clearing the Germans of their terrible historical inheritance of guilt," the moral indifference in public discussion gives way to nervousness. At the same time, literature and films from Germany deal with this topic in a way that remains clumsy, without connections to what Biller vaguely names "the final things," and especially without connection to the "souls" of his readers ("Feige das Land, schlapp die Literatur. über die Schwierigkeiten beim Sagen der Wahrheit" Cowardly the Country, Listless the Literature. About the Problems of Telling the Truth) (*Die Zeit*, 13 April 2000: 47–49). From this beginning, Biller presupposes that most of the contemporary German writers live and write in a state of political and moral oblivion, whereas in his eyes literature should have a moral task.

Bibliography

Primary Sources

Wenn ich einmal reich und tot bin (*When I Am Wealthy and Dead*). 1990.

Die Tempojahre (*"Tempo"-Years*). 1991.

Land der Väter und Verräter (*Land of Fathers and Traitors*). 1994.

Harlem Holocaust. 1998.

Die Tochter (*The Daughter*). 2000.

Kühltransport. Eui Drama (*Cold-Storage Van*). 2001.

Secondary Sources

Eke, Norbert Otto. " 'Was wollen Sie? Die Absolution?' Opfer- und Täterprojektionen bei Maxim Biller." In *Deutsch-jüdische Literatur der neunziger Jahre. Die Generation nach der Shoah*. Edited by Sander L. Gilman and Hartmut Steinecke. Berlin: Erich Schmidt, 2001, pp. 89–107.

Feinberg, Anat. "The Issue of Heimat in Contemporary German-Jewish Writing." *New German Critique* 70 (1997): 161–181.

Köppen, Manuel. "Auschwitz im Blick der zweiten Generation. Tendenzen der Gegenwartsprosa (Biller, Grossman, Schindel)." In *Kunst und Literatur nach Auschwitz*. Edited by Manuel Köppen. Berlin: Erich Schmidt, 1993, pp. 67–82.

Nolden, Thomas. *Junge jüdische Literatur. Konzentrisches Schreiben in der Gegenwart*. Würzburg: Königshausen and Neumann, 1995.

Remmler, Karen. "The 'Third Generation' of Jewish-German Writers after the *Shoah* Emerges in Germany and Austria." In *Yale Companion to Jewish Writing and Thought in German Culture 1096–1996*. Edited by Sander L. Gilman and Jack Zipes. New Haven, Conn.: Yale University Press, 1997, pp. 796–804.

Schruff, Helene. *Wechselwirkungen. Deutsch-Jüdische Identität in der erzählenden Prosa der 'Zweiten Generation'*. Hildesheim, Germany: Georg Olms, 2000.

HALINA BIRENBAUM

(1929–)

MONIKA ADAMCZYK-GARBOWSKA

HALINA BIRENBAUM WAS born in 1929 in Warsaw. Her survival trajectory comprises the Warsaw ghetto until liquidation in the spring of 1943, the Nazi camps of Majdanek and Auschwitz from whence she was sent on a death march to Ravensbrück and on to Neustadt-Glewe, where she was liberated in 1945. After the liquidation of the ghetto, she was taken from the *Umschlagplatz* and deported with other Jews to Majdanek. During a Majdanek selection she was separated from her mother, who was gassed. Halina miraculously avoided death in the gas chamber because on that particular day the supply of gas was depleted. She stayed in the camp with her sister-in-law Hela, who became a surrogate mother for her and initially helped her gain strength to fight for survival when they were transported to Auschwitz. A large part of her autobiographical book *Nadzieja umiera ostatnia* (*Hope Is the Last to Die,* 1967) is devoted to the growing bond between the two and a later reversal of roles as Halina, in turn, made efforts to save Hela's life. Her efforts were, however, unsuccessful as, sick and weakened, Hela died in the camp at the end of 1943 (her rapidly deteriorating condition is depicted in a heart-breaking way). When the time of liberation came, Halina had no strength left to rejoice: "I wanted to rejoice feverishly like others at our miraculous liberation. But I could not" (New York: M. E. Sharpe, 1996, p. 240). Only on the next day is she able to "take a deep breath and know that at last, at last, [they] were free" (p. 241). From her large family, only her older brother, Marek, survived. In 1947 she settled in Israel.

Commemoration by Testifying

In her paper on literature of the Holocaust presented at a conference at Majdanek in April 1989, Birenbaum states that she tried to reconstruct the atmosphere of those times in a clear way and above all to give a faithful account of the facts without inventing anything ("Literatura—a okres zagady," Lublin, p. 71). The Eichmann Trial was an inspiration for her. While listening to the witnesses, Birenbaum felt that their testimonies lacked something significant—the atmosphere of the constant threat of living in horror. She felt that she should write about her personal experience in order to commemorate those who perished experiencing such horror.

Hope Is the Last to Die

Halina Birenbaum's writing debut of 1967 with *Nadzieja umiera ostatnia* (*Hope Is the Last to Die*) is a shocking testimony because of its authenticity and the emotional intensity conveyed by means of simple language and first-person narration. Describing each step of her ordeal, she struggles with the question of how it was possible to survive and remain human. Many scholars of the Holocaust raise the issue that it is impossible to describe and express what seems inexpressible. To this she responds that everything a human being has experienced can be described and that one individual is able to grasp things experienced by another.

The book differs from other Holocaust memoirs written by women in terms of perspective. In a number of such memoirs (for instance, those by Nechama Tec or Janina Bauman) the authors assume, at least partly, the child's point of view and tend to present a somewhat idealized vision of their prewar lives. Birenbaum does not stylize her language to that of a child, nor does she refer to her prewar childhood years. Instead, she focuses directly on the outbreak of the war, stating explicitly that in the summer of 1939 she realized that the imminent war would be much worse than previous ones and that it would be especially hard for Jewish people.

In her depiction of life in the Warsaw ghetto, Birenbaum underlines the social and financial divisiveness in the community and the different fates of the poor versus the privileged. Birenbaum came from a working-class family and lived in a Warsaw Jewish neighborhood. Thus, paradoxically, she was spared the shock of dislocation typical of individuals from assimilated families; her social background may also explain the lack of idealization sometimes expressed in accounts of middle-class memoirists. She is very critical of the *Judenrat*, or Jewish council, that formally governed life in the ghetto presenting their members as "totally subservient to the Nazis" and depicting their "shameful acts and bribery" (p. 12). She accuses the *Judenrat* of suppressing the spirit of resistance and of deluding people that resistance did not make sense:

> All financial contributions, deliveries of supplies and of human beings for slave labour later also for extermination—were obtained by the Nazis from the Judenrat (5) . . . [The council] was feeble and subservient to the orders of the German Nazis, deaf to our cries and insensible to people's tears. Its members only wanted to please their executioners and to save their own skins, the lives of their families . . . also those who could repay them well for help (p. 14).

On the other hand, she writes about the members of the resistance in the ghetto presenting them as their "pride" deserving great admiration (p. 65).

Halina Birenbaum's other books include *Powrót do ziemi praojców* (Return to the land of the forefathers, 1991) in which she describes her difficult adaptation to life in Israel, the process of learning how to function in a new country, and of building her personal life from scratch. *Ka dy odzyskany dzien* (Each day regained, 1998) is a memoir containing her contemporary observations juxtaposed with war memories, which she started writing in the 1960s. In *Wotanie o pamieć* (A call for memory, 1999), she describes the vicissitudes of twenty Jewish survivors who, after many years of silence, finally decided to speak about their lives.

Birenbaum has also published three volumes of poetry and her essays and poems have appeared in various periodicals in Poland (*Akcent*, *Więź*) and Israel (*Kontury*). She translated a number of Polish poems on the Holocaust into Hebrew. In her poetry she expresses in different generic forms, albeit as devoid of literary embellishments as her prose, a number of issues and motifs that she discussed in her nonfiction. Her first volume of poems bears the significant title *Nawet gdy sięŚmieję* (Even when I laugh, 1990) in which she writes of the omnipresence of her Holocaust experience in her later existence and declares that she never forgets and never moves far from what happened then; this is not the past for her because whatever happened in those times persists in her and grows more intense with the passage of time. She calls herself the proof of her family's existence, their tombstone. As she always repeats during her frequent lectures and readings at schools, universities, and other institutions in Israel, Poland, and Germany, she feels compelled to talk about her Holocaust experience and what happened to her family because when she remembers them she brings them back to life. Although the memory of her mother occupies a special place in those recollections, she also remembers anonymous victims who, on the verge of death, asked those still living to remember, to tell their story, and to give witness.

In spite of the horrible experience she tries to find sparks of light in the Holocaust night. In her poem "My Life Started from the End" she states that she got to know death before learning about birth. Her life started from the end and only then did it return to the beginning. She rose from death, which was not in vain because good is as strong as evil. In the Preface to *Wotanie o pamieć* she states that there is a world after Auschwitz as well as after life. In honor of the fruition of a prophetic observation by a woman who knelt beside her in a Birkenau roll call and foretold that their suffering would be commemorated by future generations, Birenbaum feels obliged to carry on her mission to record and teach and takes pleasure in the proliferation of books and films about the Holocaust. As she stated in a letter to M. E. Sharpe, who published the second revised edition of *Hope Is the Last to Die* in 1996:

> We have to remember the Holocaust because of the people who didn't survive. They wanted to stay alive to tell the world all that I have told, their last dream was to be remembered. We all, the whole humanity, owe them that. When I speak about those who did not survive, describe them, I am trying to give them another hour of life so they can live in the minds and hearts of those who hear me. The murderers, the Nazis, didn't want anybody to know what they did to us. If we do not remember today—forever—we do what *they* wanted! (p. vii).

Halina Birenbaum is well known in Poland as a Holocaust survivor, poet, and powerful speaker and educator; she seems relatively little known in the English-speaking world.

Bibliography

Primary Sources

Nadzieja umiera ostatnia (*Hope Is the Last to Die*). 1967. 1st English edition 1971; expanded edition 1996.

Nawet gdy si miej (Even when I laugh). 1990.

"Literatura—a okres zaglady." In *Swiadectwa i powroty nieludzkiego czasu* (Testimonies and returns of the inhuman time). Ed. Jerzy Świêch. Wydawnictwo UMCS: Lublin, 1990, 71–77.

Powrót do ziemi praojców (Return to the land of the forefathers). 1991.

Nie o kwiatach (Not about flowers). 1993.

Jak mo na w s owach (How can words express). 1995.

Ka dy odzyskany dzie (Each day regained). 1998.

Wotanie o pamieć (A call for memory). 1999.

Secondary Source

Gross, Natan. *Poeci i Szoa: Obraz Zagtady Żydów w poezji polskiej*. Offmax: Sosnowiec, 1993.

LIVIA BITTON-JACKSON

(1931–)

MARLENE HEINEMANN

BORN 28 FEBRUARY 1931 in Bratislava, Czechoslovakia, to Marcus and Laura (née Roth) Friedman, Livia was deported from Somorja, in Hungarian-occupied Czechoslovakia, with other family members on 18 April 1944 to Nagymagyar Ghetto; one month later to Dunaszerdahely, then to Auschwitz, in Poland; Płaszów; Auschwitz again; Augsburg, Germany; and Waldlager, near Dachau. She was liberated on 30 April 1945 in Seeshaupt, Germany, by American soldiers. Having emigrated to the United States in 1951, she received a B.A. in 1961 from Brooklyn College; she earned an M.A. in 1963 and a Ph.D. in 1968 from New York University. She married Leonard G. Jackson on 23 August 1977, a second marriage for Bitton-Jackson. She has two children from her first marriage and two stepchildren.

Significance

Bitton-Jackson is the author of the memoir *Elli: Coming of Age in the Holocaust*, 1980, which was praised by reviewers for its lack of rhetorical excess, its detail, and its emotional immediacy. Her memoir is a contribution to the documentation on Jewish families and especially children during the Holocaust. Her family's story is part of the fate of Hungarian Jews. *I Have Lived a Thousand Years: Growing Up in the Holocaust*, published in 1997, is a near-duplication of *Elli* intended for a child audience. She also wrote *My Bridges of Hope: Searching for Life and Love after Auschwitz*, 1999, also for young people, describing her experiences immediately following World War II. She served as a consultant for a motion picture based on her books. Bitton-Jackson has written scholarly articles on the *Shoah* and other Jewish topics, including "The Nazi 'Blood Myth' and the Holocaust," 1988.

Elli: Coming of Age in the Holocaust

This memoir describes the thirteen-year-old author's life in Somorja and the deportation of her entire family, including an older brother and a widowed aunt, to nearby ghettos, then to Auschwitz. Her father is deported before the others to a nearby forced labor camp, Komarom. He dies shortly before liberation. At Auschwitz, arriving deportees are divided into those who will be sent to the gas chamber and those who will enter the camp. Elli's brother, Bubi, is separated from the women (he survives). Dr. Josef Mengele, the man who is dividing the deportees, is impressed by Ellie's blond hair, so he tells her to go with her mother into the column that is entering the camp. He sends the aunt to the other column, probably because she is frail and unfit for hard work. After twelve days in Auschwitz, Elli and her mother are sent by train (cattle car) to Camp Płaszów, where they do mainly outdoor labor for seven weeks. The brutal supervisor of the hilltop leveling work group kills prisoners who dare to rest for a moment. After being returned by train to Auschwitz for a few more weeks after the evacuation of Płaszów, mother and daughter are sent by cattle car to Augsburg, Germany, where Elli helps assemble bomb-control devices in a factory (Michelwerke), while her mother does cleaning work. Living conditions are much better than in Auschwitz, though their food is still inadequate.

After seven months, Elli and her mother are evacuated from Augsburg in order to escape the advance of the Americans and the English and are sent to Waldlager, near Dachau, where they are reunited with Bubi, who has been reduced to a barely living skeleton. They then spend five days in a train, moving from Mühldof to Seeshaupt, Germany, without food or water, occasionally fired upon by the SS, who want to hide the evidence of their evil deeds from the approaching Allies, or strafed by American planes, until liberation in Seeshaupt on 30 April 1945. They return to their hometown in Czechoslovakia in June and, having learned that Elli's father has died, travel to Hungary in search of surviving relatives. Most of them have perished.

The most distinctive stylistic feature of the narrative is its emotional immediacy. This is achieved by the primary use of the present tense throughout, combined with the first person narrator and the point of view of a thirteen-year-old child who reacts strongly to each stage of the ordeal. At Camp Płaszów, Elli's outdoor work commando is threatened with decimation for stopping work to seek shelter from a sudden downpour. ("Decimation" is the shooting of every tenth prisoner in a line.) Elli is more terrified of losing her mother than of dying herself. She is certain that one of them will die. "If Mother dies, I die. Oh God, let me rather be tenth!" (Times Books, 1980, p. 103), Elli cries hysterically and insists on staying awake at night to be together with her mother as long as possible. The threatened punishment is never given because the SS are preoccupied with Polish partisans fighting in the vicinity. The other inmates react to the threat by reciting the Psalms the night before the punishment is expected. The reader experiences the threat through the mind of a terrified child for whom death and separation from her mother are unimaginable.

Elli's fear of losing her parents is equal to her fear of death, both of which are extremely intense. She suffers the permanent loss of her father and a temporary separation from her mother. Separated from her father and brother, she experiences her fate as dependent on her mother's survival, which is sometimes in doubt. In Auschwitz, her mother becomes partly paralyzed and is knocked unconscious after a falling bed plank hits her. Elli exerts heroic efforts to save her from a selection in the infirmary, then to get both of them into a transport bound for a labor camp in Germany. An SS officer does not notice the mother's paralysis, so she passes selection. He does notice a festering wound on Elli's leg and, not believing she will be able to work, selects her for gassing. Elli expresses her desperation as she searches for a way to sneak into her mother's transport: "I must go after Mommy. She is out in the pouring rain. She cannot stand without support. She cannot put on her dress. Out there alone. She might have fallen by now. In the cold, pouring rain. Naked" (p. 132). Elli expresses no concern for herself, only for her mother, and refuses the protection offered by another woman. When all seems lost, she finds her mother being attacked by a female SS guard. Afraid that the guard will break her mother's arm, Elli commits "sabotage": she jumps at the guard and shoves her against a wall. The guard then viciously punches and kicks Elli, but the young girl exults that she has not been killed. It is not known why the guard did not kill Elli; she did not know Elli had been selected for gassing.

The expression of gratitude to God for survival and other good fortune is a recurrent motif in *Elli*. It is an aspect of the Orthodox Jewishness that forms part of the identity of Elli, her mother, and her companions. Occasionally, however, Elli expresses the pain of personal and communal suffering and loss. Like other inmates, she has heard rumors of the gas chambers throughout the ordeal but has not believed them. She has clung to a myth of a special camp for children and the elderly. Near liberation, when Bubi tells her the rumors are true, she declares she has been robbed of her freedom because she must now live in a world in which small children are gassed with their mothers. Elli's dawning awareness of human destructiveness in the camps enhances the value of the memoir.

I Have Lived a Thousand Years: Growing Up in the Holocaust

Elli: Coming of Age in the Holocaust (1980) and *I Have Lived a Thousand Years: Growing Up in the Holocaust* (1997) are very similar, although the former is for adults while the latter is intended for children. There are a few additions to the plot in the children's book and only one notable subtraction: the first train ride to Auschwitz is no longer described in the 1997 edition. However, all the horrors of the various camps are described in exactly the same way with almost identical words. A glossary and two appendices of chronology show the progression of family and historical events. Because these changes are slight, reviews of the later book may be read for their commentary on the content of the earlier book.

Most of Bitton-Jackson's reviewers have been positive in their assessments of both books. Often these reviews focus on one or more of the incidents narrated in the books to illustrate how Jackson uniquely handles her experience. Two of them, one by Hanna B. Zeiger, the other by a reviewer from *The New Yorker*, relate an incident in the book occurring right after liberation in which a local German citizen is shocked to discover that Elli is not an elderly person of sixty but a child of fourteen. This incident conveys the degree of disfigurement wrought by starvation, filth, and forced labor in Nazi camps that Elli and the others have endured. Hazel Rochman finds the book distinctive in that it shows the victims preserving their humanity. Although this theme is common in autobiographical and some fictional Holocaust works, others emphasize the horror and amorality of the victims.

Although Rochman criticizes the book for its "occasional overwriting," which dwells on pain and suffering too much, several reviewers praise the memoir for its style. Elizabeth Devereaux and Diane Roback mention the "personal and immediate" observations of camp brutality that avoid "sweeping rhetoric." Similarly, Dorothy Rabinowitz notes the lack of "rhetorical excess" and the focus on details of daily life. Rabinowitz also comments on the "overpowering emotional immediacy" of the narrative (Rabinowitz, p. 12). Kari Jo Verhulst says that "the reader stands by helplessly as each unfathomable horror is realized" because the narrative is limited to the child's awareness (Verhulst, p. 55).

My Bridges of Hope: Searching for Life and Love after Auschwitz

In this work, Elli, her mother, and her brother return to their home and try to have a normal life, but, failing in the attempt, make preparations to emigrate to the United States. Although Elli wants to go to Palestine, her mother and brother prefer the United States, where a brother of Elli's father is living and ready to help them. The family decides to stay together. Echoing a recurrent theme of Holocaust memoirs addressing the survivor's sense of separation or difference from people who were spared direct Holocaust experience, a gulf divides Elli from her new classmates; she feels comfortable only with survivors. When her uncle in America sends student certificates to Bubi and Elli that qualify them for expedited visas to the United States, the family decides to send Bubi only, so Elli can stay with her mother and wait for their turn in the regular emigration system. With the takeover of Czechoslovakia by the Communists in 1948, the U.S. Embassy is closed. In a hurry to leave the country before the new regime closes the borders, Elli carries out a dangerous escape plan for her mother and herself. They join an illegal transport of Jewish refugees being sent to Palestine via Vienna. Military police have been bribed to allow these transports. Elli and her mother must maintain disguises as Hungarians because no Czechs are allowed in the transports. Since Elli has been working as a facilitator of these transports, she is in danger of being recognized by her former colleagues who are in the same building as the refugees being processed. Although two do recognize her, they let her and her mother pass all the checkpoints and they manage to get to Vienna. From there they must go to Germany to wait for visas to the United States. They arrive in New York City in April 1951.

This book is more objective and less personal than the previous memoirs, but it is still told in the present tense. Karen Simonetti finds that the fluctuation between "passionate entries and detached observations" is a reflection of the continuous separations in Elli's life. The reviewer is probably referring to the abrupt transitions from the end of one chapter to the beginning of the next. For example, on page seven, Elli, her mother, and Bubi learn that Elli's father died shortly before liberation. They all express their mourning, especially Elli, who screams out her grief. Thus ends the chapter. The next chapter begins dispassionately: "The long, hot summer days are over, and the leaves on our acacia tree have turned golden bronze" (Simon and Schuster, 1999, p. 8). Bitton-Jackson describes her return to school, and does not mention her father again until much later. Another example of an abrupt transition occurs where Elli ends a chapter describing with sadness some survivor children at her summer teaching job: "I am suddenly overwhelmed with pain as Rivka concludes the prayers, and all the others chant amen. So many tragedies. So many young, promising, ravished souls." The next chapter begins: "It is the first full week of August, and no counselor has arrived as replacement for Frieda" (p. 92). She is referring to a counselor who has resigned, leaving her in charge, despite her lack of experience.

The book is likely to appeal to both adolescent and some adult readers.

"The Nazi 'Blood Myth' and the Holocaust"

Bitton-Jackson's article "The Nazi 'Blood Myth' and the Holocaust" is a piece of scholarship that traces the development of the Nazi idea of race and blood in the antisemitic writings of medieval Christians and late-nineteenth- and early-twentieth-century French and German essayists and novelists. Introducing the essay with the question of how the German people were made to carry out the annihilation of their neighbors, Bitton-Jackson studies major precursors of Nazi propagandists who had an effect on German society. These writers derived the idea of the destruction of Aryan blood by Jews from early medieval Christian ideas of murder by Jews of Christ and of Christian children every Easter. Modern antisemites added to this blood libel myth the idea of a Jewish racial need to destroy Christians and, later, "Aryans." Bitton-Jackson cites Arthur Dinter, the author of the best-selling novel *Sin against the Blood*, who charged Jews with pollution of Aryan blood through sexual contact between Jews and Aryans. Similarly, she isolates Alfred Rosenburg, the main Nazi ideologist who publicized the idea of Jews as disease-producing germs which suck the blood of the weak not only to strengthen themselves, but also to bring death to their victims. These and other writers developed the concept of racial antisemitism expressed as contamination by Jews through intermarriage of the superior blood of Aryans, a central theme of Nazi propaganda.

Bitton-Jackson also locates the origin of the paired concepts of Jewish destruction of pure blood and Jewish greed in the story of the Crucifixion. "The dual accusation of deicide and betrayal-for-money" represented by Judas had been a central part of the deicide myth since the early Christian writers (Garber et al., p. 317). According to Bitton-Jackson, the Judas myth was reincarnated and integrated with the blood libel canard in the latter half of the nineteenth century by equating the Jew as a monstrous moneylender who drained the Gentile world of its money as of its life blood. Thus, she brings together two motifs of the antisemitic myth: blood and money. She also links the Christian and the racist concepts of Jewish destruction of non-Jewish blood, yoking together the somewhat disparate ideas of murder and contamination.

Livia Bitton Jackson has won several awards, including the Christopher Award, the Eleanor Roosevelt Humanitarian Award from United Jewish Appeal, and the Jewish Heritage Award from Jewish Teachers Union.

Bibliography

Primary Sources

A Decade of Zionism in Hungary (Under name Livia Elvira Bitton), *1918–1928*. 1971.

Elli: Coming of Age in the Holocaust. 1980.

Madonna or Courtesan: The Jewish Woman in Christian Literature. 1982.

"The Jew as Literary Hero." In *Fields of Offerings: Studies in Honor of Raphael Patai*. 1983.

"The Nazi 'Blood Myth' and the Holocaust." In *Methodology in the Academic Teaching of the Holocaust*. 1988.

"Returning to Tradition: *The Contemporary Revival of Orthodox Judaism* by M. Herbert Danzger," review. spring 1991.

"Miriam Akavia: Redeeming the Past." In *Hebrew Literature in the Wake of the Holocaust*. 1993.

I Have Lived a Thousand Years: Growing Up in the Holocaust. 1997.

My Bridges of Hope: Searching for Life and Love after Auschwitz. 1999.

Secondary Sources

Cunningham, Jennifer. "Last of the Witnesses." *The Herald (Glasgow)*, 16 July 1999: 21.

Devereaux, Elizabeth, and Diane Roback. "I Have Lived a Thousand Years: Growing Up in the Holocaust," *Publishers Weekly*, 244, no. 5 (3 February 1997): 108.

"Elli: Coming of Age in the Holocaust," *The New Yorker*, 56, no. 13 (19 May 1980): 162–163.

Fine, Ellen S. "Women Writers and the Holocaust: Strategies for Survival." *Reflections on the Holocaust in Art and Literature*. Edited by Randolph L. Braham. New York: Columbia University Press, 1990.

Garber, Zev. *The Paradigmatic Genocide: Essays in Exigesis and Eisegesis*. Lanham, MD: University Press of America, 1994.

Heinemann, Marlene E. *Gender and Destiny: Women Writers and the Holocaust*. Westport, Conn.: Greenwood Press, 1986.

Hershenson, Sarah. "Books on My Mind." *The Jerusalem Post*, 67, no. 20365 (21 October 1999), Features, 9.

"My Bridges of Hope: Searching for Life and Love after Auschwitz." *Publishers Weekly*, 246, no. 4 (25 January 1999): 97.

Rabinowitz, Dorothy. "The Lessons of the Past." *New York Times Book Review*, 85, no. 12 (29 June 1980): 12–13.

Rochman, Hazel. "I Have Lived a Thousand Years: Growing Up in the Holocaust." *Booklist*, 93, no. 14 (15 March 1997): 1233.

Rochmis, Dorothy H. "Elli." *West Coast Review of Books* (July 1983): 36.

Simonetti, Karen. "My Bridges of Hope: Searching for Life and Love after Auschwitz." *Booklist*, 95, no. 17 (1 May 1999): 1584.

Sommer, Allison Kaplan. "The Holocaust—As It Was." *Jerusalem Post*, 66, no. 19846 (4 February 1998): Features, 11.

Verhulst, Kari Jo. "Stories Not Forgotten: Young Girls Tell of the Holocaust." *Sojourners* (November–December 1997): 55.

Zeiger, Hanna B. "I Have Lived a Thousand Years: Growing Up in the Holocaust." *Horn Book Magazine*, 73, no. 4 (July–August 1997): 472–473.

Zvirin, Stephene. "Elli: Coming of Age in the Holocaust." *Booklist*, 76, no. 21 (1 July 1980): 1587.

HEINRICH BÖLL
(1917–1985)

STEPHAN BRAESE

HEINRICH BÖLL, WHO received the Nobel Prize in literature in 1972, is among the world's most famous German authors. In addition to his numerous literary works, Böll's involvement in public acts of protest, particularly during the last two decades of his life, contributed to this status. Böll repeatedly intervened in national debates in the Federal Republic of Germany and, like a sort of "remembrance laborer" (Vogt, p. 105), he insistently pointed toward the historical mortgage of National Socialism, World War II, and the Holocaust that continued to shape social and cultural life in West Germany as well as in Europe as a whole. Recent research has revealed, however, that although Böll's literary writings refer to the experience of the war, they do not actually recognize the Holocaust as the core event of National Socialism. This leads to some problematic consequences for Böll's representations of Jewish figures as well as for the interpretation of World War II in his writings as a whole.

Biographical Sketch Until 1945

Heinrich Böll was born on 21 December 1917, in Cologne, the son of the artisan carpenter Viktor Böll and his wife, Maria, whose maiden name was Hermans. Life at home was middle-class, Catholic, and antimilitaristic. Originally well-off, the family fell into poverty during the global economic crisis of 1929. Böll attended school until 1937. Backed by an anti-Nazi attitude that was upheld at home as well as by individual teachers, Böll successfully refused to become a member of the Hitlerjugend, the National Socialist Party youth organization; membership was more or less a duty for every youngster in Nazi Germany. Reading Adolf Hitler's *Mein Kampf* at the age of seventeen gave Böll an early understanding of the fundamental political points of view and the long-term perspective of National Socialism. After graduating, Böll started an apprenticeship at an antiquarian bookstore, where he had the opportunity to read banned authors, such as Karl Marx and Sigmund Freud. After discontinuing his apprenticeship and absolving his obligatory service in the Reichsarbeitsdienst, an agricultural and industrial organization of the National Socialist Party, Böll was drafted into the army shortly prior to the outbreak of World War II.

After basic training, Böll was transferred to Bromberg, Poland. The campaign against Poland was already finished. In an interview held in 1976, Böll recalled that it was there that he witnessed the terror of Hitler's SS against the Polish civilian population. In the summer of 1940, he went to France, where he was stricken with dysentery. He recovered in army barracks in Germany before again being transferred, this time to the French coast of the English Channel. During a vacation in March of 1942, he married Annemarie Cech, a teacher. In August of 1943, Böll was sent to Russia, where he spent months in trench warfare. Later he was sent to Rumania. With the aid of forged documents, Böll was able to return to Germany, where he hid with his family for a short time. They hoped to be liberated by the American forces that were rapidly advancing, but the Americans did not immediately claim this region, and Böll rejoined a German troop out of fear of being discovered and being executed as a deserter. He was taken captive by the Americans on 9 April 1945, was released in September of the same year, and returned home.

Decades later, Böll maintained that he had hardly witnessed antisemitic crimes. Coming from an explicitly Catholic background, he was, of course, familiar with "theological controversies between Christianity and Judaism, between different confessions . . . but I never experienced the racist" (p. 636). Böll had known about concentration camps, and "from time to time one met someone, who had escaped such an existence, was condemned to silence, but nonetheless made hints" (p. 635). In the middle of the 1970s, Böll recounted that he had "also not seen any transports. Once, at night, as I was driving home from eastern Europe as a soldier, and the train halted at a small train station in the middle of Germany, I did see thousands of shaven-headed people. But that wasn't just Jews, also soldiers, civilians, communists or whatever. Saboteurs, as one called them" (p. 635). In the same discussion, Böll commented on his assignment in the west: "As an army soldier in the roll of an interpreter, I felt no guilt, but many things were simply embarrassing, it was embarrassing" (p. 626).

War and Holocaust in the Early Texts

In his extensive oeuvre, Böll made two attempts at depicting episodes of the extermination politics inflicted by the Nazis on the Jews from a witness's perspective. The short tale "*Todesursache*: *Hakennase*" (Cause of Death: A Hooked Nose), written in 1947, relates a German lieutenant's attempt to rescue his Russian, non-Jewish landlord from mass executions that are being carried out in the village. The lieutenant is informed by the Russian landlord's wife that her husband was mistakenly taken away. "No sir, not a Jew, no. Sir! Sir!" Lieutenant Hegemüller rushes to where the executions are underway: "A line of the death-bound leads from the collecting place up to the highest level edge of the stone quarry, from whence the steadily whipping crack of machine pistols rang into the afternoon" (*Erzählungen*, Kiepenhauer & Witsch, 1994, pp. 71, 73). But precisely at the moment when Hegemüller reaches the location of the massacre, the Russian landlord is shot and falls to the ground. Hegemüller drags the man to an army doctor. Upon seeing the now dead landlord, the doctor, with a stiffly laughing voice, dictates to an assisting nurse: " 'So then, write down: Cause of death—a hooked nose'." Lieutenant Hegemüller subsequently goes insane.

For many years, this tale, which is only a few pages long, remained unpublished. An editor, to whom Böll had sent three texts, selected a different one, referring to the paper shortage as a reason for not publishing more. "Todesursache: Hakennase" did not appear until 1983. Readers today may tend to miss a certain degree of analytical precision in the story. The murderers are contrasted as "imbecilic clods" against the victims, who appear "raised in a delightful manner up out of the masses and placed in the loftiness of the human personality" (p. 73). The fact that the rescue attempt in the tale relates to a non-Jew can be read ambivalently as a critical gaze at the specific, narrow disposition of the German lieutenant or as a shortcoming of the author's own perception of the scope of events. But the position of this text in literary history is to be assessed by recognizing that it focuses on a mass execution of Jews by Germans at an unusually early point in time in German postwar literature.

Other factors were to be decisive for Böll's literary reflections on the National Socialist past. His conviction that there is a close relatedness between the victims of the Nazi extermination politics and the small pawns of the army, the Landsers, was highly consequential for his poetic work. In an opening speech held in connection with the Week of Brotherhood in 1956, Böll said:

> My brother got lost in history. Where, at what point in this history did he get lost? Was he murdered in Maidanek, did he starve in a prison camp, was he attacked in Russia, or was he hanged as a deserter? . . . We, we survived: we barely escaped murder in the places of extermination, fled shortly before the trap closed itself—or we saved our lives from one day to the next during the last months of the war, through this hell, that is not yet described: headlong, disbanded prison camps, evacuated concentration camps, rivers of refugees, evacuated city populace, soldiers, driven by execution squads, collected up again and again, randomly tossed from trap to trap—all, who are seated here belonging to one of these groups, we stood under the terror of a horde of rats, that had the law on its side (*Essayistische Schriften und Beden I*, Kiepenhauer & Witsch, 1978, pp. 69, 72).

And shortly thereafter, Böll places the honor of the various deaths in an equivalent relation: "Each death has its nobility, each dead one his honor, the dignity of a dead man is inviolable, that of the young murdered Jew from Lemberg, that of the same-aged SS-man, who was misled" (p. 73). In these lines, Böll parallels the experiences of the Jewish survivors of the Holocaust with those of the German soldiers and the populace of the German cities. A precarious "blurring of borders" (Serrer, p. 50) comes about, which entered Böll's literary work on various levels. In the short tale "Im Käfig" (In the Cage), for instance, which Böll wrote in 1947, the author depicts the misery of a man in captivity during the war. It remains unclear whether this man is being held in a camp for prisoners of war or in a Nazi concentration camp. The text ends with the words: "He was just a human being—anyone" (*Erzählungen*, p. 63). It is evident that this line is intended to evoke a universal perspective, one that proposes ignoring any specific characteristics of the protagonist in order to frame a general outlook. The problem that derives from such a perception of the Nazi extermination politics was soon to become particularly acute in Böll's novel *And Where Were You, Adam?*

This novel was published in 1951. The many episodes focus on the destinies of various persons affected by the war. But it is most markedly the tale of the German soldier Feinhals, who experiences the war as utterly senseless. This assessment deepens when Feinhals befriends a Jewish woman, Ilona Kartök, whom he meets at a girl's school in Hungary, where his quarters have been established. Ilona is one of the two major Jewish figures to appear in Böll's oeuvre. She appears to be a "construction of various stereotypes" (Serrer, p. 53): She is beautiful, smart, fond of children, altruistic, and blue-eyed, and beyond that, she is a converted, ardent Catholic. Yet even her conversion does not protect her from being deported to a concentration camp. The sadistic commander of the camp, Obersturmführer Filskeit, is a perverted music lover, who forces newly arriving deportees to audition for him; good singers have slightly better chances of survival. But when Ilona begins to sing Catholic litanies too beautifully for him, he shoots her in an outburst of rage.

In this episode, Böll accomplishes the above mentioned blurring of borders not only by "christianizing" the Jewish figure but also by paralleling Ilona's deportation and Feinhals's transport to the front. Both travel in furniture trucks, clearly marking a symbolic equivalence between the Jewish victim and the German soldier. It seems that it was difficult for Böll to represent Jewish figures sui generis. In subsequent texts, he refrained from depicting episodes of Nazi mass extermination comparable to the events related in "Todesursache: Hakennase" and *And Where Were You, Adam?*

Billiards at Half Past Nine/Group Portrait with Lady

The critical perceptions of West German postwar society that Böll advances in his high-profile novels, such as *Billiards at Half Past Nine*, *Group Portrait with Lady*, and *The Clown*, are linked to reflections on German history prior to 1945 and in many cases prior to 1933. Rainer Nägele has observed that it is typical of these reflections that "precisely the specific aspects of National Socialism . . . move into the background to favor the more universal experience of war" (p. 184). Lawrence Langer nevertheless reads *Billiards at Half Past Nine* as a specific contribution to Holocaust fiction:

> The extraordinary relevance of Böll's novel to Holocaust fiction and *l'univers concentrationnaire* is nowhere clearer than here: for the failure of the retrospective imagination to find meaning in history or in the consolations of tragedy dramatizes the absurd position of man as Survivor: the act of recollection, instead of forging links with the past, only widens the exasperatingly impassable gulf between the dead and the living, creating a void which makes new beginnings for the future equally impossible (p. 270).

The main theme of the novel *Billiards at Half Past Nine* seems to substantiate this argument most impressively. The book tells the story of a family of architects, whose founder, Heinrich Fähmel, constructed an abbey in the 1920s. During the last days of the war, his son, who is a demolition expert, blows up the building under the orders of a crazed general. The tale is told from a point in time at which the grandson is rebuilding the abbey. Numerous additional episodes render a wide depiction of an era ranging from the Second Empire (1871–1918) through 1958. In alliance with Nägele and in critical opposition to Langer's contention, one determines that the jolting of historical understanding central to the novel's reconstructions does not have its source in a recognition of the Nazi mass annihilation as a core catastrophe. On the contrary, an occasionally quite ominous order made up of evil "buffalos" and good "lambs" seems to determine history in the book.

> A static order beyond history is hinted at, that is at once of a decidedly religious nature, but then more closely related to a vague, general notion of historical transcendence. The permanence of the "buffalos" from the age of Wilhelm through the present day of the Federal Republic can be read, on the one hand, as a continuity of certain historical tendencies, but on the other hand, a static reading imposes itself more strongly, that is strengthened by the religious nature of the symbolism and the leitmotiv technique: The order of the buffalos and lambs as permanent transhistorical structure (Nägele, p. 195).

The big topics of Böll's literary retrospectives with regard to the Nazi years are opportunism and the willingness to adapt, the suppression of the workers' movement, and the resistance of the "little people." Much like *Billiards at Half Past Nine*, the novel *Group Portrait with Lady*, which was published in 1971, paints an extensive mural of the era, documenting the manifold entanglements of the present with the past, particularly the war years. At the center of numerous recollections and eyewitness accounts collected from various involved persons by an *aut* (author), a woman who attempted throughout her life to avoid adapting to social conventions is remembered. Viewing this novel by way of example, Klaus Briegleb notes:

> Böll's naive literary humanism illuminates the methodological problem of NS-reflexive literature, the representation of the 'victims', in as much as it solves the problem

> morally and a widespread community at home is grateful for its doing this: Here we have an author, who writes in constant worry about the possibility of empathizing with the experiences that his figures have, also and especially if they are resistant figures. The NS-continuum is attacked as if it were the wilhelminian Germany of Heinrich Mann (obsession with order, opportunism etc.) (p. 82).

In *Group Portrait with Lady* the "confrontation with the *Shoah* is not a 'theme', the personnel is oriented in the worst of it to war and breakdown." Beyond that, Böll again advances a problematic representation of a Jewish figure in this novel. The second vital Jewish figure in Böll's writings is Rachel. Like Ilona Kartök in *And Where Were You, Adam?* Rachel is a nun, converted to Catholicism. She seems to share some traits with Simone Weil and Edith Stein who were of Jewish descent, had a close connection to Catholicism, and were persecuted by the Nazis. In an interview that Böll gave in 1973, he responded to some criticism of *Group Portrait* that had come to his ears in the United States.

> I was recently in America, . . . and they all said, my God, you don't write anything about Hitler and the war, about the great murders and these stories. I told them, when I know that it could mean punishment by death to give a Jew or a Soviet prisoner of war a cigarette, then I know everything about the Nazi period. . . . I just name the cigarette in order to illustrate 12 years of German history. I don't really need to know more. Then I don't need to write about the KZs, because they're already in there, aren't they? (Interviews I, p. 25).

With these sentences, Böll formulated the notion that only a few reminiscences, even mildly hinting at the years of Nazi rule, are potentially sufficient to summon up the entire catastrophic cosmos in the mind of the reader, particularly the mass annihilation ("KZs"). But actually, Böll's writing refrained from leading to the " 'pits of terror', that would open up to a historical reflection of the victimizers" (Briegleb, p. 82). This may be one of the reasons for the great success that Heinrich Böll experienced in Germany.

Reception in Germany and Abroad

In West Germany, Heinrich Böll's literary works were generally received ambivalently. Although he had already been honored with the prize of the Gruppe 47, one of the most important prizes for a literary work in Germany at the time, in 1951, it was not until 1953 that he achieved commercial success with the volume *And Never Said a Word*. The scandalous dimension of Böll's texts was not constituted by the rare representations of mass annihilation but by the increasingly insistent representation of immediate continuities between the Nazi period and the early days of the Federal Republic. Böll's repeated criticism of the official Catholic Church also caused displeasure in church-related media. Renowned critics, such as Karl Korn, Marcel Reich-Renicki, Hans Schwab-Felisch, and Joachim Kaiser, critically appraised Böll's writings for decades, always trying to make sure that heightened debate about the content didn't prohibit a discussion of formal questions. In 1968, Theodor W. Adorno referred to Heinrich Böll as representative of the spirit of people who share his language.

The fame that Böll enjoyed outside of Germany was more unanimous. After a slow start, Böll's novels gained increasing acclaim among readers in France and in the United States, and they were soon translated regularly. Böll attained an exceptional position during the 1960s in eastern Europe, most remarkably in the Soviet Union, as well as in Israel. In these countries, he enjoyed the reputation of a German who knew how to convincingly combine national self-criticism with personal integrity. This helped to build bridges before the political rehabilitation of international relations had begun to make headway. Böll's appointment to receive the Nobel Prize in literature in 1972 commemorated these achievements both implicitly and explicitly.

Being recognized as a voice of the nation's conscience did not protect Böll from a large-scale campaign launched against him by the influential media company Springer in the 1970s. Böll had attempted to call for calm public discussion at a time when a militant underground group that sought an end to social injustice had abducted, and sometimes murdered, members of the social elite. Soon thereafter, the novelist was publicly denounced for allegedly sympathizing with the murderers. Even up until shortly before his death (16 July 1985, in Langenbroich/Eifel), Böll participated in various protests, such as opposing the attempt to station American Pershing II missiles in West Germany. Without a doubt, one perceives an increasing radicalization of the citizen Böll in these activities, which must also be viewed in connection with his literary work. What was determinant for his literary work seems to hold true for his concrete social engagement: Böll's writing and social involvement were most fundamentally motivated and structured by his own experiences of German power relations, beginning with those before 1933, when the Nazis came into power, and followed by those gathered as an army soldier at war on the European fronts. They are far less informed by a recognition of the Holocaust as a singular rupturing of history.

Bibliography

Primary Sources

Und Sagte Kein einziges Wort (And Never Said a Word). 1953.
Wo warst du, Adam? (*And Where Were You, Adam?*) 1951.
Billard um halb zehn (*Billiards at Half Past Nine*). 1959.
Gruppenbild mit Dame (*Group Portrait with Lady*). 1971.
Ansichten eines Clowns (*The Clown*). 1963.
Essayistische Schriften und Reden I 1952–1963 (Essays and Speeches). 1978.
Erzählungen (Stories). 1994.

Secondary Sources

Briegleb, Klaus. "Vergangenheit in der Gegenwart." In *Gegenwartsliteratur seit 1968*. Edited by Klaus Briegleb and Sigrid Weigel. Munich, Vienna: Hanser, 1992, 73–116.

Butler, Michael. *The Narrative Fiction of Heinrich Böll: Social Conscience, and Literary Achievement*. Cambridge, New York: Cambridge University Press, 1994.

Langer, Lawrence L. *The Holocaust and the Literary Imagination*. New Haven and London: Yale University Press, 1975, pp. 265–284.

Nägele, Rainer. "Heinrich Böll. Die große Ordnung und die kleine Anarchie." In *Gegenwartsliteratur und Drittes Reich*. Edited by Hans Wagener. Stuttgart: Reclam, 1977, pp. 183–204.

Reid, J. H. *Heinrich Böll—A German for His Time*. Oxford, New York, Hamburg: 1988.

Serrer, Michael. "Parallelisierung und Grenzverwischung—Zur Darstellung von Juden im Werk Heinrich Bölls." In *Vom Umgang mit der Schoah in der deutschen Nachkriegsliteratur*. Edited by Norbert Oellers. Berlin: Erich Schmidt, 1995, pp. 50–64.

Vogt, Jochen. "Der Erinnerungsarbeiter–Zur Charakteristik des Publizisten Böll." Ju: Jochen Vogt 'Erinnerung ist unseve Aufgabe'—über Literadur Moral und Politik 1945–1990. Opladen, 1991.

White, Ray Lewis. *Heinrich Böll in America, 1954–1970*. Hildesheim, New York: Olms, 1979.

Interview

"Eine deutsche Erinnerung," *Heinrich Böll: Werke–Interviews I 1961–1978*. Köln: Kiepenheuer & Witsch 1980, 504–665.

JORGE LUIS BORGES

(1899–1986)

ILAN STAVANS

THROUGHOUT HIS LIFE, Jorge Luis Borges, an Argentinean non-Jew, was infatuated with Jewish motifs and symbols. This led him to seek to trace a Jewish ancestor in his genealogical tree, one who would make him, finally, *un judío*. Among the plethora of essays, stories, interviews, lectures, and reviews he left behind that address this interest, one of the most emblematic pieces is a small composition, barely six paragraphs long, titled "I, a Jew." In it Borges reacted, with enviable concentration and stalwart conviction, to a 1934 claim by the magazine *Crisol* that he was indeed a Jew. The accusation came from an antisemitic faction of the Argentine intelligentsia whose objective was to discredit him in public opinion. Borges, in turn, took it as a compliment. To get a sense of his response, a quote from the translation by Eliot Weinberger will suffice:

> Like the Druzes, like the moon, like death, like next week, the distant past is one of those things that can enrich ignorance. It is infinitely malleable and agreeable, far more obliging than the future and far less demanding of our efforts. It is the famous season favored by all mythologies.
>
> Who has not, at one point or another, played with thoughts of his ancestors, with the prehistory of his flesh and blood? I have done so many times, and many times it has not displeased me to think of myself as Jewish. It is an idle hypothesis, a frugal and sedentary adventure that harms no one, not even the name of Israel, as my Judaism is wordless, like the songs of Mendelssohn: *Selected Non-Fiction*, edited by Eliot Weinberger, New York: Viking, 1999, pp. 110–111).

One year earlier, Hitler had achieved power in Germany. The Ashkenazic population of Hispanic America had arrived, between roughly 1880 and 1930, so that by 1934 Jews, mostly poor and uneducated, were a fixture in Argentinean society. Before this wave of immigration another one across the Atlantic into the Spanish-language regions had taken place: dozens, perhaps hundreds, if not—as some historians want us to believe—even thousands of crypto-Jews had arrived from Spain, Portugal, the Netherlands, and North Africa in the colonial era, between 1525 and 1810. But for a variety of reasons the slow disappearance of these crypto-Jews, and of the New Christians who came at the same time, was all but consummated by the time the Yiddish-speaking *shtetl* dwellers arrived in the same landscape. Argentina in particular had been a magnet for large-scale philanthropists and organizations imbued in the project of the exodus of Jews from Europe. The French benefactor Baron Maurice de Hirsch (1831–1896), as well as the *Alliance Israélite Universelle*, had put immense resources into the objective of making the pampas a suitable habitat—by means of socialist agricultural communes—for poor Jews escaping pogroms in Poland, Lithuania, and the Ukraine. The early immigrants, thus, had settled in rural milieus where gaucho life prevailed. This explains the lore of the Jewish gaucho at the turn of the twentieth century. But life in the countryside lasted only one, at the most two generations. Immigrants and their children slowly moved, en masse, to urban centers, especially to Buenos Aires. By the time Hitler came to power in Germany, a large concentration of Jews was already not only fluent in Spanish but also active in Argentinean society. Still, anti-Jewish sentiment, a fixture in Latin America from the time of the Spanish conquistadores and the first Catholic missionaries, remained rampant, and to this day refuses to vanish altogether.

Antisemitism, supported by the Catholic Church and by conservative factions in the government, permeated every aspect of life in Argentina. This, after all, is the only country in the Americas that has had a full-fledged pogrom: the *semana trágica* of 1919. As a Semitophile, Borges was a rarity. In fact, his love for Jews and Jewishness only increased as his career developed. It was constantly tested by events, such as the formation of the State of Israel in 1948 and acts of terrorism during Argentina's Dirty War in the 1970s and 1980s. More than anything, it was tested during World War II, from the time he wrote "I, a Jew," to the moment the Allies liberated the camps, when Borges was forty-six. The fascist sympathies that had infiltrated Argentina in the 1930s then became quite popular among conservative artists and intellectuals. Their liberal counterparts, for fear of inciting their foes even more, generally abstained from any involvement in debates that included the theme of the Jewish contribution to Western Civilization in general and to the nation's culture in particular. This state of affairs was reflected at the political level. In 1930, a military regime led by General José F. Uriburu had overthrown President Hipélito Irigoyen in a coup d'etat, inaugurating an era of ultranationalism. Anti-Jewish literature was produced and disseminated easily in that period. There were a number of defamatory books published, including the novels *El Kahal* and *Oro* by Adolfo Martínez Zuviría, a well-known figure who served as the director of the National Library, a job Borges would eventually hold. In them Martínez Zuviría literally called for the extermination of the Jews. Buenos Aires, the country's capital, perceived itself as a European bastion—an Enlightened City—in the Southern Hemisphere, and so, although the strident noises of the war were far away, the mood in Argentina as a whole was one of involvement, at least at the psychological level. Since the political establishment supported the German cause, Borges often found himself attacked for his beliefs. He and his friends responded by organizing conferences and lectures to counterattack the fascist trend, but the effort, by all accounts, was marginal. For instance, a PEN Club event in support of freedom took place in the mid-1930s in Buenos Aires; but even there the voices in favor of Franco, Mussolini, and Hitler garnered attention. Relevant too is the formation of the *Comité contra el Racismo y el Antisemitismo en la Argentina*, an organization that gathered prestigious Jewish and non-Jewish personalities, among them Borges, and whose mission was to confront antisemitism in the public arena. Again, its stand was more a sign of resistance than a practical move, for, by the time World War II started, pro-Nazi forces were everywhere visible in Argentina.

The general view among biographers and critics is that Borges was deeply apolitical and that, throughout his life, he remained disengaged with—even apathetic toward—local, national, and international affairs. There is some truth to this position, but taking it at face value runs the risk of oversimplifying his position. Borges, who in adolescence had been a dilettante à la Oscar Wilde (minus the ornamental outspokenness), invariably managed to volunteer sarcastic and parodic comments about current events; they were forceful, not to say acerbic. For instance, he denounced Hitler almost from the start, decrying the arrival of Nazism as a catastrophe for German culture. A partial yet enlightening record of his opinions is to be found in *Selected Nonfiction* (1999), which includes a full section devoted to the years 1937–1945. Although Borges's writing from this period rarely addressed events in Europe directly, he trenchantly debunked nasty stereotypes. In "A Pedagogy of Hatred," he attacks the German publication of the children's book *Trau keinem Fuchs auf gruener Heid und keinem Jud bei seinem Eid* (Don't Trust Any Fox from a Heath or Any Jew on His Oath), which, he says, "has already sold 51,000 copies." He adds: "Displays of hatred are even more obscure and denigrating than exhibitions," then proceeds to dissect the volume:

> Take any page: for example, page 5. Here I find, not without justifiable bewilderment, this didactic poem—"The German is a proud man who knows how to work and struggle. Jews detest him because he is so handsome and enterprising"—followed by an equally informative and explicit quatrain: "Here's a Jew, recognizable to all, the biggest scoundrel in the whole kingdom. He thinks he's wonderful, and he's horrible." The engravings are more astute: the German is a Scandinavian, eighteen-year-old athlete, plainly portrayed as a worker; the Jew is a dark Turk, obese and middle-aged. Another sophistic feature is that the German is clean-shaven and the Jew, while bald, is very hairy. (It is well known that German Jews are *Ashkenazim*, copper-haired Slavs. In this book they are presented as dark half-breeds so that they'll appear to be the exact opposite of the blond beasts. Their attributes also include the permanent use of a fez, a rolled cigar, and ruby rings.) (*Selected Non-Fiction*, pp. 199–200).

Borges concludes: "What can one say about such a book? Personally, I am outraged, less for Israel's sake than for Germany's, less for the offended community than for the offensive nation."

The list of Borges's anti-Nazi rejoinders includes another piece drafted in 1938, in which he complains that in a revised edition of A.F.C. Vilmar's *Geschichte der deutschen National-Literatur*, edited by Johannes Rohr, entries on Goethe, Lessing, and Nietzsche have been mutilated, and the catalogue that includes seven hundred authors "incredibly, silences the name of Heine." Borges was an unequivocal admirer of German literature, and was distressed by its decline. "I don't know if the world can do without German civilization," he wrote in the highbrow magazine *Sur*, edited by his loyal friend and admirer, Victoria Ocampo; and, in another issue of the same journal, he stated: "It is unarguable that a [German] victory would see the ruin and debasement of the world." Obviously, this type of judgment could have only a limited impact on public opinion. Still, Borges regularly denounced the excesses of fascism. And yet, the outside world succeeded in reminding him that Germanophilia was on the rise in Argentina. In 1939, the crew of a German ship cornered by British forces found refuge in Argentina, confirming the country's endorsement of Nazism. This openness to Germans would continue until after World War II, when former officers such as Adolf Eichmann, and other soldiers carrying fake passports, were allowed entrance and protection, at times making a life in the same neighborhoods where survivors of concentration camps and other Jewish refugees lived. In an essay of 1940 that is probably the most important one—surely the most discussed—by Borges on the topic, called "Definition of a Germanophile," he openly ridiculed the *germanófilos* in his country. He portrayed them as monstrous people whose knowledge of German civilization is sketchy at best, who indulge in acts of the most egregious form of censorship of their own culture, and who often verge on Anglophobia as they foolishly describe the excesses of the English people in Europe. These Germanophiles, Borges states, are nothing but admirers of Hitler, "not in spite of the high-altitude bombs and the rumbling invasions, the machine guns, the accusations and lies, but because of those acts and instruments." He then adds:

> He is delighted by evil and atrocity. The triumph of Germany does not matter to him; he wants the humiliation of England and a satisfying burning of London. . . . [T]he offenses I ascribe to Hitler are, for him, wonders and virtues. . . . The Hitlerist is always a spiteful man, and a secret and sometimes public worshiper of criminal "vivacity" and cruelty. He is, thanks to a poverty of imagination, a man who believes that the future cannot be different from the present, and that Germany, till now victorious, cannot lose. He is the cunning man who longs to be on the winning side ("Definition of a Germanophile," *Selected Non-Fiction*, p. 205).

Borges greeted the news of the liberation of Paris with exhilaration in an essay that has been insufficiently read, much less studied in detail: "A Comment on August 23, 1944." In it he discusses the numerous contradictions of the many Argentineans who supported Nazism, listing what he prefers to call "incoherences." Among these, "they adore the German race, but they abhor 'Saxon' America; they condemn the articles of Versailles, but they applaud the wonders of the *Blitzkrieg*; they are antisemitic, but they profess a religion of Hebrew origin; . . . [and] they idolize San Martín, but they regard the independence of America as a mistake." The last paragraph of the essay reverberates in Borges's fiction:

> For Europeans and Americans, one order and only one is possible; it used to be called Rome, and now it is called Western Culture. To be a Nazi (to play the energetic barbarian, Viking, Tartar, sixteenth-century conquistador, gaucho, or Indian) is, after all, mentally and morally impossible. Nazism suffers from unreality, like [John Scotus] Erigena's hell. It is uninhabitable; men can only die for it, lie for it, wound or kill for it. No one, in the intimate depths of his being, can wish it to triumph. I shall risk this conjecture: *Hitler wants to be defeated.* Hitler is blindly collaborating with the inevitable armies that will annihilate him, as the metal vultures and the dragon (which must have known that they were monsters) collaborated, mysteriously, with Hercules ("A Comment on August 23, 1994," *Selected Non-Fiction*, p. 211).

The sentence italicized—by Borges himself—is a paradigm: Hitler wanted to succeed in his campaign to dominate the planet, Borges argues, yet, upon realizing that the endeavor was impossible, he deliberately sought to be crushed—indulged in an effort that could only culminate in his own defeat. For this defeat Hitler saw as a triumph: a triumph of evil over good, a triumph of barbarism over civilization.

Fiction

While in his nonfiction Borges regularly discussed the impact of fascism at home, in his stories he took a different route: every tale on the subject is set in Europe, from Czechoslovakia to Germany itself. Why is this so? Perhaps because it allowed him to tackle the issue frontally, to go to the source; and because he knew well that, since these pieces were in Spanish, their immediate impact would be felt in Argentina. Also significant is that none of these fictions take place inside a concentration camp, nor do they make reference to gas chambers or any other method of extermination. Yet they tackle the Holocaust fearlessly, in a fashion far more overt that almost anything produced by Argentine literati in those decades. (He also, throughout his career, used poetry to reflect on Jewish currents past and present, as in poems to Spinoza and on the Six Day War and the Golem. References to Hitler, though, are nonexistent in it.)

Borges's two brief stories about the *Shoah*, "The Secret Miracle" and "*Deutsches Requiem*," share a single, unifying theme: the last hours of a prisoner about to be executed by the Nazis; and the two focus, although from different perspectives, on a single concept: self-redemption. The former has a Jew as its protagonist, but it is told by an omniscient third-person narrator; the latter, instead, has a Nazi as its main character, and it is he who delivers the tale. "The Secret Miracle," written during the war and collected in *Ficciones* (1944), forms a triptych with Borges's other Jewish tales: "Emma Zunz" and "Death and the Compass." A subliminal tribute to one of Borges's intellectual heroes, Franz Kafka, dead by then for approximately two decades, it takes place in Prague in 1943. In the first scene Jaromir Hladik, a translator and playwright, is arrested by the Nazis for being Jewish. In his cell Hladik communicates with God, and this communication is the centripetal force in the argument. Hladik is the author of an unfinished drama called *The Enemies*, and he knows that, if his life is to have any meaning, it is because of his authorship. So he requests that God grant him a miracle—a secret miracle, since only he and he alone will know about it. In the final scene, as Hladik faces a German firing squad, the universe comes to a stop:

> The guns converged on Hladik, but the men who were to kill him stood motionless. The sergeant's arm eternized an unfinished gesture. On a paving stone of the courtyard a bee cast an unchanging shadow. The wind had ceased, as in a picture. . . . He had asked God for a whole year to finish his work; His omnipotence had granted it. God had worked a secret miracle for him; German lead would kill him at the set hour, but in his mind a year would go by between the order and its execution (*Labyrinths: Selected Stories and Other Writings*, edited by Donald A. Yates and James E. Irby, New York: New Directions, 1964, p. 93).

In the very last line, Hladik is shot to death on 29 March, at 9:02 A.M. Edna Aizenberg reads this story as an effort to grapple with the question of the limits of Holocaust representation by a synthesis of "historical anchoring . . . as a way of indicating the unmistakable circumstances and suspension of reality." She writes, "Borges tests the agonizing tensions between reality and representation . . . to at once articulate and evade the terror" (Aizenberg, p. 258). Elsewhere she argues that "the dichotomy Borges delineates here is clear-cut: on the one hand stands the Judaically-inspired culture of the Occident with which are aligned the virtues of the mind and the laws of morality; on the other, an uninhabitable Nazi hell of mental and moral vacuity and brute force" and that the story's thesis is the "miracle of mind over matter" (pp. 124–125), which she interprets as a "reaffirmation of Western culture and a celebration of Jewish intellect" (p. 125). Even though no evidence of a finished manuscript of *The Enemies* can be found, the prisoner dies satisfied: his life has been justified. Its justification, obviously, has to do with immortality. Borges's statement is clear: a writer's raison d'être is to leave behind the better part of his talent, and to struggle so that his contribution is finished, even if only "ideally." It is clear also that Borges understood what Jews in Europe were about in the face of tyranny and death: faith, endurance, and posterity.

"*Deutsches Requiem*," published only months after the Nuremberg Trials, is also, curiously, about faith, endurance, and posterity—but of a different sort. As fiction it is flawed, yet it contains the seed of a viewpoint more mature and developed than that of the majority of the nonfiction pieces about the war. Borges drafted it a bit later than "The Secret Miracle," and it was collected in his subsequent collection of stories, *The Aleph* (1949). The importance of "*Deutsches Requiem*" is that it is a mass in German for Germany. According to Evelyn Fishburn, "Behind the funeral lament for Judaism lies the lament for Germany itself. . . . The twin role that Judaism plays in this story of Nazi persecution is to represent centripetally its separateness from Germany and centrifugally its absorption into the main body of Germany's cultural history" (p. 149). Here, too, the philosophic and dramatic confrontation is between Jewish mind and German physicality, each represented by an emblematic character. The narrator Otto Dietrich zur Linde is a former German officer, an avid reader in youth of Schopenhauer and a devotee of Brahms, who joined the Nazi party and was elevated in 1941 to become subdirector of the Tarnowitz concentration camp. Linde, from his cell, offers a diatribe about the battle for Nazi control of the globe and, thus, delivers a justification for Hitler's actions. Borges, of course, uses the character as a springboard to explore the psyche of a "Germanophile."

Toward the last third of the story, though, Linde comes across a camp inmate who changes forever his views: the famous German Jewish poet David Jerusalem, representative of many Jewish intellectuals tortured and murdered by the Third Reich. Is it emblematic that none of these characters, Linde or Jerusalem—or Jaromir Hladik, for that matter—are real-life individuals? By all means: Borges prefers to work on composites, seeking to define archetypal figures that represent not one person but humanity as a whole. This quality of unreality is, in fact, what he is after: a sense that people are not as different from one another as they might believe themselves to be; that they are instead versions of, or at best variations on, a Platonic ideal. The following lines, in a footnote by an anonymous editor (Borges himself, of course) in "*Deutsches Requiem*" support this assumption:

> In neither the files nor the published work of Sögel does Jerusalem's name appear. Nor does one find it in the histories of German literature. I do not, however, think that

this is an invented figure. Many Jewish intellectuals were tortured in Tarnowitz on the orders of Otto Dietrich zur Linde, among them the pianist Emma Rosenzweig. "David Jerusalem" is perhaps a symbol for many individuals. We are told that he died on March 1, 1943; on March 1, 1939, the narrator had been wounded at Tilsit (*Labyrinths: Selected Stories and Other Writings,* p. 145).

In any event, Linde says of Jerusalem that he was "the prototypical Sephardic Jew, although he belonged to the depraved and hated Ashkenazim." He becomes obsessed with his victim, with the talent of his hexameters, his capacity to consecrate his genius to hymns of happiness. Linde's obsession and admiration accentuate his repulsion. In due time, he drives Jerusalem insane, and forces him to commit suicide. Linde trusts that he will thus be able to eradicate his own compassion, the Judaically associated realm of mind and morality. But he soon realizes that what we must detest in Jerusalem's world has a chamber in our own soul; that those we hold as victims are actually an essential part of ourselves. To become a new Man of Iron, Linde realizes, he must obliterate the Jewish soul. Here the italicized sentence from Borges's abovementioned essay "A Comment on August 23, 1944" acquires its full meaning. *Hitler wants to be defeated*: as Linde ponders his own destiny, he acknowledges that everything in the universe has its opposite: evil is the reverse of good and, therefore, Nazism and Judaism are two sides of the same coin. He also admits that Hitler not only hastened but also wanted his own ruin. Worse even, he announces that the Führer fought not for the German nation only but for all nations—since every man represents all men, each of us simultaneously beautiful and abominable.

It is an attractive idea, which, unfortunately, history often corroborates. Hitler's demise, for instance, coincided, on the Argentinean front, with the ascent to power of Juan Domingo Perón, another brutal dictator, one with deceitful socialist aspirations; thus, the era of *Peronismo* began, and Borges once again was, willy-nilly, an active participant. Perón emulated Mussolini and other European tyrants by instigating rowdy youthful groups and channeling their impetus against Jewish targets, from student groups to full-fledged institutions. During the first of his two regimes, between 1943 and 1945, a series of antisemitic events orchestrated by the *Alianza Libertadora Nacionalista* took place, in Buenos Aires in particular. The endorsement of Nazi values by Perón and his followers was disturbing to Borges, by then a celebrity among a small but solid intellectual elite, with a following also in France. In a series of declarations, he showed signs of deep concern: "The situation in Argentina," he said,

is very serious, so serious that a great number of Argentines are becoming Nazis without being aware of it. Tempted by promises of social reform—in a society that undoubtedly needs a better organization than the one it now has—many people are letting themselves be seduced by an outsize wave of hatred that is sweeping the country. It is a terrible thing, similar to what happened at the beginning of fascism and Nazism [in Europe] (Quoted in Emir Rodriguez Monegal, *Jorge Luis Borges: A Literary Biography,* New York: E. P. Dutten, 1978, p. 391).

It was during this period that Borges not only suffered public affront, as one *peronista* after another attacked or ridiculed him, but was also was the target of personal humiliation. His mother and sister were arrested and put in prison for a brief period of time, and he himself was demoted from librarian at the Miguel Cané Public Library to the job of inspector of poultry and rabbits in the municipal market of Calle Córdoba, a gesture by the tyrant's entourage indicating the kind of respect they felt a figure like Borges truly deserved. Borges's reaction, in return, was, as expected, nothing short of dignified: he never lost his composure as he pursued his desire to transform the affront, through metaphor, into a lucid assemblage of essays and stories. Among them was a collaboration with his friend Adolfo Bioy Casares under the pseudonym of H. Bustos Domecq, called *Monsterfest* (*La fiesta del monstruo*) and published in 1955. A handful of Perón's supporters saw their idol equated to Hitler and, at a time of international remorse about the excesses of Nazism, were offended by it. But they were more offended by the man of letters himself, who, in their view, refused to recognize Perón as the progenitor of *una nueva Argentina*. None of this deterred Borges in his quest to unveil the brutal side of the populist leader, nor did it diminish his love for one group of Perón's victims: the Jews. In a conversation of 1978, Borges, by then old and blind, stated:

The preeminence of the Jews in Western Civilization has to do with the fact that a Jew, aside from being English, French, German or whatever, is always a Jew. He is not tied by any form of loyalty or especial tradition, which allows him to innovate in science and the arts. To be an Argentinean offers a similar advantage.

By this Borges meant that Argentineans might be Hispanic Americans but also and more emphatically, citizens of the world. To which he added the following in a conversation with Antonio Carrizo four years later: "There are some people that see the Jew as a problem. I see in him a solution." (Irma Cairoli, "Algunos viven obsesionados," *Nueva Información*, 5 (1978), p. 8).

Bibliography

Primary Sources

The work of Jorge Luis Borges is collected in Spanish in four volumes published by Emecé. Various translations into English, of disparate quality, are available. The most comprehensive, unified selection is listed below:

Collected Stories. Translated by Andrew Hurley. 1998.
Selected Poems. Edited by Alexander Coleman. 1999.
Selected Nonfiction. Edited by Eliot Weinberger. 1999.

Secondary Sources

Aizenberg, Edna. *The Aleph Weaver*. Potomac, M.: Scripta Humanistica, 1986.

———. " 'Nazism is Uninhabitable': Borges, the Holocaust, and the Expansion of Knowledge." In *Jorge Luis Borges: Thought and Knowledge in the Twentieth Century*. Edited by Alfonso de Toro and Fernando de Toro. Frankfurt and Madrid: Vervuuert—Iberoamericana, 1999.

Balderston, Daniel. *Out of Context: Historical Reference and the Representation of Reality in Borges*. Durham and London: Duke University Press, 1993.

Fishburn, Evelyn. "Reflections on the Jewish Imaginary in the Fiction of Borges." *Variaciones Borges 5* (1998): 145–156.

Lindstrom, Naomi. *Jewish Issues in Argentine Literature: From Gerchunoff to Szichman*. Columbia: University of Missouri Press, 1989.

Sarlo, Beatriz. *Borges: A Writer on the Edge*. London: Verso, 1993.

Stavans, Ilan. "Borges's Jewish '*Yo*.' " In *The Inveterate Dreamer: Essays and Conversations on Jewish Culture*. Edited by Stavans. Lincoln: University of Nebraska Press, 2001.

———. "The Impact of the Holocaust in Latin America." *The Chronicle of Higher Education*, 27 May 2001.

Woodall, James. *Borges: A Life*. New York: Basic Books, 1996.

Interviews

Cairoli, Irma. "*Algunos viven obsesionados*." *Nueva Información*, Buenos Aires, no. 5, April 1978.

Carrizo, Antonio. *Borges el memorioso*. Mexico: Fondo de Cultura Económica, 1982.

TADEUSZ BOROWSKI

(1922–1951)

DANIEL R. SCHWARZ

TADEUSZ BOROWSKI WAS born in 1922 to Polish parents in the Russian Ukraine and received his early education there. After being declared class enemies, his parents were deported to Siberia in 1926. He remained with an aunt until his parents were released in 1932, exchanged for communists imprisoned by the Polish government. Borowski and his parents were reunited and settled in Poland. When the Nazis invaded Poland in 1939 he continued his education underground. In 1943, a few weeks before he and his fiancée were arrested for opposing the Nazis, Borowski mimeographed his first book of poems, *Wherever the Earth*, which, as Jan Kott has written, "predicted in classical cadences the extermination of mankind. Its dominant image was that of a gigantic labor camp" (pp. 14–15). Sent first to Auschwitz and then to Dachau, Borowski survived because he was an Aryan and worked his way up the camp hierarchy. Like the Italian writer Primo Levi, Borowski went through repatriation camps following the liberation of the concentration camps by the Allies, Levi in the USSR, he in Germany. After the war, he settled in Poland, embraced social realism, and became a prominent writer, before becoming disillusioned and committing suicide on 1 July 1951.

Borowski's stories about Auschwitz began to appear when he was 26. As Piotr Kuhiwczak writes,

> When Borowski's two collections of short stories appeared, *Pozegnanie z Maria* (Farewell to Maria) and *Kamienny 'Swiat* (World of Stone), in 1948, and later in other European languages, they caused considerable sensation. Here was a writer who, as Jan Kott writes, "judged European tradition and its level of civilization in the context of Auschwitz, while everyone else described and judged Auschwitz in the context of European tradition and its level of civilization." For Borowski, Auschwitz was neither a historical anomaly nor a temporary breakdown of civilized customs (p. 401).

The collection *Kamienny 'Swiat*, titled *This Way for the Gas, Ladies and Gentlemen* (1967) in English, derives from two collections that appeared in Poland in 1948. Borowski's stories of the camp are grim, spare, searing, and honest in self-revelation. He is a witness, a Daniel, speaking to all those who need to be alerted about Holocaust horrors. Aware of how Auschwitz and Birkenau turned fellow prisoners into murderous accomplices, and perhaps aware of Polish complicity in anti-Jewish horrors in the world outside the camps (violence that continued after the war's end) Borowski stresses how inhumanity and violence are contagious. Indeed, in the grim anecdote titled "Silence," when the prisoners are liberated, the prisoners turn on their tormentors and one of the oppressors is trampled to death.

The voice of *This Way for the Gas, Ladies and Gentlemen* is Borowski's fictional surrogate, a Polish prisoner, who, while suffering indignities, is not immune to antisemitism. As Jan Kott has written, "Borowski's Auschwitz stories are written in the first person. The narrator of three of the stories is a deputy Kapo, Vorarbeiter [*Vorarbeiter* translates as Foreman] Tadeusz. The identification of the author with the narrator was the moral decision of a prisoner who has lived through Auschwitz—an acceptance of mutual responsibility, mutual participation, and mutual guilt for the concentration camp" (pp. 21–22).

While sharing a common bond of having lived through the Holocaust, Borowski's speakers are somewhat different in each story. His speaker can be a labor kommando or an orderly. His speakers often remind us that they are not Jewish and therefore not in the same jeopardy as those they observe. At some points, Borowski's speaker seems hardened and cynical as when, in the title story, he is a predatory kapo—a labor kommando—meeting the incoming train and complaining that "dammit, they'll run out of people" (New York: Penguin, 1976, p. 31). What they have in common is that they are camp functionaries somewhat insulated from the worst deprivations. They are also Borowski's surrogates who express his guilt and disgust with what he observes. Borowski's despair is the result of the events his speakers describe.

In the final story, "The World of Stone," the narrator explains how he has become inured to emotional feeling and reductively insensitive to difference.

> Sometimes it seems to me that even my physical sensibilities have coagulated and stiffened within me like resin. . . . Through half-open eyes I see with satisfaction that once again a gust of the cosmic gale has blown the crowd into the air, all the way up to the treetops, sucked the human bodies into a huge whirlpool, twisted their lips open in terror, mingled the children's rosy cheeks with the hairy chests of the men, entwined the clenched fists with strips of women's dresses, thrown snow-white thighs on the top, like foam, with hats and fragments of heads tangled in hair-like seaweed peeping from below. And I see that this weird snarl, this gigantic stew concocted out of the human crowd, flows along the street, down the gutter, and seeps into space with a loud gurgle, like water into a sewer (p. 178–179).

Yet, in the last sentence, the speaker eloquently, if hyperbolically, turns his back on despair: "For I intend to write a great, immortal epic, worthy of this unchanging, difficult world chiselled out of stone" (p. 180).

The opening of the first and title story, "This Way for the Gas, Ladies and Gentlemen," takes us into a world where the fortunate who meet the transports thrive at the expense of those who arrive to be gassed or impressed into service as slave laborers. Words are deprived of their expected meaning and a frightening new language is created. The first story introduces us to a world where words metamorphose into new words. Terms like "Muslim" and "Canada" indicate the special camp discourse. "Canada" designates the state of well-being in camp; a special subdivision of "Canada" is the kommandos who help unload the transports of people heading for the gas chambers and thus are in a position to take many of the arrivals' possessions. By contrast, "Muslims" are those who lacked the strength or the wiles to survive.

The speaker, Vorarbeiter Tadeusz, is part of the "Canada" crew and wonders aloud what happens if there are no more transports; his friend Henri responds: " 'They can't run out of people, or we'll starve to death in this blasted camp. All of us live on what they bring' " (p. 31). Humans are reduced to predatory animals. Hearing an arriving Rabbi "wailing, loudly, monotonously," one of the fortunate prisoners who meets the transports exclaims: " 'Can't somebody shut him up? He's been raving as if he'd caught God himself by the feet' " (p. 32). Informed by his memory of the situation, the speaker's tone is unmitigated cynicism. The most narrow kind of self-interest motivates human behavior because the alternative *is* the gas chamber. Despite his desire to repress, the speaker remembers and narrates: "Motor cycles drive up, delivering SS officers, bemedalled, glittering with brass, beefy men with highly polished boots and shiny brutal faces. Some have brought their briefcase, others hold thin, flexible whips. This gives them an air of military readiness and agility" (p. 35). It is the juxtaposition of normality with the reality of what is actually happening that makes the horrifying story so compelling.

The drama of language—the "veraboten" of power versus the helplessness of the victims—comes through even in translation. Just as power corrupts the Germans, so it corrupts the prisoners of "Canada." Borowski wants us to understand the mentality of those who survive in this closed universe. The camp functionary-speaker sees the camp as a "haven," where "one is somehow alive." Note the impersonal pronoun "one" that distances the first-person involvement. Yet the speaker also understands the terrible ironic distinction between, on the one hand, the victims' plans for a future and, on the other, their life expectancy of a few minutes; he understands, too, the reduction of victims to a material resource for treasure hunters who will extract valuables for shipment to Berlin.

In the title story, "This Way for the Gas, Ladies and Gentlemen," "Zeugma" is the trope that Borowski's narrator, Vorarbeiter Tadeusz, uses to describe the transport systems. Interchangeably, trucks take lumber, cement, and people to the crematoria: "Trucks drive around, load up lumber, cement, people—a regular daily routine" (p. 34). When the transport cars open, the narrator describes the dehumanizing process:

> People . . . inhumanely crammed, buried under incredible heaps of luggage, suitcases, trunks, packages, crates, bundles of every description (everything that had been their past and was to start their future). Monstrously squeezed together, they have fainted from heat, suffocated, crushed one another. Now they push towards the opened doors, breathing like fish cast out on the sand (p. 37).

In this horrifying context, the cliché and childlike metaphor of "fish cast out into the sand" functions well.

In this story we see words deprived of their communicative function. The Polish narrator passively—almost catatonically—responds to a question of one of the Jews: "What's going to happen to us" with "I don't know. I don't understand Polish" before adding: "It is the camp law: people going to their death must be deceived to the very end" (p. 37). But the very use of the present tense in the retrospective telling illustrates his crises of conscience and belies the casualness of his response.

Borowski's narrator, Vorarbeiter Tadeusz, speaks in the present as if memory erases the past and creates a searing present. At first he writes as if he were one of the victims, but gradually we see that as one of those who meets the transports, he is one of the perpetrators—a prisoner, to be sure, but one who, in the grim survival of the fittest economy of the death camps, lives at the expense of others.

In a collection that questions the very possibility of the aesthetic, Borowski makes aesthetic choices for his imagined witness based on his potential to awaken his audience to what they may have ignored, repressed, or never known. Giving a story the shocking title "This Way for the Gas, Ladies and Gentlemen" is an aesthetic choice. Narrating the first (and three other major stories, "A Day at Harmenz," "Auschwitz, Our Home (A Letter)," and "The World of Stone") in the present, as if his "I/eye" were a camera, is another.

We see the metaphoric nature of the narrator's imagination, the reduction of feeling, and the apparent objectivity that struggles with memory's horror. Inhumanity grows by accretion; guards shoot recalcitrant children. As they relentlessly transport those who go to the chambers, trucks become etched in the narrator's mind as interchangeable with their death mission: "Trucks, loaded with people, start up with a deafening roar and drive off amidst the wailing and screaming of the women separated from their children, and the stupefied silence of the men left behind" (p. 38). The blonde woman who moves the speaker's humanity recalls the recurring topos in Holocaust narratives of human sounds punctuating and anticipating the silence of death: "In the silence that settles over nature at this time of day, the human cries seem to rise all the way to the sky" (p. 45).

The story titled "A Day at Harmenz" begins on a pastoral note that soon becomes ironic: "The shadows of the chestnut trees are green and soft. They sway gently over the ground. . . . The trees form a high palisade along the road" (p. 50). The story includes seven anecdotes of greed, pettiness, and self-survival in spare journalistic prose; the brief paragraphs resemble newspaper reporting and illustrate how the camps depend on a cycle of violence. The speaker, whose name is Tadek, a diminutive of Borowski's own first name, is judgmental and belligerent to Becker, a man who committed crimes at another camp but is starving. The speaker gets sixteen loaves of bread from Warsaw and is clearly far better off than the Jews. The *Unterscharfuhrer* abuses the Kapo, who in turn abuses other prisoners. The narrator closes this seven-part tale with the observation that the writing of his story confirms as much as the selection of Jews to be gassed: "What a curious power words have . . . Here in Auschwitz even evil words seem to materialize" (p. 80).

Perhaps the crucial insight, one that for a moment undermines the telling, is the last line of by far the longest story "Auschwitz, Our Home (A Letter)," a kind of grim parody of the Tristan-Isolde correspondence that takes the form of letters written from the men's to the women's barracks of Auschwitz. The story is an epistle to the writer's beloved, who is in the women's camp. The choice of the epistolary technique in "Auschwitz, Our Home (A Letter)," by which the persona Vorarbeiter Tadeusz frames his response as a letter to his beloved—a Polish woman partisan whom he had last seen in prison—gives the speaker a human voice. Even in the intimacy of love letters, accompanied by the almost tactile memory of physical presence and past touches, the camp cannot be left behind for a moment of tenderness or passion. Indeed, the memory of her presence gives way to an image of physical degradation.

In his letter, the narrator sees Auschwitz as a kind of parody of Western history and culture evoked only to remind us that ancient Greek and Egyptian cultures, which he regarded as European antecedents, also had a human cost and might be more of a foreshadowing of the current terrors than we readers would admit. Questioning the shibboleths of Western culture, he concludes with a dismissal of the aesthetic as a category; for Borowksi's surrogate and our narrator, the concepts of beauty and ethical ideals are anachronistic in the face of what he has learned about human nature, and the terrible *silence* that supports it. After he has heard a grotesque fantasy of a new way to burn people, the narrator concludes his epistle with an optative disguised as a declarative: "But this is a monstrous lie, a grotesque lie, like the whole camp, like the whole world" (p. 142).

Within Borowski's stories, the organization of Auschwitz replicates the hierarchy of the Nazis, but here the snobbery belongs to those who have the old numbers. The speaker is bitterly ironic about the jealousy of those who speak of "Auschwitz, our home" (p. 100), and yet he acknowledges that Birkenau may be worse than Auschwitz: "[Y]ou would understand why [Auschwitz prisoners] look down with contempt and pity on their colleagues from Birkenau—where the barracks are made of wood, where there are no pavements, and where, in place of the bathhouses with out running water, there are four crematoria" (p. 101). Barely disguised is Borowski's outrage at the psychological conditions—the traumatized state where one looks for external correspondences for chaotic internal feelings—that would enable people to make such a comparison. That in the above passage he uses the personal second-person pronoun acknowledges, even in his retelling, the need for an oasis of feeling.

It is a characteristic of Holocaust narratives to oscillate radically between, on one hand, the harsh realities of the outer world and descriptions of dehumanization, and, on the other, an effort to find a space for interiority, feeling, spaces of human feeling. Such oscillation creates a space between the telling and the told—an ethical and emotional space, and yet that momentary space is always threatened by the invasion of the actual. Borowski's detachment and distance reveal as they conceal his outrage. As Langer writes: "However extraordinary the imaginative efforts of the writer to disguise his theme with the garments of literary invention. . . . He can never totally conceal the relationship between the naked body and covering costume, the actual scars of the Holocaust and the creative salves that often only intensify pain" (Langer, p. 91).

In Borowski's Auschwitz, humans become cogs in a machine, a commodity to be used and discarded. Words become instruments to survive, not a means to express feelings. Figures of speech become luxuries, but luxuries that when introduced are often all the more effective. As in the brief anecdote "The Supper," in which prisoners are forced to watch while Russian soldiers are murdered by the SS under the auspices of a sadistic commandant, the metaphors are drawn from the Holocaust experience:

> A dark, gusty wind, heavy with the smells of the thawing, sour earth, tossed the clouds about and cut through your body like a blade of ice. . . . Several bluish lamps, swaying to and fro on top of high lamp-posts, threw a dim light over the black, tangled tree branches reaching out over the road, the shiny sentry-shack roofs, and the empty pavement that glistened like a wet leather strap. The soldiers marched under the circle of lights and then disappeared again in the dark. The sound of their footsteps on the road was coming nearer (pp. 152–153).

Note the language of terror from the "wind's cutt[ing] through your body," to the threateningly anthropomorphized trees, the brutal "leather strap," and, finally, the ominously approaching soldiers.

According to his fellow prisoners, Borowski himself actually behaved heroically. Because he sees himself as a collaborator in a world where human life is reduced to a struggle for survival in which teeth and talons dominate, his fictional narrators bear the burden of a searing guilt. In "The People Walked On," Borowski's narrator understands that wiliness and the accident of birth that makes him Polish rather than Jewish enable his own life to continue as countless thousands walk to their death. While the motion of the camp moves almost magnetically to the gas chambers we feel his grim self-hatred and guilt for surviving. In all the stories, Borowski demonstrates how each human, as he or she moves toward the crematorium, is reduced to a caricature, a phrase, and a number to be counted among the dead.

Bibliography

Primary Sources

Gdziekolwiek ziemia (Wherever the earth). 1942.
Imiona nurtu (The name of the current). 1945.
Poszukiwania (Tracing, coauthored with K. Olszewski). 1945.
Bylimy w Ówiqimiu (We are in Auschwitz, coauthored with K. Olszewski and J. Nel Siedlecki). 1946.
Kamienny 'Swiat (The world of stone). 1948. *This Way for the Gas, Ladies and Gentlemen, and Other Short Stories*. 1967.
Pozegnanio z Maria (A farewell to Mary). 1948.
Utwory zebrine (Collected works). 1954.

Secondary Sources

Bosmajian, Hamida. "The Rage for Order: Autobiographical Accounts of the Self in the Nightmare of History." In *Metaphors of Evil: Contemporary German Literature and the Shadow of Nazism*. Iowa City: University of Iowa Press, 1979, 27–54.
Ezrahi, Sidra DeKoven. *By Words Alone: The Holocaust in Literature*. Chicago: University of Chicago Press, 1980.
Kott, Jan. "Tadeusz Borowski: A European Education." In *The Theater of Essence: and Other Essays*. Evanston: Northwestern University Press, 1984, 167–178.
Kuhiwczak, Piotr. "Beyond Self: A Lesson from the Concentration Camps." *Canadian Review of Comparative Literature/ Revue Canadienne de Littérature Comparée* 19, no. 3 (September 1992): 395–405.
Langer, Lawrence L. *The Holocaust and the Literary Imagination*. New Haven and London: Yale University Press, 1975.
———. "Auschwitz: The Death of Choice." *Versions of Survival: The Holocaust and the Human Spirit*. Albany: State University of New York Press, 1982, 67–129.
Milosz, Czeslaw. "World War II and the First Twenty Years of People's Poland." *The History of Polish Literature*. Berkeley: University of California Press, 1983, 441–532.
Parmet, Harriet L. "Images of the Jew Focused on in the Translated Polish Works of Tadeusz Borowski, Jerzy Adrzejewski, and Czeslaw Milosz." *Shofar* 18, no. 3 (spring 2000): 13–26.
Schwarz, Daniel R. "Haunted by History: Tadeusz Borowski's *This Way for the Gas, Ladies and Gentlemen*." *Imagining the Holocaust*. New York: St. Martin's Press, 1999, 129–142.
Walc, Jan. "When the Earth Is No Longer a Dream and Cannot Be Dreamed Through to the End." *The Polish Review* 32, no. 2 (1987): 181–194.
Wirth, Andrzej. "A Discovery of Tragedy (The Incomplete Account of Tadeusz Borowski)." *The Polish Review* 12, no. 3 (1967): 43–52.

KAZIMIERZ BRANDYS

(1916–2000)

MONIKA ADAMCZYK-GARBOWSKA

BRANDYS WAS BORN in 1916 in Lodz, Poland. From 1934 to 1938 he studied law at the University of Warsaw and was involved with left-wing student groups as a member of the Independent Socialist Youth organization; he contributed articles to leftist student journals. Because his family was Jewish, Brandys spent the war years in Warsaw hiding on the Aryan side together with his mother, Eugenia, at the home of a Polish doctor who, among other things, forged documents for Jews volunteering under false identity for slave labor in Germany. His father, Henryk, had died in a prison in Warsaw in 1940; Brandys and his mother went into hiding in 1941. Brandys was also helped during the war by Maria Zenowicz, his future wife.

After the war, in the late 1940s and 1950s, Brandys was editor of the influential cultural journals *Kuźnica* and *Nowa Kultura* and one of the representatives of social realism in Polish prose. He was awarded the State Prize in Literature in 1950 and 1955. During the so-called October thaw in 1956 he became part of the revisionist group of writers who critically evaluated their own former involvement with Stalinist cultural dogmas. Gradually disillusioned with the policy of the Communist government, he left the Polish United Workers Party in 1966 after more than a twenty-year-long membership. In 1970 and 1971 Brandys taught Slavic literatures at the Sorbonne. In the late 1970s he got involved in the dissident movement and, therefore, could not publish most of his works officially in Communist Poland. Since martial law in 1981 and until his death in 2000, he lived abroad, mainly in Paris.

Overview of Work

Brandys described himself as a Polish rather than a Polish-Jewish writer, and only in the decade before his death started focusing more on the question of his identity. Earlier, although he did not avoid Jewish topics and introduced some characters with Jewish names and biographies, he tended to focus on universal human experience. Generally, Brandys's fiction can be described as psychological realism. One of his concerns is presenting moral and ideological dilemmas of individuals entangled in social and historical circumstances, emphasizing their difficult choices and decisions. A number of his protagonists are members of the Polish intelligentsia exposed to the experience of the prewar, war, and early postwar period. His style is characterized by sharp irony and his provocative works had an important influence on Polish intellectual life in the 1960s and 1970s, as he often challenged moral and intellectual weaknesses of the Polish intelligentsia. Among others, he questioned the validity of Polish attachment to romanticized versions of national history. In this respect he followed in the footsteps of the well-known Polish translator and critic of the prewar years, Tadeusz Boy-Żeleński (Brandys did not deny his fascination with him), famous for his sharp critique of philistine morality.

Samson

One of Brandys's best known works directly connected with the Holocaust is the novella *Samson* (1948), part of the tetralogy *Miêdzy wojnami* (*Between the Wars*) (other parts included *Antigone, 1948, Troy, the Open City, 1949*, and *Man Does Not Die, 1951*) in which he draws a portrait of Jakub Gold, a young Jewish man from a partly assimilated family. Unfortunately, the novella bears traces of the period in which it was written, which explains its simplifications; in 1962 the writer published a revised version with numerous changes. In *Samson*, young Jakub, who identifies strongly with Poland and Polish culture, becomes a target of antisemitic attacks during the late 1930s, largely due to his stereotypically Jewish looks. His physiognomy has a symbolic significance in the novella. Because of his strength and handsome dark face crowned with black curly hair he resembles the biblical Samson, but for Polish nationalists of the prewar period and later for the Nazis, he is an epitome of the hated Jew. He believes that people find his looks suggestive of the characteristics they hate in Jews.

Before the war Jakub is first arrested for a few days for urinating at the tomb of the unknown soldier in his hometown after he had become drunk at a party, and later for killing a Polish nationalist student at an anti-Jewish riot at the University of Warsaw. Jakub acts in self-defense, unaware of his enormous strength. During the war he is released from prison and spends a couple of years in the Warsaw ghetto and later in hiding on the Aryan side, sheltered by a man he befriended in prison. After the man dies and his wife and daughter have to leave Warsaw, Jakub must depart. When he comes out of hiding, he is approached by a *szmalcownik* (an informer making a profit by blackmailing Jews during the war), who wants to denounce him to the Gestapo, but is miraculously saved by members of an underground organization (most probably of Communist orientation). Jakub does not want to die as a victim, but in battle. As he explains to his comrades, he is not afraid of death but he does not want to die simply for being a Jew because it seems to him "that a man should not perish only for being what he is . . . man is not a hare. Man in such times as we have now should die for what he does" (Czytelnik, 1962, p. 159; translation by Monika Adamczyk-Garbowska).

The novella ends with Jakub casting grenades at the Germans and then jumping from the building that houses the secret organization's headquarters. With his last gesture he tears down a veil which forms a kind of wing over him:

> That's how the story of Jakub Gold ended. He fell on the edge of the sidewalk. He lay peacefully, prostrate, with his left arm stretched towards the street; in his right hand he held the curtain, its end covered his face (p. 167).

This image follows the sociorealist aesthetics of Stalinist paintings and sculptures presenting workers and Communists in the pompous poses of ancient heroes. In 1961 Andrzej Wajda, the leading Polish film director, adapted the novella for the screen.

Other Literary Forms

In later years Brandys turned to essayistic and diaristic forms (for example, his cycle of *Miesiâce* [*Months*], which he continued to publish for a couple of decades), where he reflects occasionally on the Holocaust. In his diary *Zapamiêtane* (*The Things Remembered*, 1995), in which he included references that he considered particularly important, among them some recollections from World War II, he recalls among others the Polish Jewish writer Adolf Rudnicki and compares his fate during the war to his own. As miraculous as it may seem, they both "emerged from the abyss untouched, shaved and decently dressed" (Wydawnictwo Literackie, 1995, p. 23). He contrasts his and Rudnicki's situation with that of other Jews. For example, he remembers how, during the Warsaw uprising of August 1944, he passed two Jewish survivors who probably had just come out of hiding because they looked as if they had stayed in a cellar for a long time:

> I passed them by, on that day I could not help any Jew in the world. I did not stop, I turned into Foksal Street, and then I ran bent along the barricade placed across the New World Boulevard unaware that the sight of that couple and me passing them by without a word would survive all those years and would wake me up in various houses and cities (p. 37; translation by Monika Adamczyk-Garbowska).

Passages such as this reveal his survivor guilt.

Brandys included some memories of hiding in Warsaw in *DŻoker* (1966, *Jockey*), where he also reflects on the question of how the war affected the Poles, to what extent it was a purifying shock for the society, and whether it affected them deeply. He sees this question in a larger context: the extent to which societies change, not under the influence of some reforms or other civilizing efforts, but while being exposed to death for longer periods of time. Referring to the Holocaust, he says that it was like a night falling when "Poles fell into silence then, only the mob gibbered in darkness" (*Jockey*, PIW, 1996, p. 211; translation by Monika Adamczyk-Garbowska).

To illustrate what he calls "a certain mystery," he describes (in *Jockey*) an event he heard of; a story of two brothers, both equally poor and even physically alike. When in 1943 a group of Jews was hiding in their village, one brother gave shelter to a family of a Jewish tailor while the other denounced a Jewish storekeeper's family and they both did it *disinterestedly* (by Brandys):

> When I say "Poles versus Jews" I cannot forget about either of the two brothers, I have to speak about both at the same time. So who am I talking about in fact? About Poles and Jews or about the puzzle of human light and human darkness? Of the unexplainable source of good and evil? (p. 212, translation by Monika Adamczyk-Garbowska)

This quotation illustrates the writer's basically universalist views. On the whole, because of his mixed identity and neutral position, and his lack of any direct exposure to the Nazi atrocities, he was more interested in registering different responses to the Holocaust, especially on the part of non-Jews, than in detailed depiction of Jewish experiences during the war.

Bibliography

Primary Sources

Drewniany koń (The Wooden Horse). 1946.
Miasto niepokonane (The Unvanquished City). 1946.
Antygona (Antigone) 1948.
Samson. 1948.
Troja, miasto otwarte (Troy, the Open City). 1949.
CzŁowiek nie umiera (Man Does Not Die). 1951.
Sprawiedliwi ludzie (Upright People) [a play]. 1953.
Obywatele (*Citizens*). 1954.
Czerwona czapeczka (A Little Red Cap). 1956.
Matka Królów (Mother of Kings, *Sons and Comrades* published in English, 1967). 1957.
Listy do pani Z. Wspomnienia z teraźniejszości, vol. 1–3 (*Letters to Mrs Z.; Recollections from the Present Times*). 1958–1962. English edition, 1987.
Wspomnienia z teraźniejszości (Recollections from the Present Time). 1959.
Romantyczność (Romantic Spirit). 1960.
Opowiadania (Stories). 1963.
Sposób bycia. Bardzo starzy oboje (The Style of Life. Both of Them Very Old). 1963.
DŻoker (*Jockey*). 1966.
Rynek. Wspomnienia z teraźniejszości (The Market: Recollections from the Present Time). 1968.
Jak być kochanâ i inne opowiadania (How to Be Loved and Other Stories). 1970.
MaŁa ksiêga (A Little Book). 1970.
Wariacje pocztowe (Mail Variations). 1972.
PomysŁ (An Idea). 1974.
Nowele filmowe (Film Novellas). 1975.
Nierzeczywistość (Nonreality). 1977. English edition: *A Question of Reality*, 1980.
Miesiâce. Wspomnienia z teraźniejszości (Months: Recollections from the Present Time). 1980. English edition: *A Warsaw Diary 1978–1981*, 1983.
Miesiâce. Dziennik (Months. A Diary). 1978–1979, 1981.
Kazimierz. Rondo (Kazimierz. Rondo). 1982. English edition: *Rondo*, 1989.
Miesiâce 1980–81 (Months 1980–1981). 1982.
Miesiâce 1982–1984 (Months 1982–1984). 1984. English edition: *Paris, New York: 1982–1984*, 1988.
Miesiâce 1985–87 (Months 1985–1987). 1987.
Sztuka konwersacji (The Art of Conversation). 1990.
Charaktery i pisma (Characters and Writings). 1991.
Zapamiêtane (The Things Remembered). 1995.
Przygody Robinsona (Robinson's Adventures). 1999.

Secondary Sources

CzyŻak, Agnieszka. *Kazimierz Brandys*. Poznań: Rebis, 1998.
Flaker, Aleksandar. "A Polemics with History: Kazimierz Brandys's *Rondo*." In *History: Another Text*. Edited by M. D. Birnbaum and R. Trager-Verchovsky. Ann Arbor: Michigan Studies in the Humanities, 1988, pp. 7–27.
Maciâg, WŁodzimierz. *Kazimierz Brandys* (in English). Warsaw: Authors' Agency, 1990.
Ziomek, Jerzy. *Kazimierz Brandys*. Warszawa: Wiedza Powszechna, 1964.

Bertolt Brecht

(1898–1956)

EHRHARD BAHR

Bertolt Brecht was born on 10 February 1898, in the city of Augsburg in southern Germany, and was baptized as Eugen Berthold Friedrich. His father, Berthold Friedrich Brecht, was Catholic, but his mother, Wilhelmine Friederike Sophie Brezing, was Protestant, and therefore their son was raised as a Protestant. He attended high school in Augsburg from 1908–1917. In October 1917, he enrolled as a student of medicine at the University of Munich, but in early 1918 he was drafted into the army and served as a medical orderly in a military hospital in Augsburg. After World War I, he returned to the University of Munich and changed his major from medicine to literature, but he never completed his university education. While earning his living as a dramaturge at a Munich theater and as a theater critic for Munich and Augsburg newspapers, he wrote his first antiwar poems, among them his well-known "Legende vom toten Soldaten" (The Legend of the Dead Soldier). As a writer, he was especially attracted to the theater. He wrote his first plays, *Baal* and *Trommeln in der Nacht* (Drums in the Night), between 1918 and 1920. The plays were performed in Munich, Berlin, and Leipzig in 1922 and 1923. With his career as a playwright well under way, Brecht moved to Berlin in 1924 where he had his greatest success in 1928 with the *Dreigroschenoper* (Threepenny Opera), based on John Gay's *Beggar's Opera*. The music for Brecht's opera was composed by Kurt Weill.

Toward the end of the 1920s, Brecht became strongly influenced by Marxism, studying the writings of Karl Marx and Friedrich Engels. During this same time, Brecht developed an avant-garde form of theater, called "epic theater," that was non-Aristotelian and was based on a narrative form of stage presentation. Throughout his life, Brecht sought to refine his theory of avant-garde theater, for which he coined many names, such as "dialectic theater" and "theater for the scientific age," but his dramatic theory is best known under its original name, "epic theater."

Although Brecht sympathized with the Communist Party, he never joined the party. In 1929, he married Helene Weigel, an actress, who came from an assimilated Jewish family from Vienna.

His early antiwar poetry and his identification with Marxist political and aesthetic theories made Brecht a target for Nazi persecution. On 28 February 1933, a day after the burning of the Reichtag, the building of the German parliament in Berlin, Brecht left with his wife and his two children, Stefan and Barbara, for Prague. After stops in Vienna, Zurich, and Paris, the Brecht family finally settled in exile in Denmark until April 1939, when they fled to Sweden. They were again on the move in April 1940, escaping to Finland and finally settling in Los Angeles in 1941. In 1947, Brecht appeared before the U.S. House Committee on Un-American Activities in connection with the hearings on the alleged communist infiltration of the motion picture industry. Brecht was questioned about his pro-Marxist writings, but since he was a cooperative witness and left the United States immediately after the hearings, he was never indicted, unlike the Hollywood Ten, a group of screen writers, motion-picture actors, and directors who refused to testify before the committee. Brecht and his family returned to Europe in 1947, first to Switzerland and Austria and then to East Berlin, where both Brecht and his wife had successful careers as directors at the newly founded theater of the Berliner Ensemble at the Schiffbauerdamm Theater. Brecht's productions were celebrated as models of his "epic theater." Although his theater was celebrated as a showpiece of East German culture, Brecht had conflicts with the government of the German Democratic Republic, which considered his writings too avant-garde and in violation of the state-prescribed aesthetics of Socialist Realism. Brecht died at his home in East Berlin on 14 August 1956.

Works

Brecht's importance to the field of Holocaust literature is displaced by his Marxist stance that addressed the oppression of Hitler's dictatorship and the war of aggression conducted by his armies, but neglected the German genocide of the Jews. Although Brecht's works deal with the racial doctrines of the Nazis in his play, *Die Rundköpfe und die Spitzköpfe* (Round Heads and Pointed Heads) and present the fates of victims of persecution, as in his one-act play *Die jüdische Frau* (*The Jewish Wife*), Nazi racism is presented as a capitalist ideology designed to camouflage the class struggle in the first play, while the Jewish protagonist in *The Jewish Wife* is shown to display the ideology of the ruling class. Three of the twenty-four scenes of *Furcht und Elend des Dritten Reiches* (The Private Life of the Master Race) take place in concentration camps, but not one of the inmates is Jewish; there are only a communist, a social democrat, and a Jehovah's Witness in "Moorsoldaten" (Peat Bog Soldiers), and in the other two scenes ("Dienst am Volke" [In the Service of the People] and "Die Internationale" [The International]), nondescript inmates are flogged by SS men. Brecht's "Ballade von der 'Judenhure' Marie Sanders" (Ballad of Marie Sanders, the Jew's Whore) is a poem illustrating the effects of the racial doctrines promulgated by the Nuremberg Laws of 1935 that outlawed marriage and nonmarital sexual relations between Jews and non-Jews. But the poem's focus is on the plight of the gentile woman—who is driven through the town with a sign around her neck, designating her as the "Jew's Whore"—rather than on her Jewish lover. Another poem, entitled "Der Jude, ein Unglück für das Volk" (The Jew, a Misfortune for the Nation), exposes the crude manipulation of public opinion by the Nazis, who employed this age-old antisemitic slogan, coined by the German historian Heinrich von Treitschke (1834–1896). But instead of exposing vulgar antisemitism, Brecht's satire targets the capitalists, the military, and the Nazi regime that exploit the people and are the real "misfortune for the nation."

The best example of the displacement of the Holocaust by Marxism is Brecht's play, *Die Rundköpfe und die Spitzköpfe* (Round Heads and Pointed Heads), written in 1931–1934 and first produced in Danish in 1936. Commissioned by a Berlin theater, Brecht began the play in 1931 as an adaptation of Shakespeare's *Measure for Measure*. The basic message of the adaptation was that the Nazi leaders and the rich Jews would join forces, regardless of race, and exploit the working class. The adaptation was rejected because in 1932 it was already too dangerous to produce such a play. Nazis had gained strength in the recent elections and would use violence to prevent the staging of such a play. While in exile in Denmark, Brecht revised the play but not its central message, and it was finally put on stage in Copenhagen in 1936.

The play takes place in the fictional country of Yahoo with its capital, Luma. All characters have Spanish names. The plot presents the Round Heads as the majority population and the Pointed Heads as a minority with a differing physical characteristic. Both groups are referred to as "races." The parallels to antisemitism are just as obvious as the allusions to Franco Spain and Nazi Germany. Angelo Iberin, a strongman politician and demagogue, provides the ideology that is designed to protect the ruling class, conceal the economic crisis, and direct national attention to a nonissue, namely the difference between the Round Heads and the Pointed Heads. Iberin's ideology glorifies the Round Heads as the indigenous people and the Pointed Heads as foreigners, responsible for exploitation and the economic crisis. This Marxist interpretation of Nazi racism totally obscures the goals of Hitler's antisemitism to eliminate Jews from Germany. Although the Nuremberg Laws were not yet formulated in 1934, when Brecht completed the play, and the extermination program of the "Final Solution" was not yet developed, there could be no doubt about Hitler's intentions. But Brecht's anti-Fascism was stronger than his relative disinterest in the persecution of Jews in Nazi Germany. His Marxist commitment prevented any radical change of his opinions, as far as his works were concerned.

Brecht's one-act play *Die jüdische Frau* (*The Jewish Wife*) is part of the twenty-four scenes of the cycle, *Furcht und Elend des Dritten Reiches* (The Private Life of the Master Race) that he wrote from 1935–1938 and that was first produced in Paris in 1938, then in New York in 1942, and in Los Angeles in 1945. The play is the most sympathetic and moving of Brecht's writings about the early stages of the Holocaust. It is a psychological study of a Jewish woman leaving her husband and Nazi Germany in 1935, before the most brutal events of persecution begin. She leaves her husband under the pretense of a short vacation abroad, but she is fully aware that she will not return and that her husband is glad to see her go, because their mixed marriage has affected his professional standing as a surgeon at the local hospital. Her husband, although aware of the real purpose of the vacation, fully participates in the pretense. While the wife hopes that there will be a moment of truth between them before she departs, this hope vanishes when her husband hands her a winter fur coat, although it is spring, and she had said that she would go to Amsterdam for only a couple of weeks. Both know that she is leaving for good and will need the fur coat for the next winter, but neither is able to face the truth. In her previous monologue, the Jewish wife has anticipated this final leave-taking word-by-word. But when it occurs exactly as she anticipated, both husband and wife silently acknowledge the shame of ending their relationship without telling each other the truth.

But even here, Brecht refers to the failings of upper-class ideology, as expressed by the Jewish wife who considers herself uninterested in politics and "thoroughly bourgeois" (Brecht, p. 14). She admits to herself that she has agreed that there were valuable people and less valuable people. "The valuable people get insulin, when they have sugar in the blood, the less valuable don't" (Brecht, p. 14). She realizes that she now belongs to the less valuable, according to Nazi categories, and the only redeeming feature is that she accepts this categorization as punishment for her failure.

Reception

As a writer of Holocaust literature, Brecht must be considered marginal because his Marxist stance casts a doctrinaire shadow on his writings dealing with events of the persecution of Jews. The only exception is *The Jewish Wife*—perhaps the most performed play of Brecht's works in response to the Holocaust. *Die Rundköpfe und die Spitzköpfe* (The Round Heads and the Pointed Heads) and its message that the Nazis and the rich Jews would unite against the working class, regardless of the race issue, was a failure already in 1936. Although there is no doubt about his anti-Fascist commitment—there are numerous poems and plays to document it—he never thematized the German genocide of the Jews in his writings.

Bibliography

Primary Sources

Baal. 1922.
Trommeln in der Nacht (*Drums in the Night*). 1923.
Die Dreigroschenoper (*The Threepenny Opera*). 1929.
"Ballade von der 'Judenhure' Marie Sanders" (Ballad of Marie Sanders, The Jew's Whore). 1937.
"Der Jude, ein Unglück für das Volk" (The Jew, a Misfortune for the People). 1938.
Die jüdische Frau in *Furcht und Elend des Dritten Reiches* (The Jewish Wife in The Private Life of the Master Race). 1938.
"Dienst am Volke," "Die Internationale" and "Moorsoldaten" in *Furcht und Elend des Dritten Reiches* (In the Service of the People, The International, and The Peat Bog Soldiers in The Private Life of the Master Race). 1938.
Die Rundköpfe und die Spitzköpfe (Round Heads and Pointed Heads). 1956.
Werke: Grosse kommentierte Berliner und Frankfurter Ausgabe (Comprehensive Collected Works with Commentary: Berlin-Frankfurt Edition). 1988–1998.

Translations

The Jewish Wife and Other Short Plays. 1965.
Collected Plays. 1970–1976.
Poems 1913–1956. 1976.

Secondary Sources

Bentley, Eric. *The Brecht Commentaries, 1943–1980*. New York: Grove, 1981.
Cook, Bruce. *Brecht in Exile*. New York: Holt, Rinehart & Winston, 1983.
Dickson, Keith A. *Towards Utopia: A Study of Brecht*. Oxford: Clarendon, 1978.
Esslin, Martin. *Brecht: Choice of Evils: A Critical Study of the Man, His Work and His Opinions*. Rev. ed. London: Methuen, 1984.
Ewen, Frederic. *Bertolt Brecht: His Life, His Art, and His Times*. New York: Citadel, 1967.
Gray, Ronald. *Brecht the Dramatist*. Cambridge: Cambridge University Press, 1976.
Hayman, Ronald. *Brecht: A Biography*. New York: Oxford University Press, 1983.
Hecht, Werner. *Brecht Chronik 1898–1956*. 2d ed. Frankfurt: Suhrkamp, 1998.
Hill, Claude. *Bertolt Brecht*. Boston: Twayne, 1975.
Knust, Herbert. "Bertolt Brecht." In *Twentieth-Century German Dramatists, 1919–1992, Dictionary of Literary Biography*, ed. Wolfgang Elfe and James Hardin, vol. 124. Detroit, London: Gale Research, 1992.
Lyon, James K. *Bertolt Brecht in America*. Princeton: Princeton University Press, 1980.
Mews, Siegfried, ed. *Critical Essays on Bertolt Brecht*. Boston: G. K. Hall, 1989.
Mews, Siegfried, and Herbert Knust, eds. *Essays on Brecht: Theater and Politics*. Chapel Hill: University of North Carolina Press, 1974.
Morley, Michael. *Brecht: A Study*. London: Heinemann, 1977.
Völker, Klaus. *Brecht: A Biography*. Translated by John Nowell. New York: Seabury Press, 1978.
Weber, Betty Nance, and Hubert Heinen, eds. *Bertolt Brecht: Political Theory and Literary Practice*. Athens: University of Georgia Press, 1980.
Willet, John. *The Theatre of Bertolt Brecht: A Study from Eight Aspects*. 3d ed., rev. New York: New Directions, 1968.

LILY BRETT

(1946–)

SIMONE GIGLIOTTI

NO OTHER WRITER has had so a dramatic and visible an impact in making memories of Holocaust pain and extremity speakable to Australian audiences as German-born, Australian-raised, New York–based poet, novelist, and essayist Lily Brett. The daughter of parents—Rooshka (Ruth) Spindler and Moniek Brajsztajn (Max Brett)—who had spent most of World War II incarcerated in the Lodz ghetto, with subsequent briefer internments in Auschwitz and Stutthof, Brett was born in the German Displaced Persons Camp of Feldafing, and migrated to Australia with her parents in 1948.

Interpretive Context and the Post-Genocide Generation

Brett's contribution to the growing field of Holocaust-inspired literature is somewhat unusual given that she is a so-called second-generation survivor of the Holocaust. The semantic connotations of the "first-" and "second-generation" are inadequate in Brett's case, for her work negotiates both the unspeakability of the first-generation experience in the years of Hitler's Germany, and the position of bearing witness to her parents' fragmented stories, heard in the years immediately after the event. The position of bearing witness is complicated by Brett's birth in 1946, a moment in German history when closure of the Nazi period was forestalled by the aftermath of atrocity: displaced persons' camps, hundreds of thousands of refugees, and attempts to fix accountability for crimes against humanity.

In *Children of the Holocaust* and *In the Aftermath of the Holocaust: The Second Generation*, Helen Epstein and Aaron Hass, respectively, gave a classifying label to the experiences of those burdened with their parents' memories. Subsumed under the category of "second-generation" experience were two consistent patterns: the silence of overprotective parents afraid of rousing painful memories, and alternatively, the repetitive telling of stories by parents (Fine, p. 191). Epstein and Hass's discussion is in need of fleshing out, however. Though Brett is a second-generation member, her work is acutely contemporary in addressing the loss of the testimony of survivors, which returns us to the narrative possibilities during and immediately after the event: who will tell the stories, and how will they be told?

Ellen S. Fine, in her study of recent French literature by children of survivors, renames theirs the "post-genocide" generation. This generation did not directly experience the Holocaust but has come to endure the psychic imprint of the trauma (Fine, p. 186); they retain an absent memory of the event, that is, their account is inherited as a collective and transmitted memory through the memories of the survivors themselves. Fine asks, How does the Holocaust shape the identity of those living in its aftermath—"the self's sense of itself"—and how is the burden of memory then assumed? How does the post-genocide generation respond psychologically and imaginatively to the legacy bequeathed it? (Fine, p. 185). The work of Lily Brett allows a consideration not simply of writing as producing truth and knowledge about the Holocaust, but also of obsession with the self's sense of itself.

Major Works and Themes

Brett's published writing includes poetry, fiction, and autobiographical essays or vignettes. Holocaust themes permeate each genre: strains in the parent-child relationship, the unfathomability of the parents' experiences, nostalgia for the lost culture and language of prewar Poland, and the obsessive quest to wrest the speakable from unspeakable memories. The nature of the event energizes and banalizes the production of cultural memory in national and individual projects. The metaphors commonly employed to describe it, like "conundrum," "black hole," and "earthquake," are equally problematic in paralyzing the moral conscience to continuing instances of genocidal activity. The central task of Brett's writing appears to be portraying the Holocaust world without popularization yet with some element of horror—an implicit acknowledgment of the inaccessibility of the Holocaust to those without direct experience.

Brett's poetry represents her first attempt to confront the Holocaust memories of her parents, and to bear witness to their stories. In *The Auschwitz Poems* (1986), the body, so central a metaphor in describing the Holocaust in terms of starvation, degradation, inhumanity, and injury, becomes a gendered subject of trauma. Poems such as "Their Bodies" and "Breasts" detail the assault on women. "The Toilet" and "Canada" examine the assault on and expropriation of the body in Auschwitz. The banalities of everyday life after the war in "Everything Looked Normal" are refuted with the her mother's inescapable identity in "I Wear Your Face." In *Poland and Other Poems* (1987) Brett revisits the geography of her parents' trauma and her own birth by imaginative return to such addresses as Pomorska Street. Brett mourns for her mother, who has since died, with this collection. She writes about her mother's entry into the Lodz ghetto with "At Seventeen," and in the section "Kaddish for my mother" eulogises her mother's beauty, physicality, and elegance in "Last Week" and "My Mother Is Dying."

Subsequent volumes of poetry include *After the War* (1990) and *Mud in My Tears* (1997). *After the War* considers themes of identity, guilt, and the possession of her parents' past as her own. "When I Began" alludes to the early invasion of Holocaust memories into her world and the consequent restlessness and anxiety. "Leaving You" documents the painful breach in her connection to Auschwitz that surfaces after her mother's death, while "I Keep Forgetting" is a relentless reminder to maintain the inventory of life and death in the camps. *Mud in My Tears*, her most recent volume of poetry, represents an intensification of the anxieties—how to remember and record her parents' experiences—pervasive in earlier works. The longer, narrative poems present a more reflexive treatment of the self's sense of self. The title poem struggles with the boundaries created by the words "victim" and "survivor"; clearly, Brett identifies herself as one of each. Her obsession with the Nazis is played out in "I Can't Leave Them," and the culture they destroyed is recalled with nostalgia in "We Spoke Languages" and "The Yiddish Songs."

Fiction

Brett's fiction continues the conversation with Holocaust memories. *Things Could Be Worse* (1990), *What God Wants* (1991), and *Just Like That* (1994) chart the varying effects of cultural, familial, and social alienation from Europe. Fragile relationships, family dramas, and Holocaust pasts are the dominant topics in stories of assimilated characters adapting to the unfamiliar world of Australia. The metaphors of adjustment that recur in these vignettes of social banality analogize the impossibility of escaping memories of incarceration in the first generation to the reminder of these in the second. This is particularly so in the character of second-generation Rosa Cohen in *What God Wants*. Her parents' Lodz and Auschwitz experiences persist as ominous clouds over her ability to articulate a Jewish identity separate from the Holocaust. The story "We Are All Brothers and Sisters" depicts the inherent difficulty of this notion, and offers an anatomy of dysfunctional family interaction: unresolved conflict between the first and second generation, the threats posed to Jewish tradition and continuity through intermarriage and assimilation, and the use of plumbing as a trope for the excavation and cleansing of history and the unearthing of memory.

Too Many Men (1999) presents an explicit confrontation with themes of perpetration, survival, and frustrated identities, asking the reader to revisit the landscapes of Jewish death in Poland with New York–based letter writer Ruth Rothwax and her Australia-based father, Edek. The book allows Brett the opportunity to savage the touristic theme park that Auschwitz has become and to comment on the futile attempts to rehabilitate Jewish communities in Poland, and is a tempestuous but ultimately endearing tribute to the resilience and endless appetite of her eighty-something father. Brett juxtaposes the contemporary theme of recovering one's past in Poland with a device that is limited in effect—the inclusion of Rudolf Hess, former commandant of Auschwitz, now a resident in Hell, or the so-called *Zweites Himmels Lager*, as a main character. Hess intervenes in Ruth Rothwax's journey of recovery; she conducts intense and extensive conversations with him about motivation, perpetrators, remorse, guilt, and knowledge—in fact, the issues at the center of much recent historiographical debate.

This device is only intermittently effective: some of the topics of conversation, such as Jewish resistance, attempt to animate long-standing controversies on definitions of active and passive resistance, while the tone of sarcasm and disbelief in which Rothwax delivers her soliloquies on Nazi terror distracts from the more affecting and morally gripping narrative of Edek's hesitant trips with her to the addresses and fragments of his past in Lodz, Krakow, Warsaw, and Auschwitz. Indeed, much of Brett's fiction is set in three places: Poland, Australia, and America. The scenes of wartime incarceration in Poland are revisited through the urban yet stifling cosmopolitanism of Melbourne and the vibrant ethnic diversity of New York. *Too Many Men*, in particular, travels between the two cities with ostensible ease, yet an undercurrent is that the return journeys of second-generation expatriate Australian Jews repeatedly seek a presence or cultural visibility in a society that is still defining its multicultural experiment.

Brett's autobiographical writings are *In Full View* (1997) and *New York* (2001). While *New York* offers vignettes of an expatriate gaze at New York, *In Full View* warrants further examination for its confessional reflections on the project of writing about the Holocaust, which has consumed much of the last fifteen years of her life. A dominant trope in Brett's work is the obsession with bodies: the Holocaust body, her mother's body, and her own body. In many ways, Brett's ballooning weight is the site of denying and admitting the links to her mother's history:

> I created this havoc with myself because of a complicated confluence of history and family. Death camps, starvation, greed, a beautiful mother who'd lost everything except her looks. It was a heady brew. I took my regular, symmetrical, attractive features, and I huffed and puffed until I distorted myself and resembled somebody else. And in that other person, I felt free to be peaceful ("Ageing," in *In Full View*, p. 10).

The persistent invasion of Holocaust memories in the lives of the post-genocide generation is obvious in Brett's writing. More important are the effects of these memories on conflated identities. Brett comments on her tendency to possess and inhabit her parents' world: "The fantasy of just being another statistic was one of the symptoms of my inability to separate my life from my parents' life. Particularly from my mother's life. Were we both in the Lodz ghetto? Were we both in Auschwitz?" ("The Writing Life," in *In Full View*, p. 346).

National and Critical Reception

When *The Auschwitz Poems* introduced her family's Holocaust past to Australian audiences in 1986, Brett received literary prizes and fame for traumas that were not necessarily her own. That she gave speech and elegant form to the muteness of her parents made her a pioneer in contributing to Holocaust consciousness at a time when World War II was a national topic of controversy because alleged Nazi war criminals were living comfortably in the suburbs. Though Australia is home to the highest proportion of Holocaust survivors per capita outside of Israel, consciousness about the Holocaust has lived mainly through the writings of children of survivors such as Brett and Arnold Zable, Mark Raphael Baker, and Ramona Koval. This is as much a consequence of the disappearance of the first generation as a reflection on the readiness of Australian audiences to listen.

The critical reception of Brett's writing has ranged from popular admiration to scholarly qualification. In many ways, Brett appeals to readers with recycled stereotypes of Jewish anxiety, tense relationships between parents and children, and stories of a paralyzing and unending Holocaust. In Germany, Brett's success has been credited with helping younger generations to confront the legacies of their Nazi past (Simon Mann, "Breaking the Wall of Silence," in *The Age* Saturday Extra, 7 April 2001, p. 8). In the scholarly arena, in contrast, Brett's work has remained relatively unscrutinized except for one psychoanalytic interpretation of her work. Esther Faye asserts that "Lily Brett leaves us in no doubt that her grossly overweight body is bound in a very particular way to her mother's traumatic history, that it is precisely in her body where the history of what was most indigestible about her mother's experience of the Holocaust got registered" (Faye, "Impossible Memories," unpublished version, p. 5).

In sum, the significance of Brett's writing should not be underestimated, though hers should not be taken as the only voice addressing post-genocide trauma in Australia. In addition to the writers mentioned above, sons and daughters of survivors, not because they possess any particular talent or prodigious literary energy, but because of the imperative enshrined in the words "never forget," are remaking the genre of transmitted histories. Doubtless this command, coupled with other more personal and intimate motivations, has produced both affecting and questionable versions of Holocaust trauma, conflated identities, and ever more personal reckonings with the self's sense of itself.

Bibliography

Primary Sources

Fiction
Things Could Be Worse. 1990.
What God Wants. 1991.

Just Like That. 1994.
Too Many Men. 1999.

Autobiography and Essays
In Full View: Essays. 1997.
New York. 2001.

Poetry
The Auschwitz Poems. 1986.
Poland and Other Poems. 1987.
After the War: Poems. 1990.
Unintended Consequences. 1992.
In Her Strapless Dresses. 1994.
Mud in My Tears. 1997.

Secondary Sources

Baker, Mark Raphael. *The Fiftieth Gate*. Sydney: Flamingo, 1997.

Epstein, Helen. *Children of The Holocaust: Conversations with Sons and Daughters of Survivors*. New York: G.P. Putnam's Sons, 1979.

Faye, Esther. "Impossible Memories: Lily Brett as Essayist." *Meridian* 17, no. 1 (May 1998): 63–72.

———. "Enjoying Traumatically: The Holocaust as the Second Generation's Other." *British Journal of Psychotherapy* 16, no. 2 (Winter 1999): 184–196.

Fine, Ellen S. "Transmission of Memory: The Post-Holocaust Generation in the Diaspora." In *Breaking Crystal: Writing and Memory after Auschwitz*. Edited by Efraim Sicher. Chicago: University of Illinois Press, 1998, pp. 185–200.

Hart, Alexander. *Writing the Diaspora: A Bibliography and Critical Commentary on Post-Shoah English-Language Jewish Fiction in Australia, South Africa, and Canada*. Ph.D. Diss. University of British Columbia, 1996.

Hass, Aaron. *In the Aftermath of the Holocaust: The Second Generation*. Ithaca: Cornell University Press, 1990.

Koval, Ramona. *Samovar*. Melbourne: Minerva, 1996.

Mann, Simon. "Breaking the Wall of Silence." *The Age* Saturday Extra (7 April 2001): 8.

Zable, Arnold. *Jewels and Ashes*. Brunswick (Melbourne): Scribe, 1991.

MAX BROD

(1884–1968)

MARK H. GELBER

MAX BROD WAS widely respected as a major European *homme de lettres* before the Nazis came to power in Europe. He was highly acclaimed for his numerous cultural achievements as a novelist, poet, critic, editor, religious thinker, philosopher, composer, and Jewish activist. Based in Prague, he was a key figure, if not the dominating personality, of a Prague circle of writers and intellectuals, which included Franz Kafka, Franz Werfel, Felix Weltsch, and others. Not only did he encourage and support Franz Kafka decisively on his path to fame as one of the most important writers of the twentieth century; he also played an important role in the discovery of young Czech and German poetical and musical talent. Influenced strongly by his friend, Hugo Bergmann, as well as by the thought and writings of Martin Buber, Brod gravitated to Zionism before World War I and he helped found the National Council of Czech Jews in 1918. Brod may be placed within the general category of Central European humanist Zionism with a strong cultural Zionist orientation. His affiliation with Martin Buber's journal *Der Jude* and Brod's authorship of numerous Zionist essays and collections between the World Wars elaborate this aspect of his thinking. With the takeover of Czechoslovakia by the Nazis, however, Brod left his native Prague and sought refuge in Tel Aviv. He worked as the dramatical adviser to the Habimah National Theater, while he continued to write in numerous genres and compose music until his death.

Brod's intellectual response to the Holocaust may be divided into two separate areas. The first may be labelled philosophical, while the second one is more strictly literary. Brod's religious-philosophical system, which he had articulated boldly in *Paganism, Christianity, Judaism* (1921), underwent some revision following the Holocaust. In this early work, Brod differentiated between two basic concepts: "noble misfortune" and "ignoble misfortune." The former derives from the finiteness of human beings and their metaphysical imperfection. It thus consists of the inescapable limitations of the human condition, such as death, illness, and moral imperfection. "Noble misfortune" is unchangeable, given that it inheres in the structure of human existence. The latter concept, "ignoble misfortune," derives from human behavior itself. It includes war, baneful social conditions, and hatred. Within the domain of "ignoble misfortune" human acts can make a significant difference. In this sense, the human condition can be improved upon. Humankind and God become partners within this framework, as political action provides a key to human amelioration.

Although the Holocaust does not appear to have caused Brod to alter radically his understanding of these fundamental categories, his reappraisal of his thought in the wake of the Holocaust led him to elaborate a new concept, which he called DSC in his two volume work *Diesseits und Jenseits* (Here and Beyond, 1947–1948). DSC is the abbreviation of the Latin name he gave this concept: *disruptio structurae causarum*, which means the disruption of causal structure. Brod identified heroic human actions, which tended to break through the natural causal structure of human life. By doing so, he supported his argument that human beings were ultimately free to achieve morality and a certain kind of immortality, especially in the face of pernicious evil. Human acts could thus reduce "ignoble misfortune" and lessen human suffering caused by evil in the world. Brod articulated a tragic theodicy, in that he saw divine suffering as an intimate component of the finite world. Accordingly, the world was created in order that all being and becoming would face their own negation. However, human acts of loving kindness and morality that disrupted the causal structure of nature could at the same time lead to the banishment of "ignoble misfortune" from the world and usher in a messianic age. In his last work, *Das Unzerstörbare* (The Indestructible, 1968), which is a revision of part of *Diesseits und Jenseits*, Brod repeated and emphasized his strong belief in the triumph of good over evil in the world, as well as his belief in a loving and caring God, despite the Holocaust and despite the human condition of "noble and ignoble misfortune."

Brod did not devote an entire work explicitly to the Holocaust. However, aspects of his religious-philosophical thought, refined by his attempt to accommodate the Holocaust in his scheme of things, find their way into his post-Holocaust fiction. Interestingly, most of his major novels from the postwar period are historical novels set in the distant past, for example his first novel following the Holocaust, *Galilei in Gefangenschaft* (Galileo in Prison, 1949), or his novels that focus on the historical Jesus (*Der Meister*, The Master, 1951), the Roman Cicero (*Armer Cicero*, Poor Cicero, 1955), and the humanist Reuchlin (*Johannes Reuchlin, und sein Kampf*, Johannes Reuchlin and His Struggle, 1966). This distance in time allowed Brod to address pressing issues of human morality, spirituality, individual heroism, and ethical action in times of adversity without naming the Holocaust explicitly, although these issues certainly pertain to his attempt to accommodate the Holocaust in his own understanding of the human condition.

In one postwar novel, *Unambo* (1949), the Holocaust assumes a place of real importance in terms of the plot, although this work is essentially concerned with understanding and defending the morality of the Zionist struggle to establish a Jewish state, following the War for Independence and the founding of the State of Israel in 1948. The fact that some of the Jewish freedom fighters in the novel are Holocaust survivors whose families were annihilated in Europe, or that one of the protagonists of the novel, a young fighter for the Zionist cause, lost his parents in the ovens of Auschwitz, tends to lend urgency and justice to the Zionist struggle. The death camps are mentioned time and again, although the work is set in Palestine/Israel. At one point during a savage battle, the hero of the novel attempts to bolster morale among the small group of Jewish combatants pitifully outnumbered by their Arab enemies. The notion is bruited that the world cannot comprehend at all the fact that together with each Jewish fighter there march hundreds of souls destroyed by Hitler in Auschwitz. While the Holocaust provides Brod with a convincing, and in his terms necessary, background for the establishment of the Zionist state, it is at the same time not sufficient according to his own conception. For Brod, especially following the Holocaust, the Jewish state must also be a living model of justice for its Arab residents. Brod provides a rather utopian answer to this problem in his fiction, arguing that love between Jews and Arabs will guarantee justice and serve ultimately to heal the wounds between these two peoples. However, how exactly that love shall establish itself as a potent force in the national lives of these enemy peoples is not explicitly thematized in the novel.

Bibliography

Primary Sources

Tod des Toten, 11 Novellen (Death of the Dead. 11 Novellas). 1906.
Experimente, 4 Novellen (Experiments, 4 Novellas). 1907.
Der Weg des Verliebten (The Path of the Beloved). 1907.
Schloss Nornepygge (Nornepygge Castle). 1908.
Ein tschechisches Dienstmaedchen (A Czech Servant Girl). 1909.
Erziehung zur Hetaere. Ausfluege ins Dunkelroete. Novellen (Education as a Courtesan: Excursions into the Dark Red). 1909.
Tagebuch in Versen (Diary in Verses). 1910.
Abschied von der Jugend (Farewell from Youth). 1910.
Juedinnen (Jewesses). 1911.
Arnold Beer. 1912.
Die Hoehe des Gefuehls (The Height of Feeling). 1912.
Der Braeutigam. Novellen (The Groom: Novellas). 1912.
Ueber die Schoenheit haesslicher Bilder (On the Beauty of Ugly Images). 1913.
Weiberwirtschaft. Novellen (Female Economy: Novellas). 1913.
Die Retterin (The Savior). 1914.
Tycho Brahes Weg zu Gott (Tycho Brahe's Path to God). 1915.
Die erste Stunde nach dem Tod (The First Hour after Death). 1916.
Das gelobte Land (The Promised Land). 1917.
Eine Koenigin Esther (A Queen Esther). 1918.
Das grosse Wagnis (The Great Dare). 1918.
Sozialismus im Zionismus (Socialism in Zionism). 1920.
Im Kampf um das Judentum (Struggling for Jewry). 1920.
Heidentum, Christentum, Judentum (Paganism, Christianity, Judaism). 1921.
Adolf Schreiber. Biographie. 1921.
Das Buch der Liebe (The Book of Love). 1921.
Die Erloeserin (The Redemptress). 1921.
Franzi, oder eine Liebe zweiten Ranges (Franzi, or a Second Rate Love). 1922.
Leben mit einer Goettin (Life with a Goddess). 1924.
Reubeni. Fuerst der Juden (Reubeni: Prince of the Jews). 1925.
Zionismus als Weltanschauung (with Felix Weltsch) (Zionism as a World View). 1925.
Leos Janacek, Biographie. 1925.
Die Frau nach der man sich sehnt (The Woman One Yearns For). 1927.
Zauberrreich der Liebe (Magic Kingdom of Love). 1928.
Lord Byron kommt aus der Mode (Lord Byron Goes out of Fashion). 1929.
Stefan Rott, oder das Jahr der Entscheidung (Stefan Rott or the Year of Decision). 1931.
Die Frau, die nicht enttaeuscht (The Woman Who Does Not Disappoint). 1933.
Heinrich Heine. Biographie. 1934.
Annerl. 1935.
Novellen aus Boehmen. 1935.
Rassentheorie und Judentum (Racial Theory and Jewry). 1936.
Franz Kafka. Biographie. 1937.

Das Diesseitswunder. 1939.
Diesseits und Jenseits (Here and Beyond). 2 Vols. 1947–1948.
Franz Kafkas Glauben und Lehre (Franz Kafka's Belief and Teaching). 1948.
Galilei in Gefangenschaft (Galileo in Prison). 1948.
Unambo. 1949.
Der Meister (The Master). 1951.
Die Musik Israels (The Music of Israel). 1951.
Der Sommer, den man zurueckwuenscht (The Summer One Wishes Back). 1952.
Beinahe ein Vorzugschueler (Almost a Star Pupil). 1952.
Briefwechsel mit Janacek (Correspondence with Janacek). 1953.
Franz Kafka als wegweisende Gestalt (Franz Kafka as a Pathbreaking Figure). 1953.
Fuenf Novellen (Five Novellas). 1955.
Armer Cicero (Poor Cicero). 1955.
Rebellische Herzen (Rebellious Hearts). 1957.
Mira, ein Roman um Hofmannsthal (Mira, a Novel about Hofmannsthal). 1958.
Verzweiflung und Erloesung im Werk Franz Kafkas (Despair and Redemption in the Work of Franz Kafka). 1959.
Jugend im Nebel (Youth in the Fog). 1959.
Die verbotene Frau (The Forbidden Woman). 1960.
Streitbares Leben. Autobiographie (Contested Life. Autobiography). 1960.
Die Rosenkoralle (The Pink Coral). 1961.
Der Prager Kreis (The Prague Circle). 1966.
Johannes Reuchlin und sein Kampf (Johannes Reuchlin and His Struggle). 1966.
Gesang einer Giftschlange (Song of a Poisonous Snake). 1966.
Ueber Franz Kafka (On Franz Kafka). 1966.
Das Unzerstoerbare (The Indestructible). 1968.

Secondary Sources

Baersch, Claus-Ekkehard. *Max Brod im Kampf um das Judentum. Zum Leben und Werk eines deutsch-juedischen Dichters aus Prag*. Wien: Passagen Verlag, 1992.
Gelber, Mark H. *Indifferentism, Anti-Semitism, the Holocaust, and Zionism*. Tel Aviver Jahrbuch fuer deutsche Geschichte, 1991, pp. 327–337.
Gold Hugo, ed. *Max Brod. Ein Gedenkbuch*. Tel Aviv: Olamenu, 1969.
Kayser, Wolfgang, and Horst Gronemeyer. *Max Brod*. Hamburg: Hans Christians Verlag, 1972.
Pazi, Margarita. *Max Brod*. Bonn: Bouvier, 1970.
———. ed. *Max Brod 1884–1984. Untersuchungen zu Max Brods literarischen und philosophischen Schriften*. New York: Peter Lang, 1987.

Melvin Jules Bukiet

(1953–)

ANDREW FURMAN

MELVIN JULES BUKIET (pronounced boo-KET) was one of the most important and prolific Jewish writers in the United States in the late twentieth and the early twenty-first century. Between 1985 and 2001 he published four novels, two collections of stories, and many essays and reviews in such publications as the *New York Times*, the *Washington Post*, the *Los Angeles Times*, the *Nation*, *Antaeus*, and the *Paris Review*. He also edited the anthology *Neurotica: Jewish Writers on Sex* (1999) and an anthology of writing by the children of Holocaust survivors, *Nothing Makes You Free*. A collection of stories is scheduled to be published in 2002.

Biography

Bukiet was born in New York City on 21 September 1953. His father, Joseph, was born in Proszowice, Poland, a village outside Kraków. He survived the Holocaust and World War II and immigrated to the United States in 1948. Bukiet's mother, Rose, grew up in Norma, New Jersey. The Bukiets raised their son in New York City, Long Island, and New Jersey. By his own account, Bukiet excelled in school out of a deep sense of responsibility for his parents and their extended community of Holocaust survivors. He graduated from Sarah Lawrence College in 1974 and published his first novel, *Sandman's Dust*, in 1985. Bukiet began writing the stories that would appear in his breakthrough collection, *Stories of an Imaginary Childhood*, in the late 1970s. When the book was finally published in 1992, it won the Edward Lewis Wallant Award and was a finalist for the National Jewish Book Award. In 1993 he became the fiction editor of *Tikkun* magazine and joined the faculty of Sarah Lawrence College, where he was still teaching fiction writing in 2001. In 1995 his second collection of stories, *While the Messiah Tarries*, was published to wide and favorable reviews; it was followed by the provocative novels *After* (1996), *Signs and Wonders* (1999), and *Strange Fire* (2001). In 2001 Bukiet was living in Manhattan (which he calls a small island between America and Europe) with his wife, Jill Goodman, a public-interest attorney, and their three children, Madelaine, Louisa, and Miles.

Major Themes and Concerns

Bukiet's work demonstrates that the Holocaust continues to influence contemporary Jewish American fiction writers. The European catastrophe serves as the referent around which his precocious imagination whirls. In four powerful works—*Stories of an Imaginary Childhood*, *While the Messiah Tarries*, *After*, and *Signs and Wonders*—Bukiet transports his readers to a pre-Holocaust shtetl in Poland, to contemporary Orthodox and secular Jewish milieus in the United States, and back to the European Jewish terrain after the Holocaust. The international reach of his artistic vision and the theological quandaries that permeate his work suggest that Bukiet feels a greater affinity with eastern European Jewish literary predecessors than with American ones. According to Bukiet the writers who have most profoundly influenced his writing include Jerzy Kosinski, Isaac Babel, and Bruno Schulz.

Bukiet's first collection, *Stories of an Imaginary Childhood*, might best be understood as an allusive stylistic treatment of the Holocaust. Through the perspective of an unnamed twelve-year-old narrator (on the precipice of manhood, according to Judaic belief), Bukiet brings to life the Polish shtetl, Proszowice, the setting for each of the twelve interrelated stories. The year is 1928, and the rapidly approaching Holocaust thus looms throughout the collection. Bukiet carefully constructs the stories to evoke the Holocaust allusively and to elicit responses like the following from the renowned Holocaust scholar Lawrence L. Langer: "As a member of the post-Holocaust generation, I was unable to banish from consciousness the sense that I was reading about a doomed people. . . . In a very subtle way, Bukiet builds this complicated response into his fiction" (p. 75). Even the title of the collection evokes the Holocaust; these are stories, Bukiet suggests, of an imaginary childhood in Europe that might have been his own if not for the "cunning of history."

Some critics have read *Stories of an Imaginary Childhood* as an endeavor to retrieve a world torn asunder by the Nazis: "Bukiet attempts to inscribe his life as it might have been in a Jewish world now vanished. In so doing, he retrieves a portion of that world, with all its hopes, illusions, and prayers" (Berger, p. 72). As Alan Berger suggests, Bukiet re-creates the Jewish pre-Holocaust Proszowice with scrupulous care. He peoples the shtetl with unique Jewish characters, including Zalman the grave digger; Rebecca the whore; Shivka Bellet, a shrew who bestows all her pent-up loving-kindness on a stray dog; Jacob Lester, a brainy rebel who yearns for America; and Isaac, a fraudulent but thoroughly winning "millionaire." By the time one finishes the collection, one intimately knows the Jews of Proszowice, their idiosyncratic religious rituals and superstitions. What is more, one cannot help but bemoan the imminent decimation of Bukiet's shtetl and the countless other Jewish villages in Europe whose characters and stories have yet to be "imagined."

Of the stories in the collection, the last one, "Torquemada," most provocatively engages the Holocaust. Psychologically wounded by an antisemitic assault, the adolescent narrator revisits, in a delirium, several especially virulent episodes of antisemitic persecution and occupies the persona of the persecutors, from the Egyptian pharaoh, to "Nebuchadnezzar sacking Jerusalem," to a disciple of Muhammad's vowing "eternal enmity" toward the Jews, to the grand inquisitor in Spain, Torquemada (pp. 192, 193). The narrator's father ultimately draws him out of his trance, comforting him with the words, "We have each other and it's the twentieth century of civilized man. There, there. What harm could possibly come to us in 1928?" (p. 197). In these final lines Bukiet alludes eerily to the impending Holocaust, the horrific culmination of Jewish persecution in Europe that his narrator glimpses in a protracted moment of both disorientation and stark lucidity.

Were the narrator of Bukiet's first collection to survive the Holocaust, he might write a book like *While the Messiah Tarries*. The stories in this collection are not as closely related as those in the first (for example, the author does not limit himself to a single narrator or locale), allowing Bukiet to touch on a broader range of concerns. Of particular relevance here, Bukiet explores the increasingly vehement (and morally ambiguous) attempts to record, catalog, and preserve survivor testimony and other audiovisual materials of the genocide. In "Himmler's Chickens" a nominally Jewish protagonist—who "took obscure pride in Barbra Streisand's career, and peppered his conversation with words like *hondle* [bargain] and *shvartz*" [black]—must decide what to do when a Nazi offers to sell him a home video of Heinrich Himmler madly executing chickens with a pistol (pp. 164–165). Should one pay a Nazi for such material? Preserve the film? Destroy it? These are the questions Bukiet poses for his protagonist and for his readers. In "The Library of Moloch" Bukiet betrays his deep skepticism about the documentation and preservation of Holocaust-survivor testimony. The story revolves around a fastidious American librarian, Dr. Arthur Ricardo, who is obsessed with his project to "preserve their suffering, to remit immortality in return for the chronicle of their woe" (p. 185). Although Ricardo is driven by what he perceives as the ethical imperative of his work, an implacable Holocaust survivor whom he interviews for the project charges that an insidious victim envy besmirches such American endeavors.

Stories of an Imaginary Childhood and *While the Messiah Tarries* are clearly the works of a mischievous imagination, and Bukiet ups the mischief ante significantly in *After*. The mordant humor that pervades this novel makes it Bukiet's most daring artistic approach to the Holocaust. The book opens just after Isaac Kaufman's liberation from Aspenfeld, a sub-camp of Buchenwald. By having an American "liberator" pop out of his tank in the middle of Aspenfeld asking, "Hey youse. Is this the way to the Grand Concourse?" (p. 4), Bukiet signals that he has written a Holocaust novel with a tone that is markedly different from the solemnity of, say, Saul Bellow's *Mr. Sammler's Planet*, Edward Lewis Wallant's *The Pawnbroker*, and Arthur A. Cohen's *In the Days of Simon Stern*. As Sanford Pinsker notes, "Bukiet upends the apple cart of piety that has until now attached itself to hushed discussions of the Holocaust" ("Dares," p. 285).

Indeed, Bukiet seems intent on making several contemporary Jewish and non-Jewish readers squirm. In one of the novel's more surreal scenes, for example, an emcee on board a party ship warms up the crowd with the following joke: "So what did Hitler say to Mussolini when the Italian premier paid him a surprise visit? . . . If I'd known you were coming, I would have baked a kike" (p. 262). What is more, Bukiet's survivor protagonist, Isaac Kaufman, veers dramatically from the "wounded" or "enraged" type to which readers of Holocaust literature have grown accustomed. Having just been liberated, Isaac does not search tirelessly for lost relatives, nor does he take up the Zionist struggle ("Eighty million Arabs and a desert: who needs it?") (p. 237). Rather, Isaac and his cohorts—most notably, Marcus Morgenstern, a dentist before surviving Dachau, an expert forger after, and Fishl, a saintly schlemiel who "retained every line of liturgy, history, and commentary he had ever heard"—set off to score big on the black market (p. 52). They turn over sizable profits by manufacturing and distributing straw-filled cigarettes; they somewhat incredulously scare up a market for Dead Person Identification Cards (DPIDs); and they even manage to sell broken watches by entombing into the mechanism live buzzing bees, which simulate the sound of a functioning timepiece for just long enough before suffocating.

This type of resourcefulness enables Isaac and his partners in crime to survive the *lager* (camp), and one hesitates to judge them for acting on their survival instincts after the Holocaust. Still, their resourcefulness often comes across as just plain greed. Marcus will only supply forged travel documents to fellow Jewish survivors for the right price; Isaac wishes to use Jewish skin, flayed by the Nazis, to forge more persuasive worker IDs, and, most disturbingly, he plans to confiscate eighteen tons of golden ingots created from fillings ripped out of Jewish mouths by the Nazis. On discovering the tightly guarded ingots, Marcus reacts as one might expect: "Think of all the pain" (p. 101). Isaac, however, has little patience for such sentimentality and replies, "Screw the pain. Think of the money" (p. 102).

Bukiet creates his motley crew of Holocaust survivors and tracks their impious exploits to explore the theological crisis after the Holocaust. The rootless, dizzying, surreal, and profoundly amoral postwar zeitgeist, he suggests, is what a world suddenly devoid of redemptive possibilities looks like. Bukiet's sardonic take on human motives permeates the novel. The American "liberators" of Aspenfeld, including one Jewish American soldier, treat the survivors "like pets . . . It was obvious that the Jews were no more people in their eyes than they were to the Germans. The substantial difference was that they were objects of sympathy rather than malice" (pp. 13, 16). The American public at large exhibits a voyeuristic rather than humane fascination with the European atrocity. Even worse, American newspapers happily slake the public's morbid thirst by printing graphic photographs of the dead and near dead, and leading American intellectual quarterlies scurry to discover and publish the "authentic voice of despair" (p. 181). Evidently, wrenching Holocaust memoirs make for good copy (that is, sales). Bukiet even casts an acerbic eye on Jewish volunteer relief workers, hopelessly naive and, above all, late.

Indeed, there are few good people in *After*. Still, God is the novel's real villain. The reader should not hunt for Nazi villains, for none exists (interestingly, a Ukrainian Kapo, not a German Nazi, sadistically offers Isaac a cup of scalding coffee that shatters his frozen teeth into enamel bits). The most memorable, if not the only, Nazi portrayed is Sturmmann Hans Lichter, who does not manage to flee Aspenfeld before the Americans arrive. An American soldier discovers Lichter hiding in terror amid the stench of his own defecation. Subsequently the Jewish survivors parade him around on an upraised chair in an eerie revision of a Jewish celebration ritual (commonly practiced at weddings and bar mitzvahs), and then hang him.

But Bukiet's intent here is not to vilify the Nazis; in fact, Isaac reflects that Lichter "was a quiet fellow who hardly ever killed any of the prisoners. He had even been known to give leftover bread from his sandwich to a hungry child" (p. 25). Instead, Bukiet focuses on the spiritual descent of Judaism after the Holocaust. He refuses to offer up the easily digestible, even cathartic, scene of good triumphing over evil, for the big question "after," Bukiet implies, is not so much whether the Nazis were evil but whether the atrocity marks the irreparable rupture of Jewish continuity. There certainly seems to be little hope of Jewish renewal, or *t'shuvah*. A synagogue in Ostrowiec "had been transformed into a variety store that sold sundries arranged in piles set upon the cardboard cartons in which they had been shipped: spinning tops, mirrors, thimbles, sponges" (p. 63). More hauntingly, on his mission to locate a paper source for their forging schemes, Fishl visits a museum-turned-paper-factory where the workers are melting down the archives of the Jewish community of Lodz:

> The acid hit the covers and turned them to a mash the consistency of oatmeal, and [Fishl] felt his heart clutch. He could almost feel the release of the words within. "Shma Yisroel" rising from the pulp to the heavens as the same words had risen from the owners of those books as they were placed into a different processing center. . . . Large wooden paddles sloshed the brew around, and the letters floated off the surface of the pages to the surface like the noodles in alphabet soup (p. 210).

Despite Fishl's immediate shock, the destruction of these quintessential Jewish texts seems hardly to rattle him: "The fact that the stuff was to be made into more paper to be covered with more words was a comfort" (p. 210). The reconstitution of, say, *Tanakh* (Hebrew Bible) into travel visas disturbs the reader a good bit more than it disturbs Fishl, so deeply religious "before." Small wonder that Isaac himself ponders whether any Jews actually survived the Holocaust: "Did Jews survive? I don't know what a Jew is anymore. I don't think that I bear any resemblance to my father or my grandfather or some ancestor with camels. Things are different now" (p. 157).

Bleak as the novel may be, Bukiet intimates during several magical moments that the flame of the Jewish soul will never be extinguished. Jewish continuity survives in the birth of Fishl and Rivkeh's baby, who is initially reluctant to enter the world; in the surreal manifestations of Isaac's indomitable brother, Alter; in the tale of the Last Jew on Earth, who becomes the First Jew; in the unfolding of the plot concerning the golden ingots; and in Isaac's mercy (*rachmones*) toward the son of a Nazi from Aspenfeld. Isaac resists his urge to murder the Nazi's son so that he may achieve a "perfect emptiness . . . create himself anew" (p. 83). The scene illustrates, however, that he cannot empty himself of his Jewish soul, which (though Isaac refuses to acknowledge it) is what precludes his act of ruthlessness. This moment, and the other moments mentioned above, burst on the eye like flashes of light from this canvas of seemingly inexorable darkness.

Bukiet treats the Holocaust less directly in his novel *Signs and Wonders*, but it looms as a powerful presence nevertheless, the focal point from which his moral vision originates. The novel is set in Germany, on the cusp of the new millennium. During a fierce storm that recalls the biblical flood, a barge holding the most heinous criminals is swept loose of its moorings. The gang of twelve unrepentant prisoners seems doomed to perish until the silent and mysterious Ben Alef ensures their escape through what appears to be a miracle. Ben Alef's cell mates declare him the Messiah, and the gang roams around Germany—a modern-day Sodom and Gomorrah—enlisting true believers, or "Alefites," as Ben Alef enacts one apparent miracle after the other. The novel culminates at Euro Disney on New Year's Day 2000 as a disciple's betrayal precludes salvation and marks the continued reign of evil. Through this darkly comic, apocalyptic novel Bukiet delivers a fierce indictment of the moral depravity of human civilization, which reached its nadir, Bukiet suggests, in the Holocaust.

Tragically, for example, *Kristallnacht* seems to repeat itself as the Alefites spread their "redemptive" message throughout Germany:

> The message was redemption. Absolved of all sins, the New Jews no longer had to mortify their own flesh. Instead, they struck outward, and the old Jews, that stubborn, stiff-necked people who refused to accede to the right world order, were the first to feel the sting of the lash of salvation. . . . Windows were smashed and fires were lit elsewhere in the city, wherever a store front had the gall or ill-fate to bear a Jewish surname (p. 263).

Bukiet's depiction of a Holocaust survivor in *Signs and Wonders*, Asher Rose, modeled loosely on Elie Wiesel, illustrates his scrutiny of the various ways in which the Holocaust continues to be exploited. Through his description of Rose's worldwide popularity, Bukiet offers a harsh indictment of both Rose and the culture that transforms him into "the emblematic figure of the Holocaust" (p. 242). "He continued to produce books," Bukiet writes of Rose, "but long before the turn of the century he had become more of a statesman than a writer, and was frequently called upon to lend his gravitas to multiple issues of international tragedy, be they Jewish, Rwandan, Tibetan, or whatnot. Asher Rose, the avatar of catastrophe and resurrection, spoke, and people listened" (p. 242). The pope thus enlists Rose to discredit Ben Alef. Rose's gruesome fate bespeaks Bukiet's cynicism about the way in which Rose/Wiesel has cultivated his persona and perhaps betrays a touch of resentment at the moral authority that first-generation survivors wield over second-generation witnesses.

Critical Reception

Critical discussion of Bukiet's work has been carried out mostly in book reviews in national and international publications, such as the *New York Times*, the *Los Angeles Times*, the *Village Voice*, the *Times Literary Supplement*, and the *Washington Post*. However, at the turn of the twenty-first century, Bukiet began to garner more lengthy scholarly consideration. In *Children of Job: American Second-Generation Witnesses to the Holocaust*, Berger devotes considerable attention to Bukiet's *Stories of an Imaginary Childhood* and *While the Messiah Tarries*. He considers Bukiet one of the most important second-generation writers to address the Holocaust in his work. In *Contemporary Jewish-American Writers and the Multicultural Dilemma: The Return of the Exiled*, Andrew Furman devotes a chapter to Bukiet's work, paying particular attention to the theological concerns that drive his imagination and situating his work against that of his Jewish American literary predecessor Philip Roth. In an intriguing article, "Dares, Double-Dares, and the Jewish-American Writer," Pinsker lauds the "relentless . . . fury toward God and history" in Bukiet's work, as well as the "tone of deliberately disconcerting humor" (p. 285). He argues that Bukiet outrages not for outrage's sake but "to re-humanize Holocaust survivors by allowing them to make jokes, make love, and, yes, connive for money just like other human beings" (p. 285).

Reviews of Bukiet's work have generally been favorable. In his review of *Stories of an Imaginary Childhood*, Langer argues that Bukiet's distinct and original voice "emerges from the world the author imagines and remains faithful to that world and the characters who dwell there" (p. 75). Michael Dirda, writing for the *Washington Post*, lavishes even higher praise on *While the Messiah Tarries*, concentrating on the assurance of Bukiet's prose. Bukiet's stories, Dirda argues, "leave you shaken or wonder-struck." Elizabeth Hand called *Signs and Wonders* "the Real Thing—a daringly original millennial novel, horrific and hilarious by turns, brilliant, black, bitterly funny." There have been dissenting views among reviewers. The few critics who have reacted unfavorably tend to disapprove of Bukiet's use of black humor to address the Holocaust. Reviewing *After*, for example, Deborah H. Sussman admires Bukiet's intentions to deploy black humor but faults him for not achieving "perfect pitch and perfect balance . . . to sustain the tension on the tightrope between hilarity and utter despair."

Conclusion

In 2001 Bukiet was at work on a long, complex novel set in, and narrated by, Manhattan Island. Through his fiction and his many reviews of Holocaust-related books, Bukiet has established himself as a leading voice on the European atrocity. No doubt, his mischievous imagination will continue to raise the hackles of many. The Holocaust, after all, has been the one subject relatively off-limits to the Jewish American mischief maker. But perhaps as a new century begins, readers are ready for a writer as daring as Bukiet to take center stage and scrutinize the ways in which the atrocity has been thought and written about.

Bibliography

Primary Sources

Sandman's Dust. 1985.

Stories of an Imaginary Childhood. 1992.

While the Messiah Tarries. 1995.

After. 1996.

"Machers and Mourners." *Tikkun* (November–December 1997): 44–46, 76.

Neurotica: Jewish Writers on Sex. Edited by Melvin Jules Bukiet. 1999.

Signs and Wonders. 1999.

Strange Fire. 2001.

Secondary Sources

Berger, Alan L. *Children of Job: American Second-Generation Witnesses to the Holocaust*. Albany: State University of New York Press, 1997.

Cheyette, Bryan. "Within the Borders." Review of *Stories of an Imaginary Childhood*. *Times Literary Supplement* (26 June 1992): 21.

Dickstein, Morris. "Ghost Stories: The New Wave of Jewish Writing." *Tikkun* (November–December 1997): 33–36.

Dirda, Michael. "Of Demons and Delights." Review of *While the Messiah Tarries*. *Washington Post*, 13 August 1995, WBK 2.

Furman, Andrew. *Contemporary Jewish-American Writers and the Multicultural Dilemma: The Return of the Exiled*. Syracuse, N.Y.: Syracuse University Press, 2000.

———."The Return of Moses Bellybutton." Review of *After*. *Midstream* (January 1997): 36–38.

Hand, Elizabeth. "The Fire This Time." Review of *Signs and Wonders*. *Washington Post*, 28 March 1999, 4.

Langer, Lawrence L. "Home, Before Dark." Review of *Stories of an Imaginary Childhood*. *Tikkun* (November–December 1994): 75, 79.

Pinsker, Sanford. "Dares, Double-Dares, and the Jewish-American Writer." *Prairie Schooner* 71, no. 1 (spring 1997): 278–285.

———."Melvin Bukiet." In *Contemporary Jewish-American Novelists: A Bio-Critical Sourcebook*. Edited by Joel Shatzky and Michael Taub. Westport, Conn.: Greenwood Press, 1997.

Sicher, Efraim. "In the Shadow of History: Second Generation Writers and Artists and the Shaping of Holocaust Memory in Israel and America." *Judaism* 47, no. 2 (spring 1998): 169–185.

Sussman, Deborah H. "From Horror to Humor." Review of *After*. *Washington Post*, 21 November 1996, C2.

Andreas Burnier

(1931–)

PASCALE R. BOS

Andreas Burnier, pseudonym of Catharina Irma Dessaur, was born into an assimilated, highly educated "Liberal" Jewish family in The Hague, the Netherlands. She survived World War II while hidden separately from her parents from the summer of 1942, until May of 1945, at the age of eleven to thirteen, at more than fifteen different addresses throughout the country. Some of the families she stayed with were Protestant and quite religious, and others believed in Communism or anthroposophy, an ideology centered on human development; while she made a concerted effort to fit in, the constantly changing locale and family situations in which she ended up made this difficult. She was betrayed and forced to flee a number of times, and lived for years in fear and loneliness.

Coming Out of Hiding: Andreas Burnier's Jewish Quest

Most Dutch Jews lost the majority of their family members, but Dessaur's immediate family managed to survive the war intact, and in 1945 she returned to live with them and a number of other surviving relatives. Returning home, however, proved problematic in many respects, for Dessaur's war experience made her loathe her Jewish identity. She had internalized both the negative Protestant and Marxist views on Jews of the families with whom she had stayed, and some of the Nazi rhetoric, and thus decided she no longer wanted to be Jewish:

> In the first years after the war I was a Calvinist. My parents, forming with their parents a strange nucleus left over by the German holocaust, accepted this. . . . Before many years had passed, the later almost incomprehensible tolerance of my parents—they lost a dreadful lot of face when, having their scarce Jewish friends to dinner, I said grace before and after—resulted in a silent decline of my faith. After all, Calvinism wasn't simply a way of life left over from years I had spent in hiding; it was also a protest against my once more so obviously Jewish environment. Being a Jew is being guilty, is expecting to be murdered by giant blond creeps ("Volgend jaar in Jeruzalem," ["Next Year in Jerusalem"] in *De verschrikkingen van het noorden*, translated by James Brockway).

Dessaur avoided engaging with or participating in anything Jewish for the next three decades, and terrified of renewed persecution, even denied being Jewish. Thus, as she would later note, she in effect remained in hiding for many decades after the war. Judaism and being Jewish became entirely taboo.

Dessaur went on to study law, received a Ph.D in criminology, and quickly rose within the academic ranks to become a full professor at the Catholic University of Nijmegen. She became highly respected in her field, and also made a name with her controversial and influential essayistic work, which focused on an array of ethical and criminological controversies, among which were euthanasia and genetic manipulation. She retired early in 1988, discontented with the increased bureaucracy of her academic life.

Literary Career

Concurrently with her academic career, Dessaur became a noted novelist. In order to separate the two careers and to protect her academic reputation she used the literary pseudonym Andreas Burnier. The choice of a masculine first name was deliberate: she was convinced that readers—audience and critics—dealt differently, and unfairly, with writing by women. Her first novel, *Een tevreden lach* (A Content Smile, 1965), deals explicitly with such issues of gender inequality, and deals in an open and lighthearted tone with the (im)possibility of living as a lesbian. While in her next work, a volume of short stories entitled *De verschrikkingen van het noorden* (The Terrors of the North, 1967), she would touch on the question of postwar Jewish identity and the experience of living in hiding briefly, it was in her 1969 novel *Het jongensuur* (The Boy's Hour) that Burnier would write most strongly autobiographically and thematize her war experience explicitly.

This story, Burnier's most acclaimed publication, recounts her war experiences in hiding in five chapters, each of which recounts one year during the war, but which are in reverse order (from 1945 back to 1940). The book is a harrowing story of displacement, betrayal, and Nazi terror, as well as the moving account of an adolescent trying to come to terms with her sex (the young protagonist would rather be a boy and tries in vain to stop her physical development into womanhood) and her (lesbian) sexuality.

What is unusual is that the story also recounts her intensely mixed feelings about the hiding experience. For not only were they as *onderduikers* (literally, "those who ducked under") supposed to feel "lucky" compared to the majority of Dutch Jews, who had been deported and murdered by the Nazis, they did not dare to express the reproach or anger they often felt toward their Dutch rescuers, as they owed them their lives. Burnier's text, however, focused precisely on the intense and painful conflicts that many hidden children experienced in these families:

> Was I grateful that Veendorp, too backwards and unimportant for the Germans to station troops or Dutch helpers there, saved my life? Did I feel gratitude towards "uncle" and "aunt" for their notion of Christian duty: to provide, in their poverty, free lodging for a Jew child, tribal member of the murderers of Christ? (The Jewishness of Jesus Christ himself dated in a way from before the murderousness, and was accentuated little) . . . They risked their lives, for nothing, and certainly not for money . . . My understanding and gratitude, in as far it even existed, were mixed with contempt and disgust (*Bellettrie 1965–1981*, Amsterdam: EM Querido's Uitgeverÿ, 1985, p. 207, translated by Pascale R. Bos).

Writing about her confrontation with small-town ultraconservative Protestantism in a light tone, her many references to the oppressive climate nevertheless reveal how deeply prejudice (in general, but in particular that which was directed against women and Jews) affected her:

> It took a long time before I understood their worldview. What "sin" was, the kind of sin for which you had to ask God for forgiveness every night kneeled at your bed, I couldn't imagine at first. But after half a year I got used to it. . . . He was also very merciful. For while all heathens, Jews, Catholics, . . . Muslims, Lutherans . . . and members of the Socialist Party were damned, the Reformed were not (pp. 203–4).

Most of the Jewish children in hiding came from large, progressive urban areas such as Amsterdam, and they were often placed in the homes of conservative Christian farmers in the rural northwest or south of the country. These families expected the children to leave their old, dangerous, identities behind and become active members of a new family with different values and customs, which often included a significant degree of Christian antisemitism. This imposed clash of culture and class—the conflict in identity, values, and religion—caused a sense of deep confusion and resentment in many of the hidden children. After the war, these conflicts were heightened by the divided loyalties they felt, to their foster and their biological parents.

Het jongensuur offered a view of the war experience that was entirely new in the Netherlands of the late 1960s: it suggested that while some of the Dutch had been willing out of religious duty to help Jewish people, many more simply did not care, or were willing to betray them if this proved to be opportune. While some non-Jewish Dutch authors had suggested as much, few Jewish survivors had dared to write critically of their experiences, and few were capable of doing so in so accomplished a style as Burnier. The result was a bombshell of a book. It was critically acclaimed in 1969, and over three decades later *Het jongensuur* is still seen as one of the most important Dutch works on World War II.

Over the next two decades, Burnier published over a dozen more collections of essays, poetry, and novels, whose common themes are the problematic lives of women and lesbians under patriarchy (which she dubs *seksefascisme*, "gender fascism"), the need to find spirituality and enlightenment in a progressively more rationalized and material world, and a host of other cultural-philosophical, literary, religious, and psychological topics. While much of this work is very personal, and some of it deals directly or indirectly with Nazi crimes (her objections against lenient euthanasia laws in the Netherlands, for instance, stem from her fear of Nazi-style eugenics), few of these essays and novels, unlike *Het jongensuur*, deal directly with Burnier's own Jewish background or her traumatic wartime hiding experiences, even when this background seems relevant to the topic at hand. (The 1986 novel *De trein naar Tarascon* is an exception, as the male protagonist is Jewish and it is precisely the memory of the war that is thematized. However, this is not an autobiographical book.) Thus, in a 1989 essay on a visit to the Dutch transit camp Westerbork and the German concentration camp Dachau, she muses in academic tones on the German national psyche, but leaves her own Jewish identity and war experiences out of the picture ("Muenchen en Dachau: vierenveertig jaar later," in *De achtste scheppingsdag*).

As her later works *De achtste scheppingsdag* (The Eighth Day of Creation, 1990) and *De wereld is van glas* (The World Is Made of Glass, 1997) suggest, visits to these Nazi camps brought about an intense psychological crisis in Burnier. She finally came to face her continued fear of persecution and of being Jewish; eventually (after she attended a Dutch national conference for formerly hidden children in 1992). This resulted in a sense of profound personal liberation. In the following years, she "returned" to Judaism, in the form of membership in the Dutch Jewish Liberal community, intensive study of Hebrew and the Torah and Talmud, and deep engagement with Jewish themes.

Burnier now states in interviews that she has "come home" in Judaism, and her latest novel, *De wereld is van glas* indeed suggests how central this new-found Jewish life and knowledge has become. The novel consists of a narrator's letters to an unknown Rabbi, in which she explains her return to Judaism, while still struggling to come to terms with her intense anger over the Nazi crimes and other injustices in the world. She attempts to work out this conflict through the writing of a story about three fictional characters who all represent parts of her own personality and quest for Jewishness: a young Jewish man who knows little of his background who is searching for spiritual answers; his mother, a Holocaust survivor who cannot let go of the past; and his father, an embittered assimilated classicist.

Critical Reception

Burnier's work has, for the most part, had positive reception in the Netherlands; even her debut, *Een tevreden lach*, with its somewhat controversial lesbian subject, was seen as impressive. While *Het jongensuur* was received with somewhat less enthusiasm than her short stories in *De huilende libertijn* a year later (critics missed the "fierceness"), it has over time come to be seen as a much more accurate description of life in wartime Holland than many of the novels written before it, and as a moving autobiographical document. While some critics consider Burnier's later work (and in particular her essays) too heavy in its philosophical tenor, it is universally acclaimed for its impeccable style. Her latest novel had somewhat mixed reviews: its fragmentary structure was seen by some as too convoluted, but others considered this her best work yet.- The Dutch press showed a great deal of interest in Burnier's personal saga of Jewish return, and *De wereld is van glas*'s publication received elaborate media attention.

Bibliography

Primary Sources

"Waar Kan men onde namen vinden, wie kent de naam die mÿ verlict?" *Lust en Gratie*. 1933.

Een tevreden lach (A Content Smile). 1965.

De verschrikkingen van het noorden (The Terrors of the North), short stories. 1967.

Het jongensuur (The Boy's Hour). 1969.

De huilende libertijn (The Crying Libertine). 1970.

Poezie, jongens en het gezelschap van geleerde vrouwen (Poetry, Boys, and the Company of Learned Women), essays, short stories, poems. 1974.

De reis naar Kithira (The Journey to Cythera). 1976.

De zwembadmentaliteit (The Swimming Pool Mentality), essays. 1979.

Na de laatste keer (After the Last Time), poems. 1981.

De droom der rede (The Dream of Reason), essay. 1982.

De litteraire salon (The Literary Salon). 1983.

Essays, 1968–1985. 1985.

Belletrie, 1965–1981. 1985.

Driestromenland (Land of Three Rivers), poems. 1986.

De trein naar Tarascon (The Train to Tarascon). 1986.

Gesprekken in de nacht (Conversations in the Night). 1987.

De rondgang de gevangenen (The Walk-Round of the Prisoners), essays. 1987.

Mystiek en magie in de literatuur (Mysticism and Magic in Literature), lectures. 1988.

De achtste scheppingsdag (The Eighth Day of Creation), essays. 1990.

De wereld is van glas (The World is Made of Glass). 1997.

Secondary Sources

Etty, Elsbeth. "Ik hoor altijd bij de tegenpartij." *NRC Handelsblad* Zaterdags Bijvoegsel, (8 October 1988): 3.

Schutte, Xandra. "Andreas Burnier: 'Wij zijn eendagsvliegen'." *De Groene Amsterdammer*, (19 February 1997): 20–22.

Sinnema, Pauline. "Vijftig jaar in de onderduik." Interview with author. *Het parool*, (12 February 1994): 17.

Vermeij, Lucy T. *Women Writers from the Netherlands and Flanders*. International Feminist Book Fair Press, 1992.

Wester, Rudi. "Er zijn nog heel nuttige taboes: De wereld volgens Andeas Burnier." *Opzij*, (October 1990): 13–15.

ALBERT CAMUS

(1913–1960)

SHOSHANA FELMAN

WITNESS TO HISTORY and spokesman for resistance, Albert Camus was born on 7 November 1913 in the French colony of Algeria. A year after Camus's birth, his father died of a World War I wound; his mother and her two sons moved into her mother's home in the impoverished, working-class Belmont district of Algiers. Camus attended the Grand Lycée on scholarship. In 1932, after an attack of tuberculosis, Camus received his baccalaureate degree; he then entered the University of Algiers, where he studied philosophy. Observing the rise of fascism in Europe and having worked with the Algerian Federation of Young Socialists, Camus joined the Communist Party in 1934; he and other antifascists also joined the Popular Front, which pressed for voting rights for Muslims. Camus worked politically through cultural venues: he established the Théâtre du Travail (Labor Theater), changing its name to Théâtre de l'Équipe when he was expelled from the party in 1937. Camus then reported on politics for the opposition newspaper *Algér-Républicain.* In 1940, after the newspaper was banned, Camus worked in Paris for the mass-marketed newspaper *Paris Soir.* He was, however, critical of the content and of the editor, who would soon join with the Vichy government. When Camus lost his job, he and his second wife, Francine Faure, moved to Oran, Algeria, where he worked as an editor and taught in private schools. In August 1942, Camus returned to France for respite from tuberculosis, and while recuperating, began writing *La Peste.* Camus joined the Resistance in late 1943. His greatest contribution was his work for the underground newspaper *Combat.* After the liberation, it became, with Camus as editor-in-chief, the leading newspaper in Paris (Gay-Crosier, p. 127). In his position as a *lecteur* at Gallimard publishing house, he met Jean-Paul Sartre, Simone de Beauvoir, Arthur Koestler, André Malraux, and Raymond Aron. Within the next two years he saw his plays *Le Malentendu* and *Caligula* performed. In 1947, Camus called for an international boycott of Franco's Spain, and later cofounded the Groupe de Liaison Internationale, aiding political refugees regardless of ideology (Bronner 75). By 1947, the year in which *La Peste* was published, Camus diverged politically from others directing *Combat* who aligned with de Gaulle, and thus discontinued production of the journal. Camus and Sartre also now disagreed: Sartre, Marxist, focused on the proletariat and hesitated to criticize Stalin for political purges; Camus, humanistic, spoke for the dispossessed. The differences between the two ignited into an unreconciled public argument with a negative review of Camus's *L'Homme révolte* (1951), in *Les Temps modernes*, which Sartre edited (Bronner, pp. 95–96). When the Algerian revolution erupted in 1954, Camus, appalled by French use of torture and Arab use of terrorism, called both sides to moderation, asking in *L'Express* editorials for conditions that he believed would ensure democracy in Algeria. In 1956 *La Chute* was published. Three years before his death in 1960, Camus received the Nobel Prize.

Historically, Camus's artistic productivity extends from 1942 to 1960, that is, from the last phase of the Second World War through the decade and a half that form the war's immediate aftermath. During those postwar years, Camus held a position of intellectual leadership, attested by the 1957 Nobel Prize for literature he was awarded (at the age of 43, three years before his accidental death in a car crash) for illuminating, as the prize citation goes, "the problems of the human conscience in our time." By virtue of his intellectual leadership and of the ethical stance he occupied throughout the war and after it, Camus's work indeed exemplifies "the problems of the human conscience in our time" as the problems of a radical and necessary transformation: the radical and necessary transformation of the very categories both of ethics and of history, in their relation to the function of the writer. "The writer's function," said Camus in his Nobel acceptance speech, "is not without its arduous duties. By definition, he cannot serve today those who make history; he must serve those who are subject to it." History as holocaust has affected those subjects of history who were, however, neither its perpetrators nor its most immediate and most devastated victims, but its historic onlookers: its witnesses.

The relationship of narrative to history evolves in two novels by Camus, crucially situated at the beginning and at the end of his career as writer: *The Plague* (1947) and *The Fall* (1956). Both those novels, although separated by a nine-year interval, were written subsequent to the trauma of the Second World War. Both are endeavoring, each in its own way, to assimilate the trauma. Both are explicitly preoccupied by the very possibilities—and impossibilities—of dialogue between history and language.

Promptly after the war's end, Camus published *The Plague*, the story of a town stricken by a ravaging bubonic epidemic. . . . When the first signs of the plague have been discovered in the city, the narrator of the novel, a doctor in his profession, tries to envision the forthcoming horror of the spread of the contagion.

> . . . Figures floated across his memory, and he recalled that some thirty or so great plagues known to history had accounted for nearly a hundred million deaths. But what was a hundred million deaths? When one has served in a war, one hardly knows what a dead man is, after a while. And since a dead man has no substance unless one has actually seen him dead, a hundred million corpses broadcast throughout history are no more than a puff of smoke in the imagination (pp. 36–37).

It is obviously not any war that is here implicitly evoked by Camus's narrator, but one whose historical atrocities are quite specific. How is it possible, indeed, to read about a hundred million corpses in connection with the singularly chosen metaphor of "a puff of smoke" without immediately associating it with the millions of corpses that were literally transformed into smoke in the Nazi death camps' crematoria? . . . It is not hard to understand why it has become, indeed, a commonplace to read the novel as an allegory of the Second World War: the horror of the epidemic constantly suggests that of the war through the plague's potential for a massive killing. What the plague, above all, means is a mass murder of such scope that it deprives the very loss of life of any tragic impact, reducing death itself to an anonymous, depersonalized experience, to a statistical abstraction. . . . To recognize in the dramatic allegory of the epidemic the recent history of the struggle against Nazism, readers did not need to know that Camus was himself during the war a member of the French Resistance, that he edited the French underground newspaper *Combat*, and that a long extract of *The Plague* had appeared clandestinely in Occupied France in a collection of Resistance texts. But in the context of the question of the dialogue between history and narrative, it is instructive to take notice of the fact that the novel was initially produced as an underground testimony, as a verbal action of resistance, which, as such, is not a simple statement or description of the historical conflict it narrates, but an actual intervention in this conflict. Camus's narrative intends to be not merely a historic witness, but a participant in the events it describes.

Emerging out of the very urgency of history, *The Plague* nonetheless presents itself as a pure "chronicle," an objective reproduction of historical events. Thus, the opening chapter reads: "The unusual events described in this chronicle occurred in 194- at Oran" (p. 3). In the opening chapter of *The Plague*, the relationship of narrative to history seems to be direct and entirely unproblematic: if history is of the order of a "happening"—of an "acting" and a "seeing"—and if narrative is of the order of a "telling," the two orders are conflated in the discourse of the *testimony*, through which language is transmitting the direct experience of "eyewitnessing." As testimony, the account of *The Plague* is thus itself a firsthand document, situated at the level of primordial data, closely adhering to historical perception. Joining events to language, the narrator-as-eyewitness is the testimonial bridge that, mediating between narrative and history, guarantees their correspondence and adherence to each other. This bridging between narrative and history is possible since the narrator is both an informed and an honest witness ("témoin fidèle"). Once endowed with language through the medium of the witness, history speaks for itself. All the witness has to do is to efface himself, and let the *literality* of events voice its own self-evidence. "His business is only to say: this is what happened, when he knows that it actually did happen." The "subject of history" can thus voice its presence to the history of which it was a part in articulating, in a single, unified and homogeneous utterance, history's presence to itself.

If the narrative is testimony, a historiographical report whose sole function is to say "This is what happened," why, however, does Camus have recourse to the metaphor of the plague? If the literality of a historical event is what is here at stake, why not designate this historical event by its literal, referential name? Why not refer directly to the Second World War as the explicit subject of the testimony? A superficial answer to this question could invoke the political necessity of disguise stemming from the initial underground testimonial status of the first published excerpt of the novel, that sees the light still under Nazi occupation.

But beyond this circumstantial explanation, what is striking in Camus's choice of metaphor in lieu of the historic referent is that the plague designates not simply a metaphorically substitutive event, but an event that is historically impossible: an event without a referent. "It is impossible," say the doctors at the first signs of the plague, "everybody knows that it has vanished from the Western world" (translated from the French by Shoshana Felman, p. 36).

There is thus a certain tension, a certain aporia that inheres between the allegorical and the historical qualities of the event: the allegory seems to name the vanishing of the event as part of its actual historical occurrence. Camus's testimony is not simply to the literality of history, but to its unreality, to the historical vanishing point of its unbelievability. In much the same way as the doctors think the plague historically impossible because it does not fit into the frame of reference of their science (their knowledge of medical history), the victims of the plague do not believe in the foreshadowing disaster because it contradicts their "humanism," their ideological beliefs and expectations.

In much the same way as Camus's victims of the epidemic, the victims of the Holocaust in turn did not believe in the information that was forthcoming about the Nazis' final aims. "The majority of Jewish leaders in Eastern Europe did not yet realize that this was the beginning of a systematic campaign of destruction. The whole scheme was beyond human imagination; they thought the Nazis incapable of the murder of millions. . . . Any rational analysis of the situation would have shown that the Nazi aim was the destruction of all Jews. But the psychological pressures militated against rational analysis and created an atmosphere in which wishful thinking seemed to offer the only antidote to utter despair. . . . Only a relatively small minority tried to hide or to escape, aware that deportation meant death" (Lacqueur, pp. 198–199). The unreality that strikes, thus, the event before and during its occurrence through the victims' own refusal to believe in its historic referentiality, is matched and reenacted on another level by the way in which the relief at the war's end is immediately accompanied by a denial and forgetfulness of the war's horrors. The event (the plague, the Holocaust) occurs, in other words, as what is not provided for by the conceptual framework we call "history," and as what, in general, has no place in, and therefore cannot be assimilated by or integrated into, any existing cultural frame of reference. Since we can literally witness only that which is within the reach of the conceptual frame of reference we inhabit, the Holocaust is testified to by *The Plague* as an event whose specificity resides, precisely, in the fact that it cannot, historically, be witnessed.

It is precisely because history as holocaust proceeds from a failure to imagine that it takes an imaginative medium like the plague to gain an insight into its historical reality, as well as into the attested historicity of its unimaginability. Rambert does not believe in the reality of a "total condemnation," as people failed to believe in the reality of the gas chambers. This is why Camus's own testimony, as opposed to the journalist's, cannot be simply referential but, to be truly historical, must be literary. If the failure to imagine out of which history as holocaust proceeds stems, precisely, from the witnesses' (Rambert's) failure to imagine their own implication and their own inclusion in the condemnation, Camus's own literary testimony must, above all, wrench the witnessing away from this historical failure of imagination. Literature bears testimony not just to duplicate or to record events, but to make history available to the imaginative act whose historical unavailability has prompted, and made possible, a holocaust.

The specific task of the literary testimony is, in other words, to open up in that belated witness, which the reader now historically becomes, the imaginative capability of perceiving history—what is happening to others—in one's own body, with the power of sight (of insight) usually afforded only by one's own immediate physical involvement. It is thus that the literary testimony of *The Plague* offers its historical eyewitnessing in the flesh. Rambert has to learn on his body what a holocaust—a situation of "total condemnation"—is: a situation that does not—cannot—except the witness; an experience that requires one to live through one's own death, and paradoxically, bear witness to that living through one's dying; a death experience that can be truly comprehended, witnessed only from inside (from inside the witness's own annihilation); a radical experience to which no outsider can be witness, but to which no witness can be, or remain, outsider.

> "Until now I always felt a stranger in this town, and that I'd no concern with you people," Rambert says. "But now that I have seen what I have seen, I know that I'm from here, whether I want it or not. This business is everybody's business [Cette histoire nous concerne tous] (translated from the French by Shoshana Felman, p. 174).

Bearing witness to the way in which "this history concerns us all," *The Plague* partakes of an apprenticeship in history through an apprenticeship in witnessing. The historical apprenticeship takes place only through a crisis in, and a consequent transformation of, the witness. And it is only through the medium of that crisis that the event can speak, and that the narrative can lend its voice to history.

"All a man could win in the conflict between plague and life," Rieux reflects, "was knowledge and memories."

> Knowing meant that: a living warmth, and a picture of death [une chaleur de vie et une image de mort, c'était cela la connaissance] (pp. 270–271).

The task of the testimony is to impart that knowledge: a firsthand, carnal knowledge of victimization, of what it means to be "from here" (from quarantine), wherever one is from; a firsthand knowledge of a historical passage through death, and of the way life will forever be inhabited by that passage and by that death; knowledge of the way in which "this history concerns us all," in which "this business" of the plague "is everybody's business"; knowledge of the way in which history is the body's business; knowledge of a "total condemnation."

The story of the plague amounts, thus, to the historical determination to bear witness, a determination that is lived at once as an artistic and as a political decision, and that functions at the novel's end not as a true closure, but as a signature, of Camus's work. Without quite yet exhausting its significance, the ending of *The Plague* announces the new awareness and the new moral and political imperative of an Age of Testimony: an age whose writing task (and reading task) is to confront the horror of its own destructiveness.

If, in the wake of Nazism, *The Plague* (1947) inaugurates the Age of Testimony as the age of the imperative of bearing witness to the trauma and the implications of survival, *The Fall*, appearing nine years later (1956), rewrites the problematic of an Age of Testimony in a different manner, since its dilemma and its drama do not so much bear witness to survival as they obscurely struggle through the question: how does one survive the witnessing?

Some years ago, the narrator was the chance witness of a suicide: a woman he had just passed by suddenly jumped off the bridge into the Seine. Stunned, the narrator froze for a brief moment, then continued his itinerary: this involuntary witnessing was not part of his life. But the scene has kept haunting him and, in its very absence, has brought about a radical disorientation and a gradual disintegration of everything that, in his life before it, had seemed safe, familiar, given.

At first sight, the subject of *The Fall* seems altogether different from that of *The Plague*. And yet, in much the same way as *The Plague, The Fall* in turn revolves around a scene of witnessing. And *The Fall* in turn seems to be alluding, though far less explicitly than did *The Plague*, to European history:

> Still let us take care not to condemn [our Parisian fellow citizens] . . . for all Europe is in the same boat. I sometimes think about what future historians will say of us (p. 6).

Whatever the relation of *The Fall* to European history might be, however, the scene of witnessing that it embodies differs radically from the historical scene of witnessing narrated by *The Plague*.

The Fall [may be considered] as, fundamentally and crucially, a transformation of *The Plague*, a narrative of critical rethinking of the stakes of witnessing in history and a recapitulation, at a distance of nine years, of the relation between testimony and contemporary history, in a retrospective commentary on his own highly successful novelistic wartime writing, by a Camus whose transformation and whose difference from himself and from his own successful image has not yet begun (I would suggest) to be appreciated.

In reflecting on his role as a key witness of historical events, Dr. Rieux insisted in *The Plague*: "The narrator's business is only to say: this is what happened, when he knows that it actually did happen, that it affected the life of a whole populace, and that there are thousands of eyewitnesses who can appraise in their hearts the truth of what he writes" (p. 6). In *The Plague*, the scene of witnessing is thus the scene of the historical recording—and of the historical documenting—of an event. In *The Fall*, the scene of witnessing is, paradoxically enough, the scene of the non-recording and of the non-documenting of an event: "The next day, and the days following, I didn't read the papers" (pp. 70–71). In *The Plague*, the event is witnessed insofar as it is fully and directly experienced. In *The Fall*, the event is witnessed insofar as it is not experienced, insofar as it is literally missed. The suicide in effect is *not seen* and the falling in itself is not perceived: what is perceived is the woman before the fall, and the sound of her body striking the water after the fall; there is a seeing that takes place before the occurrence and a hearing that takes place after it, but too late. *The Fall* bears witness, paradoxically enough, to the missing of the fall.

While the narrator of *The Plague* thus naturally feels, from his key position as "a faithful witness" (p. 270) that, "decidedly, it was up to him to speak for all" (p. 281), the narrator of *The Fall*, though formerly, in his profession as a defense attorney, spokesman for the victims and an eloquent champion of "noble causes" (16), does not speak to anyone about his witness of the suicide but is rather, paradoxically, reduced to silence by his very role as witness. "I informed no one."

> I must admit that I ceased to walk along the Paris quays. When I would ride along them in a car or bus, a sort of silence would descend on me (p. 42).

Rieux can "speak for all" because he understands—and shares in—the explosion of the cry that he is witnessing. Jean-Baptiste Clamence (as the narrator of *The Fall* chooses to call himself) does not understand, and does not share in, the reverberation of the cry that he is witnessing, but which—in contrast to Rieux—he believes precisely not to be of his concern because *not his own*. Met with silence and reduced to silence, the unacknowledged cry emitted by the other's voice is thus perceived as the voice of no one, coming from nowhere. But this nowhere from which the other's voice has at the same time reached and failed to reach his ears will henceforth lie in wait for the narrator everywhere, as the obsession of a vocal echo and in the form of visual and acoustic hallucinations.

Having missed his chance encounter with the real, having failed to witness both the suicide and the other's cry, the narrator paradoxically will turn into an obsessive witness of an outside world totally confused with his own delusions.

The delirium of the witness in *The Fall* picks up precisely on the vision of the sniper in *The Plague*.

> "Sorry doctor," a policeman said, "but I can't let you through. There's a crazy fellow with a gun, shooting at everybody" (pp. 281–285).

The madness of the sniper communicates both with the madness of the woman jumping and with that of the narrator of *The Fall*, in breaking through the layers of apparent resolution of the former novel and in shooting through the "calm" of those who "deny in the teeth of evidence that we had ever known a crazy world."

Because what has been witnessed cannot be made whole and integrated into an authoritative telling, *The Fall* has lost at once the narrative consistency of *The Plague* and the claim of the former novel to historical monumentality. What is witnessed, here as in *The Plague*, is the Other's death. But the scene of witnessing has lost the amplifying resonance of its communality, the guarantee of a community of witnessing. It is no longer a collective, but a solitary scene. It does not carry the historical weight, the self-evident significance of a group limit-experience, but embodies, rather, the in-significance, the ineffectuality of a missed encounter with reality and of a non-encounter between two solitudes. Unlike *The Plague*, whose testimony celebrated and recorded the significance of the dead, *The Fall* bears witness to the failure of the Other's death to claim significance. And yet, this very insignificance claims the narrative, since it decenters and defocalizes the significance of all the rest.

Camus now realizes that the very moral core that gave its momentum to *The Plague*—the establishment of a community of witnessing—was itself in some ways a distortion, a historical delusion. Inasmuch as the authentic feeling of community helped in fact to fight against the plague, the fight against the plague was itself already a distraction from what history as plague (as Holocaust) was really like. The plague is such that, by its very nature, it cannot be testified to by any alliance. Camus now understands that, in the face of history as plague, the witness, like the victim, has no ally.

What is at stake in *The Fall* is the significance of silence insofar as it defines in and of itself an act, a political behavior that is both a symptom of, and a crucial factor in, historical developments. There is indeed a deeper allegorical significance to the silence with which the narrator shrouds the scene of the suicide.

> I had already gone some fifty yards when I heard the sound—which, despite the distance, seemed dreadfully loud in the midnight silence—of a body striking the water. I stopped short, but without turning around. Almost at once, I heard a cry, repeated several times, which was going downstream; then it suddenly ceased. The silence that followed, as the night stood still, seemed interminable . . . I informed no one (pp. 69–70). I must admit that I ceased to walk along the Paris quays. When I would ride along them in a car or bus, a sort of silence would descend on me (p. 42).

Silence here is not a simple absence of an act of speech, but a positive avoidance—and erasure—of one's hearing, the positive assertion of a deafness, in the refusal not merely to know but to acknowledge—and henceforth respond or answer to—what is being heard or witnessed. In this defeat of the presence of the witness to reality, silence is the active *voiding of the hearing*, the voiding of the act of witnessing of a reality whose transmission to awareness is obstructed and whose content is insistently denied as known—insistently asserted (reasserted) as *not known*—because essentially remaining *unacknowledged*.

The relation between silence and not knowing, and the question of what knowing and not knowing mean in practice and in theory—in the practice and the theory of history—is what the drama of *The Fall* is, in fact, profoundly all about. The narrator of *The Fall* reflects, indeed, at once upon how history is made by, and rewritten through, the silence of the censor, and how massacres historically repeat themselves through history's replaying of its subtle oscillation between knowing and not knowing. Thus, *The Fall* reflects upon how "knowing" and "not knowing" are translated into actions, and what they in effect mean in the practice and the theory of history.

The central status of the suicide scene is established, paradoxically, both through the effort to recover it and through the effort to avoid it and to turn away from it. There is, however, yet another silent center that is inscribed outright at the beginning of the book, a center, it is true, which the reader is most likely to bypass and that appears to be itself disorientingly peripheral ("you understand then why I say that the center is here, although we stand at the tip of the continent," p. 15), but which is nonetheless alluded to as somehow crucial. It is presented, quite significantly, at the opening of the novel, as a topography that the narrator and his listener will precisely go around. This center of avoidance, and yet also of encounter, appears when the narrator, who has just met his listener in a bar in Amsterdam, offers to show his guest the way back to his hotel:

> Your way back? [Votre chemin?] . . . Well . . . the easiest thing would be for me to accompany you as far as the harbor. Thence, by going around the Jewish quarter [en contournant le quartier juit] you'll find those fine avenues with their parade of streetcars full of flowers . . . Your hotel is one of them (*The Fall*, p. 10).

The "Jewish quarter" is thus mentioned at the outset of *The Fall*, as though in passing, with the subtle, but full charge of the historical implications of the movement of bypassing—of turning away from, and of going round—something that is nonetheless the center. The geographical or topographical guidance the narrator offers could itself be emblematic of a larger search and of an allegorical/historical attempt to get one's bearings: to find in history one's way—the right way; to find in history a way back home. We might choose, *The Fall* seems to suggest, to bypass certain quarters of our history or not to look at history from hell. And yet, the way back home passes through that one place—that one hell—we want most of anything to avoid: the Jewish quarter.

> I live in the Jewish quarter [Moi, j'habite le quartier juif] or what was called so until our Hitlerian brethren made room. What a cleanup! Seventy-five thousand Jews deported or assassinated; that's real vacuum cleaning. I admire that diligence, that methodical patience. When one has no character one has to apply a method. Here it did wonders incontrovertibly, and I am living on the site of one of the greatest crimes in history [J'habite sur les lieux d'un des plus grands crimes de l'histoire] (pp. 10–11).

It is therefore the Jewish concentration camps that, like the innermost circle of hell, are implicitly at the center of the novel: a center that remains, as such, unspeakable. The Jewish quarter "or what was called so" is itself a name that is no longer valid, a displaced, anachronistic designation that names—improperly—only an absence and a silence. Unlike the silence with which Sartre has surrounded Soviet concentration camps by not talking about them, by not avowing them, the silence of the Jewish concentration camps can no longer be dispelled by an avowal. The last circle of hell is inhabited by those who are no longer there, those who, from within the very center of the circle, have precisely been obliterated. The Jewish quarter—or the ultimate concentric circle—is inhabited by silence, a silence we can no longer dispel, denounce, deplore, or simply understand. "When one comes from the outside, as one gradually goes through those circles, life—and hence its crimes—becomes denser, darker" (p. 14).

What is the connection, the question now arises, between this denser, darker, and unnameable center of silence in the midst of Amsterdam's concentric circles, and the other silent center of the plot's concentric movement—the scene of the woman's drowning? What is the relation between the conspicuously marginal narrative divagation on the Jewish quarter at the opening of the novel and the inconspicuously pivotal episode of the suicide? I would suggest that the opening remark, in creating a significantly audible subtext of the very silence of extermination, is meant to cue the reader to the fact that the real subject of the novel (of the testimony) is, precisely, this subtext: what does it mean to inhabit the (exterminated) Jewish quarter of Amsterdam (of Europe)? What does it mean to inhabit history as crime, as the space of the annihilation of the Other?

Framed by such a question, the suicide episode—in its insistent evocation of the bystander's silence and of the narrator's failure to become a responsive witness—can be interpreted as an allegory of the deafness and the muteness of the world facing the extermination of the Jews. Despite the shock that swept the world when the Nazi death camps were first liberated in 1945, information about the extermination had been communicated to the Allies since at least 1941. The Polish Underground had played a key role in the transmission of the news about the Nazi gas chambers to the West, but its information—like the testimony, later, of some rare escapees of concentration camps—had been met with "disbelief" and accused of "exaggeration." The Nazi genocide occurred by virtue of the fact that all sides of the war maintained a terrible but universally shared secret: "the fact of a concentration-camp universe." Thus, Camus's allegory in *The Fall*, unlike that of *The Plague*, addresses, in what turned history into a Holocaust, not the magnitude of the event but, on the contrary, the tendency to its minimization that allowed it to occur through systematic deafness, silence, and suppression of information. Camus's allusion to the betrayal of the "allies" would thus have this further connotation and further historical allusion to the Western Allies—and to their failure to become responsive and effective witnesses vis-à-vis the Nazi genocide. The "plague" is such that it cannot be testified to by any alliance.

The narrator witnessing the suicide scene without response, in much the same way as the Marxist intellectuals accepting Stalin's labor camps and the Western Allies witnessing the genocide with a conspiracy of silence, become, in fact, historical participants, accomplices in the execution of the Other. Unlike *The Plague, The Fall* revisits thus contemporary history as a story not of resistance but of complicity. *The Fall*, indeed, enacts the Holocaust as a radical failure of representation, in both senses of the word: failure of representation in the sense of making present the event; failure of representation in the sense of truly speaking for the victim, whose voicelessness no voice can represent. In bearing witness to the witness's inability to witness—to the narrating subject's inability to cross the bridge toward the Other's death or life—*The Fall* inscribes the Holocaust as the impossible historical narrative of an event without a witness, an event eliminating its own witness. Narrative has thus become the very writing of the impossibility of writing history. Narrative, Maurice Blanchot writes elliptically, "from before Auschwitz' [récit d'avant Auschwitz]."

> At whatever date it might have been written, each narrative henceforth will be from before Auschwitz (*Aprés-coup,* Paris: Minuit, 1983).

I would suggest the cryptic forms of modern narrative and modern art always—whether consciously or not—partake of that historical impossibility of writing a historical narration of the Holocaust, by bearing testimony, through their very cryptic form, to the radical historical crisis in witnessing the Holocaust has opened up.

Reprinted excerpts from Shoshana Felman's studies, "Camus' *The Plague*, or a Monument to Witnessing" and "The Betrayal of the Witness: Camus' *The Fall*." The integral studies constitute chapters 4 and 6 of *Testimony: Crises of Witnessing in Literature, Psychoanalysis, and History*. Shoshana Felman and Dori Laub, M. D. New York: Routledge, 1992.

Bibliography

Primary Sources

Books

Révolte dans les Asturies. 1936.
L'Envers et l'endroit. 1937. "Betwixt and Between" in *Lyrical and Critical.* 1967.
Noces. 1939. "Nuptials" in *Lyrical and Critical.* 1967.
L'Etranger. 1942. *The Stranger.* 1946.
Le Mythe de Sisyphe. 1942. *The Myth of Sisyphus.* 1955.
Le Malentendu suivi de Caligula. 1944. *Caligula and Cross Purpose.* 1947.
Lettres à un ami allemand, 1945. "Letters to a German Friend" in *Resistance, Rebellion and Death.* 1961.
La Peste. 1947. *The Plague.* 1948.
L'Etat de siége. 1948. *State of Siege* in *Caligula and Three Other Plays.* 1958.
Actuelles: Chroniques 1944–1948. 1950. In part in *Resistance, Rebellion and Death.* 1961.
Les justes. 1950. *The Just Assassins* in *Caligula and Three Other Plays.* 1958.
L'homme révolté. 1951. *The Rebel.* 1953.
Actuelles II: Chroniques 1948–1953. 1953. In part in *The Myth of Sisyphus and Other Essays.* 1955.
Les esprits. 1953.
L'eté. 1954. "Summer" in *Lyrical and Critical.* 1967.
Réquiem pour une nonne. 1956. Adapted from William Faulkner's novel.
La chute. 1956. *The Fall.* 1956.
L'exil et le royaume. 1957. *Exile and the Kingdom.* 1958.
Réflexions sur la peine capitale. With Arthur Koestler. 1957. Camus's contribution translated as *Reflections on the Guillotine: An Essay on Capital Punishment.* 1959.
Actuelles III: Chronique algérienne 1939–1958. 1958. In part in *Resistance, Rebellion and Death.* 1961.
Discours de suéde. 1958. Nobel Prize Acceptance Speech. 1958.
Les possédés. 1959. Adapted from Fyodor Dostoyevski's novel. *The Possessed.* 1960.
Carnets, mai 1935—février 1942. 1962. *Notebooks, 1935–1942.* 1963.
Théâtre, récits, nouvelles. 1962.
Carnets, janvier 1942–mars 1951. 1964. *Notebooks, 1942–1951.* 1965.
Essais. 1965.
La mort heureuse, Cahiers Albert Camus, no. 1. 1971. *A Happy Death.* 1972.
Le premier Camus, suivi d'é Ecrits de jeunesse d'Albert Camus, Cahiers Albert Camus, no. 2. 1973. *Youthful Writings.* 1976.
Fragments d'un combat: 1938–1940, Alger Républicain, Le Soir Républicain. 1978.
Journaux de Voyage. 1978.
Caligula, version de 1941, suivi de La Poétique du premier Caligula. 1984.
Le premier homme, Cahiers Albert Camus, 7. 1994.

Prefaces, Introductions, and Other

Maximes et anecdotes, by Nicholas-Sébastien Roch [de] Chamfort. 1944.
Le combat silencieux, by Andre Salvet. 1945.
L'Espagne libre, by Jean Camp and others. 1946.
Dix estampes originales, by Pierre-Eugéne Clairin. 1946.
Laissez passer mon peuple, by Jacques Méry. 1947.
Devant la mort, by Jeanne Héon-Canone. 1951.
"Herman Melville," in *Les écrivains célèbres*, volume 3. 1952.
Contre-amour, by Daniel Mauroc. 1952.
Moscou sous Lènine—Les origines du communisme, by A. Rosmer. 1953.
Désert vivant: Images et couleurs de Walt Disney, adapted by Camus, Marcel Aymé, Louis Bromfield, Julian Huxley, François Mauriac, André Maurois, and Henry de Montherlant. 1954.
L'allemagne vue par les écrivains de la résistance française, by Konrad Bieber. 1954.
"L'Enchantement de Cordes," in *Cordes-en-Albigeois*, edited by C. Targuebayre. 1954.
Ballade de la gêole de Reading, by Oscar Wilde. 1954.
Œuvres completes, by Roger Martin du Gard. 1955.
La vérité sur l'affaire Nagy. 1958.
La posterité du soleil, by Henriette Grindat. Text by Camus. 1965.

Translations

La derniére fleur, by James Thurber. 1952.

La Dévotion à la croix, by Pedro Calderon de la Barca. 1953.

Un cos intéressant, Avant-Scène, no. 105 (1955): 1–25, by Dino Buzzati.

Le Chevalier d'Olmedo, by Felix Lope de Vega Carpio. 1957.

Secondary Sources

Abbou, André. "*La Chute* et ses lecteurs: I. Jusqu'en 1962." *Albert Camus* 3, "Sur *La Chute*." Ed. Pierre-Louis Rey. Paris: Hatier, 1970.

Amiot, Anne-Marie. "*La Chute*, ou, de la prison au labyrinth." *Annales de la Faculté des Lettres et Sciences Humaines* no. 2 (1967): 121–130.

Barnett, Richard L. "Nothing but Difference: Of Poetic Rescission in Camus's *La Peste.*" *Symposium: A Quarterly Journal in Modern Literatures* 41 (fall 1987): 3, 163–173.

Bartfeld, Fernande. "Le monologue séducteur de *La Chute.*" *Revue des lettres modernes*, nos. 904–10 (1989): 119–128.

Barthes, Roland. "De l'eïvre au texte." *Revue d'esthétique* 3 (1971): 225–232.

Bernard, Jacqueline. "The Background of *The Plague:* Albert Camus' Experience in the French Resistance." *Kentucky Romance Quarterly* no. 2 (1967): 165–173.

Bloom, Harold, ed. *Albert Camus: Modern Critical Views.* New York and Philadelphia: Chelsea House, 1988.

Braun, Lev. *Albert Camus: Moralist of the Absurd.* Cranbury, N.J.: Associated University Presses, 1974.

Bree, Germaine. *Camus.* New Brunswick, N.J.: Rutgers University Press, 1959.

———. *Camus and Sartre, Crisis and Commitment.* New York: Delta, 1972.

———, ed. *Camus: A Collection of Critical Essays.* Englewood Cliffs, N.J.: Prentice-Hall, 1962.

Bronner, Stephen Eric. *Camus: Portrait of a Moralist.* Minneapolis: University of Minnesota Press, 1999.

Cruickshank, John. *Albert Camus and the Literature of Revolt.* London: Oxford University Press, 1959.

Cryle, Peter. "Espace et éthique dans *La Peste.*" *Roman 2* (December 1986): 47–56.

———. "*La Peste* et le monde concret: étude abstraite." *Albert Camus* 8, "Camus romancier: *La Peste.*" Edited by Pierre-Louis Rey. Paris: Hatier, 1976, pp. 9–25.

Davis, Colin. "Altericide: Camus, Encounters, Reading." *Forum for Modern Language Studies* 33 (April 1997): 129–141.

———. "Interpreting *La Peste.*" *The Romanic Review* 85 (1994): 125–142.

De Rycke, Robert M. "*La Chute:* The Sterility of Guilt." *Romance Notes* 10 (spring 1969): 197–203.

Duvall, William E. "Camus' Fall From Nietzsche." *Historical Reflections/Reflexions Historiques* 21 (fall 1995): 537–552.

Ellison, David R. *Understanding Albert Camus.* Columbia: University Press of South Carolina, 1990.

Felman, Shoshana. "To Open the Question." *Literature and Psychoanalysis: The Question of Reading: Otherwise.* Edited by Shoshana Felman. Baltimore: The Johns Hopkins University Press, 1980, pp. 5–10.

Finkelstein, Bluma. "Jean-Baptist Clamence entre Job et l'Ecclésiaste." *Albert Camus 15: Textes, intertextes, contextes autour de "La Chute."* Edited by Raymond Gay-Crosier. Paris: lettres Modernes, 1993, pp. 9–62.

Fitch, Brian. "Locuteur, délocuteur, et allocataire dans *La Chute* de Camus." *L'Analyse du discours/Discourse Analysis.* Edited by Pierre R. Léon and Henri Mitterand. Montréal: Centre Educatif et Culturel, Inc., 1976, pp. 48–57.

———. "Narcisse interprète: *La Chute* comme modèle herméneutique." *Revue des Lettres Modernes* nos. 632–36 (1982): 89–108.

———. *The Narcissistic Text: A Reading of Camus' Fiction.* Toronto: The University of Toronto Press, 1982.

Fletcher, John. "Camus, the Liberation, and *La Peste:* A Fresh Look." *The International Fiction Review* 21, nos. 1–2 (1994): 32–38.

Gay-Crosier, Raymond. "Albert Camus." *Dictionary of Literary Biography* 72. Detroit: Gale Research Inc., 1988, pp. 110–135.

———, ed. *Albert Camus 15: Textes, intertextes, contextes autour de "La Chute."* Paris: Lettres Modernes, 1993.

———. "Renegades Revisited: From Jonas to Clamence." *Albert Camus'* L'Exil et le royaume: *The Third Decade.* Edited by Anthony Rizzuto. Toronto: Paratexte, 1988, pp. 19–33.

Greene, Robert W. "Fluency, Muteness, and Commitment in Camus' *La Peste.*" *French Studies* 34 (October 1980): 421–433.

Grenier, Jean. *Albert Camus, souvenirs.* Paris: Gallimard, 1968.

Grenier, Roger. *Albert Camus, Soleil et Ombre: Une biographie intellectuelle.* Paris: Gallimard, 1987.

Hewitt, Nicholas. "*La Chute* and *Les Temps Modernes.*" *Essays in French Literature* 10 (1973): 64–81.

Hoven, Adrian van den, and Basil D. Kingstone. "Amsterdam as a Source of Symbols for Camus' *The Fall.*" *Canadian Journal of Netherlandic Studies* 14 (Fall 1993): 33–38.

Hughes, Edward J. *Le Premier homme; La Peste.* Glasgow: University of Glasgow French and German Publications, 1995.

Johnson, Robert B. "Camus' *La Chute* ou Montherlant s'éloigne." *French Review* 44 (May 1971): 1026–1032.

Jones, Rosemarie. *Camus'* L'Etranger *and* La Chute. London: Grant and Cutler, 1980.

Keefe, Terence. "Camus's *La Chute:* Some Outstanding Problems of Interpretation Concerning Clamence's Past." *Modern Language Review* 69 (July 1974): 541–555.

Kellman, Steven G. *The Plague: Fiction and Resistance.* New York: Twayne, 1993.

King, Adele. "Structure and Meaning in *La Chute.*" *PMLA* 77, no. 5 (December 1962): 660–667.

Knapp, Bettina L., ed. *Critical Essays on Albert Camus.* Boston: G. K. Hall, 1988.

Krapp, John. "Time and Ethics in Albert Camus's *The Plague.*" *University of Toronto Quarterly: A Canadian Journal of the Humanities* 68 (spring 1999): 655–676.

LaCapra, Dominick. "Rereading Camus's *The Fall* after Auschwitz and with Algeria." *History and Memory after Auschwitz.* Ithaca: Cornell University Press, 1998, pp. 73–94.

Lacqueur, Walter. *The Terrible Secret.* New York, Penguin Books, 1983.

Lévi-Valensi, Jacqueline. "*La Chute* ou la parole en procés." *Revue de Lettres Modernes* nos. 238–44 (1970): 33–57.

———. *"La Peste" d'Albert Camus.* Paris: Gallimard, 1991.

Lottman, Herbert R. *Albert Camus: A Biography.* Garden City: Doubleday, 1979.

Maier, Charles. "A Surfeit of Memory? Reflections on History, Melancholy and Denial." *History & Memory* 5 (1993): 137–152.

Maillard, Claudine et Michel. *Le langage en procés: structures et symboles dans "La Chute" de Camus.* Grenoble: Presses Universitaires de Grenoble, 1977.

Nguyen Van-Huy, Pierre, and Mai Phan Thi Ngoc, with Jean-Rene Peltier. *"La Chute" de Camus; ou, le dernier testament: Etude du message camusien de résponsabilité et d'authenticité selon "La Chute."* Neuchatel: La Baconni6re, 1974.

Palmer, R. Barton. "The Novel of Revolt: Humanism and Style in *The Plague.*" *Renascence: Essays on Value in Literature* 32 (1980): 67–78.

Porter, Laurence M. "From Chronicle to Novel: Artistic Elaboration in Camus's *La Peste.*" *Modern Fiction Studies* 28 (winter 1982–1983): 589–596.

Remak, Henry H. H. "Comparative Value Judgements: Integration and Isolation in Camus' *La Peste* (1947) and Grass' *Die Blechtrommel;* Melanges offerts a Albert Gerard." *Semper Aliquid Novi: Litterature comparee et litteratures d'Afrique-d'Afrique.* Edited by Janos Riesz and Alain Ricard. Tubingen: Narr, 1990, pp. 167–174.

Rey, Pierre-Louis. *Camus: La Chute.* Paris: Hatier, 1970.

Sartre, Jean-Paul. "Reponse a Albert Camus." *Les Temps modernes* 82 (August 1952): 334–353.

Thody, Philip. *Albert Camus: 1913–1960.* London: Hamish Hamilton, 1961.

Tucker, Warren. *"La Chute,* voie de salut terrestre." *The French Review* XLIII 5 (April 1970): 737–744.

Viggiani, Carl A. "Camus and the Fall from Innocence." *Yale French Studies* no. 25 (spring 1960): 65–71.

Weyembergh, Maurice. "La Memoire du Juge-Penitent." *Albert Camus 15: Textes, intertextes, contextes autour de "La Chute."* Edited by Raymond Gay-Crosier. Paris: Lettres Modernes, 1993, pp. 63–78.

Zepp, Evelyn H. "The Generic Ambiguity of Albert Camus's *La Chute.*" *French Forum* 7 (September 1982): 252–259.

ELIAS CANETTI

(1905–1994)

KRISTIE A. FOELL

ELIAS CANETTI WAS born on 25 July 1905, the son of Mathilde (née Arditti) and Jacques Canetti, in Ruschuk, Bulgaria, at that time still part of the Austro-Hungarian Empire. The multiethnic Danube port city was populated by Bulgarians, Turks, and Sephardim, the neighborhood of Spanish Jews in which the Canetti family lived. In 1911, the family moved to Manchester, England, where father Jacques died suddenly in 1912, an event Canetti relates to his own lifelong opposition to death. A year later, mother Mathilde relocated to Vienna with her three sons, teaching Elias German in just three months en route. From 1916 to 1921, Canetti attended school in Zurich, receiving his *Abitur*, the German diploma required for admission to the university, in Frankfurt (Germany) in 1924. Canetti thus experienced a Pan-European, polyglot childhood, in which his acquisition of German came late.

The small family returned to Vienna in 1924. That same year, Canetti met his future wife, Veza Taubner-Calderon (1897–1963), who was at first a more successful writer than he. In 1929, Canetti earned a doctorate in chemistry from the University of Vienna; after this "delaying tactic" (his term), he embarked on his full-time literary career. After spending summer 1928 in Berlin, where he met Bertolt Brecht, Georg Grosz, and Isaac Babel, Canetti set out to write a "human comedy of the insane," projected as a series of eight novels, each based on a figure with just one main characteristic. His later collection of brief portraits, *Earwitness: Fifty Characters* (1974), continues this basic idea.

The Novel *Auto-da-Fé*

Canetti completed only one novel in the series: *Die Blendung* (*Auto-da-Fé*), about the reclusive, book-loving sinologist and misanthrope, Peter Kien. Completed in 1931 but not published until 1935, the novel confronts this creature of the mind with a series of "commoners" for whom he is no match: his housekeeper, Therese, whom he mistakenly marries; the self-styled chess "genius," Fischerle, an underworld denizen who is also a humpbacked, long-nosed Jewish caricature; and the "Hausbesorger" (Viennese apartment manager) Benedikt Pfaff, a former policeman who lives by his fists. Exploited and terrorized by each of these figures in turn, Kien finally burns to death with his books, which he ignites in a paranoid delusion of protecting them. The novel has been read as a study of mental illness, a critique of psychoanalysis, an exercise in expressionist aesthetics, an illustration of the theories Canetti later developed in *Crowds and Power*, a reflection of contemporary personal and intellectual issues, and a prophetic apprehension of the barbarism and destruction of World War II and the Holocaust. The published interpretation Canetti himself most appreciated was David Roberts's *Kopf und Welt* (*Head and World*), originally written in English.

Canetti was clearly troubled by the possibility that Fischerle, the novel's problematic Jewish character, could be read as a confirmation of antisemitic stereotypes. In the third and final volume of his autobiography, Canetti offered a third-party justification for the figure, delivered by the Hebrew poet Avraham been Yizchak, whom Canetti called "Dr. Sun" ("Sonne"):

> It would be argued that my portrayal of the Jew Fischerle lent itself to misuse by racist propaganda. But, said Sonne, the character was true to life, as true to life as the narrow-minded provincial housekeeper or the brutal janitor. When the catastrophe had passed, the labels would fall from these characters, and they would stand there as the types that had brought about the catastrophe. I am stressing this particular, because in the course of subsequent events I often felt uneasy about Fischerle. And then I found comfort in what Sonne had said that day (*The Play of the Eyes*, translated by Ralph Manheim, New York: Farrar, Straus and Giroux, 1986, p. 209).

Nicola Riedner's recent monograph on Fischerle places this figure within a historical context, noting that Fischerle's physical appearance (long nose, sad eyes, hunchback), his lust for money, his apparent occupation as a pimp, his intelligence, his ability to transform or "assimilate" himself, and many other features reflect antisemitic stereotypes. Riedner follows each of these topoi back to the European Middle Ages and claims that Fischerle is the only figure in the novel with a historical background that points beyond the individual. She concludes that Fischerle is to be read as a "warning to those assimilated Jews who believed themselves completely secure and unendangered and did not relate antisemitic tendencies to themselves. In fact, precisely this deceptive feeling that antisemitism did not apply to them would seal the fate of many Jews. Canetti demands memory of the sources of one's origins" (Riedner, p. 143).

In 1934 Elias and Veza married, keeping the marriage a secret from Canetti's mother, toward whom he carried a double burden of guilt: not only had he "betrayed" her by marrying, he also outlived her. Although Mathilde Canetti died in her bed of tuberculosis (1937), Canetti seems to have felt a kind of survivor guilt; throughout his autobiography, Canetti insists that the writer expiates his guilt toward the dead by preserving them in his text. In the fall of 1938, Elias and Veza Canetti fled Vienna via Paris, settling in London in 1939; Veza's posthumously published novel, *Die Schildkröten* (*The Turtles*), reflects this experience.

Crowds and Power: Exploring the Roots of Fascism

In England, Canetti forswore "any other and especially a purely literary work" (*The Human Province*, translated by Joachim Neugroschel, New York: Seabury Press, 1978, p. v) to concentrate on the anthropological study *Crowds and Power*. "My main work at this time was investigating the roots of fascism, that was the purpose of *Crowds and Power* . . . even if the word [fascism] may not appear there, still, the book's 500 pages are really about nothing else" (Bienek, p. 36). Critics Petra Kuhnau and Bernd Widdig have both placed *Crowds and Power* in the context of historical Holocaust studies, emphasizing how Canetti's view of German history makes a direct link between the Weimar inflation and the mass murder of Jews.

Crowds and Power attempts an empirical classification of crowds and "Machthaber" ("wielders of power," or rulers). By basing many of his observations on ethnological research among primitive peoples, on myths and religious beliefs, and on historical events from a wide variety of times and places, Canetti stakes his claim to a universally valid discussion of the subject, as Michael Mack has shown. Nonetheless, the influence of his specific historical experience is evident. Canetti did not begin to equate survival with power and view death as the basis of power until the 1940s, apparently in response to the Holocaust, writing in 1944: "Do we not see them, people, being sent to death by the trainload. . . . Who would want to kill then, who would even dream of killing *if nothing could be killed?*" (*The Human Province*, p. 52). In 1952, Canetti struggled with a generalized notion of survivor guilt: "There are many things one shouldn't be, but the only thing one must *never* be is a victor. Yet one is a victor over every person one knows well and survives. Victory is surviving. How can one keep living and yet not be a victor? The moral squaring of the circle" (*The Human Province*, p. 138). In *Crowds and Power*, Canetti warns his readers: "The larger and more frequent the heaps of dead which a survivor confronts, the stronger and more insistent becomes his need for them. . . . The significance of his victories is measured by the number of the dead" (*Crowds and Power*, translated by Carol Stewart, New York: Farrar, Straus and Giroux, 1984, p. 230). Canetti connects this need to kill to confirm one's power with the mechanisms of paranoia, often discussed by others as a driving motive of Hitler's personality; Canetti himself would make this parallel explicit in his 1971 essay "Hitler, according to Speer" (reprinted in *The Conscience of Words*). In the conclusion to *Crowds and Power*, Canetti merely alludes to the Holocaust when he writes that the survivor's "most fantastic triumphs have taken place in our own time, among people who set great store by the idea of humanity" (p. 468).

Canetti's Aphorisms (*Aufzeichnungen*)

During his work on *Crowds and Power*, Canetti began writing "Aufzeichnungen," or "jottings," as a spontaneous counterbalance to his concentrated effort on the larger work. Interspersed in these notes and aphorisms, one finds Canetti's few direct reactions to the Holocaust, which he does not otherwise make an overt focus of his work, perhaps because of his pessimistic analysis of the meaning of the *Shoah* for the Jewish people: "People do not hate them [the Jews] any less, but they no longer fear them. For this reason, the Jews can make no greater mistake than to continue the laments at which they were masters and to which they now have greater inducement than ever before" (*The Human Province*, p. 71). Canetti rejects the idea that the Holocaust was unique in history; indeed, an aphorism from 1992 pleads for a form of remembering separate from specifically German culpability:

> The ongoing assignment of guilt, with no end in sight, leads to hatred. Endless blame is monstrous. Even the taking of one life for another made more sense, though it has ceased to do so for our current temperament.
>
> The more monstrous the guilt, the less it can be upheld.
>
> But should what has happened be forgotten? It should remain as something incomprehensible, not as guilt.
>
> Can the incomprehensible be separated from guilt? The incomprehensible is anonymous. It is not related to any one people. It is something inhuman that threatens *everyone* and can erupt from anywhere. One must tackle it with assembled forces, like a monster (*Aufzeichnungen 1992–1993*, Munich: Hanser, 1996, p. 7).

Probably because of Canetti's unorthodox views, his work has not often been included in the category "Holocaust literature," though his concept of the survivor certainly addresses a central phenomenon of Holocaust studies.

Although Canetti's life was deeply influenced by Hitler's insistence on a racial Jewish identity, the extent to which Canetti's own cultural identity should be called "Jewish" remains an open question. In 1944, he wrote in his diary, "The greatest intellectual temptation of my life, the only one I have to fight very hard against is: to be a total Jew. Should I harden myself . . . against the Germans because they are possessed by the devil? Can't I still belong to all [peoples of the world] . . . and nevertheless be a Jew?" (*The Human Province*, p. 51). Confirming his own dual identity as both a Jew and a participant in German culture, Canetti wrote in 1945, "Come spring, the grief of the Germans will be an inexhaustible well, and little will distinguish them from the Jews. Hitler has turned the Germans into Jews in just a few years, and 'German' has become as painful a word as 'Jewish' " (*The Human Province*, p. 57). In his 1967 reflections on a trip he took to Morocco in 1954, Canetti would write of the Jewish faith with a sense of loss: invited to celebrate Purim with a family he admired, "I declined with cordial thanks. I could imagine his father's disappointment at my ignorance of the old customs. I would have got most of it wrong and could only have said the prayers like a person who never prays" (*The Voices of Marrakesh*, translated by J. A. Underwood, New York: Seabury Press, 1978, p. 76). In 1992, he again affirms his own humanist universalism: "My stubborn resistance to the Bible, which kept me away from it for decades, has to do with the fact that I never wanted to submit to my origin" (*The Agony of Flies*, translated by H. F. Broch de Rothermann, New York: Farrar, Straus and Giroux, 1994, p. 157).

Elias Canetti received the Nobel Prize in literature in 1981; he died on 14 August 1994, in Zurich.

Bibliography

Primary Sources

Über die Darstellung des Tertiärbutylcarbinols. Dissertation, typescript. 1929.

Hochzeit (*The Wedding*). 1932.

Die Blendung (*Auto-da-Fé*; in the United States, originally translated as *The Tower of Babel*). 1935.

Komödie der Eitelkeit (*Comedy of Vanity*). 1950.

Fritz Wotruba. 1955.

Masse und Macht (*Crowds and Power*). 1960.

Die Befristeten (*The Numbered*). 1964.

Aufzeichnungen 1942–1948. Rede auf Hermann Broch. 1965.

Die Stimmen von Marrakesch (*The Voices of Marrakesh. A Record of a Visit*). 1967.

Der andere Prozess (*Kafka's Other Trial: The Letters to Felice*). 1969.

Die Provinz des Menschen (*The Human Province*). 1973.

Der Ohrenzeuge (*Earwitness: Fifty Characters*). 1979.

Das Gewissen der Worte (*The Conscience of Words*). 1975.

Die gerettete Zunge (*The Tongue Set Free: Remembrance of a European Childhood*). 1977.

Die Fackel im Ohr (*The Torch in My Ear*). 1980.

Das Augenspiel (*The Play of the Eyes*). 1985.

Das Geheimherz der Uhr: Aufzeichnungen 1973–1985 (*The Secret Heart of the Clock: Notes, Aphorisms, Fragments 1973–1985*). 1987.

Die Fliegenpein: Aufzeichnungen (*The Agony of Flies: Notes and Notations*). 1992.

Nachträge aus Hampstead. Aufzeichnungen 1954–1971 (*Notes from Hampstead. The Writer's Notes, 1954–1971*). 1994.

Aufzeichnungen 1992–1993. 1996.

Aufzeichnungen 1973–1984. 1999.

Secondary Works

Atze, Marcel, ed. *Ortlose Botschaft: der Freundeskreis H.G. Adler, Elias Canetti und Franz Baermann Steiner im englischen Exil*. Marbach am Neckar: Deutsche Schillergesellschaft, 1998.

Barnouw, Dagmar. *Elias Canetti zur Einführung*. Hamburg: Junius, 1996.

Bienek, Horst, and Elias Canetti. "Elias Canetti." *Borges—Bulatovic—Canetti. Drei Gespräche mit Horst Bienek*. Munich: Hanser, 1965, pp. 31–40.

Darby, David, ed. *Critical Essays on Elias Canetti*. New York: G.K. Hall, 2000.

Falk, Thomas H. *Elias Canetti*. Twayne's World Authors Series. New York: Twayne, 1993.

Foell, Kristie A. "July 15, 1927: The Vienna Palace of Justice is burned in a mass uprising of Viennese workers, a central experience in the life and work of Elias Canetti." *Yale Companion to Jewish Writing and Thought in German Culture, 1096–1996*. Edited by Sander L. Gilman and Jack Zipes. New Haven, Conn.: Yale University Press, 1997, pp. 464–470.

Hanser Verlag, *Essays in Honour of Elias Canetti*. Translated by Michael Hulse. New York: Farrar, Straus and Giroux, 1987.

Hirschfeld, Gerhard. *Exile in Great Britain. Refugees from Hitler's Germany*. Leamington Spa, England: Berg, 1984.

Ishaghpour, Youssef. *Elias Canetti: Métamorphose et identité*. Paris: La Différence, 1990.

Kuhnau, Petra. *Masse und Macht in der Geschichte. Zur Konzeption anthropologischer Konstanten in Elias Canettis Werk "Masse und Macht."* Würzburg: Verlag Koenigshausen & Neumann, 1996.

Lawson, Richard H. *Understanding Elias Canetti*. Columbia: University of South Carolina Press, 1991.

Mack, Michael. "Representing the Holocaust. Power, Death and Metamorphosis. An Examination of Elias Canetti's Use of Anthropological Literature in *Masse und Macht*." *Germanisch-Romanische Monatsschrift* 48 (1998): 317–335.

Riedner, Nicola. *Canettis Fischerle: Eine Figur zwischen Masse, Macht und Blendung*. Würzburg: Königshausen & Neumann, 1994.

Roberts, David. *Kopf und Welt. Elias Canettis Roman 'Die Blendung'*. Munich: Hanser, 1975.

Widdig, Bernd. *Culture and Inflation in Weimar Germany*. Berkeley: University of California Press, 2001.

Archive

Elias Canetti's "Nachlass," containing his personal library and manuscripts, is located at the library of the University of Zurich, Switzerland. The library will be accessible to scholars beginning in 2002, the manuscripts in 2024.

Paul Celan
(1920–1970)

AMY COLIN

According to Wolfgang Emmerich, author of the most recent Paul Celan biography (1999), Celan is considered today the most important German-speaking poet since 1945. Celan's *Shoah* poem "Todesfuge" ("Death Fugue," probably written in 1944) has gained such significance that it was compared to Picasso's *Guernica* and read by Ida Ehre in the German *Bundestag* (parliament) on 9 November 1988 in commemoration of the *Reichskristallnacht* (Night of the Broken Glass). The rapidly growing number of critical studies published since Celan's death in 1970, the international conferences, the relatively recent publication of two critical editions of his works, several annotated editions of his correspondence, and a yearbook all testify to his worldwide recognition.

As numerous Celan readings, including the biographies by Israel Chalfen, John Felstiner, and Wolfgang Emmerich reveal, the author's native cultural background and life experiences, in particular the murder of his parents in a death camp, shaped his poetic development, leaving an imprint on his concept of poetry and choice of themes. So important was his hometown Czernowitz, capital of the Bukovina, for the poet, that he referred to himself as a modern "Villon from Czernowitz near Sadagora" (Hasidic market-town and birth place of his mother). Time and again Celan's work invokes a return to his Bukovina, a region of "people and books," where different ethnic groups—primarily Romanians, Ruthenians, Germans, Jews, Magyars, Poles, Armenians, Hutzuls, and Lippovanes—coexisted relatively peacefully for decades. In this former Habsburg crown-land, situated the northeastern Carpathian Mountains, the river Dnjester, and Moldavia (Romania), the diversity of cultural traditions contributed to the development of a multifaceted Austro-German, German-Jewish, Romanian, Ukrainian, and Yiddish literature, producing poets who were fluent in several different languages. The influence of the Austro-German culture was so strong that Romanian, Ruthenian, and Yiddish authors wrote their first texts in German. Under the impact of growing nationalism they later turned to their mother tongue, but continued to use motifs from German literature. In the nineteenth- and twentieth-centuries, the main representatives of the Austro-German literature in the Bukovina were Jews, who often believed in the existence of a German-Jewish symbiosis, precisely because they had experienced the peaceful days of the Habsburg monarchy. Among them was an older generation of Celan friends and contemporaries, including Alfred Margul-Sperber (1898–1967), who was Celan's mentor; Alfred Kittner (1906–1991); Moses Rosenkranz (1904); and Rose Ausländer (1901–1988). After the downfall of the Habsburg monarchy in 1918, when the Bukovina became part of the Romanian Kingdom (Saint Germain Treaty, 1919), German-speaking writers became increasingly insulated in the Romanian environment, but "paradoxically", the Austrian Jewish component of Bukovina's culture reached its culmination precisely in this interwar period. In the late 1930s, the rise of nationalism, fascism, and antisemitism in the Bukovina shattered dreams of intercultural understanding. World War II and the *Shoah* destroyed Bukovina's biotope of peaceful coexistence. The experience of the persecution and the genocide of the Jewish people stigmatized a younger generation of Bukovinian Jewish poets, including Paul Celan, Immanuel Weißglas (1920–1979), and Alfred Gong (1920–1981).

In his seminal poetological text, "The Meridian" (in *Collected Prose*), Celan emphasizes that any actual journey back to his homeland was not possible, although Celan's Bukovina continued to exist on his imaginary poetic map. It is not only the wealth of images, themes, and memories, ranging from Bukovina's peaceful hills with beech woods to the genocide of the Jewish population (in particular the murder of his parents in a death camp), that invokes the inextricable link between his poetry and his native contextuality.

Celan's poetry transforms the main characteristic of Bukovina's culture into a structural principle. It is the legendary Bukovinian receptivity to heterogeneous ethnic traditions with which Celan infuses the rich intertextuality of his entire oeuvre.

Selected Poems and Themes

In his early poem "Espenbaum" ("Aspen Tree"), written probably in 1945 or 1946, Celan carries motifs, metaphors, and structure of the Romanian *doină*, a folk elegy, over into German verses lamenting the murder of his beloved mother:

> Aspen tree, your leaves glance white in darkness.
> My mother's hair never turned white.
> Dandelion, so green is the Ukraine.
> My blond mother did not come home.
> Rain cloud, above the well you linger?
> My gentle mother is weeping for us all
> Golden star you swing your golden sling.
> My mother's heart was wounded by lead.
> Oaken door, who did unhinge you?
> My sad mother cannot return (*Gesammelte Werke*, Frankfurt am Main: Suhrkamp Verlag, 1983, vol. 3, p. 40).

A *doină* starts with an address to nature, often a leaf or a tree, which is called upon as a witness or as a compassionate listener. In the Romanian folk elegy, nature mirrors the speaker's sadness. Like a *doină*, Celan's poem, written in couplets, begins with an appeal to nature, but metaphors such as the aspen tree gazing at darkness and the image of the rain cloud lingering over the fountain project the sadness of the lyrical "I" upon nature. Paralleling the *doină*'s lamentation, the second line in each of Celan's couplets speaks of the mother's suffering. The mother, whose heart is wounded and who weeps for all, becomes a symbol of mourning.

Breaking away from the *doină* tradition, the poem's last couplet no longer invokes motifs characteristic of the Ukrainian and Bukovinian scenery, but the violently broken oak door, a metaphor of the mother's deportation from her Czernowitz home. Celan's mother, along with many other Bukovinian Jews, was transported in cattlecars to Transnistria (eastern Ukraine), forced to do hard labor, and later shot dead by members of the Nazi organization Todt.

In the poem "Dornenkranz" ("Crown of Thorns"), Celan interweaves heterogeneous stylistic devices and motifs, ranging from allusions to the New Testament to expressionist metaphors of violence, from Germanic myths to verses recalling Rilke's "Der Ölbaum-Garten" ("The Olive Garden"), linguistically enacting the poem's master trope: a wreath. "Let go the purple. // The night / hammers the hour's heartbeat into place / the clock hands, two spear points, it bores burning into your eyes" (p. 42). Celan's poem embeds the references to Christ's suffering (the crown or rather wreath of thorns) as well as to the Roman soldiers, who wrapped Christ in a scarlet cloak in order to mock him, in an unusual configuration of expressionist metaphors denoting an entirely different time and scene: "The snow-light went out. All the naked are alone. . . . I rode into the night, I will not return" (p. 42). The extinguished light associated with the idea of bareness and deprivation brings to mind images of murdered Jews thrown naked into mass graves. In the poem's metaphorical netting, *Shoah* motifs are tied to the metaphor of a maternal embrace: "In the ash trees, your delicate image; // take me with the night wind into your arms. / At your ashen breasts I light you stars goodbye" (p. 42). Without explicitly naming or narrating its key idea, the poem links memories of the mother killed during the *Shoah* to Christ's passion. The unusual association also recurs in a first version of Celan's "Winter" (1944): "There falls now, Mother, snow in the Ukraine: / Receive the Saviour's crown of thousand grains of grief". In the final version, Celan concealed his idea: "There falls now, Mother, snow in the Ukraine: / the Saviour's crown of thousand grains of grief."

In his famous "Todesfuge" ("Death Fugue," in *The Poems of Paul Celan*), probably written in 1944, Celan created one of the most intricate structural and metaphorical wreaths. Celan's programmatic poem calls upon the entire tradition of European literature in order to vivify the sufferings of Jewish deportees in the death camp. As the title suggests, the poem is a fugue, but its abruptly ending lines also invoke another musicality and rhythm: Petre Solomon, who first translated the poem into Romanian, called Celan's early master poem a "Death Tango" ("Tangoul Mortii"), and Celan approved of this translation yet the poem also captures the rhythm and incantation of a Kaddish:

> Black milk of daybreak we drink it at sundown
> we drink it at noon in the morning we drink it at night
> we drink and we drink it
> we dig a grave in the breezes there one lies unconfined (*The Poems of Paul Celan*, Anvil Press, 1995, p. 61).

The "Death Fugue" is Celan's Kaddish for his murdered parents and the victims of the *Shoah*.

As literary critics have pointed out time and again, Celan's "Death Fugue" inextricably links, but also sets against one another, a variety of literary traditions ranging from the Old Testament to European romantic poetry, French symbolism, and German expressionism. One of the poem's master tropes, the "black milk of dawn," enacts an unusual linguistic wreath of juxtapositions and affinities: the milk, a symbol of nourishment, whose whiteness denotes purity and innocence is black, suggesting the idea that the speakers in this poem no longer drink milk, but death. A multiplicity of literary citations are interwoven in this key metaphor: Rose Ausländer's "black milk," Alfred Margul-Sperber's "dark milk of peace," Georg Trakl's "black frost" and "black snow," Franz Werfel's "black mother milk of the end," and Jean-Arthur Rimbaud's "milk of the morning and of the night."

The metaphorical wreath becomes a powerful means of vivifying the dynamics between perpetrators and their victims, but Celan's poem goes a step further. It undermines the elusiveness of metaphors by embedding in his Kaddish explicit references to the atrocities in death camps and to the sadism of the perpetrators who forced some of their victims to sing and play music, and others to shovel their own graves.

> A man lives in the house he plays with the serpents he writes
> he writes when dusk falls to Germany . . .
> he whistles his Jews out in earth has them dig for a grave
> he commands us strike up for the dance (p. 61).

No image of this poem conveys the annihilation of the Jewish people in more powerful a way than the metaphor of "a grave in the air": "We dig a grave in the breezes there one lies unconfined" (p. 61). Celan's verse conveys not only a somber reality, but also his kinship to the Russian Jewish poet Osip Mandelstam, who wrote a poem titled "Im Luftgrab" ("In the Air Grave"), published in 1913. It is his requiem for the victims of Stalin's terror. In the concluding lines of his "Death Fugue," Celan rips the intertextual weaving apart: "your golden hair Margarete / your ashen hair Shulamith" (p. 63). The juxtaposition of the name "Margarete," invoking the Faustian tradition, to the name Shulamith, which stands for the Song of Songs, discloses the abyss between the German and Jewish cultural tradition, between Nazi perpetrators and Jewish victims.

Celan's programmatic "Death Fugue," and in particular its dense intertextuality, triggered a problematic debate about poetic influences in Celan's work. Some critics attacked Celan for plagiarizing the work of Bukovinian poets, while others accused him of misusing the tragic fate of his parents in order to draw attention to his own work. But many scholars hailed the "Death Fugue" as one of the most important *Shoah* poems and a refutation of Theodor Adono's verdict: "After Auschwitz, to write poetry is barbaric." The poem, which represents both a culmination point and poetic closure of Celan's Bukovinian period, entered literary history and became part of the German *Vergangenheitsbewältigung* (coping with the past). Celan, however, felt so frustrated and embittered by the entire debate about his poem that he changed his style radically.

In his later poetry, Celan alienated more and more familiar syntactic and semantic structures, literary allusions, and citations from their habitual context. His texts came to explode cultural traditions, combining the residues of the linguistic destruction with words from other languages, technical terms, and neologisms. The poet encrypted the meaning of his verses, but his linguistic upheavals still created an innovative wreath, a language-grille ("*Sprachgitter*"), which scholars identified with his concept of poetry. The term "*Sprachgitter,*" whose second component "*Gitter*" derives from the Indo-European verb "*godh,*" meaning, "to unite, or to bind tightly," invokes a multiplicity of often contradictory meanings, ranging from a cloister window with a grille and a prison to a metaphor for a divine sphere. "*Sprachgitter*" is a metaphor of communication in spite of barriers, but also a symbol of the impossibility of communication. In the poem with this term as its title, the central verses illustrate the dynamics of separation and ties:

> (If I were like you. If you were like me.
> Did we not stand
> under one trade wind?
> We are strangers.) (*The Poems of Paul Celan,* Anvil Press, 1995, p. 105).

It is via the pronoun "we" that Celan's language-grille achieves the proximity of the disparate "I" and "You." Celan's poems from the volumes *Von Schwelle zu Schwelle* (1953), *Sprachgitter* (1959), and *Niemandsrose* (1963) both thematize and enact language-grilles, linking and juxtaposing leitmotifs of his earlier work to his later innovative language games. The *Shoah* remains the central topos.

In his programmatic "Engführung" ("The Straitening," in *The Poems of Paul Celan*), words carry the reader into a scenery of deprivation, ashes, and night.

> Driven into the
> terrain
> with the unmistakable track:
> grass, written asunder. The stones, white, with the shadows of grassblades: Do not read any more—look!
> Do not look any more—go! (p. 117).

It is a place of unmistakable traces: stones, grass, and writing. The subsequent unusual command to cease reading, that is, to stop interpreting the semantic significance of words, has the opposite effect: it prompts readers to try to interpret the enigmatic text. Since familiar approaches to interpretation are doomed to fail, a mindful reader inevitably returns to the opening commands, which replace reading first with seeing and then with walking. Cognition of the materiality of traces and words still implies interpretation, but walking through writing denotes an entirely different approach to the text. The poem speaks of a coming, going, and falling, referring such movements to the words themselves:

came, came.
Came a word, came
came through the night,
wanted to shine, wanted to shine.

Ash.
Ash, ash.
Night (p. 118).

The words' journey through the thicket of language leads to tears and sadness, but also to a nonplace, where language itself turns to "whirls of particles" and silence. Time and again the poem repeats the line: "Nowhere / does anyone ask after you" (p. 117). Celan's intricate poem, which invokes a multiplicity of literary traditions from the Old Testament to surrealism, ends with the same words as it began, suggesting a closure and the idea that the journey to the nonplace is inherent in language itself. Unlike the "Death Fugue," this poem no longer names what happened, but sets words free, allowing them to enact a movement toward silence. The poem drives the German language to its own margins the way the Nazis pushed the Jewish people to the border of existence.

Poetry and Biography: An Inextricable Bind

Celan's unusual poetic development is inextricably linked to his biography. His knowledge of different languages and literatures, his openness to different cultural traditions, his attachment to German as his poetic language, and his strong interest in political events were shaped by both his native contextuality and his education. Celan, alias Antschel, was born into an assimilated, but relatively observant, Jewish family on 23 November 1920. His mother, Fritzi (Frederike) Schrager, motivated her son's strong interest in German literature, while his father, Leo Antschel, a religiously observant Zionist, insisted on giving Paul a Jewish education. After attending a private school, where he learned both German and Romanian, Antschel moved to a Hebrew school, the Ssafa Iwrija, but later transferred again to a Romanian elite school. There he was confronted with growing antisemitism, which forced him to move again to a Ukrainian gymnasium attended by other Jewish students.

In Czernowitz, at the age of sixteen, Antschel wrote his first German poems, turned into an avid reader of literature, and developed a strong interest in botany as well as politics. As a member of the illegal communist youth organization, he translated some of Bakunin and Marx into Romanian, and published these adaptations in an illegal leftist pamphlet *Elevul Roșu* (*The Red Student*) distributed among workers. During his medical studies in Tours (1938), Celan familiarized himself with French surrealism, which had a strong impact on his poetic development. At the start of World War II, Celan, on holiday in Czernowitz, could no longer return to Tours. Because Czernowitz University had no medical school, he studied French and German literature.

Soviet occupation of the Bukovina (following the ultimatum of 26 June 1940) opened Antschel's eyes about communist dictatorship, for the Soviets persecuted Bukovina's population and deported all potential opponents to Siberia including social democrats and other leftist intellectuals. Celan turned away from communist ideology, but continued to stand up for social justice and political freedom, inscribing his political engagement in his work. His poems reflect upon key political events, ranging from the Spanish Civil War to the Soviet occupation of former Czechoslovakia, but the most significant tragedy that marked his life and work was the *Shoah*.

In 1941 Antschel experienced how Romanian fascist troops reconquered the Bukovina, killing thousands of Jews within the first forty-eight hours. They forced the Jewish population of Czernowitz, including him and his parents, to move into a ghetto from where they deported their victims in cattle wagons to the death camps in Transnistria (eastern Ukraine). The mayor of Czernowitz, who tried to save at least a part of the city's large Jewish population, obtained Marshall Antonescu's permission to exempt certain professionals from deportations. Jews who received permits signed by the influential General Calotescu were allowed to return to their plundered homes. When winter came, deportations were temporarily interrupted because the trains could no longer run. The mayor issued the ghetto survivors, including the Antschel family, their own permits. In the spring and summer of 1940, when deportations resumed again, all Jews in possession of the mayor's rather than the general's permit were deported to Transnistria. Antschel, who recognized the looming danger, went into hiding, but could not persuade his parents to join him. Antschel's father died of typhoid fever in the camps, and his mother was shot dead. Among the deportees were several poets, including Antschel's friends and classmates Immanuel Weißglas and Alfred Gong, but also his talented seventeen-year-old cousin Selma Meerbaum-Eisinger (1924–1942).

Later, Antschel was sent to forced labor in the Romanian labor detachment Tăbărești (in Buzău, southern Moldavia), but in the winter of 1944 he was allowed to return to Czernowitz, which was soon retaken by the Red Army. Under the Soviets, Antschel continued his studies at the University of Czernowitz. In 1945 he received Soviet permission to leave for Romania. In Bucharest, the poet made a living as a translator from Russian into Romanian for the publishing house *The Russian Book*, frequented the circles of Romanian avant-garde poets, and wrote German as well as Romanian surrealist texts. At that time, Antschel's texts appeared first under the Romanian pseudonym Paul Aurel, and then Ancel, the Romanian spelling. His uneasiness about the communist regime and attachment to the German poetic language motivated his decision to leave the country.

In 1947 he braved the dangers of crossing the borders illegally and got to Vienna. Otto Basil, the pope of surrealism, and Ingeborg Bachmann helped the poet, who was once again confronted with the difficulties with refugee life. In February 1948, the journal *Plan* published seventeen of his poems under his new pseudonym, Celan. In 1948 Celan's prose text, "Edgar Jené und Der Traum vom Traume" ("Edgar Jené and the Dream about Dreams"), and first volume of poems, *Der Sand aus den Urnen* ("Sand from the Urns"), appeared. In the course of the same year, Celan decided to settle in Paris. He found new friends among French poets, scholars, and artists; later he married the painter Gisèle Lestrange (1927–1991), whose etchings and lithographs inspired some of his neologisms and stylistic devices. He wrote titles for her images, and she translated some structural principles of his texts into her drawings. Their son, Eric, later became a magician.

In Paris, Celan obtained a *Licence ès Lettres* in 1950 and taught German (in particular translation) at the Ecole Normale Supérieure (1959–1970), while continuing to write poetry in German and produce a remarkable number of German adaptations of works by the futurist Velimir Khlebnikov, the Russian poet Osip Mandelstam, and the modern French poets Henri Michaux, André du Bouchet, and René Char. Both his translations and the intertextual density of his poetry inscribe themselves in the Bukovinian tradition of cultural mediation; they helped him preserve an intellectual bond to his lost, but still present, Bukovina.

Only gradually did Celan's significance as one of the foremost poets of the German tongue become fully recognized. Important literary awards and invitations to lecture followed: the Bremen Literary Award (1958) and the Georg Büchner Award (1960) for which he wrote his seminal poetological text "Der Meridian." But Celan, at the height of his career, also became the target of a malicious libel campaign started by Claire Goll. Her unjust accusation of Celan's having plagiarized the work of her husband, Yvan Goll, was picked up by the German press and infused with neo-fascist tones, and Celan became increasingly aware of the presence of the Nazi past in contemporary Germany. In some of his letters he warned his friends of a rising antisemitism of the left. The incident overshadowed his life, brought back memories of persecution during the war, and plunged him into depressions. It prompted him to change his style of writing and document the genesis of his poems. The impact of his suffering on his poetry is documented in his published correspondence with Petre Solomon, Nelly Sachs, and Franz Wurm. In 1969 Celan visited Israel, addressed the Hebrew Writers' Association, and met with survivors from his home city. Back in Paris, severe depressions, obsessive anxieties, and persecution mania still haunted him. Celan tried to kill himself several times, and beginning in 1962 Celan was hospitalized a number of times in different psychiatric clinics. At the end of April 1970 he set an end to his life, drowning himself in the Seine.

A Double Bind

Like the *Shoah* poets of his homeland, Celan defiantly continued to write poetry in German, in spite of his traumatic experiences during World War II and the fact that he lived in a non-German linguistic environment. As a result, he was confronted with the dilemma of being a victim of the *Shoah* and a poet writing in the language of those who murdered the Jewish people. Unlike most other Bukovinian Jewish poets who continued to write in a German classicist style in order to prove that they, the persecuted Jews, were the true heirs of German culture, Celan followed another route. As early as 1944, in his poem "Near the Graves," which also uses the structure and motifs of the Romanian *doină* to lament the mother's death, Celan questions the possibility of writing in the mother's tongue: "And mother, you bear it, as once, oh, at home, / the quiet, the German, the heart-wrenching rhyme?" (*Gesammelte Werke, Collected Works*, 1983, vol. 3, p. 20).

Years later, in the poetological text "Edgar Jené and the Dream about Dreams (1948), Celan explicitly emphasizes that history and political developments have transformed the essence of language, leaving traces which can no longer be erased. Moreover, as his "Bremen Speech" (1958) documents, Celan believed in the strength and resilience of the German language. In his view, the German language had gone through "terrifying silence, through the thousand darkness of murderous speech . . . It went through and could resurface, 'enriched' by it all" ("Bremen Speech," *Gesammelte Werke*, vol. 3, pp. 185–186; *Collected Prose*, Carcanet Press, 1985, p. 5).

In his volumes of poetry from *Niemandsrose* (1963) and *Atemwende* (1967) to *Schneepart* (1971) and *Zeitgehöft* (1971), Celan structures his poems in such a way that their tropes and metaphors in and of themselves subvert their semantic coherence, enacting a fundamental idea of Celan's poetological text *Der Meridian*, the oscillation of language from a "still-here" to an "already-no more." Celan's poems call and pull themselves back from a "ceasing to be" to a "still possible existence" ("The Meridian," *Collected Prose*, p. 49). Celan later associated this process of renewal and assertion of meaning through self-effacement with his key poetic concept: the "Atemwende," the turn of breath. So important was this notion that he used it as the title of a volume of poems published in 1967. Such turns of breath are not only structural principles of his work, but also a crucial means of inscribing his key ideas into his unusual poetic idiom.

It is through such turns of breath that Celan's poems unmask the consequences of language abuse, disclosing the wounds that history had inflicted upon language. One of the most powerful examples is his late poem "Leuchtstäbe" ("Flashlights," 1968, found in *Gesammelte Werke*, vol. 2), which resembles a surrealist collage. Disparate figurative clusters clash with one another in this text: "Flashlights, their / conversation, / on traffic islands, / with finally dismissed / emblem-pleasures, // meanings / straddle in the torn-up pavement" (p. 402). The poem's syntactic and semantic structures are broken apart, but the poem maintains its political context. These unusual linguistic configurations, written in 1968, dramatize the students' uprising in Paris as well as the Soviet occupation of Prague.

In the second part of "Flashlights," Celan confronts the reader with a strange scenario: "a sucker-arm snatches / the jute bag full of / decision-mumblings, from / the CC" (p. 402). Although his innovative language game frees words from the constraints of familiar connotations and allows them to interact freely, the reference to both the Soviet Central Committee and the concentration camps encrypted in the abbreviation "CC" (in German "ZK") reveals that no linguistic upheaval can change the meaning of these two letters: the wounds of language do not heal.

One of the focal ideas of Celan's poetry is the poem's dialogical nature. Following the lead of German Romantic philosophers, Martin Buber, and in particular Osip Mandelstam, Celan believed that poems could not come into being without addressing a "You." Like the Russian Jewish poet, Celan conceived his poems as "letters in a bottle," carrying the hope, but also the doubt of reaching an Other. In "The Meridian," Celan emphasizes: "But the poem speaks, . . . True, it speaks only on its own, its very own behalf. . . . But I think . . . the poem has always hoped . . . to speak also . . . on behalf of the other. . . . Only the space of this conversation can establish what is addressed, can gather it into a 'you' around the naming, speaking I" ("The Meridian," *Collected Prose*, pp. 48, 50). Celan's poems enact such movement toward an "Other," which constitutes itself within the dialogue between an "I" and a "You." Such "Other" assumes different forms, ranging from the memory of the mother to a divine Other and even "U-topia." But for Celan, poetic language is also actualized language under the sign of individuation; each poem carries the signature of its author. It is for this reason that his poems explore, time and again, the imaginary map of his childhood, embarking on a journey of the impossible, a voyage back to a "non-place," his homeland, the Bukovina. The exploration of such "topos" in light of "u-topia" led the poet to the discovery of yet another key dimension of poetic language, the "meridian," the "immaterial though terrestrial line," connecting past, present, and future. Celan's poetry discloses several meridians. One of them connects his homeland, the Bukovina, to other places on the map of his life. Another meridian discloses itself in the dialogue between his early and late poetry, in particular between his substantially different ways of responding to the *Shoah*.

The *Shoah* themes in his work are often connected to his reflections on Jewishness. His poetry invokes a multiplicity of connotations associated with this term, ranging from religious and political status, intellectual affinity, emotional bond to the movement toward an Other, and an understanding of Judaism as an aspect of humanness. Celan's work bears the signature of an author who was well aware of his multiple identity as a European Jewish poet, as a Villon from multiethnic Czernowitz, as a Jew stigmatized by the *Shoah* writing in the language of those who murdered his people, and as a poet who posed hope and conceived his poems as "letters in a bottle." Celan's work vivifies all of these and many more dimensions of being a Jewish poet writing in German, but also transgresses them, setting language free to disclose the unutterable inherent in its metaphors.

Critical Reception

A substantial number of critical Celan studies (Alvin Rosenfeld, Otto Pöggeler, Clarise Samuels, Amy Colin) examine the dynamic interrelations between Celan's response to the experience of Jewish persecution during World War II and his poetics, including his use of different literary traditions to convey a vision of being-in-the world shaped by the *Shoah*. These discussions are often inextricably linked to a controversy about language, especially German as an appropriate poetic means to vivify the Jewish tragedy. Under the impact of Celan's poetry, Theodor Adorno, who had initially rejected all poetry invoking the *Shoah* as barbaric, changed his view. Adorno, in his *Negative Dialectics*, no longer condemned poetry itself, but rather the attempt to restore a culture that had failed to prevent the Holocaust. For Adorno and many other readers, Celan's work was a powerful example of verses that succeeded in expressing the ineffable.

Scholarly studies of *Shoah* themes in Celan's work often give special attention to the poet's Jewishness, associating the term with a predetermined cluster of themes rather than the multiplicity of potential meanings evoked by his poems. Consequently, some scholars (Heinz Michael Krämer, Peter Meyer) identify Celan as a religious Jew while others point to Celan's strains of Jewishness (Jerry Glenn, John Felstiner). Several experts (Stéphane Moses, Joachim Schulze, and John Felstiner) perceive Celan as a Jewish poet per se, while others (Edith Silbermann) emphasize Celan's double allegiance to the German language and to Jewishness.

The multifaceted representation of Jewishness in Celan's poetry has prompted some critics, such as Dietlind Meinecke and Theo Buck, to argue that Celan transcends "Jewishness," revealing that *conditio judaica* is a *conditio humana*. Other interpreters reject such a view because it establishes a hierarchical relationship between universalism and Judaism, regarding the first as the "higher epistemological strata" of Celan's poetry. Stéphane Moses reverses the hierarchy, uncovering how references to Judaism emanate even from so-called universal themes. Rather than judging Celan's interpretations of "Jewishness" according to preconceived ideas of its essence, some literary critics (Otto Pöggeler, Philippe Lacoue-Labarthe, Emmanuel Levinas) explore the intricate ways in which certain concepts of Jewishness come into being through Celan's poetic language and interact with other crucial aspects of his poetics.

Not only Celan's response to the *Shoah*, but his enigmatic poetic language fascinates readers. Hans-Jost Frey, Werner Hamacher, and Rainer Nägele analyze his work primarily from a theoretical and linguistic point of view. Peter Szondi, and later Jean Bollack, reveal how personal experiences, political events, and literary traditions contribute to the genesis of his enigmatic poems. Hans-Georg Gadamer transgresses the particular in Celan's images as a means of reaching out to the poem's *Sinneinheit* (semantic unity). Other critics shed light on the intertextuality of Celan's work, uncovering allusions to literary, psychoanalytic, and philosophical traditions ranging from Friedrich Hölderlin and Jean Paul to Sigmund Freud and Martin Heidegger (Böschenstein, Nägele, Pöggeler). Beda Allemann uses Wittgenstein's language game theories as a means of uncovering semantic patterns in Celan's idiom, while Jacques Derrida discloses the intricate interaction of legibility and illegibility in Celan's work. A substantial number of Celan readings are inscribed in the translations of his work, including the remarkable English adaptations by Margaret Guillemin, John Felstiner, Michael Hamburger, Joachim Neugroschel, Rosmarie Waldrop, and Katherina Washburn. In spite of these and many other readings, which illuminate a variety of aspects of Celan's multifaceted work, his poetry still retains its enigma and constitutes a challenge to readers.

Bibliography

Primary Sources

Critical and Annotated Editions

Gesammelte Werke (Collected Works). 1983.

Das Frühwerk (The Early Works). 1985.

Werke. Historisch-Kritische Ausgbe (Works. Historical and Critical Edition). 1990–1997. (Includes *Atemwende, Fadensonnen, Schneepart* and *Lichtzwang*.)

Werke. Tübinger Ausgabe (Works. Tübinger Edition). 1996. (Includes *Sprachgitter* and *Die Niemandsrose*.)

Die Gedichte aus dem Nachlaß (Posthumous Poems). 1997.

Individual Works

Sprachgitter. 1959, 1996. (Included in *Werke. Tübinger Ausgabe*.)

Die Niemandsrose. 1963, 1996. (Included in *Werke. Tübinger Ausgabe*.)

Atemwende. 1967, 1990. (Included in *Werke. Historisch-Kritische Ausgbe*.)

Schneepart. 1971, 1994. (Included in *Werke. Historisch-Kritische Ausgbe*.)

Fadensonnen. 1991. (Included in *Werke. Historisch-Kritische Ausgbe*.)

Lichtzwang. 1997. (Included in *Werke. Historisch-Kritische Ausgbe*.)

Selected Letters

Dischner, Gisela. *Paul Celan an Gisela Dischner. Briefe aus den Jahren 1965–1970.* (Letters from the years 1965–1970). Edited by Runkehl and T. Siever. 1996.

Einhorn, Erich. "Paul Celan—Erich Einhorn. Briefe (Letters). Comments and annotations by M. Dmitrieva-Einhorn." *Celan-Jahrbuch* 7 (1998).

Sachs, Nelly. *Paul Celan–Nelly Sachs. Briefwechsel* (Correspondence). Edited by Barbara Wiedemann. 1993.

Solomon, Petre. "Briefwechsel mit Paul Celan" Correspondence with Paul Celan, 1957–1962. *Neue Literatur* (Bukarest) 32 (1981); die Stimme Nr. 26 (1970).

Szondi, Peter. *Briefe.* Edited by C. König and T. Sparr. 1993.

Wallmann, Jürgen P. "Auch mich hält keine Hand" (No hand holds me back either). *die horen* 16, no. 83 (1971).

Wiedemann, Barbara, and Franz Wurm, eds. *Paul Celan—Franz Wurm—Briefwechsel* (Correspondence). 1995.

Paul Celan–Gisèle Celan-Lestrange. *Correspondence (1951–70)*, 2 vols. 2001.

English Translations of Celan's Works

Glottal Stop: 101 Poems by Paul Celan. Translated Nikolai Popov and Heather McHugh. Hanover and London: Wesleyan University Press, 1967.

Speech-Grille and Selected Poems. Translated by Joachim Neugroschel. New York: E. P. Dutton and Co., 1971.

Collected Prose. Translated by Rosmarie Waldrop. Manchester: Carcanet Press, 1985.

Last Poems. Translated by Katherina Washburn and Margaret Guillemin. San Francisco: North Point Press, 1986.

Poems of Paul Celan. Translated by Michael Hamburger. New York: Persea Books, 1988, 1980; London: Anvil Press, 1995.

Threadsuns. Translated by Pierre Joris. Los Angeles: Sun and Moon Press, 2000.

Fathomsuns and Benighted. Translated by Ian Fairley. New York: The Sheep Meadow Press, 2001.

Selected Poems and Prose of Paul Celan. Translated by John Felstiner. London: W. W. Norton, 2001.

Secondary Sources

Bibliographies, Documentation, Yearbooks

Bohrer, Christiane. *Paul Celan-Bibliographie.* Frankfurt am Main: Peter Lang, 1989.

Emmerich, Wolfgang. "Bibliography." In *Paul Celan.* Reinbeck: Rororo, 1999, pp. 181–186.

Glenn, Jerry. *Paul Celan: Eine Bibliographie.* Wiesbaden: Otto Harrassowitz, 1989.

Hamacher, Werner, and Winfried Menninghaus. *Paul Celan.* Frankfurt am Main: Suhrkamp, 1988, pp. 345–359.

Ivanovic, Christine. *"Kyrilisches, Freunde, auch das . . ." Die russische Bibliothek Paul Celans im Deutschen Litearturarchiv Marbach.* Deutches Literaturarchiv, Marbach, 1996.

Lorenz, Otto. "Paul Celan: Bibliographie." *Kritisches Lexikon zur Gegenwartsliteratur.* München: Beck, 1998.

Speier, Hans-Michael. *Celan-Jahrbuch.* Heidelberg: Universitätsbuchhandlung, 1987–2001.

Selected Memoirs

Barasch, Moshe. "Über Paul Celan. Interview mit Cord Barkhausen." *Sprache und Literatur in Wissenschaft und Unterricht* 16, no. 1 (1985): 93–107.

Basil, Otto. "Wir leben unter finsteren Himmeln." *Literatur und Kritik. Österreichische Monatsschrift* 52 (1971): 102–105.

Baumann, Gerhart. *Erinnerungen an Paul Celan.* Frankfurt am Main: Suhrkamp Verlag, 1986, 1992.

Bollack, Jean. *Herzstein. Über ein unveröffentlichtes Gedicht von Paul Celan.* Translated by F. v. Wögerbauer. München, Wien: Hanser Verlag, 1993.

Bonnefoy, Yves. *Le nuage rouge: Essais sur la poetique.* Paris: Mercure de France, 1992.

Böschestein, Bernhard. "Gespräche und Gänge mit Paul Celan." *Paul Celan.* Edited by B. Böschenstein and G. Bevilacqua Marbach. Marbacher Literaturarchiv, 1990, pp. 7–19.

Cameron, Esther. "Erinnerungen an Paul Celan." *Park. Zeitschrift für neue Literatur* 10, no. 27/28 (1986): 50–52.

Cioran, E. M. "Encounters with Paul Celan." *Acts: A Journal of New Writing* no. 8/9 (1988): 151–155.

Dor, Milo. *Auf dem falschem Dampfer. Frangmente einer Autobiographie.* Wien/Darmstadt: P. Szolnay Verlag, 1988.

Huppert, Hugo. "Spirituell. Ein Gespräch mit Paul Celan." In *Paul Celan.* Edited by Hamacher, Werner, and Winfried Menninghaus. Frankfurt am Main: Suhrkamp, 1973.

Krolow, Karl. "Paul Celan." *Jahresring.* Stuttgart (1970): 338–346.

Leiser, Erwin. *Leben nach dem Überleben. Dem Holocaust entronnen—Begegnungen und Schicksale.* Königstein/Ts.: Athenäum, 1982.

Lenz, Hermann. "Erinnerungen an Paul Celan." In *Paul Celan.* Edited by Werner Hamacher and Winfried Menninghaus. Frankfurt am Main: Suhrkamp, pp. 315–318.

Mayer, Hans. "Erinnerungen an Paul Celan." *Merkur* 24, no. 12 (1970): 1150–1162.

Michaux, Henri. "Sur le chemin de la vie." In *Paul Celan. Etudes Germaniques* 25 (1970). Vol. 3, 250.

Reinfrank, Arno. "Schmerzlicher Abschied von Paul Celan." *die horen* 16, no. 83 (1971): 72–75.

Schmueli, Ilana. "Denk dir. Paul Celan in Jerusalem." In *Jüdischer Almanach 1995.* Edited by J. Hesing. Frankfurt am Main: Suhrkamp, 1994, pp. 9–36.

Schocken, Gershom. "Paul Celan in Tel Aviv." *Neue Rundschau* 91, Heft 2/3 (1980): 256–259.

Schwerin, Christoph Graf von. *Als sei nichts gewesen. Erinnerungen und Interpretation.* Berlin: Edition Ost, 1997.

Silbermann, Edith. *Begegnung mit Paul Celan. Erinnerung und Interpretation.* Aachen: Rimbaud Verlag, 1993.

Solomon, Petre. *Paul Celan. Dimensiunea Rom neasca.* Bucharest: Kriterion, 1987. L'adolescence d'un adieu. Paris 1990. Die Stimme 26 (1970).

Wurm, Franz. "Erinnerungen an Paul Celan." *Neue Züricher Zeitung*, no. 24/25 (November 1990).

Selected Critical Studies

Adorno, Theodor. *Negative Dialectics.* Translated by E. B. Ashton. New York: Continuum, 1973.

———. "Engagement." In *Noten zur Literatur III, Gesammelte Schriften.* Edited by Rolf Tiedemann. Frankfurt am Main: Surhkamp, 1974.

Allemann, Beda. "Das Gedicht und seine Wirklichkeit." *Etudes Germaniques* 25 (1970).

———. "Paul Celans Sprachgebrauch." In *Argumentum e Silentio.* Edited by Amy Colin. Berlin: Walter de Gruyter, 1999.

Bollack, Jean. " 'Eden encore,' *L'acte critique: Un colloque sur l'oeuvre de Peter Szondi.*" *Cahiers de Philologie* 5 (1985).

———. "Paul Celan und Nelly Sachs. Geschichte eines Kampfes." *Neue Rundschau* 108, no. 18 (1994): 119–134.

———. "Vor dem Gericht der Toten. Paul Celans Begegnung mit Martin Heidegger und ihre Bedeutung." *Neu Rundschau* 108, no. 1 (1998): 127–156.

———. *Paul Celan. Eine Poetik der Fremdheit.* Translated by F. v. Wögerbauer. Wien: Szolnay Verlag, 2000.

Böschenstein, Bernhard. *Leuchttürme. Von Hölderlin zu Celan: Wirkung und Vergleich.* Frankfurt am Main: Insel Verlag, 1982.

Böschenstein, Bernhard, and Sigrid Weigel, eds. *Ingeborg Bachmann und Paul Celan. Poetische Korrespondenzen.* Frankfurt am Main: Suhrkamp, 1997.

Böttiger, Helmut. *Orte Paul Celans.* Wien: Paul Zsolnay Verlag, 1996.

Buck, Theo. *Muttersprache, Mördersprache.* Aachen: Rimbaud, 1993.

Chalfen, Israel. *Paul Celan: Eine Biographie seiner Jugend.* Frankfurt am Main: Insel Verlag, 1979.

Civikov, Germinal. *Interpretationsprobleme moderner Lyrik am Beispiel Paul Celans.* Amsterdam: Rodopi, 1984.

Colin, Amy. *Holograms of Darkness.* Bloomington: Indiana University Press, 1991.

———. *Argumentum e Silentio. Ein Internationales Paul Celan Symposium.* Berlin: Walter de Gruyter, 1987.

Colin, Amy, and Alfred Kittner. *Versunkene Dichtung der Bukowina.* München: Wilhelm Fink Verlag, 1994.

Corbea, Andrei. *Czernowitz: Jüdisches Städtebild.* Frankfurt am Main: Jüdischer Verlag, 1998.

Corbea, Andrei, and Michael Astner. *Kulturlandschaft Bukowina. Studien zur deutschsprachigen Literatur nach 1918.* Jasi: Editura Universitatii Al. I. Cuza, 1990.

Derrida, Jacques. *Schibboleth.* Paris: Editions Galilée, 1986.

Emmerich, Wolfgang. *Paul Celan.* Reinbeck: Rororo, 1999, pp. 181–186.

Fackenheim, Emil. "The Holocaust: A Summing up after Two Decades of Reflection." In *Argumentum e Silentio.* Edited by Amy Colin. Berlin: Walter de Gruyter, 1987.

———. " 'Ziv, that light': Translation and Tradition in Paul Celan." *New Literary History* 18 (1986–87).

Felstiner, John. *Paul Celan: Poet, Survivor, Jew.* New Haven: Yale University Press, 1995.

Frey, Hans-Jost. "Zwischentextlichkeit von Celans Gedicht: Zwölf Jahre und Auf Reisen." In *Paul Celan.* Edited by Werner, Hamacher, and Winnifred Menninghaus. Frankfurt am Main: Suhrkamp, 1973, pp. 139–135.

Gadamer, Hans-Georg. *Wer bin Ich und wer bist Du? Ein Kommentar zu Celans Gedichtfolge "Atemkristall."* Frankfurt am Main: Suhrkamp, 1986.

Gellhaus, Axel, and Andreas Lohr, eds. *Lesarten. Beiträge zum Werk Paul Celans.* Köln/Wien: Böhlau, 1996.

Glenn, Jerry. *Paul Celan.* New York: Twayne, 1973.

Ivanovic, Christine. *Das Gedicht im Geheimnis der Begegnung. Dichtung und Poetik Celans im Kontext seiner russischen Lektüren.* Tübingen: Niemeyer, 1996.

———. *Zur Poetik Paul Celans: Gedicht und Mensch. Die Arbeit am Sinn.* Heidelberg: C. Winter Universitätsverlag, 2000.

Jacob, Michael. *Das Andere Paul Celans, oder, Von den Paradoxien relationalen Dichtens.* München: W. Fink Verlag, 1993.

Jamme, Christoph, and Otto Pöggeler. *Der glühende Leertext. Annäherungen an Paul Celans Dichtung.* München: Fink Verlag, 1993.

Janz, Marlies. *Vom Engagement absoluter Poesie. Zur Lyrik und Ästhetik Paul Celans.* Königstein/Ts.: Athenäum, 1976.

Koelle, Lydia. *Paul Celans pneumatisches Judentum. Gott-Rede und menschliche Existenz nach der Shoah.* Mainz: Matthias-Grünewald Verlag, 1997.

Lacoue-Labarthe, Philippe. *Poésie comme expérience.* Breteuil-sur-Iton: Christian Bourgois, 1986.

Lehmann, Jürgen, ed. *Kommentar zu Paul Celans "Die Niemandrose."* Heidelberg: C. Winter, 1997.

Lehmann, Jürgen, and Christine Ivanovic. *Stationen. Kontinuität und Entwicklung in Paul Celans Übersetzungswerk.* Heidelberg: Universitätsbuchhandlung, 1997.

Lévinas, Emmanuel. "De l'être à l'autre." In *Noms Propres.* Montpellier. Fata Morgana, 1976.

Lyon, James K. "Die patho-Physiologie des Ichs in der Lyrik Paul Celans." *Zeitschrift für deutsche Philologie.* 106, no. 4 (1987): 591–608.

———. "Judentum, Antisemitismus, Verfolgungswahn: Celans 'Krise' 1960–62." *Celan-Jahrbuch* 3 (1989): 175–204.

Mayer, Peter. "*Paul Celan als jüdischer Dichter.*" Diss. Heidelberg, 1969.

Meinecke, Dietlind. *Über Paul Celan.* Frankfurt am Main: Suhrkamp, 1970.

Moses, Stéphane. *Spuren der Schrift: Von Goethe bis Celan.* Frankfurt am Main: Jüdischer Verlag, 1987.

Nägele, Rainer. "Paul Celan: Konfigurationen Freuds." In *Argumentum e Silentio.* Edited by Amy Colin. Berlin: Walter de Gruyter, 1987, pp. 237–265.

Neubauer, John, and Jürgen Wertheimer. "Celan und/in Europa." *Arcadia* 32, no. 1 (1997):

Olschner, Leonard. *Der feste Buchstab. Erläuterungen zu Paul Celans Gedichtübertragungen.* Göttingen/Zürich: Vandenhoeck and Ruprecht, 1985.

Pöggeler, Otto. *Die Spur des Worts: Zur Lyrik Paul Celans.* München: Karl Albert, 1986.

Reichert, Klaus. "Hebräische Züge in der Sprache Paul Celans." In *Paul Celan.* Edited by Werner Hamacher and Winfried Menninghaus. Frankfurt am Main: Suhrkamp, 1973, pp. 156–169.

Roselfeld, Alvin. *A Double Dying.* Bloomington: Indiana University Press, 1980.

Samuels, Clarise. *Holocaust Visions: Surrealism and Existentialism in the Poetry of Paul Celan.* Columbia, S.C.: Camden House, 1993.

Schulz, Georg-Michael. *Negativität in der Dichtung Paul Celans.* Tübingen: Niemeyer, 1977.

Schulze, Joachim. *Celan und die Mystiker: Motivtypologische und quellenkundliche Kommentare.* Bonn: Bouvier, 1976.

Shoham, Chaim, and Bernd Witte. *Datum und Zitat bei Paul Celan. Akten des Internationalen Celan-Colloquiums.* Haifa: 1986, New York, Frankfurt: Peter Lang, 1987.

Steiner, George. *After Babel. Aspects of Language and Translation.* London: Oxford University Press, 1975.

Strelka, Joseph P. *Psalm und Hawdalah. Zum Werk Paul Celans. Akten des Internationalen Paul-Celan-Colloqiums.* New York: Peter Lang, 1987.

Szondi, Peter. *Celan-Studien.* Edited by Jean Bollack, Henriette Beese, et al. Frankfurt am Main: Suhrkamp, 1972.

MICHAEL CHABON

(1963–)

LEE BEHLMAN

MICHAEL CHABON IS a young Jewish-American novelist and short story writer who has risen to prominence as one of the leading writers of his generation. His work has received substantial critical acclaim, particularly the novel *The Amazing Adventures of Kavalier & Clay* (New York: Random House, 2000), for which he won the 2000 Pulitzer Prize for fiction. Much of Chabon's early writing features precise, John Cheever–like slices of contemporary, middle-class Jewish-American life, but with *Kavalier & Clay*, a sweeping work of historical fiction, Chabon widened his thematic scope to dramatize the significance of America as a place of real and imaginary escape for Jews. In this novel set at midcentury, America is both the goal of escape for refugees of the Holocaust and the place where escapist popular fantasy is born, often at the hands of those same refugees.

Early Life and Career

Michael Chabon was born on 24 May 1963 in Washington, D.C. and was raised in Columbia, Maryland. His Brooklyn-born father, Robert, has worked as a pediatrician, lawyer, and hospital manager and his mother, Sharon, is a lawyer. After his parents divorced when he was twelve years old, he spent his summers and holidays with his father in Pittsburgh, the city where he would eventually attend college and that would become a frequent setting for his novels and stories.

After a year at Carnegie-Mellon University in Pittsburgh, Chabon transferred to the University of Pittsburgh, where he graduated with a B.A. in English in 1984. He received an M.F.A. in creative writing from the University of California at Irvine in 1987. While at Irvine he submitted as his master's thesis, an early manuscript version of his first novel, *The Mysteries of Pittsburgh* (1988). Upon reading the manuscript over a weekend, his thesis adviser, MacDonald Harris, immediately contacted an agent in New York, who soon sold the manuscript to William Morrow. The novel is narrated by Art Bechstein, a recent college graduate, who tells of his adventures in Pittsburgh with a set of colorful, unpredictable friends during the summer following his college graduation. *Mysteries* explores some dark territory in its evocation of Art's difficult family history, but for the most part it is a sunny, affecting comedy of sexual confusion and self-awakening.

The Mysteries of Pittsburgh made Chabon an "instant success at age twenty-three" (*Publishers Weekly*, 1995, p. 44). He went on to write short stories for the *New Yorker* and *GQ*, as well as travel essays for *Vogue* and the *New York Times*. His short stories were eventually collected in *A Model World* (1991), an enthusiastically received book featuring tales about a wide range of young Jewish-American figures, most notably a boy named Nathan Shapiro. The five Nathan Shapiro stories follow this character through early and late adolescence, as he bears painful witness to his parents' separation and divorce, suffers an unlikely crush on one of his mother's friends, and awkwardly (and unsuccessfully) attempts his first sexual experience.

Fountain City and Beyond

From 1987 to 1992, Chabon worked on his second novel, the ill-fated *Fountain City*. Although the frame of the story described a love affair between a young American man and an older Parisian woman, Chabon incorporated much more, including what appear to be more explicitly Jewish themes than had previously appeared in his fiction. As he describes it,

> [*Fountain City*] was a novel about utopian dreamers, . . . an Israeli spy, a gargantuan Florida real estate deal, the

> education of an architect, the perfect baseball park, Paris . . . and the crazy and ongoing dream of rebuilding the Great Temple in Jerusalem. It was about loss—lost paradises, lost cities, the loss of the Temple, the loss of a brother to AIDS; and the concomitant dream of Restoration or Rebuilding ("Wrecked." http://www.michaelchabon.com/FC.html).

Chabon's experience growing up in the experimental community of Columbia, Maryland, was an acknowledged influence on his depiction of architectural (and other) utopianism in the manuscript. The fourth draft of *Fountain City* grew to fifteen hundred pages before Chabon, exhausted and unhappy with the shape of the work, put it aside for good in early 1993 in favor of writing the short, hilarious campus novel *Wonder Boys* (1995). This novel's hero is Grady Tripp, a shaggy, middle-aged writer and teacher of creative writing at a Pittsburgh college. Tripp can't ever seem to finish the two-thousand-page manuscript of his own seemingly disastrous second novel. *Wonder Boys* guides its readers through a weekend of slapstick-filled, progressively more disastrous adventures involving Tripp, his bizarre but very talented student James Leer, his anything-goes literary agent Terry Crabtree, and the pernicious manuscript itself. Curtis Hanson recently adapted the novel into a successful Paramount movie starring Michael Douglas.

During the five-year period in which he worked on *Fountain City*, Chabon was divorced from his first wife, the writer Lollie Groth, then met and eventually married his second wife, the mystery novelist and lawyer Ayelet Waldman. They were married in 1993 and now live in Berkeley, California, with their three children. In 1999 Chabon published his second short story collection, *Werewolves in Their Youth*, that includes several stories of suburban dread including "House Hunting," a tale of real estate and sexual perversity, and the title story, which concerns the failure of a small child to come to the aid of an unpopular classmate. Chabon has also written several unproduced scripts for television and the movies, including "House of Gold," a pilot for a series about three generations of a Jewish-American family, as well as a script proposal for the movie *X-Men*. He is currently writing the screenplay for a movie version of *Kavalier & Clay*, and in October 2002 he will publish a children's book, *Summerland*.

Kavalier & Clay and the Holocaust

After several months of research and years of writing, in 2000 Chabon released his most important work thus far, *The Amazing Adventures of Kavalier & Clay*. This sprawling, picaresque narrative tells the story of two Jewish comic-book artists, Josef Kavalier, a refugee from German-occupied Czechoslovakia, and his cousin Sam Clay (formerly Klayman), Brooklyn-born and bred. We follow their combined careers from youth, when they join forces to create comic books in late-1930s New York City, to middle age in early-1950s suburban Long Island. As he narrates this friendship, Chabon creates a broad canvas that accommodates renderings of prewar Czech-Jewish life, American corporate culture, the bohemian life in 1940s Greenwich Village, gay life and homophobia, and long digressions on the merits of comic books.

In its capaciousness, the novel seeks to incorporate the Holocaust as an essential American experience, a necessary part of a twentieth-century bildungsroman, and much of the power and interest of the novel derives from the tensions that result. The essential optimism of the American novel tradition of social advancement and moral education that informs this novel is disciplined and even challenged by the harsh realities of twentieth-century European history. The two strands are ultimately incommensurate but the novel tries a number of ways to make them meet, and the central vehicle for this meeting is the form of the comic book. Through the art of this quintessentially American popular medium, Josef, a man scarred by his memories and the awareness of his family's danger, seeks to represent his rage and his dreams of personal and collective escape. His major creation, done in collaboration with Sam, is the Escapist, a costumed, Nazi-bashing superhero who, like Houdini, can overcome any confinement. Through its exploration of this classic American popular art form, the novel stages a defense of American imaginary and real-life "escape" from the Holocaust and other modern European horrors, while also detailing the limits of this gesture.

The novel begins in 1939, describing the first meeting of Sam and Josef as teenagers in Sam's mother's apartment in Brooklyn, but then quickly flashes back to the story of Josef's childhood in 1930s Prague before the German invasion of Czechoslovakia. Josef is a stern, brilliant son of two secular Jewish doctors. A curious child, he receives an education in escape artistry from a wizened, eccentric local master of Eastern European origin named Kornblum. After a daring attempt at escape from a sealed bag dropped in the Moldau River nearly kills him, Josef is forced to end his training, but he never forgets Kornblum's *ausbrecher* (escapist) artistry, his "Baltic smell," and the satisfactions of escape (p. 25). The growing Nazi threat to the Jews of Prague is developed slowly in the narrative, through increasing references to new restrictions on

Jews that inhibit Josef's family's freedom of movement, but the wider story of Jewish subjugation increases in urgency and pace, if not in detail, after the March 1939 German invasion. Once Prague falls to the Nazis, Chabon focuses even more on the story of Josef's family as a microcosm of Jewish experience, as he describes their efforts to make good Josef's escape. They succeed in gaining an exit visa for Josef through well-placed bribes, but soon after leaving Prague, Josef discovers that his papers are not in order. Unwilling to return and face his family, he turns up at the doorstep of his former teacher, Kornblum. Together they hatch a miraculous plan to effect Josef's escape—by hiding in a sealed coffin that contains the lifeless clay form of the golem of Prague, Rabbi Loew's famous creation.

By introducing Rabbi Loew's golem into the text, Chabon invokes a classic story of Jewish resistance to gentile oppression. According to what was at first a nineteenth-century oral tradition, and then appeared in a series of accounts that have proliferated since Leopold Weisel's version in *Sippurim* (1847–1856), Rabbi Judah Loew Ben Bezalel of Prague, an accomplished Torah and Kabbalah scholar, created a golem in 1600—a figure made of clay brought to quasi-living form by the power of God's holy name—in order to protect the Jewish ghetto from the threat of a pogrom (Bilski, p. 14; Scholem, "Golem of Prague," pp. 335–336; Goldsmith, pp. 21–37). Rabbi Loew was responding to an immediate threat, a dark rumor that was spreading that a Christian child had been killed by Jews in order to salvage his blood to make matzoh. The golem, silent and robotlike, performed his task of patrolling the streets of the ghetto until he was no longer needed, whereupon Rabbi Loew returned him to inanimate form and had his clay remains placed in the attic of the *Altneuschul* (the "Old New Synagogue") until he was again needed. This tale has been retold and developed by many writers since 1856, and was preceded by centuries of golem lore dating back to the Babylonian Talmud (Sanhedrin 65b) and an important early kabbalistic text, the *Sefer Yezirah* (*Book of Creation*). In *Kavalier & Clay*, Chabon is concerned chiefly with the later Rabbi Loew tradition of the golem as a figure of Jewish resistance.

Although Rabbi Loew's golem is a figure of resistance, it is also based on fantasy and wish fulfillment: though Rabbi Loew was a real historical figure, there is no real evidence that he ever created a golem. As he invokes the golem legend, Chabon initiates a long process of pairing apparently irreconcilable narrative modes in the novel: he begins by matching the desperate reality of Jewish life in Nazi-occupied Prague with a fantastical folk tradition of survival and hope. This pairing suggests the juxtapositions to come between realistic narrative and comic-book narrative, and between a story of Jewish-American optimism and opportunity with the systematic elimination of the Jews in Europe. The effect of these juxtapositions, as seen in the Prague section, is deliberately jarring and often unsettlingly funny. We are told, in tones reminiscent of a bad spy novel, of how Josef comes to be a stowaway in the golem's coffin: The leaders of Prague's Jewish community chose to remove the golem to a safer place for the duration of the war. Kornblum has been appointed by a secret committee to locate the golem, which has been lost since it was removed from the *Altneuschul* early in the century. By means of dedicated detective work, Kornblum and Josef discover the golem's new location in a sealed-off tenement apartment in the Josefov district, disguise its lifeless husk as a "dead *goyische* giant" (p. 52), and then hide Josef in a secret compartment at the bottom of its coffin. The coffin is shipped to the "safe place" (p. 15), Vilna, Lithuania, and from there Josef manages to escape to the United States via a roundabout Pacific route through imperial Japan.

As the golem becomes, quite literally, the vehicle for Josef's escape to America, so comic books become the means of his imaginary escape from his past. Chabon takes pains to draw connections for the reader between the golem itself as a physical presence and the fanciful heroes of comic-book art. Early on, the narrator likens the golem's crude mud construction to the crudely drawn heroes of early comic-book artists: The golem's hands and feet are "poorly proportioned, as is often the case with the work of amateur artists, and much too large for its body" (p. 61). Along with Harry Houdini, the golem is described in the novel as a historical precursor to golden-age comic-book heroes such as Superman, and indeed, Josef's first stumbling effort at drawing a superhero figure to sell is a golem. This idea is predictably dismissed by a potential buyer as "too Jewish" (p. 86). Chabon takes evident pleasure in narrating the Jewish origins of early comic books and their creators, drawing on interviews with such key early figures as Stan Lee and Will Eisner (whose 1986 autobiographical graphic novella *The Dreamer*, about the early days of comic books, is a clear precursor text to *Kavalier & Clay*) and on the example of Jerry Siegel and Joe Schuster, the teenage Jewish cocreators of Superman. Late in the novel, Sam humorously makes these connections clear: "What, they're all Jewish superheroes. Superman, you don't think he's Jewish? Coming over from the old country, changing his name like that. Clark Kent, only a Jew would pick a name like that for himself" (p. 585).

Sam and Josef's most successful creation, the Escapist, is a barely disguised figure of Jewish hope, and more specifically a vehicle for Josef's most fervent fantasies of personal revenge and family deliverance. In one issue of "The Escapist," in what the narrator describes as "a transcendent moment in the history of wishful figments," the Escapist captures Hitler and frees all of Europe from bondage. "The war was over; a universal era of peace was declared," and as a result, "the Kavalier family of Prague . . . [was now] free" (p. 166). This victory in the comic book proves to be illusory (it was not the real Hitler after all), but Chabon repeatedly emphasizes the value of such escapist fantasy in the face of the limitations of historical truth. In an important passage near the end of *Kavalier & Clay*, he presents a full defense of escapism from Josef's perspective:

> Having lost his mother, father, brother, and grandfather, the friends and foes of his youth, his beloved teacher Bernard Kornblum, his city, his history—his home —the usual charge leveled against comic books, that they offered *merely an easy escape from reality*, seemed to Joe actually to be a powerful argument in itself. He had escaped, in his life, from ropes, chains, boxes, bags, and crates, from handcuffs and shackles, from countries and regimes. . . . The escape from reality was, he felt—especially right after the war—a worthy challenge (p. 575).

The harsh reality that Josef faces in the course of the novel is the eventual murder of his entire family. In the first half of *Kavalier & Clay*, Josef struggles to save members of his family, in particular his young brother Thomas, through a series of increasingly frustrating meetings with a representative from the German consulate and the sneeringly condescending and transparently antisemitic representatives at the U.S. State Department. Meanwhile, receiving only intermittent letters from his family, he hears of their forced removal from their home, their "resettlement" in a crowded new house with another large Jewish family, and the illness and death of his father. Hope intervenes briefly when it seems that Josef is going to be able to at least save Thomas, but the ship carrying the boy and other young Jewish refugees is sunk by a German U-boat. In a rage of guilt and anger at this unbearable loss, Josef enlists in the army and promptly disappears from the lives of his lover, Rosa Saks Luxemborg (who is carrying his unborn child), and his dear friend Sam. While serving at a military post in Antarctica, Josef hears a faint radio broadcast from Germany, a promotional report on the wonders of the "model" concentration camp, Theresienstadt. For a fleeting moment, through the static Josef hears the voice of his maternal grandfather singing a Schubert strain, and he realizes the completeness of his loss—all his remaining family will die in Theresienstadt. The pathos of Josef's helpless distance from his family's story and their eventual fate is evoked here through his struggles to hear this ghostly voice from the ether. Years later, after all these disasters, Josef returns to reunite with son, partner, and former lover in a dramatic scene set at the Empire State Building. In the passage quoted previously, Josef still manages to defend the art he had once abandoned, an art of fantasy and escape.

Although Josef himself comes to affirm the value of fantasy and escape, the novel at irregular intervals exhibits uncertainty about the appropriateness of these gestures in the face of the Holocaust. One important moment in which the novel appears to be critiquing its own position on escape occurs early on, when Kornblum and Josef are attempting to locate the missing body of the golem in a Jewish tenement in the Josefov. The two characters disguise themselves as census takers for the Nazis, as they work door to door, trying to find the missing, unoccupied room that will contain the hidden golem; when this methodical approach doesn't work, they ask all the Jewish tenants to place Stars of David on their windows in order to isolate the missing room. In what was at first a comedic, fantastical scene of disguise and role-playing, Kornblum and Josef end up taking on the roles of the Nazis and their servants in perpetuating the abuse of the Jews. Soon after their plot succeeds, in a moment of excruciating self-consciousness for Kornblum and the novel itself, Kornblum tears up the cards they had used for their fake "census":

> "Contemptible," he said, but Josef was not sure, then or afterward, whom or what he was talking about—the ruse itself, the occupiers who made it plausible, the Jews who had submitted to it without question, or himself for having perpetrated it (p. 45).

The last option, "himself for having perpetrated it," marks a fault line in the novel between the machinery of picaresque, escapist suspense that enriches the novel's narrative drive and the inescapable facticity of the Holocaust, which challenges all attempts at representation, and all attempts to escape it. In this fleeting but important gesture of self-criticism—a gesture that is wholly absent from an "escapist" movie about the Holocaust, *Life Is Beautiful*—the plot machinery of the novel grinds to a halt.

Still, despite these jarring contrasts, and despite the frequent impression that Josef's escapism is at minimum a response to his own survivor's guilt, for the most part *Kavalier & Clay* affirms the inherent value of escapist art: great pain and loss can be represented and even transformed through an indirect, seemingly ridiculous episodic narrative form. Just as, in *Maus II*, Art Spiegelman's eponymous narrator questions and then ultimately affirms his use of serious "commix" art to tell the story of his parents' Holocaust history, Chabon uses Josef to defend the genre of inherently *unserious* superhero comics and its attendant escapism as a response to the loss faced in the Holocaust and as a viable alternative to an explicit Holocaust narrative. Near the end of the novel, Josef reveals that for several years he has been secretly writing just such a story, a 2,256-page comic book called *The Golem.* (Interestingly, golems have appeared numerous times in comics, including a short series in Marvel's *Strange Tales* [1974], in *The Incredible Hulk* [no. 134, 1970], in a Lubavitcher-produced series called *The Adventures of Mendy and the Golem*, and even in *Superman* [no. 134, 1972] [Bilski, p. 48; Goldsmith, p. 151].) For his giant comic book, Josef invents a hero, Josef Golem, a "wayward, unnatural child," who reverses Josef's own story of oppression and flight by nobly sacrificing himself for the sake of his community (p. 577). Where and when his character lives and the full nature of his story is unclear—Chabon gives us few details—but we are given one important piece of information: this new golem tale avoids the tendency of most modern golem stories to address the moral cost of creating a new being and the trouble that can ensue. (Indeed, the theme of what Josef calls "overweening human ambition" [p. 582] persists in recent golem fictions as diverse as Isaac Bashevis Singer's children's book *The Golem* [1981], Cynthia Ozick's Bartleby-like short story "Puttermesser and Xanthippe" [1982], and Marge Piercy's novel of interlocking golem stories set in the future and the past, *He, She and It* [1991].) To Josef, the "shaping of a golem" is an act of imaginative if not political will, "a gesture of hope, offered against hope, in a time of desperation," as in the story of Rabbi Loew's use of the golem to rescue the Jews of Prague from the threat of pogrom (p. 582). Though Josef's golem tale is set in a recognizably Jewish milieu, and hence seems to allow him to confront his life and his loss more directly than before, this story remains "the voicing of a vain wish, when you got down to it, to escape" (p. 582).

Critical Reception

There has been only one peer-reviewed article on Michael Chabon's work, Douglas Fowler's "The Short Fiction of Michael Chabon: Nostalgia in the Very Young." In this perceptive 1995 essay, Fowler describes how the "young and bright and socially advantaged Jewish males" of Chabon's early fiction evince a deep longing for the "sustenance" they once drew from their fractured families. Fowler finds exceptional among his contemporaries, Chabon's compassion for his often misguided characters and his mastery of seemingly effortless, polished prose. Many reviewers of Chabon's books from *The Mysteries of Pittsburgh* to *Werewolves in Their Youth* have celebrated this combination of formal skill with generosity of voice. In marking these qualities and in seeking to establish Chabon's growing significance as a writer, critics have often compared him to John Cheever and the early Philip Roth (in *Goodbye Columbus* mode).

Chabon has remarked that some words of advice from the *Washington Post's* Jonathan Yardley issued at the end of his review of *Wonder Boys* spurred his ambition to write *Kavalier & Clay*: "He said, you know how to do this, you've written two novels with a very limited scope, now go out there and let's see what you can do" (Buzbee, p. 7). Many critics of *Kavalier & Clay* have in turn responded to its great scope: the *New York Times'* Janet Maslin called it a "big, ripe" narrative that finds "success in reaching for big settings . . . big creative leaps . . . and big historical relevance without strain" (p. E10), and the *Washington Post*'s Michael Dirda (p. 15) called it "absolutely gosh-wow, [and] super-collosal." In crediting it for its size and ambition, some critics have judged it a candidate for the title of "Great American Novel," and indeed, with its sprawling story line, its thematic breadth, and its Melvillean use of archival (or pseudo-archival) material, the novel seems a likely candidate. It is surprising, in this case, that the novel has not been compared more often with Saul Bellow's *Adventures of Augie March*, a book frequently given the designation of "Great American Novel" that also tells a story of energetic young Jewish men making their way in the world of American commerce.

Much of the most perceptive critical writing on *Kavalier & Clay* has concerned its reworked history of the dawn of comics and its treatment of comics as a valid popular art form. Brian Doherty in *Reason* has well-evoked Chabon's defense of the form and his careful re-creation of the Jewish influence on comics' origins, especially the origins of the superhero. Like some other critics, Doherty acknowledged how the publication of *Kavalier & Clay* demonstrates the growing respect accorded to comic-book art and early comic-book creators in late-1990s America.

In focusing on the novel's epic American sweep and its celebration of American popular culture, nearly all critics have failed to adequately address it as a story about the Holocaust. Admittedly, the chapters set in Jewish Prague are few and appear early in the novel, and for much of the novel the characters are physically distant from events going on in Europe, but the story of Josef and his attempts to help his family escape from the Holocaust and to effect his own, quintessentially American "imaginative" escape is the dominant story in the novel. The only critic who has fully confronted the novel's attempts to combine American cultural fantasy with a story about the Holocaust is John Podhoretz. In a 2001 *Commentary* review, Podhoretz is quite critical of Chabon's attempts to mirror Josef's use of the fantastic in his own narrative. In particular, Podhoretz criticizes Chabon's use of the golem as "a symbol of the murdered European diaspora":

> There is nothing offensive in this conversion of the *Shoah* into metaphor; but there is something off about it. The Jews of Central Europe, both those who were murdered and those who escaped murder, were ordinary people. In attempting to memorialize them and pay tribute to their suffering, Chabon descends into a false mysticism. It is true that their tradition featured a certain mystical strain, but it is also horrifically true that mysticism was among the forces that led to their extermination—an evil mysticism that promised the world would be purified by their removal (pp. 71–72).

Podhoretz fails to credit Chabon with any self-consciousness about the inadequacy of his own gestures at fantasy and escapist modes of writing, but his critique is nevertheless valuable for beginning what it is hoped will be a fruitful critical debate on the representation of the Holocaust in Michael Chabon's writing.

Bibliography

Primary Sources

Novels and Short Story Collections

The Mysteries of Pittsburgh. 1988.
A Model World and Other Stories. 1991.
Wonder Boys. 1995.
Werewolves in Their Youth. 1999.
The Amazing Adventures of Kavalier & Clay. 2000.
Summerland. Forthcoming, October 2002.

Uncollected Fiction

"The First Chapter of *Fountain City.*" http:/www.michaelchabon.com/FC1.html
"Revenge of Wolverine" (Unproduced screenplay for the movie *X-Men*). *Harpers* (October 2000): 32–38.
"House of Gold" (Unproduced television script). 1996. http://www.michaelchabon.com/houseogold.html
"The God of Dark Laughter." *The New Yorker* (9 April 2001): 116–128.

Nonfiction Essays and Articles

"Travel: Footloose." *Vogue*, May 1989, 266ff., pp. 379–381.
"The Recipe for Life." 2000. http://www.michaelchabon.com/golem.html
"It's in the Cards." *New York Times Magazine*, 21 July 1991.
"Prague: Lost Era's Last Survivor." *New York Times*, Current Events Edition, 26 September 1993.
"Las Vegas: Glitz and Dust." *New York Times Magazine*, Part 2: The Sophisticated Traveller, 13 November 1994.
Introduction to *Julius Knipfl: Real Estate Photographer*, by Ben Katchor. New York: Little, Brown, 1996.
"Guidebook to a Land of Ghosts." *Civilization*, June 1997, 67–69.
"The Hand on My Shoulder." *Vogue*, October 1997: 379–381.
"Michael Chabon: The Writing Life." *Washington Post Book World*, 16 July 2000.
"Fred Kelly: Teaching Ike to Tap." *New York Times Magazine*, 7 January 2001.
"Talk Delivered at the Nabokov Museum, St. Petersburg, 1 June 2000." http://www.michaelchabon.com/VN.html
"Wrecked." [Undated] http://www.michaelchabon.com/FC.html
"Maps and Legends." [Undated] http://www.michaelchabon.com/columbia.html

Secondary Sources

***Kavalier & Clay* Book Reviews**

Caldwell, Gail. *Boston Globe*, 19 November 2000, third edition.
Dirda, Michael. *Washington Post Book World*, 17 September 2000, final edition.
Doherty, Brian. "Comics Tragedy." *Reason* 33, no. 1 (2001): 48–55.
Hoorspool, David. "Sam and Joe Take on the Nazis." *Times Literary Supplement*, 6 October 2000.
Kalfus, Ken. "The Golem Knows." *New York Times*, 24 September 2000.
Maslin, Janet. "A Life and Death Story Set in Comic Book Land." *New York Times*, 21 September 2000.
Patterson, Troy. "Comics Genius." *Entertainment Weekly*, 29 September 2000, 123ff.
Podhoretz, John. "Escapists." *Commentary* 111, no. 6 (2001): 68–72.
Shepard, R. Z. "Biff! Boom! A Super Novel about the Golden Age of Comics." *Time*, 25 September 2000: 103[C]ff.

Interviews

Arana, Marie. "Michael Chabon: Touched by Fortune." *Washington Post*, 16 July 2000, final edition.
Binelli, Mark. "The Amazing Story of the Comic Book Nerd Who Won the Pulitzer Prize for Fiction." *Rolling Stone*, 27 September 2001, pp. 58–62, 78.
Buzbee, Lewis. "Michael Chabon: Comics Came First." *New York Times Book Review*, 24 September 2000.
Eberhart, John Mark. "The High Art of Escapism." *Kansas City Star*, 9 September 2001.
Holzel, David. "Michael Chabon Pulls Off a Sleight of Hand." *CNN.com Book News*, 22 September 2000. http://www.cnn.com/2000/books/news/09/22/michael.chabon/index.html
Hubbard, Kim. "Natural Wonder." *People Weekly*, 26 June 1995, 63.
See, Lisa. "Michael Chabon: Wonder Boy in Transition." *Publishers Weekly*, 10 April 1995, 44.
Tobias, Scott. "Michael Chabon." *The Onion AV Club*, 22 November 2000, http://avclub.theonion.com/avclub3642/avfeature-3642.html
Walton, David. "PW Talks with Michael Chabon." *Publishers Weekly*, 21 August 2000, 45–46.
Weich, Dave. "Michael Chabon's Amazing Adventures." 2001. www.powells.com/authors/chabon.html

Sources on the Golem Legend

Bilski, Emily D. *Golem! Danger, Deliverance and Art*. New York: The Jewish Museum, 1988.

Bloch, Chayim. *The Golem: Legends of the Ghetto of Prague*. [1919] Translated by Harry Schneiderman. Blauvelt, N.Y.: Rudolf Steiner Publications, 1972. Reprint of the 1925 Vienna edition.

Goldsmith, Arnold L. *The Golem Remembered*. Detroit: Wayne State University Press, 1981.

Idel, Moshe. *Golem: Jewish Magical and Mystical Traditions on the Artificial Anthropoid*. Albany: SUNY Press, 1990.

———. "Elie Wiesel, Rabbi Judah Lowe, and the Golem of Prague." *Studies in Jewish American Literature* 5 (1986): 15–28.

Rosenberg, Yudl. "The Golem or the Miraculous Deeds of Rabbi Liva." [1909] Translated by Joachim Neugroschel. In *Yenne Velt: The Great Works of Jewish Fantasy and the Occult*. New York: Stonehill Publishing, 1976, 2: 162–225.

Scholem, Gershom. "The Golem of Prague and the Golem of Rehovot." *The Messianic Idea in Judaism*. New York: Schocken, 1971.

———. "The Idea of the Golem." *On the Kabbalah and Its Symbolism*. Translated by Ralph Manheim. New York: Schocken, 1985, pp. 158–204.

ALBERT COHEN

(1895–1981)

JUDITH KAUFFMANN
(Translated by Ruth Morris)

ALBERT COHEN WAS born in 1895, the only child of Marc and Louise Coen (Cohen changed the spelling of his family name when he began his law studies in Geneva in 1914), in the ghetto of Corfu, the lost paradise of his early childhood. To the end of his days he spoke the Judeo-Venetian language of the ghetto. His formative years in Marseilles (1900–1914) were marked by the discovery of antisemitic hatred: on his tenth birthday a street vendor publicly called him a "dirty Yid." This traumatic encounter sent him "to an invisible concentration camp" (*O vous, Frères humains* [O you, Human Brothers], Paris: Gallimard-Folio, 1972, p. 73), and "twisting his soul for ever," acted as a decisive factor in turning him into a warrior for the Jewish cause. He took up residence in Geneva in 1914 and acquired Swiss citizenship in 1919. Until his death in 1981 he lived in Switzerland, with a number of periods abroad: a year in Egypt, Parisian interludes during the 1920s and 1930s, and his long exile in London during the war (1940–1947).

A Tale of Three Careers: Lawyer, Militant, Writer

As an attorney, Albert Cohen held senior positions as a lawyer-diplomat at the international institutions in Geneva, in particular the International Labor Office, and played a major role in assisting stateless persons. During the war, when he was appointed legal adviser to the Intergovernmental Committee for Refugees in London, he initiated an improved version of the Nansen passport (an internationally recognized identity card for stateless persons): in 1946, the original single sheet became a thirty-two-page booklet that enabled refugees to travel, and above all guaranteed the possibility of returning to the country that had signed the document. Cohen used to say that this little white book was "his most beautiful book."

He became actively involved in the Jewish and Zionist cause early in his life, and established and ran *La revue juive*, produced by major publisher Gallimard. This cultural and political magazine, which had a brief (1924–1925) but important existence, had a prestigious board, including figures such as Sigmund Freud, Albert Einstein, and Martin Buber. A close colleague of Chaim Weizmann, Cohen was appointed adviser to the Jewish Agency in Paris in 1939. He worked on establishing a French Jewish Legion, an initiative that unfortunately came to a sudden end. Because of French political reasons, such as the desire to avoid disrupting British Middle Eastern politics, the project never progressed beyond the planning stage. Similarly, an initiative designed during the "phoney war" (a term describing the period between September 1939, when the Allies declared war against Germany, and June 1940, when the war took serious shape with the German invasion of France) to establish a committee of intellectuals called *Pro Causa Judaica* to support persecuted Jews, failed to materialize despite the expressed desire of leading figures, including scientists (Frédéric Joliot-Curie) and writers (Georges Duhamel, Jules Romains, François Mauriac, and Paul Claudel), to join. In contrast, Cohen was successful in his liaison assignments with exiled governments in London.

Active as a writer from his youth to his last breath, Cohen worked in many genres: poetry and theater briefly in his early stages (*Ezéchiel* won the Comoedia prize for the best one-act play of 1930), war journalism during World War II, autobiographical writing, and finally novel writing, which was the great passion of his life. It took some forty years to write *Solal* (1930), *Mangeclous* (*Nailcruncher*, 1938), *Belle du Seigneur* (1967, Grand prix de l'Académie française) and *Les Valeureux* (The Valiant, 1969). This quartet of novels relates the rise and fall of Solal, the son of the rabbi of the Jewish community of Cephalonia, Corfu's literary twin. Solal, who becomes Under-Secretary-General of the League of Nations toward the end of the 1930s, is also the tragic hero of an all-consuming passion for his lover, Ariane. His cousins, collectively known as "the Valiant"—ludicrous clowns known for their ill-timed pranks—strike discordant notes of Jewish marginality and exclusion in this four-part heroic symphony. The inventive and voracious clan leader, Mangeclous (Nailcruncher), in the eponymous 1938 novel, provides his comic—and gastronomic—version of the future "Cohen passport": a "Franco-British-American-Czecho-Scandinavian-Swiss passport" with "a variegated nationality, like a vanilla and strawberry ice cream" (*Nailcruncher*, London: Routledge, 1940, p. 230). While fiction sometimes anticipates reality, the fighter and the writer are never far from each other, for the artist, like the man, is profoundly involved in the history of his time. This quartet of novels attains universality by drawing its lifeblood from the experience of Jewishness as an extreme.

Speaking Silently

While antisemitism haunts Cohen's literary universe as much as it did his life, the *Shoah* does not, at first glance, appear to be a major component of his writing. There are however, a few passages in his autobiographical texts where the death camps are presented as the ultimate development of anti-Jewish racial hatred.

In his novels, most of which were published after the war, direct reference to the Holocaust would be anachronistic because the novels are set before those events. Genocide is referred to in some brief asides by the author, or in Solal's dream sequences and apocalyptic hallucinations (Goitein, p. 90). These "oblique forms," which refer to the *Shoah* (Schaffner, p. 98), are scattered throughout the text and represent Cohen's humble contribution to the monument to Jewish memory (Goitein, p. 85). These few signs, however, make their appearance at strategic moments.The novelist's digression about the death of close relatives who were deported goes hand in hand with questions about literary creation as a practice of aesthetic distancing as opposed to ethical commitment, a series of questions that lie at the heart of all thinking on *Shoah* writing:

> Suddenly I am haunted by the German horrors, the millions of those burned by the wicked nation, those of my family in Auschwitz, and their terrors, . . . my uncle and his son arrested in Nice, gassed in Auschwitz, . . . my mother's terror, how every day she expected a knock, a bang on the door, banging by the Gestapo, German banging, wicked banging . . . and what is the point of writing, and how is it possible to continue telling the story of the Valiant, how can one smile? (*Les Valeureux*, Paris: Gallimard-Folio, 1969, p. 255).

He replied in advance to this question by writing that the book *The Valiant*, about his cousins, is a "farewell to a species which is dying out" (p. 91). He thus explicitly raises the issue of the relationship between writing—he refers to his book as a "trace" (p. 255)—and mourning and memory.

Other significant allusive passages are to be found in the hero's long internal meditation on his destiny (in *Belle du Seigneur*, Paris: Gallimard, 1967, pp. 849–887). Solal calls upon his "lovely Jews," to whom he "speaks in silence" (p. 879). This formula seems to apply to his *Shoah*-related discourse wherein he expresses, in a paradoxical nutshell of an oxymoron, the desire to air his "crazy truth" about Jewish existence and the need to take refuge in muteness, for fear of being misunderstood. This "speaking silently" highlights the fragility of literary communication, which is always at risk of failure because of the speaker's incapacity to account for the unspeakable, and the problematic presence of a responsible partner (George Steiner's "responsible" reader) ready to assume his/her share of responsibility for an authentic exchange. Cohen's work requires the cooperation of a reader capable of identifying the subtext and decoding his oblique and disjointed writing. I have selected three texts that illustrate my point.

From "Germanimality" to Nazi Abjectness

In Solal's monologue the novelist reproduces, almost word for word, part of texts he wrote in 1942 under a pseudonym in *France libre*, one of the magazines published for the exiled French community in wartime London. In one such text, "Combat pour l'homme" ("Fighting for Man"), Cohen defines the roots of Nazism in an overall view of the human species, which he divides into two groups: "people who live under the sway of nature" and the Jewish people, "a people who live under the rule of anti-nature" (*Belle du Seigneur*, p. 876). The former tell how "nature's law is arrogant might and rampant egoism and rude health . . . the sacred right of the strong in other words of those best equipped to commit murder" (p. 878). In order to describe the behavior of the German population, which developed an extreme affinity with "the great apedom of the primeval forest," Cohen invents the portmanteau term "Germanimality." The second group is the embodiment of "the people of the Holy Law and the prophets the people who strove to establish the reign of the human on earth . . . the people who combat the laws of nature and the bearer of a crazy hope which nature abhors" (p. 878). As the incarnation of the people "which upon Sinai's top did declare war upon the natural upon the animal in man," Jews represent the absolute negation of Nazism: their total elimination is a necessity.

Cohen develops his thinking about what is human and what is inhuman in the framework of a history of mankind in which the unique struggle of the Jewish people occupies an exemplary position:

> It is our glory as primates sprung from time without memory . . . to be metamorphosed into the gnarled and twisted but miraculous bent-backed wanderer a creature monstrous and sublime . . . this twisted miraculous divine-eyed being this non-animal non-natural monster that is man the product of our own heroic handiwork (p. 880).

Toward the end of this long introspective exercise, Solal drifts off to a nightmarish world. The suggestive denseness of the description is inversely proportional to its length:

> The room full of gesticulating bodies piled high one up on top of the other in a pyramid in a hullabalooing mound the tongues of those below lick the heels of those above while the heels tread on the heads of the lickers below (p. 886).

This scene arouses a vague feeling of déjà vu for the reader who is familiar with pictures of the extermination camps. The focusing on anatomical details—tongues, heels, skulls—emphasizes the dismantling of bodies into dehumanized puppets. The reference to "licking" introduces an incongruous note of sensuality into this image of horror. The gesture of life in a death scene confers an abject dimension on this camouflaged representation of the Final Solution, with its intermingling of the familiar and the terrifying. The inappropriate terminology—"hullabalooing mound"—strips the cries of any sound. Petrified in space, the mute shrieks are the metaphorical expression of the impossible communication of a horror that is unspeakable and inaudible.

A Little Irreverent Digression: A Prayer for a Passport

A number of lightweight, silly anecdotes, published before the Holocaust, take on new meaning with hindsight. Little Uncle Saltiel specializes in making up prayers for famous people: Léon Blum, Einstein, Freud, the president of the United States—and Hitler:

> "Oh Eternal," he said, the palms of his hands turned towards heaven, "if this Hitler is good and acts according to Thy principles, let him live in happiness for a hundred and six years. But if Thou deemest that he acts evilly, then turn him into a Polish Jew without a passport!" (*Nailcruncher*, p. 230).

The canceling of a passport does not, a priori, assume the dimensions of major punishment. The prayer, expressed before Nazism's genocidal phase, demanding a punishment made ridiculous by its incongruity and inadequacy, represents a joke in very bad taste and an insult to the real victims of the Final Solution. But should one go beyond this basic interpretation of the literal message?

To turn Hitler into a Slavic Jew is to humiliate him by casting him to the very bottom of the racial ladder. The tyrant, reduced to what he most despises and hates, is symbolically stripped of all greatness, even that of a prince of evil. Condemned to insignificance and anonymity, he is hoist upon his own petard.

By minimizing his suffering, the victim also indirectly rejects the mythology of the martyr, which is so dear to Western culture. By stripping it of any redeeming cosmic dimension, he helps set the record straight about the glorification of suffering. It is also an understatement to the effect that punishment is always at a lower level than the atrocities perpetrated. In a world where the struggle of the helpless community is lost in advance, escaping into the realm of the derisory makes it possible to indirectly criticize the actual scandal of persecution. At the same time, when specifically contextualized as Nazi genocide, resistance should not be measured by its actual success. In the ghettos or the camps, fighting to survive is already an act of resistance. In his monologue, Solal sings an ode to "a people who stood firm and resisted not for a year not for five years not for ten years but a people who stood firm for two thousands years" (*Belle du Seigneur*, p. 873).

Mourning, Memory, Writing

The literary text represents a cenotaph. Erected in memory of the deceased but not containing their bodies, the verbal monument records the diffuse traces of the dead in the memory of words. By writing, one is expressing the pain caused by the absence of his nearest and dearest and his efforts to prevent their final vanishing into the muteness of infinity.

By enumerating the persecutions, Solal recites the lament of past deaths and lauds the martyrs. With the litany of the dead—"O my dead of ancient days" (*Belle du Seigneur*, p. 880)—the fictional memory of the *Shoah* takes its place in the long history of Jewish martyrdom. Cohen's text is part of the traditional Jewish lamentation, the *kinna* (lament), but in a grotesque variation which, through its incongruous ravings, departs from the familiar ritual of consolation, because in his view, absurdity and derision rule over a universe lacking "any meaning beyond its pointless existence in the stark eye of the void" (p. 880). The flamboyant tale of Solal the conqueror, sophisticated mixture of exaltation and mockery of passionate love, is undermined by the antisemitic discordant rumblings of the repressed history of Western civilization.

Bibliography

Primary Sources

Paroles juives (Jewish Words). 1921.
Solal (*Solal*). 1930.
Ezéchiel (Ezechiel). 1930.
Mangeclous (*Nailcruncher*). 1938.
Le livre de ma mère (*Book of My Mother*). 1954.
Belle du Seigneur (*Belle du Seigneur*). 1967.
Les Valeureux (The Valiant). 1969.
O vous, frères humains (O You, Human Brothers). 1972.
Carnets 1978 (Notebooks 1978). 1978.

Secondary Sources

Goitein-Galpérin, Denise. "La *Shoah* dans l'œuvre d'Albert Cohen." *Yod* Publications Langues'O, no. 25 (1987): 85–100.

———."Albert Cohen et l'Histoire: son action politique et diplomatique." *Cahiers Albert Cohen*, no. 9 (September 1999): 17–31.

Kauffmann, Judith. "Albert Cohen et la 'parole silencieuse' ou comment (ne pas) écrire un roman sur la Shoa." In *Albert Cohen et la guerre*. Edited by Catherine Milkovitch-Rioux. Clermont-Ferrand: Centre de Recherches sur les Littératures Modernes et Contemporaines, 1998.

———. *Grotesque et marginalité. Variations sur Albert Cohen et l'effet-Mangeclous*. Bern: Peter Lang, 2000.

Milkovitch-Rioux, Catherine. "Préface." In *Albert Cohen et la guerre*. Edited by Catherine Milkovitch-Rioux. *Clermont-Ferrand*: Centre de Recherches sur les Littératures Modernes et Contemporaines, 1998.

Schaffner, Alain. " Un écrivain en guerre. Littérature et polémique dans 'Salut à La Russie.' " In *Albert Cohen et la guerre*. Edited by Catherine Milkovitch-Rioux. Clermont-Ferrand: Centre de Recherches sur les Littératures Modernes et Contemporaines, 1998.

———. *Le Goût de l'absolu. L'enjeu sacré de la littérature dans l'œuvre d'Albert Cohen*. Paris: Honoré Champion, 1999.

ARTHUR A. COHEN

(1928–1986)

S. LILLIAN KREMER

ARTHUR COHEN CONTENDS that all Jews, whether physically harmed in the Holocaust or not, are psychological survivors. He maintains "the generation that bears the scar without the wound," is obligated "to describe a meaning and wrest instruction from the historical" (*The Tremendum: A Theological Interpretation of the Holocaust*, Crossroad, 1981, p. 2). Theologian, publisher, editor, rare book dealer, art historian, essayist, and novelist, Cohen was born on 25 June 1928 to Isadore and Bess (Junger) Cohen and died of cancer 31 October 1986. He earned a B.A. in 1946 and an M.A. in 1949 from the University of Chicago. Additional graduate studies took him to the Union Theological Seminary, the New School for Social Research, Columbia University, and the Jewish Theological Seminary of America. Philosophy and theology, the subjects of Cohen's academic studies, are the passions evident in his fiction. Cohen had a successful publishing career as cofounder and managing director of Noonday Press, founder and president of Meridian Books, vice president of World Publishing Company, editor-in-chief and vice president of the General Books Division of Holt, Rinehart & Winston, and managing editor at Viking Press. He served as chairman of the board at the YIVO Institute for Jewish Research, advisory board member at the Institute for Advanced Judaic Studies at Brandeis University, as a member of the board PEN American Center, and lectured at Brown University. *In the Days of Simon Stern* (1973) received the Edward Lewis Wallant Prize and *An Admirable Woman* (1983) won the National Jewish Book Award in fiction and the Janice Epstein Award.

Recognition "that Western culture is a Christian culture, that Western values are rooted in the Greek and Christian tradition(s)" (quoted by Cole, p. 36) led Cohen to a religious crisis and contemplation of conversion to Christianity. With the guidance of philosopher Milton Steinberg, Cohen embraced Judaism, an experience described in his essay "Why I Choose to Be a Jew." Jewish theology is at the heart of Cohen's scholarship and creative writing. Among his most important works is *The Natural and the Supernatural Jew* (1962), wherein he distinguishes between the Jew who is shaped by history and environment and the Jew whose messianic faith transcends history. In *The Tremendum: A Theological Interpretation of the Holocaust* he wrestles with recognition of radical evil and argues for a new theological language in which the concept of God is redefined by taking the Holocaust into account.

An American Midrash

In the Days of Simon Stern, a rich, culturally textured, complex philosophic novel, incorporates biblical legend, theological, Talmudic, and kabbalistic discourse. The European Jewish experience is examined through testimony by public figures and the post-Holocaust perspective of refugees, survivors, and American Jews who escaped the conflagration by virtue of geography, but are bound to it by virtue of their Jewish identity. Beginning with the prophetic announcement of the marriage of Stern's parents and their future son's messianic destiny, the novel traverses their immigration to America, Simon's extraordinary rise to wealth and influence, his efforts to rehabilitate a group of death camp survivors, and his departure from the confines of the Lower East Side to extend his messianic influence.

The novel is a compendium of Jewish religious thought, history, and sociology presented in modes ranging from expository essay to tales within tales, dream-drama, sermon, letters, and meditations and commentaries narrated by the blind scribe, Nathan of Gaza, descendant of a long line of rabbis and scribes, chronicling the life and times of Simon Stern, messiah. A survivor of Auschwitz and Buchenwald, Nathan's authenticity stems from his witnessing of the Holocaust and his prewar career as Torahic scribe. Blinded in the Holocaust, he is a Tiresias figure, endowed with extraordinary moral insight, despite the loss of physical sight.

Akin to many European Jewish authors, Cohen situates the Holocaust within the context of Jewish persecution history from the medieval to the modern era. One of the novel's set pieces, a narrative within the narrative, "The Legend of the Last Jew" structurally foreshadows its Holocaust sequence and thematically reveals both the similarities and distinctions between Church and Nazi antisemitism. Set in modern Spain at a time when the church has achieved "the conversion of all the world to the Catholic faith" (*In the Days of Simon Stern*, Random House, 1972, p. 119) it relates the trial of Don Rafael Acosta, who is nominally Catholic, but is actually a secret Jew, the last survivor of many generations of the forced Conversos of Iberia. Acosta's martyrdom simultaneously evokes the persecutions of the fifteenth-century Spanish Inquisition, public humiliation, torture, and murder, and heralds the novel's Holocaust subject. With his dying breath, the last Jew repudiates Christianity and affirms loyalty to the God of his ancestors. His final words at his Vatican exhibition enunciate a post-Holocaust argument for the continuation of Jews and Judaism despite God's silence in the face of destruction. The redemptive legend concludes with the narrator's report of the regeneration of Jewry by Acosta's followers and his view that Simon Stern's support of the Society for the Rescue and Resurrection of the Jews places him among those followers. The metaphoric *Shoah* annunciation is prologue to dramatic presentation of Simon Stern's attendance at the 1943 Madison Square Garden rally in support of European Jewry. The address by Chaim Weizmann, future president of Israel, delineating the massive Jewish losses and the international indifference to the plight of Jews, is the overt inspiration for Stern's rescue mission.

Allied abandonment of European Jewry and the failed efforts of the American Jewish leadership to bring the tragedy to public attention, or to convince government officials of the need to counter its progress, complements the story of Stern's rescue mission. Prologue to the Weizmann speech is a woman carrying a placard with the grim admonition to "Remember the St. Louis." The reference is to the fate of 907 Jewish refugees from Germany aboard the ship *St. Louis*, who were denied asylum while waiting offshore, first in Cuban waters and then within miles of Florida; they were returned to Europe and thereby condemned to death. President Roosevelt's telegrammed assurance to the rally audience that the Nazis will fail rings hollow compared to Weizmann's observation that a "conspiracy of silence" (p. 153) is facilitating the destruction of the Jews.

Cohen depicts Roosevelt's deficient response in a dream sequence based on the only meeting he had with Jewish leaders, a futile talk between a pleading minority constituency and an unfeeling president disputing the authenticity of the petitioners' report of massive Jewish deaths. Echoing the report on Theresienstadt by duped Red Cross observers, Roosevelt quotes the organization's finding "the camps to be clean, no maltreatment, no disease, and few deaths. Excellent medical facilities. . . Talk of liquidation is regarded as irresponsible" (p. 155). Members of the Jewish delegation counter the Red Cross reports with witness testimony, but to no avail. In a rare use of irony by Cohen, the president asks the delegation whether he should cable the Pope, a fitting conclusion to a despairing dream, for Roosevelt's moral failure to act on behalf of the Jews was matched by that of Pius XII.

Cohen's documentary approach is evident in his critique of the American press for its failure to report the magnitude of Jewish losses and U.S. State Department's suppression of reliable casualty reports. Only the Yiddish press covered the Holocaust with the urgency it required. The confluence of the Weizmann speech, the Roosevelt dream, realization that nothing will be done to stop the genocide, and revelation of his messianic identity, inspires Stern's postwar mission to rescue a remnant of the remnant. He envisions and builds a Bene Brak, a complex modeled on the ancient Hebrews after the destruction of the Holy Temple. In this Jewish community, the survivors will heal each other in body and spirit.

At war's end, Stern travels to Dachau, Bergen-Belsen, Mauthausen, Auschwitz, and other camps to find survivors who will help realize his mission to ensure the endurance of Judaism and Jewry. Parodying the Nazi death selections, the messiah makes restoration selections, choosing Jews of many nationalities, classes and backgrounds, professions, and capacities; Jews united by their passion for renewal.

The Austrian, Russian, and Hungarian survivor histories cast as retrospective passages inscribe wide-ranging Holocaust experiences and interpretation. An Austrian refugee distinguishes the real Vienna from the romantic illusion, contrasting the storybook aristocratic Vienna of concert, opera, ballrooms, and cafés with the Nazi-welcoming Vienna of 1938 that tolerated daily riots, "Jews . . . being assaulted, humiliated, and harassed" (p. 187). The Holocaust history of the novel's narrator begins with his ironic return to Hungary from the safety of Palestine. Three months later, he is at a detention camp with other victims awaiting transfer to Auschwitz. Nathan characterizes his Auschwitz experience as "ordinary"—ordinary starvation, ordinary illness, and ordinary brushes with arbitrary death.

Most enigmatic of the survivors is a figure introduced to further Cohen's post-Holocaust theological interests. Janos Baltar is a self-hating half-Jew, half-Romanian shaped by a grotesque sexually abusive childhood and European anti-Jewish pathology. Born into a society that establishes life opportunities on the basis of religious and ethnic identity, he was at a constant disadvantage. A victim of violence, he becomes a guard in a concentration camp, a perpetrator of violence against the helpless. Despite the caution expressed by his aides, their warnings of the "indefinable contagion of Baltar," and his own reservations, Simon Stern accepts Baltar's plea to join the survivor remnant in America, explaining his decision in kabbalistic terms that characterize Cohen's post-Holocaust theodicy, a perception of God as the creator of good and evil. Simon concludes that Baltar comes to them because he senses in them the counter to his own villainy and they must therefore accept him.

Cohen weaves theological concerns expressed in *The Tremendum* into the narrative through the meditations of the scribe, dialogues between the messianic redeemer and his staff, and in a biblical play. Striving to undermine Stern's rehabilitation project, Baltar devises a Job drama calculated to subvert the survivors' faith in a just and benevolent deity. In addition to playing the satanic role, his commentary veers sharply from traditional Jewish Jobian interpretation. As the drama progresses, Baltar contrasts the restitution God made to Job and the irretrievable losses of Holocaust victims. Baltar challenges Judaic acceptance of suffering by the just, either as a test of their fidelity to God or acceptance that man's finite mind cannot probe the depths of divine omniscience. He urges the audience to counter this view because as Holocaust survivors they know tragedy without divine reversal. Their children, he reminds them, "are buried beneath the earth of Europe, . . . are not restored . . . And there is no less righteousness in you" (p. 283).

Cohen's post-Holocaust theology is expounded in the novel by Rabbi Lazare Steinman, a Russian-born survivor who has "been on the losing side of every major conflict of the century." Wrong in transient matters, he has always been morally correct. Steinman departs from the ancient rabbis in his perception of deity and covenant. He grieves for God because "He wants so much and can affect so little" (p. 255). Steinman has arrived at a position that marks the Holocaust as an event so different from the previous Jewish disasters that it must change our theological perceptions. He rejects the views of pious Jews who judge God guilty of failing to uphold the covenant for, in his view, expecting a participatory covenant is to expect God to respond to human petition, a condition disproved in the *Shoah*. The passage assessing Holocaust evil is analogous to Cohen's *tremendum* philosophy positing a "transforming caesura," a break in interpretation of Jewish theology and history that denies the symmetry of Sinai and Holocaust: "it annihilates for us the familiar categories by which we have read and decoded our past . . . the *tremendum* disallows traditional memory, obliging it to regard all settled doctrine anew, all accepted principle afresh, all closed truths and revelations as open" (p. 80). Steinman insists on a break from past theology similar to that in the *Tremendum*, where Cohen argues, "the traditional God has no connection with the Holocaust despite the palpable fact that the immensity of the *tremendum* implies a judgment upon God" (p. 81). Simon Stern and Steinman foreshadow Cohen's later insistence that Jewish reality must account for the *Shoah* "in its view of God, world, and man; it must constellate Jewish facts of practice and belief in such a way as to enable them to endure the *tremendum* and withstand it and a God who creates a universe in which such destructiveness occurs" (p. 82). Since evil's source is in divine creation it contributes to the complexity of creation and must be approached with the goal of repair. The vital question is how to affirm God meaningfully in a world where evil enjoys dominion.

In keeping with the restorative and regenerative approaches to Holocaust tragedy espoused by philosopher Emil Fackenheim, Cohen's Jews, aside from Baltar, respond to Holocaust loss by undertaking a major project of repair (*tikkun*) to strengthen Judaism and Jewry. They seek to build a new Jewish civilization responsive to the threat of the disappearance of the Jews from history and assign this task to American Jewry and the Holocaust survivors. They follow the tradition of the ancients who refrained from blaming God for the destruction of the temples and exile. Simon's comprehension that God embodies good and evil is manifested in his salvific effort to create a Bene Brak for the regeneration of the survivors as well as in his response to Baltar's destruction of the center. He restores the building and moves uptown to assume an even larger messianic role. The blind scribe's assessment of Simon's decision echoes Cohen's acceptance of contradictions in his nonfictional exploration of post-Holocaust theodicy, his understanding of the necessity of distinctions: ". . . first by separating the *tremendum* from all things and descending into the abyss, then by rejoining the *tremendum* to the whole experience of mankind as endpoint of the abyss and new beginning of the race" (p. 26).

Critical Reception

Reviewers for *Book World* and *Books and Bookmen* objected to the encyclopedic scope and discursive qualities of the *In the Days of Simon Stern*, exhibiting little patience for its digressions into Jewish history and textuality. It is precisely that erudition that delights its partisans. In the *New York Times Book Review*, Cynthia Ozick wrote, "In its teeming particularity every vein of this book runs with a brilliance of Jewish insight and erudition to be found in no other novelist. . . . Arthur Cohen is the first writer of any American generation to compose a profoundly Jewish fiction on a profoundly Western theme" (p. 6). M. J. Bandler was equally complimentary in *Commonweal*, proclaiming *In the Days of Simon Stern* "a jewel to be treasured; a majestic work of fiction that should stand world literature's test of time, to be read and reread in search for new meanings and interpretations." For Edward Alexander, among the novel's significant contributions to American Holocaust literature is its unique exploration of "the bearing of the Holocaust upon the ancient Jewish idea that messianic redemption will come through historical catastrophe." Alexander applauds its suggestion of "a new future for American Jewish writing," exploration of "how to reorganize Judaism in the Diaspora after the European Diaspora has been destroyed" (p. 330). Diane Cole concludes that the "erudition, invention, and passion" of Cohen's work "have established him as one of American Judaism's foremost men of letters" (p. 35). Arthur Cohen is clearly foremost among the authors who grapple with the meaning of post-Auschwitz Jewish identity and the search for post-Auschwitz Jewish affirmation.

Bibliography

Primary Sources

Nonfiction

Martin Buber. 1957.
The Natural and the Supernatural Jew. 1962.
The Hebrew Bible in Christian, Jewish, and Muslim Art. 1963.
The Negative Way: A Collaboration. Lithographs by Paul Brach. 1964.
Arguments and Doctrines: A Reader of Jewish Thinking in the Aftermath of the Holocaust. 1970.
A People Apart: Hasidism in America. With Garvin Phillip. 1970.
The Myth of the Judeo-Christian Tradition and Other Dissenting Essays. 1970.
The Delaunays, Apollinaire and Cendrars. 1972.
The Book Stripped Bare: A Survey of Books by 20th Century Artists and Writers: An Exhibition of Books from the Arthur Cohen and Elaine Lustig Cohen Collection. 1973.
If Not Now, When? Toward a Reconstitution of the Jewish People: Conversations between Mordecai M. Kaplan and Arthur A. Cohen. With Mordecai M. Kaplan. 1973.
Osip Emilevich Mandelstam: An Essay in Antiphon. 1974.
Sonia Delaunay. 1975.
The Jew: Essays from Martin Buber's Journal "Der Jude: 1916–1928." Translated by Joachim Neugroschel. Alabama: University of Alabama Press, 1980.
The American Imagination after War. 1981.
The Avant-Garde in Print. 5 vols. 1981.
Piet Zwart. 1981.
The Tremendum: A Theological Interpretation of the Holocaust. 1981.
Herbert Bayer: The Complete Works. 1984.

Fiction

The Carpenter Years. 1967.
In the Days of Simon Stern. 1973.
A Hero in His Time. 1976.
Acts of Theft. 1980.
An Admirable Woman. 1983.
Artists and Enemies: Three Novellas. 1987.

Books: Edited

Handbook of Christian Theology: Definition Essays on Concepts and Movements of Thought in Contemporary Protestantism. With Marvin Halverson. 1958.
Anatomy of Faith. Milton Steinberg. 1960.
Humanistic Education and Western Civilization: Essays for Robert M. Hutchins. 1964.
The New Art of Color: The Writings of Robert and Sonia Delaunay. 1978.
Contemporary Jewish Religious Thought: Original Essays on Critical Concepts, Movements, and Beliefs. With Paul Mendes-Flohr. 1987.
Contemporary Jewish Religious Thought: Original Essays on Critical Concepts, Movements and Beliefs. With Paul Mendes-Flohr. 1988.

Selected Articles and Essays

"The Encounter of Judaism and Christendom." *Cross Currents* 3 (March 1951): 91–95.
"Revelation and Law: Reflections on Martin Buber's Views on Halakhah." *Judaism* 1, no. 3 (July 1952): 250–256.
"Messianism and the Jew." *Commonweal* 62, no. 15 (July 1955): 367–369.
"Religion as a Sacred Ideology." *Partisan Review* 23, no. 4 (fall 1956): 495–505.
"Our Present Situation." *Conservative Judaism* 11, no. 2 (winter 1957): 13–19.
"The Jewish Press." *Commonweal* 67, no. 3 (October 18, 1957): 65–68.
"The Problem of Pluralism." In *Religion and Free Society*. Edited by William Lee Miller, et al. New York: The Fund for the Republic, 1958.
"The Natural and the Supernatural Jew: Two Views of the Church." In *American Catholics: A Protestant Jewish View*. Edited by Phillip Sharper. New York: Sheed and Ward, 1959, pp. 127–257.
"Why I Choose to be a Jew." *Harper's Magazine*, April 1959, 63–66.
"On Judaism and Catholicism." *Reconstructionist* 25, no. 8 (29 May 1959): 3–8.
"On Judaism and Catholicism, II." *Reconstructionist* 25, no. 9 (15 June 1959): 19–24.
"An Analysis of Milton Steinberg's *Anatomy of Faith*: A Reply to the Critics." *Conservative Judaism* 14, no. 4 (summer 1960): 14–21.

"The God of Israel—Pursuer and Pursued." *Judaism* 10, no. 4 (fall 1961): 296–297.

"Of Books, Readers and Writers." With Arthur Hertzberg and Ruth Hyman. *Our Age* 3, no. 2 (12 November 1961): 3–6.

"Judaism and the Academy: The Philosopher and the Jew." *Judaism* 11, no. 4 (fall 1962): 309–319.

"Notes toward a Jewish Theology of Politics." *Commonweal* 77, no. 1 (28 September 1962): 10–11.

"Jewish Theology for the Interregnum." In *Living Legacy: Essays in Honor of Hugo Hahn*. Edited by Bernard N. Cohn. New York: Congregation Book Reviews and Letters Habonim, 1963, pp. 69–79.

"Reflections on the History of Jewish Thought." In *Religion and Contemporary Society*. Edited by Harold Stahmer. New York: Macmillan, 1963.

"A Theology of Jewish Existence." *The Christian Century* 80, no. 4 (23 January 1963): 104–107.

"The Jew, Secularity, and Christian Culture." *Ramparts* 2, no. 2 (autumn 1963): 49–56.

"Discussion: Comments on Paul Weiss's 'The Religious Turn.' " *Judaism* 12, no. 1 (winter 1963): 3–27.

"Between Two Traditions." *Midstream* 12, no. 6 (June/July 1966): 26–35.

"Further Reflections on the Natural and Supernatural." In *Varieties of Jewish Belief*. Edited by Ira Eisenstein. New York: Reconstructionist Press, 1966, pp. 29–42.

"Silence and Laughter." *Jewish Heritage* 8, no. 4 (spring 1966): 37–39.

"The Retrieval of the Human: Some Reflections on Morality." *American Judaism* 16, no. 1 (fall 1966): 10–11, 24.

"The Myth of the Judeo-Christian Tradition." *Commentary* 48, no. 5 (November 1969): 73–77.

"Theology as Creative Art: Franz Rosenzweig's *The Star of Redemption*: An Inquiry into Its Psychological Origins." *Midstream* 18, no. 2 (February 1971): 13–33.

"Beyond Politics, Vision." *Congress Bi-Weekly* 39, no. 5 (10 March 1972): 33–47.

"Franz Rosenzweig's *The Star of Redemption*: An Inquiry into Its Psychological Origins." *Midstream* 18, no. 2 (February 1972): 13–33.

"The Last Jew on Earth: A Fable." *Commentary* 54, no. 5 (November 1972): 48–59.

"Willing a Messianic Marginality." *Sh'ma* 3, no. 44 (22 December 1972): 29–30.

"The Birth of Simon Stern." *Response* 16, no. 16 (winter 1972–73): 43–52.

Introduction to *Judaism and Tragic Theology*, by Frederick S. Plotkin. New York: Schocken Books, 1973.

"The Play of Job—1945." *Midstream* 19, no. 1 (January 1973): 35–40.

"Arthur Cohen." In *Self Portrait: Book People Picture Themselves*. New York: Random House, 1976, p. 136.

"Aggadah and the Fictional Imagination." *Sh'ma* 6, no. 106 (23 January 1976): 45–46.

"Human Fraternity: The Liturgy of Theological Enmity." In *Modern Jewish Thought: A Source Reader*. Edited by Nahum Glatzer. New York: Schocken Books, 1977, pp. 175–180.

"Paradisical Origins and Disenchantments." In *All Our Sons and Daughters*. Edited by John Garvey. London: Templegate Publishers, 1977, pp. 102–113.

"Our Narrative Condition." *Present Tense* (summer 1980): 58–60.

"The Tremendum as Caesura: A Phenomological Comment on the Holocaust." *Cross Currents* 30, no. 4 (winter 1980–1981): 421–440.

"Franz Rosenzweig's *The Star of Redemption*: Mystic Epistemology without Kabbalah." In *Unfinished Essays in Honor of Roy L. Hart*. Edited by Mark C. Taylor. *Journal of American Academy of Religion* 48: 65–81.

"Kafka's Prague." *Partisan Review* 4 (April–May 1981): 552–563.

"Mysterium Tremendum." In *Judische Theologie des Holocaust*. Edited by Michael Brocke and Herbert Jochum. Munich: Kaiser, 1982.

"The Religious Center of the Jews: An Essay in Historical Theology." In *Religion in America*. Edited by Mary Douglas and Steven M. Tipton. Boston: Beacon Press, 1982–1983.

"Autobiographical Fragment: The Holocaust." *Forthcoming* 1, no. 3/4 (1983): 27.

"The Last Word from Berlin." *Present Tense* 10, no. 4 (summer 1983): 43–47.

"Life amid the Paradigms or the Absence of a Jewish Critique of Culture." *Journal of the American Academy of Religion* 54, no. 3 (fall 1986): 499–519.

"The Holocaust and Christian Theology: An Interpretation of the Problem." *Judaism and Christianity under the Impact of National Socialism, 1940–1945*. Edited by Otto Dov Kulka and Paul R. Mendes-Flohr. Jerusalem: The Historical Society of Israel and The Zalman Shazar Center for Jewish History, 1987, pp. 473–497.

"Observations on the Danish Rescue." In *The Rescue of the Danish Jews: Moral Courage under Stress*. Edited by Leo Goldberger. New York and London: New York University Press, 1987, pp. 191–194. (Adapted from paper given at Conference on the Rescue of Danish Jewry, Sutton Place Synagogue, New York City, 23 October 1983.)

"On Judaism and Modernism." *Partisan Review* 3 (1987): 437–442. (Paper originally delivered at the National Jewish Book Awards, New York City, 17 May 1984.)

"Myths and Riddles: Some Observations about Literature and Theology." *Prooftexts* 7, no. 2 (May 1987): 107–122.

Selected Book Reviews

Review of *The Eclipse of God*, by Martin Buber. *Judaism* 2, no. 3 (July 1953): 280–283.

Review of *Religion and Humanity*, by Eugene Kohn. *Judaism* 3, no. 3 (summer 1954): 275–282.

"The Polemicist and the Professor." Review of *The Professor and the Fossil*, by Maurice Samuel. *Jewish Frontier* 23, no. 11 (December 1956): 28–35.

"Revival in Judaism, Too: A Review Article." Review of *American Judaism*, by Nahum Glazer. *The Christian Century* 74, no. 42 (16 October 1957): 1232–1233.

"Martin Buber." Review of *Martin Buber: The Life of Dialogue*, by Maurice Friedman. *Conservative Judaism* (winter 1958): 29–33.

"The Philosophy." Review of *Hasidism and the Modern Man*, by Martin Buber. *Saturday Review*, 7 June 1958, 18.

"The Westernization of Judaism." Review of *The Course of Modern Jewish History*, by Howard M. Sachar. *Saturday Review*, June 1958, 27.

"Selected." Review of *Between God and Man: An Interpretation of Judaism. From the Writings of Abraham J. Heschel*, edited by Fritz A. Rothschild. *The Christian Century* 76, no. 24 (24 June 1959): 751.

"Americans Confront the Past: History in the Guise of Drama." Review of *The Deputy*, by Rolf Hochhuth. *Christianity and Crisis* 24, no. 5 (30 March 1964): 51–53.

"The Jewish Intellectual in an Open Society." Review of *Confrontations with Judaism: A Symposium*, edited by Phillip Longworth. London: Anthony Blond, Ltd., 1967, pp. 17–34.

"Commentary." Review of "Homeland and the Holocaust: Issue in the Jewish Religious Situation." *The Religious Situation: 1968*, edited by Donald L. Cutler. New York: Beacon Press, 1968, pp. 87–91.

"The Metaphysics of Survival." Review of *The Chocolate Deal*, by Chaim Gouri. *Midstream* 14, no. 9 (November 1968): 77–79.

Review of *The Religious Imagination: A Study in Psychoanalysis and Jewish Theology*, by Richard L. Rubenstein. *New York Times Book Review* 73 (1968): 8–9.

"Job and the Modern Imagination." Review of *The Dimensions of Job: A Study and Selected Readings*, by Nahum N. Glatzer. *Congress Bi-Weekly* 36, no. 7 (12 May 1969): 21–22.

"Judaism and Metaphysics." Review of *Jewish Philosophy in Modern Times*, by Nathan Rotenstreich. *Midstream* 15, no. 4 (April 1969): 73–76.

"The Gift of the Human." Review of *Adam Resurrected*, by Yoram Kaniuk. *Congress Bi-Weekly* 38, no. 13 (10 December 1971): 19.

Review of *The Holocaust and the Literary Imagination*, by Lawrence L. Langer. *New York Times Book Review*, (18 January 1976), 19.

"Passionate Scholar." Review of *Jews and Judaism in Crisis*, by Gershom Scholem. *New York Times Book Review*, 11 September 1977, 40.

"On Emil Fackenheim's *To Mend the World*: A Review Essay." Review of *To Mend the World: Foundations of Future Jewish Thought*. *Modern Judaism* 3, no. 2 (May 1983): 225–236.

"God the Implausible Kinsman." Review of *Against the Apocalypse: Responses to Catastrophe in Modern Jewish Culture*, by David G. Roskies. *New York Times Book Review*, 17 June 1984, 28–29.

"On Theological Method (A Response on Behalf of *The Tremendum*)." *Journal of Reform Judaism* 31 (spring 1984): 56–65.

"An Uncontentious Responsum to Will Herberg." *Judaism* 12.4 (Fall 1963): 487–492.

Secondary Sources

Articles, Reviews, and Letters about Arthur Cohen

Aksler, Samuel M. "Work in Judaica, 1970–72: A Sampling." *American Jewish Yearbook* 74 (1973): 244–263.

Alexander, Edward. *Resonance of Dust: Essays on Holocaust Literature and Jewish Fate*. Columbus: Ohio State University Press, 1980, pp. 142–146.

"Arthur A. Cohen: In Memoriam." *Orim: A Jewish Journal at Yale* 2, no. 2 (spring 1987): 109–115.

Bandler, Michael J. Review of *In the Days of Simon Stern*. *Commonweal* 98 (28 September 1973): 530–513.

Berger, Alan A. "Arthur A. Cohen." *Crisis and Covenant: The Holocaust in American Jewish Fiction*. Albany: State University of New York, 1985, pp. 42–48.

Bilik, Dorothy Seidman. *Immigrant-Survivors: Post-Holocaust Consciousness in Recent Jewish-American Fiction*. Middleton, Conn.: Wesleyan University Press, 1981.

Cain, Seymour. "Semite Also." *Christian Century* 74, no. 42 (16 October 1957): 1236–1237.

Cohen, Jacob. "Third Generation: Choosing or Chosen." *Jewish Frontier* 26 (October 1959): 10–14. (Response to "Why I Choose to Be a Jew." *Harper's* (April 1959): 63–66).

Cole, Diane. "Profession: Renaissance Man, Arthur A. Cohen." *Present Tense* 9, no. 1 (autumn 1981): 32–35.

Daiches, David. "Symbolic Dimensions." *Commentary* 44 (April 1967): 94–96.

Eckardt, A. Roy. "The Jew." Review of *The Natural and Supernatural Jew*. *The Journal of Bible & Religion* 31, no. 3 (July 1963): 240–242.

Gertel, Elliot B. "Visions of the American Jewish Messiah." *Judaism* 31 (spring 1982): 153–165.

Gottschalk, Alfred. "The Wisdom of the Moderns." Review of *Contemporary Jewish Religious Thought*, edited by Arthur A. Cohen and Paul Mendes-Flohr. *New York Times Book Review*, 29 March 1987, 6–7.

Halpern, Ben. "A Theological Jew." Review of *The Natural and Supernatural Jew*. *The Jewish Frontier* (February 1964): 11–13.

Haupt, Christopher-Lehman. Review of *In the Days of Simon Stern*. *New York Times*, 5 June 1973, 39.

Heer, Friedrich. "The Future Needs the Past." Review of *The Natural and Supernatural Jew*. *The Christian Century* 81, no. 20 (13 May 1964): 635–638.

Katz, Steven T. " 'The Tremendum': Arthur Cohen's Understanding of Faith after the Holocaust." *The Journal of Jewish Thought and Philosophy* 1 (1992): 28–303.

Kremer, S. Lillian. "Eternal Faith, Eternal People: The Holocaust and Redemption in Arthur A. Cohen's *In the Days of Simon Stern*." In *Witness through the Imagination: Jewish American Holocaust Literature*. Detroit: Wayne State University Press, 1989.

Maccoby, Hyam. Review of *The Jew*. *Commentary* 171, no. 4 (April 1981): 77.

Malin, Irving. "Acts of Faith." Review of *Acts of Theft*, *The Carpenter Years*, *In the Days of Simon Stern*, and *A Hero in His Time*. *Congress Bi-Monthly* 47, no. 4 (May 1980): 15.

McDowell, Edwin. "Was That Hannah Arendt or Not?" Review of *An Admirable Woman*. *New York Times*, 9 December 1983, C31.

McGary, Michael B. Review of *Arguments and Doctrines*. *American Jewish Historical Quarterly* 60 (June 1971): 395.

———. *American Judaism: Adventures in Modernity*. New York: Prentice-Hall, 1972. (A discussion of Cohen's work appears on pages 121–127, 155, 156.)

———. Review of *The Tremendum*. *Commonweal* 108 (31 July 1981): 439.

———. Review of *The Tremendum*. *Journal of Ecumenical Studies* 18, no. 4 (fall 1981): 675.

Ozick, Cynthia. "A Library of Rediscoveries." *Writers' Choice*. Edited by Linda Sternberg and Bill Katz. Reston, Va.: Reston Publishers, 1986, p. 26.

Rosenfeld, Alvin H. "Arthur Cohen's Messiah." *Midstream* (August–September 1973): 72–75.

Satlof, Claire R. "Arthur Allen Cohen." *Contemporary Jewish-American Novelists*. Edited by Joel Shatzky and Michael Taub. Westport, Conn.: Greenwood Press, 1994, pp. 46–53.

Stern, David. "Theology into Art: An Appreciation of Arthur A. Cohen." *Response* 21 (spring 1974): 63–71.

ELIE COHEN

(1909–1993)

DICK VAN GALEN LAST

ELIE ARON COHEN was born in the Jewish quarter of Groningen, Netherlands, on 16 July 1909. His parents were killed in Auschwitz. The son of a waiter, Cohen was sensitive to class differences at a young age. After his final exams the high school director called him and said: "Cohen, I have just the job for you. You are a son of the chosen people, so you know everything about doing business: I have a job for you on a cotton plant in Africa." Cohen, however, chose to study medicine at the University of Groningen in one of the northern provinces of the Netherlands. In 1936 he became a general practitioner in a small village outside Groningen.

The War Years

Less than a year after the Nazis invaded Holland in May 1940, all Jews had to report to the authorities and were issued identity cards stamped with a black letter J. The German policy of excluding Jews from Dutch society and separating them from non-Jews included a regulation of 1 May 1941 whereby Jewish doctors could only have Jewish patients. As a result, Cohen was forced to give up his practice. After the isolation came deportations, which began in Holland in July 1942. Cohen tried to escape with his family to Sweden but was betrayed and arrested by the SD (the security and intelligence service of the SS) on 13 August 1942.

In the camps, first in Amersfoort, then in Westerbork (from 12 December 1942 to 14 September 1943) and later in Auschwitz, Cohen owed his life to the fact that the Nazis needed his services as a physician. In this privileged position Cohen could help a lot of people, but at the same time he felt guilty because of the death of too many others whose lives he could not save. There were limits. Although he was held in Westerbork for more than nine months, Cohen's skills could not protect him when his wife unintentionally insulted a German Jew—the German Jews held crucial positions in the camp bureaucracy—and both he and his family were immediately put on the next transport. In Auschwitz he waved goodbye to his wife and four-year-old son as they, just after their arrival, went to the gas chambers.

As a physician in Auschwitz assigned to the psychiatric room of Block 9, Cohen underwent other traumatic experiences that were to haunt him for the rest of his life. He was better treated than most prisoners, but in return he was forced to help the SS during the selections and to send patients back to work as soon as possible if they were not sent to the gas chamber. Sometimes he had to kill psychiatric patients by giving them lethal phenol injections in the heart, in order to protect other patients in the block. Later, in the preface of his memoirs (*De afgrond* [*The Abyss*], 1971), he asked for his reader's understanding of the moral dilemmas he faced:

> Those who would condemn me should realize that only those who have traveled the same road, or almost the same road, are qualified to do so. Those who have not experienced the unimaginable suffering in the German concentration camps, who have never known what it is to be filthy, lice-ridden, hurt, humiliated, and starved, who have not lived in "the kingdom of the dead," lack all right to judge (*The Abyss: A Confession*, New York: Norton, 1973, p. 59).

Elie Cohen was marched out of Auschwitz on 18 January 1945: "A miracle had happened: we left Auschwitz by foot and not through the chimney, we were happy, we were marching as if we were going on holiday." But the optimism was short-lived. Little did he know that worse was still to come. In his 1992 book *Beelden uit de nacht* (Images of the Night), Cohen describes the so-called death marches, on which hundred of thousands more Jews were killed during the last months of the war:

> The road ahead was full of horror. Everywhere we walked, we saw traces of the transports that had gone before us.

> Anxiously we looked at the corpses along the road: uncovered, with bashed-in skulls, with craniums shot away, with mutilated faces, sometimes no more than a pool of blood, men and women. . . . In the beginning we counted the corpses, but very soon we lost count (*Beelden uit de nacht,* p. 119).

By the time Cohen finally arrived in the concentration camps of Melk and Ebensee, he had become practically a *Muselman* (someone on the threshold of death). When he was liberated by American troops on 6 May 1945 he weighed a mere thirty-five kilos—less than eighty pounds. Only 150 out of the 3,000 Jews who had been deported returned to Groningen. Cohen's wife, their child, his sister, his parents, and his parents-in-law, had all perished.

After the War

In 1947 Cohen established himself as a neurologist in Arnhem, Netherlands. He remarried and, as if trying to exorcize his camp experiences by treating them in an "objective scientific" spirit, in 1952 he published his dissertation *Het duitse concentratiekamp: Een medische en psychologische studie* (*Human Behavior in the Concentration Camp*), which had an immediate impact and was soon translated into many different languages. The *New York Times* of 13 April 1952 called it "a cool, dispassionate inquiry into the mentality of the camps, why the Nazi masters and the prisoners acted as they did." Cohen's study joined those of other concentration camp survivors who wrote in the immediate postwar period, such as Primo Levi, Viktor Frankl, Eugen Kogon, David Rousset, and Robert Antelme, and placed him among the pioneers who recognized and had an interest in the concentration camp as a social laboratory. Cohen was the first who analyzed the psychological defense mechanisms that enabled prisoners to resist oppression, thanks to a process of "depersonalization." "Acute depersonalization," Cohen believed, "causes a personality split that enables one to distance oneself when reality is too terrible to be experienced directly."

In 1968, Cohen introduced the notion of "post–concentration camp syndrome" (his research on this phenomenon was eventually published in the journal *Science and Public Policy* in June 1981) and in 1973 he contributed to the founding of Centrum '45, a center for psychological help for victims of the former German concentration camps. Although he never had literary pretensions, Cohen described his experiences in the concentration camps extensively in newspaper articles and books. In 1972 he published *De Afgrond (The Abyss)*, an autobiographical account of the Holocaust experience. In this memoirs he painted an unflinching—and disconcerting—image of the behavior of the Jews in the camps, including himself. He was also one of the first to write about the Sobibor extermination camp, where more than 34,000 Jews from Holland were killed in the years 1942 and 1943. In his book *De negentien treinen naar Sobibor* (The Nineteen Trains to Sobibor, 1979), Cohen interviewed fifteen of the thirty people who survived Sobibor after a rebellion of October 1943. (A more academic study on this relatively unknown camp was to be published in 1993 by a Dutch survivor of Sobibor, Jules Schelvis.) As a newspaper reporter Cohen attended several trials of German criminals of war, and even interviewed some of them. One of his newspaper articles describes his encounter with one of the executioners of Sobibor, Gomerksi, who received him in his neat appartment in Frankfurt. His last book, *Beelden uit de nacht*, published one year before his death, was Cohen's attempt to give an account of his deeds in the concentration camps. With his irrepressible need to testify and with his emotional involvement, Elie Cohen played an important role making the horrors of Sobibor and Auschwitz known to the wider Dutch public.

Historical Perspective

The systematic destruction of the Jews and other groups only gradually became the focus of collective remembrance in the Netherlands, as elsewhere. In the decades after the war, the fate of the Jews was seen by Gentiles primarily as an illustration of German evil. Their focus was on the suffering of the Dutch people. Until the late 1960s, the heroes of World War II had been celebrated while its victims had been more or less disregarded But as the younger generation began to criticize the older for its behavior during the war, the Jews were "discovered" as victims, not only of the Nazis but also of Dutch collaboration; 95 percent of the Jews deported from the Netherlands never returned.

Jewish victims of persecution came to be identified as traumatized people who needed psychiatric help and were often encouraged to liberate themselves from the burden of their traumatic memories by writing them down, a process that resulted in a flood of publications. Historical research and debates gradually moved from studying impersonal power structures toward exploring the roles and experiences of individuals during the war. One could call the last two decades of the twentieth century the "era of the witness."

In the midst of this the unparalleled interest in the persecution of the Jews, and the demand for books about the Holocaust—for book in which cause and effect are clearly articulated, books that explain what actually happened and what it was like to have been a victim—historians clearly have had a problem integrating the survivors' voices and the veritable flood of survivor memorial literature into their narratives. In Holland, however, historiography and psychiatry became closely connected. Historical studies on the persecution relied partly on eye-witness testimonies, some of which were written by psychiatrists like Elie Cohen. He and other psychiatrists also played a role in the implementation of government policy, since they were asked to estimate the extent to which war pension claimants were disabled due to events related to war or persecution. The Dutch historian Ido de Haan points to Cohen and his fellow psychiatrists as prominent cultural critics in postwar Holland. As a result of their work in making the interconnection between the domains of history, psychiatry, and politics, says de Haan, the persecution of the Jews is now understood as a Dutch national trauma. By the 1970s, Dutch society's negligence and indifference toward the Jews during as well as after the war was viewed with a sense of guilt, and the trauma of the Holocaust experience was treated with ever-increasing consideration and attention due to the relentless efforts of people like Cohen.

Elie Cohen died in Arnhem on 22 October 1993.

Bibliography

Primary Sources

Het duitse concentratiekamp: Een medische en psychologische studie (*Human Behavior in the Concentration Camp*). 1952.

De afgrond: Een egodocument (*The Abyss: A Confession*). 1971.

De negentien treinen naar Sobibor (The Nineteen Trains to Sobibor). 1979.

"The Post–Concentration Camp Syndrome: A Disaster Syndrome." 1981.

Foreword. *Hitler or Hippocrates: Medical Experiments and Euthanasia in the Third Reich.* Paul Hoedeman, 1991.

Beelden uit de nacht: Kampherinneringen (Images of the Night). 1992.

Secondary Sources

Galen Last, Dick van, and Rolf Wolfswinkel. *Anne Frank and After: Dutch Holocaust Literature in Historical Perspective.* Amsterdam: Amsterdam University Press, 1996.

Haan, Ido de. *Na de ondergang: De herinnering aan de Jodenvervolging in Nederland, 1945–1995* (After the Destruction: The Memory of the Persecution of the Jews in the Netherlands, 1945–1995). The Hague: Staatsdrukkerÿ/Uitgeverÿ, 1997.

Jong, L de. *Het Koninkrijk der Nederlanden in de Tweede Wereldoorlog,* vol. 8, *Gevangenen en gedeporteerden* (The Kingdom of the Netherlands in World War II, vol. 8, Prisoners and Deportees). The Hague: Staatsuitgeverij, 1978.

Archives

Relevant letters and other documents can be found in the NIOD, the Netherlands Institute for War Documentation in Amsterdam.

LEONARD COHEN

(1934–)

MICHAEL GREENSTEIN

LEONARD COHEN WAS born in Montreal in 1934 to Nathan and Masha, and graduated from McGill University in 1955. He attended Hebrew school at the Shaar Hashomayim Synagogue. His family was prominent in Montreal's Jewish community. He attended Columbia University from 1956 through 1957, but failed to complete his graduate course of studies, completing instead his first book of poetry, *Let Us Compare Mythologies* (1956). A series of Canada Council grants enabled him to buy a house in Greece, where he has lived intermittently since 1960, and where he has done much of his creative writing. In 1969 Cohen received the Governor General's Award for Poetry but turned it down due to his association with friends in Quebec's separatist movement. In addition to writing poetry and novels, Cohen has turned to singing in more recent years, and divides his time between Montreal and a Zen retreat in California.

Poetry

Cohen has identified the Holocaust as the "central psychic event in his life," saying he "never recovered" from its "illumination of human behavior" (quoted in Dorman, p. 66). Although there are hints of the Holocaust in his first two collections of poetry, *Let Us Compare Mythologies* and *The Spice-Box of Earth* (1961), his third volume, *Flowers for Hitler* (1964), focuses more directly on the Holocaust. Cohen supplies a note on the title: "A while ago this book would have been called SUNSHINE FOR NAPOLEON, and earlier still it would have been called WALLS FOR GENGHIS KHAN." His note points to the banality of evil or relativism of historic periods, as well as his own black romanticism that balances nature's positive attributes of flowers and sunshine against wicked personalities throughout history. Adolf Hitler, Hermann Goering, Joseph Goebbels, and Adolf Eichmann are the focus of Cohen's satiric vision. A quotation from Primo Levi supplies the epigraph to Cohen's volume of poems: "If from the inside of the Lager, a message could have seeped out to free men, it would have been this: take care not to suffer in your own homes what is inflicted on us here." What intrigues Cohen in Levi's passage is the contrast between extreme conditions in the concentration camps and ordinary domestic situations. By juxtaposing those two extremes—flower garden and Hitler's camps—Cohen highlights the absurdity of *l'univers concentrationnaire* but also demonstrates its universal potential, its ability to resonate a generation after liberation.

Surrealism dominates the poem "Congratulations" in its blending of pronouns, senses, particulars, and universals, innocence and evil. The present tense brings history home in each of the poem's three stanzas. "Here we are eating the sacred mushrooms / out of the Japanese heaven" (p. 15). Cohen's surreal metaphor domesticates the horrors of Hiroshima before turning to other examples of "our time's adventure" in the second stanza: "the jeweled house of Dachau / Belsen's drunk fraternity" (*Flowers for Hitler*, Toronto: McClelland and Stewart, 1964, p. 15). The domestic irony of Dachau appears in the jewelry taken from murdered Jews. After invoking the boats of Marco Polo and Arthur Rimbaud, which cover space and time, Cohen ends the poem with a rhetorical question about their boats that seem "like floating violins/ playing Jack Benny tunes?" (p. 15). Beginning with the atomic bomb floating over Japan and ending with floating Jewish music, the sailing craft in "Congratulations," like Rimbaud's and Marco Polo's, alights upon Holocaust sites. Cohen congratulates the modern century on its ability to survive after the Holocaust.

"Goebbels Abandons His Novel and Joins the Party" also points to the absurdity of the Nazis with the glib shift from writing poetry to entering the politics of destruction. This poem also ends with rhetorical questions: "Will favourite hair favourite thighs . . . drive him to adventurous cafés?" (p. 29) After this allusion to the Aryan race, the final question addresses "bestial beauty" that is capable of turning off Goebbels' "religious electric exlax light". The six rhyming stanzas of "It Uses Us!" create a more formal Gothic effect. The poet and his lover confront a heap of corpses "exposed to camera leer"—photography both distancing the immediacy of horror and making accessible the past through newsreel effect. Cohen's black humor arises from his alliteration, "snatch a skull," as well as the rhyming of "leer" and "dear," for the personified camera contrasts with the dehumanized victims (p. 31). In the second stanza he furthers his line of inquiry, asking his lover if she could wear a cape or claim the burned for herself. If not, he asks if this death is "unusable/ alien and new." Unusable helps to explain the poem's title: the past or death uses us, challenges us to confront all the horrors. The poet exchanges faces with the dead, his eyes are burnt and free. In the final stanza the museum ovens whisper: "All things can be done," and attest to the "war that Freedom won" (p. 31). In the post-Holocaust world, Freedom has won a Pyrrhic victory.

"The Invisible Trouble" deals with covering up the tattooed numbers from a concentration camp. "Hitler The Brain-Mole" lists a number of leading Nazis who enter the poet's body: Hitler stares out the poet's eyes, Goering boils gold in his bowels, and Goebbels pushes out from his Adam's Apple. In Cohen's grotesque vision he makes a lampshade out of his lover's kiss. "The Failure of a Secular Life" describes the daily routine of a Nazi torturer who comes home with his black bag and tongs to a wife who cannot bear his "trade." She cries out with "real-life Dachau," ruins his career, and he falls to pieces, as Cohen portrays the banality of evil. Similarly "All There Is to Know about Adolph Eichmann" delineates his ordinary physical features and ends with a series of rhetorical questions concerning the banality of evil: "What did you expect? / Talons? . . . Madness?" (p. 66).

"A Migrating Dialogue" opens with a description of a Hitler-like figure: "He was wearing a black moustache and lather hair. / We talked about the gypsies" (p. 72). Cohen's dialogue allows him to wander through European history, juxtaposing Hitler and his victims. The poet treats Hitler as a child, telling him not to bite his nails, not to eat carpets, not to watch parades on the Late Show, and not to "ka-ka" in his uniform. The surreal dialogue migrates between European history and contemporary pop culture in America. After inquiring about the fate of aristocratic Junkers who resigned in 1941, the poet commands his listener to "wipe that smirk" off his face, before listing cartoon characters who torture: Captain Marvel, Joe Palooka, Li'l Abner, and the Katzenjammer Kids.

"Peekaboo Miss Human Soap," with its childlike and horrific associations, introduces a stanza that declares that the Holocaust never happened, and that one cannot believe everything in museums—from castles on the Rhine to blond SS. In the penultimate stanza the poet believes with a perfect faith in World War II, though he is not so certain about earlier events in history. In the final stanza he attributes his education to a special photogravure section of a 1945 newspaper that displays the victims' gold teeth as well as Eva Braun, Geli Raubal, and Hitler. The last line, "I can't get their nude and loving bodies out of my mind" (p. 74), confuses victims and perpetrators.

"Opium and Hitler" is less meandering with its nine clipped quatrains and rhyme scheme. "Several faiths / bid him leap— / opium and Hitler / let him sleep" (p. 78). If the Holocaust denies the poet any Kierkegaardean leap of faith, at least opium will let him sleep through history's nightmare. This escape from reality concludes with the "Leader" starting a racial speech in the final stanza. Cohen recreates a drugged version of history.

The four quatrains of "Hitler" are more orderly in their unsuccessful attempt to put history to sleep, for the post-Holocaust mind continues to be filled with images of horror. The poet imagines Hitler and his henchmen asleep among poppies, resists Nazi parades, and stuffs their microphones with "old chaotic flowers / from a bed which rapidly exhausts itself" (p. 125). The poem concludes with the prosaic "Never mind," for the historic images turn up as poppies in the libraries of the real world. The final two lines are ironic in their approach to the banality of evil: "The leader's vast design, the tilt of his chin / seem excessively familiar to minds at peace" (p. 125). Hitler's macrocosmic plan shrinks to the tilt of his chin, fate reduced to synecdoche, even as the oxymoronic "excessively familiar" leads to minds that can never be fully at peace long after Hitler's death. Cohen's poetry offers catharsis and denies it at the same time.

Fiction

Cohen's first novel, *The Favorite Game* (1963), pits children's games of torture against the Nazis' methods of torture, and home movies against the newsreels of the war. Pop culture focuses on torture: "Imaginations were released to wander on a reconnaissance mission from Calvary to Dachau" (*The Favorite Game*, Toronto: McClelland and Stewart, 1970, p. 16). Impersonating the Nazis, protagonist Lawrence Breavman plays war games with his girlfriend, Lisa, who watches the "Krauts" coming. "*Achtung. Heil Hitler*! You are a prisoner of the *Third Reich*" (p. 18). Cohen's chronological disorder in the novel blurs and brings into relief his childhood understanding of events in the 1930s and 1940s filtered through his retrospective adult understanding after the war. The children's innocence he had in Montreal contrasts with universal guilt. From the safety of his transatlantic distance, Breavman "would love to have heard Hitler or Mussolini bellow from his marble balcony" (p. 51). Composing postcards to Hitler, Cohen invents iconoclastic "games" that infiltrate his imagined Gestapo and destroy his fascist enemies.

Where *The Favorite Game* is a coming-of-age novel, a portrait of the Jewish artist coming to terms with the legacy of the Holocaust and the predicament of growing up Jewish in Montreal, Cohen's second novel, *Beautiful Losers* (1966), a novel of intersecting narratives exploring the interaction of past and present, is more experimental and postmodern, reaching back to Indian mythology and Canadian history to collocate Indian suffering and Jewish suffering during the Holocaust. In this obscene, hallucinogenic novel, the *Shoah* appears alongside other catastrophes, and Cohen tries to deny comparisons, insisting that each tragedy carries its own unique suffering.

The first part of the novel, "The History of Them All," juxtaposes tribal sufferings, including Jewish history. The second part, "A Long Letter from F.," describes an episode in Argentina when the narrator's friend F. takes the narrator's wife Edith on a sordid sexual vacation. This section begins with the words, "Among the bars in my soap collection" (*Beautiful Losers*, Toronto: McClelland and Stewart, 1966, p. 164) before Edith discusses their waiter, a man with a moustache and raincoat who turns out to be Hitler. After the orgy between F. and Edith, which includes "a complete movie of the Second World War" (p. 174) and scenes reminiscent of Kafka's Penal Colony, "There was a professional knock on the bland door" (p. 181). The waiter enters with his passkey, and when asked if he likes Argentina, he replies in his heavy accent that he misses the newsreels and parades. He takes out a bar of soap derived from melted human flesh and lathers F. and Edith in the bathtub, dries them, and comments without a trace of nostalgia that he had millions of such anatomical parts at his disposal. He spends time before a full-length mirror playing with his moustache and slanting his hair across his forehead, this fetish overlapping with sexual fetishes. Before he exits he reminds them to inform the *Police Gazette*, and leaves with "the vague stink of his sulfurous flatulence" (p. 183). Nowhere in the narrative does his name appear, and Edith briefly thinks that he might be an A—(a member of an almost-extinct Indian tribe).

Although some, like Norman Ravvin, read *Beautiful Losers* "as an examination of the role of the Holocaust in contemporary culture, and as a call to heed the lessons learned from the Nazi victimization of the Jews," the novel's central concern with suffering "is figured not through the prism of Jewish history, but through . . . a Mohawk tribe . . ." (Ravvin, "Writing Around the Holocaust," pp. 22–23). Cohen's purpose in introducing this unnamed Hitler is unclear. In the midst of the most depraved sexual scene, Hitler's appearance suggests the most depraved sense of history, the most extreme form of degradation and dehumanization. Although the oxymoronic *Beautiful Losers* centers on the extinction of Indian tribes, there are frequent parallels with the extermination of Jews. F. compares the martyrdom of Catherine Tekakwitha in 1678 to "newsreel Belsen" (p. 194) and a Nazi medical experiment (p. 196). F. is world weary and war weary: "I knew what they were doing to the Gypsies, I had a whiff of Zyklon B. . . . In perfect sleep we took the soap and waited for the showers" (pp. 162–163). F. deconstructs history through his obsession with soap, its paradoxical ethnic cleansing made possible by the melting down of human fat. The orgiastic scene with Hitler in the Argentinian hotel bedroom is a grotesque parody and parable of post-Holocaust kitsch culture that shows its fascination with Nazism. Cohen indulges riskily in the excesses of this ethos in order to criticize its insanity. Ultimately there is a moral purpose in confronting an ongoing Nazi legacy.

Bibliography

Primary Sources

Let Us Compare Mythologies. 1956.
The Spice-Box of Earth. 1961.
The Favorite Game. 1963.
Flowers for Hitler. 1964.
Book of Mercy. 1964.
Parasites of Heaven. 1966.
Beautiful Losers. 1966.
The Energy of Slaves. 1972.
Death of a Lady's Man. 1978.
Stranger Music. 1993.
Dance Me to the End of Love. 1995.

Secondary Sources

Dorman, L. S., and C. L. Rawling. *Leonard Cohen: Prophet of the Heart*. London: Omnibus, 1990.
Greenstein, Michael. *Third Solitudes: Tradition and Discontinuity in Canadian-Jewish Literature*. Montreal: McGill-Queen's, 1989.

Hutcheon, Linda. "Leonard Cohen and His Works." *Canadian Writers and Their Works*. Toronto: ECW Press, 1989, 1992.

Nadel, Ira. *Various Positions: A Life of Leonard Cohen*. Toronto: Random House, 1996.

Ondaatje, Michael. *Leonard Cohen*. Toronto: McClelland and Stewart, 1970.

Purdy, A. W. "Leonard Cohen—A Personal look." *Canadian Literature* 23 (winter 1963): 7–16.

Ravvin, Norman. *A House of Words: Jewish Writing, Identity, and Memory*. Montreal: McGill-Queen's, 1997.

———."Writing Around the Holocaust: Uncovering the Ethical Centre of *Beautiful Losers*." *Canadian Poetry* 33 (fall 1993): 22–31.

Carlos Heitor Cony

(1926–)

JOSEPH ABRAHAM LEVI

During the first three hundred years of European expansion/migration to the Western Hemisphere, early Jewish presence in Brazil (1500–1822) was mainly Sephardic, consisting of *conversos*, otherwise known as new-Christians, *marranos*, or crypto-Jews—Jews forced to convert to Catholicism. At a later date—as early as 1822, with the proclamation of the independent kingdom of Brazil, and since the establishment of the Brazilian republic in 1889—their descendants were finally able to declare Jewish identity without the fear of being persecuted either for their religion or for their ethnic background.

During the first decades of the nineteenth century, the Amazon region saw a wave of Sephardic immigration, mainly from North Africa and the Levant. At the same time, Alsatian and French Jews established themselves in Rio de Janeiro and surrounding areas, soon after losing their ties with Judaism. Over the last two decades of the nineteenth and the first four decades of the twentieth century, Brazil witnessed massive Jewish immigration from northern and eastern Europe, first from Germany, until 1886, then followed by Jews from Austria and Eastern Europe who established themselves in the metropolitan areas of Rio de Janeiro, São Paulo, and Pôrto Alegre.

During and after the Holocaust, Brazilian Jews managed to set aside their occasional insurmountable differences to come together as a group. The same happened during the Vargas regime (1930–1945) and the dictatorship (1964–1988). Though assimilation has always been a factor in the loss of Jewishness—either for lack of interest in keeping the old faith, through intermarriage, or, as it often was the case, for fear of rejection by the rest of Brazilian society—cultural awareness, at least, has always remained a constant in the literary expression of Jewish writers, regardless of their ethnic backgrounds. This would apply to writers like Carlos Heitor Cony who, despite his lineage, did not have or proclaim any tie with Judaism.

The third and penultimate son of Ernesto Cony Filho and Julieta de Morais, Cony was born in Rio de Janeiro on 14 March 1926. His paternal grandfather, Augusto Cândido Xavier, was the descendant of French Moroccans and assimilated, nonpracticing Jews. In 1938, Cony entered the Seminary of São José, where he spent seven years studying religion, Latin, Greek, Hebrew (which he detested), philosophy, logic, as well as, by his own initiative, some Brazilian, British, French, and Portuguese authors. During his last two years in the seminary, Cony wrote his first novel, *Informação ao crucificado* (Information to the Crucified, 1961), as well as a few articles for the local journal *O Seminário* (1942–1944). In 1945, he enrolled in the Faculdade Nacional de Filosofia, where he studied Romance literatures. Disenchanted with the system, Cony dropped out of school the following year and, by accident, discovered journalism. In 1955, Cony published his autobiography, *Cadernos do Fundo do Abismo* (Copybooks from the Bottom of the Abyss). In the same year, he wrote his first novel, *O Ventre* (The Womb, 1958). His second novel, *A verdade de cada dia* (The Truth of Every Day, 1957), won the Rio de Janeiro *Prêmio Municipal de Literatura* (Municipal Prize of Literature), (1959). His novel *Matéria de Memória* (Matter of Memory) (1962) was made into a movie by Paulo Gil. Cony also wrote a novella for a prime-time television soap opera, *Os sete pecados capitais* (The Seven Capital Sins) called, "Luxuria: Grandeza e decadencia de um cacador de rolinhas" (Lust: Greatness and Decadence of a Turtle-Dove Hunter), broadcast in 1965. Since 1960, Cony has been a journalist for the *Correio da Manhã* as well as a very prolific and accomplished author. He is married to Maria Aparecida and has two daughters, Regina Celi and Maria Verônica.

Pessach: a travessia (Passover: The Crossing) (1967)

Despite his disinterest in Jewish religious observance, Cony's writing evidences cultural awareness of Jewish ethnicity and history. Cony entered the arena of the Jewish question with *Pessach: a travessia*. In this semi-autobiographical novel, he combines his interest in Judaism with the themes of political and social justice.

Pessach: a travessia is semi-autobiographical mostly because of its parallels with Cony's personal predicament. Paulo Simões, the main character, a writer, is forty years old and is living under a Brazilian dictatorship, which is mainly characterized by a lack of freedom. Aside from dictatorship, religion and the family are seen as part of the oppressive and endemic patriarchal system. He denounces: "the family, religion, society, governments, dictatorships, capitalism, imperialism, all the evils" (Rio de Janeiro: Civilização Brasileira, 1967, p. 253).

Just like Paulo Simões, perhaps Cony wanted to explore his own Jewish roots, always from a secular and ethnic point of view, and determine if they could lead him to a full understanding of his "racial" and cultural place within Brazilian society: "It is possible that I have Jewish blood, diluted someplace . . . but I am not a Jew . . . Ok, let's admit that we are Jews, in the racial sense" (Cony, pp. 7, 79). The misuse of the word "racial" as it applies to Jews is not confined to Cony alone; it is in fact shared by many Mexicans and Central and South Americans. Centuries of racial and ethnic miscegenation has, at times, caused the distinction between "racial" and "ethnic" to rest purely on a semantic choice rather than an accurate characterization of the group in question. Unlike most twentieth-century Brazilian Jews, Cony's Jewish origins date back to the first two decades of the nineteenth century. This could explain his detachment from Judaism. Assimilation to Brazilian society had become a reality, or a necessity, for people like Cony and his family even before the end of the nineteenth century. In *Pessach: a travessia*, Paulo Simões's father recalls, with great regret, his own denial, his crypto-Jewishness, as well as his father's complete assimilation to the new environment: "It was a mistake, my son . . . I see that I made a mistake . . . a few years ago I said the same thing to your grandfather . . . an assimilated Jew [who] also decided not to be a Jew" (Cony, pp. 79, 81).

The remoteness of Paulo Simões's/Cony's Jewish ancestry, with its almost one-hundred-year presence on Brazilian soil, is most likely responsible for this feeling of detachment from what could be perceived as a "Jewish identity." Coming from a French Moroccan and already secularized, nonpracticing Jewish background, Cony's family had, if not an easier, at least a better, chance of assimilating to Brazil than any East-European *Ashkenazi* ethnic group. The Portuguese language and Brazilian society, though different, was, for linguistic, historical, and cultural reasons, easier to understand and to assimilate to for Mediterranean people than for Eastern European Jewish ethnic groups who, understandably enough, resisted and even resented assimilation, at least in the beginning. What is left, then, is the social/ethnic aspect of Judaism that might have intrigued Cony and possibly still intrigues him today. Paulo Simões's father perhaps is foreshadowing Cony's own intentions, preoccupations, and internal dilemmas when he declares his intention to assert his Jewish identity.

The year in which *Pessach: a travessia* was published, 1967, marked General Artur da Costa e Silva's presidency/dictatorship (1967–1969) and the creation of a new constitution, which intensified the authoritarian power of the president; and for the Brazilian-Jewish author it signaled his rediscovering of his secular Jewish roots, and his concern for the possible genocide that the new state of Israel could suffer as a result of the Six-Day War (5–10 June 1967). Syria, Egypt, Jordan, and Iraq were threatening a second Holocaust. The confluence of these two historic events may be at the heart of the novel's exploration of Jewishness and Brazilianess as a metaphorical "Crossing of the Red Sea" (Cony, p. 139) leading to a union of his Jewish-Brazilianess.

Though the book suggests an obvious denunciation of Nazism and Brazilian dictatorship, there are no direct overt references to either. Since the novel was written during the dictatorship, any direct allusion to the latter would have resulted in Cony's imprisonment and the work being censored. Fascism and Nazism are directly linked to each other and openly discussed, but no direct connection is made to the current Brazilian regime. Both ideologies are seen as an eternal enemy, not confined by nationality or relationship. As for Nazism, Paulo Simões's father remarks: "Nazism was something transitory, it lasted a little, less than twenty years, and what is that for a people who, since the Egyptians, since the Assyrians, have been encountering their executioner in their own neighbors, in last night's friend?" (Cony, p. 78). Perhaps with this quote, Cony and the Simõeses are also alluding to the fact that their former rejection of their "Jewish identity" was influenced by Brazilian antisemitism. Being relatively young and still not very aware of the political situation around him, Paulo Simões does not consider the Jews living in Brazil and Latin America as being at risk or in any particular danger. Though recognizing the existence of a fascist government, Paulo Simões is convinced of the relative safeness that this part of the world can offer, and has offered, to all people, including the Jews. His father, though, is also aware of the people's hysteria and determination to find a scapegoat in times of distress. This, coupled with the role of the media, instigated and controlled by the government, could lead to a new Holocaust, or rather, yet another form of Nazism: But

> when the government, through massive propaganda, begins to say that the Jews are responsible for the high cost of living, that the Jews are responsible for famine and deaths in the northeast [of Brazil]—then things change. We were already accused for the rain and the drought. History repeats itself, either as a tragedy or as a farce. For the Jews it is never a farce: it is always a tragedy (Cony, p. 82).

The novel is narrated in the first person by Paulo Simões—the last name being the Portuguese anagram of *Moisés* (Moses), though his real name was Paul Simon Gorberg, of German/Polish Jewish descent. The story is divided into two parts: *Pessach (a Passagem por Cima)*, (Pesah) (The Passing Over)—the literal translation of the Hebrew word *Pesach*, to pass over—and *A travessia* (The Crossing). While in the first part, the emphasis is on Paulo Simões, his life, and his manuscript "*Pessach*," foreshadowing epiphanic events to come, the second part is the portrait of Paulo Simões's gradual change, his "passing over" from a state of complete indifference to one in which he is fully aware and conscious of his political persona and, ultimately, his ethnic identity. Throughout the novel, there are small glimpses of his future *travessia*, his double crossing and acceptance of his Jewish roots, as well as his role within Brazilian society as a politically responsible citizen, one who faces evil (dictatorship) and its consequences. From being a symbol of neutrality, of simple "passing over," and of non-commitment, *Pessach* transforms itself into real and personal involvement. Ensuing political events simply lead him to "pass over." He feels compelled to act: "My dad would be proud to know that the old plan was not abandoned, it is here, by my side, as an offer, perhaps more than that, as an imposition" (Cony, p. 159). Paulo Simões's father, and his grandfather before him, had already had a similar awakening, which affected his final and, this time, public acceptance of his Jewish heritage: "if there were to be a persecution [in Brazil]. Then, I would make a point of going to the streets with the Star of David on my shoulder" (Cony, p. 81). Now it is the time for his son, Paulo, to become aware of who he is and to live accordingly.

Captured by rebels, most of whom have been victims of a dictatorship, Paulo Simões eventually understands their reasons for wanting to overthrow the government. In addition to political commitment, he also has to make some personal choices, predominantly concerning the question of his Jewish identity, which he ultimately accepts when he remains the only survivor of the clandestine movement that wanted to reform the government. He is the only member of the guerrilla group who manages to cross the Uruguayan border into freedom. Now that he is free from the burdens of dictatorship, his crossing is also his awakening: he becomes a new Moses. Imbued with his newfound courage and identity, he turns around and heads back into Brazil: "May each one of us be a Moses, may he cross the river and, later, when he can, return to fight again. After all, Moses also ran away. The important thing is to return, after" (Cony, p. 288). This novel falls within the parameters of post-Holocaust Jewish literature of the Diaspora, although the atrocities of the Holocaust are transposed to Brazilian society. The issues at hand and the individual choices eventually lead the main character to opt for the survival of Jewish values, even at the possible cost of his life.

Given his personal involvement with, and interest in, the political events of the time, Cony's novel should therefore be seen through a double lens: first as a political insurrection against oppression (dictatorship) and then as a personal epiphany, one in which the Jewish identity of the main character is born as he finally crosses the border, twice, passing the spiritual/ethnic and the physical/political thresholds. Brazil and Uruguay thus become the ground for Paulo Simões's personal Exodus: freedom from slavery and a lack of fear in facing the consequences of evil. The title is thus instrumental for understanding the outer (political persona) and the inner (ethnic-religious identity) conflicts of the main character and, perhaps, of Cony himself. The Passing Over is at the same time an Exodus and a re-crossing, this time returning recharged and ready to face reality: "There is a wild, strange happiness when I abandon the *travessia* and I return to the margin" (Cony, p. 301).

The novel within the novel, which is being written by Paulo Simões, is the key to this double awakening. This book within a book called *Pessach* reflects Paulo Simões's fascination with the Exodus and the enslaved people freed by Moses. The "episode of the Exodus, whose social, political, and religious vestiges are obvious, was born from a strictly personal motivation . . . an existential motivation" (Cony, p. 204). Freedom generated his response to an existential moment when he observed one too many lashes against a Jewish slave. Just like Moses, Paulo Simões has reached his limit and is now determined to free his people, the Brazilians, the Jews, or both: "the personal motivation gave way to the social motivation" (Cony, p. 204). The political exodus is necessary for the "awakening" of Paulo Simões's Jewish soul. The atrocities of dictatorship, torture and castration, just like those of the Holocaust, will be conquered by determination, by rejecting silence and indifference, and, most of all, by acting, so that future generations will never forget.

Cony's importance in the field of post-Holocaust literature should therefore be evaluated within the framework of the political events of his time. Cony's response and contribution to the understanding of historical phenomena like genocide and dictatorships are thus incorporated in his representation of the "awakening" of his characters who, through a personal epiphany, "cross the boundary" and (re)claim their Jewish identity. Unlike his father and his grandfather, both crypto-Jews until almost the end of their lives, forty-year-old Paulo Simões finally decides to claim his heritage publicly, with no fear of repercussions, just as he is not afraid of possible repercussions when he returns to Brazil, where he could be arrested for associating with revolutionaries.

Among the many scholars who have examined Cony's ties with Judaism and the Brazilian political arena, Nancy T. Baden, Paulo Francis, Heitor Martins, Cohn W. Parker, Daphne Patai, and Nelson H. Vieira have provided a most comprehensive analysis of the author's *travessia*. Baden, for example, emphasizes Cony's symbolism of the personal, gradual change and commitment to the political scene and the gradual "awareness and acceptance of himself as a Jew," as well as the important role of the writer, Cony/Paulo Simões, in times of censorship: "the writer feels it his role to continue to pique the reader's consciousness and provide alternative opinions—despite the confines of censorship" (Baden, pp. 115, 116). For Patai, looking at the metaphor/myth of the Exodus as a key to the promised land, Cony succeeded in transforming "a static image into a dynamic one: the idea of a promised land is replaced by an image of human action and determination in ever new conditions" (Patai, p. 162). Vieira continues along these lines, underscoring the decisive role of the individual and his ethnic persona as civic models. In this case, the ethnic/secular "Jewish experience is offered up as an example from which Brazilians on the whole can learn" (Vieira, "Judaic Fiction in Brazil," pp. 35–36).

Perhaps the multiplicity of approaches could be appreciated if readers take into consideration the fact that besides a crossing, they are also witnessing an awakening, an epiphany of some sort, the birth of a new Brazilian Prometheus, one who is carrying his Jewish roots with pride, regardless of the consequences: "I am at the vertex of the enormous irregular triangle which is the promise of a people, a mission of a man" (Cony, p. 301). The people are the Jews/Brazilians. The man is Moses/Paulo Simões/Cony: "The night of the Exodus, when the Jews ate unleavened bread, the . . . people [of Israel] left towards their own destiny. As people—in a generic term—that night was also a special night, though, much later, it became the seed of the great social and political thing" (Cony, pp. 204–205).

Bibliography

Primary Sources

Hino das Férias (Hymn of the Holidays). 1944.
Cadernos do Fundo do Abismo (Copybooks from the Bottom of the Abyss). 1955.
O ventre (The Womb). 1958.
"Sobre todas as coisas" (Above All Things). 1959.
A verdade de cada dia (The Truth of Every Day). 1960.
Informação ao crucificado (Information to the Crucified). 1961.
Matéria de memória (Matter of Memory). 1962.
Da arte de falar mal, Crônicas (On the Art of Badmouthing, Chronicles). 1963.
"Luxuria: Grandeza e decadencia de um cacador de rolinhas" (Lust: Greatness and Decadence of a Turtle-Dove Hunter). 1964. Featured in a prime-time television soap opera, *Os sete pecados capitais* (The Seven Capital Sins). 1965.
Antes, o verão: romance (Before, the Summer: Romance). 1964.
O ato e o fato: crônicas políticas (The Act and the Fact: Political Chronicles). 1964.
Tijolo de segurança: romance (Security Brick: Romance). 1965.
Pôsto 6, Crônicas (Post 6, Chronicles). 1965.
Balé branco (White Ballet). 1966.
Chaplin: ensaio-antologia (Chaplin: Essay-Anthology). 1967.
Pessach: a travessia (Passover: The Crossing). 1967.
Sôbre tôdas as coisas: contos (Above All Things: Short Stories). 1968.
Quem matou Vargas: 1954, uma tragédia brasileira (Who Killed Vargas: 1954, a Brazilian Tragedy). 1974.
Pilatos: romance (Pilate: Romance). 1974.
O caso Lou: assim é se lhe parece (The Lou File: So It Is, if You Think So). 1975.
A noite do massacre (Paranóia): cine-romance (The Night of the Massacre, (Paranoia): Movie-Novel). 1976.
Babilônia! Babilônia! Contos (Babilon! Babilon! Short Stories). 1978.
Marina Marina. 1978.
Nos passos de João de Deus (Along the Steps of John of God). 1980.
JK, memorial do exílio (JK, Memorial of Exile). 1982.
"A Brazilian Passover." 1984.
Orlando Teruz, painter. 1985.
"Da morte de Brito Broca" (On the Death of Brito Broca). 1991.
Rio 92. 1992 [1991].
Quase memória: quase-romance (Almost Memory: Almost-Romance). 1995.

O piano e a orquestra (The Piano and the Orchestra). 1996.
Lagoa: história, morfologia e sintaxe (Lagoon: History, Morphology, and Syntax). 1996.
A Casa do poeta trágico (The House of the Tragic Poet). 1997.
O burguês e o crime e outros contos (The Burgess and the Crime and Other Short Stories). 1997.
Os anos mais antigos do passado: crônicas (The Most Ancient Years of the Past: Chronicles). 1998.
Romance sem palavras (Romance without Words). 1999.
O harém das bananeiras (The Harem of the Banana Trees). 1999.
Novel *Matéria de Memória* (Matter of Memory) made into a movie by Paulo Gil.

Secondary Sources

Critical Response to Author's Work

Baden, Nancy T. "The Brazilian Revolution of 1964 as Depicted in Selected Novels of Antônio Callado and Carlos Heitor Cony." In *Proceedings [of the] Pacific Northwest Council on Foreign Languages, Twenty-Seventh Annual Meeting, April 22–24, 1976*. Edited by David P. Benseler. 27 Part I, Foreign Languages. Corvallis: Oregon State University, 1976.

———. "Cony, Carlos Heitor," In *A Dictionary of Contemporary Brazilian Authors*. Edited by David Foster and Roberto Reis. Tempe: Center for Latin American Studies, Arizona State University, 1981.

Francis, Paulo. "A travessia de Cony." *Revista Civilização Brasileira* 3, no. 13 (1967): 179–183.

Igel, Regina. "La inmigración judía en la ficción de Brasil." *Judaica Latinoamericana Estudios Histórico-Sociales II* (1993): 265–274.

Lockhart, Darrell B. "Introduction." In *Jewish Writers of Latin America. A Dictionary*. Edited by Darrel B. Lockhart. New York: Garland, 1997.

Martins, Heitor. "Quarup e Pessach." *Minas Gerais (Suplemento Literário)* (May 25/June 1, 1968): 4–5.

Parker, John M. "The Novels of Carlos Heitor Cony." *Luso-Brazilian Review* 10, no. 2 (1973): 163–186.

———. "Rumbos de la novela brasileña contemporánea: 1950–1970." *Revista de Cultura Brasileña* 38, no. 12 (1974): 5–28.

Patai, Daphne. "Carlos Heitor Cony: Moses as Everyman." In *Myth and Ideology in Contemporary Fiction*. Rutherford: Fairleigh Dickinson University Press, 1983.

Vieira, Nelson H. "Jewish Resistance and Resurgence as Literary Symbols and Metaphors for Brazilian Society and Politics." In *Proceedings of the Ninth World Congress of Jewish Studies, Jerusalem, August 4–12 1985*, Division B, vol. 3, *The History of the Jewish People (The Modern Times)*. Jerusalem: World Union of Jewish Studies, 1986.

———. "Judaic Fiction in Brazil: To Be or Not to Be Jewish." *Latin American Literary Review* 14 (July–December 1986): 31–45.

———. "Post-Holocaust Literature in Brazil: Jewish Resistance and Resurgence as Literary Metaphors for Brazilian Society and Politics." *Modern Language Studies* 16, no. 1 (1986): 62–70.

Interviews

Antônio, João. "Inquérito: o romance urbano." *Revista Civilização Brasileira* 7 (1966): 190–220.

Interviewed by Nelson H. Vieira, Rio de Janeiro: Manchete Television Station, June 1983.

Brazil, Antisemitism, Dictatorship, and the Holocaust Experience

DiAntonio, Robert. "Redemption and Rebirth on a Safe Shore: The Holocaust in Contemporary Brazilian Fiction." *Hispania* 74 (December 1991): 876–882.

———. *Brazilian Fiction: Aspects and Evolution of the Contemporary Narrative*. Fayetteville: University of Arkansas Press, 1989.

Horowitz, Irving Louis. "Jewish Ethnicism and Latin American Nationalism." *Midstream* 18 (November 1972): 22–28.

Lesser, Jeffrey. *Welcoming the Undesirables, Brazil and the Jewish Question*. Berkeley: University of California Press, 1994. 2d edition, 1995.

———. *O Brasil e a questão judaica: imigração, diplomacia e preconceito*. Translated by Marisa Sanematsu. Rio de Janeiro: Imago, 1995.

Levine, Robert M. "Brazil's Jews during the Vargas Era and After." *Luso-Brazilian Review* 5, no. 6 (1968): 45–58.

Milgram, Avraham. "The Jews of Europe from the Perspective of the Brazilian Foreign Service, 1933–1941." Translated by Naftali Greenwood. *Holocaust and Genocide Studies* 9, no. 1 (1995): 94–120.

ADAM CZERNIAKOW
(1880–1942)

JOSHUA D. ZIMMERMAN

THE HEAD OF the Judenrat (Council of Jewish Elders) in the Warsaw ghetto until his death in July 1942, Czerniakow was born in 1880 in Warsaw to a middle-class assimilated family. After completing his studies in chemistry at the Warsaw Politechnik, he received an engineering degree from the University of Dresden, Germany, in 1908. Shortly before World War I, Czerniakow became involved in Jewish public life, and, in independent Poland, took up the cause of defending the interests of Jewish artisans, who made up one-third of the gainfully employed Jewish population. From the early 1920s, Czerniakow was chairman of the Association of Jewish Artisans in Poland, a Zionist-affiliated organization. During that time, he published several articles outlining his ideas for a comprehensive program of vocational training and technical schools for Jewish youths. Between 1927 and 1934, he represented Jewish artisans on the Warsaw city council, and he ran for election to the Polish senate in 1928 and 1931, representing the Jewish national camp on the National Minorities Bloc list. Czerniakow's activities also included a regular teaching post in Jewish community schools.

Career

Although he fought publicly for Jewish rights in the period between the two world wars, Czerniakow wrote very little and, as a result, was not widely known. He was raised in the spirit of general European and Polish culture and remained aloof from internal struggles between Jewish political parties. Czerniakow's low visibility began to change in the late 1930s when he was appointed vice-chairman of the Warsaw *Kehillah* at a time when this Jewish leadership body was no longer elected but chosen by the Polish government. The position set the stage for Czerniakow's rise to the leadership of Warsaw Jewry during the Holocaust.

Czerniakow's activities from the outbreak of World War II until his suicide on 23 July 1942 were closely scrutinized after the war both by underground ghetto activists and by those who knew and worked with him, and they created controversy. That controversy began with the events surrounding the appointment of Czerniakow, a relatively unknown figure, to head of Warsaw's Council of Jewish Elders (*Judenrat*) under the Nazi occupation. The eminent Polish Zionist leader, Apolinary Hartglas, accused Czerniakow of careerism and self-aggrandizement in attaining the post, but scholars and contemporaries who knew and worked with him have cast grave doubt on such an interpretation.

When the Germans invaded Poland on 1 September 1939, causing wholesale chaos and panic, many Jews fled the capital city. Among the many Jewish leaders who chose to flee was the head of the Warsaw *Kehillah*, Maurycy Mayzel. Czerniakow remained in Warsaw and on 6 September began to keep a diary. After heading an ad hoc Jewish citizen's committee, Czerniakow reportedly visited the mayor of besieged Warsaw, Stefan Starzynki, requesting that he replace the absent Mayzel. On 23 September Mayor Starzynski formally appointed Czerniakow as head of Europe's largest Jewish community. "A historic role in a besieged city," Czerniakow wrote in his diary on 23 September. "I will try to live up to it." Thus, as Israel Gutman emphasizes, Czerniakow was not appointed head of the Warsaw *Kehillah* by the Germans but rather by the Polish authorities when Warsaw was still under Polish control.

Shortly after the surrender of Warsaw to the Germans, Czerniakow fell victim to Nazi Jewish policy in occupied Poland, which mandated the creation of councils of Jewish elders in every Polish Jewish community of over 500 members. These councils, consisting of between twelve and twenty-four men, were headed by chairmen chosen by the local German authorities. Thus, on 4 October 1939, just one week after the German occupation of Warsaw, Czerniakiow records that he was stopped by the police, driven to the office of the Nazi security police headquarters, ordered to find twenty-four men to sit on the new Warsaw Judenrat, and instructed that he was to assume its leadership. The first Warsaw *Judenrat* was a continuation of the prewar Jewish *Kehillah*. It included all those members of the prewar *Kehillah* who had remained in Warsaw as well as key figures of the various Polish Jewish political parties, senior officials of the welfare institutions and public organizations.

The Diary

From September 1939 until his death, Czerniakow ran the affairs of Europe's largest Jewish community. During this time he kept a daily diary that Raul Hilberg has characterized as "the most important Jewish record of that time" (Raul Hilberg and Stanislaw Staron, Introduction to the *Warsaw Diary of Adam Czerniakow*. New York: Scarborough Books, 1982, p. 25). The diary was presumed lost until 1964, when Yad Vashem (the Israel Holocaust memorial and archive) acquired the original notebooks from a Polish-Jewish immigrant in Canada, herself a survivor of the Warsaw ghetto, who had purchased Czerniakow's diary from an unknown person before leaving Warsaw in 1959. (Only the fifth notebook, covering the period 14 December 1940 to 22 April 1941, was missing and has never been found.) Czerniakow's daily chronicle, consisting of 1,009 small notebook pages, is written in a sparse style with brief, simple sentences similar to an office diary kept for quick reference. Scholars agree that the diary was not intended for publication but rather as raw material for a book to be written after the war. Fearing that the diary might fall into Nazi hands, Czerniakow, the most visible and exposed Jewish personality in Warsaw, wrote cautiously and selectively. It is thus often a bare-bones chronicle of daily events, omitting those facts and opinions that may incriminate the author or other community members. Unlike other chroniclers and diarists of the Warsaw ghetto who had time to write and reflect on the events around them, Czerniakow's work is written in the quick, impatient hand of an extraordinarily busy man.

As head of Warsaw Jewry during the Holocaust, Czerniakow's diary provides a wealth of information about how Nazi policy was applied to the ghetto, and how the ghetto's leader attempted to balance carrying out Nazi orders with improving the living conditions of Warsaw Jewry. In increasingly horrible conditions, Czerniakow desparately struggled to soften the impact of Nazi decrees. He consistently fought for higher food rations, relief for the poor and orphans, the rights of children to education, the vocational training of Jewish youths, the promotion of cultural and religious activities, and saving of Jews from Nazi persecution.

In the first three months of occupation, Czerniakow recorded the imposition of several anti-Jewish laws. These included the demand for a complete census of the Jewish population in Warsaw, the closing of Jewish primary and secondary schools, the compulsory white armbands with blue Jewish stars, the demand for daily forced labor battalions, and the ban on public prayer.

By the end of December 1939, the heavy burden placed on Czerniakow was beginning to take its toll. With the capriciousness of Nazi edicts and of German property and monetary expropriations that depleted the community's funds, Czerniakow complained of headaches, anxiety, and sleep problems. Working seven days a week from morning until evening, Czerniakow was known to take home files to work on at night. In January 1940, Czerniakow tried to resign from his post, writing, "In view of all these tribulations I asked the SS to be released from the chairmanship since I find it impossible to manage the Community under these abnormal conditions. In reply I was told that this would be inadvisable" (26 January 1940). In the summer of 1940, Czerniakow noted, "I had a dream that I handed over my responsibilities to Mayzel. What a beautiful illusion" (2 July 1940), adding later, "I would not care to be born a second time. How tiring all this is!" (30 November 1941).

Czerniakow's clear sense of commitment to the community is revealed in his attitude to emigration. While it was still possible to emigrate, Czerniakow refused to accept a certificate to Palestine (12 February 1940). Shortly after, a certain Kirszblum, who was leaving for Palestine, tried to get out of paying the emigration tax to the community. Czerniakow recorded his reply: " 'I will not forget you, you louse, how you pretended to act as a leader and are now running away with others like you, leaving the masses in this horrid situation' " (20 February 1940). Later, after several prominent prewar leaders had resigned from the *Judenrat* or emigrated, the famous historian, Dr. Ignacy Schipper, reportedly complained to Czerniakow that the *Judenrat* no longer represented the authentic leadership of Polish Jewry. Czerniakow took great offence at such a remark: "I asked him where these 'mentors' were? Should we not look for them among those who have fled or among those who tried to leave but did not succeed (he himself had a passport in his pocket)" (5 October 1941).

In mid-October 1940, the Nazis summoned Czerniakow to the SS offices and announced, after several postponements and rumors, that a walled ghetto would be created in Warsaw. The Jewish community, with its own money and by its own hands, would have to build walls that would close it in on 1 December. Henceforth, Czerniakow's diary is preoccupied with the details of the ghettoization process. Amid general panic and utter confusion around the question of the precise boundaries, which continued to change based on the whims of the authorities, the decree called for the displacement of 104,000 Poles and 700 ethnic Germans living inside the Jewish quarter, and the addition of 110,000 Jews, along with Catholics of Jewish origin, to the ghettto. The Jewish population would now be completely isolated from the so-called Aryan side of Warsaw, and the *Judenrat* would conduct all internal affairs. A Jewish police battalion of 2,000 men was established and, in May 1941, Czerniakow was invested with the responsibilities and powers of "Mayor of the Jewish District."

With the establishment of the Warsaw ghetto—a central phase in the process of destruction—the situation of the Jews in Warsaw deteriorated dramatically as the *Judenrat*'s activities considerably widened. It performed the functions of a city government, dealing with food, work, health, housing, and sanitation. At the height of its activity, the *Judenrat* oversaw twenty-five departments and 6,000 workers. Czerniakow, noted by his colleagues for his tremendous energy and organizational talent, displayed raw courage in his fearless negotiations aimed at easing restrictions and edicts, increasing food rations, and gaining the release of Jewish prisoners. In a meeting with district governor of Warsaw, Ludwig Fischer, Czerniakow was assured that starving the Jews was not the Nazis' objective. He pleaded for increases in food supplies, to which Fischer replied that he would look into the matter (21 May 1941).

By July, when the results of his labors to remedy the urgent problem of malnutrition and starvation had not yielded concrete results, Czerniakow began to suspect that Polish Jewry was doomed. "The ring will be tightened more and more and the whole population will slowly die out" (8 July 1941). By the fall of 1941, Czerniakow began to feel that all his efforts were in vain: "All this toil, as I see it, bears no fruit. My head spins and my thinking is getting muddled. Not one single positive achievement. The food rations were to be increased. The mountain gave birth to a mouse" (1 November 1941). One result of his frustration was that Czerniakow became more bold and was not afraid to reproach the Nazi authorities. When Heinz Auerswald, the Nazi ghetto commissar in Warsaw, maintained that a Jewish worker should labor all day for a bowl of soup, Czerniakow recorded his reply: "I remarked that he could also have a wife and children. Auerswald retorted that 2 bowls of soup might be made available. And how is he going to have his shoes repaired?" (1 November 1939). When, later, Commissar Auerswald reproached Czerniakow for failing to extract the required taxes from the ghetto population, Czerniakow responded, "I said in turn that it is difficult to exact taxes from people who had everything taken away from them. As usual the conversation came to nothing" (8 April 1942).

The beginning of a new policy of Nazi terror reached the Warsaw ghetto in the form of an announcement in November 1941 that the death penalty would be imposed on any Jew found illegally outside the ghetto. The first victims of the draconian decree were executed that same month. Emmanuel Ringelblum noted in his diary that the executions had "set all Warsaw trembling" (p. 236).

It is at this point that Czerniakow began to raise pointed questions, in the form of inconspicuous sentences hidden between unconnected paragraphs, about the Nazis' overall aim. Already in October 1941, Czerniakow noted, "Alarming rumors about the fate of the Jews in Warsaw next spring" (27 October 1941). In December, Czerniakow buried the following sentence inside a paragraph of unrelated things: "A possible deportation of 120,000 Jews from Warsaw" (22 December 1941). Days before the secret Wannsee conference in January 1942, at which the Final Solution was presented for the first time to the entire German bureaucracy outside of Berlin, Czerniakow had a premonition of evil when Auerswald, his direct superior, was summoned to Berlin: "I heard that Auerswald had been summoned to Berlin. I cannot shake off the fearful suspicion that the Jews of Warsaw may be threatened by mass resettlement" (19 January 1942). Four days later, after Auerswald's return, Czerniakow ominously wrote, "I went to see Auerswald and asked him whether he had received any new instructions from Berlin. He answered that his trip to Berlin was private" (23 January 1942).

With the increasing prominence of rumors of mass deportation, Czerniakow fluctuated in his evaluation of their truthfulness. While on 18 May 1942 he referred to such rumors as "not without foundation," on 1 July 1942 he appeared to change his mind, writing, "Both yesterday and today rumors about deportation of 70,000 Jews. The rumors are groundless (so far)." By 19 July, panic gripped the Warsaw ghetto, and Czerniakow recorded that he drove around the ghetto and visited three playgrounds, all the time with a smile on his face to calm the populace. The following day, Czerniakow pressed the Nazi authorities for answers. They assured Czerniakow that the rumors were "utter nonsense." Czerniakow then went to the offices of two SS leaders, who "expressed their indignation that the rumors were being spread and promised an investigation" (20 July 1942). Reassured, Czerniakow gave the order to inform the ghetto population that all rumors of deportation were false.

On the morning of 21 July 1942 the SS arrested all the Judenrat members in the community building with the exception of Czerniakow. Ominously, the SS also entered Czerniakow's apartment looking for his wife, who was eventually found and detained. On 22 July 1942, at 10 A.M., Nazi officials surrounded the community building and entered Czerniakow's office to announce the order for the mass deportation of Warsaw Jewry "to the East." Czerniakow was ordered to provide 6,000 Jews for "resettlement" by 4 P.M. that same day. Czerniakow was frankly informed that if he did anything to impede the deportation process, his wife would be the first to be shot. Czerniakow questioned the Nazi authorities about where "in the East" these people were being resettled, but the question remained unanswered. Hillel Seidman, a *Judenrat* member who entered Czerniakow's office immediately after the SS officials departed, recorded the following impressions in a diary entry for 23 July 1942: "One look at him was enough—the chalk white face, shaking hands, and staring eyes that see nothing. Until then Czerniakow had firmly believed . . . that we would outlive the German oppression. . . . All his plans and hopes collapsed in front of this cruel reality." The last two entries, on 22 and 23 July 1942, reveal that Czerniakow tirelessly negotiated for the release of Judenrat members from prison as well as campaigned to exempt orphan children from deportations. On the following day, after being informed that the daily quota would be increased and that orphan children would be included in the deportation, Adam Czerniakow committed suicide. His last words, written on a note found at his desk, cried out, "I am powerless, my heart trembles in sorrow and compassion. I can no longer bear all this" (*Encyclopaedia Judaica*, Vol. 5, p. 1211).

Reactions

Czerniakow's last act has been interpreted in conflicting ways. Some chroniclers and underground activists, such as Emmanuel Ringelblum and Itzhak Katzenelson, characterized Czerniakow's suicide as an act of weakness, while Hartglas maintained after the war that Czerniakow had failed to warn the public before his death or call for resistance. Alexander Donat's postwar memoir reflectes these views: "If he had been given a glimpse of the bottomless abyss to which we were consigned, he did not pass his knowledge on to us. His suicide only intensified our despair and our panic. . . . We felt it was desertion, not leadership" (pp. 60–61).

Others, including those who knew him personally, considered Czerniakow's suicide an act of courage. "Rather than become a mere tool of the enemy," Hillel Seidman wrote just hours after Czerniakow's suicide, "he took his life and died with honor" (p. 58). "His end proves conclusively," wrote the diarist Chaim Kaplan three days after Czerniakow's suicide, "that he worked and strove for the good of his people" (p. 384). A colleague of Czerniakow's during the interwar period, Aryeh Tartakower, wrote after the war of Czerniakow's "boundless devotion" to Warsaw Jewry and to his "nobility" in the face of Nazi brutality (p. 64). Warsaw ghetto historian Israel Gutman, reflecting a broad consensus among Jewish historians, likewise concluded, "Today we can emphatically state that the denunciation of Czerniakow at the time of his death was neither just nor pertinent" (1982: p. 207).

The Warsaw Diary of Adam Czerniakow, published both in the original Polish as well as in Hebrew, English, German, and French translations, is one of the most important Jewish records of the Holocaust. It sheds light on the personality and character of Warsaw Jewry's leader as well as on the nature of Nazi rule in occupied Poland.

Bibliography

Primary Sources

Dos tsekhn-gezets (The Artisan's Law). 1925.

The Warsaw Diary of Adam Czerniakow: Prelude to Doom. Edited by Raul Hilberg, Stanislaw Staron, and Josef Kermisz. 1982.

Secondary Sources

"Adam Czerniakow." In *Encyclopaedia Judaica*, vol. 5. Jerusalem: Keter Publishing House, 1971.

Blumental, Nachman. "A Martyr or a Hero? Reflections on the Diary of Adam Czerniakow." *Yad Vashem Studies* 7 (1968), 165–171.

"Czerniakow, Adam." In *Nowa encyklopedia powszechna PWN*, vol. 1. Edited by Barbara Petrozolin-Skowronska. Warsaw: Wydawnictwo Naukowe PWN, 1998.

Gutman, Israel. "Adam Czerniakow: The Man and His Diary." In *The Catastrophe of European Jewry*. Edited by I. Gutman and L. Rothkirchen. New York: Ktav, 1976, pp. 451–489.

———. *The Jews of Warsaw, 1939–1943: Ghetto, Underground, Revolt.* Bloomington: Indiana University Press, 1982.

Hartglas, Apolinary. "How Did Czerniakow Become Head of the Warsaw Judenrat?" *Yad Vashem Bulletin* 15 (1964): 404–407.

Kohansky, Mendel. "The Last Days of Adam Czerniakow." *Midstream* 15.3 (1969): 61–67.

Leksikon fun der nayer yidisher literatur, vol. 4. New York: Congress for Jewish Culture, 1961.

Tartakower, Aryeh. "Adam Czerniakow—the Man and his Supreme Sacrifice." *Yad Vashem Studies* 6 (1967): 55–67.

Tushnet, Leonard. "Chairman Adam Czerniakow." *Pavement of Hell*. New York: St. Martin's Press, 1972, pp. 73–138.

Noted Warsaw Ghetto Memoirs and Diaries That Shed Light on Czerniakow's Character and Leadership

Donat, Alexander. *The Holocaust Kingdom: A Memoir*. New York: Holocaust Library, 1978.

Hirszfeld, Ludwik. *Historia jednego życia*. Warsaw: Czytelnik, 1946.

Kaplan, Chaim A. *The Warsaw Diary of Chaim A. Kaplan*. Translated and edited by Abraham I. Katsh. Revised edition, New York: Collier Books, 1973.

Lewinski, Jerzy. "The Death of Adam Czerniakow and Janusz Korcak's Last Journey." *Polin* 7 (1992): 224–252.

Ringelblum, Emmanuel. *Notes from the Warsaw Ghetto*. Translated and edited by Jacob Sloan. New York: Schocken Books, 1974.

Seidman, Hillel. *The Warsaw Ghetto Diaries*. Translated by Yosef Israel. Southfield, Mich.: Targum Press, 1997.

Tenenbaun, Mordechai. *Dappim min ha-deleka*. Tel Aviv, Israel: Hotsaat ha-Kibuts ha-meuhad, 1947.

CHARLOTTE DELBO

(1913–1985)

DAVID MESHER

CHARLOTTE DELBO WAS born on 10 August 1913, in the French town of Vigneux-sur-Seine, in Seine-et-Oise, south of Paris. The daughter of a riveter, she joined the Young Communists organization in 1932, and two years later met her future husband, Georges Dudach, a leader of that organization and editor of the communist journal of the arts, *Cahiers de la Jeunesse* (Notebooks of Youth). Later, while studying at the Sorbonne, Delbo wrote articles and reviews for the journal, including an interview with the actor and director Louis Jouvet, which led to a stint as his assistant beginning in 1937. Delbo was on tour with his theatrical company in South America when Germany occupied France, but in 1941 she left Jouvet's employ and risked her own safety to return to Paris and work with Dudach in the French Resistance. Dudach and Delbo were arrested by French police at their apartment in March 1942, and turned over to the Gestapo. She was allowed to visit him once before he was executed by firing squad on 23 May 1942, at Mont Valérien. Delbo herself was imprisoned at La Santé and Romainville before being transported to Auschwitz from the train station at Compiègne in January 1943, in a convoy of 230 French women who, like Delbo, were mostly non-Jews, arrested for their active opposition to the German occupation. Delbo spent her first months in Birkenau, the death camp of Auschwitz, before being transferred to Raisko, a satellite labor camp, in June 1943. A year after arriving at Auschwitz, in January 1944, Delbo was sent to Germany, where she was held at the Ravensbrück women's camp until liberation was arranged by Count Bernadotte and the Swedish Red Cross in April 1945. After recuperating in Sweden, Delbo returned to Paris, one of only forty-nine women who survived from the group originally transferred from Compiègne to Auschwitz.

Back in France, Delbo began to work on a memoir of Auschwitz and completed the first volume, *Aucun de nous ne reviendra* (*None of Us Will Return*, 1965), in 1946, before putting the manuscript away for nearly twenty years; parts of the second volume, *Une Conaissance inutile* (*Useless Knowledge*, 1970), were also written in the first years after the war. At the same time, Delbo returned to work for Jouvet, before joining the United Nations in Geneva, from 1947 to 1960. Even after her first books began to be published in the 1960s, Delbo held a position at the National Center for Scientific Research (CNRS), working with Henri Lefebvre.

Beginning with *La Théorie et la pratique* in 1969, Delbo became active as a playwright, publishing seven other plays in the next ten years; two of these are concerned with atrocities committed during the war, *Qui rapportera ces paroles*? (*Who Will Carry the Word*?, 1974) and *Kalavrita des mille Antigone* (Kalavrita of the Thousand Antigones, 1979). Her other plays pursue the themes of heroism and victimization by dealing with more contemporary events, including the 1956 Hungarian uprising in *La Capitulation* (The Capitulation, 1977), and the 1968 "Prague Spring" in *La Ligne de demarcation* (The Line of Demarcation, 1977). Delbo's last work involving the camps, *La Mémoire et les jours* (*Days and Memory*, 1985), combines wartime memories and contemporary concerns by interweaving stories told by and about women in the camps with others about suffering in Argentina, Greece, Spain, and the Soviet Union; it was published posthumously in 1985, the year of her death. A third Holocaust-related drama, "Une Scène jouée dans la mémoire" (A joyous scene from memory), was published in 1995.

Auschwitz and After

Despite this considerable record of publication, Charlotte Delbo's reputation rests primarily on her remarkable trilogy, *Auschwitz and After*—though to call it a "trilogy" is perhaps misleading. Of its three volumes, the first two are quite similar in most respects, while the third is, in many ways, very different. *None of Us Will Return* and *Useless Knowledge* were both written, in whole or in part, by the end of 1947, though they were not published until 1965 and 1970, respectively. Both works are first-person, impressionistic accounts of Delbo's experiences at Auschwitz. The first, *None of Us Will Return*, is limited to those experiences at Auschwitz, beginning with the arrival at the death camp's train station, and ending on a warm spring day a few months later. The second, *Useless Knowledge*, broadens the scope to cover her entire incarceration, beginning with two or three sections set in France before transportation to Auschwitz, and ending back in Paris after her liberation. The third book of the trilogy, *The Measure of Our Days* (1971), though still written mostly in the form of a first-person narrative, is no longer Delbo's own autobiography but the stories of thirteen other women survivors, many of whom were transported with her from Romainville in 1943, and whose names serve as the titles for most of the chapters of the volume. The author, who held interviews and exchanges with each of them, relates their memories of Auschwitz, as well as their experiences on returning to France. Not surprisingly, this duality of theme and duplication of subject mirror "the kind of 'parallel' personality assumed by Delbo," according to Nicole Thatcher (p. 46), so that the structure of the trilogy can be seen as a projection as well as a creation of the author's post-Auschwitz psychology.

If the third volume makes the trilogy seem imbalanced in matters of narrative persona, chronology, and setting, it nevertheless offers an important clue to understanding Delbo's underlying themes: the development of the trilogy moves from re-creating Auschwitz in the first book, to chronicling Delbo's complete wartime experience in the second, and finally to discussing the difficulties the survivors faced in postwar France in the third. When Delbo began to write her memoirs of Auschwitz in 1946, while still recuperating from the effects of that and other camps in which she had been incarcerated during the war, it is likely that her intention was to bear witness to the horror that was the Holocaust. Later, however, her focus changed to encompass the problematic attitude of the French people in accepting the survivors, and the underlying French acquiescence and involvement in atrocities committed by the Germans. A story that Lawrence L. Langer relates in his introduction to *Auschwitz and After* helps make this point. After arriving back in Paris, Delbo was determined to find the two French policemen who arrested her and Dudach, feeling that they "were indirectly responsible for his execution and her deportation." But it turned out that, "about a year after they had arrested Delbo and her husband," the two men "had switched allegiances and joined the resistance. . . . Under the circumstances, the authorities informed Delbo, they could not be prosecuted" (p. xii). Many of Delbo's subjects in the final volume had similarly frustrating experiences, whether seeking justice or merely anonymity in France after the war.

Significantly, most of Delbo's published nondramatic, testimonial writing concerns the women who were transported to Auschwitz with her, in one way or another. Those women, including Delbo herself, are not only the subject of all three volumes of *Auschwitz and After* but also of Delbo's two other testimonial works, *Convoy to Auschwitz* (1965) and, indirectly at least, *Days and Memory* (1985). *Convoy to Auschwitz*, published in the same year as volumes of the trilogy began to appear, is a kind of companion piece to the trilogy. However, for example, where *The Measure of Our Days* provides a generally subjective and impressionistic account of the experiences of thirteen of Delbo's fellow survivors, *Convoy to Auschwitz* is more objective reportage, including a ten-page summary of their experiences followed by, in the words of John Felstiner in his introduction to this book, "a collective biography of the 230 Frenchwomen who were deported from Compiègne to Auschwitz on January 24, 1943" (p. xi). Except in a few instances where mothers and daughters, or sisters, are treated together, each of the 230 is given a separate entry with vital statistics and a personal sketch, followed by her Auschwitz number and descriptions of her life in Auschwitz, her death (for all but the forty-nine who survived), and the way Delbo came by that information. Delbo herself is alphabetized as Charlotte Dudach, and hers is the only entry written in the first person. Hers, too, is the only entry in which such vital statistics as date and place of birth are given after the Auschwitz number. The sketch that precedes it covers the period from September 1941, when Delbo decided to return to occupied France from South America, until her arrest with her husband in March 1942, his execution that May, and her own transfer from La Santé to Romainville in August. In addition to the individual accounts, there are also half a dozen commentaries by Delbo, placed at the end of entries that prompt them, most coming at the beginning of the book. The commentaries cover such topics as the difference for survivors in being designated a "political" or "resistance" deportee (p. 21), "Canada," the "sorting house for booty" taken from new arrivals at Auschwitz (p. 25), and "the race" in which inmates were forced to run through a vicious gauntlet of male and female guards and kapos on 10 February 1943 (p. 26). As stunning and powerful as

Convoy to Auschwitz is in its own right as a historical and sociological study, it is also an invaluable source for readers of *Auschwitz and After*, since many of the women described in the latter (where they are identified only by nicknames or first names) can be cross-referenced. For example, three of the survivors, Gilberte, Poupette, and Germaine, whose tales are told in *The Measure of Our Days* (pp. 242, 271, 309), can be identified in *Convoy to Auschwitz* as Gilberte Tamise (pp. 205–206), Simone Alizon (pp. 16–19), and Germaine Renaudin (pp. 185–186).

None of Us Will Return

The first volume of *Auschwitz and After* begins, significantly, at the Auschwitz train depot, but just as significantly, Delbo herself is not present in the opening scene. Instead, she presents a general arrival, an image of *all* arrivals, and begins by contrasting this train station with "normal" ones where "there are people who arrive and people who leave" (p. 3). The reader might anticipate an obvious contrast—at Auschwitz there are only arrivals—but Delbo is much more subtle than that. As she explains, the depot at Auschwitz

> is a station where those who arrive are those who are leaving a / station where those who arrive have never arrived, where / those who have left never came back (p. 3).

The straightforward truth, that there were only arrivals, is not sufficient for Delbo because it reveals nothing, expresses nothing. Her description, in which "those who arrive are those who are leaving," re-creates the confusion of those arriving in the mind of the reader, whose sense of orderly language is undercut. And though the victims "think they've arrived in Hell" (p. 4), they resist that certain knowledge, preferring to remain in denial. They arrive without knowing "there is no arriving in this station" (p. 4). How can that be? Because they expect things to make sense, as does the reader. "They expect the worst—not the unthinkable" (p. 4). In discussing this line, Lawrence Langer argues that " 'they' include not only new arrivals at Auschwitz, but all those who seek meaning in the human condition despite the gloomy poignance of her narrative" (1978, p. 202). Primo Levi's first insight into Auschwitz, the recognition that "language lacks words to express this offense, the demolition of a man" (p. 26), is similar to Delbo's description of the arrival, but instead of analyzing the experience as Levi does, Delbo attempts to evoke it for the reader through language that borders on the irrational yet conceals the darker logic of mass murder.

Delbo's experimental narrative style continues, after the characteristically impressionistic prose of the arrival scene, with five pages of verse, either directed outward to Christians ("You who have wept two thousand years / for one who agonized for three days and three nights," p. 10), and to the complacent ("O you who know," p. 11), or describing the initial selection, the tattooing, and the anonymity of the setting. It is only with the next section, "Dialogue," that we hear Delbo's own voice for the first time, and then at first in conversation with another woman. Though they are both from Paris, there is an important difference between Delbo and this stranger because "she has no F on her chest. A star" (p. 15). The impact of all the suffering that Delbo is about to describe, all the suffering endured by her and her French countrywomen, is subtly predicated on this first individualized scene in which it is clear that whatever the deprivations experienced by gentile inmates, the Jews had it worse. As Delbo herself explains in *Convoy to Auschwitz*, early in 1943 "conditions for Jews and non-Jews were nearly the same. Nearly. But that slight difference led to a higher mortality rate among the Jews" (p. 9). The first "Dialogue" in *None of Us Will Return* details this difference in seemingly small but important elements, such as clothing (Delbo is wearing a warmer striped uniform, the Jewish woman a tattered, ill-fitting civilian coat, because Jews were generally made to wear discarded clothing instead of uniforms at Birkenau). When Delbo attempts to encourage the other women by saying "it's the same odds for both of us," the reply is accompanied by a gesture of the hands mimicking rising smoke from the chimneys. "For us," the woman says, meaning Jews, "there's no hope" (p. 15). The same point, about the greater strictures and worse conditions faced by Jews, is made two sections later in "The Men," when the French women give a column of Jewish men their surplus bread, provoking a desperate fight for the food.

Significantly, Delbo mentions in the first conversation that she has already been at Birkenau for five weeks. Unlike most other memoirs of Auschwitz, which place great emphasis on the horror of initial impressions, *None of Us Will Return* begins at that point, about one-quarter of the way through the author's period in the death camp. From there, the memoir proceeds with chapters describing features of the camp, daily rituals, memorable events, and personal reactions. As Rose Yalow Kamel explained, Delbo's diary style underscores "the tension between the narrative text on the one hand and on the other the tortured reiteration and not-so-obvious silences of the survivors' drive to order that which resists ordering" (p. 66). For example, Block 25, the camp morgue, is described in "The Dummies" (pp. 17–19), both deflating and hallowing the passage from life to death. The daily but excruciating routine of standing in an interminable "Roll Call" is described in two chapters with that title. "Daytime" is a composite description of Delbo's unit at work in the fields; "Night" is a stream-of-consciousness narrative full of the horrors of a terrified mind within an exhausted body, too tired to sleep and tormented by hunger and fear. Rare, individualized memories may be affirmative, such as the glimpse of a flower in the chapter titled "Tulip"—though this brief reverie, too, is ultimately ruined when the women discover that the house where the tulip is growing is owned by an SS officer, leading them to "despise this memory and the tender feelings which had not yet dried up" (p. 61). Recalled events are more often examples of extreme cruelty, such as witnessing a man punished by fifty blows of a club, in "Up to Fifty," or running a violent gauntlet of their keepers one Sunday, "the day everyone feared the most" (p. 90), in the chapter "Sunday."

There is no clear chronological order to the memories in *None of Us Will Return*. Lea Wernick Fridman has suggested that narrative time in the volume "unfolds within the subjective logic and temporal rhythms of the wounded body" (p. 123). For example, that terrible Sunday is identified as "a Sunday in March" (p. 94), which should place it close in time to the first "Dialogue," but instead it is positioned late in the memoir. And, though the title of the last chapter, "Springtime," suggests some sort of conventional closure—of a natural rebirth from the death and destruction of humanity's moral winter into some possibility of continuance—the ending only reinforces the memoir's intentional lack of development and hope. In "Springtime," recognizable memories of nature, such as "the blackbird in the acacia tree" from Delbo's former life (p. 112), are dashed against the grim truth of Auschwitz. *None of Us Will Return* does not end with Delbo's June transfer to Raisko, which helped ensure her survival. Instead, "Springtime," like so much of the trilogy, is a meditation on memory. Spring in Auschwitz is "the stink of diarrhea and corpses. Above this stink a blue sky." Delbo admits, however, that in her "memory spring was singing" (p. 111), and she sees this as a kind of betrayal—an indication of what suffering has done to her memory. Delbo can recall "only clichés," which devalue experience, because in Auschwitz "we lost our memory." And thus, even for Delbo and the other women who eventually returned to France, the last lines of the volume reiterate its title in a new and more horrifying way: "None of us will return. . . . None of us was meant to return" (pp. 113–114).

Useless Knowledge

Strikingly, because its component volumes assiduously avoid any semblance of chronological or thematic development, there is a very clear pattern to the trilogy as a whole, which carries the reader between two points of focus. One is Auschwitz itself, the subject of the first volume; the other is France, the subject of the third, the changed and, in many ways, indifferent home to which the changed and, in some ways, fragile survivors, like Delbo, were repatriated. Bridging these two locales is the purpose of the second volume of the trilogy, *Useless Knowledge*, which begins in the prison at Romainville—in the first chapter, there is a reference to "that morning at the Santé" (p. 121), as an earlier experience—and ends with Delbo's return to Paris. Addressing her countrymen in the final section of *Useless Knowledge*, Delbo speaks of "unlearning" the lessons of Auschwitz, but, as the reader and Delbo will discover in the final volume, "unlearning" —by disavowing one's own memories—is no easy task.

Because *Useless Knowledge* recounts the various transfers from prisons, camps, and hospitals, which are, themselves, a sort of calendar for Delbo and the others, the second volume has the clearest sense of chronology in the trilogy. But this should not be taken to represent order or thematic development, especially in Auschwitz, the "world beyond knowledge." Indeed, this is one of the greatest challenges for Delbo and other Holocaust writers—creating art without order may seem like making bricks without straw, but any imposition of order on Auschwitz and its senseless routine of death would be an intolerable falsification of the experience.

The volume begins with two brief episodes set in the fortress prison at Romainville, separated by a verse elegy for Delbo's husband, Georges Dudach. The scene of their last meeting, which took place before Delbo was transferred to Romainville, is narrated in "The Farewell," one of the last chapters of the volume; and so memories of Dudach help bracket *Useless Knowledge*, which like the other volumes of the trilogy, has memory as its theme. Following chronologically on the Romainville sections, Delbo narrates the arrival at Auschwitz in verse:

> This dot on the map
> This black spot at the core of Europe
> this red spot
> this spot of fire this spot of soot
> this spot of blood this spot of ashes
> for millions
> a nameless place . . .
> Today people know
> have known for several years

that this dot on the map
is Auschwitz
This much they know
as for the rest
they think they know (pp. 137–138).

Because both volumes recount Delbo's experiences in Auschwitz, some sections of *Useless Knowledge* may necessarily seem similar to passages in *None of Us Will Return*. An early example of this is the chapter on "Thirst" (pp. 142–145), which may or may not refer to the same general period already detailed in a chapter also titled "Thirst" in *None of Us Will Return* (pp. 70–75). In the earlier chapter, thirst is a measure of the concentrationary process of dehumanization: "On the edge of insanity," Delbo writes, "I gauge the full extent of the madness to which thirst has driven me" (p. 71). Thirst drives her to break ranks, despite SS guards and their dogs, and to throw herself into a stream; only then "lucidity returns" (p. 72). That respite is brief, and Delbo ends this earlier chapter by cataloguing her daily obsession with hydration: "There is the thirst of the day and the thirst of the evening. . . . There is the thirst of the evening and the thirst of the night, the very worst" (p. 74). That thirst is the worst because at night she dreams of drinking.

Though apparently similar in subject, the chapter on "Thirst" in *Useless Knowledge* is quite different in function. It begins, as does the earlier section, with a sense of how extreme deprivation has worked to dehumanize her. As Delbo recalls, "All my senses had been abolished by thirst" (p. 142). This time, the thirst is slaked by drinking an entire bucket of water, and in the rare moment of satiety that follows Delbo can focus on the mind, not the body. The quenching of thirst thus becomes a passageway to memory—the memory of a life where one could "step into a café and order a beer" (p. 141)—creating a transition on multiple levels to the next chapter, "The Stream," in which the author challenges the very notions of memory and memoir, as if asking whether the thirst for that remembered life will be sated or drowned in a post-Holocaust stream of all-too-painful consciousness.

"The Stream" begins with this attack on memory. "Strange," Delbo writes, "but I don't recall anything about that day" (p. 147). Even for those familiar with the workings of the unreliable narrator of postmodern fiction, being confronted with the same narrative technique in a Holocaust memoir can be disconcerting—especially because of the continuing challenges of deniers and revisionists. For Delbo, however, the issue is not the unassailable truth of her experiences, but the best way to convey them. This chapter, then, purports to be her recollection of a day she cannot remember—certainly, a logical impossibility. But there is no logic in Auschwitz, and even some of those details she thinks she has accurately recalled, Delbo herself knows cannot be true: "In my memory—try as I do with all my might—there is only the stream and me. This is wrong, absolutely wrong. No one was there alone, except in solitary, and I knew no one who was imprisoned in this way. No one from our group, I mean" (p. 148). Finally, the memoirist tries to imagine what she must have been thinking during a washing she knows happened but cannot remember—the memoir itself several times removed from "memory" per se. All this is symbolized by the streams of water and consciousness. As the chapter ends, Delbo concludes, "It must have happened like this, but I have no memory of it. I only recall the stream" (p. 153).

"Thirst" and "The Stream" reveal the disparate burdens of memory and suggest how *Useless Knowledge* functions in transition between *None of Us Will Return* and *The Measure of Our Days*. In *Days and Memory* Delbo herself used this motif of thirst to introduce an important distinction in her conception and utilization of memory. There she differentiates between "deep" memory, based on sense-data, and "external" or "intellectual" memory, based on thought and reflection:

> Because when I talk to you about Auschwitz, it is not from deep memory my words issue. They come from external memory, if I may put it that way, from intellectual memory, the memory connecting with thinking processes. Deep memory preserves sensations, physical imprints. It is the memory of the senses. For it isn't words that are swollen with emotional charge. Otherwise, someone who has been tortured by thirst for weeks on end could never say again, "I am thirsty" (pp. 3–4).

Deep memory is a burden for Delbo both in Auschwitz during the war, where tantalizing thoughts of prewar France were more torment than comfort, and in postwar France, where survivors found Auschwitz memories debilitating among people eager to ignore the reality of atrocities and suffering greater than their own. But there are also the "external" memories of the ideals of culture and humanity when trapped in a concentrationary universe, and of the experience of inhumanity once freed from it. As Delbo herself explains, "Since Auschwitz, I always feared losing my memory. To lose one's memory is to lose oneself, to no longer be oneself" (p. 188). Such memories will remain bottled up inside them, however, because though the survivors "have much to recount, . . . we can't speak of the nature of our anguish" (p. 168). This, then, is the irony of the title, because memories are, to some extent, "useless knowledge" both in the death camp and after it. As the volume ends with Delbo's repatriation to France, she makes this point in verse:

I have returned
from a world beyond knowledge
and now must unlearn
for otherwise I clearly see
I can no longer live (p. 30).

The Measure of Our Days

Having bridged the abyss between Auschwitz, that "world beyond knowledge," and postwar France, the world of her readers, Delbo uses the final volume of her trilogy to assess the treatment of the survivors on their return home, and the lasting effects of their experiences. Delbo's decision to present the world of the death camp solely from her own point of view, and the process of reintegration into French society from the points of view of thirteen fellow survivors, is certainly the most striking element in this part of *Auschwitz and After*. Lawrence Langer suggests that "the monologues of *Mesure de nos jours* are the perfect form to express the hermetic world of the survivors, a world they seek to break out of in vain" (p. 235). On the surface, it might indicate the author's greater interest in the psychological effects of Auschwitz and the social problems of postwar France, but there are many other possible interpretations—including the likelihood that French readers would require greater substantiation than a single, subjective account if the cruelty and complicity of French society were to be found credible.

The volume begins with Delbo's own story of the shock she experienced once back in France. By the time she arrived in Paris, Delbo had been out of Birkenau for two years, including six months at the satellite labor camp of Raisko, still part of the Auschwitz complex, fifteen months in Germany at Ravensbrück, and a short period of recuperation in Sweden. But the physical and psychological impact of Auschwitz-Birkenau was such that she had never recovered a sense of well-being in mind or body. Her reaction to friends who came to visit, and to the books that they left, was the same. "Everything was false, faces and books, everything showed me its falseness and I was in despair at having lost the faculty of dreaming, of harboring illusions; I was no longer open to imagination, or explanation. This is the part of me that died in Auschwitz" (p. 239). For Delbo as for the other women whose stories are told in *The Measure of Our Days*, it is a part never to be resuscitated.

One of those women is Ida, a French Jew who was not among the 230 women in the convoy to Auschwitz with Delbo. Ida was transported to Auschwitz after only three days at Drancy, and so she "hadn't had time to get to know anyone" (p. 289). She had been turned in by the poor French couple with whom her parents had boarded her, in a small village, before her mother and father had gone separately into hiding. When it became clear to Ida that she was in danger of being arrested, she announced her decision to leave; Alice, the wife, dissuaded her, saying that if Ida escaped the gendarmes would detain Emile, the husband, instead. Ida's survival in Auschwitz, like that of so many others, can be attributed at least in part to her early transfer to a work camp, in her case Buna. After the war, with no surviving relatives, she returned to France and was taken in by a family friend, eventually marrying and having a daughter. "And then," Ida says, "I don't know what happened. One day, just when everything was going well—one day I was seized by an insurmountable anguish" (p. 298). She was briefly institutionalized but soon returned to her family. Ida's story ends with an update on Alice, whom she visited several times after returning from Auschwitz. "Now," says Ida, "we won't be going to Alice for the holidays any longer. Last year, one winter evening, she hanged herself in her kitchen. Winters are sad in the country" (p. 300).

Ida, overcome only briefly by insanity, is one of the better-adjusted survivors in *The Measure of Our Days*. Another is Marie-Louise, who tells the visiting Delbo, "As you can see, I've got everything I need. I'm happy" (p. 279). Yet Marie-Louise is a voracious reader of wartime deportation accounts—her shelves are full of books and there are stacks of them on the floor. With her husband, Pierre, she makes pilgrimages to the various camps where she was once interned, including Auschwitz. Pierre, incidentally, has read and heard so much testimony about the camps that he seems to be a survivor himself, and Rose Kamel makes an incisive point about gender roles in the trilogy when she suggests that Pierre "has taken it upon himself to appropriate [Marie-Louise's] deep memory—for which, she reiterates, she is deeply grateful" (p. 74). Otherwise, the couple remain isolated in their suburban home, rarely going out except to attend ceremonies and commemorations, and to see old comrades like Delbo. One such ceremony is described in the chapter titled "The Funeral." This is not, in fact, Germaine's funeral but the conversation among the survivors traveling together on a train to attend it, which is covered in the chapter. Like so much of *The Measure of Our Days*, that conversation is filled with ironic and even spiteful remarks. Employing a concentrationary perspective, one of the women on the train explains, "After Auschwitz, I no longer cry at funerals. . . . People are lucky to have a funeral" (pp. 339–340). Most of the survivors carry with them such deep memories of the Auschwitz dead—uncommemorated, but not unremembered.

Conclusion

Delbo's testimonial writings are themselves intended to commemorate the victims and honor the survivors. In her introduction to *Convoy to Auschwitz*, the author claims that the high survival rate for her group of French women—"and for Birkenau in 1943, fifty-seven out of two hundred and thirty after six months was exceptional, unique in the history of the camp"—was due to the fact that they had time, in Romainville, "to form small, tightly knit units within a large, homogeneous group, helping each other in all sorts of ways, often quite small" (p. 9). Recently, however, Anna Hardman has countered that, despite the sense of "support and solidarity [Delbo] received from a small group of French women, the negation of human solidarity, given the conditions in Birkenau, dominates her writing" (p. 59). Though Hardman is primarily interested in interrogating gendered interpretations of both text and experience, she conflates here the ultimate isolation of individual survival with the supportive sense of community—both of which figure into Delbo's memoir. The sense of interdependence and camaraderie cannot erase the brutal realities of the death camp, but it nevertheless informs every page of *Auschwitz and After*, a tribute to the human spirit in the most inhumane of conditions.

Bibliography

Primary Sources

Les Belles Lettres (Beautiful Letters). 1961.

Aucun de nous ne reviendra (*None of Us Will Return*). 1965.

Le Convoi du 24 janvier (*Convoy to Auschwitz: Women of the French Resistance*). 1965.

La Théorie et le pratique (Theory and Practice). 1969.

Une Conaissance inutile (*Useless Knowledge*). 1970.

Mesure de nos jours (*The Measure of Our Days*). 1971.

La Sentence (The Judgment). 1972.

Qui rapportera ces paroles? (*Who Will Carry the Word?*). 1974.

Maria Lusitania (Maria Lusitania). 1975.

Le Coup d'état (The Coup d'état). 1975.

La Ligne de démarcation (The Line of Demarcation). 1977.

La Capitulation (The Capitulation). 1977.

Spectres, mes compagnons (Ghosts, My Companions). 1977.

Kalavrita des mille Antigone (Kalavrita of the Thousand Antigones). 1979.

La Mémoire et les jours (*Days and Memory*). 1985.

Auschwitz and After. 1995.

"Une Scène jouée dans la mémoire." (A Joyous Scene from Memory). 1995.

Secondary Sources

Felstiner, John. Introduction to *Convoy to Auschwitz: Women of the French Resistance*, by Charlotte Delbo. Boston: Northeastern University Press, 1997, pp. xi–xv.

Fridman, Lea Wernick. *Words and Witness: Narrative and Aesthetic Strategies in the Representation of the Holocaust*. Albany: State University of New York Press, 2000.

Hardman, Anna. "Representations of the Holocaust in Women's Testimony." In *The Holocaust and the Text: Speaking the Unspeakable*. Edited by Andrew Leak and George Paizis. New York: St. Martin's Press, 2000, pp. 51–66.

Kamel, Rose Yalow. "Written on the Body: Narrative Re-Presentation in Charlotte Delbo's *Auschwitz and After*." *Holocaust and Genocide Studies* 14, no. 1 (2000): 65–82.

Langer, Lawrence L. *The Age of Atrocity: Death in Modern Literature*. Boston: Beacon Press, 1978.

———. Introduction to *Auschwitz and After*, by Charlotte Delbo. Translated by Rosette C. Lamont. New Haven: Yale University Press, 1995, pp. ix–xviii.

Levi, Primo. *Survival in Auschwitz: The Nazi Assault on Humanity*. Translated by Stuart Woolf. New York: Collier Books, 1993.

Thatcher, Nicole. *A Literary Analysis of Charlotte Delbo's Concentration Camp Re-Presentation*. Lewiston, New York: Edwin Mellen Press, 2000.

HANA DEMETZ

(1929–)

S. LILLIAN KREMER

BORN IN NORTHERN Bohemia (Sudetenland) in 1929, Hana Mueller was the child of a Czech-Jewish mother and a German-Catholic father. Her father, an attorney, was employed by the state until 1938, when he had to relinquish his job for refusing to divorce his Jewish wife. Her mother died for lack of medical care, banned from seeing German doctors and prevented, by curfew, from seeing a Jewish doctor when she suffered a sudden acute intestinal obstruction. Demetz remained in Czechoslovakia through the war, but was spared the fate of full Jews. When the school expulsion edict for Jewish half-castes was issued in 1943, she had to leave school. After she spent a year in a private school for Jews, that institution was also closed and she was sent to compulsory factory labor manufacturing grenades. Although she either witnessed or heard reports of her Jewish family's *Shoah* suffering, which included confiscation of property, Gestapo torture of an uncle, and transfer of some members to Theresienstadt, it was only after the war that she learned of their deportation and murder in Auschwitz.

Raised Catholic and designated by Nazi law as a *Mischlinge*, a half-caste, the author brings a distinctive perspective to her autobiographical novel, *The House on Prague Street* (1980), written to celebrate her family and record the tragedy they suffered. In 1949 Demetz became an editor for Radio Free Europe, broadcasting in German and writing children's programs. She married the eminent German scholar Peter Demetz in April 1950 and came to the United States in 1952. They lived in New York for two years and then moved to New Haven, where Peter Demetz was a graduate student at Yale. Both had long careers at Yale, where the novelist taught Czech for twenty-five years. After thirty years, her marriage ended in divorce and she married a fan of her novel whose family hailed from the same region as hers, but had lived safely in America during the war.

A *Mischlinge's* Life

The House on Prague Street is structured as the Holocaust era experience and reflection of a young *Mischlinge*, Helene Richter. Set entirely within a family context, the narrative alternates between reports of hardships borne by Jewish relatives and her own comparative ease. The main distinction of this Holocaust text is its struggle with the ethical complexity of the divided self confronted with an uncommon history. Continually shifting from first- to third-person perception, from youthful perspective to superimposed adult retrospective, Demetz balances a young girl's Holocaust era ambivalence with the mature author's psychological and moral reflection. The progression of stages in Helene's understanding of the Nazi violation of her family and neighbors and their transformation from valued citizens to disenfranchised pariahs, parallels her metamorphosis from assimilated Czech to despised half-caste.

Demetz conveys the chaotic nature of life under hostile German rule by careful juxtaposition of prewar and Nazi-occupied Europe, evoking life as it was for newly enfranchised and assimilated European Jewry from the mid-nineteenth century through the Holocaust. The prewar peace and prosperity enjoyed by the assimilated middle-class Jewish population before the advent of Nazism is evident in the family's prominent civic role and their prosperity evidenced by the spacious house on Prague Street with its ample domesticity and generous hospitality. Paralleling historic accounts of escalating Nazi anti-Jewish legislation, Demetz shows how various categories of Jews were deprived of civil rights and isolated from the general population and how Aryan spouses were humiliated and intimidated.

Demetz focuses solely on affluent Jews' diminishing prospects in a series of ritualistic birthday celebrations marking the family patriarch's transformation from citizen to pariah. The first party, set in the prewar era, is a tableau of serenity. Abundant flowers and fruit from the family garden and orchard symbolize the Edenic quality of pre-Holocaust life, a scene exuding high spirits emblematic of the good relations between Czechoslovakian Jews and Gentiles. Surrounded by a large, exuberant, and prosperous family, Max Löwy plays the role of charming host and paterfamilias basking in the warm greetings of the town dignitaries. Portending the end of the paradisal peace is the after-dinner discussion by the men as they linger over coffee and cigars, conversing about the specter of German anti-Jewish demonstrations. Yet, despite the anxious undercurrent, these Jews insist that Czechoslovakia will not tolerate German style antisemitic injustices, a credible view in their circumstances. By the early occupation-era birthday celebration, the impact of anti-Jewish legislation is already evident in the Löwy uncles' diminishing prosperity: the banker has sold all his stock; the manufacturer is reconciled to the loss of his factories; and Max has lost the warehouse and yards. Max Löwy's decision to sell his car, lest this possession offend powerful antagonists, and his insistence that the women of the family refrain from wearing elegant clothing and dress modestly reflect the malaise of assimilated Jews. By the time of the third birthday gathering, Czechoslovakia is a police state, manifested by the guarded demeanor of gentile neighbors. Thus, the Jew who thought he could make himself a Czech among Czechs by the eradication of his name from a Jewish congregational register has, under the Nazi regime, become a ghetto Jew once again. Requisition of the ancestral Jewish home and deportation to Theresienstadt of its displaced residents help readers understand the effects of sharp curtailment and eradication of every facet of hard-won European Jewish emancipation.

Demetz charts the progress of the *Shoah* by listing the departures and disappearances of full Jewish family members through emigration, deportation, murder, suicide, Gestapo torture, and SS murder. Marie Richter's plight mirrors the debasement of the semi-privileged Jew married to an Aryan. She must carry identity papers marked *Jude*, add the name Sara to her own, and wear the infamous yellow star marked with the word *Jude* whenever she leaves home. Subjected to relatively minor forms of discrimination, denied access to transportation, public buildings, entertainment, and adequate diet, she eludes the deportation that her parents and close relations experience, but dies by Nazi decree when she is deprived of medical care, as was the author's mother. By 1944, all the family members "were gone now with the transports" (*The House on Prague Street*, translated by Hana Demetz, New York: St. Martin's Press, 1980, p. 107). From Theresienstadt, grandparents, aunts, and uncles are sent to Birkenau. Classified hierarchically between the disfranchised "full Jew" and the valued German *Volk*, Helene is exempt from much of the worst discrimination. She is humiliated by a pro-Nazi teacher who insults her by ignoring her and refusing to allow her to participate in class discussion, then by pulling her hair, and finally by sexually molesting her prior to her expulsion from school, the counterpart of the adults' dismissal from professional and civic realms. Although the occupation is relatively comfortable for Helene, she is drawn more deeply into the war near its end for, like Demetz, she is conscripted into a labor unit to manufacture hand grenades and experiences the tension and fear of victims working in close proximity to Nazi masters.

Illustrative of Helene's identity ambivalence are juxtaposed scenes of her accommodation to Jewish family and German friends and associates. First, we encounter her surreptitiously garbed in a borrowed dirndl dress and white knee socks looking "very Aryan" (p. 100) and feeling very self-satisfied while singing sentimental songs about the homeland for hospitalized German soldiers; then we see her outraged by the advances of a Nazi cadet or feeling guilty about being in the company of these Germans. She is torn between the wish to enjoy security as a German and occasional pangs of guilt for the suffering of her Jewish relatives. She quickly discovers that a Jewish family is a liability, a hindrance to life's pleasures and good fortune. As a young teenager, she shares with some other Holocaust chroniclers, such as the unincarcerated Anne Frank, an overwhelming desire to lead a normal life despite the dire times. Her adolescent response to increasingly severe Jewish deprivations leads to her resolve to resist entrapment in the dreariness of Jewish existence and to participate instead in the German world. Unlike the attic-sequestered Jewish Anne Frank, Helene escapes existentially by virtue of her half-German identity. In the company of her German father, the soldier who has become her lover, and a maiden aunt, the one paternal relative who acknowledges her, she enjoys privileges her mother is denied; she rides on public transportation, eats in restaurants, and attends public entertainments.

Demetz, who sought to counter the failure of German schools to teach Holocaust history adequately (Kremer interview), is among the ranks of those who contend that forgetting the Holocaust compounds the tragedy. She addresses the theme of Holocaust memory explicitly in Marie Richter's dialogue and implicitly in Helene's character. In an effort to assure that future generations know what the Nazis did to their victims and that the atrocities be seen from the victims' point of view, Marie insists that Helene accompany her to witness the results of German crimes and implores her to bear witness at war's end. Marie Richter argues, "Let her see it all, . . . Just let her see everything. Someone will have to know about it later on" (p. 91). After years of alternating between Holocaust evasion and confrontation, Helene encounters Holocaust reality, the quintessential *Shoah* image—a cattle car filled with skeletal Jewish prisoners. Although she refrains from commentary, it is clear that Helene is at the threshold of comprehension of the catastrophe, at the threshold of understanding. When she realizes that she is her family's sole survivor, that no one will return, her innocence is shattered.

The Journey from Prague Street

Like its predecessor, *The Journey from Prague Street* (1990) is highly autobiographical and chronicles Helene's postwar odyssey from Communist Czechoslovakia to Germany and eventually to freedom and prosperity in America. References and memories of the war years are circumscribed and play a subordinate role in this domestic novel recording Helene's unhappy marriage to a brilliant, egocentric academic and her second marriage to an American Jew. Written in the first and third person, as Helene is approaching sixty and taking stock, she claims to "have had too many lives" (*The Journey from Prague Street*, New York: St. Martin's Press, 1980, p. 3) with a past that occasionally overwhelms and disorients her: "Events overlap, reference points disappear, people who belong to one life suddenly appear out of context, in another" (p. 3). The German-Jewish ambivalence that marked the younger character persists in the postwar reflections, generated by her discovery that her first love, a German soldier, survived the war. Her initial inability to forgive him for "being part of it" is followed by a mark of her postwar consciousness. She sheds her reservation and shares a brief adulterous reunion with him while her philandering husband is otherwise occupied.

Of particular interest to readers of Holocaust literature is the sequel's relation to *The House on Prague Street*: the adult narrator's more earnest connection to her Jewish family's Holocaust history, culminating in her reflections on the girl that was, the family that was no more, "the family [that] had been lost in many transports, had been gassed, had died of broken hearts, of crushed hopes . . ." (p. 11). More sustained *Shoah* thought enters Helene's life with her marriage to the American, with whom she travels to Europe to visit his family's ancestral village. Helene's most thoughtful lament for her family appears on this site, where the synagogue and Jewish cemetery remain intact. This visit leads to her elegiac contemplation of the divergent roads the great-great grandfathers traveled and the consequences for their progeny, one who had the good fortune to emigrate to America in the nineteenth century and the other who remained in Europe, resulting 140 years later in his family's demise.

Critical Reception

Aside from a chapter in Lillian Kremer's *Women's Holocaust Writing: Memory and Imagination*, Demetz has not attracted the interest of academic critics. She has, however, enjoyed the praise of book reviewers and columnists such as George Will, who wrote, "*The House on Prague Street* comes as close as art can, and as close as only art can, to making the terrible truth universally accessible." Helen Epstein, author of the acclaimed *Children of the Holocaust*, shares George Will's enthusiasm, describing the book in her *Washington Post* review, as "a tiny gem. . . . so artfully constructed that without a single explicit reference to mass murder and only a few allusions to public figures or events, the reader is made to feel and understand the comprehensive and corrosive power of Nazi Germany" (p. 1).

Bibliography

Primary Sources

The House on Prague Street. 1980.
The Journey from Prague Street. 1990.

Secondary Sources

Ascherson, Neal. "Survivors." *New York Review of Books* (12 June 1980): 34–36.

Epstein, Helen. "Living at the Fringe of Nightmare." *The Washington Post Book World*, 3 August 1980, 1, 14–15.

Kendall, Elaine. "A Fortuitously Timed 20 Century Odyssey: *The Journey from Prague Street* by Hana Demetz." *Los Angeles Times*, 6 April 1990, E4.

Kremer, S. Lillian. "Hana Demetz." In *Women's Holocaust Writing*. Lincoln: University of Nebraska Press, 1999, pp. 100–118.

Tucker, Martin. "Demetz, Hana." In *Literary Exile in the Twentieth Century: An Analysis and Biographical Dictionary*. New York: Greenwood, 1991, p. 202.

Will, George. "Review of *The House on Prague Street.*" *Washington Post*, 3 August 1980, Books Section, p. 1.

Williamson, Barbara Fisher. "*The Journey from Prague Street.*" *New York Times Book Review*, 1 July 1990, 7, 15.

Interview with S. Lillian Kremer. 20 May 1988.

ALCINA LUBITCH DOMECQ

(1953–)

ILAN STAVANS

PERHAPS THE MOST accurate adjective to describe the oeuvre of Alcina Lubitch Domecq is frugal: she is known as a writer of few, well-chosen words; her stories and a novel are brief in length and laconic in plot, and the landscape she evokes in them is one of desolation and austerity. In an autobiographical essay, part of which is available in English translation under the title "Résumé Raisonné" (in editor Sadow, *King David's Harp*) she states that silence is her authentic mode: "Silence," she argues, "is my true language." She then adds: "And yet, I write . . . Alone, to myself. I write in spite of all the suffering it unravels. . . . [L]iterature places me firmly on the ground. It gives weight to my being" (Sadow, p. 184).

Rumored for years to be at work on a *magnum opus*, Lubitch Domecq is the author of several slim volumes: the novel *El espejo en el espejo* (*The Mirror's Mirror*, 1983) and the collection of stories *Intoxicada* (Intoxicated, 1984). Their leitmotif is revenge: reprisal against others for crimes committed in a time of war, especially in concentration camps; and vengeance against oneself for failing to live up to one's own expectations. In the novel and several of the stories, the characters return to a series of questions: What is bravery? How does one react against evil? Is one justified in perpetuating horror when horror has been inflicted on us? For about a decade after the publication of her two books, the critical reception was limited to book reviews, but interviews and panoramic critical studies of Lubitch Domecq's motifs and *weltanschauung* have begun to appear, especially in the United States.

She is a native of Guatemala and for long stretches has also lived in Mexico and Israel. The Holocaust played a major role in her upbringing and appears everywhere in her literature. After the war her father immigrated to Guatemala, but his experience in Auschwitz proved to be devastating; he was unable to handle his professional and family affairs and was ultimately hospitalized in a mental institution. This apparently had a profound impact on his two children, who found a bastion of sanity and continuity in their mother, a non-Jewish *mestiza* (i.e., a person of mixed Spanish and Indian blood). Indeed, Lubitch Domecq manifests psychological traumas borne of the response of the so-called second generation, the children of Holocaust survivors, exposed to the ghosts of the past through the instability of their parents. Hers is doubtlessly a survivor's syndrome. Her fiction is populated by troublesome parent/child relationships: the protagonist of *El espejo en el espejo*, for instance, lives in constant fear that what her eyes see is only a façade behind which demons, goblins, witches, and monsters live; and the female narrator of "Simple Thoughts," which takes place in a prison cell in Argentina during the so-called "Dirty War," devises a magical method through which to enter the mind of a torturer who has repeatedly raped her. Her objective, it seems, is not to stop him but to understand why he is so inclined to perform evil. Indeed, the author's family path not only illustrates the journey of Eastern European Jews to the Americas in World War II but also the scar inflicted on their successors:

> After the liberation of Auschwitz, Papa spent a few weeks wandering around the Pale. He stayed briefly in Lodz (where he met an idol of mine, Isaiah Spiegel, at the time retrieving from memory the stories included in *Ghetto Kingdom*), then made his way to Lyon, worked a few weeks in a Paris shoe factory, and eventually sailed across the Atlantic. His arrival point was Havana, where he lived for three months toward the end of 1946. Then his cousin managed to bring him to Guatemala, where Papa's name changed from Ya'acov Yehoshua Lichtenshtein to Jacobo Lubitch and where, willy-nilly, he began working as an assistant in an optician's office. My mother, Josefina Domecq Pérez, a non-Jew, was from a wealthy Spanish family with ties to Mexico's wine industry ("Résumé Raisonné" in Sadow, p. 173).

In the same autobiographical essay, Lubitch Domecq's conversation with another Jewish-Mexican writer, Angelina Muníz-Huberman, is reproduced. "Is writing worth the effort?" asks the author of *Intoxicada*:

> "Perhaps not," she replied. "But do we have a choice?"
> "Silence," I responded.
> "Nature is silent . . . words are human. And only words can be *personalized*."
> [Muníz-Huberman] is right: To write is to erupt (Sadow, pp. 174–175).

Exceptional among writers of the Spanish-language Americas, for whom the Holocaust has not been an important source of literary inspiration, Lubitch Domecq has internalized the tribulations of the *Shoah* to such a degree that she no longer perceives behavior as civilized. While Latin American writers like Moacyr Scliar (Brazil), Simja Sneh (Argentina), and Mauricio Rosencof (Uruguay) address the Nazi destruction of European Jewry directly, using personal anecdotes and historical research to re-create the Nazi atrocities, Lubitch Domecq takes many liberties. She approaches the Holocaust tangentially, from the impressionistic perspective of a daughter. In her fiction she turns the experiences between 1939 and 1945 into haunted and haunting allegories. Critic Stephen A. Sadow says that she

> looks at writing as something she must do, as a way to hand[le] her pain. Her novel and stories are filled with sharp-edged images, are populated by the ghosts of her past, and possess a strong dose of the surreal. Every word, every comma is eked out. Putting enormous care into each work, she has produced a number of veritable "jewels" (p. 171).

Most of Lubitch Domecq's stories take place in nameless locations. Sometimes these locations have a European feel, others appear to be set in Latin America or at least display religious and mythical elements of it. In one of these tales a little boy whose parents have given him a set of toy soldiers as a Hanukkah present spends his afternoon hours building a battlefield, then a refugee camp, then barracks, and finally an incinerator. The boy steals a handful of dolls from his sister, and the soldiers ultimately place them in the makeshift incinerator. In the background while the boy plays are the voices of his parents and other unnamed relatives, who every so often check on the boy to make sure he is "enjoying himself as only 6-year-olds might."

> The matches lay on the ground. The dolls were dismembered, their plastic skin burnt. A circle of exhausted toy soldiers, in defiant Aryan attitude, stood around a bonfire made of scrawny sticks. *Estás bien, quedido?* The boy's innocent smile was the best reply: yes, yes, yes . . . I'm full of joy, Mom! (*Intoxicada*, Joaquin Mortiz, p. 76; translation by Ilan Stavans).

Lubitch Domecq's work is influenced by the mathematical style of Jorges Luis Borges and Italo Calvino. She uses allegory and metaphor to invoke solitude and alienation. Mysticism, as filtered through Kabbalah and pre-Columbian cultures, is an inspiration in her tales, as is Yiddish literature, especially the oeuvre of the triumvirate Mendele Mokher Sforim, Sholem Aleichem, and Isaac Leib Peretz. (She taught herself Yiddish to read her father's correspondence.) *El espejo en el espejo* is a haunting post-Auschwitz meditation that again takes place in a battlefield, this one filled with real corpses. The images used are those of children of Holocaust victims, whose sense of dignity has been shattered by the experience of their parents. Characters are presented in a dehumanized fashion: they are "bestial," "instinctual," even "cannibalistic." Chaos prevails as a woman, sleepless, roams in search of a home. She is convinced a *dybbuk*—e.g. a foreign soul – has taken control of her body. Mutations take place: she becomes, among other fabulous creatures, a wolf, eager to devour human flesh. At one point in the novel, a lieutenant speaking in an almost undecipherable tongue similar to old German interacts with the protagonist. He tells her that the Jews were a demonic race. The protagonist listens coldly, quietly, processing the information without emotion. Suddenly, she transforms herself into a jaguar that jumps on the old German, turning him into her prey. She devours him in a matter of minutes.

> Blood-thirsty jaws, astute sight, the *yaguára* wildcat, his yellowish-brown coat carefully tinted with black spots, observes with menacing clinical eyes. He is king and his appetite is inexhaustible. A force within drives him forward. Nothing scares him. Suddenly, the carnivorous quadruple jumps on his victim, carrying it on. It is a sanctifying act: the German must die, be gobbled, returned to its infernal source (*El espejo en el espejo*, Joaquín Mortiz, p. 103; translation by Ilan Stavans).

This particular scene has prompted a few critics to point out the impact of Shamanism in *El espejo en el espejo*, but the impact of the Holocaust is also evident: humans abused by oppressors become mythical beasts that devour their enemy in the religious act.

Several of the stories in *Intoxicada* are also about social types taken from popular culture, such as the mythological hollering woman, La Llorona. A few are relocated against an agonizing Holocaust backdrop, such as the barracks in a concentration camp and a gas chamber. Interior rupture is at center stage in "Bottles," a story told from the viewpoint of a boy whose mother suffers a nervous breakdown. A Poe-like effect of "being possessed by a superior force" is tangible. The reader gets the impression the mother is unable to cope with the family, largely as a result of her personal experiences. Elsewhere in this collection the characters are overcome by desires to sin: to loot, to attack, to rape, to kill.

Arguably Lubitch Domecq's most famous story—surely the most personal—is "Ur." It is typical of her obsession with revenge. Its central theme is the Holocaust as perceived by a survivor's daughter. In it the narrator attempts to understand her psychologically fragile paternal figure, who was enslaved by the Nazis and forced to be the primary caretaker of a sick Gestapo *kommandant* diagnosed with a terminal illness.

> "In Ur I kept my little secret."
>
> Father never wanted to talk about Ur. Yet he appeared forever lost in it.
>
> In Spanish, he pronounced the word uneasily but with meticulous care: Ooh-rrh. Inquisitive as I was, I relentlessly asked myself: where is the place? And is it really a place? Has anyone ever lived in it?
>
> At one point, Father evasively described Ur: it was, I was told, a location, *un lugar,* complete with buildings, a hospital, a collective bath, and a huge fence. But he refused to go any farther (*Nothing Makes You Free: Writings by Descendants of Jewish Holocaust Survivors.* ed. Melvin Jules Bukiet, New York: W.W. Norton, 2002, p. 328).

It is left to the father to accompany the Nazi commander through his agony and last days, and he does so dutifully . . . until he decides to take revenge against him and the German people by substituting urine for his medicine. In spite of his courage, the father's act cannot bring back the innocence and happiness lost in the war. Lubitch Domecq never questions the moral behavior of the narrator's father. In fact, "Ur" eulogizes it: the message is that making the *kommandant* drink urine instead of medicine is insignificant in the larger ethical picture; the abuse he sustains is a well-deserved token of retribution. It might not bring redemption, but it brings spiritual satisfaction. In the end, though, that satisfaction doesn't match the aggression against the Jews, and so the question remains: Should the father have applied his antagonistic feelings more usefully, confronting not only the Gestapo officer but the German army as a whole with a formal, more effective form of resistance?

Revenge without fulfillment is a typical Lubitch Domecq twist: the frugality of our options to respond against barbarism makes our human condition almost intolerable. An enlightening passage highlights her reaction against Nazism:

> On one occasion [while still young] . . . I saw a portrait of Adolf Hitler in a history book. Mama explained to me he was the leader of the Nazi army that killed all of Papa's family. I was mesmerized. Somehow, it didn't seem possible that a man so gallant would perpetrate so much evil. Hitler's facial expression was enigmatic: he smiled at me. Was his smile stolen? Had he taken it away from Papa? I vividly remember telling myself that if I ever saw Hitler walking on a downtown street, I would first ask him ("Résumé Raisonné" in Sadow, p. 175).

Bibliography

Primary Sources

El espejo en el espejo: o, La noble sonrisa del perro (The Mirror's Mirror: or, the Noble Smile of the Dog). 1983.

Intoxicada (Intoxicated). 1984.

"Résumé Raisonné." *King David's Harp: Autobiographical Essays by Jewish Latin American Writers.* Edited and with an introduction by Stephen A. Sadow. Albuquerque: University of New Mexico Press, 1999, pp. 171–185.

Anthologies that Include the Works of Alcina Lubitch Domecq

Bukiet, Melvin Jules, ed. *Nothing Makes You Free: Writings by Descendents of Holocaust Survivors.* New York: W.W. Norton & Co, 2002.

Poey, Delia, ed. *Out of the Mirrored Garden: New Fiction by Latin American Women.* New York: Anchor Books, 1996.

Stavans, Ilan, ed. *The Oxford Book of Jewish Stories.* New York and London: Oxford University Press, 1998.

Secondary Sources

Sadow, Stephen A. *King David's Harp: Autobiographical Essays by Jewish Latin American Writers.* Albuquerque: University of New Mexico Press, 1999.

Stavans, Ilan. "On Separate Ground." *Passion, Memory, and Identity: Twentieth-Century Latin American Jewish Women Writers.* Edited by Marjorie Agosín. Albuquerque: University of New Mexico Press, 1998.

———. "The Impact of the Holocaust in Latin America." *The Chronicle of Higher Education* (May 25, 2001): B7–B10.

Interviews

"It Just Isn't Right [On Being a Freak]: Conversation with Alcina Lubitch Domecq." *Albany Review* 4 (summer 1990): 54–61.

Lubitch Domecq's stories, in English translation, have appeared in *The Literary Review* and *Fiction.*

SERGE DOUBROVSKY

(1928–)

JULIETTE DICKSTEIN

JULIEN SERGE DOUBROVSKY was born in Paris in 1928. He holds a *doctorat d'état* in French letters and is a former student of the prestigious Ecole Normale Supérieure. For almost fifty years Doubrovsky has split his time between France and the United States, where he is a professor of French literature at New York University. His scholarly pursuits span the fields of seventeenth-century literature and theater, the modern novel, literary theory, psychoanalysis and literature, and autobiography. He has authored hundreds of critical essays and works on these subjects as well as on Proust and Sartre. He has also written seven novels, one collection of short stories, and is responsible for having invented the term "autofiction" to describe the novels he writes, which can be characterized as hybrid texts that rely almost exclusively on material from his own life.

Doubrovsky is one of the most important figures in the field of French letters. His writing, fiction and nonfiction, has received an enormous amount of critical and academic attention. He was awarded a Guggenheim in 1965, and his novel, *Le Livre brisé* (The Broken Book, 1989), won the acclaimed Médicis prize. The Department of French Studies at the University of Birmingham has established a Web site on his life and work. Several scholars have devoted much of their time to publishing bibliographic material by and on Doubrovsky that is also available on the Internet (see Professor Renee Kingcaid's "Bibliography of Primary and Secondary Sources on Serge Doubrovsky"). Doubrovsky's biography interests scholars precisely because of the strong relationship that exists between the written text and his life experiences, especially his relationships with different women and his family's experiences during World War II.

Life and Work

Doubrovsky's father, Israel, came to France from the Ukraine in 1912. His mother, Renée Weitzmann, was born in France. Her mother was from an assimilated Alsacian family, while her father had emigrated from Dombrowicz, Poland. The Doubrovskys survived the war years in hiding outside Paris. Indeed, this dark chapter surfaces in much of Doubrovsky's written work, but it is most pronounced in *La Dispersion* (The Scattering, 1969), *Fils* (Son or Threads, 1977), *Le Livre brisé* (The Broken Book), and *Laissé pour conte* (1999, Wordplay on "Laissé-pour-compte," or "reject" in English. "Conte" in French means a tale or narrative. Unless otherwise mentioned, all translations from the French are my own).

"How did I escape, come back?" the narrator asks in *Le Livre brisé*, "I cannot get over it" (Paris: Bernard Grasset, 1989, p. 15). In *Fils*, Doubrovsky's wartime experience is brought to the fore in a passage that restages a session with his analyst. "*What did your situation during the war reproduce*?" asks the analyst.

> 10 June 40 to the 25 August 44. A block of time. In my life. Without precedent. Never had anything like it. Before, after . . .
>
> *situation during the war*   what was it   imprisoned little by little   shut out
>
> shrinking world   *it is forbidden to it is prohibited to*   the four walls of our garden   four walls   of   the kitchen
>
> family circle   cooped up quadrature   how to resolve it   claustrophobia we are smothering   prison suffocates   one sole room one year   when we were in hiding   in   Villiers   without going out (pp. 214–216).

As the above-cited passage linguistically and thematically expresses, the Doubrovsky family was in hiding in the Parisian suburb of Villiers-sur-Marne. Luckily, they were taken in by Doubrovsky's uncle's gentile sister-in-law, Nénette, her husband, Riri, their daughter, Solange, and Nénette's father (see *Laissé pour conte*, Paris: Bernard Grasset, 1999, pp. 403–429). Doubrovsky refers to them as the family's "saviors." At one point, they were fortunate enough to be warned by a neighborhood policeman, who told them that he would have to return to arrest them at a later time (*Fils*, p. 203). Doubrovsky describes himself during these years listening to the radio, sneaking glances out the window, lusting after Solange, doing exercises for his back, and writing in his journal. While his parents were able to go out for a few hours during the day, he was advised always to remain inside the house, like a caged animal.

Doubrovsky's subsequent incredulity over his survival translates into total obsession simply with his existence and with the details that comprise his own life. "Why am I always talking about myself in my books . . .?" (*Le Livre brisé*, p. 16). Doubrovsky writes about himself and his marriages, his love affairs, his daughters, and his critical work on Sartre and Proust. He writes, also, to make sense of a world that at times is difficult to understand: "The meaning of our lives escapes us," he states, "we therefore have to reinvent it through writing. This is what I call 'autofiction' " (Célestin, p. 400).

Autofiction

Doubrovsky describes autofiction as a staging of the self and a reconstruction of the self through writing. Although he invented the term, he did not create the phenomenon, for as he points out, autofiction characterizes the writings of many authors who fictionalize themselves in their work, including Proust, Céline, and Colette. Specific to Doubrovsky's entire oeuvre, however, is the representation of his childhood experience during the war, and the impact these years have had on his life and on his scholarly and artistic choices. In his most recent novel, *Laissé pour conte*, which presents Serge Doubrovsky as he approaches old age, the relationship between his survival during the war and his ensuing career as a writer is articulated rather urgently in the following passage.

> IF I must live, one thing is sure, continue this black notebook in another form, which, no idea, one day, WRITE, novel, essay, dunno, but IF by miracle I survive, more than a desire, a must, WRITE MY SURVIVAL (May 1944) (p. 429).

Written in 1944, this journal entry is taken from the diary he kept while in hiding during the war. That these lines conclude the novel not only underscores the impact of the war on his psyche and on his work, but also communicates to the reader what Doubrovsky himself wants to make heard: that this experience was, to a large extent, responsible for his choosing to be a writer. In *La Dispersion*, Doubrovsky includes his reflections on the period of the war, and includes clippings from the French press and from antisemitic journals such as *Le Pilori* (The Pillory), *Je suis partout* (I Am Everywhere), and *La Gerbe* (The Sheaf), and his own pastiche of the type of vitriol that is spewed by such racist periodicals.

> . . . the founder of Marxism is the bourgeois Karl Marx Jew from Germany Stalin is at the beck and call of Jews New-York has become Jew-York Jew-York
>
> is the last citadel of Mamon of Hiram and Yahwe called Jehovah Churchill and Roosevelt are creatures of Israel . . . we are confronted with a racial problem not simply a religious one Jews have a particular smell explaining their ancient negroid roots dirty nails kinky hair nose in the shape of a banana . . . (Paris: Mercure de France, 1969, p. 224).

The violence of this passage, which reproduces the appalling language typical of antisemitic invective, brings to our attention the role of the extreme-right French press in disseminating fanatical propaganda during the Occupation and Vichy Regime. It also brings to the fore the heinous, racist acts committed by the French state against its Jews: "FRANCE CAPITAL DRANCY, camp with its barbed wire, its republican guards and its gendarmes in faction, mass arrest of the Vel d'Hiv July 42, parents came back with the thin bundle they quickly buckled . . ." (*Laissé pour conte*, p. 410).

Drancy was the French internment camp located outside Paris near the present Charles de Gaulle airport. It was used as a holding station for Jews and members of the Resistance before they were deported to concentration or death camps in the east. The "rafle," or mass arrest of Jews in Paris and their subsequent arrest in the Vel d'Hiv (the Vélodrôme d'Hiver was a sports stadium in the fifteenth arrondissement in Paris) took place on 16 and 17 July 1942. The French police arrested approximately 13,000 men, women, and children. This was the first time that women, children, and the elderly among French-born and naturalized Jewish citizens were rounded up for deportation.

By writing about French antisemitism and French antisemitic practices, Doubrovsky not only struggles to come to terms with the horrific past of his republican nation, but also tries to work through his relationship to Judaism: "I am not a secular Jew, I am a non-Jewish Jew! I feel no ideological, spiritual, or intellectual attachment whatsoever to Judaism" (Hughes). Despite this negative statement, a lot of text is devoted to his Jewish identity and to what befell him and other French

Jews during the war: "The yellow star was stuck onto me, I was destined to disappear, by miracle I escaped. It is in this sense that I completely assume my Jewish identity. What I mean is that in my mind I feel that I have a Jewish affiliation as well as a French one. I am Jewish and French" (Hughes).

Jewish and French, Doubrovsky is also, and perhaps most importantly, a writer who explores what he calls "the adventure of language." His fiction is experimental in nature, at times difficult to follow precisely because there is no chronological ordering of events, and no plot or character development that respects the conventions of the realist novel. Doubrovsky also manipulates the design of the page: blank spaces figure prominently, and the arrangement of text is sometimes configured into columns or even lists (see *La Dispersion*). In addition, there are often shifts in the narrative voice, as in *La Dispersion* for example, where it switches between the first- and the second-person singular. Although Doubrovsky enjoys playing with words and the structure of his texts, their inherent experimental nature is not simply the result of a gratuitous act or an aesthetic exercise. The breakdown of form translates Doubrovsky's experience of history as something that not only has failed him (Nazi Germany and Vichy France's collaborationist role), but also as something he has failed through his nonparticipation in the war and resistance (Régine Robin makes this argument in her article "Trou de mémoire: le travail de la judéité" ["Memory Hole: The Work of Jewishness"]). Indeed, Doubrovsky expresses rather strongly his frustration at having been too young to take part in any battles or in any resistance groups:

> I would have wanted to so much, machine gun fire right in the face, here's my response to the mass arrests, I have a bilious after-taste of hatred in my mouth, fight in the name of God, BE A MAN (*Laissé pour conte*, p. 419).

Doubrovsky must live with the frustration of never having participated in the war; his engagement remains on the textual level. Writing, however, does not replace action; it neither sets him free of what he feels were his responsibilities, nor does it completely deliver him psychologically from the trauma of what he endured. "Writing never delivered me. I was never liberated. Words are not acts. . . . I was spit on for four years, in French, by the French, in the press each morning. . . . One can give an account of the past, write it. One cannot rewrite it" (*Le Livre brisé*, pp. 20–21).

By clearly stating the limitations of words and writing, which can neither change the past nor take the place of armed resistance, Doubrovsky maintains something quite different from what Sartre posits in his short essays on the Occupation (see "La république du silence," *Situations, III*, Paris: Gallimard, 1947) whereby, in the context of the war and Occupation, the feat of writing can be considered an act of resistance and defiance. Sartre, however, was not in hiding. Doubrovsky, who was in hiding, acknowledges the important and powerful role of language, which finally does serve some kind of liberating function: "[W]riting fills, replaces, it's an opening to another world" (*Laissé pour conte*, p. 421).

Critical Reception

Doubrovsky's writing has received an enormous amount of critical attention. Academics and scholars continue to debate the problematics of the term "autofiction" codified by Doubrovsky (see works by Alex Hughes, Marie Miguet-Ollagnier and Hélène Jaccomard, Renee Kingcaid, Philippe Lejeune, and so on). Web sites and chat rooms devoted to Doubrovsky's work provide up-to-date resource material and virtual venues for discussion (see the Web site of the French Department of the University of Birmingham, which has also set up a chat room to discuss autofiction). Indeed, Doubvrosky has made a huge impact in the field of literary studies precisely because his autofictions encourage others to explore the relationship not only between fiction and autobiography, but also between the self and the creative process, whereby one's identity can also be something that is invented—or reinvented.

Bibliography

Primary Sources

Fiction

Le Jour S, nouvelles (The S day). 1963.
La Dispersion (The Scattering). 1969.
Fils (Sons/Threads). 1977.
Un amour de soi (Self-love). 1982.
La Vie, l'instant (Life, Present). 1985.
Le Livre brisé (The Broken Book). 1989.
L'Après-vivre (After-Living). 1994.
Laissé pour conte. 1999.

Critical Works

Corneille ou la dialectique du héros (Corneille or the Dialectic of the Hero). 1964.
Pourquoi la nouvelle critique: Critique et objectivité (New Criticism in France). 1966.
La Place de la Madeleine: Ecriture et fantasme chez Proust (Writing and Fantasy in Proust). 1974.
Parcours critique. 1980.
Autobiographiques: de Corneille à Sartre. 1988.
Autofiction & Cie (Editor). 1992.

Secondary Sources

Burgelin, Claude. "Serge Doubrovsky: profession professeur. Autoportrait de l'artiste dans la salle de cours." *Le Temps modernes* (December 2000–January 2001): 115–127.

Célestin, Roger. "Autofiction and Beyond: An Interview with Serge Doubrovsky." *Sites*, no. 1 (1997): 397–405.

Grenver, J. "La France, capitale Drancy." *Le Nouvel Observateur* 262 (17–23 November 1969): 40–41.

Hughes, Alex. "Entretien avec Serge Doubrovsky, à l'occasion de la parution de *Laissé pour conte*." The University of Birmingham, (9 July 1999). artsweb.bham.ac.uk/artsfrenchstudies/sergedou/intervw.htm.

Ireland, John, ed. "Monstrous Writing: Serge Doubrovsky's Autofiction." *Genre: Forms of Discourse and Culture* 26, no. 1 (spring 1993).

Kingcaid, Renee. "Serge Analysand." *Genre: Forms of Discourse and Culture* 26, no. 1 (spring 1993): 51–83.

Kotin Mortimer, Armine. "The Death of Autobiography in Doubrovsky's Broken Novel." *Genre: Forms of Discourse and Culture* 26, no. 1 (spring 1993): 85–108.

———. "Mort de L'autobiographie dans *Le livre brisé*." *Le Temps modernes*, December 2000–January 2001.

Nourissier, François. "Le seul écrivain français de l'école juive de New York." *Figaro Magazine* 494 (21 October 1989): 46.

Robin, Régine. "Trou de mémoire: le travail de la judéité." *Le Temps modernes*, December 2000–January 2001. 192–209.

———. *Le Golem de l'ecriture: De l'autofiction au cyber-soi*. Montreal: Editions XYZ, 1998.

Spatz, Erwin. "Serge Doubrovsky, Boris Schreiber: Autobiographes juifs." *Communuaté Nouvelle* 47 (January–February 1990): 153–155.

Judith Strick Dribben

(1923–1977)

SUSAN LEE PENTLIN

IN 1965, JUDITH STRICK Dribben (also known as Danuta Skowronska, Marie-Josephine Menard, Marie Alexandrovna Arsenyeva, Ditta Alexandrovna, and Susan Pisiuk) began writing the memoir of her life from the time of the German invasion of Russia through the establishment of the State of Israel and her marriage. In 1969 it was published (in English) in Jerusalem as *And Some Shall Live*, and one year later in New York, as *A Girl Called Judith Strick*. Golda Meir pointed to the significance of this Israeli Holocaust account in a forward, explaining that Dribben describes "not only the stages of an extraordinary life, but the stages of the history of her people, from the terrible prelude to national revival in Israel" (New York: Cowles, 1970, p. 2).

Life

Dribben was born to Alexander and Rachel (Pisiuk) Strick on 5 November 1923, in Rovno, Ukraine. She attended Hebrew gymnasium in Lvov [Lwow, Lemberg] and was studying law at the University of Lvov when the Germans reached the city in 1941. Her father, an industrialist, was murdered by the Germans shortly after the occupation, on the anniversary of the death of Petlyura, a Ukrainian hero. Her older brother Misha was mobilized into the Red Army in 1940. Her mother, who had fought in the underground against the czar, went into hiding on a farm with her younger son, Arthur. Both were betrayed and murdered near the end of the war. Only two uncles and cousins, living in Tel Aviv, survived the Holocaust. Escorted at her wedding by Ben Gurion and his wife Pola, Strick married Ed Dribben, an American, in 1954. They lived on Kibbutz Sde Boker and later in Moshav Orot. Her husband remembers her as "a first-class Jewish lady."

After the Six-Day War in 1967, Israel experienced a surge of elation and self-confidence. It was the right timing for Dribben's work to be published. She was not writing primarily with the motives common to most Holocaust memoirs: to remember family lost, to warn the next generations of the dangers of racism and hate, or to record events for history. She wrote to give meaning to her experiences, to help build Israeli national identity, and to give Israeli youth the model of a scrappy fighter to replace the common stereotype of the passive Holocaust victim.

Among Israeli writers, two viewpoints regarding the Holocaust predominate. Omer Bartov explains that in the early years in Israel, "the dominant image was of the heroic Israeli, fighting against overwhelming numbers, with 'it is good to die for our land' on his lips" (Bartov, p. 123). Gershon Shaked adds that, "What was for most of the native Israelis a historical event with collective significance was for most of the survivors a traumatic childhood memory" (Shaked, pp. 276–277). Dribben's memoir bridges both groups. She had been a partisan, a survivor of Auschwitz, and an armed fighter for the Israeli state. She was the model of a hero, bursting with youth and self-esteem, ready to face danger with sardonic wit, intelligence, and obstinate bravado, and she was a victim.

Dribben's Memoir

The memoir is divided into four sections. Each section title indicates her motivation for writing it. The first, "Hardening Steel," is an account of her early work in the underground. In 1941 Dribben joined the Ukrainian nationalist underground, with the help of a university friend, and continued her fight in the Lvov ghetto. At seventeen she was assigned to flirt with SS men and brought them to underground agents who interrogated and killed them. She described herself as cruel, "hard like steel," when she brought the "target" to their killers. After her family went into hiding, she continued her partisan work in Cracow.

For cover, she took a position as a maid. Her boss reported her for taking his German police uniform. She was held in the notorious Gestapo Montelupich prison in Cracow and interrogated by the Gestapo for many months. Her interrogations are the subject of the section titled "The Big Joke." With the Gestapo, she played a game of wit and intelligence and successfully hid her Jewish background, drawing on her language skills in German, French, and Russian. To buy time she strung them along, using different identities and weaving elaborate details about her fictitious life into confessions. Giving fake intelligence to entice the Gestapo further, she showed an almost unbelievable lack of fear. "You're a disgusting Nazi lackey," she recalled saying to a high-ranking Gestapo interrogator (*A Girl Called Judith Strick*, p. 123). Later, after a beating, she insisted: "I was so angry I hardly felt the blows. I poured out on them all the insults I have ever heard in my life" (p. 156).

"In the Shadow of the Chimneys" is about her time at Auschwitz-Birkenau. Curiously, this chapter is the shortest, but also appropriately more solemn and frank in tone. On 1 October 1943, she was sent to Auschwitz as a political prisoner, receiving tattoo number 63578. On that day, the record shows that numbers 63553 to 63603 were issued to fifty-one female prisoners sent by the Sipo and the SD (the Nazi Party's intelligence service) from Cracow (Czech, p. 497). There she emphasized her desire for solidarity with other inmates, telling an SS sergeant, "But I wouldn't like to be an exception," when she escaped the short haircut at registration (p. 180).

In quarantine, she and a friend encountered a group of Greek Jews covered with scabs. When spoken to, the women protested, "but you are Christian and we are Jewesses." Dribben protested that she and her friend were prisoners themselves. The Greeks replied that, as Jews, they were different, explaining: "they can put us in the chimneys any time they want" while Christians do not share this fate (p. 187). After she saw Sabbath candles burning in a Jewish block she recalled: "I felt like one of these women and I didn't feel like one" and confessed "I would have despised anyone who had advised me to confess my Jewishness. I wasn't ashamed of it, but they wanted to exterminate us and I had to defend myself as best I could" (pp. 208–209).

Dribben wrote about her will to live and described the victims of selections as those who "passively awaited their fate" (p. 189). With help from the camp underground, she eventually survived typhus, pneumonia, and work in penal detail 117. In the summer of 1944 she was sent to Hirtenberg, a subcamp of Mauthausen, where prisoners worked at the Gustloff Werke ammunition factory, and became camp interpreter. She escaped during the evacuation from the camp and was liberated by the Russians.

The final chapter, "Homecoming," is about how she achieved the Zionist dream of reaching Palestine. After reaching the Russian front, she donned a Red Army uniform, having apparently recovered from the effects of starvation and disease, and fought as a machine gunner in a tank unit at the battle of Vienna. After armistice she stayed with the Red Army, serving as an interpreter. She helped kidnap a former Nazi in Vienna and brought him into Russian territory. Although aware of the threat of the Soviet secret police, she dreamed of training as a Soviet diplomat until a friend explained that such a career was not open to a Jew. Shortly afterward she met two soldiers from the Palestine Brigade who encouraged her to reach Palestine. When discharge orders arrived for her return to Ukraine, she fled to the Russian zone.

Using the immigration permit issued for her cousin Susan Pisiuk, who perished in Rovno, she arrived in Tel Aviv in February 1947. Against her uncle's advice she joined the Irgun and began hiding dynamite in his library. She fought in dangerous actions against the British and, after independence, overcame bias against women in the army and trained as an artillery gunner. Later, with the support of Moshe Dayan, she became the first woman to serve as an army intelligence officer. In 1952 she was one of the founders of her kibbutz in the Negev, where she also did duty as a shepherd and manager.

Critical Response

The publication of Dribben's memoir received generally positive reviews, but there has been little critical, literary response since its publication. Marlene Heinemann's study is the only extensive literary analysis available. She includes Dribben's as one of the memoirs she analyzes in *Gender and Destiny*. She discusses Dribben's "role as sexual temptress" with the partisans and the choice she faced in Birkenau of prostitution or punishment battalion (Heinemann, pp. 29–30). She also criticizes "her denial of physical suffering" and points out how this creates "a self-dramatizing portrayal" (p. 45).

Heinemann raises issues regarding the authenticity of the work, pointing out that the dialogue is stilted, the sequence of events often unconvincing, and the tone so unemotional it makes the text seem "fictionalized," like "*reportage* within semi-fictional text" (p. 126). She finds that Dribben de-emphasizes the survival advantages she had due to her intelligence, her fluency in languages, her "Aryan" appearance, and her privileged position, and characterizes the account as one that "portrays Birkenau as a place where much suffering could be avoided through special status, disguise, and solidarity" (p. 131). On the other hand, she also notes that personal photos and Golda Meir's foreword and its details about Birkenau add authenticity. David Patterson describes Dribben as having written "as though in a state of delirium," as she witnessed the mass murder of her people and he is moved by the intensity of her feelings of solidarity (Patterson, p. 45).

Bibliography

Primary Sources

And Some Shall Live. 1969.
A Girl Called Judith Strick. 1970.

Secondary Sources

Bartov, Omer. *Murder in Our Midst. The Holocaust, Industrial Killing, and Representation*. New York: Oxford, 1996.
Contemporary Authors, vols. 37–41. Gale Research, 1970.
Czech, Danuta. *Auschwitz Chronicle, 1939–1945*. New York: Henry Holt, 1989.
Dribben, Ed. Telephone interview with Susan Pentlin. 13 February 2001.
Heinemann, Marlene E. *Gender and Destiny: Women Writers and the Holocaust*. New York: Greenwood, 1986.
Shaked, Gershon. Afterword in *Facing the Holocaust: Selected Israeli Fiction*. Edited by Gila Ramras-Rauch and Joseph Michman-Melkman. Philadelphia: Jewish Publication Society, 1985.

Roberto Drummond
(1933–2002)

JOSEPH ABRAHAM LEVI

Roberto Drummond, pseudonym of Robert Francis, the son of Francisco Alvarenga Drummond and Ricarda de Paiva, was born on 21 December 1933, in Minas Gerais, Brazil. At age thirteen—influenced by Giuseppe Ghiaroni, Eurico Silva, and Otávio Augusto Vampré (particularly his popular radio-novels)—Drummond started writing short stories and feuilletons for the radio station Rádio Nacional. In 1957, Drummond began reporting for Belo Horizonte's daily *Folha de Minas* and shortly thereafter joined the controversial and leftist weekly *Binômio*. In 1963, Drummond became editor of the magazine *Alterosa*. With the 1964 coup d'état and the establishment of a dictatorship, Drummond worked in Rio de Janeiro for the *Jornal do Brasil*, by far the most important newspaper in Brazil. The following year, he returned to Belo Horizonte where he became a freelance journalist. At the beginning of the twenty-first century, Drummond was a columnist for Belo Horizonte's two dailies *Hoje em Dia* and the *Estado de Minas*.

In 1975, Drummond published his first collection of stories, *A morte de D.J. em Paris* (The Death of D.J. in Paris), which was also considered his debut in "pop literature," and which, together with his *A outra margem* (The Other Side), and *Isabel numa 5.ª feira* (Isabel on a Thursday), won first place in the 1971 IV Concurso Nacional de Contos do Paraná (Fourth National Competition on Short Stories from the State of Paraná), as well as the 1975 Prêmio Jabuti (Jabuti Prize), offered by the Câmara Brasileira do Livro (The Brazilian Chamber of the Book) as the best book in the category of new authors. On 21 June 2002, Roberto Drummond died in São Paulo of complications resulting from a heart attack.

Roberto Drummond and Jewish Themes

Roberto Drummond has no ties with either Judaism or crypto-Judaism. His interests in Jewish issues are thus tied to his desire for expressing freedom from any kind of oppression, particularly Nazism and Brazilian dictatorship. Drummond's socialist ideals—a constant in all of his literary works and, at times, very controversial—coupled with his desire to explore the popular aspect of society, are responsible for this attention to Judaic themes, such as the Holocaust and its repercussions in Brazil. Evil, especially its effect upon human behavior, thus becomes his focus. It is within this setting that his only work on Holocaust/post-Holocaust experiences should be placed and analyzed.

Hitler manda lembranças (Hitler Sends His Best Regards) (1985)

In this work dedicated to Holocaust survivors in Brazil, Drummond weaves together local folklore, popular culture, magic, and the multilayered syncretic nature of religion in an exploration of post-Holocaust evil in Brazil. Though a fictional work, the historical accounts are all well documented. The Holocaust enters the work gradually: first in generic and short references to Adolf Hitler and Josef Mengele, the camps at Auschwitz and Buchenwald, the Nazis, and finally, with personal experiences and nightmares. Drummond's characters move from the occasional flashback to the constant pain triggered by the simple act of remembering, to personal solutions for everyday survival and adaptation to life after the Holocaust. Illustrative of the novel's facticity are references to life in Berlin, the creation of the Warsaw ghetto, numerous details of life in a concentration camp, references to socialists Rosa Luxemburg and Olga Benário Prestes—a Brazilian Jewish woman handed over to the Gestapo—and heartbreaking excerpts from diaries kept by concentration camp prisoners, all establishing the novel's realistic evocation of Holocaust evil. The many references to the Warsaw ghetto and life in a concentration camp are always intermingled with personal, vivid accounts peculiar to that moment.

Against a backdrop in which chaos is dominant, reflecting Brazil's political situation of the time, as well as the turmoil caused by the Holocaust, a vast gallery of characters, waiting for a new event to happen, move relentlessly, with an occasional happy moment, into the unexpected and the unknown, which is almost always negative. Life can change for the good or nothing at all can happen (Stroun, p. 197). What is known and felt is that evil is everywhere, assuming every shape and form imaginable, from Hitler and Mengele to the Brazilian "Dictator with blue eyes as the myosotis"—implying that blue eyes, because of their rareness, are hard to forget—to censorship, which eventually "silenced Brazil" (Stroun, p. 56).

Hitler manda lembranças is divided into seven rounds and six intervals, intermittently, thus resembling a boxing match. Paulo Franz, a narrator of German descent, recalls the events that occurred between 15 October—the day in which he discovered that 417 of the 4,813 employees of the fictitious multinational American company, Brazil Corporation, would soon be laid off—and 21 December 1983. Adam Cohen, the main character, also among those to become unemployed, is a former Auschwitz and Buchenwald prisoner. "His arm was tattooed with the number 184.467 as soon as he entered Auschwitz" (Drummond, *Hitler manda lembranças*, 4th ed., Rio de Janeiro: Editera Nova Fronteira, 1984, p. 15). He has lost his loved ones: his brother was shot at Buchenwald; his sister died in Ravensbrück; his sweetheart perished in Auschwitz's gas chambers; his friend was castrated in a medical experiment. Cohen, obsessed with capturing Auschwitz's Angel of Death, Josef Mengele, who since 1945 has been frequently spotted in South America, is convinced that he is being followed by either a former SS guard or an officer from Auschwitz. The imaginary and the real, the occasional hallucination and the recurring nightmare, bring Hitler, Mengele, the Gestapo, as well as Nazism to life. More than once, both Hitler and Mengele appear as ghosts before some of the characters, such as Aunt Miriam, who "saw Hitler in her restaurant ordering a currant juice" (Drummond, p. 37). Stela, a Polish-Jewish Holocaust survivor who personifies "the pain of the world" (Drummond, p. 21), voices the message of the novel when she says that Hitler is alive and that he simply uses other names and disguises.

The many episodes dealing with life in the concentration camps, whether reenacted as day incubi or introduced as factual events, are either a door to the understanding of the pain of the postwar period as relived by the narrator(s), or to the many flashbacks and memories of particular events that occurred before or during their capture. Hence, every night Aunt Miriam would shut the windows of her house, her recurring nightmare being that the Gestapo would come and take her to Ravensbrück. Aunt Miriam's scream in the night is "her memory" (Drummond, p. 48). A letter written eight years after the events by a woman revealing the cruelty she endured in Ravensbrück, as well as her humiliation when she was arrested, stripped naked, and beaten in one of Berlin's squares, expresses the anguish of remembering and eventually telling oneself, as well others, events that happened and the things that were witnessed.

Like most Holocaust survivors worldwide, Drummond's Brazilian Holocaust survivors suffer from what has been generally called "survivor syndrome." Drummond's Jewish characters feel the pain of survival: "Cohen would often feel an almost incurable feeling of guilt, for being alive when his entire family and the only woman he really loved were dead" (Drummond, p. 16). To honor those left behind, he inflicts pain on himself: "Cohen would walk around with a needle stuck in the collar of his jacket. Whenever he felt happy he would prick a finger of his right hand and let the blood flow. More than a penitence for the sin of being alive, it was a homage to his dead" (Drummond, p. 16). Stela experiences survivor guilt differently. During the day, she feels resigned, passive: "Hitler is alive. Inside of me, Hitler is alive, because he did everything bad that ever happened to me" (Drummond, p. 48). At night, however, she dreams of self-destruction or of self-identification with Berlin on fire: "every night I dream that I am a building on fire . . . my hope was that Berlin be caught on fire . . . it has to be this way" (Drummond, p. 49). Fire would put an end to Stela's suffering, though it would destroy her beloved city.

Among all uncertainties, Drummond's survivors only know one reality: they cannot—and should never—forget, regardless of the consequences. "Certain things, you just can't forget, you can't anesthetize yourself" (Drummond, p. 48). Some renew their commitment to memory when shocked by reality. For example, toward the end of the novel, Cohen receives a letter from Germany. Anticipating a note from someone beloved, he finds a color photograph of Hitler, inscribed: "With my best regards, a hug from Adolf Hitler" (Drummond, p. 427). This message, sent by the Chain of Hitler's Friends, suggests that, despite the advent of democracy in former West Germany (1945) and Brazil (1983), evil still exists. Overcoming his panic, Cohen reminds himself to never forget and to be happy. He tears the photo and remembers that his sweetheart, Eva, is "immortal and that not even Hitler can kill her memory" (Drummond, p. 427).

Drummond's view of the Holocaust—an analogue of Brazilian dictatorship—is typical of Brazilian Holocaust/post-Holocaust literature. Brazilian reality is intermingled with, or rather, is indeed necessary to explain and finally help the survivors cope with survival and allow them to bear witness. Since some Nazis found refuge in Brazil, the duty of Holocaust survivors is then "never to be ashamed" of being Jewish but rather to remember, to bear witness, particularly in Brazil, where "Freedom, Justice, Brotherhood, Human Compassion, Love, [and a] rebel Dream" reign(ed) sublime (Drummond, p. 42).

Drummond's narrative method according to Luis Fernando Emediato is enriched not only by the gravitas of the subject matter but also by the use of stream of consciousness writing, the inclusion of poetry, the insertion of personal diary excerpts, and, most of all, the feeling that the readers are witnessing a story with a beginning, a middle, and almost an end. The novel consists of many sub-stories that help readers comprehend the historical events and eventually to recognize and fight evil. There is no end because the end is the present, it is action reinvigorated and freed by the memory of the past.

Hitler manda lembranças is an important contribution to the field of Brazilian letters; however, more important, it shows a dynamic and proactive response to genocide, one that falls within the parameters of all post-Holocaust and survival literatures. It represents the oppression associated with Hitler and Nazism and simultaneously portrays characteristics and features peculiar to Brazilian reality, reflecting a national collective consciousness against oppression, privileging freedom from any kind of dictatorship and physical and mental abuse. Brazilian "reality of authoritarianism," coupled with the events of the Holocaust and its aftermath, provide the "ready-made symbols and metaphors for a disquieting, absurd, and often irrational evil" (Vieira, "Hitler and Mengele in Brazil," p. 429). The human will to remember and the need to tell what happened, as well as the determination to continue, are therefore the best legacy that Holocaust survivors can bequeath to the new generation of the Diaspora.

Critical Reception

The critical reception of Drummond's work has been exceptionally favorable. Drummond has been recognized by both Jewish and non-Jewish critics in Brazil as well as worldwide. Nelson Vieira views Drummond's invectives against oppression "as a sociopolitical commentary on the effects of Brazil's former authoritarian regime" (Vieira, "Hitler and Mengele in Brazil," p. 429). Drummond succeeded in making those well-known icons of evil—Hitler and Mengele, as well as Nazism—as "blatant pop metaphors for the rampant evil in today's world," especially in Brazil (Vieira, "Hitler and Mengele in Brazil," p. 429). Similarly, Robert DiAntonio views these "pop fantasies" as a fictional device that delves into "the nature of evil in the post-Holocaust years" (DiAntonio, p. 878). Drummond calls for a reflection upon the consequences of evil rather than concentrating on the mere symbols of evil that in more modern times have become trivialized and devoid of any emotional feeling. Drummond's talent lies in exposing the Nazi genocide and the uncontested torture and sheer sadism and in making topics like repression and human subjugation accessible and understandable to a wider audience. Vieira contends, "With this novel, Drummond confirmed his artistic inventiveness as a sophisticated writer" (Vieira, " 'Closing the Gap' Between High and Low," p. 116).

Brazilian critics have often called Drummond's work(s) "pop" or "underground," both terms used interchangeably as synonyms for popular and challenging. Though easily understandable, Drummond's message subverts authoritarian claims. "Pop" or "underground" literature, as in the case of *Hitler manda lembranças*, is, for Drummond, a conduit to vent his social and ideological frustrations against the many faces of evil, which is oftentimes associated with a certain political system or administration. By bringing together the effects of the Holocaust and Brazilian dictatorship, Drummond is showing "how *any* authoritarian regime must be fought via knowledge and resistance" (Vieira, "Hitler and Mengele in Brazil," p. 437).

Bibliography

Primary Sources

"Ignácio de Loyola, ou quando um santo de casa não faz milagre" ("Ignatius of Loyola, or When a House Saint Does Not Perform a Miracle"). 1974.

A morte de D.J. em Paris (The Death of D.J. in Paris). 1975.

Isabel numa 5.ª feira (Isabel on a Thursday) in *Os melhares contos brasileiros de 1974* (The Best Brazilian Short Stories of 1974). 1975.

A outra margen (The Other Side). 1975.

"Vicissitudes vividas por um certo James Joyce" ("Vicissitudes Lived by a Certain James Joyce"). 1975.

O dia em que Ernest Hemingway morreu crucificado (The Day in Which Ernest Hemingway Died Crucified). 1978.

"Resposta à TFP literária" ("Response to the Literary TFP"). 1978.

Sangue de Coca-Cola (Blood of Coca-Cola). 1980.
Quando fui morto em Cuba (When I Was Killed in Cuba). 1982.
Hitler manda lembranças (Hitler Sends His Best Regards). 1985.
Ontem à noite era sexta-feira (Last Night Was Friday). 1988.
Hilda Furacão. 1991.
Inês é morta (Inês Is Dead). 1993.
O Cheiro de Deus (God's Smell). 2001.
Novel *Hilda Furacão* made into a prime-time soap opera for the television station Rede Globo.
Sports columnists for the *Jornal dos Sports*, the *Estado de Minas*, and *Manchete Esportiva*.
Presenter of a daily sports show on one of Brazil's national channels, TV Bandeirantes.
Various articles for *Nova, Placar, Ele e Ela, Status*, the *Suplemento de Cultura* of the *Jornal de São Paulo*, and *Doçura*.
Journalist for Belo Horizonte's dailies *Hoje em Dia* and the *Estado de Miras* (1968–2002).

Secondary Sources

Critical Response to Author's Works

Barbosa Filho, Hildebrando. "Uma narrativa do medo." *Minas Gerais, Suplemento Literário* (21 September 1986): 10.
Bulhões, Antonio, ed. *Os melhores contos brasileiros de 1974* (The Best Brazilian Short Stories of 1974). Pôrto Alegre: Editora Globo, 1975.
DiAntonio, Robert. "Redemption and Rebirth on a Safe Shore: The Holocaust in Contemporary Brazilian Fiction." *Hispania* 74(4): 876–882.
Emediato, Luís Fernando. "Roberto Drummond, desarmando os detratores." *Jornal da Tarde* (January 22, 1985): 5.
Foster, David, and Roberto Reis, eds. "Drummond, Roberto." In *A Dictionary of Contemporary Brazilian Authors*. Tempe: Center for Latin American Studies, Arizona State University, 1981.
Medina, Cremilda. "Roberto Drummond: De Radical 'Pop' à Serenidade Realista." *Minas Gerais, Suplemento Literário* (20 April 1985): 8.
Souza, Marco Antônio. "A escrita pessoalíssima de Roberto Drummond." *Minas Gerais, Suplemento Literário* (February 4, 1989): 13.
Stern Irwin, ed. "Drummond, Roberto." In *Dictionary of Brazilian Literature*. New York: Greenwood Press, 1988.
Stroun, Isabelle. *Roberto Drummond*. Paris: Éditions L'Harmattan, 1993.
Vieira, Luiz Gonzaga. "A propósito da literatura de Roberto Drummond." *Minas Gerais, Suplemento Literário* 26 (1992): 2–4.
Vieira, Nelson H. " 'Closing the Gap' Between High and Low: Intimations on the Brazilian Novel of the Future." *Latin American Literary Review* 20(40): 109–119.
———. "Hitler and Mengele in Brazil: The Testimony of Roberto Drummond." *Modern Fiction Studies* 32, no. 2 (1986): 427–438.
———. "Jewish Resistance and Resurgence as Literary Symbols and Metaphors for Brazilian Society and Politics." In *Proceedings of the Ninth World Congress of Jewish Studies, Jerusalem, August 4–12 1985*, Division B, vol. 3, *The History of the Jewish People (The Modern Times)*. Jerusalem: World Union of Jewish Studies, 1986.
———. "Judaic Fiction in Brazil: To Be and not to Be Jewish." *Latin American Literary Review* 14(28): 31–45.
———. "Post-Holocaust Literature in Brazil: Jewish Resistance and Resurgence as Literary Metaphors for Brazilian Society and Politics." *Modern Language Studies* 16, no. 1 (1986): 62–70.
———. "Bruxaria [Witchcraft] and Espiritismo [Spiritism]: Popular Culture and Popular Religion in Contemporary Brazilian Fiction." *Studies in Latin American Popular Culture* 15 (1996): 175–188.

Interviews

Ponce, J. A. de Granville, "Roberto Drummond." Roberto Drummond, *A morte de D.J. em Paris*, 1975. São Paulo: Ática, 1983.
Ribeiro, Rosângela, "Roberto Drummond de romance novo: 'Começou a valorização do autor brasileiro.' Roberto Drummond está com livro novo na praça: Ontem à noite era sexta-feira. 'Comparo esse livro ao pai que casou com outra mulher'." *Minas Gerais, Suplemento Literário* 1, no. 109 (5 November 1988): 1; 8–10.

ANNE DUDEN

(1942–)

HARTMUT STEINECKE
(Translated by Della Couling)

ANNE DUDEN DID not experience the Holocaust as a contemporary and she is not Jewish. But she has contributed to German-language Holocaust literature to an extent matched by scarcely any other non-Jewish German writer of her generation: not through dealing in literary form with aspects of the actual persecution and murder of Jews, but through a penetrating understanding of the consequences for life in the country of the perpetrators and in a world in which violence and murder on this scale were possible and perhaps could even be possible again.

In the story "Transition" in her first book, *Opening of the Mouth* (1985), she wrote: "I saw the shovelling away of mountains of corpses in *Night and Fog*, the film by Alain Resnais and knew, if that has happened once, it can happen again at any time, in fact to anyone." (translated by Della Couling, London and Sydney: Pluto Press, 1985, pp. 64–65). In a conversation in 1996 Duden alluded to the autobiographical origins of this traumatic obsession: "For me, those piles of corpses became from that moment on the measure of the human body. Whenever afterwards I saw a naked body, I thought first of those bodies." Since then for her "partly only in shock-like flashes, partly as a creeping process," Germany has come to be conceived as "hunter's lair and murderers' den; bombsite and mountain of rubble, control centre and mass grave" (*Zungengewahrsam. Kleine Schriften zur Poetik und zur Kunst.* Koln: Kiepenheuer and Witsch, 1999, p. 26).

Duden was born on 1 January 1942 in Oldenburg, spent her childhood in Berlin and in the German Democratic Republic (GDR), and in 1953 fled with her mother to the Federal Republic of Germany (West Germany). From 1962 she lived, studied, and worked in publishing in West Berlin. Like many others of her generation, since the time of the student revolts of 1968 she has occupied herself intensively with the German history that most older Germans have repressed. Very early on Duden started to write, but only after she went to London in 1978, where she has since made her home, did she publish her first works—with the encouragement of Austrian-Jewish author Erich Fried.

Das Judasschaf: "Slaughterhouse" Germany

In her book *Das Judasschaf* (1985), Duden gives the main character her own date of birth, which becomes the starting point for dealing with the Holocaust: "Nineteen days after her birth, in the same place, the resolution was drawn up during a conference to eliminate eleven million people. . . . It was her raw brain, which had now for over twenty years been living in a slaughterhouse. More precisely, it was sticking on the ceiling there. Cold air and draughts were the worst, but noise too contributed to the gradual derangement" (Berlin: Rotbuch, 1985, pp. 38–39).

For Duden, the Wannsee conference became the key to her view of history and an essential trigger for her writing: at the core of the texts stands the question of how one can continue to live after the *Shoah* and with an awareness of it, in the midst of repressions and scraps of memory, images of violence, and nightmare. Violence dominates history, is quite concretely experienced in many of Duden's texts, and is metaphorically written onto the body. Between life and death—"not-living and not being-able to die"—"something else" is released: The body, site of violence, of memory, also becomes "the battleground for writing" (Kramatschek, p. 23).

The body as site of memory becomes at the same time the place in which language arises anew. For the main character in *Das Judasschaf*, who is referred to alternately as "I," "she," and "the person," the areas of inner and outer, of one's own body and the outside world, merge with one another like those of present and past. Memories, dreams, historical documents, descriptions of old paintings overlay one another; the "I" dissolves, fails to find an identity. The title metaphor of *Das Judasschaf* reflects this ambiguity. It is an actual creature from the context of the slaughterhouse ("*Judasschaf*" was the term for the sheep that led an arriving flock up to the door of the slaughterhouse), and at the same time a metaphor; it links the victimizer and the victim in one term. Alexander von Bormann summarizes this indissoluble dialectic: "The book is not a historical study on the holocaust, its presuppositions and implications, but is based on the intertwining of the aspects of perpetrator/victim, as might be experienced for those born directly during it and just after it, or—much more profoundly—might not be experienced" (von Bormann, p. 263).

This ongoing ambivalence is summarized by her penetrating analysis of Vittore Carpaccio's *The Dead Christ*: the dead man, "a man hanged, pierced, stabbed," his head—soon "to be indistinguishable from the four skulls under the table—skin-, hair- and fleshless component," next to it "bones, animal and human skulls . . . half-decomposed flesh just held together by skin" (p. 119). Signs of violence dominate, as in early history so too in older art—the description and the book end with the sentence: "It is beautiful and I am afraid" (p. 125). A main problem for any literary writing after and on the Holocaust, for Duden as for many other Germans, is the use of the language in which mass murder was ordered, organized, administered, and recorded. She makes the subject come graphically alive by introducing into the text of *Das Judasschaf* long quotations from the actual words of Himmler and the Auschwitz commandant, Rudolf Hoess, or from documents contained in the catalogue *Dachau Concentration Camp 1933–1945* (1978), a circular to the "commandants of concentration camps": "Re: utilization of cut off hair" and a report on "Experiments in warming up chilled humans" (*Konzentrations lager Dachau 1933–1945*, edited by Comité International de Dachau, 1978, p. 127). It is significant that the only direct images of the Holocaust occur in the form of quotations, for Duden's approach is not to depict the concentration camps, the sites of the murders, the fates of individuals, and identification with the victims. She writes with the consciousness of belonging to the perpetrating nation. From a distance in time she shows the continued violence whose origin in the Holocaust is, however, constantly recalled—if only with a single word ("extermination"). Hence her works do not fall under the broad category of "memory culture" and the moralizing phrase "Never again!"

A New Language: "Barrage of the Unbearable"

For her own aesthetic access Duden seeks out a new language that not only distances itself from the deformed language of National Socialism but also from what has meanwhile become the largely ritualized language of Holocaust discourse in Germany. She describes this process later in her poetry lectures *Zungengewahrsam*: "The mother tongue exposed the fatherland, by distancing itself from it, separating from it. The language went into the tongue, to become writing" (pp. 25–26). Duden's long-lasting distancing of herself from German-speaking regions has served to render her sensitivity to the German language more acute: both to the historical problems of the language as a whole and to hidden etymologies and daily usage. The poems, prose, and essays written during the 1990s show a radicalism in images and word construction seldom met with in the German language, the reduction of syntax to its most essential. Words are examined regarding their origin and components, sounded for subtones and associations. Parts of words are combined to form previously unknown, unheard, often unheard-of forms. Such "end- and bound-less labour of perception" leads to a "barrage of the unbearable" (*Wimpertier*, Koln: Kiepenheuer and Witsch, 1995, p. 113). In many of these texts—above all, the poems—pain, torture, blood, violence, and murder are dealt with; images of tortures and murders in the annihilation camps remain leitmotifs:

> No path leads past the labour camp
> and only once per shift may the latrine be used.
> . . .
> Words curl inwards
> and are stuck crouching in the dead
> in the wake of such a night
> ("Rockfall," translated by Elsie Callander, in "Introducing Anne Duden," *In Other Words*, no. 6, 1995, pp. 28–29).

Images of a history of violence are inscribed in every present; the name of a concentration camp becomes the cipher of their origin:

> Only those with unscathed bones
> the residents
> get their resurrection
> on fringed country roads
> in Esterwegen for example
> noon

and again only striated cloud
and a few orders to fire.
("Trifolium Tetrachord," in *Steinschlag,* Koln: Kiepenheuer and Witsch, 1993, p. 51).

The concrete words garnered from reality penetrate ever more tellingly in more general contexts: they capture the impossibility and the paradox of still living and writing after such a violation of history, which was of course also a violation of culture.

Duden's work is regarded as difficult; its readership is limited, and the difficulty in translating it has until now hampered international impact. Literary criticism and literature studies have, however, increasingly recognized its importance and originality. Duden has consequently won a number of important literary prizes. They are in homage to an oeuvre that again and again undertakes the attempt to tackle the fundamental problems of present-day existence—among them the violence of man against man, which culminated in the Holocaust—in a new aesthetic of perception, expressed in a personal, suggestive language.

Bibliography

Primary Sources

Übergang (Opening of the Mouth). 1982.
Das Judasschaf (The Judassheep). 1985.
Steinschlag (Rockfall). 1993.
Der wunde Punkt im Alphabet. 1995.
Wimpertier. 1995.
Zungengewahrsam. Kleine Schriften zur Poetik und zur Kunst. 1999.
Hingegend. Gedichte. 1999.

Secondary Sources

Bird, Stephanie. "Desire and Complicity in Anne Duden's Das Judasschaf." *Modern Language Review* 93 (1998): 741–753.

Von Bormann, Alexander. " 'Besetzt war sie, durch und durch'. Traumatisierung im Werk von Anne Duden." *Deutsche Nachkriegsliteratur und der Holocaust.* Edited by Stephan Braese et al. Frankfurt: Campus, 1998, pp. 245–267.

Briegleb, Klaus. "Negative Symbiose." *Gegenwartsliteratur seit 1968.* Edited by K. B. Weigel and Sigrid Weigel. Munich: Hanser, 1992, pp. 117–150.

Steinecke, Hartmut. "Green Man, Hydra und Dichtung. Anne Dudens Kunst der Wahrnehmung." *Bayerische Akademie der Schönen Künste. Jahrbuch 14*, vol. 2. Donauwörth, Germany: Oreos, 2000, pp. 725–733.

Weigel, Sigrid. *Bilder des kulturellen Gedächtnisses. Beiträge zur Gegenwartsliteratur.* Dülmen-Hiddingsel: Tende, 1994.

Interviews

Interviews by Anne Duden and Sigrid Weigel. "Schrei und Körper—Zum Verhältnis von Bildern und Schrift. Ein Gespräch über *Das Judasschaf,*" *Laokoon und kein Ende: Der Wettstreit der Künste.* Edited by Thomas Koebner. Munich: 1989: edition text + kritik, 1989, pp. 120–148.

Interview by Claudia Kramatschek. "Gespräch mit Anne Duden. In den Faltungen der Sprache." *Neue deutsche Literatur* 2000, no. 2, pp. 32–44.

Interview by Martin Lengwiler. "Das Gedächtnis des Körpers ist die Kunst." *Neue Zürcher Zeitung*, October 29, 1996.

GERHARD DURLACHER

(1928–1996)

DICK VAN GALEN LAST

GERHARD LEOPOLD DURLACHER was born on 10 July 1928 in Baden-Baden, Germany, the only son of liberal Jewish parents, Arthur Joseph and Erna Sofia Solomonica Durlacher. In 1937 the Durlachers fled to take refuge with family in Holland, and they established themselves in Rotterdam, where Arthur was offered a job as a sales representative. When the Germans bombed Rotterdam on 14 May 1940, the family moved to the city of Apeldoorn. In October 1942, they were arrested and deported to Westerbork. Gerhard Durlacher arrived in Theresienstadt in January 1944 but was moved to Auschwitz in May of the same year. The Red Army liberated him at Gross-Rosen on 8 May 1945. When he returned to Holland he discovered that his entire family had perished in the death camps. He stayed with an aunt, who told him to forget about his camp experiences. Later he wrote about this period: he was seventeen years old, "without a profession, and without an education. The camps were a training camp for dying, not for living" (*Quarantaine, Verhalen*, Amsterdam: Meulenhoff, 1993, p. 87). Everything had to start all over again.

After studying medicine in Utrecht, the Netherlands, for some years, he studied sociology in Amsterdam. He married and had three children. From 1964 to 1983 he was a researcher at the Sociological Institute of the University of Amsterdam. It was only in 1983 that Durlacher started collecting documentation about the survivors of the Holocaust and began publishing regularly on this topic in *De gids*. In 1991 he published a collection of this material under the title *De zoektocht* (*The Search*), and the book became the basis of a documentary by the Dutch filmmaker Cherry Duyns, whose film *Laatste getuigen* (Last Witnesses, 1991) follows Durlacher's journey to meet his fellow camp inmates, a journey that concludes with their reunion in Israel. In 1994 Durlacher received the Anne Frank Award for his 1987 book *Drenkeling* (*Drowning*) and the AKO Literary Award for his 1993 book *Quarantaine*. In 1995, he received an honorary doctorate in the social sciences from the University of Amsterdam. His work has been translated into German, English, and Italian. He died on 2 July 1996 in Haarlem; his collected writing was published posthumously, in 1997.

Writing After Auschwitz

By the end of the twentieth century, the Holocaust was regarded as pertinent to almost every disturbing contemporary event—ethnic cleansing, the refugee problem, and the daily toll of human rights violations throughout the world. But it was not until after the end of the Cold War, which had created growing interest in human and civil rights and in international law, that public attention focused on the Holocaust in a way that caused a greatly increased sensitivity toward the victims. Haunted by "scorching emotions" himself, Durlacher played an inestimable role in the process of bringing the Holocaust into public consciousness in the Netherlands.

Writing, though, did not extinguish Durlacher's own grief: "One can not console the inconsolable, one can not beseech what can not be beseeched." Writing for him had the function that it relieved, as he once said, the hard disk of his personal computer, his memory: "I put my memories on a floppy, to relieve my memory." He wrote his memoirs as accurately as possible, checking every detail, and he mistrusted literary pretensions, as if one could not read a literary text also as a document. Often he felt uneasy when people praised his books for their literary qualities, because he found it hard to associate literature with war and persecution. At this time he disagreed with Sem Dresden in his 1991 study *Persecution, Extermination, Literature*. Rather, Durlacher shares the discomfort expressed by Theodor Adorno about the propriety of aesthetic representations in Holocaust writing, namely, the limitations one confronts in writing about Auschwitz after Auschwitz. For example, in *Niet verstaan* (Not Understanding, 1995) Durlacher writes that he will never be able to describe the transports in the cattle cars to Auschwitz, because of the inadequacy of language. The idea that someone who had never been in such a cattle car would attempt to write about it would have shocked him. Only at the end of his life did Durlacher start to write fiction, but death prevented him from finishing the novel he had started.

Breaking the Silence: Durlacher's Work

It took Durlacher almost forty years to break his silence and give up "the suppression of the unsuppressable past." As a sociologist Durlacher had always been especially conscious of the fact that poverty, hunger, and disasters had resulted in the excesses of fascism, nazism, and terrorism. Anxious to understand the entire social and political backdrop of his experience during the Holocaust, he undertook a great deal of research before writing each of his five small autobiographical books: *Strepen aan de hemel: Oorlogsherinneringen* (*Stripes in the Sky*, 1985), *Drenkeling: Kinderjaren in het Derde Rijk* (*Drowning: Growing Up in the Third Reich*, 1987), *De zoektocht* (*The Search: The Birkenau Boys*, 1991), *Quarantaine* (Quarantaine, 1993), and *Niet verstaan* (Not Understanding, 1995).

Stripes in the Sky refers to "the white stripes of hope" that were drawn by the Allied airplanes in the sky above Auschwitz in 1944. Durlacher and the other camp inmates saw the Allied bombers appear above Birkenau, but only on their way to industrial targets. "The feeling that the world more or less discreetly turns the other way or watches unmoved while hundreds of thousands of people are systematically being killed all around you, and that you yourself know that every day you are still alive is a cruel trick of fate, is something that cannot adequately be expressed in words" (p. 24). Before he wrote these lines, Durlacher had done thorough research regarding the passive attitude of the Allies, which has not only been attributed to incomprehension and indifference but also to traditional antisemitism.

In *Stripes in the Sky*, Durlacher describes his journey from Westerbork to Theresienstadt and, finally, Auschwitz. He writes about the Nazi propaganda movie made in Theresienstadt, *Der Führer schenkt den Juden eine Stadt* (The Führer Gives the Jews a City), which he calls a "cynical comedy." The movie was never officially released, although it was shown by the SS to visiting members of rescue committees in early April 1945. Durlacher comments:

> During the weeks of the filming, between 16 August and 11 September 1944, Theresienstadt was a grotesque movie studio with spectators in black uniforms and caps with death head insignias commanding the movie-makers and actors and admonishing them to remember their mortality. The priviliged artists believed themselves safe and indispensable. For two weeks, the black uniformed illusionists of mercy kept the fantasy alive by granting gifts and favours. In the weeks between 28 September and 28 October 1944, 17,520 film-makers, actors and extras journeyed to the terminus that was Auschwitz. Only 1,496 returned (p. 69).

Upon his arrival in Auschwitz, Durlacher was assigned to stay in the Männerlage Birkenau B II D, in front of the Rampe where the selections took place and where Josef Mengele decided over life and death: "With every rejection, I stand straighter, my fists at my side, my head made of granite" (p. 56). The fourteen-year-old Durlacher survived Mengele's selections together with eighty-eight other boys between the ages of thirteen and sixteen.

Like Robert Antelme (L'espèce humaine) and Primo Levi (Se questo è un uomo), Durlacher gives a precise description of the different stages of dehumanization that the SS imposed upon the Jews. After registration and the tattooing of a number on their left arm ("Every prick burns in our brains, and, woe be unto him who does not know his new 'name' perfectly," p. 58), the prisoners undergo one more moment of degradation: the shaving.

> The razor scrapes cruelly across my lower abdomen. Our pubic hair and the hair from the heads of some of the boys falls to the floor. On a sign on the wall, I read: "Eine Laus, dein Tod" (A louse means your death). Our shame dies. Even the order "Bücken und Arsch hoch" (Bend over with your ass in the air) doesn't matter any more. Only the fear of pain remains. We enter the showers and hear the bath Kapos utter their crude jokes about gas or our physiques (pp. 57–58).

Durlacher remembered how, just before the liberation of the camp, he ate rations that were meant for others who had no use for them anymore:

> . . . when a disembodied hand proffers a piece of bread, I take my neighbour's portion as well, for he's gone to a place where food doesn't count anymore. From the land of the dead, he saves my life. I play this game of resurrection two or three times, but when only a few of my companions in the lower bunks are still alive, I flee this underworld, and with my last ounce of strength I hoist my lice-infected and scabies-ridden body to the upper bunk (p. 74).

Durlacher differed from another inmate of Auschwitz, Primo Levi, in that he never saw life in the camp as a war of all against all. He preferred to remember the spirit of sacrifice: "at the nadir of every civilization," he wrote, "a residue of decency is left" (Interview, *NRC-Handelsblad*, 30 April 1991). But even he was forced to admit that under these extreme circumstances only very few stayed human like the anonymous Peter, whom he met at Auschwitz, who could recite Schiller's *The Robbers* from memory.

In *Drowning*, Durlacher describes how the noose around the neck of the Jews was gradually tightened in a little town in Nazi Germany where he grew up. The great events are described from the perspective of a child—as in Jona Oberski's *Childhood*—so that the brutal violence of the persecution remains in the background without being understood. It is through the eyes of the small Gerhard that one learns what it meant to be a Jewish boy in a school where the rest of the class, former friends, suddenly became hostile, because he did not belong to the "superior" Aryan race.

Quarantaine starts where *Stripes* ends: Durlacher's return home. But home is not his home anymore after his parents have perished. Unlike Primo Levi, who wrote in *The Truce* about "the liberating joy of recounting my story," Durlacher had quite different experiences when he returned to Holland in the summer of 1945: "Highly principled friends of my parents and neighbours, some decent and some not, each had their story of the hardships of the occupation, which made me choke back the unspeakable. I was the near stranger who had to listen to everything that everyone else had heard over and over again, and I bought acceptance with my willing ear and discrete silence" (*Quarantaine. Verhalen*, Amsterdam: Meulenhoff, 1993, p. 127). In the Netherlands, camp survivors had to listen to long stories about the hunger winter of 1944–1945 or about German "atrocities" ("Do you know what happened to me? Germans stole my bicycle"). Incomprehension and, worse, denial made it painfully clear to the returned Jews that they could not take their presence in the Netherlands after liberation for granted. Durlacher once despaired that his returning home was even worse than his experience in the concentration camps.

In one of the stories in *Quarantaine*, Durlacher recalls what happened to him when he discovered a picture of his father one day in a photograph album of Westerbork: "Half of a century shrivelled up to half a second. With a magnifying glass I look at my father and I realize that at that time he was only forty-one years old . . . the memory of my childhood that was overshadowed by his harsh regime, all of a sudden looses its sharp contours. I realize the relativeness of the sorrow of my youth and I feel resignation. Pity takes the place of resentment" (p. 46). This absence of resentment is a characteristic feature of Durlacher's writing. Durlacher's autobiographical recollections of the Holocaust instead reflect his desire (as one Dutch critic said in summarizing Durclacher's work and life) "to record, to understand, to hand on."

Bibliography

Primary Sources

De laaqstbetaalden (The Lowest Paid). 1965.

Strepen aan de hemel: Oorlogsherinneringen (*Stripes in the Sky*). 1985.

"A Comment on the Speakers from Israel." 1987.

Drenkeling: Kinderjaren in het Derde Rijk (*Drowning: Growing Up in the Third Reich*). 1987.

De zoektocht (*The Search: The Birkenau Boys*). 1991.

Quarantaine (Quarantaine). 1993.

Niet verstaan (Not Understanding). 1995.

Verzameld Werk (Complete Works). 1997.

Met haat valt niet te leven: Krantestukken door G. L. Durlacher & Gesprekken met G. L. Durlacher door Ageeth Scherphuis, Adriaan van Dis e.v.a. (One Can Not Live with Hatred. Newspaper articles by G. L. Durlacher & Conversations with G. L. Durlacher by Ageeth Scherphuis, Adriaan van Dis a.o.). 1998.

Secondary Sources

Dresden, Sem. *Vervolging, Vernietiging, Literatuur* (*Persecution, Extermination, Literature*). Amsterdam: Meulenhoff, 1991.

Galen Last, Dick van, and Rolf Wolfswinkel. *Anne Frank and After: Dutch Holocaust Literature in Historical Perspective*. Amsterdam: Amsterdam University Press, 1996.

MAREK EDELMAN

(1921–)

KATARZYNA ZECHENTER

MAREK EDELMAN, THE only surviving commander of the Warsaw Ghetto Uprising of 1943, was born in Warsaw on 1 January 1921 (or 1919). His mother, Cecylia, and father, Natan, came from Homle (Gomel, today in Byelorussia). Marek had an older brother who died before he was born. His father died in 1924 or 1926, his mother most probably in 1934. Eventually Edelman was raised by his mother's friends from the BUND (General Jewish Workers Union of Poland). He attended high school in Warsaw, and after the beginning of World War II, began to work as a messenger in a pediatric hospital. He was a member of the BUND, and after November 1939 was engaged in the production of underground publications, including the monthly publications *Za wasza i nasza wolność* (For Your and Our Freedom) and *Yugnt Shtime* (The Voice of Youth), the weekly *Der Werker* (The Worker), and the political magazine *Tsait Fragn* (Problems of the Times). From 1941 to 1943, he was a member of the BUND's first resistance unit in the Warsaw ghetto, kept contact with the Polish underground army, and sent reports about the extradition of the Jews from the Warsaw ghetto and the first resistance actions of the ŻOB (Jewish Fighting Organization).

Edelman and the Resistance

The ŻOB started an uprising in the Warsaw ghetto after 400,000 Jews were deported and only 60,000 people remained at the beginning of 1943. Edelman became a deputy commander and was active in the resistance from the beginning of the uprising on 19 April 1943 (he was responsible for Toebbens' Sheds and the Brush Factory region). After the suicide death of the leader of the uprising, Mordchai Anielewicz, on 8 May 1943, Edelman became the last commander. After the uprising was suppressed, Edelman, assisted by the Polish underground, escaped through the sewers to the center of Warsaw, where one year later he fought in the Warsaw Uprising (1 August 1944 to 2 October 1944). Although considered a hero after the war both in Poland and abroad, Edelman remained silent about his experiences with the exception of publishing *Getto walczy* (*The Ghetto Fights*) in 1945 in Warsaw.

After the war, Edelman married Alina Margolis, a courier for the BUND and Polish underground nurse, whom he met during the uprising in 1944. They have two children, Anna and Aleksander. He began to work in the Pirogow's Hospital in Łódź, where he became a distinguished cardiologist and authored a book on cardiac arrest. Despite the antisemitic campaign of the communist government in 1968, Edelman decided to remain in Poland so "the official powers would have someone to be ashamed of."

Since 1976 he has actively participated in the creation of the Committee of the Defense of Workers (KOR) and later the independent workers' union, Solidarity, which eventually led to the fall of Communism in Poland. He was one of 101 intellectuals who, in 1976, signed a letter of protest against the changes in the Polish constitution forced by the Communist government, which would have formally stated Poland's political subordination to the Soviet Union. In 1981 he became a Solidarity delegate to the government and was interned (1981 to 1982) after the imposition of marshal law on 13 December 1981. After his release, Edelman began working in the underground Solidarity Union. Because the authorities were afraid to arrest him as he was widely recognized as the symbol of Jewish heroism during World War II, they tried to force him into early retirement. This generated protests, both in Poland and abroad (especially in France), and Edelman remained at his post. After Poland regained independence, Edelman became the chairman of the Social Committee on Minorities in Poland (1988 to 1990). On 17 April 1998, Edelman was decorated with Poland's highest honor: the Order of the White Eagle. He received honorary doctorates from Yale University and Université Libre in Brussels. He is still politically active, and has written open letters to Presidents Clinton and Chirac seeking help for persecuted nations, including Kosovo.

The Ghetto Fights

Although Edelman is the author of only one short Holocaust book, *The Ghetto Fights*, several books and films, as well as a play, are devoted to him. In 1977, Hanna Krall, a journalist and herself a Holocaust survivor, conducted a series of interviews with Edelman that later led to her book *Zdążyć przed panem Bogiem (Shielding the Flame: An Intimate Conversation with Dr. Marek Edelman, the Last Surviving Leader of the Warsaw Ghetto Uprising)*. A year later, Krall produced a documentary drama, *To Steal a March on God*, based on interviews with Edelman and his book, *The Ghetto Fights*. In 1999, Rudi Assuntino and Włodek Goldkom published a book based on talks with Edelman titled *The Guardian: Marek Edelman Talks*, in which Edelman discusses his youth, work in the ghetto, and the Warsaw Ghetto Uprising.

The Ghetto Fights: The Participation of BUND in the Defense of the Warsaw Ghetto was originally published in Poland in 1945 and one year later in New York by the BUND. It was republished in 1983 for the fortieth anniversary of the uprising and translated into English in 1990. Edelman's book, or rather booklet, for it contains only sixty-seven small-format pages, was introduced by respected Polish writer Zofia Nalkowska. According to Nałkowska, Edelman's work accomplishes what many masterpieces fail to achieve: it documents the collective suffering of a nation without escaping into pathos. John Rose, the translator of Edelman's book into English, praises Edelman's work in a similar manner and does not hesitate to call it "brilliant" (Introduction to *The Ghetto Fights*, 1990, p. 11). Lucidity is one of the major assets of Edelman's extraordinary account not only of the ghetto uprising, but also of the social, moral, and human causes leading to it.

More importantly, however, Edelman's book is the first account of the uprising published almost immediately after the end of World War II, and as such it documents the emotions prevalent in the ŻOB that were responsible for its decision to begin desperate struggle in spring of 1943. Edelman dedicated his account to the memory of Abrasza Blum, the "ideological father of armed resistance" (p. 85), who was killed on 3 May 1943, fighting the Germans without a weapon. This reflects both the sentiment of Edelman's work and that of the ŻOB: pronouncements that the only way of acting toward Germans in occupied Poland was to undertake intense resistance "before being led to death" (p. 43) and "that always, under all circumstances, one should oppose Germans" (p. 70).

Edelman's account is written from the perspective of one of the soldiers of the Warsaw Ghetto Uprising rather than one of its leaders. He barely mentions his own role, although he mentions his duties and refers to himself in the third-person singular, believing, as he said many years later, that "it is not important who was shooting and where"; he prefers to "be a witness to certain values" (Assuntino and Goldkom, p. 88). He begins his account with a description of the situation of the Warsaw Jews after the city fell to the German army in September 1939. He stresses the feeling of being lost and the fear of the Jewish population as a result of its gradual isolation from the general Polish population through the erection of the wall separating the "Aryan" side from the ghetto in November 1940. Edelman documents the general mood after the introduction of collective punishment in early November 1939, when "the fear of the Germans took on unequaled forms" (p. 36), as well as the growing difficulty in surviving the hunger and deteriorating sanitary conditions due to the persistent addition of large Jewish populations (deported from villages and towns) to the ghetto. Special attention is paid to the role of fear, especially that of starvation, which, according to him, prevented the general population from believing the news that so-called deportations to the east were, in fact, mass slaughters—"why would they be giving bread away if they intended to murder them? . . ." (p. 58). He carefully documents the desperate efforts of the ŻOB to convince the ghetto population of the ruse, including sending Zalmen (Zygmunt) Frydrych to the death camp in Treblinka, who returned to deliver an eyewitness account later published in the magazine *Ojf der Wach* (On Guard). The often-repeated phrase, sometimes accentuated by the usage of bold type, "the Ghetto does not believe" (pp. 43, 50, 57), emphasizes the desperation of Edelman and the ŻOB fighters at their inability to convince the population about the true nature of deportations and the need for action. It is from this point of view that Edelman condemns the death of Adam Czerniakow, the head of the Judenrat (Council of Jewish Elders), who, realizing the approaching fate of the Warsaw ghetto, decided to commit suicide:

at the time, however, we thought that he had no right to act as he did. We thought that since he was the only person in the ghetto whose voice carried a great deal of authority, it was his duty to inform the entire population of the real state of affairs, and also to dissolve all public institutions (p. 56).

He presents the gradual change in the ghetto's attitude toward the ŻOB, beginning with the first street battle on 18 January 1943, when "for the first time the Jew in the street realized that it was possible to do something against the Germans' will and power" (p. 71) and "when the entire Polish Underground was full of praise for us" (p. 71), which resulted in receiving fifty large pistols from the Home Army Command. From this point of view, Edelman presents the ghetto uprising as a desperate act of choosing one's way of dying, an attitude stemming from the romantic belief in value of heroic death and dying "honorably" (p. 69), which had earlier prompted the ŻOB to feel "ashamed of the Chelmno Jews' submissiveness, of their failure to rise in their own defense" (p. 43). In this context, *The Ghetto Fights* is an essential account of the mood prevalent in the Warsaw ghetto and in the ŻOB before the uprising, as well as documentation of the heroic struggle of those who "had done their duty to the end" and, most importantly, an attempt "to keep them alive—forever" (p. 87).

Bibliography

Primary Source

Edelman, Marek. *Getto walczy. Udzial Bundu w obronie getta warszawskiego* (*The Ghetto Fights: The Participation of BUND in the Defense of the Warsaw Ghetto*). 1945, 1946, 1983, 1990.

Secondary Sources

Assuntino, Rudi, and Wlodek Goldkom. *Strażnik. Marek Edelman opowiada*. Kraków: Znak, 1999.

Bartoszewski, Władysław. *Polish-Jewish Relations in Occupied Poland, 1939–1945. The Jews in Poland*. Edited by C. Abramsky, M. Jachimczyk, and A. Polonsky. Oxford: Basil Blackwell, 1986, pp. 147–160.

———. *The Warsaw Ghetto. A Christian's Testimony*. Translated by S. G. Cappellari. London: Lamp Press, 1987.

Grupińska, Anka. *Ciagle po kole. Rozmowy z żolnierzami getta warszawskiego*. Kraków: Twój Styl, 2000.

Gutman, Yisrael. *The Jews of Warsaw, 1939–1943: Ghetto, Underground, Revolt*. Bloomington, 1982.

Karski, Jan. *Story of a Secret State*. Boston: Houghton Mifflin, 1944.

Korboński, Stefan. *The Jew and the Poles in World War II*. New York, 1989.

Krall, Hanna. *Shielding the Flame: An Intimate Conversation with Dr. Marek Edelman, the Last Surviving Leader of the Warsaw Ghetto Uprising*. Translated by J. Stasińska and L. Wechsler. New York: Henry Holt, 1986.

———. *To Steal a March on God*. Translated by Jadwiga Kosicka. Amsterdam: Harwood Academic Publishers, 1996.

Ringelblum, Emmanuel. *Notes from the Warsaw Ghetto: The Journal of the Warsaw Ghetto*. Edited and translated by J. Sloan. New York: Schocken, 1974.

———. *To Live with Honor and Die with Honor! . . . Selected Documents from the Warsaw Ghetto Underground Archives*. Edited and annotated by J. Kermish. Jerusalem: Yad Vashem, 1986.

Rotem, Simha (Kazik). *Memoirs of a Warsaw Ghetto Fighter*. Translated by B. Harshav. New Haven: Yale University Press, 1994.

Stroop, Jurgen. *The Stroop Report: The Jewish Quarter Is No More*. Translated by S. Morton. New York: Pantheon, 1979.

Szczęsna, Joanna. *An Interview with Dr. Marek Edelman. Magazyn: A supplement to Gazeta Wyborcza*, 22 April 1999.

Zuckerman, Yitzak (Antek). *A Surplus of Memory. Chronicle of the Warsaw Ghetto Uprising*. Translated by B. Harshav. Berkeley: University of Califonia Press, 1993.

Films

Edelman, Marek. *Memory*. Interview with Simon Wiesenthal and members of the ŻOB who took part in the uprising. Documentary footage and photographs. English narration. Film Unit TOR, 1992.

Chronicle of the Warsaw Ghetto Uprising According to Marek Edelman. Dir. Jolanta Dylewska. Nazi footage and Edelman's recollection. Poland, 1993.

YEHUDA ELBERG

(1912–)

ESTHER FRANK

YEHUDA ELBERG WAS born into a prestigious rabbinic family on 15 May 1912 in Zgierz, Poland. His father, Abraham Nathan Elberg, was rabbi in Zgierz when Yehuda was born and later in Sonik and Blashki, towns where Yehuda grew up and was educated. Yehuda's maternal grandfather, Tsvi Yekheskal Mikhelson, was an important rabbi in Warsaw and was widely regarded for his scholarship in rabbinic and Hasidic texts. Elberg emphasizes that this background was influential in his formation as a writer. In his view, his upbringing represents the "truth" about the vanished life in Poland, and this truth is what he loves as a writer. Retrospectively, it seems clear that throughout his long career, Elberg's heritage shaped his imaginative vision and gave him the cultural confidence to continue as a Yiddish writer. In spite of the discontinuities in his life, he found in the spirituality of his background a psychological and moral focus for his work.

Life and Career

Elberg was educated in the most traditional Jewish institutions. He attended a *kheder* at the age of three; he later studied at the Yeshiva in Warsaw, where his grandfather was rabbi, and was himself ordained as rabbi in his teens. He was also attracted to secular learning. Access to a large library in the home of a very learned Zionist *maskil* (progressive scholar) changed the young Elberg. In his late teens he turned from his calling as a rabbi to a career as a writer. Elberg wanted to bring his worlds together in his writing, and in order to do so he chose to write in Yiddish, which was rich in the idioms of the culture. Spoken by his ancestors, it was the language of sermons and traditions, of world literature, and of a growing literary tradition.

In the 1930s Elberg left home in search of work and of a literary milieu. Modern Yiddish literature had, by this time, developed strong literary centers in Warsaw and Lodz, where writers experimented with various literary subject matter and styles, and demonstrated the resourcefulness of Yiddish as a literary language. Elberg chose to settle in Lodz. He quickly became a textile engineer and worked at writing Hasidic tales, a genre familiar from his youth. Elberg did not publish these tales but returned to this form when he was in his eighties. Elberg's return to earlier forms and tried themes became a pattern in his postwar writings. They provided him with the resources he required for his writing and gave him the opportunity to preserve the world he had lost.

Elberg appeared in print for the first time in 1932. "Ber Lep" was published in the newspaper *Lodz Folks Blat*. Impressed with the type of character Elberg created, critics praised his skills in presenting the "*proster yid*" (common Jew, known in Jewish society for his lack of religious learning and piety), and noted his ability to portray crudeness in combination with sensitivity and refinement. "Ber Lep" won Elberg acclaim as a writer. Elberg had found a focus in his fiction for his interest in depicting the strength of the ordinary Jew. He developed his skills at character portrayal by making the instinctual the key to character, and infused it with value to show that crudeness in human nature could become a source of ethical responsibility in a social world in the process of becoming unmoored. For example, Elberg shows in "Ber Lep" that the main character's vulgarity is a life-giving force under conditions of duress. Looking back on Elberg's literary output, Yiddish critics saw "Ber Lep" as a precursor to his postwar writings. N. B. Minkoff noted that Elberg's choice of narrative style provided the foundation for his later exploration of the brutish aspects of human nature and the dissolution of Jewish life.

In 1940, under Nazi occupation, conditions in Lodz worsened. Elberg moved to Warsaw, married, and became more involved with Zionist activities. That year Elberg and his family were forced to live in the Warsaw ghetto, where his wife eventually perished. While some Yiddish writers produced in the ghetto, Elberg wrote only sporadically. In 1942 he left the ghetto and went underground. He lived in hiding with a Polish couple, smuggled goods in and out of the ghetto, and saw events and acts that fueled his postwar fiction. His postwar writing is closely fashioned on actual events, fiction in which his characters exhibit the instinctual and psychological aspects of human nature; his complicated plots involve the collapse of a multileveled but coherent world.

Elberg survived the war by remaining underground, living in various places in Europe until 1945. After the war, he devoted all his energies to restoring Jewish life. In Lublin he organized the first Yiddish Committee; in Lodz he worked with others to found the Yiddish Press Agency and set up the Historical Institute. He was engaged as secretary-editor by the Lodz newspaper *Dos nye lebn* (The New Life). He wrote articles for the newspapers *Dvar* (The Word) of Tel Aviv, and *Morgn zshurnal* (Morning Journal) of New York. For one year in Paris he worked at the monthly journal *Kyum* (Existence). In 1948 Elberg emigrated to New York, remarried, had two children, and became an American citizen. Elberg later moved to Florida and worked for the *Histadrut*. After the death of his second wife, he married a Canadian, and moved to Montreal.

Holocaust Writing

A collection of stories, *Unter kuperne himlen* (Under Copper Skies, 1951), was the first work Elberg published after the war. It was given the Fefer Prize by the Congress for Jewish Culture in Brazil. Most of the stories in this collection are set in Poland during the war and share common thematic concerns. All depict human behavior under duress and draw attention to the sexual, to the erotic, and to varying lusts and loves—anarchic forces that come to be understood as valued forces for life. The stories show Elberg introducing new character traits to the Jewish world and trying to find ways to combine or relate them to values in Jewish culture.

The story "873" in this collection won critical acclaim. It was singled out for praise by the prominent Yiddish critic Shmuel Niger, rescripted by writer Pinchus Bisberg, and staged by the Young Yiddish Theatre in Buenos Aires. Niger noted Elberg's success in capturing the brute destruction of Jewish life and drew attention to his strength in portraying Jews of character who did not succumb to debasement. "873" paints a wide canvas of life during the Nazi occupation in Poland and ends in Warsaw after the war. Although the story introduces Jewish life in the ghetto and in Polish and Jewish resistance groups, the main focus of the story is on the psychological and moral dilemma of the Jew who hides his Jewishness. Little attention is paid to the larger tragedy of events.

The story focuses on an assimilated Jew who passes as an Aryan in the Polish section of Warsaw, and centers on the two wars he experiences: the war within himself and the war against the Nazis. The two wars come together when the Gestapo forces him to turn spy on the very groups he grows to admire, the resistance fighters in the ghetto and the Polish underground. As the story traces his growing affinity for Jewish life it analyzes the pressure his affections exert on his conscience. His fear of being discovered and repudiated by his group grows as strong as his fear of dying, a fear that pressures him into becoming spy number 873 from the start. The story suggests that his fear of dying is primary; it is linked to his rejection of community and of Jewishness. In the void this creates, his instinct acts on him as an anarchic force and brings out the brutish aspects of his nature. His fear works as a force for life but also works to destroy him. Eventually the secret of his spying is exposed, and a return to community and tradition is made possible. Elberg, however, destroys the potential for the sentiment of forgiving. When the protagonist repents and recovers his sense of belonging he loses his fear of dying, but the recovery of his spiritual side makes it impossible for him to stay alive. At the story's end he hangs himself.

Elberg draws on structures of character portrayal he developed but restructures the relation between the instinctual and the spiritual and empties the instinctual of its valued force. In the context of the destruction of Jewish life during and after the war, the denial of the Jewish spirit is more threatening to the self than the instinctual struggle for survival. To survive by passing is portrayed as a form of self-rejecting violence, which is more violating than the threat of the Gestapo. Through a return to Judaism, the main character overcomes his brute instinct to stay alive. He takes charge of his own death by hanging and counters the fear that degraded him. The recognition of his spiritual strength as a Jew is what ultimately allows the character to recover his own self-respect. It enables him to face his fear of death and to recover his dignity as a man.

Publishing after the war, Elberg was acutely aware of the importance of recovering cultural continuities. Focusing on life in and out of the ghetto, on forests in the Polish countryside, on Jews and non-Jews, they indicate his efforts to find a way to balance his commemorative needs with his needs as a modern writer—a balance he continued to seek through his career, to his most recent writings. Not surprisingly Elberg experiments with different styles and genres, stretching and adjusting his language to probe his concerns.

Until the 1970s Elberg experimented with character portrayal; in the 1970s and 1980s he broadened the scope of his writing. Interested in exploring the larger tragedy of events and its impact on human nature, Elberg turned to the novel as a form. He published several novels and stories in rapid succession, among which *Oyfn shpitz fun mast* (On the Tip of the Mast, 1976) was most celebrated by his critics. It won the prestigious Manger Prize for literature in 1977, and was republished in English (1997) as *The Ship of the Hunted.* Its two central story lines, set in Nazi-occupied Poland, are those of a mother and son, each fighting separately for survival. It describes life in the ghetto and in the Polish countryside, and the horrors of life in Treblinka through the struggles of a large and complex family. The narrative voice is close to the material narrated, and the use of flashbacks through time and space adds intensity to the multilayered vision of Poland before, during, and after the war. The novel is fashioned on actual events and looks forward to restored Jewish life in Palestine, but the vision of the future is problematic; it is symbolized at the novel's end in the image of a shoreline, a border not yet reached, and is embodied in the portrayal of the mother in the throes of giving birth to a son. The two images gather together the narratives that structure the novel, which centers principally on the story of a mother and her son both fighting separately for survival in a doomed Warsaw.

The story of the mother is of her effort to preserve her life and the life of her family in the Warsaw ghetto up to and beyond its liquidation. The son's story concerns his struggle to survive outside the ghetto in the Polish countryside. The mother's story provides a rich portrait of prewar Jewish life in Warsaw and details the tragedy of its destruction. It draws attention to the horrors of Treblinka and sets up a contrast between her life before and during the occupation. The son's story provides a detailed depiction of rural life in Poland and introduces interactions between Poles and Jews, and Jews and Germans, and draws attention to the varying ways the "natural" works as a force in human nature and in life. Each story details a desperate struggle for survival. The mother's story traces her changing understanding of what it means to love. It tells of her acceptance of a relationship based on lust, as she is deprived of a blissful one based on marriage and tradition and of her recognition of it as a force for survival. The son's story traces his adaptations to a life that enables him to stay alive. He learns to live with Poles in nature, becomes adept at smuggling and disguise, and develops the brutish aspects of his character as he finds survival strategies. The two stories come together after the war when mother and son prepare for illegal emigration to Palestine. At the novel's end the son is killed while hoisting a new Zionist flag to the ship's mast, while the mother gives birth to another son. Elberg brings the stories together to find a redemptive focus for the brutish aspects he describes, but the future at the end of the novel is not a viable or visible reality. It is a promised hope that underscores the very losses the vision is meant to counter. Elberg's novel recovers the vanished world and reminds us of its values, but unwittingly invites us to recognize the tragedy of its destruction.

It was not an easy task for Elberg to imagine a future. In the years that followed, Elberg slowly shifted his writing focus. He stopped writing about the ghetto and the war and concentrated on the prewar world, returning to the tales of his youth. There he found a preserve of a vanished Jewishness and new resources. Retelling the legends and fables, he recovers an oral mode, a rich idiomatic Polish Yiddish, and returns to Yiddish the treasures of the world he loves.

Bibliography

Primary Sources

Unter kuperne himlen (Under Copper Skies). 1951.
Oyfn shpitz fun mast (On the Tip of a Mast, *The Ship of the Hunted* published in English, 1997). 1974.
Tsevorfene Zangen (Scattered Stalks). 1976.
Mayses (Stories). 1980.
A mentch is Nor a Mentch (A Person is Only a Person). 1983.
Kalman kalikes imperya (The Empire of Kalman the Cripple). 1983, 1997.
In leymene hayzer (In Clay Houses). 1985.
Tsvishn morgn un ovnt (Between Morning and Evening). 1987.
Ship of the Hunted. 1997.
Khasidic Tales. 2001.

Secondary Sources

Niger, Shmuel. "Farbrekhn un Shtrof." *Yehuda Elberg: essayen vegn zayn literarishn shafn.* Bena Costa Chair in Yiddish and the Joseph A. Berman Fund. Jerusalem: Bar Ilan University, 1990.
Vayner, Gershon. *Yehuda Elberg:essayen vegn zayn literarishn shafn.* Bena Costa Chair in Yiddish and the Joseph A. Berman Fund. Jerusalem: Bar Ilan University, 1990.

Interview and Archives

Yehuda Elberg, interviews by Esther Frank, May–July 2001.
Critical material on Yehuda Elberg can be found in archival collections housed in Montreal at The Jewish Public Library and The Canadian Jewish Congress.

YAFFA ELIACH

(1937–)

ALAN ROSEN

YAFFA ELIACH WAS born in 1937 to Moshe and Zipporah Katz Sonenson. Her family lived for a number of generations in the Lithuanian town of Eishyshok, the residents of which were mostly Jewish. Along with other institutions of note, Eishyshok featured a yeshivah that had among its students and faculty some of the greatest figures in Lithuanian Jewry, including Yisrael Meir Hakohen (the Haphetz Hayyim) and Chaim Ozer Grozinski.

The nine-hundred-year history of the Jews of Eishyshok came to an end when, in the days following *Rosh Hashanah* (25 and 26 September) of 1941, the Nazi *Einsatzgruppen* murdered virtually all (nearly 5,000) of the town's Jews. Yaffa was four and one-half years old. Most of Eliach's family survived the massacre by first hiding in a bunker and then fleeing to the neighboring town of Radun. However, a baby brother, Shaul, was killed when, in order to keep his cries from betraying their location, the occupants of the bunker suffocated him.

Along with a number of other Jews from the region, the Sonenson family were hidden by a Christian family named Korkuc for much of the duration of the Nazi occupation. After the Nazis retreated and Russian troops occupied the area in 1944, the Sonenson family returned to Eishyshok. The return to Eishyshok, however, proved deadly: Eliach's mother and a second baby brother, Hayyim, were murdered by local Poles in a pogrom.

Eliach's father, Moshe, was soon arrested for alleged subversive activities and was imprisoned in Siberia from 1945 until 1953. Eliach herself was sent to live with her aunt and uncle, who soon emigrated to Israel. Her older brother, Yitzhak, joined her there, as did her father after his release from the gulag. In Israel she also met her future husband, Rabbi David Eliach, who was her high school principal.

She emigrated to the United States in 1954 and became a naturalized citizen in 1957. She earned a B.A and M.A. from Brooklyn College and a Ph.D. in Jewish History from the Graduate Center of the City University of New York. In 1969 Eliach joined the faculty of Brooklyn College, where she served as professor of history and literature in the Department of Judaic Studies. In 1974 Eliach founded the Center for Holocaust Studies, Documentation and Research in Brooklyn, one of the earliest institutions of its kind. Housed at the Yeshiva of Flatbush, the center provided a library, spearheaded interviews with liberators of concentration camps, and, most importantly, drew on the special population of the borough to assemble a singular repository of interviews with religious survivors. These interviews formed the basis for a number of Eliach's publications on the Holocaust, including her collection, *Hasidic Tales of the Holocaust* (1982).

Eliach continued as director of the Brooklyn center until it was incorporated into the Museum of Jewish Heritage in New York City in 1991. In the 1980s and 1990s, she also played a pivotal role in the design of the Holocaust museum in Washington. Her contributions there included supplying the photographs of Eishyshok, which she used to construct the museum's "Tower of Life." In recent years, Eliach has taken this elegy to a vanished town several steps further. In 1998 she published a massive book, *There Once Was a World*, which chronicles the nine-hundred-year history of Eishyshok, including its destruction in the Holocaust. Moreover, Eliach is currently at work on constructing a model of the town to be based in Israel.

The Last Jew (1977)

Many of Eliach's preoccupations appear in her 1977 play, *The Last Jew* (written in collaboration with Uri Asaf). "The last Jew" is one Avraham Schneiderman who, in this fictionalized historical drama, alone remains of the Jews of Eishyshok. His daughter, Bluma, has married a converted Jew, Vladimir, with whom she debates the proper means of Holocaust commemoration. More importantly, Vladimir turns out to be the son of a Lithuanian collaborator, Vassily, who played a central role in the murder of the Jews of Eishyshok. The play concludes with Schneiderman condemning Vassily to death and apparently carrying out the sentence himself off-stage.

Set in Israel in 1970, the play explores issues of memory, revenge, collaboration, and the complex legacy of the Holocaust that devolves upon children of survivors and persecutors alike. In terms of dramaturgy, Eliach and Asaf use techniques reminiscent of Durrenmatt and Brecht—particularly a chorus of two madmen, who recite liturgy and sing religious songs. Such techniques infuse the play itself with a sense of ritual commemoration of the events. *The Last Jew* served as one of Eliach's earliest elegies to her hometown.

Hasidic Tales of the Holocaust (1982)

From approximately 1974 to 1981, Eliach and her students at Brooklyn College interviewed religious Jewish survivors of the Holocaust. Eliach then translated, edited, and rewrote the material of the interviews into a "unified form" of eighty-nine tales. She arranged the tales in four sections, the first three narrating events that took place during the Holocaust, the final section in its aftermath. Most of the tales are set in Poland, Russia, Germany, and Austria, with a smaller number in the last section taking place in postwar America and Europe. Though the interviews were conducted in multiple languages, Eliach rendered the tales derived from the interviews exclusively in English.

Almost uniquely among literary works in English on the Holocaust, these tales place in the foreground how the spiritual media of the Eastern European Jewish tradition confronted the Holocaust. These spiritual dimensions included the saving merits of deceased ancestors; the wisdom of saintly men and women and the holy objects they used and bequeathed; the redeeming power of prayer, dreams, blessings; and the active role played by miracles. Eliach's collection shows the continued potency of these spiritual forces, even in the grim circumstances of ghettos and concentration camps, but it also chronicles the failure or reconception of these forces in the unique situation that, according to a number of tales, the Jews faced.

Most facets of the Holocaust (decrees, deportation, ghettos, labor, concentration and DP camps) are at least touched on in these tales. Among ghettos, Bochnia and Lvov figure prominently. Among concentration camps, Auschwitz, Bergen-Belsen, and Janowska are the setting of several tales. Eliach refers to many distinguished personages of Hasidic Jewry during the war years. However, a number of tales feature one particular master and his family: the Rebbe of Bluzhov, Rabbi Israel Spira. A renowned figure in postwar Brooklyn, Rabbi Spira was interviewed by Eliach's students; she herself developed a warm personal relationship with him.

Most of the stories in *Hasidic Tales of the Holocaust* are short, ranging in length from one to four pages. Each tale bears a title emphasizing a certain dimension. Some tales adhere more strictly than others to the genre of Hasidic tales, which almost always focus on the relationship between a disciple (hasid) and a master (rebbe). This is true, for instance, of the first tale in the collection, "Hovering over the Pit," where the Blushover rebbe and a companion survive miraculously by jumping over a bomb crater in the Janowska camp. Yet even this tale is somewhat unconventional, focusing not on the master's relation to a Hasidic disciple, but instead to a "freethinker," someone who was not part of the Hasidic orbit.

Other tales deviate more radically from convention, frequently excluding reference to a master or disciple. These stories highlight the power of other spiritual resources. In "The Grandson of the Arugat Ha-Bosem," for instance, one man dreams he should go and tell his friend, who has already been consigned to the piles of corpses, that his grandfather says that he will live. After having the dream the third time, he carries out the charge and brings his friend back from the land of the dead. Here, a supernatural dream and the merit of a distinguished ancestor combine to bring about the miracle.

Still other tales emphasize the impotence of these traditions in the face of the unique conditions of the Holocaust. In "The Vision of the Red Stars" and "No Time for Advice," for example, disciples, according to convention, turn to masters for advice and wisdom; but in the former the advice turns out to be destructive, and in the latter the master refuses to give advice, stating conclusively: "Don't ask me any questions. This is no time for advice" (New York: Oxford, 1982, p. 49). Condensed by Eliach into a single statement by a great Hasidic figure, the words imply that the continuity of tradition no longer succeeds. As another authoritative figure expresses later in the tale, "It is a time such as we have never experienced before" (p. 50). What might appear to be truisms in other settings, here, in the context of devotion to tradition, carry immense weight.

The failure of tradition among those who were its flagbearers is brought home most pointedly in the story "Puff," where a devout Hasidic butcher shows up one day at the door of a former friend, caressing a non-Jewish German woman and declaiming, "I had a wife, six children, a hundred and fifty years of Hasidic ancestors, and hundreds of years of illustrious rabbinic grandfathers, but, puff . . . all went up in smoke" (p. 205). In Eliach's narration, the friend recognizes his visitor only at the end of the tale, highlighting for the reader the distance between the pious Hasidic butcher and this iconoclastic survivor who now stands at the door. Although the same person, the distance between what he was and what he has become marks the traumatic consequences of the Holocaust for the world of traditional Jewry.

The collection concludes with a two-part narrative of almost ten pages—the longest by far. This two-part story chronicles the success, traditions, and eventual annihilation of the Backenroth family of Schodnica in Galicia. Attending to the details of family customs and narrating the step-by-step destruction of the family's beauty and wealth, this concluding narrative bears a formal resemblance to the great family sagas of nineteenth-century realism, epitomized by Thomas Mann's *Buddenbrooks*. Whereas in these sagas the family usually undergoes disintegration from within over a number of generations, in Eliach's concluding tale the destruction comes from without and happens in a matter of days. Eliach may have chosen to conclude with this very different kind of tale to highlight the contrast between the world past and the world in the wake of the Holocaust.

Eliach's own story of survival enters only indirectly. It appears most poignantly, if enigmatically, in "The Telephone Operator." A set of several of the stories tell of the destruction of Eliach's town, Eishyshok (spelled in this volume as Eisysky). A number of the later stories derive from Eliach's experience in America after the war or as a member of President Carter's Commission on the Holocaust, visiting relevant sites in Europe. She thus obscures her own fate as a child survivor, perhaps to ensure that her story will not overshadow the work of scholarship and of storytelling that she has assembled.

Critical Responses

Criticism of *Hasidic Tales* has focused on several points. First, *Hasidic Tales* recovers a world that the catastrophe of the Holocaust tends to obscure. Leon Wieseltier, noting the special contributions that *Hasidic Tales of the Holocaust* makes to the literature of the Holocaust, speaks of restoring the vital context of Eastern European life: "Eliach has recovered the destruction of the Hasidim of Poland as it was for those who were being destroyed, and she has done so because she knows who they actually were. She knows their philosophical and social and religious particulars, and how they appeared in adversity" (Wieseltier, p. 38). As Wieseltier implies, *Hasidic Tales* can be appreciated as a work of cultural anthropology.

Michael Berenbaum adds an appreciation for Eliach's marriage of historical scholarship and literary artistry. In *Hasidic Tales*, Berenbaum suggests, "each tale is beautifully written and has narrative vitality. Yiddish and many other foreign tongues are captured and transmitted in a literate English that carries a trace of the original language but does not read like an awkward translation" (Berenbaum, p. 237). Even Eliach's style, recasting the tales for New World readers, remains faithful to Old World cadences.

In terms of theological response, however, Berenbaum voices a misgiving that some readers commonly express regarding Eliach's emphasis on miraculous survival. Most victims did not survive. According to this view, to highlight miraculous survival in the face of such losses distorts the event and falsifies the response to it. As I have suggested, however, a number of the tales do not emphasize miraculous salvation but rather show that traditional responses cannot accommodate the extreme losses suffered in the Holocaust.

Other critics see the fusion of historical scholarship and literary artistry not as a strength but as a weakness. James Young believes that Eliach's attempt to provide factual confirmation for the events related in the tales weakens the force of the collection. Eliach's detailed historical footnotes and indication of the place, time, and people involved in the interview actually compromise the nature of the tales. According to Young, the tales are legends and should be looked at exclusively in that light. It should be noted that Young supports this argument by citing a single tale (the first in the collection). Taking account of the varied nature of the eighty-nine tales, including the realism of the concluding one, might yield a different conclusion.

Bibliography

Primary Sources

Books

Eshet Ha-Dayag (The Fisherman's Wife). 1965.
HaYehudi Ha-Acharon: Drama b'Chamesh Timunot (*The Last Jew: A Drama in Five Scenes*). With Uri Asaf. 1977.

The Liberators: Oral History Testimonies of American Liberators, from the Archives of the Center for Holocaust Studies. Editor, with Brana Gurewitsch. 1981.
Hasidic Tales of the Holocaust. 1982.
We Were Children Just Like You (Editor). 1990.
Holocaust Oral History Manual. With Brana Gurewitsch. 1991.
There Once Was a World: A Nine-Hundred-Year Chronicle of the Shtetl of Eishyshok. 1998.

Selected Articles

"The Holocaust and New Hasidic Tales." 1982.
"The Holocaust and New Hasidic Tales." *Tradition* 20 (1982): 228–234.
"Defining the Holocaust: Prospectives of a Jewish Historian." *Jews and Christians After the Holocaust.* Edited by Abraham Peck. Philadelphia: Fortress, 1983, pp. 11–23.
"Jewish Tradition in the Life of the Concentration Camp Inmate." *The Nazi Concentration Camps.* Proceedings of the Fourth Yad Vashem International Historical Conference, Jerusalem, January, 1980. Jerusalem: Yad Vashem, 1984, pp. 195–206.
"Survivors of a Single Shteltl; Case Study: Eishyshok." *She'erit Hapletah, 1944–1948: Rehabilitation and Political Struggle.* Proceedings of the Sixth Yad Vashem International Historical Conference, Jerusalem, October, 1985, eds. Yisrael Gutman and Avital Saf. Jerusalem: Yad Vashem, 1990.
"Private and Public Commemoration of the Holocaust: In Search of 'The Perfect Rest.' " *What Have We Learned? Telling the Story, Teaching the Lessons of the Holocaust.* Edited by Franklin Littell, Alan Berger, and Hubert Locke. London: Mellen, 1993, pp. 392–402.
"Popular Jewish Religious Responses during the Holocaust and Its Aftermath." *Jewish Perspectives on the Experience of Suffering.* Edited by Shalom Carny. Northvale, New Jersey: Aronson, 1999, pp. 297–329.
"Primo Levi and His Concept of Time: Time of the Gun, Time of the Spirit." *Memory and Mastery: Primo Levi as Writer and Witness.* Edited by Roberta Kremer. Albany: SUNY, 2001, pp. 21–34.

Secondary Sources

Berenbaum, Michael. Review of *Hasidic Tales and the Holocaust. Simon Wiesenthal Annual* (1983): 235–239.
Rosen, Alan. " 'The Language of Dollars': Multilingualism and the Claims of English in *Hasidic Tales of the Holocaust.*" In *Witnessing the Disaster: Essays on Representation and the Holocaust.* Edited by Michael Bernard-Donals and Richard Glejzer. Madison: University of Wisconsin Press, 2002.
Wieseltier, Leon. "The Life Before the Death," Review of *Hasidic Tales of the Holocaust. The New Republic* 188 (1983): 38, 40.
Young, James. *Writing and Rewriting the Holocaust: Narrative and the Consequences of Interpretation.* Bloomington: Indiana University Press, 1988.

Archives

The Museum of Jewish Heritage in New York houses a number of audio tapes of the interviews that form the basis for the tales of *Hasidic Tales of the Holocaust.*

RICHARD ELMAN

(1934–1997)

S. LILLIAN KREMER

THE SON OF Edward and Pearl Elman, Richard Elman was born in New York on 23 April 1934. He received a B.A. from Syracuse University in 1955 and an M.A. from Stanford, where he studied with Yvor Winters and Malcolm Cowley, in 1957. Elman's career has included writing for the media and academic positions as a visiting writer at several universities including Bennington, Columbia, the University of Pennsylvania, and the State University of New York at Stony Brook, in addition to writing fiction and poetry. His awards include a CAPS Fellowship in 1976 and three PEN syndicated short-story awards. A prolific writer, Elman has written both under his own name and pseudonyms.

Holocaust Trilogy

Richard Elman's Holocaust writing is distinctive in American annals for its appearance at the beginning of increased cultural interest in the Holocaust, and particularly for its trilogy construction and his focus on the tragic plight of Hungarian Jewry in 1944. The first volume, *The 28th Day of Elul* (1967), offers a detailed account of the Aryanization of Hungary from the dehumanization of a subject people to the eve of deportation to the concentration and death camps. Given the peculiar Hungarian circumstances of gradual, piecemeal diminution of Jewish freedom in contrast to non-Axis occupations characterized by swift ghettoization and deportation, Elman is able to elaborate the "temporizations and accommodations to the Nazi threat . . . the way the victims were forced to cooperate in their own humiliation and destruction" (Slavitt, pp. 7–8). The second volume, *Lilo's Diary* (1968), is the 1944 journal of a young female ward of the family, a quintessential victim. The third, *The Reckoning* (1969), narrated from the perspective of the paterfamilias, Newman Yagodah, is a moral and historic accounting, a fusion of subjective personal moral assessment and objective analysis of the economic and political forces contributing to the Holocaust. After several failed attempts to write a fourth volume from the perpetrator's point of view, Elman abandoned the project (Kremer interview). While the breadth of the trilogy and its use of multiple perspectives have much to recommend it, the inverted chronology is problematic. The tripartite configuration and backward glance from the post-Holocaust era to the 1920s was not Elman's original intent.

A Survivor's Retrospective

The survivor's tale of *The 28th Day of Elul* is initiated by an attorney's request that a Holocaust survivor named as beneficiary of an American uncle respond to questions about his post-Holocaust religious identity. Responding to the inquiry in epistolary form, Alex Yagodah relates a retrospective chronicle of his family's social and political destruction; he reviews the cataclysmic event that changed his life, but confines his story to the advent of the *Shoah* rather than the concentration camp universe.

Paralleling the historic patterns of harassment of Jews by pro-Nazi governments and citizens standing to benefit economically in a *Judenrein* society, Elman charts an incremental pattern of economic and civic abuse and oppression: Jewish public life is curtailed, police expropriate Jewish property, special taxes are imposed on the Jewish population, and Gentiles are encouraged to renege on their debts to Jews. These oppressive measures are calculated to render the victim populace docile before its deportation to the killing centers. Analogous to government-sanctioned theft of Jewish property is the fictional collaborator's systematic attempts to have the Yagodahs legally transfer their wealth to him. Elman translates these policies to the dramatic level in the business rivalry of the Jewish Yagodah and gentile Skirzeny, as the Jew agrees to sign over all his family property to his antagonist in exchange for assistance in the escape of all nine family members. Once the Yagodah estate exchange is negotiated, Skirzeny betrays the family, claiming that there are only papers for eight and Lilo, the beautiful ward of the family, must remain behind for she is most likely to survive by passing as a Gentile, a ruse to provide his step-son with the woman he wants. To save eight, Newman Yagodah must abandon one, a clear analogy to the decisions Jewish councils had to render. That the entire escape plan was a ruse to have the property legally transferred is clear from Skirzeny's musings about the Yagodahs' eventual destination. The older generation's economic antagonism is compounded by the psychosexual rivalry of the younger generation. Jewish vulnerability is emblematically and dramatically represented in Lilo's rape. The rapist taunts the Yagodah cousins, daring them to report his attack to the police, whose job and inclination it is to protect the rapist and condemn the Jewish victim for seduction and race mixing. Aptly naming the chief villain, who clearly enjoys the Nazi inversion of justice, Miklos Skirzeny, Elman alludes to two pro-Nazi Hungarian officials, Admiral Miklos (Nicholas) Horthy, whose authoritarian regime reflected his sympathy for Italian Fascism and German Nazism, and *Oberstrumbannführer* Skorzeny, who installed an even more pro-Nazi force after overthrowing Horthy.

The family drama is played alongside a philosophic debate raging during the time of *Elul's* 1960s composition; namely, Hannah Arendt's attribution of success of the Nazi genocide to misguided and incompetent Jewish leaders. Thus, the novel's moral dilemma turns not only on the German crime against Jewry, not only on Christian Europe's ready acquiescence to Germany's genocidal goal and profiting from betraying Jews into the hands of their persecutors, but on post-Holocaust judgment of the victims. The survivor repudiates blaming the victims, warning his American correspondent to distinguish between the criminals and their victims. Although Alex finds fault with everyone, he recognizes degrees of guilt and raises critical distinctions between sins of commission and sins of omission. Aware of the human predilection for life and hope, even in the face of disaster, he cautions post-Holocaust contemporaries to desist from condemning the victims because their illusions "grew out of the very life we were leading. Unarmed and ill prepared, beset by murderers" (*The 28th Day of Elul*. New York: Charles Scribner's Sons, 1967, p. 112). The American "code of ethics [which is] for free men in a free society" (p. 133) does not apply to the Nazi universe. The novel's dual Holocaust era/post-Holocaust perspectives complicate the discussion of victim responsibility by juxtaposing the narrator's wartime denunciation of his father and the Jewish Council of Elders for failing to save Jewry with his criticism of postwar exaggerations of Jewish Council Holocaust complicity. Elman enters the fray in opposition to Hannah Arendt by having his narrator reject her council culpability thesis on the grounds that "It confuses victims with victimizers" (p. 157).

Diary: A Victim's View

Whereas the trilogy's first and third volumes address the collective Hungarian Holocaust experience from anticipatory and retrospective analytical points of view, *Lilo's Diary* charts the psychological trauma of a victim in the clutches of Hungarian Nazi collaborators. Accordingly the novel's diction emphasizes psychosexual imagery and metaphor to convey desecration of Jewish life. The journal is a captive young woman's assessment of female and Jewish vulnerability, reflected first in her role as ward in the Yagodah household and secondly as fugitive/prisoner in the household of an extortionist and a rapist. Lilo is a paradoxical creature: suspicious and trusting, passionate and cold, aggressive and meek; more profoundly complex and calculating in her self-portrait than she was in her cousin-fiancé's guilt-induced memoir. With a sharper eye and more caustic tongue than Alex, Lilo observes and comments on the trilogy's major players, on the disintegrating family, and the corruption of public institutions. Ironically, the likelihood of Lilo's survival increases as she undergoes a Holocaust metamorphosis from the son's sex slave to the elder's political pawn when he recognizes her value as his "safe-conduct" when the liberators enter Hungary.

Ledger: Analytic Observations

The trilogy's final volume, *The Reckoning: The Daily Ledgers of Newman Yagodah, Advokat and Factor* (1969), elaborates on the process of maintaining Hungary in the Nazi orbit by installing pro-Nazi officials and the progression toward the annihilation of Hungarian Jewry. Through the vehicle of the elder Yagodah's ledger, Elman demonstrates the evolution of Nazi influence in and control of Hungary, the impact of the erratic political climate marked by periods of relative safety and peril for the Jewish population, and the successive cycles of hope and disappointment, from relaxation of restrictions to aggressive persecution that preceded the final slaughter.

The ledger parallels the moral accounting of a corrupt bourgeois parvenu and the society that shaped him with that society's collaboration in the destruction of Jewry. The personal ledger complements the first-person narrative of the first two volumes, substituting a prewar point of view for the hindsight of the survivor account and adding economic and sociological analyses of a chronicler educated in the twin crucibles of World War I and the Depression. Deception is an integral part of Yagodah's daily existence: deceptions in his personal relationships, self-deceptive belief in the Enlightenment myth that he is a European among Europeans, and disbelief in the significance of European antisemitism. Yagodah's most tragic failures, limited vision and courage, account for his decision to remain silent about German intentions for Hungarian Jewry.

Newman Yagodah is, as his first name implies, the new man, the post-Enlightenment assimilated Jew, emblem of European betrayal of the Enlightenment ideals that were supposed to grant Jews full citizenship sharing in the political, cultural, and economic life of their respective countries. Instead, Jews discovered that to achieve the status of tolerated European, the Jew was free to become a nominal Jew, never free to be a devout and observant Jew and a European. The Jew was free to fight in Europe's wars, free to work in a restricted capacity in its economy, and, most particularly, free to disassociate from Jewish life; but never free enough to enjoy social acceptance and full rights of citizenship.

Newman Yagodah shares many traits of Hannah Arendt's Jewish pariah—the Jewish social outcast whose political emancipation was incomplete. According to Arendt, "During the 150 years when Jews truly lived amidst, and not just in the neighborhood of Western European peoples, they always had to pay with social insult for political success" (Arendt, quoted by Feldman in Introduction, p. 18). Unlike Arendt's noble pariah, who "tried to make of the emancipation of the Jews the ideal it should have been—an admission of Jews as Jews to the ranks of humanity" (Arendt, p. 68), Yagodah, like most assimilated European Jews, was content with limited acceptance, and opportunity to play the parvenu. Thus Elman makes evident that the antisemitism rife in Viennese society of Yagodah's university years was part of the established antisemitic European tradition and implies that this foundation was instrumental in Germany's successful conduct of its genocide program, an implication underscored by references elsewhere to the Vatican's efforts to save baptized Jews in utter disregard for the lives of observant Jews.

Deportation Assemblies

Elman avoids representation of the concentration camp universe, but he constructs a deportation assembly that rhetorically forecasts Auschwitz. The assembly scene in *Elul*, the strongest single scene of the novel, combines contemporary terror with post-Holocaust knowledge. Stripped of their watches, rings, and coins, the Jews are kept standing in the broiling sun for hours while German soldiers, bayonets in position, encircle them. An officer's announcement that the able-bodied will work and "the unfit can expect special treatment at camps so designated" (p. E132), a rhetoric of "resettlement" and "special treatment" (p. E132) bespeak hope for survival to the naïve victims and Auschwitz to the post-Holocaust narrator and reader. *The Reckoning* reconstitutes the deportation assembly in a different key, adding economic and historic nuance and analysis. As survivor memoir and reflection, the *Elul* account is coherently delivered and benefits from a twenty-year historic perspective. Conversely, *The Reckoning's* presentation is fragmentary and diffuse, conveying the confusion and terror of the victims who must make judgments based on Nazi deception, Hungarian duplicity, and worldwide disinterest. Newman's assembly representation dramatizes the victims' frustration, impotence, and fear. Unlike the survivor's acerbic commentary and gallows humor imitating Holocaust irrationality, Newman's questions suggest prewar concepts of rational consequence: "*How have we deserved any of this*?" His statements convey moral indignation: "To be herded like so many cattle, to be branded like so much scorched and writhing flesh—*why us*? For what purpose?" (*The Reckoning: The Daily Ledgers of Newman Yagodah Advokat and Factor*. New York: Charles Scribner's Sons, 1969, p. 111). In sharp contrast with the survivor's bitter understanding of world indifference to Jewry's slaughter is the victim's desperate hope for deliverance. Consistent with the third volume's larger sociological and historic approach, its assembly scene becomes a memorial tableau of those to be lost in the Holocaust, a pre-funerary elegy for lives about to be vanquished.

Theological Implications

The trilogy is an early American example of Holocaust-wrought theological and philosophic conjecture and reconfigurations. Elman asks whether ideas about human nature should be revised in light of Holocaust knowledge, and whether traditional Jewish thinking about the covenantal connection survived *Shoah* disruption. God stands accused of dishonoring the covenant. Simultaneously accepting God and protesting divine inaction, Yagodah, like the believers in the fictional worlds of Elie Wiesel and I. B. Singer, holds God accountable for Holocaust passivity. He wrestles with the terrifying realization of the coexistence of a just and merciful God and an evil creation. Although he cannot explain the inexplicable, Alex confesses, "I believe" (p. E24), echoing "*Ani Ma'amim*," the traditional affirmation of faith victims recited as they entered the gas chambers. In post-*Shoah* Israel, Yagodah casts his lot with Jewry: "I am one of them for sure. What other meaning would my life have? I am a Jew" (p. E276). Yagodah's response is void of the erudition or even basic principles of Jewishly educated characters. Instead, he shifts from a theological to a sociological discourse and equates group identity with religious identity.

Alex Yagodah's post-Holocaust denunciation of God for crimes against the covenant parodies the psalmist's mournful supplicating tone: "Only He betrayed us. He profaned us. He took our prayers in vain. He mocked us. He rewarded us with cruelty. He listened but did not hear. He was there and he was not there when we needed Him. He led us into injustice" (p. E24). By reformulating the psalm, the survivor's protest conforms to Jewish literary tradition of radical reinterpretation by means of textual inversion that may be interpreted as a means of articulating faith despite the terror of separation from God. Here, the sacred text is put to irreverent use to issue a protest. "The technique of imitating the breach of God's promise in the parody of Scripture . . . [using] 'symbolic inversion,' and 'countercommentary' " is a basic form of Jewish response to catastrophe for "to mimic the sacrilege allows the individual to keep faith even as the promise is subverted" (Roskies, p. 20). The technique is more convincing in terms of Elman's ability to construct such passages than it is a believable attribution to Alex Yagodah and his cousin Lilo, neither of whom appear to be sufficiently Judaically educated to formulate such constructions.

The volume's title and its epigraphs from Jeremiah provide interpretive guidelines. Elul, the sixth month of the Jewish calendar, is the period of preparation for repentance. The Hebrew letters for the word *Elul* suggest a phrase from the Song of Songs referring to the love between God and his people. Since the Holocaust compromised that relationship and occasioned the reexamination of the covenantal bond, the combined Elul allusion and Jeremiah epigraphs of Jewish defeat followed by redemption, and the novel's Israeli setting reinforce Yagodah's commitment to the continuity of Jewish identity.

Similarly, the Jeremiah epigraph for Book Two corresponds with the period of Jewish exilic suffering under Babylonian captivity and the novel's treatment of Nazi invasion, occupation, and genocide. At the same time, the passage includes an intimation of redemption in its concluding line, "in the peace thereof ye shall have peace," foreshadowing the promise in Jeremiah 30 predicting return to and rebuilding of Jerusalem, "The city shall be rebuilt" (30:10) "and they shall come back from the land of the enemy" (31:10). Jeremiah's polar functions, threatening judgment and promising restoration, suit Elman's treatment of the spiritual return of the individual sinner and the Elul implications of spiritual restoration as well as the historic manifestation of collective Diaspora suffering and regeneration in the Israeli homeland.

Although Elman introduces the theological theme overtly in the survivor's memoir, he concludes *Lilo's Diary* with a prayer parody addressing similar issues in the thoughts of an equally unconvincing candidate. Nonetheless, the device effectively unites the two volumes. In anger and confusion Lilo prays a horrid fused pastiche of lines from "Hear O Israel," the central prayer of the Jewish liturgy; *Avinu Malkenu*, the hauntingly beautiful high holiday supplication; the twenty-third psalm, attesting to God's goodness and mercy; and concludes the Hebrew portion with words from the mourner's *Kaddish*.

> Dear God, Dear Murderer, thy will be done
> Thy Kingdom come
> Our Father, Our King
> Give us this day our Daily Hunger
> Our Father which art in Heaven Curse us, despise us, murder us, betray us
> O Lord Our God Thou hast set up a table before us
> In the presence of our enemies
> My cup runneth over . . .
> *Yisgadal . . . V'Yisgadal . . . V'yisroman* (*Lilo's Diary*, New York: Charles Scribner's Sons, 1968, pp. 153–154).

Elman thereby concludes the volume with a brilliant allusion evoking the traditional prayers, and at the same time again suggesting through their brutal fragmentation the disruption of Jewish life wrought in the Holocaust and, in their unseemly fusion, an echo of Alex's biblical countertext. Furthermore, in an addendum, Elman reminds us of the instigator of the calamity necessitating the parody by shifting to German, a language Lilo believes appropriate to sentimental poetry and carnage, and therefore appropriate for prayer to God, the murderer. Lilo's prayer-parody formally echoes the survivor's indictment of God for Holocaust passivity and his poetics of sacrilege.

The trilogy gains substance from the manifold ways in which the three volumes interlock. Elman advances American Holocaust literature in his explicit inclusions of Holocaust history. Moving past delineation of the existential Holocaust experience, he explores the Holocaust's implications for Jewish religious and political survival.

Critical Reception

Perhaps because the trilogy appeared during the war in Vietnam and before the Holocaust gained a foothold in literary circles and popular culture in America, it has not garnered the critical attention it might otherwise have earned. Sidra DeKoven Ezrahi discusses the trilogy briefly in terms of the incompatibility of documentary and artistic approaches, "the incompatibility between the probing psychological approach of the artist-as-creator and the informational, collective overview of the artist-as-historian" (p. 46). Alan Berger presents the most sustained negative critique, condemning Elman's "massive failure to come to grips with the Holocaust" and for making "metaphors of both Judaism and the Holocaust" (p. 163). David Slavitt considers the first volume "an extraordinary tour de force, an amazing achievement for an American," but he also claims that "the trilogy does not sustain itself" (p. 9). The *Times Literary Supplement* reviewer regarded *The 28th Day of Elul* as "remarkable . . . an exercise in moral restraint which 'tells us more' than many head-on confrontations with the abyss" ("After the Deluge," p. 833). Holocaust survivor and noted author, Elie Wiesel wrote that Elman's "ideas are provocative, his outcry uncompromising, . . . [that he] touches on the most important human and philosophical questions of our time" (p. 4).

Bibliography

Primary Sources

Novels

A Coat for the Tsar. 1959.
The 28th Day of Elul. 1967.
Lilo's Diary. 1968.
The Reckoning. The Daily Ledgers of Newman Yagodah, Advokat and Factor. 1969.
An Education in Blood. 1970.
Freddi and Shirl and the Kids: The Autobiography in Fables of Richard Elman, A Novel. 1972.
Taxi Driver (based on screenplay by Paul Schrader). 1976.
Little Lives (under pseudonym John Howland Spyker). 1978.
The Breadfruit Lotteries. 1980.
Smokey and the Bandit (under pseudonym Delmar Hawks). 1981.
Gangster Chronicles (under pseudonym Michael Lasker, with Richard A. Simmons). 1981.
The Menu Cypher. 1982.
Disco Frito. 1988.
Tar Beach. 1992.
Love Handles. Forthcoming.

Poetry

The Man Who Ate New York. 1976.
Homage to Fats Navarro. 1978.
In Chontales. 1981.
Cathedral-Tree-Train and Other Poems. 1992.
Love, Richard: Last Poems and Translations. Forthcoming.

Collected Short Stories

Crossing over and Other Tales. 1973.

Memoir

Namedropping: Mostly Literary Memoirs. 1998.

Biographies

Eric Linklater: A Critical Biography (under pseudonym Michael Parnell). 1985.
Laughter from the Dark: A Life of Gwyn Thomas (under pseudonym Michael Parnell). 1988.

Reportage

The Poorhouse State: The American Way of Life on Public Assistance. 1966. Excerpted and reprinted in *Aspects of Poverty*. Edited by Ben Seligmann, 1968.
Ill-at-Ease in Compton. 1967.
Uptight with the Rolling Stones. 1973.
Cocktails at Somoza's: A Reporter's Sketchbook of Events in Revolutionary Nicaragua. 1981.

Editing

Charles Booth's London: A Portrait of the Poor at the Turn of the Century. Edited with Albert Fried. 1968.

Selected Articles, Short Stories, Reviews, and Poems

Under pseudonym Eric Pearl. "Learning the Cannoneer's Hop." *Nation* 186 (10 May 1958): 415–417.
"A Word for Yvor Winters." *Commonweal* 74 (14 July 1961): 401–402.
"Publisher for Poets." *Saturday Review* 44 (22 July 1961): 33–34.
"Malamud on Campus." *Commonweal* 75 (27 October 1961): 114–115.
"For Ivan Mestrovic, 1883–1962." *Commonweal* 75 (9 February 1962): 506–507.
"Post Time: Poem." *Commonweal* 77 (28 September 1962): 18.
"Song in Friendship." *Commonweal* 78 (24 May 1963): 252.
"The Legacy of Louis MacNiece." *New Republic* (26 October 1963): 19–21.
Interview with Isaac Bashevis Singer. *Commentary* 36 (November 1963): 364–372.
"Beckett's Testament." *Commonweal* 80 (26 June 1964): 416–418.
"Institution of Blacklisting." *New Republic* 149 (5 December 1964): 17–18.
"Educational TV." *Nation* 200 (1 March 1965): 217–221; inside cover (19 April 1965): 421.
"Poet of Plainness." *Commonweal* 82 (14 May 1965): 250–251.

"Antic Arts." *Holiday* 38 (August 1965): 83–87.
"Books." *Commonweal* 82 (6 August 1965): 573–575.
"Puerto Ricans." *Commonweal* 83 (7 January 1966): 405–408.
"The Kerensky Complex." *Evergreen Review* 10 (February 1966): 44 passim.
"Singer of Warsaw." Review of *In My Father's Court* by Isaac Bahevis Singer. *New York Times Book Review* (8 May 1966): sec. 7, 1.
"Hell's Angels." *New Republic* 156 (25 February 1967): 30–32.
"Biafra in Dixie." *Nation* 208 (13 January 1969): 55.
"Tit for Tat." *My Name Aloud: Jewish Stories by Jewish Writers*. Edited by Harold U. Ribalow. New Brunswick: Thomas Yoseloff Ltd., 1969, pp. 92–100.
"If You Were on Welfare." *Saturday Review* 53 (23 May 1970): 27–29.
"Brief Life Is Best in the End, I Suppose." *Atlantic* 230 (December 1972): 62–66.
"Lichen Painter." Poem. *New Yorker* 51 (9 February 1976): 36.
"*Journals: Early Fifties, Early Sixties*, by Allen Ginsberg." *Nation* 225 (1977): 500–501.
"Down at La Casa Tropica." *Nation* 228 (28 April 1979): 460–461.
"Memo." Poem. *Nation* 231 (27 December 1980): 710.
"Reading Gil Sorrentino." *Review of Contemporary Fiction* 1, no. 1 (spring 1981): 155–156.
"Films." *Nation* 233 (5 September 1981): 188–189.
"Un Entretien avec Isaac Bashevis Singer." *L'Arc* 93 (1984): 4–11. With Joel Blocker.
"Unfinished Business." *Nation* 243, no. 4 (16 August 1986): 118–119.
"Yvor Winters, Wallace Stevens, and 'Thanatopsis.' " *Under Open Sky: Poets on William Cullen Bryant*. New York: Fordham University Press, 1986, pp. 58–59.
"Cool Lightning over Tucson." Poem. *New Yorker* 63 (25 May 1987): 87.
"John Ciardi and 'Treat It Gentle.' " *John Ciardi: Measure of the Man*. Edited by Vince Clemente. Fayetteville: University of Arkansas Press, 1987, pp. 79–81.
"On William Bronk." *Sagetrieb: A Journal Devoted to Poets in the Imagist-Objectivist Tradition* 7, no. 3 (winter 1988): 66–67.
"Bashevis." *Tikkun* 9, no. 1 (January 1994): 63–68.
"Homage to William Bronk." *Columbia Library Columns* 43, no. 2 (February 1994): 3–14.
"The Many Forms Which Loss Can Take." *The Critical Response to Tillie Olsen*. Edited by Kay Hoyle Nelson and Nancy Huse. Westport, Conn.: Greenwood, 1994, pp. 113–114.

Broadside

"May from My Bluff." St. James, Long Island: Everett Press & Publishers, Inc., 1983.

Secondary Sources

"After the Deluge." Review of *The 28th Day of Elul*. *Times Literary Supplement* (21 September 1967): 833.
Arendt, Hannah. "Anti-Semitism." Quoted by Ron H. Feldman in Introduction to *The Jew as Pariah: Jewish Identity and Politics in the Modern Age*. Edited by Ron H. Feldman. New York: Grove Press, 1978.
Berger, Alan L. "Symbolic Judaism." *Crisis and Covenant: The Holocaust in American Jewish Literature*. Albany: New York State University Press, 1985, pp. 160–164.
———. *Crisis and Covenant: The Holocaust in American Jewish Fiction*. Albany: State University of New York Press, 1985.
Cronin, Gloria L., Blaine H. Hall, and Connie Lamb. "Richard Elman." *Jewish American Fiction Writers, an Annotated Bibliography*. Garland Reference to the Humanities, vol. 972. New York: Garland Publishing Co., 1991, pp. 215–224.
Delbanco, Nicholas. "Nicholas Delbanco on Richard Elman's *The 28th Day of Elul*, *Lilo's Diary*, and *The Reckoning*." In *Rediscoveries II: Important Writers Select Their Favorite Works of Neglected Fiction*. Edited by David Madden and Peggy Bach. New York: Carroll, 1988, 71–77.
Ezrahi, Sidra DeKoven. *By Words Alone: The Holocaust in Literature*. Chicago: University of Chicago Press, 1980, pp. 46–47.
Gilmore, Michael T. "The Moral Vacuum." Review of *The Reckoning*. *Congress Bi-Weekly* (23 January 1970): 17.
Hochman, Baruch. "The Jewish Vogue." Review of *The 28th Day of Elul*. *Commentary* (September 1967): 107–110.
Koch, Christopher. Review of *Lilo's Diary*. *Commonweal* (17 January 1969): 504–505.
Kremer, S. Lillian. "The Trial of the Damned: Richard Elman's Holocaust Trilogy." In *Witness through the Imagination: Jewish American Holocaust Literature*. Detroit: Wayne State University Press, 1989, pp. 142–180.
Leonard, John. "Complicity and Consequences." Review of *Lilo's Diary*. *New York Times* (13 September 1968): 45.
Lieber, Joel. "The Bartered Bride." Review of *Lilo's Diary*. *Saturday Review* (7 September 1968): 46.
———. "The Fruits of the Holocaust." Review of *The 28th Day of Elul*. *Saturday Review* (15 April 1967): 36–37.
———. "Fiction." Review of *The Reckoning*. *Saturday Review* (11 October 1969): 39–40.
O'Brien, John. "Keeping Literary Company: Working with Writers since the Sixties." *Review of Contemporary Fiction* 18, no. 3 (fall 1998): 261–265.
Riemer, Jack. "Three Tales of 'Madness.'" Review of *Lilo's Diary*. *Hadassah Magazine* (October 1968): 16.
Roskies, David G. *Against the Apocalypse: Responses to Catastrophe in Modern Jewish Culture*. Cambridge: Harvard University Press, 1984.
Sigal, Clancy. "Hell Came for a Visit." Review of *Lilo's Diary*. *New York Times Book Review* (25 August 1968): 4.
Slavitt, David R. "Richaleh: Richard Elman: April 23, 1934–December 31, 1997." *Hollins Critic* 37, no. 2 (April 2000): 1–20.
Weinberg, Helen. "Before the Fatal Moment." Review of *Lilo's Diary*. *Congress Bi-Weekly* (22 May 1967): 22–23.
———. "A Sequel in the Present Tense." Review of *The 28th Day of Elul*. *Congress Bi-Weekly* (25 November 1968): 21–22.
Wiesel, Elie. "Legacy of Evil." Review of *The 28th Day of Elul*. *New York Times Book Review* (28 May 1967): 4, 34.
Winegarten, Renee. "A Powerful, Imaginative Novel." Review of *The 28th Day of Elul*. *Hadassah Magazine* (May 1967): 16.
Zeitlin, Naomi. "Strange Document." Review of *The 28th Day of Elul*. *World Jewry* (November–December 1967): 29.

Interview

Interview by S. Lillian Kremer, 6 April 1987. Unpublished.

AMOS ELON

(1926–)

ROGER FRIEDMANN

AMOS ELON WAS born on 4 July 1926 in Vienna, Austria, to Max and Marie Elon, who immigrated to the Jewish community in Palestine with their two-year-old son in 1928. He served as an officer in the Israeli army during Israel's War of Independence in 1948, attaining the rank of first lieutenant.

After receiving a B.A. from Hebrew University in Jerusalem, Elon became a reporter for the Tel Aviv daily *Ha'aretz*, where he worked as a foreign correspondent, editorial writer, and columnist from 1952 to 1983. His social and political commentaries have earned him a reputation as one of Israel's most distinguished journalists. He has also authored a number of meticulously researched historical studies in both English and Hebrew that examine the legacy of the modern Jewish state. *Herzl* (New York: Holt, Rinehart and Winston, 1975), his biography of Theodor Herzl, the patriarch of the Zionist movement, has been acclaimed by Arthur Miller (in *Contemporary Authors*) for its "warts and all" portrayal and "better yet the mysterious dialectical interplay between his personality, his obsessions and his fears, and the underlying menace of pre–World War I Vienna . . . and Europe." Another work, *The Israelis: Founders and Sons* (New York: Holt, Rinehart and Winston, 1971) examines the historical origins of Arab-Israeli conflict and questions many of the assumptions that inform public sentiment in Israel regarding the righteousness of the Jewish position toward the neighboring Arab states and the Palestinians. Elon also criticizes Jews in Palestine during World War II for having done too little to aid Jews in Europe in their time of extreme distress. The extent to which the Jewish community in Palestine was not maximally engaged in rescuing European Jews during the Holocaust is explored in Elon's only foray into literary fiction, his novel *Timetable* (Garden City: Doubleday & Co., 1980).

Timetable

Timetable reconstructs in meticulous detail the story of Joel Brand, who delivered to members of the Palestine-based Jewish Agency the particulars of a proposal by the Nazi official Adolf Eichmann to trade the lives of one million Jews for trucks and other items in short supply in the German army's inventory. The affair was already well known to the Israeli reading public as a result of the 1961 trial of Eichmann and an earlier (1954) libel trial, involving a minister in David Ben-Gurion's government, who alleged he had been falsely accused of betraying Hungary's Jewish population during World War II. While that trial did not specifically concern the Brand mission to save Hungarian Jews, Brand had been called to testify on behalf of those in Hungary who had spearheaded the effort. In his novel, however, Elon uses the figure of Joel Brand, a member of the Hungarian Jewish Committee for Rescue and Relief, as a vehicle for portraying the sense felt by some of Europe's Jews of betrayal by their brethren fighting for a Jewish state in Palestine. The novel exposes a terrible paradox for twentieth-century Zionists living in British-controlled Palestine: On the one hand, the rationale for the Jewish national homeland in Palestine proposed by Zionists was that only through its existence could such a catastrophe as the one befalling European Jewry be averted; on the other hand, the decimation of European Jewry ensured that the dream of a homeland would be realized. Indeed, more than once, officials from Winston Churchill to Lord Moyne, Britain's pro-regent in the Middle East, consoled those lobbying British officials to do more to rescue Europe's Jews by assuring them that the crimes being committed against the Jewish people guaranteed them that their state would be "the biggest plum of the war" (p. 250).

Timetable is more interested in reconstructing a historical episode than asserting a literary theme. It is more noteworthy for its careful journalism than its imaginative use of language, and unfolds as a high form of popular fiction driven by suspenseful narrative. It is, however, scrupulously researched and confined to relating just those events for which an abundance of documentation exists, leading some critics to wonder whether it should not have been written as a history. Elon (quoted in the *Contemporary Authors* essay cited above) says the novel is "not fiction, it's faction. The events described in the book actually happened; the conversation is reconstructed." He adds that while "the historian must stick to the dry facts," he "decided to develop the dialogue freely" because he was interested in "trying to fathom [the] motive and character" of the protagonists.

The novel concerns the real-life characters involved in the most infamous of Nazi efforts to barter Jewish lives. After Germany invaded Hungary in March 1944 to keep the Hungarian government, an ally of Germany, from striking a separate peace with the Allies, Adolf Eichmann met in Budapest with representatives of the Hungarian Jewish Committee for Rescue and Relief, and proposed exchanging the one million surviving Jews in Europe, most of whom lived in Hungary, for ten thousand trucks and unspecified quantities of staples, including coffee and soap. Those attending the meeting agreed that Joel Brand, a member of the rescue committee, would bring the offer to the attention of the Allies by traveling to Istanbul, Turkey, where he would meet with representatives of the Jewish Agency, headquartered in Palestine and responsible for smuggling Jews there from Europe. They would put him in touch with the Zionist leader Chaim Weizmann, who had the ear of Winston Churchill. Several conditions, however, were placed on the offer: first, Eichmann insisted that none of the ransomed Jews be sent to Palestine, so as not to harm Nazi relations with the Arabs; second, Eichmann promised that the trucks would be used only on the Eastern front, and not against British or American troops; third, he insisted that Brand return with a reply two weeks after leaving; and finally, Eichmann insisted that a converted Jew who went by the name of Gyorgy and worked for the Gestapo as well as other intelligence services accompany Brand on his mission.

When Brand arrived in Istanbul on 18 May 1944, his mission was immediately compromised by his lack of a visa. Eichmann's agents had supplied him only with a German passport. He was arrested by Turkish authorities, who were persuaded by Jewish Agency representatives not to deport him while they tried to arrange a meeting with the head of the Agency's political department, Moshe Shertok (later Sharett, Israel's first foreign minister and second prime minister). In this episode, Elon introduces one of the novel's few fictional characters, Teddy Mark, who appears to be based at least in part on the real-life figure of Ehud Avriel. Mark is instrumental both in persuading Turkish authorities not to deport Brand and in persuading representatives of the Jewish Agency of Brand's sincerity and the possible authenticity of his mission. The mission, however, is compromised further by the agent Gyorgy, who informs British Intelligence that Brand's mission is merely a diversion, while the real mission is an offer he bears to open negotiations toward a separate peace between the Germans and the Western Allies, Great Britain and the United States.

While Brand remains under house arrest and Jewish Agency representatives desperately try to arrange a meeting with Shertok, valuable time passes; the deportation of Hungarian Jews to Auschwitz accelerates, and the two-week deadline approaches. Even though the Hungarian rescue committee has never believed that the Allies would accede to the Nazi ransom demand, they had hoped Brand would return with a reply leading to a prolonged negotiation that might halt or slow the deportation of hundreds of thousands to Auschwitz. Brand has also carried with him maps the Allies might use to bomb Auschwitz and rail lines leading there. Nevertheless, inexplicable periods of time pass, scuttling the slim hope that Brand may alter the course of events. The Turkish government repeatedly denies Shertok an entrance visa, preventing him from meeting Brand, and finally the Jewish Agency concludes that Brand must go to Jerusalem to meet him. On Brand's trip there, however, on which he is accompanied by Teddy Mark, he is arrested—a week after Eichmann's deadline expires—by British intelligence agents at Aleppo, in the northern tip of Syria. Brand spends the next five months in British custody, first in Aleppo, then in Cairo, being interrogated to ensure he isn't a German agent.

How the British took custody of Brand remains controversial. Much of Elon's novel is informed by Brand's ghostwritten recollection, *Desperate Mission* (1958). In it, Brand contends that he was lured into a trap by the Jewish Agency, that it had apprised the British of his activities at every step. Brand's account, though, has been disputed by some participants in the affair, and some Holocaust historians, such as Yehuda Bauer, writing in *Jews for Sale?* (1994), contend that Brand's memory is self-serving, that he, in fact, desired to travel to Jerusalem for his own safety rather than return to Budapest at great peril to himself. While Elon does not ostensibly take sides in the controversy, and does not directly accuse the Jewish Agency of perfidy, his treatment of the sequence of events leading up to Brand's arrest in *Timetable* leaves that impression. On the train from Istanbul to Aleppo, Mark almost clairvoyantly cautions Brand not to talk to the British should they become separated, which indeed happens, leading to his arrest by the British. Elon describes Brand spending the next four months detained by the British at Aleppo and then in Cairo, where he is interrogated by British Intelligence about his mission. Brand, according to Elon, is certain that Mark and the Jewish Agency have conspired with the British to prevent his mission from bearing fruit. Satisfied that Brand is not a German intelligence agent, the British eventually allow him to travel to Jerusalem, too late to carry out his mission, too late to buy time for the Jews of Hungary.

Even though Elon's descriptions of Brand's experiences are faithful to Brand's recollection of the events in *Desperate Mission*, his portrayal of the deliberations of the Jewish Agency representatives, based on records housed in the Central Zionist Archive, does not agree with Brand's interpretation of the events. Rather, in the novel, Elon suggests that the Jewish Agency did not conspire with the British, but was simply powerless to affect policy decisions at the high levels that would have been needed to open a negotiation with the Germans. Contemporary Holocaust historians Yehuda Bauer, in *Jews for Sale?* and David Wasserstein, in *Britain and the Jews of Europe, 1939–1945*, agree on the futility of Brand's hope of negotiations that might have saved Jewish lives by purchasing time. As the date for the invasion of Normandy approached, the risks posed to Britain and the United States would have been too great; entering into any kind of negotiation with the Germans would have been interpreted by Soviet leader Josef Stalin as an attempt to broker a separate peace, threatening the alliance. While Elon's novel does not reconstruct the deliberations among British authorities that led to Brand's arrest, it illustrates that the Jewish community in Palestine was as powerless as the Jewish community in Europe when it came to saving the lives of Jews, shattering their illusion that they were "young heroes, blond new Jews" while the Jews "of Europe [were] cowards" (p. 340).

Journey through a Haunted Land

The product of Elon's 1965 travels throughout Germany, *Journey through a Haunted Land* (New York: Holt, Rinehart and Winston, 1967) contrasts the country's robust economic recovery from World War II with its spiritual impoverishment. Elon's account opens in Auschwitz during a trial of twenty Germans accused by the German government of crimes they committed during the Holocaust. The trial venue has been moved temporarily to Auschwitz to "check the veracity of expert opinions and testimony of witnesses" (p. 2). The inquiries include measuring the dimensions of the camp's various facilities, as if the "Frankfurt court [had] sent them there to measure an outrage with a yardstick." Elon's travelogue on the Germany of the mid-1960s takes him to all quarters of the country, but what he really surveys is the intellectual landscape of a country triumphant in an economy having risen from the rubble of Allied bombing. Sweeping away the ashes of its moral ruin, however, has proven a much more difficult, almost impossible, task for the German people.

One means of ascertaining the "new" Germany's willingness to acknowledge culpability for Hitler's crimes, Elon argues, is examining the way citizens talk in reconstructing the past. For example, he notes that the phrase "the worst of all times" is used to refer "to the immediate postwar period . . . when German cities were in ruins," not the "time when smokestacks belched at Auschwitz" (p. 24). Who was responsible for the decimation of European Jewry? he asks. According to the new German vernacular, he says, "Everything happened merely 'in the name of the German people' as if perpetrated by foreign mercenaries." This attitude is illustrated in an explanation offered by the public relations officer showing Elon the reconstructed Krupp factory in Essen. This man says of Alfred Krupp, a convicted Nazi war criminal, that "it is true '[he] supported the Nazi machine, but not voluntarily . . . it was the dreadful result of a tragic entanglement of fate,' not unlike the 'tragic entanglement that forced the Jewish elders to collaborate with the Nazis' " (p. 54).

Elon turns to Germany's intelligentsia, particularly the country's writers, to find evidence of the nation's spiritual rehabilitation. He discovers that German poets' "preference for extremely avant-gardistic abstractions . . . may be a flight from the contaminated language . . . of the Nazi period" (p. 235), and that the heavily subsidized German theater depends on revivals of English, American, and French playwrights. While all of Europe suffers culturally from the loss of its Jewish population, Germany has become more parochial than the others as a consequence. Only in the work of Günter Grass does Elon recognize an authentic recounting of Germany's past, an intellectually honest exorcism of her demons.

The book ends with Elon back in Frankfurt, where he began, covering the Auschwitz trial, which he says became almost as famous as the Nuremberg trials, not for its size, or because "Germans were sitting in judgment on each other, but rather because those mass murderers seemed like the average clientele of almost any West German barber shop" (p. 254). He wonders, however, what this trial and the many others like it will accomplish if they cannot spur a moral awakening among Germans. On the trip he reports in *Journey through a Haunted Land*, he has seen little evidence of such a development. At the trial, Elon reports, a journalist asked one of the police officers assigned to guard the defendants what he would do if he were ordered to shoot at the people attending the trial; he answered, " 'An order is an order. When you get an order to shoot, then you just have to shoot' " (p. 259).

Critical Reception

Both Elon's contributions to Holocaust literature received a favorable reception in the English-language press. While Jean Strousse, writing in *Newsweek*, questioned his decision to present Joel Brand's story in a novel, arguing that as nonfiction "it would have had the full force of history behind it," Judith Walzer and Frederic Morton praised the choice. Walzer, writing in the *New Republic*, argued, "In the way that only fiction can, his book prompts us to reflect, to become witnesses to the unresolved problems of history." In a review for the *New York Times*, Frederic Morton concluded that "Elon's powerful documentary novel indelibly renders both the courage and hopelessness of Brand's ordeal [in a form] that is likely to give Brand's anguish the audience that it deserves." Reviewing *Journey through a Haunted Land* for the *New Republic*, Stanley Kaufman praised Elon's account of his travels as "intelligent" and "probing . . . intent on learning, rather than substantiating preconceptions."

Bibliography

Primary Sources

Journey through a Haunted Land, The New Germany. 1967.
The Israelis: Founders and Sons. 1971.
Herzl. 1975.
Timetable: The Story of Joel Brand. 1980.
Flight into Egypt. 1980.
Jerusalem: City of Mirrors. 1989.
Jerusalem Battlegrounds of Memory. Rev. ed. of *Jerusalem: City of Mirrors*. 1995.
Founder: A Portrait of the First Rothschild and His Time. 1996.
A Blood-Dimmed Tide: Dispatches from the Middle East. 1997.

Secondary Sources

Bauer, Yehuda. *Jews for Sale? Nazi-Jewish Negotiations, 1933–1945*. New Haven, Conn.: Yale University Press, 1994.
Brand, Joel. *Desperate Mission: Joel Brand's Story*. Translated by Alexander Weissberg-Cybulski. New York: Criterion Books, 1958.
Contemporary Authors. 2001. Online.
Kaufman, Stanley. "Haunted and Haunting." *New Republic*, 11 March 1967: 20ff.
Morton, Frederic. "Doing Business with Eichmann." *New York Times*, 7 September 1980.
Strousse, Jean. "Failed Savior." *Newsweek*, 11 August 1980: 71–72.
Walzer, Judith B. "Eichmann's Emissary." *New Republic*, 22 November 1980: 36–37.
Wasserstein, David. *Great Britain and the Jews, 1939–1945*. Oxford: Oxford University Press, 1979.

HELEN EPSTEIN

(1947–)

JANET HANDLER BURSTEIN

HELEN EPSTEIN HAS published five books of nonfiction, three of them *New York Times* Notable Books of the Year. Born in Prague to parents who had survived imprisonment in the camps, Epstein grew up in New York City and graduated from Hebrew University in Jerusalem and Columbia University's School of Journalism. For twenty-five years she worked as a freelance reporter and critic for the Sunday *New York Times*, the *Washington Post*, the *Boston Globe*, and many magazines. Married and the mother of two sons, she lives outside Boston and is affiliated with the Center for European Studies at Harvard and the Hadassah International Research Institute on Jewish Women at Brandeis.

The Second Generation

Only eight months old when her parents fled to the United States after the Communist coup in Czechoslovakia, Helen Epstein has had a life that—as her biography sums it up—reads like a paradigm of a goal-oriented American success story. It seems to trace a straight, deliberate path from the liberal arts into journalism, research, publishing, and family life. But her work has become a cornerstone of the growing literature of the second generation chiefly because of the turnings concealed in that path. Generally credited as one of the earliest works on the experience of children whose parents survived the Nazi camps, Epstein's first book, *Children of the Holocaust*: *Conversations with Sons and Daughters of Survivors* (New York: G. P. Putnam's Sons, 1979), introduced to public awareness a group of young people who shared significant memories of Hitler's war—whose lives had been shaped and were still shadowed by a traumatic European past that was not theirs, for they had all been born after the war, and all of them had grown up in the United States.

These young people were children of those who had survived Hitler, and the effect upon them of their parents' suffering was, for several decades after the war, largely unacknowledged. This silence enclosed the story of the Holocaust in what Epstein called an "iron box buried so deep inside" (*Children of the Holocaust*, p. 9) that she could never be sure what it was, or what it contained. Among the ghosts that lay within it, she gradually discovered not only terrifying images of skeletons, barbed wire, shattered glass, mountains of children's shoes, and missing relatives, which belonged to the inadequately told stories of her parents, but also the feelings evoked in her by those images and by her parents' suffering—feelings that had been buried, together with the story of the terrible past.

Feeling the vulnerability of these traumatized parents, whose occasional outbursts of rage were troubling—and incomprehensible—to their children, Epstein and others of the second generation had often curbed their own aggressions and buried their own negative feelings, and had grown up believing that anger was a privilege one had to earn by suffering as their parents had suffered. Epstein's own effort to earn that privilege took her to Israel for three years, where she not only completed work on her first college degree but also lived out unconscious desires to both rescue her parents—or their surrogates in others who needed to be helped—and experience what they had suffered.

In the mid-1970s, while teaching journalism at New York University—where she would become the first tenured woman in her department—Epstein began to interview Holocaust survivors for an oral history project. She interviewed her own parents shortly thereafter, and eventually undertook conversations with children of survivors that led to publication of *Children of the Holocaust*. As she interviewed dozens of other children whose parents had survived the camps, she discovered that their experiences and hers were similar in some important ways. Like her, many of them were scarred by their parents' silences or efforts to disguise the pain of their memories. The process of listening, as a journalist, to other people telling the story that had been so fragmentary and elusive, so detached from emotions during her childhood, liberated feelings of sadness that she had not, earlier, allowed herself to feel. Like many of those whom she interviewed, moreover, she realized through these conversations with them that they belonged to a community; they shared a traumatic past which had shaped them in similar ways. Though they were "strikingly different people . . . who would not have met under ordinary circumstances" (p. 340), though their parents had lived out very different versions of survival, their stories intersected and overlapped in a way that embodied, collectively, the legacy of the Holocaust.

Although some research on survivors had begun when the process of demanding and calculating reparations from the German government began, and a therapy group in Boston for children of survivors, organized by Eva Fogelman, had begun to meet in the mid-1970s, Epstein's 1977 piece in the *New York Times Magazine* and her 1979 memoir, *Children of the Holocaust*, brought national and international recognition to a phenomenon that had, like the recollections of survivors themselves, gone largely unexpressed in the years after the war.

Much of Epstein's own biography is threaded through this first memoir, together with the recollections of other children of survivors and research on psychological studies of the aftermath of the Holocaust.

Where She Came From

A later work, *Where She Came From: A Daughter's Search for Her Mother's History* (Boston: Little, Brown, and Company, 1997), develops more deeply not only the story of her mother's and grandmother's and great-grandmother's European past, but also the crucial process of the "search" itself, which enables Epstein to loosen her bond to her mother, but also to acknowledge the ways in which that bond continues to inform her life and work. Reviewers have generously praised the range and scholarship of this work, which traces the migration of her mother's family from Brtnice to Vienna and Prague. Both the lives of these gifted, energetic women and the places themselves—the high-fashion salons in which they dressed the elite of Prague, the culture of the great cities that taught and inspired and ultimately assimilated them—are wonderfully vivid in this memoir.

Seized and deported to Terezin (Theresienstadt) (then later to Auschwitz) when her mother Franci was just twenty-two, on the day after she had had her tonsils removed, this family moved straight from the busy cosmopolitan streets and shops of middle Europe into the squalor, hunger, filth, and desperate uncertainty of what Franci would call "*koncentrak*"—the world of the lager (camp). Franci's own story of that experience "was so compelling," Helen testifies, that it "eclipsed her family history" and became "the center of rather than the interruption in her life" (*Where She Came From*, p. 234). Surviving the loss first of her parents, then of her husband, then of the young orphan girl she had "mothered"; starved, abused, but nurtured occasionally by other prisoners; later, in a memoir that Helen would eventually incorporate into *Children of the Holocaust*, Franci casts herself in the third person when she describes herself as a prisoner signaling to her daughter the psychic wound that split her sense of herself as the Nazis had interrupted the trajectory of her life.

Within the daughter's account of her mother's family's journey through Europe and Hitler's camps to America, however, is the story of Epstein's own journey—not just to Europe to recover her mother's past, but inward, to confront the complexities of her connection to this mother. After Franci's death, Epstein begins this "search" by looking at her mother's now empty room, perceiving for the first time her mother's world through Franci's eyes, and reflecting deeply upon the bond that had connected them. "So intense was our bond that I was never sure what belonged to whom, where I ended, and she began. . ." Epstein realizes. "I shared my life with her, half-understanding that I was her anchor and that, through me, she lived out alternatives to what had been her own life"(*Where She Came From*, p. 10). This search begins, thus, with a recognition deeply felt but long delayed: that a daughter's life may try to compensate for the damage and losses sustained by a mother who survived the camps.

Beyond this recognition, Epstein discovers that her own work as a journalist owes much to her mother's work. She remembers her mother telling stories at day's end as she "stood at her cutting table, considering cloth." Unlike the scraps of cloth her mother carefully seamed together, the stories were fragmented, disjointed. "My mother was a master at joining parts. . . . If necessary, she would . . . rip everything apart and fix it in the morning. But she never fixed the way she told her past. The parts never fit. They remained separate and discrete." As a child, Epstein "collected threads and scraps of stories, hoarding them, mulling them over. . . . Each was distinct. There were no seams, only wide gaps in the fabric"(p. 13). As she shapes a metaphor from this childhood memory, the adult writer's voice emerges from the child's recollection and yields its own insight: fascinated once by the "disjunctures" in her mother's story of the past, the journalist undertakes in this memoir the work of repairing them.

Conclusion

Part of the work of mourning, this reparation can never restore, of course, what has been lost—any more than a child's life can compensate for a parent's suffering or deprivations. But the insight adds a dimension to the importance of Epstein's work for contemporary American readers. On one hand, her memoirs carry forward into the vernacular of American experience the legacy, borne by the second generation, of remembering Jewish life, and work, and suffering in Europe. These memoirs also show us, however, that memory is not the only legacy. In a personal sense, Epstein's work deepens our understanding of a child's troubled but enduring relationship to a beloved parent whose strengths and scars weigh equally in its complexity. In a collective sense, her work suggests that our own cultural strengths may grow partly from the troubled but enduring bond between American Jews and those who carry scraps of the European story to us.

Bibliography

Primary Sources

Children of the Holocaust: Conversations with Sons and Daughters of Survivors. 1979.
Companies She Keeps: Tina Packer Builds a Theater. 1985.
"Holocaust Was my Parents' Defining Story," in *The Independent* (London). (2000).
Editor, "Jewish Women 2000: Conference Papers from the HRIJW International Scholarly Exchanges, 1997–1998." 1999.
Joe Papp: An American Life. 1994.
Music Talks: Conversations with Musicians. 1994.
Editor, "Study in American Pluralism through Oral Histories of Holocaust Survivors: A Final Report." 1977.
Where She Came From: A Daughter's Search for Her Mother's History. 1997.

Secondary Sources

Barthel, Joan. "Urgent Things to Say" review of *Children of the Holocaust. New York Times Book Review* (29 April 1979): 7, 52.
Benedek, Elissa P. Review of *Where She Came From. The American Journal of Psychiatry* (August 2000): 1351–1352.
Berger, Alan L. *Children of Job: American Second-Generation Witnesses to the Holocaust*. Albany: SUNY Press, 1997.
Burstein, Janet. "Traumatic Memory and American Jewish Writers: One Generation after the Holocaust." *Modern Jewish Studies* 11: 188–197.
Clegg, Ellen. "In the Motherland: A Daughter's Quest to Find Her Mother's History" (review of *Where She Came From*). *The Boston Globe* Book Section (December 14, 1997): H1.
Gay, Ruth. "Lost World" (review of *Where She Came From*). *New York Times Book Review* (Sunday, November 2, 1997): section 7, page 18.
Sicher, Efraim. "In the Shadows of History: Second Generation Writers and Artists and the Shaping of Holocaust Memory in Israel and America." *Judaism* (Spring 1998): 169–185.
Singer, David. "Vicarious Suffering" (review of *Children of the Holocaust*). *The New Leader* (18 June 1979): 20–21.
Walker, Gina Luria. "Pieces of the Past" (review of *Where She Came From*). *Women's Review of Books* XV:7 (April 1998): 20–21.

LESLIE EPSTEIN

(1938–)

S. LILLIAN KREMER

ONE OF THE most controversial novelists of the Holocaust, Leslie Epstein was born in 1938 to Hollywood screenwriter Philip Epstein and Lillian (Targen) Epstein. He received his B.A. in 1960 from Yale University and studied as a Rhodes Scholar at Oxford University, receiving his diploma in 1962. While overseas, he traveled to Israel and read much about the *Shoah* (Goldman, 1997, p. 82). Returning to the United States, he earned an M.A. in theater arts from the University of California at Los Angeles (1963) and a D.F.A. from the Yale Drama School in 1967. From 1965 to 1978, Epstein taught in the English department of Queens College of the City University of New York, while there earning a National Endowment for the Arts grant (1972), a Fulbright Fellowship to lecture in the Netherlands (1972–1973), a CAPS grant (1976–1977), and a Guggenheim Fellowship (1977–1978). In 1978 he accepted a professorship at Boston University, where he now teaches and directs the creative writing program. He has pursued his interest in drama by adapting some of his fiction into short plays for the Boston Playwrights' Theatre. Invited to lecture at schools such as Lane College, Yale University, and Johns Hopkins University, he has also taught writing workshops at the artistic community Yaddo and in New Delhi, India (Goldman, p. 82), and has held a residency at the Rockefeller Institute in Bellagio. Epstein has continued to earn National Endowment for the Arts grants, and his writing has garnered many awards including the Playboy Editor's Award for nonfiction (1971); the American Academy and Institute of Arts and Letters' Distinction in Literature Award (1977); and for *The King of the Jews* (1979), a National Book Critics Circle nomination for Most Distinguished Work of Fiction (1979) and the American Library Association Notable Book citation (1980). His novel *Pandaemonium* (1997) was a 1997 finalist in fiction for the National Jewish Book Award; *Ice Fire Water* (1999) was a 2000 finalist in fiction for the Koret Jewish Book Awards. For creation of the fictional character Leib Goldkorn, the American Academy and Institute of Arts and Letters cited him for distinction in literature.

Documentary Fiction

King of the Jews fuses history and art to convey the essential evil of the Nazi universe, particularly the insidious way it coerced its Jewish victims to do its bidding. The vicissitudes of a slave labor ghetto based on the Lodz ghetto—with its Nazi overlords, Jewish police, bureaucrats, political factions, heroes, rebels, and victims—take center stage. Epstein presents a panoramic grouping of public voices representing various social and political factions, including that of a young narrator, a survivor who attained maturity in the ghetto world. Much of the novel's authenticity stems from Epstein's representation of the *Judenrat's* management of employment assignments, food and housing distribution, police operations, prevention of sabotage, and, most tragically, its role in implementing selections for deportations to concentration and death camps.

True to his belief that Holocaust fiction often commands insufficient authority, Epstein has appropriated documentary evidence from Emanuel Ringelblum's *Notes from the Warsaw Ghetto*, Gerald Reitlinger's *The Final Solution*, Isaiah Trunk's *Judenrat: The Jewish Councils in Eastern Europe under Nazi Occupation*, and Leonard Tushnet's *Pavement of Hell*. Reitlinger's book, which was Epstein's introduction to the enigmatic Chaim Rumkowski, is most likely his source of several incidents, character relationships, and names. Epstein modeled his Baluty Suburb primarily on the Lodz ghetto with some Vilna ghetto grafts applied, and fictionalized historic figures, thereby constructing a highly provocative synthesis.

Situated between documentary and art, and further complicated by its irreverent ironic tone, *King of the Jews* continues to provoke controversy and critical debate. Like scholars, diarists, and other novelists, including Jurek Becker, Primo Levi, and Saul Bellow, who try to comprehend and delineate the Rumkowski figure, Epstein shows us his sharply polarized feelings. Acknowledging the unprecedented evil under which the elder functioned, the novelist dramatizes the dilemma of balancing loyalty to one's people with obedience to the enemy who sustains one's position and authority. Epstein's Trumpelman oscillates between sympathy and condemnation, for the ghetto leader embodies the tension of men whose Holocaust tragedy was compounded by the morally ambiguous role Germans thrust upon them: complicity with the enemy in the hope of saving as many Jews as they could. True to historic portraits, Epstein casts Trumpelman as a complex and contradictory figure: a sinner-savior, a charismatic healer, a persuasive speaker, a charlatan, a dictator, a gullible victim. His noble effort to save Jews through their slave labor is contradicted by his autocratic dispersal of food and deportation of smugglers, strikers, and saboteurs. Epstein's judgment against Trumpelman lies in three areas: his self-delusion; his exultation in power (illustrated in the issuance of ghetto currency and postage bearing his likeness and his flamboyant style); and, most tragically, in his betrayal of Jews through compliance with Nazi "resettlement" orders. The superimposition and revision of speeches by Jacob Gens, leader of the Vilna ghetto, on the biographical detail and manner of Rumkowski invests Trumpelman with an authentic aura, while the invented material heightens his megalomania.

Unlike the ensuing chapters, which faithfully adhere to events in several ghettos and the actions of their leaders, the novel's first chapter aptly titled "The Golden Age" is set in the two decades preceding German occupation of Poland, and relies heavily on literary invention to establish character motivation. Epstein's invented biographical detail exaggerates Trumpelman's egocentrism at the expense of the complexity of his model's (Rumkowski) social and communal role, rendering the fictional character opportunistic, unethical, buffoonish, and arbitrary, lacking his model's community service record and political activism. Rumkowski was vice president of the *kehillah*, a Jewish community council elected by the populace to administer philanthropic institutions, organize Jewish schools, and license ritual officials. Rumkowski fought Polish antisemitism through accommodation, and when that failed turned to Zionism. Trumpelman is apolitical prior to ghettoization, engaging in spontaneous heroism rather than disciplined political action. Epstein also takes liberties with Rumkowski's personal life to further demean the Trumpelman character by replacing Rumkowski's courtship and marriage to a respected young lawyer with Trumpelman's tawdry liaison with a caberet singer.

Among the most successful stylistic components of the work are its literary genre adaptations. While some argue that traditional literary forms and conventions are unequal to Holocaust representation, Epstein has demonstrated how conventional forms can be successfully adapted to Holocaust subject matter and ironic commentary on the subject. He evokes classical forms to access previously unknown experience and to elucidate western civilization's role in the creation of a social and political context fostering and supporting the Holocaust. The parallel between Christian and Nazi persecution of European Jewry is illuminated by means of the medieval morality play metamorphosed as a contemporary Nazi-sponsored street drama that is prologue and transition from the "golden age" to the iron age of Nazism. Adhering to medieval form, a wagon stage appears on which actors perform an antisemitic diatribe in the town square for an audience of soldiers, *Volksdeutschers* (ethnic Germans), Poles, and reluctant Jews. The narrator advises the audience that it will see an accurate portrayal of a historic event and then verbally sets the scene at the Jewish cemetery in Prague where the alleged Elders of Zion conspire against Christian Europe in a diabolic plan of world domination. Predictably, a Rothschild stereotype speaks of financial control; and other tribal heads address tactical matters of pestilence, famine, and economic upheaval. As the stage Jews perform the Christian slander of the Jewish ritual bloodletting of an innocent Christian youth, the audience is encouraged to take vengeance against local Jews once the play has concluded—the gallant Nazi rescue of Christian Europe from the Jewish menace.

The cheering audience provides the play's epilogue, beating local Jews and plundering their property with impunity, a *Kristallnacht* to the tune of pageant cart bells and peeling church bells. The street play not only coalesces pernicious medieval blood libel and modern *Protocols of the Elders of Zion* propaganda, it introduces images of flame, smoke, and grave foreshadowing the crematoria and smokestacks of the death camps.

The morality drama's insistence on the canard of a secret Council of Jewish Elders is an ironic transition to the actual German establishment of its *Judenrat*, the Jewish Council of Elders forced to administer German law in the ghetto. The Nazis were particularly skillful in drawing on existing Jewish community structures to perpetuate their criminal goals. The community *kehillah* lent itself to such misappropriation. The Nazis order the Jews to choose from "The most intelligent, the most resourceful among you" (*King of the Jews*, W.W. Norton, 1993, p. 42) intending thereby to identify, humiliate, and murder the best and brightest to induce the submission of the remainder. Hoping to outwit the Nazis by electing the dissolved *kehillah* to the *Judenrat*, the Jews play into the hands of their oppressors who kill the elected leadership and install their own appointees.

Despite the critical charge, Epstein fails to present the true villainy of the Germans and focuses instead on Jewish collaboration, thereby making the Holocaust appear "an internal Jewish matter" (Wisse, p. 76). Epstein dramatizes the Germans in a manner that reveals their duplicity and barbarism in debilitating, exploiting, brutalizing, and murdering six million European Jews. The novel's designations of the Germans as "Brave Ones," "Warriors," "Others" is a source of considerable critical ire (Milton, p. 76), but might appropriately be read as an allusive reference to Nazideutsch, the perversion of language to conceal criminal behavior. Rather than absolving the Germans of guilt, Epstein's parody of Nazideutsch echoes George Steiner's thesis that there is a straight line from corruption of language to corruption of power; from designating people as vermin to the extermination process.

More than most American novelists, Epstein dramatizes Nazi corruption and evil. Just as the Jewish elder is modeled on Rumkowski, so too, the German administrator is based on the Lodz chief officer, Hans Biebow. Beyond the influence of Gerald Reitlinger's presentation of Biebow, Epstein draws on the work of Hannah Arendt, particularly her assessment of Nazis as bourgeois businessmen, ordinary jobholders, and family men. F. X. Wohltat, like Biebow, saw in a productive ghetto an opportunity for personal financial gain and consequently tried to stall its liquidation.

Like many Polish Jews who thought isolation from a violent public would guarantee their safety, Trumpelman and the novel's Jews initially welcome the ghetto as a haven from oppressive mobs and sporadic government-sponsored antisemitic violence. Like Rumkowski, Trumpelman envisioned the ghetto as an autonomous Jewish enclave, a miniature state with a large measure of self-rule, directing its own administrative bureaucracy, police force, fire brigade, postal service, currency exchange, school system, and health care. Like Rumkowski, who led the longest surviving ghetto in occupied Europe, Trumpelman aspires to be the Moses of the ghetto, keeping his people alive until liberated from slavery by ruling dictatorially, arguing that the only means the Jews have to achieve *lebensrecht* is to make the ghetto indispensable to German needs. To that end, he transforms the ghetto into a major manufacturing unit. Like his historic model, Trumpelman solidifies his power by controlling the ghetto's food supply. He frustrates smuggling, which he perceives as a threat to his economic control, by instituting ghetto currency (Rumkies) to curtail the power and corruption of the ghetto police, who no longer find it profitable to deal with smugglers. The Trumpelman/Wohltat alliance, far-fetched as it seems, is based on the historic Rumkowski/Biebow association.

While Holocaust literature amply records Jewish impotence in the face of Nazi atrocity, only recently have there been recognition and documentation of Jewish resistance efforts in the ghettos and concentration camps. Epstein poignantly captures the tenacious struggle to stay alive in the operation of a clandestine ghetto nursery defying the German ban on Jewish births, food smuggling, large-scale work stoppages, and sabotage operations. Guided by the same principles of fusion that shape his character constructs, Epstein supplements the historic Lodz strikes and leftist opposition with events borrowed from the Jewish resistance movements in the Vilna and Warsaw ghettos, events that could not have been duplicated in the sealed Lodz ghetto. "The Five Day Strike," in which the textile workers are emblematic of all ghetto laborers, is based on evidentiary material from Lodz.

Nothing better demonstrates the moral dilemma of the *Judenrat* than the demand imposed on its members to provide the Nazis with deportation lists, and no section of the novel better illustrates the strengths and weaknesses of Epstein's fusion strategy and ironic tone. The starvation and mounting death tolls produced by ghetto food rationing, work schedules, and police actions had sorely tried the council members. The "resettlement" order devastates them. Their impotence to cope with radical evil or to resist German orders is manifest as they weigh dismal alternatives. As its dilemma grows more painful, there is a decided shift in tone from Jewish compassion to Nazi diction and advocacy for the expendability of "anti-social elements" and jail inmates, rather than of productive workers. In a Nazideutsch self-deceptive parody, an unnamed victim argues: "that we look at things this way. Not who should go but who should stay. The biologically sound material. The socially valuable elements" (p. 161). Epstein incorporates details and lines from Reitlinger's and Tushnet's reports of an exchange between Vilna's Jacob Gens and a rabbinic council that sought to advise him on deportations. However, he so embellishes the exchange that tragedy descends into farce. The artistic failure of the fiction's debate lies in Epstein's unfortunate fusion of the Talmudic arguments that the Vilna ghetto rabbis used to dissuade

Jacob Gens from cooperating with the deportation and misappropriated arguments irrelevant to the issue leading one critic to charge that the debates read like "snappy one-liners" of a "hyperactive Jewish moral imagination" (Wisse, p. 76). Similarly, Trumpelman responds to the council's disapproval of his leadership by offering himself for postwar trial, as did Jacob Gens, but with an oratorical flourish more consistent with Rumkowski's personality.

Bearing Witness: The Arts

An exception to the novel's frenetic tone appears in the Yellow Bus chapter bearing witness to the Chelmno destination of the deportees, where they were awaited by mobile gas vans. Hidden under the transport railcar, the novel's central consciousness is witness to the victims' screaming, gassing, and mass burial, and to preparations for additional extermination contingents. Epstein renders the scene with Germanic precision: the victims disrobe, enter the waiting vans; mechanics supply the carbon monoxide; the bodies are removed; and the next group is processed. The following day, the Jewish slave laborers work among the corpses removing their hair and other items of value.

Epstein develops resistance and witnessing themes through his fictive rendition of the secret work of historians and archivists who recorded ghetto history at grave risk to their own safety. He introduces three minor characters, a mature painter and two youthful photographers, who risk torture and death to visually document ghetto history. The model for the boy photographers is Mendel Grossman, whose book *With a Camera in the Ghetto* was published two years prior to *King of the Jews* and appears to be the source of several descriptive passages in the novel. Grossman took thousands of photographs of the Lodz Jews, their illnesses, their hunger, their degradation. He recorded the distribution of food rations, workshop industries, domestic life, human beasts of burden pulling excrement wagons, deportations, and public executions—scenes documented by the novel's photographers. Epstein thus honors ghetto and concentration camp witnesses who recorded Holocaust history in diaries, histories, and drawings, and testifies to the power of art to respond to the human condition.

Ghetto residents simultaneously resisted the Nazi effort to dehumanize them and covertly criticized their oppressors through participation in veiled cultural events. Based on the Vilna model of a play overtly set in a previous historic period, but deeply analogous to and critical of the contemporary ghetto leadership, Epstein's *Makbet* uses the Shakespearean study of political corruption to highlight that of Trumpelman's administration, a scheme that is not lost on Madame Trumpelman. Throughout the play, Epstein emphasizes the role external evil plays in the moral decline of the ambitious flawed monarchs. A Shakespearean-style prologue, delivered by a comedian, alluding both to the Elizabethan fool's freedom to speak the truth and World War II–era anti-Nazi humor, offers the tale of a distant city's "resettlements" that mocks the *Judenrat* and the elder for their compliance with deportation orders. A terrible dramatic irony prevails as the ghettoites weep for the legendary Scots while their own police force assembles to herd them into deportation transports. The chapter expresses Epstein's belief in the power of art to influence and interpret human behavior. The Baluters, themselves victims of unprecedented persecution, empathize with the theatrical bleeding Scots. Implicit in the audience's reaction is Epstein's criticism of an unresponsive, uncharitable international audience that watched knowingly and idly as the Nazis and their collaborators performed their drama and the Jews suffered their tragedy. The theater scene concludes with a historic usurpation drama. Trumpelman came to power by Nazi whim and is just as arbitrarily replaced by his ghetto rival as the usurper Macbeth came to his crown criminally.

Haunted Survival in a Comic Voice

Although *King of the Jews* is Epstein's only protracted Holocaust work, Holocaust survivor Leib Goldkorn is a recurring figure in Epstein's work, appearing initially in the critically acclaimed "The Steinway Quintet," (1976), then in *The Goldkorn Tales (1985)*, and most recently in *Ice, Fire, Water* (1999). Epstein approaches these works in two time frames, the present of Goldkorn's hilariously rendered New York life and eternal *Shoah* time as lived in memory. Goldkorn managed to escape to the United States in 1943. His family perished in Dachau following his thwarted effort for their escape, a memory that haunts him.

The most recent Goldkorn incarnation and most ambitious presentation is in *Ice, Fire, Water*, a retrospective of the ninety-four-year-old survivor's Holocaust memories and fantasies narrated against the backdrop of his contemporary comically rendered aging physicality. Foremost in Goldkorn's Holocaust memories are the loss of family and his aborted efforts to encourage public resistance to the Nazi genocide. The memory of his betrayed family that haunted Goldkorn in "The Steinway Quintet" is fleshed out in the novel, as is his contempt for Hans Maltz, the colleague whom he paid to arrange his family's escape, who is, in fact, a Nazi. Convinced during the war years that art could make a difference, Goldkorn composes an opera based on the legendary figure of Queen Esther—who saved Persian Jews from mass murder in the ancient world—hoping that the Haman/Hitler analogy would be evident and lead to the defeat of the Nazis. This scheme brings Goldkorn into hilarious proximity with 1940s movie stars whom he sees as potential stars of his opera. In "Ice" he and his sister, dressed as an Austrian rifleman, try to assassinate Hitler at the 1936 Olympics where Goldkorn encounters Sonia Henie. Mistaken for composer Erich Korngold, he is invited to write the score for Henie's movie, which he tries to rework as his Purim play. In "Fire" he meets Carmen Miranda and famed conductor Arturo Toscanini on a ship bound for Rio and tries again to have "A Jewish Girl in the Persian Court" performed this time for the pro-Axis Brazilian president in the hope of denying Hitler an ally. In "Water" he is in Hollywood directing a film of his operetta starring Esther Williams.

Given that Goldkorn was a witness only to the early phase of the Nazi operations, direct witness of the *Anschluss*, and indirect witness of *Kristallnacht*, Epstein's Holocaust canvas is limited and dependent on news bulletins that Goldkorn encounters. Goldkorn learns of the night of broken glass in the Paris press, the headlines referring to Berlin's grand synagogue in flames, Berlin in a sea of crystal, Germany in a war against the Jews. Whether the French journalists reported *Kristallnacht* as Germany's war against the Jews may be in doubt, but Goldkorn's perception is real as the language shifts from headline to the protagonist's reckoning:

> One hundred Jews murdered. Thousands sent off to the camps. Two hundred synagogues burned to the ground. How many businesses destroyed? Seventy-five hundred. The broken glass! Equivalent to half the output from Belgium for an entire year. . . . The cost: five million marks. And who would bear this expense? The insurance companies of the Reich? The brown-shirted perpetrators? Do not force me to laugh. The answer is—and here we see, in the master race, diabolical cleverness—the victims themselves! For creating a public disturbance. Special tax: one million marks. The Jews would pay for their own pogrom! *Kristallnacht*! (*Ice, Fire, Water: A Leib Goldkorn Cocktail*, W.W. Norton, 1999, p. 24).

This passage fusing the pained and angry response to the violence of *Kristallnacht* and the satiric observation of the further insult of ordering the Jews to pay for the destruction is typical of the novel's tone. This apt juxtaposition is compromised, however, for Epstein lapses into farce in the following section of a post-*Kristallnacht* embassy scene beginning with Goldkorn's perception of a crowd of the doomed outside the French embassy awaiting visas. Inspection of the valued documents reveals the crowd to be comprised of film enthusiasts who had been waiting for tickets to an American film premiere.

Undergirding Goldkorn's hilarious and ridiculous wartime misadventures in Hollywood is Epstein's critique of the film capitol's failure to produce work during the war years that addressed Holocaust tragedy. While Hollywood movies advanced Allied war interests and provided escapist films for relief from the horrors and deprivations of war, it consciously avoided any mention of Germany's war on the Jews. Typical of Epstein's acerbic censure is his juxtaposition of a catalogue of German victories in the Sudetenland, the seizure of Bohemia and Moravia, Slovakia, the fall of Poland and France, with a satiric note on Hollywood's production for the masses, "A film in which a man stuffed with straw dances with a man made of metal" (p. 106).

Having grown up in the Hollywood culture as son and nephew of the twin screenwriters who wrote *Casablanca*, Epstein is comfortable with re-creating the Hollywood of the 1940s, but he is profoundly uncomfortable with Hollywood's cinematic evasion of the Holocaust, in its capitulation to the likes of Ambassador Joseph Kennedy who warned of an antisemitic backlash if films addressed the persecution of European Jewry. In his critique of Hollywood contrasted with Goldkorn's persistent wartime effort to use art to reveal the *Shoah* and postwar remembrance, Epstein argues for the morality of bearing witness. Thus the man who finds "the horror is in the quietness and the routineness with which . . . [the Holocaust] actually happened" (Brownlow, p. 71) has devoted much of his writing to charting the absurdity and moral corruption of the Nazi system and the world that tolerated the Holocaust.

Critical Reception

Critical assessment of *King of the Jews* has been sharply divided between those, such as Edith Milton, Ruth Wisse, and Alvin Rosenfeld, who condemn Epstein for belittling tragedy with farce and those who commend the work as a serious historical narrative. He has drawn the ire of these critics for his pastiche of Lodz, Warsaw, and Vilna ghetto experiences, his amalgam of Rumkowski and Jacob Gens (the Vilna ghetto leader) in I. C. Trumpelman's characterization, as well as his fictional invention and comic tone. Yet the work has also garnered the praise of Robert Alter who applauds the narrative mode and observes that "No work of fiction has opened up so fully the unbearable moral dilemma in which the *Judenrat* members found themselves, governing with a pistol at their heads, administering the processes of death, corrupted of course by their awful power, yet trying to preserve life when there was no real way to preserve it" (Alter, pp. 44–45). Terrence Des Pres offers the strongest defense of Epstein's comic approach for its authenticity as it iterates Emanuel Ringelblum's incorporation of ghetto humor in his chronicle of the Warsaw ghetto and theoretically Bakhtinian terms of the "carnival laughter"—"laughter that attacks all rules, regulations, and hierarchies, . . . laughter that celebrates the regenerative powers of community" (p. 222). I argue elsewhere that "Epstein's is a moral voice that does not spare the Nazis. It is one which accurately recreates the hellish system they devised, dramatizes its physical and moral victims as well as its spiritual and moral victors, and in that process confronts the twentieth century's calamity through a superb fusion of documentary and creative imagination" (Kremer, p. 141).

Bibliography

Primary Sources

Novels

P. D. Kimerakov. 1975.
King of the Jews: A Novel of the Holocaust. 1979.
Regina. 1982.
Pinto and Sons. 1990.
Pandaemonium. 1997.
Ice, Fire, Water. 1999.

Short Stories

The Steinway Quintet Plus Four. 1976.
Goldkorn Tales. 1985.

Selected Publications in Periodicals and Books

"Playground." *Yale Review*, December 1967, 222–235.
"Arithmetic of Silence." *Nation*, 11 August 1969, 119–121.
"Lessons." *Yale Review*, October 1972, 1–42.
"Review." *Atlantic*, September 1975, 53–61.
"The Reality of Evil." *Partisan Review* 13 (1976): 639.
"Skaters on Wood." *Esquire*, September 1977, 109–111.
"The Steinway Quintet." *Antæus* 23 (autumn 1976): 42–100. Reprinted in *The Best American Short Stories, 1977: And the Yearbook of the American Short Story*. Edited by Martha Foley. Boston: Houghton Mifflin Co., 1977.
"Eichmann and Other Matters." Review *Jew as Pariah*, by Hannah Arendt. *New York Times Book Review*, 21 January 1979.
Review of Cynthia Ozick's *Levitation. New York Times Book Review*, 14 February 1982.
"Music of the Spheres." *Georgia Review* 38, no. 4 (winter 1984): 765–823.
"Micro Motion." *Omni*, January 1985, 72–77.
"Atrocity and Imagination." [adaptation of address, April 1985] *Harper's*, August 1985, 13–16.
"The Novel's Grip upon Reality." *TriQuarterly* 65 (winter 1986): 39–45.
"Writing about the Holocaust." In *Writing and the Holocaust*. Edited by Berel Lang. New York: Holmes & Meier, 1988, pp. 261–270.
"Huey, Duey, Louie and Other Classics." *New York Times Book Review*, 7 December 1997, 28–29.
"The Undead." *New York Times Book Review*, 12 April 1998, 7.
"From *Fire Ice Water*: Hip Hop." *TriQuarterly* (fall 1999): 105–117.
"Odessa in the Bronx." *New York Times Book Review*, 9 July 2000, 7, 13.

Secondary Sources

Alter, Robert. "A Fable of Power." Review of *King of the Jews. New York Times Book Review*, 4 February 1979, 45.
Ascherson, Neal. Review of *King of the Jews. New York Review of Books*, 5 April 1979, 28–29.
Bernstein, Michael. "A Hollywood Cast Coping with Hitler's Menace." Review of *Pandaemonium. New York Times*, 2 June 1997, C13.
Busch, Frederick. "Even the Smallest Position." *Georgia Review* 38, no. 3 (Fall 1984): 525–541.
Crain, Jane Larkin. Review of *King of the Jews. Saturday Review*, 31 March 1979, 53.
Des Pres, Terrence. "Holocaust Laughter?" In *Writing and the Holocaust*. Edited by Berel Lang. New York: Holmes and Meier, 1988, pp. 216–233.
Evanier, David. "Disaster á la Carte." Review of *Goldkorn Tales. New York Times Book Review*, 7 April 1985, 8.
Goldman, Irene C. "*King of the Jews* Reconsidered." *Midstream* (April 1986): 56–58.
———. "Leslie Epstein." *Contemporary Jewish-American Novelists: A Bio-Critical Sourcebook*. Edited by Joel Shatzky and Michael Taub. Westport, Conn.: Greenwood Press, 1997, pp. 81–86.
Grossinger, Harvey. "*Ice Fire Water: A Leib Goldkorn Cocktail.*" *Houston Chronicle*, 13 February 2000, Zest 14.
Grossman, Mendel. *With a Camera in the Ghetto*. Edited by Zvi Szner and Alexander Sened. New York: Schocken Books, 1977.
Kakutani, Michiko. Review of *Goldkorn Tales. New York Times*, 3 April 1985, C24.
Kremer, S. Lillian. "Chaim Rumkowski and the Lodz Ghetto in Leslie Epstein's *King of the Jews*." In *Witness through the Imagination: Jewish American Holocaust Literature*. Detroit: Wayne State University Press, 1989, pp. 103–141.
Krome, Sidney. "Power and Powerlessness in the Judenrat: Chairman M. C. Rumkowski as King of the Jews." *West Virginia University Philological Papers* 38 (1992): 258–269.
Kunow, Rudiger. " 'Emotion Recollected in Tranquillity'? Representing the Holocaust in Fiction." In *Emotion in Postmodernism*. Edited by Gerhard Hoffmann and Alfred Hornung. Heidelberg, Germany: Carl Winter Universitatsverlag, 1997, pp. 257–269.
"Leslie Epstein." *Contemporary Authors Online*. The Gale Group, 2001. http://galenet.galegroup.com/servlet/LitRC?c = 1&ai = 27752&ste_6&docNum = h100002959. 14 April 2002.
Milton, Edith. "Looking Backward: Six Novels." *Yale Review* 69 (October 1979): 89–103.

Reitlinger, Gerald. *The Final Solution: The Attempt to Exterminate the Jews of Europe 1939–1945*. New York: A.S. Barnes, 1961.

Ringelblum, Emanuel. *Notes from the Warsaw Ghetto*. Ed. Jacob Sloan. New York: Schocken Books, 1979.

Rosenfeld, Alvin. *A Double Dying: Reflections on Holocaust Literature*. Bloomington: Indiana University Press, 1980.

———. "The Holocaust as Entertainment." Review of *King of the Jews*. *Midstream* (October 1979): 55–58.

Schiff, Ellen. "American Authors and Ghetto Kings: Challenges and Perplexities." In *America and the Holocaust*. Edited by Sanford Pinsker and Jack Fischel. Greenwood, Fla.: Penkevill, 1984, pp. 7–34.

Schwarz, Daniel R. *Imagining the Holocaust*. New York: St. Martin's Press, 1999.

Trunk, Isiah. *The Jewish Councils in Eastern Europe Under Nazi Occupation*. New York: Macmillan, 1972.

Tushnet, Leonard. *The Pavement of Hell*. New York: St. Martin's Press, 1972.

Wisse, Ruth. Review of *King of the Jews*. *Commentary* 67 (May 1979): 76–77.

Yogev, Michael. "The Fantastic in Holocaust Literature: Writing and Unwriting the Unbearable." *Journal of the Fantastic in the Arts* 5, no. 2 (1993): 32–49.

Selected Interviews

"Publishers' Weekly Interviews." Edited by G. Stuttaford. *Publishers' Weekly*, 8 January 1979, 8–10.

Interview with S. Lillian Kremer. 6 June 1985. Unpublished.

"From the Modocs to Marlene Dietrich," by Judith Shulevitz. *New York Times Book Review* 4 November 1990, 3.

"An Interview with Leslie Epstein," by Mark Brownlow. *Agni* 39 (1994): 64–82.

"The Man Who Rode Away: What D. H. Lawrence means to today's readers." Epstein and forty-three other novelists respond to Gary Adelman's query. *TriQuarterly* (winter 2000).

ELŻBIETA ETTINGER

(1925–)

S. LILLIAN KREMER

IT IS NOT surprising that when Polish-born (19 September 1925) political scientist and *Shoah* survivor Elżbieta Ettinger turned to creative writing, she explored the implications of political upheaval in the lives of her characters. Whereas most Polish Holocaust survivors left the land that became the unmarked grave of millions of fellow Jews, Ettinger remained in Poland after the war. She earned her M.A. and Ph.D. at the University of Warsaw, and another advanced degree at the Academy of Political Science. She was employed in the foreign trade ministry and as a translator for the Polish government. Ettinger represented the government abroad until Communist-driven antisemitic policies led to wholesale dismissal of Jews from government positions during the 1960s as part of the official anti-Zionist campaign. At this time, Ettinger undertook a Ph.D. in literature and embarked upon a second career in hope of encountering less political interference. Antisemitism became increasingly prevalent, leading her to immigrate to the United States in 1967. There she was associated with Radcliffe, where she had been a Bunting Fellow prior to her immigration and later, a senior fellow at the Radcliffe Institute from 1972 to 1974. From 1973 until her retirement, Ettinger was professor of humanities and Thomas Meloy Professor of Rhetoric at the Massachusetts Institute of Technology.

During her Bunting Fellowship period exploring the theme of law in American literature, Ettinger devoted her nights to writing a *Shoah* novel, *Kindergarten* (1970), to counter American misperceptions of the genocide, Polish antisemitism, and Jewish passivity (Kremer interview). Her fictional account of postwar hardship and anxiety-ridden existence for Jewish Holocaust survivors in Poland is the subject of an autobiographical novel, *Quicksand* (1989). Ettinger's method of writing the lives of prominent political women through the lens of their correspondence and personal relationships with influential political philosophers is at the heart of her three books, *Comrade and Lover: Rosa Luxemburg's Letters to Leo Jogisches* (1979), *Rosa Luxemburg: A Life* (1986), and *Hannah Arendt/ Martin Heidegger* (1995). She is the coeditor of *Studies in Poetics: Commemorative Volume Krystyn Pomorska (1928–1986)*, author of numerous Polish-language critical essays and book reviews, and translator of works from English and German into Polish.

Hiding in Aryan settings and serving as a partisan engaging in sabotage, Ettinger spent the years of the *Shoah* in and out of the Warsaw ghetto, with four months in the Majdanek concentration camp. Her contribution to Holocaust testimony began with the reports she filed while imprisoned in the Warsaw ghetto. A student in underground classes taught by one of the contributors to Emanuel Ringelblum's clandestine chronicle of ghetto life, *Oneg Shabbat*, she shared reports on education and daily life and death in the ghetto that became part of her teacher's report to Ringelblum. After her escape from the ghetto, Ettinger lived on the Aryan side of Warsaw and fought in a resistance unit that "blew up bridges and killed a number of German officials" (Kremer interview).

The Holocaust Crucible

Kindergarten is a third-person narrative presented from the point of view of Elli Rostow, who comes of age during the Holocaust under an assumed Christian identity. The brief prologue frame, dated 1962, introduces Elli as a *Shoah*-haunted survivor brushing imagined gas away from her child's crib. Compelled by history and a promise given to her grandfather to remember and to bear witness, memories of dead relatives and fragments of key events that will be developed in the central recollected narrative flood her consciousness. The novel's focus is the battle for survival and victims' responses to Nazi oppression and Polish complicity. Within the settings of the Warsaw ghetto and Aryan Poland, the major characters experience Holocaust-wrought transformations: from housewife to resistance fighter, from innocent school girls to experienced fugitives, from antisemite to benefactor of Jews, and from self-confident partisan to paranoid suicidal victim.

Ettinger adopts a discourse of discontinuity that interrupts narrative flow to evoke Holocaust rupture in the lives of European Jewry. Rather than employing a linear, chronological progression, she presents a complex series of juxtaposed dramatic scenes, flashbacks and flashforwards, meditations, and diary entries. The text loops back and forth on itself, juxtaposing dramatic presentation and diary meditation to illuminate political and psychological themes. The novel's intricate structure counterpoints ghetto incarceration through dramatic action and Elli Rostow's diary accounts with scenes of the fugitive experience in Aryan Poland. The diary segments record the incremental stages of occupation and ghettoization, Warsaw ghetto administrative edicts, and the impact on private lives. It also provides a record of the characters as they were before catastrophe struck and thereby suggests the magnitude of their transformations. Entré to Elli's thoughts and emotions, to her metamorphosis from free citizen to ghettoized pariah, from innocent girl to instant adult, is realized in the diary's discourse as well as the events it charts.

The novel's action begins in *medias res*, in a narrative style imitative of *Shoah* displacement and disorientation, thrusting the reader into a violent ghetto deportation action. Not until a later diary entry, quoting and dating the deportation edict, do readers understand that the novel's setting is the Warsaw ghetto. Iteration of the edict conditions allows readers to see the documents through dual perspectives of residents ignorant of their true import, and from a post-Holocaust frame of reference. In contrast to the highly charged language and brutal action of the deportation, the edict's diction reflects the Nazis' manner of lulling victims into acquiesence to assure orderly deportations from the ghettos to the concentration and death camps. The ghetto's prominent members, whose survival depended on carrying out German orders against the Jewish population, were exempt. The promise of survival through labor and the inducement of food enticed the suspicious but starving ghetto populace to volunteer for the transports. Choral voices in the dramatic scene speak ofg forced labor battalions, temporary reprieves through essential labor passes, and roundups. References abound to Jewish efforts to survive through work, bribery, and hiding, and the German counterplan for population control and depletion through the use of Jewish police, starvation, disease, and deportation to the extermination camps. The Rostow diary passages echo themes of historic testimonies: early trust resulting from isolation among fellow Jews (for they were too isolated from the non-Jewish Polish population to get news) the ensuing starvation, disease, and deportations; criticism of the ghetto leadership; and the rise of Jewish resistance.

A resister herself, Ettinger refutes the myth of Jewish passivity and offers dramatic representation of Jewish organized and executed resistance inside and outside the ghetto among men, women, and children of all circumstances, effectively linking the themes of resistance and Holocaust-wrought character transformation. The active resistance theme is centered in Elli's mother, Maria, a member of a partisan group operating from the Aryan side. She is representative of the women Emanuel Ringelblum celebrates as heroines, relying on their "Aryan" looks and forged Aryan papers identifying them as Poles or Ukrainians, who travel through the cities and towns of Poland as couriers.

The resistance of the teenage protagonists is initially limited to surviving as "Aryan Jews," surviving outside the law, moving from place to place, obtaining false papers, "passing" as Christians. They must blend with their surroundings, adopt Polish customs, habits, and mannerisms, be convincing Catholics in and out of church. They must watch every word, every gesture, lest they betray nervousness or unfamiliarity with the adopted routine. The characterizations focus on individuals' psychic stress generated by the sustained risk of discovery and denunciation. Elli is transformed from an assured young woman facing dangerous ghetto situations with ingenuity to a fear-obsessed victim; her sister, Lili, plummets from high-spirited optimism into madness. Drawing on her own experience, Ettinger masterfully represents the anxiety associated with open hiding—eluding blackmailers, the constant need to alter identity and relocate, and the need to be faithful to the assumed character, coupled with the incessant fear of discovery.

The second half of the novel shifts from reports of Maria's activities to dramatic presentation of active resistance by Elli and her associates. In the privileged position of Polish worker in a German office dealing with "the Jewish problem," Elli garners information useful to the resistance and stays abreast of developments in the ghettos. She learns of the liquidation of the "Jewish Quarter" of Chelm and the murder of those who tried to evade deportation, and the historic Warsaw Ghetto Uprising, much as Ettinger herself did when she worked in a German office (Kremer interview). Overcoming her concern that because she is unable to fire a gun or dress a wound she will be useless, Elli leaves her job without permission and returns to the ghetto where she witnesses many corpses, mortar shells exploding, detonations, fire, "monstrous piles of charred bricks, melted iron, broken pipes, smoldering wood" (*Kindergarten*, Boston: Houghton Mifflin, 1970, p. 174).

Ettinger presents the uprising through Elli's report of ghetto losses to an underground leader and her expression of regret that the insurrection had not begun a year earlier. Her communication is characterized as "dry and terse with no adjectives and no comments. So many killed, so many wounded, no arms, no medicine, no food, no water" (p. 182). Ettinger suggests the heroism of the ghetto fighters in a single brief reference to the changed function of the ghetto wall. Not only is it a symbol of Jewish imprisonment, it now "kept off the Germans who wouldn't enter the ghetto except through cleared paths and in close order; and it became instead a bulwark and passage for the insurgents" (p. 171). Thus, while Ettinger intimates the historic circumstances of the makeshift ghetto army holding off Hitler's forces and causing them to retreat, regroup, and enter the ghetto with trepidation previously unheard of, she forgoes the anticipated dramatic representation of the insurgency.

Ettinger shares the focus other women writers give to women's experience, although her fiction does not enter the gender-segregated world of the camps. Her women are, nevertheless, vulnerable, and occasionally empowered, by virtue of their gender. Sexual assault is present from the early occupation period, as Maria discovers when she is caught in a roundup for humiliating manual labor and then suffers harassment by a Nazi officer who finds her "*So jung . . . so schön*" ("so young, so beautiful"), and expresses his admiration in a manner that implies rape. When she returns home, Maria sits, "staring blankly ahead" (p. 34), and talks of an acquaintance who committed suicide with her two daughters. Similarly, a Polish extortionist hiding a group of fugitives insists on payment in cash and sexual favors, forcing himself upon the women. Conversely, because Ettinger's women are relatively free, opportunity presents itself for them to use men's sexual appetites to their own advantage. When the refugees decide to kill the extortionist, who has promised to betray them, they not only ply him with liquor, the women are assigned to distract him by playing to his lust.

The fate of children in the *Shoah*, a common theme among women writers, finds thorough explication in Ettinger's universe, in the ghetto realm as well as on the Aryan side. Ettinger is particularly adept at delineating the special precariousness and precociousness of children whose parents have had to leave them, children who learn adult behavior and assume adult responsibilities early. The four year old, who "is always ready for the road" (p. 129), knows how to refrain from asking embarrassing questions, knows how to promise that she will be good so her cousins will want to keep her, knows how to conceal her identity in the presence of a German soldier. When the teenagers are at work, the child is left alone for twelve hours in an unheated room with prepared breakfast and lunch, meals she eats in reverse order. After weeks of this routine, the precocious child leaves her food uneaten, and clings desperately to her cousins upon their return in the evenings.

Madness and suicide loom throughout the novel. Madness is Ettinger's central metaphor and objective correlative for the Nazi world. Ettinger charts the disrupted lives of major and minor characters, either by introducing them when they have already lost reason or life and following with exposition of the route that led to the catastrophe, or by delineating the progressive transformation from clarity to derangement, the movement from fighting for survival to rejecting existence that is externally controlled and persistently degraded. Lili's madness is the culmination of Gestapo torture. Elli's madness progresses incrementally with subjection to ever-increasing violence beginning with participation in the gruesome assassination of a self-declared informer, a Pole who is bleeding the ghetto escapees for all the money he can while threatening them with denunciation, followed by the execution of a Nazi who interferes with a resistance mission, whom she kills rather than allow him to deliver her to the Gestapo. Another factor contributing to her paranoia is fear that Adam, her ethnic German lover, a reformed antisemite and fellow partisan, whose loyalty she doubts and from whom she conceals her Jewish identity, will either lead her into captivity through his resistance work or betray her to the Nazis. Ettinger concludes *Kindergarten* with Elli's surrender to madness and her attempted suicide triggered by her belief that Adam has betrayed her.

Quicksand

Immediately following the Warsaw ghetto insurrection in *Kindergarten*, Elli addresses the subject of maintaining historic memory, anticipating a time in the future when those who abandoned the Jews of the ghetto will come by the hundreds of thousands to bury the dead and care for the living: "I believe they will never forget what happened to us. They will tell it to their children and impose on them a burden never to forget" (*Quicksand*, London: Pandora, 1989, p. 190). At the time, it is unclear whether the mourners she has in mind are Poles or Jews. *Quicksand*, a far more bitter novel than *Kindergarten*, resolves the question. The new Poland chooses not to remember its lost Jews. After temporarily accepting its invisible Jews to rebuild the nation, it returns to outright antisemitic persecution.

For the most part, *Quicksand* is composed in a straightforward realistic mode. Flashbacks are easily recognized and share none of the looping quality of those in *Kindergarten*. *Shoah* matter enters the postwar fiction subjectively and subconsciously through dreams, or directly in survivors' dialogue. Representations of survivor angst through dreams and nightmares are conventions Ettinger shares with native-born American novelists. Elli's beloved Lili and Maria emerge in dreams and memories confirming the pain of her solitary survival. Maria appears in a surrealistic vision emerging from a wall, which opens to facilitate her arrival, and then changes to a barbed wire fence. The survivor's response is schizophrenic: "she did not know whether it was safe to call her 'mother' or use her wartime pseudonym" (pp. 307–308).

Political criticism is at the heart of *Quicksand*. Beyond the rhetorical convention of integrating political debate into the dramatic context, the underlying theme of *Quicksand* is fundamental similarity of Soviet and Nazi totalitarian regimes and the central role antisemitism plays in each. Holocaust memory is profaned in Communist Poland, which follows the Soviet directive on obscuring Jewish Holocaust losses through strictly imposed silence. Reflective of postwar Poland's antisemitism are the characters' concealment of their Jewish identity and adoption of Polish names. Ettinger starkly contrasts frightened, socially diminished Polish Jews with their Israeli survivor counterparts, self-confident nation builders, valued fellow citizens. Poland is a Jewish mass grave; Israel is the site of Jewish regeneration. Virulent postwar Polish antisemitism convinces Elli to declare herself a Jew. She will no longer maintain her silence when the old hatred pollutes the body politic of the country she fought for in the Polish uprising of 1944. The novel concludes with images of bright flowers that lose their luster, shrivel, and die when they are brought home, as has the brief season of Jewish acceptance in postwar Eastern Europe. Poland is again mired in the quicksand of antisemitism. Elli Warska willingly returns to her Jewish identity by resuming her rightful name, Elli Rostow, thereby symbolically separating herself from the land of her birth, the center established by the Nazis for the genocide of European Jewry.

While the critics have largely neglected Ettinger's Holocaust works, her controversial nonfiction has received considerable attention. The works on Luxemburg and Arendt each have their ardent advocates and detractors. Praised for bringing Luxemburg to life as a subject, Ettinger was faulted by some critics for her psychohistorical analysis. Garnering even more attention, from prominent critics and scholars such as George Steiner, is *Hannah Arendt/Martin Heidegger*, a reconstruction of the adulterous, star-crossed love affair of the assimilated Jewish philosophy student and her famous pro-Nazi professor, and their long-term correspondence through the mid-1970s. The furor the book provoked among scholars was fueled by Ettinger's singular access to the formerly sealed letters of the lovers. The interest generated by the Arendt/Heidegger book may inspire critics to examine Ettinger's autobiographical and authoritative contributions to *Shoah* narrative, for it is in her fictional rendition of the dynamics of Jews in open hiding and the resistance that she contributes significant social and psychological insights to our understanding of the *Shoah* and its aftermath in Poland.

Bibliography

Primary Sources

Novels

Kindergarten. 1970.
Quicksand. 1989.

Nonfiction

Comrade and Lover: Rosa Luxemburg's Letters to Leo Jogisches. 1979.
Rosa Luxemburg: A Life. 1986.
Hannah Arendt/Martin Heidegger. 1995.
Studies in Poetics: Commemorative Volume: Krystyna Pomorska (1928–1986). Coedited. 1995.

Secondary Sources

Fernandez, Dòminique. "Vies d'emprunt." *L'Express* (5–11 July 1971).
Fleisher, Leonard. "Review of Kindergarten." *Saturday Review* (23 May 1970): 49–50.
Kremer, S. Lillian. "Elżbieta Ettinger." In *Women's Holocaust Writing: Memory and Imagination*. Lincoln: University of Nebraska Press, 1999, pp. 66–99.
"On the Aryan Side of the Wall." *Times Literary Supplement*, 16 July 1971.
Rawicz, Piotr. "Les Enfants de Varsovie." *Le Monde*, 25 June 1971.
Reed, John. "Kindergarten." *The New York Times Book Review*, 8 February 1970.

Roazen, Paul. "Soft-Hearted Hannah." *American Scholar* 65, no. 3 (summer 1996): 455–459.

Romano, Carlin. "The Nazi and the Schoolgirl—*Hannah Arendt/Martin Heidegger* by Elżbieta Ettinger." *Nation* 261, no. 11 (9 October 1995): 390–394.

Steiner, George. "The New Nouvelle Heloise?—*Hannah Arendt/Martin Heidegger* by Elżbieta Ettinger." *Times Literary Supplement*, 13 October 1995, pp. 3–4.

Wistrich, Robert S. "A Fine Romance." *Commentary* 101, no. 2 (February 1996): 58–60.

Wolin, Richard. "Hannah and the Magician—*Hannah Arendt/Martin Heidegger* by Elżbieta Ettinger/*Love and Saint Augustine* by Hannah Arendt, edited with an interpretive essay by Joanna Vecchiarelli Scott and Judith Chelins Stark." *New Republic* 213, no. 15 (9 October 1995): 27–37.

Interview with S. Lillian Kremer. 23 May 1988.

EMIL FACKENHEIM

(1916–)

SUSAN E. SHAPIRO

EMIL FACKENHEIM WAS born in Halle, Germany, in 1916. His father, whose family's presence in Germany traced back to the Thirty Years War, was a lawyer. His mother came from a long line of rabbis. He was the middle child of three brothers, one of whom was not able to leave Germany with the rest of his immediate family on the last plane out in 1939, and died there.

Fackenheim grew up in a liberal Jewish home and attended the famous rabbinical seminary in Berlin, the *Hochschule Fuer die Wiessenschaft des Judentums*, between 1935 and *Kristallnacht*, 10 November 1938. His father was arrested by the Gestapo in Halle on *Kristallnacht*, the very last day that Fackenheim formally attended the *Hochschule*. After being locked out of the vandalized *Hochschule*, Fackenheim returned home to Halle to help his mother win his father's release. Instead, he too was arrested on the morning of 11 November 1938 and was deported to Sachsenhausen concentration camp, along with approximately 4,000–5,000 other Jewish prisoners. When Fackenheim was released on 8 February 1939, three hundred men remained, a number of whom were imprisoned for the duration of the war.

Fackenheim won his release from Sachsenhausen because he could prove that he would be leaving Germany. While at Sachsenhausen, Fackenheim had applied to graduate schools in America in philosophy, and Harvard responded by arranging that he receive a scholarship to study at the University of Aberdeen in Scotland. Two months after his release, Fackenheim passed his rabbinical exams at the *Hochschule* and, on 12 May 1939, with the Gestapo closing in, Fackenheim emigrated to Scotland. He had only one year of peaceful study there before the war, once again, disrupted his life. After the Nazis invaded Holland, Fackenheim was interned for a year and a half in Britain because they regarded him as a German national, even though, as a Jew, he was no longer regarded as a citizen by the German government. Fackenheim was then deported to Canada, where he was put in an internment camp for several months in Sherbrooke, Quebec. He and his fellow Jewish internees were treated as German prisoners-of-war. It was at the prisoner-created "camp university" where Fackenheim first taught philosophy and where he and his friend, Henry Fischel (later a professor at Indiana University), served as rabbis for the prisoners.

When he was finally released from the internment camp, Fackenheim went to Toronto where he was sponsored by a family originally from Vienna. By this time, Fackenheim had already been accepted for graduate study in philosophy at the University of Toronto, where he was warmly welcomed, and after receiving his Ph.D., he taught as Professor of Philosophy until 1983, when he made *aliya* to Israel with his wife Rose, whom he married in 1958 and their three children, Suzy, David, and Yossi. Fackenheim then taught at the Hebrew University Rothberg School for Overseas Students. In June 2001, Yad Va-Shem, Hebrew Union College, and Hebrew University co-sponsored an international conference in Jerusalem in honor of Fackenheim's eighty-fifth birthday.

Fackenheim has published nearly two hundred scholarly articles and twelve philosophical books. Six of these books pertain either fully or to a significant degree to the *Shoah*. In order of publication, these texts are *Quest of Past and Future: Essays in Jewish Theology* (1970), *God's Presence in History: Jewish Affirmations* (1970), *Encounters Between Judaism and Modern Philosophy: A Preface to Future Jewish Thought* (1973), *The Jewish Return into History: Reflections in the Age of Auschwitz and a New Jerusalem* (1978), *To Mend the World: Foundations of Post-Holocaust Jewish Thought* (1982), and *The Jewish Bible after the Holocaust: A Re-reading* (1990), two of which have been most influential, *God's Presence in History* and *To Mend the World*. Fackenheim continued, in his eighties, to write articles related to the Holocaust and philosophy. His autobiography, *Epitaph for German Judaism*, was scheduled for publication in November 2002 by University of Wisconsin Press.

God's Presence in History

Written in the aftermath of the 1967 Six Day War, *God's Presence in History* (1970) marks a turning point in Fackenheim's thought. Philosophy and Judaism are both seen as vulnerable to and informed by history to a degree not previously registered—and, indeed even resisted—in his thought (see *Metaphysics and Historicity*, 1961). This turn is evidenced as well in the introduction to Fackenheim's collection, *Quest for Past and Future*, also written in the aftermath of the 1967 war:

> Until this century the Midrashic framework, while subject to external challenges, has remained internally unbroken. But because it is open, and open not to fancied occurrences but to actual events, this framework is not wholly invulnerable. Today, vulnerability is no mere theoretical possibility. For the Jewish theologian of today cannot continue to believe, or continue to engage in theological thought, as though the events associated with the dread name of Auschwitz had not occurred (Bloomington: Indiana University Press, 1968, p. 17).

In his introduction to *The Jewish Return into History*, Fackenheim further elaborates on this earlier decisive change in his thought in *Quest*:

> The earlier book climaxed with the one major change in my thinking . . . in more than thirty years of literary activity . . . Philosophical and religious thought widely take themselves to be immune and indeed indifferent to the "accidents" of "mere" history. The conscious repudiation of this view, first in abstracto and subsequently in relation to the events of our age, is the major change in my thinking to which I have referred. . . . For the events to which Jewish thought is required to make itself vulnerable today are enormous, unprecedented, and ineluctable: the Holocaust and the rise of a Jewish state after two thousand years of Jewish statelessness (New York: Schocken Books, 1978, pp. xi–xii).

While it is primarily the rabbinic tradition that is examined in *God's Presence in History*, Fackenheim's manner of inquiry in this text is philosophical. The dialectic of (formative and affirming) "root-experiences" and (challenging and negating) "epoch-making events" through which he characterizes the Jewish tradition, the tension between God's "Saving Presence" in history and God's "Commanding Presence" and, even, the "Commanding Voice of Auschwitz," as well as the broken middle of "mad midrash" in which contradictions remain unresolved, are all characteristically marked by Fackenheim's post-Hegelian style of reflection. Fackenheim's claim that the *Shoah* is historically unprecedented and, thus, unique, raises a challenge to the rabbinic tradition of theodicy in which suffering is justified as "because of our sins." He utterly rejects such a blaming of the victims.

Instead, a unique historical event requires, Fackenheim argues, a unique philosophical and religious response, the 614th commandment: "Thou shall not grant Hitler posthumous victories." This command, according to Fackenheim, is evidenced in the very life-choices made by Jews after the Holocaust both on the level of the family and the nation. While fully aware of the threat of extermination, Jews chose to bear children. Fackenheim regards the addition of the 614th commandment to the traditional 613 commandments not only as determined by, and as a negation of, Nazism but as an affirmation of Jewish life. This resistance to Nazi genocide and the affirmation of life through generation becomes, for Fackenheim, paradigmatic. For him, Zionism and support for the continued existence of the State of Israel is an analogous post-Holocaust affirmation, one that unites secular and religious Jews as well as Zionist non-Jews. These responses, however, are fragmentary. In *God's Presence in History*, this fragmentation is troped through rabbinic *midrash*. It is not until *To Mend the World*, however, that Fackenheim develops these themes and approaches from within the Western philosophical tradition as such.

To Mend the World

In his major work, *To Mend the World*, Fackenheim argues that the Holocaust represents a total break with the history of Western thought, action, and belief. The greater part of this text is devoted to a retrospective reenactment of this break. The last section is focused on the recovery of the foundations of thought, action, and belief after this rupture. This text begins in radical negation and, yet, concludes in affirmation.

One of the significant characteristics of Fackenheim's writings after the 1967 war and, especially, in *To Mend the World* is his beginning from within the claim of radical negation emerging from the *Shoah*. He raises the question of recovery, of affirmation, only from within this testimony of radical negation. As a consequence, he deliberately weights our attention toward negation and suffering; the possibility of hope and comfort must, for Fackenheim and for those upon whose testimony he draws, be justified in the face of the priority of the claims of massive suffering and its negating effects. Thus, he does not assume that recovery of the Jewish tradition or of the Sacred or Holy is possible after the *Shoah*; nor, however, does he think that such recovery is impossible. In this way, Fackenheim is in principle able to attend to the dual claims of "rupture and recovery," of negation and affirmation, without necessarily effacing one claim or the other.

The argument of *To Mend the World* implicitly dramatizes the turn in Fackenheim's thinking after the 1967 war in which thought became vulnerable to, even refutable by, historical events. As he notes in the introduction to *To Mend the World*,

> The present work is made necessary by events not in the history of philosophy but in history. And since one of these—the Holocaust—ruptures both history and the history of philosophy, there can be no question here of a system [as in Hegel] or even an antisystem [as in Franz Rosenzweig] (New York: Schocken Books, 1982 p. 22).

Fackenheim, thus, begins by demonstrating how Western philosophy has moved from a view of thought's transcendence of history to its engagement with history, to, finally, its utter finitude and loss of transcendence in its disastrous confrontation with one historical event in particular: the Holocaust. As Fackenheim states, "Where the Holocaust is, thought is not, and where thought is, the Holocaust is not confronted" (p. 200). For him, the foundations of reason have been destroyed in the *Shoah*, and thought may now only uncover this disaster in its own thinking. But if, as Fackenheim argues, the Holocaust and thought displace each other, how may they be brought together in order to demonstrate this displacement? If the Holocaust negates Western reason, what sort of argument may be used to demonstrate or prove this negation?

When he juxtaposes the Holocaust and reflection in order to articulate the displacing effects of their encounter, his writing takes a pronounced rhetorical turn. It is primarily through testimony and example that the turning points in Fackenheim's argument are most persuasively and powerfully made. For example, the displacement of thought by the *Shoah* is rhetorically accomplished in the disruptive inclusion of pieces of documentary narratives—such as selections from Holocaust and post-Holocaust diaries and memoirs—in the middle of his examination of the logic of the philosophical arguments under consideration, including those of Spinoza, Hegel, Rozenzweig, and Heidegger, among others. These "documentary pieces" of the event break into and paralyze thought. One such account is that of the *Muselmänner* from Primo Levi's *Survival in Auschwitz*; it is placed by Fackenheim in the midst of a philosophical argument, whose testimony it ruptures, both in its content and with its very performance.

The argument performatively being made by Fackenheim is that such a return to the foundations of Western thought after the Holocaust is impossible just as, in one's reading, a return to the argument dropped earlier (when interrupted by the account of the Muselmänner), as if now to complete it, is impossible. The failure of thought in confronting the Holocaust, thus, is rhetorically demonstrated.

If the ruin of the foundations of Western thought by the Holocaust is demonstrated through testimony and example, so is Fackenheim's reorientation to the future made possible rhetorically. He relies on the astonishing testimony of physical and spiritual resistance to the Nazis within the Holocaust itself in order to move beyond the utter collapse of Western thought. Examples cited, described, and documented by Fackenheim are the Warsaw Ghetto Uprising, the continued maintaining of the *mitzvot* by the Buchenwald Hasidim (even though they considered the Holocaust as *both* historically and theologically unprecedented), and the paradigmatic resistance of Pelagia Lewinska, a Polish noble woman who, in Auschwitz, recognized its total and deadly logic and who, in response, "felt under orders to live" and so to resist (p. 217; see Lewinska, 1968, pp. 141ff., 150).

Like the account of the *Muselmänner* that ruptures the foundations of reason, the powerful testimonies of resistance disrupt the totally negative logic of the arguments leading up to it in *To Mend the World*. In both cases, the documentary effect of testimony breaks the logic of the discourse preceding it, although with opposite results. If with the first testimony we are plunged into despair, the second testimony makes possible hope. Indeed, in perhaps the darkest moment of the text, the testimony of resistance appears, offering the possibility of a reorientation toward the future, which until that point had been unimaginable.

In moving from rupture to recovery, however, Fackenheim preserves and privileges the testimony of resistance by translating the grounds of its persuasiveness into a logic that effaces the rhetoricity of his argument. He shifts the weight of his argument from negation to affirmation not only then, during the *Shoah*, but for us now; because resistance was possible then and there, resistance is necessary for us here and now, both logically and morally. Recovery, thus, is surprisingly to be found from within the rupture itself, for if within the Holocaust the abyss was crossed in resistance, then it has already, in principle, been closed and the process of *tikkun*, i.e., mending, begun. We are mandated to continue this process of recovery now through resistance, reconnecting our past and present in anticipation of the future.

Does this affirmative conclusion efface the negations of the first part of *To Mend the World*? By making resistance logically necessitate and morally legislate for us now Fackenheim risks excising the very characteristic that makes this testimony so moving, astonishing, and reorienting. On one hand, then, rhetoric makes possible the uncovering of the disaster that the Holocaust is within Western thought, making evident the collapse of the foundations of action and belief. On the other hand, it is precisely this rupture that is covered over in the logical and categorical guaranteeing of recovery. The contradictions between a rhetoric of rupture and a logic of recovery in *To Mend the World*, however, are due not only to his privileging of the testimony of resistance; they issue from his interpretive assumptions as well.

Throughout his writings, Fackenheim employs a somewhat idealist hermeneutic in which experience and perception are understood to precede and, thus, be separable from language. In *God's Presence in History* (1970), for example, he links both the certainty of and the capacity to reenact miracles to their being matters of perception and experience and not interpretive events. Experience and perception are treated as primary when it comes to God's presence in history, whereas language and interpretation are considered secondary. The miracle at the Red Sea, as witnessed by the maidservants, is paradigmatic. Just as the maidservants are authoritative witnesses, so the Holocaust has its canon of testimony. These later witnesses, furthermore, allow the facts to speak for themselves, and do not speak for—i.e., interpret—them. Indeed, the claim to authoritativeness is dependent upon that of the immediacy of their perception, experience, and understanding and as prior to language and interpretation.

It is the tone, but not the syntactical, grammatical, or rhetorical coherence of language that for Fackenheim is in principle marked by the Holocaust. In this way, although Western thought is ruptured in the Holocaust, language has been left unmarred. Both the rupture and recovery of thought may then, at least in principle, be enacted without either breaking or mending language. Thus, the startling recovery of the last part of *To Mend the World* is made possible, indeed is prefigured, by the text's hermeneutical assumptions. Whereas Fackenheim proclaims that the Holocaust breaks the continuity between past and present and totally ends philosophical intelligibility, his interpretive assumptions and method seem to assume the continuity he explicitly declares to be ruptured.

By narratively emplotting the contradiction between the claims of total break or rupture and the recovery of Western thought, Fackenheim makes possible a temporal mediation between them. The "middle" of the text seems to offer something new in the testimony of resistance: a new category, a new departure for thought. But the novelty of this testimony in part is eclipsed. Despite Fackenheim's having "dwelled in the broken Hegelian middle ever since [the 1967 war]" ("A Retrospective,"*Jewish Philosophers and Jewish Philosophy*, p. 222), the work of the "middle" of the text becomes that of suturing and closing its rupture.

This failure to linger in the broken middle, however, perhaps says less about the limits of Fackenheim's enterprise than it does about the contradictory demands and aporetic situation of post-Holocaust writing and thought generally, for the attempt to write and think rupture and recovery together in the same work issues in a series of contradictions that pull apart post-Holocaust discourse. Almost inevitably, one function is figured as subservient to the other in such thought. Of all his many works, *To Mend the World* most eloquently embodies these contradictory claims upon post-Holocaust thought as it moves between rupture and recovery. This monumental work thus illuminates our post-Holocaust situation for future Jewish—but not only Jewish—reflection.

Bibliography

Primary Sources

Paths to Jewish Beliefs: A Systematic Introduction. 1960.
Metaphysics and Historicity. 1961.
Quest for Past and Future: Essays in Jewish Theology. 1968.
The Religious Dimension in Hegel's Thought. 1968.
God's Presence in History: Jewish Affirmations and Philosophical Reflections. 1970.
Encounters Between Judaism and Modern Philosophy: A Preface to Future Jewish Thought. 1973.
The Jewish Return into History: Reflections in the Age of Auschwitz and a New Jerusalem. 1978.
To Mend the World: Foundations of Future Jewish Thought. 1982.
The Jewish Thought of Emil Fackenheim: A Reader. 1987.
German Philosophy and Jewish Thought. 1992.
Jewish Philosophers and Jewish Philosophy. 1996.
The God Within: Kant, Schelling, and Historicity. 1996.

Secondary Sources

Braiterman, Zachary. "Why Is the World Today Not Water? Revelation, Fragmentation, and Solidarity in the Thought of Emil Fackenheim." In *(God) After Auschwitz: Tradition and*

Change in Post-Holocaust Jewish Thought. Princeton: Princeton University Press, 1998, pp. 134–160.

Cohn-Sherbok, Dan. "Revelation and Mass Murder: Emil Fackenheim." In *Holocaust Theology*. London: Lamp Press, 1989, pp. 43–55.

Katz, Steven T. "Emil Fackenheim on Jewish Life after Auschwitz." In *Post-Holocaust Dialogues: Critical Studies in Modern Jewish Thought*. New York: New York University Press, 1983, pp. 205–247.

Morgan, Michael L. "Philosophy, History, and the Jewish Thinker: Jewish Thought and Philosophy in Emil Fackenheim's *To Mend the World*." In *Dilemmas in Modern Jewish Thought: The Dialectics of Revelation and History*. Bloomington: Indiana University Press, 1992, pp. 111–124.

Seeskin, Kenneth. "Emil Fackenheim." In *Interpreters of Judaism in the Late Twentieth Century*. Edited by Steven T. Katz. Washington, D.C.: B'nai B'rith Books, 1993, pp. 41–57.

ELAINE FEINSTEIN

(1930–)

CLAIRE M. TYLEE

ELAINE FEINSTEIN (NÉE COCKLIN), an only child, was born in 1930, in the depressed industrial northwest of England like her parents, Isidore Cocklin and Fay (Compton) Cocklin. They were the children of Russian Jewish immigrants from Odessa, where one of her grandfathers had studied at yeshiva and enjoyed a reputation as a *Tzaddika* (a holy man to whom it was customary to turn for advice). However, she was raised and educated in the more prosperous English Midlands, in Leicester where her father ran a small wood factory and was president of the local synagogue. She read English at Newnham, Cambridge, graduating in 1952. The individuality of her writing stems from her examination of what Olga Kenyon calls her "dual cultural heritage," Anglo-Jewish and Russian (*Writing Women*, 1991, p. 39); she is often praised for her lack of parochialism. Having married Dr. Arnold Feinstein in 1956 and been occupied with three sons, she did not begin publishing books until 1966 when her first collection of poems, *In a Green Eye*, appeared. She has since achieved distinction as a poet, translator, dramatist, and biographer, with seven collections of poetry and four biographies. Her reputation as a writer of fiction was achieved more gradually, although she has now published fourteen novels and a collection of short stories, *The Silent Areas* (1980).

Fiction

Feinstein's first novels were unremarkable, although successful, examples of the English woman's novel about female self-discovery: *The Circle* (1970), *The Amberstone Exit* (1972), and *The Glass Alembic* (1973). Since then she has dealt more overtly with issues of Jewish identity and European history across a variety of fictional genres. These range from the spoof science fiction of *The Ecstasy of Dr. Miriam Garner* (1976) and the family saga of *The Survivors* (1982), through the "condition of England" novel, *All You Need* (1989), to an example of women's romantic fiction, *Lady Chatterley's Confession* (1995)—a sequel to D. H. Lawrence's novel, written from the point of view of Lady Chatterley. Such subversion of popular forms to deal with serious political issues has been a feature of women's writing since the 1960s, but Feinstein idiosyncratically uses feminist issues to raise questions about perceptions of Jewish difference. For instance, Nell in *All You Need* is brought out of her self-absorption by watching Lanzman's *Shoah* on television. It prompts her to reassess her own mixed identity. Connie, in *Lady Chatterley's Confession*, living unhappily with Mellors in fascist Italy, only loses her political indifference when she gets to know a German Jewish refugee. Sarcastically he tells her his father died in Dachau of a heart attack brought on by taking part in an obstacle race.

These straightforward works enable Feinstein to reach a mass audience, but critics have been more impressed by her more sophisticated modernist novels, such as *The Border* (1984), *Mother's Girl* (1988), and *Loving Brecht* (1992). Although these, too, deal with central concerns of the women's movement (women's relationships with men as lovers, husbands, fathers, and the rewriting of biographies of famous men through the lives of women close to them), they use unconventional narrative forms to situate such concerns within crucial moments of European Jewish history. While *The Border* deals with prewar Vienna and Paris, and *Loving Brecht* is set in Berlin and Moscow, *Mother's Girl* more unusually investigates wartime resistance in Hungary. Jewish identity and history are also themes of Feinstein's poetry, especially in *The Celebrants and Other Poems* (1973), but it is within her prose fiction that she extensively interrogates the significance of the Holocaust.

Autobiographical Statements

Feinstein has produced two explicitly autobiographical works. In "A Legendary Hero" (in *Fathers: Reflections by Daughters*, 1983) she portrays the powerful influence of her father. He is also closely depicted in *The Amberstone Exit*, and much of *The Survivors* is based on her own family background, as are sections of *Mother's Girl*. This was confirmed in an interview by Olga Kenyon in 1984 (where she was anxious to distinguish herself from the character of Diane in *The Survivors*). "A Legendary Hero" begins with Feinstein's claim: "I am still glad to be one of those who at least began life with a general trust of men" (p. 159). It was to her strong love for her father that she attributed being "instinctively monogamous, in an age where such a condition is rare and may even become comic" (p. 167). The importance to her of the marriage partnership, the productive tensions of a committed relationship, not only gave her a distinctive position among feminist writers, it provided a narrative dynamic for exploring different responses to the dilemma of being Jewish.

The autobiographical essay she contributed to a collection in 1985 has been much cited by critics ("Elaine Feinstein Writes," in *The Bloodaxe Book of Contemporary Women Poets*, Newcastle: Bloodaxe, 1985). There she identified certain key points in her development as an Anglo-Jewish writer. The first of these occurred at the end of World War II when she learned exactly what had been done to so many children of her own age in Hitler's camps. The event exploded her childhood sense of security. "You could say that in that year I became Jewish for the first time. Not something I regret. But no doubt the knowledge of human cruelty damaged me." A second key point occurred when she discovered the Russian poet Maria Tsvetayeva, whose work she went on to translate and publish in 1971. Tellingly, she called her 1987 biography of Tsvetayeva *A Captive Lion*. Feinstein claimed that without Tsvetayeva she would "never have written novels, still less plays" (p. 116). From her and from other Russian women poets such as Anna Akhmatova she learned the value of self-exposure and how to explore fear, pain, and suffering with courage. They also confirmed her refusal to be an insular "little Englander," in either the form or the content of her own writing.

The Children of the Rose

A further key point in Feinstein's development took place after both her parents died in 1973. She went with her husband to Poland and met his one surviving cousin, who had been saved as a hidden child by several Polish families. While there, she visited Warsaw and Krakow where she had an experience in a Jewish cemetery that became the climax of her fourth novel, *The Children of the Rose* (1975). This novel marked a departure in her work wherein she began retrieving Jewish history and writing it into English cultural memory. She does not attempt to fictionalize persecution directly, unlike, say, Bernice Rubens in *Brothers*. Instead, Holocaust episodes are conveyed to us through the reactions of those with secondhand experience, and through the knowledge and memories of those who got away, who were bystanders, or who were too young to fully comprehend. In fact, her major focus has been on the ways in which later generations, both Jewish and non-Jewish, have been haunted by a history repressed in mainstream culture. That history reemerges vividly through the dreams, memories, and visions of her sensitive characters. It is also inscribed in the physical world those characters inhabit, whether the harsh, brutal landscapes where savage acts of history were actually committed, or the rooms they recreate for themselves where characters scent the aroma of a dead past. "All Europe tastes of blood" as Mendez states in *The Children of the Rose*. In fact, while the commonplace world of the present is composed of conversations and activity to keep despair at bay, the past is summoned more vividly through taste ("sweet herrings and poppyseed bread," "honeycake, cherry, aniseed," "birch woods in the rain") or smells that evoke past emotions.

In *The Children of the Rose*, Lalka's breakdown, or breakthrough, commences in Warsaw when she is asked if she remembers at all how it was before the war. Against her will her mind then flows with memories of hiding in a village outhouse as a child, waiting to escape on a hay cart; she relives odors of moldy potatoes, onions, kerosene, of horses pungent and sweating with fear, and the smell of a baby's wet knickers—"She must have been carrying Clara," her baby sister. This involuntary reliving of past experience releases her ability to feel authentically and leads to her willing visit to the synagogue and cemetery at Kasimiersh. At first she marvels and even feels envy for the bodies lying quietly under their old stones. She focuses on a single red rose. It is then explained to her that on this spot one of the German massacres of local Jews took place; an unknown number, maybe hundreds were shot. At once the place appears sinister as though there were still blood in the soil and the weeds, the grass, even the rose, all grew from that blood. She suffers a collapse. She has come home to herself by returning to Poland and found only death and silence at her core.

Critical Responses

The previous passage illustrates how Feinstein brings to life a metaphor that has been latent throughout *The Children of the Rose*. For instance, in a conversation between Mendez, Lalka's husband, and his younger girlfriend, Lee, about being European, he accuses her of "only skating on the topsoil." She responds, "Well, I don't want to dig up the whole bloody graveyard, thank you." As the title suggests, the marriage of Mendez and Lalka has, like the rose, been rooted in a cruel past. Yet despite their long estrangement, he jeopardizes his dearest dream in order to fly to Poland and take care of Lalka. Against the odds, love flourishes. It was presumably this poetic strategy of using a character's heightened vision to revivify a metaphor as literal truth that inspired critics to link Feinstein's work with that of her contemporaries, Angela Carter, J. G. Ballard, and Emma Tennant. According to Peter Conradi, her work was seen as part of the "New Gothic" movement in English literature, forwarding a program of antirealism designed to undercut social illusions fostered by the realist novel. Feinstein rejected this categorization, however, seeing that movement as denying humanism, and disowned its "fashionable resistance to compassion which I believe is as much a luxury of our English innocence as the euphoria of the flower generation."

She clearly shared the project of disrupting English complacency, although not out of any postmodern agenda. As other critics such as Michael Schmidt have noted admiringly, hers is "a richly moral art." It is more appropriate to place her work (as Cheyette and Kenyon have done) alongside other Jewish women, particularly those of her own generation: Anita Brookner and Bernice Rubens. They too write novels that are grounded in historical time and stress the reality of ethical dilemmas, although offering no pat solutions. In spite of the dissimilarity of their work in terms of style, there is another feature Feinstein, Brookner, and Rubens have in common: the dialectical mode of dealing with the Holocaust and the resultant problems posed for Jewish identity. Both the topic and the dialectical structure of *The Children of the Rose*, concerned with the later lives of two Jewish child refugees who arrived in England in the 1930s, are shared with Brookner's *The Latecomers* and Rubens's *Madame Sousatzka*. Unlike the typical English novel (which they are all also capable of writing), these post-Holocaust novels do not feature a single protagonist but alternate between two. They are constructed to demonstrate alternative responses to the Jewish past, disregarded but fundamentally influential on their characters' lives.

Phyllis Lassner, in a perceptive study of Feinstein's fiction, takes her story "The Grateful Dead" as "pivotal" in Feinstein's work. She argues that Feinstein resolves the tension between the rational perspective of her male characters and the emotional response of her females, in favor of the women and against the weight of patriarchal authority. However, it seems that Feinstein, while showing sympathy to her female characters, as do Brookner and Rubens, refuses to favor the intuitive over the intellectual, but holds them in balance. Their novels are modernist in their ironic withholding of "an answer" to the angst they delineate. Nevertheless, they are adamant that British culture is not immune from the events that took place in Continental Europe.

Bibliography

Primary Sources

Books

In the Green Eye. 1966.
The Circle. 1970.
The Magic Apple Tree. 1971.
Selected Poems of Maria Tsvetayeva (editor). 1971.
At the Edge. 1972.
The Amberstone Exit. 1972.
The Celebrants and Other Poems. 1973.
The Glass Alembic (published in the United States as *The Crystal Garden*). 1973.
The Children of the Rose. 1975.
The Ecstasy of Dr. Miriam Garner. 1976.
Three Russian Poets—Translations. 1976.
Some Unease and Angels: Selected Poems. 1977.
The Shadow Master. 1978.
The Silent Areas: Short Stories. 1980.
The Feast of Euridice. 1980.
The Survivors. 1982.
"All Writers Are Outcast." *New Statesman* (26 February 1982): 22–23.
"A Legendary Hero." In *Fathers: Reflections by Daughters*. Edited by Ursula Owen. London: Virago, 1983, pp. 159–168.
The Border. 1984.
Contemporary Authors Autobiography Series. Volume 1. 1984.
"Elaine Feinstein Writes." In *The Bloodaxe Book of Contemporary Women Poets: Eleven British Writers*. 1985.
Bessie Smith: a Biography. 1986.
A Captive Lion: Life of Maria Tsvetayeva. 1987.
Badlands. 1987.
Mother's Girl. 1988.
All You Need. 1989.
City Music. 1990.
Loving Brecht. 1992.
Lawrence's Women. 1993.
"Making Dailiness Exotic." *Jewish Quarterly* (autumn 1994): 64–65.
Dreamers. 1994.
Lady Chatterley's Confession. 1995.
Daylight. 1997.
Pushkin. 1998.
Dark Inheritance. 2000.
Gold. 2000.

Unpublished Plays

Breath (teleplay). 1975.
Echoes (radioplay). 1980.
Lunch (teleplay). 1981.
Lear's Daughters (theatreplay). 1982
Diary of a Country Gentlewoman (teleplay in twelve parts). 1984.

Secondary Sources

Cheyette, Bryan. *Contemporary Jewish Writers in Britain and Ireland: an Anthology*. London: Peter Halban & University of Nebraska Press, 1998.

Conradi, Peter. "Elaine Feinstein: Life and Novels." *Literary Review* (April 1982): 24–25.

———. "Elaine Feinstein." In *Dictionary of Literary Biography 14*. Edited by Jay L. Halio. Detroit: Gale, 1983, pp. 292–297.

———. "Elaine Feinstein." In *Dictionary of Literary Biography 194*. Edited by Merritt Mosley. Detroit: Gale, 1998, pp. 292–297.

Couzyn, Jeni, ed. *The Bloodaxe Book of Contemporary Women Poets: Eleven British Writers*, Newcastle: Bloodaxe, 1985.

Kenyon, Olga. *Writing Women: Contemporary Women Novelists*. London: Pluto 1991, pp. 39–50.

Lassner, Phyllis. " 'Witness to Their Vanishing': Elaine Feinstein's Fictions of Jewish Continuity." In *British Women Writing Fiction*. Edited by Abby H. P. Werlock. Tuskaloosa: University of Alabama Press, 2000, pp. 107–124.

IRVING FELDMAN

(1928–)

JOSHUA L. CHARLSON

IRVING FELDMAN HAS never been a household name. Over the course of his fifty years as a published author, however, he has steadily built a reputation as an innovative, committed poet whose deft and ironic linguistic touch often limns the absurdities of American life. Now in his seventies, Feldman continues to write productively, having published his tenth collection of poems, *Beautiful False Things*, in 2000. Indeed, his stature seems to have grown quickly in the latter part of his career, as reflected in the MacArthur Foundation Fellowship ("genius grant") he was awarded in 1992. He has also been the recipient of fellowships from the Guggenheim Foundation, the Academy of American Poets, and the Ingram Merrill Foundation.

Feldman's verse ranges across centuries, cultures, languages, and voices, but his biography reveals him as a New Yorker first and foremost, and his origins proclaim themselves in the prominence of the city in his writing. Born in Brooklyn to striving middle-class Jewish parents, William and Anna Feldman, Irving Feldman received his bachelor's and master's degrees from the City College of New York and Columbia University, respectively. After brief stints teaching in Puerto Rico and France and in Ohio (at Kenyon College), he returned to New York State to teach at the State University of New York at Buffalo, where he has been a faculty member since 1964 and now holds the title of Distinguished Professor of English.

Presence of the Holocaust in Feldman's Poetry

Irving Feldman is not a Holocaust poet in the sense of someone whose imagination and works focus on representations of the event. Rather, he has over the course of his career authored several poems that make valuable contributions to American poetry of the Holocaust. Significantly, these poems self-consciously acknowledge the distance between his position as a second-generation Jewish American and that of the European Jews who were Holocaust victims. Rather than attempt to unproblematically narrate or imagine events of the *Shoah*, Feldman qualifies his stance, even as he does attempt to confront the horror. The power of such poems derives at least in part from the tension between the desire to reconstitute the tragic past and the recognition that such an endeavor may be nothing more than a self-serving illusion.

Despite their rarity, however, these poems are not aberrations in Feldman's career; they fit within two broader themes that are consistent preoccupations. One is a concern with Jewish history and identity. Feldman at times approaches this subject within the framework of family, producing memory poems that range in tone from sardonic to nostalgic (for example, "Family History," "Our Father"); at other times, he delves into the past through the literary-historical avenues of biblical allusions or reworkings of traditional Yiddish folk tales ("The Lost Language," "A Tale of a Needler and a Nailer"). Modern Jewish identity is a complex phenomenon for Feldman; tensions between self and community run throughout the poet's work.

Feldman's consideration of the Holocaust also derives from his concern with atrocity and suffering in the twentieth century. While the Holocaust is obviously the century's paramount example of industrialized evil and mass suffering, especially for Jews, the poems often meditate on catastrophe and disaster in more generalized ways, imbued with elegiac sentiments while the *Shoah* lingers as a barely discernible background presence. In other cases, such as the long, phantasmagoric "Flight from the City," fascism and Nazism assume a more allegorical resonance. Increasingly, too, Feldman has taken a sharply satiric stance toward the trivialization and exploitation of tragedy in American society; this comes to bear on his consideration of the Holocaust in several poems that acknowledge the aesthetic and moral risks inherent in any representation of mass trauma.

Specific Works

The two poems for which Feldman is best recognized as a poet of the Holocaust are "The Pripet Marshes" and "To the Six Million," the final works in the collection *The Pripet Marshes* (New York: Viking, 1965). Each poem attempts a kind of imaginative leap across time and geography back into the *Shoah*—what Sidra Ezrahi calls "an act of mystical transference in an effort to engage history" (p. 212)—but they collapse in the end from the weight of that historical burden on the speaker's persona. Before examining those two works, it is important to note the brief poem that precedes them, "Scene of a Summer Morning." This opens with a nostalgic recollection of a childhood walk with the speaker's mother to the store of Yankel the butcher. In the second stanza, though, the speaker shifts from the vibrant memory of "the mazes of that morning" to the jolting admission: "Who writes these lines / I no longer know, but I believe him / to be a coward, that only one who escaped" (*New and Selected Poems*, New York: Penguin, p. 50). Feldman appears to associate this fragment of memory with the Jewish community, "The Ten Tribes there, lost forever," of the final line. The sense of guilt so poignantly expressed here seems key to understanding the two poems that follow. For Feldman, as an American Jew, there is a sense of rupture between the present and past, between the Jewish world of his childhood and the post-Holocaust world of his adulthood, along with a profound sense of guilt that he has "escaped"—a word that calls to mind the escapes of actual survivors, though Feldman's is an accident of birth.

In "The Pripet Marshes," the speaker is spurred by this guilt to place himself at the site of the atrocity he has been exempted from. He imagines that he takes his Jewish friends ("seize" is the word he tellingly chooses) and places them in the Pripet Marshes—the site of a massacre in 1942—"which I have never seen," among buildings "I have only heard of" (p. 50). He then launches into a detailed, moving catalog of the friends and family he imagines he will send back, only to modify these descriptions as the characters are "transfigured" by the impending arrival of the Germans. The truly audacious conceit comes at this point, when the speaker announces, "I snatch them all back, / For, when I want to, I can be a God" (p. 52). This hubristic claim cannot be backed up, however, and indeed, in the final stanza the speaker acknowledges his failure to complete his rescue, as he himself sinks to the ground "as though drugged or beaten." Here, as throughout the poem, Feldman walks a fine line, suggesting that a modern Jew may belatedly become a kind of victim, but then undercutting the claim with the conditional "as though." This vein of self-critique, which runs through Feldman's Holocaust poems, has been described by Alicia Ostriker as a "palpable theatricalization of the scenario of holocaust as a form of pleasure" (p. 110).

The speaker of "To the Six Million" engages in a similarly quixotic effort to transport himself to the past and recover the victims of the Holocaust. In the poem's first part, the speaker identifies himself as an archetypal survivor: "Who I am I do not know, / but I believe myself to be one / who should have died" (*New and Selected Poems*, p. 55). With its epigraph from Jonah and atmosphere of barrenness, this section presents a chilling picture of the loneliness of the survivor. Although the figure represented could well be an actual Holocaust survivor, this notion is again tied to Feldman's position as an American Jew who has avoided the fate he would have encountered across the ocean. In part II, the tone and direction shift; using the *Song of Songs* as his dominant motif now, the speaker tries to effect a kind of erotic-spiritual merging with the dead, mixing marital and deathly images in a way that evokes the ambivalence at the heart of Feldman's writing:

> Sweetness, my soul's bride,
> come to the feast I have made,
> my bone and my flesh of me,
> broken and touched,
> come in your widow's raiment of dust and ashes,
> bereaved, newborn, gasping for
> the breath that was torn from you,
> that is returned to you (p. 57).

Two later poems, "The Bystander at the Massacre" (in *All of Us Here*, New York: Viking, 1986) and "Outrage Is Anointed by Levity" (in *The Life and Letters*, Chicago: University of Chicago Press, 1994), also deserve notice for their treatment of the Holocaust. Reflective of a shift in Feldman's poetic tendency from an earlier prophetic voice to a more reflexive stance, these two poems treat the Holocaust in more oblique fashion, concerning themselves instead with the slippery ethics of aestheticizing atrocity. "The Bystander at the Massacre" is one of a sequence of poems that take as their ostensible subject the strange white figures of the sculptor George Segal—one of whose notable creations is installed at the San Francisco Holocaust memorial. The poem may also refer to Brueghel's painting *The Slaughter of the Innocents* (or to a photograph of the painting), and in this sense clearly signals skepticism toward the layers of distance that may separate an artist from the atrocity depicted in his or her work. While "bystander" in the context of the Holocaust typically refers to civilians who failed to intervene to protect victims, here Feldman transfers the label to the modern-day consumer of atrocity—whether as spectator or as artist—and speaks of "the spectator's essential doubtfulness" (p. 14). The "evasion" of our commercialized consumption of human tragedy, he suggests, is dangerous because it "expands to enormous complicity" (p. 16). From spectator to complicit participant, whether in meditations on violence today or on the *Shoah*, Feldman argues that the trivialization of atrocity can only lead ultimately to our own loss of perspective, to the "demented scream" the poem describes.

In "Outrage Is Anointed by Levity, or Two Laureates A-Lunching," Feldman again addresses the ways artists can go wrong in thinking about the Holocaust. The poem serves as a sharp riposte to a conversation between two acclaimed poets, Joseph Brodsky and Mark Strand, regarding Theodor Adorno's comment on Holocaust poetry: "How can one write poetry after Auschwitz?" Feldman mocks the two poets for their flippant approach to Adorno's serious concerns (Brodsky reports Strand's rejoinder: "And how can one eat lunch?"). Rather than a defense of Adorno, though, the poem constitutes a critique of the self-importance of artists who risk trivializing or marginalizing atrocity:

> And all we shall know of apocalypse
> is not the shattering that follows but
> brittleness before, the high mindlessness, the quips (p. 49).

In the poem's last section—a series of short, clipped lines—Feldman turns inward, attempting to write verse that embraces silence. He finds, however, that the effort is fundamentally misguided:

> This
> poem
> doesn't silence
> silence
> one or the other—this poem
> or silence—interrogates one or the other (p. 50).

Silence may seem preferable to exploitative visions of atrocity, but Feldman suggests that silence itself is illusory, and that in the end the committed artist cannot help but turn his eye—and his artistic vision—toward catastrophe.

In each of his poems on the Holocaust, Feldman engages with the tensions inherent in confronting a historical tragedy in which the author took no part; to his credit, he neither avoids the responsibility to consider the past nor sheds the self-consciousness that allows him to monitor his own words and imagination for any breaches of the ethical and aesthetic demands of the *Shoah*. Sidra Ezrahi remarks that for Feldman this "historical remove . . . constitutes the boundary and the resource as well as the ultimate challenge for the imagination," and she regards the poems from *The Pripet Marshes* as among "the most radical attempts to possess the universe of camps and ghettos by a kind of literary fiat" (p. 180). Such a leap of imagination necessarily risks critical censure, but Feldman's readers, like Ezrahi, have usually deemed him successful. Alicia Ostriker, for instance, labels the poem "The Pripet Marshes" a "masterpiece" for its evocation of "divine and human good and evil" (p. 110) and though not everyone might make the same judgment, few would dispute that Feldman has produced Holocaust poems of lasting value. Also contributing to Feldman's achievement is his ability to frame the subject of the Holocaust within larger contexts of Jewish life and history. As John Hollander writes, "Feldman has a full sense of the problematic role . . . of *zakhor*, 'memory,' in place of any traditional historiography in Judaism" (p. 59).

Bibliography

Primary Sources

Works and Days. 1961.
The Pripet Marshes. 1965.
Magic Papers. 1970.
Lost Originals. 1972.
Leaping Clear. 1976.
New and Selected Poems. 1979.
Teach Me, Dear Sister. 1983.
All of Us Here. 1986.
The Life and Letters. 1994.
Beautiful False Things. 2000.

Secondary Sources

Elman, Richard. "Three Varied Talents." *The New York Times Book Review*, 15 August 1965: 4. Review of *The Pripet Marshes*.

Ezrahi, Sidra DeKoven. *By Words Alone: The Holocaust in Literature*. Chicago: University of Chicago Press, 1980.

Gitenstein, R. Barbara. *Apocalyptic Messianism and Contemporary Jewish-American Poetry*. Albany: State University of New York Press, 1986.

Hollander, John. "All of Us Are Here." *The New Republic*, 14 July 1986: 28–30. Review of *All of Us Here*.

———. "Creative Hate and Lifelines of Love: Some Thoughts on Irving Feldman's Poetry." In Schweizer (1992): 47–61.

Ostriker, Alicia. "My Name Is Laughter: Irving Feldman and the Replaying of the *Akedah*." In Schweizer (1992): 101–125.

Rosenthal, M. L. "Some Thoughts on Irving Feldman's Poetry." In Schweizer (1992): 29–39.

Schweizer, Harold. "Lyric Suffering in Auden and Feldman." *English Language Notes* 31, no. 2 (1993): 66–74.

———, ed. *The Poetry of Irving Feldman*. Lewisburg, Pa.: Bucknell University Press, 1992.

Fania Fenelon

(1909–1983)

HOLLY M. BURMEISTER

WHILE PERHAPS BEST known as the 1980 Emmy-winning television movie of the same name, Fania Fenelon's *Playing for Time* (1976) deserves scholarly attention in its own right as a Holocaust memoir that eloquently addresses many issues of surviving the death camps. Woven into Fenelon's narration of life as a principal member of the Auschwitz women's orchestra are such themes as gender-specific body anxieties, rape and sex within the camps, and the role of music both as a method of resistance to the Nazi agenda of mass annihilation of the Jewish people and as a a mode of concession to wishes of the death camp administrators.

Life

Born in Paris in 1909 to a Jewish father, Leonide Goldstein, and a Catholic mother, Marie Bernier, Fanny graduated from the Conservatoire de Paris as a soprano vocalist and a pianist. She became a cabaret singer and took the name Fania Fenelon. According to an interview, she used her position as a cabaret singer to shield her involvement in the French Resistance, which began in 1940. "I sang in cabarets where German officers went," she recalled. "When they were drunk, I would photograph the contents of their briefcases and pass the film along" (Anderson, p. 10). After her arrest in 1943, Fenelon was transported from Paris to Drancy, where she was interrogated and tortured for nine months, and then transferred to Birkenau. There, Fenelon was rescued from the cremation ovens by her ability to sing *Madame Butterfly* (a favorite of camp subcommander Maria Mandel) and placed in the Auschwitz women's orchestra. Finally, she was transferred to Bergen-Belsen, where the British liberated her on 15 April 1945.

After the war, Fenelon continued her career as a musician, living for many years in East Germany, where she became a professor of music at East Berlin, Leipzig, and Dresden conservatories. Later she toured Europe broadly as a concert vocalist. Fenelon died of cancer on 21 December 1983 at the age of seventy-four in Paris.

Playing for Time: The Memoir

Curiously, there has yet to be any substantial scholarly treatment of Fenelon's single work. At the time of its publication, many critics lauded the work, proclaiming that Fenelon's story was "particularly well-told, with a minimum of self-pity" and "raises the unanswerable questions of personal morality in the abyss" (Sokolov, p. 10). However, in the favorable reviews of the memoir (as in those of the television movie and subsequent theatrical productions around the country), the critical attention has been on the author herself, not on her finely crafted story. Such emphasis might better be placed on the text itself, for *Playing for Time* richly rewards the careful reader.

One of the most striking features of Fenelon's memoir is the candid and varied representations of female prisoners' sex and sexuality within the camps. As many feminist scholars of Holocaust literature have noted, female camp inmates experienced the concentration camps in gender-specific ways, ways that are profoundly different from the more frequently portrayed male prisoners' experience of the Holocaust. Gender-specific experiences included, but were not limited to, female prisoners' vulnerability to sexual assault and pregnancy and the complications associated with menstruating. Fenelon's text certainly reflects such experiences. In one example, Little Irene, a Jewish Russian inmate, explains that she decided to have sex with a male inmate while incarcerated at Drancy because she "didn't want to go off to a work camp or a deportation camp without some degree of experience to arm me against the possibility of rape" (p. 149). In other passages, the orchestra women speak of their dual anxiety surrounding menstruation—fear that while they still menstruated, the blood would call attention to them and lead to their deaths, and fear that their periods, ceased from severe malnutrition and physical strain, would never return.

However more vulnerable women prisoners were because of their gendered bodies, Fenelon's memoir also makes clear that at least some women prisoners used their bodies as negotiating tools for better conditions, more food, and a relatively more secure position. Clara, Fenelon's early companion, quickly determines that she is able to supplement her rations by agreeing to become a "kapo's girl," trading sex with the largely Polish male block guards in exchange for food. Fenelon links Clara's willingness to trade sex for food with a general deterioration of her moral character. The trajectory that begins with Clara's prostituting herself to kapos ends with her becoming a kapo as well. Expressions of sexuality as moral degradation also appear in *Playing for Time*'s depiction of the black-triangled prostitutes' secret dance. In this scene, the "orchestra girls" (as they are referred to throughout the text) "hire" themselves out to play for an explicitly lesbian dance party. The orchestra players are as stunned by the lavish amounts of food present as by the overt displays of lesbian sex: "there were just little squeaks from the 'girls' and condescending laughter from the fake 'fellows' as they stood around the table stuffing themselves, preposterously lady-like withal, fingers crooked, gobbling genteely" (p. 218).

Contrasting this scene of sexual and gourmand debauchery is the blooming love interest between Little Irene and Marta. Whereas the other lesbian scenes provide proof of the degraded morality of the participants, this love interest sparks renewed hope in Fenelon of the goodness inherent in humanity. She writes: "[w]hat was wrong to love here? If I believed in God, I would say that to feel a pure clean feeling in this place, where evil reigned supreme, was a sign of His blessing" (p. 147). The inclusion of this consensual, noncoerced sexual relationship in the memoir expands the ways in which women prisoners' sexuality is portrayed in Holocaust literature.

While Fenelon draws a fairly clear line between good (redemptive) sexuality and bad (corrupting) sexuality, her depictions of complicity in, and resistance to, the Nazi regime are far more complicated. Music becomes a sort of character in its own right, personifying the moral choices the women in the orchestra must make. Over and over again, Fenelon is caught between her sheer pleasure in making music and the knowledge that her music is also pleasurable to her predominantly SS audience, including Mengele and Himmler. The charge of prostitution she levels at Clara she also inveighs against herself: "[f]or me, singing was a free act, and I was not free; it was, above all a way of giving pleasure, giving love, and I felt a frantic desire to see those three SS men stuck like pigs, right here, at my feet" (p. 93).

Music is both an instrument of covert resistance and overt cooperation. On one occasion, Fenelon orchestrates familiar Yiddish anthems to play for the prisoners as they daily march out for work duty and incorporates forbidden Gypsy music into the concerts given for camp administration; on other occasions she sings *Madame Butterfly* in the middle of the night at the behest of SS officials who want comfort after a hard day of gas chamber selections. The portrait Fenelon paints of conductor and violinist Alma Rose, German Jewish niece of Gustav Mahler, provides another example of the troubling relationship the orchestra women conduct with their music and their audience. Rose, a rigorously trained musician, subjects the largely amateur musicians to exhausting rehearsal schedules and abusive punishment for the dual purpose of keeping the women in the orchestra alive by pleasing the camp administration and of gratifying her own ego as the conductor.

Fenelon never reaches a comfortable truce over the moral dilemma of whether it was right or wrong to, as *New York Times* reviewer Raymond Sokolov put it, "fiddl[e] while one's people burned" (p. 10). In fact, Fenelon accomplishes something more difficult, something which has broader, more lasting impact. She vows, journal in hand, to "remember everything of this stinking horror" (p. 24).

Playing for Time: The Film

In 1980, Arthur Miller adapted Fenelon's text for television, and CBS cast Vanessa Redgrave, an outspoken supporter of the PLO (Palestinian Liberation Organization), in the lead role over Fenelon's (and other Holocaust survivors') objections. The ensuing furor landed both Fenelon and Redgrave in the media spotlight. The critics' main objection to the film was the political affiliation of Redgrave—a legitimate concern, as critic Richard Cohen notes, given the propensity of television portrayals to supplant the public identity of the person portrayed with that of the actor portraying her (p. C1). Perhaps what can best be said for Miller's television script (as well as his subsequent play version) is that it does assist Fenelon in meeting her stated goal in writing *Playing for Time*: keeping the Holocaust in the forefront of her audience's consciousness.

Bibliography

Primary Source

Sursis pour l'Orchestra (*Playing for Time*). 1976.

Secondary Sources

"Fania Fenelon." In *Encyclopedia of the Holocaust*, vol. 1. Edited by Israel Gutman. New York: Macmillan, 1990.

Interviews

Anderson, Susan Heller. "Memories of a Nazi Camp, Where a Musical Gift Meant Survival." *New York Times*, 7 January 1978, 10.

Safer, Morley. "The Music of Auschwitz." Carousel Films, 1978.

BERTHA FERDERBER-SALZ

(1903–1997)

HOLLY M. BURMEISTER

BERTHA FERDERBER-SALZ was born in 1903 in Kolbuszowa, Poland, to Israel Zvi and Reivel Rachel Frost. She married Moses Ferderber and gave birth to two girls, Rachel and Rehava. In 1941 the Ferderbers were forced to enter the Cracow ghetto. Bertha escaped the ghetto and attempted to hide with her daughters and sister in Grodzisk, an isolated village on the edge of the Black Forest. However, after a few years, Nazi invasion forced the girls and then their mother to return to the ghetto. Although the Ferderbers managed to smuggle their children out of the ghetto and hide them with Polish-Catholic acquaintances shortly before the ghetto was sealed, Bertha Ferderber-Salz and her husband were transferred to the Plaszow labor camp in March 1943.

Bertha Ferderber-Salz survived Plaszow and was transferred to Auschwitz in November 1944. Upon the liquidation of the Auschwitz camp, she was moved to Bergen-Belsen. Following the liberation of the Bergen-Belsen death camp, Ferderber-Salz returned to Poland to retrieve her own children and the children of relatives who had not survived the death camps. She lived for several years in Poland after the war and emigrated to the United States with her daughters in 1946. Bertha Ferderber-Salz died in Brooklyn, New York, in 1997.

Critical Attention

Ferderber-Salz's memoir, *And the Sun Kept Shining* (1980), is frequently featured in bibliographies of survivor testimony or those that gather texts on women's experiences in the Holocaust, so it is clear that scholars are aware of her work. This awareness has not yet spurred critical investigation, or even any lengthy book reviews. The scholar seeking secondary material on Ferderber-Salz's work will come away from the research table utterly empty-handed. There are, however, several aspects of *And the Sun Kept Shining* that may interest scholars of Holocaust literature in general, and especially those interested in Polish accounts of the *Shoah.* Ferderber-Salz's "record of [her] sorrow and suffering" is notable for illustrating the financial and emotional costs of sheltering her children with Gentiles during the war (p. 13). It also provides firsthand details of the actions (and inactions) of Gentile Poles during the war which, given the abysmal survival rate of Polish Jews, makes *And the Sun Kept Shining* a useful text. Finally, scholars may appreciate the way in which Ferderber-Salz's testimony's structure reflects her survival experience.

Testimony

Ferderber-Salz's testimony details not only the savagery of the Nazi regime, but also the fortune-seeking opportunism of fellow Poles who exploited the desperate situation of the Jewish refugees. She writes, "one of the peasants had promised to conceal us when the time came . . . [but] our savior was no different from the others. He, too, wanted only our money and had no intention of endangering his life for us" (p. 55).

This peasant's treachery is not the first or last that Ferderber-Salz records. She writes in great detail of the process of hiding her children among Gentiles, the emotional and psychic toll this took on her children and herself, and the financial compensation extracted from her by the families that hid her children. Ferderber-Salz reflects several times on the unfair burden her eldest child, Rachel, bore in assuming a parental role for her infant sister, Rehava. Rachel endures abuse from her guardians and employers, and is forced to turn over all of her wages to her guardians in exchange for their continuing protection (p. 78). Ferderber-

Salz's recollection of her last covert meeting with her daughter (until after the liberation) illustrates the stolen childhoods of the Holocaust, and is particularly demonstrative of the premature adulthood forced on child victims of the Holocaust. Marching past her daughter in a forced labor procession from the Cracow ghetto, Ferderber recalls that "during the seconds when our glance met I also saw immense sorrow in my daughter's eyes . . . . How much she needed me, how she longed to find comfort in my arms! But she understood that she must not even look at me for very long"(p. 76). Though quite young, Rachel understands that she must vigilantly monitor all of her body movements, including the length of her gaze, in order not to betray herself, her sister, or her mother. When Ferderber-Salz is reunited with her two daughters, Rehava immediately falls to her knees and prays to the Virgin Mary figure hanging on the wall, causing the Gentile guardian to note, "because you asked the Virgin Mary to help you every night your mother has been saved and come back to you" (p. 178). The price of the children's survival is the eldest daughter's emotional health and the youngest daughter's understanding of her Jewish heritage.

The author makes it clear that children were saved by their rescuers for self-aggrandizing reasons, be it money, possessions, or the opportunity to convert young Jewish children to Catholicism. In contrast to the story of Oskar Schindler and other "righteous Gentiles" who acted to save Jewish people during the Holocaust, Ferderber-Salz's testimony asserts that assistance from Gentiles most often came at very steep prices. At another point, she describes a Polish Gentile's despair at the murder of her Jewish neighbors as "shed[ding] crocodile tears over our catastrophe" (p. 208).

Narrative Structure

While scholars will likely remember Ferderber-Salz's Holocaust memoir far more for its *Shoah* content than its literary artistry, the organization of *And the Sun Kept Shining* is worth investigation. The narrative opens with the author's jumbled, frenzied account of her and her family fleeing invading Nazi troops in Cracow. Ferderber-Salz's account is studded with encounters with friends and loved ones. The telling of this event includes complicated descriptions of familial relationships and affinity networks—a tightly knit circle of family and friends. As the narrative progresses, these references winnow away. Loved ones are cleaved out of her story as she journeys from Cracow to Plaszow, Auschwitz to Birkenau. Ferderber-Salz's frenetically populated opening family scene is dialectically counterbalanced with her description of her tiny remaining camp family: herself and her niece: "I am in Bergen-Belsen, my last station. Death is raging all around. Our strength is drained: we are afflicted with hunger and epidemics. The dead and the quick lie intermingled in the dark block" (p. 154). The complex sentences and florid language that characterize the beginning of her narrative are stripped away, leaving the barest staccato language of reporting, which linguistically reflects her experience.

Also noteworthy is the memoir's achronologic structure. Ferderber-Salz begins her story straightforwardly enough, at the moment when she and her family first felt the terror of Nazi rule in Poland. However, shortly into the text, Ferderber-Salz jumps to her internment in Bergen-Belsen, leaps backwards in time to her stay at Plaszow, and intermixes these tales with memories of her refuge in Grodzisk and Cracow, Poland. Ferderber-Salz takes the reader through her story not according to the calendar, but rather by the linking of one memory to another. While Ferderber-Salz's organizing strategy can be frustrating for the reader, it is also one of the text's strengths, for it illustrates the disorder and chaos of the Holocaust experience.

In her introduction, Ferderber-Salz writes: "I have managed to fulfill my deepest desire of my brothers and sisters in suffering—to remain alive and tell what the murderers of our people did to us" (p. 13). *And the Sun Kept Shining* reads like a product of deep desire—organization sometimes jumbled, language sometimes tortuous or overwrought, analysis sometimes delivered in broad sweeping strokes. Despite these so-called flaws (or perhaps because of them), Ferderber-Salz's autobiographical account holds the reader's attention and realizes the author's stated intent—to ensure that a survivor's voice, and a survivor's memory, contribute to the chronicling of the Holocaust.

Bibliography

Primary Source

And the Sun Kept Shining. 1980.

Lion Feuchtwanger

(1884–1958)

WULF KOEPKE

LION FEUCHTWANGER WAS born in Munich, Germany, on 7 July 1884, the oldest son of Sigmund Feuchtwanger and Johanna née Bodenheim, wealthy Orthodox Jews settled in Bavaria for centuries. Lion declined to take over the family business; after studies in German literature and history, he received a Ph.D. from the University of Munich in 1907. His dissertation dealt with Heinrich Heine's unfinished novel *Der Rabbi von Bacharach* and questions about Heine's Jewishness.

Early Career

Feuchtwanger became a successful writer and translator of plays. In 1918, a number of German theaters produced his historical play *Jud Süß* (published in England as *Jew Suess* and in the United States as *Power*), dramatizing an episode in the history of Württemberg in southwest Germany. Its duke, Karl Alexander, had relied on his "court Jew," his financial adviser Joseph Süß Oppenheimer, to finance his lavish tastes, and the many tariffs imposed by the government but blamed on Süß made the Jew the most hated man in Württemberg, so that in 1738 Süß was indicted, tried, and sentenced to public hanging, a clear miscarriage of justice and an incidence of aggressive antisemitism. This complex story intrigued many writers and historians, and Feuchtwanger realized that his play did not do justice to it. He withdrew the play and rewrote it as a large novel, but he could not find a publisher until 1925, at which time it became an instant hit and a best-seller in the Anglo-Saxon world.

Feuchtwanger became known from then on as the author of widely read historical novels, and he was identified with Jewish concerns. *Jud Süß* was re-adapted by Ashley Duke in 1929 as a play often performed in Britain and served as the basis for the British movie *Jew Suess* (1934), directed by Lothar Mende. But in 1940 things took an ugly turn when the Germans used the story of Oppenheimer, but not Feuchtwanger's novel, for one of their infamous antisemitic movies, *Jud Süß*, directed by Veit Harlan. Stung by this coincidence and by the fact that the major actors were former friends, some of whom had performed in Feuchtwanger's play of 1918, Feuchtwanger wrote an open "Letter to Seven Actors," first published in *Atlantic Monthly* in 1941, reminding them of their past affiliation and of what he saw as the inevitable future—Germany's defeat and the end of National Socialism.

Feuchtwanger was a secular adherent of Spinozism, a philosophy that developed a consistent system of pantheism: God equals nature; God and nature are one. He was also influenced by the writings of Sigmund Freud and Karl Marx, yet as the descendant of Orthodox Jews, he was deeply concerned about the fate of the Jews in the Diaspora. He considered nationalism an anachronism and did not agree with the idea of establishing a Jewish homeland in Palestine, even after the Nazis came to power in 1933, but he knew that the fate of Jewish minorities would remain precarious until the day when a rule of reason and peace would make matters of race obsolete. To explore the issues of this precarious Jewish existence, he chose as his focus the life of Flavius Josephus, or Joseph ben Mathitjahu (A.D. 37–100), a prominent historian and unreliable ally of the Jews in first-century Roman politics, close to the emperors Vespasian and Titus, but in disgrace under Domitian. The writing of this trilogy intertwined with the events leading to Feuchtwanger's exile. The first volume, *Der jüdische Krieg* (*Josephus*), appeared in 1932; the second, *Die Söhne* (*The Jew of Rome*), in 1935; and the last, *Josephus and the Emperor*, in 1942, but only in English; the German version, *Der Tag wird kommen*, had to wait until the end of World War II in 1945. *Josephus* became a key document of Feuchtwanger's exile. In one of his last novels, *Die Jüdin von Toledo* (*Raquel, the Jewess of Toledo*), published in 1955, Feuchtwanger returned once more to the crucial issue of the precarious condition of the Jew in a gentile society.

Feuchtwanger used the technique of the historical novel also to narrate contemporary events. In Munich he had witnessed the attempted coup by Adolf Hitler and his followers in 1923 and their subsequent trial for treason. He incorporated this into a panorama of the Bavarian capital after 1918 with the dominant theme of justice, entitled *Erfolg* (*Success*, 1930), a first literary depiction in German of Hitler, the fanaticism of his followers, and the political corruption that gave them their chance. This book earned Feuchtwanger the enduring resentment of his native city.

Die Geschwister Oppermann

Jews and antisemitism were minor themes of *Success*, but when Hitler rose to power in 1933 and the Nazi terrorism was organized against German Jews, Feuchtwanger realized the true face of this ideology. He was on a lecture tour in the United States when the Nazis took over. His house in Berlin was ransacked and his manuscripts were destroyed. He never returned to Germany. Feuchtwanger was in Sanary-sur-Mer in southern France trying to rebuild his life when a messenger came from British Prime Minister Ramsay MacDonald asking Feuchtwanger for a (fictional) story on the events in Germany that could be used for a film. He complied and even collaborated with a screenwriter on a script, but the British government entered into its policies of appeasement and the movie was never made. Feuchtwanger took the story and, with uncharacteristic speed, finished the novel, *Die Geschwister Oppermann* (*The Oppermanns*) by September 1933 to be published by Querido in Amsterdam. However, a competitor of Feuchtwanger's brother Ludwig in the publishing industry and high-ranking Nazi named Oppermann protested against the misuse of his "good" German name in the novel and threatened Ludwig with a concentration camp. As a result, the German edition in Amsterdam appeared first as *Die Geschwister Oppenheim.*

The Oppermanns was the first novel of wide distribution, translated into many languages, to describe the fate of the German Jews in 1933. The Oppermanns are a wealthy Berlin family who own a furniture factory and furniture stores. Martin Oppermann manages the business, while Edgar is a respected professor of laryngology, and Gustav is a writer and critic in the process of writing a biography of Gotthold Ephraim Lessing, the friend of Moses Mendelssohn and author of *Nathan der Weise*, a play dear to the hearts of many German Jews. Their sister, Klara, is married to the East European Jewish businessman Jacques Lavendel. The action takes us from November 1932 to summer 1933 and moves along four main plot lines: 1) Martin's futile attempts to save the firm for the family, which cause him to be arrested and tortured by the SA (Nazi Storm Troopers) at one point, an experience that brings back an awareness of his Jewishness; 2) Edgar's dismissal from the hospital where he works amid the hatred of Nazi colleagues and students; 3) Gustav's late political "awakening," his ineffectual attempts to act against the regime, his incarceration in a concentration camp, and his death soon after his release, not without having left his account of the atrocities; and 4) the increasing problems that Berthold, Martin's son and a "half-Jew," faces in his gymnasium (high school) with his Nazi teacher and classmates, that lead to his suicide. There is no place for the Oppermanns in Germany; they have no choice but to emigrate, an outcome predicted by Lavendel but resisted by the patriotic Oppermanns. In his realistic description of the fictitious concentration camp Moosach in southwestern Germany, Feuchtwanger used the reports and documentations available to him at the time.

What is significant in this novel is Feuchtwanger's insistence on the entwining of the political and the personal, the economic and the cultural spheres. The Jews were envied as successful competitors, but the Nazis turned the Germans' envy into hatred. Ordinary Germans were drawn in and, often against their will, participated in the terror. The nature of the regime was terroristic, and already in 1933, totalitarian.

The book had a huge commercial and considerable critical success. It was translated into fifteen languages, and the total international sales were already 257,000 copies in 1934. The novel was hotly debated by the public, especially in leftist circles. The early debate among German exiles dealt exclusively with the political issues, particularly whether antisemitism was not stressed enough or was overemphasized. In other countries, such as the United States and Switzerland, critics saw a well-constructed novel with exciting scenes, and the political issues were considered secondary. Later, it was recognized that Feuchtwanger had offered a comprehensive view of German society in 1932–1933. The novel appeared in the Soviet Union in 1935. Its success in the Soviet Union and elsewhere prompted a film version in 1937, though, for political reasons, the plot was substantially altered in the film and the Jewish dimension was all but eliminated. The novel immediately became a widely recognized model for other novels on the subject. In 1983, the television film *Die Geschwister Oppermann* by Egon Monk, in two parts, two hours each, was broadcast on the fiftieth anniversary of the Nazis' coming to power, in Germany, Great Britain, Italy, and Sweden, a late confirmation of Feuchtwanger's accurate depiction of the events of 1933 in Germany.

Feuchtwanger insisted that antisemitism had not infected "the German people" as such; even after 1945 he maintained the distinction between "Germans" and "Nazis." In 1933 he was also much more optimistic than was justified about the chances of an indigenous German resistance to the Nazis. Yet he already made it quite clear that Nazi boycotts, threats, book burnings, and concentration camps were not merely "excesses" but revealed the true nature of the regime.

Feuchtwanger in France

From his exile in southern France, Feuchtwanger participated in the attempts to enlighten the world about the regime in Germany. To cite one of many examples: In 1936, after the passage of the Nuremberg racial laws, the Editions du Carrefour in Paris, one of the exile presses, published a documentary book with the ominous title *Der gelbe Fleck. Die Ausrottung von 500,000 deutschen Juden* (*The Yellow Spot. The Eradication of 500,000 German Jews*), with a preface by Feuchtwanger. It is a painstaking documentation of individual incidents of terror and murder, of local ordinances and resolutions of professional groups to exclude Jews, to deny them the necessities of life, and to separate them from Germans, a process that reached its first climax in the Nuremberg laws. Jews could not be Germans—the existence of "German Jews" had ended. At this point, the "solutions" were local and not centrally organized, but everything was designed to drive out or kill the Jews, many of whom had lived in Germany for centuries. Feuchtwanger's name was important for a wider distribution of the book. His short preface pointed out that this was the true nature of the regime, but not that of the German people as a whole. He called for active participation in the struggle against inhumanity.

In 1940, Feuchtwanger published his long novel *Exil* (*Paris Gazette*), about the life and political struggle of the German emigrants in Paris. One of its subplots involved the kidnapping of an emigrant journalist from Switzerland to Germany and his incarceration in a concentration camp. With the outbreak of World War II in 1939, the French government placed all emigrant men of present and former German, Austrian, or Czech nationality in internment or concentration camps; the women and many children were incarcerated in May 1940. After the armistice in 1940, the non-Jewish inmates were given the opportunity to return to their country of origin, but the vast majority were anti-Nazis and chose to remain in France. The camps were maintained during the Vichy regime, and from these camps, in 1942–1943, the Jewish inmates were deported to Auschwitz. Because of his advanced age, Feuchtwanger was interned only in May 1940 and was smuggled out in July by his wife, Marta, with the help of the American Vice-Consul from Marseille.

Feuchtwanger in the United States

Feuchtwanger and his wife escaped to the United States and settled in Los Angeles in 1941, moving to Pacific Palisades in 1943, where Feuchtwanger spent the rest of his life. In 1941 he published an account of his camp experiences in Les Milles, near Aix-en-Provence, *Unholdes Frankreich* (*The Devil in France*), describing the chaos following the German invasion and the general indifference of the French authorities. His first novel written in America, *Die Brüder Lautensack* (*Double, Double, Toil and Trouble*, 1943), drawing on the tragic fate of Hitler's astrologer, Erik Jan Hanussen, whom Hitler had executed, and involving Hitler himself and the events of 1933, is remarkable insofar as it ignores the crucial fact that Hanussen was a Jew and marginalizes the issue of antisemitism.

Feuchtwanger never obtained U.S. citizenship, because the U.S. government suspected him of being friendly to communism. The theme of persecution recurs in his works written after 1945, especially in his play *Wahn oder der Teufel in Boston* (*The Devil in Boston*, 1948), and his novel *Goya oder der arge Weg der Erkenntnis* (*This Is the Hour. A Goya Novel*, 1951). He never wrote about the Holocaust, but there is a short story of 1942, "Das Haus am Grünen Weg" (The House in the Shady Lane), which describes once more the moral degradation accompanying the Nazi takeover of Germany and raises a crucial moral question: is it a duty or even possible to do justice to the perpetrators and to regard them as human beings instead of simply hating them and wishing them dead?

Feuchtwanger died on 21 December 1958, in Los Angeles. He remained without citizenship, which prevented him from seeing his native Munich once more and visiting his closest friend, Bertolt Brecht, in Berlin. At the time, Feuchtwanger was one of the best-known writers in the world. The significance of his work for Holocaust studies is threefold: 1) he described and analyzed the precarious condition of Jews in the Diaspora between assimilation and exclusion in *Jud Süß*, the *Josephus* trilogy, and *The Jewess of Toledo*, a testament to the dilemma of the last generation of German Jewish writers; 2) he traced the beginning of the end of the German Jews and the initial Nazi terrors of "Schutzhaft" ("protective custody") and concentration camps in *The Oppermanns*, pointing out the true nature of the regime when the West wanted to ignore it; and 3) he documented the character of the French internment / concentration camps whence many thousands of Jews were deported in his account *The Devil in France*. Feuchtwanger never wavered in his faith in the eventual advent of the rule of reason and peace. Therefore, he called the trilogy of his contemporary novels—*Success, The Oppermanns*, and *Paris Gazette*—"Der Wartesaal" (The Waiting Room).

Bibliography

Primary Sources

Heinrich Heines "Rabbi von Bacharach." Eine kritische Studie. 1908.
Julia Farnese. 1915.
Warren Hastings. 1915.
Die Kriegsgefangenen (*The Prisoners of War*). 1918.
Thomas Wendt / 1918 (*1918*). 1919.
Der holländische Kaufmann (*The Dutch Merchant*). 1920.
Die Petroleuminseln (*The Petrol Islands*). 1923.
Die häßliche Herzogin (*The Ugly Duchess*). 1923.
Wird Hill amnestiert? (Amnesty for Hill). 1923.
Jud Süß (*Jew Suess; Power*). 1925.
Erfolg (*Success*). 1930.
Der jüdische Krieg (*Josephus*). 1932.
Die Geschwister Oppenheim/Die Geschwister Oppermann (*The Oppermanns*). 1933.
"Nationalismus und Judentum," in *Die Aufgabe des Judentums* (*The Task of the Jews*), with Arnold Zweig. 1933.
Die Söhne (*The Jew of Rome*). 1935.
Moskau 1937 (*Moscow—1937*). 1937.
Der falsche Nero (*The Pretender*). 1937.
Exil (*Paris Gazette*). 1940.
Unholdes Frankreich (*The Devil in France*). 1941.
Die Brüder Lautensack (*Double, Double, Toil and Trouble*). 1943.
Simone. 1944.
Der Tag wird kommen (*Josephus and the Emperor/The Day Will Come*). 1942/1945.
Stories from Far and Near. 1945.
Venedig (Texas), und andere Erzählungen. 1946.
Waffen für Amerika/Die Füchse im Weinberg (*Proud Destiny*). 1947/1948.
Wahn oder der Teufel in Boston (*The Devil in Boston*). 1948.
Die Witwe Capet (*The Widow Capet*). 1949.
Goya oder der arge Weg der Erkenntnis (*This Is the Hour. A Goya Novel*). 1951.
Narrenweisheit oder Tod und Verklärung des Jean-Jacques Rousseau (*'Tis Folly to Be Wise, or Death and Transfiguration of Jean-Jacques Rousseau*). 1952.
Centum Opuscula. 1956.
Spanische Ballade/Die Jüdin von Toledo (*Raquel. The Jewess of Toledo*). 1955.
Jefta und seine Tochter (*Jephta and His Daughter*). 1957.

Letters

Lion Feuchtwanger–Arnold Zweig Briefwechsel 1933–1958. 2 vols. 1984.
Lion Feuchtwanger. Briefwechsel mit Freunden 1933–1958. 2 vols. 1991.
Briefe an Eva von Hoboken. 1996.

Film and Television Adaptations

Jew Suess. England. 1934.
Die Geschwister Oppermann. Soviet Union. 1937.
Die Geschwister Oppermann. Television Series. 1983.
Erfolg. Film and television Series. 1990.

Secondary Sources

Fernsehfilm "Die Geschwister Oppermann" von Egon Monk nach dem Roman von Lion Feuchtwanger, ed. ZDF Information und Presse. Frankfurt: Fischer Taschenbuch Verlag, 1982.
Feuchtwanger, Marta. *Nur eine Frau. Jahre. Tage. Stunden.* Vienna: Langen-Müller, 1983.
Feuchtwanger, Martin. *Ebenbilder Gottes.* Tel Aviv: Olympia, 1950.
Huder, Walter, and Friedrich Knilli, eds. *Lion Feuchtwanger "... Für die Vernunft, gegen Dummheit und Gewalt."* Berlin: Publica, 1985.
Jaretzky, Reinhold. *Lion Feuchtwanger.* Reinbek, Germany: Rowohlt, 1984.
Kahn, Lothar. *Insight and Action. The Life and Work of Lion Feuchtwanger.* Rutherford, N. J.: Fairleigh Dickinson University Press, 1975.
Köpke, Wulf. *Lion Feuchtwanger.* Munich: C. H. Beck, 1983.
Koepke, Wulf. "Lion Feuchtwanger." *Encyclopedia of Literary Biography*, vol. 66 (1988): 115–138.
Schneider, Sigrid. *Das Ende Weimars im Exilroman. Literarische Strategien zur Vermittlung von Faschismutheorien.* Munich: K. G. Saur, 1980.
Spalek, John M., ed. *Lion Feuchtwanger. The Man—His Ideas—His Work.* Los Angeles: Henessey and Ingalls, 1972.
Spalek, John M., and Sandra H. Hawrylchak, eds. *Lion Feuchtwanger. A Bibliographic Handbook*, vol. 1, The German Editions. Munich: K. G. Saur, 1998.
Sternburg, Wilhelm von. *Lion Feuchtwanger. Ein deutsches Schriftstellerleben.* Königstein / Ts., Germany: Athenäum, 1984.
——. *Lion Feuchtwanger. Materialien zu Leben und Werk.* Frankfurt: Fischer Taschenbuch Verlag, 1989.
Thalheim, Peter. *Lion Feuchtwanger. Die Geschwister Oppermann. Oldenbourg Interpretationen*, vol. 68. Munich: Oldenbourg, 1994.
Zerrahn, Holger. *Exilerfahrung und Faschismusbild in Lion Feuchtwangers Romanwerk zwischen 1933 und 1945.* Bern: Peter Lang, 1984.

Jerzy Ficowski

(1924–)

THEODOSIA ROBERTSON

JERZY FICOWSKI (born in Warsaw, Poland) is a distinguished poet, prose writer, scholar, and translator. He has received literary awards in Poland, England, the United States, and Israel. Both linguistically and thematically, he is one of the most original Polish poets of the twentieth century, and his work contributes significantly to Holocaust literature. During the German occupation of World War II Jerzy Ficowski served in the Home Army (AK) and took part in the Warsaw Uprising of 1944. After the war he studied journalism, sociology, and philosophy at the University of Warsaw and lectured there on the subject of the gypsies. He did direct field research from 1948 to 1950, traveling with the gypsy camps in Poland and conducting linguistic research among the Hungarian and Romanian gypsies.

Jerzy Ficowski began publishing in the Polish press in 1946, and his debut volume of poetry appeared in 1948, *Ołowiani żołnierze* (Leaden Soldiers); twenty collections of poems followed. He has written poetry for children, a collection of prose pieces, *Czekanie na sen psa* (Waiting for a Dog's Dream, 1970), as well as essays. During the years of Solidarity and Martial Law, Jerzy Ficowski coedited the literary quarterly *Zapis* (The Record) in the late 1970s and was a member of KOR (Komitet Obronny Robotników, the Workers Defense Committee). From 1977 to 1989 his collections appeared either underground or abroad. He lives in Warsaw, Poland.

Scholarship and Translation

Jerzy Ficowski's work deals with several facets of Hitler's genocide in Poland. As the major postwar scholar on Polish gypsies, his nonfiction studies, as well as his poetry and prose have salvaged the culture of this people, decimated in the Holocaust. Among his several books on gypsy history and culture, *Cyganie w Polsce. Dzieje i obyczaje* (*Gypsies in Poland. History and Customs*, 1989) contains a chapter on the extermination of the gypsies in the Holocaust.

Jerzy Ficowski is also the major scholar and critic of the life and work of Bruno Schulz (1892 to 1942), a Polish-Jewish artist and writer murdered in the Holocaust. Ficowski began researching Schulz's life and artistic legacy in 1946; his study of the writer (entitled *Regions of the Great Heresy*) was first published in 1967 and has since had two revised editions (1975 and 1992). In addition to his evocation of Schulz's unique creative world, Ficowski traced the course of Schulz's life, which ended in his starvation and murder in his Nazi-occupied town, Drohobycz (now in western Ukraine). Ficowski's meticulous and determined efforts preserved information about Bruno Schulz for several decades until the subject of the Jews in Poland and their fate in the Holocaust could be openly discussed in the 1980s. Bruno Schulz also inspired two of Ficowski's poems: "Mój nieocalony" (My Unsaved One; 1968) and "Drohobycz 1920" (1981).

Jerzy Ficowski is also one of the most active translators of Yiddish literature into Polish remaining in Poland. He has translated the 1964 anthology of Yiddish folk poetry, its title taken from a lullaby, *Rodzynki z migdałami. Antologia poezji ludowej Żydów polskich* (Raisins with Almonds: An Anthology of the Folk Poetry of Polish Jews), *Antologia poezji żydowskiej* (An Anthology of Jewish Poetry, 1983), and *Pieśni o zamordowanym żydowski narodzie* (Songs of the Murdered Jewish Nation, 1982) by Yitzak Katzenelson, a Yiddish poet killed in Auschwitz in 1944. He has translated parts of the volume *Archiwum Ringelbluma—getto warszawski* (The Ringelblum Archive—Warsaw Ghetto, 1980) as well.

Poetry

Above all, Jerzy Ficowski is a poet whose creative work presents unusual examples of Holocaust subject matter. His unique combination of poetic art and knowledge of gypsy life combine in the unusual poem, "Modlitwa do świętej wszy" (Prayer to the Blessed Louse) in the 1981 collection, *Śmierć jednorożca* (Death of a Unicorn). The poem carries an explanatory note that the action takes place in spring 1944, during the delousing of the gypsy barracks in Auschwitz-Birkenau. The poem evokes the poignant image of a gypsy woman clutching a louse in her fist as she is forced to enter a supposed delousing shower. Stripped of her once vibrantly colorful skirt, she is now naked and helpless. She sings in her gypsy language to the louse in her tightly clenched fist, because in gypsy lore, lice leave the human body at death. As long as she clings to the louse, she will live.

Jerzy Ficowski's 1979 collection, *Odczytanie popiołów* (*A Reading of Ashes*, 1981), comprises twenty-five poems devoted entirely to the Holocaust. The opening poem, known by its first line, "nie zdolałam ocalić" ("I did not manage to save"), illustrates the compression and paradox that mark Ficowski's Holocaust poetry. In "I didn't manage to save," the poet shifts the well-known theme of rescue (in Polish, *ocalenie*) from its earlier postwar association with the miraculous survival of poetry or the individual poet to the grim reality of incalculable human loss:

I did not manage to save
a single life
I did not know how to stop
a single bullet

and I wander round cemeteries
which are not there
I look for words
which are not there
I run

to help where no one called
to rescue after the event

I want to be on time
even if I am too late (*A Reading of Ashes*, Menard Press, 1981, p. 7).

The following poems in *A Reading of Ashes* often recall details, images, and places connected with Jewish communities and with names and voices of individuals. Fragments of the past survive deliberate devastation because they are preserved in the poet's memory and in his poetry, but the situation in "I didn't manage to save" is painfully ironic—the poet survivor remains in a hopeless position of death in life.

The theme of death in life involves multiple time frames that are present in the poetic voice of the survivor. In "Krajobraz pośmiertny" ("Posthumous Landscape"), the survivor recalls names along a railway line familiar from childhood, places of summer vacations that later were seen by victims peering out through cracks between boards of cattle cars as they crossed the same landscape to their deaths. The poet sees the death of his childhood, as well, while the landscape survives. The final strophe of the poem reads:

Oh long since the wagons the wagons, the wagons
have run over that landscape and killed it
but posthumous it lasts unpunished to this day
there are no witnesses they have perished
the corpse of my childhood
was traveling with them (p. 22).

"Próba czasu" ("Test of Time") carries an explanatory note, itself a powerful image:

Où est très . . . très belle . . . treblinká?
the wagon asked, inside were about two hundred.
And my mother was walking loaded with bundles.
She halted. She had forgotten her French.
—the railway siding in Malkinia, c. 1942/43 (p. 36).

The poem that follows is a single strophe of twenty-one lines composed of disjointed dialogue. Its phrases seem to roll forward until the strophe comes to a halt in the final three words or voices of the last line: Gdzie Treblinka Tutaj (Where Is Treblinka Here).

Years of terror in youth appear as if in another lifetime in "Epitafium żywcem umarłego" ("Epitaph of One Dead while Alive"), which concludes:

he was scared to death
of the book of Moses
his own ten fingers
and curly mount sinai fear
yet he survived

yet he survived
himself (p. 10)

Several poems in *A Reading of Ashes* mingle the entire historic past of Jews in Poland with fragments of prewar Jewish life and culture, images from everyday ghetto reality, details of Jewish religious observance (Torah, candlesticks, *talith* [prayer shawl]), and Jerusalem as a place and a people. Like his master, Bruno Schulz, Ficowski invents a unique poetic time. The speaker of the poem fuses centuries of Jewish life with the time of Holocaust destruction in striking oxymoronic combinations, such as an "airy *kirkut*" (Jewish cemetery), "the *kahal* (Jewish community) of eternal sleep," or "salwa ciszy" ("salvo of silence"). In dense and compact lyrics, images intersect, sometimes seeming to hurtle forward, as people of the past and of the present are being pushed on, toward death. In "Do Jeruszalaim" ("To Jerusalem"), for example, the *talith*, candles, folk sayings, and pogroms jumble together as people both dead and living are pressed forward in an eternal movement through gas chambers and "airy cemeteries" to "Jerusalem." In "Co jest" ("What Is") voices of past conversation, local Jewish characters, and old quarrels pierce strophes describing "the dense crowd of nobody" and the noisy "hubbub of such silence." Amid references to "sabbath," "candlestick," "*kahal*," and "kabbalah," Jewish names waft into empty space and are known only to forgetfulness.

Compression is signaled through verbal paradox in the poem title, "Egzekucja pamięci" ("The Execution of Memory"). Here, outside a small town when the first patches of early winter snow are seen, we hear the onomatopoetic sounds of "spats splash" ("chlupoczą kamasze") of grey-bearded Hasids treading on the ground to their deaths, their blood in pools on the muddy earth. While poems such as "Posthumous Landscape" record specific place names, "The Execution of Memory" evokes a generalized landscape of eastern Poland, its rivers and forests, birds and sky. The landscape was once dotted with the little domes of synagogues surrounded by poplars, their branches raised to the sky, like hands greeting the salvo of silence.

Poems also capture unbearable sights connected with the Warsaw ghetto, particularly its suffering children, to whom passersby become inured. A starving child begs in "Sześcioletnia z getta żebrzaca na Smolnej w 1942 roku" ("A Girl of Six from the Ghetto Begging on Smolna Street in 1942"). In "5 VIII 1942," Ficowski contributes to the enormous number of poems inspired by the death in 1942 of Janusz Korczak, the famous physician, pedagogue, and director of the Warsaw Children's Orphanage. At the close of this poem, the children grow as grey as the ash they will become, while the Old Doctor becomes a child, smaller and smaller, until he is not even born. In the end "nowhere is full of them."

Two long poems, "List do Marc Chagalla" ("Letter to Marc Chagall") and "Postscriptum listu do Marc Chagalla" ("A Postscript to the Letter to Marc Chagall") contrast children's testimony of the Holocaust with the fairy-tale beauty of Chagall's landscapes and his reminiscences of Jewish life in Vitebsk. The poet speaks in an ironic, even painfully sarcastic voice, as he contrasts the suffering of children with the ethereal landscapes of the artist. Finally, "Twoje matki obie" ("Your Two Mothers") records the miraculous story of Jerzy Ficowski's wife, Elżbieta, who survived as an infant smuggled out of the ghetto in a little coffin, sedated with luminal so as not to cry before reaching the Aryan side. She was found there, her orphanhood washed away, swaddled in the love of a second mother:

> That was how
> both your mothers
> taught you
> not to be surprised at all
> when you say
> *I am* (p. 41)

In "Pożydowskie" ("Jewish Effects"), others benefit from the Holocaust. Clothes, furniture, housewares left behind are picked over, the lives of their Jewish former owners emanating from the objects. Time remains encased in a dress, a chair, or a platter. A pot belonging to the starved will feed others to satiety.

In "Muranów góruje" ("Muranów crops out"), Holocaust death fuses with postwar reconstruction and forgetfulness, as a district in the old ghetto is rebuilt. Upon the dead the living rise up, repeating their appalling refrain: "było nie było jest jak jest" ("What's past is past things are as they are"). An immense rubble of fragile human bone and ash is a surprisingly strong foundation; after all, "most letters reach their destination." The poem suggests the piles of ashes, which the poet tries to read:

> Muranów crops out
> on strata of dying
> its foundation supported by bone
> its cellars in craters
> emptied of cries (p. 25)

Like Muranów, the poet has been set up upon a pile of ash. If he is silent, he lies. Simply walking, he treads upon the dead.

Several of Ficowski's poems (in other volumes) refer to Jews in Poland who emigrated, people who left before the war or those were forced to leave decades afterward. Another form of time emerges: those absent continue to remain present as a part of life missing for those who remain. In "Spis abonentów" (The List of Subscribers, 1981), the poetic voice contemplates the prewar Warsaw telephone book. In the speaker's reverse phrase, what was once flesh has now become word. People of the past stand in the lines of printed letters; everything in alphabetical order. In the 1979 poem, "Dworzec Gdański 1968" (The Gdańsk Train Station 1968), friends are wrenched away from those who remain. Doors close in the train for departure—in the heart; those forced to depart are overdue for their death.

Critical Reception

Fellow poet Zbigniew Herbert has written that memory is the native realm for Ficowski. He fulfills the obligation of his generation, because "poets who live in storm zones have a sense of responsibility for the collective destiny, and assume a duty of bearing witness to the truth" (Preface, *A Reading of Ashes*, 1981). Herbert's implication is that Ficowski does manage to "rescue after the event." *A Reading of Ashes* carefully collects fragments of a life irretrievably gone, examines the ashes of its human beings, buildings, and places with respect and tenderness, even if they cannot be deciphered or explained. Another poet, Anna Kamieńska, notes that the seemingly straightforward quality of Ficowski's language plays upon an elaborate cultural reference system. The lack of punctuation in the poems contrasts with the horror and outrage they express. Ficowski is passionate for the individual, often named, their small tokens of identity, and their personal effects. A younger poet and critic, Piotr Sommer, characterizes Jerzy Ficowski's poetry linguistically, emphasizing its verbal inventiveness. Ficowski's distinctive time, memory, silence, and sound emerge through his language. Piotr Sommer describes it as a "living system of signs that organize past and present anew and enable past and present to converse" ("Wszystko, co trochę, wiem [Everything that I Know a Little]. Posłowie. Afterword to *Wszystko to czego nie wiem* [*Everything I Don't know*]. Sejny, Poland: Pogranicze [Seria Meridian], 1999, p. 179). This hallmark of all of Jerzy Ficowski's poetry is powerfully effective in *A Reading of Ashes.*

Bibliography

Primary Sources

Poetry in Polish

Moje strony świata (My Sides of the World). 1957.
Makowskie bajki (Poppyseed Tales). 1959.
Amulety i definicje (Amulets and Definitions). 1960.
Pismo obrazkowe (Picture Writing). 1962.
Ptak poza ptakiem (Bird beyond Bird). 1968.
Odczytanie popiołów (*A Reading of Ashes*). 1979, 1981, 1993.
Gryps (Smuggled Message). 1979.
Errata. 1981.
Śmierć jednorożca (Death of a Unicorn). 1981.
Inicjał (Initial). 1994.

Poetry in English

Polish Poetry of the Last Two Decades of Communist Rule: Spoiling Cannibals Fun. 1991.

Folktales in English

Sister of the Birds and Other Gypsy Tales. 1976.

Non-fiction in English

Gypsies in Poland: History and Customs. 1989.

Secondary Sources

Gross, Natan. *Poeci i szoa. Obraz zaglady żydów w poezji polskiej.* Sosnowiec, Poland: OFFMAX, 1993.
Herbert, Zbigniew. Preface to *A Reading of Ashes* by Jerzy Ficowski. Translated by Keith Bosley and Krystyna Wandycz. Introduction by Zbigniew Herbert. London: Menard Press, 1981.
Kamieńska, Anna. "To moja rzecz, bo pospolita." *Res Publica* 6(1980).
Odczytanie popiołów. A Reading of Ashes (dual language edition). Translated by Keith Bosley and Krystyna Wandycz. Łowicz, Poland: Browarna, 1993, pp. 44–47.
Sommer, Piotr. *Wszystko, co trochę, wiem* (Everything that I Know a Little).
Posłowie. Afterword to *Wszystko to czego nie wiem.* (Everything I Don't Know [a selection of the poetry of Jerzy Ficowski]). Sejny, Poland: Pogranicze (Seria Meridian), 1999, pp. 179–218.

IDA FINK

(1921–)

SARA R. HOROWITZ

IN "TRACES," A story so brief it occupies a scant three pages, a survivor of the Nazi genocide examines a photograph of the market square of a ghetto where she had resided many years earlier. In circumstances deliberately left vague, the story focuses on the woman during an interview during which she is called upon to bear witness to the events of the Holocaust. Perhaps to jog her memory, she is shown a photo of a small market street in the ghetto in winter—a street she immediately recognizes as "Meat Street," because of its butcher shops. The ghetto had been made progressively smaller and smaller, until only that one street remained, and the ghetto became known as "the butcher shop ghetto" (*A Scrap of Time and Other Stories*, translated by Madeline Levine and Francine Prose, New York: Random House, 1987, p. 136), a name with obviously ominous resonances. After identifying the photo, she pushes it away, in order to stave off unwanted memories. The vignette couples the photograph with the reluctant memory of the survivor. The photo depicts an empty street, with the snow marked by "traces of footprints" (p. 135). The woman immediately recognizes not only the photograph, but the circumstances under which it was taken. She understands, in other words, why the street was empty and who made the footprints. The prints in the snow are indeed traces, three times removed, of Jewish children who looked like "little gray mice" (p. 137) as they went silently to their deaths, refusing to reveal the whereabouts of their parents. The ephemeral nature of memory is symbolized by the snow, long ago melted, the children, long ago murdered, the ghetto, long ago destroyed, and the meaninglessness of the photo without the presence of the survivor to explain it: "A trace of those children. And only she can leave that trace, because she alone survived" (p. 137). Prompted by the barely discernible presence of the children's death march in the photo, the woman overcomes a reluctance to probe the past. Ultimately in the story, the survivor remembers the past; she knows how to read a photo of blankness and white, to make a sliver of memory speak volumes. Having heard her remembrance, the unnamed and undepicted interviewers now will look at the enigmatic photograph with new eyes. The story "Traces" can serve as an emblem of Ida Fink's art—slivers that open up on a destroyed world, fragments that speak to the whole. Fink's narratives enable the reader to notice some small detail, and through that detail, to see the nightmare world in its complexity.

Life

Ida Fink was born in Poland in 1921 to an educated, professional family, well integrated into Polish culture. Her father was a physician, and her mother had completed graduate work. As secular Jews, they had a strong sense of Jewish identity but were not religious. At home, they spoke Polish and German, but not Yiddish.

Fink did not encounter antisemitism as a child, although she knew it existed. Part of the Polish intelligentsia, her family socialized with both Jews and non-Jews. Many of her friends were Polish, as well. By the time she entered high school, however, things had changed. The German presence in Poland influenced the way people behaved. Antisemitism became more blatant, and she began to hear frequent antisemitic comments. Although Fink did not look identifiably Jewish, being fair, blond, and blue-eyed, she did not attempt to hide the fact that she was Jewish. As antisemitism increased it became important to her to assert her Jewishness, to tell people she was Jewish.

Early on, she understood that the changing political climate would affect her future in radical ways. For example, she was interested in studying literature at the university but realized being a Jew would stand in her way. She began to study music, intending to become a pianist. The Nazi invasion of Poland in September 1939, when Fink was eighteen years old, interrupted her studies. Together with her family, Fink resided in the ghetto until 1942, when she and her younger sister left together by using false identity papers. The two sisters survived the war in hiding, by concealing their identities. A fictionalized account of the war years appears in her novel *The Journey* (1992). After the war, Fink married; in 1957, she moved to Israel with her husband and daughter. She had never studied Hebrew, so in Israel—at the age of thirty-six—she began to learn the Hebrew alphabet.

Although before the war Fink had begun preparation for a career as a pianist, she always wanted to write, and took a creative writing course in Poland. Even then, she had a marked preference for very short forms of writing. As the academic year progressed, her friends put together increasingly thick manuscripts—writing lengthy novels—while she had perhaps eight to ten pages to show for her efforts at the end of the term. She wrote slowly, with a surety that short stories were her métier.

Even during the war years, while she was in hiding, she was already determined to write about her experiences. But she did not write about the war right away—indeed, not until more than a decade had passed. In the late 1950s, Fink began to compose the stories that would find their way into her published collections. Her initial attempts at publication, however, did not meet immediately with success. She was told her writing was "too quiet" and subdued for its subject, that she should write more dramatically. However, she did not change her style, and eventually her work was published to glowing reviews. A collection of her stories was published in Polish in 1983. In 1989, *A Scrap of Time and Other Stories* was published in English. Following its 1990 publication in Polish, her novel *The Journey* was published in English translation in 1992. *Traces*, a second collection of stories and short plays in English translation, appeared in 1997. Although she has lived in Israel since 1957 and has become fluent in Hebrew, Fink continues to write in Polish. In some measure, her writing comes out of Polish literary tradition and shares the rhythm of that language. Her works have been well received in Polish and have also been translated into Hebrew, English, French, Dutch, German, Italian, and other languages. Fink's writing has garnered many prestigious international awards, including the first Anne Frank Prize for Literature (1985), the Moravia Prize, and the Yad Vashem Prize (1995).

Fink has explained that the events detailed in her stories "actually happened," that they are "authentic" and "true" stories about her own life and the lives of people she knew during the war years, but she chooses to write fiction rather than autobiography, memoir, or reportage, in part because fiction is the genre in which she feels most comfortable. In addition, the vehicle of fiction offers a necessary distance, so that her own privacy and that of others is respected. Most important, perhaps, fiction offers a writerly freedom to give a narrative the artistic shape that enables it to communicate the unspeakable—the experience of living through (or dying in) Nazi atrocity, and the implications and aftereffects of the Nazi genocide.

Domestic Life in the Shadow of Atrocity

Fink has proven herself a consummate writer of very short stories, some of them no longer than two to four pages. These very short stories present slices—one might say slivers—of life under the Nazi program of genocide. Like all of her writing, these fragments isolate revealing moments that point to the complexities not only of victimization and survival, but of memory and narrative. Many of Fink's narratives focus on intimate moments, such as those between siblings, spouses, lovers, or parents and children. Her writing reveals the ways in which atrocity insinuates itself into the structure of domestic life, imprinting itself and reshaping even one's closest relationships. For example, "The Key Game"—perhaps her most famous story—focuses on parents attempting to train their young child to help the father hide, in the event that Nazis come to their apartment to take him away. The family has been eluding the genocidal net in a series of hasty moves to different apartments. The mother and son appear confident that they can move about safely, perhaps under assumed identities. The son is blue-eyed, and the mother feels secure enough to work. Perhaps, like her son, she does not look distinctly Jewish; perhaps she is not Jewish. The father's life, however, is endangered, and the family must not let on that he lives with them (or indeed, that he lives at all). The father has devised for himself a hiding space behind a false panel in the bathroom. In order to allow him time to secret himself, the boy must delay opening up the door to the soldiers who will come to the apartment door, and he must do so in a manner that will not arouse suspicion. Trying, presumably, to quell the boy's fears about the imagined scenario, and to help him learn what he must do, the parents devise what they term a "game"—the "key game" to which the title refers. The boy must run through the small apartment, loudly opening and slamming closed drawers and cabinets, all the while proclaiming that he cannot find the key. This charade of a key hunt is intended to allow the father the time he needs to save himself. When the boy finally opens the door, he is to tell the soldiers who have come for his father that Papa is dead. The parents repeatedly drill the boy, timing his efforts, and evaluating his performance. The father complains that he will require more time than the boy has managed to provide.

By means of this window on domestic life during the *Shoah*, the story reveals something of the duress for Jews living on borrowed time under Nazism. That murder lurks around every corner, that the doorbell may toll a death knell, is presented as part of the ordinary for this family, whose inner dynamics have been radically altered by the present circumstances. The story emphasizes the son's extreme youth. He is referred to as "the boy" and "the child," and when his mother speaks to him, she refers to herself in the third person "when Mama is at work," for example, as parents often do with small children. Nonetheless, responsibility for his father's life rests on his three-year-old shoulders when his mother is not at home. The child's presence in the apartment, concealing his father's existence and lying to those who might seek the man, places him in further jeopardy. For his part, the father's fear of danger diminishes him, disabling him from acting as a father to his small child. When the drill has been completed, he appears ashen, covered with the dust and plaster of his makeshift hiding spot, but also resembling the corpse he fears he will become should the ruse fail. When prompted by his wife to praise the boy for playing his part in their doomsday rehearsal—to offer some fatherly reassurance to the child—the father can barely manage to utter a sentence of wooden praise. In essence, the story depicts a reversal of roles, wherein the son performs the role of father, protecting and defending, while the father assumes a childlike passivity and anxiety.

Whatever the ultimate fate of this man (and the text grimly suggests that he is "already long dead" to those who hunt him), something significant has been altered. His identity as a man and a father has been eroded. Indeed, her stories depict a range of parent-child behaviors, each of which have profound psychological ramifications. The narrator of "Crazy," for example, longs for the onset of some form of dementia to help distance him from the excruciating memory of what he sees as fatherly betrayal. He looked on from a hiding space as his three small daughters were placed on a truck and taken to their deaths. When the children noticed their papa and began to call out to him, "I put my finger to my lips and shook my head at them, they shouldn't cry out, they should be quiet. Sha!" (*Scrap*, p. 109). Although in actuality the man was powerless to save his children, and joining them would have meant dying with them, the memory festers in him. In the ironically titled "A Spring Morning," a father desperately attempts to save his small daughter as the Jews of their town are marched to their death in a nearby forest. Seizing what seems to be an opportune moment, he urges his daughter to run out of the line, into the yard of a church, and throw herself on the kindness of strangers. But the child is noticed and shot. The man is permitted to pick up her lifeless body and carry her to his own death. Thus, the last moments of his life are marked by an additional anguish: "he understood that they would not kill him here, that he had to keep on walking, carrying his dead child" (*Scrap*, p. 47).

Conversely, the boy in "Splinter" recollects his mother's cool-headed heroism, which saved his life. He and his mother had been living together in a small room after his father had been transported, waiting for the preparation of the false documents that would have allowed them to pose as Christians. When the roundup of Jews began, the mother quickly folded up the boy's cot, tossed his bedding into a closet, placed the boy in a corner near the door to the room, and opened the door to the soldiers in such a way that it hid the boy from their vision. The mother's desperate ruse succeeded. As far as the soldiers could see, the boy tells his girlfriend after the war, "There was only one bed and one person in the room" (*Scrap*, p. 126). The mother is beaten and dragged off to her death, but her son survives, as she had hoped. Looking back, the son admires his mother greatly. "How did she do it? It was unbelievable. . . . She must have rehearsed that moment beforehand, she acted so quickly and efficiently" (p. 125). At the same time, however, the boy is tormented by the memory of that night, by what he sees as filial betrayal. "Because you know, when my mother pressed me against the wall with the door, I grabbed the handle and hung on to it, even though it wouldn't have shut on its own" (p. 126). In all these stories, and in others, the very love that one has for one's parents or one's children is turned into a vehicle for torment.

These stories also hint at the psychological connection between power and selfhood. The mother in "The Key Game," who feels safe enough to seek out work while her husband hides in their apartment, manages to continue to function as the boy's mother. She praises him sweetly for his performance and urges her husband to do so, as well. The father, however, seems to have been robbed of a sense of agency. A similar dynamic shapes the relationship between the two Jewish sisters in *The Journey*, who together survive the war posing as Aryan Poles. The young women, in their late teens or early twenties, acquire false identity papers, then hire themselves out for labor in German factories and farms. One sister is fair-haired and blue-eyed, easily taken for a young Polish woman. The other, olive-skinned, with dark hair and eyes, fears that she looks too Jewish for safety and sees herself as a liability to her more Aryan-looking sister. This difference in appearance—which, in essence, represents different degrees of endangerment—affects their personalities and their performance in crisis. The blond sister is energetic and clever, repeatedly devising plans on the fly that save their lives. The younger sister plays a more passive role, always looking to her fairer sister for direction and decisions. That this difference in personality is an outcome of their relative positions of danger during the war, rather than an essential characteristic of the women, becomes clear toward the end of the war. The women make their way south to the border between Germany and Poland. There, because Poles are darker featured than elsewhere, everyone sees the sister as "the perfect specimen of Polish womanhood" (*The Journey*, translated by Joanna Weschler and Francine Prose, New York: Farrar, Straus, Giroux, 1992, p. 230), and no one suspects her of being Jewish. More secure in her ability to "pass," the younger sister suddenly takes a more active role in their planning, becoming an equal partner to her sister for the remainder of their time in hiding.

When the World Unravels

Many of Fink's stories isolate the moment when the world unravels—the moment, that is, that one realizes that Nazism has radically changed the nature of things, or the moment when one knows that death awaits imminently. In "The Garden That Floated Away," for example, the narrator sees the lush garden of the neighbor next door, a non-Jewish childhood friend, "float away, slowly and majestically, into the distance far beyond our reach" (*Scrap*, p. 11). As the narrator's father negotiates the purchase of false identity papers, the neighbors pick ripe russet apples from their trees. They notice that the tree on the Jewish property has been picked bare while the apples were still green. "They were saying . . . that we were right to do so, because who knows what would happen to us by winter" (p. 13). While the father attempts to secure the life of his children, the neighbors note the likelihood that he will fail. Although the two adjoining properties had always been as one, without the "intrusion" of fence to separate them, only the neighbor's garden floats freely. The difference in the destiny of the two families under Nazism—and the ability of the neighbors to accept that difference calmly, however sadly, is symbolized by the differences in the gardens in the narrator's vision—the one, bare and earthbound, prematurely consumed; the other lush and soaring. Other examples of such piercing moments may be found in "A Spring Morning" and "The Threshhold." In "A Spring Morning," a man roused from a deep sleep by the sound of a persistent fly, realizes he has been hearing the approach of trucks, the beginning of a roundup. "A terrible feeling of regret tore through him when he remembered the dream, that buzzing fly, and he understood that he had overslept his life" (*Scrap*, p. 44). In "The Threshhold," a fifteen-year-old Jewish girl stubbornly denies the insistence of her elders, at the start of the German occupation of Poland, that Jewish life was doomed. Against the advice of her aunts and uncles, she continues to see friends, to take long walks. She "kept her distance from them, just as she distanced herself from their incessant concern with all the frightening and incomprehensible events. She locked herself in her own world" (*Traces*, translated by Phillip Boehm and Francine Prose, New York: Henry Holt, 1997, p. 11). But when a twenty-year-old SS soldier cold-bloodedly shoots a Russian boy at close range in her presence, telling her "it's so simple" to kill (p. 15), she understands that her family's vision was correct.

The themes enfolded in "The Garden That Floated Away" resonate in other stories, as well. The special poignance of the premature death of young people—those no longer children but not yet adults—informs "*Jean Christophe*," for example. In this story, a Jewish girl working in a labor detail is absorbed in a novel that she reads during every break. Her concentration is not broken by her knowledge that Jews are being deported that day. The novel is about love, and the girl fears she will not have time to finish it by the time she herself is killed. In "An Afternoon on the Grass," a young Jewish woman questions her friends about their boyfriends, about love, she says, "I'll never know" (*Traces*, p. 35), acknowledging that she will likely die without ever having experienced youthful romance. In "Behind the Hedge," a housebound Polish dowager chases away a young couple she spies halfnaked in the bushes on her property. The girl, she later learns, was shot during an *aktion*, after being forced to strip naked with other Jews and help dig a mass grave. Belatedly, the older woman understands "that moment of love and happiness, which they tried greedily to save from their broken life" (*Scrap*, p. 22). She recollects the girl's explanation of her behavior: "We're not allowed to do anything. We're not even allowed to love each other, or make each other happy. All we're allowed to do is die. 'At your age,' you say. And will we get any older?" (*Scrap*, p. 22).

In addition, Fink's narratives trace the range of attitudes evinced by those not under threat of genocide, attitudes ranging from rare instances of intervention and rescue, to resignation and indifference, to exploitation. A complex and disturbing picture of rescuers, for example, emerges in "Shelter," a story that depicts a Jewish couple who visit the Polish couple who had secreted them in a small, bricked-in corner in the cellar of their dilapidated hut five years earlier. Although they had nothing to offer at the time in exchange for the hiding place, the Jewish couple promised to pay for a new house, should they survive the war. Three years after the war, the Jewish couple fulfill their promise. When they visit their rescuers, they are given a tour of the new house, complete with a hidden, windowless room underground, "just in case," their rescuer explains, "something happens" (*Scrap*, p. 133). Later, the Jewish man reflects on the moral blindness of the Polish couple who had put themselves at risk to save them, even if for uncertain profit. "Sentenced to a hiding place, sentenced to death once again? And by whom? By good people who wish us well. To build a hiding-place out of the goodness of one's heart!" (p. 134). The rescuers chillingly anticipate a future time of antisemitic persecution, when one couple might be saved, but the genocidal machinery would go on unimpeded. In *The Journey*, a friend of the narrator offers to take her in during the war—at great personal risk—but insists that the younger, dark-haired sister be left to fend for herself. The Polish neighbors in "The Garden That Floated Away" comment on the fate of the Jews but do not offer to intervene. "Aryan Papers" focuses on a sixteen-year-old girl who buys false documents for herself and her mother, using her virginity as currency. The man who extracts this price denigrates her coarsely and laughingly, describing her to a friend as both a "whore" and a "virgin" (*Scrap*, p. 68). "A Conversation" presents a reversal of this traditional mode of gendered exploitation. In this story, a Polish woman desires the sexual favors of a Jewish man who lives with his wife on her property during the war. Taken together, the two stories indicate that the politics of power that shape gender relations is itself subject to shift in power. That she has life and death power over the Jewish couple places the Polish woman in a position traditionally occupied by men.

Interior Transformations: Identity and Memory

Fink's work also explores the psychological dimension of hiding under false identities—an experience regarded as relatively "easy" by survivors of concentration camps and forest bunkers, as the boy in "Splinter" reflects to his girlfriend. But through Fink's writing, one comes to realize the toll of such posing and passing, particularly as one's family, friends, and community go to their deaths. The protagonist of *The Journey*, for example, takes on a succession of false identities as she and her sister move through Germany as hired laborers during the war. She experiences a dangerous blurring of identity boundaries as the self she was before the war dissolves into the series of invented selves of her masquerade. This blurring of identities is indicated structurally, by a movement back and forth between third and first person. She must, of course, embrace each of these new identities, must internalize these invented biographies, in order to be convincing to others. But as time wears on, she finds herself losing her real self to these new selves. While working on a farm, for example, she gives herself over to the peasant life. Seduced by the sun in the fields, the simple farming life, the outdoor air, while posing as "Maria," she notes that her pseudo-self "virtually took on a life on her own; sometimes . . . she actually dominated me! . . . riding in the cart out to the field, I would feel a blissful calm, and it would occur to me that later I could live just like this: simply and peacefully, without all the things I used to need, in a world defined by fields, meadows, rakes, and cows. . . . I didn't like Maria gaining on me, even though I was working so hard to become her" (p. 231). At the same time, however, she feels intermittently pulled by a dangerous internal urge to rebel. For example, when German soldiers condescend to her, mocking the illiterate peasant girl she pretends to be, she seethes inwardly. Once, against her better instincts, she takes them on, almost revealing her secret life. Several German scientists are discussing racial theory at a local bakery turned pub, commenting on "Maria" and the other Poles: "Primitive, lazy, dirty" (p. 234). Presuming she had never heard a piano being played, one of the German's assistants plays a few isolated notes on an old, out-of-tune piano, attempting to impress her. Battling her own instincts for survival—"Stop, don't do it," she tells herself (p. 235)—she cannot resist showing them up by playing a Chopin polonaise.

While Fink's writing treats the wartime experience and its aftermath, her work also is concerned with exploring the act of memory itself, and the transposition of memory into narrative and into imaginative literature. The short narrative "A Scrap of Time," for example, begins with an elaborate prelude about the narrator's ability to recollect the events she wishes to narrate. She informs the reader that she must reach into what she terms "the ruins of memory" to relate the story of the "first action" in her city—that is, the first massive roundup of Jews for murder. The narrator, a Jewish survivor of the *Shoah* who grew up in Poland, recollects what occurred on that day. But rather than plunge into the heart of the matter, she beings by interrogating the very act of memory, and her own ability to translate it into narrative. "I want to talk about a certain time not measured in months and years. For so long I have wanted to talk about this time, and not in the way I will talk about it now, not about this one scrap of time. I wanted to, but I couldn't, I didn't know how. I was afraid, too, that this second time, which is measured in months and years, had buried the other time under a layer of years, that this second time had crushed the first and destroyed it within me" (*Scrap*, p. 3). Fearful of the fragility of memory, she feels the need to reassure both herself and her reader or listener that "digging around in the ruins of memory, I found it fresh and untouched by forgetfulness" (p. 3), its details "still fresh; its colors and aromas have not faded" (p. 5). Despite this affirmation, however, she has difficulty relating this "scrap of time," and instead embarks on a series of circumlocutions that run counter to the desire to bear witness.

From the contemplation of memory and its reliability, the narrator moves into an extended consideration of the definition of war jargon—for example, the distinction between the terms "action" and "round-up." Yet here, too, she refrains from plunging directly and straightforwardly into discussion. Instead of defining the terms, she muses, "I don't know who created this technical term [action], who substituted it for the first term, 'round-up' . . . Round-ups were for forced labor" (p. 4). The narrator never actually says outright what "action" means; the reader comes to understand, through omission, that it connotes outright murder. "We called that first action . . . a round-up although no one was rounding anyone up" (p. 4). This indirection and circularity mirror the beginning of the narrative and its equivocation regarding memory. The missing definition corresponds to the missing "scrap of time," still not revealed to the reader. Both the word "action" and the memory that the narrator wishes tocall upon contain the horror of mass slaughter. Like the definition of "action," the memory at the center of the "scrap of time" will be disclosed through indirection, perhaps because Holocaust atrocity cannot be faced head-on.

The postponed disclosure, when it finally begins, thwarts the reader's expectations. The narrator has promised to reveal a "fresh and untouched" story unearthed from the "ruins of memory." But it quickly becomes clear that what she wants to talk about has not happened to her and thus belongs, rightly, to someone else's memory, complicating her claim. She recollects, "In the middle of the marketplace . . . we were ordered to form ranks. I should not have written 'we,' for I was not standing in the ranks" (p. 4). From an unobserved vantage point, she sees the action on the marketplace, yet remains unseen. Since she wishes to relate the fate of the Jews rounded up and murdered—in particular, the fate of one specific Jew, her cousin David—it is precisely her absence from the scene that allows her to relate what occurred, even though her knowledge is severely limited. Because the dead cannot relate their own stories, her narration shifts into what Primo Levi has referred to as "a discourse 'on behalf of third parties,' the story of things seen at close hand, not experienced personally." But the narrator soon flees from the square, hiding among the bushes on a hillside. Much later, when she returns home, she learns that her cousin David was among the crowd of Jews gathered at the market square and marched off with the others to an unknown fate.

David's story comes to her only in bits and pieces, and not until after the war does she learn it in its entirety. The fragments of David's story reach the narrator through a number of different sources: people who spoke to him at the square, a note that he writes to his mother, the peasant who delivers the note and adds information of his own, postcards from people who were rounded up with David, and anonymous rumors. The narrator first learns what happened in the square during her absence: "the women had been told to go home . . . only the men were ordered to remain standing there" (p. 7). She learns also that David believed that he had done "violence to his own fate"—moving out of hiding and into the crowd. Later that evening, an unnamed peasant delivers a note that David wrote to his mother and tossed from a truck packed with human cargo. The note begs his mother's forgiveness. But the peasant withholds full disclosure. "The peasant that evening brought the note that said, 'I myself am to blame, forgive me,' was somber and didn't look us in the eye. He said he had found the note on the road to Lubianki and that he didn't know anything else about it; we knew that he knew, but we did not want to admit it" (p. 9). Soon postcards begin arriving from some of the men who were with David. The cards indicate that the men have been taken to a labor camp somewhere in the Reich, where they are alive and well. At the same time, unsubstantiated rumors "told a different story altogether—of soggy earth in the woods by the village of Lubianki, and of a bloodstained handkerchief that had been found. These rumors came from nowhere; no eyewitnesses stepped forward" (p. 10). These two sets of evidence—postcards, rumors of handkerchiefs—contradict one another. Only after the war, with the completion of the peasant's truncated narrative, does the narrator learn what actually occurred. "It happened just as rumor had it, in a dense, overgrown forest, eight kilometers outside of town, one hour after the trucks left the marketplace. The execution itself did not take long, more time was spent on the preparatory digging of the grave" (p. 10). Thus, belatedly, the narrator arrives at the "scrap of time" announced at the beginning of the narrative—David's death. Like the execution, which "itself did not take long," the actual telling of the story takes far less time than the "preparatory digging"—in earth and in memory.

Why does the narrator employ so circuitous a narrative path to impart David's story? First, because death remains always unarticulated, outside of narrative. Second, the narrator is attempting a dual story—of both living and dying in the Holocaust. She tells the story of her own survival, but at the same time, she wishes to tell that of David, because he cannot tell it himself. To accomplish this, she must imagine David's last moments, supplementing the bits and scraps of memory available to her. She traces in her mind the route by which David reaches the square, his solitary ruminations while in hiding, his sense of his impending death. The narrator temporarily places herself alongside her cousin in order to imagine—and to save from oblivion—his last moments, last feelings, before he falls victim to mass slaughter.

Similarly, "A Spring Morning" argues for the place of imaginative narrative in Holocaust memory. The story begins by recounting a restaurant conversation where a Polish petty municipal official entertains his friends with an anecdote about the roundup of local Jews. He remembers overhearing, with amusement, how a Jewish man crossing the bridge over the Gniezna River "with his wife and his children for the last time in his life" compared the murky river to beer. "Listen to this: Here's a man facing death, and all he can think about is beer" (*Scrap*, p. 39). After recounting the crass dinner exchange between the Polish official and his friends, the narrative shifts. An elaborate interior monologue recounts precisely what the Jewish man thought, did, and felt, from the moment he rises on the morning of his death, through his stunning realization that he has "overslept his life," his desperate attempt to save his toddler, and finally, his last moments—carrying his child's corpse to his own death at the mass grave in the forest. With these two points of view—the Polish official's and the dead Jewish man's—Fink's story presents two versions of the day's event. The Polish official's recollections may well have been spoken after the event, but do not adequately take in the experience of the Jewish man or the fate of the Jews. The man's interior monologue, in contrast, does service to the murdered Jews of Europe, but would be impossible to retrieve in actuality. Fink's story makes clear that without the fiction—without the narrator's imaginative intercession into historical reality—the tragic indignity of the murdered man and the superfluous cruelty of his suffering would remain untold. Instead, it would be left to callous functionaries and indifferent bystanders—like the Polish official whose Aryan ancestry leaves him safe to watch the death march with indifference. "Thanks to him and to people like him, there have survived to this day shreds of sentences, echoes of final laments, shadows of sighs of the participants in the marches funébres, so common in those times" (p. 39), the narrative cynically notes. Fiction, imaginative engagement with history, then, becomes the means to retrieve impossible narratives, to give voice to the murdered dead.

Fink's writing also examines the refusal of memory and the limitations of testimony. In "The Table," a one-act play inspired by radio broadcasts of war crimes trials, Fink raises questions about the nature of survivor memory and the needs of historians and juridical processes. The play brings four survivors to testify in court after the war about an "action" they witnessed. These four different testimonies agree in essence about the violence of the "action." But they differ in the details. The prosecutor asks whether there was a table in the marketplace where the murdered Jews had been rounded up. He demands to know the dimensions of the table, its precise position in the square, and whether there were chairs, as well. He explains that such details are necessary because the court requires "something concrete" to validate their memories. He tells them that an agreement on the details would allow their recollections to corroborate one another. But the prosecutor succeeds only in undermining their testimony. The four witnesses cannot agree on the specifics of the table. They all testify that the marketplace was covered in snow and that the snow was drenched with blood. The prosecutor tells them that "snow doesn't constitute proof for judges, especially snow that melted twenty-five years ago" (*Scrap*, p. 156).

Not only juridical procedures but also individuals—even sympathetic individuals—may refuse to listen to and absorb survivor testimony. For example, when the boy in "Splinter" relates his anguished story of being saved by his mother, his girlfriend falls asleep. When the Polish woman in "Night of Surrender" tells the American soldier who has fallen in love with her that she has been living for years under an assumed identity, that she is really Jewish, he does not reject her as she expected. But when she explains that her entire family was murdered during the war, he advises her to come with him to America and begin life anew, forgetting her past, her people, even her name. " 'Klara,' he repeated. 'Clear one . . . but you'll always be Ann to me' " (*Scrap*, p. 101). The refuge and future he offers her comes with a price—the erasure of her own history and identity.

Critical Assessment

The power of Fink's understated writing, and the importance of detail and perspective, have been noted by critics and reviewers of her work. Her work has been well received in Poland, and she has received many invitations to speak and read there. In other countries and other languages, the power of her work has also been recognized. After the publication of her novel, *The Journey*, in Hebrew translation (1993)—five years after the publication of her first collection of short stories in Hebrew translation (1988)—the Israeli critic Gershon Shaked noted her extraordinary contribution to Holocaust literature. Unlike writers who mythologize the Nazi genocide, Fink neither demonizes the perpetrators nor idealizes the victims, but restores to all their human face. Thus, according to Shaked, her writing explores antisemitism not as an abstract ideology but as a hatred grounded in human culture, history, and behavior. Similarly, rather than eulogizing martyrs, she places the living and dying victims in the contexts of their lives. Shaked argues that she is among the finest writers to create literature about the Holocaust, and he argues for her significance as an Israeli writer, reshaping that country's understanding of the past.

The English translations of her novel and two short story collections have received glowing reviews. Reviewing *A Scrap of Time* for the *Times Literary Supplement*, Jayne Pilling praised the "immediacy" of Fink's stories, astutely noting not only the brilliance of the stories individually, but the skillful orchestration of their sequence in the collection, which serves "as the framework for an unspoken interpretive commentary," all the more effective for being unspoken but implied. Johanna Kaplan, in her *New York Times* review, found many of the stories in that collection "truly shocking" for their plunge into "a moment of the most extreme, frenzied, precisely catastrophic anguish." Fink's novel and subsequent collection received similar accolades. In a *New York Times* review, Herbert Mitgang argued for the broad, contemporary relevance of Fink's work, describing *The Journey* as "singular in its details, yet universal in its memories." Fernanda Eberstadt praised *Traces* in her *New York Times* review, noting Fink's "gift . . . for the delicate miniature, the oblique detail that freezes the reader's heart." Other reviews reflect similar responses to the volume, and critical attention to her work has grown. Shaked and Marek Wilczynski note her sophisticated use of language—and in particular her interpolation of foreign tongues—to convey the ongoing assault of Nazi atrocity. Fink's short fiction has been anthologized in several collections of Holocaust literature.

The narratives and plays that comprise Fink's oeuvre are characterized by an unsentimental, incisive look at ordinary people whose lives—and sometimes whose deaths—have been marked by encounters with Nazi atrocity. Her depictions of the minute and spare details of everyday existence during the Nazi genocide powerfully convey, through apparent understatement, the profound and lasting effects of the Holocaust on its victims and survivors. Through the vehicle of fiction, with lean prose, Fink's writing speaks the unspeakable.

Bibliography

Primary Sources

A Scrap of Time and Other Stories. Translated by Madeline Levine and Francine Prose. 1987. First appeared in Polish in 1983.

The Journey. Translated by Joanna Weschler and Francine Prose. 1992. First appeared in Polish in 1990.

Traces: Stories. Translated by Phillip Boehm and Francine Prose. 1997.

Secondary Sources

Eberstadt, Fernanda. "Images of an Extinguished World." *New York Times*, 24 August 1997, p. 12. Review of *Traces*.

Horowitz, Sara R. *Voicing the Void: Muteness and Memory in Holocaust Fiction*. New York: State University of New York Press, 1997.

Kaplan, Johanna. *New York Times Book Review*, 12 July 1987, p. 7. Review of *A Scrap of Time*.

Levi, Primo. *The Drowned and the Saved.* translated by Raymond Rosenthal, New York. Summit, 1986.

Mitgang, Herbert. "Words as a Shield Against the Nazis." *New York Times*, 19 August 1992, p. 18. Review of *The Journey*.

Pilling, Jayne. *Times Literary Supplement*, 26 August 1988, p. 928. Review of *A Scrap of Time*.

Shaked, Gershon. "Shem ha-mis'ḥak: hisradut" (The Name of the Game: Survival). *Yedi'ot Aharonot*, 6 August 1993, p. 26.

———."Lesaḥek b'te'atron absurd" (Playing in the Theater of the Absurd). *Yedi'ot Aḥaronot*, 13 August 1993, p. 31.

Wilczynski, Marek. "Trusting the Words: Paradoxes of Ida Fink." *Modern Language Studies* 24, no. 4 (fall 1994): 25–38.

Interviews

Interview by Katarzyna Bielas. "Zawsze chcialam pisac" (I've Always Wanted to Write). *Gazeta Wyborcza* 160 (12 July 1994): 11.

Interview by Eva Hoffman. "Fantasy Is Harmful." *New York Times Book Review*, 12 July 1987, p. 9.

BARBARA FINKELSTEIN

(1937–)

VICTORIA AARONS

BARBARA FINKELSTEIN'S HOLOCAUST novel, *Summer Long-a-Coming* (1987), is set at a remote distance from the ghettos and death camps of eastern and central Europe. Rather, its setting, a small rural town located on the outskirts of the wooded New Jersey pine barrens, would seem to distinguish this novel from the urban backdrop generally characteristic of fiction by American Jewish writers, especially those of Finkelstein's own "second generation" of Holocaust writers. But Finkelstein's remote setting, Jake's Poultry Farm, on the "outermost rim of the Jersey Pine Barrens," encircled by "No Trespassing" signs, and "removed . . . from city influences," managing only "dim contact with the world outside" (*Summer Long-a-Coming*, Sarasota, Flo.: Disc-Us Books, Inc., 1987, pp. 1–3) is an important locale for the desolate events that determine the fate of Finkelstein's characters and for the estranged voice of the narrator, Brantzche Szuster, who recounts this story of defeat, endless loss, and inevitable ill-fate.

Barbara Finkelstein, born in 1937, received her Ph.D. in Education from Columbia University in 1970 and in 1983 obtained the position of Professor of the Department of Education Policy, Planning, and Administration at the University of Maryland. An American-born daughter of Holocaust survivors, Finkelstein has combined her professional interests in cross-cultural studies and education with her personal interests in oral histories, especially those of Holocaust survivors documented in Yad Vashem, Israel's Holocaust memorial museum and archive.

In Finkelstein's only Holocaust novel, *Summer-Long-a-Coming*, the events of the Holocaust define the characters' responses to one another and dictate their actions, circumscribing their lives just as the New Jersey woods enshroud and encircle their poultry farm. In this atmosphere of festering isolation, the novel's range of vision can only turn inward. Rukhl and Yankl Szuster, Auschwitz survivors from Poland, can only return to the haunted memories and constant reminders of the devastation of the *Shoah*: the Nazi labor camps, the train tracks of Poland, and the Ukrainian forests in which Jews were held captive and massacred. The pine barrens of Finkelstein's remote New Jersey poultry farm become for her narrator, the second eldest of the three American-born Szuster children, a reenactment of her parents' Holocaust experiences, a legacy bequeathed to her: "Hiding in the Polish woods from the Nazis, from Christians, and now hiding in America . . . All they know how to do is hide, and now that's all I know how to do . . . a family of survivors—all of us, not just my parents" (pp. 8, 15). But the narrator's identification with her parents' trauma is thwarted by her resistance to their continued piety and belief in the divine presence of God, a position that Brantzche struggles with throughout the novel. Her refusal to accept her parents' pious life of Jewish ritual and traditional belief is further kindled by their stilled silence about their experiences during the Holocaust. Brantzche's position of antagonism, protest, and judgment against her parents and against God undergoes numerous and difficult transformations as she comes, finally, by the novel's close, to acknowledge her Jewish identity through a gradual, personalized awareness of the horrors of the Holocaust.

Summer Long-a-Coming is a story of post-Holocaust relocation and renewed life in America. For Rukhl and Yankl Szuster, America remains an alien land, "a planet," as their disaffected daughter puts it, "where the spaceship crash-landed . . . life in exile . . . untouched by the territory beyond the farm's borders" (p. 97). The novel's epigraph, a passage from Daniel Defoe's *Robinson Crusoe*, is a fitting preface for the sense of desolation that permeates the voice of Finkelstein's narrator. For the central part of the novel, Brantzche Szuster, a fifteen-year-old girl, envisions herself, much as does Defoe's narrator, held captive paradoxically by her perceived sense of abandonment, her exile a reenactment of Crusoe's unprotected and unanswered bewilderment: "where are the rest of you? . . . Why were not they saved and you lost? Why were you singled out?" In prefacing the novel with Crusoe's lament, Finkelstein inscribes a eulogy to the dead, to those long dead and to others who inexplicably survived only to inscribe the past onto their children, children, like Brantzche Szuster, who respond with anger and resentment at their sense of imprisonment by the unsolicited presence of a veiled but unrelenting past bequeathed to them. Finkelstein, like her narrator an American-born child of Holocaust survivors, has remarked that the "Holocaust casts a shadow too wide . . . to escape" (quoted in Berger, ed., p. 48). And thus, for Brantzche Szuster, Finkelstein's adolescent character who narrates this coming-of-age, post-Holocaust novel, her parents' experiences in the *Shoah* define her. Their past horrors establish the perimeters of her vision.

Instead of the hoped-for promise and freedom of America, the adult Szusters find themselves alienated from and suspicious of the cultural norms and the social vernacular of their new home. In their newly constructed refuge, Rukhl and Yankl Szuster find themselves blindsided by American racism and antisemitism and bludgeoned by a past they cannot escape. So they retreat, as their daughter resentfully puts it, "refus[ing] nourishment from the outside world" (p. 97), insulating themselves from anyone outside the family. But Finkelstein shows that it is not at all clear that the Szusters would find emotional sustenance in America. The picture Finkelstein paints of the United States in the tumultuous years of the late 1960s is one of heightened anxiety, suspicion, easy anger, ostracization, and a carnivalesque atmosphere of unrestrained patriotic gaiety that barely hides its menacing undercover. While one might expect the dislocated, haunted refugees to find shelter in the insulation of the family, there is no solace there either. The American-born children, Sheiye, Brantzche, and Perel, find their parents barely acceptable relics of an archaic and distasteful past that they would rather deny, a past exemplified by their parents' habitual use of Yiddish, "with its strictures and death tallies . . . a poison" (p. 48). The very language is a measure of the distance between them. America is not the promised land, nor are the Szuster children an anticipated covenanted future, a compensation for the suffering of the past, "children, who were supposed to vindicate the crimes of the past by being happy" (p. 163). Instead, the three children, at war among themselves and with their pious, restrictive, unyielding parents, are ill-fated, "a repeat of [their] parents' past" (p. 15). This generational conflict allegorizes the feared destiny of *Yiddishkeit* in post–World War II America.

This climate of decline, ruin, and ill-fate is established early on in Finkelstein's novel, long before the exact circumstances of the Szusters' undoing are made explicit. There is an uneasy, foreboding tone from the novel's inception that the very conditions that delineate the Szusters' lives are not right. Even nature seems to be at odds with the Szuster family, the environment and the natural world complicitous against them from the very start. The novel's opening lines set the scene for impending calamity with an unprecedented and inauspicious infestation of hornets that besiege their yard, an omen of things to come. And the weather—marked by a storm so unusual for a New Jersey summer, "thunder, lightning, and rain . . . hoping to steal their way unnoticed"—seems intentionally to plague the Szusters, an echo of the unnatural state of affairs of another time. Although the injurious and ruinous ways of nature are set in direct contrast to the human wreckage and devastation of the *Shoah*, the undercurrent of evil that permeates the novel's unfolding becomes an echo of that time and place and a harbinger of ill to come. "History," as this embittered daughter of survivors resentfully acknowledges, "wasn't finished abusing us" (p. 163). When finally Sheiye, the Szusters' eldest child and only son, "accidentally" kills his youngest sister, Perel, the event is seen, because of the intentional ambiguity of its motivation, as an act of evil no less than that experienced by the narrator's parents in Nazi-occupied Poland: "the new holocaust in the Szuster family . . . extended the old one" (p. 169). The death of Perel is, finally, the family's not-unanticipated undoing. The Szusters are severed: the narrator is sent to live with another family of survivors, Sheiye is left to run the poultry farm on his own; and the elder Szusters renounce America, a country that had long since failed them, for Israel.

The generational tension is heightened by the novel's theological debate, framed by the conflict between the narrator and her parents, especially her father, who here represents a centrist Orthodox view toward the Holocaust. The Job-like Yankl Szuster fears God and maintains his faith in the midst of adversity. He views the ways of God as beyond the ken of human comprehension. The Holocaust, for him, represents the human capacity for evil. It most certainly does not suggest, as it does for his daughter, the absence or malfeasance of God. The Szusters' piety, however, instead of enriching their lives, further isolates them in recurring patterns of grief and despair, as witnessed by their daughter, who, for most of the novel, blames God for her parents' continual suffering and her own misery. It is only when Brantzche learns indirectly of her parents' experiences in Poland during the Holocaust, through their testimonies to the Yad Vashem historian, that she can appreciate the scope of their suffering. Yankl and Rukhl's shared silence, their refusal to tell their "stories" to their children but rather to shield them from the atrocities they experienced, is not atypical of Holocaust survivors and is the source of considerable tension in the literature of second-generation Holocaust writers. The parents' "public" testimony, while circumventing the treacherous terrain of probing questions from their daughter, distances their histories from life in America, placing them instead in Israel's history and linking them to a community of survivors. It is, however, when Brantzche emerges from the exile of her own adolescence and hears her parents' voices on the tapes recorded by the Yad Vashem historian that she can accept their history as her own. By the novel's close, the narrator goes on her own quest for restorative Jewish identity (*tikkun atzmi*). The novel's final words, "Gedenk . . . Remember," suggest the healing powers of shared memory and is a collective expression of Jewish identity. And so the narrator, through the course of the novel's narration, experiences expiation and redemption.

Sadly, however, Brantzche's parents' *aliyah* to Israel is made less in reparative celebration than in defeat. The cataclysmic events that assault the Szuster family are, disturbingly, contrived as a kind of microcosm of the Holocaust, conditions from which they can never recover. Summer, here a metaphor of reprieve, is, indeed, for them "long-a-coming." Finkelstein, in attempting to justify this uneasy parallel, points to the difficulty in writing about the unspeakably immense scope of the Holocaust for one who was not a witness to the events, so that, in her words "I had to make it smaller, bring it down to me" (quoted in Berger, p. 48). In choosing this microcosmic narrative strategy, Finkelstein points to the central conflict in imagining the Holocaust, particularly for fiction writers. In negotiating the difficulties of fictionalizing the Holocaust, Finkelstein intersperses the narrative of her novel with testimonies given by her fictional characters, Rukhl and Yankl Szuster, to an oral historian, testimonies that form part of the collection for the survivor's archives at Yad Vashem. (Finkelstein has suggested that the taped interviews are drawn from her own parents' testimonies of the Holocaust.) Ultimately, however, the central conflicts in *Summer Long-a-Coming*, conflicts between past and present, between generations of survivors and their children, between conflicting notions of God, family, and obedience, and between direct witnessing and being told about the Holocaust, can, as Finkelstein sees them, never be adjudicated. For even at the novel's close, when the narrator comes at least partially to realize the nature of her parents' obsessions and the scope of their suffering, there is neither reconciliation nor reprieve, only the recognition of unrelenting pain.

Bibliography

Primary Source

Summer Long-a-Coming. 1987.

Secondary Sources

Berger, Alan L., ed. *Children of Job: American Second-Generation Witnesses to the Holocaust*. New York: State University of New York Press, 1997. Contains lines from the text of a lecture by Finkelstein at Syracuse University, 5 October 1987.

Bukiet, Melvin Jules. "Unto the Next Generation." *The Washington Post* (4 May 1997).

Collins, Douglas. "Shadows Cast on the Wall of a Cave." *Syracuse Jewish Observer* 26 (October 1987): 9–13.

Steinberg, Sybil. "Review of *Summer Long-a-Coming*, by Barbara Finkelstein." *Publishers Weekly* (20 March 1987): 69.

Alain Finkielkraut

(1949–)

JONATHAN JUDAKEN

ALAIN FINKIELKRAUT IS one of the most prominent intellectuals in France today. His cultural and political interventions inevitably return to the crisis in modernity that culminated in the Holocaust: the contradictions between the core values of the modern West—liberty, equality, human rights, democracy, national sovereignty—and modern identity, whether racial, national, religious, or ethnic. Finkielkraut's work explores this crisis in terms of the legacy of the Enlightenment and the French Revolutionary tradition, the *Shoah* and its denial, and the politics of memory and history in general.

Biography

Alain Finkielkraut is a child of survivors (of the Holocaust from Poland). His father arrived in Paris from Warsaw in the 1930s and was subsequently deported to Auschwitz for three years. His mother moved from Lvov to Berlin, escaped and survived the war with false papers in Belgium, and then moved to Paris in 1948 where she met her future husband and gave birth to Alain in 1949.

Finkielkraut was raised with a strong Jewish identity, albeit with little religious content. Although his parents sought to lay their traumatic past to rest and embraced the French assimilationist tradition, their persecution as Jews had lasting impact. As the tumultuous period of the late 1960s reached its crescendo, Alain was studying at the prestigious Lycée Henri IV to enter the École Normale Supérieure de Saint Cloud in French literature. Attracted to the New Left's emancipatory politics, he was one of the anonymous militants in the mass student uprising in May 1968 and a fellow traveler of the radical Left in the early 1970s. Like the cohort of young former militants, the Nouveaux Philosophes, Finkielkraut was skeptical of the lyrical illusions of his generation by the late 1970s, and broke with the New Left over their widespread anti-Zionism.

He taught for a period at the École polytechnique until he achieved enough notoriety from his success as an engaged essayist by the 1980s to work full-time as an *homme des lettres* in the mold of Voltaire. His interventions reflect on struggles from the Israeli incursion into Lebanon to Holocaust denial, from the Klaus Barbie trial to polemics over the Third Balkan War, from debates about multiculturalism in France to the fecundity of the humanist tradition. His meditations on these topics are widely disseminated in regular appearances in the French media, including *Répliques*, his own radio show; as the editor of the now defunct journal *Le Messager européen*; on the cultural pages of many French newspapers; and as the author of a large and expanding number of books.

The Imaginary Jew

Finkielkraut first addressed the impact of the *Shoah* in *Le Juif imaginaire* (*The Imaginary Jew*, 1980), a brilliant analysis of the Jewish condition in a post-Holocaust world. The Final Solution eliminated Jewish socialists of the Bundist tradition and secular Yiddish culture, leaving nonreligious Jews like himself without a living culture to sustain their identity. This abyssal absence structures his conception of his Jewishness: "What makes me a Jew is the acute consciousness of a lack, of a continuous absence: my exile from a civilization which, for 'my own good,' my parents did not want me to keep in trust" (*The Imaginary Jew*. Translated by Kevin O'Neil and David Suchoff. Lincoln, Neb.: University of Nebraska Press, 1994, p. 114).

Finkielkraut recognizes that his early conception of authentic Jewishness, based on Jean-Paul Sartre's notion that the Jew is a product of the antisemite's gaze, was grounded in family stories of the "Final Solution" (p. 11) and that ultimately it was a fiction of his own family romance. To lay claim to the ostracism and exile of Jewish identity on the basis of his father's generation's experience in Auschwitz was bad faith, a "drama without a fateful event" (p. 6). The "imaginary Jew" is the name he gives to those Jewish "mama's boys" (and girls), protected from the horrors of the persecution of Jews, who are "cowards in life, martyred in dreams" because "they have not performed their apprenticeship to Judaism under the gaze of the Other" (pp. 14–15).

Finkielkraut examines the inherent dilemmas of modern Jewish identity from assimilation to Jewish observance and considers the ruses of memory in an effort to reconnect with a pre-Holocaust past permanently and irremediably lost as a result of the *Shoah*. His critical self-analysis ranges from Jewish social activism to Zionism. Ultimately this leaves him straddling the double binds of the French-Jewish social contract that has preoccupied his many political engagements acutely summarized by David Suchoff in his introduction to the 1994 translation: "*The Imaginary Jew* thus imagines a Jewish politics that is anti-assimilationist but committed to the Enlightenment, supportive of Israel while it argues for the Diaspora, and a proponent of ethnic particularism rooted in history, yet that aspires to remain in critical tension with universal ideals" (Suchoff, p. 20). Like so many contemporary Jews, Finkielkraut's Jewishness exists in opposition to what it is not. This negativity animates his resistance to the many forms of contempt aimed at Jews, but leaves him empty when it comes to Judaism.

The Future of a Negation: Reflections on Holocaust Denial and the Question of Genocide

This negation has guided Finkielkraut in other texts he has published, first in his castigation of Holocaust deniers in *L'Avenir d'une négation (The Future of a Negation*, 1982). Holocaust denial has an infamous history in France, dating back to the immediate postwar period. Unlike Deborah Lipstadt or Pierre Vidal-Nacquet, who historicize its evolution and demolish the arguments of what Vidal-Nacquet calls the "assassins of memory," Finkielkraut reflects on the ideological and historical factors that lead people *not* to dismiss them. The danger of the deniers, who refer to themselves as "revisionists," to legitimize their position, is that they remain in the debate, positing their denial as a viable alternative theory. Finkielkraut's general intent is "to study the modalities of this obliteration [of the past by the deniers] by examining the question of the genocide of the Jews" (*The Future of a Negation: Reflections on the Question of Genocide*. Translated by Mary Byrd Kelly. Lincoln, Neb.: University of Nebraska Press, 1998, p. xxxiv).

Like racism and fascism, the origin of Holocaust denial is a phenomenon of both the Left and the Right in France. However, Finkielkraut focuses much of his analysis on the extreme Left and explores its convergence with the deniers' *Weltanschauung*. He first examines the failures of various Marxist strands to grasp antisemitism and the uniqueness of National Socialism from the Dreyfus Affair to the present. In the contemporary context, dogmatic extremists like the group La Veille Taupe (who publish the works of Robert Faurisson, the most infamous of the French deniers), depict Hitlerian antisemitism as a veil that prevents recognition of the suffering of our society at present. Their claim to the truth of history as the history of class struggle leads them to deny the facts of the gas chambers, which do not fit their historical model.

Critiquing Noam Chomsky's defense for writing a preface to one of Robert Faurisson's books (that he was merely defending free speech), Finkielkraut explores how the predilection among contemporary intellectuals with unmasking the manufacturing of consent created by the media and multinationals leads to a propensity to deny the truth of facts themselves. What remains is a "war of images" where "power is not content to make history: it manipulates it" (p. 51). This results in what Finkielkraut calls "the Holocaust effect" (produced by the miniseries *Holocaust*), which leads to a generalized skepticism. Finkielkraut contends that this skepticism is particularly prevalent in the 1960s generation, both because of its emphasis on demythologization and because its own revolutionary gods proved false.

For Finkielkraut, however, anti-Zionism is at the core of Holocaust denial, which he explored at greater length during the Lebanon War in *La Réprobation d'Israël* (The Reprobation of Israel, 1983): "Formerly, Israel was untouchable because of the proximity of the genocide. Today the genocide is subject to dispute due to the alleged behavior by Israel" (p. 89). As a result, in the present battle of images, there is a systematic effort to make the Palestinians the Jews of the Middle East and the Israelis into a Nazi occupying power.

Finkielkraut also considers the historical sources of the construct "genocide," arguing that since its inclusion in the U.N. convention in 1948, the specificity of the notion as it was originally defined by Raphaël

Lemkin has given way to a banalization of the concept. This has led a number of oppressed groups and those who speak for them to associate their victimization with genocide, which not only eviscerates the concept, but leads to a denial of the unique elements of the genocide against the Jews.

Remembering in Vain: Crimes against Humanity

Finkielkraut's subsequent texts move beyond the extermination of memory evident in Holocaust denial, to an emphasis on its fragility evident in contemporary debates that inevitably concern how we remember history, most palpably in his assessment of the Klaus Barbie trial, *La mémoire vaine* (*Remembering in Vain: Crimes against Humanity*, 1989). Barbie, known as the "Butcher of Lyon," was head of the Gestapo in Lyon during the Nazi occupation. Two acts of murder that compete for symbolic priority in French consciousness make Barbie metonymically stand for the entire Vichy period: his torture and killing of Jean Moulin, de Gaulle's representative in France responsible for unifying the Resistance, and his deportation of forty-four Jewish children who were sheltered in a children's home in Izieu.

Complicating the anguished competition between remembering the "Franco-French" conflicts during the Nazi occupation and the French complicity in the Final solution was how Barbie's lawyer, Jacques Vergès, decided to defend his client. Choosing a defense team of ex-colonials and himself half-Cambodian, Vergès used the trial and the media to interrogate the category of "crimes against humanity" as the charge against Barbie by comparing the genocide against the Jews to the systematic oppression, expropriation, and mass murder of French colonial subjects and the ongoing mistreatment of Palestinians by Israel. Moreover, the United States assisted Barbie in escaping France because of his supposed expertise in combating communism. In South America he was allegedly involved with dictators, terrorists, and gun runners.

The dark history of the twentieth century (colonialism, communism and the Cold War, fascist genocide and dictatorships) was thus condensed in this single trial. The Barbie trial was, therefore, to Finkielkraut and France what the Eichmann trial was to Hannah Arendt and to Israel and Germany. Finkielkraut uses it as a foil to focus on justice in the age of mass media, the distortions of the past in the present, and the frailty of universal humanity in the face of the competing interests of particular communities. His evaluation examined three aspects in particular: (1) the fallacies of analogic thinking by considering the comparisons made between the Holocaust and colonization, Nazi genocide and communist purges, and the deportation of Jews vs. Resisters; (2) the notion of "crimes against humanity" deployed in the case against Barbie, who was important to bring to justice precisely because he was unimportant in the Nazi hierarchy, thus insuring that individual responsibility would be ascribed to each cog in the death machine; and (3) the failure of the media adequately to represent history and its contribution to acting out rather than working through the traumatic past. Alice Kaplan's excellent introduction summarizes Finkielkraut's essential point:

> We once thought that individuals died, but humanity itself continued unimpaired. The Holocaust taught us that humanity itself is mortal. The notion of crimes against humanity is the juridical trace of the coming to consciousness of humanity's mortality, the legal protection that is going to safeguard what law for individuals can't do. Finkielkraut wants crimes against humanity to be defined, clarified, and ready and waiting to protect humanity (*Remembering in Vain*, p. xxviii).

Remembering to Forget: The Holocaust and the Politics of the Past

Following his examination of the frailty of memory and the need to reevaluate our conception of humanity dramatized by the Barbie trial and extrapolated in *L'humanité perdue* (*In the Name of Humanity*, 1996), Finkielkraut's subsequent interventions are condensed in his most recent book, *Une Voix vient de l'autre rive* (A Voice Comes from the Other Bank, 2000), which analyzes references to the *Shoah* made in the midst of contemporary political debates. The title refers to a quote by Emmanuel Levinas, who is perhaps the greatest influence on Finkielkraut and whose ideas he explicated in *La Sagesse de l'amour* (*The Wisdom of Love*, 1984). Levinas enjoins us to accept the responsibility of hearing the voices from the other side, who include the ghosts of the past who demand a response that expresses fidelity to the significance and particularity of their deaths. How to respond responsibly is not a foregone conclusion. We are charged to "never forget" as an ethical obligation to the victims of the Holocaust, but Finkielkraut explores how what precisely must be remembered remains ambivalent.

Finkielkraut's critique of certain modes of antiracist politics elaborated in *La défaite de la pensée* (*The Defeat of the Mind*, 1987) is revisited in his critique of how leftist intellectuals intervened in the debates about immigration in the late 1990s. In response to new immigration laws, renowned philosopher Alain Badiou and famous sociologist Pierre Bourdieu sought to unveil institutional racism and to show the discriminatory nature of the national-social state, in part by making references to the legislation against the Jews in the Nazi period. Finkielkraut's criticism emphasizes that their references ultimately serve to minimize the horrors of Hitler in order to maximize the horrors of the present.

In a chapter critical of Régis Debray's criticism of the NATO bombing of Serbia in 1999, Finkielkraut continues his analysis of allusions to the Nazi genocide in the context of the debates about the Third Balkan War developed in his book *Comment peut-on être Croate?* and in his subsequent writings on the war in the former Yugoslavia (*Dispatches from the Balkan War and Other Writings*, 1991–1996). Finkielkraut charges that Debray was among a multitude of intellectuals whose analysis telescoped their understanding of the Balkan War directly from the Nazi apocalypse, forgetting all of the intervening years from Tito to the present.

If he condemns equivalences that are too facile, Finkielkraut also denounces intellectuals like Claude Lanzmann who insist on not comparing the *Shoah* to other historical events like those that occurred in the former Yugoslavia. Lanzmann has denied *any* analogy between the siege of Sarajevo and the Warsaw ghetto or ethnic cleansing and the extermination of the Jews. Citing a manifesto signed by him during the Franco-Algerian war in October 1961, however, Finkielkraut shows that Lanzmann once used the Nazi occupation as a legitimate foil for his political commitments. He argues, therefore, that both positions (Debray's and Lanzmann's) result in a "forgetting, in the name of memory" (*Une voix vient de l'autre rive*, p. 48) that can only be overcome by focusing on the specificities of historical events rather than turning the Holocaust into a symbolic site to justify any number of incompatible positions.

Finkielkraut also explores some lessons from the Holocaust, what they teach us about pedagogy, and what we can learn about remembering this traumatic past in general. In discussing the theater, lectures, poetry, and concerts produced at the camp at Terezin, he argues that these artists impose upon those of us who encounter their work a double obligation: first the imperative to guard the memory of those who did not survive, but also that those who did survive (and the works of art that live beyond death) should *not* be reified as embodiments of Auschwitz. Finkielkraut's concrete example is of a magazine's photoshoot in Atlanta, a city where there are still several survivors, where the chosen model was a Jew (who spent the war in the Pacific) because he represented the "survivor look" that the publication sought. This is one of several examples he gives of ceding to memorialization what belongs to memory.

He also discusses the work of Philippe Meirieu, director of the National Institute on Pedagogical Research, who draws lessons from the Holocaust in reevaluating pedagogy in a number of books. Meirieu argues that the example of Germany as a highly civilized nation who perpetrated the genocide of eastern European Jewry should caution us to move away from education based on the indoctrination of a uniform culture to a posthumanist pedagogy. Instead of standardizing individuals, education should furnish them with the tools that will enable them to master their environments and to defend their identities, thereby contributing to a shift from hegemony to heterogeneity with the ultimate goal of intercultural communication. Meirieu insists that the Holocaust enjoins us to eliminate two models of pedagogical totalitarianism: the teacher as *dominus* (lord) who hierarchizes being or as the *magister* who homogenizes it. Instead, we are ordained to help reveal the humanity of each child. In countries like France, where universal education is one key to inculcating shared republican values, the implications are enormous. Clearly intrigued by Meirieu's arguments, Finkielkraut is nevertheless wary of any pedagogy animated by the politics of identity.

Finkielkraut concludes by discussing two opposed approaches to the irreparable and traumatic past: those represented by writers Albert Camus and René Char as opposed to that of Jean-Paul Sartre. Sartre and his followers learned from the war that there is no outside of history and that we must remember, in the spirit of Marx, that history is the story of human liberation and the struggle for universal fraternity. This is forgotten whenever we fail to recognize that inequality is the result of human actions and choices and not part of the natural order of things. Sartre thus condemned Camus's *La Peste*, which was an allegory of the Nazi occupation, because it considered the occupation through the extended metaphor of the plague, thus representing the period as a natural rather than a human catastrophe.

For Camus as opposed to Sartre, memory is a corrective to utopia on the basis of experience. What Camus stressed in remembering the past was the absurdity of existence, uncertainty, and confusion. In the post-Holocaust world, as all of Finkielkraut's writing suggests, ambivalence and ambiguity are impossible to avoid. This demands that we hear the summons of the past attuned to its nuances and singularities, which always makes the manner in which we remember complex. In short, Finkielkraut suggests that remembering the past responsibly should be a critical activity that questions dogmatism.

Bibliography

Primary Sources

Le Nouveau Désordre amoureux, with Pascal Bruckner (The New Love Disorder). 1977.

Ralentir: mots-valises! (Slowdown! Portmanteau Words). 1979.

Au coin de la rue, l'aventure, with Pascal Bruckner. (At the Corner of the Street, Adventure). 1979.

"Préface: Les larmes et le fontionnaire" ("The tears and the functionary"). In Haïm Gouri, *Face à la cage de Verre: Le procès Eichmann*. Jérusalem, 1961. 1995.

Le Juif imaginaire (*The Imaginary Jew*, 1994). 1980.

Le Petit fictionnaire illustré (Little Illustrated Fictionary). 1981.

L'Avenir d'une négation (*The Future of a Negation*, 1998). 1982.

La Réprobation d'Israël (The Reprobation of Israel). 1983.

La Sagesse de l'amour (*The Wisdom of Love*, 1997). 1984.

La défaite de la pensée (*The Defeat of the Mind*, 1995). 1987.

La mémoire vaine: Du crime contre l'humanité. (*Remembering in Vain: Crimes against Humanity*, 1992). 1989.

Le mécontemporain: Péguy, lecteur du monde moderne (The Non-Contemporary: Péguy, Reader of the Modern World). 1991.

Comment peut-on être Croate? (*Dispatches from the Balkan War and Other Writings*). 1991–1996.

L'ingratitude: *Conversation sur notre temps avec Antoine Robitaille* (Ingratitude: Conversations on Our Epoch). 1999.

L'humanité perdue: Essai sur le XXe siècle (*In the Name of Humanity*, 2000). 1996.

Préface to *Le XXe siècle en France: Art, politique, philosophie* (Preface: The Twentieth Century in France). 2000.

Une Voix vient de l'autre rive (A Voice Comes from the Other Bank). 2000.

Secondary Sources

Auron, Yaïr. *Les juifs d'extrême gauche en mai 68: Une génération révolutionnaire marquée par la Shoah*. Translated from Hebrew by Katherine Werchowski. Paris: Albin Michel, 1998, pp. 92–100.

Friedlander, Judith. "The Lithuanian Jewish Enlightenment in French Translation: Emmanuel Lévinas and His Disciple Alain Finkielkraut." In *Vilna on the Seine: Jewish Intellectuals in France since 1968*. New Haven & London: Yale University Press, 1990, pp. 80–106.

———. "Translator's Introduction." In *The Defeat of the Mind* by Alain Finkielkraut. New York: Columbia University Press, 1995, pp. ix–xix.

Golson, Richard. "Introduction: Negationism in France: The Past and Present of an Illusion." In *The Future of a Negation: Reflections on the Question of Genocide*. Translated by Mary Byrd Kelly. Lincoln & London: University of Nebraska Press, 1998.

Judaken, Jonathan. " 'To Be or Not to Be French': Soixante-Huitard Reflections on '*la question juive*.' " *Modern Jewish Studies* (forthcoming).

Kaplan, Alice. Introduction to *Remembering in Vain: The Klaus Barbie Trial and Crimes against Humanity* by Alain Finkielkraut. Translated by Loxanne Lapidus with Sima Godarg. New York: Columbia University Press, 1992, pp. ix-xxxvi.

Kritzman, Richard. "Critical Reflections: Self-Portraiture and the Representations of Jewish Identity in French in *Auschwitz and After: Race, Culture and "the Jewish Question" in France*. Edited by Lawrence D. Kritzman. New York and London: Routledge Press, 1995, pp. 98–118.

Schneider, Judith Morganroth. "Albert Memmi and Alain Finkielkraut: Two Discourses of French Jewish Identity." *Romantic Review* 81 (1990): 130–136.

Suchoff, David. Introduction to *The Imaginary Jew*. Translated by Kevin O'Neill and David Suchoff. Lincoln & London: University of Nebraska Press, 1994, pp. vii–xviii.

———. Introduction to *The Wisdom of Love*. Translated by Kevin O'Neill and David Suchoff. Lincoln & London: University of Nebraska Press, 1997, pp. ix–xxi.

Wolitz, Seth. "Imagining the Jew in France: From 1945 to the Present." In *Yale French Studies 85: Discourses of Jewish Identity in Twentieth-Century France*. Edited by Alan Astro. New Haven: Yale University Press, 1994, pp. 119–134.

Erica Fischer

(1943–)

PHYLLIS B. LASSNER

In *Aimee and Jaguar: A Love Story* (Berlin 1943), Erica Fischer combines two genres of Holocaust writing, the narrative of experience and historical analysis, to offer a new perspective on Holocaust and post-Holocaust representation and consciousness. The book's narrative drama is intended to focus on the story of Felice Schragenheim, twenty-year-old daughter of upper middle-class, liberal, assimilated German Jews. Felice perished, probably in the Bergen Belsen concentration camp, on 31 December 1944, after being held at Theresienstadt, Gross-Rosen, and Auschwitz. In effect, the story foregrounds Elisabeth (Lilly) Wust, nine years older than Felice, the wife of a German soldier, and a mother of four, who was awarded the Reich's Mother's Cross. For sixteen months, from 2 April 1943 until Felice's arrest on 21 August 1944, the two women lived together as lovers in Lilly's apartment in Berlin, where Felice concealed her activities with the Jewish underground from Lilly.

Contribution to History of Women's Holocaust Experience

Aimee and Jaguar makes a valuable contribution to our understanding of women's sexual relationships during the Holocaust, a subject only beginning to come to light as authors like Fanya Gottesfeld Heller and Edith Hahn Beer, aging and haunted by these experiences, feel the importance of disclosure. We have had even less access to accounts of lesbian experiences at the time. *Aimee and Jaguar* explores one such relationship in the context of Berlin, the center from which Nazi racialist and sexist laws reverberated. Equally significant is the attention to Lilly's wartime and postwar experience, which shapes "another story behind this first one, namely the transformation of a Nazi sympathizing antisemite into a prosemite savior of four Jewish women, and then the story became even more interesting. It became a very German story, capable of symbolizing the eternal German dilemma" (Erica Fischer interview, p. 2).

Interpretation

This dilemma is further complicated by the fact that the story of Felice is told, not as her own recorded testimony or memoir of victimization, not as a singular narrative of one individual's struggle, but as a work involving a complicated three-way relationship. Deeply invested in the story and emerging as another dramatic presence is the researcher, compiler, and narrator, Erica Fischer, a journalist whose own half-Jewish identity (through her mother) becomes part of her emerging consciousness about what it means to write this book. The story, therefore, does not belong to Felice alone, or even to Lilly. As Fischer reflects in her epilogue, the book is an investigation and meditation on what it means for a contemporary writer who did not directly experience the Holocaust to be drawn into the historical, emotional, and moral questions that shape a Holocaust political and sexual relationship—in this case, between Felice, or Jaguar, as she called herself, and her lover, whom she nicknamed Aimee.

Erica Fischer was born in England in 1943, but returned with her parents to their homeland of Austria in 1948. In 2001, she worked as a journalist, writer, and translator in Berlin. Her epilogue articulates questions about the difficult process of piecing together a typically fragmented Holocaust experience. In this case, the lack of the subject's own reconstruction or input into the pieces of her writing saved by Lilly is significant. That Fischer, a third party with her own interests, performs this reconstruction highlights the fact that any attempt to shape what can be known into a coherent structure involves an interpretive process that risks constructing contestable meanings. Fischer acknowledges that the social contexts of Felice's story were gleaned not only from her interviews with Lilly between 1991 and 1993 (some of which are captured in the documentary film *Love Story*). She also used interviews and writing by others who, like Felice, became known as "U-boats,"—Jews who went underground in Berlin—as well as interviews with three of Lilly's sons. Whatever valuable perspectives their recollections contribute to our knowledge of wartime Jewish life in Berlin, our only access to Felice's voice and experience is through letters, poems, photographs, and diary entries Lilly shared with Fischer. Fischer reproduces portions of these, but despite Felice's own language of expression, we are left knowing that she must remain an elusive presence in her own story. For example, the book offers little information about Felice's underground activities except through interviews with her friend, Lola Sturmova, who reports that Felice worked as a journalist in several newspaper offices and so was able to glean and pass on news of the war. According to Sturmova, Felice also wrote articles under pseudonymous initials and had them smuggled to England through an officer friend in homosexual circles, "Kaleu" Henschel. Similarly, from fellow "U-boat" Gerd Ehrlich, we learn that it was probably the infamous Stella Goldschlag, "the Jewish Lorelei" who worked for the German police, who denounced Felice.

While Felice's other underground activities are concealed by lack of witness and written testimony, the gap is filled by Lilly's anxieties. On the one hand, she reports that Felice protected her by telling her nothing; on the other, she protests that she would have preferred to help protect Felice by sharing any knowledge that might have prepared her for danger. By all accounts, however, Felice not only wishes to protect Lilly and her sons from any incriminating information, her ambiguity and secrecy reflect Felice's independent and adventurous spirit. Felice's move into Lilly's apartment signals not only her attraction to Lilly, but the tightening vise of the Gestapo, and yet even after moving in with Lilly, Felice disappears for days at a time.

The book's combined and partial testimonies become even more complex through Fischer's relentlessly doubting questioning of Lilly. The self-conscious presentation of that doubt creates a narrative tension that both highlights the story of Felice's struggle and insists on sharing its emotional and moral terrain. As Fischer engages her readers in the personal odyssey of constructing her Holocaust narrative, she openly registers doubts, impatience, even fury with Lilly, her primary informant. In turn, Lilly's ability to survive has been both undermined by her obsession with Felice and strengthened by a sense of moral stature achieved through the relationship. Lilly's dire pursuit of Felice after her capture, when she illegally takes food and clothes to her at Theresienstadt, confirms the devotion she has previously expressed. When Felice is forced by escalating danger to confess her Jewish identity, Lilly responds not only with expressions of love but by denouncing her own selfish politics in the past. Years later, in her interviews with Fischer, as though she has to legitimize her transformation, Lilly effusively credits the liberal profile of her family, whose genealogy includes her brother's Jewish biological father. Despite Lilly's personal risks, Fischer suggests that her attempts to rescue and succor Felice may have angered the Gestapo and further endangered her Jewish lover. Ever the bereft lover, Lilly assumes a tragic stature that not only obscures questions about her political affinities in the ten years before she met Felice, but also threatens to overshadow Felice's tragic death with its living emotional presence. The urgency with which Lilly continues to search for her lover even after she receives official notice of Felice's death and the isolating choices she makes afterward create a disturbing sense of a willed desolation.

Lilly's total immersion in grief and mourning goes beyond tragic loss. While Fischer gives full credence to Lilly's undying love for Felice, she also sees it as a blueprint for the construction of Lilly's postwar life. For example, instead of rebuilding her life as part of Germany's postwar prosperity, Lilly chooses an abusive marriage and passively accepts her impoverished condition. For Fischer, this behavior signifies how Lilly's depressed state reflects her tragically unfulfilled love for Felice. More complicated yet, while Fischer assesses Felice's character as sexually adventurous and suspects that she might not have remained faithful to Lilly had she survived, Lilly's almost ritualistically repetitious testimony and her grieving "book of tears" become memorials to the equally faithful love Lilly believes Felice would have sustained for her. More significant from the perspective of post-Holocaust identity politics are Lilly's relentless, if thwarted, efforts to convert to Judaism and to raise her sons as Jews. Although Lilly registered her boys at school as Jewish and her son Eberhard studied Judaism and eventually immigrated to Israel, Lilly's son Bernd reports that she "imposed herself" by joining the Jewish Community which may have "tolerated her, but blocked any serious efforts on her part to convert." Lilly's unrelenting desire to identify as Jewish not only draws her closer to the lost Felice; it is as though for Lilly, Jewish identity will rescue both of them. Lilly's conversion would mark her with the identity the Nazis decreed indelibly poisonous and confirm Lilly's empathy with suffering as a significant part of Jewish historical identity. Conversion would not only represent an act of reparation, but a symbolic restoration of Felice within her transformed self. It would fulfill Lilly's statement to Fischer that Felice "was my counterpart, my complement, literally. I felt I was both myself and Felice. We were a mirror image. . . ." (p. 34). At the same time, Jewish conversion would also rescue Lilly from her own destructive cultural legacy and identity as a German.

Fischer reflects on her own immediate and written responses to Lilly—her frustration with Lilly's elusive denials that she had ever been antisemitic, that a bust of Hitler had adorned her living room, or that she did not know Felice as well as she had assumed—and takes responsibility for her judgments as reflections of her own developing moral and historical consciousness:

> [Lilly] expected me to accept her view of herself without question, of course: Lilly at Felice's side as a victim of Nazism. But once I had broken through her resistance, which was exhausting to us both, we got along better. I tried to make it clear to her that she did not have to be a heroine to be my friend, and that I could not be her friend if untruth stood between us (p. 271).

So compelled is Fischer by this love story that even as she recounts Lilly's fierce and sometimes self-destructive attachment to Felice's memory, her own voice betrays such an intense passion for her subject that it begins to reflect Lilly's obsession and forces Fischer "to face an important chapter of [her] own life: flight, foreignness, life on the edge, exile" (p. 272). While Fischer's Austrian husband Martin is doing penance for his parents' indifference to Hitler's victims by working to subvert "Germany's restrictive refugee policy" on behalf of Bosnian refugees, Fischer finds not only an emotional tie to her subject, but the painfully moral one of questioning the value of her work: can writing about the Holocaust compare in moral seriousness to activism (p. 273)? The denouement of her book remains as significantly ambiguous as the question of Lilly's righteousness: in the time Fischer devoted to completing her book, "living without the benefit of his love, Martin, the moralist, saved the lives of fifteen hundred people" (p. 274).

Contribution to Nazi Social History

Despite Fischer's frustrations, her recounting of Felice's and Lilly's story begins to fill an important gap in Nazi social history. Claudia Schoppmann's *Days of Masquerade* (1996) examines the experiences of ten lesbians persecuted by the Nazis, but otherwise there is scant available information about the fate of lesbians during the Third Reich. Unlike gay men, lesbians were not labeled illegal or deviant and were not sent to concentration camps unless they were caught as Jews. Instead of wearing pink triangles, under Himmler's December 1937 Preventive Combating of Crime decree they wore those marking them as "political" or "antisocial." With its weave of racist and sexist ideologies, Nazism denigrated lesbians as unnatural women who rejected their biologically determined fates to become wives and mothers. As the German feature film *Aimee and Jaguar* shows so graphically, despite immediate dangers, Felice's lesbian social circle continued to be a thriving part of the Berlin café and cultural society that in the interwar period had nourished a cosmopolitan gay community, including magazines, activist organizations, and athletic clubs. Following closely the book's interweave of political, social, and psychological implications, a New Year's Eve party in the film dramatizes the lesbians' sense of heightened danger as the Nazis legislated cross-dressing as a sign of degenerate sexuality.

Critical Reception

Aimee and Jaguar has been received as an important contribution to the social history of lesbian experience in the Third Reich, especially because the juxtaposition of photos with Lilly's and Felice's writing adds complexity and humanity to an otherwise vague sense of little known historical subjects. Some critics, however, find that the narrative style suffers occasionally from a clumsy translation and some lapses into soap opera prose. More importantly, Fischer fails to analyze sufficiently the relationship between Lilly's selective and constructed memory and a collective past. The lack of primary and secondary bibliography also makes it difficult to use the book as a work of comprehensive research. Nonetheless, the emotional intensity expressed by an endangered but vibrant lesbian community experience in the Third Reich successfully emerges from Fischer's representation of a singular relationship within its wider social and political nexus.

Bibliography

Primary Source

Aimee and Jaguar: A Love Story, Berlin 1943. 1994.

Films Based on Erica Fischer's Work

Aimee and Jaguar: The Film. Max Farberbock, Director and Screenwriter. Gunther Rorhbach, Producer. Hanno Huth, Producer, 1999.

Love Story: A Documentary Film. Catrine Clay, Producer and Director. BBC Education, 1998.

Secondary Sources

Annan, Gabriele. "Felicity with Felice." *Times Literary Supplement* (15 December 1995): 32.

Beer, Edith Hahn, and Susan Dworkin. *The Nazi Officer's Wife: How One Jewish Woman Survived the Holocaust.* New York: William Morrow, 1999.

Belzberg, Leslie. "*Aimee and Jaguar: A Love Story, Berlin 1943.*" *Advocate* (6 February 1996): 60.

Bock, Gisela. "Racism and Sexism in Nazi Germany." *Different Voices: Women and the Holocaust.* Edited by Carol Rittner and John K. Roth. New York: Paragon House, 1993, 161–186.

Bridenthal, Renate, Atina Grossman, and Marion Kaplan, eds. *When Biology Became Destiny: Women in Weimar and Nazi Germany.* New York: Monthly Review Press, 1984.

Heller, Fanya Gottesfeld. *Strange and Unexpected Love: A Teenage Girl's Holocaust Memoirs.* Hoboken, N.J.: Ktav Books, 1993.

Horsley, Joey. "*Aimee and Jaguar: A Love Story, Berlin 1943.*" *The Women's Review of Books* 14:2 (November 1996): 9–11.

Jull, Peter. "All Are Punished." *Arena Magazine* 31 (October–November 1997): 42–43.

Koonz, Claudia. *Mothers in the Fatherland: Women, the Family, and Nazi Politics.* New York: St. Martin's Press, 1987.

Owings, Alison. *Frauen: German Women Recall the Third Reich.* New York: Rutgers University Press, 1995.

Sayce, Liz. "*Aimee and Jaguar.*" *Off Our Backs* 26.10 (November 1996): 18.

Schoppmann, Claudia. *Days of Masquerade: Life Stories of Lesbians during the Third Reich.* Translated by Allison Brown. New York: Columbia University Press, 1996.

Shuttaford, Genevieve. "Forecasts: Nonfiction." *Publishers Weekly* 242:44 (30 October 1995): 51.

Stimpson, Catharine R. "Where the Boys Aren't." *Voice Literary Supplement* 141 (December 1995): 7.

Interview

"An interview with Erica Fischer." Zeitgeist Films, Ltd. 2000–2001. http://zeitgeistfilm.com/current/aimeejaguar/ajintef.html

MOSHE FLINKER

(1926–1944)

DICK VAN GALEN LAST

MOSHE ZE'EV (MAURICE Wolf) Flinker was born on 9 October 1926 in The Hague, Netherlands, the son of Lazjer Noech Flinker (1898–1945) and Mindla Rochanini (1895–1945), an Orthodox Jewish family who had fled the pogroms in eastern Europe. It was probably the remembrance of these pogroms that made the Flinkers more alert than their much more confident Dutch coreligionists to the unmistakable signs of an approaching catastrophe. Once the Germans occupied the Netherlands in May 1940, they started their policy of the isolation and exclusion of Jews. In 1941 Moshe along with other Jewish children had to attend Jewish schools, where they were taught by Jewish teachers, a form of segregation gradually introduced in all spheres of social life. In July 1942 it took young Moshe an hour and a half to get to school: bicycles had become the property of the Reich, and Jews could no longer use public transportation. That same summer deportations to the east started. On 2 August 1942, a member of Reichskommissar Arthur Seyss-Inquart's staff called the Jews "the biggest enemy of Germany" and announced that they would be sent eastward "just as poor and full of lice" as they had come to the west earlier. "They are in for difficult times," the German concluded his speech, which was widely quoted in the Dutch press, and many Jews, especially those who had come recently from the east, understood the consequences. In September 1942 Moshe fled with his parents, five sisters, and small brother to Brussels because the family hoped to have a better chance for survival in Belgium than in the Netherlands.

In Holland the Germans had set up a so-called *Aufsichtsverwaltung* (supervisory civil administration) under the leadership of the Austrian Dr. Arthur Seyss-Inquart, who was given the title of Reichskommissar (high commissioner). This civilian administration left more room for the SS (*Schutzstaffel*, literally "protection echelon") to determine policy toward the Jews and greater authority to execute it. Conversely in Belgium, as in France, the Germans had established a *Militärverwaltung* (military administration). The existence of the SS regime in Holland and the very deferential attitude of Jews and non-Jews alike helps explain why only twenty-five percent of Dutch Jewry survived World War II, in contrast to Belgium and France, where, respectively sixty percent and seventy-five percent of all Jews survived. This was by far the highest percentage of victims in the western European countries occupied by the Germans, and it gave birth to the ongoing discussion among Dutch historians about the reasons for the discrepancy. In addition to these factors, Moshe's father had extensive business relations in Brussels, and social networks were an important factor in Jews being able to survive the occupation. From Brussels the Flinkers hoped to have a better chance of going on to a neutral country, such as Switzerland.

In the beginning everything went relatively well for the Flinker family, who were not known as Jews in their new environment. "So we ventured out into the streets without wearing our Jewish badge and did other things forbidden to Jews," Moshe wrote in the first entry of the diary he started in Brussels on 24 November 1942 (*Young Moshe's Diary*, Jerusalem: Yad Vashem, 1958). But more and more, Moshe was gripped by "terrible sensations of loneliness, isolation, and dejection" (7 April 1943). And just like Etty Hillesum (*Etty, A Diary 1941–1943*), Moshe Flinker felt guilty about being safe, "carefree, and lacking nothing," while "his brothers" were being deported. He wrote in the first month of 1943: "I, too, wish to suffer with my brothers, with my people, whom I love so much. My people, my people!" Far from feeling that he had been saved to be a hope for the "future of [his] people," he convinced himself that he was a traitor "who fled from his people at the time of their anguish" (p. 65). He imposed various restrictions on himself so he would feel at least a part of the suffering that his brethren were undergoing, and he even considered volunteering for work in one of the labor camps. Eventually betrayed by a Jewish informer, the Germans arrested the family in April 1944, on Passover Eve, the holiday that celebrates the Jews' deliverance from Egyptian slavery. In his final, undated diary entry, Moshe wrote: "Pity us, have mercy, Lord, on Thy people, do not tarry, do not wait, for soon it will be too late." From the Mechelen transit camp, he and his family were deported to Auschwitz on 19 May 1944, where they arrived on May 21, and where Moshe was probably killed immediately on arrival. His parents also perished, but all his sisters and his brother survived the camp. When his sisters returned to their apartment in Brussels, they found the diary that Moshe had started in November 1942. His diary—in very colorful Hebrew—was published in 1958 in Israel by Yad Vashem, and in 1965 they published an English edition. A Dutch translation was published in the Netherlands in 1973.

His contemporary Anne Frank started her famous diary in her hiding place in Amsterdam in the same year as Moshe Flinker began his diary in Brussels, on 24 November 1942. However, their diaries have little in common. Moshe Flinker, an adolescent confronted with growing Nazi pressure, was obsessed with the question of faith. As a bright religious boy, he spent all his time learning and reading the Talmud, while Anne Frank belonged to a family of liberal, assimilated Jews who had little affinity with observant Judaism. In contrast to many other Jews, the Nazi persecution brought Moshe closer to his faith. On 26 November 1942, he wrote:

> I feel certain that further troubles will not bring any Jew back to the paths of righteousness; on the contrary, I think that upon experiencing such great anguish they will think that there is no God at all in the universe, because had there been a God He would not have let such things happen to His people. It seems to me that the time has come for our redemption, or rather, that we are more or less worthy of being redeemed.

Living in exile, Moshe believed his true country was "the Holy Land, the Land of Israel." He was a fervent Zionist who believed that with a state of their own in Palestine, Jews would be able to deal with non-Jews as equals and no longer be merely a "nation of victims"—"dead live people or the living dead." He dreamed of one day being "a Jewish statesman in the Land of Israel" (p. 36), and he even started learning Arabic. Moshe was sure that Jews had suffered more than was necessary to deserve redemption. Being Orthodox, he was convinced that only God could bring real salvation, not the Allies. In December 1942 Moshe heard that "a hundred thousand Jews were dying in the East." He did not believe that the downfall of the Third Reich would be the end of all the problems for the Jews, as he was not convinced of the good intentions of the Allies. "The way to redemption will not be measured by England's victories but by Germany's," he wrote in February 1943. He predicted the Cold War and, as far as the Jews were concerned, an apocalyptic end with the "destruction of the largest part of the world, because everybody has tormented our people. . . . It is as if everyone is laughing at our plight."

Moshe Flinker was often indignant not only about what he saw as the sins of the Allies, for example, their bombing of defenseless German towns, but also about the indifference of those now referred to as "bystanders"

> I don't know what to think, what to say, what to do. I see in the streets that the gentiles are happy and gay, and that nothing touches them. It is like being in a great hall where many people are joyful and dancing and also where there are a few people who are not happy and who are not dancing. And from time to time a few people of this latter kind are taken away, led to another room, and strangled. The happy, dancing people in the hall do not feel this at all. Rather, it seems as if this adds to their joy and doubles their happiness (p. 71).

In fact, in Belgium as in other German-occupied countries, the dance halls and stadiums were full. Cinema attendance was higher than ever, allowing Moshe to believe that people were not aware of the suffering of the Jews. It was after watching the German antisemitic propaganda film *Jew Süss* in a Belgian cinema on 14 December 1942, that Moshe "realized the nature of the fiend"(p. 43).

Moshe noticed the estrangement that led to a form of depersonalization: "The terrible events of these days make everything seem tiny, as if viewed through the wrong end of the microscope; the greater the troubles, the smaller everything seems" (p. 50). In a situation like this, keeping a diary becomes a means of compensating for one's smallness. About his motivation Flinker wrote: "It is because I hate being idle that I have started this diary so that I can write in it every day what I do and think" (p. 23). Intellectually and psychologically, writing a diary is a method of self-preservation and self-assertion, especially under extreme oppressive circumstances. Thus, in a sense, the individual regains his or her rights. By keeping a diary, Moshe hoped to get to know himself better and improve himself ("to better my soul") and to get control over things. His diary is a moving monument to faith and exemplifies the complete identification of a religious boy with the suffering of his brethren, in which he wrote that the anguish was not "the physical affliction of my people [but] their spiritual anguish, which may well be greater than their physical pain. . . . I feel a burning love for my poor people which, because of my not being involved physically, makes me more aware of its troubles" (p. 84).

Bibliography

Primary Source

Hana'ar Moshe—Yomano shel Moshe Flinker (Young Moshe's Diary: The Spiritual Torment of a Jewish Boy in Nazi Europe). 1958.

Secondary Sources

Boas, Jacob. *We Are Witnesses: Five Diaries of Teenagers Who Died in the Holocaust.* New York: Henry Holt, 1995, pp. 80–113.

Galen Last, Dick van, and Rolf Wolfswinkel. *Anne Frank and After: Dutch Holocaust Literature in Historical Perspective.* Amsterdam: Amsterdam University Press, 1996.

Heebing, Sonja. "Anne, Esther en Mozes. Jonge dagboekschrijvers in oorlogstijd." In *Een halve eeuw geleden. De verwerking van de Tweede Wereldoorlog in de literatuur* (Half a Century Ago: The Coming to Terms with the Second World War in Literature). Edited by Hans Ester and Wam de Moor. Kampen, Netherlands, Kok, 1994, pp. 230–241.

Holliday, Laurel. *Children in the Holocaust and World War II.* New York: Pocket Books, 1995, pp. 209–217.

Anne Frank

(1929–1945)

MARTHA A. RAVITS

THE MOST BELOVED of all Holocaust writers, Anne Frank, through her diary, has exerted unparalleled influence on the literary, educational, and human rights legacy of the Holocaust. Thanks to the postwar discovery of her family photo album, her sympathetic young face has become a twentieth-century icon that is recognized around the world.

Life

Anne Frank was born in 1929 in Frankfurt, Germany, to assimilated Jews, Otto and Edith Frank. With the rise of Hitler, her family emigrated to Amsterdam, Holland, where her father had established a business in pectin and cooking preparations. The vivacious girl's normal life of friends and school ended abruptly when the Nazis seized Holland in 1940. Fearing such an invasion, her father had prepared a hiding place in the upper stories at the rear of his office building on Prinsengracht, and the family quickly moved there in 1942, when Anne's older sister, Margot, received a notice to report for labor camp. Through Anne's writing, the family quarters became known as the "Secret Annex." Loyal office workers and friends in the business below the hiding place sheltered the Franks and four other Jews for two years.

Anne's diary gives a vivid account of that time, the relationships among family members and their co-inhabitants—the Van Pels family and a dentist named Pfeffer—as well as a portrait of her own adolescent development under the psychological pressure of war, privation, and intensified searches for Jews. Anne records the daily reports from the family's protectors on the worsening situation for all Dutch citizens and watches the round-ups of Jews for deportation.

Betrayed by an anonymous informant, the Frank family and those in hiding with them were arrested by the Gestapo on 4 August 1944 and sent to Westerbork transit camp. Their names appear on a list of prisoners on the last train to leave Holland for Auschwitz. At Auschwitz, Anne's mother, Edith, died. Anne and Margot were later sent to Bergen-Belsen in Germany. Amid squalid conditions, first Margot, then Anne succumbed to typhus fever in March 1945, just weeks before the Allied liberation. Anne was fifteen. Only her father survived to return from Auschwitz to Amsterdam, where the Frank family's Dutch protector, Miep Gies, presented him with Anne's diaries and papers, which Gies had salvaged from the floor of the ransacked annex at the time of the Jews' arrest.

The Diary

Originally published in Europe, the diary was translated from Dutch into English and released, in 1952, in the United States as *Anne Frank: The Diary of a Young Girl*. It became a surprise bestseller. The popular reception of Frank's diary in the United States—before the publication of most Holocaust literature in English—signaled the role that personal narratives and testimony would play in arousing public consciousness about Hitler's extermination of Europe's Jews. The subsequent adaptations of the diary for stage and screen in the 1950s sentimentalized much of the substance of the diary for popular consumption and stirred a debate about the merits of historical versus popularized representations of the Holocaust and the blurring of distinctions between the two.

The diary, however, remains preeminent in literary history. It still serves for many readers—augmented by the story of Anne Frank's arrest and murder—as a prolegomenon to the subject of the *Shoah*. It became the first memoir to gain widespread international attention. John Hersey's novel *The Wall* had appeared one year before the publication of Anne's diary, but most Holocaust literature in English—novels, plays, or memoirs—would follow by nearly a decade. Elie Wiesel's *Night* appeared in English translation in 1960, just after the translation of Primo Levy's autobiography. Their books, along with works by André Schwarz-Bart, Leon Uris, and Jerzy Kosinski (and the publicized trial of Eichmann in Israel) raised the tide of Holocaust awareness. It was not until the 1980s—three decades after the dramatization of Anne Frank's diary—that movies on the Holocaust again attracted a mass audience, and television programs like "The Wall," "The Holocaust," and the dramatization of Fania Fenelon's "Playing for Time" fired the international conscience.

The diary of Anne Frank attained historical canonization across categories: in women's autobiography, in adolescent life-writing, and in human rights memoirs. The popularity of the attractive, spunky teenager invited infantilization and romanticization, qualities that distort her image and disregard the penetrating literary style of her text. The diary, addressed as letters to a fictional confidante named "Kitty," is an epistolary autobiography that begins with Anne Frank's thirteenth birthday, 12 June 1942, when she received the red-plaid diary as a gift. Approximately one month later, she records the move into the secret annex and begins the account of her family's difficult years in hiding. The diary is broken off just days before their arrest in August 1944. During those two years of captivity, Anne honed her writing skills. She regarded the cramped attic as a laboratory for the study of human nature, especially her own, as she matured rapidly into adulthood.

In one dramatic episode of the diary (not depicted in either the play or the film), Anne describes the eight Jews listening at their forbidden radio on 28 March 1944, to a London broadcast by the Dutch government in exile. They heard the Dutch minister of education, art, and science announce plans to collect and publish after the war, accounts written by ordinary Dutch citizens, to document their lives under the occupation. He mentioned, in particular, letters, sermons, and diaries. "Of course," Anne writes, "they all made a rush at my diary immediately. Just imagine how interesting it would be if I were to publish a romance of the 'Secret Annex' " (*The Diary of Anne Frank*, the Critical Edition, Doubleday, p. 578). With this goal in mind, Anne began systematically to revise and reshape her diary for publication.

Her revisions on supplemental loose-leaf pages show the writer's concern for future readers: "No one will grasp what I'm talking about if I begin my letters to Kitty just out of the blue, so, I'll start by sketching in brief the story of my life" (p. 182). Anne crafts a literary exposition in which she lays out her family origins, explains the tightening anti-Jewish measures in Holland, and attaches a list of pseudonyms to shield the identities of the Jews in hiding and their Dutch protectors. On 11 May 1944 she wrote: "My greatest wish is to become a journalist someday and later on a famous writer. Whether these leanings towards greatness (insanity!) will ever materialize remains to be seen. . . . I want to publish a book entitled *Het Achterhuis* [the house behind] after the war" (p. 647).

That chosen title was used when the diary was first edited and published in Holland in 1949. In the 1980s, The Netherlands State Institute for War Documentation thoroughly researched, ran forensic tests on, and published the full diary along with authenticating evidence and background essays by historians. *The Diary of Anne Frank: The Critical Edition* is a scholarly, variorum edition and a history of the young woman who is now Holland's most famous author.

Despite, or perhaps because of, the hardships of confinement with enforced daytime hours of silence, Anne Frank matured as a writer with time to think and to practice her craft. Her stylistic technique displays innovation and variety, while the content ranges from social satire to philosophic reflection to stark terror. She understood writing as a means of psychological exploration and a therapeutic strategy to ward off despair. Inside the front cover of the diary she wrote, "I hope that I shall be able to confide in you completely . . . and that you will be a great support and comfort to me." On the back cover she inscribed in French, "Be good and steadfast in courage." In between, she forged a document of searing intellectual independence that weaves together social and historical commentary with psychological and spiritual astuteness.

Books, reading, and education loomed large for the cultured German Jews in isolation. Under their father's guidance, Anne and Margot kept up their studies and added correspondence courses in French, English, Latin, algebra, shorthand, German literature, history, classical mythology (Anne's favorite subject), geography, and the Bible. Margot's academic brilliance inspired the younger, more rebellious sister to keep pace. When Anne fastened her romantic hopes on the only target available, Peter Van Pels, her writing swelled with adolescent pathos, frustration, and sexual curiosity.

The diary builds through scenes of everyday life and internal bickering among the eight trapped Jews to suspenseful scenes of late night break-ins to the office below that threaten to disclose them. Anne records the news they received from their protectors on the worsening conditions for friends and Jews rounded up and sent to Westerbork transit camp where they "are branded as inmates by their shaven heads" (p. 273). On 9 October 1942, she wonders, "If it is as bad as this in Holland whatever will it be like in the distant and barbarous regions they are sent to? We assume that most of them are murdered. The English radio speaks of their being gassed" (p. 273). Thus, the diary disproves the myth that the fate of European Jews was not known outside the camps during the war.

Anne's meditations on human suffering, antisemitism, and injustice raise the diary to the level of serious literature. Her thoughts reach a crescendo in 1944 when Allied bombers rend the night skies, and Anne hopes that liberation is approaching. Unfortunately, the vice of terror tightens, as Anne witnesses through the attic windows during the day the Gestapo roundups of Amsterdam's Jews, and thus fears her own fate:

> In these times, ideals, dreams and cherished hopes rise within us, only to meet the horrible truth and be shattered. It's really a wonder that I haven't dropped all my ideals, because they seem so absurd and impossible to carry out. Yet I keep them, because in spite of everything I still believe that people are really good at heart.
>
> I simply can't build up my hopes on a foundation consisting of confusion, misery, and death, I see the world gradually being turned into a wilderness, I hear the ever approaching thunder, which will destroy us too, I can feel the sufferings of millions . . ." (p. 694).

Thus, Anne Frank's often-quoted pronouncement on human goodness is embedded in a dialectical context that shows her battling to retain hope amid traumatic circumstances. Her thoughts in hiding fluctuate between hope and despair. In the 1950s, the adaptations of the diary suppressed the complexity of the writer by using her words on human goodness out of context to conclude both the play and the film. Anne Frank's idealism was simplified and emphasized to gain audience sympathy for an innocent "young girl" crushed by brutal totalitarianism, an unfair portrait of the insightful, many-sided writer.

Controversy

When the diary was first published in America in 1952, a brief introduction signed by Eleanor Roosevelt was included that praised Anne Frank as a heroic young victim of war and the diary as an antiwar document. This set the keynote for treatment of the diary during the Cold War. No mention was made of antisemitism or the Franks being targeted by the Nazis as Jews. Anne Frank's Jewish identity was purposely downplayed to serve the purposes of the times. The diary was interpreted as pleading for universal human rights, especially in the diary's popularized adaptations as a Broadway play in 1955 and then as a Hollywood film in 1959. A controversy was precipitated by the American Jewish writer Meyer Levin, who had helped Otto Frank find an American publisher for the diary and who wrote a glowing review for the *New York Times Book Review* when it appeared. Levin wanted to dramatize the diary as a way of bringing the fate of the six million Jews to world attention, and he started work on a script that aired briefly on radio, but his efforts were rejected by Broadway producers. Otto Frank then turned to Lillian Hellman for advice, and she recommended the husband-and- wife team of Frances Goodrich and Albert Hackett, Hollywood non-Jewish screenwriters, for the project. Their Pulitzer Prize-winning play was such a hit on Broadway that it went on to success in Europe and was then transformed into a Hollywood movie directed by George Stevens, bringing international renown to Anne Frank. These popularized versions of the diary ingratiated Anne with popular audiences but eliminated her reflections on antisemitism and specific mention of Hitler's brutality toward the Jews. Hackett and Goodrich deleted Anne's outcries against antisemitism near the end of the diary and invented a speech on the generalized nature of oppression in a speech to cheer up Peter: "We're not the only people that've had to suffer. There've always been people that've had to . . . sometimes one race . . . sometimes another . . ." This travesty distorts Anne Frank's thinking as well as her incisive and articulate manner of expression. The story of an innocent young girl unjustly hunted by a totalitarian regime was a marketable message in the 1950s, when American political fears had shifted from fascist Germany to Communist Russia. The 1955 stage play directed by Garson Kanin and Stevens's 1959 film both concluded with Anne's line on human goodness and hope.

The play set off a dispute with Meyer Levin, who was infuriated by the suppression of the diary's Jewish content. In his book, *The Obsession*, Levin claims that his goal was to translate Anne's words faithfully onto the stage and to portray her victimization as a Jew. He was appalled by the pablum of the Broadway production. Charging that the Broadway team had stolen material from his script, Levin sued Otto Frank and Kermit Bloomgarden, producer of the play, in court. The unfortunate case led to years of legal battles that resolved little but provided fodder for Holocaust deniers and revisionists. Levin died in 1981 without seeing his play produced.

A 1997 Broadway revival of the Goodrich-Hackett play, "The Diary of Anne Frank," re-ignited the controversy. Some reviews were favorable, but others objected to the now-dated, bowdlerized and popularized 1950s version. Cynthia Ozick in the *New Yorker* lamented the retrograde dramatization ("infantalized, Americanized, homogenized, sentimentalized") and dared to wonder if history would have been better served had the famous diary been lost (6 October 1997, p. 87).

The debate about whether the diary stands for universalism or Jewish particularism often boils down to the question: How Jewish was Anne Frank? Her case highlights the elasticity of the very term *Jewish identity* and the fallacy of trying to evaluate retrospectively the temporal and shifting inclinations of a human sensibility. The controversy is particularly vexed in the case of a teenager, whose diary is marked by the fluctuations and questionings of adolescent development. Furthermore, life-writing as a genre records the flux and pulse of a writer's thinking rather than decisive ideological stands. Anne Frank embraced her own multiplicity, referring to herself as "quicksilver Anne," and a "bundle of contradictions" (pp. 696–697). She desired an active life but instead was locked away, a confinement that forced her to consider the meaning of the Jewish identity that caused her oppression. Both the universalists and the Jewish particularists who wish to claim her are able to point to passages in the diary that validate their points.

She was not a practicing Jew nor had she received a religious education, but two years of accelerating terror intensified Anne Frank's sense of what it meant to be a Jew. She began to chart her personal suffering on the historic spectrum of antisemitism. With increased maturity, her sense of Jewish identity becoming stronger until toward the end of the diary, where she mentions God and the persecution of the Jewish people more frequently.

> Who has made us Jews different from all other people? Who has allowed us to suffer so terribly up till now? It is God that has made us as we are, but it will be God, too, who will raise us up again. If we bear all this suffering and if there are still Jews left when it is over, then Jews, instead of being doomed, will be held up as an example. Who knows, it might even be our religion from which the world and all peoples learn good. . . . We must remain Jews, but we want to, too (p. 600).

In other passages, Anne expresses a desire above all else to become a Dutch citizen after the war. Themes of universalism and Jewish ethnicity are intermingled throughout the diary. Unlike the stage Anne, the diarist astutely recognizes and disapproves of Peter's internalized antisemitism, but she also dreams of the wider world, Paris, and a career as a contemporary journalist. In reading the full diary readers are confronted by the transformation of Anne's character as she passes through the dark isolation imposed by the Nazis. Her ability to look horror in the face and record it honestly makes the diary a moving indictment of antisemitism. Her own victimization causes her not only to empathize with all Jews caught in the Nazi reign of terror but also to speak of human suffering.

In promoting the play and in founding the international Anne Frank Foundation in Amsterdam with proceeds from the diary, Otto Frank intended to use his daughter's fame to further the cause of universal tolerance and human rights. He chose to emphasize the broadest possible interpretation of Anne's writing. Who can legitimately claim that Anne Frank, had she lived, would have disagreed with that purpose? Her sense of political morality and compassion stemmed from the German-Jewish legacy instilled by her father: "My feeling for justice is immovable" she wrote just months before her arrest (p. 601), as a corollary, she pledged, "If god lets me live, I shall not remain insignificant, I shall work in the world and for mankind!" (p. 601).

The story of this beleaguered, cosmopolitan, and lucid writer, murdered in her youth, helped to focus world attention on the Holocaust at a time when many American Jewish leaders hesitated to raise that issue for fear of arousing antisemitic sentiment. Anne Frank's voice was praised for its courage, an acknowledgment that the voice of resistance most readily accepted by the public was that of a nonthreatening, assimilated young woman. The diary is not graphic and does not describe the atrocities the concentration camps inflicted on victims but its reception must be credited with opening the way for other Holocaust writing and public understanding on a large scale. The diary overcame barriers of time, culture, ethnic bias, and popular indifference to initiate the historical process of memorializing and universalizing the Jewish victims of Hitler's Final Solution.

Bibliography

Primary Sources

Anne Frank: The Diary of a Young Girl. 1952.

The Diary of Anne Frank: The Critical Edition. 1989.

Anne Frank: The Diary of a Young Girl: The Definitive Edition. 1995.

Secondary Sources

Brenner, Rachel Feldhay. *Writing as Resistance: Four Women Confronting the Holocaust, Edith Stein, Simone Weil, Anne Frank, Etty Hillesum*. University Park, Penn.: Pennsylvania State University Press, 1997.

Enzer, Hyman Aaron, and Sandra Solotaroff-Enzer, eds. *Anne Frank: Reflections on Her Life and Legacy*. Urbana, Ill.: University of Illinois Press, 2000.

Geis, Miep, and Alison Leslie Gold. *Anne Frank Remembered: The Story of the Woman Who Helped to Hide the Frank Family*. New York: Simon, 1987.

Goodrich, Frances, and Albert Hackett. "The Diary of Anne Frank." New York: Random, 1956.

Lee, Carol Anne. *Roses from the Earth: The Biography of Anne Frank*. London: Viking, 1999.

Levin, Meyer. *The Obsession*. New York: Simon and Schuster, 1973.

Melnick, Ralph. *The Stolen Legacy of Anne Frank: Meyer Levin, Lillian Hellman, and the Staging of the Diary*. New Haven, Conn.: Yale University Press, 1997.

Muller, Melissa. *Anne Frank*. Translated by Rita and Robert Kimber. New York: Metropolitan Books, 1998.

Novick, Peter. *The Holocaust in American Life*. Boston: Houghton Mifflin, 1999.

Ozick, Cynthia. "Who Owns Anne Frank?" *New Yorker* (6 October 1997): 76–87.

Ravits, Martha. "To Work in the World: Anne Frank and American Literary History." *Women's Studies: An Interdisciplinary Journal* 27 (1997): 1–30.

Rittner, Carol, ed. *Anne Frank in the World: Essays and Reflections*. Armond, N.Y.: Sharpe, 1998.

Thurman, Judith. "Not Even a Nice Girl." *New Yorker* (18 December 1989): 166–120.

Waaldijk, Berteke. "Reading Anne Frank as a Woman." *Women's Studies International Forum* 16 (1993): 327–335.

VIKTOR FRANKL

(1905–1999)

TIMOTHY E. PYTELL

VIKTOR FRANKL WAS born on 26 March 1905 in Vienna, and died there on 2 September 1997. His parents were Gabriel Frankl and Elsa Lion. Frankl received both his M.D. (1930) and his Ph.D. (1948) from the University of Vienna. He also founded his own school of psychotherapy—logotherapy. Logotherapy is a form of existential psychotherapy that is conceived as "therapy through meaning" (Frankl, *Man's Search for Meaning*, 1984, pp. 101–137). Although Frankl promoted logotherapy as the successor to Freud's psychoanalysis and Adler's individual psychology and, therefore, the "third Viennese school of psychotherapy" (Frankl, *Was nicht in Meinen*, 1995, p. 44), recognition of his work stemmed from his Holocaust testimony, *Man's Search for Meaning* (1946), which was ranked by "Library of Congress in Washington . . . as one of the ten most influential books in America" (Frankl, 1995, p. 99). *Man's Search* has been translated into twenty languages, including Chinese and Japanese, and sold over ten million copies worldwide.

The renowned Harvard psychologist Gordon Allport wrote a preface for the first English translation of *Man's Search* (1959). Like many readers, Allport was impressed with how Frankl rendered "hunger, humiliation, fear and deep anger at injustice . . . tolerable by closely guarded images of beloved persons, by religion, by a grim sense of humor, and even by glimpses of the healing beauties of nature." Allport was also moved by Frankl's ability to make "larger sense out of his apparently senseless suffering" by facing "fully the ubiquity of suffering and the forces of evil," and thus deriving "a surprisingly hopeful view of man's capacity to transcend his predicament and discover an adequate guiding truth" (*Man's Search for Meaning*, New York: Simon and Schuster, 1984, pp. 7–10).

Unlike Allport, the highly regarded specialist on Holocaust testimonies, Lawrence Langer, was extremely critical of Frankl. Langer criticized *Man's Search* for not recognizing that Auschwitz represented a rupture in the values of Western civilization. According to Langer, Frankl relied on philosophers Baruch Spinoza, Arthur Schopenhauer, Friedrich Nietzsche, and others "to transform his ordeal in Auschwitz into a renewed encounter with the literary and philosophical giants" and thus preserved "the intellectual and spiritual traditions they championed, and his own legacy as an heir to their minds" (Langer, "The Literature of Auschwitz," 1994, p. 64). Langer also claimed that Frankl's testimony "avoids the difficulty of altering the reader's consciousness so that it can contend with the moral uncertainties of the Holocaust" (Langer, *Versions of Survival*, 1982, p. 24). In sum, Langer rejected the uplifting rendition of the Holocaust that Allport so admired. Instead, Langer claimed that the heroic version of meaningful suffering denied the moral and physical terror of the Holocaust.

It is easy to comprehend the mass appeal of Frankl's version of survival, but given what we know about the horrific reality of Auschwitz, the optimism is perplexing. It is especially odd because Frankl, like so many survivors, lost his entire family except his sister. Perhaps the best explanation for his heroic rendition is found in an examination of his actual camp experience. Frankl, his wife (Tilly), and his parents (Elsa and Gabriel) were all deported to the "model ghetto" of Theresienstadt on 25 September 1942 (*Totenbuch Theresienstadt*, p. 32). Frankl was interned in Theresienstadt for two years before being transported to Auschwitz. In 1991, Frankl told the American preacher Robert Schuller: "I was in Auschwitz only three or four days . . . I was sent to a barrack and we were all transported to a camp in Bavaria" (Frankl, 1991, p. 10). This fact is substantiated by the prisoner's log from the sub-camp of Dachau, Kaufering III, which listed Frankl's arrival on 25 October 1944, exactly six days after his deportation from Theresienstadt. The usual travel time was two days from Theresienstadt to Auschwitz, although in *Man's Search* Frankl described the journey as lasting "several days and nights" (*Man's Search*, p. 226). He also described his journey out of Auschwitz to Kaufering III as lasting "two days and three nights" (p. 44), later in the same text. At Kaufering III, Frankl eventually volunteered as a doctor and was transported to Türkheim. The prisoner logs from Kaufering III show no. 119104 being transported to Türkheim on 8 March 1945. Frankl therefore spent just under five months (25 October to 8 March) in the work camp at Kaufering III. Frankl gave the date of his liberation from Türkheim as 27 April 1945 (Gruber, 1974, p. 224). In Theresienstadt, Frankl worked in the public health department and ran a suicide prevention service; at Kaufering III he was on a work crew and spent much of the winter digging a tunnel; at Türkheim he was a block warden in charge of a typhus ward. Therefore, it seems that his confrontation with the terror of the concentration camps (he described numerous near death experiences) lasted for about six months (19 October 1944 to 27 April 1945).

Any reader of *Man's Search* will be stunned to discover that Frankl spent only a few days in Auschwitz. In the book, Frankl made no reference to his two-year internment in Theresienstadt, but instead begins his testimony with his arrival in Auschwitz, movingly describing the details of his experiences there at great length. He conveys "the circumstances of [his] admission" and described how a "cry broke from the ranks of anxious passengers, . . . Auschwitz!" (p. 22). He then related the initial selections, shaving, numbering, delousing, and showers that occurred upon admission to Auschwitz. The reader is led to believe that Frankl spent a great deal of time in Auschwitz through descriptions such as those of enduring sleep deprivation; the inability of prisoners to clean their teeth (yet they "had healthier gums than ever before"; and the wearing of "the same shirts for half a year" (pp. 30–32). He claimed "the prisoner of Auschwitz, in the first phase of shock, did not fear death. Even the gas chambers lost their horrors for him after the first few days" (p. 31). Because Frankl was in Kaufering III after the first few days, the horror of the gas chamber certainly disappeared for him. On the opening page of *Man's Search*, he honestly asserted that "most of the events described here did not take place in the large and famous camps, but in the small ones where most of the real extermination took place," but he spent the first third of the book describing his experiences in Auschwitz. It is also not clear why Frankl made the questionable claim that "the real extermination took place" in the work camps and ghettos. Any concentration camp experience was certainly horrendous, but the incomprehensible reality is that 1.3 million people were systematically murdered in Auschwitz; survival was both rare and exceptional. Frankl gives the impression that he experienced the reality of Auschwitz, and although Frankl's experience was no doubt atrocious, the truth is that he spent limited time in Auschwitz.

In combination with this limited experience was Frankl's need to come to terms with surviving. Aharon Appelfeld claimed: "The survivor's testimony is first of all a search for relief; and as with any burden, the one who bears it seeks also to rid himself of it as hastily as possible" (p. 82). The fact that Frankl quickly dictated *Man's Search* in nine days shortly after the war suggests the need for relief, but dictation, combined with his psychological state, did not allow for measured reflection. For example, the opening page of *Man's Search* made the profoundly incorrect claim that "this tale is not concerned with great horrors, which have already been described often enough." At the time (1946) the magnitude of the Holocaust was nowhere near being understood. *Man's Search* is full of such contradictions. Langer pointed out the contradictions in Frankl's testimony between the "myth" of heroic survival and descriptions of atrocities. On this issue, a questioning Langer stated it is "as if Frankl himself were unconsciously committed to a dual vision, torn between how it really was and how, retrospectively, he would like to believe it had been" (Langer, 1982, p. 19). Similarly, when reflecting on the pervasive "Christian vocabulary" in Frankl's testimony, Langer puzzled that it is "as if Frankl secretly yearned for a transfiguration of Auschwitz into nothing more than a test of the religious sensibility" (Langer, 1982, pp. 22–23).

On the latter issue, Frankl did not hesitate to use his survival of Auschwitz to justify his belief in God. It is well known that many intellectuals questioned theological conceptions of the world after the Holocaust. In contrast Frankl argued "my personal experiences offer evidence—religion did not die in Auschwitz, nor 'after Auschwitz,' to allude to the title of a book that was authored by a rabbi (who incidentally had not been there)" (*Man's Search for Ultimate Meaning*, 1997, p. 152). Frankl's disparaging remark was directed at Richard L. Rubenstein's controversial *After Auschwitz*, which rejected "the traditional biblical theology of covenant and election" in the name of a "death-of-God theology." Frankl also tied belief to psychological health and logotherapy when he claimed: "It is self-evident that belief in a super-meaning—whether as a metaphysical concept or in the religious sense of Providence—is of the foremost psychotherapeutic and psychohygienic importance" (*The Doctor and the Soul*, 1965, p. 33).

The logotherapist Haddon Klingberg deflected criticism that Frankl wasn't forthcoming about his actual camp experience, and that he subsequently used his "survival" of Auschwitz to promote logotherapy on the grounds that "when he referred occasionally . . . to the three years he spent in Auschwitz and Dachau . . . he used these names as the ones his audience likely would recognize." Klingberg then added, "in every instance his point 'in context' was something other than naming or chronicling camps" (p. 234). Whether or not one finds Klingberg's defense of Frankl convincing, the question remains why Frankl never fully disclosed his actual camp experience, leaving himself open to criticism that he exploited his survival of Auschwitz.

On the issue of using the Holocaust, Langer stated that Frankl made "survival a matter of mental health" (Langer, 1982, p. 24). Langer took specific issue with Frankl's statement that surviving was a challenge that "one could make a victory of" or "simply vegetate, as did a majority of the prisoners." Langer recognized that Frankl's self-congratulatory tone leads to the suggestion that he had the mettle to survive, and concluded "that the real hero of *Man's Search for Meaning* is not man, but Viktor Frankl" (p. 24).

Klingberg has defended Frankl on this issue with the claim "that what he was saying is: all other things being equal, the attitude one took and the meaning one found could make the difference between life and death" (pp. 235–236). However, we know the reality of Auschwitz is that attitude mattered little for survival. The vast majority were killed, a lucky few survived. Klingberg's defense reflects the appeal of Frankl's mythical view and leads to the continuing distortion of our understanding of Auschwitz. For the interested reader, a more accurate portrayal of "surviving" Auschwitz is Primo Levi's *Survival in Auschwitz*.

In sum, Frankl was a peculiar representative of the Holocaust. His testimony, one of the most popular, is a questionable version. He used his survival, misrepresentations, and falsifications, to promote his logotherapy. To what degree his deceptions were intentional or stemmed from a psychic trauma is difficult to gauge, but he never publicly clarified the details of his survival. However, as Langer recognized, it seems as if Frankl was torn between how it really was and how retrospectively he wished it had been. Apparently, Frankl's psychological state, in combination with his limited experience, led him to present elements of atrocity as only a backdrop to his heroic and mythical view of survival. This approach was certainly useful; the majority of Frankl's followers, Donald Tweedie, Robert Leslie, and Reuven Bulka, are pastoral psychologists and theologians who find Frankl's transfiguration of Auschwitz into a test of religious sensibility appealing. As Langer pointed out, however, such a view profoundly misrepresents both the reality and cultural significance of Auschwitz.

Bibliography

Primary Sources

Ein Psycholog erlebt das Konzentrationslager, 1946; *From Death-Camp to Existentialism: A Psychiatrist's Path to a New Therapy*, 1959; *Man's Search for Meaning*, 1962; *Man's Search for Ultimate Meaning*, 1997.

Arztliche Seelsorge. 1946. *The Doctor and the Soul*. 1965.

. . . trotzdem Ja zum Leben sagen (Nevertheless Say Yes to Life). 1946.

Die Psychotherapie in der Praxis. Eine kasuistische Einführung für Ärzte (Psychotherapy in Practice. A Casuistic Introduction for Physicians). 1947.

Der unbewusste Gott (*The Unconscious God: Psychotherapy and Theology*). 1949, 1975.

Der unbedingte Mensch (Unconditional Man). 1949.

Homo patiens. 1950.

Logos und Existenz (Logos and Existence). 1951.

Theorie und Therapie der Neurosen. Einführung in Logotherapie und Existenzanalyse (Theory and Therapy of Neuroses. An Introduction to Logotherapy and Existential Analysis). 1956.

Psychotherapy and Existentialism: Selected Papers on Logotherapy. 1967.

The Will to Meaning: Foundations and Applications of Logotherapy. 1969.

The Unheard Cry for Meaning: Psychotherapy and Humanism. 1978.

Die Sinnfrage in der Psychotherapie (The Question of Meaning in Psychotherapy). 1981.

Man's Search for Meaning. 1984.

Logotherapie und Existenzanalyse (Logotherapy and Existential-analysis). 1987.

"Dr. Robert Schuller Interviews Viktor Frankl: How to Find Meaning in Life." *Possibilities: The Magazine of Hope* (March/April 1991).

Was nicht in meinen Büchern steht (*Viktor Frankl—Recollections: An Autobiography*). 1995.

Secondary Sources

Adler, H. G. *Theresienstadt 1941–1945*. Tuebingen: 1960.

Appelfeld, Aharon. "After the Holocaust." In *Writing and the Holocaust*. Edited by Berel Lang. New York: Holmes and Meir, 1988.

———. *The Story of Theresienstadt*. Boston: Branden Books, 1993.

Berkley, George. *Vienna and Its Jews: The Tragedy of Success*. Boston: Madison Books, 1988.

Fabry, Joseph. *The Pursuit of Meaning: Viktor Frankl, Logotherapy, and Life*. Boston: Beacon Press, 1968.

Gould, William Blair. *Viktor E. Frankl: Life with Meaning*. Belmont, California: Brooks/Cole, 1993.

Gruber, Marianne. "Der Wille zum Sinn." *Die Pestsäule* (December 1974).

Halperin, Irving. *Messengers from the Dear*. Philadelphia: Westminister Press, 1972.

Klingberg, Haddon. *When Life Calls Out to Us: The Love and Life Work of Elly and Viktor Frankl*. New York: Doubleday, 2001.

LaCapra, Dominick. *Representing the Holocaust*. Ithaca: Cornell University Press, 1994.

Langer, Lawrence. *Versions of Survival*. Albany: State University of New York Press, 1982.

———. "The Literature of Auschwitz." In *Anatomy of the Auschwitz Death Camp*. Edited by Yisrael Gutman and Michael Berenbaum. Bloomington and Indianapolis: Indiana University Press, 1994.

Lederer, Zdenek. *Ghetto Theresienstadt*. New York: Fertig, 1993.

Rubenstein, Richard. *After Auschwitz: History, Theology, and Contemporary Judaism*. Baltimore, Md.: Johns Hopkins University Press, 1992.

Totenbuch Theresienstadt. Wien: 1971.

ERICH FRIED
(1921–1988)

KRISTIE A. FOELL

ERICH FRIED WAS born in Vienna on 6 May 1921, the son of Hugo Fried (1890–1938) and Nellie Fried née Stein (1896–1982). The young Erich showed intellectual and artistic aptitude at an early age; during 1926–1927, which he called his "wunderkind time," Fried was the leading child actor in plays by Ferdinand Raimund, but his father insisted that he give up theater once he started school. The culmination of Fried's formal education, however, was to be the Wasagymnasium (*Bundesgymnasium*) in Vienna's 9th district. Shortly after the *Anschluß* in early 1938, Fried's school became an office for the SS and he was abruptly dismissed with a diploma (*Abgangszeugnis*). Fried reacted to the annexation by founding a small youth resistance group that distributed antifascist literature.

On 24 April 1938, Fried's parents were arrested by the Gestapo for conspiring to export currency; during the interrogation, father Hugo received a deadly kick in the stomach. In more than one recollection, Fried pointedly notes the name of the murderer, a Mr. Göttler, and the fact that he was later a customs official in Düsseldorf. Hugo Fried died in Vienna's public hospital (*Allgemeines Krankenhaus*) on his forty-eighth birthday; he was buried in the "new Israelite section" of Vienna's Zentralfriedhof on 27 May 1938.

Exile and Hardship in London

On 4 August 1938, Fried fled to England via Belgium, arriving in London on 5 August. A great-uncle, Franz Kalina, who lived in the Netherlands, provided the financial guarantee for his immigration, then promptly died. In London, Fried founded a refugee self-help group that brought more than seventy people to England before the war, including his mother. Until 1940, Fried worked as an office assistant for the German Jewish Refugee Committee, then supported himself with a series of menial jobs. He joined two communist refugee organizations: the Austrian Centre and its youth wing, Young Austria; and the Free German League of Culture (Freier Deutscher Kulturbund). These gave him contact with writers and artists such as Joseph Kalmer, Theodor Kramer, and Georg Eisler; he first published in the Austrian Centre's journals, *Zeitspiegel* and *Young Austria*, and in a 1941 anthology published by the Free German League.

Fried's grandmother, Malvine Stein (1866–1943), was deported to Theresienstadt on 10 September 1942, and murdered in Auschwitz on 26 March 1943. (She had remained behind in Vienna because she was blind.) The losses of this time would stay with Fried throughout his life: until his death, he kept in his office a piece of barbed wire from the concentration camp Esterwegen, where the German pacifist Carl von Ossietzky had been tortured to death in 1938, as well as a knife blade he found on his first visit to Auschwitz in 1967. Fried's poem "The Survivor (after Auschwitz)" raises the issue of survivor guilt:

> How often
> must I die
> to atone
> for the fact that I
> did not die there? (Volker Kaukoreit and Klaus Wagenbach, eds., *Gesammelte Werke*, edited by Voker Kaukoveit and Klaus Wagenbach, Berlin: Wagenbach, 1993, vol. 2, p. 522).

In the autumn of 1943, Fried withdrew from the group Young Austria because of conflicts with the doctrinaire attitudes of the party. He was further isolated from the exile community when it embraced the theory of German collective guilt that prompted Ilya Ehrenburg's statement that "the only good German is a dead German." Fried found it absurd that German and German Jewish exiles could subscribe to such a notion, and suggested that the entire group throw itself into the Thames to demonstrate its self-hatred. His 1960 novel, *Ein Soldat und ein Mädchen* (A Soldier and a

Girl), a love story between an American antifascist soldier and a condemned female concentration camp warden, is another example of Fried's unwillingness to write off any individual human being on the basis of race or national origin.

The year 1944 saw the publication of two very different works by Fried, the English-language resistance pamphlet "They Fight in the Dark," and his first volume of poetry, *Deutschland* (Germany). In the same year, he married his first wife, Maria Marburg, with whom he had a son, Hans. Fried's second volume of poetry, *Österreich* (Austria), followed quickly in 1945. The postwar years were a time of economic struggle; in addition to freelance work for the British Central Office of Information, Fried earned his living in a glass factory. He still found time to assemble a group of Jewish exile writers that included Franz Baermann Steiner, Hans W. Cohn, Hans Eichner, and H. G. Adler. By 1946, his first marriage had effectively ended, although the divorce was not finalized until 1952.

Success and Protest

In 1952, the BBC German Service hired Fried to write for its German Soviet Zone Programme. Fried broadcast political and cultural commentaries, as well as English literature in German; Steven Lawrie gives a full account of Fried's work for the BBC. Fried's second marriage, to Nan Spence-Eichner, coincided with the beginning of this employment; after bearing him two children, David and Katherine, Nan would leave the marriage in 1962. David later became a graphic artist who collaborated with his father on several projects.

Also during this time, Fried began the slow, never-completed process of "return" to the German-speaking countries, traveling to Berlin in 1953. He became a prolific and sought-after literary translator from English to German; his versions of twenty-seven Shakespeare plays were staged at leading theaters throughout Germany and are still in print. Fried made his first official postwar visit to Vienna in 1962, but his application to have his Austrian citizenship reinstated went unacknowledged. From 1963 until its dissolution in 1967, Fried participated in the meetings of the Gruppe 47 (Group 47).

In 1965 Fried entered his third, apparently successful, marriage, with photographer and graphic artist Catherine Boswell; she would document their life together in photographs, drawings, and paintings, and has contributed to several biographical works since Fried's death. The couple had three children, daughter Petra (b. 1965) and twin sons Klaus and Tom (b. 1969); Fried would also live to see three grandchildren. The family's residence at 22 Dartmouth Road in London (from 1969) became a domestic haven where Fried kept a notoriously book-strewn office, his *Schriftstellererker*.

Fried became increasingly politically active during the 1960s, publishing his controversial poetry volume *Und Vietnam und* (and Vietnam and, 1966) with Klaus Wagenbach, who would remain his primary publisher. The Vietnam poems show that he drew universal conclusions from World War II and the Holocaust. But Fried's criticism was not confined to the actions of the superpowers; his poem "Hear O Israel," from his 1967 volume, *Anfechtungen* (Temptations), angered many who saw things differently:

When we were the persecuted
I was one of you
How can I remain one
when you become the persecutors?

Your longing was
Is to become like other nations
who murdered you
Now you have become like them

You have outlived
those who were cruel to you
Does their cruelty
live on in you now? (*100 Poems without a Country*,
translated by Stuart Hood, p. 36).

Fried recalled the controversy surrounding this poem: "I was attacked by some people who knew me, 'How can you, as a Jew, say anything against Israel? Have you never heard of the voice of the blood?' 'Yes,' I replied. 'I heard of this once, from Hitler, and once was enough for me' " ("Ist Antizionismus Antisemitismus [Is anti-zionism anti-semitism]?" *Anfragen und Nachreden*, edited by Volker Kaukoreit; Berlin: Wagenbach, 1994, p. 160).

Fried initially admired the young journalist Ulrike Meinhof, though he did not support her later "career" as a Red Army Faction terrorist. When authorities prematurely declared Meinhof's 1976 death in solitary confinement a suicide, Fried was not the only one who found the circumstances suspicious; even before her death, the concluding stanza of his poem "The Query" had made a provocative comparison between postwar Germany's treatment of idealistic, if misguided, terrorists such as Meinhof, Gudrun Ensslin, and Horst Mahler, and that same society's lenient attitude toward ex-Nazis:

But one question for the justice system
about the length of their sentences:
How many thousands of Jews
must a Nazi have murdered
in order to be condemned
to such a long confinement today? (*Gesammelte
Werke*, vol. 2, p. 260).

Fried sent a telegram to Meinhof's funeral, calling her the "greatest German woman since Rosa Luxemburg."

By the late 1970s, the German press increasingly (and wrongly) classified Fried as a supporter of left-wing terrorism. There were repeated calls to remove his works from schoolbooks; most spectacularly, a Christian Democratic politician declared that he would like to see Fried's works burned, an echo of the past that was not lost on the writer. The 1977 collection of poems, *So kam ich unter die Deutschen* (How I Came Among the Germans), a reference to the nineteenth-century poet Friedrich Hölderlin's diagnosis of "the German misery," is only one expression of Fried's critical stance at this time.

Writing about the Holocaust

Fried frequently expressed his outrage at the silent acceptance of former Nazis in postwar German society, as in his poem "A Question of Tact":

In
the
house
of
the
hanged
man
do
not
mention
the
rope
because
that's
where
his
hangman
now
enjoys
his
retirement (*Last Honours,* translated by Georg Rapp, p. 9).

For all his political engagement, Fried never accepted the idea that literature was "dead" or superfluous, or that, as the philosopher Theodor Adorno said, there could be no poetry after Auschwitz, a thought Fried addresses in his poem, "Questions about Poetry since Auschwitz":

Whether it rose up as a small brown bird
out of the smoke of cremation ovens
and then rested in one of the birchs [sic]
of Birkenau

whether it flew closer
drawn by the screams of the girls
and saw them raped
and then sang
. . .
whether at last in a tree
stripped by defoliants
it built its nest of hair
of paper shreds of rags and bloody feathers

and now waits for mating
for the time to sit on its eggs
and for the hatching of
its eternally innocent young

that only lyric poets know
who steadfastly call
for wild bird protection
in a world soon to be whole again (*100 Poems without a Country,* translated by Stuart Hood, pp. 67–69).

As for portraying the Holocaust itself in art, Fried reflected after his first visit to Auschwitz in 1967:

> If the unbearable remains unmitigatedly unbearable, then that is for most people no reason not to bear it any longer and, perhaps, change the world in such a way that there is nothing unbearable any more. It is just a reason to forget the unbearable as quickly as possible and to no longer think about it, even if much that is likewise unbearable continues to exist or is even threatening ("My Doll in Auschwitz," *Children and Fools,* translated by Martin Chalmers, p. 57).

Fried himself wrote both prose and poetry about the Holocaust, including the following vivid portrayal that combines personal and historical elements:

My Girlfriends

Slowly in three to four weeks
or suddenly over night
my girls turn into
my aunts and elderly cousins

I see them anxiously
chewing their false teeth
and with arthritic fingers
wipe their spat-at faces

They arrive at Theresienstadt
with suitcases and bundles
They fall out of the window
still groping for their glasses

When they stretch in my bed
they are trying to stand to attention
in order to be spared
when the sick are picked out

I see them discoloured blue
when I kiss them in the morning
stacked in sixes
—the shit and vomited bile

washed off with garden hoses—
ready for transfer
from the gas chamber
to the incinerators (*On Pain of Seeing: Poems by Erich Fried,* translated by George Rapp, p. 38).

The transformation of the speaker's "girlfriends" into older female relatives, as well as the conflation of his bed with the concentration camp bunks of the women, simultaneously alienate and involve the reader. Drawing on the literary motif of a young man who finds his beloved transformed into a hag, the juxtaposition of sexuality with the cruel degradation of the body in the Holocaust protests against this transformation of women capable of love and enjoyment into disfigured bodies disposed of like trash.

Although this unflinching portrayal might be read as despairing, Fried's response to the unbearable past was always to attempt to prevent the unbearable present and future; his opposition to the war in Vietnam, to nuclear arms, to military interventions that served the interests of ruling powers was intimately linked to the Holocaust. Fried states as much, with an ironic twist, in his 1983 poem "Debt of Gratitude" (subtitled "Fifty years after Hitler's accession to power"):

Much too used
to shake with anger
at the crimes
of the swastika times

we forget
to be just a little thankful
to our predecessors
that their deeds

might still help us
to recognise in time
that *we* are planning
a far greater crime today (*Love Poems,* translated by Stuart Hood, p. 219).

Recognition and Reflection

Fried was finally reinstated as an Austrian citizen in 1982; that same year, the Viennese literary workshop Alte Schmiede devoted a seminar to his works. But 1982 also saw Fried's first operation for cancer; the terminal illness seemed to spur him on to even greater activity. He remained controversial. There were debates when he received the Großer Österreichischer Staatspreis (Great Austrian State Prize) in 1985, and again when he received the Georg-Büchner-Preis in 1987. In 1986, when Fried accepted the Österreichischer Staatspreis für Verdienste um die österreichische Kultur im Ausland (Austrian State Prize for Promoting Austrian Culture Abroad), he simultaneously campaigned against presidential candidate Kurt Waldheim, then "honored" Waldheim's election with limericks like the following:

In all the world this man is known
He's a president full of renown.
But the source of his fame
and his shameful nickname
Could finally bring Austria down (*Gesammelte Werke,* vol. 3, p. 541).

During his final decade, Fried continued to reflect on his Holocaust experience with the 1983 collection, *Angst und Trost. Erzählungen und Gedichte über Juden und Nazis* (Fear and Comfort: Stories and Poems about Jews and Nazis), and the 1986 *Mitunter sogar Lachen* (Almost Funny); some of these essays can be found in English translation in *Children and Fools.* The autobiographical stories in these volumes evince a clear view of the implications of Nazi racial theories along with an ability to see the motivations of individual sympathizers and party members in a human light. In "Hitlerjunge Papanek," for example, Fried relates the painfully humorous story of Hitler Youth Papanek, who discovers that he has Jewish ancestors and dutifully resigns from the party. His Nazi friend Bertel, acknowledging the racial laws but not willing to end the friendship abruptly, locates a pub that is not off-limits to Jews and throws Papanek a farewell party. Fried notes that "none of the arguments I had brought forth against Hitler's racial theory on our walks to and from school during the last three years seemed to have made as great an impression on him as the case of Papanek" (*Mitunter sogar Lachen,* p. 51).

After giving an interview for the German television network ARD on 3 November 1988, Fried was admitted to the hospital in Baden-Baden, where he died on 22 November; he was buried in London on 9 December 1988.

Bibliography

Primary Sources

"They Fight in the Dark: The Story of Austria's Youth." 1943.
Deutschland (Germany), poems. 1944.
Österreich (Austria), poems. 1945.
Gedichte, poems. 1958.
Ein Soldat und ein Mädchen (A Soldier and a Girl), novel. 1960.
Reich der Steine (Empire of Stone), poem cycle. 1963.
Warngedichte, poems. 1964.
Überlegungen (Conversations). 1964.
Kinder und Narren (*Children and Fools*). 1965.
Und Vietnam und (and Vietnam and), poems. 1966.
Anfechtungen (Temptations), poems. 1967.

Arden muss sterben (*Arden Must Die*), opera libretto. 1967.
Zeitfragen (Questions of Time), poems. 1968.
Befreiung von der Flucht (Deliverance from Flight), poems. 1968.
Intellektuelle und Sozialismus (with Paul A. Baran and Gaston Salvatore). 1968.
Last Honours (selected poems translated by Georg Rapp). 1968.
Die Beine der größeren Lügen, poems. 1969.
Gedichte, poems. 1969.
On Pain of Seeing: Poems (Selected poems translated by Georg Rapp). 1969.
Unter nebenfeinden, poems. 1970.
Aufforderung zur Unruhe (Invitation to Unease), poems. 1972.
Die Freiheit den Mund aufzumachen, poems. 1972.
Höre, Israel! (Hear, O Israel!) poems and footnotes. 1974.
Gegengift (Antidote), poems and a cycle. 1974.
Fast alles Mögliche. Wahre Geschichte und gültige Lügen. 1975.
Kampf ohne Engel (Struggle Without Angel). 1976.
So kam ich unter die Deutschen (How I Came Among the Germans), poems. 1977.
Die bunten Getüme, poems. 1977.
100 Gedichte ohne Vaterland (*100 Poems Without a Country*). 1978.
Liebesgedichte (selected poems translated in *Love Poems*). 1979.
Lebensschatten, poems. 1981.
Zur Zeit und zur Unzeit. 1981.
Das Unmaß aller Dinge. 1982.
Das Nahe suchen. 1982.
'Ich grenz noch an ein Wort und an eine anderes Land'. Über Ingeborg Bachmann. 1983.
Angst und Trost. Erzählungen und Gedichte über Juden und Nazis. 1983.
Es ist was es ist. Gedichte (selected poems translated in *Love Poems*). 1983.
Kalender für den Frieden, poems. 1984.
Und nicht taub und stumpf werden, speeches. 1984.
Beunruhigungen, poems. 1984.
Und alle seine Mörder, verse drama. 1984.
In die Sinne einradiert. Gedichte zu Radierungen von Catherine Fried-Boswell. 1984.
Um Klarheit. Gedichte gegen das Vergessen. 1985.
Von Bis nach Seit. Gedichte 1945–58. 1985.
Fall ins Wort. Ausgewählte Gedichte 1944–1983. 1985.
Die da reden gegen Vernichtung. Psychologie, bildende Kunst und Dichtung gegen den Krieg (with Erwin Ringel and Alfred Hrdlicka). 1985.
Wächst das Rettende auch? Gedichte für den Frieden. 1985.
Mitunter sogar Lachen (Almost Funny). 1986.
Die Umrisse meiner Liebe. Lyrik, Erzählungen, Essays. 1986.
Was bist du mir? Gedichte von der Liebe. 1986.
Vorübungen für Wunder, poems. 1987.
Am Rand unserer Lebenszeit, poems. 1987.
Gegen das Vergessen, poems. 1987.
Wo liegt Nicaragua? (Where Is Nicaragua?) (with Heinrich Albertz). 1987.
Nicht verdrängen, nicht gewöhnen. Texte zum Thema Österreich. 1987.
Gedanken in und an Deutschland. Essays und Reden. 1988.
Unverwundenes, poems. 1988.
Gründe. Gesammelte Gedichte. 1989.
Mißtrauen lernen. Prosa, Lyrik, Aufsätze, Reden. 1989.
Als ich mich nach dir verzehrte. Zweiundsiebzig Gedichte von der Liebe. 1990.
Zwischen Tür und Amsel, poems. 1990.
Einbruch der Wirklichkeit. Verstreute Gedichte. 1990.
Gesammelte Werke, four vols. (Edited by Volker Kaukoreit and Klaus Wagenbach). 1993.
Anfragen und Nachreden. Politische Texte. (Edited by Volker Kaukoreit). 1994.
For reasons of space, Fried's translations, journalistic pieces, and essays are omitted here.
For a complete bibliography, see Kaukoreit, *Frühe Stationen*, and Lawrie.

Secondary Sources

Alter, Nora M. ". . . und . . . Fried . . . und . . . : The Poetry of Erich Fried and the Structure of Contemporaneity." *Studies in Twentieth Century Literature* 21:1 (Winter 1997): 79–109.
Dressler, Christine. *"Nach dem Landlos greift des Landlosen Hand." Erich Fried, ein Exilautor? eine Untersuchung seines nach 1945 entstandenen Werkes.* Vienna: Edition Praesens, 1998.
———. *Erich Fried.* München: Edition Text + Kritik, Heft 91. 1997.
Fried-Boswell, Catherine, and Volker Kaukoreit, eds. *Erich Fried. Ein Leben in Bildern und Geschichten.* Berlin: Wagenbach, 1996.
Glenn, Jerry. "Erich Fried." *Major Figures of Contemporary Austrian Literature.* Edited by Donald G. Daviau. New York: Peter Lang, 1987, pp. 163–183.
Heimann, Angelika. *"Bless thee! Thou art Translated." Erich Fried als Übersetzer moderner englischsprachiger Lyrik.* Amsterdam: Grüner, 1987.
Jessen, Christiane, Volker Kaukoreit, and Klaus Wagenbach, eds. *Erich Fried: Eine Chronik. Leben und Werk: Das biographische Lesebuch.* Berlin: Wagenbach, 1998.
Kane, Martin. "From Solipsism to Engagement: The Development of Erich Fried as a Political Poet." *Forum for Modern Language Studies* 21:2 (April 1985): 151–169.
Kaukoreit, Volker. *Frühe Stationen des Lyrikers Erich Fried: vom Exil bis zum Protest gegen den Krieg in Vietnam. Werk und Biographie 1938–1966.* Darmstadt: J. Häusser, 1991.
——— ed. *Einblicke, Durchblicke: Fundstücke und Werkstattberichte aus dem Nachlass von Erich Fried.* Vienna: Turia & Kant, 1993.
——— and Wilhelm Urbanek, eds. *Am Alsergrund: Erich Frieds Jugendjahre in Wien (1921–1938). Texte und Dokumente mit einem Wiederabdruck der Londoner Exilbroschüre, "They fight in the dark, the story of Austria's youth."* Vienna: Turia & Kant, 1995.
Kaukoreit, Volker, and Heidemarie Vahl. *Einer singt aus der Zeit gegen die Zeit. Erich Fried 1921–1988. Materialien und Texte zu Leben und Werk.* Darmstadt: Jürgen Häusser, 1991.
Lampe, Gerhard. *Ich will mich erinnern an alles was man vergißt. Erich Fried, Biographie und Werk.* Cologne: Bund-Verlag, 1989.
Lawrie, Steven W. *Erich Fried: a Writer Without a Country.* New York: Peter Lang, 1996.
Mayer, Hans. *Über Erich Fried.* Hamburg: Europäische Verlagsanstalt, 1991.
Schäfer, Katrin. *Die andere Seite: Erich Frieds Prosawerk. Motive und Motivationen seines Schreibens.* Vienna: Edition Praesens, 1998.
Wellbery, David E. "Death as a Poetological Problem: On Texts by Erich Fried and Ernst Meister." *Argumentum e Silentio.* Edited by Amy D. Colin. Berlin: de Gruyter, 1986, pp. 87–98.

Saul Friedländer

(1932–)

JULIETTE DICKSTEIN

Saul Friedländer was born in Prague, Czechoslovakia, in 1932. He holds the Maxwell Cummings Chair of European History at Tel Aviv University and the 1939 Club Chair in Holocaust History at the University of California at Los Angeles. He has a doctorate from the University of Geneva (1963), and taught at the Graduate Institute of International Studies in Geneva from 1964 to 1988 and at the Hebrew University in Jerusalem from 1969 to 1975. Friedländer is one of the most important historians of World War II. His scholarship has received numerous awards and prizes, most recently the MacArthur ("genius") Fellowship in 1999. He is the author of *Nazi Germany and the Jews, Vol 1: The Years of Persecution, 1933–1939* (1997), *Memory, History, and the Extermination of the Jews of Europe* (1993), *Reflections of Nazism* (1984), *When Memory Comes* (1979, first published in French as *Quand vient le souvenir* [1978]), *History and Psychoanalysis* (1979), *Kurt Gerstein* (1969), and *Pius XII and the Third Reich* (1965). In 1992, he also edited a seminal work on Holocaust historiography titled *Probing the Limits of Representation*. Friedländer is one of the founders of the prestigious journal *History & Memory*, as well as its former editor-in-chief. He serves on the Independent Experts Commission investigating Swiss policies during World War II, and is a member of several scientific advisory boards at academic institutions in Israel and in Europe.

Friedländer is not only a scholar of the Holocaust, but also a survivor of this dark chapter in European history. As a boy in 1939, he fled with his parents from Czechoslovakia to France. Several years later, in 1942, during the mass arrests of foreign-born Jews, Friedländer was sent into hiding in a French Catholic monastery under the name of Paul-Henri Marie Ferrland. He was baptized, became a devout Catholic, and for a while, actually considered becoming a priest. His parents were aware that he would receive a Catholic education and "were at peace with themselves, for their first and foremost objective, from this point on, was to save their child" (*When Memory Comes*, p. 78). Friedländer's parents tried to escape to Switzerland, but were stopped at the border and sent back to France. In October they were deported to Auschwitz and never came back.

Friedländer's autobiographical memoir, *When Memory Comes*, chronicles these catastrophic years as it moves between his memory of his experiences as a young boy in France during the 1940s, and the experience of writing these memories while a young professor of history in Israel during the 1970s. The movement back and forth creates an important connection between the present act of writing and the events recounted in the narration.

> I sometimes feel a profound sense of discouragement while thumbing through these pages: I will never be able to express what I want to say; I know these awkwardly written lines are very distant from my recollections. They will cover only scattered fragments of my parents' existence, and what had been their world, and what had been my childhood (*Quand vient le souvenir*, Paris: Éditions du Seuil, 1978, pp. 125, 126. Unless otherwise noted, all translations from the French are my own.).

Friedländer nonetheless expresses that by writing about the past, he is able to establish a connection to it, especially to his parents who were suddenly and violently taken from him. He also articulates his personal task as a historian/survivor to "recapture the meaning of an epoch, and to re-establish the coherence of a past, [his] past" (p. 134).

> The war was over; my parents had not returned. The Red Cross thought they had identified, in Theresienstadt, a couple whose names corresponded to those of my mother and father, but we had to wait because a typhus epidemic had imposed a quarantine. Unreal wait: the days passed without a sign, and during all this time, I would ask myself: how am I going to welcome my parents? Will I simply be able to express my happiness? (p. 121).

Without falling into excessive sentimentality or nostalgia, *When Memory Comes* poignantly conveys the emotions of the adult Friedländer looking back at his childhood. His language is rich and provocative, yet unadorned and straightforward:

> Today, at this moment as I write, here I am at the age of my father when he disappeared . . . I contemplate [my parents] from far away, very far away, and I ask myself: what blindness drove them in such a way from one mistake to another until the end? What obscure destiny? I try to understand, to put myself in their place, to imagine what I would have done, but I cannot . . . even today, I can only see them through the eyes of a child (p. 54).

Friedländer includes in his memoir excerpts of letters written by his parents from the late 1930s to 1942. The most wrenching is the last letter written by his mother on 5 October to an acquaintance; it was thrown from the train deporting her and her husband to Germany.

> The first lines are written in ink, then an almost empty pen had tried to trace lines that had subsequently been filled in with pencil:
>
> "Madame, I am writing to you from the train taking us to Germany. At the last moment, I sent you 6,000 francs and a charm bracelet through a Quaker representative. Through a lady, I sent a file with stamps. Keep it all for the little one, and for the last time, accept our infinite thanks and warmest wishes for you and your entire family. Do not abandon the little one! May God reward you and bless you and your entire family. —Elli and Jan Friedländer" (p. 87).

When Memory Comes not only relates the experiences of Friedländer as a child during the war in France, and the tragic fate that befell his parents, it also narrates how Friedländer suddenly became aware of his Jewish identity, and how he then began to move away from his Catholic education and toward Judaism, especially the Zionist cause. At the end of the war, Friedländer learned what happened to his parents and 6,000,000 European Jews through a Jesuit priest from Saint-Etienne whom he had befriended. "Didn't your parents die in Auschwitz?" he asked. The adolescent Friedländer was thus informed about the precise nature of the Nazi destruction of the European Jews, about "Auschwitz, the trains, the gas chambers, and the crematoria, the millions of dead" (p. 129). For the first time in his life, Friedländer completely accepted who he was as a Jew. "Something had changed, a connection was reestablished, and an identity emerged" (p. 129).

Friedländer became involved with Zionist activities. At the age of sixteen he clandestinely left France for the newly established state of Israel aboard an arms-smuggling ship called the *Altalena*. The *Altalena* was directly involved in battle during the Arab-Israeli war. While there were many casualties on board, there were also a good number of survivors, among them Friedländer and Menachem Begin, who was to become prime minister of Israel. In Israel, Friedländer stayed with his uncle and studied to be an agronomist until he realized his true vocation as a historian.

As a historian of the Holocaust, Friedländer has made fundamental contributions to the field. According to him, the task of the historian of the Holocaust is to render "as truthful an account as documents and testimonials will allow, without giving in to the temptation of closure" (*Memory, History, and the Extermination of the Jews of Europe*, Bloomington: Indiana University Press, 1993, p. 131). By closure he means a simplistic, positivist notion of what happened and why. Indeed, Friedländer refers to the "excess" the Holocaust carries, which confirms the problematic nature of traditional historiographic methodology:

> Whether one considers the *Shoah* [Israeli term for Holocaust which means catastrophe] as an exceptional event or as belonging to a wider historical category does not affect the possibility of drawing from it a universally valid significance. The difficulty appears when this statement is reversed. No universal lesson seems to require reference to the *Shoah* to be fully comprehended. The *Shoah* carries an *excess*, and this excess is the something which remains to be phrased which is not, which is not something determined (p. 133).

According to Friedländer, the Holocaust is a watershed, for it constitutes an epistemological shift that forces us to reconfigure a progressive, positivist notion of history and time based on successivity. Scholars like Friedländer (also Dominick LaCapra, Henry Rousso, Cathy Caruth, and others) conceptualize the "past" as more connected to the present than traditional historians. The past—the war years—carries a different historiographic status, not only because its memory is still alive, but because our contemporary moment has not finished contending with its legacy. Indeed, the war years (1939 through 1945) extend well beyond the moment of German surrender. This perspective, which upsets the chronology of the Second World War, is precisely the historical view of Vichy historian, Henry Rousso, who is affiliated with one of France's most prestigious social science research centers, the Institut d'histoire du temps présent (Institute of the History of Present Time). In an unpublished article on the conception of the institute, Rousso, its current director, explains the term "present time" as a particular perspective on contemporary history that includes the historian's testimony.

Saul Friedländer has not only contributed volumes of invaluable research on the Nazi era and its aftermath to the field of Holocaust historiography, but also his own experience and witnessing. As a (Jewish) historian who bears direct witness on the Nazi era, Friedländer argues that the "discrete" categories of history and memory, with respect to "the representation of the recent past or a past considered to be of cardinal relevance for the identity of a given group," are far from definite opposites (*Memory, History, and the Extermination of the Jews*, 1993, p. viii). The inclusion of personal experiences within the historical narrative reintroduces "individual memory into the overall representation of the epoch" (p. 132), and helps us all to learn and to remember, for we are continuously reminded of what happened through individual testimony.

Toward the end of *When Memory Comes*, Friedländer asks himself, "Isn't what I have succeeded in saying only just a small part of what I wanted to express?" (p. 166). Perhaps. Nonetheless, Friedländer's "quest, his incessant confrontation with the past is, in and of itself, a sufficient reason and a necessary undertaking" (p. 166), for in the words of the philosopher Gustav Meyrink, whom Friedländer quotes, "When knowledge comes, little by little, memory comes as well." And in his own words, "when memory comes, little by little knowledge comes as well" (pp. 166,167).

Bibliography

Primary Sources

Le rôle du facteur américain dans la politique étrangère et militaire de l'Allemagne, Septembre 1939–Décembre 1941 (The Role of the American Factor in Germany's Foreign and Military Policy). 1963.

Pius XII and the Third Reich. 1965.

Réflexions sur l'avenir d'Israël (Reflections on the Future of Israel). 1969.

Kurt Gerstein, The Ambiguity of Good (Translated by Charles Fullman). 1969.

Hussein, Mahmoud, and Saul Friedlander. *Arabs & Israelis: A Dialogue* (With Mahmoud Hussein; translated by Paul Auster and Lydia Davis). 1975.

History and Psychoanalysis. 1979.

When Memory Comes. 1979.

Quand vient le souvenir. 1978.

Reflections of Nazism: An Essay on Kitsch and Death (Translated by Thomas Weyr). 1984. 1993.

Hitler and the Final Solution. 1984.

Visions of Apocalypse: End or Rebirth? (editor). 1985.

La Politique étrangere du général de Gaulle (General de Gaulle's Foreign Policy) (editor). 1985.

Probing the Limits of Representation (editor). 1992.

Memory, History, and the Extermination of the Jews of Europe. 1993.

The Jews in European History: Seven Lectures. 1994.

Nazi Germany and the Jews, Vol 1: The Years of Persecution, 1933–1939. 1997.

CARL FRIEDMAN

(1952–)

EFRAIM SICHER

BORN IN EINDHOVEN, Holland, in 1952, to Holocaust survivors, Carl (Carolina) Friedman grew up in a Jewish milieu in her hometown and later in Antwerp. She trained as a translator and interpreter, and worked for some years as a journalist. After her marriage broke up, she moved to Amsterdam. Friedman has lectured extensively on the Holocaust. She made her literary debut in 1991 with the short autobiographical novel *Tralievader (Nightfather)*. *Nightfather* is a young girl's memoir of growing up, experiencing the Holocaust through her father's incessant stories. The traumatic effects of hearing these nightmarish stories on a daily basis are expressed in a narrative that attempts to define what it means to be a child of the Holocaust, a narrative that is immediately recognizable to other children of Holocaust survivors.

Holocaust Daughter

The father in Friedman's novel relives his hiding, deportation, and incarceration in a concentration camp. His stories of the past are of bestiality and horror. The child in the novel is led to believe at an early age that "camp" is the normal condition of human existence to which she has not been personally subjected, and she begins to feel ungrateful for her stroke of good fortune. "Camp" is what her father has in common with the wolf at the zoo.

In an attempt to emulate their father's memory of smuggling stolen dog food into the camp barracks and swallowing the moldy, nauseating filth, she and her brothers drink from a dirty water puddle. But the secret of "camp" that sets the parents apart from other families remains elusive. The secret is in the father's every word and expression, and in that sense the Holocaust has never ended. It is "camp" that makes the family different, and that is all the girl knows about Judaism and the Jews. She identifies so much with her father's daily torment of living after Auschwitz, his restless prowling and unbearable memories, that she transposes them into her own imagination. She cannot see what is wrong with drawing pictures of the hangings of starving prisoners in art class at school instead of drawing pictures of pixies. Hangings are, after all, true, while pixies are not.

At night, as he sleeps, the father, Ephraim, relives camp roll call, and while his dream can be dismissed, the blood on his face, the result of his knocking his head against a closet, cannot be denied. The Holocaust is likewise a truth that cannot be denied, and by adopting it as universal and absolute the girl divides the world into those who are Holocaust survivors and those who are not. She also assumes that those who are not survivors are thus in some way in denial of the horror. As a daughter of the Holocaust, she feels inadequate when faced with her father's knowledge of hunger and suffering. In her dreamworld, electrified barbed wire fences and the SS or the sadistic *kapos*, orderlies drawn from camp inmates who were often notorious for their brutality, threaten her existence. Even when her father is persuaded to tell a children's story, as opposed to a story that really happened, he alters the details. In his version of the tale of Red Riding Hood, for instance, he has the girl visit the hospital block where her grandmother is sick with typhus. On her way, Red Riding Hood is attacked by dogs trained by the Nazis to tear prisoners apart.

The girl in Friedman's novel seems unaware of her father's love and imagines him as a burning, wounded animal surrounded by a world devoid of salvation. It does not occur to her that camp survivors might nurture their children while coming to terms with the traumatic past. The novel is set in the time of the Eichmann trial, and the presence of the balding man in the defendant's box on the television screen makes the Holocaust both more real and less understandable, because the girl has internalized her father's stories so thoroughly into her perception of herself and the world around her that she cannot detach herself from this awesome event that lies beyond comprehension.

The transference of the survivors' traumatic experience leaves a burning imprint on a childhood lived in the shadow of the Holocaust: the boycott of German cars and goods, obsession with food, the reenactment of escape in the woods (instead of picnicking), and the prohibition of joining the Girl Scout Brownies, which is too reminiscent of the *Hitlerjugend* (Hitler Youth) and could result in being sent away to "camp." The transposition, nevertheless, seems at times excessive. The girl imagines Native Americans in Western movies are being hunted down for extermination by Nazi cowboys.

There is, however, a compelling pathos in the child's naive credulity. The cruelty of Grimm's *Fairy Tales* appears truer to her than the humane values of Western civilization. And the Holocaust continues to affect her life when she watches her father being taken away to a sanitarium. The sickness of the camps will never be healed. The affliction is not to forget anything, because to forget is to deny, and as a result, instead of normal love and affection, the father has filled his children's lives with his searing tales of degradation and inhumanity.

Friedman has stated in her "Afterword" that she had little ambition to be an author, and writes that she does not know why she wrote *Nightfather* but hopes it may make people kinder to each other when they understand the results of the Nazis' racist hatred. That is a very small, idealistic hope, however much it is sustained by the record of Dutch resistance during World War II. The resurgence of neo-Nazism and Holocaust denial is countered by writing the memory of the Holocaust in a bare style that restores meaning and emotional impact to the usual grand phrases about the war. Growing up to believe it might happen again at any moment, however, can lead to paranoiac insecurity, and the resulting self-awareness might be based on a void that contains a mute scream.

Left Luggage

Friedman's 1995 novel *Twee koffers vol* (*The Shovel and the Loom*) is better known in its adaptation as Jeroen Krabbé's award-winning film, *Left Luggage*, which premiered at the 1998 Berlin Film Festival. Starring Isabella Rossellini, Maximilian Schell, Jeroen Krabbé, Marianne Sägebrecht, and Laura Fraser, and with Chaim Topol as the wise Mr. Apfelschnitt, the film's title gives a powerful metaphor to the burden of the past as explored in the novel. The left luggage comprises two suitcases that the father in the story buried at the time of the German invasion. The violin and the photos in the suitcases are not only symbols of the past but are an essential recovery of a prewar life in Berlin that has been irretrievably lost. The dead leave no memory except through the items in the suitcases.

The father's pathetic obsession with digging up this lost treasure is symptomatic of living in the past. The mother, on the other hand, denies the past and remains silent about her Holocaust experience. In contrast to the shovel, her symptomatic emblem is the loom, a huge wooden instrument of torture in which she imprisons herself. The loom is an escape from the horror with which she cannot deal.

The novel is set in Antwerp in the aftermath of the 1968 student revolt, amid demonstrations against the Vietnam war, when the younger generation looked to Marxism for solutions to the world's problems. Chaja, the protagonist, finds no answers in her philosophy course or in radical politics. She is appalled by the antisemitism of the New Left and the hatred or indifference of her fellow students and townspeople. She is estranged from her parents and cannot accept her mother's rejection of the past. Chaja looks to the past because it holds the memory of the dead, and she believes the past has value.

In the past is hidden the secret of the Jews' suffering and survival. Chaja discovers this unexpectedly. After despairing of the disgusting conditions at the restaurant where she works, Chaja finds a baby-sitting job with a Hasidic family in Antwerp's Jewish quarter. What makes her overcome her prejudice against this outdated way of life, cooped up behind chicken wire and ancient laws, is an attachment to the Kalmans' problem child, Simcha. His name means "joy," and soon Simcha fills Chaja's life. She begins her return to the sources of Judaism, reading through the night and consulting with the local Jewish oracle, Mr. Apfelschnitt. There are no clear-cut answers to Chaja's search for G-d and the mystery of the Jews' survival, but she does find meaning in her own life through her relationship with Simcha.

Although regarded by Mr. Kalman as an immodestly dressed secular woman, Chaja wins a place in Simcha's heart and helps him to stop wetting himself by taking him on walks to the pond in the local park, where he is fascinated by the ducks and starts to imitate their quacking. In Edwin de Vries's script of the story, there is an insight into what is only latent in the novel: the affinity between Simcha's and Chaja's situations. Chaja's excursions to the duck pond bring Simcha to speak his first words. Later, Chaja teaches Simcha to recite the *Ma Nishtna?* the questions asked at the Passover feast by the youngest son of the father about the meaning of the ritual retelling of the Exodus story of Israel's redemption from Egypt. Mr. Kalman fails to respond to Simcha's achievement and reveals to Chaja that Simcha is a "memorial candle" conceived to replace a child lost in the Holocaust. In the novel, the Passover preparations and Chaja's present to Simcha of the toy duck serve no more than to emphasize the emotional starvation caused by the family's strict adherence to Hasidic rules and the father's inability to connect emotionally with his family. The father distances himself further while on commercial trips for his chocolate business. The Kalman family situation clearly parallels Chaja's own home, where her mother has distanced herself in the loom, while her father can only think about his shovel. She too, like Simcha, must break out of an autistic isolation.

As the story comes to an end, two policemen bring Chaja's father home and confiscate his shovel, but, unlike the novel, the film concludes with Chaja joining her father in his futile digging for lost luggage. The loss can perhaps never be recuperated or redeemed, but the search for the past gives meaning to present lives and enables Chaja to break out of her own psychic envelope and come to terms with her Jewishness. This comes out most forcibly in her dogged resistance to the antisemitic concierge who torments her and blocks her way in and out of the Kalmans' apartment building. In one skirmish, Chaja rips the concierge's coat, and Mrs. Kalman sends Chaja on paid leave until things have calmed down. While she is away, Simcha is fatefully drawn to the duck pond, where he drowns. Chaja for the first time has to face loss in her own life. She goes to comfort the bereaved family and nearly gets thrown out by the Hasidim who blame her for her part in the tragedy. But Mrs. Kalman rents a ritual tear in Chaja's jacket in a gesture of solidarity in mourning and in recognition of a true daughter of Israel, an *eshet chayil* (woman of valor), who has stood up for her people and accepted the meaning of the past.

Conclusion

Friedman's contribution to Dutch Holocaust literature added to the widening circle of writing that emerged in the 1980s about children of the war (*Kinderen van de oorlog*), which included not just child survivors but also children of collaborators and victims of Japanese occupation of the Dutch East Indies. This literature also boosted a national preoccupation with the troubled history of the war and with its memory of both heroism and collaboration. Moreover, the rupture in Dutch Jewish life and the destruction of the prewar community have forced second-generation Dutch Jews to reimagine the Jewish past and reinvent their Jewish identity, as is apparent in the themes of conversion, messianism, dysfunctional families, and death in Friedman's 1996 short story collection, *De grauwe minaar* (*The Gray Lover*), which won the Aristeion Prize.

Because Friedman addresses the latent aftereffects of the Holocaust, she attracts an international audience who can readily empathize with the formative influence of inherited trauma and the rediscovery of Jewishness. Rather than the up-beat note of the Broadway production of *Anne Frank's diaries*, with its icon of a child who has not lost faith in humanity and whose diary does not record the horror of the camps, Friedman's writing joins a growing trend to voice the unspeakable and undiscussable presence in one's own family of the Holocaust past.

Bibliography

Primary Sources

Tralievader (*Nightfather*). 1991.
Twee koffers vol (*The Shovel and the Loom*). 1995.
De grauwe minaar (*The Gray Lover: Three Stories*). 1996.

Secondary Sources

Last, Dick Van Galen, and Rolf Wolfswinkel. *Anne Frank and After: Dutch Holocaust Literature in Historical Perspective*. Amsterdam: Amsterdam University Press, 1996.

Taylor, Jolanda Vanderwal. *A Family Occupation: Children of the War and the Memory of World War II in Dutch Literature of the 1980s*. Amsterdam: Amsterdam University Press, 1997.

Rebecca Camhi Fromer

(1927–)

DIANE MATZA

REBECCA CAMHI FROMER is a poet, playwright, Holocaust scholar, and co-founder of the Judah Magnes Museum in Berkeley, California. Educated primarily in New York and California, she has a master's degree in literature and linguistics from San Francisco State University.

Biography

When the Jews of Spain were expelled in 1492, they dispersed throughout the Ottoman world. In the most hospitable of these communities, Salonika and Monastir among them, Sephardi rabbis and writers produced extensive creative work, advancing the prominence of Sephardi culture. Salonika, in fact, became a distinctly Sephardi city, where even non-Jews spoke Ladino, fifteenth-century Spanish with a mixture of Turkish and Hebrew, and where the Sephardi liturgy replaced that of the indigenous Jewish community.

Fromer was born in New York in 1927 to parents from two great centers of Sephardi life. Her mother, Sarah Castro, of Salonika, Greece, and her father, Jack Camhi, of Monastir, Macedonia, immigrated to the United States separately after World War I. They met and married in New York, where Rebecca and her brother, Morris, were born into the Ladino-speaking community. The family later moved to Los Angeles, where they again lived in the Sephardi community. In this atmosphere, where pride of heritage affects the contours of individual identity, Fromer developed a distinctive artistic sensibility that infuses her illuminations of Sephardi experiences with an insider's knowledge of the rich, multicultural nature of a little-known Jewish culture. Fromer's devotion to interpreting the Sephardi experience of the Holocaust can be traced to her own family's history. In the crucible of family tragedy—in particular, the desperate but failed attempt of her father's brother-in-law to save his family in 1939—the Jewish injunction to remember and to memorialize the lost world of the Sephardim became Fromer's imperative.

Overview of Published Works

Fromer has always written extensively. Her many plays and poems attest to an eclectic interest in a broad range of subjects. However, it is Fromer's prose, and one anthologized play, that reveals her passionate commitment to illuminating individual Sephardi stories of the Holocaust. In a poignant, unpublished piece called "Para Ti" (For You), readers learn about the Auschwitz survivor Dario Gabbai's agonizing past (Gabbai is a close friend to Daniel Bennahmias, also an Auschwitz survivor, and both men are from Salonika), about Fromer's first intuition regarding his story, and how this intuition foretells her future as metaphorical midwife who "delivers" tales of the survivors' terror. In this capacity, she has written two books, *The Holocaust Odyssey of Daniel Bennahmias, Sonderkommando* (1993) and *The House by the Sea: A Portrait of the Holocaust in Greece* (1998), and co-authored, with Rene Molho, the memoir *They Say Diamonds Don't Burn: The Holocaust Experiences of Rene Molho of Solonika, Greece* (1994), and, with Lucille Eichengreen, *Rumkowski and the Orphans of Lodz* (2000). Numerous shorter works, including a story and play collected in my *Sephardic American Voices, Two Hundred Years of a Literary Legacy*, are based on extensive conversations with Holocaust survivors. As of 2002, Fromer's contributions to the literature of the Holocaust had been reviewed primarily in library journals and Jewish and Sephardi newsletters. Her interviewing method alone is worthy of wider attention by scholars and lay readers.

Fromer's writing is genuinely collaborative. The tools of her trade are not, however, the usual tape recorder, paper, and pencil of the oral historian. Instead, Fromer enacts the storytelling traditions of Sephardi culture. This means she participates in the survivor's narrative (here and there asking for clarification or expressing a personal reaction) and in the survivor's journey sometimes through reticence, other times through eloquence. In the story "Erika," for example, a survivor tells how she unwittingly participated in trading her sister's life for the life of another camp inmate. The first-person narrative, with its emphasis on direct address to an unnamed listener, firmly includes the reader in the storyteller's continuing moral agony. The one-act play, "The Inquiry," also based on survivors' recollections, mixes fiction and fact to construct a postwar conversation between an anonymous interrogator and Larissa, wife of the Salonikan traitor Albala (called Albino in the play), who is said to have collaborated from a position of awareness. Self-justification undercuts the truth of Larissa's testimony, and the interrogator's refusal to pronounce absolute judgment leaves her facing her own complicity in evil.

The Holocaust Odyssey of Daniel Bennahmias

In Fromer's full-length works, the collaborative technique works somewhat differently, because readers actually hear Fromer's voice. This is most apparent in *The Holocaust Odyssey of Daniel Bennahmias, Sonderkommando*, a work that is a genuine achievement in history and psychology. Fifteen years of friendship are the foundation for this complex and difficult project. In addition, three full years pass from the time Fromer actually begins the writing of *The Holocaust Odyssey* to its completion. Structurally, the book accents the moments of Danny's reluctance to continue the storytelling project. At times he struggles to reach beyond silence and face the past and its pain. The first four chapters dramatize the repeated shocks of the Italian, and then the German, invasion of Greece, the journey to Auschwitz, and the camp experiences prior to Danny's selection as a *Sonderkommando*, one assigned to empty and clean the crematoria. However, just as Danny is about to tackle the more devastatingly traumatic material, he finds he cannot proceed. Work on the book stalls.

Fromer is patient. Respecting the survivor's interior turmoil, she uses the hiatus strategically; her own voice takes over the narrative in the next chapter. With grace and clarity, she then raises some fundamental issues to understanding the Holocaust. The central question for so many Holocaust writers concerns language: How can mere words possibly describe the toll of the Holocaust's daily horrors? Though Fromer grants the arts a special role in this task, she agrees, as stated in *The Holocaust Odyssey*, with many other commentators that "the depths of anguish cannot be plumbed; not now, not ever. Not in this case" (Fromer, University of Alabama Press, p. 28). Still, Fromer persuades readers that this inability to accurately portray the Holocaust victim's suffering can, under no circumstances, be an impediment to speaking the most elementary truth: The Nazis were preoccupied with death. The victims were conditioned for it, and the perpetrators mastered it. Fromer continues to write, even though, at times, she must work alone. When she tells Danny that she is continuing the project without him, however, something happens. Perhaps it is a sudden desire for release that makes it possible for Danny to speak. Perhaps it is the survivor's mission, Danny quietly acknowledges, to challenge the revisionists; in any case, the impasse is breached.

In the concrete and specific testimony that follows, Danny describes the *Sonderkommando*'s grim day-to-day experiences—the disentangling of bodies, the removal of hair and gold, the cleaning and whitewashing of the gas chambers. This is Hitler's vision, in all its malign efficiency: a world without Jews and without Jewish memory. Readers also learn of the camp inmates' desperate challenge to this vision, the failed revolt at Auschwitz in the closing days of the war. More than four hundred inmates are swiftly executed in retaliation, but the confusion after this complex attempt allows Danny to mingle with other prisoners and escape the death sentence meant for all *Sonderkommandos*.

For Fromer, one purpose drives her work. This is to ensure that the "obscene slaughter of the Jews of Europe by the Nazis would not be the final word on the 'final solution' " (letter to Diane Matza). To be sure, desperate loss inevitably shadows the survivors. Danny, as is Elia Aelion in Fromer's *The House by the Sea*, is nearly overwhelmed by the total destruction of his centuries-old community and the almost complete disappearance of family, friends, and a distinct Jewish way of life. Both Danny's and Elia's survivor guilt is unmistakable. Fromer honors this reality by interweaving, within the text, an accurate representation of both the Holocaust's disturbing legacy and the survivor's deeply rooted desire for hope and continuity. One lovely example is the romantic spin Fromer gives the penultimate chapter of *The Holocaust Odyssey*. Here is her last line: Danny meets "the love of his life" when he works at the Joint Distribution Center helping refugees after the war (p. 111).

The House by the Sea

What readers encounter in *The House by the Sea* is Elia Aelion's memorial to friends and relatives who were swallowed by a world they could not imagine existed. Those people, like Daniel Bennahmias who could not or would not leave Salonika, were summarily deported; some others were betrayed in Athens by the traitorous Jew, Recanati (a reference to the Salonikan Recanti brothers, Costa and Pepo). In this poignant tribute to the past, Fromer describes the dramatically different circumstances facing the Jews of Greece. Occupied by the Germans, Salonika is a death trap. However, the Italians have never interfered with the freedom of the Jews living under their occupation. Thus, as long as the Italians govern Athens, Jews like Elia could live openly as Jews in the Atlas hotel. After the Italian defeat, hiding becomes imperative and especially difficult for Salonikans, whose highly distinctive Greek accents immediately mark them as Jews. This "disability" means that Elia and more than a dozen compatriots could not use their ration cards, thus making them more dependent on the support and protection of various Athenian Christians. During one harrowing period, a sympathetic "madam" hides Elia and several friends in a "pleasure house" frequented by German soldiers. Yet this suffering seems so completely inconsequential to Elia when he faces his postwar losses. Devastated by the deaths of family and friends, he is prevented for a while from marrying his fiancée, Rachel, and moving on with his life. Rachel does not press him but urges him to return to Salonika, where he can face his "great but mistaken notion that [he] lived in an ordered, safe, and relatively sane world" (Fromer, San Francisco Mercury House, p. 21). Fromer's and Elia's literary collaboration effectively renders that idealized life and the reality that destroyed it.

Like many other Holocaust scholars, Fromer insists that survivors who write Holocaust history implicitly challenge the Nazis' planned erasure of an entire people. Their vivid recollections of places and people memorialize a world that no longer exists. Not only that, by concentrating on tales of compassion in a world where violence and betrayal had become expected, Daniel Bennahmias and Elia Aelion affirm that Nazism's brutality did not so thoroughly dehumanize its victims. Of course, Danny in Auschwitz and even Elia, who hid in Athens, learned far too quickly that their former stable world was just a dream. Yet in these narratives, both men demand a place for simple decency. In *The House by the Sea*, Elia describes numerous acts of kindness and courage by Greek and Italian Christians. These acts show that the Jews were not universally reviled, that not everyone bowed so readily to the Nazis. In Danny's account, the defiant heroism of the *Sonderkommando* Albert Errera, who is killed after striking his SS guards with a shovel, the *Sonderkommandos*' efforts to protect one another, and the prisoners' revolt speak to a resilient humanity among the victims. Fromer contends, too, that Danny's decades-long preoccupation with the moral implications of his experience is the telling measure of his own empathy and integrity.

Toward the end of *The Holocaust Odyssey*, Danny tells the following story. One of the first Greek returnees from Auschwitz is a man named Bati. Just as the Jews in Athens are emerging from hiding, Bati reenters the city. When he tells the truth of the crematoria, no one believes him, and he spends two weeks locked up as a madman. This is hardly a unique occurrence, and often it was the price of speaking the truth at that time.

It is not difficult to imagine that once Danny became used to silence, each passing year made it even more difficult to communicate his experiences. Fromer's primary contribution to Holocaust literature has been to bring so much heretofore unrecorded testimony such as Danny's to light. To make this particular work as complete as possible, Fromer frames *The Holocaust Odyssey* with an introduction by historian of Greek Jewry, Steven Bowman. She also includes, in both *The Holocaust Odyssey* and *The House by the Sea*, pertinent documents and photographs from the pre- and postwar periods. The final effect is to create a comprehensive account that compels the reader toward identification not only with individuals but also with a fully realized portrait of a Sephardi world confronting the shocking upheaval of war.

Bibliography

Primary Sources

The Holocaust Odyssey of Daniel Bennahmias, Sonderkommando. 1993.

They Say Diamonds Don't Burn: The Holocaust Experiences of Rene Molho of Salonika, Greece. 1994. (co-written with Rene Molho)

"The Inquiry" and "Erica." 1996.

The House by the Sea: A Portrait of the Holocaust in Greece. 1998.

Rumkowski and the Orphans of Lodz. 2000. (co-written with Lucille Eichengreen)

Secondary Sources

Reviews

The following critique and response address Rebecca Fromer's method in *The Holocaust Odyssey*.

Katzmann, Pat. "Memoir of Becoming the 'Living Dead.' " *San Francisco Chronicle Book Review* (June 12, 1994). Also see Rebecca Fromer's response in the June 19th edition of the *Book Review*, p. 5.

Altsech, Moses B., and Y. Afrieronon. "Greek Jews and the Holocaust." *Journal of the Hellenic Diaspora* 23, no. 2 (1997): 29–60.

Bedford, Robert. *An Introduction to Literature on the Holocaust in Greece*. New York: Sephardic Historical Committee, 1994.

Bowman, Steven. *Jews in Wartime Greece*. New York: Conference on Jewish Social Studies, 1986.

Fleischer, Hagen. *Greek Jewry and Nazi Germany: The Holocaust and Its Antecedents*. Athens: Gavrielides Publishing, 1995.

Kabelli, Isaac. "The Resistance of the Greek Jews." *YIVO Annual of the Jewish Social Sciences* 8 (1953): 281–288.

Kampanellis, Iakovos. *Mauthausen*. Athens: Kendros Publishers, 1995.

Levy, Dr. Isaac Jack. *And the World Stood Silent: Sephardic Poetry of the Holocaust*. Chicago: University of Illinois Press, 1989.

Matsas, Dr. Michael. *The Illusion of Safety: The Story of Greek Jews During the Second World War*. Athens: Pella Publications, 1997.

Mazower, Mark. *Inside Hitler's Greece: The Experience of Occupation, 1941–1944*. New Haven, CT: Yale University Press, 1993.

Nahon, Dr. Marco. *Birkenau, The Camp of Death*. Tuscaloosa: University of Alabama Press, 1989.

Sevillas, Errikos. *Athens-Auschwitz*. Athens: Lycabettus Press, 1983.

LADISLAV FUKS

(1923–1994)

DAVID MESHER

LADISLAV FUKS WAS BORN in Prague on 24 September 1923. His surname indicates that he was probably an ethnic German whose ancestors came from the so-called Sudetenland, whose inclusion in Third Reich was demanded by Adolf Hitler—a demand appeased by the European powers in the Munich Pact of 1936. Fuks's personal reaction to the murder of Jewish friends and the fate of Prague Jews was a lifelong study of things Jewish and a writing career largely devoted to portrayals of the Holocaust; yet, as a Gentile, his emotional distance from those events helped to produce his distinctively quirky fictions about the destruction of European Jewry.

After the war, Fuks was a student of philosophy and psychology at Charles University in Prague, receiving his doctorate in 1949. He was then employed in the paper industry until 1956, when he began working at the Czech Institute for Preservation of Historical Monuments. While there, Fuks published his first book, a nonfiction study of the historical Kynzvart Chateaux. In 1959 Fuks moved on to a position at the National Gallery, which he left in 1963, after the success of his first novel, *Mr. Theodore Mundstock* (1963), to devote himself to writing full time.

Mundstock was a success, both in Czechoslovakia and abroad. At home, it appeared at a time when Jewish themes had become popular in Czech literature, and its relatively rapid publication in English translation suggests the interest with which the novel was greeted in Britain and the United States. A decade later, in his seminal study *The Holocaust and the Literary Imagination* (1975), Lawrence Langer discussed *Mundstock* at greater length than any other work of Holocaust literature. Shortly thereafter, however, Sidra DeKoven Ezrahi, in *By Words Alone* (1980), termed *Mundstock* "the consummate execution of the form" of the "survivor-novel" (p. 87)—apparently mistaking Fuks for a Jewish survivor of the Holocaust. Thus a writer, who in his native Czechoslovakia gained attention specifically for his Czech viewpoint on the Jewish question, has been treated as exceptional abroad, as well as misidentified as unassuming elderly Jew.

Fuks's first completed work of fiction was probably *Mí cernovlasí bratri* (My Dark-Haired Brothers), which he only published in 1964 after the success of *Mr. Theodore Mundstock*. The semiautobiographical narrator of the stories—like Fuks, the son of a police official—describes the suffering of his Jewish classmates at the hands of an antisemitic teacher during the prewar German occupation of Prague. Though these stories also operate as a metaphor for the Holocaust, their realistic presentation marks them as journeyman efforts in the author's remarkable development of a surreal, or perhaps magically real, re-creation of the Jewish experience in German-occupied Prague.

Mr. Theodore Mundstock

It is all the more surprising, then, that Fuks found his characteristic voice so early in the novel *Mr. Theodore Mundstock*, his first published fiction. *Mundstock* begins shortly before the 1942 assassination of Reinhard Heydrich, chief of Reich security who had been sent by Hitler to ruthlessly suppress any opposition to the German occupation of Bohemia and Moravia, and ends with the mass transportations that same year, when more than half of Prague's Jews were removed, many to the "model" concentration camp at Theresienstadt (Terezin), before eventually being sent on to death camps. Yet against the background of such historical data, Fuks creates a surreal foreground in which his protagonist, an unassuming elderly man formerly employed as a clerk in a string and rope business, can act out delusions of salvation in the midst of the Holocaust.

Those delusions are evident, if not entirely clear, from the first page of the novel, when Mundstock returns to his apartment where his shadow retrieves the mail. A few paragraphs later, Mundstock is greeted by his pet "creature," which he thinks is a chicken, but which turns out to be a pigeon. Later in the novel, Mundstock walks through the city while under the influence of a strong sedative, endures bouts of hallucination and insanity, imagines himself a savior-like prophet of the Jews, and even attempts suicide (only to be saved, ironically, by Gestapo agents investigating the attack on Heydrich).

Though eyewitness accounts of Holocaust victims sometimes invoke a surreal atmosphere, surrealism in Holocaust literature is often decried as undercutting the horrible reality of the destruction of European Jewry. In *Mr. Theodore Mundstock*, however, surrealism is only an expression of the devastating stress under which Jews lived at the time. Mundstock can trace his shadow's separate identity, for example, to the day when he was fired by a brutal, uniformed German, from the job he had held since his youth. Outside the office, in the rain, the devastated Mundstock weeps until he feels that "something inside him *split in two*." Then, "from the rain and tears at his feet there rose a *shadow*" (p. 75). Calling the shadow "Mon" reinforces the notion of a split personality or an alter-ego, as if the name were formed from the first part of Mundstock. It is the shadow's role to keep Mundstock in touch with reality, whether the subject is the ingredients for blancmange or the likelihood of transports, while Mundstock seeks escape through the rejection or falsification of reality with lies, dreams, hallucinations, and attempted suicide.

This seems to change when Mundstock sets himself the task of training to survive the Holocaust. He convinces himself that "method and a practical approach could save him" (p. 111), and not just him, but all Jews. So he asks himself, "Who could survive the concentration camp?" His answer is, "The man who thoroughly, properly prepared for everything in a logically planned manner" (p. 112). In fact, this is no change at all, but instead Mundstock's crowning fantasy. From the relative safety of Prague, Mundstock imaginatively follows his former coworker Vohrjahren onto the train and into the camp. Mundstock practices carrying a heavy suitcase to devise the best method for changing hands; he reflects on forced marches in ranks and realizes that the inner positions are less subject to abuse. He even tries to pick a fight with a butcher to test out his theory on the efficacy of seeming to have a few teeth knocked out in curtailing an attack, and asks the baker—incredibly—for a job next to the ovens, in order to get used to their heat.

Though Mundstock tells others, "The whole secret, you see, is not to have any illusions. If you go about with your eyes open there's nothing to be afraid of" (p. 162), he is self-deluded until the very end. Walking to the assembly point for transportation in Prague, and carefully switching his suitcase from hand to hand according to his method, in a final irony Mundstock is run down and killed by a military truck while crossing the final street. Fuks could not have allowed his protagonist to test out his preparations for survival in practice, because of the resulting implication that victims who did not survive as long as Mundstock were themselves at fault for not having prepared better. Simply put, the vast majority of Jews were not in control of their own destinies, and neither was Mundstock, his delusions notwithstanding.

The Cremator

Karel Kopfkringl, the protagonist of Fuks's *The Cremator* (1967), his only other work to be translated into English, could be Mundstock's mirror image. Both are quiet, unassuming, introspective men, and both novels deal primarily with their characters' inner lives. Kopfkringl is an official at the Prague crematorium, a family man living a comfortable life, thanks in part to the support of his wife's aunt. But where Mundstock fancies himself a savior of the persecuted and powerless, Kopfkringl's secret world is considerably more sinister, for Kopfkringl becomes a murderer. At first, Fuks's protagonist is merely a worshipper of death, who obsessively reads a Tibetan book of the dead, religiously tends his crematorium, and as Sonia I. Kanikova shows, "views people primarily as corpses awaiting their burning ceremony" (p. 2947). Under the influence of his friend Willi Reinke, however, who is a member of the Sudeten German National Party, Kopfkringl begins to see Lakmé, his "beautiful, blackhaired" wife (London and New York: Marion Boyars, 1984, p. 7), and their sixteen-year-old son, Mili, as liabilities because of their "Jewish blood." Willi plays Mephistopheles to Kopfkringl's Faust, offering, in the Aryan mythology of National Socialism, a historical correlative for Karel's worship of death; Sonia Kanikova has traced the chronological development of Nazi ideology in arguing that the parallel structures of Tibetan and Nazi myths in the novel have their antecedents in an Aryan messianism. Kopfkringl, while a monster, is more an opportunist than a Nazi. He bashes in his own son's head with an iron rod in the basement of the crematorium, while wearing his ethnic German outfit of "high black boots and Tyrolean hat with the braid and the feather," but then hides the murder by cremating Mili's body with the corpse of an SS officer. "There's no difference in human ashes," Kopfkringl thinks. "It doesn't matter whether they are the ashes of a German Bannführer or of a quarter-Jewish boy" (p. 166). In a bizarre twist, that sentiment of postmortem egalitarianism separates Kopfkringl from Willi, whose own worship of death takes the form of Nazi racial fanaticism.

In the special calculus of Fuks's Holocaust, where no evil deed goes unrewarded, Kopfkringl prospers after the murders, becoming the director of the crematorium, and is asked to consult with a high German official about "an experiment which was important to them" involving "gas furnaces for the future" (pp. 168–169). The novel ends with a touch of the surreal: Kopfkringl imagines himself as the reincarnation of the Dalai Lama; begins to detail plans for the murder of his daughter, Zina; and is finally led away by "three men in white," to be institutionalized.

Even in the irony of its ending, *The Cremator* seems to have been created with *Mundstock* in mind. The characters of Mundstock, Kopfkringl, and Willi Reinke are all affected by what is, for Fuks, the destructive madness of messianism. Mundstock dies before his "method" can save (or harm) anyone, Willi's Thousand Year Reich collapses in 1945, and the insane Kopfkringl, looking out from the window of a hospital train at end of the war, takes credit for all survivors: "Happy mankind. I've delivered it. There certainly won't be any more persecution, injustice or suffering in the world. No more, for certain, not even for horses . . . Gentlemen, the new order is now beginning" (p. 176).

For Fuks and his fellow Czechs, that "new order" would involve Communist rule. After the ruthless Soviet suppression of the liberalizing "Prague Spring" in 1968, Fuks seemed to become, in his next three novels, something of an apologist for the Communist regime, before returning to more familiar themes in his last works. Stagings of two of his books were produced for Czech television, and four of his works have been made into films, including *The Cremator* (*Spalovac mrtvol,* 1968, directed by Jurai Herz) and a 1985 Polish adaptation of *Mr. Theodore Mundstock*, directed by Waldemar Dziki and titled *Kartka z podrozy* (Postcards from a Journey). Lavislav Fuks died in Prague on 19 August 1994.

Bibliography

Primary Sources

Zámek Kynzvart; historie a prítomnost (Kynzvart Chateaux: History and Presence). 1958.

Pan Theodor Mundstock (*Mr. Theodore Mundstock*). 1963.

Mí cernovlasí bratri (My Dark-Haired Brothers). 1964.

Variace pro temnou strunu (Variation for a Sombre Spring). 1966.

Spalovac mrtvol (*The Cremator*). 1967.

Smrt morcete (Death of the Guinea Pig). 1969.

Myši Natalie Mooshabrové (Natalie Mooshaber's Mice). 1970.

Pribeh kriminálního rady (Story of an Inspector-in-Chief). 1971.

Neboztíci na bále (Deceaseds at the Ball). 1972.

Oslovení z tmy (A Voice from the Dark). 1972.

Navrat a zitného pole (Return from the Rye Field). 1974.

Pasácek z doliny (Rider from the Dale). 1977.

Kristálový pantoflícek (The Crystal Slipper). 1978.

Obraz Martina Blaskowitze (The Picture of Martin Blaskowtiz). 1980.

Vévodkyne a kucharka (The Duchess and the Cook). 1983.

Cesta do zaslíbené zeme a jiné povídky (Journey to the Promised Land and Other Stories). 1991.

Let' myšlenko na zlatých krídlech vánku (Flight: Thought on the Golden Wings of the Breeze). 1994.

Moje zrcadlo: vzpomínky, dojmy, ohlédnutí (My Mirror: Memories, Impressions, and Reflections). 1995.

Secondary Sources

Ezrahi, Sidra DeKoven. *By Words Alone: The Holocaust in Literature*. Chicago: University of Chicago Press, 1980.

Kanikova, Sonia I. "The Jews in the Works of Ladislav Fuks." In *Remembering for the Future*. Edited by Yehuda Bauer, et al. Oxford: Pergamon Press, 1989, pp. 2946–2957.

Langer, Lawrence L. *The Holocaust and the Literary Imagination*. New Haven: Yale University Press. 1975.

Skvorecky, Josef. "Some Contemporary Czech Prose Writers." *Novel: A Forum on Fiction* 4 (1970): 5–13.

Slaba, Dora. "Ladislav Fuks." *Panorama* 7 (1985): 29–49.

Winner, T. G. "Czech Avantgarde Prose of the Sixties." *Mosaic* 6.4 (1973): 107–119.

———."Mythic and Modern Elements in the Art of Ladislav Fuks: *Natalia Mooshaber's Mice*." In *Fiction and Drama in Eastern and Southeastern Europe: Evolution and Experiment in the Postwar Period.* Edited by Henrik Brinbaum and Thomas Eekman. Columbus, Ohio: Slavica Publishers, 1980, pp. 443–461.

ROMAIN GARY
(1914–1980)

JUDITH KAUFFMANN
(Translated by Ruth Morris)

ROMAIN GARY'S LIFE is an example of true fiction, where reality and imagination meld, giving rise to a fictitious world more authentic than the concrete universe of bare facts and figures.

The Bare Facts

Born Roman Kacew in 1914 in Moscow to a Jewish mother with Lithuanian roots, Nina Owczinski, Romain Gary never knew the identity of his real father. In 1927, after a Russian-Polish childhood (Moscow, Vilnius, Warsaw), he and his mother made their home in France, in Nice. In 1935 he acquired French nationality. He had a three-part career: as soldier, diplomat, and writer. During World War II he served as a navigator-bomber in the Free French Air Force, was made a Companion of the Liberation, and was decorated several times. From 1946 to 1961 he served as a high-ranking French career diplomat (Sofia, Berne, La Paz, New York as a spokesman at the United Nations, and Los Angeles). In 1963 he married actress Jean Seberg by whom he had a son, Diego. From the mid-1960s onward, after several forays into the film-making world, he focused largely on writing, settling down for good in Paris.

The author of some thirty books, mainly fiction, Gary is a best-selling author. After being awarded France's Critics' Prize for his first novel, *Education européenne* (*A European Education*, 1945), he has, uniquely, twice been the laureate of the Goncourt, the most prestigious French literary prize, for *Les Racines du ciel* (*The Roots of Heaven*, 1956) and *La Vie devant soi* (*The Life before Us*, 1975). The latter was the culmination of a new career on which he embarked in 1972 under the pseudonym of Emile Ajar, in order to escape his public persona and the indifference of "lazy critics" who, in his view, did not pay his books the attention they deserved. When Ajar had to show up, for public relations purposes, one of Gary's relatives played the part. Though Gary felt he was losing control of the situation, the secret of this hoax did not emerge until six months after his suicide in 1980.

The True Fiction

A man of a thousand faces, Gary enjoyed inventing stories and facts. Who was his father? The famous Russian silent movie actor, Ivan Mosjoukine, as he sometimes claimed, ostentatiously exploiting a certain degree of physical resemblance, or Lejba Kacew, his mother's ex-husband, whom he scarcely knew. The reason he ultimately acknowledged this filial relationship was because of a "particularly revolting detail" in this man's tragic end at Auschwitz. Lejba Kacew was said to have "dropped dead of fright" a few steps away from the gas chamber: "The man who died in this way was a perfect stranger to me, but that day he became my father for ever" (*Promise at Dawn*, New York: Harper, 1961, p. 107). This deportee's extreme fragility made him stand out amidst the anonymous crowd who experienced mass extermination. For Gary, the "epitome of the minority figure," whose books address the topic of "irreversible, overwhelming weakness" (*La nuit sera calme* [The Night Will Be Calm], Paris: Gallimard-Folio, 1976, p. 102), solidarity with all forms of marginality, exclusion, and persecution is a deep-seated, gut reaction. In Gary's life, this essential affinity, stronger than reality, is a substitute for kith and kin. Refusing to be conditioned by natural filiation and circumstances, he goes against the objective appearance of the bare facts and opts for the inward truth—the subjective authenticity—of personal experience.

Inventing one's own patronym is a way of escaping genealogical constraints. In Russian, the pseudonyms Gary and Ajar are associated with a fire motif: the former is the imperative of the verb "to burn," while the latter means "embers." By deliberately making a covert link between his persona and the Promethean hero snatching life from fire, the artist suggests he plays a dangerous game, at risk of burning himself. Although man never has the upper hand in the struggle against his mortal condition, by choosing the circumstances of his death, he is able to assert a certain degree of control—however derisory—over his fate. Among all the possible reasons for suicide, this extreme challenge is by no means the least plausible hypothesis. Gary concludes his farewell note with a posthumous smile: "I have finally expressed myself completely" (Bona, p. 440). He finishes his confession about the Ajar mystery with a clown's pirouette: "I have had a good time. Goodbye and thank you" (*Vie et mort d'Emile Ajar* [Life and Death of Emile Ajar], Paris: Gallimard, 1981, p. 43). In his life, or rather through his death, he embodies black humor, that form of self-aggressive derision where, having the last provocative word, one melds laughter and death.

Resisting/Writing

Two categories of texts may be identified in Gary's body of work on the Nazi period. His first and last novels, *Education européenne* and *Les Cerfs-volants* (The Kites, 1980), fall into the category of books focusing on the struggle against Nazi barbarity from the perspective of resistance to oppression. The primary topics of these stories—racial persecution and exclusion—underlie this entire body of work. *La Danse de Gengis Cohn* (*The Dance of Genghis Cohn*, 1967), a disturbing, aggressive novel that relates the posthumous relationship of a deportee with his SS hangman, reveals the other face of Nazism—the *Shoah* and its radically new forms of horror.

The Spirit of Resistance or the Power of Imagination

Education européenne and *Les Cerfs-volants* share a common structure: the first experiences of the adult world and love of two adolescents, Janek the Polish partisan, and Ludo the French Resistance fighter.

Written between dogfights, between September 1940 and the fall of 1943, *Education européenne* made a big splash in England and in France, rated as one of the first—and according to Sartre, perhaps one of the best—works of fiction to be published about the Resistance.

The novel has a mirror-like structure, presenting the author of a book, whose title (also *A European Education*) has an ironic dimension, explained as follows: "A European education . . . means bombs, massacres, hostages who are shot, men forced to live in holes, like animals" (*A European Education*, New York: Simon and Schuster, 1960, p. 76). The fictive novelist reads one of his tragic and pathetic tales to his companions, while a partisan is dying, but fiction transforms the banal and sordid death of the tuberculosis sufferer into a heroic struggle. Gary argues fiction is distinguished from falsehood by "the difference between authentic creation and the skill to disguise and misrepresent reality" (p. 322). As "pirates of the Unreal" (*La nuit sera calme*, p. 323), realist writers rewrite history while searching for a more profound truth.

The book, which adopts the fairly loose framework of a realistic chronicle about the underground war, tells some significant stories and includes a number of symbolic portraits, including the child martyr and the invincible leader. Wunderkind, the Jewish boy prodigy, uses his violin to wrest the world out of chaos: "In the beginning hatred died, and with the first chords hunger, scorn and ugliness were fled, like larvae of the dark whom light destroys and kills" (*A European Education*, p. 161). Nadejda, the partisan, is invulnerable because as pure fiction he exists only through the words of an elusive, fugitive rumor. While music makes it possible to wipe out the horror of the world, imagination, that "fragment of poetry" (*La nuit sera calme*, p. 229) encourages resistance by rising above the totalitarian constraints of the concrete world in order to achieve the impossible.

Gary's last novel, *Les Cerfs-volants*, provides an original metaphor for men's fight for freedom: kites made by young Ludo's uncle. In their varied designs, these toys act as a symbolic response to events. An example is the yellow stars, "the seven stars of shame," which sent their protest soaring into the July 1942 skies at the roundup of Jews at the Paris Vélodrome d'Hiver. These childish ephemeral objects represent "life like a relay race in which each of us, before falling in, must carry further the challenge of being a man" (*Promise at Dawn*, p. 246).

As books that relate a number of little stories taken from a broader chapter of history, these novels also reflect society's shifting perception of events. The historian Henry Rousso has defined a four-phase chronology of the "Vichy syndrome" (*Vichy, un passé qui ne passe pas*, Folio-Histoire, 1996, pp. 22–35). After the years of "unfinished mourning," a period of "repression" began around the mid-1950s, encouraging people to forget the widespread collaboration with the Germans and endorsing a portrayal of occupied France in which the population was aligned with the Resistance. This was followed at the beginning of the 1970s by the "broken mirror" phase, with the crumbling of wartime myths and the uprising of various forms of revisionism. Since then, an "obsessive memory" has focused on those dark years.

The somewhat Manichean view of the immediate postwar period, "this routine which involves reducing Germany to its crimes and France to its heroes" (*Les Cerfs-volants*, p. 269), is replaced by an ambivalent perspective, which emerged in the course of the 1970s and 1980s, when new and ambiguous representations arose of the occupation years: "Enough of black and white. The only thing that's human is gray" (p. 332), as one of the characters puts it.

The elliptical dedication, "To memory," marks the novel as a locale for the collective expression of fighting against weakness and despair, and a place for recording the individual traces of the heroes of this revolt. The book, as a symbolic "lieu de mémoire" (locus of memory), is at once a "shelter" (*A European Education*, p. 65) for endangered values and a verbal memorial for dead heroes.

The Power of Humor

With *La Danse de Gengis Cohn*, a change in perspective comes about. After a visit to Warsaw in 1966, an extremely violent experience that was, for him, a "descent into hell" (Huston, p. 68), Gary launched the picaresque adventures of Genghis Cohn, a character with whom he frequently identifies.

The book was favorably received in the United States, in contrast to lukewarm reactions in France, where its deliberate blasphemous excesses seemed unacceptable. (It would be another thirty years until the book was published in paperback.) Gary deliberately seeks to shock. In order to describe the horrors of Nazi persecution, he makes use of sexual metaphors, and he unflinchingly assigns blame for the extermination of the Jews to the Western Christian world, by showing how antisemitic Nazi ideology was steeped in what historian Jules Isaac calls "the teaching of contempt."

In the 1980s, the world of academe began to reconsider the book critically. *La Danse* was largely viewed as a premonitory symptom of the split personality and identity crisis to which the Ajar riddle gave rise (Huston, Bayard, Mehlman, Robin). For the scholars working on literary representations of the *Shoah* (Wardi, Klein, Dayan Rosenman, Rinn), the importance of *La Danse de Gengis Cohn* lies in the way it addresses the problem of the aesthetic treatment of evil and the trivialization of horror.

By using the combined effect of the comic, whose satirical and ironic tones entail an unusual view of things, and the unreal—the hero is a ghost untroubled by excesses or incongruities of any kind—the writer establishes procedures of distancing and connivance that promote an oblique and demystifying way of looking at the world and people. Thus is disclosed Western culture's repressed side, including its violent roots and the shocking ways that suffering is exploited by art.

Genghis Cohn, alias Moishe Cohn, a comedian on the Yiddish burlesque circuit, famous for his savage humor in Berlin, Warsaw, and Auschwitz, has for some twenty years been the dybbuk of his executioner, "Hauptjudenfresser" Schatz. The Hebrew root of dybbuk means "to stick." In Jewish folklore, a dybbuk is "an evil spirit, a demon who . . . gets within you and starts to reign and lord it over you, as master" (*The Dance of Genghis Cohn*, p. 67). Demon of a dead person, it possesses the body of a living person, most often in order to seek revenge for an unjust death. When the former SS officer opens his mouth, you never know who is speaking, the Nazi hangman or his Jewish victim.

Now a police commissioner, Schatz ("Honey" in German) is investigating a series of mysterious deaths. In a remake of *Lady Chatterley's Lover*, Baroness von Pritwitz is suspected, together with her accomplice, the gamekeeper Florian, of murdering her impotent lovers. Gary proposed some symbolic readings of his novel: Lily incarnates a ravening Germany, side by side with Florian, "German Death, impassive and fiendish," while Schatz, possessed by his Jew, exhibits German bad conscience, weighed down by six million corpses. Or maybe Lily, confronting Genghis her impassioned lover, represents humanity as a nymphomaniac in search of the Absolute, while the world is overwhelmed by obscene violence.

The nickname of Genghis Cohn couples extremely discordant notions in an explosive fusion/tension relationship: the punning bisociation of bloody barbarian Genghis (Khan) with Cohn the scapegoat brings to a climax the macabre encounter of dead and alive. The heterogeneous combination of the pun speaks at once of revolt and the impossibility of such revolt. What can a naked man achieve as he faces the firing squad? He associates a trivial insulting gesture with the verbal obscenity—"*Kush mir in tokhes!*" (p. 25)—in one of those innovative but ineffective outbursts of Jewish humor, which Genghis defines as "a sort of unarmed aggression."

Elsewhere, the condemned comedian, who wishes to survive in posterity by virtue of a last *khokhme* (joke), proposes a wisecrack on culture. While standing on the edge of the collective grave, he offers this final witticism: "Culture is when mothers who are holding their babies in their arms are excused from digging their own graves before being shot" (p. 53). By shifting attention away from the mass execution, the victim keeps the drama at distance, thereby making it possible to "defuse the real" (*Promise at Dawn*, p. 160), and to short-circuit violent emotional reactions. Because of Cohn's refusal to adopt a masochistic accommodating attitude, his witticism becomes "a declaration of dignity, an affirmation of man's superiority over what happens to him" (p. 160). The verbal self-defense helps to demystify the concept of redemptive sacrifice dear to the Western world. At the same time, it highlights the (apparently) chivalrous behavior of a gentleman protecting the weak and describes, without any hint of protest, the collective martyrdom of the victims and their implied participation in the process of their own slaying. This powerful condensed definition of culture summarizes the perverted alternating between violence and civility and the abject proximity of the executioner to his victims, which characterizes SS barbarity.

The description of culture—the digest of a society's dominant values that are often regarded as sacred—becomes the instrument of indirect and subtle criticism of the people who, beneath a mask of morality, conceal barbarity behind human faces. Genghis Cohn is a clown, one of the "sacred fools who are the only ones able to make us feel what is sacred, what is sham" (*La nuit sera calme*, p. 242).

Black humor, a tried and tested tactics for resisting oppression, is practiced by persecuted minorities, often disrupts the boundaries of good taste, and is a major constituent of Jewish humor, but a recurrent image, which provides a counterpoint to Genghis Cohn's black symphony, takes us even further. There is a famous photograph taken in a Polish ghetto of a laughing German soldier pulling the beard of an elderly Hasid who "is also laughing" (*The Dance of Genghis Cohn*, p. 136). In the novel's final carnivalesque turmoil, the "immortal" smile of the old man, being dragged along by his beard "toward posterity," attracts the observation: "we must be approaching eternity" (p. 189). Counterbalancing the hangman's cynical triumph, the old man's smile opens the door to the absolute. Novelist and philosopher Michel Tournier advanced the concept of *rire blanc* (white laughter) for the laughter that accompanies, beyond the blasphemies of black humor, "the emergence of the absolute in the midst of the fabric of relativity in which we live" (*Le vent Paraclet*, Paris: Gallimard-Folio, 1977, p. 198). Mankind confronts the abyss—infinity or nothingness—with this paradoxical laughter.

A Story of Love and Fury

The final picture in the novel shows Genghis Cohn, bent double under the weight of "His heavy Cross" at the intersection of the horizontal *comic* and the vertical *cosmic*. Instead of the figure of the Christlike martyr set for posterity in the immobility of a monument, he embodies a new metamorphosis of the eternal pariah, the comic Jew wandering forever on his *via dolorosa*, "indestructible" (*The Dance of Genghis Cohn*, p. 192). A grotesque and pathetic hero of a story of fury and of love—fury against the violence that human beings perpetrate on other human beings, and love for humanity—*Genghis Cohn* is one of those men "who know how to get beyond hatred . . . to the place where there is laughter" (*La nuit sera calme*, pp. 128–129).

Bibliography

Primary sources

Education européenne (*The Forest of Anger* and *A European Education*). 1945.
Tulipe (Tulip). 1946.
Le Grand Vestiaire (*The Company of Men*). 1949.
Les Couleurs du jour (*The Colours of the Day*). 1952.
Les Racines du ciel (*The Roots of Heaven*). 1956.
L'Homme à la colombe (The Man with the Dove). 1958.
La Promesse de l'aube (*Promise at Dawn*). 1960.
Les oiseaux vont mourir au Pérou (*Hissing Tales*). 1962.
Lady L. (*Lady L.*). 1963.
Pour Sganarelle. Recherche d'un roman et d'un personnage (For Sganarelle: Research on a Novel and a Character). 1965.
Les Mangeurs d'étoiles (*The Talent Scout*). 1966.
La Danse de Gengis Cohn (*The Dance of Genghis Cohn*). 1967.
La Tête coupable (*Guilty Head*). 1968.
Adieu Gary Cooper (*The Ski Bum*). 1969.
Chien blanc (*White Dog*). 1970.
Europa (Europa). 1972.
Les Enchanteurs (*The Enchanters*). 1973.
La nuit sera calme (The Night Will Be Calm). 1974.
Les Têtes de Stéphanie (*Flight to Allah*). 1974.
Gros-Câlin. 1974.
Au-delà de cette limite, votre ticket n'est plus valable (*Your Ticket Is No Longer Valid*). 1975.
La Vie devant soi (*The Life before Us*). 1975.
Pseudo (Pseudo). 1976.
Clair de femme. 1977.
Charge d'âme (*The Gasp*). 1978.
L'Angoisse du roi Salomon (*King Solomon*). 1979.
Les Cerfs-volants (The Kites). 1980.
Vie et mort d'Emile Ajar (Life and Death of Emile Ajar). 1981.

Secondary Sources

Bayard, Pierre. *Il était deux fois romain Gary*. Paris: PUF, 1990.

Bellos, David. "Ce que Momo veut dire. La mémoire de la *Shoah* dans *La vie devant soi* de Romain Gary." *Perspectives*, no. 6 (1999): 55–66.

Bona, Dominique. *Romain Gary*. Paris: Mercure de France, 1987.

Catelain, Valérie. "*Education européenne*: de la conscience de soi à l'universel: réalité ou utopie?" *Roman 20/50*, 32 (December 2001).

Catonné, Jean-Marie. *Romain Gary / Emile Ajar*. Paris: Belfond, 1990.

Dayan Rosenman, Anny. "Des cerfs-volants jaunes en forme d'étoiles: la judéité paradoxale de Romain Gary." *Les Temps modernes*, no. 568 (November 1993): 30–54.

Douzou, Catherine. "Récit et récits dans *Education européenne*." *Roman 20/50*, 32 (December 2001).

Huston, Nancy. *Tombeau pour Romain Gary*. Arles: Actes Sud, 1995.

Kauffmann, Judith. "La danse de Romain Gary ou Gengis Cohn et la valse-horà des mythes de l'Occident." *Etudes littéraires* 17, no. 1 (April 1984): 71–94.

———. "Gallows Humor and Jewish Humor: A Reading of *The Dance of Genghis Cohn* by Romain Gary." In *Jewish Humor*. Edited by Avner Ziv. Tel Aviv: Papyrus, 1986.

———. "Littérature, humour et expérience des limites. Réflexions sur *La danse de Gengis Cohn* de Romain Gary." *Humoresques*, no. 9 (1998): 101–112.

———. "Horrible, humour noir, rire blanc: quelques réflexions sur la représentation littéraire de la *Shoah*." *Humoresques*, no. 14 (June 2001): 207–224.

Klein, Judith. *Literatur und Genozid. Darstellung der nationalsozialistischen Massenvernichtung in der französischen Literatur*. Wien-Köln-Weimar: Böhlau Verlag, 1992.

Lecarme, Jacques. "Relire *Education européenne* (1945) à travers *Les Cerfs-volants* (1980)." *Roman 20/50*, 32 (December 2001).

Mehlman, Jeffrey. "On the Holocaust Comedies of 'Emile Ajar.' " In *Auschwitz and After: Race, Culture and the "Jewish Question in France*." Edited by Lawrence D. Kritzman. New York: Routledge, 1995.

Östman, Anne-Charlotte. "*Education européenne* et la résistance à la réalité." *Roman 20/50*, 32 (December 2001).

Pfeffercorn, Eli. "The Art of Survival, Romain Gary's *The Dance of Genghis Cohn*." *Modern Language Studies 10*, no. 3 (fall 1980).

Renard, Paul. "Fourmis et rossignols: *Education européenne* d'une version à l'autre." *Roman 20/50*, 32 (December 2001).

Rinn, Michaël. *Les récits du Génocide. Sémiotique de l'indicible*. Lausanne: Delachaux et Niestlé, 1998.

Robin, Régine. *Le Golem de l'écriture. De l'autofiction au Cybersoi*. Montreal: XYZ, 1997.

Sungolowsky, Joseph. "La judéité dans les œuvres de Romain Gary. De l'ambiguïté à la transparence symbolique." *Etudes littéraires* 26, no. 1 (summer 1993): 111–128.

Tassel, Alain. "Réverbérations du titre dans *Education européenne*." *Roman 20/50*, 32 (December 2001).

Wardi, Charlotte. *Le génocide dans la fiction romanesque*. Paris: PUF, 1986.

PIERRE GASCAR
(1916–1997)

CLAUDIA HOFFER GOSSELIN

PIERRE GASCAR (PSEUDONYM of Pierre Fournier) was born in Paris in 1916 and died in the Jura mountains of France in 1997. He spent his childhood years in Gascogny, from which he took his nom de plume. Raised in extreme poverty by a peasant grandmother who spoke only the local dialect, he attended secondary school on scholarship and worked at several jobs before joining the army. Although he spent the whole of World War II in German prisoner-of-war camps, his Holocaust-related literary work was most influenced by his experience in the Rawa-Ruska "disciplinary" camp on the Polish/Ukrainian border. Built by the Russian cavalry in 1939, this isolated camp held French and Belgian prisoners of war who had made repeated attempts at escape. Approximately twelve to thirteen thousand prisoners occupied Rawa-Ruska between April and November 1942 when, in violation of the Geneva Convention, they were returned to Germany to work for the Reich.

Rawa-Ruska, renamed "Brodno," is the setting for Gascar's novella *The Season of the Dead* (1953). A factual description of the camp is to be found in his *Histoire de la captivité des Français en Allemagne 1939–1945* (A History of French Captivity in Germany, 1939–1945, 1967) as well as in his posthumously published *Le Temps des morts: le rêve russe, texte définitif* (*The Season of the Dead*: *The Russian Dream, Definitive Text*, 1998). In his introduction to this work, Gascar states that he quickly regretted having fictionalized his experience at Rawa-Ruska. He felt that the ornate style and overly literary elements of the novella prevented the reader from perceiving it as a true act of witness. Although Rawa-Ruska continued to dominate Gascar's memory, he believed that forty years later everything had already been said; his memoir would no longer be of great interest.

The Season of the Dead, combined with six shorter texts collectively titled *Les Bêtes* (*Beasts and Men*) received the prestigious Prix Goncourt in 1953. Seemingly destined for a glorious literary career, Gascar's modesty and alienation from the bourgeois world of the *literati* caused him to fade from public notice. Extraordinarily prolific, he published approximately seventy works in many genres, including short stories, novels, biographies, essays, plays, film scripts, and travel literature. As a journalist he wrote for international agencies such as the World Health Organization. In the 1970s, aware of the dangers of environmental degradation, Gascar turned to writing about nature; he struggled to convince society of man's need for a harmonious relationship with the natural world.

Rawa-Ruska

In his book on French captivity, Gascar points out that in spite of German threats, the discipline in Rawa-Ruska was only slightly worse than experienced by prisoners of war in camps located in Germany. However, the French and Belgians held in Rawa-Ruska were subject to more extreme physical deprivation (the camp was called "le camp de la goutte d'eau," the "one-drop-of-water camp," because there was in fact only one faucet shared by all the prisoners). Most importantly, Rawa-Ruska was different from all other stalags in that the prisoners sent there were direct witnesses to genocide. The Belzec extermination camp, unnamed in the novella, was no more than twenty kilometers from Rawa-Ruska; the months when the French prisoners of war occupied the camp coincided almost exactly with those of mass murders at Belzec, where 500,000 to 600,000 deportees were killed.

Upon arriving at the camp, prisoners encountered local Jews who were forced to work there; they met others when they themselves were allowed to work for food in the town. Soon afterward they began to see the trains passing through the town's railroad station;

for weeks they listened to the desperate cries of the deportees. Finally they became witnesses to the round-ups and disappearance of the local Jewish population. Although Gascar regretted having turned his experience into "literature," *The Season of the Dead* nonetheless remains an act of witness.

The Season of the Dead

A lengthy and brilliant analysis of *The Season of the Dead* can be found in Lawrence Langer's *The Holocaust and the Literary Imagination*. Death is at the center of Langer's text, which begins with an image of death and ends with the fact of death. The controlling metaphor is the cemetery established by the German authorities next to the camp, in which French prisoners are to be "decently" buried; even those shot attempting to escape are honored with a German salvo. The cemetery is created before the first death occurs; each time there is a death, the cemetery detachment digs a new grave, which remains open, awaiting the next corpse. The prisoners occupy themselves by beautifying the graves with transplanted grass and flowers. They become a group apart from the rest, "workers in death's garden" (*Season*, New York: Meridian Books, 1960, p. 185), making the spot so beautiful and idyllic that eventually German soldiers come on Sundays to take photographs. The narrator underlines the irony of the prisoners' efforts: in the midst of massacres they spend their days "busily working over the dead as over some piece of embroidery" (p. 233).

The dominion of death is further extended when Gascar allows the narrator and his German guard—a pastor who will ultimately be punished for trying to save a young Jewish girl with whom he has fallen in love—to explore the ancient Jewish cemetery located in the nearby woods. The dominant symbol is the broken branch, with its message of never-ending death carved on the burial stones. The discovery by the prisoners of an anonymous Jew, his face buried in the grass but identified by his armband, points as well to the difference between the dead in the cemetery, whose names are known, and the Jewish victims whose deaths will go unmarked. The horror of anonymous and brutal death is further reinforced when the gravediggers stumble across a group of bodies, probably those of assassinated Jews, thrown helter-skelter into the ground. This is "uncivilized" death:

> these liquefying muscles, this half-eaten eye, those teeth like a dead sheep's; death, no longer decked with grasses, no longer ensconced in the coolness of a vault, no longer lying sepulchered in stone, but sprawling in a bog full of bones, wrapped in a drowned man's clothes, with his hair caught in the earth (pp. 220–221).

According to Langer, even the beauty and rebirth of nature cannot bring hope to this place marked by death. The narrator is in a world where everything becomes its opposite, where waking is dreaming, light is darkness, life is death. In Gascar's *univers concentrationnaire*, death has become the vital force that drains the vitality from life.

An important figure in *The Season of the Dead* is Isaac Lebovitch, a village Jew who exchanges a few words with the narrator toward the beginning of the text. Lebovitch reappears later as the man who lives in the "extra" grave during the night, only to disappear during the day. The cemetery workers do their best to feed and protect the unseen occupant of "their" grave. Although he is a man already in hell, experiencing the inconceivable loneliness of having lost all his companions, Lebovitch still hopes for an "exemption"; perhaps he will be able to survive. One day, however, he is gone; the narrator's hope disappears with him. Making one last attempt to reaffirm the dominion of life over death, he has a brief encounter with the Polish girl Maria. The intensity of his gestures frightens her and, after giving him a fleeting kiss, she runs away. The dominion of death is the only one left to him: "Within me and without me a great silence had fallen. After a moment, I wiped my tears and went back to my dead" (p. 249).

Beasts and Men

For Langer, Gascar has successfully led the reader into the *univers concentrationnaire* where nothing truly exists outside of death. The short stories in *Beasts and Men* titled "The Horses," "The House of Blood," "The Animals," and "The Dogs," which Langer analyzes in detail, are less apparently Holocaust related and yet they are filled with torture, slaughter, and persecution. Often referred to by critics as "Kafkaesque," although Gascar claimed that he had never read Kafka before writing them, the stories reflect such an acute sense of anguish and unrelieved misery that the reader is thrown into despair.

In "The Horses," a soldier becomes the keeper of an enormous herd of horses being held behind the lines for future battles in an unnamed war. Mad with hunger and dying of disease, they become almost uncontrollable; the soldier reacts to their overwhelming numbers and strength by constantly beating them. His cruelty is gratuitous, a form of insanity born of merciless conditions. Although the victims are horses, they are living in the perfect *univers concentrationnaire*. Unable to bear the situation any longer, the soldier frees them all and deserts the army.

In "The House of Blood," a young adolescent becomes a butcher's assistant and must participate in the slaughter of a series of animals. The butcher himself slowly descends into madness when he is required by a new law to do his job in a freshly built "antiseptic" slaughterhouse rather than in his own shop. In defiance of the law, he flees into the woods and continues slaughtering. The animals are killed one after the other until, like the soldier, the boy can no longer bear their suffering and runs away, thinking "O God, O God, don't let them kill any more sheep!" (Meridian Books, 1960, p. 56). Although Gascar points to his peasant childhood as the source of this butchery, which continued to haunt his dreams for many years, in the context of the Holocaust the slaughter of innocent animals takes on a symbolic meaning.

"The Animals" returns the reader to the torments experienced by prisoners of war. In this story they are Russians held in a barn by their German captors, who also have under their supervision a displaced zoo menagerie. The prisoners acquire tobacco and exchange it for part of the meat given to the animals. The starving creatures howl furiously and claw desperately at the floors of their cages. Gascar creates another *univers concentrationnaire* in which men and beasts have become indistinguishable. The prisoners are about to give the zookeepers the corpses of two men shot for foraging in exchange for the animals' meat, when the German front is broken by the Russian army. In this universe, human beings can never be certain to what bestiality desperation will drive them and all faith in human nature is forever lost.

Gascar's lengthiest story, "The Dogs," is perhaps his most Kafkaesque work. It takes place in a military camp after the war, as preparations are being made for the next possible conflict. Here dogs are trained to attack men who, although dressed in protective clothing, are not entirely safe from their teeth. In spite of their apparent obedience, the camp is dominated by the dogs; the narrator concludes that it is in fact "kennels for men" (p. 136). The use of attack dogs cannot fail to bring to the reader's mind the vicious animals trained to kill by the Nazis. Thus, Gascar's postwar world continues to reflect the darkness and cruelty of the Holocaust. Always lurking beneath the surface of "normalcy" are the threatening shadows of the not-so-distant past.

Among other critics who have recognized the contribution of Pierre Gascar is Sidra DeKoven Ezrahi. In her book *By Words Alone*, she analyzes *The Season of the Dead*, emphasizing the ubiquitous presence of death and the narrator's encounter with the horror of death in its "uncivilized" anonymous form. She also points to his "act of witness," an imaginative leap into the cattle cars transporting Jewish victims, which takes the form of a brief narrational shift from first to second person. In a 1961 article titled "The Concentrationary World of Pierre Gascar," Chester W. Obuchowski praises Gascar's ability to communicate "cosmic suffering," with his powerful use of "poetic evocation" (p. 334). Gascar for Obuchowski is both an insider and an outsider, a victim of the myriad forms of dehumanization inflicted on prisoners of war but nevertheless not a concentration camp survivor. The critic considers Gascar's work an extremely "effective fictional portrayal of the concentrationary universe" at a time when many writers were struggling with the near-impossible task of fictionalizing the Holocaust. While Obuchowski includes analyses of both *The Beasts* and *The Season of the Dead*, other critics, among them Judith J. Radke, Marcel Thiébaut, and Alain Robbe-Grillet, focus their attention on *The Beasts*. Thiébaut argues that Gascar, consciously or not, is a literary heir to Kafka, one who has seen that author's imaginary world transformed into reality. Gascar's stories create a hell where animals, like men, are subject to blind forces, but in addition are threatened by man's ever-present capacity to transform himself into their executioner. Radke speaks of the end of companionship between man and animal, of the "cruel metamorphosis which has transformed them both" (p. 89). Robbe-Grillet summarizes the overriding theme of the stories in *The Beasts*, each one about a man who has previously lived in ignorance and "who finds himself suddenly plunged into a 'subterranean world whose importance he had underestimated' " (review translated in *Modern French Literature*, Ungar, p. 429).

Pierre Gascar's early work remains as a *témoignage* to the senselessness and terror of the *univers concentrationnaire* and to man's seemingly endless potential for dehumanization. At the same time, Gascar survived Rawa-Ruska with a profound admiration for the solidarity and spirit of resistance shown by the French prisoners who shared his fate. Their courage inspired him to fight against human injustice and indifference. Throughout his long career, writing was his quintessential act of witness.

Bibliography

Primary Sources

Les Meubles (The Furniture). 1949.

Le Visage clos (The Closed Face). 1951.

Les Bêtes suivi de Le Temps des morts (*Beasts and Men Followed by The Season of the Dead*). 1953.

Le Temps des morts (*The Season of the Dead*). 1953.
Les Bêtes (*Beasts and Men*). 1953.
Chine ouverte (China Opened Up). 1955.
Les Femmes (Women). 1955.
La Graine (*The Seed*). 1955.
L'Herbe des rues (The Grass in the Streets). 1956.
La barre de corail suivi de Les Aveugles de Saint-Xavier (*The Coral Barrier Followed by the Blind Men of Saint Xavier*). 1958.
Les pas perdus (Waiting at the Station). 1958.
Voyage chez les vivants (Voyage among the Living). 1958.
Soleils (*Women and the Sun*). 1960.
Le Fugitif (*The Fugitive*). 1961.
Chambord. 1962.
Vertige du présent (The Vertiginous Present). 1962.
Les Moutons de feu (*Lambs of Fire*). 1963.
Le Meilleur de la vie (*The Best Years*). 1964.
Les Charmes (*Charms*). 1965.
Auto (Automobile). 1967.
Histoire de la captivité des Français en Allemagne, 1939–1945 (A History of French Captivity in Germany). 1967.
Les Chimères (The Chimeras). 1969.
L'Arche (The Ark). 1971.
Rimbaud et la Commune (Rimbaud and the Commune). 1971.
Le Présage (The Omen). 1972.
Quartier Latin (The Latin Quarter). 1973.
L'Homme et l'animal (Man and Animals). 1974.
Les Sources (The Springs). 1975.
Dans la forêt humaine (In the Human Forest). 1976.
Charles VI. Le Bal des ardents (Charles the Sixth: The Flaming Ball). 1977.
Un jardin de curé (The Priest's Garden). 1979.
L'Ombre de Robespierre (Robespierre's Shadow). 1979.
Les Secrets de Maître Bernard (The Secrets of Master Bernard). 1980.
Gérard de Nerval et son temps (Gérard de Nerval and His Times). 1981.
Le Règne végétal (The Vegetable Kingdom). 1981.
Buffon. 1983.
Le Fortin (The Fort). 1983.
Le Diable à Paris (The Devil in Paris). 1984.
Genève (Geneva). 1984.
Humboldt l'explorateur (Humboldt the Explorer). 1985.
Du côté de chez Monsieur Pasteur (Mr. Pasteur's Way). 1986.
L'Ange gardien (The Guardian Angel). 1987.
Pour le dire avec des fleurs (Say It with Flowers). 1988.
Montesquieu. 1989.
Portraits et souvenirs (Portraits and Memories). 1991.
La Friche (The Fallow Land). 1993.
Aïssé: récit (Aïssé: Narration). 1998.
Gascogne (Gascony). 1998.
Le Temps des morts : le rêve russe, texte définitif (*The Season of the Dead: The Russian Dream, Definitive Text*). 1998.
Transsibérien (The Trans-Siberian Railway). 1998.
"*Du temps des morts à La Barre de corail*." *Annales politiques et littéraires*, 1960.

Secondary Sources

Albérès, R. M. *Le Roman d'aujourd'hui, 1960–1970*. Paris: Éditions Albin Michel, 1970.
———. "Le réalisme onirique de Pierre Gascar." In *Littérature horizon 2000*. Paris: Éditions Albin Michel, 1974.
Bernold, André. "Le Silence de la Résorption." *La Nouvelle Revue française* 539 (December 1997): 42–47.
Clerval, Alain. "Interview avec Pierre Gascar." *La Nouvelle revue française* 279 (March 1976): 72–75.
Ezrahi, Sidra DeKoven. *By Words Alone*. Chicago and London: The University of Chicago Press, 1980.
Fabre-Luce, Anne. "Incidences de l'imaginaire dans les nouvelles de Pierre Gascar." *French Review* 41 (1968): 839–848.
Langer, Lawrence. *The Holocaust and the Literary Imagination*. New Haven and London: Yale University Press, 1975.
Nourissier, François. "Quel est le prix de la probité?" *La Nouvelle revue française* 539 (December 1997): 31–41.
Nyssen, Hubert. "Le pouvoir incantatoire: propos de Pierre Gascar recueillis et commentés." *Synthèse* (Brussels) (1967): 86–95. *Les Voies de l'écriture*. "Pierre Gascar: le pouvoir incantatoire." Paris: Mercure De France, 1969.
Obuchowski, Chester W. "The Concentrationary World of Pierre Gascar." *French Review* 34 (1961): 327–335.
"Pierre Gascar." In *Dieu dans la littérature d'aujourd'hui*. Edited by Gérard Mourgue. Paris: Éditions France-Empire, 1961.
"Pierre Gascar." In *Dictionnaire de littérature contemporaine, 1900–1962*. Edited by Pierre Boisdeffre. Paris: Éditions Universitaires, 1962, pp. 123–142.
"Pierre Gascar." In *Modern French literature*: *A Library of Literary Criticism*. Edited by Debra Popkin and Michael Popkin. New York: Ungar, 1977.
Radke, Judith L. "The Metamorphoses of Animals and Men in Gascar's *Les Bêtes*." *French Review* 39 (1965): 85–91.
Robbe-Grillet, Alain. "Pierre Gascar: *Les Bêtes*." *La Nouvelle revue française* 7 (1953): 141–144. Translated in *Modern French Literature: A Library of Literary Criticism*. Compiled and edited by Debra Popkin and Michael Popkin. New York: Ungar, 1977, p. 429.
Rohou, Guy. "Solitaire et fraternel." *La Nouvelle revue française* 539 (December 1997): 35–41.
Thiébaut, Marcel. "*Les bêtes* ou le sillage de Kafka." *Annales* 60 (1953): 17–21.
Veraldi. Gabriel. "*Les bêtes*." *Lettres nouvelles* (1953): 456–462.
Willard, Nancy. "The Grammar of Water, the Syntax of Fire." *Chicago Review* 22 (1971): 104–118.

PETER GAY

(1923–)

RUTH A. STARKMAN

THE EMINENT AMERICAN historian Peter Gay was born Peter Joachim Fröhlich in Berlin on 20 June 1923. In 1939, he emigrated from Nazi Germany to the United States with his family. After a long and distinguished academic career first at Columbia University and then at Yale, Gay became Sterling Professor of History Emeritus at Yale University, and director of the Center for Scholars and Writers, New York Public Library. His many publications begin with his dissertation, *The Dilemma of Democratic Socialism: Eduard Bernstein's Challenge to Marx* (1952) and include the widely read *Weimar Culture* (1968), *A Godless Jew* (1987), and *The Freud Reader* (1989), as well as the five-volume historical work, *The Bourgeois Experience: Victoria to Freud* (1984–1998). *My German Question* (1998) is among his most recent publications.

The preface to *My German Question* opens with the words "This is not an autobiography," for Gay intends his memoirs as more than a story of the "outrages and insults" he "swallowed" (p. ix) during the six years from 1933 to 1939 that he and his family lived under the Third Reich. Instead, Gay endeavors to record what he "brought to that experience and the deposits it left on [him]" (p. ix), portraying himself not as a passive victim, but as a young German Jew coping with life under the Nazis. Such agency is important to Gay's narrative because he hopes that his own experiences will have a "more general application" (p. ix) with respect to German-Jewish responses to the rise of the Third Reich.

Gay frames his memoirs with an epigraph from Christopher Marlowe's *Dr. Faustus*, "Why, this is hell, nor am I out of it," which asserts from the outset the unremitting trauma of his experience. Such persistence of memory manifests itself in the narrative's form as well as substance. Not merely content to retell the experience in a straightforward manner, *My German Question* proceeds asynchronically according to the important events and psychic epiphanies that occur as the author revisits the past. The effect is an unsettling self-discovery beginning with Gay's first, decisive visit back to Berlin at the height of the Cold War in 1961. The narrative then turns to Gay's early years with his family in Berlin after 1933, showing the Fröhlich family's growing awareness of their peril. Each step of the journey from Germany to America is punctuated by memories and commentary from later periods, so that the reader slowly pieces together the events with the various traumas that shaped the historian. The end result presents a convincing personal profile of a German Jewish family and the predispositions, cultural limitations, and traumas they shared with other German refugees. This latter aspect of shared experience is important to Gay's narrative, for *My German Question* pauses in many places to speculate on the reasons Jews such as the Fröhlichs remained as long as they did in Hitler's Germany.

With intimate detail, the first part of *My German Question* presents Gay's family, the Fröhlichs, as typical German Jews, who, like Germany's larger Jewish population after more than a century of emancipation and assimilation, viewed themselves as modern liberal Germans rather than as Jews. Socializing and working among Gentiles and a group of equally assimilated Jews, they retained only a vague sense of belonging to a distinct German subculture or minority religion. The Fröhlichs had their infant son Peter circumcised, but in every other respect, their Jewishness was marked only by a few Yiddish words and a sort of quizzical noncomprehension of the Germanic fads of the era—mountain climbing for one—which they referred to as "g.n." or "goyim nasches," Gentiles' pleasure. In general, Gay's parents made no outward demonstration of their Jewishness, transmitting to their son an "uncompromising rejection of any tribal identification . . ." (p. 50). He remarks: "the idea of attachment to a social community or a common heritage was virtually meaningless . . . Jewish awareness? Jewish identity?

These were empty slogans to them—and hence to me . . ." (p. 49).

In 1933, the Fröhlich family's world radically changed. That year, they "had suddenly become Jews" (p. 47) by German decree. This transformation of their world remained, however, deceptively oblique, for the early years of the Nazi regime remained relatively benign for Gay's family. He relates the "mixed signals" of the times: As a schoolboy at the enlightened and liberal Goethe Gymnasium he endured no particular affront, as late as 1936 his father's business prospered, and most of the family's non-Jewish friends remained supportive. Amid the foreboding political atmosphere, Gay still enjoyed his childhood pleasures, though in retrospect he views them as "survival strategies": stamp collecting, watching soccer, attending the 1936 Olympics, and making jokes about the Third Reich.

Kristallnacht, the night of broken glass, the pogrom of November 9, 1938, finally forced the Fröhlich family to confront the necessity of their departure from Germany. Quoting his friend and fellow historian Peter Loewenberg, Gay describes the violence of the Nazis on *Kristallnacht* as part of a "degradation ritual" (p. 133) designed to publicly brutalize, intimidate, and impoverish the Jewish population. From then on, what the Fröhlichs had intimated and feared, but not fully accepted, was apodictically clear: They had to leave Germany, and the sooner the better. Gay describes the suspense and disappointments of their efforts to emigrate and the Nazis' bureaucratic schemes, as well as the rejection of passage to England. All of these were counterbalanced by the bravery and resourcefulness of his father in working out the thorny emigration process, and by the courage of the non-Jewish friends who helped his family. Most striking is his father's prescient success in booking transatlantic passage two weeks earlier on the *Iberia*, instead of their original plans, which had been to take the infamously ill-fated *St. Louis*, whose passengers were refused entry in the United States, Cuba, and every other port in the New World. For the 284 *St. Louis* passengers who landed back in England, Gay tells us, "the country's humane action meant deliverance . . . of the 623 who landed on the Continent only forty survived the war" (p. 158). Having lived in proximity to these statistics but survived by dint of pure luck, is an existential state that Gay shares with many émigrés. He therefore refuses to call himself a "survivor," never having been incarcerated in any of the Nazi camps nor having experienced any direct physical danger.

Gay's family arrived in Cuba in 1939, and two years later settled in the United States. Then, following the lead of an émigré cousin, the Fröhlich family Anglicized its name. Peter Joachim Israel Fröhlich became Peter Jack Gay—the "Israel" part inserted by the Nazis and visible on the copy of his passport, which appears on the cover of his book, he officially and permanently removed. The process of becoming an American began immediately, though there were constant financial and social roadblocks to becoming the highly successful historian he would eventually become. Having been forced from his gymnasium by Nazi racial laws, Gay found that in America the laws of economics soon ended his efforts to finish high school. Kindness prevailed, however; teachers recognized his potential, and he eventually moved from manual labor, for which he remained ill-equipped and dispositionally ill-suited, to the university. For the author's father, meanwhile, displacement and emigration took a greater toll. Too old to embark on a course of reeducation, culturally adrift in a new land, Gay's once highly able, socially keen businessman father had trouble finding a new vocation and would struggle to the end of his days in America. Of this failure to adapt completely Gay comments, "Hitler had broken him. . . . It is not sentimental to say that he died of a broken heart" (p. 176). In moments such as these, as elsewhere throughout the memoir, Gay vents his anger at those who have chided the German Jews for remaining in their beloved Germany, which failed to return their love. Conjuring an image of his father performing manual labor for which he was too old and unsuited, Gay remarks, "I think of those who have nagged at German refugees for more years than I care to remember—'Why didn't you leave earlier' and 'why didn't you realize that though you loved the Germans, the Germans didn't love you?'—and could cheerfully throttle them" (p. 176). This source of animus arises frequently, though apart from a passing reference to Gershom Scholem, it is not entirely clear who, or which "other Jews," have questioned the German-Jewish inability to part with Germany.

Where Gay reserves anger for the non-German commentators, he has achieved a certain rapprochement with postwar Germany—a personal perspective unique to the experience of the émigré. Through frequent trips to his native land, through the experience of those who aided his family and the discovery of "good Germans," Gay believes he has managed to reintegrate Germany into his personal and professional life. He accomplishes this at a price, however.

Gay notes his less successful effort in confronting the Holocaust itself. He remarks that he has avoided seeing Claude Lanzmann's documentary *Shoah*, has not wanted to visit the United States Holocaust Memorial Museum in Washington, and has refused to accompany his wife on a visit to Auschwitz. The question remains whether such an avoidance is personal, whether other German-Jewish refugees share this sensibility, or whether it arises in resistance to the growing American interest in the Holocaust.

Gay focuses instead on the "German question" of his emigration, relating the liberating effect of finally being able to discuss his own experience of Kristallnacht at an international summer seminar in college, where he first became able to "rethink [his] feelings about [his] German past" (p. 184). Far from exorcizing the past, such confrontations have confirmed the intractable nature of his experience, showing him "that Peter Fröhlich of 1938 and 1939 is still alive in Peter Gay in 1997" (p. 206). In the end, Gay suggests his personal judgment of Germany may evolve and that he will continue in the next installment. He concludes, as newspaper serials in German say, "Fortsetzung folgt"—to be continued . . . (p. 206).

Bibliography

Primary Sources (Books)

The Dilemma of Democratic Socialism: Eduard Bernstein's Challenge to Marx. New York: Collier Books, 1962.
Age of Enlightenment, by Peter Gay and the editors of Time-Life books. Revised edition. New York: Time, 1966.
A Loss of Mastery: Puritan Historians in Colonial America. Berkeley: University of California Press, 1966.
The Enlightenment: An Interpretation. New York: Knopf, 1966–1969.
Deism: An Anthology. Princeton, N.J.: Van Nostrand, 1968.
Weimar Culture: The Outsider as Insider. New York: Harper & Row, 1968.
The Bridge of Criticism: Dialogues Among Lucian, Erasmus, and Voltaire on the Enlightenment. New York: Harper & Row, 1970.
The Party of Humanity: Essays in the French Enlightenment. New York: Knopf, 1971.
Modern Europe. Peter Gay; R. K. Webb. New York: Harper & Row, 1972–1973.
The Enlightenment: A Comprehensive Anthology. New York: Simon & Schuster, 1973.
Modern Europe to 1815. Peter Gay, R. K. Webb. New York: HarperCollins, 1973.
Style in History. New York: Basic Books, 1974.
Art and Act: On Causes in History—Manet, Gropius, Mondrian. New York: Harper & Row, 1976.
Freud, Jews, and Other Germans: Masters and Victims in Modernist Culture. New York: Oxford University Press, 1978.
The Bourgeois Experience: Victoria to Freud. New York: Oxford University Press/Norton, 1984–1998.
Vol. 1: *Education of the Senses.* New York: Oxford University Press, 1984.
Vol. 2: *The Tender Passion.* New York: Oxford University Press, 1986.
Vol. 3: *The Cultivation of Hatred.* New York: Norton, 1993.
Vol. 4: *The Naked Heart.* New York: Norton, 1995.
Vol. 5: *Pleasure Wars.* New York; London: Norton, 1998.
Freud for Historians. New York: Oxford University Press, 1985.
A Godless Jew: Freud, Atheism, and the Making of Psychoanalysis. New Haven, Conn.: Yale University Press; Cincinnati, Ohio: Hebrew Union College Press, 1987.
Freud: A Life for Our Time. New York: Norton, 1988.
Voltaire's Politics: The Poet as Realist. New Haven, Conn.: Yale University Press, 1988, ca. 1959.
Sigmund Freud and Art: His Personal Collection of Antiquities. Binghamton, N.Y.: SUNY. Binghamton, University Art Gallery, 1989.
Reading Freud: Explorations and Entertainments. New Haven, Conn.: Yale University Press, 1990.
My German Question: Growing Up in Nazi Berlin. New Haven, Conn.: Yale University Press, 1998.
Mozart. New York: Lipper/Viking Books, 1999.

Edited Works, Translations, Introductions

Cassirer, Ernst. *The Question of Jean-Jacques Rousseau.* Edited and translated with an introduction and a new postscript by Peter Gay, 2nd ed. New Haven, Conn.: Yale University Press, 1989.
The Columbia History of the World. Edited by John A. Garraty and Peter Gay. New York: Harper & Row, 1972.
Eighteenth Century Studies: Presented by Arthur M. Wilson. Edited by Peter Gay. Hanover, N.H.: University Press of New England, 1972.
Engelman, Edmund: *Berggasse 19: Sigmund Freud's Home and Offices, Vienna 1938. The Photographs of Edmund Engelman.* Introduction by Peter Gay; captions by Rita Ransohoff. New York: Basic Books, 1976.
Freud, Sigmund: *An Autobiographical Study.* Translated and edited by James Strachey; with a biographical introduction by Peter Gay. Standard ed. New York: Norton, 1989.
———. *Civilization and Its Discontents.* Translated and edited by James Strachey; with a biographical introduction by Peter Gay. Standard ed. New York: Norton, 1989.
———. *Five Lectures on Psycho-Analysis.* Translated and edited by James Strachey; with a biographical introduction by Peter Gay. Standard ed. New York: Norton, 1989.
———. *The Freud Reader.* Edited by Peter Gay. New York: Norton, 1989.
———. *Group Psychology and the Analysis of the Ego.* Translated and edited by James Strachey; with a biographical introduction by Peter Gay. New York: Norton, 1989.
———. *Introductory Lectures on Psycho-Analysis.* Translated and edited by James Strachey; with a biographical introduction by Peter Gay. New York: Norton, 1989.
———. *An Outline of Psycho-Analysis.* Translated and edited by James Strachey; with a biographical introduction by Peter Gay. New York: Norton, 1989.
Friedman, Martin L. *A View of a Decade.* Museum of Contemporary Art, Chicago, Illinois. Essays by Martin Friedman, Robert Pincus-Witten, and Peter Gay. Chicago: The Museum, 1977.
Historians at Work. Edited by Peter Gay and Gerald J. Cavanaugh. New York: Harper & Row, 1972–1975.
Voltaire. *Candide.* Translated and edited by Peter Gay. A bilingual ed. New York: St. Martin's Press, 1963.
———. *Philosophical Dictionary.* Translated, with an introduction and glossary by Peter Gay. Preface by André Maurois. New York: Basic Books, 1962.

Transcript/Lecture

"My German Question." *New York Review of Books* 47, no. 2 (10 February 2000): 21–23.

Secondary Sources

Goodnick, Benjamin. "Jews, Freud and Gay." *Judaism: A Quarterly Journal* 38, no. 1 (Winter 1989): 103–112.

Green, Martin. "A Love Affair with German Culture." *New York Times Book Review*, 29 January 1978.

Herf, Jeffrey. "My German Question." *Wall Street Journal*, 3 November 1998: A20.

Kermode, Frank. "Displaced Person." *New York Times Book Review*, 25 October 1998.

Rosenfeld, Alvin H. "My German Question: Growing Up in Nazi Berlin." *New Leader* 81, no. 13 (30 November 1998): 15.

Schwartz, Amy E. "My German Question." *Wilson Quarterly* 22, no. 4 (Autumn 1998): 100.

ÁGNES GERGELY

(1933–)

RITA HORVÁTH

ÁGNES GERGELY, POET, novelist, translator, and literary scholar, was born on 5 October 1933 in Endrőd, a village on the Great Hungarian Plain. Her parents were Róza Fenákel and György Guttmann. She spent much of her early childhood in Zalaegerszeg, a town in western Hungary, where her father worked as a journalist. She attended school in Budapest, Endrőd, and Szeged. As was characteristic of the so-called "Fifties" in Hungary, she acquired a laborer's certificate for turning iron, as well as an elementary- and high-school education. At Eötvös Loránd University in Budapest she majored in Hungarian and English language and literature, graduating in 1957. Between 1957 and 1963 she taught in an elementary school and then in a high school in a Budapest suburb. She then took an active part in the literary life of Hungary. She worked for Hungarian Radio, for important literary magazines, and for a publisher. In 1973–1974 she was a member of the International Writing Program at the University of Iowa. In 1979 she received her Ph.D. from Eötvös Loránd University. Her dissertation, written on the Nigerian poet Christopher Okigbo, was published in 1986. In 1992 she began teaching in the postgraduate program of Eötvös Loránd University's English-literature department. She received numerous prizes for literature, including the Attila József Prize (1977 and 1987), the Tibor Déry Award (1985 and 1996), the Milán Füst Prize (1994), the Salvatore Quasimodo Prize (1995), the Soros Prize for creativity (2000), and the highest national prize in Hungary, the Kossuth Prize (2000).

Works

Gergely and her mother survived the Holocaust in the ghetto of Pest. Her father was taken to forced labor and perished in Günskirchen. Many of her relatives were murdered, and most of those who survived left Hungary after the Holocaust. Not surprisingly, Holocaust-related notions and images, such as marches, gas chambers, and people who let themselves be taken away, frequently surface in both her abstract and her personal writing. Allusions to personal losses are also omnipresent. Her continually frustrated need to come to terms with the Holocaust as a historical fact, as a personal experience, as a part of her life, and as a theological-existential reality acts as an organizing force in her work, which is remarkably diverse in terms of both genre and theme.

By following the fate of one image in particular in Gergely's work, we can see the transformation of her ideas about the role of personal memories of the Holocaust and of witnessing. The image is of the last time she saw her father stepping out the door of a hiding place to report for forced labor. In one of her autobiographically inspired novels, *A tolmács* (The Interpreter), she writes: "I see a tall man disappearing from the door into the November fog. This is the only picture that I guard from the war. All else is merely scraps" (p. 45).

Gergely continues to rewrite an elegy for her father, of which there are four versions. The first version appeared in her first volume in 1963, and the last, the 1998 version, had not been published in any collection as of 2001. The early versions—"Ajtófélfámon jel vagy" ("You Are the Sign on My Door Jamb"), its slightly rewritten variant bearing the same title, and "Apu" ("Daddy")—are based on the scene of her father leaving his hiding place. This scene is presented with many details. The poet angrily includes all the objects that were supposed to aid survival: knapsack, thermos, warm underclothes, pocketknife, and prayer book. She legitimizes the centrality of this witnessed scene by contrasting it with the notion that she merely imagines/invents her father's fate afterward. She calls the facts of forced labor—"the march / the bars, the bridge, the sludgy road / the gorging of grass, the fatal empty weakness"—"freak inventions of the mind" (*Requiem for a Sunbird* 20).

"You Are the Sign on My Door Jamb" and "Daddy" significantly differ in their representations of personal memories. "You Are the Sign on My Door Jamb" opens with a denial—"I do not cherish memories/and those I have I do not safeguard"—and regards the rise of memories as involuntary and unwelcome:

I do not seek forgotten graveyards.
Bio-chemistry does not move me.

Yet at times like this towards November
when fog-damped windows seal my room
and I gasp for air and long for relief,
beyond a sense of space I sense your rise
as from the waters of the mind
and odd gestures of yours re-emerge.
Requiem for a Sunbird 19).

"Daddy," on the other hand, forcefully negates the negation of the previous poem and asserts the importance of remembering:

His memory in a honey-coloured wall.
The wall's crying absence in the Sun.
It keeps growing, with no reason to hide.
Graves are no biochemistry at all.
The air is turning glassy.

Moisture and fog won't delay
till a November day.
. . .
It is not vegetative to recall.
(*Requiem for a Sunbird* 66).

The hierarchy favoring personal memory over imagination is reversed in the 1998 version of the elegy, titled "Őrizetlenül" ("Guardless"). The poem, which opens by stating, "All of a sudden there are no more eyewitnesses/neither for the good nor for the bad," represses the image witnessed by the poet and is entirely concerned with the father's march toward death. The "freak inventions of the mind," which are not hers and which one can only know from witnesses' accounts and from the imaginative/inventive acts of literature, are more real than the "real" image she safeguarded as the symbol of the horrors of the Holocaust. The poem drastically unsettles established notions of reality and witnessing.

It is emblematic of Gergely's controlled, low-key poetics that we learn less from her own poetry about the gaping wound caused by losing her father than from her strong reaction to Sylvia Plath's poem "Daddy." Gergely translated Plath's poem and included it in her 1973 volume *Valogatott szerelmeim* (My Selected Loves). Most probably, the feelings induced by Plath's poem influenced her decision to name the third variant of the elegy "Daddy." The vigor of her wound also accounts for the shift from memory to imagination. By concentrating on her father's march rather than on his departure, the poet does not have to abandon him until his death.

The title of the first version of the elegy, and of Gergely's first book of verse, "You Are the Sign on My Door Jamb," voices a crucial sentiment of highly assimilated Jews in Hungary. By turning her murdered father (a symbol of the Holocaust itself) into a sign of her Jewishness, the mezuzah (a highly visible religious symbol), she identifies the Holocaust as the only, or most important, constituent of Jewish identity. The Holocaust replaces religion in determining Jewish identity. This title also contains a theological and historical accusation: the sign that is supposed to save a Jewish household from destruction actually singles it out for destruction.

Gergely frequently returns to the question of identity in poems such as "Keserű-gyökerű" ("Bitter-Rooted"), "Halak" ("Fish"), "A 137. Zsoltár" ("Psalm 137"), "Pannon ég alatt" ("Beneath Pannonia's Sky"), versions of "Legenda" ("Legend"), and "Az 'Ágnes Asszony' Költőjéhez" ("To the Poet who wrote 'Agnes Asszony' "). She finds herself in a double bind, which she calls a "double minority existence." Such an existence means that a person belongs to an oppressed minority and lives its historical fate, but at the same time he or she identifies with the cultural heritage of the oppressive majority. Gergely, who so proudly identifies with the fate and heritage of the European Jews, is also committed to Greco-Roman based Western culture and to Hungarian culture within it. She believes it is a terrible mistake to reject the values of Western culture because of the disastrous history in which Western civilization is hopelessly entangled and implicated.

Gergely's sense of this double bind has made her aware of other artists in similar situations. A feeling of kinship inspired many of her translations and scholarly works. She views, for example, the Irish poet and playwright William Butler Yeats (1865–1939), Christopher Okigbo (1932–1967), and the Japanese writer Akutagawa Rjūnosuke (1892–1927) as being worn away by trying to synthesize antagonistic cultures and historical fates. One pays an exorbitant price for being an interpreter in such a situation: solitude. However, Gergely interprets and connects the hitherto-isolated pain of individuals caught up in similar struggles. Aware of her constant failure as cultural interpreter, she creates a community of artistic loneliness.

Bibliography

Primary Sources

Ajtófélfámon jel vagy (You are the sign on my door jamb). 1963.
Glogovácz és a holdkórosok (Glogovácz and the sleepwalkers). 1966.
Johanna. 1968.
Azték pillanat (Aztec moment). 1970.
A tolmács (The interpreter). 1973.
Válogatott szerelmeim (My selected loves). 1973.
A chicagói változat (The Chicago version). 1976.
Kobaltország (Cobalt state). 1978.
Hajóroncs (Shipwreck). 1981.
Huszonegy: Magyar művészarcok (Twenty-one: Portraits of Hungarian artists). 1982.
Stációk (Stations [of the Cross]). 1983.
Fohász lámpaoltás előtt (Prayer before turning off the light). 1985.
Árnyékváros: Válogatott versek (Shadowtown: Selected poems). 1986.
Költészet és veszélytudat: Feljegyzések egy afrikai költő portréjához (Poetry and consciousness of danger: Notes on the portrait of an African poet). 1986.
Riportnapló Északról (Report diary from the North). 1988.
Nyugat magyarja: Esszénapló William Butler Yeatsről (The Hungary of the West: Essay diary about William Butler Yeats). 1991.
Királyok földje: Válogatott és új versek (Land of kings: Selected poems and new poems). 1994.
Közép-Európa ígéret volt (Central Europe was a promise). 1994.
Absztrakt tehén: Tárcanapló (Abstract cow: Feuilleton-diary). 1995.
Necropolis: Százhuszonhat vers, 1993–1996 (Necropolis: One hundred and twenty-six poems). 1997.
Requiem for a Sunbird: Forty Poems. Edited by Tótfalusi, István. Budapest: Maecenas, 1997.
A barbárság éveiből: Huszonöt régebbi és huszonöt újabb vers, 1988–1997 (From the years of barbarity: Twenty-five older and twenty-five newer poems, 1988–1997). 1998.
Őrizetlenek (The unguarded ones). 2000.

Secondary Sources

Faragó, Vilmos. "Könyvek a kirakatban: Lírikusok prózája, és egy prózaíró lírája." *Élet és Irodalom* 12 (1966): 4.
Koczkás, Sándor. "A történelmi 'kímélet' poétája: Gergely Ágnes: Árnyékváros." *Jelenkor* 12 (1986): 1139–1142.
Lengyel, Balázs. "Közvetlenül és áttételesen." In *Verseskönyvről verseskönyvre: Líránk a hetvenes években*. Budapest: Magvető, 1982. pp. 234–244.
Lengyel, Balázs. "Mozgásterek." In *Verseskönyvről verseskönyvre: Líránk a hetvenes években*. Budapest: Magvető, 1982, pp. 353–360.
Poór, Péter. "Gergely Ágnes: Glogovácz és a holdkórosok." *Életünk* 2 (1966): 157–159.
Rónay, György. "Az olvasó naplója." *Vigilia* (November 1964): 686–688.
Sinka, Erzsébet. "Gergely Ágnes Azték pillanat." *Kritika* 10 (1970): 53–54.

Interviews

Interview by Gyula Batári. "Beszélgetés Gergely Ágnes írónővel legkedvesebb olvasmányairól." *Könyv, könyvtár, könyvtáros* (September 1993): 52–54.
Interview by Katalin Budai. "Az író nem lehet fegyelmezetlen." *Magyar Napló* 3 (1993): 9–11.
Interview by Károly Csala. "Beszélgetés a tagadásról." *Népszabadság* 299 (1991): 23.
Interview by Zsolt Koppány. "Ágnes, hisz a feltámadásban?" *Jel* 3–4 (1989): 52–54.
Interview by Katalin Liptay. "Magritte rózsája," *Magyar Napló* 10 (1993): 7–8.
Interview by András Lukácsy. "Gergely Ágnes: A hallgatás is lehet játék—de mindenképpen ítélet: Sem kenyérrel, sem kővel." *Magyar Hírlap* 299 (1993): 30.
Interview by Ágnes Osztovits. " 'A múlt héten megszerettem Budapestet': Gergely Ágnes születésnapi történetei." *Magyar Nemzet* 230 (1993): 19.
Interview by Szabolcs Szunyogh. " 'Egy nyelven beszélnek az álmok': Kerekasztal-beszélgetés Gergely Ágnes költészetéről." *Köznevelés* 9 (1999): 14–16.
Interview by Lajos Márton Varga. "Budapestből az emlékét szeretem." *Népszabadság* 44 (1994): viii.

KAREN GERSHON
(1923–1993)

PETER LAWSON

KAREN GERSHON WAS born Kaethe Loewenthal on 29 August 1923. Her hometown was Bielefeld, in the province of Westphalia, Germany. Kaethe had two older sisters, Lise (one year older) and Anne (two years older). Her parents were Paul, an architect, and Selma (née Schoenfeld), a housewife.

Childhood under Nazism

Gershon's autobiographical narratives, *A Lesser Child* (1994) and "A Tempered Wind" (1992, unpublished), provide poignant accounts of the refugee life of children fortunate enough to escape Nazi Europe. *A Lesser Child* details the impact of the rise of Nazism on the private life of an assimilated German Jewish child, while "A Tempered Wind" picks up her story of adjustment to English life. Similarly, Gershon's novel *The Bread of Exile* (1985) narrates the experiences of a *Kindertransport* (children's transport) youth, while *We Came as Children* (1966) provides a platform for the collective recollections of *kinder* in Britain.

When Hitler came to power, Kaethe was ten. Three years later, Aryanization at the local school led to her expulsion. As Jewish schools were established in response to institutional antisemitism, Kaethe entered a non-Aryan boarding school in 1937. The following year she joined a Zionist program designed to select those best suited for immigration to Palestine. Both Kaethe and her sister Lise passed the course. Five weeks after *Kristallnacht* (organized anti-Jewish riots that took place on 9 and 10 November 1938), Kaethe and Lise were sent by their parents on a *Kindertransport* to England. They arrived in Harwich, Essex, on 15 December 1938. The psychological consequences of this uprooting are evoked in Gershon's *Selected Poems* (1966).

Refugee in England

From Dovercourt reception camp, the Loewenthal girls were sent to Scotland in February 1939, where they stayed in the stately home of the Balfour family. "They were here to prepare themselves for life in the homeland which had been promised to the Jewish people by the British Government in the Declaration issued in 1917 when Arthur Balfour was Foreign Secretary" ("A Tempered Wind," p. 56). Seventeen-year-old Lise left for Palestine before war broke out, but Kaethe was too young to join her. By the time the British government made fresh entry permits available in June and July 1940, "the idea of [my] . . . leaving England just then had been abandoned" (p. 80). From January to May of 1941, Kaethe lived in a Zionist community, or *hachsharah*, in Wales; she chose to leave the *hachsharah* to enter domestic service in Leeds.

The unsettled nature of refugee life had effects at the most intimate level. For example, it was homesickness that spurred Gershon's marriage to a distant cousin in 1942; they separated the following year. In 1944 Kaethe passed a scholarship examination for Edinburgh University, but felt a degree "was altogether irrelevant to what I wanted to do with this life which my parents and the British people had preserved for me" (p. 197), and left after only one term.

At the war's end, Kaethe discovered that her parents had not survived the concentration camps. Gershon writes: "I found the [Red Cross] list headed *Westfalen* (Westphalia); it consisted of only one page. I looked down it; there was not even a name beginning with L" (p. 194). Kaethe learned that her parents had been deported to the Riga ghetto in December 1941: "The Jews worked there as slaves for the Wehrmacht and . . . my father, after a year or so, was one morning found dead in his bed—he had a weak heart. . . . My mother was known to have survived until the autumn of 1944, when the Germans put an end to the ghetto" (p. 195).

In 1948 Kaethe married a Gentile art teacher, Val Tripp. They had four children: Christopher, Anthony, Stella, and Naomi. Having previously anglicized her name to Karen, Kaethe assumed the nom de plume Karen Gershon in 1957. "Gershon" was Paul Loewenthal's Hebrew name, meaning "stranger in a strange land."

In 1968 the Tripps emigrated to Israel. Although they returned to Britain in 1973, three of Gershon's four children—Christopher, Anthony, and Naomi—later chose to raise families in the Jewish state. Gershon's reasons for returning were twofold: first, she discovered that Israelis tended to favor Hebrew over Anglophone poetry; second, she did not feel completely at home in Israel. As she explained: "I feel more at home in Israel than I do in England, but I don't feel at home there either, and that is worse, because there I still expect to be able to feel at home. Here [in England] I am reconciled" (*We Came as Children*, London: Papermac, 1989, p. 9).

Gershon did not resume her novelist's career until 1980, when *Burn Helen* appeared. She wrote several further novels, only two of which were published: *The Bread of Exile*, which is semiautobiographical, and *The Fifth Generation* (1987) about Hitler's son. In 1990, a documentary about Gershon's life, *Stranger in a Strange Land*, aired on British television.

Poetry

From the age of thirteen, Gershon was "a convinced Zionist and a bit of a propagandist" (*A Lesser Child*, London: Peter Owen, 1994, p. 129). For the 1936 "communal Hanukkah celebration," she was inspired to create her first complete poem:

> Writing in pencil on scrap paper, she put the words down, one, two, or a line at a time, once she had considered them and recognized them as right. . . . The poem began, 'Wake up, Jews!' and went on to say that they ought not to leave it to others to decide what their Jewishness meant, that they should learn to see it as an asset instead of as a burden, that they should decide to emigrate to the Land of Israel not because they were no longer wanted in Germany but because that was where they should want to be (p. 130).

After emigration to England, Gershon's Zionism and poetry remained intertwined. At Dovercourt reception camp, the refugee children expected to leave for Palestine very soon. Gershon explains:

> Needing material about the Land of Israel, I began to write stories, and essays, and poems, and a whole sequence of "Letters from Jerusalem"; in my imagination I lived there. . . . Recognition mattered to me far less than that the thoughts of all of us should be occupied as much as possible with the Land of Israel. Feeling so involved in what I thought was the most important activity in the camp, having the incentive to be writing, writing, I almost stopped feeling homesick and began to feel almost happy ("A Tempered Wind," pp. 49–50).

What remains of Gershon's German poetry was published in *Mich nur zu trösten bestimmt* (Only Meant to Comfort, 2000). She burned the bulk of it in 1941, before (she states) "setting out to turn myself into an English-writer" ("A Tempered Wind," p. 97).

Selected Poems (1966)

Gershon was driven by a survivor's sense of guilt. She felt it her duty to bear witness: "The terrible past is not an adversary but my greatest asset: I will not fight against it but put it to work. I cannot alter what has happened but by making a tool of it I can at least give it a purpose," she asserted (*We Came as Children*, pp. 159–160). The consequence of this decision was her acclaimed collective autobiography of *Kindertransport* refugees, *We Came as Children* (1966), and her simultaneously published *Selected Poems*. Of the 10,000 *kinder* sent to Britain, 254 were chosen to contribute to *We Came as Children*. Gershon assembled their recollections without attribution, thus foregrounding the shared over the solipsistic experience of these castaway Jewish youngsters. She divided the book into sections with titles such as "The Reception Camps" and "Institutions." In what is clearly her own entry (describing Gershon's return to Bielefeld in 1963), she writes: "My Jewish childhood in Nazi Germany and my orphan exile at the age of fifteen must remain a part of my life always" (pp. 159–160). Elsewhere, she states: "It has taken me twenty-five years to learn to accept what I am: a German Jew" (p. 149). Together, *We Came as Children* and *Selected Poems* established Gershon as a pioneer in the field of Holocaust literature.

Four of Gershon's *Selected Poems*—"The Children's Exodus," "Cast Out," "The Town," and "To My Children"—appear as a coda to *We Came as Children*. All affirm the fact that the communal refugee experience was also intensely personal. For example, in "The Children's Exodus" Gershon writes:

> When we went out of Germany
> carrying six million lives

that was Jewish history
but each child was one refugee
we unlike the Egyptian slaves
were exiled individually
and each in desolation has
created his own wilderness
(*We Came as Children*, p. 171).

By using the analogy of the Egyptian Exodus, she implies the Haggadic tradition of remembering Jewish history and the injunction to read the collective as personal narrative. Thus, the participant in the Passover service is enjoined to consider him- or herself as present at Sinai to receive the Law.

Like her fellow poets and *kinder* Gerda Mayer and Lotte Kramer, Gershon is keen to record her gratitude to Britain for providing a refuge: "At Dovercourt the winter sea / was like God's mercy vast and wild" (p. 172).

Collected Poems

In the introduction to her *Collected Poems* (1990), Gershon comments on the poetic form employed in "The Children's Exodus." "A style I discovered for myself," she writes: "an eight-line stanza with movable rhymes or half-rhymes" (*Collected Poems*, London: Papermac, 1990, p. 2). Just as "The Children's Exodus" owes a debt to Hebrew liturgical tradition, so, too, "Monologue" may be related to Hebrew lamentation. Here the poet refuses to be consoled for her parents' murder, because mourning is all she now has of them; following her beyond the immediate historic loss, it remains as part of her own identity:

Now I am glad to be alone
What is unspoken is my own
I do not want to be consoled
because this grief is all I hold
I will not let my parents rest
and I will not be reconciled
I mourn them and I mourn this child
I have returned and I am lost
("Monologue," *Collected Poems*, p. 33).

Similarly, Gershon echoes many Jewish writers in pursuing the theme of survivors' guilt. Unlike traditional elegists, the Holocaust writer describes a survivor's guilt that is particular to communal loss of historic proportions, rather than the microcosm of circumscribed, personal grief. "In the Park" addresses such guilt explicitly in the wake of the *Shoah*: "This was no suitable setting for one in mourning / I thought of my dead and felt guilty to be alive" (p. 32).

Necessarily, *Selected Poems* also contains direct reflections on Gershon's deceased parents: the nightmare of not being with them at their death ("I Was Not There"), the terrible disavowal of Gershon's mother ("I have disowned her for life's sake"—from "My Mother"), and the yearning expressed in "My Father": "I search my childhood continually for my father / as I searched the town for him on the day our synagogue burned" (p. 34).

Other poems, such as "To My Children," celebrate Gershon's new family. Coupling the Jewish theme of repair (*tikkun*) with English imagery, Gershon celebrates life and Jewish continuity in a poem admonishing her children to understand their history. The poet has borne her refugee status with pride, and now looks to regeneration in a family to be tended as lovingly as an English garden. Gershon's disclosure that "the first poem in the English language which made an impression on me was 'The force that through the green fuse drives the flower' [by Dylan Thomas]" ("A Tempered Wind," p. 107) is significant here:

Be proud of the beginning you have in me
be proud of how far I have wandered with this burden
I would value you less if I were not a refugee
your presence changes my wilderness to a garden
("To My Children, *Collected Poems*, p. 55)

Having lost her parents in Hitler's Europe, Gershon continues to express her love of family, and restoration through family, in subsequent collections such as *Legacies and Encounters* (1972) and *My Daughters, My Sisters* (1975). The latter volume boasts a particularly fine epithalamium in "Married Love":

I sought a home it would not hurt to lose
which would outweigh for me the one I lost.
Now that you have been closest to me longer
than anyone else, much longer than my parents
(and all the time I have been renewed and changed)
you lie green in the membranes of my senses
and rise like sap in my experiences
(*Collected Poems*, pp. 100–101).

Coming Back from Babylon (1979)

In *Coming Back from Babylon* (1979), Gershon turns to biblical characters and narratives. Still, her own responses as a Jewish child under Nazi tyranny are given voice, for example, in "Samson in Gaza," where she evokes the heroic fortitude of her father in the Riga ghetto:

My father too was made a slave—

God spoils good tools to mend the world;
mourn every hero as a man.
To himself Samson wasn't brave,
I see him with my father's face;
the hands that brought the pillars down
(*Collected Poems*, pp. 116–117).

Similarly, Gershon writes of a fictional father in *The Bread of Exile*: "[He] did not look like one humbled, persecuted, bereft: but rather like Samson about to take hold of the pillars" (London: Gollancz, 1985, p. 13).

In like manner, "Esther" recounts: "All the girls wanted to play the queen: / Haman was Hitler when I was young" (*Collected Poems*, pp. 119–120). Gershon's novel "The Historical and Legendary Esther" (1980, unpublished) reasserts the resemblance between Haman and Hitler:

> In the twelfth year of King Xerxes' reign [474 BCE], Memucan's seal, a francolin between two lotus blossoms, was replaced by Haman's sauvastika: the wheel of the swastika widdershins to the course of the sun—symbol of the forces of evil. His followers, members of the secret organisation called the Pishtra, came out into the open as an elite military force ("The Historical and Legendary Esther," p. 74).

Thus, Gershon narrates biblical tales of victory over evil forces designed to bring humiliation and annihilation to the Jewish people, with clear Nazi resonances.

Joshua Poems (1990)

In her *Joshua Poems* (1990), Gershon deploys a post-Holocaust perspective to chart the life of Jesus the Jew. By exploring the pre-Passion experiences of "one tortured Jew" ("A Tempered Wind," pp. 177–178), Gershon's sequence domesticates Jesus in Jewish geography, culture, and history. "Cheder Boy" is typical in its wit, intensity, and typological purpose:

If he sat opposite the rabbi
he did his reading upside down:
a boy in cheder has his place;
when he was old enough to study
he learned to take his place among
the centuries of Jewish boys
who have no time for being young
and sometimes are killed for their faith.
(*Collected Poems*, p. 160).

If Christians have traditionally insisted on typologically interpreting the Old Testament as presaging the New, Gershon, in the *Joshua Poems*, rereads the New Testament as presaging the Holocaust. Among the other poems sharing a trajectory with the *Shoah* are "The Flight into Egypt" and "The Bethlehem Babies": tales of "refugees" and "the mess of bodies in the common grave" (pp. 156–157), respectively.

Notes of a Heart-Patient (1993)

Shortly before her death on 24 March 1993, Gershon was working on a new collection of poems, "Notes of a Heart-Patient" (forthcoming as *Grace Notes*, 2002).

In the last poems, Gershon reconsiders the themes of earlier volumes—refugees and Jewish trials, family, Israel, and the Bible—while now facing her imminent death. In "Afterwards," the poet imagines her verses as refugee children:

When I am dead my orphaned memories
will squat about the world like refugees,
unable to help themselves, depending on
total strangers treating them like their own (p. 9).

Gershon considers explicitly Jewish experiences in several poems, including "The Death of Jews," "On Being a Jew," and "Yad Vashem." In the first of these, she confides: "To me, the death of a Jew/is a death in the family" (p. 40). "On Being a Jew" goes further in attempting a definition of Jews by neither "nation, race, or creed," asserting that "ineluctably, / a Jew is a Jew by his history" (p. 20). "Yad Vashem" returns to the scene of Gershon's "Israel Notebook 1966" (in *Legacies and Encounters*). Of the Holocaust memorial in Jerusalem, Gershon maintains:

It makes a family of all the dead,
making who mourn here all one family:
it is the Jewish people's family grave.

We suffer from a famine of relations;
here, in community of memory,
we find the closest family we have (pp. 48–49).

Critical Reception

Karen Gershon's poetry has been well received in her adopted home. As C. B. Cox astutely remarks:

> It shouldn't be implied that they [the poems] are memorable only because of their subject-matter, for Karen Gershon has developed a highly original technique. Usually each line forms a single rhythmic unit, the movement of the poem proceeding without conventional syntax, in a kind of litany of pain (p. 180).

Cox goes on to venture that Gershon is one of the "major war poets" of 1939 to 1945. Certainly, Gershon was influenced by the poets of 1914 to 1918. "My English mentors were the poets of the First World War," she states elsewhere, "especially Wilfred Owen" (*Collected Poems*, p. 2). John Smith notes that in Gershon's verse "a lot depends on how much one agrees with Owen: *the poetry is in the pity*" (p. 13). To be sure, Gershon's poetry follows Wilfred Owen's in urging pity, and the reception of poems as one would compassionately welcome "refugees / unable to help themselves" ("Afterwards," "Notes of a Heart-Patient," p. 9).

It is difficult not to read Gershon's lines autobiographically. Family proved a blessing for the poet in her adult life, yet she remained haunted by the parents she had lost: "the dead are beyond reach and reason: / they haunt us and we feel alone" ("Grace Notes," "Notes of a Heart Patient," pp. 24–25). Although Gershon claimed to have lost her religious faith, she also felt that faith ineradicably within her: "As some dead stars are plain to see / my childhood faith remains in me. ("The Death of Jews," "Notes of a Heart Patient," p. 40). The poet associated grace and faith with the home from which she had been uprooted, as well as the home she made in England. Indeed, home itself, for this German-Jewish refugee, was akin to holiness. As Gershon writes in "The City of David" ("Notes of a Heart-Patient"): "and we call holy where he was at home."

Bibliography

Primary Sources

Poetry

The Relentless Year: New Poets 1959, with Christopher Levenson and Ian Crichton Smith. 1959.
Selected Poems. 1966.
Legacies and Encounters: Poems 1966–1971. 1972.
First Meeting. 1974.
My Daughters, My Sisters. 1975.
Jephthah's Daughter. 1978.
Coming Back from Babylon. 1979.
Collected Poems. 1990.
Mich nur zu trösten bestimmt (Only Meant to Comfort). 2000.
Grace Notes. 2002 (forthcoming).

Novels

The World Was Old (as Karen Loewenthal). 1956.
Burn Helen. 1980.
The Bread of Exile. 1985.
The Fifth Generation. 1987.

Other

We Came as Children: A Collective Autobiography, (editor). 1966 and 1989.
Postscript: A Collective Account of the Lives of Jews in West Germany since the Second World War (editor). 1969.
"Journey to the Past." *The Jewish Quarterly* 144 (winter 1991–1992).
A Lesser Child: An Autobiography. 1994.

Secondary Sources

Baer, Edith. "Book Reviews." *Jewish Frontier* (May 1967): 36–39.
Berger, Alan L. "Jewish Identity and Jewish Destiny, the Holocaust in Refugee Writing: Lore Segal and Karen Gershon." *Studies in American Jewish Literature* 11, no. 1 (spring 1992): 83–95.
Carey, John. "Digging in the Sand." *New Statesman* (20 May 1966): 736–737.
Cox, C. B. "Patriots and Exiles." *The Spectator* (5 August 1966): 179–180.
Cunningham, Valentine. "Yesterday's Children." *The Observer* (10 April 1994): 19.
"Karen Gershon: Obituary." *Jewish Chronicle* (2 April 1993): 15.
"Karen Gershon: Obituary." *The Times* (London, 15 April 1993): 23.
Hartnett, David. "Traces of Darker Times." *The Times Literary Supplement* (London, 21 September 1990): 1007.
Longley, Michael. "Book of the Day." *Irish Times* (23 July 1966): 15.
Neuberger, Julia. "A Growing Disquiet." *The Observer* (11 March 1990): 61.
Pett, Vicky. "Karen Gershon: Obituary." *The Guardian* (22 April 1993): 17.
Smith, John. "Tragedy and Poetry." *The Tribune* (8 July 1966): 13.
Unterecker, John. *New York Times Book Review* (26 March 1967): 4.

Archives

Manuscripts of *A Tempered Wind* (1992), *Notes of a Heart-Patient* (1993), and Gershon's unpublished novels are housed at the poet's last address: The Coach House, Coach House Lane, St. Austell, Cornwall, United Kingdom.

AMIR GILBOA
(1914–1984)

HANOCH GUY

AMIR GILBOA WAS born Berl Feldman 26 September 1914 in Radivil, Ukraine. He eventually changed his name to leave behind the diasporic Jewish identity and assume an Israeli one, as many in his generation did. As a youth, he attended both a Jewish religious school and a Polish school. He avidly read texts of Jewish history and political Zionist books, and at the age of ten he composed a play and wrote diaries in Hebrew. From 1932 to 1937 he spent time in Poland; he joined a pioneer training camp at Lutsk in 1933. There he learned several labor skills that would be useful in Israel, including carpentry, logging, and quarrying. He remained active in Zionist organizations throughout this time. Leaving his parents and seven older siblings behind in 1937, he boarded an illegal ship in Cyprus that was sailing to Palestine, defying the British requirement for a certificate of entry into Israel. In 1938 he spent a year in the kibbutz of Givat Hashlosha. He published his first poem "*Ki Elzaak*" (When I Shout) in 1941, and Orkha published his first collection, *Laint* (Tiredness) in 1942. He volunteered in the British army from 1942 to 1946; he was first stationed in Egypt in a transportation unit. He traveled with the unit across North Africa, then to Italy, where his unit joined with the Hebrew brigade and traveled through Belgium and the Netherlands. After his return to Europe, he helped to smuggle Holocaust camp survivors from Austria, Germany, and Italy into Israel. Gilboa later worked for about thirty years in Tel Aviv as an editor in a publishing house.

Gilboa cherished his family that perished in the *Shoah* and wrote about his childhood, and his fond memories of time with his family, as well as his feeling of having been uprooted. In his *Shoah* poems he expresses grief, loss, and guilt over not having been able to recognize the impending catastrophe: "in those years of horror before we found out about that atrocity that was in our homes," he said, "I wrote . . . while awake and in a dream" (quoted in Barzel, p. 21).

In recognition of his literary achievements Amir Gilboa was awarded the Shlonsky Award for literature (1961), the Usishkin Award (1964), the Brenner Award (1970), the Bialik Award (1971), and the Dov Chomsky Poetry Award (1977). He was also honored with the State of Israel Award for Poetry (1982), and the New York University Neuman Award (1984). He died of a heart attack 2 September 1984.

Mourning His Family

Gilboa's book *Kehulim va-Adumim* (Blue and Red, 1963) is a compilation of many Gilboa collections. The book is dedicated to his parents and siblings, who perished in the *Shoah*, and included in the volume is a poem that serves metaphorically as a memorial candle for his family. The poet's pain is intense, and he is torn between his urge to extinguish the candle and the feeling that the candle is the only remnant he has of his family. Looking at the twisted candle he cries, mourns, and merges with the candle and his dying family:

> Let me extinguish it;
> It is not only a memorial soul candle.
> It is the twisted body candle
> Of my father and mother,
> Of my little sister,
> Of Esther.
> . . . . .
> The candle weeps incessantly
> . . . . . .
> It ferments in
> blood and tears
> (*Kehulim va-Adumim,* Tel Aviv: Am Oved, 1963, p. 58).

Gilboa blames himself for being blind to the ominous portents of the devastation that awaited his family and the Jews as a people; the signs that appeared, he says, as a scorching fire instead of the miraculous burning bush:

> I was standing at the threshold of my father's house
> when the world was burning
> and all eyes saw the fire
> and there was nobody to send the fire
> as a burning bush . . . (pp. 84–85).

The poet remembers that his father used to tell the family that the massacres of Jews by the Cossacks in 1648–1649 were the very last. Gilboa writes bitterly that his father said the Levites would sing again in the temple in 1928, when

> There will be no more abusers of children of Israel
> And no more Israelites slaughtered
> And no more burned Jewish houses (p. 311).

He writes that his father together with the prophet Daniel will lead a multitude of Jews as well as prophets to the slaughter. Daniel, who is the prophet of salvation, is portrayed by Gilboa as a helpless victim (Roskies, p. 20). The poet implies that the naïveté and faith in redemption gave the Holocaust's victims false hope. Gilboa ends the poem by recalling the biblical injunction to wage unceasing war on the biblical Kingdom of Amalek, in repayment for the Amalekites' cowardly and unprovoked attack on the feeble Israelites marching out of Egyptian bondage, and he asserts that so, too, do the Nazis merit punishment for their atrocities against innocent civilians. The Nazis are like biblical enemies, and it is incumbent upon the poet and his generation to remember and avenge the Holocaust.

Later in the poem, the poet helplessly knocks with his fists on the imaginary gates surrounding the Holocaust's many victims. The gates allude to the concluding prayer that is recited as part of the observance of Yom Kippur:

> Open for us the gate
> when the gate is locked . . .
> Let us come through your gates.

The Jewish faithful believe that during this most important prayer of Yom Kippur, God determines who will live and who will die. Therefore the congregation asks God to open the gates of compassion. Evoking a Hebrew literary convention whereby a sacred text is used irreverently—as a way of imitating an enemy's sacrilege, in a form of "counter commentary" that overturns the traditional text in the same way that the enemy disrupts the order of the world (Roskies, p. 20)—Gilboa thus reverses the outcome of the prayer of Yom Kippur. The gates of compassion remain closed. Indeed, God is not even mentioned in the poem.

The last night of 1942 haunts Gilboa. This was the night when his parents and siblings were murdered by the Nazis. It happened to be the eve of the Jewish holiday *Simchat Torah* (joy of the Torah).

> I see—
> a wall of red liquid
> rising and transparent.
> Through it an axe
> Smashing the crowns of glory
> Of my brothers (p. 55).

Hillel Barzel comments that the poem presents a reversal of the story of the Red Sea crossing as chronicled in the biblical book of Exodus, in which God parts the sea to save the Jews and destroy their pursuing enemies. Gilboa's expressionist "red liquid" heralds the demise of fallen twentieth-century Jews (p. 23). Instead of the wall of water that facilitated the crossing of the Red Sea of the Israelites, there is a wall of blood devouring them.

The poet realizes he was awarded the power of imagination but feels it is a false substitute for the loss of his family:

> This is our devoured soul and our madness ascending in a holy song. This is our umbilical connection in the cruel severing from the precious parents' home.
> This is a pain flown to heaven and the essence of our imagining power that is a disappointing compensation (p. 118).

This pain is incessant. It darkens his days, choking him. Because he is an orphan, he is unable to find happiness.

Guilt, Hate, and the Refusal to Forgive

In a two-line poem titled "A poem for the world," Gilboa states bluntly: "If my people forgive their murderers/there will be no atonement." Then the poet cries: "My mother, my mother!" (p. 287).

The poet is especially enraged by the idea of reparations offered by Germany, to *Shoah* victims and in another poem, he asks:

> How can we settle the account with them
> If they hand us thirty shekels.
> How will we keep the hate
> If we sell it
> And inherit the lie for our sons (p. 306).

Later in the same poem, Gilboa speaks for all the sons who feel guilty that they did not know about the horrible atrocity and:

> We did not come to rescue them from death
> we will not seek ransom of death
> We will keep the hate till a day
> Of settling the account.

As he waits to "settle the account," the poet lives in a duality of joy and sad memories that keep him up at night. He is waiting with other sons for their fathers to return. In one ballad, Gilboa imagines an eerie scene of the slain fathers emerging at a night's end:

> They came up
> from under every thick root, from the leaves'
>   thicket . . .
> These are our fathers
> We recognized them by the pupils of fire.
> By the sealed lips that became a black line
> And by the waxen parchment face . . . (p. 112).

The metaphor of cut trees is used to depict the victims of the *Shoah*. The butchered fathers rest on tree trunks, and the third part of the poem conveys the purpose of their return:

> We heard without voice, without anything said
> As a hatchet striking the rocks
> The command of: revenge
>   And hope (p. 113).

The sons rise to fulfill the command by burning their lips with embers in a prophetic initiation. An ax above every cut tree symbolizes the fathers calling for a day of reckoning for the murderers. According to Yosef Seh-Lavan, the poem calls the Jewish people everywhere to avenge the genocide, to punish the Gentiles responsible for the *Shoah* (p. 281).

"Isaac"

While in most poems Gilboa writes in the first person about the *Shoah*, in the poem "Isaac" he takes the persona of Isaac, taking on one of the most traumatic and evocative stories in the Bible. The poet subverts the Akedah, the story of Abraham's binding of his son Isaac in order to offer him as a sacrifice—and God's merciful intercession—to narrate a chilling tale of murder. Gilboa begins the poem with an idyllic scene of a father and son taking a stroll through the woods:

> Toward morning the sun strolled in the forest
> Together with me and my father,
> My right hand was in his left (Finer-Mintz, p. 248).

The early morning seems a testimony of good will. The hand-holding is reminiscent of the deep devotion described in the biblical Song of Songs, the long, lyrical love poem that reads as an allegory of the relationship between God and Israel. But the next stanza smashes any illusions about the unity between father and son: "Like a lightning flash, a knife between the trees / And I fear the terror of my eyes opposite the blood on the leaves."

The child calls to his father. Then the father's voice comes as an echo through the wood: "It is I who am slaughtered, my son, / And my blood is already on the leaves."

The father is the one who is butchered and the son wakes up (Tsalka 8). The sun is the co-conspirator of the murderer who is hiding, increasing the terror. God is missing from the poem, which alludes to his consent to the murder of the father.

Critical Assessment

Amir Gilboa's *Shoah* poetry, with its vivid imagery and inversions of sacred Jewish symbols, is distinguished by clarity, directness, and a profound expression of loss. Gilboa's translator Shirley Kaufman views Gilboa as the voice of his generation—expressing historical continuity with the biblical tradition and simultaneously experimenting with style (p. 12). Hillel Barzel has praised Gilboa's poetry for its "uniqueness that ranks him among the top Hebrew poets" (p. 189). Another critic, Avraham Shaanan, concedes that "for many readers [Gilboa's] poems remain unclear because of their special expression." Nonetheless, says Shaanan, "undoubtedly [Gilboa's] rhythmic and tonal expressions are powerful, even if his metaphors are sometimes obscure" (p. 193).

Bibliography

Primary Sources

Be-geto Roma (In the Roman ghetto). 1948.
Sheva Rashooyot (Seven domains). 1949.
Shirim ba-Boker (Poems in the morning). 1953.
Kehulim va-adumim (Blue and red). 1963.
Ish ha-mayim shel Gili (Gili's water man). 1963.
Ketaf (Picking). 1971.
Ayalah eshlakh otakh (Gazelle, I'll send you). 1973.
ha-Kol holekh: Rishumim yomaniyim be-onah me'uheret (Everything goes). 1985.
Ratsiti likhtov 'sifte yeshenim; 12 shirim; Ayalah eshlah otakh; ha-Kol holekh (I wanted to write the lips of sleepers). 1987.
Kol ha–Shirim. (Collected Works). 1987.

Translations of Gilboa's Work into English

Abse, D. "One Hundred Hats." *European Judaism* 5 (1970–1971): 31.
Anderson, Elliot. *Contemporary Israeli Literature*. Philadelphia: JPS, 1977, pp. 137–148.
Arad, Miriam, Stephen Mitchell, and Amir Gilboa. "Poems." *Ariel* 33–34 (1973): 11–13.
Bargad, Warren, and Stanley Chyet. *Israeli Poetry*. Bloomington: Indiana University Press, 1986, pp. 13–56.
Burnshaw, S., and T. Carmi. *The Modern Hebrew Poem Itself*. Cambridge, Mass.: Harvard University Press, 1989, pp. 137–148.
Carmi, Tscharney. *The Penguin Book of Hebrew Verse*. New York: Viking, 1981.
Finer-Mintz, Ruth. "Isaac." *Poetry* 92; no. 4 (July 1958): 248.
Frank, Bernhard. *Modern Hebrew Poetry*. Iowa City: University of Iowa Press, 1980.
Kaufman, Shirley, trans. *The Light of Lost Suns: Selected Poems of Amir Gilboa*. New York: Persea, 1979.
Schwartz, Howard, and Anthony Stanley. *Voices in the Art*. New York: Pushcart, 1980, pp. 80–85.

Secondary Sources in Hebrew

Balban, Abraham. *Mivhar Maamarai Bikoret* (Selected critical essays). Tel Aviv: Am Oved, 1972.
Barzel, Hillel. *Amir Gilboa: Monografya*. Tel Aviv: Sifriyat Poaalim, 1984.
Seh–Lavan, Yosef. *Amir Gilboa*. Tel Aviv: Or-Am, 1977.
Shaanan, Avraham. *Dictionary of Modern Hebrew and World Literature*. Tel Aviv: Yavneh, 1959.
Tsalka, Dan. *Amir Gilboa: Mivkhar Shirim Umamarim al Yetzirato* (A selection of poems and articles). Tel Aviv: Mahbarot Leshira, 1962.

Secondary Sources in English

Bargad, Warren. "Binary Oppositions in the Poetry of Amir Gilboa." *Association for Jewish Studies Review* (1988): 103–127.
———. "Poems of Saul: A Semiotic Approach." *Prooftexts* 10 (1990): 313–334.
———. *To Write the Lips of Sleepers: The Poetry of Amir Gilboa*. Cincinnati: Hebrew Union College Press, 1994.
Bronstein, H. "Who Can Still Bless the Light?" *Journal of Reform Judaism* 26 (fall 1979): 1–20.
Kipnis, T. "Devotion to the Promised Land." *American Zionism* 59, no. 28 (spring 1968).
Roskies, David. *Against the Apocalypse*. Cambridge, Mass.: Harvard University Press, 1984.
Shaked, Gershon. *Hebrew Writers*. Jerusalem: Institute for Hebrew Translations, 1993, p. 49.
Yom Kippur Mahzor (Prayer book). Jerusalem: Sinai, 1960.

NATALIA GINZBURG

(1916–1991)

JUDITH KELLY

BORN IN PALERMO ON 14 July 1916, Natalia Ginzburg was the youngest of the five children of Giuseppe Levi and Lidia Tanzi. The family moved to Turin in 1919 because her father had been offered the chair in anatomy at the university. During the 1930s she came to know Primo Levi, who was a friend of her brother, Alberto, and a regular visitor to the family home. In 1938 she married Leone Ginzburg, a Jewish Marxist and active anti-Fascist who, because of his political activities, was exiled by the Fascist regime in 1940. He was sent to Pizzoli, an isolated village in the south of Italy, where Natalia joined her husband in exile. The couple moved to Rome following Mussolini's arrest in July 1943. In November of that year her husband was arrested by the authorities and died in the hospital on 5 February 1944 as a result of torture in Rome's Regina Coeli prison. Natalia Ginzburg spent the next few months in hiding with her three children, Carlo, Andrea, and Alessandra. In 1945 she returned to Turin, together with her parents and her children, and worked for the publishing firm of Einaudi. She remarried in 1950, but her husband, Gabriele Baldini, died in 1969 after an operation. In 1983 she was elected to Parliament as an Independent, and was reelected in 1987. She died in Rome on 8 October 1991.

Literary Output

Natalia Ginzburg's first published novel, *La strada che va in città* (*The Road to the City*, 1942), came out under the pseudonym Alessandra Tornimparte. As Ginzburg explains to Marino Sinibaldi (Garboli & Ginzburg, pp. 33–34), she adopted the pseudonym because in 1942 the Fascist Racial Campaign was underway, and publication of works by Jewish authors was forbidden. Inspiration for the novel came from Ginzburg's period of political exile with her husband in Southern Italy, and the manuscript was taken to Turin during a short leave of absence and subsequently published by the Einaudi publishing house, where Ginzburg worked in the postwar period. Ginzburg goes on to tell Sinibaldi that she discovered what it was to be Jewish while in exile, but that she only realized the gravity of her situation when Polish and German internees arrived with tales of the experiences they had endured.

Much of Ginzburg's literary output bears little direct relation to her experience of discrimination and exile, but her autobiographical narrative, *Lessico famigliare* (*Family Sayings*, 1963), which won the Strega literary prize in 1963, gives sharp, personal insight into the events of the Fascist period insofar as they impinged upon the author and her family. Her father was Jewish and her mother Catholic, but the difference of religious faith is initially mentioned only because of the misgivings of Ginzburg's paternal grandmother about such a union. Her doubts are quickly overcome after an evening at the theater with her future daughter-in-law, and her censure then centers upon her other son's wife, who is an actress. In conversation with Marino Sinibaldi (Garboli & Ginzburg, p. 65) Ginzburg describes herself as being both Jewish and Catholic, which she terms "una doppia cittadinanza" (a dual citizenship).

Ginzburg recounts her father's fury at seeing Fascist blackshirts in the street, or upon discovering that university colleagues had joined the Fascist ranks. She also remarks upon the ferocious family arguments about Fascism, which she was still unable to understand even in later life, given that all the family was demonstrably anti-Fascist. Her brother, Mario Levi, was arrested on the Italian side of the Swiss border for being in possession of anti-Fascist literature, but escaped his captors by jumping in a river and swimming to the safety of neutral Switzerland. Ginzburg's father was also arrested and imprisoned by the Fascist authorities for nearly three weeks, while her eldest brother, Gino, was detained for two months. Her youngest brother, Alberto, was also arrested, imprisoned in the Regina Coeli prison in Rome, and later sent into internal political exile. Ginzburg describes the family home being searched by the Fascists, but her main memory of this was that her mother secreted shop receipts in Natalia's school bag, to prevent the Nazis uncovering them and her father becoming aware of her mother's expenditures.

References in *Lessico famigliare* (*Family Sayings*) to momentous events of the period tend to be rather elliptic: this is an autobiographical narrative in which personal and family memories are recounted, rather than a chronicle of events. Thus the murder by Fascist agents of the Rosselli brothers, who were well-known members of the Italian Resistance group Giustizia e Libertà (Justice and Freedom) is mentioned in a single sentence, without any description of the reaction of other anti-Fascists or the consequences for the Resistance movement, which had lost two of its bravest representatives. The effects of antisemitic persecution in Germany and the flight of German Jews from their homeland is recorded in two sentences: "Torino, da anni, era piena di ebrei tedeschi, fuggiti dalla Germania. Anche mio padre ne aveva alcuni, nel suo laboratorio, come assistenti" (For years Turin had been full of German Jews who had fled from Germany. Even my father had a few of them in his laboratory, as assistants) (p. 130). Ginzburg mentions the start of the racial campaign in Italy only in relation to her reaction and that of some Jewish female friends who, having already enrolled before the racial laws came into effect in 1938, are allowed to continue their university studies. Universities were forbidden to accept Jewish students after 1938. Natalia's friends accept the situation "senz' ombra di panico" (without a shadow of panic) (p. 137). References to the implementation of the racial campaign continue to give personal rather than broadly historical insight into the situation. The author recounts that Jewish relatives, friends, and acquaintances were either leaving Italy for destinations in North or South America, or were preparing to leave, but that she and her husband, Leone Ginzburg, were unable to leave because the Fascist authorities had taken their passports and deprived Leone of his citizenship. She also details the fact that her father had lost his university chair, and it is implicit that this was because he was Jewish. Having taken employment in Belgium, he was then forced to flee the country following the German invasion. In a wry twist of fate, when the ambulance in which he was traveling arrived in Boulogne it was commandeered by German soldiers, to whom he volunteered his unmistakeably Jewish surname and his intention to return to Lièges, where they promptly returned him.

Natalia Ginzburg recalls the period of internal political exile as being happy and tranquil, mainly because of the friendship demonstrated toward her husband, children, and herself by the townspeople of Pizzoli. However, following the fall of Mussolini, her husband went to Rome where he resumed his clandestine anti-Fascist activities. Natalia followed later with the children when German troop movements started to make their place of exile dangerous. However, twenty days after joining her husband in Rome, he was arrested, and Natalia and the children went into hiding and never saw Leone again. She refers to the assistance she received from Adriano Olivetti, of the famous typewriter firm, and of the comfort that she felt upon seeing him, "dopo tante ore di solitudine e di paura" (after so many hours of loneliness and fear) (p. 168).

After the war the family learned of the fate of the Jewish parents of Natalia's sister-in-law, Miranda. Despite the implementation of the Fascist racial laws, which severely curtailed their freedom of association and rights as citizens, like so many Italian Jews they were unable to believe that the restrictions were any more than a bribe given by Mussolini to Hitler. Refusing to take the precaution of assuming false names or obtaining identity cards, following the occupation of northern Italy by Nazi troops they were denounced, captured, and transported to an unknown destination from whence they did not return. In *Lessico famigliare* (*Family Sayings*) Ginzburg recounts the chain of events, but does not go into detail about the emotional or psychological effect of this news upon the family. Nor does she recall other similar stories, of which there would have been many because the Jewish community in Turin lost many members in just such circumstances during the Nazi occupation. Miranda's parents are emblematic of all those family acquaintances who did not return home at the end of the war.

Lessico famigliare (*Family Sayings*) is as close as Ginzburg comes to describing the suffering that she and her family endured because of antisemitic persecution in Italy. In a foreword to the narrative she advises readers that if they attempt to read it as a chronicle they will find much missing. Critics of Ginzburg's writings rarely deal with themes such as her politics or her Jewish identity. This is because her experiences have undoubtedly in some way contributed to her formation as a writer, but have not directly informed her writings. As Bullock notes: "The persecution of Jews figures in *All Our Yesterdays* [*Tutti i nostri ieri*] as part and parcel of the horrors of war without emerging from the general background of progressive devastation . . . ; the few references elsewhere are minimal and have no bearing on plot or characterisation" (pp. 6–7, n. 5).

Bibliography

Primary Sources

La strada che va in città (*The Road to the City, Two Novelettes*). 1942.
È stato così (*The Dry Heart* in *The Road to the City, Two Novelettes*). 1947.
Valentino (*Two Novellas, Valentino & Sagittarius*). 1951; reprint 1957.
Tutti i nostri ieri (*Dead Yesterdays*, reprinted as *All Our Yesterdays*). 1952.
Sagittario (*Two Novellas, Valentino & Sagittarius*). 1957.
Le voci della sera (*Voices in the Evening*). 1961.
Le piccole virtù (*The Little Virtues*). 1962.
Lessico familiare (*Family Sayings*). 1963.
Cinque romanzi brevi (Five Short Novels). 1964. (Includes *Un'assenza* [An Absence, 1933], *Casa al mare* [House by the Sea, 1937], *Mio marito* [My Husband, 1941], *La madre* [The Mother, 1948].)
Il maresciallo (The Marshall). 1964.
Ti ho sposato per allegria e altre commedie (I Married You for Joy and Other Plays). 1968. (Includes *Ti ho sposato per allegria* [I Married You for Joy, 1965], *L'inserzione* [*The Advertisement*, 1965], *Fragola e panna* [Strawberry and Cream, 1966], *La segretaria* [The Secretary, 1967].)
Mai devi domandarmi (*Never Must You Ask Me*). 1970.
Caro Michele (*Dear Michael*). 1973.
Paese di mare e altre commedie (Seaside Place and Other Plays). 1973. (Includes *Paese di Mare* [Seaside Place, 1968], *La porta sbagliata* [The Wrong Door, 1968], *Dialogo* [Dialogue, 1970], *La parrucca* [The Wig, 1971].)
Vita immaginaria (Imaginary Life). 1974.
Borghesia (*Family*). 1977.
La famiglia Manzoni (*The Manzoni Family*). 1983.
La città e la casa (*The City and the House*). 1984.
Opere raccolte e ordinate dall'Autore (Works Collected and Ordered by the Author). 1986– .
L'intervista (The Interview). 1989.
Serena Cruz o la vera giustizia (Serena Cruz or True Justice). 1990.

Secondary Sources

Bullock, Alan. *Natalia Ginzburg: Human Relationships in a Changing World*. New York & Oxford: Berg, 1991.
Garboli, Cesare, and Lisa Ginzburg, eds. *Natalia Ginzburg. È difficile parlare di sé*. Torino: Einaudi (Gli struzzi, 508), 1999.
Hughes, H. Stuart. *Prisoners of Hope: The Silver Age of the Italian Jews 1924–1974*. Cambridge, Massachussetts, London: Harvard University Press, 1983.
Jeannet, Angela M., and Giuliana Sanguinetti, eds. *Natalia Ginzburg: A Voice of the Twentieth Century*. Toronto: University of Toronto Press, 2000.
Quarsiti, Maria Luisa. *Natalia Ginzburg. Bibliografia, 1934–1992*. Firenze: Giunti, 1996.
Simborowski, Nicoletta. "Music and Memory in Natalia Ginzburg's *Lessico familiare*." *Modern Language Review* 94, no. 3 (July 1999): 680–690.
Soave Bowe, Clotilde. "The Narrative Strategy of Natalia Ginzburg." *Modern Language Review* 68, no. 4 (October 1973): 788–795.

Archives

Relevant letters and other documents can be found in the Fondo Manoscritti (Manuscript Archive) at the University of Pavia. Other essays and articles can be found in Quarsiti, Maria Luisa, Natalia Ginzburg. *Bibliografia, 1934–1992* (see secondary sources).

JACOB GLATSTEIN

(1896–1971)

BEN FURNISH

JACOB GLATSTEIN WAS born in Lublin, Russia (now Poland), on 20 August 1896, the son of Yitskhok and Ite Rokhl (Yungman) Glatstein. As a child, Glatstein received a traditional religious education, but his father also hired private tutors for him to learn secular subjects. His father also introduced him to Yiddish literature through the works of Sholem Aleichem, Y. L. Peretz, and others. Glatstein even traveled to Warsaw as a youth to meet Peretz. Thus, unlike almost all Yiddish writers before him, Glatstein grew up familiar with the Yiddish literary tradition rather than coming to it as an adult.

During Glatstein's youth, conditions for Jews in Russian Poland were deteriorating. After two years of deliberation, Glatstein's parents agreed to his wishes to emigrate to New York City in June 1914. He left his parents behind in Europe to live with his uncle on the Lower East Side. There, he worked at what he estimated was over fifty different factories during World War I. In 1919 he married his first wife, Nettie. She supported him as he almost completed a law degree at New York University, and after he abandoned law studies to write poetry and publish the Yiddish literary journal *In Zikh* (Introspection). The couple had three children.

Early Career

Glatstein taught Yiddish for a year at a Sholem Aleichem School but had to resign after a romance with a student in 1923. He then began his lifelong career in Yiddish journalism, which eventually included regular columns in the *Morgn-Dzhurnal* (Morning-Journal) and *Der Tog* (The Day), as well as editing roles with *Der Yidisher Kemfer* (The Jewish Fighter), *Di Tsukunft* (The Future), *Folk un Velt* (People and World), and other publications.

At New York University Law School, Glatstein met two other Yiddish writers, A. Glants-Leyeles and N. B. Minkov; together, they led the way to innovations in the form and content of Yiddish poetry. Known as *Inzikhistn* (Introspectivists), after *In Zikh*, the name of their journal and title of the 1919 manifesto that stated their artistic rationale, these youthful writers were more influenced by American culture than their elders of a few years, the *Di Yunge* (young) group, who in turn were more influenced by Russian and German literary currents.

The *Inzikhistn* brought modernism to Yiddish poetry by developing such innovations as free verse and poetic syntax suggestive of actual conversation; exploration of highly personal subjective emotional states, perspectives, and symbols; and the conviction that Yiddish writers need not limit themselves to specifically Jewish topics. No matter the subject matter, they approached it from a Jewish perspective because Jewishness was integral to their identity. *Inzikhistn* maintained that each poem's form should be determined by that poem's own unique artistic needs rather than by any a priori structure. Glatstein's first book of poems, *Yankev Glatshteyn*, appeared in 1921.

In 1934 Glatstein returned for the only time in his life to Lublin, where his mother was dying. This experience inspired his two novels, *Ven Yash iz Geforn* (*Homeward Bound*, 1938) and *Ven Yash iz Gekumen* (*Homecoming at Twilight*, 1939). Although Glatstein conceived these novels as a trilogy, he never finished the third volume. At this time he also drafted notes for poems that he later considered to be his first writing about the Holocaust. In 1940 he published a book for young readers, *Emil un Karl*, about a friendship between a Jewish and a Christian boy in Vienna near the time of Austria's *Anchluss* (merger) with Germany.

The Holocaust affected Glatstein directly and deeply as a human being and artist. Glatstein lost his father and other close relatives to the Nazis. The Holocaust marks a turning point in his career as a poet, not only in its importance as subject matter for much of his later work, but also for the way in which he shifted his focus from formalistic innovation to exploring how to use poetry to express a horror so profound that it virtually defied language itself. Glatstein not only lost close family members to the Nazis, he also lost his childhood Jewish community of Lublin, virtually the whole of the Eastern European Yiddish cultural milieu, and finally, any hope for new generations of Yiddish readers for his work.

In the post–World War II years, Glatstein wrote not only about the Holocaust itself but about the subsequent evaporation of the Yiddish cultural milieu in America. His journalistic and poetic output continued unabated, and he struggled to maintain high standards for his work and for Yiddish despite the inexorable decline in the number of readers of Yiddish literature. Though as a youth he had exerted the right of Yiddish writers to explore universal (or at least not traditionally Jewish) themes, subjects, and symbols, in the later decades Glatstein relied significantly on traditional Jewish cultural source material to inform his poetic vision.

In 1952 Glatstein divorced Nettie to marry the artist Fanny Mazel, whom he met in 1933. They remained together until his death.

Among Glatstein's honors were the Lamed, Leivik, Kessel, and Kovner prizes for Yiddish literature, an honorary doctorate from Baltimore Hebrew College, and the Yizkor Prize of the World Federation of Bergen-Belsen Associations, which published his Holocaust-related poetry in a collected volume, *Kh'tu Dermonen* (*I Keep Recalling*), in 1967. Glatstein also coedited one of the first English-language anthologies of Holocaust literature in 1969. He died 19 November 1971, in New York City, at a time when a number of events were being held to celebrate his seventy-fifth birthday.

Poetry

Glatstein's first three poems published in 1919 (which he selected to reprint in his last poetry collection before his death) remain famous among readers of Yiddish literature: "Tirtl-toybn" (Turtle Doves); "In Roykh" (In Smoke); and "1919." These poems exemplify the *Inzikhistn*'s artistic principles, and were foundational to Glatstein's later work, including his poems about the Holocaust.

The first group of Holocaust-related poems are those of the late 1930s, which presage the coming catastrophe. Two of the most famous, both from 1938, are "A Gute Nakht, Velt" ("Good Night, World") and "Vegener" ("Wagons"). (These poems can be found in *Gedenklider* [In Remembrance], 1943.) With an eerie near prescience, Glatstein writes in the first poem about erasing cultural assimilation by returning to the ghetto wearing the yellow star to study sacred texts, although the self-chosen ghetto he describes in the poem differs sharply from Nazi-imposed ghettos that would follow. The poem also clearly expresses a disillusionment with Western culture as its voice offers to send back all its "would-be saviors," "the Jesusmarxes" (from *I Keep Recalling: The Holocaust Poems of Jacob Gladstein*, translated by Barnett Zumoff, Hoboken, NJ: Ktav, 1993, p. 4).

Glatstein said he wrote "Wagons" after learning about Nazi experiments on German Jews in the mid-1930s. It describes a group of sick Jews who arrive in sad wagons at a village where there is no one to meet them. Glatstein writes that the old Jewish men see in each other's eyes a prayer that "If death should come, / May I not be the only one to remain alive" (*I Keep Recalling*, p. 6).

From "A Gute Nakht, Velt" and "Vegener," *Gedenklider* traces Glatstein's growing awareness of Nazi atrocities. The book contains two sections, the latter of which, "Nem a Pinkus un Farshrayb" (Take a Record Book and Record), focuses on contemporary events in Europe. "In the Year 5699" symbolizes the events of 1939 as an inverted Passover in which Christian children's lives are spared while the yellow patch on Jewish doorposts marks those homes for death. "Birgerkrig" ("Civil War") is written in the voice of the biblical Abel addressing Cain, representing their fraternal struggle as being renewed in every generation of human conflict. The matriarch Rachel weeps for the Jewish dead in "Lublin, 1941," written in the voice of Herschel, a recently orphaned eleven-year-old boy who hears Rachel's cries. Herschel notes his community's as-yet-futile cries to the highest heavens and speculates that perhaps God has forgotten all of them.

"Tsum Tatn" ("To My Father"), written in the poet's first-person voice to his father trapped in Lublin, combines Glatstein's tender recollection of how his father raised him to be a Yiddish writer with how he imagines his father is facing death. In the 1943 poem "Milyonen Toytn" ("Millions of Dead"), Glatstein clearly grasps the scale of Jewish loss to the Nazis. This poem introduces two of Glatstein's most important responses to events: the need to sanctify the dead by eternally remembering their fate and the eternal futility of consolation in the face of their deaths. He writes, "Forever will our living people / Be dead with millions of dead." (p. 56). In "Got Iz a Troyeriker Maharal" ("God Is an Unhappy Maharal"), Glatstein inverts the legend of the Maharal Rabbi Yehuda Leyb ben Bezalel of Prague and the golem. As in the original legend, the golem monster that the Maharal creates to protect the Jewish community instead runs destructively amuck; so does God, as Maharal sees the creature he once loosed upon the world, Divine Punishment, now run out of control destroying that which God sought to safeguard.

Gedenklider closes with "Unzer Tsikhtik Loshn" ("Our Neat and Tidy Language"), in which Glatstein expresses how he is loathe to defile the Yiddish language by using it to describe the Germans' crimes against the Jews. As the poem continues, it relies increasingly on German words transliterated into the Yiddish alphabet rather than Yiddish words to show that only the Germans, in their "blood-sausage language" (the German words *blut-wurst shprache*), can roar about their insane revenge upon the defenseless innocent (for which Glatstein uses the Yiddish word *shvakhe*). Not only does blood sausage combine the *treyf* (unkosher) elements of pork and blood, but it also symbolizes the Germans' bloodthirsty behavior.

The second half of *Gedenklider* thus introduces a range of themes that remained important in Glatstein's subsequent work and in other works of Holocaust literature, including the failure of Western liberalism and the question of how Jews should respond ("A Gute Nakht, Velt"), the inconsolability of the Jewish people's loss and the sanctity of memorializing that loss, the dimensions of that loss in personal ("Tsum Tatn") and collective ("Milyonen Toytn") terms, the use of longstanding Jewish cultural images such as Cain and Abel ("Birgerkrig"), the golem, and, most significantly, God ("Got Iz a Troyeriker Maharal"). For the rest of his life, Glatstein found himself returning to these themes as he wrestled with despair and with trying to comprehend the meaning and responsibilities of his own survival.

Shtralndike Yidn (Radiant Jews) was published in 1946. Considered by many to be his finest work, this volume intensifies and expands upon the Holocaust themes introduced in *Gedenklider*. Where in *Gedenklider* Glatstein used indictment as a poetic stance against the Germans, in *Shtralndike Yidn* he levels indictment against God. Glatstein also continues to struggle with both personal and communal loss by further inverting traditional Jewish images. Beyond their evident despair and anger, his poems ultimately conclude that Jewish life in the Holocaust's aftermath has been irrevocably redefined in ways that will take time to comprehend.

A talmudic legend maintains that all Jews stood together at Sinai to accept the Torah. In "Nisht di Meysim Loybn Got" ("The Dead Don't Praise God"), Glatstein extends the legend:

> We accepted the Torah on Sinai,
> And in Lublin we gave it back.
> The dead don't praise God—
> The Torah was given for life.
> And just as we all stood together
> At the giving of the Torah,
> So indeed did we all die at Lublin (from *I Keep Recalling*, p. 92).

Here, Lublin represents not only the destruction of Glatstein's home community but all of European Jewry. As Hadda notes (pp. 83–84), the poem harshly and ironically inverts Psalm 115, in which the dead are those who do not accept the supremacy of the God of Israel. In Glatstein's poem, all those from every generation who accepted the God of Israel's Torah are now dead. The Torah, rendered useless without a people to keep it alive, disappear. "On Yidn" ("Without Jews") further explores the implications of Israel's death: "Without Jews there will be no Jewish God" (p. 108). As the last Jews of the world, the Jewish dream and reality are disappearing, soon God, too, will be gone. Who, the poem asks, will now be left to dream of, remember, deny, or leave in order to return to, the God of Israel?

Two other poems in *Shtralndike Yidn* further explore the vexing problem of God's failure to prevent the Holocaust, albeit in diverging ways. "Mayn Vogl-Bruder" ("My Fellow-Wanderer") begins with the line, "I love my sorrowful God" (p. 112) but far from being a traditional hymn of praise to God's perfection, the poem actually explores God's transformation into a fallible human being who wanders, suffers, and inflicts suffering. The speaker describes his fellow wanderer as "the God of my disbelief" (p. 114) and describes God as dear to him "now that He is human and unjust." God confides in the speaker that he now sees the Jewish people, in their present suffering, as godlier than He is. The martyred speaker of "Heyliker Nomen" ("Holy Name") proclaims that if he were Abram son of Terah he would rather "bow to all sorts of destroyers" (p. 114) than accept God's covenant. Better to accept the covenant of the machine gun or the flying fortress than that of the killer of whole peoples. No matter how much fate may reverse itself, the poem continues, heaven can never repay its debt to the murdered Jews, and no matter how greatly future generations mourn them, these Jews shall insist, even from the grave, that they never understood God's intention in permitting their deaths.

Glatstein's encounter with the divine in *Shtralndike Yidn* assembles evidence for indictment against God, but Glatstein sometimes transmits his indictments as lamentations of grief as well as proclamations of guilt. In fact, in "A Vort in Moyl" ("A Word in My Mouth"), God appears as an old, sick, ridiculed beggar. This poem's voice implores the reader not to blaspheme God, but rather to be His defender just as Rabbi Levi

Yitzkhok of Berdichev defended the Jewish people before God. Clearly in this and other poems, Glatstein mourns the loss of God and the Torah as well as the martyred Jews. What is missing from the indictment, what still mystifies Glatstein despite his own actual lack of religious belief, is God's motive for failing to stop the Germans from slaughtering the six million. Glatstein can only speculate: God has become human and therefore fallible; God has grown enfeebled; God has committed some kind of sick, incomprehensible joke; God has somehow vanished at the worst moment.

In one of *Shtralndike Yidn*'s most poignant poems, "Mayn Bruder Binyomen" ("My Brother Benjamin"), Glatstein asks God why He needed Benjamin to live forty-four destitute years. Benjamin's only happiness in life was his family, his wife and son. Glatstein asks God, "Did you really want him and his wife to live / To experience the overflowing joy / Of leading their only son / To the marriage-embrace of the ovens, / Where You cremated all of them?" (p. 132). Although Glatstein's personal loss of his brother, sister-in-law, and nephew is profound in itself, he speaks in almost a national voice as he holds God responsible for Benjamin's fate and, by implication, the fate of millions of Jews like him.

Other poems in the book deal with such Holocaust-related topics as "Vidershtand in Geto" ("Ghetto Uprising") and "Sutzkever" (about Vilna poet Avrom Sutzkever). Even in the ambitious poem "Kh'Davn a Yidish Blat in Sobvey" ("I Pray a Yiddish Paper in the Subway"), which contains no explicit mention of it, the Holocaust seems to loom constantly for the reader behind every threat that Glatstein senses around him. While the word *blat* in the subway context indicates a newspaper, the word can also refer to studying a page of Talmud—hence Glatstein *davns* (prays) the page. Glatstein demonstrates how reading a Yiddish newspaper in a New York subway is a spiritual exercise. While Glatstein's non-Jewish neighbor, who tells him to "Be a man, read American," can read his newspaper for pleasure, the Yiddish newspaper reader's news offers no such escape. The Yiddish newspaper is his daily *siddur* (prayer book), his *shakhres* (morning prayer). He notes how freely the non-Jew next to him can move throughout the world, express whatever political views are his wont, his passport quietly in his pocket. In contrast, Glatstein's passport rests uneasily in his pocket—American or not, he does not feel safe in the world, even in this New York subway.

Shtralndike Yidn closes with two poems that form their own section: "Kh'tu Dermonen" ("I Keep Recalling") and a prose poem, "Lublin, Mayn Heylike Shtot" ("Lublin, My Holy City"). The latter is a catalog listing what Glatstein describes as a sacred place, particularly the Maidenek woods where the Nazis killed thousands in the shadow of nearly one thousand years of Jewish history in Poland. Glatstein ends the poem by saying, "But my holy city, the city of my world, will never be rebuilt" (p. 160). "Kh'tu Dermonen" forms a powerful conclusion to *Shtralndike Yidn* by elegantly interweaving Glatstein's private losses and tragedies, his "individual, smaller Holocausts," with the Jewish national tragedy. The lengthy poem contains lists of details about Glatstein's early life in Lublin and how Glatstein understands their significance more deeply in light of the Holocaust. For example, he now sees his mother as the mother of the entire Jewish people, the repository of its entire Yiddish culture and language, all of which he sees passing from the world with her death and the deaths of Jewish mothers like her. Glatstein chose "Kh'tu Dermonen" as the title work for his 1967 collected Holocaust-related poems.

Glatstein's next book, *Dem Tatns Shotn* (My Father's Shadow, 1953), contains only a few Holocaust-related poems. Glatstein was entering a new period of his life and work in which he realized that the Holocaust would remain with him for as long as he lived, yet he also realized that the memory of this cataclysmic event might prove ephemeral, dying with him and his generation. In "Do Lign" ("Here Lies"), the poem's narrator realizes that the memory of the Holocaust can remain clear "only for one generation of love" (from *Dem Tatns Shotn* by Jacob Gladstein, New York: Farlag Matones, 1953, p. 144).

Glatstein continued to struggle with the problem of God, but he no longer focused on indictment. Instead, he tried various poetic means to maintain some sort of relationship with God in view of the Holocaust's irremediable fact. The narrator of "Kh'vell Zikh Ayngloybern" ("I'll Find My Faith") speaks of building a new Jewish community with a God who does not sleep and who watches over the community, even its cemetery of "worried corpses." The poem's ending reveals the speaker to be one who died at Maidenek and seeks to defy that fate by starting a new life—though sadly, the poem's ending leaves little hope for the narrator's success.

In "Der Daytsh Trakht" ("The German Thinks"), Glatstein writes in the voice of a defeated Nazi who describes the quiet that would have reigned had Germany won the war as it had planned. Then the wailing of the Nazi victims' relatives, whose continued survival in the world represents the problem of "half-finished work," would be silenced. Instead of Jewish tombstones and German guilt, Western civilization could have enjoyed German monuments and Jewish silence. The poem's chilling implication is that the greatest mistake the Germans made according to Western mores, which value victory as the ultimate virtue, was not in slaughtering millions of victims but in losing the war in which victory would have brought them moral redemption—at least according to the relativist standards of the non-Jewish world.

Glatstein's two 1960s collections, *Di Frayd fun Yidishn Vort* (The Joy of the Yiddish Word, 1961) and *A Yid fun Lublin* (A Jew from Lublin, 1966) continue the trend in *Dem Tatns Shotn* of diversification of the author's themes and images from the strong emphasis on the Holocaust found in *Gedenklider* and *Shtralndike Yidn*. However, certain themes, such as the problem of God after the Holocaust and the Jew's place in Western life after the Holocaust, recur. "Got's Dorn" ("God's Thorn-Bush") describes a bush that burns and is consumed, Moses is lost, everything is destroyed, and God weeps from a distance, bewailing "my holy clouds of smoke." The bush can be seen as the murdered Jews, many of whom were incinerated in crematoria that belched clouds of smoke. God is no longer indicted but suffers alongside the Jews. In "A Zun" ("A Son"), Glatstein again wrestles with how Jews are to respond to the Holocaust. A son of murdered millions has a right to anger, a reason to mourn, and in a world in which the "hunters" carry long swords but short memories, a responsibility to remember.

In 1967 Glatstein wrote in the introduction to his collected Holocaust poems, *Kh'tu Dermonen*, that the Jewish and German peoples face unique circumstances after the Holocaust among the peoples of the world. No other nations have experienced and perpetrated, respectively, industrial mass murder. Thus, a special account remains to be settled—perhaps can never be settled—between the Germans and Jews. Glatstein rejects the idea of a "new Germany" as sounding insane, and implores his Jewish readers—he assumed the poems would receive scant attention from Christian readers—not to forget what Germany did to the Jewish people.

Critical Reception

Glatstein won general acclaim from his critics first as a leading Yiddish writer and literary critic of the twentieth century, and particularly as the leading Yiddish modernist poet. His command and manipulation of the Yiddish language—its vocabulary and musicality—was one of the most sophisticated of all Yiddish writers. That reputation was already well on the way to being established when the events of the Holocaust occurred.

Glatstein used poetry to interpret those events and their devastating impact on his personal life and on the Jewish people. He remained largely true to his modernist artistic principles by not allowing polemics or sentimentality to overwhelm the transformative art of his poetry, yet he also unflinchingly confronted the challenge that the Holocaust posed to him as an artist and human being. He cast those challenges as the legitimate, even necessary and inescapable, subject of the Jewish poet's eye. In fact, as Harshav and Harshav suggest, Glatstein's youthful *Inzikhist* convictions, particularly in rejecting as a false "either/or," the opposition between Jewishness and universality, proved important preparation for his subsequent poetry on Holocaust themes. Glatstein's Holocaust-related poetry is thus poetry first and foremost, not mere polemic in verse form. Second, it reflects the poet's own highly personal voice, vision, and poetic structure. Third, it draws fully on a Jewish communal perspective that includes a rich vein of Jewish cultural imagery, tradition, and reference for metaphor.

Glatstein further maintained his commitment to his artistic standards by insisting to the end of his life that he and other serious Yiddish writers sought attention for their work strictly for its literary value. He rejected any attention based upon mere pity, curiosity, or sentiment (as when he reacted negatively to Cynthia Ozick's story "Envy, or Yiddish in America," which portrayed the fading contemporary Yiddish literary scene in a manner he found patronizing).

The Holocaust certainly forms a midway point dividing Glatstein's career chronologically and thematically. Hadda identifies a major split in how critics understand these two distinct periods in Glatstein's career. Some critics, like Y. Rapoport and Shmuel Lapin, maintain that Glatstein underwent a transformation as a result of the Holocaust. An artistic rebellious son, the Holocaust compelled him to recognize his Jewish responsibilities. Arn Glants-Layeles and others maintain, in contrast, that although Glatstein remained the same artist as before, the Holocaust afforded him an opportunity to write material that won him more recognition in the Jewish world. As Hadda concludes, both sides are partially correct. Howe praised Glatstein for retaining the first-person poetic voice, which he introduced into Yiddish during his early *Inzikh* period, and into his Holocaust writing as well. Howe summed up his literary merits: "Jacob Glatstein was a major, perhaps a great, poet, even though the world did not know him and is never likely to" (p. 77). Yet over thirty years later, Glatstein's work is not only still being read, but his Holocaust-related poetry in particular forms an important, creatively honest body of work through which to explore the literary and imaginative dimensions of the Holocaust.

Bibliography

Primary Sources

Poetry

Yankev Glatshteyn (Jacob Glatstein). 1921.
Fraye Ferzn (Free Verses). 1926.
Kredos (Credos). 1929.
Yidishtaytshn (Yiddish Meanings). 1937.
Gedenklider (In Remembrance). 1943.
Yosl Loksh fun Khelm (Yosl loksh from Chelm). 1944.
Shtralndike Yidn (Radiant Jews). 1946.
Dem Tatns Shotn (My Father's Shadow). 1953.
Fun Mayn Gantser Mi (Of All My Labor). 1956.
Di Freyd fun Yidishn Vort (The Joy of the Yiddish Word). 1961.
A Yid fun Lublin (A Jew from Lublin). 1966.
Kh'tu Dermonen (I Keep Recalling). 1967.
Gezangen fun Rekhts tsu Links (Songs from Right to Left). 1971.

Fiction

Ven Yash iz Geforn (*Homeward Bound*). 1938, 1969.
Ven Yash iz Gekumen (*Homecoming at Twilight*). 1939, 1962.
Emil un Karl (Emil and Karl). 1940.

Prose and Edited Works

Finf un Zibetsik Yor Yidishe Pres in Amerike (Seventy-five Years of the Yiddish Press in America). Edited with Shmuel Niger, Hillel Rogoff, 1945.
In Tokh Genumen (Sum and Substance). 3 vols. 1956, 1960.
Mit Mayne Fartogbikher (With My Morning Books). 1963.
Af Greyte Temes (In Ready Times). 1967.
Anthology of Holocaust Literature. Edited with Israel Knox, Samuel Margoshes. 1969.
In der Velt mit Yidish. 1972.
Prost un Poshet. 1978.

Glatstein Collections

Poems by Jacob Glatstein. Translated by Etta Blum. 1970.
Selected Poems of Jacob Glatstein. Translated by Ruth Whitman. 1972.
Selected Poems of Yankev Glatsheyn. Translated and edited by Richard J. Fein. 1987.
I Keep Recalling: The Holocaust Poems of Jacob Glatstein. Translated by Barnett Zumoff. 1993.

Secondary Sources

Bikel, Shloyme. "Yankev Glatshteyn: Gezamlte Lider." In *Shrayber fun Mayn Dor*. New York: Farlag Matones, 1958, pp. 108–115.
Faerstein, Chana. "Jacob Glatstein: The Literary Uses of Yiddish." *Judaism* 14 (1965): 414–431.
Fein, Richard J. Introduction to *Selected Poems of Yankev Glatshteyn*. Edited and translated by Richard J. Fein. Philadelphia: Jewish Publication Society, 1987, pp. xv–xxx.
———. "Glatshteyn's Critical Motive." *Yiddish* 9, no. 2 (1994): 5–11.
"Glatstein, Jacob." *Encyclopaedia Judaica*. New York: Macmillan, 1971, pp. 615–616.
Goldsmith, Emanuel S. Introduction to *I Keep Recalling: The Holocaust Poems of Jacob Glatstein*. Translated by Barnett Zumoff. New York: Ktav, 1993.
Hadda, Janet R. *Yankev Glatshteyn*. Boston: Twayne, 1980.
Harshav, Benjamin, and Barbara Harshav, eds., trans. *American Yiddish Poetry*. Berkeley: University of California Press, 1986.
Howe, Irving. "Journey of a Poet." *Commentary* 53 (January 1972): 75–77.
Lapin, Shmuel. "Jacob Glatstein: Poetry and Peoplehood." *American Jewish Yearbook* 73 (1972): 611–617.
Niger, Shmuel. "Dem Tatns Shotn" and "Rozhinkes mit Mandlen." In *Yidishe Shrayber fun Tsvantsikstn Yorhundert*. New York: Alveltlekhn Yidishn Kultur Kongres, 1973, pp. 9–16, 17–25.
Orenstein, Eugene. "Jacob Glatstein." In *Encyclopedia of World Literature*. Edited by Steven R. Sarafin. Farmington Hills, Mich.: St. James Press, 1999, pp. 263–264.
Tabatshnik, Avrom. "A Conversation with Jacob Glatstein." Translated by Joseph C. Landis. *Yiddish* 1 (summer 1973).
Whitman, Ruth. "The Man and His Work." In *The Selected Poems of Jacob Glatstein*. Translated by Ruth Whitman. New York: October House, 1972, pp. 11–23.

MICHAŁ GŁOWIŃSKI

(1934–)

KATARZYNA ZECHENTER

MICHAŁ GŁOWIŃSKI WAS BORN in Pruszków on 4 November 1934 as the only son of Felicja Rozenowicz and Henryk Głowiński, a clerk. After the beginning of World War II, his family first resided in the Pruszków ghetto, but was later moved to the Warsaw ghetto from which they escaped in January 1943. For some time, Głowiński and his mother hid in Warsaw while his father found a refuge in Kielce. Later, thanks to Irena Sendler, the head of the Children's Section of Żegota (Council to Aid Polish Jews), Głowiński was placed in an orphanage run by the Sisters Servants of Saint Mary, in a village of Turkowice where he survived the rest of the war. A large part of his family—his parents, grandparents, two aunts, and cousins—survived as well. After the war he studied Polish literature at Warsaw University and graduated in 1955. Since 1958 he has been working in the Institute of Literary Research at the Polish Academy of Science (IBL PAN). Głowiński has been, since 1976, a full professor of Polish literature and the chairman of the scientific council at the Polish Academy of Science. Since 1969 he has been on the editorial board of *Literary Review* (*Pamiętnik Literacki*) and collaborated with many literary journals such as *Creativity* (*Twórczość*), *Texts* (*Teksty*), and *Second Texts* (*Teksty Drugie*). He has also published widely in Polish émigré journals, especially in Parisian *Culture* (*Kultura*), and has clandestinely published journals in communist Poland such as *Independent Culture* (*Kultura Niezależna*) and *Criticism* (*Krytyka*). He is the author of numerous volumes devoted to the theory of literature, poetics, the mechanisms of communist propaganda, and, in general, the language of totalitarian systems and "newspeak" (*nowomowa*) in communist Poland. He is also the author of two slim volumes devoted to experiences in surviving the Holocaust: *The Black Seasons* (1998), which was nominated in 1999 for the Nike Award, the most prestigious literary award in contemporary Poland, and *The Madelaine Made from Whole-Meal Bread* (2001). Currently he is working on his third autobiographical book, *The History of One Poplar and Other Stories* (*Historia jednej topoli i inne opowieści*), which will, however, include elements of fiction.

Holocaust Works

Michał Głowiński belongs to the latest group of Polish writers of Jewish origin (such as Wilhelm Dichter), who did not begin writing about the Holocaust until they were in their late fifties or sixties. As such he belongs to the last generation of writers who describe the Holocaust based on their personal experiences and memories. In his documentary books, however, Głowiński openly admits his inability to remember certain facts and situations, yet chooses not to make changes, for he feels it not only "inappropriate" (p. 7) but also dangerous to make his stories literary rather than autobiographical or even documentary.

Głowiński's works devoted to the Holocaust are collections of loosely connected essays in more or less chronological order. Both volumes deal with the Warsaw ghetto, hiding outside the ghetto, the postwar years, Stalinism and communism in Poland, and certain aspects of Głowiński's reaction to contemporary Germans and to German culture in general. They are written in a simple, sometimes colloquial, Polish with each chapter devoted to one important event, often followed by a conclusion describing the psychological consequences of the experience on Głowiński's later emotional life. Głowiński often interrupts the story line to analyze what made people behave the way they did and wonders about the complexity of human nature.

The story titled "The House under the Eagles" is devoted to an almost proverbial stepmother who helped Głowiński's mother and other Jews in hiding, and who hid a small Jewish boy: "because this courageous, active woman, readily helping other people, was a domestic tyrant with a soul of a corporal, not allowing even the tiniest sign of opposition" (p. 87). Another story, "The Black Hour," is devoted to a young man who came to blackmail his mother and, being bored while waiting for the money, decided to play chess with the boy for whom "death took the image not of a Death with a scythe but a tall man with a smartly trimmed mustache" (p. 67).

The first essay of *The Black Seasons*, "The Fragments from the Ghetto," is devoted to the sensory aspects of Warsaw ghetto reality where Głowiński's family found itself after being moved from a short-lived ghetto in Pruszków. Głowiński discusses sensory inputs including the color of the ghetto as a unique grayness, the color of paper used to cover the dead bodies in the streets; the complete lack of any nature (no trees, grass, horses, dogs); the smell of poverty in the ghetto; hiding in a cellar to escape being taken to the *Umschlagplatz*, and one of its emotional results: his later inability to use the word "selection" in everyday speech. The following chapter ("The Cookie") is devoted to a minor event that took place in the ghetto, but which made him realize his complete helplessness and vulnerability in the face of the terror. After a long illness his mother promised to buy him a cookie for good behavior, yet when she finally did, a hungry child ("*ocrachmunes*," p. 22) pulled it out of his hands and ate it immediately. This event led Głowiński to a realization that "nothing will happen according to his will, that he will risk aggression and that everything that he would like to have and is important to him, can be taken away from him" (p. 22). Although giving ample evidence of the psychological trauma of ghettoization and hiding, *The Black Seasons* provides the reader with a somewhat balanced view of life: the experience of immediate danger is often balanced against another person's help and a situation seen as tragic (the house in which the family was offered a hiding place was burned) turns into a situation helping Głowiński and his mother to survive:

> so now when I look from such a long distance at the events of that day in December 1943, I wonder whether the fire on Odolańska Street was not a happy tragedy and if not for that fire, my Mother and I would not have survived the occupation. Maybe even the owner of the house owes her life to it for the Germans would have, for sure, sentenced her to death for hiding Jews in her home (p. 82).

The following four chapters concentrate on Głowiński's stay in an orphanage in Turkowice where he was one of thirty Jewish children hidden by the nuns. The danger posed by the Germans and the Ukrainian nationalists who eventually killed one of the nuns and some children, constitutes the background for an analysis of the emotional state of a Jewish child separated from his family: a situation that led him to a state of constant apathy similar to that experienced by victims of extreme hunger. The moment of danger occurs when three brothers threaten to denounce him to the Germans: "the cruelty of an epoch is concentrated and reflected in the cruelty of children" (p. 116), is offset by the behavior of Sister Róża, who not only reassured him that the three brothers would be punished for their behavior, but also gave him a piece of bread with the last piece of butter, although there was already hunger in the orphanage. Sister Róża's act is presented to restore balance; Głowiński's "indescribable fear" (p. 114) subsides because of the piece of bread, which became "something more than a portion of food able to satisfy hunger: it transformed itself into a sign that here there are people who are kind to me, and that the world is not as horrible, as I believed a few minutes before" (p. 121). Such an approach, as well as the often-expressed gratitude to the nuns, suggests an explanation for why, despite the horrors Głowiński describes, his stories still exhibit some faith in humanity.

The last four chapters of *The Black Seasons* are devoted to the early postwar years, yet are not devoid of horrors other than escaping death. Most disturbing is a chapter devoted to a priest who taught religion in Głowiński's primary school and whose antisemitism eventually led to "praising genocide" (p. 152), and to the destruction of a fragile emotional equilibrium Głowiński achieved during the first years after the war. Facing such a situation led not only to almost forgetting the orphanage in Turkowice and the people to whom "he owes his own life" (p. 154) but also to a fear of others and a realization of his vulnerability: "I felt threatened again and even more alienated than usually" (p. 153). The last chapter, "And the Germans Are People Too" (the title is reminiscent of the title of a drama by Leon Kruczkowski), serves as a far-reaching analysis of Głowiński's approach to Germans after the war: he "has not seen a good German. I saw only the executioners" (p. 170). Despite the passing of time and his intellectual understanding that not all Germans are responsible for the Holocaust, Głowiński remains uncertain how to answer the question: "but really, are they people like others? I cannot forget my doubts" (p. 182).

Out of twenty-nine essays that constitute the story line of the second autobiographical volume, *The Madelaine Made of Whole-Meal Bread*, only two ("From Ghetto to Ghetto" and "The Return") deal with the Holocaust. The majority are devoted to the early years of aggressive communism and Głowiński's studies during these years; a few (with one exception) question whether some of the people he describes might have been Jewish (they had no families), or they might have left Poland at the end of the 1960s. Despite describing concrete characters, Głowiński attempts to analyze personalities typical of the communist period, sometimes even including elements of fiction. (*The Black Seasons*, on the other hand, contains no such elements as it is intended as a documentary.) The last essay, "The Return," is devoted to Głowiński's trip to the orphanage in Turkowice where he found refuge during the war. Although he is unable to find any traces of the orphanage (after the war it was taken from the nuns and the nuns were forced to leave), his intention is not to confront reality with his memories but rather to see the place the way he was unable to see it during the war. Głowiński does not intend to "free himself completely from the past for it would equal forgetting" (p. 213), and forgetting is something that his autobiographical books intend to prevent.

Bibliography

Primary Sources

Poetyka Tuwima a polska tradycja literacka (*Tuwim's Poetics and the Polish Literary Tradition*). 1962.

Zarys teorii literatury (*Outline of the Theory of Literature*). Co-authored with A. Okopień-Sławińska and J. Sławiński. 1962.

Porządek, chaos, znaczenie. Szkice o powieści współczesnej (*Order, Chaos, Meaning: Sketches on Contemporary Novel*). 1968.

Powieść młodopolska. Studium z poetyki historycznej (*The Novel of the Young Poland: Studies in Historical Poetic*). 1969.

Wiersze Bolesława Leśmiana (*The Poems by Boleslaw Leśmian*). 1971.

Gry powieściowe (*The Literary Games*). 1973.

Słownik terminów literackich (*The Dictionary of Literary Terms*). Co-authored with T. Kostkiewiczowa, A. Okopień-Sławińska, and J. Sławiński. 1976.

Style odbioru. Szkice o komunikacji literackiej (*The Style of Reception*). 1977.

Zaświat przedstawiony. Szkice o poezji Bolesława Leśmiana (*The Other World Presented: Studies of Bolesław Leśmian's Poetry*). 1981.

Mity przebrane: Dionizos, Narcyz, Prometeusz, Marchołt, labirynt (*The Myth in Disguise*). 1990.

Nowomowa po polsku (*The Newspeak in Polish*). 1990.

"Ferdydurke" Witolda Gombrowicza (*"Ferdydurke" by Witold Gombrowicz*). 1991.

Marcowe gadanie (*The Talks in March*). 1991.

Poetyka i okolice (*The Poetics and Vicinity*). 1992.

Rytuał i demagogia. Trzynaście szkiców o sztuce zdegradowanej. (*The Ritual and Demagog: Thirteen Sketches on Degraded Art*). 1992.

Peereliada. Komentarze do słów 1976–1981 (*The People's Poland: Comments on Words 1976–1981*). 1993.

Pisamk 1863 i inne szkice o róznych brzydkich rzeczach (*The Literary Hack in 1863 and Other Sketches on Bad Things*). 1995.

Mowa w stanie oblężenia 1982–1985 (*The Speech in the State of Siege*). 1996.

Czarne sezony (*The Black Seasons*). 1998.

Magdalenka z razowego chleba (*The Madelaine Made from Whole-Meal Bread*). 2001.

Secondary Sources

Adamczyk–Garbowska, Monika. "A New Generation of Voices in Polish Holocaust Literature." *Prooftexts: A Journal of Jewish Literary History* 9, no. 3 (1989): 273–287.

Fik, M. "Czy warto pisać o socrealiźmie?" *Puls* 6 (1992).

Gawryś, Cezary. "Turkowice–śmierć i ocalenie." *Węęź* 4, no. 342 (1987).

Kornhauser, J. "Literatura na telefon." *Dekada Literacka* 9 (1993).

Leociak, Jacek. "W cieniu Zagłady. Literackie świadectwa Holocaustu." http://www.wirtualnywydawca.pl/8.09.zlpolska 2000.doc

Łukaszewicz, M. "Straszny dziadunio socrealizm." *Nowe Książki* 3 (1993).

Paldiel, Mordecai. *The Path of the Righteous: Gentile Rescuers of Jews During the Holocaust*. Hoboken, 1993.

———. "*The Rescue of Jewish Children in Poland and the Netherlands*." In *Burning Memory: Times of Testing and Reckoning*. Edited by A. L. Eckardt. Oxford, 1993.

Sliwowska, Wiktoria, ed. *The Last Eyewitnesses: Children of the Holocaust Speak*. Chicago, 1998.

Stefanowska, Z. "Michał Głowiński jako badacz nowomowy." *Teksty Drugie* 4 (1992).

Tomasik, W. "Ubizm." *Teksty Drugie* 2 (1993).

Werbowski, Tecia, and Irene Tomaszewski. *Żegota. The Council for Aid to Jews in Occupied Poland, 1942–1945*. Montreal, 1999.

LEA GOLDBERG

(1911–1970)

HARRIET L. PARMET

LEA GOLDBERG WAS born in Kovno (Kaunas), Lithuania, on 29 May 1911, where she spent her early childhood. She moved with her family to Saratov, Russia, during the First World War. When the war ended she returned to Kovno, finishing high school in 1928. She studied Semitic languages, German studies, and history at the universities of Berlin and Bonn, completing a doctoral dissertation on the Samaritan translation of the Bible (*Encyclopedia Judaica*, 1972, s.v. Lea Goldberg, p. 703).

A Zionist most of her life, Lea Goldberg arrived in Palestine in 1935. In the same year her first book of poems, *Smoke Rings*, was published. Goldberg was a member of the avant-garde writers group directed by Avraham Shlonsky, publisher of the literary magazine *Turim*. After a career as a schoolteacher, she joined the staff of the Labor Union's newspaper *Davar* as theater critic and later (1943) became editor of *Al Hamishmar*'s literary supplement. She prodigiously published poetry in Hebrew newspapers and journals and in her many books of poetry. Goldberg also wrote literature for children as well as theoretical articles on children's literature. She served on the staff of *Davar Liyladim*, a popular children's magazine, and was the editor of *Sifriyyat Poalim*. She was appointed the literary adviser to *Habimah*, Israel's national theater. In 1952 she was invited to chair the Comparative Literature Department at the Hebrew University of Jerusalem and did so until her death in 1970. In 1954 she joined a delegation of "Democratic Women" to visit the former Soviet Union. However, when it came to accepting the "Socialist realism" decreed from Moscow, she refused. Goldberg defined culture as the masterpieces of the Russian pre-Revolutionary Golden Generation, most especially Tolstoy, whose *War and Peace* (1958) she translated into Hebrew. Other classics she translated include Chekhov's stories, Gorki's *Childhood* (1943), whose titles she also translated, several plays and poems by Shakespeare (1957), selected poems of Petrarch, and Ibsen's *Peer Gynt* (1958) (*Encyclopedia Judaica*, p. 704).

Lady of the Castle

Lady of the Castle (1956), a play exploring themes of Diaspora and Israeli Jewish identity against the backdrop of Holocaust memory, was the only Goldberg play published and performed in her lifetime. It was presented in 1959 by Israel's Chamber Theater and hailed as an immediate success. Gershon Shaked, Israeli scholar and critic wrote, "*Lady of the Castle* may be the first play whose problem is a universal one: the crisis of our generation in its cultural perspective" (p. 186).

This play is neither set in Eastern Europe during the war nor does it focus on survivor problems in Palestine. The text explores the meeting of Israeli rescuers with a Holocaust survivor who was fortunate to escape the horrors of ghettos and concentration camps, but experienced tensions and anxieties associated with being in hiding. The venue is an old castle in a Central European country about two years after the Second World War (1947), the backdrop for an examination of European and Israeli locations as viable sites for rehabilitation of Holocaust survivors and Jewish continuity. Three themes, which are closely interwoven with the cultural conflict between the characters, dominate *Lady of the Castle*: New versus Old; Jew versus Christian; Israeli versus European. The dramatist never draws a clear-cut line between the polarities and does not categorically decide in favor or against them. Zabrodsky, the caretaker of the castle and former aristocratic owner is, according to Shaked, a tragic hero who vainly tries to overcome time and its destructive power, which the critic interprets as a sign of the dramatist's nostalgia for a world bound to romantic and aesthetic ideals. Thus Goldberg, who by conviction belonged to a left-wing socialist movement that aspired to better the life of the people, was emotionally and perhaps subconsciously attached to the culture of prewar Europe—the culture whose only remaining champion is the lonely old caretaker of the castle. Goldberg's German studies and dedication to teaching the masterpieces of European literature could explain this positive, even tragic portrayal of the former count. His intellectualism, conservatism, nobility, and high aesthetic sense are, after all, what produced the Goethes and Schillers of European culture (Taub, p. 17).

Through Israeli rescuers of Holocaust survivors, Goldberg juxtaposes the Zionist culture with the Diaspora. Dora Ringel, an Israeli social worker, is the agent of the new culture, on a mission to discover surviving Jewish children in Europe and transfer them to Israel. Between Dora's and the ex-count's extreme views are those of Michael Sand, a practicing Zionist committed to building a Jewish homeland in the Middle East. Sand is capable of integrating his European past, both the good and the bad, into his new life. He is the perfect example of the kibbutznick who, after plowing the fields in Galilee or the Negev, relaxes with the art of Mozart and Tolstoy. Nineteen-year-old Lena, whose name is an abbreviation for Helena, represents the Greek cultural model. She is a Holocaust survivor who remains concealed in Zabrodsky's castle, believing the lies her benefactor tells her regarding the continuation of the war and the ever-present Nazi danger. Fearing for her safety, she is reluctant and mistrustful, resisting Dora's pressure and promises of a better life. The drama foregrounds a deep emotional and conceptual disparity between the ideological new Israeli stance of the rescuer and the unmitigated anguish and loss of the survivor (p. 73).

Thus, the essence of the conflict is seen in the apparently uncompromising contrast between two different spiritual/intellectual worlds. The moribund world, which has been condemned to death with its treasures, charms, and noble sickly isolation, is a world that is no longer anything but a home for ghosts, even though it still retains remnants of its past fascination. In contrast is the world the rescuers offer, a materialistic world in lieu of the romantic; harsh conditions in place of escapist luxury; equality and a classless society in place of aristocracy and privilege for the few. It is a world that sees all ghostly castles as suspect.

Zabrodsky's ancestors belong to the highest Christian hierarchy, but he is certainly not antagonistic toward the Jews. Zabrodsky finds a commonality between his Jewish, European and Israeli ancestors, as well as of those of Dora and Sand. As Glenda Abramson observes, Zabrodsky loves Lena, but even more he reveres her as a symbol of the past, which he is unable to relinquish. She, in turn, regards him as her protector and has developed a certain affection for him; over the years the two have acted out in secret the conventions of a vanished time, a vanished world (p. 117). For Dora, he is a reminder of all she condemns: European aristocracy, Christian persecution of Jews, and his association with Nazis who used his castle as their headquarters. In actuality, he hated the Nazis because they threatened the culture he values.

A reading of the revelation of St. John is vital for an understanding of Zabrodsky's attitude toward the present and future. By deceptively prolonging the nightmare of the Nazi threat, the count creates an atmosphere conducive to Lena's conversion to his mystical vision of redemption drawn from St. John's revelation. Some of Goldberg's readers were shocked to discover the aforementioned Christian reference. In many of her poems, one finds church bells, Madonnas, and quotations from the Christian Bible. In any case, all of this is intrinsic to her European upbringing. Gradually, however, these symbols become muted as Goldberg becomes more and more enthralled with the vistas of Israel.

Dora and Sand reconcile their cultures: the old Europe and the new dynamic Israel. One of Sand's self-imposed tasks is to collect the traditional Jewish books written in Europe and make them an integral part of the new culture in Israel. Books and libraries are important, significant connections to the old world.

Literary Perspectives

Goldberg's unique treatment sets *The Lady of the Castle* apart from many Israeli Holocaust dramas. Although the meeting with the survivor, Lena, is only a few hours in duration, it nonetheless serves as a microcosm of the issues that have shaped Israeli society for many years. From Lena's perspective, the prospects of leaving the old world with its familiar and safe surroundings is frightening. As someone who has been frequently mistreated, she is suspicious of Dora's promises of a better, freer life in the Jewish state. Lena is indeed cynical. One can understand her preference for the constancy and steadfastness of the count over the uncertainties awaiting her in Dora's and Michael's promised land.

The meeting with Lena forces the rescuers to confront a world they left behind for a new life in Palestine. For Michael and Dora, Europe means persecution, humiliation, and ultimately the Holocaust. For Michael, however, these memories are ambiguous because unlike Dora, he can transcend Europe's antisemitism and elitism and appreciate its rich cultural traditions. For Dora, Palestine symbolizes a much brighter future, freedom, and hope. Even though the Europe of the immediate postwar held little hope for the remaining Jews, Dora's cliché-ridden propagandistic statements about Palestine do not ring true, challenging what she represents in the play and reinforcing the count's defense of old values and old Europe, a world the Nazis and the war have managed to destroy.

The literary style of the play is in the Gothic tradition: a castle, mistaken identity, ghosts, trap doors, mysterious keys, a shared birthplace, a locket containing poison, and so on. Obviously, the play has been written by a poet who yearns with sorrow for the magic of the dead world; an Israeli poet, however, who depicts a failure to come to terms with the full horror of the Holocaust. As Gershon Shaked reminds us, "The survivors remain vulnerable and tormented. The Zionist home saved their bodies, but could not restore their spiritual repose" ("Afterword," p. 288). This Hebrew poet will not allow herself to be totally taken in by the alien charms the castle embraces, as they are the stuff of legends and ghosts. Goldberg's stand is finally crystallized as the present is chosen; the Jewish girl is rescued from her prison by Michael and Dora (Lena is hidden in the basement and never sees the sunlight). Lena actually participates in the castle's complete liquidation.

Robert Alter writes in *Commentary* that Goldberg's play makes explicit a pattern that is implicit or has already been worked through psychologically in the best of her poems. The play deals with a young survivor of the Holocaust in a manner that tends toward melodrama and quasi-allegorical schematization. This sensitive girl has been confronted by the adult world and with personal and historic facts of terror that tempt her to choose madness, which is seen as a virtual suicide, rather than adult life. Lena ultimately chooses life. It is interesting to note that it is poetry, a children's song (shared with Dora), that Lena clings to as a talisman to help her out of the nightmare of violated childhood into a hoped-for world of light (p. 85).

Lady of the Castle is distinguished by its attempt to raise the immediate and familiar subject to another level, to add another dimension, one that is simultaneously historical, unusual, and personal.

Bibliography

Primary Sources

Pegishah 'im meshorer: 'al Avraham Ben Yitshak Sonah. 1952.

Ba'alat ha-armon: epizodah dramatit be-shalosh ma'arkhot. 1955 or 1956.

Light on the Rim of a Cloud; 14 Poems by the Hebrew Poet Leah Goldberg. 1972. English version by Ramah Commanday.

Room for Rent. 1972.

Lady of the Castle: A Dramatic Episode in Three. 1974. Translated from the Hebrew by T. Carmi.

Russian Literature in the Nineteenth Nentury: Essays. 1976. Translated into English by Hillel Halkin.

Selected Poems. 1976. Translated and introduced by Robert Friend.

ha-Gal ha-kal shel ha-shirah ha-'Ivrit: pizmonot-pirsum. 1984 or 1985.

At telkhi ba-'sadeh: shirim u-manginet / [shirim]. 1989.

Secondary Sources

Barzel, Hillel. *Shirat Erets-Yisra'el : Avraham Shlonski, Natan Alterman, Le'ah Goldberg.* Tel-Aviv: Sifriyat po'alim, 2001.

Liblikh, Amiyah. *El Le'ah.* Tel Aviv: ha-Kibuts ha-me'uhad, 1995.

Orkhot, Rut Kartun-Blum Ve-'Anat Vaisman. *Pegishot 'Im Meshoreret : Masot U-Mehkarim 'Al Yetsiratah Shel Le'ah Goldberg.* Tel-Aviv: Sifriyat po'alim, 2000.

Solgnik, Nili. *Me'afyene Ha-Humor Be-Shirat Ha-Yeladim Shel Le'ah Goldberg.* Jerusalem: N. Solgnik, 1999.

REBECCA GOLDSTEIN

(1950–)

EZRA CAPPELL

In *Mazel* my character Sasha sees a young I. B. Singer walking down the street and overhears him saying something, something which he actually had said in a story. A woman asks him: "Why are we Jews so doomed?" And he answers: "Because we love life too much." And that to me somehow says so much about our history. You know not to see us only in terms of that tragedy, and not to feel the victim because that is not about us, that is about them. That is what they did to us, but that's not what we're about. We're not about being martyred, and we're not about suffering, and we're not about victim-hood; we're about celebration" (Rebecca Goldstein, Interview, October 2000).

RENEE FEUER, THE first-person narrator of Rebecca Goldstein's novel *The Mind-Body Problem* (1983), wanders into a small restaurant in Vienna faint from hunger. Renee has been following her husband Noam Himmel, a world-renowned mathematician, across the European continent on an academic journey that doubles as their honeymoon. When Renee notices that the waitress's arm bears the blue tattoo of a concentration camp survivor, amazed to find a survivor living in Austria, she asks the waitress: "And you still live here?"

The waitress replies: "I lived in America for a few years after the war, in New York's Washington Heights . . . But I am Viennese . . . In spite of it all. In spite of the fact that I can look out into this square and remember when it flowed with blood. I am Viennese" (Penguin Books, 1993, p. 109). What was it that drew Renee Feuer to that café of all the many she and Noam had passed that afternoon? When it comes to imagining and representing the Holocaust, as well as the rich texture of Jewish history, Rebecca Goldstein cannot help but dream Jewish dreams.

Being an ethical, humanistic writer in the aftermath of the Holocaust, Goldstein repeatedly asks: How can we not attempt to represent this monumental loss to world history? As it did for Renee and for many of Goldstein's characters, the Holocaust, either through familial history or by historical import, became a centering force. Concerning the effect of the Holocaust on her work, Goldstein replies:

> I know that it looms large in my psyche. In some sense it was something I actually wanted to get past, for example, in writing *Mazel.* I think that we have been scarred, all of us collectively, the world, not just Jews, although particularly Jews, scarred by the trauma, that we forget what their lives were like before. We see them in terms of their end and the tragedy and we forget about the fullness and the richness of that culture—and the joyfulness, the sort of life-embracing, vivid, intense celebration of life" (Interview).

Until her teens Rebecca Goldstein believed that her father was a concentration camp survivor. She held this belief despite the fact that her father had immigrated to America in the early 1930s. In a recent interview she says:

> Now my father was Polish and for some reason throughout our childhoods my younger sister and I somehow connected, we thought somehow that he had gone through the camps. There was something about him that made us really think that he had . . . so if I am not a child of survivors, I think I have very much the sensibility, to a certain extent, of a child of survivors. There was such a sense of the hurt, of the betrayal, of the broken lives in our family" (Interview).

Goldstein's childhood beliefs reinforce Arthur Cohen's observation in *The Tremendum* that American Jews are the Holocaust witnesses who "bear the scar without the wound." Goldstein is a writer on the front lines of a generation of writers who in Cohen's words feel "the obligation, self-imposed and self-accepted (however ineluctably), to describe a meaning and wrest instruction from the historical" (p. 2). The nexus of ideas that animates Goldstein's lyrical prose swirls around the issue of memory, both private and historical. Thus the Holocaust, both as moral educator and as personal history, is often at the center of her short stories and novels.

Goldstein is a writer and philosopher concerned with the many ways in which people balance the competing claims of mind and body, reason and desire. It is therefore not surprising that Goldstein, as a Jewish American writer and as someone profoundly interested in her characters' personal philosophy, is drawn to the darkest aspects of humanity and the history of her own family in the Holocaust. Concurrently, Goldstein, through her philosophical and fictional universe, wrestles with the dilemma of bearing witness to the Holocaust from a generational distance. Indeed, as dramatized in much of her fiction, but perhaps most poignantly in her short story "The Legacy of Raizel Kaidish" (in *Strange Attractors*), her haunting and unparalleled evocation of the psychological consequences of Holocaust survival and the bequeathed emotional legacy with which the second generation must somehow reckon, lay bare the costs of both emotional detachment in the face of trauma and terror, as well as the perils of emotional involvement, all the time forcing the reader to contemplate the awesome demands that are a consequence of each position. In the end the reader is left pondering whether these two philosophical positions are as mutually exclusive as Goldstein's thwarted and frustrated characters would have us believe.

Concerned with the long and proud history of her people, Goldstein is not satisfied with a fictional universe that limits itself to portraying only the twelve years of the Third Reich. In her novel *Mazel* (1995), which won both the National Jewish Book Award and the Edward Lewis Wallant Award, Goldstein gives voice to the pre-Holocaust culture of the Jews, focusing on the vibrancy and culture that was largely destroyed by the Nazis. Unlike many second-generation writers dealing with the Holocaust, rather than focus entirely on the destruction of European Jewry, Goldstein attempts to reanimate that lost world by beginning in prewar Poland to show the rich and varied cultural life that flourished in Warsaw before the war. In the tradition of Aharon Appelfeld, who in *Badenheim 1939* shows the calm before the storm in a resort community in Austria on the eve of the Holocaust, Goldstein's *Mazel* chapters set in prewar Poland create almost unbearable tension within readers who are aware of what in a few short years will befall European Jewry and engulf Goldstein's characters.

Biography

Goldstein was born in 1950 into a traditionally Orthodox home in White Plains, New York. Her father was, in Goldstein's words, "a *shtickele chazzan*" (a minor cantor), who immigrated to America in the 1930s. He was to have a profound and lasting influence on Goldstein's life and work. Goldstein attended an Orthodox *Beis Yaakov Yeshiva* for girls. The Yeshiva's antifeminist teachings also left their mark on Goldstein in her dual roles as a mother and writer. After graduating from *Beis Yaakov*, Goldstein, against her mother's wishes (it was unacceptable for a traditional Jewish girl to go to college), enrolled at Barnard College where she earned her B.A., before going on to Princeton where she earned a Ph.D. in philosophy. After completing her Ph.D., Goldstein returned to Barnard where she taught in the philosophy department for ten years. Goldstein has won two Whiting Awards, a grant from the American Council of Learned Societies, and was awarded a "Genius Grant" from the MacArthur Foundation. She has two daughters, Yael and Danielle, and lives in Brooklyn, New York.

In speaking of her family's Holocaust history, Goldstein says:

> My father was born in a shtetl in Poland (Lemberg). He left before the war. He was one of the youngest in a large family, so they came over. His older sister is the only one who married and settled over there so she and her four children, four of my first cousins, of course, died. That was on the Polish side. On my mother's side, the Hungarian side, my grandmother had come over by herself from Hungary, she had a huge family, very artistic, very prominent, very wealthy, they almost all died. There were a few who managed to survive from this very large family (Interview).

Those few who did survive would often come to stay with Goldstein's family in White Plains. Memories of these immigrant survivors, the few remnants, were formative for the young Goldstein. She says:

> There was one in particular, Zanvil, who really impressed me because he was so arrogant. He would order my mother, and us girls around, do this and do that. He was a shriveled up broken little man. And my mother did not like to be ordered around [but] she did it. She picked up after him. She did everything. And I said, "He's so obnoxious, why are you doing this?" And she would say, "You don't want to know. You don't want to know." And I was always hearing this: "You don't want to know." She'd say: "He was in the camps." I'd ask: "What does that mean?" She'd say: "You don't want to know." So I got the sense of these people that something incredibly horrible and mysterious had happened to them. I remember my mother saying of this guy: "He used to ride around on his white horse, he was a prince surveying his land, and now look at him" (Interview).

Goldstein's father had been studying for his doctorate in German literature at the City College of New York before the war. Years after the Holocaust he refused to help his daughter with her German homework while she studied philosophy; he refused to speak the language calling it "*Farfluchtah* Deutsche" (accursed German).

> It was sort of an ultimate denial; he wouldn't even speak the language. I came to understand that he had such a deep sense of betrayal. One of the things about Jews, I think European Jews, and I inherited this very strongly, is a love of German culture. I mean, we love German culture: my father loved it, and we loved it. And it didn't love us back quite clearly. So there's a sense of betrayal on top of everything else that this culture had so let us down (Interview).

Work

Goldstein's voice is unique in contemporary fiction; she is able to write elegantly on any scientific or intellectual topic: quantum physics or mathematics, as well as Orthodox Judaism and philosophy. Goldstein is a writer perpetually enchanted by the ethical; she is obsessed with the issue of morality in a post-Holocaust universe. Her fiction is marked by a ceaseless interrogation of traditional Judaism and history, a history that has the Holocaust as one, but only one, of its many defining moments.

Goldstein, unlike her thwarted intellectual characters, urges her readers to embrace the ambiguities of life, to somehow forge a reconciliation between their bodies and their minds. In her numerous forays into the Gothic, for example her short story "Tales of the Dangerous Duke" (in *Strange Attractors*) and her most recent novel *Properties of Light* (2000), Goldstein reminds her readers that her roots, although transplanted from Europe, have found fertile soil on American shores.

Like Nathaniel Hawthorne in his *Scarlet Letter*, Goldstein's novels are populated by intellectuals, characters who, much like Arthur Dimmesdale, are caught between reason and passion, body and mind. Yet unlike Hawthorne's use of his Puritan past, Goldstein takes her inspiration from an even older tradition: Orthodox Judaism.

In an age of increasing relativism, when deconstruction and poststructuralism hold sway and metaphysics seems quaint, Goldstein's work stridently proclaims the human will. In Goldstein's fictional universe, truth becomes a moral imperative leading her characters and readers to ask the right questions, the big questions, those concerning faith and doubt, history and responsibility.

Goldstein's fictional universe hovers in the questioning and ephemeral space between the old world of received traditional Judaism marked by blind faith and adherence to a patriarchal worldview, and a doubting, skeptical, scientific new world order of super-string chaos theory and relativity; one inherited by birth, the other gained through rigorous and sustained rational analysis. In *The Mind-Body Problem*, Renee Feuer exhibits this twin tradition. She is named after René Descartes, the father of modern philosophy and rationality, and her maternal great-grandmother Reine, a name that connotes spiritual purity. As Goldstein tells her readers, Reine was "married at twelve and lived to have sixteen children and sixty grandchildren before she was carted off, at ninety-four, to Auschwitz" (p. 179).

Despite a wide range of fictional topics and philosophical themes, Goldstein returns time and again to the Holocaust, however obliquely. In *The Mind-Body Problem* the war seems grafted onto what is essentially an academic (Barnard, Columbia, and Princeton) satire. Renee and Noam's honeymoon in Europe seems more an opportunity for Goldstein to tentatively enter the actual European site of the Holocaust than an occasion to reflect on the consequences of the Holocaust both historically and emotionally. A reader in search of the emotional residue, still actively evolving for the second generation of not just survivors, but the victimizers' children as well, had to wait until 1989 and the publication of Goldstein's second novel, *The Late Summer Passion of a Woman of Mind*. In this novel Goldstein attempts to stretch her readers' compassion and empathy to the narratological breaking point. She demands that her readers empathize with Eva Mueller, the daughter of a Nazi theorist and musicologist, who becomes a rationalist philosophy professor and flees to New York to escape the burden of her familial history. It is only after Eva corresponds with a *Yad Vashem* Holocaust scholar in Israel and reads her father's Nazi-ideology–laced treatise on Wagner, that she can begin to fully enter the world of the living for the first time. Goldstein's novel poignantly warns of the importance of memory and an accounting of history for the second generation.

In *The Dark Sister* (1991) Goldstein burrows into the shadowy recesses of her characters' minds, ultimately reinventing both William and Henry James as literary characters and giving new meaning to the term "Jamesian" novel. Through the eccentric writer Hedda, Goldstein once again dramatizes the struggle between remaining aloof and uninvolved in the emotional lives of others, and therefore of oneself, or venturing into the world of passion and feeling and therefore compassion for others. For Hedda's sister Stella, in the conclusion of *The Dark Sister*, this empathic choice may open the way to memory and a better balance between mind and spirit.

In *Strange Attractors* (1993), Goldstein plays with voice, tone, and point-of-view; in these multilayered and often interlocking stories she shows her remarkable range as a writer. In the first two stories of this collection, "The Editor's Story" and "Dreams of the Dangerous Duke," Goldstein is primarily interested in tone and style and in representing how women's genius has been quashed in different ages. However, the strength of this collection shines in Goldstein's stories dramatizing theological questions, both moral and philosophical, which swirl and eddy around the Holocaust. Goldstein has said that she is wary of any direct aesthetic representation of the Holocaust. This is a stance to which she rigorously adheres, and her Holocaust stories are all the more powerful for her position that the ground of the martyrs is holy and not to be trod upon lightly—in fact, for someone who considers herself akin to a second-generation survivor, perhaps not to be trod on at all. Instead, Goldstein forces her readers to ponder the philosophical and moral questions left to the next generation, chief among them the questions of transmission, of the *mesorah* of Jewish history—what must be told to the next generation, and what must remain silent.

Silence in Goldstein's work (the phrase "over there" is the only Holocaust marker) often points to the "unspeakability" of the crimes against not only Jews, but against all of humanity. Goldstein's short story "Mindel Gittel" wrestles with what historian Peter Haidu has termed "The Dialectics of Unspeakability," the challenge of aesthetically representing the Holocaust. Haidu remarks that "Silence can be the marker of courage and heroism or the cover of cowardice and self-interest; sometimes it is the road-sign of an impossible turning" (p. 278). In Goldstein's complex moral fictional universe, silences are often suffused with the meaning of all that cannot, or will not, be said.

Goldstein forces her readers to account for the silence of Mindel Gittel's parents. Is it self-preservation within a hostile postwar goyish Connecticut? Is it merely expedience or personal preference that closes off intergenerational communication? Or is their silence an act of mercy, of not wanting to taint a golden child of the new world with all the unspeakable horror of the world left behind in their transatlantic flight? Perhaps their silence symbolizes the world's silence that greeted many survivor tales with both hostility and disbelief. Survivor stories were often not openly discussed until the second generation came of age, a generation somewhat removed from the horrific events of the Holocaust.

In pondering these questions, Goldstein's fiction begins a low murmuring dialogue within each of her readers, an intertextual conversation that obliterates silence—at least that part of silence that is destructive, which is filled with fear and self-hate, pity and embarrassment. Through her morally complex stories, Goldstein urges her readers never to succumb to easy answers be they stridently called forth or silently ignored.

In her dual role of philosopher and fiction writer, Goldstein recognizes that how the Holocaust will be remembered by future generations, those without a direct link to the firsthand witnesses, is the awesome responsibility of her generation. Goldstein's fiction travels the tortuous route between representing the Holocaust and its legacy, without prurient description of the unspeakable horror, but without needlessly diluting Holocaust images. Aesthetically and narratively it is a difficult road to travel, particularly in an age that demands increasingly macabre elements to satisfy its passion for blood and guts, yet Goldstein never allows her fiction to ask easy questions, and she would hope no less for her readers as well.

Methodology

> Iris Murdoch said somewhere that "False consolation is bad art." And that rang so true to me. Art is supposed to open you up to the world; it's not supposed to close you off with false, easy answers—that's morally and aesthetically wrong. I've spent most of my life thinking about things that are irreconcilable, and if they're good questions, there are no easy answers and you want to do justice to that (Interview).

Goldstein's conception of allusion and oblique representation of the Holocaust is not only an aesthetic decision, but a moral one as well. She asks:

> How can the Holocaust not dominate one's consciousness as a Jew, or . . . anybody as a citizen of a civilized world . . . how do we deal with that in fiction? The ethical problem seems to be: it seems too large, too significant, and too important to be subverted in any way for aesthetic effect. And yet you want to, part of what it means to be a Jew today is that the Holocaust lies in our path (Interview).

For a fiction writer, in addition to the ethical problem stands an equally troubling aesthetic dilemma. Goldstein asks: "How do you do justice to this? I have always been very impressed with the way that Aharon Appelfeld deals with it: he will never, ever be in the Holocaust; it will always be before or after. And that is what I did in *Mazel*" (Interview). Goldstein would never dare tread upon the ground of the Holocaust. She believes that indirection is the only way to do justice to the enormity of the Holocaust. She calls the space of Holocaust victims, both physical and aesthetic, "holy ground." "I wouldn't dare, they're martyrs. I wouldn't bring my [comparatively] trivial goals as a novelist onto that ground. But to somehow indicate how large, by skirting around it—I think it's very effective" (Interview).

This is precisely the aesthetic choice Goldstein makes in her evocation of the difficulties faced by the second generation and the nearly impossible choices that the survivors were forced to make as they Americanized their children. One of the more striking instances of this aesthetic and moral choice is glimpsed in Goldstein's powerful story "Mindel Gittel," collected in *Strange Attractors*. In referring to the horrors of the Holocaust, Goldstein's narrator Sol can't even bring himself to mention the continent that was the site of the Holocaust; instead he ominously repeats the vague phrase "over there."

Goldstein has said about Sol and his euphemistic use of "over there" that she was thinking about the silence that shut down any Holocaust discussion in her home.

> Just the enormity, the reticence. The reticence that I grew up with in my own family. It was: "You don't want to know. We can't say. We can't do justice . . ." This is where language breaks down. It's where everything breaks down: it's the black hole of all values. There is no language adequate to it. It's either "over there," or there's silence—which is what I had experienced (Interview).

Perhaps the most obvious instance of Goldstein's combining her philosophical and fictional writing modes is her short story "The Legacy of Raizel Kaidish" (which also appears in *Strange Attractors*), which dramatizes the emotional toll bequeathed by survivors to their children before being passed on to the third generation. The story is told from the perspective of the daughter of a survivor of Buchenwald, a woman named after a martyr, Raizel Kaidish, who died in an act of courage. As Raizel narrates: "My mother's moral framework was formed in Buchenwald. Forged in the fires, it was strong and inflexible. One of her central concerns was that I should come to know, without myself suffering, all that she had learned there" (p. 229). The story turns on the unbearable moral decisions survivors were forced to make in the camps, and forces the reader to suspend judgment on the mother, who at the story's conclusion reveals that far from being the hero of the episode, she was actually the informer who betrayed Raizel Kaidish.

"Raizel Kaidish" brilliantly dramatizes the weakness inherent in any ethical system not tuned to the humanistic, to the case-by-case situation. Goldstein's short story reveals the difficulties of drawing easy moral conclusions from our vantage point, three generations removed from the Holocaust. Goldstein says she wrote this story, her first piece of fiction, as a pedagogical tool for a class on ethics at Barnard College:

> I was teaching a course on ethics and I was making the claim to my students that rules often don't do justice to the ethical situation, that you often need to have the narrative, you have to have the story. A rule oriented ethics is not fine-tuned enough . . . I was trying to think of a situation that I could use to explain this to my students, and that's how that story came to me. I was trying to solve this pedagogical problem in a class of ethics. Of course the Holocaust preoccupation came out in that story (Interview).

Importance in the Field of Holocaust Literature

Being a philosopher as well as a fiction writer, Goldstein is in a position to not only write evocative and emotionally challenging works of fiction, but to codify an aesthetics of Holocaust representation as well. Consequently Goldstein, through her forays into representing the Holocaust in such stories as "Mindel Gittel" and "The Legacy of Raizel Kaidish," manages to involve her readers fully in the lives of another. This is especially true of her second novel, *The Late Summer Passion of a Woman of Mind*, where Goldstein attempts the nearly impossible: that her readers will have utmost compassion and empathy for the progeny of a Nazi theorist. Goldstein's work is vitally important in order to understand the difficult second-generation response to the Holocaust as well as its evolving moral and aesthetic difficulties.

Critical Response

Described by Cynthia Ozick as "brainy and versatile," there is no doubt that Goldstein is one of only a handful of contemporary American fiction writers engaged in dramatizing ideas. In her essay "Visits to Germany in Recent Jewish-American Writing," Susanne Klingenstein surmised: "Goldstein's novels are more interested in the philosophical positions they expose than in psychological realism" (p. 554). While this position may have some relevance to Goldstein's early work, her more recent fiction has managed to convey a deep appreciation for philosophical ideas without sacrificing any psychological realism or emotional power.

Writing about *Mazel*, Andrew Furman says that Goldstein's work affirms the notion that "Jewish identity is one that is worth both preserving through ritual and transmitting through art" (p. 99). Goldstein is a writer more in the European tradition of philosophical fiction. Because she defies easy categorization, many American reviewers and critics do not know quite what to make of her. Still, much of the reception of her work has been extremely positive. Goldstein is one of only a handful of writers engaged in asking what Harold Bloom has called "the large questions." Goldstein's philosophical fiction forces her readers, living just a few generations removed from the European carnage, to embrace the ambiguities of a post-Holocaust world. She is a writer descended from a direct line of questioning Jewish skeptics and writers of overt paradoxes. Goldstein, with her feminist challenge of orthodoxy and her ethical aesthetic principle concerning Holocaust representation, is firmly within the avant-garde of the Jewish American cultural tradition. Her work is one freshly forged link in the great chain of Jewish tradition stretching back thousands of years.

Bibliography

Primary Sources

Books

The Mind-Body Problem. 1983, 1993.
The Late Summer Passion of a Woman of Mind. 1989, 1990.
The Dark Sister. 1991.
Strange Attractors. 1993.
Mazel. 1995.
Properties of Light. 2000.

Articles and Essays

"Against Logic." *Best Contemporary Jewish Writing*. Edited by Michael Lerner. San Francisco: Jossey-Bass, 2001, pp. 367–370.
"Looking Back at Lot's Wife." *Commentary* (September 1992): 37–41.
"Writing the Second Novel: A Symposium." *The New York Times Book Review*, 17 March 1985.

Secondary Sources

Berger, Alan L. "American Jewish Fiction." *Modern Judaism* 10 (1990): 221–241.
Cohen, Arthur. *The Tremendum: A Theological Interpretation of the Holocaust*. New York: Crossroad, 1981.
Furman, Andrew. *Contemporary Jewish American Writers and the Multicultural Dilemma: Return of the Exiled*. Syracuse, N.Y.: Syracuse University Press, 2000.
Haidu, Peter. "The Dialectics of Unspeakability: Language, Silence, and the Narratives of Desubjectification." *Probing the Limits of Representation: Nazism and the "Final Solution."* Edited by Saul Friedlander. Cambridge, Mass.: Harvard University Press, 1992, pp. 277–299.
Klingenstein, Susanne. "Destructive Intimacy: The *Shoah* between Mother and Daughter in Fictions by Cynthia Ozick, Norma Rosen, and Rebecca Goldstein." *Studies in American Jewish Literature* 11, no. 2 (fall 1992): 162–173.
———."Visits to Germany in Recent Jewish-American Writing." *Contemporary Literature* 34, no. 3 (1993): 538–570.

Interview

By Ezra Cappell. Hudson Hotel, New York, October 16, 2000.

ALLEGRA GOODMAN

(1967–)

EZRA CAPPELL

WRITING ABOUT THE biblical matriarch Rachel, Allegra Goodman observes that "It does not matter how much commentary has been written; questioning and speculation are a part of reading this text. The questions cannot end, because gaps are integral to the story; the text will never be exhausted, because it can never be filled" ("The Story of Rachel," p. 174). Although Goodman is referring to the troubling episode involving Rachel's theft of her father's idols, she might just as easily have been speculating on her own representation of the Holocaust within her fiction. Goodman is a writer who is concerned with asking the right questions, if only to remind her readers of the tremendous gap that the Nazi era has left, not only within Judaism, but within contemporary culture as well.

Goodman is a discriminating observer of social mores and a chronicler of domesticity in the tradition of George Eliot. A satirical writer who relies on her readers to cut through layers of social nuance to glimpse the kernel of wisdom embedded within each of her stories and novels, Goodman is also, despite her Victorian roots, a writer with a decidedly postmodern and feminist sensibility. Her fictional universe is peopled with seekers; her characters are inevitably engaged in a cultural conflict in their attempt to transcend the quotidian of contemporary American society and connect to some deeper theological meaning. This quest often ends ambiguously because Goodman is a writer more interested in setting up a problem than in seeking a solution. Thus, much of Goodman's work focuses on the religious conflicts, alienation, and displacement of the second and third generations of assimilated Jewish Americans, many of whom are descended from Holocaust survivors. This displacement, either as a result of the Holocaust for Andras and his children in *Kaaterskill Falls* (1998), or the crippling effects of American assimilation for Ed and Sarah in *The Family Markowitz* (1996), sends Goodman's characters in search of higher spirituality. Goodman has never dealt with the Holocaust head-on in her fiction; instead she alludes to it in a troubling way, allowing her readers to view how her characters, whether they are assimilated or Orthodox, are disturbed by their personal and historical legacies.

Biography

Goodman was born in Brooklyn, New York, in 1967, but grew up in a small Jewish community in Hawaii where her parents taught at the University of Hawaii. Goodman remembers having worn a traditional floral muumuu at her *bat mitzvah*. She began publishing and gained recognition for her writing at a remarkably young age—her first story appeared in *Commentary* when she was a freshman at Harvard University, while her first book of short stories was published before her graduation at the age of twenty-one. Goodman would go on to earn a Ph.D. in English literature from Stanford University.

Much of Goodman's writing is semiautobiographical and draws upon the exoticism of her upbringing. At the end of her first story collection *Total Immersion* (1989), for example, Goodman appends a glossary of words, not only for the Yiddish and Hebrew phrases, but also for the Hawaiian words and phrases that trickle into her prose. She presently lives and writes in Cambridge, Massachusetts, with her husband, David, a computer science professor at MIT, and her two children, Ezra and Gabriel.

Work

Goodman's first book, *Total Immersion*, is a collection of stories that satirize Jewish American mores and assimilation. Goodman's sharp, witty writing showcases her remarkable penchant for cutting through layers of socialization to expose the unvarnished truth of her characters' lives. The Holocaust pervades this collection perhaps more for its absence than by its presence. One of the few references to the war in *Total Immersion* occurs when a Jewish American, who served during World War II, remembers the letters he wrote home while in the Navy. Although he weeps as he remembers that "We all had no idea whether we'd make it through the war," Goodman quickly undercuts his tears, informing her readers that Max "had a small problem with his eyesight" and that he looked "as unconcerned as a man chopping onions" (Dell, 1998, pp. 137–138). The Holocaust is never mentioned during this American Jew's World War II remembrance. Later in the story, even the rabbi emeritus of the community, while reflecting on his time as military chaplain in Hawaii during World War II, remembers "hardships and shortages" without mentioning the Holocaust or what befell the community's European brothers and sisters: the Holocaust doesn't even enter into the equation. This type of caustic, biting satire distinguishes Goodman's early stories.

Goodman's second book, *The Family Markowitz*, is a series of interlocking stories in which the Holocaust serves as subtext for many of her characters' lives. In "Fannie Mae," the first story of the collection, Rose becomes infuriated when the daughter of her deathly ill second husband comes from Israel to sleep on her sofa. Rose wants to send Dorothy back to Israel where she can no longer pester Maury about his past. She complains bitterly to her Washington Heights neighbor Esther: "I was seven years old when I came to England, and I was all alone with no one in the world to look after me. . . . And she can never know what I saw and went through." For added emphasis she explains: "My own parents sent me away. . . . In the name of safety they abandoned me" (Farrar, Straus and Giroux, p. 12).

As in all her writing, Goodman treats the Holocaust with a deft touch; through small details she reveals her characters' histories while concurrently showing the influence the Holocaust has had on the second and third generations. Goodman's fiction bears more than a passing resemblance to the work of Chaim Grade, whose work Goodman says "is always the elegiac record of times past. Even Grade's prewar work bears the shadow of the Holocaust" ("Writing Jewish Fiction," p. 269). Appropriating Grade's technique of foreshadowing the Holocaust, Goodman weaves Holocaustal images into works set in prewar Europe: the previous passage, readers find out in a later story, deals with Rose's family history during World War I; Rose's displacement is in fact not a consequence of the Holocaust.

Many of Goodman's stories dramatize the ways in which modern Americanized Jews have turned Holocaust commemoration into a cliché. If, as Francine Prose observed some time ago, the Holocaust is "the pin with which to stick yourself" (quoted in Horowitz, p. 142), that pin has begun to blunt. In Goodman's fictional universe, the Holocaust and the issue of Holocaust memory, indeed of any meaningful Jewish past history, is tied up in a larger search, often a futile search, for spirituality within the morass of assimilated America.

The following exchange is emblematic of Goodman's concerns. Henry, an aesthete who has moved to England, visits his brother Ed, an academic and terrorism expert in Washington, and they go to a *Shabbos* service at the local synagogue.

> "What did you think of Congregation S.T.?" Ed asks.
> "Not bad. Not bad at all. Except for the ghastly Holocaust sculpture. The air-conditioning was splendid."
> "I meant—you know—spiritually," Ed says.
> Henry looks at him questioning ("Fantasy Rose," *The Family Markowitz*, p. 154).

In "The Persians," Ed and his wife, Sarah, search for a suitable bat mitzvah gift for their friend's daughter. Their simple trip to the local bookstore becomes transformed into a test of wills that dramatizes the political fallout from renewed Holocaust interest among assimilated Jewish America and its literature. Sarah rejects Philip Roth's *Goodbye Columbus* as being "too 50'ish," I. B. Singer's *Collected Stories* as "too kinky," and Saul Bellow's *The Adventures of Augie March* as "too hard for a twelve year old." When Sarah proposes *The Diary of Anne Frank*, all Ed can think to say is "Oh, very original." When Ed accuses Sarah of "honing in" on Holocaust books, Sarah offended, responds: "I am not! I'm just looking for the Jewish ones" (p. 170).

In "The Four Questions," Ed, a Middle East expert, is so conscious of political correctness he ensures that the only word of the *Haggadah* that he doesn't translate into English is *Mizrayim.* Instead of saying "Egypt," Ed sticks to the ancient Hebrew so as not to taint the current political scene. Once the traditional four questions are read, Goodman really turns up the heat. When Ben reads, "But for the assimilated child . . . it is up to us to open the discussion," rather than engage in an actual conversation about the significance of the *Haggadah*, Ed says, going against the *halachic* prohibition of adding to the commandments of the Torah, "We can meditate for a minute . . . on a fifth child who died in the Holocaust" (p. 196).

Instead of this moment of silence linking the Markowitz clan to family history, or it being an occasion of genuine Holocaust commemoration, Ed's addition to the ancient Haggadah is simply self-serving. Goodman's narrator tells us: "They sit silently and look at their plates." A moment later Miriam, the *baalat teshu-*

vah (lit.: mistress of repentance; a recent returnee to Orthodoxy), the affiliated but angry Orthodox daughter says: "So much for discussion at the seder" (p. 196). It is this difficult assimilated American response to the Holocaust that Goodman invokes in her early fiction. Her treatment of the Holocaust, however, takes a decided turn in her more recent work.

In the opening pages of Goodman's first novel, *Kaaterskill Falls*, Andras, a child-survivor of the Holocaust, and his wife, Nina, argue over his responsibility to bear witness to his personal trauma. Frustrated over his inaction, befuddled by his lifelong reticence on the topic of his childhood displacement during the war, she implores him: "Survivors are witnesses, and when they are gone there will be nothing left." World-weary Andras can't even summon the energy to respond to his wife's chastisement. The omniscient narrator reports: "But how can he describe a vacancy, an absence?" (The Dial Press, 1998, p. 46).

Goodman, writing from a third-generational remove from the Holocaust, has her character Andras, although a child-survivor, epitomize the third-generational bind. Deeply affected by their grandparents' suffering, third-generation witnesses are removed from testifying to the atrocities of the Holocaust, yet are often compelled to represent those events which, even sixty years later, are at the center of their familial history and legacy. In *Kaaterskill Falls* Goodman attempts to represent the moral complexities of living an Orthodox life within the demands of modernity while being aware of the responsibilities to Jewish history, particularly the Holocaust. Goodman has said, "it was a matter of creating this moment that would make the reader think, and feel troubled" (Kreilkamp, p. 80).

In her most recent novel *Paradise Park* (2001), Goodman once again represents not the Holocaust itself, but the ways in which assimilated American Jews respond to its legacy, both in preserving its history and in marring the historical record for personal use. *Paradise Park* follows the self-absorbed, unreliable first-person narrator Sharon Spiegelman on a twenty-year journey through spiritual reversal, disappointment, and ultimate rebirth. Goodman uses the occasion of Sharon's receiving a letter from her old boyfriend Gary (who has become a *baal teshuvah* and moved to Jerusalem where he is studying at the Torah Or Institute) to satirize much of American Jewry's simple knee-jerk response to the Holocaust. Goodman explains that after Gary was "persecuted" (i.e., "dumped" by his German girlfriend), he wanders around Holland and finds himself in the Anne Frank house where he receives a spiritual epiphany: "That he was a Jew like Anne. He was Jew enough to be killed for it. As soon as he realized he was Jewish, Gary took off for Jerusalem" (The Dial Press, p. 144).

Goodman uses the seemingly innocuous occasion of Sharon's taking a religion seminar midterm to satirize her trivializing of the Holocaust. When the proctors collect the booklets before she has finished the exam, Sharon exclaims: "It was like I was in some labor camp trying to scribble out my last words, and the guards snatched away my scrap of paper" (p. 166). Goodman often has her characters abuse genuine Holocaust memory to satirize the ways in which both her Orthodox and her assimilated characters, through their debilitating self-absorption, misuse Holocaust images and history. Similarly, after Sharon has moved to Jerusalem to be with her supposed *bashert* (destined mate) Gary, and is unhappy studying *halakah* (Jewish law) with her teacher Morah Zipporah, she bitterly complains to Gary: "She's a Nazi" (p. 181).

Perhaps the most disturbing scene in the novel, from the perspective of a reader concerned with Holocaust memory and history, is the late afternoon walk Gary and Sharon take in Jerusalem's old city. Gary tells Sharon of his epiphanic moment in the Frank house. In a satirical reworking of Thane Rosenbaum's "Cattle Car Complex," in which an American child of survivors experiences a psychotic flashback to the Holocaust in a midtown Manhattan elevator car, Gary is dragged out of the Anne Frank House. Gary says: "It was a moment of sheer terror. . . . I was standing in the Anne Frank house, and I felt deep in the pit of my stomach that my identity was her identity. Her fate was my fate. We shared one blood . . . I was a Jew! I was gasping for air, and I was crying out. And the security guards came for me but I couldn't stop screaming. . . . They began to drag me away" (p. 182).

In this section Goodman mocks the easy pieties of her assimilated American Jewish character, a narcissistic man who equates his own neurosis and rootless identity with the unimaginable (and unrepresentable) suffering of Anne Frank. Through her satiric rendering of Gary's tainted Holocaust memory, a trivializing distortion of history, Goodman stridently and ironically defends true Holocaust witnessing.

Sharon's response to Gary's overwrought tale is reminiscent of Bernard Malamud's seminal grocery store debate on Jewish identity between Morris Bober and Frank Alpine in *The Assistant*. Even the unstable and self-absorbed Sharon questions Gary's simple formulations: "how could you not have realized before you were a Jew?" Gary's answer to Sharon's question is important for it begins to reveal Goodman's methodology behind her representation of the Holocaust. He replies: "No, Sharon! Don't you see? Before I had no history. I had no knowledge. I had no learning. And at that moment. In one split second in the Netherlands. My history came home to me. That was what happened" (p. 183). Goodman's short, incomplete, and staccato sentences reveal the imperfection of Gary's logic. The six years of the Holocaust cannot become a substitute for millennia of Jewish history and culture. In keeping with Goodman's caustic satire, both Gary and Sharon are blissfully unaware of the shortcomings of their distorted view of Jewish identity and culture. Goodman's characters remain ignorant of the horrific parody Gary has made of the Frank family's seizure by the Gestapo.

Methodology

Rather than probe the limits of representation in attempting a Holocaust literature, Goodman concerns herself with the ways in which American Jews have made use of the Holocaust: ethically, historically, and most of all, personally. Goodman's omniscient narrator in *Kaaterskill Falls* eerily evokes Cynthia Ozick's conception of a post-Holocaust Germany. Ozick says, "What stands in witness for Germany is not the Germans, but an emptiness, an absence—the ones who are not there" (quoted in Klingenstein, p. 546). Any writer who thematically represents the Holocaust is, in the words of Norma Rosen, "a witness through the imagination" (p. 58). Although Goodman is a third-generation witness, an outsider thrice removed from the Holocaust, she has never shied away from the innate difficulties of this situation.

Goodman's major contribution to Holocaust representation has been and continues to be her wry and often disturbing evocation of the uses—historical, personal, often selfish, and always conflicted and complicated—that her Americanized Jewish characters make of Holocaust memory. In the short story "Sarah," Goodman says of the Markowitz clan's matriarch: "Rose did not suffer in the wars directly, but she imagines she did, and in her mind's eye sees them sweeping away the world she loved" (*The Family Markowitz*, p. 217).

Numerous philosophers, including Berel Lang, have debated whether the Holocaust is beyond the limits of aesthetic representation. Goodman never probes the limits of representation discussed by Lang; her work never engages this debate. Instead Goodman turns her attention to the ways in which assimilated and affiliated American Jews, as well as non-Jews, incorporate Holocaust awareness into their bifurcated, modern identities. For example, in her story "Mosquito," a German Christian theologian attending a conference on interfaith relations asks for forgiveness from the Jews assembled in a circle around her. She says: "I do not take it for granted—I am a Christian, and a German one—what it is to sit down with you who are Jews. This is a privilege for me . . . it is a lesson to us who have residing on us the guilt of our history. So I must deeply thank you" (*The Family Markowitz*, p. 128). Never actually describing the camps or their conditions, Goodman writes obliquely of the Holocaust. She is concerned with representing the legacy of the Holocaust not just for the survivors themselves, but also for the second and third generations.

Importance in the Field of Holocaust Literature

Although Goodman has yet to write what a previous generation of Jewish American authors would call a "Holocaust literature," almost all of her work is informed by the awesome legacy that the Holocaust has bestowed on Jews living in both Israel and the Diaspora. Goodman is one of the most forceful and eloquent voices speaking for the third generation of survivors who try to warily circle the legacy of suffering bestowed on them, fifty years removed from the events of the Holocaust.

As Sanford Pinsker says, Goodman's "social realism and moral seriousness" leads her to a unique perspective on American Jewry. In her best stories Goodman manages to combine an awareness of the lingering effects of the Holocaust with a nuanced Israeli sensibility. In "One Down," the concluding story in *The Family Markowitz*, two sets of second-generation parents discuss the impending marriage of their children. The usual small talk about their children's future takes a dark turn when Zaev reflects on his own difficult upbringing raising chickens in Palestine and wonders about his third-generation son: "If anything ever happens in this country, is he going to survive?" Zaev's despairing thought leads to a recounting of his mother Ilse's Holocaust history. He continues: "People laugh when I say this, but my mother . . . she came from a very wealthy family, and they lost everything." A moment later Ilse continues her sister's story of displacement and loss as a result of the Holocaust: "one to England, one to New York, I to Palestine escaping, and one perishing in Dachau" (pp. 249–250).

Goodman's social realism assumes its full dimension in the figure of Rose, the Markowitz matriarch. While listening to Zaev and Ilse's story, Rose can't help but feel jealous. She feels that her family's displacement during World War I should take precedence in the recounting. "In her mind's eye, with her background as a reader of historical romances, she can't help believing that if there is a greater trend or larger story to be told, then it would have to be her story writ large" (p. 250). In "One Down," Goodman's retelling of the Holocaust history of one particular family becomes a modern Midrash on the nature of family stories, particularly Holocaust family stories, and the ways in which they become altered by the vagaries of time and memory.

Critical Reception

The majority of critics tend to agree with Cynthia Ozick who, while Goodman was still an undergraduate at Harvard, proclaimed: "This Goodman is a marvel." As a result of her attention to mores and her biting social satire, Goodman has often been compared to the great Victorian novelists. Generally eschewing postmodern narrative pyrotechnics, Goodman's work is indeed reminiscent of an earlier period. C. Beth Burch simply refers to Goodman as "a Jewish Jane Austen with an edge" (p. 91). Similarly, critic Sanford Pinsker said that *Total Immersion* "is a satire so delicately balanced, so precise, that one harkens back to Austen or to Eliot for its models" (p. 188). Ivan Kreilkamp, in an interview in *Publisher's Weekly*, writes: "In the tradition of authors from Balzac to Faulkner, Goodman creates the effect of a fully developed alternate world, in which her characters move from story to story like familiar acquaintances" (p. 77). Andrew Furman may be the first critic to remark on Goodman's trenchant engagement with the State of Israel, suggesting that "Although Israel emerges as a refuge for Jews in the aftermath of the Holocaust, Goodman also explores the tangled conflict between the Israelis and the Palestinians that currently divides the Jewish American community" (p. 140).

Goodman won a Whiting Award for her first book *Total Immersion*, while her widely acclaimed second book, *The Family Markowitz*, was a *Los Angeles Times* best-seller and a *New York Times* notable book of the year. Continuing her remarkable ascendancy, Goodman's third book and first novel, *Kaaterskill Falls*, was a National Book Award finalist in 1998. Goodman's second novel was praised in *Commentary*, where John Podhoretz called *Paradise Park* "a bravura performance." In the *Daily News* Sherryl Connelly says, "Goodman's aptitude for finely shaded comic writing grounded in acute observations on faith and faithlessness, makes *Paradise Park* a divine read" (p. 1).

Goodman has been praised for each new development in her career, and is almost universally considered one of the most important fiction writers of her generation. She eloquently voices the perils of unfettered assimilation, the withering of roots and the loss of memory that is often attendant with pursuing the American dream. Her morally serious work warns of the political misuse American culture has often made of Holocaust commemoration. Goodman's work continues to dramatize the complex lives of her American and Israeli Jewish characters, while powerfully rendering the conflicts that inevitably arise between tradition and modernity, memory and history.

Bibliography

Primary Sources

Major Works of Fiction

Total Immersion. 1989, 1998.
The Family Markowitz. 1996.
Kaaterskill Falls. 1998.
Paradise Park. 2001.

Nonfiction Articles

"The Story of Rachel." In *Genesis: As It Is Written: Contemporary Writers on Our First Stories*. Edited by David Rosenberg. New York: HarperCollins, 1996, pp. 169–178.
"Writing Jewish Fiction In and Out of the Multicultural Context." In *Daughters of Valor: Contemporary Jewish American Women Writers*. Edited by Jay L. Halio and Ben Seigel. Newark: University of Delaware Press, 1997, pp. 268–274.
"O.K., You're Not Shakespeare. Now Get Back to Work." *New York Times*, 12 March 2001, E1.

Secondary Sources

Berger, Alan L. "American Jewish Fiction." *Modern Judaism* 10 (1990): 221–241.
Burch, C. Beth. "Allegra Goodman (1967–)." In *Jewish American Women Writers: A Bio-Bibliographical and Critical Sourcebook*. Edited by Ann R. Shapiro. Westport, Conn.: Greenwood Press, 1994, pp. 88–94.
Connelly, Sherryl. "The Divine Miss S." *New York Daily News*, 4 March 2001, Arts and Culture, 1.
———,"The Other Side of Paradise." *New York Daily News*, 1 April 2001, Showtime, 20.
Furman, Andrew. *Contemporary Jewish American Writers and the Multicultural Dilemma: Return of the Exiled*. Syracuse, N.Y.: Syracuse University Press, 2000.
Horowitz, Sara. R. "The 'Pin with which to Stick Yourself': The Holocaust in Jewish American Women's Writing." *Daughters of Valor: Contemporary Jewish American Women Writers*. Edited by Jay L. Halio and Ben Siegel. Newark: University of Delaware Press, 1997, pp. 141–159.
Klingenstein, Susanne. "Visits to Germany in Recent Jewish-American Writing." *Contemporary Literature* 34, no. 3 (1993): 538–570.
Pinsker, Sanford. "Satire, Social Realism, and Moral Seriousness: The Case of Allegra Goodman." *Studies in American Jewish Literature* 11, no. 2 (1992): 182–194.
Rosen, Norma. "The Holocaust and the American-Jewish Novelist." *Midstream* 20, no. 8 (October 1974): 54–62.

Interviews

Kramer, Peter. *Forward*, (11 May 2001): 10–12.
Kreilkamp, Ivan. *Writing for Your Life #4*. Edited by Jonathan Bing. *Publisher's Weekly* (2000): 74–78.

HAIM GOURI

(1923–)

DVIR ABRAMOVICH

FETED AS ONE of the pillars of modern Hebrew poetry, Israel Prize recipient Haim Gouri first came into contact with the Holocaust universe in 1947 when he was sent by the Hagana, the precursor to the Israeli Defence forces, to a displaced persons camp in war-torn Europe. Dispatched to help the victims in Hungary and Austria reach Israel, the young Sabra, or native-born Israeli, became part of the "culture of remembrance," and memory thus became a recurring theme in his narrative chronicles. It was perhaps inevitable that this harrowing encounter with the remnant of the Holocaust would have a striking and indelible effect on the young man. Upon returning to Israel to fight in the War of Independence, he became determined to keep the flame of memory alive through his *ars poetica*. In a 1996 interview Gouri remarked, "I see myself as an Israeli and a poet of all generations influenced by so much of our past. Meeting the survivors of the Holocaust changed my life. There is hardly a work of mine without images of the *Shoah*" (Scheidemann interview, p. 5).

Psychological Aspects

Certainly, Gouri was one of the first Israeli artists to treat the barbaric events of the Holocaust and their aftermath, adopting as his primary concern the psychic trauma the Nazi inferno engendered within the survivors, and as secondary the role his fieldwork in Europe played in his initial literary forays. His early verse, *Pirhel Esh* (Flowers of Fire), *Ad alot ha-shahar* (Until Dawn Arose), and *Shoshanat Ruhot* (Compass Rose), is pervaded with images of young antiheroes plunged into the abyss of postwar Europe, who while trekking through the detritus of the European landscape are disoriented by the ethical bankruptcy of the perpetrators and the devastating fate of their people. The protagonist represents a collective, rather than an individual, a mythical observer for the Jewish people, whose parabolic objective through his wanderings is to collect testimonies about the deracination of Jewish life. Gouri's work reveals a naturalistic-realist template, which studs the poems with references to the historical streets, palaces, bridges, and churches of cities such as Vienna, Budapest, and Prague. The effect is to overlay the text with a mimetic, historical patina that anchors it to the specific apocalypse. Furthermore, by including accurate detail in settings and names, the writer ensures a quality of realism that intermingles with the figurative, surrealistic ingredients.

Leavened by fury, distress, and lamentation for his vanquished brothers and sisters, Gouri's personal protestations continuously reference the visceral and tragic dimension, lodging the reader in the shocking frame of history (Yaoz, p. 105). Accordingly, his vast panorama of meditations evokes the staggering horror the Sabra senses upon his exploration of genocide. In different ways, Gouri marshals the aesthetic and poetic devices to excavate the traces of the vanished dead, deftly showing how their echoes still resonate in the cities, towns, rivers, monuments, and bridges of Europe. Again and again, the poet employs the imagery of nature as a metonymy for darkness, strangeness, and collaboration with the Nazi beast. Walking alone at night among the ruins, the speaker senses a foreign landscape oozing cruelty, as the deathly snow entombs the corpses and at once masks the footprints of the merciless killers and the flowing blood of the departed.

To be sure, the pilgrimage is a somber, ordeal-laden affair, as the speaker, groping for a nexus with a cultural history from which he has been removed by time, is struck by the menacing quietness of the streets, saturated with indifference. Above and beyond that, the Israeli visitor sauntering through the barren roads that once transported his brethren yearns to establish a sense of identification and empathy that the young generation back in his homeland did not feel. The young man, the alter ego of Gouri whose kin did not perish in the camps, attempts concomitantly to wrestle with the atrocities and to incorporate their cultural identity into his being. The motif of engagement between the naïf Israeli and the survivors finds fertile ground in "Little Koti," an overtly allegorical opus. In the poem, the peripatetic hero is approached by a young girl, a phantasmagorical figure who is an archivist of all the survivors' sense of loss and pain. In the course of their encounter, the girl, who may be a virgin or a saint, details the gruesome murder of Jews, which later become nightmares, "One day, in the lamplight, in the dark December Streets / Little Koti told me about the unnatural deaths . . . Her story darkened the western sky, over the snowy streets" (*Words in My Lovesick Blood*, Detroit: Wayne State University Press, 1996, p. 29). Likewise, in the poem "Night Diary" the narrator is steered by an anonymous figure through a kaleidoscopic exploration of the horrible sites of killing, unleashing within him an anguished cry.

What is obtrusively evident to readers of Gouri's canon is that the remembrance of the victims never strikes a moralizing or condemnatory tone. The speaker never views the slain as passive weaklings who were led to their death like sheep to the slaughter. Rather, as he hurls Jobian questions (in compositions such as "Two Poems of Quarter VI" and "Until the Dawn"), the poet is engulfed by a wounding sense of guilt, not only for being alive but also because of the intimidating helplessness he feels in the face of such nameless bestiality. The young man is gripped by an overpowering desire to remember, to keep the memory alive, so as to ensure that the voices of the dead never become silent or forgotten. Gouri traverses similar ground in his semiautobiographical novel *Hachakira: Sipuro Shel Reuel* (The Investigation, 1980), a barely fictionalized collage of vignettes mirroring Gouri's confrontation with the survivors during his mission to Europe. Unsurprisingly, the author is incarnated on the page as an Israeli adolescent, trawling through Prague and Budapest as part of his assignment to rescue Jews. Everything is essayed from the standpoint of the envoy Reuel, who emphasizes his multiple interactions with the Jews who outlived the carnage.

Themes

A thematic index of Gouri's arc of the Holocaust can be found in the poem "Inheritance" (*Words in My Lovesick Blood*, 1996). Inarguably one of the writer's most noted compositions, "Inheritance" co-opts the biblical story of Abraham and Isaac to draw a link with the European terror, which Gouri asserts is the stock element in Jewish history. In the poem's final stanzas we read,

> Isaac we are told, was not offered up in sacrifice
> He lived long
> enjoyed his life
> until the light of his eyes grew dim
> But he bequeathed that hour to his progeny
> They are born
> with a knife in their heart (p. 27).

In compression, the mythical iconography of the poem encourages us to view the national narrative of Isaac's descendants as one of endless victimization and persecution, opening inevitable parallels with the wartime suffering of the modern generation. Additionally, one finds a list of charges sheet against God for an absence of divine intervention, which betrays a current of defiance and doubt about God's mercy toward his people.

The Chocolate Deal

Gouri's continuing fixation with the Holocaust was ossified in the 1965 novella *Iskat Hashokolada* (*The Chocolate Deal*). In one of the first reviews to appear after the book's publication in English, Arthur Cohen contended that "*The Chocolate Deal* is the most fully realized and moving novel of the Holocaust written by a non survivor that this reviewer has read" (p. 79). Casting his narrative net outside the recognizable social reality of the Palmach generation, Gouri zeroes in on the damaged personhood of the survivors, in the process addressing many issues to create a psychologically and symbolically driven work. Underpinning this angst-freighted tale is a first-person narration that positions the spectator to view events and emotions from the principals' stance, pulling us tightly into their interior consciousness. It is also of significance that in this gaunt, minimalist, and highly elliptical narrative, any specific referent to the Holocaust is conspicuously absent, underscoring its naked allegorical and abstract quality as well as eschewing the convention of dramatizing the senseless monstrosity. It is difficult not to be swept up by the power of Gouri's adroit and trenchant observations about the excruciating emotional fissures that torment the central characters and their disparate roads to recovery.

As the story opens, Mordechai Neuberg (Mordi) and Reuven Krauss (Rubi), who were friends before the war, chance upon each other in the train station of an unnamed European capital after surviving Hitler's devastating onslaught. Both have lost their families and friends. One immediately feels the specters of bareness haunting the book's tableaux, reinforced by the elusive, diffused nature of the narrative. The unidentified city, broken and fragmented, stands for the lingering gradational field of chaos that saturated Europe and the mental crumbling of the survivors. Explicitly mapping on this geographical canvas several of the different phases of the journey taken by the survivors, Gouri yokes the material and spiritual to enunciate and set the tone for the rest of the storyline.

Following their meeting, Rubi accepts Mordi's offer of sharing his room. It is an empty time where the ordered clock-time of civilization has been displaced by hell. In one heartbreaking moment, we see the two heroes expend valuable hours, searching the missing persons section of the newspaper for remaining family members, only to fail repeatedly in their efforts. More than anything else, Gouri's narrative strategy is to stress the differences between the two men who represent diffused philosophical inflections of how one can come to terms with inhumanity and how one can go on living in a world shorn of compassion and justice. To wit, it soon becomes clear that Mordi is the embodiment of the impotent survivor, imprisoned by scorching memories, unable to break away from the feelings of guilt and shame. His appearance early on is telling:

> A tall man. Bent a bit. Gray suited. He remains behind . . . he drifts slowly after those who are rushing, like a solitary rear guard. . . . Unless he's decided to become a statue, a monument, some sort of action, of movement is expected . . . He exploits up to the permissible limit his privilege to stand there, keep silent and make up his mind (*The Chocolate Deal,* Wayne State University Press, pp. 1–3).

Once a promising journalist and doctoral candidate in Troubadour poetry, we learn that he was saved by the kindness of his professor who arranged for him to be hidden in a convent cellar. Consequently, the teacher was captured and tortured, an event that greatly contributes to Mordi's unfolding disintegration. In a sense, the emotionally paralyzed Mordi wishes for death, for he has seen the evil that men do and has quietly decided to remain lost in his existential alienation (amid such characterization, it is worth noting that Mordi's name alludes to death in French). Afflicted with self-denial, the erstwhile journalist is fatally emasculated to the extent that he settles within the irreducible comfort of the Sister of Mercy warehouse—a lodging that is a corollary to his monastic subsistence. Eventually, Mordi's emotional disrepair crescendos when Rubi disappears for two weeks without notice to be with his lover. Without his friend to prod him toward accepting and rejoining life, dystopian as it is, the defeated hero collapses into suicide under the enormity of his broodings and spiritual stasis. Mordi's hurtling toward doom is a memorable image that punctuates the core of the novel, amplifying the path of quiet resignation that some opted to embrace.

Unlike the forlorn Mordi, Rubi is unwaveringly committed to reengaging with life. Despite the intense woundedness, the one-time math genius has not been diminished by the catastrophe in Europe, channeling his remaining reservoir of energy (perhaps also rage and vengeance) to go on living. It is a small problem that precious little is furnished in the form of a backstory to explain how Rubi endured, but from the outset it is deeply realized that hunger and action mark his every move, whether it is with women or whether it is in a new enterprise he fantasizes about. The novel underlines the sharp polarities between the two men who epitomize antithetical philosophical inflections about how to live in a post-Holocaust world. Hence, thematically the work provides a cornucopia of observations generated by an interlocking of the two sides of the survivor coin. Yet Alan Mintz notes that the writer's "investment of narrative sympathy is so evenly distributed that it is impossible to say that one is favored over the other. There is little sense of an Israeli writer making an assessment of survivors relative to the values of his own generation" (Mintz, p. 257).

Hoping to exploit distant family connections, Rubi at first actively searches for the affluent Salomons, even though Mordi, who knows they were slain, warns him against such a course. Congruent with his sensitive personality, Mordi counsels Rubi to send his uncle, a rich lawyer before the war, a letter, instead of unexpectedly appearing at their residence. Meanwhile, Rubi takes up with a former lover, Gerti, whom he meets in the streets working as a prostitute. Later he learns that her own moral rectitude is in question and that she is the secretary to a Gestapo camp doctor named Hoffman. Still, this revelation does not dissuade Mordi from seeking pleasure in this tainted woman's body, further compounding the move away from the shackling eclipse of the past.

Midway, Rubi discovers the truth about his wealthy relatives. Alone again after Mordi's sudden death, Rubi searches for new ways to actualize his dreams for wealth. He cooks up a fraudulent venture concerning chocolate. He plans on buying enormous amounts of the excess military chocolate left by the departing American troops. He then intends to blackmail the same Dr. Hoffman for whom Gerti works and whose young daughter he saved from a burning building (whether it is a daydream or fact can be debated) in order to procure a medical opinion that the eating of chocolate adversely impacts the sexual performance of men. Once the price of the chocolate is lowered, Mordi counts on buying it cheaply and then inflating the price so that he can sell it at a profit.

The specific fraud aside, it is revealed that Dr. Hoffman is not only guilty of horrendous crimes during the reign of the Nazi administration, but also of seizing ownership of Rubi's uncle's dwelling and possessions. Nonetheless, Rubi does not have qualms about taking advantage of the doctor's guilt, and the physician ultimately consents to Rubi's offer of silence and the opportunity to disappear. This gesture of authorial enunciation has Gouri making obvious nods to the Israeli acceptance of German reparations as well as considering the issue of collaboration with the murderers and their accessories. Should one forgive the agents of the "final solution" in their quest to escape the disorienting graveyard of the past and rebuild a fractured existence, even though it may be an obscene divesting of loyalty and betrayal of the victims? Or should he maintain his fidelity to the sacrificed ones? It is significant that this subplot is only interposed near the end and never reaches fruition, strongly implying that it is either a product of Rubi's delirious reveries or that he has decided not to implement the deal. On the whole, the shorthand message hammered home is that the survivors have the dilemma of either returning to life, with all its insuperable weight, or retreating from its unfathomable cruelty into oblivion.

No question, *The Chocolate Deal* has many virtues, most notably, in the words of Gershon Shaked, its ability to understand that "Even among the survivors there existed differentiation" (pp. 20–21, 46). Shaked then adds

> Gouri has given . . . a crushing answer to the question whether if and to what extent, can the Israeli born comprehend and tackle the world of the "other" . . . He does try and observe him from the outside as a narrator or temporary guest, but tries to look at him from the inside. He understood from the inside how his "dead brother" lived the reality of survivorship, the fear, the renewal and the burden of the past (pp. 20–21, 46).

Bibliography

Primary Sources

Pirhel Esh (Flowers of Fire). 1949.

Ad alot ha-shahar (Until Dawn Arose). 1950.

Shoshanat Ruhot (Compass Rose). 1960.

Iskat Hashokolada (*The Chocolate Deal*). 1965.

Hachakira: Sipuro Shel Reuel (The Investigation: The Tale of Reuel). 1980.

Words in My Lovesick Blood. Translated by Stanley F. Chyet. 1996.

Secondary Sources

Cohen, Arthur. "The Metaphysics of Survival." *Midstream* (November 1968): 79.

Gouri Haim. "A Sense of Irony." Interview by Mike Scheidemann. *Jerusalem Post*, 26 December 1996, 5–7.

Mintz, Alan. *Hurban: Responses to Catastrophe in Hebrew Literature.* New York: Columbia University Press, 1984.

Shaked, Gershon. "Ben ha'aretz vechavayat ha*Shoah*." *Iton 77* 197 (June 1996): 20–21, 46.

Yaoz, Hana. *The Holocaust in the Poetry of the State Generation.* Israel: Ekad, 1984.

Michal Govrin

(1950–)

EFRAIM SICHER

A RESEARCHER OF Jewish folklore, author, and theater director, Michal Govrin was born in Tel-Aviv, studied literature at Tel-Aviv University, and completed her doctoral dissertation at the Sorbonne, Paris. She teaches drama in Jerusalem. Govrin brings to her understanding of her mother's Holocaust experiences her interest in cabbala, Hasidism, and drama. In particular, Govrin brings the insight that storytelling is performative and that it can be a lifesaving transmission to future generations (Alexander and Govrin, p. 34). Her poetry deals with, among other contemporary themes, Holocaust memories, shadows of the past that inhabit her life and project onto it traumatic scenes of deportations and massacres, evoked in phrases drawn from prayers and biblical passages that acquire unexpected personal meaning in the search for the past: "What happened yesterday turns into a Purim mask," writes the poet as she rummages among the discarded clothes in a storeroom and dreams of indecent photos of lost relatives ("Tsurat hazikaron" [The form of memory], published in *Gufei milim*, Haqibuts hameukhad, 1990, p. 7).

Govrin grew up with the typical inability to connect the commemoration of the Holocaust at school with her mother's story, even though her school placed unusual emphasis on the study of Jewish heritage and the pupils acted out a women's revolt in a Gestapo prison. Moreover, Govrin's literature teacher was the poet and Bergen-Belsen survivor Itamar Ya'oz-Kest. A trip to Poland in 1975 galvanized her understanding of self, family, and nation, spurring her to write her first novel, *Hashem* (*The Name*), a major contribution to the second generation's coming to terms with the past and with its identity, and winner of Israel's 1997 Kugel Prize.

> The "journey to Poland" began in that journey "[over] there"—the journey every child makes to the regions of before he was born, to the unknown past of his parents, to the secret of his birth. My journey to Mother's world began long before I "understood" who my mother, Regina-Rina Poser-Laub-Govrin, was, before I "knew" that she survived the "Holocaust," that she once had another husband, that I had a half-brother. But there was the other "knowledge," that knowledge of pre-knowledge and of pre-language, transmitted in the thousand languages that connect a child and his parents without words. A knowledge that lay like a dark cloud on the horizon. Terrifying and seductive (Govrin, "The journey to Poland," *Partisan Review* 66, 4 (Fall 1999), p. 556).

Returning with this "knowledge," Govrin was forced to connect the history books with her real mother, her mother's reminiscences of prewar Kraków and its horror of genocide, the photo album hidden at the bottom of a lingerie drawer, her mother's rages, and her obsessive tidying regime with her own identity. "Poland" had been an incomprehensible fairytale land for Govrin, as it had been for Momik in David Grossman's *See Under: Love*, who similarly grew up with the Holocaust's searing presence in his childhood. Only after Govrin's visit to Poland did the meaning of what her mother had gone through in the Holocaust come home to her like an "earthquake."

Separation from her mother during a period of adolescent rebellion forced Govrin to face the truth alone. While forced to stay in Germany following an accident and then while stranded in Paris during the 1973 Yom Kippur War, she realized that

> there is no refuge in the soothing distinctions between "then" and "now," between "there" and "here." And I also understood that there is no racial difference, imprinted at birth between "them" and "us," nor can we hide behind the fences of the Chosen People. And that, in every person, the murderer and the victim potentially exist, blended into one another, constantly demanding separation, every single day, with full awareness. I understood that I could no longer hide behind the collective, ready-made definitions of memory. That there would be no choice but to embark on the journey that is obstinate, lonely, and full of contradictions (Govrin, "The journey to Poland," p. 560).

A confrontation with Western culture cannot avoid the fundamental contradiction in the juxtaposition of secular humanism with absolute evil or its justification, silencing, and corroboration in storytelling itself. And for Govrin, the pull of jazz, hedonistic bohemia, and fun-loving New Yorkers did not drown out the esoteric and eternal truths in the mystical tales of the Hasidic masters.

In *The Name*, a young woman named Amalia, studying at a well-known seminary for *khozrot betshuvah* (religious penitents) in Jerusalem, addresses herself in an agonizing search for self that verges on madness. She is seeking to exorcise a dead woman, her father's former lover for whom she has been named, and whose name she believes posesses her. This woman, Mala Auerbach, heroically committed suicide in a concentration camp rather than be executed for attempted escape. To find out who this dead woman was, Amalia must explore the dark recesses of the Holocaust and the family secrets "over there" in Europe, which together create a black pit of contaminated filth that threatens to suck her in.

The intimate diary-like narrative of *The Name*, with its fragmented flashbacks, charts the mystical process of *tikkun*, or cosmic repair, during the annual counting of the *'Omer*, the forty-nine days between the redemption from Egypt on Passover and the revelation at Sinai celebrated on Shavuot (Pentecost). The daily count parallels the levels of the cabalistic *Sfirot*, the mystical levels of creation, and leads to *tikkun*. *Tikkun* is both the repair of a broken soul and the repair of transmigratory souls from the past; *tikkun* is an individual act of repair through prayer, penitence, and good deeds that may contribute to the redemption of the nation and to the drawing in from exile of the *Shekhinah*. *Tikkun* is especially needed after the destruction caused by the Holocaust. Amalia's weaving of a Torah Ark curtain also weaves her text into a mending of a broken soul, even if the outcome is left tantalizingly unclear.

While she attempts through her writing/weaving to redeem the hidden sparks of holiness, Amalia is lured by the seductive force of the dark secrets of the past into abandonment to the evil inclination. To this agonized struggle, which is the struggle of a post-Holocaust generation for faith in the Divine covenant, are coopted an array of unnamed Jewish sources from the Talmud to the *Esh haqodesh*, a rabbinical commentary dug out of the ruins of the Warsaw ghetto, and such contemporaries as Emmanuel Levinas and Jacques Derrida. Amalia's name combines a Hebrew root meaning both "labor" and "evil" with the Name of G-d for which she is yearning. She desperately wants to believe in G-d but is defeated by her own despair and by her desire for Isaiah, a sensitive young man also seeking his path back to Torah, who was to be her bridegroom.

Amalia's feelings of total loss in a world of incomprehension and lack of understanding are best exemplified by a scene in the novel in which she grabs hold of her rabbi's jacket after class, tearing off one of the buttons. Rabbi Israel Gothelf has been preaching in a Hanukkah sermon that in every darkness there is light and that the Hellenistic war on Judaism continues in Holocaust denial. Amalia is afraid she will fail in her repentance as long as she is possessed by the dybbuk of the Holocaust victim whose name she carries:

> And as if the rest of her strength burns within the sacrifice of her confession, she sways, and her head lands on the rabbi's coat. And in a voice that is suddenly weak, like a baby's bleating, she gasps onto the sourness of wet wool: "I'm scared, I'm scared," and she holds on tighter (*The Name*, Riverhead Books, 1998, p. 44).

Amalia's process of repentance follows the classic Jewish legal codifier and philosopher Maimonides' precept that the penitent must change his or her name as if to say "I am another person [*akher*] and not the one who sinned" (*Mishneh Torah*, "Hilkhot tshuvah," 2:4). This is done to separate from the sinful past and to perfect repentance to the extent of being able to face one's former lover and, in a state of virility, to withstand the temptation to sin. Yet Amalia cannot forget the sinful past because it pursues her in the form of the sinister Ludwig Stein, who takes her back to Europe to recover on film Mala's life as a brilliant concert pianist. Amalia steals the photographs in a vain effort to possess the past, to be free of possession, and to work through the inherited trauma. But instead, she displays hostility to those who offer her help (For some reason black-coated Jewish men in the novel are invariably sour and dark and she is caught in the compulsion to repeat the past.) She has convinced herself she is not permitted to love. When she attends a memorial meeting for Mala (held improbably but symbolically on the Ninth of Av, the fast day for the Destruction of the Temple), it is clear that she has in a sense become Mala and cannot become a free woman. The stranglehold of dead ghosts is unbearable for the son or daughter of survivors named for the dead, in keeping with Jewish tradition. She must live up to the often unreasonable expectations of the parents and family, who transpose loss on such "memorial candles" (Wardi, pp. 26–47). Amalia remembers all too well her father's harsh treatment of her when she failed to match Mala's musical talents after Amalia was given a xylophone at age four. Yet torn between revulsion and fascination for the past, Amalia knows that she cannot give in to denial, for to erase the sinful past is in its way a denial of Holocaust memory.

The "Other" (*Akher*) is also the epithet of Elisha ben Abbuya, the Talmudic heretic who turned his back on Torah after he had entered Paradise. He is reincarnated in Govrin's novel into the latter-day fanatic, Abbuya Asraf. Under his influence, Amalia chooses self-sacrifice in order to do penance for the soul of the namesake who has haunted her life, to redeem the souls of the Holocaust martyrs through a mending of the defiled, broken vessels, and to achieve purification after the forty-ninth degree of profanity of Auschwitz. The mystic tells her,

> "For the destruction is G-d's concealment, the sinking of the holy in the shell. And how many torments do the nation and the *Shekhinah* have, Amaliyyyaaa . . .? And only real martyrdom, only the death of the soul for the sake of holiness can break open the blood of the mother giving birth! The death of saints, Amalia, is the beginning of redemption" (p. 105).

This presentation of the martyrdom of the six million, which explains G-d's self-concealment (*hester panim*) at Auschwitz, can only spell tragedy for an impressionable, suicidal young woman who takes these words out of context and turns her inner torments from a means of self-purification to a blasphemous end of redemption through sin.

Coming as a stranger—an Other—to her own life, she knows, as Govrin says of herself, that "after Auschwitz, there are no more stories that do not betray, there are no more innocent stories" (Govrin, "The journey to Poland," p. 562). To start over again after such rupture, to turn one's back on the past, as a group of Holocaust survivors try to do at a European resort in Govrin's short story "La Promenade" (in the collection *Leakhoz bashemesh: sipurim veagadot*), is to ask a question that Amalia asks Rabbi Gothelf: how to remember and to forget—to remember what Amaleq did, as the Bible commands, and at the same time to wipe out the remembrance of Amaleq. The rabbi's answer is that to "return to G-d" is the way to "renew our days as of old," not to adopt an alien identity but to restore a former state of purity through repentance, the only means left in the absence of Temple sacrifice (Govrin, *The Name*, pp. 196–198).

Amalia, who has confused the memory of the individual with the nation's destiny, private sin with collective punishment, cannot understand this, mainly because she cannot cope with her own failures and self-deceit. Amalia is unable to attain repentance from love as distinct from repentance out of fear, though she struggles out of the vale of tears to rise from the city of destruction set against the desolate beauty of Jerusalem's landscape. Amalia perverts her rabbi's teachings and imagines herself on the altar of repentance as a sacrificial victim who will give up her soul in mystical union with the Holy Name at the completion of the *'Omer* count. It must be apparent to the reader that, in defiance of halakhic Judaism and the various statements made by Jewish thinkers on the subject, Amalia has substituted herself for the Holocaust martyr in a deluded and mistaken attempt to redeem absolute evil.

The questions Govrin asks raise the basic existential dilemmas that torment the second generation. She confronts theological issues of faith and salvation, asking "what is the terrorizing persuasive force of tales and of their metamorphoses into theologies, ideologies? How to struggle with forgetting, with denial, without whitewashing, but also without reiterating the same stories, without inflaming the same evil instincts? How to tell responsibly" (Govrin, "The journey to Poland," p. 561).

Bibliography

Primary Sources

"Reshimot al ha-teatron ha-italk." (Notes on Italian Theater) *Bama* 64–65 (1973): 78–81.
Otah sha'ah: shirim (That very hour). 1981.
Leakhoz bashemesh: sipurim veagadot (To seize the sun: stories and legends). 1984.
"Storytelling as a Performing Art." 1989. (Co-written with Tamar Alexander.)
"La Promenade." 1985.
Seder halailah hazeh (This Night's Seder). 1989.
Gufei milim: shirim (The bodies of words: poems). 1990.
Hashem (The Name). 1995.
"The journey to Poland." 1999.
Ma'aseh hayam: khronika pirush (Tale of the sea: a chronicle/commentary). 2000.

Secondary Sources

Sicher, Efraim. "The Return of the Past: The Intergenerational Transmission of Holocaust Memory in Israeli Fiction." *Shofar: An Interdisciplinary Journal of Jewish Studies* 20, no. 2 (winter 2001): 1–25.
Moraly, Yehuda. "Vers un nouveau theatre juif" (Towards a New Jewish Theater) *Pardes* 21 (1995): 59–76.
Wardi, Dina. *Memorial Candles: Children of the Holocaust*. London: Routledge, 1992.

Chaim Grade

(1910–1982)

BEN FURNISH

Chaim Grade was born on 5 April 1910, in Vilna, Russia (now Vilnius, Lithuania). He was the only child of Shlomo-Motte Grade, a Hebrew teacher, and Vella Blumenthal Grade. Grade's father died when he was seventeen, and his mother became a fruit seller in the Vilna markets. Grade studied in several *yeshivot*, including seven years at the Novaredker Yeshiva under the Chason-Ish, Rabbi Avraham-Shaya Karelitz, a leader of the Mussar movement (an ascetic movement within Lithuanian Orthodox Judaism).

At age twenty-two, Grade left Mussar and Orthodoxy for a secular lifestyle. He also began writing poetry, publishing his first chapbook, *Yo* (Yes), in 1936. He became affiliated with the Young Vilna Group, a network of poets that included Abraham Sutzkever. His second book of poetry, *Musarnikes* (Mussarites or Ethical Ones, 1937), sold well enough for a second printing.

After the Soviets occupied Vilna in 1940, Grade was accepted into membership in the new Vilna chapter of the Soviet Writers Union and secured a Soviet passport. As he would later recall, these two affiliations helped save his life. When the Nazis invaded Vilna, Grade fled, on foot at first, deeper into the Soviet Union. His first wife, Frumme-Liebche, started out with him, but her feet were injured and she could not keep up. Convinced that only adult men, not women and children, needed to fear the Nazis, she urged Grade to go on without her while she returned to town.

After roughly a year and a half as a refugee in Ashkabad, Stalinabad, and in Tadjikistan, Grade traveled to Moscow. There, Soviet Yiddish writers from the Jewish Anti-Fascist Committee testified as to the quality of his work and he was able to live in relative stability until the end of the war. Along the way his passport protected him from arrest, and his Writers Union membership entitled him to a ration and exemption from military service. In Moscow he became acquainted with the leading circle of Yiddish writers, which Stalin would later purge, and which Grade would memorialize in his poem, "Elegy for the Soviet Yiddish Writers."

After the war, Grade returned to Vilna, only to confirm the deaths of his wife, Frumme-Liebche, and his mother. He moved on to Lodz, Poland, in 1946, where he stayed for six months. During the next two years, Grade served as chair of the Yiddish Writers Union in Paris. After traveling to America as a delegate to the Jewish Culture Congress, he and his second wife Inna Hecker Grade (whom he originally met in Moscow) chose to remain. For decades until his death, he lived in an Amalgamated Houses apartment in the Bronx (collective housing sponsored by the Jewish labor movement). Inna taught university foreign language courses and collaborated in later translations of her husband's work. Grade toured the Yiddish lecture circuit from Detroit and Miami to Johannesburg, Buenos Aires, Israel, and elsewhere. He wrote for New York's Yiddish newspapers, *Morgan-Journal*, *Forverts*, *Yidisher Kemfer*, and others.

Although Grade left Mussar, in a sense Mussar never left him. Some of his richest writing grows out of his experience with the moral and ethical struggles of the pre-Holocaust Vilna Orthodox community. In fact, toward the end of his life, Grade said he felt his calling as a writer was to describe the religiously observant milieu that once existed in Vilna. Although secular in his own lifestyle, Grade continued to study the Talmud throughout his life and wrote lovingly and painstakingly about observant Jews. His secularism was based in rational skepticism rather than in an alternate ideology.

Grade's major novels, including *Der Brunem* (*The Well*, 1967), *Di Agunah* (*The Agunah, The Abandoned Wife*, 1961), *Tsemekh Atlas* (*The Yeshivah*, 1967–1968), and the novella collection *Di Kloyz un di Gas* (*The Sacred and the Profane*, also published as *Rabbis and Wives*, 1974), all deal with ethical conflicts within prewar observant Jewish communities around Vilna. Following publication of Ruth Wisse's translation of *Der Brunem* in 1967, Grade began to acquire a readership in English.

Chaim Grade died on 8 June 1982, in New York City. His last published book, *Der Shtumer Minyan* (The Silent Quorum, 1976), short stories also set in prewar, religiously observant settings, remains untranslated; he also left a significant body of unpublished work in Yiddish. Grade's many prizes and awards include the Remembrance Award from the Bergen-Belsen Memorial Association, the Epstein Award from the Jewish Book Council, the Bimko and Lamed prizes, and honorary doctorates from the Jewish Theological Seminary and Union College.

Prose

Grade's two most widely known Holocaust-related works are the latter sections of *Der Mames Shabosim* (*My Mother's Sabbath Days*, 1955), a memoir, and the loosely fictionalized story "Mayn Krig mit Hersh Rasseyner" ("My Quarrel with Hersh Rasseyner," which was adapted as *The Quarrel*, an award-winning film, in 1991). These first prose publications grew out of autobiographical lectures he delivered about Vilna, his wartime experiences in the Soviet Union, and his life shortly after the war, and the works were first published in English in 1972 by the Bergen-Belsen Memorial Association in a volume called *The Seven Little Lanes*. In 1986, the English version of the full memoir, *My Mother's Sabbath Days*, was published.

"My Quarrel with Hersh Rasseyner" defies simple classification; it is generally considered a short story, although one could make a case for reading it as a memoir or even an essay. Written in first person and growing out of the author's own experience, the story derives its narrative force from a philosophical dialogue. Chaim Vilner (a character—clearly based on the author himself—who had appeared in Grade's early poetry) visits Paris to lecture in Yiddish. While strolling in the park he encounters his former friend, Hersh Rasseyner, with whom he had attended the Mussar yeshiva. Unlike Vilner, who walked away from the yeshiva for a secular writing career (as did Grade), Rasseyner remained in the Mussar fold. Rasseyner, as though compensating for Vilner's defection, became ever more intensely and privately immersed in religious study and the two men lost contact.

Both men survived the Holocaust. Vilner (like Grade) fled to Russia, but Rasseyner was imprisoned in the Nazi death camps. Now, in the late 1940s, they meet again by chance to find that each man's experience of the Holocaust has left him only more firmly committed to the path he had chosen. For Vilner, the Holocaust confirms his doubt in God: "You must ask God the old question about the righteous man who fares ill and the evil man who fares well—only multiplied for a million murdered children" (Himmelfarb, p. 405). For Rasseyner, the Holocaust confirms his doubt in humanity: "With the Almighty's help, I could stand the German's boots on my throat, but if I had had to put on his mask, his murderous face, I would have been smothered as though I had been gassed" (p. 399).

Eli Cohen, the film director of *The Quarrel*, displayed notable fidelity to Grade's story and spirit, but does shift the story's setting from Paris to Montreal, and in the end, the film depicts two of Rasseyner's yeshiva students whose utter hostile rejection of the secular Vilner is untempered by the bond of past friendship that links Rasseyner and Vilner.

The story unfolds as an argument between Rasseyner and Vilner, no mere altercation but an argument that, as Ruth Wisse notes, employs all the rational cross-examination of *pilpul* (dissection of talmudic legal reasoning between two study partners in yeshiva). Rasseyner states his concern for Vilner's spiritual welfare, particularly because they have both reached middle age. Rasseyner says he would find the world unbearable without God, but Vilner counters that he cannot, in light of the Holocaust, accept that God's judgment is always right. Rasseyner points out that God's purpose is shown not only in salvation but in misfortune as well.

In Rasseyner's view, Jews who embrace secularism—and even those who seek to moderate traditional Jewish observance—are trying to "dance at two weddings at the same time"—to make an impossible compromise. Vilner sees this path not as an absurd contradiction but as a worthy challenge that is, in its duality, a more rigorous responsibility than Rasseyner's uncompromising, predefined path. Vilner sees a part of Rasseyner that is self-satisfied: "You allow yourself to mock, because, after all, what you do is for the sake of heaven, isn't that so?" (p. 645). Vilner reminds Rasseyner about their study of Rabbi Jonah Gerondi, who wrote the *Gates of Repentance* in recognition that he had been wrong in his fanatical condemnation of Maimonides.

As the conversation takes another turn, Rasseyner cites the failure of educated Germans to prevent the slaughter. He has read and been impressed by the achievements of Western European philosophy, but in the end he concludes that its adherents failed their test by depending solely on thought and not action, solely on the human mind and not on God. Vilner asks what place Rasseyner sees in his divine system for Jews who were not meticulously observant, but who were martyred just the same. For that matter, Vilner asks, what about non-Jews who saved the lives of Jews? Vilner says that no amount of misbehavior justified the deaths of a million innocent Jewish children. "The same misfortune befell us all, but you have a ready answer while we [secular Jews] have not dispelled our doubts" (p. 650).

The argument ends in a draw in the sense that neither man changes the other's mind. Grade keeps the dispute between the two men as fair and rationally balanced as it is intense. Yet the vehemence of their dispute somehow reaffirms the power of their ultimate common bond. Rasseyner's statements logically dictate that he reject Vilner as a friend, that there can be no agreement to disagree between them on these fundamental matters of belief. Yet Rasseyner does not ultimately shun Vilner, nor does Vilner wholly reject Rasseyner, but rather ends the story by saying to him, "May we both have the merit of meeting again in the future. . . . Let us embrace each other" (p. 651). Grade ends the story before the reader knows how Rasseyner will respond, but behind the tension of that uncertainty lies at least the possibility that the two men will meet and speak again.

"My Quarrel with Hersh Rasseyner" stands as a highly significant work of literature about the Holocaust, even though at first glance it might seem an unlikely candidate for such status. After all, it takes place after 1945, includes little action other than dialogue between its two characters, and includes more philosophical speculation than direct description of the Holocaust itself. Although this story is not allegory—its characters are fully drawn and not mere symbols—readers can see within it a microcosm of how factions within the Jewish world have responded to the Holocaust. Readers can see how the Holocaust challenges religious and secular Jews (and, by logical extension, any believers in God and humanity) to reconcile their beliefs with the incontestable reality of evil in the world. From the story, readers can further extrapolate how, in the Holocaust's aftermath, the ideological divisions between Jews cut ever deeper, to the point that even meaningful conversation between alienated factions became nearly impossible despite their shared past, including their shared past enemy, Nazism.

Like Rasseyner, many strictly observant Jews who survived the Holocaust and remained observant found themselves becoming even more strenuous in their observance and in their communal separation from all who questioned their convictions. Like Vilner, many skeptical Jews who survived the Holocaust felt confirmed in their doubts over even the foundational principles of Judaism. Even though this division predated the Holocaust, just as Rasseyner's and Vilner's friendship and estrangement did, the Holocaust fortified that division. The alienation that this division has prompted between Jewish factions has continued to persist—even flourish—in Europe, Israel, North America, and elsewhere in the decades following World War II.

Der Mamas Shabosim falls into three sections. The first, "My Mother's Sabbath Days," renders a portrait of Grade's mother, Vella, in the years between his return home from the Mussar yeshiva and his flight from the 1941 Nazi invasion. The second section, "The Other End of the World," covers some of Grade's years in the Soviet Union, particularly Soviet Central Asia, during World War II. The final section, "The Seven Little Lanes," recounts Grade's grim return to Vilna at the war's end, where he finds the ghetto in ruins and confirms his mother's and wife's deaths at the Nazis' hands. (The title refers to the seven streets that comprised the Vilna ghetto).

The first third of this memoir is Grade's personal account of his mother's life from the years after he left Mussar until he fled Vilna in 1941. Through this memoir's lens, readers also gain a glimpse into the last days of pre-Holocaust Vilna. Grade's mother once asked him why he wrote about her (he had already written a number of poems about her selling fruit at the gate before the war), and in the book she recalls his answer: "He says he doesn't mean only me; he means all the mothers like me, all the women of my kind" (*Der Mamas Shabosim*, p. 128). In fact, Grade's mother, her piety (including years of sleepless Thursday nights preparing for the Sabbath), tenacity (including years as a street vendor), and the ultimate tragic fact of her death in the Vilna ghetto stand among Grade's most prominent and enduring themes, recurring in this work and in much of his poetry.

When Grade returns to Vilna after the war, he finds his mother's house intact but with a net of spiderwebs covering the entire entrance. A woman who tells him how she survived by hiding in the sewers recalls his mother. When Grade hears her say the first *aktion* (seizure of Jews for deportation and execution) took place on Yom Kippur, he is certain this is when she died: "All her life she had lived with the Sabbath and with Yom Kippur, and she went to Ponary [the forest on the outskirts of Vilna where Jews were murdered in mass executions] as she would go to the synagogue. While still in Asia, I had decided that my mother's Yohrzeit must fall on Yom Kippur" (p. 373).

The Vilna ghetto's streets remain, but only a few of its residents survived to return. Grade meets Balberishkin the shoemaker, who lost his entire family, and pediatrician Anna Itkin, who is living with her surviving twin son. Anna knew Grade's wife Frumme-Liebche and tells Grade how his wife remained bravely at her nursing post in the ghetto hospital children's ward during an *aktion*. At the memoir's close, Grade writes, "I have wandered across half the world, but this path, though the ruins of this handful of dead streets, is longer and harder" (p. 389).

Grade's novels and his story collection *Der Shtumer Minyan* (The Silent Quorum) deal with ethical conflicts among prewar Orthodox Jews in Lithuania and thus do not relate directly to the Holocaust. These works were written after the Holocaust, however, and do depict a world vanquished by the Holocaust. Grade deals particularly with ethical conflicts in the religious setting. *The Well*, for example, tells the story of Mende, a simple porter who out of sincere piety leads an effort to repair the Vilna synagogue's well. On his way to this goal, Mende encounters an intricate web of motivations from others who offer or decline their help mostly for their own personal, rather than purely ethical, reasons. *The Agunah* deals with the efforts of Merl, whose husband has been missing for fifteen years, to remarry under Jewish law. The novel ultimately explores the contradictory rabbinical rulings that Merl receives, one denying her remarriage and the other permitting it. *The Yeshivah* also features conflict between opposing philosophies of strictness and forgiveness as lived out in the actions of two contrasting characters.

Poetry

Grade is also the author of a substantial body of Yiddish poetry on Holocaust themes, although only a handful of these poems have been translated into English. These poems include "Der Veg fun Payn" ("The Road of Suffering"), "Der Mantl" ("The Coat"), "Der Nes" ("The Miracle"), and "A Naked Boy." "Der Veg fun Payn" is an epic lamentation based on a passage from Ezekiel, which is in fact Grade's own lamentation. The poem's voice mourns having to wander at the gates of Babylon and reminds its audience of how the horrors of the Holocaust fit within a scriptural Jewish context. The speaker addresses God in the poem, but he speaks of having waited in vain for a response while having to endure a list of hardships. In the end, the speaker asks God "why have you turned away from us?" (translated by Betsky-Zweig, p. 42).

The voice of "Der Mantl" describes being pursued by his coat, "two empty sleeves raised to choke" (translated by Howe and Greenberg, p. 338) after he had abandoned it to cover a corpse in the ghetto streets. In "Der Nes," Grade reflects on the miracle of his survival and his subsequent life: "everything I build is built on a miracle" (translated by Whitman, p. 25).

Grade's poem "A Naked Boy" opens as though addressing God ("Creator of the world in all its diverse forms!"), but the invocation is more than partly ironic. The poem describes the wandering spirit of a young boy who is looking for a place to bury his baby sister. Both were killed at Treblinka. Even as a spirit in the sky, he feels responsible for her as she clings to him. The poet wishes he could find their native land or persuade the boy to accept a Galilee grave "where all the trees will murmur sympathetically," but the boy does not trust the site, and so "he keeps wandering about/around Treblinka's altar where the fire is out" (Kramer, pp. 177–178).

Grade's untranslated volumes of Yiddish poetry on Holocaust themes include the latter two sections of *Doyres* (Generations), *Auf di Khurves* (On the Ruins), *Shayn fun Farloshene Shtern* (Light of Extinguished Stars), *Pleytim* (Refugees), and *Der Mentsh fun Fayer* (The Man of Fire). Most of the Holocaust-related poems from *Doyres, Shayn fun Farloshene Shtern*, and *Pleytim* were written between 1941 and 1945 when Grade was in the Soviet Union.

In his Holocaust-related poems in *Doyres*, Grade confronts Nazi atrocities more directly than in perhaps any of his other work. Poems such as "Chad Gadya," "Toytn-Tants" ("Death Dance"), and "Der Retseyekh" ("The Murderer") form indictments through their illustrations of Nazi brutality.

Pleytim describes the experience of Grade and other refugees in Soviet Central Asia during the war. Themes include refugees' fruitless waiting for loved ones to escape German-held areas and join them in the Soviet Union—for example, "Zi Kumt Nisht" ("She Does Not Come"); simultaneous reflection on the hardships and the wonders of the natural elements and terrain while on the road in flight, such as "In Nakht un in Vint" ("In Night and in Wind"), "Kazakhstaner Step" ("In the Kazakh Steppe"), and "In Vaytn Ashkabad" ("In Remote Ashkabad"); and death on the road, such as "Mit Dayn Guf Auf Mayne Hent" ("With Your Body in My Hands"). Although written in the Soviet Union, the poems do not bear the flavor of Soviet socialist realism, as critic Shmuel Niger states. Instead, this collection of poems is suffused with longing for Vilna, his lost home.

Shayn fun Farloshene Shtern includes poems about such Holocaust and post-Holocaust themes and issues as the 1946 pogrom in Kielce, Poland ("Kelts"); a section of poems called "Yerushim fun Geto" ("Inheritances from the Ghetto"), which includes "Der Tsurikgekumener Zun" ("The Returning Son") and other poems about returning to the ghetto after the war; and the concentration camps. Some of the poems combining Holocaust and biblical themes and imagery include "Di Merkovah in Lager Oshvientshim" ("The Chariot in Auschwitz Concentration Camp"), "Ikhzekal in Lager Oshvientshim" ("Ezekiel in Auschwitz Concentration Camp"), and "Shir Hashirim" ("Song of Songs").

Auf di Khurves ("On the Ruins") is a chapbook-length poem written about the bleak experience of returning to Vilna after the war and finding only devastation where the Jewish community and ghetto, including his own home, had once been. *Der Mentsh fun Fayer* (The Man of Fire) contains several Holocaust-related poems, including "A Toyre on Yidn" ("A Torah Without Jews"), "Di Geblibene" ("The Survivors"), and "Der Mantl" ("The Coat").

Shmuel Niger used the words "lamentation" and "scriptural" to describe Grade's poetry (pp. 110, 125), and in fact, Grade fits well within the tradition of lamentation in Yiddish and Jewish literature that David Roskies, Sidra Ezrahi, and others have described. Roskies discusses how "the survivor's tactic of inverting Scripture can be seen as a means of keeping faith." (p. 19). Like Bialik writing about Kishinev, or Sh. Ansky writing about Jewish suffering in World War I, and like Grade's Vilna contemporary Abraham Sutzkever, Grade sees catastrophe through a Jewish lens. Grade's poetic lamentations often invert traditional Jewish themes. An exception to this in his non-Holocaust-related poetry includes his sequence of Elijah poems in *Der Mames Tsavoe* (My mother's Will, 1949).

"Chad Gadya," from *Doyres* (New York: Yiddisher Kultur Farband, 1945), is named after the closing song of the Passover Seder, the festival that celebrates the Jews' delivery from slavery in Egypt. Grade's irony is bitter, because his poem mourns the Nazi enslavement of the Jews; while the traditional song describes the cycle of life, Grade's poem describes a cycle of death. The Jews have become the goat to be slaughtered, and the Nazis are the slaughterers:

The song is old, . . . oh *chad gadya,*
The Haggadah is wet with blood and tears,
And the *shoykhet* [ritual slaughterer], oh the shoykhet
  is a Gestapo,
With a loaded naked revolver (p. 145).

"Toytn-Tants" ("Death Dance"), also from *Doyres*, similarly inverts festivity into horror as it describes the Gestapo's fatal subjugation of Poland, but the poem also recalls Ezekiel's Valley of the Dry Bones as it predicts that the murdered ones will somehow witness a final judgment for the Nazis:

Sand buried us over—
You will still recognize this grave pit,
And you will have no more peace.
Each of you will carry
Thousands of dead on your shoulders . . .
We in graves will laugh . . . (p. 148).

Although Grade does not name God as the instigator of this retribution, the poem voices a Jewish conviction that evildoers will face an ultimate moral reckoning.

"The Chariot in Auschwitz" and "Ezekiel in Auschwitz" (in *Shayn fun Farloshene Shtern*) transport the apocalyptic, visionary prophet Ezekiel to the concentration camp. The four animals of the chariot vision appear, as do four Yiddish poets who lose first the flesh from their bones, then their skeletons altogether, turning to smoke. Ezekiel, who wrote of the Babylonian's conquest of Jerusalem and taking the Jews into exile and captivity, in Grade's poem exhorts the Son of Man never to forget the Holocaust. In "Song of Songs" (in *Shayn fun Farloshene Shtern*) Grade remembers a woman he calls sister as a child, a young woman, a bride, and eventually, a casualty of the Nazis.

Although much of Grade's poetry about his mother predates the Holocaust, and many poems of his 1949 collection *Der Mames Tsavoe* (My Mother's Will) do not deal directly with it, the Holocaust forms an inevitable backdrop for the entire work. Her importance as an individual figure and as a representative of all other women like her and of their simple, exacting piety and self-sacrifice, takes on added meaning when recalled in light of her murder by the Nazis. The poem "Ir Letste Yom Kippur" ("Her Last Yom Kippur") describes what Grade imagined his mother experienced on the day he believed the Germans deported her from the ghetto. "Kol Nidre" describes that day from his point of view in Soviet Tadjikistan.

Grade's poetry is also scriptural in the sense that it is more narrative than lyric, serving the almost liturgical functions of memorializing, questioning, foretelling, and extracting meaning from contemporary events by placing them in the larger context of scriptural Jewish history. The result, though secular and often inverting conventional scriptural associations, nonetheless fits squarely within the long lamentation tradition in Jewish literature.

Critical Reception

Grade is generally regarded as one of the foremost Yiddish writers of the twentieth century. Before the Holocaust came to Vilna, he was active in the influential Young Vilna group of poets and had published poetry in Yiddish publications around the world. His reputation was already sufficient to secure his membership in the Soviet Writers Union and for the Jewish Anti-Fascist Committee to affirm his skill. As early as the late 1940s, such leading contemporaries as Shmuel Niger and Jacob Glatstein praised his poetry on the Holocaust and other themes. By the 1950s, Shloyme Bickel was calling him one of the most important prose writers in Yiddish. "Grade is the most eloquent Yiddish poet," wrote Niger (p. 116). Glatstein agrees: "Chaim Grade writes some of the most beautiful description in all Yiddish poetry" (p. 53).

That Grade is not yet more widely known among English-speaking readers may be due to several factors. Though he lived in North America for over thirty years and wrote prolifically there, he never felt fully at home with English. He waited until the 1960s to permit translations of his works from Yiddish to English, a project that remains far from complete. Sidra DeKoven Ezrahi compares Grade's situation to that of Isaac Bashevis Singer, who came to America earlier and at a somewhat younger age. Grade also did not choose to promote himself and his work on the general American literary scene as Singer did. Grade was dealt the fate of a post-Holocaust Yiddish writer most of whose potential readers were either dead, inaccessible in the Soviet bloc, or no longer reading Yiddish. The critical consensus is that Grade's importance far surpasses the relatively minor, though positive, attention he has thus far received outside the Yiddish-speaking world.

Curt Leviant's positive *New York Times* review of Ruth Wisse's 1967 translation of Grade's novel *The Well* was followed by Leviant's translating Grade's novels *The Agunah* and *The Yeshiva*. Both of these titles enjoyed respectable sales and attention in English. Grade's wife collaborated on translating other works, including *Rabbis and Wives* (also published as *The Sacred and the Profane*) and *My Mother's Sabbath Days*. Most fortuitous for Grade's translated Holocaust-related writing has been Irving Howe and Eliezer Greenberg's decision to include "My Quarrel with Hersh Rasseyner" in their anthology *A Treasury of Yiddish Stories*. From there it has been anthologized elsewhere and adapted for screen and stage. Critics Edward Alexander and Milton Konvitz write in their respective articles on "My Quarrel with Hersh Rasseyner" that it merits consideration as "a minor classic of modern literature" (p. 233) and "among our writings that are considered sacred" (p. 19).

Hatred of and anger toward the Nazis is overshadowed in Grade's work by his emphasis on loving tribute to his departed family and obliterated Jewish community. In fact, most of his writing, even when it does not concern the Holocaust directly, comprises a kind of memorial to the remarkable people, place, and time that comprised Grade's home community of Vilna.

Taken as a whole, "My Quarrel with Hersh Rasseyner," *Der Mamas Shabosim*, and Grade's Holocaust-related poetry join with his numerous other writings to form an integral body of work that bridges pre- and post-Holocaust experience. While Grade wrote the greater part of his total oeuvre after the Holocaust, yet in settings that occur prior to it, those works that do directly engage the Holocaust form a remarkable sensibility. That sensibility blends the seemingly irreconcilable perspectives of a thorough Lithuanian yeshiva education with those of secular skepticism and a brilliant, cosmopolitan literary voice. Clearly, Grade's oeuvre awaits fuller critical consideration as well as complete translation into English.

Bibliography

Primary Sources

Yo (Yes). 1936.
Musarnikes (Mussarites or Ethical Ones). 1939.
Doyres (Generations). 1945.
Farvoksene Vegn (Overgrown Paths). 1947.
Pleytim (Refugees). 1947.
Auf di Khurves (On the Ruins). 1947.
Der Mames Tsavoe (My Mother's Will). 1949.
Shayn fun Farloshene Shtern (Light of Extinguished Stars). 1950.
Der Mames Shabosim (*My Mother's Sabbath Days*). 1955.
Di Agune (*The Agunah* or The Abandoned Wife). 1961.
Der Mentsh fun Fayer (The Man of Fire). 1962.
Der Brunem (*The Well*). 1967.
Tsemekh Atlas (*The Yeshivah*, 2 vols.). 1967–1968.
Auf Mayn Veg tsu Dir (On My Way to You). 1969.
The Seven Little Lanes. (1972).
Di Kloyz un di Gas (*The Sacred and the Profane*, also published as *Rabbis and Wives*). 1974.
Der Shtumer Minyan (The Silent Quorum). 1976.

Secondary Sources

Alexander, Edward. "A Dialogue of the Mind with Itself: Chaim Grade's Quarrel with Hersh Rasseyner." In *The Resonance of Dust: Essays on Holocaust Literature and Jewish Fate*. Columbus: Ohio State University Press, pp. 233–247.
Betsky-Zweig, Sarah, ed., tr. "The Road of Suffering," In *Onions and Cucumbers and Plums*. Detroit, Mich.: Wayne State University Press, 1958.
Bickel, Shloyme. "Chaim Grade." In *Shrayber fun Mayn Dor*. New York: Matones, 1958, pp. 366–377.

Bird, Thomas E. "Chaim Grade." In *Encyclopedia of World Literature*. Edited by Steven R. Serafin. Farmington Hills, Mich.: St. James, 1999, p. 289.

"Chaim Grade." In *Encyclopaedia Judaica*. New York: Macmillan, 1971–1972, p. 893.

Cohen, Eli, director. *The Quarrel*. Written by David Brandes, based on play by Joseph Telushkin, based on story by Chaim Grade. Canada: Apple and Honey Productions/Atlantis Films, 1991.

Ezrahi, Sidra DeKoven. *By Words Alone: The Holocaust in Literature*. Chicago: The University of Chicago Press, 1980.

Glatstein, Jacob. "Chaim Grade." In *In Tokh Genumen*. New York: Matones, 1947, pp. 49–56.

Gold, Herbert. Review of *My Mother's Sabbath Days*. *New York Times Book Review*, 16 November 1983, p. 12.

Hecker, Inna. "Chaim Grade: The Challenge to God." *Judaica Book News* (spring–summer 1979): 15–18.

Himmelfarb, Milton, tr. "My Quarrel with Hersh Rasseyner." In *Truth and Lamentations: Stories and Poems on the Holocaust*. Edited by Milton Teichman and Sharon Leder. Urbana: University of Illinois Press, 1994.

Howe, Irving and Eliezer Greenberg, ed., tr. "The Coat" in *A Treasury of Yiddish Poetry*. New York: Schocken, 1969.

Konvitz, Milton R. "Chaim Grade's Quarrel." *Midstream* (November 1995): 19–23.

Kramer, Aaron, ed., tr. *The Last Lullabye: Poetry from the Holocaust*. Syracuse, N.Y.: Syracuse University Press, 1998.

Leviant, Curt. "*The Well* by Chaim Grade." [rev.] *New York Times Book Review*, Vol. 72, Section VII, 22 October 1967, p. 69.

Liptzin, Sol. *A History of Yiddish Literature*. Middle Village, N.Y.: Jonathan David, 1985, pp. 417–422.

Niger, Shmuel. "Chaim Grade." In *Yidishe Shrayber fun Tsvansikstn Yorhundert*. New York: Alveltlekhn Yidishn Kultur Kongres, 1973, pp. 99–127.

Pinsker, Sanford. "Chaim Grade: The Yiddish Writer as Agunah." *Yiddish* 8, no. 2 (1992): 55–58.

Roskies, David G. *Against the Apocalypse: Responses to Catastrophe in Modern Jewish Culture*. Cambridge, Mass.: Harvard University Press, 1984.

Slotnick, Susan A. "Chaim Grade's Central Concern on the Occasion of His 70th Birthday." In *Jewish Book Annual* 37, New York: Jewish Book Council, 1979–1980, pp. 106–115.

Whitman, Ruth, ed., tr. "The Miracle," in *An Anthology of Modern Yiddish Poetry*. New York: October House, 1966.

Wirth-Nesher, Hana. *What Is Jewish Literature?* Philadelphia: Jewish Publication Society, 1994.

Wisse, Ruth R. "In Praise of Chaim Grade." *Commentary* (April 1977): 70–73.

Interviews

Hecker, Inna. "Chaim Grade: A Portrait of the Man." *Judaica Book News* (spring–summer 1979): 19–22.

Reichek, Morton A. "A Writer in Search of an Audience." *Present Tense* (summer 1979): 40–45.

Ribalow, Harold U. "A Conversation with Chaim Grade." *Congress Monthly* (February 1975): 15–18.

GÜNTER GRASS

(1927–)

JULIA F. KLIMEK

Life and Work

Günter Grass was born on 16 October 1927 in Danzig, Germany (now Gdansk, Poland). His parents, Willy and Helene Grass, owned a grocery store and were members of the petty bourgeois class. Grass attended local schools until 1944. He then volunteered as an antiaircraft auxiliary at age fifteen, and at sixteen, during the brutal winter of 1944–1945, he was sent to the Eastern Front where he was wounded and where more than half his comrades died. Before his release from an American prisoner-of-war camp in 1946, he was walked through the Dachau concentration camp as part of the American re-education effort, an experience to which he, who had been raised in the ideology of the Hitler Youth, responded with disbelief in spite of visual proof: "It took years before I began to understand: this will forever be present; our shame will neither be forgotten nor worked through" (*Schreiben nach Auschwitz*, p. 9).

After a brief and unsatisfying return to school, Grass worked on a farm and in a potash mine near Hildesheim. He refers to these years as politically formative after a youth dominated by Hitler's ideology. In 1947, Grass began an apprenticeship as a stonecutter; from 1948 to 1952 he studied sculpture and drawing first at the Academy of Art in Düsseldorf, then at the State Academy of Fine Arts in West Berlin. In 1956, he moved to Paris and published a first collection of poetry, *Die Vorzüge der Windhühner*. Later, his parallel interests of writing and drawing produced a number of works that combined Grass's poetry with his illustrations.

In 1959, Grass published *Die Blechtrommel* (*The Tin Drum*), the first part of the Danzig Trilogy, to which he added, after returning to Berlin in 1960, *Katz und Maus* (*Cat and Mouse*) and *Hundejahre* (*Dog Years*) in 1961 and 1963, respectively. *Die Blechtrommel* remains his best-known work today and was made into a film under the direction of Volker Schlöndorff (1979). During the same time period, Grass produced several plays. In the early 1960s, Grass entered the political arena as a supporter of Willy Brandt and the Social Democratic Party, for whom he campaigned and wrote speeches. After his withdrawal from politics in the 1970s and 1980s, Grass returned in 1990 to speak out against a reunited Germany, which he perceived as too strong a nation.

Although he has published poetry collections, plays, and essays, Grass is best known for his narratives. The Danzig Trilogy was followed by *Der Butt* (*The Flounder*, 1977); *Kopfgeburten, oder die Deutschen sterben aus* (*Headbirths: or, the Germans Are Dying Out*, 1980); and *Unkenrufe* (*The Call of the Toad*, 1992). The novel *Ein weites Feld* (*Too Far Afield*, 1995), his response to the German reunification, is situated in the narrative present of 1989–1990; the German past of Auschwitz continues, however, to linger beneath the surface. His recent work *Mein Jahrhundert* (*My Century*, 1999) narrates a short story for each year of the twentieth century, assembling small events into a larger historical framework.

Grass has five children with his first wife, Anna Schwarz, to whom he was married from 1954 to 1978. After travels to Israel, Poland, China, Indonesia, Nicaragua, and a six-month stay in India, Grass now lives in Northern Germany with his second wife, Ute Grunert, an organist. He continues to write both fiction and essays.

Importance in Holocaust Literature

Günter Grass engages the Holocaust on several levels. *Die Blechtrommel* is an epic narrative set in the Danzig area and centered on Oskar Matzerath, a boy who on his third birthday refuses to grow. The story makes direct reference to *Kristallnacht*, the first large-scale, open act of violence against Jews in Germany and to the Jews' forced emigration from Danzig. Related to specific characters within Grass's novels, the political history gains the power of personal experience and is indelibly woven into the German landscape. Many of his characters are complicit in the events that constitute the Holocaust. Grass's writing, deceptively simple in its word choices, yet evocative in its images, never directly condemns or evaluates the events of the Holocaust. Instead he positions the most horrific among the most quotidian descriptions to force together, again and again, past and present, as in the scene when Fajngold, sole survivor of his Jewish family, returns after the war to take over the Matzerath grocery store and finds Matzerath dead in the cellar:

> He called not only Luba his wife, but his whole family into the cellar, and there is no doubt that he saw them all coming, for he called them by name: Luba, Lev, Jakub, Berek, Leon, Mendel, and Sonya. He explained to them who it was lying there dead and went on to tell us that all those he had just summoned as well as his sister-in-law and her other brother-in-law who had five children had lain in the same way, before being taken to the crematoria of Treblinka, and the whole lot of them had been lying there—except for him because he had to strew lime on them (p. 398).

Fajngold's roll call of the dead serves not only to memorialize the victims but also to evoke their presence in the postwar context of the grocery store, which in turn is thereby more closely linked to Treblinka than the Matzerath family (and the reader) might have thought. In the comparison, Matzerath's corpse is presented to be "like" those corpses in Treblinka, not only by way of reminding Fajngold but through the rhythm of and repetitions in the passage, as John Reddick observes (p. 33). That Fajngold's ongoing remembrance of the past is soon experienced as an annoyance is voiced by the narrator Oskar, whose statement "Lysol is more important than life" (p. 413) creates precisely the emotional response in the reader that a more direct accusation of the Holocaust might fail to evoke. Oskar continues: "This Mr. Fajngold could corroborate, for he had sprinkled the dead, not one corpse but many, why bother with figures; he had sprinkled dead men and women with Lysol and that was that. And he knew names, so many that it became tedious . . ." (p. 414). Oskar's indifference reflects his lack of interest in the dead and the past. Grass's dry tone, in which he evenly narrates past and present alongside one another, emphasizes not so much the horror of what has happened but the reprehensible and incomprehensible *absence* of horror in those who know about the past and can comment on it with such indifference.

The understanding that the Holocaust not only was inseparable from quotidian life in the 1930s and 1940s but in many ways remains so today, necessitating an ongoing process of coming to terms with the past, continues to inform Grass's writing. The reference to Auschwitz serves as a touchstone for his speaking out against current issues ranging from the relationship between ethnic groups in Germany today to inequality between Europe and developing nations. Repeatedly, Grass has cited Theodor Adorno's dictum on the barbarity of poetry after Auschwitz as a point of departure for his own writing relationship with the German past; he also names his friendship with the poet Paul Celan as a decisive factor in continuing his work.

Grass has substantially influenced the political culture in Germany since the 1960s, both through his fiction and through his strong personal engagement with the political left. The Danzig Trilogy presents Germans as a gullible people who denied the evil that gradually infiltrated every aspect of their public and private lives and who created a nation of willing followers and perpetrators during the Nazi regime. Most notably among his novels, *Die Blechtrommel* engages questions of collective German guilt and the responsibility of those who supported the Nazi regime as followers. In this story, Oskar Matzerath's father warms his hands and emotions at the burning synagogue in Danzig; Oskar swipes three tin drums from the destroyed toy store of the Jew Markus, an acquaintance. Oskar's family pays for their participation in German atrocities with the loss of their home to a Jewish survivor.

Hundejahre, a later novel, depicts the brutalization of children, along with the growing antisemitism of the 1930s and 1940s, in the violent conflict between Matern and his half-Jewish childhood friend Amsel. The amorality of this generation is expressed in the response the narrator ascribes to the girl Tulla, who causes her teacher's arrest and eventual death in a concentration camp: "Why? Just because." Tulla later reports with fascination on the mountains of bones and corpses in the Stutthof concentration camp. *Hundejahre*, however, also emphasizes the importance of storytelling, for, as Grass's narrator says, "as long as we are telling stories, we are alive" (p. 536). The activity of narration, however, is not to be understood so much as a "bearing witness" (an important aspect for many Jewish Holocaust writers), as it is a reminder that humanity depends on narratives to put events in relation to each other and to create meaning, in understanding both history and human relationships and failures. Without stories, the task of questioning and speculating about meaning would be abandoned. While the extreme situation of the Holocaust may challenge the writer to reflect on the possible absence of meaning, more commonly stories serve to connect events and people.

In Grass's assessment, the postwar years failed to address the recent past. His works *Örtlich Betäubt* (*Local Anaesthetic*, 1969) and *Aus dem Tagebuch einer Schnecke* (*From the Diary of a Snail*, 1972) return to the theme of the German past from the perspective of the late 1960s and early 1970s. Written in response to actual or imagined questions from the generation of his children, they probe the continued absence of a satisfying coming-to-terms with Germany's Nazi past, and, as Grass refers to the continued presence of Holocaust consciousness in *On Writing and Politics, 1967–1983*, the "shame and grief rooted in knowledge of German crimes that cannot be wished away" and the responsibility of the writer to write "against the passage of time" (pp. 85, 87). In the 1960s, Grass campaigned against attitudes of complacency and indifference toward the German past and spoke out against Germany's postwar focus on prosperity. *Aus dem Tagebuch einer Schnecke* relates events from the narrative present of the Brandt campaign against a historically accurate report of the persecution, emigration, deportation, and murder of the Danzig Jews. The text closes with Grass's travels to Israel and Poland that bring narrative closure to the story of the few survivors and reinforce the link between past and present.

Reception

In Germany as much as abroad, the novels of the Danzig Trilogy were instant bestsellers and were also condemned by readers as pornographic, sacrilegious, blasphemous, and morally offensive. In his book *Critical Essays on Günter Grass*, Patrick O'Neill calls Grass "a poser of questions and rejector of easy answers" (p. 13). Grass and his work have been the subject of numerous books, articles, reviews, and news stories. His understanding of the writer's role between literature and politics has been met with controversy, and his adversaries have criticized his political speeches as polemic, citing the same lack of restraint, judgment, and formal education that characterizes his novels. Marcel Reich-Ranicky, one of Grass's most persistent critics since the publication of *Die Blechtrommel*, charges Grass with a lack of artistic control over his material and yet lauds his outstanding narrative talent. In his introduction to Grass's collection *On Writing and Politics*, Salman Rushdie sees in Grass a fellow migrant writer who has used his double displacement from a past dominated by Nazi ideology and from the place of his childhood to draw attention to the basic constructedness and unreliability of any reality. Rushdie's vision affirms not only Grass's importance as a postwar German writer but also his relevance in a contemporary postcolonial context. Grass has been awarded a number of prizes and honors in Germany, France, Italy, Poland, and the United States for his literary works, beginning with the immediate international acclaim of *Die Blechtrommel*. In 1999, Grass was honored with the Nobel Prize in literature.

Bibliography

Primary Sources

Die Vorzüge der Windhühner (The merits of windfowl). 1956.
Die Blechtrommel (*The Tin Drum*). 1959.
Gleisdreieck (Triangle of tracks). 1960.
Hochwasser (*Flood*). 1963.
Katz und Maus (*Cat and Mouse*). 1963.
Hundejahre (*Dog Years*). 1965.
Onkel, Onkel (*Mister, Mister*). 1965.
Die Plebejer proben den Aufstand (*The Plebeians Rehearse the Uprising*). 1966.
Ausgefragt (Interrogated). 1967.
Über meinen Lehrer Döblin (On Döblin, my teacher). 1968.
Über das Selbstverständliche: Reden, Aufsätze, offene Briefe, Kommentare (selections published as *Speak Out! Speeches, Open Letters, Commentaries*). 1968.
Briefe über die Grenze: Versuch eines Ost-West Dialogs (Letters across the border: An attempt at an East-West dialogue). 1968.
Örtlich betäubt (*Local Anaesthetic*). 1969.
Aus dem Tagebuch einer Schnecke (*From the Diary of a Snail*). 1972.
Mariazuehren (*Inmarypraise*). 1973.
Liebe geprüft (*Love Tested*). 1974.
Der Bürger und seine Stimme: Reden, Aufsätze, Kommentare (A citizen and his voice: Speeches, essays, commentaries). 1974.
Als vom Butt nur die Gräte geblieben war (When only the bones of the flounder were left). 1977.
Vatertag (Father's day). 1977.
Der Butt (*The Flounder*). 1977.
Denkzettel: Politische Reden und Aufsätze, 1965–1976 (Reminders: Political speeches and essays, 1965–1976). 1978.
Das Treffen in Telgte (*The Meeting at Telgte*). 1979.
Aufsätze zur Literatur (Essays on literature). 1980.
Kopfgeburten oder Die Deutschen sterben aus (*Headbirths, or The Germans are dying out*). 1980.
Ach Butt, dein Märchen geht böse aus (Alas, flounder, your tale won't end well). 1983.
Widerstand lernen. Politische Gegenreden 1980–1983 (Learning to resist: Political counterpositions, 1980–1983). 1984.
Radierungen und Texte 1972–1982 (*Etchings and words 1972–1982*). 1984.
In Kupfer, auf Stein (In copper, on stone). 1986, revised 1994.
On Writing and Politics, 1967–1983 (selections from *Der Bürger und seine Stimme*, *Denkzettel*, *Aufsätze zur Literatur*, and *Widerstand lernen*). 1985.

Die Rättin (*The Rat*). 1986.

Mit Sophie in die Pilze gegangen (Gathering mushrooms with Sophie). 1987.

Zunge zeigen: ein Tagebuch in Zeichnungen, Prosa und einem Gedicht (*Show your tongue*). 1988.

Skizzenbuch (Sketchbook). 1989.

Wenn wir von Europa sprechen: ein Dialog mit Francoise Giroud (Speaking of Europe: A political dialogue with Francoise Giroud). 1989.

Ein Schnäppchen namens DDR: Letzte Reden vorm Glockengeleut (East Germany at bargain prices: Last speeches before the sound of the bell). 1990.

Deutschland, einig Vaterland? Streitgespräch mit Rudolf Augstein (Germany, a single Fatherland? A debate with Rudolf Augstein). 1990.

Schreiben nach Auschwitz: Frankfurter Poetik-Vorlesung (Writing after Auschwitz: The Frankfurt Poetics Prize lecture). 1990.

Deutscher Lastenausgleich: Wider das dumpfe Einheitsgebot. Reden und Gespräche (Sharing the German burden: Against the stultifying compulsion to unify. Speeches and interviews). 1990.

Two States—One Nation? The Case Against German Reunification (transl. *Schreiben nach Auschwitz und Deutscher Lastenausgleich*). 1990.

Totes Holz: Ein Nachruf (Dead wood: An epigraph). 1990.

Kahlschlag in unseren Köpfen (The clearcut mind). 1990.

Gegen die Verstreichende Zeit: Reden, Aufsätze, Gespräche, 1989–1991 (Writing against time: Speeches, essays, and interviews, 1989–1991). 1991.

Vier Jahrzehnte: ein Werkstattbericht (Four decades: A work in progress). 1991.

Rede vom Verlust: Über den Niedergang der politischen Kultur im geeinten Deutschland (On loss: The deterioration of the political climate in the United Germany). 1992.

Unkenrufe (*The Call of the Toad*). 1992.

Novemberland (Novemberland). 1993.

Angestiftet, Partei zu ergreifen (Forced to take sides). 1994.

Ein Weites Feld (*Too Far Afield*). 1995.

Die Deutschen und ihre Dichter (The Germans and their writers). 1995.

Gestern, vor 50 Jahren (Yesterday, 50 years ago). 1995.

Rede über den Standort (A place to stand). 1997.

Mein Jahrhundert (*My century*). 1999.

Secondary Sources

Brandes, Ute. *Günter Grass*. Berlin: Spiess, 1998.

Brode, Hanspeter. *Günter Grass*. München: Beck, 1979.

Hollington, Michael. *Günter Grass: The Writer in a Pluralistic Society*. London: Marion Boyars, 1980.

Leonard, Irene. *Günter Grass*. Edinburgh: Oliver and Boyd. 1974.

Mason, Ann L. *The Skeptical Muse: A Study of Günter Grass' Conception of the Artist*. Bern: Lang, 1974.

O'Neill, Patrick. *Gunter Grass Revisited*. New York: Twayne, 1999.

O'Neill, Patrick, ed. *Critical Essays on Günter Grass*. Boston: G. K. Hall, 1987.

Reddick, John. *The "Danzig Trilogy" of Günter Grass: A Study of* The Tin Drum, Cat and Mouse, and Dog Years. London: Secker & Warburg; New York: Harcourt, Brace, 1975.

Reich-Ranicky, Marcel. *Günter Grass*. Zürich: Ammann Verlag AG, 1992.

Schwan, Werner. *Ich bin doch kein Unmensch: Kriegs- und Nachkreigszeit im deutschen Roman*. Freiburg: Rombach, 1990.

GERALD GREEN

(1922–)

HILENE FLANZBAUM

GERALD GREEN WAS born in Brooklyn, New York, and educated at Columbia University. Green's father, Samuel Green, a doctor, was married to Anna (Matzkin) Greenberg. After college, Green entered the military where he served with the U.S. Ordnance Corps until 1946. He worked as a writer and an editor for NBC news between 1947 and 1950. He has written many popular novels, four screenplays for television, and several works of nonfiction. He had moderate success with his novels *The Last Angry Man* (1957) and *To Brooklyn With Love* (1968), yet nothing he has written before or after came close to the response elicited by his screenplay and novel, *Holocaust*.

Holocaust

Holocaust (1978), as both a miniseries and a novel, was a watershed cultural phenomenon rather than a conventional literary event. Green, who had never been perceived as having much standing in the academic community, wrote the screenplay for the television program first, and then later that year wrote the novel. Most would agree that the novel has little literary merit. One of the novel's many detractors, the reviewer for the *New York Times*, Helen Yglesias, argued that "this blockbuster book unlooses a commercial aggression before which the refinements of literary judgments are simply ludicrous." Yet whether critics liked it or not, there is no disputing that the phenomenon of *Holocaust*, first as a wildly successful television miniseries and then a blockbuster novel, demands that students of the Holocaust pay attention to Green's accomplishment. *Holocaust* was a national sensation and a milestone in the popular representation of the Nazi genocide.

A four-part series that produced nine and one-half hours of television viewing, *Holocaust* first appeared on NBC between 16 April and 19 April 1978. The director, Marvin Chomsky, was following his great success in *Roots* (1977), the most-watched television miniseries in broadcast history, which chronicled an African-American family's journey from being captured into slavery in the seventeenth century to emancipation. Despite Chomsky's success with *Roots*, the network still hesitated to make *Holocaust*, a miniseries that seemed to offer nothing but unrelenting human misery. While *Roots* had ended in the triumphant return to freedom of Kunta Kinte's nineteenth-century descendants, it was unclear what human victory would be celebrated at the end of *Holocaust*. Network executives, perhaps gambling on the American public's newly reawakened interest in ethnicity and ancestry, and deciding to stress the more simplistic aspects of history (good vs. evil), overcame their initial reservations and hired Green to write the screenplay.

The Artists of Terezin

Green's credentials were not as extensive as they might have been, although in 1969 he had published *The Artists of Terezin*, a nonfiction account of life in that concentration camp also sometimes called *Theresienstadt*. Terezin had not been an extermination camp, but rather a walled fortress that Hitler claimed "protected the Jews." Important political prisoners, as well as notable musicians, writers, and artists were sent there for "safer" keeping. In actuality, of course, many prisoners were just passing through Terezin on their way to death camps further east. Still, the inmates of Terezin managed to eke out a good deal of artistic work. Composers wrote symphonies, and the children were given paper on which they could draw their experience. Green compiles over one hundred of these illustrations, as well as providing editorial comment and historical background on both Terezin and the child artists, the large majority of whom did not survive the camps. *The Artists of Terezin* is an important book, not because it has sold so many copies, but because it opened the door to a new way, especially for children, of perceiving the Holocaust. Following Green's example, other scholars and museum curators have worked hard to recover the lost art of that period.

Green's involvement in the Terezin project, and undoubtedly his successful earlier novels, proved to NBC that he had a gift for telling stories. No place did that gift serve him more fully than when he wrote the screenplay for *Holocaust*, the second most-watched miniseries in television history. After the network rebroadcast the series the following year, NBC estimated that as many as 220 million viewers in the United States and Europe had seen it. When Green decided to capitalize on the success of the series by turning his original screenplay into a novel of the same name, it became a bestseller overnight.

Critical Reception

There is nothing remarkable about either the novel or the miniseries. Green chose to depict the event by following the interlocking lives and destinies of two families in Germany during World War II. One family, the Weiss family, is Jewish; the Dorf family is not. Erik Dorf, a good German, quiets his conscience for the sake of his ambition and becomes, at the prodding of his grasping wife, an SS officer who works with the evil Reinhand Heydrich. Through the eyes of the son of the Weiss family, as well as the eyes of Erik Dorf, viewers and readers witness many of the most horrendous moments of the Holocaust: *Kristallnacht*; the plotting of the Final Solution; the mass murder at Babi Yar; the uprising in the Warsaw ghetto, and finally, the liberation at Auschwitz. Rudi Weiss, the young Jewish protagonist, is heroic beyond measure: handsome, fearless, athletic, just. Rudi will survive to live on a kibbutz in Israel. As Daniel Schwarz tells us, "the plot depends on implausible coincidences in which the two major characters and their families intersect at opportune times." The dialogue is inappropriately "Americanized" and "sometimes Green's prose is execrable" (p. 163).

Schwarz's complaints are typical. Many unhappy reviewers disliked the plot's improbability and melodrama, arguing that it was unlikely that any one family would actually witness all these events; others argued that the characters were flat and uninteresting. Still, to focus on either the plot details or the relative complexity of the characters in either version (miniseries or novel) is to miss their great cultural and historical impact on America and Europe in general, and on Holocaust studies in particular. In both cases, the impact of *Holocaust* could not have been more profound.

There is no way to precisely measure the effect that *Holocaust* had on the popular viewing public; no way to tally the conversations in classrooms, at water coolers, and at family dinner tables. There can be no doubt, however, that like *Roots* before it, *Holocaust* had a huge national impact; internationally—in Israel, Great Britain, and the Scandinavian and Benelux countries—the show excited public debate. In West Germany, almost half of all adults watched the show, and it broke a thirty-five-year taboo on discussing the topic. This renewed discussion served to highlight contemporary West German problems with antisemitism and new neo-Nazi groups (Markovits, p. 74). With the exception of *Schindler's List*, which premiered fifteen years later, no other representation of the Holocaust has reached as many people and sparked as much interest in the subject. Proof of this lay not only in the network's decision to rebroadcast the series a scant year later, but also in the immediate and enormous success of the novel version. Clearly, Green's publisher, Bantam Books, understood that the huge success of the miniseries marked the beginning of a new era in national awareness and curiosity about the Holocaust. Scholars of the Holocaust have concurred with the assessment that the miniseries and the novel marked a watershed in public discussion of the event. However they have not agreed as to whether this has had more negative or positive ramifications.

Paradoxically enough, this debate among scholars was sparked by the huge and emotional response to the airing of the series. Equally important perhaps was the fact that the debate laid out the terms that many of the debates about popular representations of the Holocaust would follow in the future. While on one hand Elie Wiesel famously declared the miniseries to be "untrue, offensive, cheap," the program won a slew of awards, several Golden Globes and Emmys, including one for Green in the category of "Best Dramatic Screenplay." Yet the very notion that the Holocaust could have popular appeal—even commercial viability—seemed offensive to some. Scholars have maintained that many (and perhaps all) representations of the Holocaust that have found a large popular audience have trivialized the true horror of the event. This argument has been reintroduced in dozens of cases, most notably in the response to *Schindler's List*, as well as the movie *Life Is Beautiful*, and even the holiest of texts in Holocaust studies, *The Diary of Anne Frank.*

Supporters of these pieces agree that popular versions of the Holocaust do often minimize horrific events, yet they believe that the benefits of wide public remembrance outweigh the liabilities of any particular rendering. Whatever the miniseries' failings, Green and the producers (knowing they would be creating a "major television event") were scrupulous in their research and in their desire for realism, even going so far as to film part of the movie in Mauthausen concentration camp. At the same time, however, they also were striving to engage a wide popular audience. Green should be credited with, at least to some degree, accomplishing both of these goals. Whatever one believes about the quality of the screenplay or novel, there can be no doubt that they triggered the beginning of a widespread public engagement with the Holocaust.

In later years, Green continued to work on controversial topics, writing a screenplay about Vietnam War student protests, "Kent State," and a docudrama about Raoul Wallenberg, the Swedish diplomat who saved many Hungarian Jews from deportation to Auschwitz. Neither of these, nor any future novel, were as successful as *Holocaust*. As of this writing, most of Green's books, including *Holocaust*, are out of print; yet as long as Green's name is synonymous with that miniseries and the controversy it engendered, he will be long remembered.

Bibliography

Primary Sources

The Artists of Terezin. 1969.
Faking It. 1972.
The Portfolio PTA. 1976.
The Heartless Light. 1976.
Girl. 1977.
Holocaust. 1978.
Cactus Pie, Ten Stories. 1979.
The Healers. 1980.
The Lotus Eaters. 1980.
Murfy's Men. 1981.
The Chains. 1981.
Not in Vain. 1984.
East and West. 1987.

Secondary Sources

Avisor, Ilan. "The Hollywood Film and the Presentation of the Jewish Catastrophe." In *Screening the Holocaust: Cinema's Images of the Unimaginable*." Bloomington: Indiana University Press, 1988, pp. 129–131.

Guild, Hazel. "Germany and the TV Holocaust." *Variety* (Los Angeles), 23 May 1979.

Huyssen, Andreas. "The Politics of Identification: 'Holocaust' and West Germany." *New German Critique* 19 (winter 1980): 117–136.

Markovits, Andrei S., and Rebecca S. Hayden. " 'Holocaust' before and after the Event: Reactions in West Germany and Austria." *New German Critique* 19 (winter 1980): 53–80.

Schwarz, Daniel. *Imagining the Holocaust*. New York: St. Martin's Press, 1999.

Wiesel, Elie. "Trivializing the Holocaust: Semi-Fact and Semi-Fiction." *New York Times*, 16 April 1978.

Yglesias, Helen. "Genocide for Everyone." *New York Times Book Review*, 16 April 1978, p. 15.

URI ZVI GREENBERG

(1896–1981)

HANOCH GUY

URI ZVI GREENBERG, a descendent of Hasidic rabbis, was born in Bialykmien, eastern Galicia, on 21 September 1896. At the age of two, he moved with his family to Lvóv, where he later received a Jewish orthodox education. In 1912 he published his first Yiddish poems in *Yiddisher Arbeiter* and his earliest Hebrew poems in *Senunit.* Greenberg published his first Yiddish collection and was conscripted into the Austrian army in the same year. Two years later he deserted the army and returned to Lvóv, where, in 1918, he witnessed the pogrom against the Jews by the Polish army.

Greenberg published three Yiddish collections of poetry in the next two years; then, in 1921, he moved to Warsaw, where he edited the anti–Europe and anti–Christianity *Albatross*, which was subsequently banned because the state censor declared it inflammatory. Greenberg was eventually forced to leave Warsaw. He moved to Berlin and remained there until December 1923 and then immigrated to Israel.

Greenberg's first Hebrew collection, *Aimah gedolah veyaraikh* (A Great Horror and a Moon), appeared in 1924. Four years later, he published *Anacreon aal Kotev ha-ltzavon* (Anacreon on the Log of Despondency) and *Hazon Ehad ha Ligyonot* (A Vision of One Legion). Three more collections appeared in 1929: *Kelev Bayit* (A House Dog) and its appendix, and *Ezor Hamagen Veneum ben Hadam* (The Girdle of Defense and the Speech of the Son of Blood). In the same year he joined the Revisionist Party as a result of the massacre of Jews in Hebron.

The poet lived in Warsaw from 1931 to 1935. There he edited the weekly newspaper *Di Velt* (The World) and participated in several Zionist congresses. In 1936, he returned to Israel and published the collection *Sefer Hakitrug Vehaemunah* (The Book of Condemnation and Faith). Greenberg went back to Poland in 1937 and barely escaped, in 1939, two weeks after the war broke out. He returned to Israel and in 1949 served as a member of the Israeli parliament. During this time, he published *Min hachachlil umin Hakachol* (Of the Ruddy and of the Blue), 1949, *Mitoch Sefer haiggul* (From the Book of the Circle), 1950, *Maahalach beeretz Rabbah* (A Walk about a Great Land), 1950, *Rehovot ha–Nahar* (Streets of the River), 1951, *Masa va-Nevel* (A Load and a Harp), 1954, and *Sirai Aspaklar behai Alma* (Poems of a Mirror and This World), 1954.

Greenberg's poetry has been praised internationally. For his literary work, he has received the Bialik Award (1947, 1954), the State of Israel Award for literature (1957), and the Talpir Award (1963). New York University granted him the Neuman Award (1965), and Israel gave him the Israel Creativity Award and the Memorial Award in 1970 and in 1973, and the Itzik Manger Award for Yiddish literature in 1978.

Greenberg was married to the poet Aliza Greenberg and lived in Jerusalem. He died in 1981.

Overview

Greenberg's poetry spans almost seven decades and was written in Poland, Germany, Austria, and Israel. He published primarily in Yiddish until 1924, when he abandoned that language and wrote only in Hebrew. Several decades later, he returned to Yiddish and occasionally incorporated Aramaic in his poetry.

Believing that the ideological force of the poem overrides traditional concerns with meter and genre, Greenberg developed a unique voice. B. Y. Michali asserts, "Like every unique artist Greenberg is not part of the poets' choir of his generation. He is different in his content, his voice and his tune" (p. 345). Benjamin Hrushovski agrees that Greenberg expanded the possibilities of his poetic expression and choice of subjects, adding that Greenberg's poetry is wild, ecstatic, and breaks through all prohibitions (p. 8). The poet's work is distinguished by long Whitmanesque lines, which move like waves, with pathos or even bathos, modernist figurative language, and the abandonment of meter indicative of expressionism (Oren, p. 335) and a prophetic language of wrath that incorporates modern technological terms with Israeli slang, creating a poetry quite different from European expressionism. Greenberg eschewed poetry for poetry's sake and symbolism, favoring instead poetry in the service of ideology where the poetic form is secondary to the content (Bahat, pp. 308–322). Greenberg argues in his book *Kelape tish 'im ve–tish'ah* (Against Ninety-Nine) that there is no place anymore for short lyrical poems, sonnets, or other classical genres (Tel-Aviv: Sadan Press 1928, p. 38). According to David Veinfeld, Greenberg was influenced by the expressionist movement, the crisis in values that it expressed, the horrors of the First World War, and the despair that followed. He was also influenced by Futurism, which emphasizes the urban setting, speed, the treatment of the human body as a machine, and modern machinery (pp. 344–358). Greenberg' s poetry is not readily accessible, even for the Hebrew speaking reader. According to Gidion Katznelson, "Facing the phenomenon of Uri Zvi Greenberg's poetry, the reader is frequently very confused and feeling [that] he is looking at a wondrous palace that has seven locks" (Katznelson, p. 137).

Holocaust Poetry

Greenberg is among the first writers to tackle the subject of the Holocaust in Hebrew, and Alan Mintz characterizes Greenberg's major Holocaust work, *Streets of the River* (1951), as "the single most important work on the Holocaust in Hebrew literature" (p. 165). Greenberg's Holocaust poetry can be divided into two categories: the poetry of prophecy, written in the years 1923 to 1930, and the poetry of lamentation, contained in *Streets of the River* and later poetry.

Common Themes

Greenberg's pre-Holocaust poetry is marked by his personal encounters with violence, the experience of a young conscript in the Austrian army on the Serbian front, and, later, his family's suffering in the Ukrainian massacres in Lvóv. A common theme of Greenberg's Holocaust poetry is the concept of a unifying history. According to Barukh Kurtzweil, Greenberg's poetry unifies all times and preserves the past as living presence (p. 99). The unifying historical theme states that Jewish history is like streets of a great river originating in Ur with Abraham and flowing through exile to the *Shoah*. The river is saturated, writes Greenberg, with blood and tears. This key is included in a short poem in *Streets of the River*, "The Poem of Avraham's Race":

> From the day we defeated the nature of water and fire
> and we exited singing to freedom and kingdom
> the fire follows us to catch us between the straits.
> The water follows us in order to drown us (*Rehovot ha–Nahar*, Jerusalem: Schocken, 1953, p. 32).

Connecting pagan and Christian antipathy toward Jews, Greenberg claims that since the Jews smashed the stone and wooden idols and taught that there is a single creator, the gentile trees cast the shadow of death on them.

Contributing to this theme of the great suffering of the Jews throughout history are three sub-themes, all explorations of the guilt of those responsible for the suffering. The gentiles are guilty, believes Greenberg, because they have hated Jews throughout history. The Jews are guilty, for they have been unprepared and too weak to resist the violence perpetrated against them. Ultimately, God is guilty because He has abandoned His people. Greenberg responds to these conditions in the Hebraic lamentation tradition, mourning and yearning for the presence of those who died in the *Shoah* and now dwell in subterranean Europe. To the lamentation tradition, Greenberg adds poems calling for revenge and redemption.

Prophetic Holocaust Poetry: Visions, Sources, and the Poet of Destruction

During the poet's stay in Germany, Poland, and Israel before the Holocaust, Greenberg wrote a series of poems predicting the Holocaust in shocking details, explaining its reasons and the outcome. Paraphrasing Jeremiah, Greenberg writes in his *Anacreon aal Kotev ha-Itzavan*: "As chapters of burning prophesy, my days burn in all the revelations and my body is in the middle as melting metal, and God the blacksmith stands above me and strikes with might" (p. 74). Conscious of the harshness of his poetry, the poet feels that God is compelling him to write the visions, however dark they are. Under the facade of the calm and cultured Europe lay the ancient hate, violence, and destruction, visible only to the one who sees the cracks in the façade. In

Condemnation and Faith he writes, "In the Horror of Prophecy":

> How did such an insane vision come to me?—
> Any one with a torn shirt
> Like a tearing sorrow, a vision comes through.
> It was a melting and bursting forth vision (*Sefer Hakitrug Vehaemunah, Jerusalem*: Sadan, 1937, p. 28).

In another context, he is at a loss to explain his visions. The poet H. N. Bialik asked Greenberg how he imagined a detailed horrific description in "Going Underground," one that reads as if it were written after the Holocaust, to which Greenberg admitted his own amazement that his early vision of the impending Holocaust appeared in 1923 in Berlin, where he published a horrific visionary poem (Bahat, p. 324). The poet probably also refers to his Yiddish book *In the Kingdom of the Idol* and his poem "Going Underground," which was published in *The Streets of the River* in 1951.

Greenberg sees the hatred toward Jews as a continuous venomous process that is well hidden from the rest of the world, waiting to erupt at any moment. He contextualizes the Holocaust within a long history of anti-Jewish persecution, as "A silence . . . burning for thousands of years in the abyss below the trees . . . a poison that lies and accumulates in the abyss" ("In the Kingdom of the Idol," *Albatross* no. 4–5, p. 15). In doing this Greenberg draws a straight line from the Jews who were butchered by the Babylonians in 586 B.C.E. to the millions of European Jews who suffered in the Holocaust in the twentieth century. The poet envisions his body added to the other victims: "It resembles a tree in our woods of agony that moves with the millions of trees in the storm" (p. 65). Greenberg drives home a vision of the continuity of hatred expressed toward the Jews from Babylonian and Roman times, through the Spanish Inquisition to modern Europe: "Rome is eating my kingdom down to its foundation and Spain is burning and cutting to pieces bodies and holy pages, up to Russia who slaughters in the reign of the Czar Nicolai and Poland and its neighbors. A Jewish poet is rising to sing from the horrible depth of blood in the middle of Europe" (*Sefer Hagrarat Haola* [Book of the Ascending Manhood], p. 64). The poet cries out that the Gentiles will not be satisfied until all Jews are exterminated. The European Christians combine the ancient pagan dark forces with the fierce murderous cross.

Greenberg points an accusing finger at the Christian church as the major guilty party of the inevitable genocide: medieval Christian hatred for the Jews will erupt and destroy all Jews. Greenberg locates an irrational fear of Jews and a belief in their having mythical powers to harm Europe as the foundation for murdering them. The Jews are doomed under the sword of the cross that is going to slaughter them, and they do not resist. In Greenberg's poem "*Tur Malka*," he writes "The big herd degenerates there under the crosses . . . We are millions for the swords and just a few heroes (*Sadan* A–B, Jerusalem, 1925, p. 47)."

According to Greenberg, in Condemnation and Faith, Christians are still seeking revenge for the crucifixion of Jesus. No country is safe for the Jews from the merciless cross that turns into a murderous knife: "because the cross will not pity. It is made out of iron which is already in the poet's heart" (p. 44). In 1926, Greenberg warns against seeing Europe as a civilized and enlightened entity. Its façade of high culture and slogans of liberty and equality hide prejudice, hate, and evil. As he is quoted in Shalom Lindenbaum's *The Poetry of U. Z. Greenberg:* "On the world surface, I presently see sixteen million Jews under the big crosses that may be our hanging places in the middle of the day . . . until the last baby is dead. Enlightened Europe is not enlightened regarding Jews" (p. 159).

Criticism of the Jews' Passivity: Jewish Martyred Sheep Waiting for the Messiah

Greenberg asserts that one of the main reasons for the coming catastrophe is the passivity of the Jews throughout the ages. While the poet lived in Berlin, in 1923, he included in his epic poem "In the Kingdom of the Idol" descriptions of the Jews as sheep, kids, lambs, and cattle who are frightened and cling to the herd without thinking or doing anything. Lindenbaum points out that Greenberg alludes to the German saying: "One who makes himself a sheep is devoured by the wolves." Lindenbaum also comments that by using the sheep and herd negatively, Greenberg reverses the traditional positive connotation of the Jews as the flock of God that is led by Moses to freedom. The descriptions of sheep, whose eyes reflect the glitter of a large knife and swords and who are surrounded by dead shepherds with kids' heads on their knees, point to total despair and certain death. The shepherds were unable to protect their flocks, and they die with them. Greenberg blames the inept Jewish leadership that did not have enough foresight and strength to lead the people to a safe place (Lindenbaum, pp. 138–139). The poet sees the situation as hopeless because the Jewish people are languishing in passivity and are indeed becoming sheep (p. 139). The poet repeats both his imagery and his warning in 1929, seeing even more clearly a shepherdless, frightened herd about to be drowned. *A House Dog* he reverses the miraculous crossing of the Red Sea by Moses and the successful crossing of the Jordan by Joshua. In contrast to the other crossings, the current one is doomed to failure. All Jews will die in the process, as the ancient Egyptians died, "trembling terribly between water and water . . ." (*Kelev Bayit*, p. 9).

In a 1924–1925 collection, A Great Horror and a Moon, Greenberg scolds the Jews who are waiting for the Messiah. He claims that they do not even know what a messiah is. Even if he comes, the poet does not want him because he will have no idea of his people's suffering, which he did not experience. In Greenberg's view, the Jews do not need a heavenly messiah but one who has been in the midst of the suffering and shame:

> there is no messiah in the world!
> I do not want a heavenly messiah whose body is fog
> and his head of onyx who does not
> know our shame and tortures.
> There is no messiah in the nation, not even his shadow (*Aimah gedolah vevaraikh*, Tel Aviv: Haidim, 1925, pp. 40–41).

Greenberg warns Jews not to be so willing to die sanctifying God's name because He is powerless and may be dead. He counsels, in The Book of the Ascending Manhood, "Leave the martyrs alone. Become heroes" (*Hagravat Haola*, Tel Aviv: Sadan, 1926, pp. 40–41). According to the poet, God is miserable and He wants to abandon His kingdom. He is no longer calm and competent. There is no wonder, then, that the feeble and indifferent God abandons the Jews. Greenberg goes even further and postulates that God is already dead. He died a bloody electric death.

In his prophetic poems, Greenberg predicts the total annihilation of the Jewish communities in Europe. He presents an image of a vengeful Europe that sought the end of Judaism for almost two thousand years. In his poem, "In the Kingdom of the Idol," Greenberg describes hundreds of thousands of Jews who are trying to escape into the woods and giving birth to dying children:

> The hundreds of thousands are fleeing back to the woods of suffering:
> And among the trees of suffering children are born
> who already have dimness and weakness in their blood to wither
> even before the roses (*Albatross*, no. 3–4, p. 15).

Greenberg describes all Jews marching into captivity as their ancestors did in the time of the Roman General Titus, who destroyed Jerusalem in 70 A.D. The past will be repeated, and Jews will be sold and will spill their blood for water and bread and the cloth on their backs. In an ironic contradiction to fairy tales, in which the woods are sites of challenge for the heroes, the European woods are the execution sites for hanging and wounding Jews. Even the trees are collaborators of the murderers, who leave their victims hanging on their branches.

> Such a thick forest is growing here on the meadow.
> The valleys of suffering and horror are so deep in Europe!
> The trees have suffering heads of wild darkness, wild darkness
> The dead with bleeding wounds are hanging on their branches (p. 15).

The vision the poet sees compels him to present the victims to heaven as testimony of destruction and accusation of God's failure: "I am hanging my naked dead on branches. / I let them rot lawless facing all the stars" (p. 15).

In his prophetic poetry Greenberg addresses the time after the total destruction of the Jewish communities and of Europe. He writes: "Ten will remain, ten hurting Jews, a bleeding remnant of survivors / in order to prove: There was once such a nation on the Christian painful soil" (p. 15).

Greenberg allows for the survival of ten for the obligatory quorum to pray in a community and recite the Kaddish, the prayer for the dead.

Post-Holocaust Poetry

Greenberg's predictions materialized, and the poet's bitterness toward the European gentiles intensifies in his post-Holocaust poetry. So do his cries against God who abandoned His people. Although Greenberg invoked the format of Yom Kippur atonement—that the Jews were killed because they have sinned by forgetting the kings, Lake Galilee, the Jordan River, and snowy Mount Hermon, to cultivate the high culture of the gentiles—after the *Shoah*, his criticism and accusatory tone against the Jews soften, and his compassion increases. He writes that the essence of his anger has broken down with the breaking of his people, and a stream of compassion runs in him (*Streets*, p. 203). Lindenbaum comments that with the shift from burning anger to tender compassion, the form has changed: the rhythm becomes more peaceful, the language softer, and metaphor less aggressive.

Reiterating the prophetic poetry, Greenberg writes that all Europe's peasant population sought to benefit from the annihilation of the Jews, every peasant waiting to get a pair of shoes from a Jew who is taking them off. In Streets of the River, a peasant throws a stone that splits a baby's eye while the infant's mother is trying to shield him (*Rehovot ha–Nahar*, pp. 42–43). Reiterating the march of antisemitic history, he identifies those of the ancient world who sought to burn Abraham in Ur Kasdim, the Philistines, the Babylonians, and the Assyrians, as well as the Romans and the Spanish Inquisitors and their descendants, observing that despite the Germans' so-called high culture of music, literature, and philosophy, they are predators feasting on a dead sacrifice:

> God's death in their bread . . . From the loftiness of their holy of holies
> comes up a vapor
> smoke of burning bodies in a fiery oven (*Rehovot ha–Nahar,* p. 171).

The Crown of Lamentation

Alan Minte writes that the publication of Streets of the River is both a chronicle of "the ordeal of personal loss" and the crown of lamentation for the *Shoah* victims (Mintz, p. 171). This wide-ranging book of narrative, dramatic, lyric, and hortatory verse, which earned Greenberg the title of the "great lamentor" (Michali, p. 345) and "records what Hebrew literature, in the main, does not: an attempt to face the Holocaust and to grapple with the enormity of the loss through stages of denial, nostalgia, and resignation. . . ." (Mintz, p. 172), signifies a turning point in Greenberg' s poetry as well as in the critical reception of his work. While critics disagreeing with his nationalistic approach and animosity toward all Gentiles continued to attack him, scholars started to evaluate his poetry in a balanced study. Textual and comparative approaches replaced the previous biographical and ideological approaches.

Representative of more recent scholarly attention is that of Mintz's commentary on the lyric passages of *Streets of the River*, which is applicable to much of Greenberg's Holocaust poetry: in its "regard to the image of the slaughtered, it is a movement from disfigurement, abandonment, and the shame of unburied nakedness to a purified radiance and to a restored relationship with the living" (Mintz, p. 199). According to the poet, the process of writing *Streets of the River* was a logical-methodological one. He describes himself as an architect of the science of mourning and defines the writing as poems of religious longing. The book revolves around six major cycles: a summary of Jewish history, mourning for the poet's close family, mourning for the European Jewish community that perished, the deep longing of the poet for the renewal of the kingdom of Israel, revenge, and redemption, which may be read in terms of its "thematic and formal opposition between two orders of discourse: bardic and lyric . . . a patterned series of public assertions, undercut by involuntary withdrawals into private concerns, followed by recoveries of public discourse" (Mintz, p. 180).

The poet describes Jewish history in sharp and tragic terms, as a great river of blood and tears that began flowing when "A supreme father's race emerged from the wild animal enemies" (*Rehovot ha–Nahar*, p. 7). The saga begins with Abraham and ends with the fiery Germans. The descendants of Abraham are always tested by God: "walk the streets of the river throughout the generations/and the gentiles' world is blooming on both banks" (p. 7).

In the first cycle of mourning, personal lamentation for the poet's own family, Greenberg feels that he sinned by leaving his holy parents. The scene of his leaving is still burning in him: "I saved my body when I fled from my mother's and father's house . . . But I did not save my soul" (p. 63). He describes the murder of his father as if he witnessed the Nazi officer striking his father with his rifle and sees the snow turning red. In his bitterness, he writes that the Gentiles' earth kicked his father, and God did not help because He belonged to the gentiles (p. 102). Next, he imagines his sister being raped in the woods after escaping from the cars of sulfur:

> and the gentiles found her there and they did not kill her:
> they all coveted her there and became her betrothed . . .
> With their horse sperm they murdered her
> and at last they buried her in that forest (p. 58).

From the anguished lyric recording of the poet's personal loss, he returns, in "*Keter Kinah le–kohl beit Israel*" (A Crown of Lament for All Israel), to the bardic voice lamenting the loss of six million Jews. The poet begins with an imagined panorama of defenseless East European Jewry marching to its death, among them his own family. In agony, he sees himself climbing up and down the high ladder of pain, reversing the miracle of Jacob's ladder in Genesis. He is a witness, although he was not there, recognizing that "Beyond pain there is no more pain!/Beyond despair there is no more despair" (p. 113). Lamenting the murdered European Jews, the poet celebrates their nobility: "Jews of the Mishnah and the Psalms" (p. 118); Jews still holy and faithful to God, "they keep on burning like the burning bush that was not consumed and the fire is covered with a prayer shawl" (p. 31). The poet reverses the miracle of the burning bush that was not consumed and writes that the Jews are burned, and there is no presence of God. The gentiles are feasting on their bread of a dead God and savor the vapor of burning Jews in the ovens:

Here they are, sitting down for a meal. We know a dead sacrifice
Their Gods' death in their bread and from the exaltation of their holy of holies
a vapor goes up:
the smoke of burning bodies in the scorching furnace (p. 171).

Greenberg envisions the death marches of the handsome and holy Jews who are nameless and dark. They are accompanied by stone-throwing young gentiles who curse them, while a Nazi promises them that the Jews will be well laundered in the furnace.

then they stood totally naked;
men and women and their . . . children
facing their killers on the verge of open pits
and they saw the horror of their death (p. 54).

The poet sees them vividly standing in gas clouds at the threshold of their death. Their arms are stamped with a number. Then they are pushed inside like sheep and chickens, watching the ones who were already gassed (pp. 54–55).

The Jewish Communities of Heaven and Hell

The poem "*Baiba makhterot*: *Khazon lail Kayitz*" (Going Underground: A Summer Night Vision), written by Greenberg in 1923 in Berlin, was included in Streets of the River in 1951. In the poem, he presents the only survivor of the *Shoah*, who meets with the poet and leads him underground to be with all the slain Jews who are now "the people of the deep earth." They are chanting Yom Kippur hymns and are safe underground because

We found a homeland below.
It is round, big and Jewish in depth . . .
The homeland of death is beautiful (*Rehovot ha–Nahar,* 1953, pp. 9–13).

In the poem "*Keilat ha–Kadesh bamarom*" (The Holy Communities in Heaven), Greenberg describes a redemptive vision of blue heavens that look like plowed fields:

They are walking together; the members of the holy communities
of all the Israeli towns that ascended to heaven
just as the towns were on earth (pp. 128–129).

The poet suggests that every Jewish town became like heavenly Jerusalem but without God or angels. He adds that heaven is like the snowy fields of the kingdom of the cross.

Out of his deep mourning and pain, the poet cries for revenge against the gentiles and the use of the royal sword. He envisions the Jewish redemption through the sword, the burning bush, Sinai, and the return of the kingdom that will build the third temple. The poet is intent on forging a new King David's sword instead of the one that was smashed. He intends to use it to avenge the murder of his people: "and anybody who threatens us, we will destroy by the sword" (*Rehovot ha–Nahar*, p. 88). Greenberg is calling for a new Hebrew Hannibal who will cruelly traverse Europe, and will plough through houses and people, and will destroy all the gentile cities, ignoring their Christian cries (p. 90).

In addition to calling for national revenge, Greenberg desires personal revenge. He writes a letter to his dead father, telling him how he avenged his death. He describes himself as a partisan who seeks out Ivan, asks him why he killed his father, and kills him with the same knife used to kill his father. Greenberg invokes the old law of blood revenge and creates his own commandment and blessing:

Blessed are thou king of the world, who sanctified us in his commandments and
instructed us to spill blood for blood,
a soul for a soul (*Rehovot ha–Nahar,* p. 371).

Jerusalem is a central symbol for the previous glory of Israel in Greenberg's poetry. He describes the revival of the city: "While Jerusalem is dark . . . all of a sudden it is light./While all the gentiles' capitals at her feet are extinguished because it is light" (p. 90).

The poet devotes the holy of holies to his mother and thanks God for teaching him to fight and to bring all the slain Jews to the wailing wall and to King David's tomb until the kingdom is revived (p. 371).

The Last Kaddish

The poet transforms the traditional orphan's prayer for the dead to focus on the revival of the dead, the uprooting of the gentile religions, and the restoration of God's kingdom in Jerusalem. His new version is written in Aramaic, as was the original prayer, to make the poem more authentic. However, he leaves intact only the first line of the prayer and adds:

In the world that He will renew
and revive the dead and elevate them

to an eternal life
and build the city of Jerusalem
and complete the temple in it
and uproot (pagan) worship from the land
and bring the worship to this place
and will crown holiness.
May he be blessed in His kingdom and its preciousness (p. 371).

Bibliography

Primary Sources

Yiddish

Ergeiz Oyf Felder (Somewhere in the Fields). 1915.

In Zeitnes Roish (The Rush of Times). 1919.

Farnachtengold (Golden Dusk). 1921.

Mefisto, 1922.

Krieg Oyf Der Erd (War on Earth). 1922.

Unzere othioth glian: Bi der toiren fun treren shtait a yid in gedenkenschaft (Our Letters are Glowing: At the Gates of Tears, a Jew Stands in Remembrance). 1978.

Hebrew

Aimah gedolah veyaraikh (A Great Horror and a Moon). 1923.

Hagravat Haola (The Book of the Ascending Manhood). 1926.

Anacreon aal Kotev ha-Itzavon (Anacreon on the Log of Despondency). 1928.

Hazon Ehad ha-ligyonot (A Vision of One Legion). 1928.

Kelape tish'im ve-tish'ah (Against Ninety-Nine). 1928.

Kelev bayit (A House Dog). 1929.

Ezor hamagen veneum ben hadam (The Girdle of Defense and the Speech of the Son of Blood). 1929.

Sefer hakitrug vehaemunah (The Book of Condemnation and Faith). 1936.

Rehovot ha–Nahar (Streets of the River). 1951.

Kol Ketavov (All His Writings). 1990.

Secondary Sources

Hebrew

Bahat,Yaakov. *Uri Zvi Greenberg*. Jerusalem: Yahdav-Dvir. 1983.

Barzel, Hillel. *Meshorerim Bigedulatam*. Makor Yahdav. Tel Aviv: Agudat Hasofrim, 1979, pp. 73–122.

Debby-Guri, Lillian. "Galut ugeulah Beshirat Uri Tzvi Greenberg." *Bikoret Uparshanut* 15 (1980): 183–200.

Friedlander, Yehudah, ed. *Uri Zvi Greenberg: A Selection of Critical Essays of His Writing*. Tel Aviv: Am Oved, 1974.

Friedlander, Yehudah. *Uri Zvi Greenberg*. Jerusalem: Schocken, 1973.

Hrushovski, Benjamin. *The Theory and Practice of Rhythm in the Expressionist Poetry of U. Z. Greenberg*. Porter Institute for Poetics & Semiotics. Tel Aviv: Tel Aviv University, 1978.

Katznelson, Gidion. "A Key to the Poetry of Uri Zvi Greenberg." In *Uri Zvi Greenberg*. Edited by Yehudah Friedlander. Tel Aviv: Am Oved, 1974.

Kurtzweil, Barukh. *Bein Hazon L'Vain Aabsurd* (Between the Vision and the Absurd). Tel Aviv: Schocken, 1966.

Landau, Dov. *Height of Poetry in the Depth of Time*. Jerusalem: Ministry of Culture and Education, 1983.

Lindenbaum, Shalom. *The Poetry of U. Z. Greenberg* (Hebrew & Yiddish) Outline. Tel Aviv: Hadar, 1984.

Michali, B. Y., ed. "Uri Zvi Greenberg Is Eighty." *Moznayim* 43.5 (October 1976). Tel Aviv: Hebrew Writers Association.

Shaanan, Avraham. *Dictionary of Modern Hebrew and World Literature*. Tel Aviv: Yavneh, 1959.

Shoham, Reuven. *Seneh Basar Vadam*. Beer Sheba, Israel: Ben Gurion University, 1997.

Veinfeld, David. *Raishit ytzirato shel Uri Tzvi Greenberg Beivrit*. Thesis. Jerusalem: Hebrew University, 1965.

Yaivin,Yehoshua. *Uri Tzvi Greenberg-Meshorer mekhokek*. Tel Aviv: Sadan, 1938.

Yudkin, Leon I. *On the Poetry of U. Z. Greenberg*. Jerusalem: Mass, 1987.

English

Alter, Robert. "A Poet of the Holocaust." In *Defenses of the Imagination*. Philadelphia: The Jewish Publication Society of America, 1978.

Arnon, Y., ed. *Uri Zvi Greenberg: A Bibliography of His Works and of What Was Written about Him*. Jerusalem: Adi Moses, 1980.

Band, A. "The 'Rehabilitation' of Uri Zvi Greenberg." *Prooftexts* 1 (1981): 316–326.

Hever, H., ed. *Uri Zvi Greenberg on His Eightieth Anniversary*. Jerusalem: Jewish National and University Library, 1977.

Mintz, Alan. *Hurban*. New York: Columbia University Press, 1984.

Miron, Dan. "Uri Zvi Greenberg War Poetry." In *The Jews of Poland between Two World Wars*. Eds. Yisrael Gutman, et al. Hanover: NH.: Brandeis University Press, 368–382.

Nash, S. "The Development of Some Key Metaphors in Uri Zvi Greenberg's Poetry." *Hebrew Studies* 24 (1983): 121–135.

Yudkin, L. "The 'Mission' of Uri Zvi Greenberg." *Modern Hebrew Literature* 3 (autumn 1976).

Penueli, S. Y. and A. Ukhanani, eds. *Anthology of Modern Hebrew Poetry in Two Volumes*. Selected by S. Y. Penueli. Jerusalem: Israel Universities Press, 1966.

Anderson, Elliot, ed.*Contemporary Israeli Literature*. Philadelphia: The Jewish Publication Society of America, 1977.

Bargad, Warren, and Stanley F. Chyet, eds. *Israeli Poetry*. Bloomington: Indiana University Press, 1986.

Frank, Bernhard, translated and introduction. *Modern Hebrew Poetry*. Iowa City: University of Iowa Press, 1980.

Mintz, Ruth Finer. Edited and translated. *Modern Hebrew Poetry*. Berkeley: University of California Press, 1966.

Burnshow, Stanley, T. Carmi, and Ezra Spicehandler, eds. *The Modern Hebrew Poem Itself*. Cambridge: Harvard University Press, 1989.

Carmi, T., ed. *The Penguin Book of Hebrew Verse*. New York: The Viking Press, 1981.

HARVEY GROSSINGER

(1948–)

DANIEL WALDEN

HARVEY GROSSINGER, BORN on the Grand Concourse in Bronx, New York, on 19 August 1948, grew up in the East Bronx, a short walk from the Bronx Zoo. After a family move, he and his younger brother attended public schools in Mamaroneck in lower Westchester County, less than a mile from the Long Island Sound; Harvey graduated from Mamaroneck High School in 1966.

After earning a B.A. in English, with a minor in philosophy, from New York University's Washington Square College (1970), Grossinger received an M.A. in English at Indiana University and an M.F.A. in creative writing at American University. His thesis project was titled "Home Burial: Five Stories." Several of these stories were published in the *New England Review* (1991), the *Chicago Tribune*, the *Western Humanities Review*, the *Cimarron Review*, the *Mid-American Review*, *Ascent*, and the *Antietam Review*. *The Quarry: Stories* was published by the University of Georgia Press, 1997.

Career and Critical Reception

Grossinger held many jobs before, during, and after graduate school. He was a trailblazer (literally cutting scenic trails through undeveloped woodland), an editorial assistant, a freelance copy editor at RR Bowker Publishing Company, and a freelance manuscript reader and reviewer for Vanguard Press. For a while he was a salesman at the largest Canadian wholesale and retail artist supply company in Toronto; he worked for a few years as a waiter in a Washington, D.C., restaurant and as a supervisor and occasional salesman for a wholesale wine and beer distributorship in northern Virginia. For the past few years he has been a regular contributor of book reviews of new fiction for *The Houston Chronicle* and a professorial lecturer at American University and Johns Hopkins University.

Although Grossinger's reputation as a writer had been growing for several years, it was with the publication of *The Quarry: Stories* (University of Georgia Press), winner of the Flannery O'Connor Award for Short Fiction (1995) and the Edward Lewis Wallant Book Award (1997), that he came to the attention of major critics. Sybil Steinberg writes in *Publishers Weekly*, "the five stories and one novella . . . center on Jewish Americans who are haunted by persecutions imagined and real, including the Holocaust. It isn't the absent victims or direct survivors of the Holocaust who are Grossinger's focus, but their children and grandchildren" (p. 48). According to Eden Osucha in the *Boston Book Review*, Grossinger is "a natural and mesmerizing storyteller from whom haunting human mysteries emerge. These are stories so good they shock" (19 June 1998). According to Lillian Kremer, in her remarks announcing the Edward Lewis Wallant Book Award, Grossinger is "a writer blessed with both a playful satiric wit as well as psychological insight. Grossinger seems to have something of Saul Bellow's eye and Philip Roth's ear" (19 April 1998, unpublished).

"The Quarry"

The closing novella in this collection, the hundred-page "The Quarry," is complexly narrated from alternating points of view of an American father, his son, and a self-defined voice of a Holocaust survivor, juxtaposing tales of personal bereavement that capture the reader's attention. What Grossinger is concerned with in "The Quarry," as in many of his other stories, is the psychological impact and transmission of traumatic personal and collective memory. In other words, he examines how the recollections of deceased loved ones affect their families and how memory of the *Shoah* affects eyewitnesses and sensitive listeners. The narrator asserts that in this imperfect memoir, with "some meager concessions for our infrequently deficient recollections . . . what we remembered about the past may, of course, be more *significant* then what had actually happened" (p. 215).

Shortly after this statement, the voice of the Holocaust survivor tells the story of her family, including that of her son who has been silenced by the Nazis through the mutilation of his tongue. Readers then learn, through the controlling trope of the quarry, that the father and son experience Holocaust epiphanic insights. The father, in liberating the death camps, sees a granite quarry holding the bodies of concentration camp victims who have been tortured, mutilated, hung, electrocuted, stabbed, shot, and experimented on. Later, in postwar America, the body of Uriel Mermelstein, Mickey's friend and a young *Shoah* survivor, is found at the bottom of a local, iced-over limestone quarry by a drunken stonecutter, as a result either of having been pushed by some antisemites or of suicide. Mickey believes it may have been the latter, that because he had not defended Uriel earlier when he was assailed by local hooligans, Uriel had given up hope. "Beyond the memory of the broken body of his friend," Kremer writes, "the narrator is haunted by his own guilt for taking the role of unresponsive bystander, a thought that resonates for the reader as an indictment of the world community of silent bystanders to the genocide of European Jewry" (19 April 1998, unpublished).

What Grossinger has done so well, writes Sanford Pinsker in the *Providence Journal-Bulletin*, is limn "the difference between memoir and the shaping hand of imagination, as well as the subtle ways in which ostensible 'truths' often disguise deeper truths" (16 November 1997). In this forceful meditation on memory and amnesia, *The Quarry* fits wonderfully in the growing body of Holocaust fiction (a phrase at once fitting yet repugnant) by contemporary Jewish-American writers belonging to a generation at least once removed from the atrocities. Given that the writers have learned about the Holocaust indirectly through survivor relatives or through relatives or friends, as in Thane Rosenbaum's *Elijah Visible* and *Second Hand Smoke* or Melvin Jules Bukiet's *Stories of an Imaginary Childhood*, the difficulty of imagining the *Shoah* has become an inescapable subject rather than a creative impediment. Grossinger's attempt to confront this subject through "The Quarry" is, in Andrew Furman's words, "the most aesthetically satisfying articulation of this emergent theme in Jewish American fiction" (p. 11).

Through several narrators and two stories set in a small Indiana town, Grossinger never allows the reader to forget that the novella is primarily about his narrators' memories concerning the events. "All I have left is my impoverished *memory* of what happened to my wife, and that is an elusive thing indeed" (p. 179), Jacob reflects. But it is through Mickey, Jacob's son, that the Holocaust—in particular the experience of his friend's mother Esther Mermelstein, in the camps—is depicted. "The Quarry" is finally about Mickey's burden, explains Furman, "as one who must grapple with the haunting strangeness of the Holocaust (p. 12)." The Holocaust exists tangibly for Mickey and those of his generation, Grossinger implicitly argues, only through the treacherous imagination. It is Jacob, who, having entered the camps as a liberator, tells Mickey all the horrific details of what he had witnessed. As the novella unfolds, Mickey becomes more and more self-conscious as a narrator. He realizes, Furman points out, "that the imagination necessary to reconstruct the Mermelstein story threatens to usurp the events themselves" (p. 12). He is not beholden then to what actually happened, because Mickey realizes that what is remembered could be more significant than what actually happened. Mickey is free to retrieve what memories he can, for, Grossinger writes, quoting William Faulkner, "the past is never dead, it is not even past" (p. 218). In the tradition of Bernard Malamud, Furman points out, Grossinger inscribes his significant dead into memory, when the preceding generation of immigrant Jews and Holocaust refugees wills this collection, especially this novella, into being. "That Mr. Grossinger draws so naturally upon such diverse literary influences," Furman concludes, "heralds a rich and vibrant future for Jewish American literature" (p. 12).

Much of the strength in this collection, especially in "The Quarry," comes from Grossinger's extraordinary descriptive powers, his superb eye for detail. His remarkable gift for description is tempered by an equally rare sense of writerly self-control. There's not a stray or indulgent line in "The Quarry," as Eden Osucha writes; every word is appropriate, essential. Grossinger has a penchant for illustrating nearly indescribable inner realities through more recognizable external realities. In "The Quarry," Grossinger shows the talent and the control that places him in the line of descent from Bellow and Malamud to Roth and Cynthia Ozick.

Bibliography

Primary Sources

"Armistice." 1985.
"Bernstein." 1986.
"Promised Land." 1987.
"Hearts and Minds." 1989.
"Dinosaurs." 1990.
"Home Burial." 1991.
"Leisure World." 1997.
The Quarry: Stories. 1997.
"Home Burial." 1998.

Secondary Sources

Dachslager, Earl. *Houston Chronicle*, 10 August 1997: 21.
Furman, Andrew. *The Forward*, 19 June 1998:11–12.
Kremer, Lillian, at the Edward Lewis Wallant Award Presentation, University of Hartford, 19 April 1998, unpublished.
Osucha, Eden. *Boston Book Review*, 17 August 1998.
Pinsker, Sanford. *Providence Journal-Bulletin*, 16 November 1997.
Stoll, Rachel. *New York Times*, 21 July 1997:17.
Steinberg, Sybil. *Publishers Weekly*, 10 March 1997:48.

DAVID GROSSMAN

(1954–)

RANEN OMER-SHERMAN

DAVID GROSSMAN IS one of Israel's most internationally acclaimed and frequently translated novelists, widely recognized as a writer of extraordinary gifts, whose structurally intricate style is accompanied by a bold social vision. He is regarded as a pioneer of innovative techniques hitherto unknown in Israeli literature, such as magic realism and other experimental narrative strategies. Injustice in its political and social forms, as well as its psychological repercussions, form the central themes of his work.

Born in Jerusalem, Grossman studied philosophy and theater at the Hebrew University, receiving his bachelor of arts in 1979. He began a twenty-five-year career at Israel Radio at the age of ten as a correspondent for youth broadcasts. David Grossman's novels have often addressed dimensions of Israel's origins neglected by Israeli writers.

Themes and Motivations

In a startling break from the relative silence of Israeli writers during the Yishuv—the pre-state Jewish community in Palestine—and the subsequent early decades of the Jewish state, Grossman has been particularly interested in the tremendous, but little-understood, impact that the Jewish state's emergence from the ashes of Europe has had on Israeli national consciousness and sense of destiny. Grossman's belief that the suppression of the European-Jewish experience has often led to unfortunate responses to the meaning of victimhood is all the more remarkable because he is neither a survivor nor the child of survivors. Yet, Grossman sees the effacement of ethical values transmitted through, and shaped by, centuries of vulnerability in the modern Jewish state. A martial ethos is allowed to substitute for Jewishness itself. Most Israeli writers whose work speaks directly to Holocaust themes have been themselves survivors, such as Aharon Appelfeld, Dan Pagis, and Abraham Sutzkever. Grossman's Sabra generation (the first generation of post-state, native-born Israelis) and those before him were raised on a strident pedagogy, described candidly by Israeli educator Karmi Yogev as one that placed its greatest emphasis "on our more, if you will, normal periods of history: the First Temple, the Second Temple, the colonization of Palestine in the past few generations. The younger generation is much more inspired by heroism and triumphs than disasters [finding] aspects of our negative history, to put it mildly, uninspiring" (Meyer, p. 102). Obviously, if for the Jewish writers of the second-generation there is a special challenge to mediate the biographical and psychological reality of the Holocaust, the burden is greater still for the Israeli writer, struggling to overcome Zionism's effacement of the past. So it is startling to find that the painful problem of "identification" with unviable Jewish types from the diasporic past, and the problematic self-image of the conqueror, are the themes addressed with such sensitivity and acute moral vision in Grossman's critically acclaimed masterpiece, *See Under: Love* (1986). Like Art Spiegelman's *Maus*, this novel takes up the unenviable burden of the second generation, to create an ethical bridge to the past while commemorating breakage and loss.

See Under: Love

In *See Under: Love*, Grossman examines the consequences of the repression of Holocaust trauma in ways that speak for an entire generation. As Naomi Sokoloff argues, the novel, while resisting the Zionist discourse of heroic redemption, instead offers the reader a memorable corrective to the fact that "Israel saw its role vis-à-vis the survivors of Nazism as one of rescue and rehabilitation, not of identification" (p. 39). Were it only for the fact that Grossman, a born Sabra, was one of the first Israelis to consider the way in which his culture was unconsciously traumatized—the consequences of repression of memory as well as the marginalization of Holocaust survivors—*See Under: Love* would be an unforgettable work, but this work of soaring prose and audacious imagination is also one of the most memorable Hebrew novels ever written. This is unusual because Grossman belongs to what is usually called the third generation of Israeli writers, who came of age only after the Yom Kippur War of 1973. As Grossman tells it, the novel's origins can be traced to his own childhood encounter with the otherness of the European Diaspora, as expressed by its preeminent narrator, Sholem Aleichem:

> my father gave me the stories of *Mottel, the Son of Peyse the Cantor* . . . incessantly I dug my tunnel to the Diaspora . . . When I was about nine and a half, in the middle of the Holocaust Day ceremony . . . suddenly it pierced me: the six million, the slain martyrs . . . they were my people. They were my secret world. The six million were Mottel and Tevye and . . . Chava . . . and Stempenys . . . On the blazing asphalt of the *Beit Hakerem* schoolyard, I felt as if I was literally disappearing, shriveling and dissolving . . . Above all, I was panic-stricken because I imagined that I might now be the only child . . . whose responsibility it was to remember all those people ("My Sholem Aleichem," pp. 4–5).

From that sunny day haunted by European ghosts, Grossman seems to have begun the journey "to understand the Diaspora" and de-marginalize the survivor in a fuller sense than any previous Sabra. In *See Under: Love* he strives for a healing reconciliation between the Sabra and the European Jew.

"Momik," by far the most accessible of the novel's four sections, also stands on its own in its psychological veracity and its profoundly moving aesthetic dimensions. The story concerns a troubled nine-year-old child growing up in the Tel Aviv of the 1950s among Holocaust survivors. This is Israel of the early years of statehood, a liminal culture still in the making. On a more intimate level, Grossman is masterful at conveying how the "normal" world is actually an incomprehensible place of sudden, shocking transformations, as the opening lines of the novel suggest:

> It was like this, a few months after Grandma Henny was buried in her grave, Momik got a new grandfather. This grandfather arrived in the Hebrew month of Shebat in the year 5317 of the Creation, which is 1959 by the other calendar (*See Under: Love*, Farrar Straus Giroux, 1989, p. 3; all quotations, unless otherwise noted, are from this work).

Like many survivors of the era, the child's parents, ironically named Neumans, say very little about their ordeal during the war. Throughout "Momik," the child, an ardent reader of Sholem Aleichem, struggles to transform the metaphoric into the literal and tangible, responding to clues such as the "Nazi Beast," which he naturally understands literally as a wild animal, perhaps capable of being called forth to reveal its mysteries and thus close the abyss between Momik and his parents. Unlike the other children he knows, Momik is discouraged from going on overnight class trips, and his father, who screams at night in his sleep, rarely speaks more than a few sentences to him at a time. For Momik, the adult world conspires against him to preserve its secrets—secrets that are apparently dark and sinister. It is highly significant that Momik locates these secrets geographically, "down below." The cellar (*makshan*) is a storeroom, but it also suggests material that has been stashed away, even repressed. Caught between the Yiddish spoken at home and the Hebrew of school, and partly because of the children's fiction he reads, Momik sees his function in life as a codebreaker and interpreter of signs. Because his survivor parents won't let him come close to their terrifying experience, he has to engage in a project of rebuilding a past, of re-creating it for himself. Like Sholem Aleichem's Mottel, with whom he fully identifies, Momik strives to rewrite life's "unacceptable scenarios" (Ezrahi, p. 129). Keeping what he thinks of as "spy notebooks," he begins a search "to put together the vanished land of Over There like a jigsaw puzzle, there's still a lot of work left on this, and he's the only one in the whole world who can do it, because who else can save Mama and Papa from their fears and silences and *krechtzes*, and the curse, which was even worse after Grandfather Anshel turned up and made them remember all the things they were trying so hard to forget and not tell anyone" (p. 18).

Much later in the novel we learn that at the beginning of the century, when the century was still innocent, Momik's grandfather, Anshel Wasserman, had been famous as the author of a popular series of childrens' adventure tales. Now he is reduced by his experiences in the Nazi camps to the incomprehensible cryptic mumblings that set off Momik's quest. In the family's cellar, Momik locates pieces of the Jewish past in Europe, a *Tsena urena*, the Yiddish translation of the Bible and commentary adapted for Orthodox Jewish girls, and other Yiddish texts that link exile and home, Europe and Israel. At the same time, Momik struggles to form a coherent narrative between the disparity of Zionist masculinity and the Jewish vulnerability he witnesses at home. The decoding here takes the form of childish, even comical translations of the horror of his relatives' experiences:

> there was a war in that kingdom, and Papa was the Emperor and also the chief warrior, a commando fighter. One of his friends (his lieutenant?) was called Sondar . . . They all lived in a big camp with a complicated name . . . Also there were some trains around, but that part isn't clear . . . And there were also these big campaigns in Papa's kingdom called Aktions, and sometimes (probably to make people feel proud) they would have really incredible parades, like we have on Independence Day (p. 30).

The child, Momik, cannot transcend the essential incoherence of the Auschwitz universe, but within the terms of his own narrative he nevertheless forges a strange form of understanding:

> Supper:
>
> It goes like this: first Mama and Momik set the table very fast, and Mama warms up the big pots from the refrigerator, and then she brings supper in. This is when it starts getting dangerous. Mama and Papa chew with all their might. They sweat and their eyes bulge out of their heads and Momik pretends to be eating while he watches them carefully, wondering how a woman as fat as Mama could come out of Grandma Henny, and how the two of them could have had a scarecrow boy like him. He only tastes what's on the tip of his fork, but it sticks in his throat because he's so nervous. This is just how it is—his parents have to eat a lot of food every night to make them strong. Once they escaped from death, but it isn't going to let them get away a second time, that's for sure . . . God help them, he says in Hebrew in his heart, and translates it into Yiddish so God will understand, *Mir zal zein far deine beindelach,* Do something to me instead and have mercy on their little bones, as Mama always says about him (pp. 48–49).

As suggested by this passage, Grossman's concern here is with the poignant inability of survivors to prevent the transmission of their agony to the younger generation. As the writer Haim Gouri has observed of the young state, "the Holocaust was nowhere and everywhere" (p. 154). Momik is agonized by the palpable fear that emanates from his parents' bodies and the memories of a hunger that haunts them as they struggle to find a viable identity and a foothold in the Zionist present. Their abnormal eating habits have been determined by their trauma, but the Sabra child has compassionately cast his parents in the heroic mold of the Israel in which he has grown up, and in his imaginative world their quotidian struggle takes on the significance of an epic endeavor. In the end it is Diasporic vulnerability and powerlessness that the child's instincts tell him he must integrate, not only to enter the adult world but to somehow be fully Jewish. Yet Grossman also seems to suggest that the parents' heroic struggle actually resists their easy absorption into Israel's stereotypes, which has encoded the *Shoah*'s survivors as pitiful victims. This gentle irony ensures that Momik's interpretations of the mysterious behavior that surrounds him is both the error of an innocent child and the heartbreakingly astute reading of a higher consciousness. For Grossman formulates Momik's childlike response as a subtle critique of the way the Zionist society, as the official centripetal force of Jewish peoplehood, reduced the condition of *Shoah* survivors to childlike innocents, beings that were somehow not capable of autonomous heroism.

As Grossman's own secular education in childhood taught him, the "Zionist-Israeli continuum" was "emphatically not the history of Jewish suffering; it is not the history of the Holocaust . . . Israeli students . . . perceive times of exile and suffering as essentially negative and periods of normality or heroism as the historical source of their own national identity" (Meyer, p. 72). But as the novelist suspects, it is the untold narrative that wields the most insidious power over the child's imagination. Hence, Grossman creates a child protagonist who would precociously contend with the gaps and silences of that official narrative. But Momik's ethical struggle with darkness leads to tragedy. For in his hunt for the Nazi "Beast," he assembles a ghoulish chamber in the cellar where he imprisons hedgehogs, lizards, kittens, and young birds, hoping to coax it to appear. After failing to conjure up the beast, Momik decides he isn't "Jewish enough" (p. 78) and determines that if he leads the neighborhood survivors into the dark basement, something will happen. It does. Surrounded by dying animals and the suffering of the old survivors, Momik suffers a shocking nervous breakdown, defeated by an evil stronger than he is. The grandfather, whose sudden arrival from Over There set Momik's agonized quest into motion, walks out of the house and never returns. The story concludes with the insatiable grief of Momik's mother, emblematic of the open wound of the Holocaust: " 'If there was at least a grave to visit, but to disappear like that?' " (p. 86).

In "Bruno," the second section, Momik is a thirty-three-year-old writer, married to Ayala, a daughter of survivors, with a son named Yariv. The remaining three sections, "Bruno," "Wasserman," and "The Complete Encyclopedia of Kazik's Life," constitute Momik's struggle to transform his childhood trauma into an artistic and moral vision of the universe. Unfortunately, despite the lessons of his anguished childhood, Momik seems on the verge of repeating his parents' mistakes by sacrificing his love for his son in training him to face the inevitable catastrophe that he himself learned is intrinsic to the Jewish condition. Each section of the novel embodies a different struggle to exorcise the Nazi "Beast." Two lost figures—the legendary writer Bruno Schulz and Grandfather Anshel—are resurrected so that Momik can merge with their identities and tell their stories. In a sense, this is the Sabra's opportunity to experience the moral world of the Holocaust victim.

In "Bruno" we meet the Polish-Jewish novelist "Bruno Schulz," who is mysteriously altered after viewing Munch's *Scream* in a Danzig art gallery. Instead of being murdered in the Drohobycz ghetto as the real Schulz was in 1942, he undergoes a literal sea change as he is transformed into a salmon. From this juncture, the story becomes a flight of fantasy through the world's oceans, an act of artistic reverence that recalls Bruno Schulz's *The Street of the Crocodiles*. At the same time, the adult writer Momik struggles to recover Schulz's lost major work, *The Messiah*, in which the myth of the coming of the Messiah would presumably redeem both Schulz and Momik. As Gershon Shaked observes of this fabulous dream, "life in the world of imagination is a refuge from life in grotesque reality" (p. 318). Initially, Momik embraces the fictionalized Bruno as intrinsic to "a fragile network of weak links across the world" (artists such as Franz Kafka, Thomas Mann, Albrecht Durer, and Francisco de Goya), dark visionaries who knew "the truth" (p. 91), but as Momik discovers, Bruno's messianic forgetfulness is a life that cannot mesh with lived experience.

"Wasserman" picks up with Momik's reconstruction of the story in which Grandfather Anshel Wasserman had been trapped when Momik was a child. It is here that Grossman's novel will most disturb some readers for its audacity in entering the taboo domain of the concentration camp universe itself, hitherto the sacrosanct fictional realm of such Auschwitz survivors as Tadeusz Borowski ("This Way for the Gas, Ladies and Gentlemen"). Readers will not only recall the philosopher Theodor Adorno's unease over poetry after Auschwitz but, more specifically, will be mindful of Elie Wiesel's warning (notwithstanding his own novelizations of the past) that a dangerous void separates fiction and the reality of the Holocaust: "A novel about Auschwitz is not a novel, or else it is not about Auschwitz" (p. 314). Perhaps for that very reason, Grossman avoids the pretense of evoking the merely documentary, struggling to place history and the imagination in a new light. The reader does not forget the novel's cautionary introduction, and Momik's own struggle to reconstruct the Holocaust's taboo realm becomes a metacommentary on Grossman's own. As Efraim Sicher observes, this is where the novel most "speaks through Bruno Schulz's surrealism in its claim to 'truth' and fantasizes experiences that the author could not have witnessed and that deliberately stretch plausibility" (p. 307). It may well be that the genre of fantastic art, precisely because of its provocative refusal of the Holocaust's official tropes and symbols, is best suited to forestall the complacency of conventional closure, drawing the reader into an inner space of permanent disruption.

In this surreal inversion of Scheherazade's struggle to preserve her life through telling stories, Anshel, beloved chronicler of the "Children of the Heart" tales, enters into a satanic covenant with the SS officer *Obersturmbannführer* Neigel (who fondly recalls the former's tales from his childhood) to elude the fate in store for him. For his part, Neigel attempts to persuade the children's writer of the beauty of the Reich, the first movement in human history to refuse to " 'compromise at every step with human weakness!' " (p. 239). Apparently, Grossman's sense of "witnessing" requires some attempt to reconstitute imaginatively the identity of the perpetrator. In an odd parallel with Bruno Schulz's patronage by a Nazi officer (until Schulz is murdered by the officer's rival), the Nazi camp commandant adopts the old Jew as his personal bard, promising him that he will be beyond the reach of destruction, though Wasserman yearns for the reward of death. This allegorical narrative seems to take seriously the notion that art can survive the Holocaust, perhaps even confront evil (in the guise of Herr Neigel), though Grossman never suggests that storytelling can lead to closure or full knowledge. What is affirmed, however, is "the narrative psyche deploying imaginative freedom. The story lives on, since it is within the power of the author to create reality. The one solace of the defeated is fiction" (Yudkin, p. 176). In one of the novel's most memorable twists, Anshel's powerful narrative succeeds in overcoming—by humanizing—his Nazi captor, with the strangely anti-epic fable of Kazik, a miraculous and tragic being in the ensuing section. Moreover, Momik, emotionally frozen since childhood by the chilling horrors of history, is shaken to his core, mysteriously "infected" by his great-uncle Wasserman's humanity, and at last freed to fulfill his buried promise, to serve, in spite of distance, incomprehension, and loss, as the witness and conduit for the older man's wounded spirit:

> The air was all aquiver. My hand began to tremble as though it had a life of its own. My fingers pulled and pressed together. I looked at them in astonishment: they started to pull, but there was nothing there. They didn't stop moving. They groped. They prodded the air to make it flow toward them in a certain pattern, they propelled it wisely, stubbornly, churned it into a thicker substance, and suddenly there was moisture on my fingertips, and I understood that I was drawing the story out of nothing-

> ness, the sensations and words and flattened images, embryonic creatures, still wet, blinking in the light with remnants of the nourishing placenta of memory, trying to stand up on their wobbly legs, and tottering like day-old deer, till they were strong enough to stand before me with a measure of confidence, these creatures of Grandfather Anshel's spirit . . . (p. 223).

The novel, and the tale that Wasserman, the "House Jew," tells his Nazi captor, culminates in "The Complete Encyclopedia of Kazik's Life." Just as "Wasserman" wove together the fragments Momik assembled from his memory of his grandfather's narrative in the Tel Aviv of Momik's childhood, the final section reveals the epic that Anshel told Herr Neigel. In Grossman's luminous gesture toward *tikkun* (healing), the encyclopedia entries struggle to redefine the fundamentals (such as "Art," "Suffering," or even "Love" to which the novel's title alludes) for the post-Auschwitz universe: "to reveal the simplicity of basic mechanisms animating all members of the human race" (p. 303). Here, the life of a strange child named Kazik, whose lifespan in the concentration camp universe is tragically compressed into a fleeting twenty-four hours, is told, expressing the desperate hopes of the survivors from Momik's childhood neighborhood: "All of us prayed for one thing: that he might end his life knowing nothing of war . . . We asked so little: for a man to live in this world from birth to death and know nothing of war" (p. 452). But this utopian dream is impossible, as the bereft reader realizes, for Grossman's novel is written for a world that cannot escape war or the strangely cyclical manifestations of the Beast, as the generations of Israelis who have faced two Intifadas (popular Palestinian uprisings against Israel occupation) know full well. Still, Kazik's legacy is a new vocabulary, reimagining what language must say after the Nazi destruction of meaning. It reinstates the most essential entry of all (left out of the encyclopedias of the Holocaust that calculate numerical losses and dates)—love.

Critical Reception

Though some critics have expressed their unease over whether Grossman goes too far in his apparent "relativism . . . that to be a potential Nazi is part of being human" (Sicher, p. 312), Grossman's novel has been more widely praised by those who see ways in which its ambitious journey through trauma suggests redemptive possibilities for those prepared to draw meaning from the past to more authentically engage the present. For instance, Gershon Shaked, one of the novel's earliest Israeli critics, appreciated how the novel's significance resides in its capacity to interrogate how the second and third generation of survivors, the mental and spiritual inheritors of their parents' anxieties and traumas, can and will come to terms with a trauma that for them was not personal experience but an inherited psychological neurosis. The trauma was no longer repressed or expressed; it has become part of . . . "the collective subconscious of the group" (p. 314).

In the American-born literary critic Sidra Ezrahi's cogent analysis of the novel's mediation between disparate Jewish destinies, "by engaging in a major act of reinventing the past, Momik reassumes some of the prerogative and burden of the Diaspora and challenges the limits of narrative as they had developed in Hebrew literature" (p. 129). Other critics share her sense that the novel represents a profound attempt to transmit the significance of the Diasporic past to young Israelis and other readers far removed from the experience of persecution and exile. As Sara Horowitz observes, though the "reconstruction of the Holocaust past" proves damaging to the child, Momik's memory work ultimately triumphs by "inscribing its own versions onto the past and rediscovering its disruptive effects in themselves . . . testimony becomes an act of love and the only steady avenue of communication between the generations" (pp. 291–292).

For other critics, it is notable that the narrative incessantly juxtaposes Yiddish, the language of Over There (the dead past), and Hebrew, the language of the heroic present and Israel's third generation of writers. (Betsy Rosenberg's superb English translation deftly preserves fragments of each.) As Leon Yudkin argues, Momik's "presentation of his world, elastic and dynamic" compels

> us into a reassessment of that past world "over there," as well as our immediate reality. That is the point of so-called Holocaust literature. Not that it remains locked in the past, regurgitating identical material, but that it must exist. The past must be part of the present and must be constantly disinterred if we are to come to terms with the present (p. 175).

In these ways Grossman's novel, while not acquiescing to the artifice of narrative closure, challenges the convention of the "unrepresentability" of the Holocaust as well as its official uses in Jewish national life. It is also noteworthy that, since Grossman's emergence, the Holocaust theme has been taken up by other Israeli writers of the post-Holocaust generation such as Tanya Hadar, Savyon Liebrecht, Oded Peled, and Nava Semel, some of whose work awaits translation. Grossman's epic has been aptly compared to other twentieth-century reworkings of myth and history such as Faulkner's *The Sound and the Fury* and Gabriel García Márquez's *One Hundred Years of Solitude.*

As a whole, Grossman's oeuvre has been dedicated to recognizing the consequences that Jewish history and memory have had for the Jewish national homeland as well as those directly affected by its triumphs. For Grossman, national redemption is a messy business, complicated by the suffering of others. Though primarily a novelist, he first came to international attention with *The Yellow Wind* (1987), his searing account of what he observed on the West Bank in early 1987. Mediating between the complex collective myths, political solutions, and animosities on both sides of the Palestinian-Israeli conflict, Grossman placed his readers in direct contact with impassioned, wounded human beings from both ends of the occupation. Grossman concludes that Palestinians, like Jews earlier in the century, have been forced to develop diasporic strategies of survival. Hence, the Jewish reader is often subjected to startling moments of unexpected "recognition." For instance, in a powerful passage, an old woman in the Deheishe refugee camp, who longs for the sweet water of her village well, evokes the author's own memory of his grandmother, an exile from Poland. It is as if Grossman, paying full heed to the trauma of the Holocaust, would have Jewish readers remember the Palestinians' past and their exilic present as if it were their own. Today *The Yellow Wind* is considered essential reading for any introduction to the Israel-Arab dispute. A second work of journalism, *Sleeping on a Wire: Conversations with Palestinians in Israel*, appeared in 1994.

David Grossman lives in Jerusalem. In addition to the two works of journalism noted above, he has written several novels, numerous childrens' books, and a play in Hebrew. His works have been widely translated into Arabic, Danish, English, French, German, Italian, Japanese, Norwegian, Portuguese, Spanish, and Swedish.

Bibliography

Primary Sources

Novels and Fiction

Ratz (Jogger). 1983.
Hiuch Ha-bedi (Smile of the Lamb). 1983.
Ayien Erech Ahavah (See Under: Love). 1986.
Sefer Ha-Dikduk Ha-Primi (The Book of Internal Grammar). 1991.
Yesh Yeladim Zig-Zag (Zigzag Kid). 1994.

Drama

Gan Riki (Riki's Playgroup). 1988.

Journalism

Ha-Zeman Ha-Tzahov (Yellow Wind). 1987.
Nochahim Nifkadim (Sleeping on a Wire: Conversations with Palestinians in Israel). 1992.

Essays

"My Sholem Aleichem." *Modern Hebrew Literature* 14 (spring/summer 1995): 4–5.

Children

Du Krav (Duel). 1982.
Ah Hadash Legamri (A Brand New Brother). 1986.
Itamar Metayel Al Ha-Kirot (Itamar Walks on Walls) 1986.
Itamar Michtar (The Itamar Letter). 1986.
Itamar Ve-Kova Ha-Ksamim Ha-Shahor (Itamar and the Magic Black Hat). 1992.
Sefer Ha-Shirim Shel Fozz (Fozz's Book of Poems). 1994.
Misher Larutz Ito (Someone to Run With). 2000.

Secondary Sources

Ezrahi, Sidra DeKoven. *By Words Alone: The Holocaust in Literature.* Chicago: University of Chicago Press, 1980.

Gouri, Haim. "Facing the Glass Booth." In *Holocaust Remembrance: The Shapes of Memory.* Edited by Geoffrey H. Hartman. Cambridge, Mass.: Blackwell Publishers, 1994.

Horowitz, Sara R. "Auto/Biography and Fiction After Auschwitz: Probing the Boundaries of Second-Generation Aesthetics." In *Breaking Crystal: Writing and Memory After Auschwitz.* Edited by Efraim Sicher. Chicago: University of Illinois Press, 1998, 276–294.

Meyer, Michael. *Jewish Identity in the Modern World.* Seattle: University of Washington Press, 1990.

Mintz, Alan. "A Major Israeli Novel." *Commentary* (July 1989): 56–60.

Morahg, Gilead. "Breaking Silence: Israel's Fantastic Fiction of the Holocaust." In *The Boom in Contemporary Israeli Fiction.* Edited by Alan Mintz. Hanover, N.H.: University Press of New England, 1997, 143–183.

Shaked, Gershon. "The Children of the Heart and the Monster: *See Under: Love." Modern Judaism 9, 3 (October 1989): 311–323.*

Sicher, Efraim. "The Holocaust in the Postmodernist Era." In *Breaking Crystal: Writing and Memory After Auschwitz.* Edited by Efraim Sicher. Chicago: University of Illinois Press, 1998, 297–328.

Sokoloff, Naomi. "David Grossman: Translating the 'Other' in 'Momik'." In *Israeli Writers Consider the 'Outsider.'* Edited by Leon I. Yudkin. Rutherford, N.J.: Fairleigh Dickinson University Press, 1993, 37–56.

Wiesel, Elie. "For Some Measure of Humility." *Shma* 5, no. 100 (1975): 314.

Yudkin, Leon I. "Holocaust Trauma in the Second Generation: The Hebrew Fiction of David Grossman and Savyon Liebrecht." In *Breaking Crystal: Writing and Memory After Auschwitz.* Edited by Efraim Sicher. Chicago: University of Illinois Press, 1998, 170–181.

VASILII GROSSMAN

(1906–1964)

ALICE NAKHIMOVSKY

IN THE BEAUTIFUL phrase of the literary historian Shimon Markish, Vasilii Grossman is a "Russian Writer of Jewish fate" ("A Russian Writer's Jewish Fate," *Commentary* 81, no. 4, 1986, pp. 39–47). Grossman began his career as a Russian novelist with Soviet sympathies and little interest in Jewish issues. He became one of Russia's best-read war reporters and one of the country's most courageous (and most repressed) writers of fiction. As his life became bound up with Jews—his mother was killed in the Berdichev ghetto and he accompanied the Red Army as it liberated the Ukraine and parts of Poland—he took on the responsibility of documenting the Holocaust, a responsibility that was qualitatively different in Stalinist Russia from anywhere else in the world. Many of Grossman's wartime articles mention the Jewish tragedy; one was used in evidence at the Nuremberg Trials.

At the war's end, Grossman worked with Ilya Ehrenburg and the Jewish Anti-Fascist Committee on the compilation of essays and eyewitness reports about Nazi atrocities against the Jews; in 1954, he also wrote a novel, *Za pravoe delo* (For a Just Cause) about Stalingrad whose main character was a Jewish physicist. As Stalin unleashed his "anti-cosmopolitan" (Jews were given the code name "cosmopolitan") campaign, both these projects were aborted, as prominent members of the Anti-Fascist Committee were arrested. In the case of thirteen prominent Yiddish writers, their complicity in the projects resulted in their execution. While Grossman's life was spared, the novel that had initially brought him acclaim was ripped apart in the press in the kind of language that could easily have presaged his arrest. Saved again by Stalin's death, he began work on his major novel, *Life and Fate* (completed 1960), which the post-Stalinist authorities heard about and tried to destroy. This novel takes on all the tragedies of Russian twentieth-century history: collectivization, Stalinist forced labor, the war. But it also takes up the Holocaust, becoming the first and still the greatest Russian work of fiction to do so.

Life

Vasilii Semyonovich Grossman was born in Berdichev, a city so full of Jews that it figured in Jewish jokes. His mother, Yekaterina Savelievna Grossman, and his father, Semyon Osipovich Grossman, separated during his childhood. His background was bourgeois bordering on upper class, with a sprinkling of antiestablishment radicalism. The combination was not in the least atypical, though Grossman in later years did his best to suppress his early upbringing in the home of a wealthy uncle. He did not know Yiddish or Jewish religious practice, and fit easily into the early Soviet state. He received a degree in chemistry and worked (unhappily) in industry before turning to fiction. His early works differ from the Soviet standard only in the surprisingly numerous characters who have Jewish names and some Jewish characteristics. Grossman at the time was interested in the phenomenon of the Jewish Bolshevik. His very first published story is called "In the Town of Berdichev." In 1967, filmmaker Aleksandr Askoldov combined it with images from the short stories of Isaac Babel and used it as a Holocaust film called "Commissar." Because of the nature of the subject, the film was only released in 1987.

While his life before the war was not cloudless—it included the arrest of a close relative who had helped him and whom he did not sufficiently help, a matter of already endemic fear—the war changed things utterly. When the Nazis invaded on 21 June 1941, it was clear that his mother, in Berdichev, was in danger. As a member of the Union of Writers, Grossman easily had the connections to get her a train ticket to Moscow. His (non-Jewish) wife objected, a refusal all the more pointed because it was standard Soviet practice to live with in-laws and she indeed later brought her own family to live with him. Grossman acquiesced, and two weeks later the Nazis were in Berdichev, where they set up a ghetto and shortly thereafter (September 1941) murdered its inhabitants. Grossman never forgot his mother's death or his own failure to rescue her. The entire story, including the acrimony between husband and wife, is told in *Life and Fate*. Characteristic of the later Grossman, he forces himself to see his mother's final moments.

Journalist

Grossman, in anguish, volunteered for the war. He was made a military correspondent for *Krasnaya zvezda* (Red Star), the army newspaper, serving over one thousand days on the frontlines. He chronicled the crucial victories at Stalingrad (fall 1942–winter 1943) and Kursk (summer 1943), which together constituted a major blow to the Nazi war machine (both battles were also terribly costly to the Red Army). By all accounts, he distinguished himself by his bravery and his insight into soldiers' lives, and by his insistence on writing about Jews. His sketch "Ukraine," published in *Krasnaya zvezda* in 1943, was the first to mention the massacre at Babii Yar that had taken place two years earlier, though true to Soviet practice, the paragraph about the Jews was deleted from all but the first edition. Censorship of another sort clouded an essay called "Ukraine Without Jews," which Soviet censors approved for publication—but only in Yiddish.

Grossman accompanied the Red Army as it went through Poland and on to Berlin. Entering Treblinka in 1944, he wrote the first account in any language anywhere of how a death camp functioned. He got his information both from surviving Jews and from S.S. officers and villagers. That the account was published at all was probably due to the fact that the death camp was on Polish soil and liberated by the Soviets; the murderers, as Grossman showed them, were exclusively German Nazis. This article was later reprinted by the Russians for use at the Nuremberg Trials.

The Black Book

Critical to this story of Holocaust documentation is the aborted project known as the "Black Book." Publication of a book of eyewitness accounts was first proposed by Albert Einstein and the American Committee of Jewish Scientists, Artists and Scholars, which was engaged in a wartime collaboration, encouraged by Stalin, with the Soviet Jewish Anti-Fascist Committee. This idea of an international project to document Nazi atrocities against the Jews was taken up by Solomon Mikhoels and Itsik Feffer on their famous visit to the United States in 1943. Around the same time, quite separately, Grossman and his fellow writer and war reporter Ilya Ehrenburg had begun collecting such documents on their own. The two projects were united, with editorship of the Soviet edition going first to Ehrenburg, and then, after his resignation, to Grossman. Issues of censorship and compromise clouded the project from its beginning. Should the compilers suppress evidence of Ukrainian collaboration in order to publish documents about Jews? Should they call Jews "Jews" or just "people"? Hope that the "Black Book" would be published continued through the summer of 1947, when the publishing house Der Emes set the type. However, by that time, Stalin no longer felt the need for American-Jewish support, and the Central Committee canceled publication on the grounds of "political error." In January 1948, Mikhoels was run over by a truck on Stalin's orders, an event that was followed that November by the arrest and eventual execution (1952) of the entire leadership of the Jewish Anti-Fascist Committee.

Novels

Two more pivotal events, both with Jewish import, befell Grossman in these years. The first is connected with his novel *Za pravoe delo* (For a Just Cause), which takes up the battle of Stalingrad and was the precursor to *Life and Fate*. Though the novel treads lightly on a number of sensitive issues, it had a hard time passing the editorial board. While it was still in the prepublication stage, the future Nobel laureate Mikhail Sholokhov asked derisively "who gave *him* the right to write about Stalingrad?"—meaning "who gave a Jew the right to record this Russian national victory?" After Grossman agreed to a number of changes, including demoting his Jewish hero by giving him a Russian superior and adding a chapter about Stalin, the novel was printed. Russian readers were hungry for truthful novels, and the book was a tremendous success. Then an article appeared in *Pravda* condemning it. Perhaps the major sin cited in the editorial was the novel's focus on Jews: the Russian family at the book's center was intermarried with one, and yet another one figured as a family friend.

While Grossman was not arrested, what did happen was perhaps worse. In the early months of 1953, the country was in the throes of the Doctors' Plot: an antisemitic frenzy casting a group of Jewish doctors as "murderers in white coats." We now know that the doctors were going to be hanged in the Kremlin, followed by a mass deportation of Jews to Siberia. In preparation for this event, highly placed Jews were called in to the editorial offices of *Pravda* and asked to sign a letter condemning the doctors and supporting the exile of Jewish citizens ("for their own protection"). The letter itself has not turned up in the archives, but the content as recorded by the writer Venyamin Kaverin, who did not sign, dovetails with what Grossman's best friend, Semyon Lipkin, recalls Grossman as saying. Grossman would later describe the incident in *Life and Fate.* Like Viktor Shtrum, the Jewish hero of that book, Grossman felt the weight of the state on him and signed. (In the novel, Victor's rival had the courage not to sign; in Grossman's life, that place was held by Ehrenburg.) Having disgraced himself in his own eyes, Grossman found Lipkin and the two of them went out of town and got drunk. Neither of them knew at first that Stalin had died. The Doctors' Plot was called off by government decree on 4 April 1953, one day after the doctors were themselves liberated and one day before the official announcement of Stalin's demise.

Life and Fate, completed in 1960, was in many ways Grossman's act of expiation. It is uncompromising. A huge realistic novel, it focuses not only on the war, but on what were then forbidden episodes of Soviet history: collectivization with its resulting Ukrainian famine, Bolshevik fanaticism, the Stalinist camps. Grossman asks if there is in fact a major difference between Nazi Germany and Stalinist Russia. Through his vast roster of characters, he studies the nature of resistance and submission. He thinks about Russian democracy, which existed in fact between the February and November revolutions of 1917, and in theory—as Grossman sees it—in the works of Anton Chekhov. He includes a discourse on antisemitism, which distinguishes the everyday, social variety from the state-sponsored version adapted by both Nazi Germany and its enemy, Stalinist Russa. He wonders if there is any ideology at all that could stop the events he witnessed, and finds no hope in anything except some individuals' inexplicable acts of kindness.

The Holocaust theme in the novel appears with reference to two characters. Viktor Shtrum's mother, like Grossman's, is trapped in the Berdichev ghetto. Her story takes the form of a letter she writes to her son. Among the painful details she recounts is the behavior of neighbors once they discover that Jews were acceptable victims; this issue of Ukrainian complicity in the persecution and murder of Jews was, throughout the Soviet period, even more untouchable than the Holocaust itself. The other Holocaust victim is a Jewish military doctor, Sofya Levinton. In *For a Just Cause*, Sofya and two companions had run into a German ambush. Now in *Life and Fate*, Grossman felt free to take up their fates: one ends up in a prisoner-of-war camp, where he remains a rigid Bolshevik and is shot without really understanding what his beliefs led to; the other, the Russian driver, is saved by a Ukrainian woman whose kindness ignores ethnic distinctions. Sofya, as a Jew, is sent to a death camp.

In following Sofya's story to its end, Grossman uses details he learned on entering Treblinka and from his work on *The Black Book.* He is interested in the psychology of those who made the Holocaust happen. As we move in the novel from Eichmann to the man who closes the gas chamber door, Grossman imagines their motivations and justifications. He also—at a time when there were no fictional models, and when, as far as he knew, he was the only writer treading on this ground—tried to imagine what it was like for the Jews all the way to death.

One of his main characters is a little boy, David, who is trapped while visiting his grandmother (Grossman's own daughter was nearly trapped in Berdichev visiting her grandmother). Grossman gives David his own birth date, and a child's awareness of certain issues he saw as critical. As David enters the gas chamber, he watches Sofya suddenly lunge at an SS guard. In this futile but humanly important attack, David understands the nature of freedom. At the same time, he understands the end of freedom in death. Throughout his journey in the cattle car, David has been holding a chrysalis in a match box, a symbol of his own emerging life (though the chrysalis, significantly, is dead). Now David throws the chrysalis away, thinking "let it live."

Even more important than David is Sofya, an energetic and rather brusque woman who never saw herself as a Jew. Thrown together with other Jews, she does become a Jew, in part because the Nazis have labeled her that way, but more profoundly because "Jew"—unlike, say, "Bolshevik" or "prisoner of war"—is indeed her core identity. By the end of her first day in the cattle car, she is addressing her fellow Jews with the words *"brider yidn,"* and although given the opportunity to put off her death by letting the Nazis know she is a doctor, Sofya refuses to single herself out.

At the same time that Sofya becomes a Jew, this unmarried, rather masculine woman becomes attached to the abandoned David. As the end approaches, she holds David close. Her last words are "I have become a mother."

When Grossman finished the novel in 1960, he showed it to a conservative journal on the theory that its editors were scoundrels but capable of a bold move. In retrospect, the idea may not have been so crazy. Krushchev had already made his speech denouncing Stalin. In 1961 Yevtushenko's "Babii Yar" was read by millions; in 1962 Solzenitsyn's *One Day in the Life of Ivan Denisovich* became the first—albeit mild—account of real life in a Stalinist labor camp. But Grossman had neither Yevtushenko's luck nor Solzhenitsyn's: his novel was confiscated (Russians like to say "arrested") by the KGB. Trying to get it back, he was told that it would not be publishable for three hundred years. When Grossman died in 1964 of cancer, he had no way of knowing whether the manuscript copies he had hidden with friends would ever make it to the light of day. Fortunately, in the late 1970s, the courageous Russian writer Vladimir Voinovich preserved the novel on microfilm. In this manner, the manuscript made its way West, where admirers of Grossman, among them Shimon Markish, worked hard to get it published. *Life and Fate* appeared in Russia itself in 1990.

Bibliography

Primary Sources

The Black Book, Ilya Ehrenburg and Vasilii Grossman, eds. 1980.

Evreiskii antifashistskii komitet v SSSR 1941–1948: dokumentirovannaiia istoriia. 1996.

Life and Fate. 1960.

Na evreiskie temy: izbrannoe v dvukh tomakh. Jerusalem: Biblioteka Aliia, 1990.

Zhizn' i sud'ba: roman. Moscow: Sovetskii pisatel', 1990.

Secondary Sources

Garrad, John, and Carol Garrad. *The Bones of Berdichev: The Life and Fate of Vasily Grossman*. New York: The Free Press, 1996.

Lipkin, Semyon. *Stalingrad Vasiliia Grossmana*. Ann Arbor, Mich.: Ardis, 1986.

Markish, Shimon. *Le Cas Grossman*. Paris: Julliard/L'Age d'homme, 1983.

Nakhimovsky, Alice Stone. *Russian-Jewish Literature and Identity: Jabotinksy, Babel, Grossman, Galich, Roziner, Markish*. Baltimore: Johns Hopkins University Press, 1992.

JEAN-CLAUDE GRUMBERG

(1939–)

EDWARD ISSER

JEAN-CLAUDE GRUMBERG was born in Paris on 26 July 1939. In March 1943, Grumberg's father, Zacharie Grumberg, who had emigrated to France from Romania in the 1930s to escape the rising tide of fascism, was arrested by the French Milice (the Vichy police force) and sent to the Drancy internment camp. He was shortly thereafter deported to the east, apparently to Auschwitz, and never returned. Living surreptitiously as Gentiles, Grumberg, his brother, and their mother survived the war, after which the postwar French government refused to pay his mother a pension or acknowledge any responsibility in the death of his father. Grumberg's mother supported her two sons by working as a seamstress.

In the 1960s, having failed at a series of jobs, Grumberg began working as a comic actor in Jacques Fabbri's company. In 1967 he wrote his first play, *Michu*, followed a year later by his first successfully produced work, *Demain une fenêtre sur rue*. Thereafter, Grumberg established himself as one of the most prolific and popular French playwrights and screenwriters of the late twentieth century, with over twenty-five plays and half a dozen screenplays to his credit. In 2001 he was a resident playwright with the Comédie-Française but continued to work independently on television and film projects. In 1974 he won the Critics Award, and the SACD Award for best playwright (for the play *Dreyfus*). In 1980 he won the Critics Award, the SACD Award, the Parisian Award, and the Ibsen Prize for best playwright (for *L'atelier* [*The Workroom*]). In 1991 he was awarded the Grand Prize of the French Academy (for *Zone libre* [*The Free Zone*]). In 1998 he won the Critics Award for best playwright (for *Rêver peut-être*), and in 1999 he won the prestigious SACD Grand Prize Award for the collected body of his work. He has won an unprecedented five Molière Prizes, for best adaptation of a foreign work (1991, 1995, 1998) and for best play (1991, *Zone libre*, and 1999, *L'atelier*).

Jean-Claude Grumberg has carved out a place in French intellectual life as the social conscience of the nation. Celebrating the intellectual and social life of French Jews, he has addressed issues of racism, oppression, and moral bankruptcy of other eras and has dramatized the crimes of Vichy France and the lasting psychic damage engendered by French action and inaction, in plays such as *Zone libre* and *L'atelier* and in screenplays such as the *Dernier métro, Les milles*, and *Le plus beau pays du monde*, and has joyfully celebrated the intellectual and social life of Jews in France, most notably in works such as *Adam et Éve*.

Grumberg is most renowned in France and best known in the United States for his so-called Holocaust trilogy consisting of *Dreyfus, L'atelier*, and *Zone libre*, a triptych representing the world of European Jews before, during, and after the Holocaust. Grumberg's characters are working-class types who are more concerned about creature comforts and interpersonal relationships than philosophizing or global affairs. When the world crashes in on them, as it invariably does, the audience sees real people being destroyed. The pure stupidity of the destruction, the utter waste of humanity, is infuriating. The effect is devastating and impressive.

Dreyfus

Dreyfus (American version, *Dreyfus in Rehearsal*; British version, *Dreyfus the Comedy*) is a comedic work that explores the failure of the European Jewish community to come to terms with the historical circumstances. The play is set in the outskirts of Vilna, Poland, in 1931. The action of the play occurs in a meeting hall where a group of amateur Jewish actors, who usually mount light comic fare, are producing an original play by a writer-director about Alfred Dreyfus, the French army officer who was unjustly condemned in an antisemitic plot for treason, sentenced to solitary confinement at Devil's Island in 1894, and exonerated in 1906. Grumberg uses the process of rehearsal, and the discussions and arguments that emerge, to explore the nature of antisemitism in France and Poland. Uninterested in antisemitism per se, Grumberg is concerned primarily with the manner in which Jews respond to such animosity. He allows each character to espouse alternate strategies. Zina believes that Jews are safest when they keep a low profile. She asserts that Dreyfus got himself into trouble by overreaching, essentially not knowing his place as a Jew in a Christian world. Arnold believes that Jews must come to terms with their own impotence and absorb the blows that invariably fall. He wonders why Dreyfus stood up to the injustice instead of trying to defuse the situation by negotiation. Nathan—a character who never appears—deserts the production to join a Jewish defense organization committed to fighting Polish antisemites. The play's author and director, Morris, believes that antisemitism must be addressed in a larger context by bringing about a fundamental change in universal consciousness:

> And what if I tell them that last week, thirty miles from here—not even thirty—a gang of Polish patriots beat up some Polish Jews . . . What will they say? "Well, that won't happen here, not to us, because we know how to stay in our place?" We have no place—anywhere—as long as this kind of stupidity and hate lives in man. A question. Why did Emile Zola defend Dreyfus? He didn't know him. He'd never seen him. He wasn't even Jewish himself. So why? For his own sake? No. He was fighting stupidity and hatred and prejudice . . . and listen—hear me out—as long as men don't do what Zola did, as long as they say, "Aaah, to hell with what happens to others"—then nothing will go right—anywhere—and not only for Jews (*Dreyfus in Rehearsal*, adapted by Garson Kanin, New York: Dramatists Play Service, 1983, pp. 14–15).

The universalistic—socialistic—position expressed by Morris is countered by the arrival of Wasselbaum, a dignitary from the Zionist Congress who has come to Vilna to exhort the Jews to prepare for *aliyah*, immigration to Israel, as the only solution to the Jewish condition. Wasselbaum's reading of history directly contradicts Morris's:

> My dear young man, you spoke of Dreyfus. Do you know that it is precisely because of this dreadful Dreyfus affair that Theodore Herzl—who chanced to be in Paris at the time—recognized the desperate necessity of an independent Jewish State? And if one day this dream is achieved we shall owe it to the ordeal, to the suffering of Captain Alfred Dreyfus (p. 29).

The one person who has no point of view is Michael, the young shoemaker who complains and worries throughout rehearsal that he is unable to wrap his mind or heart around the character of Dreyfus. Michael is by nature a pacifist and cannot envision himself as a captain in the French army. The dramatic arc of the play centers upon how Michael literally and figuratively assumes the mantle of Dreyfus.

The actual production of the play about Dreyfus is never mounted. Polish antisemites enter the Jewish neighborhood and terrorize the community; two thugs force their way into the theater and threaten the members of the company. Each member deals with the intrusion in keeping with his or her own personality and perspective. Morris attempts to embrace the thugs as fellow workers, but is thrashed for his efforts. Arnold and Zina cringe and remain out of sight, but Michael emerges from hiding in his Dreyfus costume—a military uniform with a prop saber—and courageously confronts the bullies. Michael's bravery emboldens the others who then collectively set upon the would-be attackers. The theater is left a shambles and the company is severely shaken. Confronted by stark reality of antisemitism, the actors lose their enthusiasm for a theatrical representation of it. The company disbands. In a coda, staged a few months later, Mendl, Arnold, and Zina remain in Vilna mounting a musical comedy based on the work of the writer Sholom Aleichem. The audience learns (by means of an awkward device of letter reading) that Morris traveled to Warsaw and embraced communism, and Michael and Myriam have traveled to Berlin believing that Jews are safer in Germany than in Poland.

Although the play is not technically an example of Holocaust representation, the historical event nevertheless permeates the work, just as French reaction to the Dreyfus case may be seen as a harbinger of French Holocaust era attitudes. The audience watches the unfolding action, knowing that all the members of the company are doomed. Grumberg, however, never judges his characters. He presents them as all too human figures trying to fill their mundane existence with culture and joy. The playwright celebrates the zest for life of the company members and their refusal to surrender to despair.

The Workroom

The second play in Grumberg's Holocaust triptych, *L'atelier* (*The Workroom*), divided into ten self-contained naturalistic scenes, is set in Paris between 1945 and 1952. *The Workroom* describes in grim detail the hardships that Simone, Grumberg's fictionalized mother, suffered in the aftermath of the war as she waited futilely for the return of her husband and struggled to support her two sons by working in a sweatshop run by Léon, a French Jew. Grumberg uses the dialogue of the play's ten self-contained scenes to reveal French attitudes toward Jews and the Holocaust. Simone's coworkers, gentile women from various working-class backgrounds, display a frightening level of ignorance, apathy, and prejudice as they express their opinions about the fate of French Jews. The owners of the shop, driven by survivor guilt and a sense of historical responsibility, employ Simone and a male survivor of Auschwitz who is only referred to as the Presser. The mysterious character of the Presser plays a central role in the drama, personifying the specter of the Holocaust that hangs over the entire work. The Presser, in a sincere effort to help Simone begin the process of healing, is finally able to make her realize that her husband will never return. Simone confides her pain and desperation to the Presser and, in a devastating manner, describes the bureaucratic frustration and the survivor trauma she encounters when seeking information about her husband:

> No one knows anything . . . We get shuttled from office to office. . . . Did you come through the Hotel Lutetia? (*The Presser nods.*) I was told to go there, way in the beginning, to get information—someone who might have seen him, who . . . Well, you know, by showing the photographs, . . . I only went once and I didn't dare go up to anyone. There was a woman who grabbed me by the arm and stuck a photograph under my nose—a kind of yearbook picture—I can still see the kid, he was about the age of my eldest, wearing short pants and a tie, and holding a book. "The top student in the class," she was yelling, "he's always the top student in the class." She wouldn't let me go. "Why are you crying?" She asked again and again. "Why are you crying? Look, look, they're coming back. They'll all come back. It's God's will, God's will." Then another woman started screaming and pushing her. . . . I saw her again several times in the office, crazier and crazier each time (*The Workroom*, adapted by Daniel A. Stein and Sara O'Conner, New York: Samuel French, 1982, pp. 177–178).

Simone's situation is made thoroughly pathetic because the French government refuses to provide closure. She has to fight tooth and nail to get a death certificate, and when it finally arrives, it merely states that her husband died after departing Drancy. There is no recognition that he was deported by the French Milice. As in the situation faced by the playwright's mother, there is no assumption of responsibility, and the authorities refuse to provide any compensation or pension because Simone's husband was born in Romania. The most startling scene in the play occurs when Léon and the Presser are left alone in the shop. Launching into a lengthy monologue about life in occupied Paris, Léon attempts to convince the Presser that he, too, suffered during the Holocaust though he avoided the camps, and he explains that the real enemy was not so much the Nazis, but his fellow Frenchmen who were willing accomplices. The Presser, however, simply responds "they caught me!" (p. 187). Léon ignores the pain of the Presser and continues in a self-absorbed manner. The Presser, perceiving Léon's deafness, decides that he can no longer work for him and leaves the shop, never to return. The play concludes in 1952 when Simone's son, approximately twelve years old (the same age as Grumberg in 1952), tells Léon that Simone has taken ill and has been hospitalized. Léon rants and raves, oblivious to Simone's welfare. The other women gather around the young boy and fawn over him before returning to their workstations as if nothing had happened. This scene encapsulates the French attitude—both Jewish and gentile—toward the Holocaust: a momentary distraction, worth a degree of lip service, and then a return to routine. Even Léon, the French Jew, cannot be bothered about the suffering of his coreligionists. *The Workroom* is a stinging indictment of French apathy, denial, and self-absorption. It is the first play that describes truthfully the plight of Jews in Nazi-occupied France and the attitude of the French populace toward Jews after the war.

The Free Zone

Grumberg's *Zone libre* (*The Free Zone*) is a haunting tale of survival under dire circumstances. Grumberg's dramaturgical strategy in *The Free Zone* is similar to that of *The Workroom*. The audience is swept into the situation not by empathy—since these characters are anything but sympathetic—but by getting caught up in the daily routine. The fear, anxiety, and boredom of the situation slowly and inexorably transcends the proscenium and engulfs the viewer. The action of the play occurs between 1941 and 1944 and is set in a small shack on the grounds of a farm in Corrèze, France, in the "free zone"—that area not initially occupied by the Nazis. The Zilberberg family, who managed to escape from Paris, is sheltered by an elderly farmer named Maury, a generous Gentile who provides for the family and seeks nothing in return. The Zilberbergs are a surly and petty bunch. Alienated, hungry, and angry, they live day-to-day in constant fear of discovery. The patriarch, Simon Zilberberg, a whining hypochondriac, berates his mother-in-law for speaking Yiddish, has no pride in his Jewish ancestry, and argues endlessly with his wife, nephew, and sister-in-law. Over the course of the play, however, Simon gains pride, self-respect, and humane qualities as he discovers the strength and willpower to survive. Simon plots various strategies to save members of his extended family. He wants to hide his nephew, Henri, in a Catholic boarding school, but Henri goes to Paris to seek his parents, who had been deported. While Simon searches for Henri, the French Milice appear suddenly at the farmhouse and the gentile farmer saves the family by distracting the officers by freely pouring wine. The French police are not monsters or evil incarnate, but bored civil servants merely doing their job. As they drink from Maury's bottle, the officers describe their job:

> We had a hell of a day. . . . There was this guy yelling at us because he claimed we were rounding up other people's Jews but not his. The captain kept telling him there was nothing we could do since his Jews had their papers in perfect order, but he wouldn't back off. "It's always the big guys who win out in this country," he was yelling, "It's not fair, the Marshall should only know what goes on behind his back," and so on and so forth. In the end, just to shut him up, we rounded them up anyhow (p. 84).

Toward the end of the play, Simon—now a member of the French Resistance and carrying a rifle—returns to learn that his family has returned to liberated Paris. He discovers that the farmer is sheltering a German soldier. Angry, Simon decides to effect his own justice, while Maury tries to dissuade him. The two men struggle and Simon's gun fires, scaring everyone but harming no one. Sobered by the blast, Simon leaves the gun and exits. Simon's decision to forgo vengeance is not romanticized; he has not discovered charity or forgiveness. Rather, he realizes that petty vengeance will achieve nothing. Simon's actions at the end of *The Free Zone*—his determination to rebuild and reclaim his life—encapsulate Grumberg's attitude about Jews in postwar France. He believes that Jews have a place in France and that the French must come to terms with this fact. Characters like Simone, Simon, Léon, and most especially the Presser have all paid dearly for the right to live in freedom in France.

Bibliography

Primary Sources

Stage Productions

Michu. 1967.
Demain une fenêtre sur rue. 1968.
Mathieu Legros. 1969.
Rixe. 1969.
Amorphe d'Ottenburg. 1971.
Chez Pierrot. 1974.
Dreyfus. 1974.
En r'venant d'l'expo. 1974.
L'atelier (The Workroom). 1979.
Les vacances. 1981.
L'Indien sous Babylone. 1985.
Zone libre (*The Free Zone*). 1990.
Les autres. 1991.
Linge sale. 1994.
Maman revient pauvre orphelin. 1994.
Adam et Ève. 1997.
La criée. 1997.
Les courtes. 1998.
Rêver peut-être. 1998.
Les gnoufs. 2001.
Le petit violon 2001.

Adaptations of Foreign Works

Mort d'un commis voyageur (*Death of a Salesman*) by Arthur Miller. 1987.
Le chat botté (*The gestiefelte Kater*) by Ludwig Tieck. 1988.
Les trois soeurs (*The Three Sisters*) by Anton Chekhov. 1988.
Encore une histoire d'amour (*Separation*) by Tom Kempinski. 1994.
En cas de meurtre (*Tone Clusters*) by Joyce Carol Oates. 1995.

Screenplays

Dernier métro. Screenplay with Suzanne Schiffman and François Truffaut. 1980.
Des années sandwich. Screenplay with Pierre Boutron. 1988.
La petite apocalypse. Screenplay with Constantin Costa Gavras. 1992.
Les lendemains qui chantent. Screenplay. 1995.
Les milles. Screenplay with Sébastien Grall. 1995.
Faits d'hiver. Screenplay with Robert Enrico. 1999.
Le plus beau pays du monde. Screenplay with Marcel Bluwal. 1999.
Le vicaire (working title). Screen adaptation of Rolf Hochhuth's *The Deputy*. Forthcoming.

Published Plays

The Workroom. Adapted by Daniel A. Stein with Sara O'Conner. 1982.
Dreyfus in Rehearsal. Adapted by Garson Kanin. 1983.
L'atelier. 1985.
Les autres. 1985.
L'Indien sous Babylone. 1985.
Demain une fenêtre sur rue, suivi de Chez Pierrot. 1990.
Dreyfus. 1990.
Zone libre. 1990.
En r'venant d'l'expo. 1992.
The Free Zone and *The Workroom*. Translated by Catherine Temerson. 1993.
Linge sale, précédé de Maman revient, pauvre orphelin. 1993.
Maman revient pauvre orphelin, suivi de Commémorations. 1994.

Les courtes. Collection of one-act plays. 1995.
Adam et Ève. 1997.
Dreyfus, L'atelier, et Zone libre. 1997.
Rêver peut-être. 1998.
Amorphe d'Ottenburg. 1999.
Linge sale. 1999.
Le petit violon. 1999.
Sortie de théâtre et autres pièces courtes. 2000.

Secondary Sources

de Beaumarchais, Marie-Alice. "Grumberg." In *Dictionnaire des littératures de langue française, vol 2*. Edited by Jean-Piere de Beaumarchais. Paris: 1984, p. 987.

King, Robert L. "Psychic Numbing and Grumberg's *L'atelier*." *Massacusetts Review* (winter 1985): 580–591.

Pockwell, Brian. "Jean-Claude Grumberg's Holocaust Plays: Presenting the Jewish Experience." *Modern Drama* 41, no. 3 (fall 1998): 399–410.

ARNON GRUNBERG

(1971–)

PASCALE R. BOS

ARNON GRUNBERG WAS born in Amsterdam, the Netherlands, the son of elderly Holocaust survivors. His father, a German Jew who left Berlin in 1934 and who hid in the Netherlands during World War II while passing himself off as a deserting *Wehrmacht* soldier, was sixty when Arnon arrived. His mother, already in her forties when Arnon was born, had survived Theresienstadt, Mauthausen, and Auschwitz. Grunberg grew up as if an only child; his much older sister moved to Israel when he was little. He attended high school in Amsterdam, where he was a good student who loved to write (he authored a prize-winning play at age sixteen). Arnon was nevertheless expelled during his next-to-last year for chronic truancy and increasingly odd and uncontrolled behavior. Next, he worked in a number of odd jobs and briefly operated his own Kasimir Press, publishing German, "non-Aryan" literature, before devoting himself full-time to writing.

Humor Is the Best Remedy: Arnon Grunberg's Tragic Slapstick

Grunberg published his first volume of essays, plays, and poetry, *De dagen van Leopold Mangelmann* (The days of Leopold Mangelmann) in 1993, but it was in 1994, when he made his novelistic debut with *Blauwe maandagen* (*Blue Mondays*), that he gained great success and notoriety. This seemingly autobiographical work, in which the narrator, named Arnon Grunberg, relates his adolescent life as the son of difficult parents who quarrel constantly with each other and with him, is both moving and shocking. In particular the portraits of his parents—a mother who is overbearing and prone to extremely angry outbursts, seeing everything in her life as a punishment for surviving Auschwitz, and an alcoholic father who is unable to be emotionally involved in his son's or wife's life—are disturbing. The story of Arnon's days as a lost, bored, and progressively more despondent and alcoholic teenager who spends most of his time trying to connect or disconnect from his parents, his girlfriend, and himself, working odd jobs and visiting prostitutes, is tragic but also very funny, owing to its detached manner of observation. Not one to easily feel sorry for himself, the narrator, for instance, comments about his own downward spiral, "I've always been very good at dashing the hopes and betraying the trust of others. I'm still very good at it" (*Blue Mondays*. Trans. Arnold and Evica Pomerans. London: Vintage (Random House) 1997, p. 30).

Grunberg won a number of major Dutch literary prizes for *Blauwe maandagen*; it has been translated into eleven languages and is successful in these foreign editions as well (it became a bestseller in Europe), and it made the author a phenomenon in Dutch literature. Grunberg himself moved to New York City soon after he became successful in 1995, and continues to write there while publishing in the Netherlands. He contributes essays and columns about his life in America to Dutch weeklies and newspapers.

Although he is also considered an accomplished screen and play writer (he professes that the theater was his real love, but his hopes to become an actor were dashed after repeated rejection from theater schools), Grunberg remains best known for his novelistic works. His second novel, *Figuranten* (Silent extras), came out in 1997. *De heilige Antonio* (The saint Antonia, 1998) was commissioned by the Dutch Literary Seller's Fund, which constitutes a high honor, and most recently, in 2000 *Fantoompijn* (Phantom pain) was published. All were received well in the Netherlands. These works, while less explicitly autobiographical than his first novel, remain remarkably consistent in theme. All deal with the impossibility of true connections in relationships, the inability to trust, and the seeming uselessness of the pursuit of career, status, or possessions, all in light of the Holocaust (which is nevertheless not mentioned as the explicit cause). In the Netherlands, however, Grunberg is not necessarily read as a Jewish or a post-Holocaust author, rather as an extremely talented *comic* writer. As such, he was asked by the city of Rotterdam to write a modern version of the philosopher Erasmus's *In Praise of Folly*. The result was the publication of *De Mensheid zij geprezen: Lof der Zotheid 2001* (Humanity be praised: In praise of Folly 2001).

Grunberg is also said to be the author behind *De geschiedenis van mijn kaalheid* (The history of my baldness), published in 2000, which purports to be the novelistic debut of a certain Marek van der Jagt. Stylistically and thematically the novel seems remarkably similar to Grunberg's work, and when this book won the first prize for the best Dutch debut (as had *Blue Mondays*) and the author never showed up to receive the prize, the suspicions of Grunberg's authorship under a pen name mounted. Grunberg neither confirmed nor denied his authorship.

Blue Mondays as Second-Generation Literature?

Grunberg's debut was initially seen as representative of a new Dutch and Flemish generation of writers, born after 1970, whose work is characterized by nihilistic and grotesque themes. Several more novels and collections of plays, essays, and poetry later, his work is recognized instead as highly original in both style and theme, and harder to situate. Because Grunberg is much younger than most other Dutch authors of the Jewish "second generation," his work is rarely seen as belonging to this larger genre. In part, this is probably due to Grunberg's own strong dislike for the label. He has argued in interviews that he does not see his work as part of this literature, having experienced his life with his parents as "much more disturbing" than much that this literature tends to describe. Furthermore, even though this particular background plays a big role in the lives of many of the characters in his works, it is never discussed explicitly.

In part, the problem here is one of definition, for what is second-generation literature? Often, it is defined by the cathartic function it seems to have for the author. Efraim Sicher, for example, has argued that for children of survivors, "telling the story is a form of working through trauma, which ideally ends with the separation of the second generation from the dead and their connection to a real past, to a family and people in which they are a living link, transmitting a heritage to future generations" (Sicher, p. 12). For Sicher, the protagonist's search for identity and memory is central to this literature, as are depictions of a transfer of trauma from the parents to their offspring. A serious inquiry into the nature of postwar Jewish identity cannot be found in Grunberg's work, however. His protagonists go to synagogue occasionally, fast on Yom Kippur only to please their mother, and show little genuine interest in Jewish life. Judaism is clearly tainted by the *Shoah*, as the narrator of *Blue Mondays* indicates when he is speaking of (Dutch) converts to Judaism: "It was something I couldn't fathom, why people would want to become Jewish. After all, they could always just go hang themselves if they decided things were getting too tough for them" (p. 73), but these feelings remain unexamined.

Notwithstanding Grunberg's tendency to relegate this story to the background, though, the persistent presence of the Holocaust in the lives of the protagonist's parents and himself places his work, in particular *Blue Mondays*, in the genre of post-Holocaust literature. In this work, after all, the narrator's complex and conflicted interaction with his parents, who are depressed, overprotective, and extremely distrustful of the outside world, and who tend to relate everything back to their war experience and their Jewishness, is central. In response, as is typical in this situation, the narrator feels unable to relate normally to either his parents or to anyone else he would like to feel close to. Furthermore, the war and its aftermath always play in the background of the narrator's futile attempts to escape the desperation he feels at attempting to live a normal life. Auschwitz may not be mentioned, but it is the implicit standard against which everything is measured.

Thus, while it is possible to read some of the deeply disturbing conflicts in *Blue Mondays*—for instance, Arnon's traumatic experiences in having to take care of his seriously ill father, who starts to lose his mind as well as his bodily functions—as universal, reading them in light of dysfunctional interdependent family relationships caused by war trauma explains why the illness and ensuing loss are practically insurmountable for this particular family. It is after his father's death that Arnon's life starts to unravel completely. He leaves home, is unable to hold a job, starts drinking excessively, compulsively visits prostitutes, and as good as severs his relationship, always problematic but still bearable when the father was alive, with his mother.

Critical Interpretation

Grunberg's style of writing is so distant, and his capacity for narrating the tragic in extremely detached, comical fashion so great, that some in his audience, including critics, may have (chosen to) read right past the protagonist's personal connection to the Holocaust. There is in fact a remarkable lack of serious discussion of this theme in commentary on his work, which is seen as exhibiting black humor and youthful posturing, rather than as attempts of the narrator, as Grunberg describes it, to "protect" himself from a reality that was unbearable, "for humor requires distance" In *Blue Mondays*, the narrator argues: "I wasn't being cynical, I was being truthful. It's too bad the truth can end up sounding cynical, which is why you're often better off lying. If you want people to like you, that is" (p. 130). Thus, one critic reads the novel as a Jewish coming-of-age drama in which the "main redeeming quality" of the protagonist is that "his parents were hopelessly messed up—so a lot of his problems aren't really his fault" (What the particular background of the parents is, how they got to be "messed up," is not mentioned, and perhaps not fully understood,) and the narrator's lighthearted tone is taken as an apology.

Grunberg's protagonist has thus been compared to a youthful version of Philip Roth's Portnoy, or even to the filmmaker Woody Allen (Grunberg's move to Manhattan fits the picture nicely)—that is, a neurotic Jewish man incapable of normal relationships with women owing to his disturbed relationship to his mother or parents. Grunberg's "Jewish neurosis," however, is less typically Jewish or even male than clearly an aftereffect of his parents' experiences during world War II. It is thus also possible to see his style not just as detached and comical, but as suggestive of precisely those horrors that need to be kept under wraps. Take for instance the description of his mother:

> My mother . . . asked why I treated my parents this way. I saw no point in having a discussion. For the past few years I'd stopped seeing any point in having discussions. She looked small in her red bathrobe, even smaller than me . . . The bathrobe was a good twenty years old. That's because she refused to buy new clothes. She wouldn't have anything new. . . . Her life was over, she said. Her life had been over for forty years (pp. 85–86).

Elsewhere, while the protagonist is in the midst of his commiserating about his family ("My mother lives in a world where there is neither day nor night and where there are no people left, my father waits for stock reports that I'm sure haven't been broadcast for the past twenty years"), his father suggests a toast to "the girls," after which his mother suddenly exclaims, "There were a lot of girls in Mauthausen too . . . but I was the prettiest of them all. Even without my hair I was pretty. The SS thought so anyway. I was the belle of the ball in that place" (pp. 91–92). Indeed, in interviews, Grunberg has suggested repeatedly that he chose this particular tone and style of writing not for literary effect, but because the reality of his home life was so extreme that he was unable to write about it any other way, that is, realistically, and in detail, for "if I were to write everything down, no one would believe me" The reality was worse than could be imagined.

For precisely this reason, many of Grunberg's novels make extensive use of dialogue. Grunberg has stated that he likes to write dialogue, because it allows him to say more implicitly, as there is no need to describe or explain. After all, "the most painful things that occur between people are caused by what is and what isn't said."

Bibliography

Primary Sources

De dagen van Leopold Mangelmann (The Days of Leopold Mangelmann). 1993.
Blauwe maandagen (*Blue Mondays*). 1994.
Rattewit. 1994.
Figuranten (Silent extras). 1997.
De troost van de slapstick (The Comfort of the Slapstick). 1998.
De heilige Antonio (The Saint Antonio). 1998.
Het veertiende kippetje (The Fourteenth Chicken). 1998.
Liefde is business (Love is Business). 1999.
Fantoompijn (Phantom Pain). 2000.
De Mensheid zij geprezen: Lof der Zotheid 2001 (Humanity be Praised: In praise of Folly). 2001.
De Geschiedenis van mijn kaalheid (The History of My Baldness). 2000. (Attributed to Grunberg but written under the name Marek van der Jagt).

Secondary Sources

Van Galen Last, Dick, and Rolf Wolfswinkel. *Anne Frank and After: Dutch Holocaust Literature in Historical Perspective*. Amsterdam: Amsterdam University Press, 1996.
Sicher, Efraim, ed. *Breaking Crystal: Writing and Memory after Auschwitz*. Urbana: University of Illinois Press, 1998.
Wuijts, Jos. *Serieuze poging toteen volledige bibliografie van de Zelfstaudige en verspreide geschriften von Arnon Grunberg: waarin opgenoruen diens Interview met mijn bibliographs Juieder mens Schuitt een manials*. Amsterdam: Nygh & Ditmar, 1998.
Pinsker, Sanford. "Of Broccoli, Brando and Blowing Your Parents' Money." *Forward* July 6, 2001: 11.

HENRYK GRYNBERG

(1936–)

MONIKA ADAMCZYK-GARBOWSKA

HENRYK GRYNBERG WAS born on 4 July 1936 into a religious Jewish family in the village of Radoszyna near Mińsk Mazowiecki, where his father, Abram, was a dairyman. His mother was Sura (Zofia) Stolik. His younger brother was murdered by the Nazis in 1942 and his father was killed in 1944 by local Polish villagers with whom he had left some possessions. Grynberg spent the war in hiding, using "Aryan papers," first in Warsaw and then in the region of Podlasie. After the war he settled down with his mother in Lodz, where he attended a Jewish elementary school and Polish high school. After graduating from the latter in 1954, he studied journalism at the University of Warsaw, where he graduated with a master's degree in 1958. In 1959 Grynberg started working for the Jewish State Theatre in Warsaw and simultaneously launched his writing career. *Zydowska wojme* (1965) was his first work to attract critical attention.

In 1967, while on tour in the United States with the theatre, Grynberg decided not to return to Poland as a sign of protest against censorship and the antisemitic campaign instigated by and within the Communist Party. In 1971 he graduated from the Slavic Department at the University of California in Los Angeles with a master's degree in Russian literature, and began working for the U.S. Information Agency, cooperating with the Voice of America broadcasting program. A number of Grynberg's works could not be published in Poland in the 1970s and 1980s because of censorship, although some appeared in Polish presses abroad. Only after 1989 did his works become fully available. Since the fall of communism in Eastern Europe, Grynberg has been a frequent visitor to Poland.

The Dominant Theme

In almost all his works, Grynberg deals with Jewish topics, especially in connection with the Holocaust, presenting different variants of the same life story that is marked by the protagonist's survival as a child under the most difficult conditions, gradual discovery of self identity, struggles with the imposed ideology of communism, encounters with antisemitism, and, finally, exile. Although he draws a lot of his material from his own autobiography, his stories have a universal dimension. A number of critics have called him a writer of one theme, a statement that has been corroborated by Grynberg's own declarations. For example, in an interview published in the major Polish newspaper *Gazeta Wyborcza* in 1998, he stated:

> Until something more horrible than the Holocaust takes place, there is no more important topic for mankind, but let's hope that nothing like this happens. The Holocaust is a great lesson and warning for our civilization, a turning point. Although the history of the Jews is quite unique, everybody can draw conclusions from it because it has not taken place in a vacuum and it concerns everybody who participated in it (Cichy, p. 19).

Earlier in his volume of essays, published in 1984, *Prawda nieartystyczna* (Unartistic truth), Grynberg makes a similar statement implied in the very title of the article "Obsesyjny temat" (The obsessive topic). There he calls himself a guardian of the graves—a guardian of the one, great Jewish cemetery that the Nazis had turned Poland into—and he adds that this mission has prevented him from committing suicide as his will to commemorate the dead is stronger than the repulsion to the world he knows. He claims, ironically, that he became the writer of the dead because the living had enough of their own writers. And his intention is to "guard the graves against desecration" (West Berlin: Biblioteka Archipelagu, 1984, p. 133).

Grynberg made his debut in 1959 in the bi-weekly *Współczesność* with his "Ekipa 'Antygona' " (The Antigone Crew), a story about a team that exhumed victims of the Nazi crimes in Poland. The name of the team is not coincidental; there are a number of allusions to Sophocles' play in Grynberg's story. Since then, exhumation in the literary and, eventually, also in the literal sense became Grynberg's mission and destiny. In February 1992 he exhumed his father's body, wanting to give him a proper burial and to investigate the circumstances of his death.

Themes of Identity

Another theme that is visible from the very beginning in Grynberg's works is his search for identity: national, religious, professional, and even sexual. In his story "Sielanka-Siaj" (The Siaj Idyll), included in his first book, a collection of stories also titled *Ekipa "Antygona,"* little Siaj asks his mother why he was not born a girl instead of a boy, insisting that it would have been better that way. The prewar dialogue related from the post-Holocaust perspective foreshadows the child's later awareness that being a boy in the reality of the Holocaust is a greater threat than being a girl because a circumcised boy is easily identified as a Jew. In "Buszujâcy po drogach" (Rampaging Along the Roads), published in the monthly *Twórczoić* 7 (1967), there is a similar scene, concerning not a sexual identity but a national one, when the narrator recalls how he used to insist to his mother that when the war ended he would stop being a Jew.

Grynberg's search for national identity consists of a struggle between Polishness and Jewishness: he expresses himself in the Polish language and feels quite attached to the Polish landscape and culture, but he also has a great deal of resentment and many "accounts" to settle with Poland. Some roots of Grynberg's mixed identity lie in the fact that, as a child, he had to play the role of an Aryan in order to survive. His mother even created a fictitious family for him, telling him numerous stories about grandparents of Polish stock. Her fabrications were accompanied by religious confusion, as Polishness implied Catholicism and necessitated his taking his first Communion as a preventative measure. Small wonder that in his prose, Christian symbols are often combined with Jewish religious imagery.

Death and Repercussions

Grynberg's first novel was titled *Żydowska wojna* (The Jewish War), published in English under a rather kitschy and simplified title *Child of the Shadows*. The original title alludes to the Palestinian historian and soldier Joseph Flavius and the German historical novelist Lion Feuchtwanger and bears ironic implications: the Jews who are "at war" have to constantly hide. The narrator is a child in hiding with his family and friends. He observes the gradual disappearance of people close to him.

Grynberg's next novel, *Zwyciestwo* (The Victory), covers the postwar experience of his mother and himself. As with his previous book, the title is ironic, as the war has ended, but soon after the initial exhiliration doubts arise as to who actually won. In *Życie ideologiczne* (Ideological Life, 1975) Grynberg describes the pressures of Stalinism during his youth, while in *Życie osobiste* (Personal Life) the same narrator is encountered as a young adult, deeply affected by the experience of the Holocaust. These two latter works can be read independently, but they are linked together by the narrator and his environment. The narrator lives in fear of death and with a strong sense of guilt that he survived while others have perished. As he lives in a country where his community has ceased to exist, daily events evoke in him the vision of the Holocaust. For instance, there are the damaged gas stove and the bugs that infest his apartment because they "smell Jewish blood" and come to his room because there is a young Jew hiding there (*Zycie osbiste*, Warszawa: Pokolenie, 1989, p. 44). Jewish holidays underscore the destruction of the Jewish world in Poland. The motif of death is pervasive. The Holocaust experience taught Grynberg that Jews did not die a "natural death." As he related in *Kadisz* (Kaddish), a novella, published in 1987, that takes place in America, "In our family everybody died a violent death. (Paradoxically his stepfather is shot in America by a gunman.) We didn't know another one. Both grandfathers and both grandmothers, all uncles and aunts, my half-year-old brother" (Kraków: Znak, p. 23). Therefore the fact that his mother, who survived the Holocaust because of her enormous courage, strength, and inventiveness, is now dying of cancer in sunny California seems to him like a return to normalcy, but of course this does not alleviate the pain. The contrast is even stronger since, as he recalls in the story "Plenipotenctwo" (Plenipotentiary Powers) included in *Ekipa "Antygona"* (1963), as many as ninety people would attend prewar family events. They were later to fill the gas chambers and distract attention from him, as he was "only six years old and easy to overlook" (Warszawa: PIW, p. 41).

Grynberg often uses Christian terminology in reference to death. For example, while referring to his younger brother Buciek, he says that he was betrayed while hiding from the Herod's flunkeys; his grandfather was crucified on Golgotha under the name of Treblinka; and while in hiding in Warsaw, his mother took him during Easter to show him the tomb of Jesus that in fact turns out to be the Warsaw ghetto in flames during the uprising of 1943. These allusions bear bitter implications and are an accusation against the Christian world.

Although Gynberg's prevailing motif is death, he actually writes about life, albeit life marked with death. This is visible in the very titles of his cycle: after the two works mentioned above in which the word *Życie* (Life) appears, he wrote *Życie codzienne i artystyczne* (Quotidian and Artistic Life) in which the narrator is not Jewish, "Życie jako dezintegracja" (Life as disintegration), which is included in *Prawda nieartystyczna*. Like Hanna Krall in her novel *Sublokatorka (Subtenant)*, Grynberg makes a bitter and ironic comparison in his novel *Życie ideologiczne* (1995) between the clichéd concepts of Polish and Jewish death during the war:

> It is a pity that Mother was not a resistance courier during the war and did not hide illegal leaflets or grenades but only my circumcised dinky. That my teenage aunts and thirteen year old uncle did not die in the Warsaw Old Town or Mokotów [during the Warsaw Uprising of 1944] but in the village near Dobre, and not near the wall where now one can see memorial plaques and flowers but over a dug-out in the forest, a place children of the Polish villages preferred to stay away from (London: Polsha Fundacja Kulturalna, 1975, p. 98).

Like Krall, Grynberg is concerned with explaining why the Jews could not conform to the traditional Polish stereotype of the heroic resistance fighter. Ironically, his mother, who is a real heroine prepared to make every effort to secure the survival of her son, has to conform to the stereotypes of Polish society and assume a Polish identity, as stated in his book *Zydowska wojna* (1965), inventing "a grandmother who played the piano and a grandfather who died of cancer of the stomach, the noble disease of noble people" (Warszawe: Gzytelnik, 1965, pp. 44–45).

Another important topic for Grynberg is exploring the motif of his place of birth and the death of his father. This motif reappears in a number of works in which the narrator returns to the hamlet of Radoszyna and tries to talk with his former neighbors about his father, Abram. Most people no longer remember his father or try not to remember; they especially do not want to remember the circumstances of his death. Investigating the latter becomes the son's obsession, a mission that he has to fulfill. In *Dziedzictwo* (The Inheritance, 1993), which followed the film *Miejsce urodzenia (Place of Birth)* by Pawel Loziński (the film, in which Grynberg appears, was awarded many prizes, including the Golden Gate Award in San Francisco), Grynberg documents conversations conducted with the inhabitants of the villages where his father lived in hiding and was ultimately killed. This short and extremely powerful book consists of twenty-four units. All except the last are dialogues based on recordings done by the writer in February 1992. The speakers' ages range from fifty-five to ninety; some were children and some were adults during the Holocaust. The dialogues were minimally edited to preserve authenticity, including ungrammatical expressions, dialect, and various idiosyncrasies. Grynberg does not use regular notation, so only with careful reading can the identities of the speakers and their emotional states be determined. Most dialogues are quite restrained and resemble a dramatic work, like this one consisting of Grynberg's conversation with one of the peasants:

> Do you know, what happened to my father?
> I don't know, I wasn't there.
> And what did the people say?
> They said he perished somewhere in Radoszyna or in Jaczewek.
> How did he perish?
> Sir, I wasn't there . . .
> But what did the people say?
> That he was killed.
> By whom?
> It's hard to say by whom, sir . . .
> No one knew?
> Well, you know, sir . . .
> No one knew? Really?
> Sir, people know . . . (p. 49).

The final, twenty-fourth part of the book is a monologue in which Grynberg recalls his family and the circumstances of his father's death. In the conclusion he states: "I am unable to forgive. I don't want to. I do not feel eligible to do so. Let the murdered forgive if they can. I am a weak man, you cannot demand so much from me. I don't think God who is just demands that either. I think condemnation is just. Eternal condemnation. Without reprieval" (London: Ameks, 1993, p. 90).

But this experience also has a somewhat therapeutic quality for the suffering son: "I felt a cold shudder as I stood face to face with evil," writes Grynberg at the end of his book, "but I also found in some eyes and in some words the warmth that allows me to live on" (p. 90). The milk bottle found together with the remains of his father's body, wrapped by the son in *a tallith*, serves as a holy relic.

Biographical and Autobiographical Elements

Although marked with a strong autobiographical dimension, Grynberg's work should not be treated literally as autobiography. As he stated in another interview, answering a question about the relationship between the biographical truth and the artistic truth in his works:

> My biographical truth is merely an objective material. When I find some parallel material in someone else's biography I treat it the same way. I have a fairly objective and self-distancing attitude towards material. And that is why I always stress the fact that the characters I describe should not be identified with authentic individuals nor the narrator with the author. Sometimes I mix biographical plots and equip one of my characters with adventures that happened to another one (Wróbel, p. 146).

In Grynberg's more recent works he frequently uses other biographies. And thus in his documentary drama *Kronika* (The Chronicle) he deals with the Lodz ghetto; in *Pamietnik Marii Koper* (Maria Koper's Diary), he tells the story of a Jewish woman saved by a Polish peasant family; and in *Dzieci Syjonu* (*Children of Zion*), published in 1994, he uses archival material to describe the vicissitudes of Jewish children deported to the eastern territories of the Soviet Union during the war and eventually taken through Iran to Palestine. As in *Dziedzictwo*, he lets others speak with minimum intervention. For instance, *Children of Zion* starts like a litany about prewar times, almost every sentence starting with "My father . . ." as the children recall what their parents did for their living: shoemakers and professionals, the poor and the better off, Orthodox and assimilated. The book ends with a chapter titled "Orphans, orphans" (Warszawa: Wydawnictwo Karta, 1994, p. 7).

In *Drohobycz, Drohobycz* Grynberg included a number of documentary stories whose action takes place in almost a dozen countries. His most recent book, *Memorbuch*, is a slightly fictionalized biography of Adam Bromberg, a well-known editor of the Polish Academic Publishers who was forced to resign during the antisemitic campaign in Poland in 1968 and who settled down in Sweden, where he launched a publishing career. In *Szmuglenzy* (The Smugglers) he tells the story of a family of Polish Christians who risk their lives to save their Jewish friends and whose lives are later tied together permanently due to love relationships.

In all Grynberg's books, both those autobiographical and those based on the lives of others, he tries to penetrate the psyche and emotions of the victims, the persecutors and their helpers, and the eye-witnesses who are often indifferent, usually frightened, and sometimes compassionate.

Irony and Black Humor

Grynberg's style is marked with irony and black humor. As he describes his role as a writer in *Życie ideologiczne*, "How good I am a Jew. If I were French I would die of boredom. And since I am not, my mind is always occupied" (Grynberg, pp. 105–106). In *Żydowska wojna*, Grynberg creates a child narrator and uses a very simple style as the little boy can only relate the events, unable to comment on what he experiences. As Józef Wróbel observed, the short sentences apparently devoid of emotion have a double function: psychological and artistic. The psychological function is caused by the consciousness of the child protagonist while the artistic one is caused by the feeling prevailing in postwar literature in which expression is helpless in the face of the Holocaust and therefore austerity is the best solution.

Grynberg has a talent for drawing vivid and semicomic characters, like the memorable Śliwa in "Fatherland," a Polish peasant who helped a Jewish family survive. The writer draws grotesque parallels between the situation during the Nazi occupation and that in the early 1950s, years of daily struggles with the Soviet-controlled regime:

> When a law was passed that all foreign currency had to be turned in to the state bank and that the hiding of dollars was punishable by death, Biumek handed his dollars over to Śliwa, who hid them in a mow. The same one where he had hidden Biumek under the Germans. There was the same death penalty for hiding dollars as there formerly had been for hiding Jews, but dollars sat there—quietly, didn't go out to relieve themselves, and didn't require food to be bought for them (Polonsky, p. 251).

Another grotesque situation with dramatic undertones appears in the scene when Śliwa—while visiting the narrator in Lodz—says that the latter can always hide in his place if he has problems with the Communist authorities. Soon after that conversation, the narrator, tired with the city (Grynberg's narrator often calls himself a country boy and describes in a very sensual way the pleasures of country life), decides to visit the Śliwas and to help them in the harvest. However, when he arrives at their modest dwelling, stating that "things aren't good in the city" (meaning the dirt and noise, airplanes practicing before a parade), Śliwa takes his declaration very seriously, the mention of airplanes immediately evoking in him associations with the war. The narrator compares his host's cool reception and deliberation, concerning taking in an unexpected visitor-helper, to hesitations among peasants during the war—a "calculation before hiding a Jew." The whole situation would be absurd and simply amusing if not for the fact that it evokes tragic recollections:

> When he had assured me that just in case, I could always hide out at his place, he didn't suppose it would come so soon. Neither did he know how much pleasure his deliberation gave me. Now I was completely in my father's skin, I was my father body and soul. I come to Śliwa for him to hide me and I see that same sort of deliberation, I see it with the eyes of my father, whose life is being repeated, because t-h-a-t is being repeated. And my life will be repeated and so will my son's life—as long as that is repeated. We are eternal because we exist due to our enemies. And they are stupid and don't realize it (Polonsky, p. 276).

Generally in Grynberg's prose there is much emphasis on the spoken language; he lets his characters speak, limiting commentary to a minimum. As he mentioned on various occasions, he has had problems with editors who try to polish his works while he intentionally leaves some fragments uncouth.

Other Achievements

Although best known as a prose writer, Grynberg is also a poet and dramatist. He has published two plays so far. In his poems, he often deals with the motif of survival and identity, repetitiveness of evil patterns, fragility of Jewish hope and of the necessity to stay faithful to some moral principles. A number of his poems were inspired by his visits to Israel and by his American experience. Most of his poems are very personal, like "Orpheus II," addressed to his potential Jewish wife who died before he had a chance to marry her in 1941, 1942, or 1943, "perhaps before she could walk/or talk or see/perhaps before she was born" (Polonsky, p. 296). In "Drawing in Memory" he re-creates his life before the Holocaust. The poem starts with an idyllic scene of a little boy sitting at a table waiting for a meal, but it soon turns out that the "table is gray and so is the window" and the father for whom the boy and his mother are waiting "did not come/he remained outside the window/murdered and buried/near the house" (Polonsky, p. 300). Eventually the mother disappears too, but there is a sense of hope and continuity when he serves "her favorite dish to her grandson."

For his literary achievements, Grynberg received a number of awards, including Kościelski Foundation in Geneva in 1966, "Kultura" in Paris in 1969, Jurzykowski Foundation in 1990, and Jan Karski and Pola Nirenska in 1996. His book *Drohobycz, Drohobycz* was nominated for the Nike award, the highest literary award granted in Poland.

Bibliography

Primary Sources

Prose

Ekipa "Antygone" (The Antigone Crew). 1963.
Żydowska wojna (The Jewish War). 1965. (Also published as *Child of the Shadows*)
Życie ideologiczne (Ideological life). 1975.
Zwycięstwo (The Victory). 1979.
Życie osobiste (Personal life). 1979.
Życie codzienne i artystyczne (Quotidian and artistic life). 1980.
Prawda nieartystyczna (Unartistic truth). 1984.
Kadisz (Kaddish). 1987.
Kronika (The Chronicle). 1987.
Szkice rodzinne (Family sketches). 1990.
Dziedzictwo (Inheritance). 1993.
Pamiętnik Marii Koper (Maria Koper's diary). 1993.
Dzieci Syjonu (*Children of Zion*). 1994.
Drohobycz, Drohobycz. 1997.
Memorbuch. 2000.
Szmuglerzy (The Smugglers). 2001.

Poetry

Święto kamieni (The feast of stones). 1964.
Antynostalgia (Antinostalgia). 1971.
Wiersze z Ameryki (Poems from America). 1980.
Po zmartwychwstaniu (After the resurrection). 1982.
Wśród nieobecnych (Among the absent). 1983.
Pomnik nad Potomakiem (A Monument on the Potomac). 1989.
Rysujłe w pamiłeci (Drawing in memory). 1995.
Wróciłem. Wiersze wybrane z lat 1964–1989 (I Have Returned. Selected Poems from the Years 1964–1989). 1998.
Ksigga Rodsaju (Genesis). 2000.

Secondary Sources

Brach-Czaina, Jolanta. "Kompleks." *Tygodnik Powszechny* 8 (1994): 11.
Buryła, Sławomir. " 'Życie nie jest bezpiecznâ wyspâ.' O debiucie Henryka Grynberga." *Akcent* 4 (2000): 43–52.
Cichy, Michal. "Najważniejszy temat. Z Henrykiem Grynbergiem rozmawia Michał Cichy." *Gazeta Wyborcza* 225 (1998): 18–19.
Polonsky, Antony, and Monika Adamczyk-Garbowska. *Contemporary Jewish Writing in Poland: An Anthology*. Lincoln and London: University of Nebraska Press, 2001.
Wróbel, Józef. "Nigdy nie pozwolono Żydowi zostać Polakiem. Z Henrykiem Grynbergiem rozmawia Józef Wróbel." *Teksty Drugie* 5 (1992).
Wróbel, Józef. *Tematy żydowskie w prozie polskiej 1939–1987*. Krakow: Universitas, 1991.
Zaleski, Marek. "Jeruzalem. Jeruzalem." *Tygodnik Powszechny* 25 (1997): 12.

Sonia Guralnik

(1925–)

DARRELL B. LOCKHART

Sonia Guralnik was born in Russia in 1925. She spent her early childhood in the Ukraine near Kiev before her family immigrated to Chile around the time she was ten years old. As an adult in Santiago, Guralnik married, raised a family of three children, and worked as a professional chef. She began to write later in life during the 1960s, inspired in part by the political unrest of the period. She began writing almost full-time following the 1973 coup d'état of Augusto Pinochet, which sank the country into a desperate political nightmare. To date, she has written five books of narrative, focusing mainly on the short story. Guralnik's Jewish identity is central in her life and her literature. Her stories are populated primarily by characters who seem to be constantly on the move or experiencing drastic changes in their lives, such as the geographical displacement of exile that forces them to deal with issues of assimilation and loss. Her characters often cling to tradition or cherished objects (a samovar, a candelabra) to remind them of the past and keep their memories fresh.

Overview of Work

Guralnik's stories, for the most part, describe the realities for Jewish immigrants prior to World War II; those who arrived in droves in Latin America, fleeing persecution in Russia and eastern Europe. Her first collection of stories, *El samovar* (The Samovar, 1984), relates this experience of transformation and describes the Russia left behind as well as the new and strange country of Chile; the stories are clearly based on the author's own memory and experience. Her next collection of stories, *Relatos en sepia* (Sepia Colored Tales, 1987), continue giving voice to the immigrant experience as well as describing traditional Jewish celebrations and rituals. There are two stories in particular that deal specifically with the Holocaust. In "Bajando el Rhin" ("Sailing down the Rhine"), Guralnik sets the narration in the post–World War II era. It revolves around a group of elderly German-speaking women who live together in a retirement home and who decide to take a cruise down the Rhine. The physical description of the women as well as the dialogue marks them as being concentration camp survivors. Once on the boat they soon discover, much to their horror, that the director of the trip is none other than Frau Braun, a former torturer and camp guard at Bergen-Belsen. They recognize her because of her cruelty and the fact that she repeatedly steals things from them. The women engage in an act of heroism as they begin to call out their own names as well as the nicknames they had given to other concentration camp guards. This act serves to empower the women as guardians of history and memory. The event also provides an opportunity to share stories from their collective experience in Bergen-Belsen, Auschwitz, and Dachau.

> Mustache. MUSTACHE. That's it! The jailer at Bergen-Belsen. They called her Mustache. My God. They say she shaved everyday, but even so a shadow appeared at noon. It's noon now. Hardly daring to do so, she looks over at Frau Braun, who has the sun in her face . . .
>
> "She took Annie from me," Madame Katz thinks with great difficulty. She pushes back the thick tears that come up from the pit of her stomach, the sharp-edged sobs that pierce the feelings of everything she has lived . . .
>
> Madame Katz has made up her mind. She shouts: "Frau Braun is the torturer at Bergen-Belsen! Frau Braun is MUSTACHE!"
>
> Like the rustle of dry straw, the old women's voices begin:
>
> "Where were you during the war?"
>
> "In many places. And you?"
>
> "I was also in Bergen-Belsen."
>
> "In Auschwitz."
>
> "I was in Dachau."

> The old women roll up their sleeves.
> "In Ravensbrück."
> "I was also in Auschwitz" (*In the House of Memory,* pp. 78–79).

The second story, "Es la humedad" ("It's the Humidity") is constructed around a young couple that is about to move into a new apartment. The story presents an interesting contrast when the man showing the apartment—they call him Uncle Manuel—recalls with emotional nostalgia the other couple who had come to live there after the war. They had numbers tattooed on their arms and Manuel remembers them fondly and how much they had suffered. The young couple is unconcerned with the story and seems more preoccupied with how to decorate and arrange the furniture. The story sets up a dichotomy between the need/desire to remember and the forces of time that necessarily bring about change. Tío Manuel struggles to keep the previous occupants' memory alive through the objects that remain that give testimony of them, while almost irreverently the young couple seeks to erase the past and begin their own history. The story highlights the difficulty of preserving memory from one generation to the next.

In her latest book, *Para siempre en mi memoria* (Always in My Memory, 2000), Guralnik places central importance on memory and the act of remembering. The book relates numerous stories of Jews fleeing persecution both before World War II, and during the Holocaust. The book itself is an exercise in the witnessing of human tragedy, not specifically oriented toward the Holocaust, but that is certainly a part of it. As often happens with other Jewish writers from Latin American countries, Guralnik establishes a clear link between the *Shoah* and the more recent atrocities perpetrated by neofascist military regimes in countries such as Chile and Argentina where thousands of people have been tortured and disappeared. Guralnik has written many other stories about the political violence in her country and the psychological ramifications involved for the victims of such repression. In this sense she can be compared to fellow Chilean Jewish writers Marjorie Agosín and Ariel Dorfman.

Critical Reception

Sonia Guralnik's works have begun to receive a fair amount of critical attention, and some of her stories have been published in English. Within Chile her writing has been well received and she enjoys considerable success as a writer. The majority of what has been written about Guralnik's works focuses on the feminist aspects of her writing as well as the use of humor. Elizabeth Horan, for example, states

> The work of Sonia Guralnik offers an interesting example of the means by which a member of various groups previously excluded—an older woman, just entering publishing, a Russian-Jewish Chilean—can cultivate a place in the national literary scene by combining humor with social commentary (p. 140).

Another critic, Stacey D. Skar, sums up Guralnik's writing in the following manner: "Sonia Guralnik's writing, besides being extraordinarily personal, is a fascinating remembrance and recording of these memories, many of which are related to emigration, exile, assimilation, tradition, history, identity and other Jewish concerns" (p. 251). While Guralnik cannot be considered a major figure with regard to Holocaust literature, she does make an interesting and telling contribution. Few are the voices from Latin America that bear witness to the *Shoah*, and for this reason Guralnik's stories are significant.

Bibliography

Primary Sources

El samovar (The Samovar). 1984.

Relatos en sepia (Sepia Colored Tales). 1987.

Recuento de la mujer gusano (Inventory of the Woman Worn). 1991.

"Sailing down the Rhine." In *The House of Memory: Stories by Jewish Women Writers of Latin America.* Edited by Marjorie Agosín. Translated by Martha Manier. New York: The Feminist Press at the City University of New York, 1999, pp. 76–80.

Sonata de carne y hueso (Sonata of Flesh and Bone). 2000.

Para siempre en mi memoria (Always in My Memory). 2000.

Secondary Sources

Horan, Elizabeth Rosa. "Emigrant Memory: Jewish Women Writers in Chile and Uruguay." In *Passion, Memory, and Identity: Twentieth-Century Latin American Jewish Women Writers.* Edited by Marjorie Agosín. Albuquerque: University of New Mexico Press, 1999, pp. 115–160.

Skar, Stacey D. "Sonia Guralnik." In *Jewish Writers of Latin America: A Dictionary.* Edited by Darrell B. Lockhart. New York: Garland, 1997, pp. 247–251.

TANYA HADAR

(1947–)

HANNA YAOZ

Third Generation of Hebrew Holocaust Poets: Children of Survivors

A NEW GENERATION of Hebrew poets who wrote about the Holocaust appeared in the 1970s. These writers are children of survivors who reflect an "inherited fear" in their works. Chronologically speaking, this is the third generation of Israeli Holocaust poets. The most prominent of them are Oded Peled, Rivka Miriam, Tanya Hadar, and Esther Fuchs. All were born to parents who survived the horror. In their poetry, they integrate the characteristic symbology of the two generations of poets that preceded them. They are similar to the poets of the 1940s, Uri Zvi Greenberg, Natan Alterman, and others, who write poems of outrage, protest, and lamentation and express a great measure of empathy and identification with Holocaust survivors. They also practice the conventions of modernism common to survivor poets Dan Pagis, Itamar Yaoz-Kest, and others, who began writing about the Holocaust in the early 1960s and use a complex array of "poetic codes," which makes the "time of terror" unique in Hebrew poetry.

Second-Generation Syndrome

From a thematic view, the emphasis in this poetry is on the "second-generation syndrome." This syndrome was discovered in psychological and social research studies; its first and foremost characteristic is the special relationship between Holocaust survivors and their children. Children of survivors are seen by their parents as having roles of tremendous significance. They are a kind of "memorial candle" to immortalize those family members who were killed, and a realization of hopes and plans that never materialized because of the family's fate in World War II. Many children of survivors display symptoms of fear and insecurity, lack a strong self-image, and have difficulty maintaining emotional independence, as noted in the psychoanalytic work of Ludwig Hessler, Yolanda Gempel, and Dinora Pines.

This syndrome penetrated the poetry of these second-generation writers, who took their permanent place on the literary stage beginning in the 1970s, and can be called the "third generation" of Holocaust poets in Israel. Inherited memories and a combination of attraction and repulsion toward the subject in all its facets typify the writing of the children of Holocaust survivors. The most prominent concept is that of continuity and empathy toward the parents' generation that experienced the horrors of World War II. These feelings sometimes extend to their grandparents' generation, although this is accompanied by a clear tone of protest. In contrast to the disguised protest of the poets who personally experienced the Holocaust, some third-generation poets shift from the more abstract to the concrete, execute protest that searches for new codewords, and turn to open, direct language, straightforward sentences, and a biting prosodic style.

Tanya Hadar: Holocaust and Jewish Fate

Tanya Hadar was born two years after World War II in the Szeltheim displaced-persons (DP) camp near Frankfurt-am-Mein, Germany, to parents who survived the Holocaust in the Baranowicz ghetto (in White Russia). Her father was the head doctor in the DP camp. The family came to Israel in 1948. The central image in Hadar's Holocaust poetry is that of her grandmother, who was shot to death and buried in a mass grave in the forests near Baranowicz: "To take my grandmother out of my flesh / From my eyes, my belly, the soles of my feet / My daughters' names on her forehead like plaited light," she writes in a poem titled "Now I Will Sing Like Them," which appears in her second book of poems, *In the Lands of the Living* (1991). Hadar identifies with the image of an old woman standing facing a pit and being shot into it: "Grandma still walks and a thin stream runs down her back / Just like the day she was shot and fell into the pit / A tiny bloody point in the pupil." The family's fate represents the suffering of the Jewish people. Moreover, she combines the Jewish fate in the Holocaust with that of the Jews in the days of the Second Temple, its destruction, the Emperor Titus, and the Jewish prisoners in Rome. Almost two thousand years separate these two historical eras—the Roman conquest of Jerusalem and the fate of the Jews in World War II. Tanya Hadar creates a kind of reflection, with Jewish fate at various points in time joining together in her works. In her poem "Burnt House," an anonymous woman from the "House of Katrus" in Jerusalem is linked to the grandmother's face perforated with holes from German bullets (pp. 12–14, 45). There is a clear connection in Hadar's poetry between the fire and destruction of the Second Temple in Jerusalem and the fire and ashes of Jews in Hitler's death camps. In my interview with Hadar, she said: "In 1983 I visited the Dachau concentration camp with my oldest daughter. The camp and its streets were paved with white gravel. During my visit I dug my hand into this white gravel and a few finger-lengths down I reached the burnt layer."

In the poem "The Soft Cry":

The soft cry goes on and on
Over the Roman Forum
A cry spread out in the shape of a cloud
Under the arches of the Tiber sunk in the water
Children of Jerusalem sing quietly
Titus hears them and trembles
Vespasian hears them and trembles
The wild animals wail silently.

It is the same again in the poem "Gray Jerusalem." The Emperor Titus appears, but so do images of the grandparents killed in the Holocaust. Moreover, "Jerusalem in the dream is clear and full of declivities / My forefathers wander around, Lithuanian houses on their backs / Trees grow there from Poland's forests / Children play there from the days of the Second Temple."

The phenomenon of creating links between historical periods that compare Jewish suffering in different ages characterizes a noticeable portion of Hebrew Holocaust poetry. Hadar notes, "The feeling of belonging to and identification with Jewish suffering all through the generations grew deeper over the years. One can definitely trace the process from personal, private experiences as a daughter of survivors, to a wider circle of emotional and national affiliation" (Interview). About the second-generation concept, Hadar tells us that the awareness about this grew over time, with a feeling of responsibility, of inner duty and not external duress: "We express what our parents cannot express: the scream which was silenced. I feel that our task is to experience the continuity, for ourselves and for others, to make a connection to that world which is vanishing, to make it continue, to tie it together" (Interview). In a statement for *The Holocaust in Modern Hebrew Poetry* (Hanna Yaoz, 1984), Hadar traced her response to the Holocaust at various stages and observed that her effort to address the Holocaust has been a lifelong endeavor:

> The experiences of growing up and motherhood gave me the strength and spiritual daring to deal with the subject of the Holocaust, and it is interesting that it came out through the images of grandparents. Afterwards, with my return to a religiously traditional lifestyle, the personal and poetic connection widened to include other images and periods as well. These kinds of images appear in my poems: A woman from the "House of Katrus" in the time of the Second Temple, Rabbi Hanina ben Teradyon of the Ten Martyrs, Etty Hillesom from the Holocaust period, and others (Interview).

It is interesting to note that Hadar's return to a religious lifestyle influenced her poetry, as her Jewish-religious philosophy merges with the subject of the Holocaust in the volume *In the Lands of the Living*. The "lands of the living" concept has a double meaning; hidden inside is the implication of a cemetery. (The expression is taken from Psalms 116:9.) In my interview with her, Tanya Hadar related that she saw the verse "I will go before God in the lands of the living" for the first time in iron letters over the gate to the Jewish cemetery in Frankfurt-am-Mein when she went to visit her grandfather's grave, years after the war. The various sources she uses in her book of poems run the gamut from the Psalms and homiletic interpretations of the Scriptures to quotations from authors such as Berthold Brecht and philosophers such as Bernard Henri-Levy. This also testifies to her simultaneous approach to different eras and images from various generations. The progression in the poems is from an actual, realistic picture to a much broader and, for the most part, a more abstract view, with Jewish destiny being the thread that ties them together.

Bibliography

Primary Source

In the Lands of the Living. 1991.

Secondary Sources

"Holocaust Trauma: Transmission to the Second Generation." *Journal of Social Work and Policy in Israel*, Special Issue, 1992.

Vardi, Dina. *Nosei HaKhotam* (Memorial Candles). Keter, 1990; London: Routlege, 1992; Ithaca: Cornell University Press, 1991.

Yaoz, Hanna. *The Holocaust in Modern Hebrew Poetry*. Eked, 1984.

———. *Three Generations of Hebrew Holocaust Poetry*. Eked, 1990.

———. *The Melody and the Scream—A Study of the Holocaust Poetry of Israeli Poets of the Forties*. Eked, 1995.

———. *Interviews with Writers and Poets Who Survived the Holocaust*. Forthcoming.

MICHAEL HAMBURGER

(1924–)

PETER LAWSON

MICHAEL HAMBURGER WAS born in Berlin on 22 March 1924. His father, Richard, was a physician and professor; his mother, Lili (née Hamburg), a housewife. Although Hamburger escaped the German genocide of European Jewry, he experienced early manifestations of Nazism in the form of institutional racism. In his autobiography, *A Mug's Game: Intellectual Memoirs, 1924–1954* (1973), Hamburger describes his desperation as a German Jewish schoolboy tormented by an "['Aryan'] teacher, like others before him, [who] ruled by mockery and intimidation; I was reduced to such despair," he writes, "that I could not go to sleep at night" (Cheadle, Eng.: Carcanet, 1973, p. 22). In November 1933 the family emigrated to Scotland. When they moved to London soon afterward, Michael studied at Westminster School and, beginning in 1941, at Christ Church, Oxford. From 1943 to 1947 Hamburger served in the British Army, attaining the rank of lieutenant. He returned to Oxford the following year, completing an M.A. in modern languages. In 1951 he married the musician and poet Anne Beresford. They have three children: Mary Anne, Richard Benedict, and Claire Miranda.

Hamburger began a long and distinguished academic career in 1952, initially teaching at University College London, while translating German poetry. Among his many awards are the German Federal Republic's Goethe Medal (1986), and the European Community's first European Translation Prize (1990) for his renditions of verse by the Holocaust survivor Paul Celan. He has also translated poetry by Nelly Sachs, "who for many became *the* poet of the Holocaust" (*A Proliferation of Prophets*, Manchester, Eng.: Carcanet, 1983, p. 282). In 1992 he was awarded the Order of the British Empire (OBE).

Holocaust Poetry

Many members of Hamburger's family died in the Holocaust. He laments: "Of my father's family there were no survivors in Germany except a cousin living in Hamburg, with a non-Jewish wife" (*A Mug's Game*, p. 148). Of Berlin, Hamburger states simply: "I'd rather keep away from it" (p. 145). Hamburger began writing about the Holocaust in 1961, some thirty years after his emigration from the Third Reich to Britain; mindful of the unhealed wound inflicted by Nazism:

> Branded in childhood, for thirty years he strove
> To hide the scar, and truly to believe
> In the true fundaments of that commonweal
> Which once had outlawed him beyond repeal ("Conformist," *Collected Poems 1941–1994*, London: Anvil Press, 1995, p. 89)

As Hamburger acknowledges elsewhere: "I was marked for life by the racial policies of the Third Reich" (*private correspondence*, 3 March 2001). The poet's scorn for heartless administrators pervades his oeuvre (see, for example, "How to Beat the Bureaucrats," *Collected Poems 1941–1994*, pp. 198–199). Journalistic coverage of the Eichmann Trial in Jerusalem possibly spurred Hamburger to break his silence. Two years before Hannah Arendt's *Eichmann in Jerusalem: A Report on the Banality of Evil* (1963), Hamburger's poem "In a Cold Season" (*Collected Poems*, pp. 109–112) focused on the bureaucratic mindset of this "exemplary" Nazi: "Adolf Eichmann, civil servant (retired)." Eichmann is the banal murderer incarnate,

> whose only zeal was to convert
> Real women children men to words and numbers
> Added to be subtracted leaving nothing

Section four of this five-part sequence switches from the perpetrator's bureaucratic abstractions to consideration of a specific victim, Hamburger's murdered grandmother, and her bereft family:

> They made her write a postcard to her son in England.
> 'Am going on a journey'; and that all those years
> She had refused to travel even to save her life.
> Too little I know of her life, her death,

Forget my last visit to her at the age of nine,
The goodbye like any other that was the last.

"In a Cold Season" concludes with a plea to spare Eichmann's life, to feel pity rather than anger or lust "to avenge": "But show him pity now for pity's sake/ And for their sake who died for lack of pity."

Another poem of the same year, "Security" (*Collected Poems*, p. 92), hints at the endurance of Hamburger's fears as a Jew raised in Nazi Germany, by juxtaposing his own youthful vulnerability with his children's safety in postwar England, while introducing images that evoke some of the worst atrocities of the Holocaust universe:

Also that twenty years ago now I could have been
  parchment
Cured and stretched for a lampshade,
Who now have children, a lampshade
And the fear of those winds.

In "Treblinka" (1967, *Collected Poems*, p. 113), Hamburger examines the business of the death factories: "Long we'd been dirt to be wiped off, dust to be dispersed." The images of dirt and dust carry a charge in relation to antisemitism and the *Shoah*, respectively. In "Dust" (1970, *Collected Poems*, pp. 244–246), germs are depicted mingled with ashes, possibly with reference to camp crematoria: "Matter's light breath, exhalation/That mingles pollen with down/Germs with ashes."

In "S-Bahn" (1965, *Collected Poems*, pp. 134–135), Hamburger introduces the theme of Holocaust obliteration in a postwar Berlin dedicated to rebuilding. He exposes the crimes "the dreamers of reason, the cleaners" of Germany would conceal or forget: "The corpses have been disposed of, / The gas rose up, diffused."

In the prosperous 1960s, Germany recalls the Holocaust accidentially, through absences rather than confrontation with its history: "Now that the train connects /One desolation with another."

Trees and Roots

In the "Tree Poems" section of his *Collected Poems*, Hamburger turns to nature to investigate tangible evocations of the past. Perhaps Hamburger's weeping willows serve as reminders of Jewish suffering and endurance. The willow appears in several poems, including "In October" (1950), "Anachronisms" (1957–1961), and "Oxford" (1963). In "Willow" (1978, *Collected Poems*, p. 347), the tree is imbued with a survivor's toughness and obstinacy. Such resolute strength extends beyond the fires of the Holocaust: "Chop up the dry remains, /Burn them: they'll spit."

Hamburger is fascinated with roots, and his poems about trees are often meditations on his own "transplanted" status as a German Jew with British citizenship (see, for example, "Winter Solstice 1999," *Intersections*, 2000). When he seeks his own roots ("looked for my origin") in "The Search" (1962, *Collected Poems*, p. 440), he is "Always sure of the route/ Though the people grew foreign, bizarre."

Though sure of the way back home ("route"), the searcher cannot find his roots among the "foreign, bizarre" people he encounters. He is more like the "displaced persons" of an earlier poem, "The Road" (1961, *Collected Poems*, p. 437), possibly Jewish refugees "whose nationhood is a cause." Eventually, the searcher finds his native village

Where they told me: here you were born.
An unlikely place—no petrol pump, office block,
  poster?—
Yet I could not deny it, and asked them the name.
Why, Mors, need we tell you, mors, MORS.

Nothing persists for post-*Shoah* Jews in Germany but the reminder of death ("Why, Mors, need we tell you, m o r s, MORS").

"At Staufen" (1975, *Collected Poems*, pp. 295–298) describes a cemetery where pre-*Shoah* generations of German Jews are buried:

Dark the gravestones were, too,
At Sulzburg, the Hebrew letters
Blacked out by centuries
Of moss on the oldest;
With no new ones to come,
With the last of a long line
Gassed, east of here, gone.

Hamburger contrasts the sense of social integration that German Jews enjoyed before the Third Reich—as signified by their gravestone markers—with the rejection of Jews in the Nazi era: victims of the Holocaust are granted no burial place, no inscription, no sign of their presence in the German polity. This helps explain why Hamburger's relationship with Germany remains literary—through widely praised translations—while the poet chooses not to live there. The last generation of German Jews was "gassed," and is now "gone."

Hamburger notes in the introduction to his translations of poems by Paul Celan: "With the late Nelly Sachs he shared a constant awareness of writing as a survivor and witness of the European-Jewish holocaust" (*Nineteen Poems by Paul Celan*, Oxford, Eng.: Carcanet, 1972, p. 12). "Surviving in the teeth of displacement" (*After the Second Flood*, Manchester, Eng.: Carcanet, 1986, p. 277), Hamburger resembles his fellow poets-in-exile, Sachs and Celan. As the son of highly assimilated German Jews, it is possible that Hamburger empathizes with Sachs when he states that she "was scarcely conscious of her Jewishness before the Third Reich" (*A Proliferation of Prophets*, p. 285). The Holocaust hurt Sachs, Hamburger, and Celan into a heightened awareness of Jewish survival and witness. Moreover, when Hamburger writes of Celan as "an unrepentant modernist" (*The Truth of Poetry*, Harmondsworth, Eng.: Penguin, 1969, p. 325), he might be describing his own poetic practice.

As John Mander suggests, the poet reasserts "the values of an older Germany" (as quoted in *Contemporary Authors New Revision Series*, p. 163); John Matthias qualifies such an assessment by remarking in Hamburger's poetry "the moral consciousness of the modern European Jew" (p. 46).

Bibliography

Primary Sources

Poetry

Later Hogarth. 1945.
Flowering Cactus: Poems, 1942–49. 1950.
Poems. 1950–51. 1952.
The Dual Site. 1958.
Weather and Season. 1963.
In Flashlight. 1965.
In Massachusetts. 1967.
Feeding the Chickadees. 1968.
Travelling. 1969.
Penguin Modern Poets 14 (with Alan Brownjohn and Charles Tomlinson). 1969.
Home. 1969.
In Memoriam Friedrich Hölderlin. 1970.
Travelling I–V. 1972.
Ownerless Earth. 1973.
Conversations with Charwomen. 1973.
Babes in the Wood. 1974.
Travelling VI. 1975.
Travelling VII. 1976.
Real Estate. 1977.
Palinode. 1977.
Moralities. 1977.
In Suffolk. 1981.
Variations. 1981.
Collected Poems, 1941–1983. 1984.
Heimgekommen. 1984.
Selected Poems. 1988.
Trees. 1988.
Roots in the Air. 1992.
Collected Poems, 1941–1994. 1995.
Intersections: Shorter Poems, 1994–2000. 2000.

Nonfiction

Reason and Energy: Studies in German Literature. 1957.
Hugo Von Hofmannsthal: Zwei Studien (Hofmannsthal: Three Essays). 1964.
From Prophecy to Exorcism: The Premises of Modern German Literature. 1965.
Zwischen den Sprachen: Essays und Gedichte (Between Languages: Essays and Poems). 1966.
The Truth of Poetry: Tensions in Modern Poetry from Baudelaire to the 1960s. 1969.
A Mug's Game: Intermittent Memoirs, 1924–1954. 1973.
Art as Second Nature: Occasional Pieces, 1950–74. 1975.
Literarische Erfahrungen: Aufstze (Literary Experiences: Essays). 1981.
A Proliferation of Prophets: Essays on German Writers from Nietzsche to Brecht. 1983.
After the Second Flood: Essays on Post-War German Literature. 1986.
Testimonies: Selected Shorter Prose, 1950–1987. 1989.
String of Beginnings: Intermittent Memoirs, 1924–1954. 1991.

Selected Translations

Decline: Twelve Poems (Georg Trakl). 1952.
Poems (Hans Magnus Enzensberger). 1967.
O the Chimneys. (Nelly Sachs, translated with others). 1967.
Nineteen Poems by Paul Celan (Paul Celan). 1972.
Selected Poems (Peter Huchel). 1974.
German Poetry 1910–1975. 1977.
Poems (Paul Celan). 1980.
An Unofficial Rilke: Poems, 1912–1926 (Rainer Maria Rilke). 1981.
Poems and Epigrams (Johann Wolfgang von Goethe). 1983.
Hölderlin: Selected Verse (Hölderlin). 1986.

Secondary Sources

"A Tribute to Michael Hamburger." *Agenda* 35, no. 3 (autumn 1997): 3–130.
Arendt, Hannah. *Eichmann in Jerusalem: A Report on the Banality of Evil*. New York: Viking Penguin, 1963.
Davie, Donald. "Ownerless Earth." *New York Times Book Review*, 28 April 1974, 30–31.
———. *Under Briggflatts: A History of Poetry in Great Britain 1960–1988*. Manchester: Carcanet, 1989, 223–228.
Hamburger, Michael. "Rhythm." *Agenda* 10.4–11.1 (autumn–winter 1972–1973): 25–27.
Matthias, John. "Travellers." *Poetry* (April 1974): 45–55.
"Michael Hamburger." In *Contemporary Authors New Revision Series*. Vol. 47. Edited by Pamela S. Dear. Detroit: Gale, 1995, 160–164.
"Michael Hamburger." *Who's Who 1999*. London: A&C Black, 1999, 849.
Miller, David. "Michael Hamburger: Some Remarks on His Poetry." *Agenda* 11.4–12.1 (autumn–winter 1973–1974): 139–148.
Schmidt, Michael. *Fifty Modern British Poets*. London: Pan, 1979, 339–345.
Silking, John. "Michael Hamburger." In *Contemporary Poets*. Edited by Tracy Chevalier. Chicago: St. James Press, 1996, 431–435.

SHULAMITH HAREVEN

(1931–)

DVIR ABRAMOVICH

THE FIRST WOMAN to become a full member of the Academy of the Hebrew Language and Winner of the Prime Minister's Creativity Prize for her novel *City of Many Days*, Shulamith Hareven is one of Israel's preeminent authors. Over the last forty years, her finely tuned plots and perceptive, intimate portraits of lonely, frayed individuals, as well as her commitment to civil rights, have earned her the respect of readers and critics alike. In fact, in a 1992 *New York Times* article she was acclaimed by Esther B. Fein as achieving, "a level of success and acceptance among the literary elite in Israel known by no other woman" (Fein, pp. B1(N) and C13(L)). Likewise, she was hailed by the French publication *L'Express* as one of the world's one hundred most influential women.

Hareven was born in Warsaw in 1931 and immigrated to Palestine with her parents in 1940. The family settled in Jerusalem. Oddly, Hareven has steadfastly eschewed divulging any information about her childhood in Poland, choosing in interviews to instead begin her biographical sketch with her period in the Hagana Underground during the War of Independence. In a conversation with Haim Chertok in *We Are All Close*, she was quizzed about her upbringing. In response, she charted her role in the war as a teenage medic, calmly ignoring her interlocutor's plea to elucidate on her pre-Palestine days in Europe (pp. 77–78).

At first sight, maintaining a stern silence over her past may reinforce the well-worn axiom that writers wish to reject any hermeneutical move to adopt a metatextual approach in articulating an interpretation to their work. No doubt this examination, which calls for, in part, seeing diegesic characterizations as a mirror of the author's personal life, is an attractive proposition because of Hareven's pointed reluctance to discuss her private life candidly and her literary preoccupation with the Holocaust.

Most revealingly, her stories constantly emphasize the profound estrangement and sadness of life that her immigrant principals experience as they are burdened by a stifling past and a smothering psychological legacy that cannot be shed. Lacking comforting and sustaining relationships, their inner balance is vulnerable to the assault of the indelible European tragedy that is engraved and carved onto their damaged psyche, persistently threatening to unravel their personal peace or sanity. Substantively, the fragmented, harrowing memories, foregrounded in a constellation of quotidian gestures, accents, longings, and nightmares, deeply overshadow the lives of the characters trying to reconstruct a shattered existence in Israel. Homologously, Hareven revels in exploring the irony of a people who left the Diaspora to find a home in Israel but failed to do so, emotionally severed from society and outsiders in their new adoptive country. In alliance with the sorrowful undertow of the tales, the author infuses the landscape of her settings, particularly Jerusalem, with a wounded landscape, shimmering with shadows and inescapable darkness. Turning to Hareven's words, we find she employs a pared, terse style of expression that evokes complex, breathtakingly lyrical images of melancholy and ragged souls besieged by earlier scars. And although elusive at times, the sparse language nevertheless allows a space for the readers to enter and proffer their own meaning.

Twilight

In the compact, surrealistic *Twilight* (1992) a nameless woman mystically enters a city she describes as "a city of sorrow." As the story opens, the dreamer says, "Last night I spent a year in the city where I was born. I had long known the password for getting there: Dante's line, 'I am the way to the city of sorrow' " (*Twilight and Other Stories*, San Francisco: Mercury House, 1992, p. 1). In keeping with its disturbingly apocalyptic tone, we learn that every night, after the audience watches the opera, its members are taken away to freight trains by the waiting soldiers posted in the square. Attending a Mozart concert, the protagonist asks the man who saves her and whom she will later marry why the victims never escape their grisly fate. He explains that this ritualistic rounding up is repeated every night. He goes on to say that the next evening the Jews return to the opera and again the process is repeated. However, upon their return, the victims are "a little less alive each time. They fade, like pictures in an album" (pp. 4–5). There's no denying the shocking effect of the scenes of mass arrest Hareven constructs, "The floodlights of the soldiers' trucks came on and suddenly, tearing the darkness, glaring and terrible, and with this evil light came the wails, the shouts, and the curses . . . The people in their festive clothes piled up on the trucks, and there was no more telling them apart, batch after driven batch" (p. 4). In one telling sequence that seems to offer the subtext of identification with the dead, the narrator, watching her neighbors herded onto trucks, wishes to leap from the tall roof into the courtyard and join them, even though she knows it means certain death. More to the point, it calls attention to the search for identity by the European immigrants who, though absorbed into the new society, were strangely drawn to their old homeland. *Twilight* articulates a collective, irreducible, unsettling desire to unplug repressed memories in a pilgrimage toward a clearer understanding of one's psyche and the postwar individuation.

In blurring the boundaries between reality and illusion the author is referencing the indescribable nature of the Holocaust and the limits of representation. Moreover, it is hard not to read the dream allegorically as a metaphor for the Holocaust, though the storyline is redolent with rich allegory that absorbs, mosaic-like, into its fabric multiple motifs that inform and fuel the Holocaust canon. For example, darkness as a repository of menace is deployed in an early, arresting image of the city, "The city of my birth was very dark, extinguished because the sun had left it and gone away a long, long time ago" (p. 1). And later, "All that night we wandered through the streets, as there was no telling day from night except for a slight shade of difference in the depth of the darkness; everything was shrouded in the same no-light of the extinguished city. . . . They never went so far as to break into laughter. They already knew they would live without sun from now on" (p. 6). This is a universe beyond the rational or the normal, where women and men walk aimlessly ghetto-like, where statues are smashed, a hellish incubator where people are clean as smoke. It is a nightmarish world where nothing is certain, where in a nightlong year a woman marries, becomes pregnant, and then gives birth to a child who fantastically grows up and disappears into a mantle of evil.

By the story's end, the narrator awakens from her Kafkaesque dream and flees the perpetual darkness of her hometown to the blistering sun of Jerusalem, "I lay still, waiting for my soul to flow full in me again, and I knew it was all over and completed. I would no more go back to the city of my birth, to the lightless city. . . . My past was commuted. From now on I would find nothing there but the stones of Jerusalem, and plants growing with might vigor and a vast light. I got up to make breakfast, my heart beating hard" (pp. 10–11). One does not want to make too much of the parallels between fiction and fact. Still, as of course, one could draft this observation onto the author's life story as she was spared the destruction her characters suffer by the fact her parents fled Europe for Israel. On one level, it represents the excruciating attempt by Holocaust survivors to amputate the past from the present through a cathartic revisiting of their childhood in order to lift the enormous burden that transition to a new land brought. In the words of Gila Ramras-Rauch, " 'Her return' is a final cutting of the connection cord, a reaffirmation of life and sun" (p. 12).

Loneliness

Loneliness (1992) is a highly revealing tale of sorrow and alienation. The story is structured around Dolly Jacobus, a wealthy middle-aged Holocaust survivor whose husband, a successful architect and scion of one of Jerusalem's most established families (their origins in the city, we learn, go back nine generations) is abroad at a conference in Malta. While the elegant Dolly enjoys the luxuries of a comfortable existence, she is nonetheless lonely, without love, friends, or purpose. Wrapped in ennui, she is mired in a plodding stifling marriage, frustrated at never feeling at home, despite living in the city for twenty-five years after arriving in Israel at age fourteen. Constantly wondering about the meaning of home, at one point, sitting in the car on the way home she fears that "If she were to return to it this minute, . . . the key might not fit the door, so that she would remain trapped outside in impersonal space. And if it did fit, her memories might not" (*Bedidut*, Tel Aviv: Am Oved, 1980, p. 29). Elsewhere, she reflects:

> Only somebody who had never been a refugee could dare dream of oceans and great expanses of space. And twenty five years ago Dolly Jacobus had been a refugee. To this

> day she was astonished by such things as central heating, which kept on burning warmly, really burning, while the rain remained outside. Truly outside, it wasn't just an optical illusion (p. 16).

More than once, the tormenting, rippling effects of Dolly's Holocaust trauma become evident, as in a brief throwaway passage apprising the readers that she has had four consecutive miscarriages of unknown cause. Her childless state stamps her with a never-ending frustration and a craving in her soul for a wholeness that has gradually abated. Although she dreads abandonment, it is significant that it is only when she is home alone, apart from husband, that her primary emotions emerge and that she begins to gain insight and a sense of her true self. In one episode, after a young girl intentionally brushes against her right breast (an encounter that awakens within her an obsessive erotic passion), Dolly makes up her mind to "understand everything about herself once and for all. It was time she knew" (p. 23). At home, she yearns to deepen her knowledge about her childhood and establish a nexus with a life long buried away:

> She rummaged through the closet, took out all the albums and began feverishly looking for the few rare snapshots of herself from her refugee days. None lit the faintest spark. She could not find herself in any of them. Perhaps, she thought, if only, if only, I had some pictures from my childhood, from the age of four or five, perhaps then. But such a picture was not to be had anywhere on earth. It was as if Dolly had been born twice, and her first, perhaps truer, life had ended abruptly at the age of fourteen. Afterward, another post-diluvian life had begun, with its disguises and new names (p. 35).

Ultimately, the exploration of memory and the search of her family ancestry is unsuccessful for, as Yael Feldman remarks, "Her (pre-Holocaust) childhood seems to have been erased without a trace. All that is left is a wrenching pathos, a pathos rendered all the more powerful through Hareven's circumspect style" (p. 131). It is of note, Feldman continues, that even her first name, Dolly, is a clear marker of foreignness, heightening our impression of the heroine's detachment from her surroundings (p. 133). We might also infer that the moniker hints at a woman whose childhood has been stunted during the war, which would also explain her enigmatic homosexual desire toward the teenage girl who presses her mouth against her breast while the two are in line at the post office. In a sense, Dolly's upsurge in desire for the girl underscores her attempt to reclaim a stolen childhood, typical of many survivors.

Visiting her mother-in-law, Grandmother Haya, Dolly observes the eighty-nine-year-old woman confidently gazing out of her window onto the old city, "Yes, yes, she said. It all belonged to her. She could look out on it all, she who had never been a young starving refugee with a funny family name that had to be changed in a new land" (p. 123). Yet, for the disenfranchised Dolly, the stern environs of Jerusalem exacerbate her growing sense of isolation. A crucial vignette earlier testifies to the sharply discomforting existential emptiness gnawing her solitary self. Staring from her windows, a friend from the university where she attends lectures asks her how she can go on looking without feeling nervous. As a grin ghosts around her lips, she replies, "I must be a butterfly . . . But I want you to know . . . that being a butterfly is something that I have to work at very hard" (p. 16). Quite exactly what this comment means is far from clear. Nevertheless, the glimmering symbolism of a butterfly that never lands is of such specifity that the reader cannot help but suspect that they are being nudged toward conclusions that have to do with Dolly's rootlessness.

"The Witness"

A story that exemplifies the oppressive prevailing Israeli attitudes toward the survivors in Palestine of the 1940s is "Ha-ed" ("The Witness," 1985). Manifestly, it demonstrates how, in attempting to promote the pillars of Zionist dogma, Israeli society stifled real identification and understanding of the world of the Diaspora Jews. Negotiating various elements, Hareven shows how, instead of affording the survivors the respite they so craved, as well as the opportunity for some psychological relief by listening to and believing their descriptions, the *Yishuv* and its native born dealt the survivors a crushing blow by attempting to obliterate their biography, thereby crippling any opportunity they sought to reconcile with the damaged self of the past. As Rachel Brenner contends, the tale "actually rules out the possibility of a mutually acceptable *modus vivendi* between the Israeli and the Holocaust survivor. . . . The aggressive, practically unanimous, denial of the Holocaust victim's testimony isolates him in his new home" (p. 73).

The first person narrative begins in 1941 with the arrival of Shlomek, a young Polish Holocaust refugee at the agricultural boarding school of Drom Yehuda. From the outset, Yotam Raz, the teacher who is entrusted with helping the newcomer in his integration and whose viewpoint relates the unfolding drama (thirty-five years after the event), underlines to his new pupil the importance of shedding the vestiges of the past: "You will get used to things, and soon you will look like us and talk like us and no one will feel that you are not from here . . . soon you will be a *Sabra*, Shlomo, don't worry, everything will be all right" (p. 38). In offering his assessment of the story's central tenor, Shaked labels the teacher an idiot for the way he treats the escapee from Poland, his emotional frigidity and lack of psychological perspicuity (p. 130). Indeed, Yotam, himself a Polish survivor in denial of his origins, shows acute thoughtlessness and insensitivity to Shlomek's anguish in his relationship with the young victim. He tells his pupils that he is certain, "we will all welcome him warmly and provide him with a feeling of home" (p. 35).

However, any possibility of kinship or empathy for Shlomek's past suffering is given a short shrift by the guidance counsellor from the moment the adolescent reaches the village. This topos finds fruitful embodiment in a startling sequence that takes place as Shlomek enters the class for the first time. Facing his Israeli contemporaries, he is asked by Yotam to describe the state of war. In his answer, the young man says that there is no war as no one can fight the mighty German. When Boaz, one of the students, accuses the Diaspora Jews of cowardice, the upset Shlomek rises to their defense, claiming that "it was not impotence but the simple inability to stand up to the Germans and display any kind of heroism" (p. 37). It is immediately afterward that Hareven emplots, through Boaz, the widespread and dominant view of European Jews collectively shared by Israeli culture: "I'm sure there are people who fight the Germans like one should even under occupation. I'm sure not all are cowards like some people standing here" (p. 37). Next, Shlomek describes in detail his family's massacre. His father is hanged; his mother and two brothers shot.

The group reacts with sheer disbelief to the newcomer's honest report, regarding it as an incredible flight of the imagination. One says, "What is he telling there? What is he concocting? Why would the Germans kill citizens who go out to get bread . . . what is all this nonsense" (p. 37). One girl attributes it to shock, while another complains, "Really, he shouldn't tell tales . . . it is just his inventions" (p. 37), Worse, later that afternoon, reflecting on the episode, Yotam offers the following assessment of the boy's testimony:

> Shlomek's words attested to a degree of exaggeration and an unrestrained imagination. I surmised that his family perished in the bombings, or that he was suffering from feeling of guilt for leaving them there . . . maybe he does not know of their fate, and he is making up for it by thinking up shocking stories about their strange deaths . . . here for the first time as an educator, I came across a child who imagined the killing of his parents in such a way (p. 38).

At this moment we understand that the wish to nullify and eradicate the survivor's chronicle epitomizes a psychological distance that condemns that remnant of the *Shoah* as figures that the Israeli must shun. Equally, in the same week, the mistrust continues when one of the high-schoolers protests to Yoram that Shlomek is again lying about the war, claiming that during a siege they ate nothing but potatoes for two weeks. The student pleads with his teacher to confirm for him that it is nothing but a fib, that it cannot be true. Considering the excessive resentment and the bitter reaction to his plight, it is small wonder that Shlomek chooses silence, realizing there is no way he can open a dialogue with his peers, whose human experience is far removed from his. Stung from the pressure to forfeit his past, but still yearning to mourn and memorialize his family's murder, he clandestinely keeps a diary in Polish in which he records his eyewitness accounts and heritage. Furthermore, he ubiquitously engraves a secret code for all to observe, including on the wall on top of his bed, that consists of four letters and numbers (Y39, B37, E12, Y9), which toward the end we learn represent his slayed family members and the ages at which they died.

It is no accident that Yotam construes Shlomek's subsequent curbing of his outbursts and rebuffs of the advances made by Ruta, the psychologist, to talk as a signal that he has finally adjusted: "As I predicted, with his status in class rising, and with his acclimation, the lies and the fanciful stories disappeared. . . . Maybe it's a sign that Shlomek has been born again. . . . Shlomek has buried his past and I see in this a positive development. People after all are born anew here and you know this exactly as I do" (pp. 44–45). In the end though, Shlomek does not allow the process of invalidation to continue. He suddenly flees the school and makes his way to the residence of the British Commissioner to hand over his testimony about the atrocities of the War. Half a year later, his statements (the very ones that were cruelly discredited by Yotam and his students) are published by one of the leading newspapers. Incredulously, despite his reluctant acknowledgment of Shlomek's story and despite his keeping of the clipping in a draw along with other mementos from his students, Yotam insists on reproaching Shlomek for persisting with communicating his message and for not holding off a little. The final passage reveals primarily that the teacher has not abandoned his inflexible ideological posture:

> Only Shlomek's arrogance caused him to exclude himself from the group. And why did he run away as if his conscience was not clear. . . . Don't pay attention to the fact I am angry. It is always when I remember Shlomek that I become angry, even now, years later. This boy possessed

ingratitude. . . . One needs to know how and when to tell the truth. If he had only waited a few more months, it would have been published anyway, but then he would have added some honour to our school, instead of such an irresponsible act. . . . Very simply, he did not have a measure of patience (pp. 52–53).

Bibliography

Primary Sources

Yerushalayim Dorsanit (*Predatory Jerusalem*). 1962. Poetry.
Ba-Hodesh Ha-Aharon (*In the Last Month*). 1966. Stories.
Mekomot Nifradim (*Separate Places*). 1969. Poetry.
Reshut Netunah (*Permission Granted*) 1970. Stories.
Ir Yamim Rabim (*City of Many Days*). 1972. Novel.
Ani Ohev Lehariah (*I Love to Smell*). 1976.
Bedidut (*Loneliness*) 1980. Stories.
Tismonet Dulcinea (*The Dulcinea Syndrome*). 1981. Essays.
Soneh Ha-Nisim (*The Miracle Hater*). 1983. Novella.
Leorech Hashurot (*Along the Lines*). 1985. Stories.
Ha-Huliah (*The Link*). 1986. Novel.
Mashiah. O Knesset (*Messiah or Knesset*). 1987. Essays.
Navi (*Prophet*). 1989. Novella.
Ivrim Be-Aza (*Eyeless in Gaza*). 1991. Nonfiction.
Twilight and Other Stories. 1992.
Aharei Ha-Yaldut (*After Childhood*). 1994. Novella.
Otzar Ha-Milim Shel Ha-Shalom (*The Vocabulary of Peace*). 1996. Nonfiction.
Tzimaon (*Thirst—The Desert Trilogy*). 1996.
Ma Ani Ashem She-Ani Gadol? (*So What If I'm All Grown Up?*). 1999. Children's book.

Secondary Sources

Brenner, Rachel Feldhay. "Discourses of Mourning and Rebirth in Post-Holocaust Israeli Literature: Leah Goldberg's *Lady of the Castle* and Shulamit Hareven's 'The Witness.' " *Hebrew Studies* 31 (1990): 71–85.
Chertok, Haim. *We Are All Close: Conversations with Israeli Writers*. New York: Fordham University, 1989.
Fein, Esther B. "2 writers who keep their fiction free of political realities (Tatyana Tolstaya and Shulamith Hareven's characters struggle with daily life)." *New York Times*, 17 March 1992, pp. B1(N), C13(L).
Feldman,Yael. *No Room of Their Own: Gender and Nation in Israeli Women's Fiction*. New York: Columbia University Press, 1999.
Ramras-Rauch, Gila, and Joseph Michman-Melkman, eds. *Facing the Holocaust: Selected Israeli Fiction*. New York: Jewish Publication Society, 1985.
Shaked, Gershon. *Hasiport Ha'ivrit* (Hebrew Narrative Prose) V4. Tel Aviv and Jerusalem: Hakkibutz Hameuchad and Keter, 1993.

Robert Harris

(1957–)

GARY WEISSMAN

Robert Dennis Harris was born in Nottingham, England, on 7 March 1957, the son of Dennis Harris, a commercial printer, and Audrey Hardy Harris. After earning his B.A. degree in English literature from Cambridge University in 1978, he worked for the British Broadcasting Corporation (BBC-TV) as a researcher and film director for the programs *Tonight*, *Nationwide* and *Panorama*, from 1978 to 1981; and as a reporter for *Newsnight*, from 1981 to 1985, and *Panorama*, from 1985 to 1987. Harris then turned to newspaper journalism, serving as the political editor of the London *Observer* from 1987 to 1989. From 1988 to 1989 he also worked as a political reporter for *This Week* on Thames TV. In 1989 he joined the London *Sunday Times* as a political columnist and became well known in Britain for his left-leaning commentary.

While working as a journalist Harris published five nonfiction books. In 1982 he coauthored *A Higher Form of Killing*, a history of chemical warfare, and in 1983 he published *Gotcha!*, about press coverage of the Falklands war. Harris also wrote two biographies of British politicians, Labor leader Neil Kinnock and Margaret Thatcher's press secretary, Bernard Ingham, that have not been published in America. In 1986 he published *Selling Hitler*, a detailed account of the 1983 scandal involving the sale of crudely forged "Hitler diaries" to the international press. From reading Hitler's actual writings and speeches while researching this book, Harris developed an interest in the world Hitler planned to build after the war. In 1992 he portrayed this world in *Fatherland*, a crime thriller set in Berlin twenty years after Germany has won World War II.

Fatherland was a remarkable best-seller, first in Britain and then in the United States. Translated into two dozen languages, it has sold more than four million copies worldwide. In the United States, bidding for paperback rights reached $1.8 million, setting a record for a first novel. Film rights were optioned before the book's publication (though the film was not produced; instead an unfaithful adaptation was made for HBO television). Following his success, Harris moved with his wife and two children to Berkshire and largely gave up journalism in order to write novels. In 1995 he published the best-seller *Enigma*, a World War II thriller about British codebreakers. *Archangel*, a thriller about the hunt for Stalin's long-lost private notebook, followed in 1998.

Fatherland remains Harris's most successful work. Outside of Germany, where it was attacked for trivializing the Holocaust, *Fatherland* received overwhelmingly positive reviews; a notable exception was *Publisher's Weekly*, which suggested that "readers may well question the taste of using the Holocaust as the point of departure for a rather insubstantial, derivative thriller" (16 March 1992, p. 62). Yet a number of reviewers and scholars regard the book not only as a fascinating page-turner, but as a serious engagement with the legacy of Nazism and the Holocaust.

Fatherland

In its depiction of a world in which Nazi Germany has triumphed, *Fatherland* belongs to a genre that can be traced as far back as Katherine Burdekin's 1937 novel, *Swastika Night*, which portrays Europe after seven centuries of Nazi rule. *Fatherland* has been connected to the increasingly popular genre of "counterfactual" or "alternate" history, which includes works by fiction writers and historians who contemplate what the world would be like had key historical events transpired differently. Harris imagines a Europe in which "the war had dwindled to a series of bloody guerilla conflicts at the fringes of the new German Empire" after Russia's defeat (New York: Harper Paperbacks, 1992, p. 84). By 1964, when the novel is set, the Reich extends to the

Ural Mountains, the European nations have become members of a European Community under Germany, and America and Germany have entered "a nuclear stalemate the diplomats called the Cold War" (p. 84). Moreover, whereas "Stalin's holocaust" is commemorated by memorials and museums and studied by scholars (p. 208), the fate of the millions of Jews moved East during the war remains a mystery.

In addition to being an "alternate history," Harris's novel belongs to the genre of the detective story. Its protagonist is homicide investigator Xavier March, whose job requires him to wear the black uniform and swastika armband of an SS officer although he is a loner who never joined the Party. The novel begins with March inspecting a corpse lying at the edge of a lake. When the body is identified as Josef Buhler, a founding member of the Nazi Party, the Gestapo takes over; but March, sensing a cover-up, continues his investigation with the help of a plucky American journalist, Charlotte "Charlie" Maguire. What begins as an ordinary murder case turns into an investigation of genocide when they link Buhler's death to that of other Nazis who attended a 1942 conference in Wannsee to discuss "measures for a complete solution of the Jewish problem in Europe" (p. 250).

March and Charlie find the truth of what happened to the Jews revealed in a suitcase containing railway timetables, meeting minutes, memoranda, photographs, and a map of Auschwitz-Birkenau. The reader is presented with a number of documents, some of them real (such as a memorandum on the use of female prisoners' hair to make socks for U-boat crews) and some fabricated by Harris (most notably, a high-level Nazi's handwritten account of his wartime visit to Auschwitz-Birkenau, detailing the operation of the gas chamber and crematorium). Once March and Charlie uncover this documentary proof of the Final Solution, the novel's suspense turns on the question of whether they can evade the Gestapo and sneak it out of Germany. Beyond that, there is the question of whether they will be able to "change history" (p. 328) by exposing the perpetrators. Though Charlie predicts the collapse of Hitler's Germany—claiming, "You can't build on a mass grave" (p. 329)—the novel ends without giving these questions decisive answers.

Critical Reception

Despite its popular and critical success, twenty-five German publishers rejected *Fatherland*. This rejection may have had less to do with the novel's treatment of the Holocaust than with its commentary on present-day Germany. In a *Sunday Times* article titled "Nightmare Landscape of Nazism Triumphant" (which elicited a complaint from the German embassy), Harris writes: "I spent four years writing *Fatherland*, my novel about a fictional German superpower, and, as I wrote, it started turning into fact. Germany reunited to form a state of nearly 80m people. It ceased to be a neutered giant and started throwing its weight about" (10 May 1992, sec. 2, p. 1). Daniel Nassim and Bardo Fassbender have both argued that *Fatherland* is in fact a political book taking the form of a novel to better convey a message of concern about the new Germany's role in Europe.

When a German translation of *Fatherland* was finally published, German critics did not respond to this political message. Rather, they denounced the "bad taste" and "cheap sensationalism" of Harris's novel in terms reminiscent of those used by Saul Friedländer to identify a "new discourse on Nazism." In his 1982 study *Reflets du Nazisme* (translated into English as *Reflections of Nazism*, Harper & Row, 1984), Friedländer examined popular novels and films that effectively neutralize the "worst aspects of Nazism" (*Reflections*, p. 22) by betraying an awed attraction to Nazism—not to its politics, but to its "emotions, images, and phantasms" (p. 14). Is *Fatherland*, with its fantasy of a victorious Hitler, a more recent exemplar of this "new discourse"?

In one sense *Fatherland* clearly does suggest the kind of fascination with Nazism criticized by Friedländer and others. When interviewed on the American PBS program *Charlie Rose*, Harris spoke of the "extraordinary world that [Hitler had] imagined, carried around in his head for a decade or more," adding that "this was just an amazing world which cried out to be brought to life." Harris portrays this world in his *Sunday Times* article, encouraging readers to imagine they are German tourists from settlements in the East, "travelling to the capital for a week's sightseeing" (p. 6). Readers visit the same sites in *Fatherland*'s third chapter, where March accompanies his son on a bus tour of the colossal structures Albert Speer designed for the imperial capital. These are also rendered by an annotated illustration that prefaces the novel.

But if here Harris dwells on the grandeur of Hitler's "amazing world," elsewhere in *Fatherland* he presents a fraying society at odds with the Thousand Year Reich imagined by Hitler. Indeed, Harris's depiction of a Reich transformed by 1960s protests and Cold War tension has been described as a "deliberate rejection of the glamourized version of Nazism" (Parry, p. 120). Moreover, rather than evading the worst aspects of Nazism, Harris's novel is about the very effort to confront them. *Fatherland* complicates this confrontation by having March and Charlie question not only their ability to believe the "unbelievable" fact of the extermination program (p. 328), but also the impact its revelation will have on the world. "Suppose everyone knew all the details," says March. "Who would care? Would it really make any difference?" (p. 288). These questions may move readers to ask whether Holocaust consciousness has made a meaningful difference in our world, changing how we think and act in the postwar period.

In an "Author's Note" at the end of *Fatherland*, Harris lists the real-life fates of the high-level Nazis named in his fiction and identifies which documents reproduced in his novel are authentic—adding, "Where I have created documents, I have tried to do so on the basis of fact" (p. 379). *Fatherland*'s popular success suggests that many readers will, paradoxically enough, learn most of what they know about the Nazi genocide of the Jews from reading this novel about a world in which no one has heard of the Holocaust. At the same time, the line between historical fact and Harris's fiction will be most unclear to readers not already acquainted with this history.

Bibliography

Primary Sources

A Higher Form of Killing: The Secret Story of Gas and Germ Warfare. With Jeremy Paxman. 1982.

Gotcha!: The Media, the Government, and the Falklands Crisis. 1983.

The Making of Neil Kinnock. 1984.

Good and Faithful Servant: The Unauthorized Biography of Bernard Ingham. 1990.

Fatherland. 1992.

Enigma. 1995.

Archangel. 1998.

Secondary Sources

Fassbender, Bardo. "A Novel, Germany's Past, and the Dilemmas of Civilised Germans." *Contemporary Review* 265, no. 1546 (November 1994): 236–247.

"Harris, Robert (Dennis)." In *Contemporary Authors*, vol. 143. Edited by Donna Olendorf. Detroit: Gale, 1994, pp. 184–185.

Nassim, Daniel. "Nicholas Ridley: The Novel." *Living Marxism* no. 46 (August 1992). ⟨http://www.informinc.co.uk/LM/LM46/LM46_Books.html⟩.

Parry, Ann. "Idioms for the Unrepresentable: Postwar Fiction and the *Shoah*." In *The Holocaust and the Text: Speaking the Unspeakable*. Edited by Andrew Leak and George Paizis. London: Macmillan, 2000, pp. 109–124.

Whitney. Craig R. "Inventing a World in Which Hitler Won." *New York Times*, 3 June 1992, sec. C, pp. 17, 19.

Interviews

Charlie Rose, no. 1176. PBS. 10 June 1992.

Field, Michele. "Robert Harris: Facing the Enigmas of WWII." *Publisher's Weekly* 242, no. 44 (30 October 1995): 42–43.

Geoffrey Hartman

(1929–)

MICHAEL ROTHBERG

Author or editor of two dozen books of criticism and theory, Geoffrey H. Hartman is one of the leading literary critics of the second half of the twentieth century. During the course of a nearly fifty-year academic career, Hartman has received numerous prestigious honors and fellowships, and is now Sterling Professor (Emeritus) of English and Comparative Literature at Yale University. Hartman was initially known for his scholarship on British Romanticism, and especially Wordsworth. Since the 1980s he has also been one of the most important figures in Holocaust studies in the United States, both making an intellectual contribution and playing a vital institutional role as cofounder and, since 1981, as project director of the Fortunoff Video Archive for Holocaust Testimonies at Yale University.

Geoffrey Hartman was born in Frankfurt, Germany, on 11 August 1929 to Albert and Agnes Hartman. His parents divorced when he was an infant and his father moved to South America. Hartman was nine when the *Kristallnacht* pogrom took place in November 1938. His mother was able to emigrate to the United States the following month, but Hartman himself was not able to leave Germany until March 1939, when he was evacuated on a *Kindertransport* to England. He was only able to rejoin his mother in America several years later at the age of sixteen. Since 1946 he has lived, studied, and worked in the United States. He graduated with a B. A. from Queens College in New York before receiving his Ph.D. in comparative literature from Yale University in 1953. After a stint in the army, Hartman taught first at Yale, and then at the University of Iowa and Cornell University, before returning definitively to Yale in 1967. He has also held visiting professorships all over the world, including Zurich, Bologna, Tel Aviv, and Jerusalem. During the 1970s and 1980s Hartman was a key member of the group of literary critics known as the "Yale School," which was responsible for bringing poststructuralist philosophy, and especially the deconstructive thought of Jacques Derrida, to the American audience.

Since turning with increasing urgency toward engagement with the *Shoah* and Jewish questions in the 1980s, Hartman has written a series of illuminating essays, many of which have been collected in *The Longest Shadow* (1996) and has edited three works that left their mark on the fields of Jewish and Holocaust studies: *Midrash and Literature* (1986), *Bitburg in Moral and Political Perspective* (1986), and *Holocaust Remembrance* (1994). While Hartman has written movingly of his experience as a child refugee and escapee from Nazi Germany (in "The Longest Shadow," collected in the volume of that name), his favored genre is not autobiography or memoir but the essay. The range of Hartman's Holocaust-related essays mirrors the impressive scope of his writings in general and encompasses the most esoteric and the most worldly topics. Whether he is discussing the negative dialectics of Theodor Adorno and the difficult poetics of Paul Celan or the mechanics of collecting and archiving survivor testimony and the presence of the Holocaust in popular culture, Hartman brings a heightened literary sensitivity and a penchant for philosophical reflection to his work. As all of his writings make clear, and as Hartman himself remarks in *The Longest Shadow*, his primary intellectual concern has not been to change our understanding of the events of the Nazi period, but rather to interrogate the aftermath of the Holocaust—its belated refraction in literature, politics, popular culture, and especially memory.

Criticism after Auschwitz

Recent critical discourse has focused attention on what literature and culture can tell us about the implications and aftermath of the events of the Nazi genocide. This concern with the specifically post-Holocaust quality of our times goes back at least to Theodor Adorno's famous dictum from the early postwar period that "to write poetry after Auschwitz is barbaric" (Adorno, *Prisms*, MIT, 1981, p. 34)—a dictum that echoes especially throughout Hartman's *The Fateful Question of Culture* (1997). But there can be no doubt that systematic reflection on the aftermath of the Holocaust emerges most dramatically in the last two decades of the twentieth century. Hence, Hartman's turn to these questions takes place in a context that also includes the work of critics such as Shoshana Felman, Lawrence Langer, Dori Laub, Marianne Hirsch, and James Young. Within this group, Hartman's work is distinguished by its unusual combination of rigorous philosophical speculation with a subtle poetic sensibility. His allusive and sometimes playful style, which can also be found in his writings on romanticism and other topics, received theoretical justification in Yale School deconstruction, which argued that criticism should not be considered secondary to literature. Hartman's style has sometimes met with skepticism from those who value a more objective, scholarly voice, but there is much to be gained in considering an event that defies ordinary understanding through writing that systematically refuses sentimentality, formulaic response, and messages that are easily paraphrased.

In probing the aftermath—the "longest shadow," as he aptly names it—Hartman leaves no zone of contemporary culture and politics untouched, but his focus remains the same throughout: how to assess the relationship between knowledge, representation, and ethics. The final essay of *The Longest Shadow* states the issue powerfully:

> Today the relation of knowledge to the means of representation has changed. . . . We notice, on the one hand, an excess of knowledge, a plethora of detail about the "Final Solution" furnished by the techniques of modern historiography and the punctilious and overconfident recordkeeping of the perpetrators themselves. On the other hand, powerful visual media are at our disposition to convert this knowledge into simulacra of the original event. Questions arise, therefore, about the limits of representation: questions less about whether the extreme event can be represented than whether truth is served by our refusal to set limits to representation (Bloomington, Ind.: Indiana University Press, 1996, p. 151).

Here Hartman moves the matter of representing the extreme from a question of artists' technical ability to a more ethical terrain on which knowledge and truth do not necessarily converge. As this passage also makes clear, Hartman's thought is very much engaged with the present. That is, in all of his discussions about the *Shoah* he moves back and forth between what we know of the events and the actually existing conditions of knowledge which enable—or block—that knowledge. The power of the media to simulate, and sometimes to substitute for, the real are at the center of many of Hartman's reflections on the aftermath of the Holocaust, but they are not the only factors that trouble our attempts to serve truth.

The difficulty of establishing an ethical relationship between knowledge and representation also derives from the qualities of the events themselves. The Holocaust cannot be seen as "just another calamity": "its magnitude, its blatant criminality, its coordinated exploitation of all modern resources"—the "darkness" at its core—all suggest why "understanding comes and goes" and "has not been progressive" (*Longest Shadow*, pp. 37). If historical writing is critical in advancing knowledge, it is not sufficient. The literary critic's attention to problems of representation and affect can supplement history in necessary ways:

> while no recent event has elicited more documentation and analysis, knowledge has failed to become understanding. Moreover, though historians generally do not let feelings color their research, in this case the topic is approached with a transferential complexity that makes the task of description shakier: there is a mixture of numbness (leading to over-objectification) and emotionalism" (p. 39).

For Hartman, the attempt to move from knowledge to understanding involves negotiating between these two affective poles of distancing and identification. Certain works of literature engage in precisely this kind of negotiation, Hartman believes; he is a consistent defender of the kind of understanding that derives from close engagement with literary form. In recent years, however, he has consistently pointed to survivor video testimony as a privileged site for exploring the "transferential complexity" of knowledge in the aftermath of the Holocaust.

Hartman's work with the Fortunoff Video Archive at Yale not only demonstrates a personal commitment to fostering Holocaust memory, but involves an intellectual engagement with problems of media and pedagogy, as well as the literary critic's more habitual concern with representation. His paper on "Holocaust Testimony, Videography, and Education," for instance, focuses on how witness accounts "remind us that any history of the *Shoah* must include more than information" ("Holocaust Testimony, Videography, and Education," *Occasional Papers*, Queens, N. Y.: The Center for Jewish Studies, Queens College, 2001, p. 12). Video testimonies are "[r]esolutely autobiographical," but "reject a realism based on illusion," archival footage, or "reconstruction of the scenes evoked." Instead, they highlight the complex and dynamic "relation of telling to what is told" and sometimes capture "the survivor's defining struggle with trauma or loss," all of which brings these testimonies closer to "mourning" than to the "narrative desire" of conventional realist literature (pp. 14–15). Ultimately, he argues, video testimony plays two crucial roles that mediate "between a massive historiographic realism and either ritual or fictional representation": "[a]s a collective enterprise, as plural memory, videotestimony . . . provides the most human of documents and keeps something of oral tradition alive" (p. 17). In other words, such testimony helps to restore a dignified human image to people who have experienced extreme efforts to humiliate and dehumanize them. It also provides a pedagogical link to generations with no firsthand experience or memory of the events—or even, in the near future, with no chance of encountering anyone who has had such experience or memory. Paradoxically, this process of restitution and pedagogy takes place, as Hartman is at pains to mention, via a technology and a medium that can, in the wrong hands, easily abet the simulation and evacuation of historical memory.

Hartman's engagement with questions of technology and media intersects with another signature of his work: its suspicion of the politicization of memory. Critics of the aftermath have "the essential and ungrateful task of criticizing specific aspects of a Holocaust remembrance that turns into a politics of memory" (*Longest Shadow*, p. 42). Such politicization emerges for different reasons in different places, as Hartman knows well, but the crucial problem, as he sees it, is that for a postmodern world in which media simulation threatens to dissolve all claims to reality and authenticity, memory can become a realm of nostalgic and dangerous attempts to construct pure and exclusive identities. It is no surprise that a thinker who was physically displaced from his home because of the most infamous of such attempts would write that "[t]hose who seek an identity, personal, national, or racial, with an intensity that is equivalent to religious passion, seem to have returned" to delusion (p. 51).

Closely related to the suspicion of identity is a more general suspicion of all forms of ideological closure or resolution. Indeed, when Hartman writes of "deconstruction's care in avoiding premature or forced closure, a care which has no ideological motive but is directed against an anxiety that produces shortcuts to meaning" (*Longest Shadow*, p. 8), we begin to glimpse the themes that unite his work, both in its Yale School and Yale Video Archive periods. The inevitable "indeterminacy of meaning" that Hartman alludes to in his preface to the collective volume *Deconstruction and Criticism* (edited by Harold Bloom et al., New York: Continuum, 1979, p. viii) returns with a distinct historical and ethical charge in his writings on the Holocaust. Indeterminacy is not the source of Holocaust denial, Hartman rightly responds to those who see deconstruction as a source of negationism. Rather, the resistance to closure keeps Holocaust memory alive by refusing to let it rigidify in stereotypes and clichés. Furthermore, refusing "shortcuts to meaning" can serve as a constant spur to move from factual knowledge of the Holocaust toward a deeper and more complex understanding. With an intellectual and ethical force that few writers who did not experience the camps firsthand have mustered, Geoffrey Hartman moves us toward such understanding.

Bibliography

Primary Sources

Authored Books

The Unmediated Vision: An Interpretation of Wordsworth, Hopkins, Rilke and Valery. 1954.
André Malraux. 1960.
Wordsworth's Poetry 1787–1814. 1964.
Beyond Formalism: Selected Essays. 1970.
The Fate of Reading: Literary Essays 1970–75. 1975.
Akiba's Children. 1978.
Criticism in the Wilderness: The Study of Literature Today. 1980.
Saving the Text: Literature/Derrida/Philosophy. 1981.
Easy Pieces. 1985.
The Unremarkable Wordsworth. 1987.
Minor Prophecies: The Literary Essay in the Culture Wars. 1991.
The Longest Shadow: In the Aftermath of the Holocaust. 1996.
The Fateful Question of Culture. 1997.
A Critic's Journey: Literary Reflections 1958–1998. 1999.
Scars of the Spirit: The Struggle against Inauthenticity. 2002.

Edited Books

Hopkins: A Selection of Critical Essays. 1966.
Wordsworth: Selected Poetry and Prose. 1970.
New Perspectives on Coleridge and Wordsworth. 1972.
Romanticism: Vistas, Instances, Continuities. 1973.
Psychoanalysis and the Question of the Text. 1978.
Shakespeare and the Question of Theory. 1985.
Midrash and Literature. 1986.
Bitburg in Moral and Political Perspective. 1986.
Holocaust Remembrance: The Shapes of Memory. 1994.
Archiv der Erinnerung: Interviews mit Überlebenden der Shoah. 1998.

Selected Uncollected Essays

"Nerval's Peristyle." 1976–1977.
"The Response to Terror: Introductory Notes." 1983.
"Reading Aright: Keats' *Ode to Psyche*." 1983.
"Preserving the Personal Story." 1985.
"The Lesson of Bitburg." 1985–1986.
"The War against Memory." 1986.

"The Magic of Numbers/The Realism of Numbers." 1987.
"Judaic Studies: The Third Pillar." 1987.
"Religious Literacy." 1988.
"Blake's 'Speak Silence' in Literary History." 1989.
"Looking Back on Paul de Man." 1989.
"Who Is an Educated Jew?" 1989.
" 'Was It for This . . .?' Wordsworth and the Birth of the Gods." 1990.
"Stories before Our Eyes." 1988.
"The Encounter." 1992.
"English as Something Else." 1993.
"Midrash as Law and Literature." 1994.
"Jewish Tradition as/and the Other." 1993–1994.
"On Traumatic Knowledge and Literary Studies." 1995.
"The Fate of Reading Once More." 1996.
"The Blind Side of the Akedah." 1996.
" 'Breaking with Every Star': On Literary Knowledge." 1996.
"*Shoah* and Intellectual Witness." 1998.
"Aestheticide; or, Has Literary Study Grown Old?" 1999.
"Spirit and Letter." 1999.
"Aesthetic Sensibilities." *Tikkun* (January/February 2000).
"Memory.com: Tele-Suffering and Testimony in the Dot Com Era." 2000.
"A Life of Learning." 2000.
"Scattered Thoughts on *Aufmerksamkeit*." 2001.
"Contemporary Realism, Authenticity, and the New Biographical Culture." 2001.
"Holocaust Testimony, Videography, and Education." 2001.

Interviews

"Witnessing Video Testimony: An Interview with Geoffrey Hartman," by Jennifer Ballengee. *Yale Journal of Criticism* 14, no. 1 (spring 2001): 217–232.
"Interview: The Yale University Video Archive for Holocaust Testimonies." *Alphabet City* (fall 2001).

Secondary Sources

Atkins, G. Douglas. "Geoffrey H. Hartman." *Dictionary of Literary Biography, Volume 67: Modern American Critics since 1955*. Edited by Gregory S. Jay. New York: The Gale Group, 1988, pp. 134–150.
Bernstein, Michael André. "The Lasting Injury." *Times Literary Supplement* (7 March 1997): 3–4.
Clarke, Simone. Review of *The Longest Shadow. Holocaust and Genocide Studies* 12, no. 2 (fall 1998): 345–348.
Jacobson, Joanne. "Speech after Long Silence." *The Nation* (11 November 1996): 30–32.
Kurzweil, Edith. "The Holocaust: Memory and Theory." *Partisan Review* 63, no. 3 (1996): 356–373.
Pinsker, Sanford. "Memory, between Closure and Obsession." *Salmagundi* 112 (fall 1996): 226–236.
Simpson, David. "Virtual Culture: Geoffrey Hartman, *The Fateful Question of Culture*." *Modern Language Quarterly* 60, no. 2 (June 1999): 251–264.
Sprinker, Michael. "Aesthetic Criticism: Geoffrey Hartman." In *The Yale Critics: Deconstruction in America*. Edited by Jonathan Arac, Wlad Godzich, and Wallace Martin. Minneapolis, Minn.: University of Minnesota Press, 1983, pp. 43–65.

JOHN HERSEY

(1914–1993)

ROBERT FRANCIOSI

BORN IN TIETSIN (now Tianjin), China, in 1914, where he lived until 1925, John Hersey was the son of Methodist missionaries, Roscoe and Grace Baird Hersey. He graduated from Yale University in 1933, studied at Cambridge University for a year, then worked as private secretary to the novelist Sinclair Lewis. A journalist for *Time* magazine during the 1930s and 1940s, his service as a war correspondent yielded such works as *Into the Valley* (1943), on the battle for Guadalcanal; "Survival," his famous account of John F. Kennedy and PT-109; and his first novel, *A Bell for Adano* (1944), which won a Pulitzer Prize in 1945. A year after the war ended, "Hiroshima," Hersey's long essay on Japanese A-bomb survivors, comprised an entire issue of *The New Yorker* and became a multimedia sensation. Despite continued journalistic success in the late 1940s, Hersey devoted the rest of his career largely to fiction, publishing fifteen novels, two collections of stories, and nine books of reportage or essays. Hersey died in 1993 at his home in Key West, Florida.

Besides *The Wall* (1950), his epic novel on the Warsaw ghetto, Hersey engaged the Holocaust in several wartime reports for *Life* magazine, in an early story, "A Short Wait" (1947), and in a pair of articles for *The New Yorker* based on visits to Israel in 1952 and 1974, one dealing with Holocaust survivors, the other with their children.

The Wall

Hersey's visit to Hiroshima in 1946 and his conversations with A-bomb victims impelled him, almost immediately, to begin research for a novel on another horrific chapter in the annals of the twentieth century, one he had encountered as a reporter during the war's final winter—the destruction of Europe's Jews. Published in 1950, and modeled in part on Emmanuel Ringelblum's ghetto archives, *Oneg Shabbat*, Hersey's *The Wall* is not only an epic account of the Warsaw ghetto's life and death but arguably the first American novel centered on the Holocaust. When Hersey began writing his book, a wealth of materials on the ghetto was just being published, and in the case of Ringelblum's buried archive, literally being unearthed. Based on these materials, *The Wall* details events between September 1939, when Warsaw fell to the Germans, and April 1943, when a handful of young Jews actively fought the Germans for nearly a month. Two years before Anne Frank's diary would captivate American readers and more than a decade before the Eichmann trial would at last force many Jewish American writers to address the Holocaust, Hersey had arrived at the *terminus a quo* of serious engagement with Auschwitz, especially for those without firsthand experience. By trying to imagine the unimaginable, to convey through language what seemed beyond its capabilities, Hersey faced what Alvin Rosenfeld astutely cites as the fundamental challenge posed by the "post-Auschwitz imagination": "when fact itself surpasses fiction, what is there left for the novel and the short story to do?" (Rosenfeld, p. 66).

Perhaps only a journalist would have attempted as early as 1947 to write fiction about the recent murder of six million Jews. The subject, however, ultimately pulled Hersey away from the reportage that had served him on the Russian front or in Hiroshima's ruins and pushed him toward a new type of historical fiction, what he later termed "the novel of contemporary history." Early in 1947, after finishing "A Short Wait," a story about a Lodz ghetto survivor who is reunited with her American relatives, Hersey embarked on what must have seemed a logical course for any writer hoping to understand the extermination of Europe's Jews—he spent several days interviewing an Auschwitz survivor. Not until his 1962 collection, *Here to*

Stay, though, would the piece he drafted from these conversations, "Prisoner 107,907," be published. Whereas his notes on the Lodz ghetto had led to a short story, Hersey's discussions with the camp survivor dissuaded him from attempting to write on Auschwitz or another death camp. In a 1952 essay on his writing of *The Wall*, "The Mechanics of a Novel," Hersey explained that he felt the world of the camps had so dehumanized the prisoners that it would be impossible to turn their experiences into fiction. Yet if prisoners in the camps had "been degraded by their experiences to a subhuman, animal level," those in the ghetto, Hersey realized, "had lived on as families to the very end, and had maintained at least vestiges and symbols of those things we consider civilization—theaters, concerts, readings of poetry, and the rituals of everyday human intercourse" (*Yale University Library Gazette* 7 [July 1952], p. 5). Especially for an American audience, then, a book on the Warsaw ghetto would achieve what Hersey later described as the novel of contemporary history's ability to illuminate the lives of ordinary people caught in history's snares. That he chose to write about Warsaw rather than Lodz, which had been the subject of "A Short Wait" and which would subsequently inspire Leslie Epstein and others writers, seems based on two factors: the fictional possibilities of the climactic ghetto uprising of April 1943 and the wealth of documentary materials available on the Warsaw ghetto.

Plunging into materials on the Warsaw ghetto, however, even just a few years after its destruction, was an almost overwhelming task. Hersey soon discovered "a tremendous amount of material about Warsaw and the other ghettos written in Polish and Yiddish, diaries, records of organizations, letters, statistical data, medical histories, poems, plays, songs—all sorts of testimony" ("Mechanics," p. 5). He knew these materials were unlikely to appear in English, but he also recognized how absolutely essential they were to his project. Here was the full range of the ghetto's voice in all its registers of anguish and defiance—if only he could understand it. Gaining access to those Eastern European texts, he understood, required the help of knowledgeable translators, and Hersey was especially fortunate in this respect, employing as his Yiddish expert, for instance, the young Lucy Dawidowicz, who would become a foremost Holocaust scholar, publishing among many works her acclaimed *The War Against the Jews 1933–45* (1975).

By using the Warsaw ghetto as his focus, Hersey also knew that he faced two major challenges: to convey the sweep of events within this traumatic history and, more important, to bring a human dimension to the mass death of the Hitler era. He accomplished the first by resorting to a device as old as the novel itself—the fictional archive. *The Wall* is built upon a series of dated entries from the "Levinson Archive." Recovered after the war by a handful of ghetto survivors, the archive, Hersey's fictional editor explains, "has scant precedent": "it is not so formidable as history; it is more than notes for a history; it is not fiction—Levinson was too scrupulous to imagine *anything*; it is not merely a diary; it is neither journalism nor a journal in the accepted modes" (New York: Knopf, 1950, p. 6). Indeed, Hersey's imagining of the archive—with hundreds of dated entries from November 1939 to May 1943, with every detail based on facts from the ghetto's history, with actual *Judenrat* and Nazi documents incorporated, with the full range of Jewish political and cultural life given voice—was so convincing that many readers wrote to him asking where they could view the Levinson Archive, or attacked him for so deceiving his audience.

Yet, Hersey realized as well that those many excerpts from the Levinson Archive (which, his editor tells us, represents only one-twentieth of its four million words!), their sheer unwieldiness, necessitated using another device to anchor the book, one he found by focusing on what he termed "The Family," a small group of ghetto residents whose lives are thrust together. Using this family as his dramatic focus—with the commentary of the archivist Noach Levinson serving a choric function—Hersey manages to tell the larger story of the Warsaw ghetto while retaining a sense of intimacy with the characters. Through the character of Rachel Apt, for example (based on the famous underground leader Zivia Lubetkin), he not only illustrates clandestine educational efforts in the ghetto but ultimately places us squarely within the world of the Jewish Fighters Organization, while others bring to life the *Judenrat*, the Bund, the Jewish Police, even the Jewish labor crews who built the ghetto wall. And with his persistent focus on Dolek Berson, the "drifter" figure whose life touches nearly all elements of the ghetto, Hersey also depicted the transformation of Warsaw's Jews from passivity to active resistance.

Given its author's aspirations, the complexities of *The Wall* are many. Consider a representative section, one recounting the period when Warsaw's Jews learn that "resettlement" in fact means death at the extermination camp of Treblinka. Like all entries in *The Wall*, it begins with dated headings, a source attribution, then a comment:

> Events August 5–12, 1942. Entry August 12, 1942, N.L. [Noach Levinson] An appalling week. Quite apart from the news Slonim brought us, this has been the worst week we have had in the resettlement (p. 326).

The archivist then continues with a day-by-day (and historically accurate) list of the staggering numbers of deported Jews, concluding: "Grand total to date: 149,162." Such historical specificity, though, soon yields to Levinson's own meditations on what he sees as another appalling loss. The "Small Ghetto" is being emptied and the *Judenrat* office moved: "The Germans allowed us to bring typewriters and office equipment from the Grzybowska building, but *so far I have not been permitted to bring my archive*." In a sense, Levinson's fears for his archive reflect his belief that paper records will be the Jews' "only estate." "We will leave no children," he notes. "The Germans cart away our furniture and all our personal possessions as soon as they lock us into the trains. There is nothing to leave behind but history" (p. 327). Yet within this same entry, Hersey also demonstrates his ability to depict the massive tragedy of the ghetto in intimate terms, using the mention of the furniture as a prompt for one of the novel's most unforgettable moments.

Two members of "The Family" are assigned to a German detail that loots possessions from the homes of deported Jews. (Like nearly all of Hersey's "Family," they have secure jobs exempting them from the transports, perhaps one of the book's few false notes.) Reb Yechiel Mazur reports to Levinson that in a particularly tasteful apartment, he and Rabbi Goldflamm came across a beautiful rosewood box that contained a note from its owner, Rega Farbszmul. She had received the gift from her husband just before their first child's birth, though that baby was stillborn and they never had another. The box, she writes, represents those unborn children, and by implication, all the Jewish children never to be born. She then addresses its likely future owners: "If you be a German who takes this box into your home, you must know that you have taken Jewishness into your home, you have adopted the Farbszmuls, for ever and ever. You will consider this a curse. I consider this a very great blessing, for you, though possibly not for the Farbszmuls" (p. 329). Her note ends with the Shema: "Hear, O Israel: the Lord, our God, the Lord is One!" The two men decide to leave the note in the rosewood box, though they copy it for Levinson, and finally place the box in a handcart of goods "destined for the homes of high-ranking Nazis."

The ways in which even this brief section resonates throughout the novel express both the complexity and the care of Hersey's construction. Within a few chapters Reb Mazur will disappear during a roundup, but only after experiencing the betrayal of his son, Stefan, a Jewish police officer who attempts to use his parents to fill out a deportation quota. Rabbi Goldflamm will disappear in the September 1943 roundup, called "The Kettle" by ghetto inhabitants, but not before declaring to Berson that Jewish faith will survive "because a system that is based upon love and respect will outlive any system that is based upon hatred and contempt," though in a typically sardonic note, Levinson wonders how this "benign system will remain so vigorous when all its practitioners are dead" (p. 369). And Frau Mazur, fearing for the safety of her pregnant daughter, Rutka, will volunteer to go to the *Umschlagplatz*, our last view of her (again based on an actual ghetto record) calling to mind the piety and honor of the rosewood box's owner: "She carried with her nothing but a pair of slippers, symbolizing readiness for death, and a pair of candles, to make her prayers go straight to God" (p. 483).

Although some critics of Hersey's novel have challenged his understanding of Jewish culture, the responses from American Jews in 1950 were not only largely positive but even adulatory, with one writer claiming that reading *The Wall* caused him to recover his faith. Such a response may say more about Jewish American culture than the novel, yet even if Hersey's six-hundred-page book only scratches the surface of Jewish experience during World War II, it nevertheless provided all American readers in 1950 with one of the most complete fictional treatments of the Nazis' genocidal practice: from ghettoization to extermination.

Hersey's use of the fictional archive to face the Holocaust may have exposed fiction's limitations, as the critic Alvin Rosenfeld argues, by implicitly acknowledging that "the literary imagination cannot gain sufficient authority in its own terms but must yield to the terms of legitimacy that belong to documentary evidence" (Rosenfeld, p. 66). Yet in suggesting that readers of Hersey's novel, whatever its dramatic interest, might prefer "the actual historical testimonies we do have," Rosenfeld underestimates the valuable intermediary role played by historical fictions such as *The Wall*, especially those books published during the immediate postwar years. Offering its American readers emotional entrance to the Holocaust's trauma through a fictional experience based upon scrupulous research, Hersey's novel played a crucial role in bringing this reality to American understanding. As Hersey told the *Paris Review* thirty-five years after its publication, many "more authentic works" than *The Wall* have come from survivors; but in its postwar moment *The Wall* "may have helped people to understand things they hadn't understood before" (Dee, p. 247). By building *The Wall* in such an honest and painstaking fashion, John Hersey may have also helped certain Americans in 1950 to move beyond horrific images of the liberated camps and toward a deeper understanding of the destruction of European Jewry.

Conclusion

"The Holocaust," Hilene Flanzbaum has noted, "is everywhere in American cultural consciousness today." Many have condemned this Americanization, yet as Flanzbaum wisely declares, "the pervasive presence of representations of the Holocaust in our culture demands responsible evaluation and interpretation" (Flanzbaum, p. 8). If, as many have argued, the Holocaust is the central event of our time, an era often termed the "American Century," then understanding how Americans have faced this catastrophe is especially appropriate. Emerging so early in the development of our Holocaust consciousness, Hersey's *The Wall* and its many adaptations remain a rich resource for better understanding this cultural phenomenon.

Bibliography

Primary Sources

Men in Bataan. 1942.
Into the Valley, A Skirmish of the Marines. 1943.
A Bell for Adano. 1944.
Hiroshima. 1946.
"A Short Wait." 1947.
The Wall. 1950.
"The Mechanics of a Novel." 1952.
The Marmot Drive. 1953.
A Single Pebble. 1956.
The War Lover. 1959.
The Child Buyer. 1960.
Here to Stay: Studies of Human Tenacity. 1962.
White Lotus. 1965.
Too Far to Walk. 1966.
Under the Eye of the Storm. 1967.
The Algiers Motel Incident. 1968.
Letter to the Alumni. 1970.
The Conspiracy. 1972.
My Petition for More Space. 1974.
The President. 1975.
The Walnut Door. 1977.
Aspects of the Presidency. 1980.
The Call. 1985.
Blues. 1987.
Fling and Other Stories. 1990.
Antonietta. 1991.
Key West Tales. 1994.

Secondary Sources

Ezrahi, Sidra DeKoven. *By Words Alone: The Holocaust in Literature*. Chicago: University of Chicago Press, 1980.
Flanzbaum, Hilene. *The Americanization of the Holocaust*. Baltimore: Johns Hopkins University Press, 1999.
Lampell, Millard. *The Wall, A Play in Two Acts*. New York: Knopf, 1961.
———. *The Wall, A Drama in Three Acts*. New York: Samuel French, 1964.
Rosenfeld, Alvin H. *A Double Dying: Reflections on Holocaust Literature*. Bloomington: Indiana University Press, 1980.
Sanders, David. *John Hersey Revisited*. Boston: Twayne, 1991.
Schwarz, Daniel. *Imagining the Holocaust*. New York: St. Martin's Press, 1999.

Interview and Archives

Dee, Jonathan. "The Art of Fiction XCII: John Hersey." *Paris Review* 100 (1986): 210–249.
Manuscripts are located in the John Hersey Collection, part of the American Literature Collection at the Beinecke Rare Book and Manuscript Library, Yale University.

MARCIE HERSHMAN

(1951–)

THANE ROSENBAUM

MARCIE HERSHMAN WAS born on 2 May 1951, in Cleveland, Ohio, to Eugene and Phyllis Hershman. She was the first of four children (Robert, born 1953; Clifford, born 1955; and Daniel, born 1959). She grew up in Shaker Heights, Ohio, going through the public school system and enjoying the support of a close, extended family. She was influenced by the stories told to her by her grandmother, Anna Polak Weiss, who had spent her early life in a small Hungarian village, and had immigrated to the United States in 1921. Anna Weiss's heartfelt silence about the fate of her and her husband Harry's families, taken to concentration camps and murdered during World War II, inspired Hershman's acclaimed novels, *Tales of the Master Race* (1991) and *Safe in America* (1995). Hershman is also the author of a memoir, *Speak to Me* (2001), which was inspired by the death of her brother, Robert.

Hershman's reviews and essays have appeared in many publications, including the *New York Times Magazine*, the *Boston Globe*, *Poets & Writers*, *Ploughshares*, *Agni*, and *Tikkun*, and in anthologies such as *Home: Twenty Writing Women Remember*, *Wrestling with the Angel: Jewish Meditations on Death and Mourning*, and *The Beacon Best of 1999: Creative Writing of Women and Men of All Colors*. Among her awards are those from the Bunting Institute of Harvard/Radcliffe College, the LL Winship Foundation, the St. Botolph Foundation, the Massachusetts Artists Foundation, the Corporation of Yaddo, and the MacDowell Colony. She was appointed the 1999/2001 Fannie Hurst Writer-in-Residence at Brandeis University; her regular appointment is at Tufts University. She was elected to the executive board of PEN/New England in 1997.

Hershman received her B.A. in English language and literature, and graduated summa cum laude from Boston University, in 1973. She went on to earn a master's degree in American literature from the University of Massachusetts in Boston in 1978, where she was on a full academic scholarship.

Hershman lives in Brookline, Massachusetts, with her partner, Rebecca Blunk, and is active on behalf of the Brookline Public Library and other civic concerns.

Hershman and the Holocaust

In an essay published in the November/December 1996 issue of *Poets & Writers* magazine titled "The World and the Library," Hershman explained what historical and personal impulses motivated the writing of her first novel, *Tales of the Master Race*.

> What I needed to know, the question that I spent three years trying to answer . . . was this: Who saw my great-grandmother, Frieda Polak, taken out of her house, put on a wagon, and driven to Auschwitz? Who saw that happen? Had her neighbors seen her in the doorway, or standing in the cart? Surely they must have. That's what a neighborhood is about: we do witness each other's lives, even if out of the corner of an eye.

This is the poignant, tender genesis of *Tales of the Master Race*, which is a true masterpiece of Holocaust literature. In creating this work, Hershman set a new standard by an American novelist for bringing fiction to the Holocaust without trampling on the profound sensibilities that are normally associated with Holocaust art. Aware of Theodor Adorno's dictum that no poetry should arise out of the ashes of Auschwitz, Hershman places *Tales of the Master Race* within the war years, in Germany, within the center of the murderous storm that would claim the lives of six million Jews, yet she makes no art out of Jewish mass death. The novel does not fictionalize the underworld of the concentration camps, or the open-grave ditches of the forests, but rather focuses on an imaginary Bavarian town, Kreiswald, and the Aryans who live there—peacefully, domestically, patriotically—as if nothing special or extraordinary is happening to their Jewish neighbors.

Hershman's Holocaust fiction, represented in her highly original and groundbreaking first novel, is not the story and misery of the Jews, which so many have chronicled by way of personal memoir. Instead, she is after something far more complex and unknowable. In *Tales of the Master Race*, Hershman unleashes her imagination on the Germans themselves, and not necessarily on the Nazis, but rather on middle-class townspeople. What were they thinking, how did they conduct their lives, what pressures were they under, and what imperatives guided them, ultimately fueling their indifference while their Jewish neighbors were being carted off and taken to their deaths?

In so many ways, *Tales of the Master Race* offers perfect literary companion reading to Daniel Jonah Goldhagen's *Hitler's Willing Executioners: Ordinary Germans and the Holocaust*. Both books are essential to gaining insight about, and the perspective of, the bystanders. *Tales of the Master Race* asks how Germans went about their ordinary, mundane affairs, making the necessary moral compromises and adjustments, knowing full well that the lives of their Jewish neighbors were ruthlessly and irrevocably ending. In the novel, the Germans of Kreiswald play music in marching bands in support of the war effort, they make maps and carry on affairs of both business and heart, their children try out for gymnastic teams. In the basement of their police stations, their own countrymen, other Aryans, are being beheaded, while others are killed in hospitals because they are either infirm, subhuman, or physically useless to the Reich.

All the while Jews lurk in the margins of *Tales of the Master Race*. They are the unmentionable, and therefore they are barely mentioned—even as characters. They are nothing but shadows and muffled sounds in the backdrop. They are our imaginary former friends, now forgotten and exploited—completely invisible to the good, ordinary Germans of Kreiswald. We barely see them being taken away, or discussed in passing, insulted in public, herded into wagons—all the while the life of Kreiswald goes on.

Targood Stella, the young policeman in *Tales of the Master Race* whose wife eventually runs away with his commanding officer and who is terrified and wants no part of the guillotine that operates in the basement of the police station says:

> You think because we lived in the middle of those twelve years that we didn't see hate anymore? Not so. We saw it but we pretended, with that little whisper of knowledge . . . that such slight awareness was good. The hairbreadth is what kept us safe. No more and no less. Any more awareness and we might be compelled into taking a dangerous stance: any less and we'd be screaming, *Filth out! One people! One country*!—the same phrases that blackened the pages of what once was simply a town newspaper (New York: HarperCollins Publishers, 1991, p. 9).

This is precisely the kind of "middle knowledge" that Robert Jay Lifton identified in his monumental book, *The Nazi Doctors* (New York: Basic Books, 1986). So much of the human response to atrocity is defined by the preference to remain unaware, to distance the moral mind-set so that one can go about his or her day without emotional conflict and ambivalence despite the fact that that very day is cursed with horror. The lifeblood of the bystander is the capacity to depersonalize, to embrace all the possibilities that come with distraction, to split the moral sphere of existence and private conscience from one's professional duties and public stance. Targood Stella later narrates: "History can separate the first from the second night, the first from the second fact. Memory, softhearted and perhaps not as shrewd as its more public relative, just wants to hold things intact" (p. 12).

And so Hershman shows us life among those who have surrendered to the gradual formation of history without any obligation to the emotional imperatives of memory. One character who launders wash says: "Surely the Jews understand the predicament. . . . No one wants to be where they're not wanted" (pp. 85–86). Another Aryan character mocks the fate of the Jews by imitating a Jewish response that will elicit absolutely no sympathy, even though as neighbors they once all belonged to the same community organizations: "How can you do this to us? Yes, we're Jews, but we're part of the membership" (p. 91). Much later in the novel, when Jews are being rounded up, an Aryan mother who is about to lose her half-Jewish children pleads to a unmoved SS man: "No! My children are half-Aryan, their blood is half mine. . . . They're supposed to be privileged." The SS man replies: "Please . . . think of your neighbors. They're right in front, watching" (p. 189).

The novel unfolds in a fragmented, fractured, postmodern style, with multiple narrators and equally varying points of view. The chapters are delineated as portraits of a Bavarian town in both denial and suffering from righteous complicity. Characters return in subsequent chapters, and others disappear. Some moments are merely suggestive. There is heartache throughout, and betrayal, and of course, indifference, but Hershman shows us decent Germans as well, those who are deemed traitors, who will perhaps find themselves under the blade of a guillotine, and others who are merely going along because they know of no other way to respond. They simply want the time to pass. Germany, after all, is overcome by a moral eclipse, and Hershman's fictional Kreiswald is a stunning literary representation of these moral suspensions in a time of great inhumanity and indifference.

Perhaps it's no accident that Hershman chose to write and tell this story, in this particular way. In addition to her familial connections to the Holocaust, there is also her interest in the daily occurrences of human life, and how the ordinary and mundane speaks so loudly about the larger forces and conditions that surround us. In an essay on the New England Holocaust Memorial that originally appeared in *Architecture Boston*, she wrote:

> Sometimes the truth is what we hide best from ourselves. The truth? The Holocaust occurred in the marketplace. It happened amid daily life, busy lives. You couldn't not see how other people—Jews, usually—were ordered through the center of town. . . . History happens in the center of things. It happens when you are buying flowers ("Boston's Holocaust Memorial").

These are the sounds that Hershman so frequently listens to and deploys in her fiction. It is the truth found in the everyday occurrence, the otherwise unnoticeable gesture, the unremarkable moment that one day proves itself to have always been brightly shining, coded with deep messages, so obviously indispensable.

Safe in America, Hershman's second novel, also has a Holocaust component, but from a completely different perspective and geographic setting. The novel is a quintessentially Jewish-American tale, and in telling the story of the Eichenbaums of Cleveland and their thwarted efforts to save their European relatives, Hershman introduces us to yet another dimension of paralysis and helplessness when it came to the fate of Jews during the Holocaust. In writing about her second novel, Hershman explains:

> I hoped to understand what it means to be safe when those you love are not safe at all. . . . I looked to my grandparents' generation yet again: safe in America they surely were, but they had to live each day here with the knowledge that they weren't able to save parents and siblings, back in a Europe gone mad with hate.

The novel looms with a sense of desperation and impotence as the Eichenbaums fight the combined vice grip of bureaucracy, diplomacy, and moral indifference that prevented so many from escaping the Third Reich. *Safe in America* takes its cue from Franz Kafka's *The Trial*, although the former is a far more narrative and plot-sensitive novel. The grinding realization that there are large, faceless institutional and organizational forces at work that influence most decisions over life, death, and those moments in between are unmistakable in both works. Hershman reconstructs letters, depositions, and sponsorship applications to places as far reaching as Cuba and Portugal, illustrating the numbness and madness that arises out of impotence. In *Tales of the Master Race*, there is an almost lulling, languid sensation that comes from a community distanced morally and emotionally from the horrific events that surround them. In *Safe in America*, there is an equally jarring sense that rescue has its limitations, that it's so easy to feel thwarted in such an unsafe world where family members simply cannot protect one another, no matter how well-intentioned the devotion, or grave the risk.

Critical Reaction

Hershman's Holocaust-themed novels have received great praise. Writing about *Tales of the Master Race* in the *Boston Globe*, Geoffrey Stokes said:

> It is difficult to overstate the depth of Hershman's achievement. She has created a full canvas of absolutely believable (and not always likable) characters who are feeling their way through a fog of corruption that fouls everything it touches—including them. She has such control, such delicacy, such fury and such power that it is hard to believe this is a first novel; it seems the achievement of a lifetime (p. 3).

In *Time Out* in London, England, Jane Solanas wrote:

> Let's face it, one would not expect a sensitive, utterly convincing and "slim" novel about Hitler's Third Reich to emerge from America—but Hershman's debut novel is a genuinely brilliant achievement. Hershman creates a truly disturbing portrait of a town whose very banality makes it the perfect receptacle for evil.

Writing for *Washington Post Book World*, Bob Allen wrote:

> You don't have to read far to grasp the deadly irony of this book's title. These everyday Germans, rather than members of a "master race" are, in reality, a nation of little people: ultra-conformists who are unable or unwilling to see beyond their own immediate fear and self-interest as they succumb to the institutionalized evil from on high that eventually filters down into the smallest atoms of society.

And finally, writing in the *New York Times*, Michiko Kakutani observed,

> Although Ms. Hershman rarely refers to the Nazis, the horrors of the Holocaust are never far from her characters'

> stories. Indeed, each person is in some way touched by Hitler's policy of genocide or implicated in it, even if most of them try to ignore the shocking realities by focusing willfully on the minutiae of their daily lives. . . . The reader is made to see how people like them were able to ignore or rationalize the events happening around them in Hitler's Germany, and to understand by implication how the Holocaust was made possible.

Safe in America received similar critical praise. In the *Boston Globe*, Edith Milton wrote:

> Marcie Hershman followed an honorable and rather brave impulse when she undertook to write this book, which is the necessary companion and balance to her first novel. . . . *Safe in America,* also set in a provincial city and concerned with the same wartime years, is—as its title, not entirely ironically, suggests—the American antithesis to that cataclysm, chronicling a single family's decent survival in a disintegrating world. . . . *Safe in America* plays with the resonance between those ordinary griefs and changes that time wreaks in every life and the extraordinary drama of violence in progress outside the novel's framework. . . . What is most striking about this writing (is) the extraordinary authenticity of its historical, geographical and medical detail. . . . *Safe in America* informs us that neither destruction nor salvation is ever likely to be final, and that even the Eichenbaums of Cleveland—spared by a catastrophe that has erased the rest of their world—are ultimately no safer than anyone else. It is, in Hershman's hands, an incongruously hopeful thought.

And writing for *Jewish Book World*, Shana Mauer wrote:

> Despite the myriad of literature surrounding the Holocaust and its aftermath, a conspicuous gap has remained in telling of its history. Until now the perspective of those who were outside of Europe, timidly shaking off the cultural garb of the very world that was being destroyed, the immigrant Jews of the United States, had remained elusive. . . . Hershman has managed to create people with a story rather than caricatures that lend themselves to the historical setting. . . . *Safe in America* . . . speaks to a void in modern Jewish literature.

Conclusion

Hershman's contribution to Holocaust literature is invaluable and immense. She approaches the Holocaust with the heart of a novelist and the fidelity of a historian. Actual, reproduced documents are inserted throughout her novels, as if to ground her imagination in the hard reality and real events of the times she seeks to evoke and comprehend. No other American novelist has been more original and unsparing in the treatment of the Holocaust than Hershman. She has brought to life a world that is marked only by madness and mass death, and without showing any images of death, she has re-created the lives of those who were forced to cope, compromise, and endure the moral black hole that was the Holocaust.

Bibliography

Primary Sources

Tales of the Master Race. 1991.

"No Burden to Bear." *New York Times Magazine* (4 October 1992): "Hers" column.

Safe in America. 1995.

"The World and the Library." *Poets & Writers* (November 1996).

"Boston's Holocaust Memorial." *Architecture Boston* (fall 1998). Also published as "Where Markets Converge." *The Beacon Best of 1999: Creative Writing by Women & Men of All Colors*. 1999.

Speak to Me: Grief, Love and What Endures. 2001.

Secondary Sources

Claffey, Charles E. "History in Fiction." *Boston Globe*, 18 February 1992, pp. 49, 53.

Frost, Bridget. Review of *Tales of the Master Race*. *Writers' Monthly* [London] (December 1991): 10.

Hubbard, Kim. Review of *Safe in America*. *People*, 21 August 1995, p. 29.

Kehl, D. G., and Frank Katz. "Conversation with Marcie Hershman." *Studies in American Jewish Literature: The Silver Mosaic: American Jewish Literature in the New Millenium* 19 (2000): 63–73.

Kendall, Elaine. Review of *Tales of the Master Race*. *Los Angeles Times*, 27 December 1991, E5.

Kukatani, Michiko. Review of *Tales of the Master Race*. *New York Times*, 17 December 1991, C19.

Leviant, Curt. Review of *Tales of the Master Race*. *Forward* (January 2, 1992): 9–10.

"Marcie Hershman." *Contemporary Authors*. 2002. GaleNet. http://www.infotrac.galegroup.com

Milton, Edith. Review of *Safe in America*. *Boston Globe*, 14 May 1995, pp. 48, 50.

Mojtabai, A. G. Review of *Safe in America*. *New York Times Book Review*, 10 December 1995, p. 32.

Review of *Tales of the Master Race*. *Washington Post Book World*, 3 November 1991, p. 10.

Stokes, Geoffrey. Review of *Tales of the Master Race*. *Boston Sunday Globe*, 17 November 1991, Arts/3.

Sultan, Rosemarie C. "Speaking out of the Silence: Making History Real." *Sojourner* (March 1997): 37.

Vice, Lisa. Review of *Tales of the Master Race*. *San Francisco Chronicle*, 30 July 1995, p. 5.

ABEL HERZBERG
(1893–1989)

DICK VAN GALEN LAST

> Not six million Jews were murdered, one Jew was murdered and that happened six million times. So, if one really wants to explain what the persecution of the Jews meant, one has to write six million biographies of these six million individuals (Interview, *Hervormd Nederland*, 4 May 1985, p. 41).

ABEL JACOB HERZBERG was born in Amsterdam on 17 September 1893, the only son of Russian emigrants Abraham Michael Herzberg and Rebekka Person. Herzberg's grandparents had fled the pogroms in Russia for safe haven in tolerant Holland, a country whose Jews were fully emancipated. Abraham was a diamond merchant who educated Abel and his two sisters with reverence for knowledge and sent them to a non-Jewish municipal school. At his *bat mitzvah*, Abel received 130 presents, among them the complete works of poets Johann Goethe, Johann Schiller, and Heinrich Heine.

In 1912 Abel began studying law at the Municipal University of Amsterdam, and became a lawyer in 1919. Although still a Russian citizen, he served in the Dutch military during World War I, and was naturalized as a Dutch citizen in 1922.

In 1923, Abel married Thea Loeb, the offspring of a German-Jewish family, and a law student at a time when female students were the exception. She gave birth to three children. Judith, the youngest (born 1934), became a poet and playwright.

Zionism

In 1907 Abel, aged thirteen, attended the Eighth Congress of the Zionist World Organization with his parents. The mild antisemitism he had encountered had convinced him that Jews would always be threatened as long as they lacked their own land: Only the existence of a Jewish state in Palestine could solve the "Jewish Problem." He was convinced that he would live to see a Jewish state. After the establishment of Israel in 1948, Herzberg traveled almost annually to Israel, but he never settled there, as did his two elder children.

As early as 1917, as a member of the Dutch Zionist Student Organisation (NZSO), Herzberg began propagating his Zionist views. Later he wrote for the journal of the Nederlandse Zionisten Bond, *De Joodse Wachter* (The Jewish Watch).

The Nederlandse Zionisten Bond (NZB—the Dutch Zionist Bond), founded in 1899, never had more than a few thousand members. Unlike Eastern European Jews, Dutch Jews simply did not feel threatened. Indeed, Holland's orthodox Jews were fervently anti-Zionist. From 1934 to 1939, Abel Herzberg was chairman of the NZB. His convictions burgeoned: assimilation was illusory; Zionism was both a political and cultural movement—a Jewish Renaissance.

Abel Herzberg recognized the dangers of National Socialism even before Hitler took power. Herzberg's brother-in-law, the German Jew and lawyer Wilhelm Spiegel, was one of the first victims of Nazism. He was shot dead in Kiel by two Nazis on 12 March 1933. Herzberg, deeply shocked, understood that much worse was to come. His play, *Vaderland* (Fatherland, 1934), examines spreading antisemitism and its answer, Palestine. At the time, however, he was among a very few warning against Nazism.

The German Occupation

Abel Herzberg continued to write for *De Joodse Wachter* until the Germans, who occupied the Netherlands in May 1940, forbade its publication on 20 September. The NZB was dissolved in 1941, the year in which Herzberg worked briefly with the Jewish Council, and was on the editorial board of its weekly *Het Joodse Weekblad*.

Herzberg and his family refused to go into hiding and were interned in Barneveld in early 1943. Barneveld, in central Netherlands, was a small town where hundreds of the most "valuable" Dutch Jews (the *Verdienstjuden*) were kept, exempt from deportation to Eastern Europe—at least that was what the Germans led them to believe. In reality, they were to be sent to Theresienstadt. In May 1943, the Herzberg family was put on the so-called Palestine List, making them eligible to be exchanged for Germans in Palestine. On 29 September 1943, the *Verdienstjuden* were sent to the transit camp Westerbork in northeastern Netherlands. The three Herzberg children went into hiding on the same day their parents went to Westerbork. In her play, *Leedvermaak* (Malicious Pleasure), written long after the war, Judith Herzberg wrote of the wounds this separation caused.

In Westerbork, Abel Herzberg chose to be sent to Bergen-Belsen over Theresienstadt. He still hoped to be exchanged for Germans in Palestine. He met Philip Mechanicus in Westerbork, whom he characterized as "a reporter until death." They met again in Bergen-Belsen, where Abel and his wife, Thea, arrived on 11 January 1944, in the Jewish *Sternlager*, so named for the star Jews had to wear.

Ecce Homo

It was Nazi policy at the height of the Holocaust to preserve small groups of "privileged" Jews for possible exchange with Allied-held German civilians. In the Bergen-Belsen *Sternlager*, prisoner "privilege" amounted to being kept alive—although seventy percent of the internees perished before the camp's liberation. Although two transports of Dutch Jews actually departed for Palestine, the Herzbergs did not appear on the Palestine exchange lists. Devastated, Herzberg started his diary, a chronicle of the period from 11 August 1944 to 11 April 1945. The diary was published in 1950 as *Twee stroomen land* (*Between Two Streams*)—a reference to the two incompatible streams: Jewry and National Socialism. It stands alongside the diaries of two of his compatriots: Renata Laqueur, author of *Dagboek Bergen-Belsen*, and his nephew Louis Tas, pseudonymed Loden Vogel, who wrote *Dagboek uit een kamp* (Diary from a Camp). Both were published in 1965.

In 1946 Herzberg published *Amor Fati*, seven essays about life in Bergen-Belsen. This was followed in 1950 by *Kroniek der Jodenvervolging 1940–1945* (Chronicle of the Persecution of the Jews 1940–1945). A detached, historical study, it remained the Netherlands's most important tome on the Holocaust for a long time, and stands out still as historical writing at its literary peak. These three books not only give a penetrating insight into camp life, they also clearly depict Herzberg's pessimistic view of humanity, which Bergen-Belsen only confirmed.

> And when one sees here how men, big strong men, send women and children on transport, shouting, cursing, raging, or, when one has seen just once how the SS man transports corpses with a cigarette in his snout, unmoved as if he is transporting manure—no, worse—as if he is transporting bricks, then one knows: this is man. *Ecce homo*! (*Between Two Streams: A Diary from Bergen-Belsen*, London and New York: I. B. Tauris Publishers, 1997, p. 141).

The situation worsened in December 1944, when Josef Kramer became camp commandant. Kramer's portrait appears in Herzberg's *Amor Fati*. It and those of other SS henchmen in the camp are remarkably penetrating. Although Herzberg was their victim, *Amor Fati* reveals no animosity. Herzberg was convinced that it was the Nazi propaganda that had degenerated them. Asked after the war by a Jewish woman how to ensure their children would never again become victims, Herzberg answered: "That is not the problem, madam; the problem is how can we prevent our children from becoming henchmen." Yet amid his sensitive observations, his theological meditations and philosophical analyses, the grief often breaks through, as on 11 November 1944: "At times, the distress is so great that one's heart seems full of tears. . . . They are bad people who rule over the world" (*Between Two Streams*, p. 164).

Herzberg doubted his message would come through. On December 25 he wrote:

> I do not know if there will ever be a hand capable of describing the wretchedness of four thousand starving Jews in this camp on Christmas Day 1944. But even if there will be a hand capable of it, not an eye will be capable of reading it, not a heart equal to it, not a mind willing to suffer it (p. 185).

Abel Herzberg has always said that he survived because of the support his wife, Thea, and he gave to each other. More generally, he believed that people in the camps survived because of their desire to remain alive.

Inmates enjoyed a limited self-administration in Bergen-Belsen. Herzberg, in a position comparable to that of the Jewish Council presidents he would later represent, was responsible for the organization of an autonomous judiciary. He was attorney general and sometimes judge. He worked mostly on theft cases—the "theft, particularly of bread and butter, is an attempt on the victim's life!" (p. 28). The moral decline in the camps perplexed Herzberg. "I have seen labourers as well as former big capitalists and businessmen of stature steal" (p. 28). In *Persecution, Extermination, Literature*, his study of Holocaust literature, Sem Dresden pointed out that the creation of schools, of orchestras, the organization of poetry evenings and of academic lectures in the camps "will be recognized as proof of a strong sense of dignity. This holds for the noble attitude of Abel Herzberg, who in the cesspool of Bergen-Belsen tries to maintain a kind of jurisdiction" (p. 103). Dresden ranks Herzberg with Robert Antelme and Primo Levi.

Some weeks before its liberation on 15 April 1945, the Nazis completely cut off the camp's food supply. Herzberg, already suffering from typhus and edema, had left Bergen-Belsen on 11 April. He, his wife, and 2,000 other Jews, among them Loden Vogel and Renata Laqueur, left on a train that was probably heading for Theresienstadt, to become *Austauschjuden* (exchange Jews).

In the last entry of Herzberg's diary we read: "We are all ill. Tired. How is it in Holland? Outside, the birds are chirping. I lie awake at night and count the strokes of the clock. Is this freedom?" (*Between Two Streams*, p. 220). This was written on 26 April, the day the train was liberated by the Russian Army near the village of Tröbitz. Thirteen thousand Bergen-Belsen inmates perished in the three months following the liberation of the camp.

The Herzbergs were reunited with their three children in Holland in early July. Judith Herberg later expressed her ambivalent feelings in *Reunion*, a poem that can be read as an expression of the estrangement that characterized the homecoming of many concentration camp survivors.

Postwar

In September 1945 Herzberg, having recovered, resumed his law practice. He also started writing for the weekly *De Groene Amsterdammer*. Throughout his publications and his subsequent controversies, his themes focused on the persecution of the Jews, and on human nature, specifically on what men are capable of. Although his books on Bergen-Belsen were very well received in non-Jewish circles, the Jewish press condemned his emotional detachment and his willingness to forgive the Germans. Herzberg always sought to transcend his emotions; he held no grudge against antisemites (the immediate postwar years in Holland witnessed rising antisemitism) "as long as their persuasion is platonic and they don't talk big hypocrisy" (quoted in Kuiper, p. 316).

Of more importance to him was his need to understand his persecutors. In his view, Hitler had not hated the Jews, but rather the Jewish spirit. Hitler refused to accept the moral distinction that the Jews, who had received the Ten Commandments, made between what is allowed and what is not. Herzberg, presaging the view of later historians, suggested that by getting rid of the Jews Hitler was clearing the way for the right to kill.

Herzberg's reputation in the Jewish community diminished further in 1947, when in spite of his personal antipathy, he defended the two chairmen of the Jewish Council, David Cohen and Abaraham Asscher, who were accused of collaboration in the deportations. He produced *Kroniek der Jodenvervolging 1940–1945* (Chronicle of the Persecution of the Jews, 1956) as an eloquent defense of the Jewish Council, which he had despised while in Bergen-Belsen. He sent a copy to the minister of justice who, after reading it, dropped the charges against the two men. He also defended Cohen and Asscher against the later attacks of the two famous Dutch Holocaust historians, Loe de Jong, and especially Jacob Presser, in his *Ondergang. De vervolging en verdelging van het Nederlandse jodendom 1940–1945* (*The Destruction of the Dutch Jews 1940–1945*).

Herzberg was present as a reporter at the 1961 Jerusalem Eichmann trial. He agreed with Hannah Arendt (*Eichmann in Jersualem—A Report on the Banality of Evil*, 1963), and with the Dutch writer Harry Mulisch (*De zaak 40–61: een reportage*) (*The Case 40–61*) that Eichmann was not the personification of evil. For Arendt and Herzberg it was Mankind who stood trial, not Eichmann. Herzberg, however, did not go so far as to consider Eichmann a mere cog in the bureaucratic machine. He had met Eichmann in Bergen-Belsen and considered him someone "who had acted from his conviction and according to the spirit of his time" (Herzberg quoted in M. van Rossem, p. 145). This view has since been largely confirmed by most Holocaust historians. The Eichmann trial revealed the horrors of the Holocaust to the world for the first time. Herzberg, though, never liked to speak about the cruelties he had experienced; he felt it could be contagious. This attitude reflects the profound humanism evident in all his work, and most clearly expressed in *Brieven aan mijn kleinzoon* (*Letters to My Grandson*, 1964), a depiction of a vanished Jewish world.

To Herzberg revenge was inhuman, and he regularly called for the release of the remaining German war criminals in Dutch custody: Lages, Kotälla, Fischer, and Aus der Fünten. The latter two were indeed released amid a storm of protest in 1989, three months before Abel Herzberg died, aged ninety-five on 19 May 1989.

Herzberg's books, novels, stories, and dramas, some of which have been translated into English and German, received almost every literary award in the Netherlands. More remarkable, Abel Herzberg and his daughter Judith were the only father and daughter to receive the PC Hooft Prize, the highest award in Dutch letters. Abel Herzberg won his in 1972.

Bibliography

Primary Sources

De huidige toestand der joden (The Present Situation of the Jews). 1932.
De nieuwe drankwet (The New Licensing Act). 1932.
Vaderland (Fatherland). 1934.
De weg van de jood (The Way of the Jew). 1939.
Amor Fati. 1946.
Tweestromenland (*Between Two Streams: A Diary from Bergen-Belsen*. 1950, 1997).
Herodes. 1955.
Kroniek der Jodenvervolging 1940–1945 (Chronicle of the Persecution of the Jews). 1956.
Sauls dood (Saul's Death). 1958.
Twaalf jaar Duitse jodenvervolging (Twelve Years of German Persecution of the Jews). 1961.
Eichmann in Jeruzalem. 1962.
Brieven aan mijn kleinzoon (*Letters to My Grandson*). 1964.
Pro Deo. 1969.
In de schaduw van mijn bomen (In the Shadow of My Trees). 1969.
Om een lepel soep (For a Spoonful of Soup). 1972.
De memoires van koning Herodes (The Memoirs of King Herod). 1974.
Drie rode rozen (Three Red Roses). 1975.
De man in de spiegel (The Man in the Mirror). 1980.
Twee verhalen (Two Stories). 1982.
Brieven aan mijn grootvader (Letters to My Grandfather). 1983.
Mirjam. 1985.
Aartsvaders. Het verhaal van Jakob en Jozef (Patriarchs. The Story of Jacob and Joseph). 1986.
Het joodse erfgoed (The Jewish Heritage). 1991.
Zonder Israël is elke jood een ongedekte cheque (Without Israel Every Jew Is an Unsupported Cheque). 1992.
Verzameld werk (Collected Works, 2 vols.). 1993.

Secondary Sources

De Jong, L. *Het Koninkrijk der Nederlanden in de Tweede Wereldoorlog 8: gevangenen en gedeporteerden* (The Kingdom of the Netherlands in the Second World War 8: Prisoners and Deportees). Den Haag: Staatsuitgeverij, 1978.
Dresden, Sem. *Vervolging, Vernietiging, Literatuur* (*Persecution, Extermination, Literature*). Amsterdam: Meulenhoff, 1991.
Galen Last, Dick van, and Rolf Wolfswinkel. *Anne Frank and After. Dutch Holocaust Literature in Historical Perspective*. Amsterdam: Amsterdam University Press, 1996.
Haan, Ido de. *Na de ondergang. De herinnering aan de Jodenvervolging in Nederland, 1945–1995* (After the Destruction. The Memory of the Persecution of the Jews in the Netherlands, 1945–1995). Den Haag: SDU, 1997.
———. "The Construction of a National Trauma. The Memory of the Persecution of the Jews in the Netherlands." *Netherlands Journal of Social Sciences* 34, no. 2 (1998): 196–217.
Herzberg, Judith. *But What? Selected Poems*. Oberlin, Ohio: Oberlin College Press, 1988.
Kristel, Conny. *Geschiedschrijving als opdracht. Abel Herzberg, Jacques Presser en Loe de Jong over de jodenvervolging* (Historiography with a Mission. Abel Herzberg, Jacques Presser and Loe de Jong on the Persecution of the Jews). Amsterdam: Meulenhoff, 1998.
Kuiper, Arie. *Een wijze ging voorbij—Het leven van Abel J. Herzberg* (A Wise Man Passed By—The Life of Abel J. Herzberg). Amsterdam: Querido, 1997.
Laqueur, Renata. "*Writing in Defiance: Concentration Camp Diaries in Dutch, French and German, 1940–1945*." (Ph.D. diss., University of New York, 1971). Microfilm: Ann Arbor Michigan: University Microfilms International, 1979.
———. *Schreiben im KZ. Tagebücher 1940–1945* (Writing in Concentration Camps. Diaries 1940–1945) Bremen: Donat Verlag, 1992, 108–111.
Moore, Bob. *Victims and Survivors. The Nazi Persecution of the Jews in the Netherlands 1940–1945*. London: Arnold, 1997.
Presser, Jacques. *Ondergang. De vervolging en verdelging van het Nederlandse jodendom 1940–1945* (*The Destruction of the Dutch Jews*). Den Haag: Staatsuitgeverij, 1965.
Van Rossem, M. "Eichmann in Jeruzalem. Een discussie over de banaliteit van het kwaad," In *Geschiedenis & cultuur. Achttien opstellen*. Edited by E. Jonker and M. van Rossem. Den Haag: SDU, 1990, pp. 139–148.

Archives

The archives of Abel Herzberg can be found in the Letterkundig Museum, The Hague.

Judith Herzberg

(1934–)

PASCALE R. BOS

JUDITH HERZBERG, DAUGHTER of the well-known Dutch Jewish lawyer and author Abel Herzberg and Thea Herzberg-Loeb, was born in Amsterdam to a highly educated Zionist family. Owing to her father's prominence, the family was interned during World War II in a special camp for privileged Jewish inmates, in Barneveld. While initially they were able to stay in this camp in relative safety, further deportation became imminent, and Judith and her older brother and sister were smuggled into hiding. They stayed first at a local farm, but then Judith was hidden separately and moved around repeatedly for almost two years, each time having to adapt to the local dialect, milieu, and new foster families. Her parents ended up in Westerbork and-Bergen-Belsen. After the war they returned to Amsterdam and the family reunited. While her older siblings left for Palestine in 1946, Judith stayed with her parents and entered high school. Her father started writing on his Holocaust experiences right after liberation, publishing first his autobiographical account of Bergen-Belsen (*Amor Fati*, 1947), and then *Kroniek der jodenvervolging* (Chronicle of the persecution of the Jews), which chronicles the fate of the Dutch Jews—one of the first studies of its kind anywhere—in 1950. He went on to publish several more successful novels and important essays on the Holocaust.

Even though Judith Herzberg began to write poetry while in school, she married young, had two children, and did not publish her first collection of poetry, *Zeepost* (SeaPost / Sea Mail) until 1963. Several more acclaimed volumes followed, in 1968, 1970, and 1971. Forced to earn her own living after a divorce, she started writing plays in the 1970s, and screenplays soon followed. While little of her earlier work had dealt with the Holocaust, with her own or her family's war experience, the 1981 film script *Charlotte*—on the life of German Jewish painter Charlotte Salomon, who died in Auschwitz—had her examine the Nazi past in detail for the first time. Here, Herzberg meant to create a project that would allow the audience to identify with just one victim of the Holocaust and allow for empathy, something she believed impossible with an abstract number like six million.

While she did not work on *Charlotte* out of a need to engage with her own past, she became after this project more interested in articulating the continuing influence of the wartime past on the (Dutch Jewish) present. What followed was the strongly autobiographical play *Leedvermaak* (Pleasure at One's Own Misfortune or that of Others) in 1982, which tells the story of one evening, a wedding (the bride's third, the groom's second) within a family of survivors. The shards of dialogue we are presented with (as if we are looking in on brief, chance encounters taking place not at the actual wedding, but in the back rooms and hallways at this party) suggest that most characters are still strongly affected by the past, a past that remains so unarticulated, so buried that the only character who seems to face it, the bride's mother, will leave the morning after the wedding to enter a psychiatric facility, which in turn will mean that her husband of twenty-three years will leave her.

Masterful as much in what is left unsaid as in what is said, the play reveals traces of wartime trauma that had seemed particularly taboo both to the characters and to the audience: the suspicion and conflict that emerges between the grown daughter who was hidden during the war and her parents who survived concentration camps, between the foster mother and the biological parents, and in general, between Jews and Dutch non-Jews.

The play won the Dutch critics' prize, as well as the Charlotte Köhler award for the best Dutch play of the past ten years, and was made into a film by Frans Weisz in 1989. This play, as well as the dozen that followed, none of which dealt with the war again until *Rijgdraad* (Tacking Thread), a sequel to *Leedvermaak* with the same characters, in 1995, along with nine volumes of poetry, earned Herzberg major Dutch literary honors, including the most prestigious, the P.C. Hooftprijs, for her entire work. She also won several German prizes, and many of her plays have been translated and performed with much success in Germany. Her poetry has been translated into English, German, and Turkish.

Since reconnecting with an old love in Israel in 1983, Herzberg has been living part of the year in Amsterdam, part in Tel Aviv. From Israel she continues to write plays and poetry, as well as articles for Dutch publications on the situation in the Middle East (she is a passionate but critical supporter of Israel) and on theater, art, and everyday life.

Autobiographical Writing

Much of Herzberg's writing does not deal directly with the war, and is rather understated. On the one hand, she long felt that writing about the past was her father's "task," and since the elder Herzberg was so successful at it, felt no need to do so herself. On the other hand, she had found the effort simply unsustainable. Nevertheless, she managed in *Leedvermaak* as well as in some of her later poetry to find one perspective her father had been unable to provide: that of the adult who had survived while hidden separately from her parents as a child. This experience of living with a false identity day in day out, under the threat of murder, in complete isolation, affected Herzberg's worldview in fundamental ways. Central to her more autobiographical work is the experience of persecution and of loss, and a lifelong distaste for dishonesty. Some of this writing is rather explicit, such as the poem about the ambivalent reunion with her parents:

For years I had not seen such a town
or stood at the bottom of such stairs
as on that hot day, in black Sunday best
and leather shoes. And at the top
I saw vaguely my strange mother
I'd have to give her a kiss.

Soft cuddling that night after night
I'd pretended, to creep from
the war into sleep,
was dividing us now. Too grown-up,
too skinny and countrified, I took
it all back. Was this
really my mother?

Come up, she said,
winking to put me at ease,
but with both eyes at once.
Right then I thought we should say
the goodbyes we'd delayed,
but I didn't know how to look at her
with my difficult eyes

(*But What: Selected Poems*, trans., Shirley Kaufman and Judith Herzberg, Oberlin, Ohio: Oberlin College Press, 1988, p. 34).

Judith had mourned her parents' likely deaths during the two years of their absence, and when they survived and she was reunited with them, they were thoroughly estranged from her. The language they spoke (proper Dutch as opposed to the local dialect she now used) was strange to her, as was their city life. Back in Amsterdam, she missed the country, her foster parents, and the relative simplicity of that former life.

More often, however, Herzberg, an intensely private person who rarely discusses anything personal in her work or in interviews, has allowed the past to come out in her work in more subtle ways. She writes for instance often of her distaste for dishonesty, which stems from her years in hiding, having to come up with elaborate lies about who she was and where she was from, leading a double life, constantly in fear of discovery. This theme as well as the need to say and impossibility of saying good-bye return often in her work.

In her poetry Herzberg aims for simplicity, for seeming transparency, for realism, rather than for poetic beauty, which she distrusts. She does not use metaphors, rather writes in a lucid style of things she observes. It is her seemingly simple style that makes her plays particularly powerful as well. Here she is not interested in describing the feelings or inner workings of her characters, rather in revealing something about them through the dialogues they have with others. Often, these conversations seem superficial, trivial, but this banal, even absurd dialogue hints powerfully at what the characters are unable to say. Real issues are circumvented in order to be able to survive, but at every corner the overwhelming experiences of the past threaten to swallow everyone whole. Take, for instance, the exchange in *Leedvermaak* between one of the young (non-Jewish) waitresses at the wedding and Ada, the bride's mother:

Hendrikje: I went to Auschwitz last year.
Ada: Oh really (silence) Better don't speak about it to Simon.
H: Horrible. Unimaginable.
A: Yes.
. . .
H: Do you find it painful to talk about?
A: No, not at all.
H: There was a group of Americans while I was there. They were on a Holocaust tour of Europe. [. . .] "Children of survivors," they said. Searching for their parents' past. Survivor-guilt, do you have that too? Yes, maybe

it is a bit of a strange question, but it is something I can picture really well, that you would feel guilty if you survive something like that. It is almost improper. If you don't want to answer I understand. But on the other hand, you hear so often that—

A: What does it look like, Auschwitz?

H: But you were there yourself?

A: Yes, I mean in the summer.

The questions of Hendrikje, although they seem nice enough, put Ada in an absurd position, as the listening ear for someone needing to tell her own story, and simultaneously as someone who stands accused. Ada tries to accommodate the conversation, but the young girl's understanding is so far removed from her reality that this exchange is useless.

Ada is the character in this play least able to contain her war trauma; still, it is Simon, her husband, whom she is trying to protect, just as he in turn tries to protect her, and both of them have tried to shield their daughter Lea. All of this proves to be a failure, however, when at a pivotal moment during the wedding party Lea accosts her father, suggesting that he and Ada should have taken her with them to the camp:

L: You should have taken me with you to the camp.

S: And you need to bring that up on a day like this.

L: A fitting day.

S: No one gladly talks about that.

L: I do.

S: You were too little.

L: That's precisely why you should have taken me.

S: We should have this and should have that! Of course! Come, Lea-

L: Did you ever wonder how I was doing? Not in general, but how I lay in bed at night, for instance? Did you ever talk about that?

S: It would have been much more dangerous with a small child. None of us would have survived.

L: Who wants to survive?

S: Useless. Unwise.

L: If I had a child then I would take her with me, I would keep her with me, I would always take her everywhere. I would comfort her simply by holding her. I can't imagine: shall we simply give the child to someone else?

S: (*As if to Ada, forty years ago*) Maybe we'll have a better chance of surviving.

L: What for, in God's name? There's not that much special waiting for us!

S: But we thought so at the time.

L: I would hold her in my arms. Precisely when it gets bad. What does it matter how old you get? Dying is not bad—being left behind is bad . . .

You know, sometimes I envy Dory who simply ended up in an orphanage after the war and none of this mess. (*Takes his hand*)

S: No, no, you don't have to apologize, I understand what you're saying, that would have been much easier. But you can't change that now. We are still alive.

Lea's selfish, cruel, and immature accusation is dealt with with much tenderness by her father, as he wishes to shield her and himself from the trauma of the past.

In the case of Holocaust survivors dealing with (or avoiding) the past, Herzberg's understated approach seems particularly appropriate. For if there is no way in which one can do justice to one's experiences of loss, it nevertheless shows itself in other ways, and Herzberg's play shows clearly that some experiences fail to become part of the past. For these survivors, the war experience still tends to determine everything, while at the same time it always remains in the background, unarticulated. The resulting theater is powerful, not just for a Jewish audience, but for a general audience as well, which sees the general Dutch tendency toward amnesia concerning the fate of the Dutch Jews during the war mirrored in its characters. For this reason, *Leedvermaak* was extremely important, and still stands as a benchmark of Dutch-Jewish relations in the early 1980s.

Bibliography

Primary Sources

Poetry

Zeepost. (*Sea Post / Sea Mail*). 1963.
Beemdgras (Meadow Grass). 1968.
Vliegen (Flies). 1970.
Strijklicht (Floodlight). 1971.
27 liefdesliedjes (27 Love Songs, based on the *Song of Songs*). 1973.
Ethooi. 1975.
Botshol. 1980.
De val van Icarus (The Fall of Icarus). 1983.
Dagrest (Day Rest). 1984.
Twintig gedichten (Twenty Poems). 1984.
Zoals (Like). 1987.
Doen en laten (Behavior). 1994.
Wat zij wilde schilderen (What She wanted to Paint). 1996.
Het vertelde (That Which is Told). 1997.
Landschap (Landscape). 1998.
Bijvangst (Extra Catch). 1999.
Staalkaart (Pattern Sample). 2001.

Prose / Essays

Tussen Amsterdam en Tel Aviv (Between Amsterdam and Tel Aviv). 1988.
Charlotte. Dagboek bij een film (Charlotte: Diary with a movie). 1981.
Het maken van gedichten en het praten daarover (The making of poetry and the speaking about it). 1977.

Theater

De deur stond open (The door was open). 1972.
Het is geen hond (It is not a dog). 1973.
Dat het's ochtends ochtend wordt (That the morning will come in the morning). 1975.
Leedvermaak (Malicious pleasure). 1982. Made into the *Leedvermaak* (also, *Polonaise* directed by Frans Weisz, 1989).

En / or (And / or). 1985.
Merg (Marrow). 1986.
De kleine zeemeermin (The little mermaid). 1986.
De Caracal (The caracal). 1988.
Kras (Scratch). 1989.
Een goed hoofd (A good head). 1991.
Teksten voor toneel en film 1972–1988 (Texts for theater and film). 1991.
Rijgdraad (Tacking thread). 1995.
De Nietsfabriek (The nothing factory). 1997.
Een golem (A golem). 1998.
Lieve Arthur (Dear Arthur). 2000.

Screenplays

Rooie Sien (Red Sien). 1975.
Mevrouw Katrien (Miss Katrien). 1979.
Charlotte (1981).

Screenplay Collaborations

Hopkins, Konrad, and Ronald van Roekel, eds. *Quartet: An Anthology of Dutch and Flemish Poetry*. Paisley: Wilfion Books, 1978.
Joods Amsterdam (Jewish Amsterdam).
Twee vrouwen (Two women). 1977.
Een vrouw als Eva (A woman like Eve). 1978.
But what: Selected poems. Translated by Shirley Kaufman. Oberlin: Oberlin College Press, 1988.

Secondary Sources

Daphne Meijer. *Joodse tradities in de literatuur* (Jewish Traditions in Literature). Amsterdam: De Bijenkorf, 1998.

Interviews

Interview by Ischa Meijer. "De Brieven." *Vrij Nederland* November 17, 1984: 22. Translated as "The Wedding Party" in Della Couling, *Dutch and Flemish Plays*. London: Nick Hekn Books, 1997.
Interview by Hans Beerekamp. "Ik fantaseer eerder in dialogen dan in beschrijvingen." (I imagine dialogues, rather than descriptions). *NRC Handelsblad* Cultureel Supplement (January 2, 1981), 3, 8.
Interview by Elisabeth Lockhorn. "Ik denk eigenlijk, dat ik er altijd al over heb willen praten . . ." (I actually think that I always had wanted to talk about it). *Margriet* (December 24, 1986), 44–51.

William Heyen

(1940–)

VICTORIA AARONS

WHEN THE SPEAKER in the opening stanza of William Heyen's "Poem Touching the Gestapo" (*Erika*, 1984) implores the poem's "you" to "hear" his urgent exhortation, Heyen would seem to invoke the traditional Hebrew prayer, "Hear, O Israel, the Lord is our God, the Lord is One" (Deut. 6:4). Thus the poem begins with an implicit reference to the Hebrew *shema* (hear) only to mark its absence in the silenced voices of murdered Jews. For when Heyen's unconstrained speaker in the opening lines of the poem entreats his notably silent interlocutor to "hear what you'll almost remember," his plea is more a command than it is the liturgical incantation of *shema*. His use of the word "hear," in its simplicity, evokes a legacy steeped in the hope of longevity, place, and destiny, the very possibility of a Jewish history and future that is ruptured by the cataclysmic ruin of the Holocaust, a history "packed into the showers" ("Poem Touching the Gestapo," line 35). Here as elsewhere in his Holocaust poems, Heyen's poetic voice is intentionally complicated by its openly acknowledged complicity with murder, a strikingly personal and doubled voice of collusion and of hoped for censure that would exonerate him from an inheritance of participation in the atrocities that preoccupy his poetic voice, events that he only imaginatively reinvents as "what you'll almost remember" ("Poem Touching the Gestapo," line 2).

The Reach of the Past: Heyen's Biographical Voice

Heyen's Holocaust poetry would seem to bear the unfortunate legacy of his unwanted inheritance. Born 1 November 1940, in Brooklyn, New York, William Helmuth Heyen's poetry is clearly complicated by the German ancestry of his parents, Henry Jurgen Heyen, a carpenter and bartender, and Wilhelmina Woermke Heyen. His father immigrated to the United States in 1928, leaving behind in Germany two brothers who were killed fighting for the Nazis and whose deaths the poet Heyen describes in poems dedicated to both uncles ("For Wilhelm Heyen" and "For Hermann Heyen," in *The Swastika Poems*, 1977). Moreover, during Heyen's childhood, his family was subjected to anti-German fanaticism in Brooklyn when swastikas were painted on the doors of their home, which later he writes about as the immediate and personal experience of persecution, and which he describes in his prose memoir "Erika" and in the poem "Men in History" (*The Swastika Poems*).

After completing his undergraduate education at the State University of New York, Brockport, in 1961, William Heyen, in 1962, married Hannelore Greiner, whose father, also a German immigrant, had been a Nazi. Heyen went on to receive a M.A. (1963) and Ph.D. (1967) from Ohio University, and taught at the State University of New York, Cortland (1963–1965). Since 1967, Heyen has taught at the State University of New York, Brockport, where he is a professor of English, specializing in modern American poetry. Heyen's own ancestry, coupled with that of his wife, as well as the period he spent as a senior Fulbright lecturer in Germany, 1971–1972, have informed his poetry with a preoccupation with expiation and memory. The poems reveal a need to come to terms with his inherited past in his present voice, as he puts it in his prose memoir, "Noise in the Trees," "calling out, crying for someone to tell me where I am" (*Long Island Light*, New York: Vanguard, 1979, p. 77). While his work is not strictly autobiographical, his poems and prose memoirs, "Noise in the Trees" and "Erika" (*The Swastika Poems*), are deeply personal and are distinguished by a confrontational, almost confessional, speaking voice, a voice whose haunting ambiguities and ambivalences are perhaps suggestive of the poet's conflicted response to his family's past and his own legacy within it.

In this way, William Heyen's Holocaust poems erupt in cacophonous discord, a poetic push and pull that shifts the controlling voice from inside the perspective of the SS to that of those who would oppose it. The effect of this shifting voice creates in Heyen's Holocaust poetry, as he writes in "Poem Touching the Gestapo," the kind of "willed chaos" (line 89), or structured disorder, that often shapes his poems formally and thematically. The heinous administrations of the Third Reich are typically described as ineptly fashioned, the machines of bureaucracy gone wrong in incompetent disarray: "inadequate graves," "gas chambers . . . too small," "vans" whose "engines sometimes wouldn't start" ("Poem Touching Gestapo," line 26). The irony of such chaotic incompetence is not lost on the poet, however, for the consequences of the Third Reich are always unequivocally exposed, the guilty called to account, named; there is a litany of the accused: Heinrich Himmler, Josef Mengele, Otto Ohlendorf, Hermann Göring. There is no turning from responsibility in Heyen's Holocaust poetry, from the specificity of place, action, and agent. Intoned in a kind of death knoll, a roll call of locale and sites of death and destruction is recounted, itemized, in poem after poem. He mentions Babi Yar, Auschwitz, and Birkenau. In "Poem Touching the Gestapo," the condemned, too, are marched forth in the stanzas that follow, "a cortege . . . winding toward Birkenau"(line 5). For Heyen's intention, throughout the collections devoted to the Holocaust, most notably *Depth of Field* (1970), *The Swastika Poems* (1977), *My Holocaust Songs* (1980), and *Erika Poems of the Holocaust* (1984), would seem to be, to name, to articulate the cumulative experience of the Holocaust. As Heyen puts it in *The Generation of 2000*, the poems express "a desire to touch the Gestapo itself" (Princeton, N.J.: Ontario Review, 1984, p. 118).

Thus the mode of address in these poems is necessarily accusatory, a stark indictment of the events of the Holocaust and of those who allowed it to happen or who did little to prevent it, those who turned away from the realities that Heyen determinedly recounts. Heyen speaks in imperatives such as "hear," "see," and "remember," in an attempt to freeze time, to arrest the events of the Holocaust in a willed visualization of them. With the unnerving echoes of the commandants of the Third Reich, Heyen's summons to hear, in the opening stanza of "Poem Touching the Gestapo," sets the stage for the suspension of time that defines much of his Holocaust poetry. Beginning with a still photograph of Himmler, "where he still stands," Heyen clearly links past, present, and future ("Poem Touching the Gestapo," line 3). As he does so, he admonishes and unites generations of witnesses, "you . . . you in the next century, and the next," an ongoing, continuous line of participants in memory ("Poem Touching the Gestapo, lines 1–2). Heyen not only memorializes but also personalizes the victims of that time and a specific moment in time, a moment both reduced to and enlarged by that particular period in history, a poetic utterance that spans time.

The stark, exposed, and revelatory nature of Heyen's poetry, the refusal to cloak the realities of the Holocaust in metaphors of evasion or restraint, defines the personalized voice that governs most of his poems. Heyen's poetry is deeply personal, recognizably confessional. Most of the poems begin either directly or indirectly with "I" or "My," and many poems are self-addressed dramatic monologues or are addressed to members of the poet's immediate and extended family. Heyen's "I," however, is often slippery in its reference, changing shape throughout many of the poems in order to emphasize the ambiguity of that voice, the person inside and outside the parameters of localized poetic space. For example, in "Poem Touching the Gestapo," which would seem to stand as a paradigmatic case of Heyen's Holocaust poems, the initial reference to "I" brings to life, ironically, the voice of death, of Himmler, Mengele, and the rest who "will it now," a voice pathologically driven by the certainty of racial purity's dominance, "Aryan . . . ascending the misformed skull of the beast" (lines 19, 9). At the same time, however, this first-person placement shifts, breaks out of its initially circumscribed place in the poem and becomes also the voice of the poet, who in anger and outrage indicts those with whom he was previously, deceptively, aligned. Ironically, the "I" becomes the general "we" of the German people, only to shift the burden of willingness to murder to the third-person "his," whose Christian liturgical cadence, "his will be done" ("Poem Touching the Gestapo," line 71), enlarges the scope of the incrimination in no uncertain terms. And it does so necessarily to align the "I" with, finally, the "we" of those murdered, those who "close our eyes" ("Poem Touching the Gestapo," line 87). The dual reference here to both the intentional refusal to see the atrocities of the Third Reich and the closeness to them, typically for Heyen, positions the speaker in the poem as both victimizer and victim, executioner and condemned.

The Moral Imperative of Memory

The Swastika Poems, a collection of twenty-nine poems divided into two parts and separated by a narrative prose memoir, brings to life two of Heyen's most dominant themes: the devastation of the Holocaust and the ways in which time shapes memory. In the first of these two sections of poetry, "Men in History," Heyen takes readers back in time and directly addresses his family and his uncles' participation in the Third Reich. Importantly, the section begins with "A Snapshot of My Father, 1928," in which the poet's father is arrested in time by a photographic frame, a not untypical poetic conceit for Heyen. As the poem opens, his father is standing on a ship's deck, eighteen years old, an immigrant en route to America, looking "like famine," a "hayseed," but with the look of anticipation, "new life in his eyes" ("A Snapshot of My Father, 1928," lines 16, 17, 20; in *The Swastika Poems*, New York: Vanguard, 1977). This portrait of his father as a young man, sailing to the promise of a new life in America, is, at the same time, mitigated, if not impeded, by the stationary posture of his figure on deck—the ship is moving, but he remains fixed, holding "tight to the rail" ("A Snapshot of My Father, 1928," line 23). And this movement of ship and hope is, after all, only imagined by the poet from a photograph, a "snapshot" of his father, who, at the poem's close, has been "smiling for fifty years now" with the nervous mixture of desire and urgency, as when one is about to be married, "for richer or poorer," to his new country, just as time past, present, and future are wedded in the poet's desire to wrest history from the monstrous shape of the past ("A Snapshot of My Father, 1928," line 27).

For in the poems that follow his father's flight from a Germany soon to erupt in the wreckage of Nazi violence and devastation, Heyen takes readers immediately to the battlegrounds. The second poem, "For Wilhelm Heyen," is addressed to the poet's uncle, for whom Heyen was named, and who, like Heyen's father who fled to America, is captured by a camera, on a "shaft of film" (line 1). But the film is, at the poem's opening, self-destructing, aflame, ushering in the uncle's death, who "burns" while "Holland snows" ("For Wilhelm Heyen," lines 12, 13–14). Ironically, in Part I of the poem, the figure of Wilhelm Heyen is posed waving, a gesture of kinship, the speaker's acknowledgment of his relationship to the uncle who died in the year of the poet's birth. But immediately, the wave is no longer beckoning, but instead becomes the movement of the soldier's arm, a singular motion that brings with it the recognized signal of death. For, at the close of the poem, the soldier's arm becomes a "scythe," his hands "cupped full of blood," a direct acknowledgment of Wilhelm Heyen's culpability in the murder of millions of people ("For Wilhelm Heyen," lines 35, 36). For unlike the expected attempt to wash guilty hands clean of blood, an implied allusion to Shakespeare's Lady Macbeth and her futile attempts to wash the blood of guilt from her hands, the poet's uncle cups the blood of the murdered. Seeking not to cleanse himself of the guilt he so obviously denies, he willingly holds the blood, a metonymy of the dead, in his cupped hands. And thus, in a kind of metonymic exchange, blood held for blood washed, the poet acknowledges Wilhelm Heyen's crime, the literal and metaphorical trope of blood further masking the troubled relation of kinship that suffuses these poems. In a direct address to his uncle in the fourth part of the poem, the poet denounces him. Speaking directly to him, Heyen names him "Wilhelm" and condemns him. Although dead and unable to hear the voice of his nephew, Wilhelm will not, cannot die. It is made very clear at the poem's dramatic close that to discharge his uncle as dead would be to purge the poet of a legacy he cannot forget. The poet's uncle lingers still, "a shadow" of the poet's ongoing memory, of his deliberate attempt to "understand [Wilhelm's] name" and thus his own ("For Wilhelm Heyen," line 33).

This indictment of individuals, of "Men in History" (as one of the poem's titles exhorts), of members of the poet's family as well as of other participants in the Third Reich, is characteristic of the opening poems in *The Swastika Poems*. In "Letter to Hansjörg Greiner (d. Oct. 20, 1944 at War Camp Arsk, the Urals)," Heyen "speaks" to his wife's father in a voice of utter accusation and condemnation: "Has no one written you? Then I," a direct assault on his father-in-law's moral failure (line 31). These figures are not dead, and the poet's legacy comes back to haunt him in the poem "Men in History," where he poetically reproduces the swastikas painted on the doors of his childhood home in Brooklyn. These acutely personal and almost apologetic poems are like an open wound, an inevitably incomplete atonement for crimes not his own, but crimes shared because of the haphazard and hazardous conditions of birth. While the poet's father is exonerated in the volume's opening selection, the poet's uncles, finally, are not. They are, rather, forever reinvoked, reinvented, as they are in the poem dedicated to Hermann Heyen, "my Nazi uncle," whose plane went down in 1941 and whose "ashes sifted" over "the countries you hated . . . I often curse the two of you" ("For Hermann Heyen," lines 4, 8, 26).

Bearing Witness to a Past Unburied

The intervening prose narrative, "Erika," that separates the poetry sections in *The Swastika Poems* shifts the speaking voice from Nazi Germany to Bergen-Belsen some thirty years after the liberation of the death camp. The author, visiting the site of the long since abandoned camp, where in April 1945 "eighteen thousand died," is struck by the incongruity of the language of death with the names that signify it (for instance, *Buchenwald,* which means the yellow-leafed beech wood), as he is struck by the jarring antithesis of the flowering heath plant erica that now blooms over the buried dead, "very beautiful and very terrible" ("Erika," p. 43). Bound up in the author's recollections of the camp's atrocities is the memory of his own childhood, when in the same year of mass destruction, 1945, as children were being exterminated at Bergen-Belsen, his father was painting over the swastikas drawn on the windows, steps, and doors of his German home in Woodhaven, New York. "Erika" compellingly shows that Heyen's own troubled memory lies unburied in this memoir, as do the remnants of the past found by the caretaker at Bergen-Belsen, who, at the memoir's close, finds in the soil artifacts of lives destroyed: "a pin . . . the twisted frames of . . . eyeglasses . . . a key, or a wedding band" ("Erika," p. 44).

In the remaining poetry section of *The Swastika Poems,* the complex metaphors and perspectives introduced in the first section, which transport readers to Nazi Germany of the 1940s, are extended in time and place to the Germany of another generation. In "The Numinous," the title also of the final section of this collection, the poet walks the streets of a city in Germany in seeming peace and dreamy lassitude, the antithesis of the landscape sculpted in the first section of poems. However, this tonal ease rapidly gives way when the gray smoke in the air becomes, for the poet and his companion, the desiccated air of "other terrible chimneys" ("The Numinous," line 6). The city's very ordinary architecture becomes, for the poet, portents of ruin and decay. In a metaphorical rush of wings, pigeons in the air become an acute remembrance of "hearts beating" above them ("The Numinous," line 35).

Such loss and memory's attempts at recovery consistently remain at the center of Heyen's Holocaust poems. In "The Children" (in *Erika,* New York: Vanguard, 1984), the poem's speaker dreams of a city in Germany, two years after *Kristallnacht* ("night of broken glass," the 1938 pogrom in which the windows of Jewish-owned stores and synagogues were shattered). In his dream, he tries to save those children wounded in the attack. "The last driver in this procession," the poem's speaker urgently attempts to get the children to a hospital to fix what cannot be repaired, the heart exposed, nerve and tendon ripped from the body. The speaker's anxiety, impotence, and fear are a measure of the grief and loss he so penetratingly feels, "children . . . murdered . . . graves lost . . . names lost" ("The Children," lines 52–53). But upon waking, the remembered dream of his attempts to save the children and his sure knowledge that he would do so again brings a small but not inconsequential measure of "relief," a prayer to the dead, suggested by the poem's close: "Amen" ("The Children," line 62).

Heyen's poetic closures would seem to be prayers for memory, whose liturgical cadences at once lament unrecoverable loss and memorialize the victims of the Holocaust. The poet's prayers for memory, loss, and redemption would, especially in "Poem Touching the Gestapo," seem to acknowledge the rhythms of another on earlier poetic voice, that of Allen Ginsberg, whose hymn at the close of "Kaddish," a poem in memory of his mother's death, like Heyen's, becomes a prayer for his own soul and for those persecuted by the pathological inhumanity of a civilization driven mad by self-delusion, opportunism, dissimulation, and concealment.

For Heyen, the power of poetry as the willed articulation of anguish becomes the recurring metaphor of absolution, as if the very act of writing is both diagnosis and self-protection. Writing for Heyen becomes the means for penetrating into dark recesses of unimagined motivation and will. As he expresses it in "For Hermann Heyen," "my hours writing verses that wonder" at the unspeakable capacity for abomination (lines 49–50). But for William Heyen, this remarkable poet of conscience and relentless accountability, poetry is also morally transformative, since it produces the possibility for bearing witness and for restoring an imaginary life to the dead. In his *The Swastika Poems,* he writes, "the heart beats with it . . . remember" (lines 24–25).

Bibliography

Primary Sources

Depth of Field: Poems. 1970.
Profile of Theodore Roethke. 1971. (Editor)
The Trail Beside the River Platte. 1973.
Noise in the Trees: Poems and a Memoir. 1974.
Of Palestine: A Meditation. 1976.
American Poets in 1976. 1976. (Editor)
XVII Machines. 1976.
The Elm's Home. 1977.
The Swastika Poems. 1977.
From this Book of Praise: Poems and a Conversation with William Heyen. 1978.
The Descent. 1979.
The Children. 1979.
Long Island Light: Poems and a Memoir. 1979.
The City Parables. 1980.
My Holocaust Songs. 1980.
December 31, 1979: The Candle. 1980.

Blackberry Light: Sections 19–32 of "The Chestnut Rain," a Poem in Progress. 1981.
Lord Dragonfly: Five Sequences. 1981.
The Trains. 1981.
The Generation of 2000: Contemporary American Poets. 1984. (Editor)
Erika, Poems of the Holocaust. 1984.
Eight Poems for Saint Walt. 1985.
Vic Holyfield and the Class of 1957: A Romance. 1986.
Brockport, New York: Beginning with and . . . 1988.
Falling from Heaven: Holocaust Poems of a Jew and a Gentile. 1991.
Pterodactyl Rose: Poems of Ecology. 1991.
The Shore. 1991.
Ribbons: The Gulf War: A Poem. 1992.
The Host: Selected Poems, 1965–1990. 1994.
Crazy Horse in Stillness: Poems. 1996.
Diana, Charles, & the Queen: Poems. 1998.
Pig Notes & Dumb Music: Prose on Poetry. 1998.

Secondary Sources

Gerber, Philip, and Robert Gemmett, eds. "The Individual Voice: A Conversation with William Heyen." *Western Humanities Review* 23 (summer 1969): 223–233.
McFee, Michael, "The Harvest of a Quiet Eye." *Parnassus Poetry in Review* 10 (spring–summer 1982): 153–171.
McPherson, Sandra. "The Swastika Poems." *American Poetry Review* 6 (November–December 1977): 30–32.
Stefanik, Ernist. "William Heyen: A Descriptive Checklist," *Bulletin of Bibliography* 36 (1979): 157–176.
Stitt, Peter. "The Sincere, the Mythic, the Playful: Forms of Voice in Current Poetry." *Georgia Review* 34 (1980): 202–212.

GEOFFREY HILL

(1932–)

MARK SCROGGINS

GEOFFREY HILL WAS born in rural Bromsgrove, Worcestershire, on 18 June 1932, the son of Hilda Beatrice Hands and William George Hill, a police constable. He grew up near the region memorialized in A. E. Housman's collection of verse *A Shropshire Lad* and attended Keble College, Oxford, taking a B.A. in English in 1953. Since then he has taught, first at Leeds University and for briefer stints at the University of Michigan, the University of Ibadan, Nigeria, and the University of Bristol; from 1980 to 1988, he was University Lecturer in English and Fellow of Emmanuel College, Cambridge. In 1988 he became a member of the faculty of Boston University's University Professors Program and in 1998 he became codirector of the Editorial Institute at Boston University.

Style and Importance

Hill is among the greatest English poets of the second half of the twentieth century. From the beginning, he has assumed something of the stance of a prophetic poet. His prophecy is not, however, the apocalyptic vision of Daniel or St. John the Divine, but the hurt and angry social critique of a Hosea, the lamentation of a Jeremiah. As he puts it in his book *Speech! Speech!*, parodying Walter Pater, "Poetry aspires / to the condition of Hebrew," to the condition, that is, of scripture or prophecy (Washington, D.C.: Counterpoint, 2000, p. 10). Part of Hill's importance, and much of what makes his poetry so compelling, is the manner in which he has seriously, painstakingly, and with enormous self-awareness taken upon himself and his work the full burden of European history, both political and spiritual. The Holocaust, as the central event of twentieth-century history, looms large in Hill's work, and he has addressed the *Shoah* with more intelligence, intensity, and relentless poetic craft than most other non-Jewish poets.

Hill's poetry is remarkable for its density, its sometimes harsh musicality, and its power, both intellectual and emotional. In this, his clearest precursors are T. S. Eliot and William Empson. And like that of Eliot and Empson, Hill's poetry has been attacked as both difficult and hyperintellectual, cerebral. Against the latter charge, Hill somewhat paradoxically insists that his poetry is (adapting Milton's words) "simple, sensuous, and passionate." It is a mistake, he argues, to insist that "the intellect is somehow alien to sensuousness," or that poetry must concern itself only with matter of emotion or immediately perceived reality; indeed, in Hill's work, matters that less profound poets might have left to the philosopher, historian, or theologian are embodied and treated in dramatically emotional terms. As to the charge of "difficulty," Hill readily concedes that his work is not simple. Simplicity in art, however, is too often oversimplification, and the matters with which he deals are in themselves complex. His difficulty is not a matter of elitism: "genuinely difficult art," Hill argues, "is truly democratic. . . . tyranny requires simplification."

The fact remains that Hill's poetry makes few concessions to the common reader, and even some of his most enthusiastic academic admirers confess to understanding it only in part. Like the modernists before him, Hill deploys a wide range of historical, literary, and theological reference. More daunting than his range of reference, however—for references can be always looked up—is the sheer density of Hill's poetic language. He presses English to its ultimate limits: Often the reader must struggle to untangle the clotted syntax of his verse, and the reader must be continually awake to the multiple connotations of words. In the opening line of the first of "Two Formal Elegies: *For the Jews in Europe*" (from *For the Unfallen*)—"Knowing the dead, and how some are disposed"—one is initially satisfied that "how some are disposed" refers to the "disposal" of the Holocaust's murdered Jews, "in sand graves, in clenched cinders . . ." (*New and Collected Poems 1952–1992*, Boston: Houghton Mifflin, 1994, p. 19). As the sonnet progresses, however, one realizes that this is as much a poem about the survival of the judgmental hatred that condemned the Jews as it is about the Jews themselves. One "knows" the dead, but one also knows how some of the *living* are still disposed—disposed toward hatred, denial, forgetfulness. The second of these "elegies" wonders whether a film about the *Shoah* can make any lasting impact on the "pushing midlanders" Hill sees at the beach: "Is it good to remind them, on a brief screen, / Of what they have witnessed and not seen?" Is the world indeed "witness-proof"? (*New and Collected Poems*, p. 20).

The ambiguity with which Hill handles the weighty term "witness" in this early poem is representative of the ambiguity throughout his poetry. The ambiguity of the poet's position as a "witness," however—an Englishman who has not experienced the Holocaust at first hand, who has "witnessed and not seen"—does not absolve him of his responsibility to history. "There are things," Hill states in a recent *Paris Review* interview, "one has to witness to." For Hill, the poetry of slogan and single-minded statement is part and parcel of the oversimplification, the repression of the active intelligence by which tyranny holds down its subjects. Ambivalence, ambiguity, may not be a sine qua non of poetry that engages its moment's deepest issues, but they are evidence of the human intellect resistant and at work, hemmed about though it may be by cultural, social, and political pressures. While Hill's published collections of criticism, *The Lords of Limit* and *The Enemy's Country*, only occasionally address the position of the writer in the twentieth century, they are obsessively concerned with the political and social pressures under which writers labor, the "circumstances of language" of the latter volume's subtitle.

Hill is a deeply historical poet, and the subject to which he most often returns is the matter of Europe, the parade of intolerances, cruelties, and massacres that is European history from the Middle Ages through the twentieth century. For Hill, one of the primary tasks of the poet is to remind us of history, to push back into the forefront of our consciousness that which we would sometimes prefer to repress: "I return constantly," he says, "to what I think is one of the major outrages of modern life: the neglect of the dead, and a refusal to acknowledge what we owe to them, and a refusal to submit ourselves to the wisdom of the dead. . . ." As an acknowledgment of his own responsibility to the dead, Hill has written poems dedicated to various "martyrs" (the word means, significantly, "witness"): "Domaine Public" for the Surrealist poet and resistance fighter Robert Desnos, who died in Terezin (Theresienstadt); "Tristia: 1891–1938" for the Russian Osip Mandelstam, who died in a Stalinist prison camp; "Two Chorale-Preludes" based on poems by the Holocaust survivor Paul Celan; *The Mystery of the Charity of Charles Péguy*, which recounts the life and struggles of the socialist neo-Catholic pro-Drefusard Péguy (1873–1914).

Hill writes as a Christian poet. That is, while he refuses to make outright professions of faith, and while his poetry struggles agonizingly with the question of belief and its consequences, at the heart of his work is a series of meditations on the primary mysteries of the Christian religion: the Fall, the Incarnation, the Atonement. All of his religious meditations are colored by the knowledge that Christianity has been deeply implicated in a series of barbarities, from the anti-Catholic persecutions of the English sixteenth century, to the European religious wars of the seventeenth, to the persecutions of the Jewish Diaspora and the *Shoah* itself. For Hill, the Holocaust stands as the culmination and capstone of a series of religious wars and persecutions that began with the very founding of the Christian faith. As he puts it in *The Triumph of Love* (1998), "If the gospel is heard, all else follows: / the scattering, the diaspora, / the shtetlach, ash pits, pits of indigo dye" (*The Triumph of Love*, Boston: Houghton Mifflin, 1998, pp. 8–9).

King Log

A cluster of memorable poems in Hill's second collection, *King Log* (1968), directly address the Holocaust. The much-anthologized "Ovid in the Third Reich" places the Roman love poet in Hitler's Germany and attempts to imagine the mindset of those intelligent Germans who could not bring themselves to speak out: "I love my work and my children. God / Is distant, difficult. Things happen" (*New and Collected Poems*, p. 49). The poem "I Had Hope When Violence Was Ceas'd" takes its title from *Paradise Lost* XI. 779–780, where the Archangel Michael shows Adam a panorama of the wars, degradations, and idolatries that make up human history of the patriarchal age. The voice of Hill's poem is that of a Jew on the point of being murdered, his "flesh oozing towards its last outrage." In the face of this enormity, however, the speaker has attained a certain equanimity. "That which is taken from me," he says, "is not mine" (*New and Collected Poems*, p. 54).

"September Song," subtitled "*born 19.6.32—deported 24.9.42*," is perhaps the most haunting and ambiguous of these poems. Its title, evoking a bittersweet Kurt Weill–Maxwell Anderson song about the onset of old age, seems particularly ironic when applied to this ten-year-old Holocaust victim. The poem's first six lines emphasize the sheer bureaucratic efficiency of the Nazi death factories, the fact that while the child may have been among the "undesirable" element of German society, he or she was most certainly not "untouchable" (in the sense as well of the Indian caste system). "Undesirable you may have been, untouchable / you were not. . . . As estimated, you died. . . . Just so much Zyklon and leather, patented / terror, so many routine cries" (*New and Collected Poems*, p. 55). The poem's third stanza, however, breaks into an altogether different voice: "(I have made / an elegy for myself it / is true)." As the critic Christopher Ricks has pointed out, Hill's own birth date is the day before that of this anonymous child: They are almost exact contemporaries. Hill, then, is imagining himself in the place of this Holocaust victim—"an elegy for myself." But simultaneously he is acknowledging the ambiguity, the hubris of writing—as an Englishman, a non-Jewish boy growing up far from the centers of the German death machine, far even from the Blitz—on behalf of this unknown European child. It is true, he admits, that his elegy—like every poem written by an ambitious poet—has been written "for myself." The poem's final lines compound this rueful realization, as the poet, at peace in the present, observes the Autumn around him—"September fattens on vines. / Roses flake from the wall"—where the smoke in the air and in his eyes is not that of the ovens, but of "harmless fires": "This is plenty. This is more than enough." Theodor Adorno famously claimed that "To write poetry after Auschwitz is barbaric." Hill would not, I think, entirely agree, but his great insight is that any poet in the twentieth century has become, perforce, Ovid in the Third Reich.

Later Works

The books of Hill's early and middle period, collected by Penguin in 1985 and Houghton Mifflin in 1994, are for the most part written in the traditional meters and forms of classic English poetry. (An exception is the historical prose-poem sequence *Mercian Hymns* [1971].) In his most recent collections, *Canaan* (1997), *The Triumph of Love* (1998), and *Speech! Speech!* (2000), Hill has largely turned away from traditional verse forms and has begun to write in a tense, flexible free verse. The tone of the poetry has changed as well; where the early poetry was often characterized by an elevated or distant voice, the more recent work makes far greater use of the vernacular, often descending into vulgarity and slang.

The poems of *Canaan* take the density of Hill's earlier work to a new extreme, a difficulty in many poems compounded by an urgent and angry abstraction, a sense of the poet's deep disquiet unmoored to any concrete referent—any concrete referent, that is, that the reader can make out. Hill is angry at England's rulers, as evidenced by the series of poems titled "To the High Court of Parliament"; he despairs at the lack of rectitude and probity in the European community, rushing toward union—"the liberties of Maastricht"—with a blithe disregard of the history through which it has come (*Canaan*, Boston: Houghton Mifflin, 1996, p. 30). One sequence of fractured sonnets, "De Jure Belli Ac Pacis," is dedicated to the memory of Hans-Bernd von Haeften, one of the German officers executed for his part in the 1944 plot to assassinate Hitler. Von Haeften has been forgotten, as have so many others who manifested heroism in the dark times of the war. The only name current to "Europa / in her brief modish rags" is "*Schindler! Schindler!*," resurrected in Steven Spielberg's film *Schindler's List* (*Canaan*, p. 36).

The Triumph of Love

A number of critics, among them some who had acclaimed Hill's earlier poems most enthusiastically, felt that he had descended into pointless berating and tiresome self-flagellation in *The Triumph of Love*, a 150-section long poem published in 1998. *The Triumph of Love*'s themes and motifs, however, are much of a piece with Hill's earlier work. It is the voice that is different: One hears the poet speak far more in propria persona, and much more casually. His voice is undercut not merely by his own irony, but by the voices of an unnamed editor ("—ED") and a trio of carping critics, "MacSikker," "Croker," and "O'Shem." The poem is a long, meandering, agonized, and often painfully funny meditation on Western civilization at the end of the century, directionless and devoid of rectitude, its back turned on the evidence of history and the memory of the dead. Its mode is the ancient rhetorical mode of *laus et viturperatio*, praise and vilification, "public, forensic, / yet with a vehement / private ambition for the people's / greater good . . ." (*The Triumph of Love*, p. 14). Hill presents himself in the act of striving, in the face of what his age values in poetry—the "intimate buzzing and smooth toiletry, / mingled with a few squeals" of the Nobel laureates "*N.* and *N*" (p. 39) (probably Seamus Heaney and Derek Walcott)—to achieve a *public* voice, "a noble vernacular" (p. 36) that can bear witness to the wounds and crimes of history and raise up moments of "particular grace, / individual love, decency, endurance . . ." (p. 26).

As so often in Hill's poetry, the Holocaust, and Europe's faulty memory of it, are at the heart of *The Triumph of Love*. The book of Daniel is Hill's touchstone: "It is to *Daniel*, as to our own / tragic satire, that one returns / for mastery of the business . . ." (p. 5). In one horrifying section, a German captain ("Hauptmann," with a pun on the playwright) instructs an actor (or comedian—"Schauspieler") to focus and "Run . . . through again and for ever" the film (or slide) of a Jew leaping from the roof of a burning building in the Warsaw ghetto: "You see him burning, / dropping feet first, in a composed manner, / still in suspension, / from the housetop." The young man, "Semitic ur-Engel," has taken on the fate of the three boys in Nebuchadnezzar's fiery furnace (Daniel 3): "terminal agony none the less / interminable, the young / martyrs ageing in the fire. . . ." The Nazis watch this scene, one presumes, with a sadistic satisfaction; Hill replays it—"again and for ever"—for "instruction," to remind his readers and himself (pp. 10–11).

Throughout the poem, Hill gives voice to those who would accuse him of repetitive grumbling, of pointless, self-serving instrospection and self-laceration. "What is he saying; / why is he still so angry?" "Scab-picking old scab: why should we be salted / with the scurf of his sores?" (p. 17) "Shameless old man, bent on committing / more public nuisance. Incontinent / fury wetting the air" (p. 19). Hill will not, however, be swayed from his broodings, however often his critics may call them "obsessions." He mourns the "desolation of learning," learning that might allow "understanding." "By understanding / understand diligence / and attention, appropriately understood / as actuated self-knowledge / a daily acknowledgement / of what is owed the dead" (p. 63) "I am saying (simply) / what is to become of memory?" (p. 75). Poetry alone cannot preserve or perpetuate memory. It can only mourn its loss and call for its perpetuation. Poetry is, in some of the last words of the poem, no more (or less) than "*a sad and angry consolation*" (p. 82).

Speech! Speech!

Hill's recent volume *Speech! Speech!* is yet another long poem, divided into 120 twelve-line sections—one for each of de Sade's days of Sodom. It is a harrowing poem, an incessant welter of voices: the voice of Hill himself, the voices of his critics, and the voices of our contemporary media-saturated culture—newspaper headlines, radio broadcasts, the inane pieties of politicians, the strident verse of hip-hop culture, and the empty tag lines of pages on the World Wide Web. It is an intense, difficult, and often very funny book and circles around Hill's perennial concerns: the spiritual degradation of contemporary society, the loss of the West's spiritual grounding, and Europe's deliberate refusal of historical memory. The densely concatenated free verse of *Speech! Speech!* is a far cry from the deliberate traditional prosody of Hill's earlier poetry. Indeed, it places him closer to the company of the American "Language" poets than the more traditional formalists with whom he has often been grouped. But it maintains his stance as one of the English language's most challenging and valuable poets, a secular prophet whose high seriousness and ethical scruple continue to issue forth in demands that we remember and take to heart this century's lacerations.

Bibliography

Primary Sources

For the Unfallen. 1959.
King Log. 1968.
Mercian Hymns. 1971.
Tenebrae. 1978.
Henrik Ibsen's 'Brand': A Version for the Stage. 1978.
The Mystery of the Charity of Charles Péguy. 1983.
The Lords of Limit: Essays on Literature and Ideas. 1984.
Collected Poems. 1985.
The Enemy's Country: Words, Contexture, and Other Circumstances of Language. 1991.
New and Collected Poems 1952–1992. 1994.
Canaan. 1997.
The Triumph of Love. 1998.
Speech! Speech! 2000.
The Orchards of Syon. 2002.

Secondary Sources

Agenda 17 (Spring 1979), special Hill issue.
Agenda 23 (Autumn–Winter 1985–1986), special Hill issue.
Bloom, Harold, ed. *Geoffrey Hill: Modern Critical Views*. New York: Chelsea House, 1986.
Meiners, R. K. "Mourning for Our Selves and for Poetry: The Lyric After Auschwitz." *The Centennial Review* 35:3 (Fall 1991): 545–590.
Robinson, Peter, ed. *Geoffrey Hill: Essays on His Work*. Milton Keynes, U.K.: Open University Press, 1985.
Sherry, Vincent B. *The Uncommon Tongue: The Poetry and Criticism of Geoffrey Hill*. Ann Arbor: University of Michigan Press, 1987.

Interviews

"Geoffrey Hill." in *Viewpoints: Poets in Conversation with John Haffenden*. London and Boston: Faber & Faber, 1981, 76–99.
Interview by Carl Phillips, *Paris Review* 154 (Spring 2000): 272–299.

ETTY HILLESUM

(1914–1943)

PASCALE R. BOS

IN 1981, THIRTY-eight years after its author had perished in Auschwitz, a selection of the journals of Etty Hillesum was published in the Netherlands under the title *Het verstoorde leven* (*An Interrupted Life*). The book won much acclaim and became a best-seller, and reprints quickly reached 150,000 copies. Translations into several languages followed, among which were English, French, German, Italian, and Danish, and the book was soon published in over a dozen countries. In the United States, the diary appeared in 1982 under the title *An Interrupted Life*. The collected letters Hillesum wrote to family and friends while working and later while detained in the Dutch transit camp Westerbork were published as well in *Het denkende hart van de barak* (*The Thinking Heart of the Barracks*, 1982). These letters, too, won much acclaim in the Netherlands and internationally. Finally, in 1986, a critical scholarly edition of Hillesum's writing appeared in the Netherlands under the title *Etty: De nagelaten geschriften van Etty Hillesum: 1941–1943* (*Etty: The Posthumous Writings of Etty Hillesum: 1941–1943*), which contained three hundred new pages of the diary that had previously been left unpublished and thirty newly discovered letters to friends. To date, no foreign translations have appeared of this definitive edition of Hillesum's work.

"Looking Death in the Eye and Accepting It": Etty Hillesum's Diaries and Letters 1941–1943

Owing to the work's extraordinary philosophical, spiritual, and emotional richness, Etty Hillesum has become a phenomenon, particularly in European literary circles. Symposia have discussed her work and life; prominent international scholars respond to her work; study centers have been erected based on her "life philosophy"; the Etty Hillesum Center in Dêventer, Netherlands, was founded in the 1990s; and Hillesum has been central to the overall curriculum at the Dutch University for Humanities since approximately 1996.

Considering the wealth of wartime journals already published, Hillesum's posthumous success suggests that her work is clearly something special. Compared at times to that of Anne Frank, Simone Weil, and Edith Stein, Hillesum's writing is nevertheless so original and unusual that it defies easy comparison and categorization. This speaks to the work's strength but also to the fate that has befallen it in a Dutch and wider European context, namely, it is not considered part of the Holocaust literature canon or seen as Jewish. Notwithstanding Hillesum's phenomenal critical success, in many anthologies on Dutch-Jewish literature, for example, her work is curiously absent. In Europe, Hillesum's texts are often primarily discussed, taught, and admired by non-Jewish audiences. In fact, her literature is claimed by some as a particular form of New Age or Christian spirituality. However, the very reasons for this unusual reception suggest that her work does indeed deserve a central role in Holocaust literature.

Biography

Etty Hillesum was born on 15 January 1914 in Middelburg, the Netherlands. The family moved around until they settled in Deventer in 1924, where her father, Dr. Louis (Levi) Hillesum, a classicist, became the school principal of the city gymnasium (European Secondary School). Her mother, Rebecca (Riva) Hillesum-Bernstein, had fled from pogroms in the tsarist Russian Empire to the Netherlands in 1907. Hillesum had two younger brothers, Mischa, a gifted pianist, and Jaap, a doctor, both of whom were brilliant but also had serious psychiatric problems. The family life of the Hillesums was said to be loving, intellectual, and passionate, but also extremely chaotic. The parents had a tempestuous marriage, and the mother, too, was said to have been mentally unstable.

After high school in Deventer, Etty lived in Amsterdam. She studied law at the City University of Amsterdam, then studied Slavic languages, and, finally, psychology. She finished her law degree in 1939, but her other studies were interrupted in 1940 by the German invasion. She earned a living during the early war years as a tutor in Russian and as a live-in domestic. Her living arrangements were unusual, however; while she took care of the household of Hans Wegeriff, a sixty-two-year old widower, she also became his lover.

Hillesum had been suffering from depression, major mood swings, and a host of psychosomatic illnesses (headaches, stomach pains) when in early 1941 she encountered Julius Spier, a charismatic German Jewish refugee who had studied psychotherapy with Carl Jung and founded an analytic process called "psychochirology," the reading of palm prints. Spier hosted both individual psychotherapy sessions and courses in psychochirology, and after having her hand read publicly to serve as a demonstration in his class, Hillesum went into therapy with him. Part of the therapy consisted of Spier and Hillesum engaging in unorthodox "wrestling matches." In this fashion, Spier meant to have his patients regain contact with their physical, spiritual, and mental energies, and find a renewed balance between them. Etty became Spier's friend, his secretary, and eventually his lover. Through Spier's encouragement she began writing a journal in March 1941. The remarkable journal entries show profound insights about sexuality, morality, and spirituality, and trace an elaborate process of self-discovery and transformation.

While Spier's friendship and analysis would remain an important influence on her life and her journal writing until his death from cancer in September 1942, increasingly Hillesum would also come to write about the life of her friends and herself under the pressure of Nazi German occupation. Hillesum's diaries describe the intensifying isolation and segregation Dutch Jews experienced while awaiting their impending deportation to concentration camps in Poland. They also trace her own journey working for the Jewish Council, first as a secretary and then as a social worker in Westerbork. This privileged position allowed her not only to temporarily postpone her own deportation, but also to enter and leave camp Westerbork freely for work visits.

Hillesum continued to write her journal as well as a great number of letters that describe camp life in great detail. In the camp, she also attempted to provide mental and emotional support to the deportees. As Hillesum witnessed the increasing pace of the transports from Westerbork and the rapidly deteriorating situation in the camp (massive overcrowding, illness, cold, lack of adequate food and sanitation), it became clear to her that no one would escape deportation to the east. In fact the Germans were extraordinarily effective in their deportation of Dutch Jewry: 107,000 of the 140,000 Jews living in the Netherlands were deported, over 82 percent of the Dutch Jewish population. Less than 5 percent of these deportees survived, thus leaving the Dutch with the highest relative Jewish death rate of any Western European country. Hillesum prepared for the end by giving her journals for safekeeping to a friend in Amsterdam while turning down offers to go into hiding.

Her stay in Westerbork became permanent in July 1943, after her position with the Jewish Council was terminated. She was deported to Auschwitz on September 7, 1943, with the rest of her family. Hillesum died there on 30 November 1943, twenty-nine years old. Neither her parents nor her brothers survived. She took her last journals with her to Auschwitz, where they were lost.

The Diary

Hillesum's journals, some eight to twelve separate volumes, were collectively published in 1981 as a single diary, *Hetverstoorde leven*. What is most remarkable when one first reads Hillesum's published diary entries is how strikingly modern this author sounds. Both in her language and in her subject matter, the search for an authentic self, and an introspective examination of her goals and desires in life, Hillesum sounds more like a young woman of the 1980s or 1990s than the early 1940s. Her language is direct and without embellishment, even while writing on philosophical or religious matters, and her tone is extremely open and honest.

While her language makes us feel that she is a contemporary and her search for who she is or may become is ultimately a universal one and is therefore easily recognizable, the circumstances under which Hillesum wrote and which would progressively impinge on her writing were most extraordinary. Knowing of the catastrophe to come, we cannot help in our reading but to foreshadow Hillesum's unnecessary early death. We see and feel Hitler closing in on her, even as Etty in the journal successfully wards off her fears. This contradictory pull between a profound spiritual search for self and truth and the need to come to terms with the very real destruction around her is also at the heart of the journal. While the first half of the diaries focuses on a highly internal and personal process of (self-) discovery, the second half shows us Etty struggling to come to terms with the murders occurring around her.

What makes the work so unusual and so hard to place is that her journals show that precisely when the Nazis closed in on her, Hillesum managed to gradually liberate herself from fear and hatred, to the point of complete understanding and acceptance of what was to come. Hillesum's was a highly unusual, spiritually enlightened response to the Holocaust.

March 1941–January 1942

The Etty we meet in the diary's first eight months, from March 1941 to January 1942, is a brilliant but also impulsive and self-absorbed young woman. She is full of great insights but bogged down by banality. She uses the journal to find some inner peace as she feels herself to be too wrapped up with self-pity, ever-changing moods, and minor physical ailments. Central to this early part of her diary is her intense relationship with Julius Spier, whom she identifies as "S." Spier urges her toward integration and impresses upon her the necessity of getting head and heart in balance. Her first task, however, becomes a sorting out of her feelings for him. Although he has a fiancée in England to whom he wants to remain faithful, Etty feels a strong attraction to S., which she can hardly contain, especially as it seems to her to be mutual.

While at first the erotic pull seems to dominate, soon their exchanges become of a more intellectual and spiritual nature. S. suggests that she meditate and reconcile both her inner demons and the threats from the outside world. He argues that the two are indeed connected: in the face of Nazi Germany's desire for the total destruction of the Jews, one's only way to fight back is to fight the hatred within. By examining again and again the deeper grounds for human cruelty, Hillesum struggles to find solace in reliance on a spiritual power. To remain in touch with this voice deep inside herself, however, she needs to write. While the writing centers around her, once she stops writing, she feels depressed and congested. The writing becomes the central focus of her life; she would often write for hours at a time, and several times during one day.

(Jewish) Spirituality

Beyond the therapy sessions and the writing, S. also suggests that Etty meditate, and he becomes her spiritual mentor. Together they study the Bible, and this includes what Hillesum calls, in accordance with Christian usage, the New Testament. The journal also mentions that Etty reads Saint Augustine and the Apostles. Although Hillesum reads these Christian texts and writes of kneeling and folding her hands while praying, it would be incorrect to see her as a (would-be) Christian on this evidence. She actually comments herself on her unusual posture during prayer, but suggests that she uses it despite the fact that she is a Jew (*An Interrupted Life and Letters from Westerbork*, New York: Henry Holt and Company, 1991, p. 228).

No matter how open she may have been to different religious and spiritual doctrines wherever they might be found (in Christianity or Buddhism, for example), Hillesum had no interest in conversion. Neither was she interested in Jewish religious convention. Having grown up in a secular Jewish family, Hillesum never mentions observing Jewish holidays, visiting the synagogue, or keeping kosher. This was not at all unusual in her circle, in which many Jews of Hillesum's social class in Amsterdam in the 1930s and 1940s were highly assimilated. Many of these assimilated Dutch middle-class Jews did not in fact come to redefine their Jewishness until the Nazi persecution. It is thus not surprising to see that the journal rarely mentions Jewish customs or lifestyles and that there are no references to Palestine or the Zionist movement, even though Hillesum partook in the activities of a Zionist youth group as a child. Nevertheless, Hillesum's writing suggests that her Jewish identity is central to who she is, and possibly became more so precisely because of the persecution of the Nazis. She feels connected to other Jews through fate and history.

Hillesum's religiosity, then, was neither typical Christian nor Jewish. Etty's image of God was highly idiosyncratic and personal: "When I pray . . . I hold a silly, naïve, or deadly serious dialogue with what is deepest inside me, which for the sake of convenience I call God" (p. 183).

The Nazi Trap: 1942–1943

In the second half of the diary, from January 1942 to October 1942, Hillesum increasingly describes the difficult situation of the Dutch Jews. They are isolated and segregated, and by April 1942, all so-called full

Jews are required to wear a yellow star. Even though Spier, Etty, and many in the Spier circle are Jewish, the regulations and restrictions on Jews are viewed initially as minor interruptions. Hillesum even refuses to join friends and acquaintances in bashing the Germans: "It is the problem of our age: hatred of Germans poisons everyone's mind. . . . if there were only one decent German, then he should be cherished despite that whole barbaric gang, and because of that one decent German it is wrong to pour hatred over an entire people" (p. 11). Instead, she believes that to understand and overcome the Nazis, one needs to turn inward: "I no longer believe that we can change anything in the world until we have first changed ourselves. And that seems to me the only lesson to be learned from this war" (p. 84).

As deportations begin in full swing in the summer of 1942, the reality of the persecution can no longer just be contemplated on a philosophical level, however. As it becomes clear that her deportation, too, is impending, Etty's brother Jaap urges her to find a job at the Jewish Council, which would offer her a measure of protection. Hillesum feels extremely ambivalent about this opportunity. Working for the council indeed implies respite from deportation for the time being, but it also means that others would be sent in one's place. Thus, after just fourteen days of office work at the Council, she decides to volunteer to go to Westerbork as a social worker instead. Her diaries indicate that she is convinced that she can be true to herself only if she does not abandon those in danger, and if she uses her energy to support the lives of others. Her work allows her to enter and leave the camp freely for almost a year between August 1942 and September 1943.

Hillesum arrives at Westerbork just as the deportations of Dutch Jews to Poland are beginning. Every Monday, an empty train pulls into the camp, and every Tuesday a transport of about a thousand Jews leaves for Auschwitz, Sobibór, and Theresienstadt. The list of deportees is not announced until Monday evening, and these nights before deportation are filled with despair. Hillesum spends her time confronting the bereft and those who are put on transport. Meanwhile, she keeps her diary and writes letters. During this period, she travels back and forth to Amsterdam approximately a dozen times. Most of her time in Amsterdam, however, is spent in bed; she is ill and suffers from gallstones.

The last part of her diary, written in Amsterdam, tells of the sudden illness and death of S. Finally, early in June 1943 she leaves Amsterdam for Westerbork for the last time. In these last months after the death of S. Hillesum seems to have found more serenity, despite, or possibly because of, the increasingly oppressive situation. She is profoundly aware that historical circumstances are beyond her control, and that her only responsibility is to attempt to determine her responses to them:

> Very well then, this new certainty, that what they are after is our total destruction. I accept it. I know it now, and I shall not burden others with my fears. . . . I work and continue to live with the same conviction, and I find life meaningful. . . . my life has, so to speak, been extended by death, by my looking death in the eye and accepting it, by accepting destruction as part of life and no longer wasting my energies on fear of death or the refusal to acknowledge its inevitability. It sounds paradoxical: by excluding death from our life we cannot live a full life, and by admitting death into our life we enlarge and enrich it (pp. 154–155).

Hillesum works hard to come to terms with the inevitability of her own death; paradoxically, at this moment she finds a new sense of inner peace.

Hillesum's passion, even in the face of her approaching death, is for self-examination. Her diary and letters chronicle an intellectual and spiritual development that normally would take a lifetime, but out of necessity came to fruition in only two brief years. In marked contrast to the dehumanization and disintegration around her, Hillesum creates a work of profound connection: she comes to believe in and search for the essential goodness in people, in love, in connections rather than barriers. She develops a religious sensibility that gives her writings a spiritual, and at times even mystical, character that rises above the Nazi destruction.

Reception

While the first Dutch edition of Hillesum's journal, *Het verstoorde leven*, forms the basis of all the foreign translations, this publication consisted of only a selection of her writings. The critical edition that came out in 1986 in the Netherlands changes our impression of Hillesum as it allows us to see her as more fallible, more human. The different Hillesum that emerges suggests that the contradictions present in the journal were minimized in the earlier selection. Although Hillesum seemed all too aware of the contradictory impulses within herself (the spiritual versus the sensual/sexual, greediness versus asceticism), the marketing of her work thus creates a far less ambiguous, more saintlike image. The translations of her work tend to obfuscate some of the complexity or contradictory impulses in Hillesum's own thoughts as well.

In the United States this atypical image of Hillesum has not kept her from being read as part of a larger body of Holocaust literature (relatively little emphasis has been put on the spiritual aspects of her work), but her reception in Europe has been affected by this earlier selection. In France, for instance, Hillesum is a celebrated author, but she is analyzed mostly in the context of Christian theology and mysticism. In the Netherlands, too, her work is still read more within Christian circles than elsewhere, although the publication of the critical edition has managed to change her reception considerably. What is problematic about these Christian rereadings of Hillesum's work is that her murder is seen here as a voluntary sacrifice. This makes her into a martyr, a decidedly un-Jewish figure, and denies that the historical circumstances did not leave her with many options. Furthermore, such an interpretation seeks to mitigate her horrible and senseless death in Auschwitz, and suggests that her altruism and faith would have carried her to a peaceful death. We cannot know, however, if her faith helped her in Auschwitz. All we know is that while alive, Hillesum fought to remain human despite the inhumanity surrounding her, and that she chose to share her fate with that of other Jews rather than allowing herself to be an exception. This ending may be hard to understand for postwar audiences, but it is Hillesum's story.

Bibliography

Primary Sources

Het verstoorde leven: Dagboek van Etty Hillesum 1941–1943 (*An Interrupted Life: Diary of Elly Hillesum* 1941–1943). 1981.

Het denkende hart van de barak: Brieven van Etty Hillesum (*The Thinking Heart of the Barracks: Letters by Etty Hillesum*). 1982.

In duizend zoete armen: Nieuwe dagboekaantekeningen van Etty Hillesum (*In a Thousand Sweet Arms: New Journal Entries by Etty Hillesum*). 1984.

Etty: De nagelaten geschriften van Etty Hillesum 1941–1943 (*Etty: The Posthumous Writings of Etty Hillesum 1941–1943*). 1986.

An Interrupted Life and Letters from Westerbork. 1996.

Secondary Sources

Boas, Henriette. "Present-day interest in marginal Dutch Jewish Authors." *Dutch Jewish History: Proceedings of the Symposium on the History of the Jews in the Netherlands*. Nov. 28–Dec 3, 1982 Tel Aviv-Jerusalem. Ed. Jozeph Michuran. Jerusalem: Tel Aviv University, 1984.

Brenner, Rachel Feldhay. *Writing as Resistance: Four Women Confronting the Holocaust, Edith Stein, Simone Weil, Anne Frank, Etty Hillesum*. University Park: Pennsylvania State University Press, 1997.

De Costa, Denise. *Anne Frank en Etty Hillesum: Spiritualiteit, schrijverschap, seksualiteit*. Amsterdam: Uitgeverij Balans, 1996.

———. *Anne Frank and Etty Hillesum: Inscribing Spirituality and Sexuality*. Trans. Mischa F. C. Hoyinck. New Brunswick, N.J.: Rutgers University Press, 1998.

Downey, Michael. "A Balm for All Wounds: The Spiritual Legacy of Etty Hillesum." *Spirituality Today* 1 (spring 1988): 18–35.

Gaarlandt, Jan Geurt, ed. *"Men zou een pleister op vele wonden willen zijn." Reacties op de dagboeken en brieven van Etty Hillesum*. Amsterdam: Uitgeverij Balans, 1989.

Goedegebuure, Jaap. "Kampleed voor de moderne dominee." *Haagse Post* (May 29, 1982): 86–87.

Halperin, Irving. "Etty Hillesum: A Story of Spiritual Growth." *Reflections of the Holocaust in Art and Literature*. Ed. Roudolph L. Brakhama. New York: Cseugeri Institute for Holocaust Studies of the Graduate School and University Center of the City University of New York, 1990.

Hop-Dijkhuis, Siemy, ed. *Etty Hillesum '43–'93: Teksten van lezingen gehouden in de Herdenkingsweek November 1993 te Deventer*. Deventer, Netherlands: Boekhandel Praamstra, 1995.

Jong, Lovisde. *The Netherlands and Nazi Germany*. The Erasmus Lectures 1988. Cambridge: Harvard University Press, 1990.

Jorna, Ton, Denise de Costa, and Marijn ten Holt. *De Moed hebben tot zichzelf: Etty Hillesum als inspiratiebron bij levensvragen*. Utrecht, Netherlands: Kwadraat, 1999.

Kuiper, Arie. "Het Fenomeen Etty Hillesum." *De Tyd* 7 November 1986: 53.

Moore, Bob. *Victims and Survivors: The Nazi Persecution of the Jews in the Netherlands 1940–1945*. London: Arnold, 1997.

Presser, Jacques. *The Destruction of the Dutch Jews*. Trans. Arnold Pomeraus. New York: E. P. Dutton & Co, 1969.

Todorov, Tzvetau. *Facing the Extreme: Moral Life in the Concentration Camps*. Trans. Arthur Denner and Abigail Dollak. New York: Henry Holt and Co., 1996.

Van Galen Last, Dich, and Rolf Wolfswinhel. *Anne Frank and After: Dutch Holocaust Literature in Historical Perspective*. Amsterdam: Amsterdam University Press, 1996.

Zomeren, Koos van. "Een overmaat aan vergeesteliijking: De navolging van Etty Hillesum." *Vrij Nederland Boekenbijlage* (July 29, 1989): 3.

EDGAR HILSENRATH

(1926–)

NORBERT OTTO EKE

IN 1994, EDGAR Hilsenrath was awarded the Hans-Erich-Nossack-Preis des Kulturkreises der deutschen Wirtschaft to honor his writing, which was assumed to be a "kaddish for all cultures that have become extinct in the genocides of our century" ("Alexis Canem: Totenklage mit schwarzer Ironie. Der Schriftsteller Edgar Hilsenrath wird für sein Lebenswerk geehrt," *Jüdisches Allgemeine* 49[16]). This set the scene for the recognition of a work written in a style not previously found in the rhetoric of emotion that had determined the German-language *Shoah* literature since the late 1940s. Thirty years previously, the Munich-based publisher Kindler Verlag, after initial enthusiasm for the manuscript of Hilsenrath's first novel, *Night* (*Nacht*, 1964) halfheartedly printed only a small edition that the publisher quickly removed from the market. To the management of the publishing house the novel appeared to break too extremely with conventional thinking. After receiving much recognition abroad, especially in the United States, a new edition in 1978 finally brought the novel recognition by the German public.

Night and *The Nazi and the Barber*

In shocking detail, *Night* describes how National Socialist racism is reflected in the demise of the victims' social and moral values as the victims fought for survival in the sealed world of the ghetto of the Ukrainian city of Prokow. This was a fight with every person for himself for food, warm clothes, and a safe sleeping place. Hilsenrath's ghetto is no longer the place of heroic resistance or the test of ideal heroes. Instead it is hell become reality, where the rule of terror degrades the persecuted, whose combat against each other causes their own destruction. In the ghetto society dominated by angst, hunger, violence, and uncontrolled instinct, humane values and moral integrity exist only in the form of vague moments of remembrance of a bygone time, lived and acted out only by a few exceptional characters. Although Hilsenrath concentrates on the perspective of the abandoned victims in his description of the misery of ghetto life, the marks of the perpetrator that forced them into this are present in the destruction and deformation of human nature. The crassness of the description does not denounce those fighting for survival, but, on the contrary, refers to the reverse side of the National Socialist crime: the victim transformed into a distorted figure, the "ugly" Jew, by the reign of terror.

The stereotypes in this distorted depiction also constitute the beginning of Hilsenrath's second novel *The Nazi and the Barber: A Tale of Vengeance* (*Der Nazi und der Friseur*, English translation 1971, German edition 1977). In this novel the perspective is reversed. It is told from the perspective of the perpetrator, thus shedding a grotesque light on the atrocity of extermination. In *The Nazi and the Barber* Hilsenrath arranges an unfathomable, harsh, but bitterly comical manipulation of identities that advances in the tradition of the picaresque. The novel is developed as the confession of the SS hangman and mass murderer Max Schultz, who, after the war, takes on the identity of the Jew Itzig Finkelstein, one of his childhood friends whom he murdered in a concentration camp. He immigrates to Palestine, where he not only lives in the shadows of his victim's borrowed biography but involuntarily becomes one of the heroes of the Jewish War of Independence: a patriot above suspicion. Hilsenrath supports the perfidious mimicry of his "hero" by constructing a conversion of images that satirically unmask the still existing anti-Jewish and antisemitic stereotypes. Schultz, the illegitimate son of an Aryan whore, is the spitting image of the "Stürmer"-Jew (the Jew as described in the antisemitic scandal sheet "Der Stürmer"), while his Jewish friend, Itzig, corresponds to the picture of the ideal Aryan German, both becoming the mirrored reverse of their origins. The camouflage he has adopted of a late circumcision and the replacement of his SS blood group mark with a concentration camp number to complete his identity change prove unnecessary. The transformation of the perpetrator into victim is successful because the antisemitic stereotype is still in place even in postwar Germany: Schultz is considered a Jew because he looks exactly like the stereotype of a Jew says he should. That this distortion should function also from the Jewish point of view is the surprising and scandalous coup of the novel. Additionally, the unstoppable advancement of Schultz to respected citizenship and ownership of an elegant hairdressing salon occurs as part of the antisemitic cliché—so even in Israel the Jewishness of a "typical" Jew is not doubted. The antisemitic stereotype proves to be universally valid.

In the end, no (poetic) justice is meted out for the fake Jew's crimes. At an advanced age, Schultz confesses his crimes to a long-standing friend, a retired judge, in the hope of receiving his just punishment, only to be met by disbelief. Desperately, the murderer struggles with his judge to establish truth and lies, guilt and atonement; however, the symbolic process that he so desires ends with an acquittal that neither reconciles the victim nor expiates the perpetrator: the murderer is acquitted only for the reason that there can be no punishment for his crime, because the victims of the annihilation can receive no final justice that is satisfying to both sides. Thus, the novel ends not only in perplexity at the enormous burden of guilt (in which, in the U.S. edition, the passively watching God is included), but Hilsenrath also extracts the *Shoah* from the sense-giving order of human (and divine) justice. The perpetrator is left alone with the angst of his victim and the *Shoah* finds no meaningful answers.

Biography and Style

Hilsenrath openly uses autobiographical experiences as material for memory. He was born on 2 April 1926 in Leipzig, the eldest child of the merchant David Hilsenrath and his wife Anni (née Hönigsberg). Edgar grew up in Halle (Saale), where he was the only Jewish child at secondary school. The increase in antisemitic attacks prompted David Hilsenrath to send his wife and two sons, Edgar and Manfred, in the summer of 1938 to his in-laws in Sereth (now Siret) to the supposedly safe area of Bukovina, at that time part of Romania. He himself escaped in 1939 and lived out the war in France using a false name. While still in Sereth, Hilsenrath spent his time in self-education without regularly attending school; it was, in his own words, the happiest period of his life. The supposedly safe haven proved, however, to be unsafe for the family after the German invasion of the Soviet Union in June 1941. On 14 October 1941, the Romanian allies of Germany deported the Hilsenrath family to Moghilev-Podolsk (the model for the ghetto Prokow in *Night*), a bombed-out, isolated town near the Dniester River. Edgar, his mother, and his brother survived the following years in the most difficult of circumstances until the ghetto was liberated by the Red Army in March 1944. Alone, Edgar traveled initially to Bucharest, and from there via Bulgaria, Turkey, Syria, and Lebanon to Palestine. Here, he earned a meager living by occasional labor but was unable to find a *Heimat* (emotional or symbolic "home") in the alien environment. He left the country in 1947 to meet his parents and brother. The Hilsenrath family was reunited in France, only then to emigrate to the United States: Manfred in 1950, Edgar in 1951, and Anni and David in 1953. Edgar lived mainly in New York until 1975. But even there he remained without connection and *Heimat*. He had already begun working on *Night* in France and finished it in 1954 in the United States.

Hilsenrath's literary confrontation with the *Shoah*, which begins with this novel, is bound to the German language, with which, in his own words, he had a precarious "love affair" (Kraft, pp. 13–19). German remains his medium of memory even in exile in his chosen American *Heimat* where, in 1966 and 1971, respectively, his first two novels, *Night* and *The Nazi and the Barber*, were published with great critical and financial success. This relationship to the language of his childhood was used to explain his later return to Germany. He did not consider postwar Germany his *Heimat* in the emphatic sense (for Hilsenrath this would always be the lost Bukovina). When he settled in Berlin, however, it was the vital "language *Heimat*" he required as an author. The not unproblematic love of the German language and culture was described in 1978 by Hilsenrath in the short text "We Died a Different Death" (Wir starben einen anderen Tod) in the dialogue characteristic of his writings:

> My language is German.
> The damned language.
> That I love because it is my language.
> That you always loved. Even then.
> Even then, as the synagogues were burning
> That you loved. Even in the country of the mass shootings.
> Even in the country of the mass shootings.

As your eyes scanned the distance, to there, where the ovens of Auschwitz smoked.

Even then
Even then.
(Zeitmagazin, 40, 29 September 1978: 53)

The reflection on the medium of the (German) language is part of the self-reflexive references in writings about and after the *Shoah* that accompany Hilsenrath's literary works throughout the years. This reflection gains a central meaning in the fictional biographies Bronsky's Confession (*Bronskys Geständnis*, 1980) and Ruben Jablonski's Adventures (*Die Abenteuer des Ruben Jablonski*, 1997). Both novels tell of the birth of the author and his vanquishing of the trauma of being a victim and the identity crisis of the survivors by writing about the horror. Significantly, Hilsenrath anchors his tales in *Ruben Jablonski's Adventures* in the process of memory. In the frame of an introductory retrospect of the day that the Moghilev-Podolsk ghetto was liberated, he remembers: "I began to dream and thought of my childhood in Germany. Berlin! roared the tiny slit-eyed Kirghiz on his tank and swung his machine gun around. Berlin! Berlin!" (Munich and Zurich, 1997, p. 8). Hilsenrath's prose spells out in ever changing literary styles the alphabet of genocide in the twentieth century: with hypernaturalism (*Night*), in the form of satire and the grotesque (*The Nazi and the Barber*), in autobiographical memories (Bronsky's Confession and Ruben Jablonski's Adventures), with fairy stories as models (The Last Thought's Fairy Tale), and Yiddish story traditions (Jossel Wassermann's Homecoming) that make a method out of digression.

Hilsenrath has given his own answer to the question of whether a literary depiction of the act of annihilation is possible by confessing to a type of narration that gives language to a nonhierarchic memory. "Please tell the essential" (Munich 1993, p. 136) demands the solicitor in his function as an agent for a sober judicature of his dying client in the frame story of *Jossel Wassermann's Homecoming* (1993), a novel based on Hasidic legends and humorous *shtetl* stories that, in the example of the imaginary village Pohodna am Pruth, reawakens the extinct *shtetl* culture of Eastern Europe. The answer of the dying Jew is: "The essential is that I talk . . ., for as long as I talk I am not dead" (p. 136). At the end of the novel a consoling realization is formulated: "He that preserves does not believe in doom and is not desperate. Then for whom should he preserve something if there is no continuation?" (p. 319), and the project of a poetry of memory is awakened to which Hilsenrath's confrontation with the *Shoah* gave decisive contours in the 1980s and 1990s. In his late prose, Hilsenrath sets next to the historical memory the idea of a decentralized polyphonic (also fairy tale-like memory), which additionally gives the apparently marginal, the small "chatter-boxes," a voice and thus creates for the annihilated European Jewish culture in all its facets an afterlife in the collective memory of the survivors and succeeding generations.

Hilsenrath's polyphonic narration that, as in Jossel Wassermann's Homecoming and The Last Thought's Fairy Tale, sketches the poetic hypothetical picture of all the annihilated cultures, the Jewish and the Armenian, from fragments as a counterproject to the *Shoah*, which aims for total obliteration. The idea behind this work is the belief that it is possible to "rescue" history through art that is a medium of memory and "herald of the dead" (Walter Benjamin, *Das Passagen-Werk*, Frankfurt/Main, 1983, p. 603). From here Hilsenrath concretizes the idea of art as memory through the concept of a senseless and thus irrational (seen from the point of view of rationality) and disturbing memory that makes the usual treatment of history unsafe. It is a memory that wounds, that rouses the everyday consciousness impregnated against the experience of horror and thus breaks the conspiratory cordon of silence, banishment, and obliteration erected around the policy of annihilation.

In The Last Thought's Fairy Tale in this context a pattern of meaning gains narrative stringency that understands the genocide of the Armenian minority in Turkey during World War I as a historical prelude to the *Shoah*. At the beginning of the novel that follows the historical traces of the Armenian-Turkish culture annihilated in the first genocide of the twentieth century, Hilsenrath has a German officer say that the Jews and Armenians "are nearly interchangeable" (Munich, 1989, p. 39), and this is what literally happens in the end. In 1943, an Armenian who has escaped the Turkish massacre is traveling with a Swiss passport to Poland to save Jewish property from the next genocide. In Warsaw he loses his passport, and, owing to his outward appearance, he is taken for a Jew and finally perishes in a gas chamber meant for another people in a German extermination camp. Thus, the victim of the *Shoah* is metamorphosed: from being a Jew to being a victim in general, being a part of a persecuted minority. In view of this for Hilsenrath, historical meaning cannot be fulfilled in the return to preset structures but in the form of a forward-looking redemption that takes its impulse from the power of memory. Meaning is transferred *from* history *into* narrative as a guarantee of continuation of life and survival. "Poets are our memory" (p. 460), thus is the apt statement at the end of the "tale."

Critical Response

The five novels Night, The Nazi and the Barber, The Last Thought's Fairy Tale, Jossel Wassermann's Homecoming, and Ruben Jablonski's Adventures have established Hilsenrath as one of the most important living German-language Jewish authors. After a delayed reception, hampered by the German "moral" (philosemitic) majority, his reputation has also been recognized in Germany since the 1980s. Hilsenrath's works have been published in large numbers, translated into many languages, and have received many prizes (Alfred-Döblin-Preis, 1989; Heinz-Galinski-Preis der Berliner Jüdischen Gemeinde, 1992; Hans-Erich-Nossack-Preis, 1994; Jakob Wassermann-Preis der Stadt Fürth, 1996; Hans-Sahl-Preis der Kulturstiftung der Deutschen Bank, 1998). Despite his well-earned respect, Hilsenrath is still a controversial author who has had to defend himself against accusations of "post-modern entertainment" (Sautermeister, p. 227) and the "mocking of the victims" (Klüger, p. 24).

As Hilsenrath systematically violates the conventional rules of the Holocaust discourse with his use of wit, satire, and the grotesque in his novels, in Germany his works have lost none of their explosive force that had established his special and nonmainstream position in the German-language literature of the *Shoah* since the beginning of the 1980s. Hilsenrath counters the never-ending question of whether art and literature will ever be able to place commensurable aesthetic structures, which create laughter and black humor, alongside real historical horror. His works must be necessarily irritating when the art of memory has exhausted itself in the search for self-made emotion. Even as late as 1990, he explained that his writing was incompatible with the rusty patterns of meaning and stereotypes of perception, especially in the exceptional standards of an extremely ambiguous philosemitism. "I have frightened the philo-semites, I am an outsider for both the Germans and the Jews. So I can allow myself to have a little fun" (Thomas Feibel, "Ich habe die Philosemiten erschreckt, ich bin ein Außenseiter. Ans einem Gespräch mit dem Schriftseller Edgar Hilsenrath," *Frankfurter Rundschau, 215* [15 September 1990]: 2). Hilsenrath is indisputably important for the German-language *Shoah* literature as a forerunner and pioneer of a paradigm change toward a decided literary confrontation with the *Shoah*. With the current developments in the writings of third-generation German Jewish authors (such as Maxim Biller) who on winding paths follow the cultural imprinting of the *Shoah* in the thoughts and dealings of the postwar generation, Hilsenrath's nonmainstream position has been abandoned, although some still have reservations about that. Hilsenrath still frightens the philosemites but he is no longer an outsider.

Bibliography

Primary Sources

Nacht (*Night*). 1964.

Der Nazi und der Friseur (*The Nazi and the Barber: A Tale of Vengeance*). 1971 (German version, 1977).

Gib acht, Genosse Mandelbaum (Take Care, Comrade Mandelbaum). 1979.

Bronskys Geständnis (Bronsky's Confession). 1980.

Zibulsky oder Antenne im Bauch (Zibulsky or Antenna in the Belly). 1983.

Das Märchen vom letzten Gedanken (Last Thought's Fairy Tale). 1989.

Jossel Wassermanns Heimkehr (Jossel Wassermann's Homecoming). 1993.

Die Abenteuer des Ruben Jablonski. Ein autobiographischer Roman (Ruben Jablonski's Adventures). 1997.

Secondary Sources

Bauer, Karin. "Erzählen im Augenblick höchster Gefahr: Zu Benjamins Begriff der Geschichte in Edgar Hilsenraths *Jossel Wassermanns Heimkehr*." In *German Quarterly* 71, no. 4 (fall 1998): 343–352.

Braese, Stephan. *Das teure Experiment. Satire und NS-Faschismus*. Opladen, Germany: Westdeutscher Verlag, 1996.

Brecheisen, Claudia. "Literatur des Holocaust: Identität und Judentum bei Jakov Lind, Edgar Hilsenrath und Jurek Becker." Ph.D. diss. University of Augsburg. Unpublished, 1993.

Dopheide, Dietrich. *Das Groteske und der Schwarze Humor in den Romanen Edgar Hilsenraths*. Berlin: Weißensee, 2000.

Eke, Norbert Otto. "Planziel Vernichtung. Zwei Versuche über das Unfaβbare des Völkermords: Franz Werfels *Die vierzig Tage des Musa Dagh* (1933) und Edgar Hilsenraths *Das Märchen vom letzten Gedanken* (1989)." In *Deutsche Vierteljahrsschrift für Literaturwissenschaft und Geistesgeschichte* 71, no. 4 (1997): 701–723.

Fuchs, Anne. "Edgar Hilsenrath's Poetics of Insignificance and the Tradition of Humour in German-Jewish Ghetto Writing." In *Ghetto Writing: Traditional and Eastern Jewry in German-Jewish Literature from Heine to Hilsenrath*. Edited by Anne Fuchs and Florian Krobb. Rochester, N. Y.: Camden House, 1999, pp. 180–194.

Gerstenberger, Katharina, and Vera Pohland. "Der Wichser. Edgar Hilsenrath—Schreiben über den Holocaust, Identität und Sexualität." In *Der Deutschunterricht* 44, no. 3 (1992): 74–91.

Gilman, Sander. "Jüdische Literaten und deutsche Literatur. Antisemitismus und die verborgene Sprache der Juden am Beispiel von Jurek Becker und Edgar Hilsenrath." In *Zeitschrift für Deutsche Philologie* 107, no. 2 (1988): 269–294.

Hien, Ursula. "Schreiben gegen den Philosemitismus. Edgar Hilsenrath und die Rezeption von *Nacht* in Westdeutschland." In *Deutsche Nachkriegsliteratur und der Holocaust*. Edited by Stephan Braese, Holger Gehle, Doron Kiesel, and Hanno Loewy. Frankfurt am Main: Campus, 1998, pp. 229–244.

Horch, Hans Otto. "Grauen und Groteske. Zu Edgar Hilsenraths Romanen." In *Wir tragen den Zettelkasten mit den Steckbrie-*

fen unserer Freunde. Edited by Jens Stüben and Winfried Woesler. Darmstadt: Häusser, 1994, pp. 213–226.

Kraft, Thomas, ed. *Edgar Hilsenrath. Das Unerzählbare erzählen*. Munich: Piper, 1996.

Lorenz, Dagmar C. G. "Social Darwinism in Edgar Hilsenrath's Ghetto Novel *Nacht*." In *Insiders and Outsiders: Jewish and Gentile Culture in Germany and Austria*. Edited by Dagmar C. G. Lorenz and Gabriele Weinberger. Detroit: Wayne State University Press, 1994, pp. 214–223.

Moeller, Susann. "Politics to Pulp a Novel: The Fate of the First Edition of Edgar Hilsenrath's Novel *Nacht*. In *Insiders and Outsiders: Jewish and Gentile Culture in Germany and Austria*. Edited by Dagmar C. G. Lorenz and Gabriele Weinberger. Detroit: Wayne State University Press, 1994, pp. 224–234.

Sautermeister, Gert. "Aufgeklärte Modernität—Postmodernes Entertainment. Edgar Hilsenraths 'Der Nazi & der Friseur.' " In *Wir tragen den Zettelkasten mit den Steckbriefen unserer Freunde*. Edited by Jens Stüben and Winfried Woesler. Darmstadt: Häusser, 1994, pp. 227–242.

Stenberg, Peter. "Memories of the Holocaust. Edgar Hilsenrath and the Fiction of Genocide." In *Deutsche Vierteljahrsschrift für Literaturwissenschaft und Geistesgeschichte* 56, no. 2 (1982): 277–289.

Werner, Klaus. "Die literarische und dokumentarliterarische Reflexion des transnistrischen Holocaust." In *Jüdische Autoren Ostmitteleuropas im 20. Jahrhundert*. Edited by Hans Henning Hahn and Jens Stüben. Frankfurt am Main: Peter Lang, 2000, pp. 385–427.

ROLF HOCHHUTH

(1931–)

EDWARD ISSER

THE PLAYWRIGHT, essayist, and novelist Rolf Hochhuth was born on 1 April 1931, in Eschwege, Germany. His father, Walter Hochhuth, was a shoe factory owner and an accountant. Hochhuth's mother, Ilse (Holzapfel), was a housewife. The family were members of the German Evangelical Church. During the latter part of World War II, Hochhuth was assigned to a Hitler Youth unit. After the war, he studied at a vocational school and later sporadically attended the universities of Marburg, Munich, and Heidelberg. In 1955 he became a reader and editor for the German book publisher Guetersloh and later Bertelsmann-Lesering. In 1959 he began work on *Der Stellvertreter* (*The Deputy*) and, after intensive research, finished the play in 1962. Initially no one was interested in either publishing or producing the work. Finally, in 1963, Rowohlt Taschenbuch published the play and Erwin Piscator agreed to direct the premiere at the Volksbuehne Theatre. The controversial drama was subsequently awarded the Gerhart Hauptmann Prize, Berliner Kunstpreis, the Young Generation Prize, and the Frederic Melcher Prize. As of 2002, *Der Stellvertreter* had been produced professionally more than seventy-five times in twenty-five countries.

In 1963 Hochhuth was appointed an assistant director and playwright at the Municipal Theatre in Basel, Switzerland. In 1976 he was awarded the Basler Art Prize. In 1980 his novel *Eine Liebe in Deutschland* (*A German Love Story*; 1978) won the Literary Award of Munich, the Bavarian Publishers Award, and the Scholl Prize for Literature; the next year, Hochhuth received the prestigious Lessing Prize. Hochhuth's 1990 novel *Sommer 1914* (Summer 1914) won that year's Jacob Burckhardt Prize, and in 2001 Hochhuth was awarded the Jacob Grimm Prize. In 1989, Hochhuth was appointed chief cultural correspondent for the German newspaper *Die Welt*. In the 1990s, he chaired a company that secured a purchase option on the Berliner Ensemble, generating accusations from the Ensemble's director, Heiner Mueller, that Hochhuth was plotting a hostile takeover of the theater. In 1996 Mueller died of cancer and Hochhuth's company assumed ownership of the Berliner Ensemble; Hochhuth resigned his chairmanship but retained board membership. That same year, he accepted a position as a lecturer at the Johann Wolfgang Goethe University in Frankfurt am Main.

The Deputy's Indictment of the Vatican: Inflaming a Historical Debate

The 1963 premiere of *Der Stellvertreter* (*The Deputy*) was a historical and cultural event. Rolf Hochhuth's diatribe on the moral failure of the Vatican during the Holocaust gave rise to an intense controversy that still persists decades later. Rolf Hochhuth's play about a fictional Jesuit priest who seeks redemption by sacrificing himself at Auschwitz proved offensive to many Catholics. Produced in Germany during the months leading up to Vatican II, the play—which offers a stinging indictment of Vatican policies during the Holocaust and specifically excoriates Pope Pius XII for his passivity—hit a raw nerve with a Church that was in the midst of self-reflection at the height of the Cold War. Conservative spokesmen of the Church expressed outrage at what they perceived to be slanderous and libelous charges. Rallies to oppose the drama were sponsored by Catholic Church clergy and by lay Catholics in every Western European and American city where the piece was performed.

The controversy surrounding the play prompted immediate and significant historical research. Historians such as Guenter Lewy (*The Catholic Church and Nazi Germany*, 1964) and Saul Friedländer (*Pie XII et le IIIe*

Reich, 1964) weighed in significantly on Hochhuth's behalf. In 1964 the Vatican published the first volume of *Actes et documents du Saint Siège relatifs à la seconde guerre mondiale* (ADSS) to document Church action on behalf of Jews during the war. Defenders of the Church, such as Pinchas Lapide (*Three Popes and the Jews*, 1967) and Burkhart Schneider (*Pies XII*, 1968), sought to repudiate the charges leveled by Hochhuth against the Vatican and Pius XII. In 1998, the controversy over Hochhuth's play was renewed when the Vatican issued a document titled "We Remember: A Reflection on the *Shoah*," which acknowledged the suffering of the Jews and condemned antisemitism but denied any moral failure on the part of the Church. The document defended the actions of the pope and praised "the wisdom" of Pius's diplomacy. The process for the beatification of Pius XII was begun but faltered in the face of criticism generated by John Cornwall's *Hitler's Pope* (2000) and Michael Phayer's *The Catholic Church and the Holocaust, 1930–1965* (2000). Also contributing to the debate was Susan Zuccotti's *Under His Very Windows: The Vatican and the Holocaust in Italy* (2000), which drew on a wealth of documents, archival material, and published memoirs to indict Pius for failure to act vigorously on behalf of the Jews, given the extent of his wartime knowledge of the genocide. In 2001, six historians, jointly appointed in 1999 by the Vatican and the International Jewish Committee for Interreligious Consultations to examine Vatican documents regarding World War II and the position of the pope, were forced to suspend their study when they were notified by the president of the pontifical commission that access to archival material from 1923 onward was "not possible at the present for technical reasons."

The renewed controversy over Pius XII in the late 1990s led to a critical and historical reassessment of Hochhuth's play. In 1999, Johns Hopkins University Press reissued a paperback edition of *The Deputy*, the English translation of *Der Stellvertreter* by Richard and Clara Winston. In 2001, the Berliner Ensemble revived *Der Stellvertreter*, and in 2002 Constantin Costa Gavras was planning the release of a film adaptation of the play, titled *Le vicaire*. Hochhuth's play remains an enduring, problematic work that is a lightning rod for controversy.

Synopsis

Rolf Hochhuth's *The Deputy* is a homage to the great epic dramas of Johann Wolfgang von Goethe and Friedrich von Schiller. Hochhuth borrows both style and form in his attempt to create a modern, poetic historical drama. The playwright mixes and matches historical and fictional characters in a five-act verse drama. Like all the great romantic dramatists, Hochhuth takes liberties freely with facts and circumstances to further his philosophical and ethical musings. *The Deputy* is a Christian passion play that pits evil, in the shape of the mysterious Doctor, against the goodness and faith of the young Jesuit priest Riccardo Fontana.

The action of *The Deputy* occurs between August 1942 and November 1943. Fontana, who is from a well-connected Italian family, serves in the Vatican hierarchy as a junior diplomat in the papal foreign office. He is posted to the papal nuncio in Berlin, where he meets an SS officer named Kurt Gerstein. Gerstein (based on a historical figure) arrives at the papal nuncio to testify about the mass murder of Jews and to urge a Vatican protest. Riccardo, horrified both by Gerstein's report and by the reserved, diplomatic response of the nuncio, seeks out the SS officer to offer his support and service. After giving up his passport and collar to a Jew hiding in Gerstein's apartment, Riccardo travels to Rome and appeals to the pope on behalf of the Jews.

The most controversial element of the play is the papal audience granted Riccardo Fontana. During the infamous fourth act of *The Deputy*, Pope Pius XII appears on stage to answer the charges of the young priest. Hochhuth's thesis is glaringly obvious: Pius XII is cold, impervious, and conniving. The stage directions instruct an actor how to approach the role:

> The actor who plays Pacelli should consider that His Holiness is much less a person than an institution: grand gestures, lively moments of his extraordinarily beautiful hands, and smiling, aristocratic coldness, together with the icy glint of his eyes behind the gold-rimmed glasses—these should suffice (p. 195).

Pius XII, as represented in *The Deputy*, is too preoccupied with financial and diplomatic concerns, and too obsessed with his fear of the Soviets, to do anything effective on behalf of the Jews.

> A deputy of Christ
> who sees these things and nonetheless
> permits reasons of state to seal his lips—
> who wastes even one day in thought,
> hesitates even for an hour
> to lift his anguished voice
> in one anathema to chill the blood
> of every last man on earth—
> that Pope is . . . a criminal (p. 102).

Pius has no time or patience for the pleadings of the young priest, and he defends the diplomatic nuances employed by the Church:

As long ago as July of last year
The Nuncio in Pressburg learned
That Jews from Slovakia were being gassed
In the district of Lublin. Has he
Run away from Pressburg for that reason?
No, he goes on doing his duty; and behold:
He managed to arrange that no more Jews
Are being sent away to Poland
Whoever wants to help must not
Provoke Hitler.
Secretly, as our two Jesuit fathers,
Silently, cunning as serpents—
That is how the SS must be met.
We have hidden hundreds of Jews in Rome.
Have issued thousands of passports! (p. 200).

In a wildly implausible scene imagined by Hochhuth, the young Jesuit persuades Pius XII to deliver a proclamation on behalf of the Jews. In a manner fairly typical of the play, Hochhuth melds documentary and fictional material together to further his provocative interpretation of events. The proclamation written in the play is a verbatim transcript of a famous notice that was printed in *L'Osservatore Romano* (the Vatican newspaper) on 25 October 1943, nine days after the infamous Roman roundup of 16 October. Defenders of the Church have long pointed to this document as a clear expression of papal outrage and protest about German racial persecution. Detractors of Pius XII cite the same document for its failure to mention either the word "Jew" or "Nazi" as an example of diplomatic tiptoeing. Rolf Hochhuth, in the stage directions that precede the recital of the document, makes his interpretation explicit:

> As though he had never intended to follow any other course, the POPE now acts as if he were going to protest publicly against the arrest of the Jews. . . . The coldness and hardness of his face, which Church publicists are fond of describing as "unearthly spiritualizations," has virtually reached the freezing point. He strikes the pose in which he likes to be photographed, gazing over the heads of all around him, far into the distance and high up in the air. It is inevitable that the scene suddenly takes on an unreal, in fact a phantasmagoric atmosphere. Words, words, a rhetoric totally corrupted into a classic device for sounding well and saying nothing (p. 212).

A number of historians who concur with Hochhuth's thesis concerning the moral culpability of the Church nevertheless criticize the playwright for a biased representation of Pius XII. Michael Phayer, for example, categorically rejects Hochhuth's Pius XII as a vicious caricature that "does not square with the historical record" (Phayer, p. 222).

Fontana emerges as a Christlike figure who takes upon himself the burden of preserving the moral essence of the Church. Unable to convince the pope to work actively to save the Jews of Europe, Fontana attaches a Jewish star to his priestly dress and is deported to Auschwitz—to be the deputy of the pope in the face of evil. The core dramatic question of the play is whether or not Fontana will forsake his faith and embrace the nihilism of the concentration camp universe. The SS doctor (based roughly on Josef Mengele) tempts Fontana in the dramatized hell of Auschwitz, but the young Jesuit struggles to save his soul and sanity.

Hochhuth's dramatization mixes historical personages such as Pius XII, Adolf Eichmann, and Kurt Gerstein with fictional characters in scenes that neither occurred nor ever could have occurred. Kurt Gerstein, for example, appears at both the Vatican and at Auschwitz at key moments in the drama. The "real" Gerstein, however, never visited either locale. Hochhuth aggravates the problem of textual veracity by claiming the haven of poetic license while maintaining claims of truthfulness. He acknowledges that *The Deputy* is a fictional work, yet includes in the published version a sixty-five-page addendum titled "Sidelights on History" that attempts to "prove" the historical accuracy of the play.

The Deputy is an overwrought romantic melodrama that ends in a spasm of violence and sacrifice. Good wins out over evil as the inert body of Father Fontana is slowly, ceremonially carried off stage to the Auschwitz crematorium. Fontana has completed his journey—both physically and spiritually. The Church is represented by its deputy, and Fontana has achieved a redemptive transcendent sacrifice. Death is given meaning at Auschwitz and the fate of the Jews provides an impressive backdrop for this Christian morality tale.

Staging Auschwitz has been an acute problem for dramatists, Hochhuth included. His notes to act 5 of *The Deputy* describe the dilemma:

> The question of whether and how Auschwitz might be visualized in this play occupied me for a long time. Documentary naturalism no longer serves as a stylistic principle . . . no attempt was made to strive for an imitation of reality—nor should the stage set strive for it. On the other hand, it seemed perilous, for the drama, to employ an approach such as was so effectively used by Paul Celan in his masterly poem "Todesfugue," in which the gassing of the Jews is entirely translated into metaphors, . . . metaphors still screen the infernal cynicism of what really took place—a reality so enormous and grotesque that even today . . . the impression of unreality it produces conspires with our natural strong tendency to treat the matter as a legend, as an incredible apocalyptic fable. No matter how closely we adhere to historical facts, the speech, the scene and events on the stage will be altogether surrealistic (pp. 222–223).

Critical Assessments of *The Deputy*

The Deputy has garnered a great deal of critical response both positive and negative. John Simon, who recognizes the play's shortcomings, concludes,

> What is momentous is that in an age that has progressively convinced itself that its significant dramatic form is dark comedy . . . that in this era when "the death of tragedy" has become a literary commonplace, *The Deputy* stands as a valid tragedy: not great, but good, and anything but commonplace (p. 175).

The play is also marked by stilted, tautological verse, two-dimensional characterizations, and simplistic, reductive dialogue that lectures the audience ad nauseum. Yet despite the aesthetic failings and a number of historical inaccuracies, *The Deputy* remains a potent, shocking piece of agitprop theater that is a lingering indictment of the Roman Catholic Church.

As long as the basic thesis of the play—that the Catholic Church failed to demonstrate moral leadership and refused to act on behalf of Jews—is being debated, and as long as the Church authorities refuse to provide full access to all pertinent documentation, *The Deputy* will remain a divisive, controversial work of art. The critic Susan Sontag noted the aesthetic failings of the play but emphasized the significance of the work in 1964: "some art—but not all—elects as its central purpose to tell the truth; and it must be judged by its fidelity to the truth, and by the relevance of the truth which it tells. By these standards, *The Deputy* is an extremely important play" (p. 120). In the years since Sontag made that observation, a consensus has emerged among reputable historians that Pius XII and the Vatican hierarchy do indeed bear responsibility for acts of commission and omission during the Holocaust. Hochhuth's play—and more important, his fundamental accusations—have defiantly stood the test of time.

Other Works

Rolf Hochhuth has written steadily since the 1960s on themes dealing with German history and the war experience. His play *Soldaten* (*Soldiers*; 1967) examines the morality of actions taken by Winston Churchill during the war and explores the evil of British carpet bombing. The play *Juristen* (1979) criticizes the legal system of West Germany because of the way it prevented Hitlerian judges and lawyers from being prosecuted for their actions during the war. The 1978 novel *Eine Liebe in Deutschland* tells the true story of a German woman who falls in love with a Polish worker in southern Germany during the war. The woman is betrayed by her neighbors and sent to a concentration camp, and the Pole is executed. In 2001, Hochhuth's play *Hitler's Faust* chronicled the moral entrapment of a rocket scientist who assists in the war effort. Although Hochhuth continued to write about the war, his later writing avoided the topic of the Holocaust.

Bibliography

Published Plays

Der Stellvertreter. 1963. Translated by Robert David MacDonald as *The Representative*, 1963; translated by Richard Winston and Clara Winston as *The Deputy*, 1964.
Soldaten: Nekrolog auf Genf. 1967. Staged in English as *Soldiers: An Obituary for Geneva*. 1968.
Guerillas: Tragoedie in fuenf Akten. 1970.
Die Hebamme: Komoedie. 1971.
Lysistrate und die Nato. 1973.
Zwischenspiel in Baden-Baden. 1974.
Tod eines Jaegers. 1976.
Juristen: Drei Akte fuer sieben Spieler. 1979.
Alle Dramen. Two volumes of collected plays. 1991.
Wessis in Weimar: Szenen aus einem besetzten land. 1993.
Das Recht auf Arbeit; Nachtmusik: Zwei Dramen. 2000.

Stage Productions

Der Stellvertreter. 1963. Staged in English as *The Representative*, 1963; as *The Deputy*, 1964.
Soldaten: Nekrolog auf Genf. 1967. Staged in English as *Soldiers*. 1968.
Guerillas: Tragoedie in fuenf Akten. 1970.
Judith. 1984.
Unbefleckte Empfangnis: Ein Kreidekreis. 1989.
Sommer 14: Ein Totentanz. 1990.
Wessis in Weimar. 1999.
Die Hebamme: Komoedie. 2000.
Hitler's Faust. 2001.

Novels and Essays

Krieg und Klassenkrieg. 1971.
Die Berliner Antigone: Prosa und Verse. 1975.
Eine Liebe in Deutschland. 1978. Translated by John Brownjohn as *A German Love Story*. 1980.
Tell '38. 1979.
Spitze des Eisbergs: Ein Reader. 1982.
Atlantik-Novelle: Erzahlungen und Gedichte. 1985.
Schwarze Segal: Essays und Gedichte. 1986.
Alan Turing: Erzahlung. 1987.
Tater und Denker: Profile und Probleme von Casar bis Junger: Essays, Deutsche. 1987.
War hier Europa? Reden, Gedichte, Essays, Deutscher. 1987.
Menzel: Maler des licts. 1991.
Von Syrakus aus gesehen, gedacht, erzeahlt. 1991.
Tell gegen Hitler: Historische studien. 1992.
Wessis in Weimar: Szenen aus einem besetzten land. 1993.
Julia oder der weg zur macht: Erzeahlung. 1994.
Effis nacht: Monolog. 1996.

Und Brecht sah das tragische nicht: Pleadoyers, Polimiken, Profile. 1996.
Wellen: Artgenossen, Zeitgenossen, Hausgenossen. 1996.

Secondary Sources

Adolph, Walter. *Verfälschte Geschichte: Antwort an Rolf Hochhuth, mit Dokumenten und authentischen Berichten*. Berlin: Morus-Verlag, 1963.

Bentley, Eric, ed. *The Storm over "The Deputy."* New York: Grove Press, 1964. Collected essays about the play.

Berg, Jan. *Hochhuth's "Stellvertreter" und die Stellvertreter-Debatte*. Kronberg: Scriptor Verlag, 1977.

Bosmajian, Hamida. *Metaphors of Evil: Contemporary German Literature and the Shadow of Nazism*. Iowa City: University of Iowa Press, 1979.

Bouchard, Larry D. *Tragic Method and Tragic Theology: Evil in Contemporary Drama and Religious Thought*. College Park: Pennsylvania State University Press, 1989.

Butler, James A. "*The Deputy* in Retrospect." *Florida Quarterly* 15, no. 3 (1966): 19–21.

Chickering, Roger. "History and Morality in Historical Drama: A Historian's Perspective on Hochhuth's *Soldaten*." *German Studies Review* 2 (1979): 351–361.

Contemporary Literary Criticism. Detroit: Gale, vol. 4, 1975, pp. 230–232; vol. 11, 1979, pp. 274–277; vol. 18, 1981, pp. 250–255.

Fisher, Desmond. *Pope Pius XII and the Jews: An Answer to Hochhuth's Play "Der Stellvertreter (The Deputy)*." Glen Rock, N.J.: Paulist Press, 1963.

Gong, Alfred. "Rolf Hochhuth's *The Deputy*: An Attempt at Clarification." *American-German Review* 30, no. 3 (1964): 38–40.

Graef, Hilda I. "The Play That Indicts Pope Pius XII." *New Catholic World* 197 (1963): 380–385.

Hill, Leonidas E. "History and Rolf Hochhuth's *The Deputy*." *Mosaic* 1, no. 1 (1967): 118–131.

Lindsay, J. M. "Hochhuth's Play *Der Stellvertreter*." *Forum for Modern Language Studies* 1 (1965): 17–29.

Marx, Patricia. "An Interview with Rolf Hochhuth." *Partisan Review* 31 (1964): 363–37.

Murdaugh, Elaine. "The Apostate Ethic: The Alternative to Faith in Hochhuth's *Der Stellvertreter*." *Seminar* 15 (1979): 275–289.

Patterson, Michael. "Nazism and the War in Postwar German Theatre." *Modern Drama* 33, no. 1 (March 1990): 125.

Perry, R. C. "Historical Authenticity and Dramatic Form: Hochhuth's *Der Stellvertreter* and Weiss's *Die Ermittlung*." *Modern Language Review* 64 (1969): 828–839.

Schwarz, Egon. "Rolf Hochhuth's *The Representative*." *Germanic Review* 39 (1964): 211–230.

Seltser, Barry. "Realists, Idealists, and Political Heroism." *Soundings* 68, no. 1 (spring 1985): 21–41.

Simon, John. "*The Deputy* and Its Metamorphosis." In *Singularities: Essays on the Theater (1964–1973)*. New York: Random House, 1976, pp. 169–175.

Sontag, Susan. "Truth and Documentation." In *The Storm over "The Deputy."* Edited by Eric Bentley. New York: Grove Press, 1964.

Taëni, Rainer. *Rolf Hochhuth*. München: Beck, 1977. Translated into English by R. W. Last. New York: Wolff, 1977.

Ward, Margaret E. *Rolf Hochhuth*. Boston: Twayne, 1977.

Winston, Clara. "The Matter of *The Deputy*." *Massachusetts Review* 5 (1964): 423–436.

Zipes, J. D. "Guilt-Ridden Hochhuth: *The Soldiers*." *New Theatre Magazine* 8, no. 2 (1968): 17–20.

FRITZ HOCHWÄLDER

(1911–1986)

ANAT FEINBERG

FRITZ HOCHWÄLDER IS one of the few Austrian dramatists whose plays challenge the recent Austrian past, underscoring the participation of the Austrians in the crimes against the Jews, and insinuating that the spirit of "Ur-Nazism" did not die in 1945.

Born in Vienna on 28 May 1911 to Jewish parents, Hochwälder was trained to become a wallpaper decorator like his father. In August 1938, soon after the *Anschluss* (the German invasion of Austria), he fled to Zurich, where he lived as "an emigrant up to the end of the war and as a resident with Austrian citizenship afterwards." His parents were deported to Poland in 1942 and never returned. Prohibited from practicing his profession in Swiss exile, Hochwälder took up instead his hobby of writing plays. The few plays he had written in Vienna (*Jehr*, premiered 1933, and *Liebe in Florenz* [Love in Florence], premiered 1936) were not particularly successful. His reputation rests on the stage works produced from the late 1940s to the early 1960s.

Faithful to the traditional, Aristotelian dramaturgy and to the Schillerian idea of the stage as a moral platform, Hochwälder, an inexorable moralist, concentrated on the role of violence in shaping collective experience and on the conflict between individual conviction and political reality. He often reverted to historical materials—the crushing by the Spaniards of a utopian Jesuit settlement in Paraguay in the eighteenth century in *Das heilige Experiment* (The holy Experiment [translated as *The Strong Are Lonely*], premiered 1943) or the atrocities of the French Revolution in *Der öffentliche Ankläger* (The public Prosecutor premiered 1948). His late works were dramatic experiments, among them the modern mystery play *Donnerstag* (Thursday, premiered in 1959) and the allegory of the "modern non-person" (*Nichtmensch*) titled *1003* (premiered 1964). Though far less successful than the earlier plays, the late works did not impair Hochwälder's reputation as a man of great theater whose name is inscribed in world literature.

Ironically, the dramatist who chose not to return to his native country once the war was over has always been considered an Austrian author. Prizes and honors were showered on him mainly by Austrian organizations, among them the Literary Prize of the City of Vienna in 1955, a professorhip presented by the Austrian president in 1964, and the Austrian State Prize for Literature in 1966. Hochwälder died in Zurich on 20 October 1986; his grave is in Vienna, however, the city of his birth and youth, which made him an honorary citizen.

Hochwälder's Use of the Stage as a Moral Platform

Recent history features prominently in a number of Hochwälder's plays, underlining time and again the playwright's conviction that the Austrians failed to confront their past, preferring instead to obliterate the memory of their own active support of Nazi ideology. Austria's fierce commitment to the *Aufbau* (rehabilitation) was accompanied by a lack of rigor with regard to de-Nazification, leniency toward war criminals, and an institutionalized repression of acknowledgment of the collective guilt (termed "the power of forgetting" by the legal scholar Carl Schmitt). The tradition of antisemitism was not uprooted in the new state, and the authorities, who prided themselves on the "spirit of democratic tolerance" adopted a "soft-pawed attitude against manifestations of Neo-Nazism in general" (Wilder-Okladek). The media and the arts did little to foster a collective *Bewältigung* (confrontation of the past). While the so-called *Heimkehrer* (Homecoming) drama attained a certain degree of popularity, there were only isolated attempts by dramatists to shed light on the unsavory aspects of Austrian life after the *Anschluss.*

Those few playwrights who, like Hochwälder, chose to reflect on the recent past and to debunk the myth of a "new" unburdened beginning after 1945 (for example, Hans Weigel in *Barabbas*, 1946; Ulrich Becker and Peter Preses in *Der Bockerer*, 1948; or Jewish director Fritz Kortner in *Donauwellen* [The Waves of the Danube], 1949, and later in *Zwiesprache* [The Dialogue], 1964) had gone into exile, either forced or self-imposed, and spent the war years away from their homeland. These artists were among the first to caution against the moral implications of the spirit of amnesty.

Notably, Hochwälder wrote his first play on the suffering of the Jews and the endless curse of antisemitism during the war, in 1940. It was never performed. *Esther: ein altes Märchen* (*Esther: An Old Fairy Tale*) is based on the biblical Esther story; like Walter Hasenclever's *Konflikt in Assyrien (Scandal in Assyria)*, it was performed in London under the direction of John Gielgud in 1937. While Hasenclever's comedy implicitly places the biblical figures in Hitler's Germany, Hochwälder's variation on the story of the deliverance of the Persian Jews, which he suggested should be played in the style of commedia dell'arte, is set in a timeless scene. "We are defenseless, that's why we always have been and always will be the victims," says Benjamin, Mordechai's nephew (Hochwälder's addition to the source material). Benjamin chooses to dissociate himself from his people in order to fight for the socialist cause, much to the dismay of his conservative uncle. However, Esther, the king's wife and savior of her people, decides to accompany her uncle: "in these times there is no place for me here," she informs her husband, the king, at the very end of the play.

In *Der Befehl* (The Order, premiered 1968), Viennese chief inspector Mittermayer encounters the father of a girl he had murdered in occupied Holland in 1942. Torn between guilt and horror, he travels to Amsterdam, only to discover that he was indeed the murderer. In the earlier comedy *Der Unschuldige* (The Innocent, premiered 1958), a skull is found in the villa of director Christian Erdmann. Remnants of a uniform disclose that a French soldier was murdered there during the war, but whether or not Erdmann with his shady past was indeed the murderer remains an open question. Best known among Hochwälder's plays challenging the Austrian past is *Der Himbeerpflücker* (The Raspberry Picker, premiered 1965). The dramatist, who, like the Viennese Jewish director and playwright Fritz Kortner, also chose not to return to his native Austria after the war, exposes in the comedy, tinged with the picturesqueness of a well-made *Volksstück* (folkpiece), a system of repression, "unbewältigte Gegenwart" (unmastered present), practiced by an entire village. The arrival in Bad Brauning (reminiscent of Hitler's Austrian birthplace, Braunau) of a fugitive taken by the villagers for a notorious SS officer, known to have killed hundreds of Jews, forces the townspeople to face a past they had immaculately repressed. Soon enough it becomes clear that each one of the villagers has a skeleton in the closet: the owner of the local pub (called The White Lamb) established his business by selling gold extracted from the mouths of dead Jews; the local policeman participated in the killing of Jews in Vilna; the village doctor is a renowned expert on euthanasia. These former Nazis, who still yearn for the idols and myths of their heroic past, are determined to maintain their conspiracy of silence, for the unmasking of one would inevitably prompt the unmasking of all.

The fugitive turns out to be no more than a simple *ganef*, a thief who wishes to cross the border to safety. Disappointed by the banal truth, the villagers seek consolation in a new speculation, that the thief must be a Jew. "Just think of it: who has always been to blame for everything?"—The outsider with the crooked nose, the peculiar skull and hairline. "Well then, a Jew. . . . A very ordinary Jew."

Change of Direction

Der Himbeerpflücker, a play in which the Jew exists only as a figment in the minds of people, in a way reminiscent of Max Frisch's *Andorra* (premiered four years earlier in 1961), signals the direction that Austrian drama will take in the 1970s. The Jew will disappear from view, but the clichés and prejudices associated with his image will live on, characterizing the new outsider: the *Gastarbeiter* (guest worker). (See, for example, Harald Sommer's *Triki Traki*, 1971.) The new generation of Austrian playwrights (Peter Handke, Peter Turrini) allude to the fact that a new type of antisemitism, "antisemitism without Jews," signifies a phase of total mystification whereby the imaginary Jew becomes the embodiment of everything that is to be stigmatized.

Bibliography

Primary Sources

Das heilige Experiment (The holy Experiment, translated into English as *The Strong Are Lonely*). 1947.

Donadieu. 1953.

Der öffentliche Ankläger (The public Prosecutor). 1954.

Hôtel du Commerce. 1954. (After Maupassant's novella "Boule de Suif")

Der Flüchtling (*The Refugee*). 1946.
Die Herberge (*The Inn*). 1956.
Meier Helmbrecht. 1958.
Der Unschuldige (*The Innocent*). 1958.
Esther: Ein altes Märchen. (*Esther: An Old Fairy Tale*). 1960.
Dramen I (including *Heilige Experiment*, *Herberge*, *Donnerstag*). 1959.
Dramen II (including *Ankläger*, *Unschuldige*, *1003*). 1964.
Der Himbeerpflücker (The Raspberry Picker). 1965.
Der Befehl (The Order). 1967.
Dramen (including *Experiment*, *Ankläger*, *Donadieu*, *Herberge*, *Himbeerpflücker*). 1968.
Stücke (including *Experiment*, *Herberge*, *Unschuldige*, *Himbeerpflücker*, *Befehl*). 1969.
Lazaretti oder Der Säbeltiger. 1975.
Dramen I (including *Esther*, *Experiment*, *Hotel*, *Helmbrecht*, *Ankläger*). 1975.
Dramen II (including *Donadieu*, *Herberge*, *Unschuldige*, *Himbeerpflücker*, *Befehl*). 1975.
Dramen III (including *Neugier*, *Flüchtling*, *Donnerstag*, *1003*, *Lazaretti*). 1979.
Im Wechsel der Zeit (*The Changing of Times*, autobiographical essays). 1980.
Die Prinzessin von Chimay (*The Princess of Chimay*). 1982.
Dramen IV (including *Prinzessin*, *Mond*, *Bürgschaft*). 1985.

Secondary Sources

Best, Alan. "Shadows of the Past: The Drama of Fritz Hochwälder." *Modern Austrian Writing* 1980: 44–62.

Böhm, Gotthard. "Der geborene Dramatiker: Fritz Hochwälder." In *Die zeitgenössische Literature Österreichs*, edited by Hilde Spiel, 534–546. Munich Kindler, 1976.

Bortenschlager, Wilhelm. *Der Dramatiker Fritz Hochwälder*. Innsbruck: Universitat Verlag Wagner, 1979.

Daviau, Donald G. "Fritz Hochwälder." In *Major Figures of Modern Austrian Literature*, 237–267. Riverside, Calif.: Ariadne Press, 1988.

Feinberg, Anat. "The Jewish Experience and 'Vergangenheitsbewältigung' in Post-war Austrian Drama." *Colloquia Germanica* 18, no. 1 (1985): 55–75.

Harper, Anthony J. "Tradition and Experiment in the Drama of Fritz Hochwälder." In *Time and Change. Essays on German and European Literature*, 47–54. Frankfurt: R. G. Fischer, 1982.

Holdman, M. Paula. "The Concept of Order in the Drama of Fritz Hochwälder." Ph.D. Diss. New York City University, 1976.

Lennartz, Franz. "Hochwälder, Fritz." In *Deutsche Schriftsteller der Gegenwart*, 342–344. Stuttgart: Kröner, 1978.

McDonald, Edward R. "The Classical Theatre-of-illusion Modernized—The Conflicting Messages of the Moral Imperative in Fritz Hochwälder's Drama 'Das Heilige Experiment'." *Maske und Kothurn* 31 (1985): 73–100.

Patterson, Michael. *German Theatre Today*. London: Pitman, 1976, pp. 16–18.

Robertson, J. G. "Fritz Hochwälder." In *A History of German Literature*, edited by Dorothy Reich, 631–663. Elmsford: London House and Maxwell, 1970.

Schmitt, James. "The Theme of Responsibility and Its Presentation in the Drama of Fritz Hochwälder from 1943 to 1965." "Ph.D. Diss. University of Iowa, 1973.

"The Theatre of Fritz Hochwälder. Its Background and Development." *Modern Austrian Literature* 1 (1978): 49–61.

Torberg, Friedrich. "Fritz Hochwälder." In *Der Beifall war endenwollen. Theaterkritiken und Glossen*, 159–165. Munich: Deutscher Taschenbuch Verlag, 1979.

Vogelsang, Hans. "Fritz Hochwälder." In *Österreichische Dramatik des 20. Jahrhunderts*, 189–202. Vienna: Braunmüller, 1981.

Wellwarth, George. "Fritz Hochwälder: The Drama Within the Self." In *The Theatre of Protest and Paradox. Development of the Avant-garde Drama*, 207–221. New York: New York University Press, 1971.

EVA HOFFMAN
(1945–)

MARIANNE M. FRIEDRICH

EVA HOFFMAN, NÉE Ewa Wydra, was born in Kraków, Poland, on 1 July 1945. "[Th]ese bare bits of data," the author comments, "were packed with condensed personal implication. . . . In addition, my family was Jewish; and that fact as well carried a complex cargo of meaning" (Mari, p. 340).

Biographical Data

Eva's parents, Boris and Maria, née Burg, survived World War II in a Ukrainian *shtetl* near Lvov, where local peasants hid them for nearly two years. All other members of their families were murdered by the Nazis. The author recalls: "The war seemed to be my true origin, the place from which I sprang; and its horrors shadowed my external and internal world from the beginning. . . . The signs of suffering were everywhere—in the almost palpable presence of those who perished" (Mari, p. 340).

Yet, Eva Hoffman remembers the Kraków of her childhood as paradise, "a space of happiness, born perhaps of the interplay between shadows and light." Early, at age seven, Eva started to take piano lessons, and her musical talent was discovered: "It was through music," she says, "that I received my most powerful sentimental education; it was through the political and human atmosphere around me that I imbibed some of the Polish romanticism which produced Chopin" (Mari, p. 340).

In 1959, after the lifting of an emigration ban, the family moved to Vancouver, Canada, in order to escape the still pervasive antisemitism in Poland. Young Eva was an unwilling emigrant. In summing up this traumatic experience of uprooting at age thirteen, Hoffman observes in retrospect: "[I]f my psyche was formed in Poland, my consciousness was forged through the vicissitudes of immigration and transculturation" (Mari, p. 340). Early on, the experience of living without knowing the local tongue deepened her acute awareness of the fundamental importance of language, and she became "obsessed" with absorbing English in all its nuances. After finishing high school in Vancouver, Eva left her parents and younger sister and moved to the United States to attend Rice University in Houston, from which she graduated in 1967.

Throughout her student years, "lost" between two extremely different cultures, Eastern Europe and the West, the young author came to realize that in order to become truly American, she had to "transpose [herself] into a different mode of personality, a new system of perceptions, and even emotions" (Mari, p. 340). This painful process of transculturation, of becoming "lost in the translation" not only of a foreign language but a different culture as well, is captured convincingly in Hoffman's perceptive and original account of the immigrant experience, her memoir *Lost in Translation: A Life in a New Language* (1989).

For one year Eva attended the School of Music at Yale University. In 1976, she received a Ph.D. in English and American literature from Harvard University. She married Barry Hoffman in 1971, but was divorced several years later. Subsequently, she moved to New York and, over a period of ten years (1979–1990), held the prestigious position of an editor and writer for the *New York Times*, leaving intermittently to write *Lost in Translation*. She worked for the newspaper again for approximately three years, then left to travel in preparation for her second book, *Exit into History: A Journey Through the New Eastern Europe* (1993).

In 1992, Hoffman's decision to take up the writing life prompted a move to London. The author explains:

> I wanted, for a while at least, to update and perhaps develop the interrupted, "European" parts of myself, and to disentangle my youthful fantasy of Europe from the current realities. . . . I have found London . . . a satisfying

midway point between Manhattan and Cracow (Mari, p. 341).

Eva Hoffman's nonfiction book *Shtetl: The Life and Death of a Small Town and the World of Polish Jews*, appeared in 1997. Her first work of fiction, *The Secret*, was published in September 2001. During her career, Hoffman taught literature and creative writing at Harvard University, the University of New Hampshire, Tufts University, the University of Minnesota, and Columbia University. More recently she lectured as a visiting professor at the Massachusetts Institute of Technology and as a visiting fellow at the University of California in Berkeley. In addition, she taught at the Tavistock Institute in London and at the University of East Anglia. Of particular interest, regarding questions about dealing with the Holocaust, is her recent Amnesty International lecture, "Human Rights-Human Wrongs," given at Oxford University on 28 February 2001, and to be published by Oxford University Press in the spring of 2002.

Prizes and Awards, Hoffman's Journalistic Writing

Eva Hoffman's numerous awards and fellowships include the Woodrow Wilson Fellowship (1967–1968), the Danforth Graduate Fellowship (1969–1974), the Carnegie-Mellon Post-Doctoral Fellowship (1977–1978), the American Council of Learned Society Fellowship (1985–1986), the Jean Stein Award from the American Academy and Institute of Arts and Letters (1991), the Whitling Award for Writing (1992), and the Guggenheim Fellowship (1992–1993).

The author has considered her journalistic work an excellent preparation for her more extended creative works. Her voluminous body of journalistic writing encompasses penetrating articles on many cultural issues. Incisive interviews and book reviews in the *New York Times* and in other journals including the *Atlantic Monthly* and *Civilization* reflect the author's wide range of interests and sovereign competency in many fields.

Rewriting the Past: Eva Hoffman's Trilogy of Nonfiction and the Context of the Holocaust

Although Hoffman's three major books of nonfiction—*Lost in Translation* (1989), *Exit into History* (1993), and *Shtetl* (1997)—may be read independently, they are, intimately interrelated in the author's endeavor to "rewrite the past," each time from a different perspective. "To some extent, one has to rewrite the past in order to understand it," she comments; "[i]t is the price of emigration, as of any radical discontinuity, that it makes such rereadings difficult; being cut off of one part of one's own story is apt to veil it in the haze of nostalgia, which is an ineffectual relationship to the past" (*Lost in Translation: A Life in a New Language*, New York: Penguin, 1990, p. 242). Hoffman sees *Lost in Translation* as "an attempt, to integrate . . . the Polish and the American parts of the self," whereas in *Shtetl* she focuses on "the Polish and Jewish parts of the self" (Kreisler, interview). In *Exit into History* the author rewrites that part of her life story from which she had been cut off for more than four decades; after the fall of the Berlin Wall in 1989, she decided to witness and record the end of Communist rule in Eastern Europe.

Lost in Translation: A Life in a New Language has been highly praised by critics for its candor, its graceful, poetic language, and its original narrative representation. The book has been called "one of the most complex and significant specimens" of bicultural autobiography (Durczak, p. 173), and a "cross-cultural Bildungsroman" (Zaborowska, p. 231). In this memoir the introspective development of Eva's "observing consciousness" (p. 164) moves from the division of self toward "integration." In the end Eva acknowledges the birth of her newly gained identity: "I am being remade, fragment by fragment, like a patchwork quilt" (p. 220). Hoffman achieves the "overarching intimation of a mental development" by firmly establishing the inherent dynamic properties of the paradise motif in her text (Friedrich, p. 161). This strategy counteracts the narrative fragmentation resulting from the postmodern experience of multiple perspectives.

Thus *Lost in Translation* is divided into three distinct chapters, moving from "Paradise"—the "wholeness" of self of Eva's childhood in Poland—to "Exile"—the abrupt, traumatic loss of this during her high school years in Vancouver—and finally to the newly gained "paradise" in "The New World" chapter, which describes her second emigration to the United States; her college years at Rice; her graduate years at Harvard; and her successful professional life in New York.

It is precisely Hoffman's use of the paradise motif that has raised eyebrows among critics. They claim that for Hoffman, being Jewish, a "primal unity" can never have existed, that her nostalgically presented, Edenic Poland is barely recognizable as a Communist society (Krupnick, pp. 458, 459; Hirsch, p. 77). Given that Hoffman's parents are Holocaust survivors, it is striking, indeed, how little narrative space is allotted to her parents' fate during the war. Its very silencing, a strategy of playing down the shadowy parts of her background, suggests that the author has not yet come to terms with this traumatic legacy.

References to the Holocaust in the opening "Paradise" chapter are sparse. Eva obediently keeps her mother's wartime stories in her memory like "black beads," and she admits, "I don't understand what I remember. . . . I can't go as near this pain as I should. But I can't draw away from it either. . . . Surely, there are no useful lessons I can derive from my parents' experience: it does not apply to my life"; she feels there is no point in "duplicating suffering" (pp. 24–25). In contrast, she can hardly bear her father's silence about the Holocaust: "My father almost never mentions the war; dignity is silence, sometimes too much silence" (p. 23). These brief accounts vividly illustrate the symptomatic lack of communication, documented repeatedly in the literature on the subject, within the close family of Holocaust survivors that leads to repression in their children.

These marginal hints at the shadows in Eva's Polish "paradise" develop into a camouflaged yet dominant theme in the "Exile" chapter, as her repression and immigrant trauma are projected on a conspicuously unsympathetic and negative Vancouver. Canada as an inner landscape is a vast and vacant "Western Sahara" (p. 138) to her, "the dullest country in the world" (p. 133). She is aware that "a screen has fallen before [her] eyes, a screen that obscures and blurs everything. . . ." (p. 135). Even after she emigrates to the United States, Hoffman is afraid each time she visits her parents—the guardians of Holocaust memory—that the former "big fear," the "horror vacui" may return. During one visit, she is shocked by her parents' account of another wartime story about her father's sister, whose hiding place had been disclosed by another Jew (p. 252). Thus Vancouver "becomes the locus of Holocaust memory," as Sarah Phillips Casteel has demonstrated (p. 293).

As Hoffman revisits her parents in their "*shtetl* on the Pacific" (p. 250), she perpetuates her father's silence about the Holocaust. She is painfully and acutely aware that these traumatic wartime memories resist narration:

> There's no way to get this part of the story in proportion. It could overshadow everything, put the light of the world right out. . . . I try to slough off the excess darkness. . . . Paradoxically, it's not an easy adjustment to make; our first knowledge is the most powerful, and the shadows cast by it on the imagination, can be more potent than the solid evidence of our experience (p. 253).

This revealing confession explains a major function of the "Exile" chapter: it provides the narrative space in which these shadows of "the unnarratable can be bracketed, contained" (Phillips Casteel, p. 296). Hoffman thus enables herself to move on and reconstruct her new "paradise," her identity, in "The New World" chapter.

"Poland—and by extension Eastern Europe," Hoffman writes in her introduction to *Exit into History: A Journey Through the New Eastern Europe*, "remained for me an idealized landscape of the mind. . . . I wanted to see 'my' Eastern Europe before it disappeared, but to see it, this time, without my childhood fantasies and projections" (pp. x–xi). *Exit into History* traces the Eastern European "meta-narrative" of her personal history ("Life Stories, East and West," p. 3). In this account of two journeys through Eastern Europe, shortly after the collapse of Communism (1990–1991), Hoffman traveled through five Eastern European countries, Poland, Czechoslovakia, Hungary, Romania, and Bulgaria.

Above all, Hoffman is interested in observing and recording the impact of Communism on individuals, how their characters appear to have been "formed" and "deformed" under its pressures and how they cope with the new conditions (p. xv); *Exit into History* offers a rich sampling of the Eastern "politico-historical" mode, described by Hoffman, as opposed to the Western psychoanalytic mode, of biographical writing ("Life Stories, East and West," in *The Yale Review* 88.1, January 2000, at p. 3).

Questions of Jewishness are marginal in this book, and there are only two explicit references to the Holocaust. One is the long and gripping biography of a Jewish literary couple in Budapest, Anna and Gábor, both ex-Communists and described by Hoffman as "archetypal Central European" (pp. 239–248). The second reference to the Holocaust foreshadows the complexity of Hoffman's Jewish-Polish identity, at the core of *Shtetl,* her third work in rewriting the past:

> I find that the Polish and Jewish parts of my history, my identity—my loyalties—refuse either to separate or to reconcile. At the very moments when my attachment to Poland . . . is strongest, I upbraid myself for insufficient vigilance on behalf of those who suffered here—on behalf, really, of my parents, who survived the Holocaust in awful circumstances. Every time I hear Poland described reductively as an antisemitic country, I bridle in revolt, for I know that the reality is far more tangled than that (p. 101).

The word *shtetl* (Yiddish for a small market town in Eastern Europe) has become a trope, "a metaphor frozen in time" for the rich and self-contained Jewish world that died in the Holocaust (p. 80). In *Shtetl: The Life and Death of a Small Town and the World of Polish Jews* Hoffman rewrites the lost world of her parents and tries simultaneously to "disentangle" her own identity as a Jew and as a Pole (p. 19). In addition, this powerfully written and thoroughly researched historiography of Jewish-Polish relations is an invaluable contribution to a still highly charged dialogue about the Holocaust. The best-seller has been called a "manifest of historical honesty and probity" and praised widely for its dispassionate approach and clarifying contents (Breitenstein, Lipton, et al.). One critic, though, claims that, beyond achieving her "historical lesson," Hoffman does not offer anything new (Bernstein). In 1997 *Shtetl* was nominated for the Pulitzer Prize.

Hoffman points out that in post-Holocaust memory Poland holds a special place. One has to realize the magnitude of the caesura in Poland. Before the war "most of the world's Jewish population," "three million," lived in Poland (p. 2). Most concentration camps were built in Poland and it was primarily in Poland where the extermination of European Jewry took place. At the end of the war, only 240,000 to 300,000 remained in Poland.

To this day the Holocaust in Poland, the responsibility of Poles toward Polish Jews, and Polish-Jewish history continue to be highly "embattled terrain." In Jewish memory Poland is seen essentially as antisemitic, as "the heart of darkness, the central symbol of the inferno"; in the Polish response to the Holocaust, defensiveness and rancor are aggravated by amnesia (*Shtetl*, p. 3). In addition, in the memory of the West the Iron Curtain has contributed to a high degree of reductiveness. It is Hoffman's goal in this book to initiate a "dialogue that is healing rather than divisive" (p. 180). She insists that "[i]f cross-cultural discussions of difficult histories are to be at all fruitful, they need to start with acknowledgment of complexity rather than insistence on reductiveness" (p. 15).

Hoffman emphasizes her intent to counter the notion that ordinary Poles participated in the genocide "by virtue of their congenital antisemitism . . . and that Poles even today must be viewed with extreme suspicion or condemned as guilty for the fate of the Jews in their country" (p. 5). Hoffman asserts it is not her aim to absolve or condemn but "to complicate and historicize this picture" (p. 5). To achieve this goal she tracks the Holocaust not retroactively but rather within the much wider historical frame of Polish-Jewish relations that preceded it. In doing so she focuses primarily on one shtetl near the Russian border, called Bransk. The book is derived partly from Marian Marzynski's *Shtetl*, a 1996 *Frontline* documentary about Bransk: a highly selective montage, which strongly suggests that Poles were and still are antisemites. In contrast to Marzynski, Hoffman focuses on the *Shoah*'s "complexity" (p. 15), its paradoxes and ambiguities, which resist reductive remembering.

The first chapter provides a general background of six hundred years of Polish-Jewish relations. It amply proves the point Hoffman wants to make: In Poland the horrors of the *Shoah* were by no means predictable as an inevitable outcome of antisemitism. On the contrary, Hoffman argues, for centuries Jews and Poles lived side by side, sharing times of prosperity and deprivation, of war, of turmoil and of peace. During this "long experiment in multiculturalism *avant la lettre*" (p. 9), there were instances of violent hostility, but also times of symbiosis and collaboration.

For about six hundred years Poland was one of the most important centers of Jewish life in the world. Jews as the largest minority were a "highly visible and socially significant presence," culturally and politically (p. 8). From the middle of the seventeenth century, however, the relationship between the two peoples deteriorated into "suspiciousness and economic competition" (p. 10); it was particularly tried by a succession of disasters for Poland: the Cossack invasion, the Swedish invasion, the Turkish war, and Russian incursions. During these times of shared suffering, Hoffman states, the relationship between Poles and Jews prefigured the complexities of their relations during World War II (pp. 57–58). Against this historical background Hoffman focuses on life in the shtetl of Bransk. Among other sources, she draws to a large extent on the written chronicle of *Jewish Bransk*, started in 1816, and the *Bransk Yizkor Book* or *Book of Memory*, written by Jewish laypersons in 1947. The latter was compiled, shortly after the war, in a "great act of collective commemoration" (p. 89). In Bransk, also, Hoffman interviews survivors of the war. To guarantee a Jewish-Polish double perspective, she collaborates closely with an expert in the history of Bransk, the Polish historian Zbigniew Romaniuk. The highly detailed chapter about the *Shoah* vividly evokes the bestiality with which the once rich and self-willed world of the *shtetl* was erased. Bransk was suddenly turned into a place where perversion was legalized, where one was rewarded for selling the lives of neighbors but executed for helping them.

In September 1939 the Germans bombed Bransk; the Jewish neighborhood was hit hardest. Only a week later, German tanks rolled into the town. Executions followed, and the Old Synagogue was set on fire. Two weeks later the Germans left, and the Russians took over. The Jews welcomed the Soviets and their slogan of ethnic equality with flowers and banners. These actions angered the Poles, who had traditionally viewed the Russians as their enemy. In November, deportations to Siberia began; ironically, since the intelligentsia and aristocracy were targeted most, a number of Jews escaped certain death.

In June 1941, Hitler launched an attack on the Soviet Union, and once again German troops invaded Bransk overnight. Antisemitism reached its peak; an inverted morality changed the entire social structure of the town: "[T]he worst were given power and encouraged to do their worst. Cruelty was condoned, while decency was punished" (p. 219). The dehumanizing ghettoization of 2,400 Jews started immediately. The Germans appointed a *Judenrat* whose cruel task was to carry out all Nazi policies and make selections for the deportations of their own people; members of the Judenrat complied, under the illusion they could thereby save others. But there were also those who thought they could save their own lives by cooperating, like Isaiah Cukier, who was responsible for giving away seventy people (p. 224).

On 1 November 1942, the ghettos were suddenly liquidated. Only several hundred people were able to escape into the woods. A few found refuge with Polish farmers. Many were turned away by Poles who were constantly threatened, over loudspeakers and through posters everywhere, with execution for helping Jews. Within three days 2,000 Jewish people were transported to the concentration camp Treblinka; they were murdered there in the gas chambers.

In Bransk the range of Poles' responses to the *Shoah* can hardly be assessed in unequivocal terms. There were many examples of unleashed, monstrous cruelty (p. 223). A substantial number of Poles closed their eyes to the atrocities around them, or showed indifference. The official devaluation of Jewish lives, Hoffman theorizes, may have made it easier for some Poles to identify with the aggressors (p. 227); she is struck, however, by a noticeable impulse of ordinary compassion (p. 224) and by the number of those who helped, like the pharmacist Woinska (pp. 204–208). Jack Rubin's long and gripping account of his survival (pp. 225–233) exemplifies "the impossible calculus" of that time: "[I]t took at least several people to save a Jewish life; it took only one person to cause the deaths of many" (p. 244). In several respects Rubin's story parallels that of Hoffman's parents, whose survival had depended repeatedly on those who, risking their own lives and those of their families, offered to hide them (p. 6). Hoffman also points out that the gap that still divides the two communities today is the most persistent fact of their common history (p. 247).

The Holocaust was not the ultimate reason for the failure of the "experiment in multiculturalism *avant la lettre*" (p. 9). It failed, according to the author, because Polish-Jewish identity politics lacked the foundation of a strong sense of solidarity (p. 256). For too long the two group memories have remained insulated, and it is time for mutual understanding and gestures of "synthesis and reconciliation." Hoffman concludes: "[W]e need to stop splitting our own memories and perceptions in half, and pushing away those parts, which are too distressing for owning or acknowledgment. As for those who perished the time may have come to let them rest in our full remembrance, and in peace" (pp. 56–57).

Rewriting the Past in Hoffman's first Novel: *The Secret*

This novel about a mother-daughter bond is a tragicomical fable about the future of humankind; it touches on ultimate questions about human nature. The theme of the dividedness of the self, so central to all of Hoffman's writing, is removed from its autobiographical context and placed in a "post-postmodern" setting.

The narrative perspective is autobiographical. The plot is streamlined like that of a detective tale. In a desperate search for the identity of her father, Iris, the protagonist, discovers the horrifying secret her mother has hidden from her for seventeen years: Iris is a clone, a replica, of her mother. She is devastated by this violation of the most basic laws and values, and decides she must leave home to rediscover, and to reinscribe in her psyche, a lost family history. She must reclaim her relatives and grandparents, who are still unknown to her, in order to determine her own questionable identity, her "ontological status," her human, natural origins (pp. 108, 256).

The quest for her personal history, the only guarantee that will make her "human," takes Iris on a long, adventurous journey with encounters in New York, Florida, her Midwestern hometown, a small town in France, and Chicago. The gripping experience of the death of her grandparents, however, abruptly closes off her only means of entry into a continuous personal history. This sudden "Great Interruption" (p. 215) of her quest propels her, in an explosion of accumulated feelings of fury and revenge, almost to strangle her mother (pp. 165, 166). This terrifying act, signifying her closeness to the underworld (p. 228), initiates her final separation from her mother and the subsequent gradual process of finding her "ontological status," her "real reality"(p. 256). In concluding her story, Iris acknowledges that her sense of self will always remain divided, veering between suspicions about her origin and the "wrenching hope" for a truly human heart that would embrace "a psyche, a soul, a spirit" (p. 262).

In this future novel, the Holocaust appears only as a faint, almost forgotten echo of the past; the word "Holocaust" is never used. Iris's Eastern European friend Piotr introduces her to his book project about the past century. He shows her pictures, which are evidently about the Holocaust. They haunt him at night, and he considers it his difficult task to "unlock their meaning" (p. 116).

Iris elaborates on her incapacity to understand the concept of guilt. When Piotr is talking about his family history, he makes it a point that he feels guilty for what his ancestors have done. Iris cannot identify at all with the way he "relishes" his conscience. As she has no family history herself, feelings of guilt do not make sense to her. Guilt, she recalls from her Human Education class, is specific to humans; it is one of their strangest emotions, and supposed to be a sign of higher development. At an even higher stage of development, however, guilt may start to disappear, "like the appendix or other atavistic body parts" (p. 113).

There is one more remote allusion to the Holocaust in the book, as Hoffman touches on the potential for racism as a result of cloning. Iris visits a website about "Clone Power" on the Internet. The "echt-humans," she learns, see clones as a "hidden disease" comparable to the Jews in Nazi Germany. Others, by contrast, think that clones feel dangerously superior, as the Nazis did, and that the clone goal is the extermination of the human race (p. 191).

Bibliography

Primary Sources

Lost in Translation: A Life in a New Language. 1989.
Exit into History: A Journey Through the New Eastern Europe. 1993.
Shtetl: The Life and Death of a Small Town and the World of Polish Jews. 1997.
Human Rights, Human Wrongs, 2002.
The Secret. 2001.
"Warsaw Days," *The Yale Review* 80.3 (July 1992).
"The Soul He Threw Away," *The New York Times* 31 Jan. 1993.
"Let Memory Speak," *The New York Times* 23 Jan. 1994.
"The Uses of Illiteracy," *New Republic* 23 Mar. 1998.
"The New Nomads," *The Yale Review* 86.4 (Oct. 1998).
"True to Life?" *Time South Pacific* 30 Aug. 1999.
"Life Stories, East and West," *The Yale Review* 88.1 (Jan. 2000).
"The Uses of Hell," *New York Review of Books* 9 Mar. 2000.

Secondary Sources

Bernstein, Richard. "Updating the Jewish Image of Poles," *The New York Times*, 15 October 1997, 7.

Breitenstein, A. "Szenen einer Schicksalsehe: Eva Hoffman seziert die polnisch-jüdische Geschichte," *Neue Zürcher Zeitung*, 19 August 2000, 83.

Durczak, Jerzy. *Selves Between Cultures: Contemporary American Bicultural Autobiography*. San Francisco: International Scholars Publications, 1999.

Friedrich, Marianne M. "Reconstructing Paradise: Eva Hoffman's Lost in Translation." *Modern Jewish Studies* 11, Yiddish 11, 3–4 (1999): 159–165.

Hirsch, Marianne. "Pictures of a Displaced Girlhood." *Displacements: Cultural Identities in Question*. Edited by Angelika Bammer. Bloomington: Indiana University Press, 1994.

Krupnick, Mark. "Assimilation in Recent American-Jewish Autobiography." *Contemporary Literature* (1993): 451–474.

Lipton, Eunice. "Unknowing Neighbors." *The Nation* 3, Nov. 1997, 26–27.

Mari, Christopher. "Hoffman, Eva." *World Authors 1990–1995*. New York: H. W. Wilson, 1999 ed.

Phillips Casteel, Sarah. "Eva Hoffman's Double Emigration: Canada as the Site of Exile in *Lost in Translation*." *Biography* 24.1 (2001): 288–301.

Savin, Ada. "Passage to America or When East Meets West—Eva Hoffman's *Lost in Translation: A Life in a New Language*." *Caliban* 31 (1994): 57–63.

Zaborowska, Magdalena J. *How We Found America*. Chapel Hill: North Carolina University Press, 1995.

Interview by Harry Kreisler. "Conversation with Eva Hoffman," *Conversations with History: Institute of International Studies*, Univ. of California at Berkeley, 5 Oct. 2000.

YOEL HOFFMANN

(1937–)

RICHARD CHESS

YOEL HOFFMANN WAS born in Brasov, Transylvania, in 1937 to a Jewish-Austrian family. His father's name was Abraham and his mother's name was Gitta. When he was one year old, Hoffmann moved to Palestine with his family. His mother died when he was young; consequently, Hoffmann boarded with family members and in a children's home until his father's second marriage. He spent two years in a Buddhist monastery and earned his doctorate in Japan before becoming a professor of Japanese poetry, Buddhism, and philosophy at Haifa University in Israel. He has written numerous books on Zen philosophy and Japanese death poems, and for his fiction he has received the Koret Jewish Book Award and the Neuman Prize for Hebrew Literature. He lives in Haifa.

Major Work

Of Yoel Hoffmann's four works translated into English, *Sefer Yosef* (*Katschen: The Book of Joseph*, 1988) deals most directly with the Holocaust. Set in Berlin between 1928 and 1945, the novella tells the story of Joseph Silverman, a tailor, and his son, Yingele, refugees from Russia, where Cossacks murdered Chaya-Leah, Joseph's wife. Joseph's prolonged mourning over the loss of Chaya-Leah continues for nearly a decade, until he meets Miriam. The consummation of their virtually mystical love immediately precedes the murders of both Joseph and Yingele on 9 November 1938, the night of the anti-Jewish riots known as *Kristallnacht*. Father and son are murdered by Siegfried Stopf, a member of the Nazi Youth Party. Siegfried's story is told parallel to Joseph's and Yingele's stories until, on the fatal night, the two narrative lines converge.

Published in Hebrew in 1988 and then in English translation in 1998, Hoffmann's *The Book of Joseph*, like other works of Israeli Holocaust fiction, is "exploratory" as it "pursu[es] [the] existential implications" of the Holocaust (Morahg, p. 144). The text explores the psychological, spiritual, cultural, literary, and linguistic implications of the Holocaust. Hoffmann does this by writing an experimental text, one in which narrative prose and lyric poetry, as well as realistic and fantastical writing, are juxtaposed. Despite its fragmented surface, the text is unified by its voice, which is by turns tender, melancholic, satirical, charmed, erotic, horrified, and mournful. The writing moves almost seamlessly across boundaries of genre and diction (prose and poetry; realism and mysticism; myth, fable, and fairy tale; biblical and liturgical; historical and philosophical). Ultimately, Hoffmann uses all the resources of language to create a fiction that, as he says in his foreword to the novel, is "intact, like the suits sewn by Joseph," and that, despite its "few unwoven threads" is all the better for its inclusion of "many movements." Indeed, the final product is a text "fit to be made a prayer book for the devout" (*Joseph*, trans. by Eddie Levenston and Alan Triester, New York: New Directions, 1998, p. x).

Following the narrative's realistic thread, we find familiar but nonetheless compelling representations of character and event. A simple Jew from the East, Joseph is represented as a pious, mystically oriented, unsophisticated, sensitive, kind, and compassionate man, not unlike his father. "Your father's a good man," Joseph's mother once said to her son, "but his head is in the clouds" (p. 4). Joseph regards everything that happens as God's will: from his escape from Russia to the deterioration of Jewish life in Germany (p. 7). Indeed, as conditions of Jewish life in Berlin become increasingly difficult—non-Jews cease doing business with Joseph, and later, suspected of being an anarchist with designs to kill a king visiting Berlin, Joseph himself is arrested and briefly detained by the police—

Joseph's thoughts turn messianic: "In Berlin, Redemption has drawn nearer," he thinks (p. 39).

Joseph's piety and mystical leanings as well as his simple and unworldly behaviors are set into sharp relief against the backdrop of two other characters: Herr Cohn, a wealthy, cultured, assimilated German Jew who expresses a condescending attitude toward "Jews from the East," recent arrivals "who . . . have not acquired 'Kultur' like the Jews of Germany" (p. 45), and Pomeranz the watchmaker, a Spinozan-rationalist friend of Joseph's in Alexanderplatz, the area in Berlin in which the Jews from the East live. With this range of Jewish characters, Hoffmann suggests the complex social and cultural makeup of the Jewish community in Berlin at the time of the Holocaust.

In contrast to the Jewish characters, who collectively represent a range of intellectual, spiritual, economic, and cultural orientations to the world, the German characters are represented either as uneducated nationalists whose merits are predominantly physical, manifest as both brute force and sexual prowess, or as academics practicing pseudoscience to legitimize their persecution of the Jews. Siegfried Stopf's conception is represented as a crude act: "in Berlin, Hans Stopf [Siegfried's father] mounted his wife . . . pushed her onto the bed . . . and stuck the member that was between his legs into her body. Then he said, 'Na! Jetzt geh'nwir mal schlafen' (German: That's it. Now let's go to sleep)" (p. 5).

Siegfried, the novella's main German character, prides himself on his sexual aggressiveness and his cruelty to bugs and Jews. His limited insight into human nature is suggested by the following passage: " 'That's how life is. Sometimes you're happy, sometimes you're not happy. But you're usually not sad and not happy.' Siegfried was filled with pleasure at having such serious thoughts" (p. 50). If the text depended solely on the starkly contrasting characterizations of Jew and German, one might justly criticize it for stereotyping. But *The Book of Joseph* should not be read merely as a representation of sociological, cultural, and historical tensions. Rather it should be read as an exploration of clashes of conflicting, opposing forces and of the interpenetration of these forces. For instance, as the conflict between Aryan Germans and Jews, both refugees and German-Jews, speeds toward its catastrophic conclusion, the text subtly shifts from realistic to fantastical modes of writing, as in the crucial scenes with Miriam, the character with whom Joseph falls in love near the tragic end of his life.

Miriam is more a mythical or biblical character than a realistic one—precisely the type of figure toward which Joseph, with his messianic inclinations, would be drawn. Miriam's story is modeled loosely on the biblical narrative of Moses. Like Moses, Miriam is abandoned as an infant. She is found by Pomeranz "in a cradle on the paving stones of Alexanderplatz" (p. 67). Also like Moses, Miriam functions as a redeemer: she redeems Joseph from his extended period of grief over the death of Chaya-Leah, and she redeems Yingele from the condition of motherlessness. In Miriam's company, Joseph has a series of mystical experiences. For instance, at the zoo Joseph perceives that the leopard "looks at [him] with Miriam's eyes" (p. 71). Held in the leopard's / Miriam's gaze, Joseph thinks, "when all the animals entered the ark . . ., the leopard remained alone. . . . And when the world was renewed, only the leopard remembered that once birds had flown in the depths of the ocean and fish had swum in the skies" (p. 70). Thus, Joseph is transported back to the pre- and post-deluge world, to the destruction of the first world of God's creation and the creation of the second. Then, because Joseph "understands the leopard's secret," "the leopard looks at Miriam with Joseph's eyes" (p. 70). Regarding her thus, Joseph "understands that she dwells in both worlds"—the phenomenal and the transcendent—"at the same time" (p. 70). Miriam functions as a character who redeems Joseph from his own historical, fleeting, imminently tragic moment and aligns him with cosmic cycles of catastrophe and renewal.

Miriam also serves as a redeemer for Yingele. At the conclusion of a game of cat (Yingele) and mouse (Miriam), during which they playfully and passionately bite each other, Yingele "forgets that he is a cat and imagines his body being devoured limb by limb until all of it is in [Miriam's] stomach" (pp. 72–73). The introduction of Yingele's rebirth fantasy is followed by a short poem in which Yingele is transformed into a savior, a Christ figure. First "planted inside Chaya-Leah," Yingele "emerges / From the body of Miriam" (p. 73). Astrologers predict that this child, "created from the seed of man without a woman's womb," will, in a year, "rise to the heavens" and take with him "all our sins" (p. 73).

By means of this miraculous birth, Yingele is united with both his birth mother and his spiritual mother. Furthermore, the boy's birth is represented as perhaps the second coming of Christ. He returns to the world to bear upon himself its sins. But lest readers mistakenly conclude that Hoffmann is, through Yingele, suggesting that the Holocaust is the means by which God's children, the Jews, are transformed into Christ figures and sacrificed to redeem a fallen world, the poem continues with mundane, comic details that temper its mock-prophetic vision:

> And in exchange for the effort made
> (But first he must trim his fingernails)

He will be God for about
Three thousand years.
And his mother who did not bear
Him will become a saint
And his father will be (with a percentage of the take)
Patron of the tailors (pp. 73–74).

Other juxtapositions of sacred and profane texts suggest that Hoffmann is not simply undercutting the sacred but rather intertwining sacred and profane in order to create a new sense of the liturgical for our time. In one poem, Hoffmann combines the language of the biblical Song of Songs with details of a love affair set in the present of the story. Elsewhere, Hoffmann interlaces passages from Ecclesiastes into the story of the death by freezing of a disobedient boy named Peter.

The shock and delight that comes of these juxtapositions is felt nowhere more strongly than in the final words of the text. In the final scenes of the novella, following the magical consummation of Joseph's relationship with Miriam—Joseph is represented first as a satyr-butterfly and then as a male seahorse; Miriam is represented first as a nymph-butterfly and then as a female seahorse—Joseph experiences God's sheltering presence. As he sews, Joseph recalls the Twenty-Third Psalm: "surely goodness and mercy, he sews, shall follow me all the days of my life. And I will dwell in the house of the Lord, he sews, forever" (p. 78). His moment of peace and perfect faith occurs, as the text informs us, on 9 November 1938, *Kristallnacht*.

Immediately after Joseph finishes the psalm, Yingele, with a single blow to the head by Siegfried, is clubbed to death, causing Joseph to say, in Yiddish, "Mayn got, mayn got, farvos hastu mikh farlozn" (My God, My God, why has thou forsaken me? p. 79). In a moment, Joseph has gone from feeling protected to feeling inexplicably abandoned by God. Then Joseph himself is clubbed to death.

The chaos and destruction of Jewish life in Berlin that follows *Kristallnacht* is suggested by the longest poem in the text, a quasi–blank verse poem lacking narrative or lyric continuity:

They push the sun as it passes over
Alexanderplatz. Someone sells cheap soap.
A child cries; they took something
from him. People pretend the merchandise
is flawed. When the fan makes a noise,
they drip butter into it . . . (p. 80).

The closing scene, just after the end of the war, marks the return of another character, Gurnisht, to Berlin. A refugee from Hungary, Gurnisht had befriended Joseph and Yingele and worked in Joseph's tailor shop on Alexanderplatz until he fell in love with an English woman and followed her, prior to the beginning of the war, to London. After the war, Gurnisht returns to Berlin to search for his beloved friends. On Friedrichstrasse, Gurnisht finds just one house left standing. Inside, in the basement, is a bar with four patrons: two men, named Cut-Foot and Gouged-Eye; a German woman; and Gurnisht himself. This scene reads as a kind of script of an absurdist play. While Cut-Foot and Gouged-Eye converse on the nature of God—"He comes when you cry;" "He cries himself;" "He invented wine, got drunk, and now he beats his wife;" "He's a bastard;" "He created the world by spitting; "—the German woman invites Gurnisht to have sex with her. *The Book of Joseph* concludes with the two of them lying on the floor, when, "without knowing what he [is] doing, Gurnisht [comes] upon her and shout[s]: Yisgadal . . . aaah . . . vayiskadash . . . aaah . . ." (p. 93).

Throughout the novella, Gurnisht has been characterized as a man driven by an insatiable sexual desire. This intense desire was apparently triggered by two traumatic events in Gurnisht's childhood: a pogrom that he experienced with his family in Poland and then, after they had relocated in Hungary as refugees, the imprisonment of his twin brother, Lajos, in 1919, for his involvement with the Communist Party in Hungary. In this scene, having encountered yet another devastation, Gurnisht, now married, engages in intercourse with yet another woman and, as he does, begins chanting the traditional Jewish mourner's prayer, the Kaddish, uttering its first two words, which translate as "May His name be magnified and sanctified." This is Gurnisht's prayer for his murdered friends and, implicitly, for all of the exterminated Jews. It can also be read as his response to the bitter, even blasphemous characterization of God offered by the two drunks in the bar. But the prayer isn't presented in its entirety. Furthermore, Gurnisht cannot utter even two consecutive words without adding after each an emotive, inarticulate, animalistic cry—an ambiguous "aaah," an expression at once of existential pain and physical relief.

Challenging the Limits of Language

Writers on the Holocaust routinely speak to the limitations of language when it comes to representing adequately the full nature of the Holocaust experience. By drawing together many kinds of languages—prose and poetry, narrative and lyric, folk song and scripture, articulate speech and inarticulate sounds—Yoel Hoffmann in *The Book of Joseph* not only extends the reach of language in attempting to represent the fullest range of Holocaust experience possible—cruelty, suffering, madness, tenderness, eros, faith, betrayal, grief—but also suggests the impact of the Holocaust on language itself. Traditional boundaries of language do not hold. "Many movements," as Hoffmann writes in the foreword, "are better than a single movement" (p. x). Thus, the final four breaths of the text, spoken by Gurnisht (whose name is a Yiddish word meaning "nothing")—*yisgadal . . . aaah . . . vayiskadash . . . aaah . . .*—suggest at once an emptying out of meaning—what can a prayer praising God's magnificence mean in the ruins of postwar Berlin?—and its restoration: Only when language represents every kind of loss imaginable and expands to include every kind of discourse, from animalistic grunts to lofty terms of praise, can it offer a modicum of solace and become again, as in this magnificent work, a medium of authentic prayer.

Bibliography

Primary Sources

Sound of the One Hand: 281 Zen Koans with Answers. 1975. Translated with a commentary by Yoel Hoffmann.

Every End Exposed: The 100 Koans of Master Kid o: With the Answers of Hakuin-Zen. 1977. Translated with a commentary by Yoel Hoffmann.

Radical Zen: The sayings of Joshu. 1978. Translated with a commentary by Yoel Hoffmann.

Idea of Self, East and West: A Comparison between Buddhist Philosophy and the Philosophy of David Hume. 1980.

Japanese Death Poems: Written by Zen Monks and Haiku Poets on the Verge of Death. 1986. Compiled and with an introduction and commentary by Yoel Hoffmann.

Sefer Yosef (Katschen: The Book of Joseph). 1988.

Bernhart (Berhard). 1989.

Kristus shel dagim (The Christ of Fish). 1991.

Gutapershah. 1993.

Mah shelomekh Dolores (How Do You Do, Dolores?). 1995.

ha-Lev hu Katmandu (The Heart Is Katmandu). 2000.

Secondary Sources

Institute for the Translation of Hebrew Literature. "Hebrew Authors: Yoel Hoffmann." 30 September 2001. *http://www.ithl.org.il/authors.html*

Morahg, Gilead. "Breaking Silence: Israel's Fantastic Fiction of the Holocaust." In *The Boom in Contemporary Israeli Fiction.* Edited by Alan Mintz. Hanover, N.H.: Brandeis University Press, 1997.

Yudkin, Leon I. "Fill That Gap: The Space Sage, Yoel Hoffmann." *Arabic and Middle Eastern Literatures* 3, no. 1 (2000): 77–85.

Gert Hofmann

(1931–1993)

ERNESTINE SCHLANT

Gert Hofmann was born on 29 January 1931 in the town of Limbach in Saxony/Germany, where he also went to school until the family moved to nearby Leipzig in 1948. Leipzig was, at that time, situated in the Soviet zone of occupation; one year later, with the founding of the German Democratic Republic, it became part of East Germany. It should, therefore, not be surprising that when young Hofmann went for certification as translator and interpreter, he focused on Russian, but also on English. After completing his university qualifying exams (his *Reifezeugnis*), he started his studies at the University of Leipzig, but within a year moved to Freiburg/Breisgau in the Federal Republic of Germany. There he continued in the tradition of the "eternal student," embracing a wide field of studies with emphasis on English, Romance, and Germanic languages, and on sociology and political science. On occasion he had to interrupt his studies, forced to earn money, particularly because he married in 1955 and in the course of his married life had four children. In 1957 he obtained his Ph.D. with a dissertation on Henry James. During the 1960s he was professor of German studies teaching at various universities abroad, including Toulouse, Bristol, Edinburgh, Yale, Berkeley, and Austin. From 1971 to 1980 he lived in Klagenfurt/Austria and taught at the nearby Yugoslav university of Laibach (Lyublyana). In 1980 he settled in Erding, near Munich, where he lived until his death on 1 July 1993.

Career

Hofmann's career as a writer was unusual: He did not start to write prose works until 1979, when he was nearly fifty years old. This long process of gestation allowed him to present immediately mature works with a distinctive and unmistakable voice. (Literary criticism notes similarities with the early work of Austrian Thomas Bernhard; while this is true in relation to their disrupted stylistic presentations, Hofmann's repertoire encompasses a more diversified cast of characters and a wider geographic range.) From 1960 on, as he assumed the life of a wandering scholar/professor, he wrote seven plays for the theater that were performed at playhouses in Germany and Austria. More important, he concentrated on writing radio plays, forty-five of which were aired between 1960 and 1992. Many of these radio plays foreshadow and, from 1979 on, rework, themes, voices, and characters from his prose narratives. Thus, for example, *The Parable of the Blind* (1986) expresses his concern with blindness and his attempt to understand the reorientation of a life deprived of sight; this preoccupation is also evident in his radio plays—plays that are not seen but only heard, and for which he was awarded the Prize of the Blind War Veterans (*Preis der Kriegsblinden*).

Themes and Style

The novella *The Denunciation*, published in 1979, set the stage for the astonishing production of practically one prose volume per year, some of them lengthy novels, some of them collections of novellas and shorter prose writings, in addition to his continued output of at least one radio play per year. This amazing productivity is, perhaps, only slightly less formidable when one considers that Hofmann drew from a reservoir of traumas that needed to be voiced, contextualized, and reworked in ever new variations. All of Hofmann's protagonists are traumatized figures even though they cope with their traumas in different ways. These traumas are recognizable to the reader, though not necessarily to the protagonist, and usually connect to childhood experiences. In *The Denunciation* (1979), *Our*

Conquest (1984), *Veilchenfeld* (1986), *Our Forgetfulness* (1987), and *The Film Explainer* (1987), these formative childhood experiences occur during the Nazi regime and the events are often presented from the narrow perspectives of a child (or of siblings or some other combination that works with a "double") and reflect, eagerly and precociously, the opinions of the adult world and their own concomitant brutalization.

Hofmann inhabits a language commensurate with the traumatized lives of his protagonists, but on a wider level his is a language profoundly marked by the shattering experience of the Nazi regime and its legacy in the ruptured lives of his figures. Hofmann is heir to the legacy of the perpetrator generation of the Nazi regime, marked by the realization of the genocide, and his language exhibits the marks of this shattering even when he focuses on other subjects (for example, on the protagonists of the four novellas collected in *Balzac's Horse*, 1988). Broken sentences, interrupted thoughts, fragmented perspectives, gaps like black holes that suck up events never to return them to consciousness, fissures in body and mind, and images of the world drowned in another flood dominate his discourse.

The Novels

In *The Denunciation* the non-Jewish Hecht family is destroyed in the last year of the war. Because of an anonymous denunciation, the father is sent to a penal battalion on the retreating eastern front and, as predicted, is killed within a month. Soon thereafter the mother commits suicide by drowning and the fourteen-year-old twin sons are metaphorically torn from each other to grow up separately. While one of them, Karl, coopts the economic "miracle" of postwar West Germany and becomes a successful lawyer respected by the like-minded part of town, the other twin, Wilhelm, is driven across the world in an attempt to find the source of the anonymous denunciation. He dies, broken in spirit, mind, and body, in the insane asylum of New York's Bellevue Hospital. The narrative consciousness (the recipient of Karl's nightlong ruminations) registers Karl's interrupted and disjointed responses to the arrival of Wilhelm's "legacy," that is, to fragmented drafts, snippets of imaginary correspondence, notes, and bills in which Wilhelm wonders whether the denunciation had to do "with the fate of our half-Jewish neighbor L. Silberstein, who for such a long time and in such a miraculous manner had evaded the attention of the bureaucrats and who around this time had been removed from our city for the purpose of liquidation" (*Die Denunziation*, Darmstadt Neuwied: Luchterhand, 1989, p. 16). Embedded in the chaos of fragmentations and ruptures, of severance and a warped continuity (in the ill treatment of a "radical" young German there are suggestions that the postwar period continues the practices of harrassment and persecution, forerunners of the genocide) there lies hidden at its core the silence about and absence of the neighbor L. Silberstein.

While in *The Denunciation* a fragile, elderly Jew is a background figure who nevertheless determines the narrative perspective, in *Veilchenfeld* a similarly fragile, elderly Jew occupies center stage. As in *The Denunciation*, ruptures, fragmentation, silence, and the victims' presence-as-absence dominate a complex narrative. *Veilchenfeld* explores the demise of Professor Bernhard Israel Veilchenfeld, a university professor of philosophy in Leipzig, now retired (i.e., no longer allowed to teach) in the narrator's small town. The narrative perspective is that of a young boy, Hans, who watches with intense interest the town's accelerating scapegoating of Veilchenfeld and his gradual diminution. It is a complex perspective because Hans tells more than he understands, repeating what he hears adults say, registering their silences and rationalizations. In the early part of the narrative, Veilchenfeld is invited for dinner to the house of Hans' parents. The boy registers without quite comprehending, his parents' displaced, inappropriate, and ultimately self-serving responses to Veilchenfeld, who only in this scene appears as his own agent. From then on, deprived of his status as a subject (thereby reflecting society's consensus on the status of Jews) he becomes the object of observation by others, encrusted with their fears and prejudices. As Hans watches, the town closes in on Veilchenfeld in an ever more threatening circle: the space in which Veilchenfeld can move is increasingly constricted; he is losing weight and his body is shrinking; he is subjected to cruel practical jokes; he is physically abused by Nazi hoodlums, and by the police when he complains; his apartment and his books are vandalized; his passport is torn up; and finally he commits suicide for which Hans buys the poison.

Veilchenfeld presents the anatomy of a town that allowed, encouraged, and cooperated in the ostracism and persecution of a human being foreshadowing, in this one specific example, the attitudes and behavior that would lead, two years after Veilchenfeld's suicide, to the Holocaust. Hofmann gives, in Veilchenfeld's demise, the moving portrait of a victim's struggle to maintain his dignity and humanity in the midst of vicious attacks, indifference, or the frightened silence of bystanders.

In *Our Conquest*, Hofmann's attention concentrates on the behavior, opinions, and attitudes of the adults on the day of "our conquest" (the day of the end of World War II). Here, two children reveal in their distanced accounting, as they take their clues from the adults, the calloused brutality and hypocrisy of the adults and unconsciously lay bare a mentality that made the genocide possible. The frequent doubling of a protagonist into two split personalities (or into two complementary siblings) also carries over into *Our Forgetfulness*, where the protagonist has two conflicting vocations and lives, being a masseur and a writer, a husband and a recluse. On the way to his editor (a trip that spreads over the entire length of the novel), he ruminates on the horrors and calamities of the Nazi regime that have been forgotten and are buried beneath the ground he walks on. Figuratively and literally, the past has yet to be excavated.

Critical attention wondered whether Hofmann was breaking new ground with the publication of *The Film Explainer* because the novel is dedicated to his grandfather and the first sentence refers to him working as a "film explainer" in a silent film movie house. Similarly, the relationship between grandfather and grandson, their frequent walks together and the grandfather's expounding on film aesthetics (the novel offers a fairly comprehensive discussion of films from the silent into the Nazi era) have been viewed in a positive light. Yet the hidden text of the *Film Explainer* is the disappearance of the Jews, in particular of the movie theater owner S. Theilhaber, the grandfather's boss, and the grandfather's joining the Storm Troopers. Rather than seeing *The Film Explainer* as an anomaly in Hofmann's oeuvre because of its autobiographical aspects, one can argue that it is the hitherto hidden, yet driving force of all of Hofmann's explorations into the behavior of ordinary citizens and their corruption during the Nazi regime.

Critical Reception

As demonstrated by the many domestic and international awards, critical reception of Gert Hofmann's oeuvre has been favorable, although some of the major German literary awards have eluded him. Reviewers and scholars alike have been much taken with his astute and shrewd psychological presentations, with the enactment of a broken world in broken perceptions and a broken language, with the subtext forever challenging the text. Although these characteristics have elevated Gert Hofmann to a revered icon among those who appreciate his efforts, they defy acceptance by a wider audience.

Gert Hofmann was the recipient of many literary prizes and awards. In 1965 he received the Harkness Award, followed in 1968 by the International Radio Plays Award of "Kritik Prag," and in 1973 the International Radio Plays Award Ohrid. In 1979 he was awarded the prestigious Ingeborg Bachmann Prize, in 1980 the Prix Italia/Prix de la RAI, and in 1982 he received the Alfred Döblin Prize as well as the Prize for the Support of Contemporary Authors. The Radio Play Award of Blind Veterans was given to him in 1983, and three years later he received the Media Award for anti-Fascist Youth granted by the SPD (Social Democratic Party) Charlottenburg and the SPD Zehlendorf. In 1993, the year of his death, the city of Munich awarded him its Literary Prize. From 1987 on he was also a member of the German Academy of Language and Literature (Deutsche Akademie für Sprache und Dichtung).

Conclusion

Hofmann always writes from the point of view of a successor to the perpetrator generation. He "performs" in his writings the haunting preoccupation of that generation with the genocide, but also the elders' various levels of complicity in these crimes and their self-defensive "forgetfulness" in the post-Holocaust years. He accomplishes what few non-Jewish German writers manage to convey: while maintaining (and indicting) an "objectivizing" and dehumanizing narrative perspective, the victims (in *The Denunciation* and *Veilchenfeld*) retain in their suffering and persecution their dignity and humanity.

Bibliography

Primary Sources

Prose

Die Denunziation (The Denunciation). 1979.
Die Fistelstimme (The Falsetto Voice). 1980.
Fuhlrotts Vergeßlichkeit (Fuhlrott's Forgetfulness). 1981.
Die Überflutung (The Flood). Four radio plays. 1981.
Gespräch über Balzacs Pferd (*Balzac's Horse and Other Stories*). 1981.
Auf dem Turm (*The Spectacle at the Tower*). 1982.
Unsere Eroberung (*Our Conquest*). 1985.
Der Blindensturz (*The Parable of the Blind*). 1986.
Veilchenfeld. 1986.
Die Weltmaschine (The World Machine). 1986.
Unsere Vergeßlichkeit (Our Forgetfulness). 1987.
Vor der Regenzeit (*Before the Rainy Season*). 1988.
Der Kinoerzähler (*The Film Explainer*). 1990.
Tolstois Kopf (Tolstoi's Head). Stories. 1991.
Das Glück (Happiness). 1992.

Die kleine Stechardin (The Little Stechard Woman). 1994.

Theater Plays (Selected)

Der Sohn (The Son). 1965.
Bakunins Leiche (Bakunmin's Corpse). 1980.
Der Austritt des Dichters Robert Walser aus dem Literarischen Verein (Robert Walser's Leaving the Literary Club). 1983.

Radio Plays (Selected)

Die Beiden aus Verona (The Two from Verona). 1960.
Tod in Miami (Death in Miami). 1968.
Vorschläge zur Selbsterhaltung (Suggestions for Self-Preservation). 1972.
John Jacob Astors letzte Fahrt (John Jacob Astor's Last Trip). 1973.
Balzacs Pferd (Balzac's Horse). 1978.
Unser Schlachthof (Our Slaughter-House). 1985.
Jean Paul Marat (Jean Paul Marat). 1989.
Letzte Liebe (Last Love). 1991.

Secondary Sources

Butler, Michael. " 'Ein hoffnungsloser Moralist': Some Observations on the Narrative World of Gert Hofmann." *German Life and Letters* 47, no. 3 (July 1994): 375–384.

Gehrke, Ralph. " 'Es ist nicht wahr, daß die Geschichte nichts lehren könnte, ihr fehlen bloβ die Schüler.' 'Veilchenfeld': Gert Hofmanns Lehrstück über Auschwitz und Fremdenhaβ und sein Bezug zur Gegenwart." *Der Deutschunterricht* 3 (1992): 92–102.

Grünzweig, Walter. "Die vergebliche Enttrümmerung beschädigter Kinderköpfe: Nationalsozialismus in den Werken Gert Hofmanns." *German Studies Review* 12, no. 1 (February 1989): 55–68.

———. "Gert Hofmann." In *Kritisches Lexikon zur deutschsprachigen Gegenwartsliteratur.* Edited by H. L. Arnold. Munich: edition text + kritik, stand vol 1. April 1995.

Kosler, Hans Christian, ed. *Gert Hofmann. Auskunft für Leser.* Darmstadt and Neuwied: Luchterhand, 1987.

Moser, Samuel. "Zu Gert Hofmann," *Schweizer Montashefte* 5 (1985): 436–439.

Perusek, Darshan. "The Value of Life, the Price of Art." *Kaleidoscope* 35 (summer–fall 1997): 4–5.

Roscher, Achim. "Nach Lebensmaterial graben. Ein Gespräch mit Gert Hofmann," *Neue Deutsche Literatur* 6 (1992): 33–42.

Scheffel, Michael. "Jenseits von Tradition und Experiment. Zu Texten Martin Grzimeks und Gert Hofmanns." *Text und Kritik* 113 (January 1992): 38–51.

Schlant, Ernestine. "Gert Hofmann's 'Die Denunziation.' " *German Studies Review* 19, no. 3 (October 1996): 415–432.

———. *The Language of Silence.* New York: Routledge, 1999: 149–165 and 180–187.

Schumacher, Heinz. "Gert Hofmann: Veilchenfeld." In *Erzählen, Erinnern. Deutsche Prosa der Gegenwart.* Edited by Herbert Kaiser and Gerhard Kopf. Frankfurt/Main: Diesterweg, 1992.

Schwartz, Leonore. "Komik in der Katastrophe. Zum Tode des Schriftstellers Gert Hofmann." In *Deutsche Literatur 1993. Jahresüberblick.* Edited by Franz Josef Görtz, Volker Hage, et al. Stuttgart: Reclam, 1994.

Steinlein, Rüdiger. "Gert Hofmanns Erzählung 'Veilchenfeld' und der Nationalsozialismus im fiktionalen Jugendbuch." In *Die Darstellung des Dritten Reiches im Kinder- und Jugendbuch.* Edited by Malte Dahrendorf and Zohar Shavit. Frankfurt/Main: dipa Verlag, 1988.

Wendt, Gunna. *Zerlegen und Zusammensetzen: Gert Hofmanns literarische Welten*, 1995.

Barbara Honigmann

(1949–)

KAREN REMMLER

UNLIKE THE DIRECT Holocaust based work of the first generation of German-Jewish writers who either survived the concentration and extermination camps, escaped Germany, or lived there in hiding under an assumed identity, the writing of second-generation Jewish writers published in Germany is marked by a "distinctively diasporic consciousness" (Morris and Remmler, p. 1). Writers such as Barbara Honigmann draw from imagination and the fragmentary stories of family members. One of a growing number of second-generation, and more recently, third-generation, self-identified Jewish writers who write in German and for whom remembrance of the Holocaust is but one of the major themes in their work, Barbara Honigmann writes of the genealogies broken by the cataclysmic impact of the Holocaust, exile, and displacement in the aftermath of World War II.

Honigmann complicates the conventional dichotomies between "Germanness" and "Jewishness" and between perpetrator and victim by placing her figures in more complex constellations of multiple identities. The Holocaust as a historical event is less evident in her work than the pervasive desire to retrace the lines of her family history at memory sites such as cemeteries, borders, and texts left behind by those who have died. Honigmann's work places the remembrance of the Holocaust within the context of European colonialism, the division of the two Germanys after the war, and the lives of Jewish characters, who share a sense of "depaysement," of not having a home (Bondy, p. 33). Her highly autobiographical work consists of semi-fictional accounts of her own leave-taking of the German Democratic Republic (GDR), her painful attempts to reconnect with her parents, and her newfound existence as a practicing Jew in Strasbourg, France.

Background

Barbara's German-Jewish father, Georg Honigmann, a descendant in a long line of distinguished German-Jewish families, and her mother, Lizzy, a Vienna-born Jew of Hungarian background, met in England, where they were both refugees and activists in antifascist organizations during World War II. After settling in East Germany because of their socialist convictions, Georg and Lizzy Honigmann remained reticent about their past, and their political views overrode any connection to their Jewish background. Nevertheless, their daughter Barbara, who was born in 1949 and grew up in a secular home, recalls being different from most of her non-Jewish contemporaries:

> I believe, that we children of the Jews in my parents' generation, perhaps everywhere, but in Germany for an especially long time, have remained our parents' children because it was difficult to free ourselves from the history and stories of our parents. Others heard other stories, about the front, about Stalingrad, about the flight from East Prussia and Schlesia, about prisoner of war camps and about the bombs falling on German cities (*Damals, dann und danach,* Munich: Carl Hanser Verlag, p. 11, translation by Karen Remmler).

Like her father, Honigmann became a dramaturge, and her experiences in provincial theaters and in East Berlin are only partially veiled in her most recent book, *Alles, alles Liebe* (Above All, Love, 2000). Honigmann reconnected to her Jewish roots, as did a number of East German intellectuals from reemigré families, by joining the small East German Jewish community in 1976. The dissatisfaction with the status quo of the Jewish community in East Germany and the oppressive circumstances of a society that recognized its status as sons and daughters of those persecuted by the Nazis yet did not offer the freedom of choice that was sought led some children of émigrés in the early 1980s to claim their Jewish identity, despite the fact that an organized Jewish community in the East barely existed. This turn to Judaism was fashioned in part by a desire to create a community in which those who already felt out of place could learn about Jewish religious practice. In 1984, Honigmann decided to leave the GDR in search of a more viable Jewish community, which she found in Strasbourg.

Career

Honigmann discovered early in her career that her creative expertise was better expressed through writing and painting than through theater, and she began writing radio plays for children and adults before she published her first collection of short stories *Roman für einem Kinde: Sechs Erzählungen* (Novel of a child: six short stories) in 1986. The different stories trace Honigmann's separation from her life in the GDR and her odyssey to find a Jewish community that would enable her to practice Judaism and to become part of a larger community, unburdened by the constant reminder of strained German-Jewish relations. In her stories, the protagonists struggle to save remnants of Jewish identity from the ruins of the past. "Doppelter Grab" (Double Grave), a story in the collection, gives a poignant description of a visit with the Jewish scholar, Gershom Scholem, to his parents' graves in the largest and most prominent Jewish cemetery in Berlin-Weissensee.

> We freed the grave from the old leaves and twigs, branches and half-grown trees, and from the boundless ivy that crept over all the graves, from one to the other, from tombstone to tree and from tree back to tombstone, taking and swallowing everything, until the entire stony order grew back to a forest and not only the body of the dead, but also this entire work of remembering the body, became earth again (Frankfurt: Luchterhand, 1989, p. 89, translation by Karen Remmler).

This text is an allegory for the losing battle that the remaining survivors face when trying to trace family roots or to mourn the victims of the Holocaust. As Scholem remarks, "one needs an ax to cut a path through the overgrowth of time" (p. 89). This attempt to clear away the debris in order to work against a rapid consolidation of Jewish memory within German postwar culture, characterizes Honigmann's subsequent publications.

Honigmann's works include a novel, a novella, an epistolary novel, and many essays. Reproductions of her paintings often adorn her book jackets, and, like her writing, they are often self-portraits, situated in settings that express a longing for home as much as they reveal the unsettledness associated with the experience of exile. At the same time, her paintings and literary narratives display a "naiveté" that instills her work with a directness and a sense of simplicity despite also communicating the burden of remembering the Holocaust and forced exile (Lorenz, p. 215).

In her second book, *Eine Liebe aus Nichts* (A love made of nothing, 1991), the narrator seeks to overcome the estrangement from her father, a feat she accomplishes only after his death. Shortly after she leaves East Germany and arrives in Paris, her father dies. In an attempt to interpret his life through the few clues left behind in his room in Weimar, she returns to East Germany, where she finds her father's appointment book and reads his entries depicting his return to Germany after the war. The narrator reconnects with her father by entering her own notes in the remaining pages, thus writing a genealogy that connects his life to hers:

> Because I didn't want to take the calendar back to Paris simply as a memento and because so many pages were left blank, I wrote in it myself and dated the weekdays according to the present year. I entered the date of my father's death and the date of his funeral and the date in which we saw one another for the last time, and then I began to fill the empty pages, so that our entries ran together in the English calendar that was long out of date anyhow (Berlin: Rowohlt, 1991, pp. 99–100; translation by Karen Remmler).

Death and visits to gravesites are frequent themes in Honigmann's subsequent collection of essays and travel prose, *Am Sonntag spielt der Rabbi Fußball* (On Sunday the rabbi plays soccer, 1998), and *Damals, dann und danach* (Back then, then and after, 1999). In one of the essays in the latter, "Gräber in London" (Graves in London), Honigmann describes her search for her maternal grandparents' graves in London: "There is only an empty spot, where the gravestone is supposed to be, a gap between the other gravesites, just sand, gravel on a slight hill, no large or small stone, absolutely no stone, only dirt and a few weeds" (p. 37). In another essay, "Der Untergang von Wien" (The downfall of Vienna), she recalls her visits with her mother in Vienna and her mother's grave. The contrast between the two sites reveals the recurring dilemma in Honigmann's work: How does one remember the dead when their memory remains fragmented and those who knew them are dispersed throughout the world and refuse to or cannot speak of the past? Honigmann's narrators commemorate the dead by recalling their lives. The genealogies will never be intact, but their memories may serve to liberate coming generations, so that their lives are not solely dominated by the Holocaust, even as they will always be a part of that legacy.

Like her fictional texts, these essays interweave the possibility of a thriving Jewish community despite the destruction of genocide and forced exile. Honigmann's essays also tell of her life in Strasbourg, her Torah reading group, her encounters with non-Jews and Jews, her walks along borders and in cemeteries, and her travels to the United States, where she became a writer in residence at Washington University in St. Louis and was invited to speak at Brandeis University and Wellesley College, among others. Thus the remembrance of the Holocaust takes place as life goes on, even as the specter of antisemitism and racism continues to haunt Europe. Honigmann's work is a reminder that recovering silenced genealogies can lead to a sense of Jewish identity not solely determined by the Holocaust.

Honigmann won the coveted German literary award, the Kleist Prize, named after the prolific German writer of the Romantic period, because her writing displays this drive to recover lost identities and histories, even as continued exile, forced or chosen, remains the major theme of her work. Given her decision to take the leap from East to West, from a German-speaking to a French-speaking country, and from a socialist ideology that eclipsed Jewish identity to a thriving orthodox community in Strasbourg, Honigmann's writing must be understood within the context of a chosen exile, an exile made more permanent by the fall of the Berlin Wall and German unification.

Honigmann's assessment of her life in East Germany is the subject of her latest work, *Alles, alles Liebe*! (Above all, love). She describes the narrowness of East German society through the eyes of a group of mostly young Jewish artists, whose critique of the status quo includes dismay at the persistent antisemitism, the state ideology, and lack of innovation in the official cultural institutions. Written as a series of letters, the allusions to motifs from German Romanticism, such as tragic love, misunderstood genius, friendship, and alienation, abound. The main protagonist, Anna, corresponds with friends and family both within and outside of East Germany, while working at a provincial theater and living in a dismal, spartan room above a bar. As in most of Honigmann's works, the focus is not on the experience of the Holocaust but rather on the rootlessness of the second generation and the search for a sense of home outside of the German realm.

Response to the Holocaust and Post-Holocaust Antisemitism

The Holocaust appears, in Honigmann's work, to be secondary to the experience of exile, even as the consequences of this exile are clearly intertwined with the destruction left in the wake of the Holocaust. Honigmann's response to the Holocaust is complex. The Holocaust is not the focus of her work, yet its remembrance continues to color not only the relationships between Germans and Jews but also the internal struggle of German Jews to establish an identity in the present that moves beyond a homage to the victims. Second-generation German Jews have multifaceted histories, just as do their non-Jewish German counterparts. In her writing, Honigmann strives against any reduction of these histories to a dichotomous perpetrator/victim scenario. In essays, she emphasizes her indebtedness to German culture and language for enabling her to be the writer that she is today:

> It sounds paradoxical, but I am a German writer, although I don't perceive myself to be German and haven't lived in Germany for years. I think, however, that a writer is that which he writes, and he is above all the language in which he writes. I don't only write in German. The literature that has formed and educated me, is the German literature, and I refer to it in everything that I write, to Goethe, to Kleist, to Grimm's fairy tales and to German Romanticism, and I know very well that the gentlemen writers were all more or less antisemitic, but that doesn't matter (*Damals, dann und danach*, pp. 17–18).

Honigmann refuses to dwell on the consequences of the Holocaust, especially as it disrupts any hope for "normal" relations between Germans and Jews. Rather, she seeks to bypass the troubled relations by observing them from across the French-German border in Strasbourg. This position gives her a vantage point from which to observe Germans, Jews, and others, whose lives and memories are unthinkable without the conspicuous references to the failure of politics or education to hinder post-Holocaust antisemitism, another major theme in her work.

Honigmann's portrayal of antisemitic stereotypes in *Soharas Reise* (Sohara's journey, 1996), for example, can be read as ironic depictions of prevalent antisemitism throughout Europe, not just in Germany. By incorporating these stereotypes into a more complex vision of what Jewish identity means in post-Holocaust Europe, Honigmann reminds the reader that the ongoing remembrance of the Holocaust does not assure that antisemitism has been eradicated. Rather, the experience of second-generation Jews living in Europe must be recorded in all its complexity.

Honigmann's most successful attempt to present a more complex vision of what Jewish identity might look like in present-day Europe is portrayed in *Soharas Reise*. The novel diminishes the troubled relation between Germans and Jews that Honigmann laments, again and again in interviews and essays, by creating an Algerian Jewish Orthodox female protagonist, Sohara, whose relationship to the Holocaust is all but non-existent. The book describes the trauma of Sohara, an immigrant to France during the Algerian War of liberation, when her husband, Simon, who identifies himself as the Rabbi from Singapore, kidnaps their six children. In her despair, Sohara seeks the help of her neighbor, a German-Jewish Holocaust survivor, Mrs. Kahn. The two characters live in Strasbourg, a border city, whose proximity to Germany, both historically and culturally, makes it a symbol for the intersection of multifaceted ethnic and cultural identities (Sephardic, Ashkenazic, Algerian, French, and German). Mrs. Kahn refuses to speak German and refers to the Germans as "cannibals" (*Sohara's Journey*, Berlin: Rowohlt, 1996, p. 22). The Holocaust takes shape for Sohara through Mrs. Kahn's tearful recollection of her deportation, the murder of her husband in Italy, the loss and recovery of her son, and her illness after returning from a trip to Auschwitz with a group of survivors, years after the Holocaust has ended. Thus Sohara's personal tragedy, which ends once her children are returned to her through the "torah connection"—a loose group of rabbis who trace the whereabouts of her children to London—is juxtaposed with Mrs. Kahn's memories of the Holocaust.

It is through Mrs. Kahn's presence in the narrative that the presence of the Holocaust, otherwise absent, becomes visible. In fact, Sohara's distance from the Holocaust is countered by the memory of another atrocity of which she is a bystander and, as she sees it, a victim: the French occupation of Algeria and the subsequent bloody war that led to Algeria's independence. Sohara's journey from her childhood home, Oran, to France and her emotional journey from a repressed wife to an independent single mother appear to displace the centrality of the remembrance of the Holocaust for European Jews. The displacement of the Holocaust by Sohara's historical and personal trauma can be read as a narrative device to relocate the memory of the Holocaust outside of Germany's borders and to place it within the context of a broader colonial and post-colonial history. The focus shifts from the impossibility of reconciliation, or "normalization," between Germans and Jews to the differences within post-Holocaust Jewish communities and memories in Europe.

Critical Reception

The reception of Honigmann's work in the English-speaking realm is sparse. Translations of her work are in process and excerpts of her novel *Soharas Reise* and other writings will appear in *Jewish Writing in Germany*, a volume in a series on international Jewish writing to be published July 2002 by the University of Nebraska Press. Most of the secondary work on Honigmann has appeared in German newspaper reviews of her six publications to date. She has received mention in longer works considering contemporary Jewish writing in Germany, but her work has yet to be discussed in a full-length monograph. Scholars such as Karen Remmler, Thomas Nolden, Leslie Morris, Dagmar Lorenz, and Guy Stern have noted the centrality of family ties in her work and the directness of her prose style. Lauding Honigmann as the fall 2000 recipient of the Kleist Prize, Luc Bondy praised her writing for its "tactile narrative art," an immediacy of language that reveals the precariousness of Jewish identity in the aftermath of the Holocaust (Bondy, p. 33).

Dagmar Lorenz traces Honigmann's development as a writer to her detachment from her father, who represented the socialist state, toward "the construction of a positive Jewish position under the auspices of motherhood and women's spirituality" (p. 209). Lorenz defends Honigmann against Stern's claim that Honigmann has forsaken the political for a postmodern style by pointing out Honigmann's clear stance to disengage herself from the "negative symbiosis" between Germans and Jews (Lorenz, p. 209). Honigmann's disengagement is not a sign of escape, per se, but rather an attempt to fashion a positive Jewish identity that is neither solely mired in German Jewish relations nor determined by the memory of the Holocaust.

Bibliography

Primary Sources

Roman von einem Kinde. Sechs Erzählungen (Novel of a Child: Six Short Stories). 1986.
Eine Liebe aus nichts (A Love Out of Nothing). 1991.
Soharas Reise (Sohara's Journey). 1996.
Am Sonntag spielt der Rabbi Fußball (On Sunday the Rabbi Plays Soccer). 1998.
Damals, dann und danach (Back Then, Then and After). 1999.
Alles, alles Liebe! (Above All, Love). 2000.

Secondary Sources

Bondy, Luc. " 'Hier ist es zu schön, da können wir nicht bleiben.' Laudatio für den Kleist-Preis an Barbara Honigmann." *Neue Züricher Zeitung*, no. 247, October 23, 2000.
Feinberg, Anat. "Abiding in a Haunted-Land. The Issue of Heimat in Contemporary German Jewish Writings." *New German Critique* 70 (1997): 161–181.
Fries, Marilyn Sibley. "Text as Locus. Inscription as Identity: On Barbara Honigmann's *Roman von einem Kinde*." *Studies in Twentieth Century Literature* 14, no. 2 (1990): 175–193.
Herzog, Todd. "Hybrids and Mischlinge: Translating Anglo-American Cultural Theory into German." *German Quarterly* 70, no. 1 (1997): 1–17.

Lorenz, Dagmar C. G. "From Antifascism to Judaism." In *Keepers of the Motherland: German Texts by Jewish Women Writers*. Lincoln, Nebraska: University of Nebraska Press, 1997: 208–215.

Morris, Leslie, and Karen Remmler, eds. *Jewish Writing in Germany*. Lincoln, Nebraska: University of Nebraska Press, 2001.

Nolden, Thomas. "Contemporary German Jewish Literature." *German Life and Letters* 1 (1994): 77–93.

Peck, Jeffrey M. "Telling Tales of Exile, (Re)writing Jewish Histories: Barbara Honigmann and the Novel *Soharas Reise*." *German Studies Review* 24, no. 3 (October, 2001): 557–570.

Remmler, Karen. "En-gendering Bodies of Memory. Tracing the Genealogy of Identity in the Work of Esther Dischereit, Barbara Honigmann and Irene Dische." In *Reemerging Jewish Culture in Germany: Life and Literature since 1989*. Edited by Sander L. Gilman and Karen Remmler. New York, London: New York University Press, 1994, 184–209.

Stern, Guy. "Barbara Honigmann: A Preliminary Assessment." In *Insiders and Outsider Jewish and Gentile Culture in Germany and Austria*. Edited by Dagmar C. G. Lorenz and Gabriele Weinberger. Detroit, Michigan: Wayne State University Press, 1994: 329–349.

Archives

Reviews of Honigmann's work are archived in the Zentralarchiv zur Erforschung der Geschichte der Juden in Deutschland at the University of Heidelberg, Heidelberg, Germany. For more information refer to http://www.uni-heidelberg.de/institute/sonst/aj/PERSONEN/HONIGMAN.

JUDITH MAGYAR ISAACSON

(1925–)

MARTHA A. RAVITS

JUDITH MAGYAR WAS born 3 July 1925 in the town of Kaposvár, Hungary, the only child in a cultured Jewish family. Her parents were Jeno Magyar and Rózsi Vágó Magyar. During World War II Judith, along with her mother and aunt, was sent to Auschwitz and then moved to various labor camps. All three women survived and, after the war and release from the camps, Judith married an American rescuer, attorney Irving Isaacson, in December 1945. The couple immigrated with Judith's mother and aunt to Maine. Judith Isaacson became a naturalized U.S. citizen and received a B.A. from Bates College in 1965 and an M.A. in mathematics from Bowdoin College in 1967. After teaching mathematics at a high school, she taught at Bates College, where she became dean of students from 1969 to 1977. The Isaacsons reside in Auburn, Maine, and have three children and seven grandchildren. Since the publication of her memoir *Seed of Sarah* in 1990, Judith Isaacson has received honorary degrees from three New England colleges.

Seed of Sarah: Memoirs of a Survivor

In accord with the writing of other women, Judith Magyar Isaacson, in *Seed of Sarah*, describes her experience during the *Shoah* with reference to the special terrors the situation held for young women, especially the fear of rape and other sexual brutality. Like many women of her generation, in writing about sexualized trauma she is torn between refinement and frankness, between her poetic sensibility and her commitment to accuracy. She exposes obscene conditions with poignant honesty.

Literary by nature and nurture, Isaacson in her youth hoped to study comparative literature at the Sorbonne, and as a school girl she was proud to be selected to recite poetry at the patriotic festivities of the girls' *gymnazium* (private school) she attended. When her performance was interrupted by antisemitic jeers, she stood her ground and finished, suddenly aware of the intensifying Nazi threat in her society. Her literature teacher, Dr. Biczó, comforted her with a gift of Plato's *Gorgias*, citing Socrates: "It is better to suffer an injustice than to commit one." Judith would apply this motto later at Auschwitz, where she would decline the privileged position of *kapo*, a prisoner who assists the camp guards.

In her memoir Isaacson recalls her father's aborted plan to take his family to the United States, where one of his brothers lived, before the Nazi roundups. After both grandfathers died of natural causes and her father and paternal and maternal uncles were impressed into labor battalions for Jews, Judith was left in a circle of women. It is at this point in her memoir that the focus on gender terror begins. She explains that she received a warning from her youngest uncle, Imre Vágó, who told of seeing young Jewish women shipped to the Soviet front, where they were mass-raped then buried alive after being forced to dig their own graves. Judith promised that she would risk her life to avoid such a fate.

With the imposition of anti-Jewish laws in 1938 and eventual confinement to the ghetto in Kaposvár after the German occupation in 1944, Judith's world began to collapse, until as a nineteen-year-old she marked her birthday in the municipal stables awaiting deportation along with relatives and townspeople to Auschwitz. Because Hungarian Jewry was among the last population that the Nazis rounded up during World War II, Judith spent only nine months in the camps. Her brief, poignant tale unfolds in spare, graceful prose punctuated with allusions to remembered literature that helped her sustain mental equilibrium amid emotional turmoil.

Like many survivors' accounts, Isaacson's memories of the shock of the *Shoah* begin with the dehumanization of the crowded transport train that carried her remaining family members with their townsfolk away from their native city. The disorientation of the cramped cattle-car ride with two buckets in the center—one for water, one for a toilet—ended in the horror of unloading at Auschwitz, where Judith saw the old, the disabled, and the deranged, including women from her village, thrown screaming onto a heap of corpses beside the tracks. Her attention to the dispatch of the weak and disabled introduced her to the terror of the concentration camp world.

Seed of Sarah goes on to tell how, at the first selection, Judith's mother lied about her age to remain in the line with her daughter and her younger sister Magda. The three clung together resolutely throughout their ordeal, as they made their way through a "a new world, a different planet" (Urbana, Ill.: University of Illinois Press, 1990, p. 63). Arriving on one of the last transports to Auschwitz-Birkenau, the women had red crosses hurriedly painted on their backs—no time for tattooing—and were assigned to an unfinished barracks, Birkenau Lager B III, called by the inmates "Mexico" because it was considered the poorest of the poor. Judith, her mother, and her aunt endured the showers and shaving, deprivation of food and water, and long "*Zähl Appell*" (roll calls) in the July sun. Judith picked up survival tactics from experienced inmates in hurried exchanges at the latrines, along with news about missing friends. Isaacson even survived what in retrospect she believes was a selection by Dr. Joseph Mengele of prisoners to die in the crematoria because she pushed forward with her mother, as did her aunt, into a rushing crowd despite the officer's order directing her toward a transport of girls. The women ended up instead on a train headed to Lichtenau, Germany, and a camp outside a munitions factory where 1,000 Hungarian Jewish women worked beside forced laborers from many other parts of Europe.

In one particularly suspenseful episode, Isaacson recounts being singled out at a roll call to follow the camp commandant outside the gates. She trailed him through the village streets with rising panic. "Do women inherit memories of rape?" she wondered, recalling the Sabine women and the Magyar mothers of Hungarian lore (p. 90). At the commandant's residence, she was relieved beyond measure when he ordered her to scrub floors as a servant for his mistress. On her return to the barracks, she revealed a piece of pie she had received as a reward, and an envious *kapo* immediately reassigned the plush job to another inmate.

Within the vast underground munitions factory, Judith served as a "horse," dragging heavy wagons of filled grenades. When her aunt Magda lost a finger in a machine accident, Judith's mother boldly intervened with the commandant, persuading him to allow the women to seek medical care in town. In December, the three women volunteered for lighter duty but were pulled from the ranks to watch fellow inmates depart on a transport, which they later learned was destined for the death camps in Poland. Their familial bond helped them survive the winter of food shortages, for Magda worked in the dining hall and could pilfer food. Isaacson records how the women prisoners suffered from heavy manual labor in the factory as well as the exhausting trek in the cold to and from work each day. Like other Holocaust women writers, she describes how inside the barracks the women consoled one another by singing, exchanging recipes, talking of men, and occasionally marking holidays.

When supplies for factory operations ran out in the spring of 1945, the women were sent on makeshift work details into the mountains. There, luxuriating in nature, Judith was surprised by a sadistic female guard whose vengeful outburst gives the book its title:

> Dreaming is all that's left for you, bitch. After the war, you'll be transported to a desert island. No males—not even natives. Much use'll be your fancy looks, with snakes for company. Do you suppose the Americans will win the war? That would be your death sentence. We'll shoot you Jewish bitches before the Americans come—it's the Führer's decree. Your fate is sealed either way: no men. No sex. No seed of Sarah (p. 108).

In dedicating her book to "our children and our children's children," Isaacson reaffirms the generational links that confound the expressed Nazi goal of Jewish destruction.

By spring of 1945, as the Allied bombers approached their campsite, the women were moved by cattle car to Weimar, on route to Buchenwald concentration camp, where their sealed train stood on the tracks for days. They were finally released at Leipzig for a march to half-destroyed camps. When the guards ordered another evacuation, Judith and her aunt chose to hide in the infirmary with her mother, whom they feared could not survive a forced march. As the Allied bombs fell, the Jews in the infirmary were transported to a forced labor camp where they cowered in a cellar awaiting liberation.

On 20 April 1945, the U.S. army liberated the women inmates in Leipzig. At U.S. military headquarters, Judith met Irving Isaacson, an American captain with the Office of Strategic Services, who helped her family move out of the path of the approaching Soviet army to Berneck-am-Fichtelgebirge in Bavaria. There, on Judith's twentieth birthday, she and Isaacson became engaged. Their smiling engagement photo is one of several family photographs that grace the volume.

An epilogue describes Isaacson's return to Kaposvár in 1977 with her adult daughter. It was only then she learned that of the inhabitants deported from her village, only 5 percent survived.

Altogether, from two-thirds to three-fourths of Hungarian Jewry perished in the *Shoah*, most upon disembarking at Auschwitz.

Isaacson ends her narrative with the story she gleaned about her school friend Marika Erdös, who went to the university in Budapest and successfully hid there throughout the war, only to emerge during liberation festivities, when she was seized by Soviet soldiers who raped and shot her on the bank of the Danube. Because survivors of rape seldom write about the ordeal in their memoirs, Isaacson observes, she offers hers in their honor. The themes of gender terror, fear of rape, and fear of murder are interwoven with survival tactics of female solidarity, mutual concern, and female courage throughout the book. She exposes the pain of grotesque events tempered by the optimism learned from her mother, which she credits with enabling her to retain a sense of decency in a world of brutal humiliations.

Invitations to speak on New England college campuses about her Holocaust experiences prompted Isaacson to begin work on her memoirs at the age of 52. She composed *Seed of Sarah* slowly over the course of ten years, conducting extensive research by traveling to her hometown in Hungary with her daughter to revisit sites and meet old friends, to Auschwitz with her son to visit the camp and museum, and to Hessisch Lichtenau with her husband for a reunion of slave labor survivors. The visits, oral accounts of fellow survivors, and scholarly books on the *Shoah* helped her to fill in the gaps in her memory, to reconstruct the chronology and geography of her war years as a teenager, and to uncover the fate of other Jewish friends. A hometown friend and survivor, Dr. Péter Hanák, and his fellow historians referred her to works on the Hungarian Holocaust that "confirmed my memories and placed them into a historical context, others inspired my writing" (p. 157). A former teacher turned librarian, Béla Kellner, provided access to old Kaposvár newspaper archives to verify dates and the sequence of local events during 1944. Isaacson links her book, which has become a best-seller for its publisher, to the line of Holocaust literature and testimony, even as she adheres to a strongly personal narrative point of view, admirable for its simplicity, apolitical in its design.

Bibliography

Primary Sources

Seed of Sarah: Memoirs of a Survivor. 1990.

Related Works in Other Media

Seed of Sarah, a Chamber Opera by Mark Polishook.

Seed of Sarah, a video documentary based on the opera, directed by Andrea Weiss, produced by Jezebel Films, Ltd., London and New York; distributor: The Cinema Guild, New York.

Secondary Sources

Comstock, Gary L. *Religious Autobiographies*. Belmont, Calif.: Wadsworth, 1994, pp. 186–211.

ELFRIEDE JELINEK

(1946–)

DAGMAR C. G. LORENZ

ELFRIEDE JELINEK was born on 20 October 1946 in Mürzzuschlag in Styria, Austria, the daughter of the Jewish chemist Friedrich Jelinek and his non-Jewish wife, Hilde. While she was still a high school student, Jelinek studied recorder, organ, and later composition at the Vienna Conservatory. In 1964 she enrolled as a student of theater and art history at the University of Vienna and completed her studies with an organist diploma in 1971. In the early 1950s her father, who had survived the *Shoah* because his research was considered vital for the war effort, began to suffer from a psychological disorder that also affected his daughter. A nervous breakdown in 1968 caused her to interrupt her studies, and she began to write poetry. She spent the year in virtual isolation, unable to leave her parents' home. In 1969 her father died in a mental ward. At about that time she became interested in politics and the debates in the literary journal *manuskripte*. In 1972 she lived in Berlin and 1973 in Rome. In 1974 she married Gottfried Hüngsberg, a computer scientist formerly associated with Rainer Werner Fassbinder's circles, and she joined the Communist Party and moved to Vienna.

Career

The child of a near-victim of the Holocaust, Jelinek first acknowledged her Jewish background after the collapse of the Eastern Bloc and the Austrian Communist Party. These events and the 1986 Waldheim scandal, in which the former member of the Nazi military Kurt Waldheim was elected to the Austrian presidency, represented a turning point for her. Before this point Jelinek did not emphasize her Jewish background. Rather, her writing expressed her reservations against the dominant culture by espousing leftist and feminist views. Jelinek was an oppositional writer from the start and cultivated a public image as a cynical nonconformist and a literary enfant terrible. In 1991 she was one of the last to leave the Austrian Communist Party, but her sympathies for the left continued and in an interview she denounced the "colonialization of the former GDR [German Democratic Republic] and other socialist countries" by the West (Winter, p. 18). She had supported the political left, which she considered a bastion against antifeminism and neofascism. Losing her political frame of reference caused her to construct a new oppositional identity involving her father's Jewishness. She stands at the forefront of the initiatives against the right-wing, xenophobic Freedom Party as an orator, polemicist, and an eloquent critic of the party's ideological leader, Jörg Haider. Her penetrating, highly literary political pamphlets appear in collections and on the Internet. Through the use of imagery and chains of associations she exposes the mentality of those who try to vindicate National Socialism. Jelinek's awards include the Poetry and Prose Awards of the Youth Culture Week (1969), the Poetry Prize of Austrian Students (1969), the Austrian State Stipend for Literature (1972), the Roswitha-Medal of the Town of Bad Gandersheim (1978), the Prize of the Federal Ministry for Education and Art (1983), the Heinrich Böll Prize (1986), the Prize of the City of Vienna (1989), the Peter Weiss Prize (1994), the Walter Hasenclever Prize (1994), the Bremen Literature Prize (1996), and the Georg Büchner Prize (1998).

Jelinek is not a Holocaust author in the strict sense of the word, but her work—theater and radio plays, novels, short narratives, poetry, polemics, and cultural criticism—deals with the effects of the Nazi genocide on her family and larger society. Jelinek first became known as a writer of stylized avant-garde texts that configured human characters as mere receptacles and conveyors of mass culture, for example, *Lisas Schatten* (Lisa's Shadow, 1967), *Wir sind Lockvögel, Baby!* (We Are Decoys, Baby, 1970), and *Michael: Ein Ju-*

gendbuch für die Infantilgesellschaft (Michael: An Adolescent Novel for the Infantile Society, 1972). Later, her taboo-breaking use of language and portrayal of brutal expressions of sexuality startled the public and outraged the press. Her novels, and even more so her dramas, give regular rise to scandals and controversies.

Themes of Exploitation and Oppression

Jelinek's foremost interest is in the perpetrators of the Holocaust and their children, and she examines sadomasochistic personal and social relationships that mirror Nazi practices. Austria as she describes it has inherited the dynamics that made the *Shoah* possible: authoritarianism, misogyny, xenophobia, and crass materialism. The novel *Die Liebhaberinnen* (*Women As Lovers*, 1975) thematizes the exploitation of women and children as the weaker members of society in the private and public sphere. Jelinek's tightly knit, fast-paced prose is void of sentimentality and her tone is cynical. The characters and their depressing stories are portrayed with scientific detachment, as types and case studies, reserving for the narrator a position apart. This perspective of separateness in conjunction with detailed insider knowledge is also the position that the intellectual Jelinek has forged for herself. The petty bourgeois despots' holding sway over their enslaved families in *Die Liebhaberinnen* and *Die Ausgesperrten* (*Wonderful, Wonderful Times*, 1980) epitomizes the claustrophobic atmosphere in a country whose dissenting voices were silenced and whose cultural diversity was destroyed under Nazism. Jelinek foregrounds pornography, prostitution, battery, and rape in her scathing analysis of gender relations, revealing the ineffectiveness of humanism against the pervasive legacy of fascism. Showing the oppression of women among obscure fictional characters, as in the novel *Die Klavierspielerin* (*The Piano Teacher*, 1983), as well as the oppression of prominent historical figures, as in the drama *Clara S.* [Schumann] (1984), she establishes a continuity between the pre-and post-Nazi era.

In *Die Ausgesperrten*, the reader sees how the social dilemma left after National Socialism affects all social groups: the lumpenproletarian Witkowski family, former Nazis; the disenfranchised Mrs. Sepp, a working-class woman, and her son, Hans; and the Pachofens, rich industrialists. The rigid class structure in a supposedly democratic society is barely noticed by the underprivileged. Yet, the way class determines the future of the younger generation calls to mind the concentration camp hierarchy. There are no real opportunities for the ambitious Witkowski twins, Rainer and Anna, nor for the working-class lad Hans, despite the promise of equality in the public discourse. Recognizing the impasse, Rainer Witkowski goes on a rampage and slaughters his entire family. Jelinek's characters call to mind the characterization of the fascist personalities by the anti-fascist intellectuals Theodor Adorno and Wilhelm Reich. Old Mr. Witkowski, formerly a Nazi henchman, now abuses his wife and forces her to model for pornographic photos. Mrs. Witkowski, a passive and conciliatory housewife and mother, submits to every imaginable humiliation. Their twin son and daughter consider themselves anarchists and existentialists, but they conform to their parents' model, the only model they know. They, too, engage in and accept violent and abusive behavior.

Jelinek's Austria is a society without options, a concentration camp without barbed-wire fences. The new totalitarianism, the product of mind control by the media, is imperceptible. The effects of U.S.-style advertisement and the pop culture are conveyed in seemingly automatic associative language patterns that create the impression of an impenetrable mass mentality. Jelinek uses a modified stream-of-consciousness technique to describe an artificially created collective mindset overpowering the individual. In *Die Klavierspielerin* the central character is Erika Kohut, an obsessive-compulsive woman and the daughter of a controlling mother. In this novel, too, there is no escaping from the prisons of deceptive speech and stimuli, from a popular culture that fosters a sadomasochistic heterosexuality. Erika tries to make misogynist institutions—peep-shows and prostitution—work for her and then tries to alleviate her emotional distress through self-mutilation and self-denigration. The same issues are thematized in *Lust* (*Lust*, 1989), a novel employing images and motifs of pornographic literature in such a way as to unmask the terrors of sexual subjugation practiced within and outside of marriage.

In the mid-1980s, when Kurt Waldheim was elected president of Austria, Jelinek became a major participant in the newly forming secular Jewish presence. Appropriating her father's Jewish and socialist legacy she positioned herself in the tradition of Jewish satire and criticism. In an interview she defined the specifically Jewish quality of her writing in opposition to the prevailing political conservatism and xenophobia fostered by reawakened nationalism, and to a president whose involvement with Nazi special military units and the deportations in the Balkans was publicly known. She noted that satirical writing was unappreciated in contemporary Austria "because the Jews are dead" (Löffler, p. 18). In 1993 she characterized "work with language, and criticism of existing conditions with the help of language"—that is, her own literary enterprise—as a Jewish undertaking (Berka, p. 129).

Crimes Past and Present

The theme of Austria as a crime scene remained a constant in Jelinek's writing. In *Die Kinder der Toten* (The Children of the Dead, 1995), a cozy country inn, the setting of the novel, turns out to be the site of mass murders, populated by ghosts and vampires. The front matter contains a Jewish reference, the Hebrew invocation "Let them come, Spirits of the Dead that were not seen for years, and bless their children." In light of Holocaust history, Jelinek associates rural Austria with the numerous concentration camp sites located there. However, her allusions to crimes transcend historical boundaries. Past and present seem inextricably linked—images of mutilated bodies and body parts everywhere call to mind images from *Shoah* films while the sports imagery associates certain casualties with the present. Similarly, *Stecken, Stab, und Stangl* (Stick, Staff, and Rod, 1997), a drama written in response to attacks on Gypsies by right-wing extremists, blurs time frames and calls to mind the *Shoah* as the radicalism and callousness of contemporary xenophobes is revealed. The hostilities against so-called foreigners by neo-Nazis is explored in a phraseology that indicates a continuity between past and present. Similarly, the minidrama *Das Lebewohl* (The Farewell, 2000), a monologue satirizing Haider's diction and mentality, suggests that whatever is preserved in language remains accessible in the past and in the future.

Bibliography

Primary Sources

Lisas Schatten (Lisa's Shadow). 1967.
Wir sind Lockvögel, Baby! (We are Decoys, Baby). 1970.
Michael: Ein Jugendbuch für die Infantilgesellschaft (Michael: An Adolescent Novel for the Infantile Society). 1972.
Die Liebhaberinnen (*Women As Lovers*). 1975.
Bukolit: Hörroman (*Bukolit*: Novel for Listening). 1980.
Die Ausgesperrten (*Wonderful, Wonderful Times*). 1980.
Die endlose Unschuldigkeit (Never-ending Innocence). 1980.
Was geschah, nachdem Nora ihren Mann verlassen hatte; oder, Stützen der Gesellschaft (*What Happened After Nora Had Left Her Husband; or, Pillars of Society*). 1980.
Die Klavierspielerin (*The Piano Teacher*). 1983.
Burgtheater: Posse mit Gesang (Burgtheater: Burlesque with Songs). 1984.
Clara S. 1984.
Theaterstücke (Dramas). 1984.
Oh Wildnis, oh Schutz vor ihr (Oh Wilderness, oh Protection Against It). 1985.
Begierde und Fahrerlaubnis (eine Pornographie) (Desire and Permission to Drive). 1987.
Präsident Abendwind (President Evening Breeze). In *Anthropophagen im Abendwind*, 1988.
Die Klavierspielerin: Melodrama in einem Akt (The Piano Teacher: Melodrama in One Act). 1989.
Lust (*Lust*). 1989.
Wir sind Lockvögel, Baby! Theaterexperiment nach dem gleichnamigen Roman (We Are Decoys, Baby! Theatrical Experiment Based on the Novel by the Same Title). 1990.
Wolken: Heim (Clouds: Home). 1990.
Körperliche Veränderungen/Der Wald: Mini Operas nach Texten von Elfriede Jelinek (Physical changes/The Forest: Mini-Operas Based on Texts by Elfriede Jelinek). 1991.
Totenauberg. 1991.
Unruhiges Wohnen: Tanztheater (Residing Restlessly: Dance Theater). 1991.
Krankheit; oder, Moderne Frauen (Disease; or, Modern Women). In *Theaterstücke*, 1992.
An den, den's angeht: Zusatztext zu Wolken: Heim (To Whom It May Concern: Addition to Clouds, Home). 1993.
Raststätte; oder, Sie machen's alle (*Services; or, They All Do It*). 1994.
Die Kinder der Toten (The Children of the Dead). 1995.
Sturm und Zwang: Schrelben als Geschlechter Kampf (Storm and Coercion). Interviews. 1995.
Stecken, Stab, und Stangl (Stick, Staff, and Rod). 1997.
Er nichts als er: Zu, mit Robert Walser (He, Nothing But He: For, with, Robert Walser). 1998.
Jelineks Wahl: Literarische Verwandschaften (Jelinek's Choice: Literary Relations). 1998. With Brigitte Landes.
Ein Sportstück (A Sports Piece). 1998.
Elfriede Jelinek. 1999.
Erlkönigin (The Erlqueen). 1999.
Macht nichts: Eine kleine Trilogie des Todes (It Doesn't Matter: A Short Trilogy of Death). 1999.
Ende: Gedichte von 1966–1968 (Ending: Poems 1966–1968). 2000.
Gier: Ein Unterhaltungsroman (Greed: An Entertaining Novel). 2000.
Das Lebewohl: Drei kleine Dramen (The Farewell: Three Short Plays). 2000.
Peter Eschberg, Theatermacher, was sonst (Peter Eschberg, Theater Maker, What Else). 2001.

Secondary Sources

Arens, Katherine, and Jorun B. Johns. *Elfriede Jelinek: Famed by Language*. Riverside, Calif.: Ariadne Press, 1994.
Bartens, Daniela, and Paul Pechmann, eds. *Elfriede Jelinek: Die Internationale Rezeption*. Graz, Austria: Droschl, 1997.
Bartsch, Kurt, and Günter Höfler, eds. *Elfriede Jelinek*. Graz, Austria: Droschl, 1991.
Berka, Sigrid. "Ein Gespräch mit Elfriede Jelinek." *Modern Austrian Literature* 26, no. 2 (1993): 127–155.
Eigler, Friederike. *Rewriting Reality: An Introduction to Elfriede Jelinek*. Oxford: Berg, 1994.
Gilman, Sander. *Jews in Today's German Culture*. Bloomington: Indiana University Press, 1995.
Gürtler, Christa, ed. *Gegen den schönen Schein: Texte zu Elfriede Jelinek*. Frankfurt: Neue Kritik, 1990.
Hoffmann, Yasmin. " 'Noch immer riecht es hier nach Blut': Zu Elfriede Jelineks Stück Krankheit oder Moderne Frauen." *Etudes germaniques* 20 (1991): 191–204.

Konzett, Matthias. *The Rhetoric of National Dissent in Thomas Bernhard, Peter Handke, and Elfriede Jelinek*. Rochester, N.Y.: Camden House, 2000.

Löffler, Sigrid. "Spezialistin für den Hass." *Die Zeit* 4, no. 11 (1983): 18.

Lorenz, Dagmar C. G. *Keepers of the Motherland: German Texts by Jewish Women Writers*. Lincoln: University of Nebraska Press, 1997.

———. "Elfriede Jelinek (1946–)." *Contemporary Jewish Writing in Austria: An Anthology*. Lincoln: University of Nebraska Press, 1999, pp. 255–272.

Marcuse, Herbert. *A Critique of Pure Tolerance*. Boston: Beacon, 1965.

Meyer, Imke. "The Trouble with Elfriede: Jelinek and Autobiography." In *The Fiction of the I: Contemporary Austrian Writers and Autobiography*, edited by Nicholas J. Meyerhofer, 116–137. Riverside, Calif.: Ariadne, 1999.

Schmid, Georg. "Das Schwerverbrechen der fünfziger Jahre." In *Gegen den schönen Schein*, edited by Gürtler, 44–55.

Schmid-Bortenschlager, Sigrid. "Gewalt zeugt Gewalt zeugt Literatur . . . *Wir sind Lockvögel, Baby!* und andere frühe Prosa." *Neue Kritik* (1990): 30–43.

Schmitz-Burgard, Sylvia. "Body Language As Expression of Repression: Lethal Reverberations of Fascism in *Die Ausgesperrten*." In *Elfriede Jelinek: Framed by Language*, pp. 194–228.

Sichrovsky, Heinz. "*Die Ausgesperrten*." *Arbeiter Zeitung* (Vienna) 17 November 1979, pp. 8–9.

Wilke, Sabine. "The Body Politic of Performance, Literature, and Film: Mimesis and Citation in Valie Export, Elfriede Jelinek, and Monika Treut." *Paragraph* 22/3 (1999): 228–247.

Winter, Riki. "Gespräch mit Elfriede Jelinek." In *Elfriede Jelinek*, edited by Bartsch and Höfler, 9–20.

Young, Frank W. " 'Am Haken des Fleischhauers': Zum politokonomischen Gehalt der *Klavierspielerin*." In *Gegen den schönen Schein*, edited by Gürtler, 75–80.

YORAM KANIUK

(1930–)

ROGER FRIEDMANN

THE SON OF Jewish immigrants from the Ukraine to the Yishuv (the Jewish community) in Palestine, novelist, journalist, and theater critic Yoram Kaniuk was born in Tel Aviv in 1930. At the time of his birth, his mother and his father, who later became a cofounder of the Tel Aviv Museum, had become friends of the great modern Hebrew poet Hayim Nahman Bialik, who suggested the name Yoram for their *sabra* son. When Kaniuk turned eighteen, he participated eventfully in Israel's War of Independence in 1948, suffering a serious leg wound. Kaniuk had his own nightmarish experience during that conflict. In a battle north of Jerusalem, he and the other members of his unit ran out of ammunition while surrounded by a superior force of Arabs. Exposed and believed dead by their enemies, they endured two hours of terror as their attackers took practice shots at what they thought were corpses. "I was executed every two minutes," Kaniuk explained years later. "I couldn't even move an eyelash. . . . The Arabs thought we were dead but didn't want to pick up the bodies because there was an unexploded bomb among us" (Kaganoff, p. 70).

Kaniuk's experiences as a fighter during Israel's independence war place the author squarely among a group known as the Palmach generation, Israeli writers who "derived . . . their authority and their themes from their participation in the War of Independence in 1948" (Mintz, p. 10). Nonetheless, he speaks of his work after 1948 as a sailor aboard a refugee ship bringing Holocaust survivors to the new State of Israel as the most profound influence on his literary career. "This was after I had been wounded in battle, and after I had witnessed how cruel human beings can be to each other, and how senseless and wasteful war is," he explains. "Nevertheless, my encounter with the refugees was by far the most traumatic event I have ever experienced. Europe was still ravaged, and the refugees had arrived from transitory camps in Italy. From that point on the Holocaust became an obsession for me. . . . I spent four years thinking myself to be a [H]olocaust survivor" (Fuchs, pp. 74–75).

Kaniuk did not originally aspire to be a writer. In 1951 he went to New York City seeking medical treatment for the leg wound he had sustained during the War of Independence. While being treated, he developed an appreciation of abstract expressionist art and took up painting. He spent the next ten years in New York seeking to make a career as an artist. Enjoying only minor success, he was forced to support himself washing dishes at a jazz club in Harlem, where he met many of the musicians, including jazz's celebrated Charlie Parker. Eventually the need to relieve the trauma accumulated during his experiences of war and aboard the refugee ship compelled Kaniuk to turn to writing while in the United States. Abstract expressionism's capacity to startle and shock and jazz's to transform suffering into bliss left their mark on his writing style and approach to fiction. He has said he writes with his eyes, not his ears, but he is also acutely aware of the influence of jazz in his writing. "Charlie Parker would take funeral music and make a celebration," Kaniuk has stated. "I transform evil spirits into fairytales" (Kaganoff, p. 70). He has also noted that the eclectic nature of his young adult experience has contributed to his creation of fiction that defies the classifications normally applied to Israeli literature. "My work does not belong to the Palmach, and not quite to the State's generation," he says. "It contains elements of both trends, and probably European and American influences" (Fuchs, p. 76). Nevertheless, the subject matter of his fiction expresses his concerns as an Israeli.

Kaniuk wrote his first novel, *The Acrophile* (1961), while he was in the United States. Although he wrote the novel in Hebrew, he paid to have it translated into English, the language in which it was published originally. The novel recounts the endeavors of an Israeli veteran of the 1948 war who comes to New York City hoping to become a scholar so he can escape reliving the trauma of war. Kaniuk has said of the novel's protagonist that he "wants to be all alone—without ideology, without Israel, without Judaism, without Jewishness" (Kaganoff, p. 70). After spending ten years in the United States, Kaniuk returned to Israel—where he currently resides—to write his second novel, *Himmo, King of Jerusalem*. That work concerns a paraplegic Independence War veteran convalescing in a Jerusalem hospital. Despite his gross disfigurement, he becomes the object of affection of one of the nurses caring for him, who falls in love with his lips.

In *Adam Resurrected* (1971), his third novel, Kaniuk finally addressed his preoccupation with the Holocaust. The work recounts the struggle of a survivor—who escaped Hitler's furnaces because of his prewar fame as a circus clown—to come to terms with his existence. The Holocaust reappears thematically in two later works—a novel entitled *The Last Jew* (1986) and a piece of literary nonfiction, *Commander of the Exodus* (1999). Kaniuk's writing career spans four decades, and includes many other works that have been translated into twenty languages. Only late in his career was his work recognized with two major awards: the 1998 President's Prize in Israel and the prestigious French Prix Méditerranée Étranger for 2000.

Adam Resurrected

When *Adam Resurrected* was first published in Hebrew as *Adam, Ben Kelev* (Adam, Son of a Dog) in 1968, it received little critical notice—a scant four reviews in the Hebrew press (Fuchs, p. 75). However, as the novel was translated into other languages—French, Danish, Swedish, and English—its reputation as a major Western literary treatment of the Holocaust was steadily enhanced. In 1976 Susan Sontag hailed it as one of the greatest novels published in the last twenty years, and by 1978 the Swedish press proclaimed Kaniuk a candidate for the Nobel Prize in literature.

But the question remains: Why did a novel now considered Kaniuk's tour de force, a seminal work in Israeli Holocaust fiction, and a work that nearly earned its author a Nobel Prize in literature, at first receive relatively faint praise from Israel's literary community? The answers vary. Perhaps an Israeli public in 1968, still giddy from the miraculous victory of the Six Day War in 1967, did not want to be reminded of recent Jewish history when Jews were nearly annihilated because of their inability to defend themselves.

The ambivalence that Israelis feel toward literary treatments of the Holocaust is grounded, in part, in their belief that the atrocities of the concentration camp universe defy representation in language. As a consequence, reverential silence has become the proper tribute to the Holocaust's victims—a recognition that the horror and suffering they endured is unimaginable. Aharon Appelfeld, himself a major Israeli author of Holocaust fiction, explains the difficulty in breaking the silence as the result of a "secret covenant [that] was created between the survivor witness and the one to whom the testimony . . . was directed." He says, "just as the witness could not continue to stand in the space of this terror, neither could the Jew who had not experienced it" (Abramson, p. 146). In this light, Kaniuk's use of fantastic, broad satire and black humor in his fictional account of a concentration camp survivor may have struck many Israelis as too irreverent, further exacerbating the anxieties they already felt with respect to public discourse on the Holocaust.

In *Drama and Ideology in Modern Israel* (1998) Abramson argues that the discomfort Israelis feel toward a literature of the Holocaust reflects guilt and shame over the inability of the Yishuv in pre-Israel Palestine to rescue Jews in Europe during World War II. To assuage their guilt, many of Palestine's Jews learned to blame "the victims for marching like sheep to the slaughter" (p. 148) and regard Diaspora Jewry with disdain. In an essay on contemporary Israeli Holocaust fiction, Gilead Morahg concurs. He argues that Israeli discourse has been defined largely by the cultural codes of ideological Zionism, which regarded the Holocaust as "the ultimate pathology of the Diaspora mentality." Within this context, he says, "the Holocaust was the epitome of everything Zionism sought to reject" (p. 149). Kaniuk has observed that until his work aboard a Holocaust refugee ship, he had shared similar sentiments: "As a native Israeli I had very little in common with European Jews. Like many others, I was taught to reject the Diaspora" (Fuchs, p. 74).

However, Kaniuk's novel was not the first Israeli work to break the code of silence. Poet Yehuda Amichai's novel *Not of This Time, Not of This Place*, was the first, published in 1963, two years after the conclusion of the ten-week trial of Adolf Eichmann, a trial that Israel's prime minister, David Ben-Gurion, believed was necessary not only because justice demanded that Eichmann be tried and held accountable for his crimes, but because he also believed that a trial was needed to educate the Israeli public about the Holocaust. As a consequence, public discussion of the Holocaust in Israel was legitimized, at least for a time. After Amichai, novels dealing with the Holocaust were also published by Hanoch Bartov (*The Brigade* [1965]) and Haim Gouri (*The Chocolate Deal* [1965]), and Ben Amotz's *To Remember, to Forget* (1968) was published in the same year as *Adam Resurrected*. However, Kaniuk's is the first to examine so directly the concentration camp experience and the psychic scars it left on survivors. Born out of his intense identification with Holocaust survivors during his experience working aboard the refugee ship, the novel is also the first Israeli work to thematically make the Holocaust the reason for the creation of the Jewish state.

The view of the Holocaust presented in *Adam Resurrected* is telescopic, not panoramic. It focuses on the consciousness of a concentration camp survivor, Adam Stein. A renowned circus clown in Germany before World War II, he was spared death by Commandant Klein of Auchhausen, who had Adam entertain Jews as they were sent to the gas chambers. Adam also survived by eating scraps of food from a bowl left by the commandant for his dog.

Nevertheless, the novel alludes to the broader view of the Holocaust as an episode among other catastrophes in Jewish history. Its epigraph taken from Flavius Josephus, who chronicled the Jewish revolt against the Romans, culminating in the destruction of the Temple in Jerusalem in C.E. 70, quotes Josephus asking why God was "so totally absent, during the Great Destruction." This allusion, which refers to the birth of the Jewish Diaspora, creates an interpretative framework for reading the novel, in which the destruction of European Jewry in the Holocaust marks a rebirth in Jewish history. In the novel's scheme of metaphors and symbols, this new era is a time when the need for sanctuary has replaced the Jewish need for sanctification.

When the novel opens, years after Adam had been liberated from Auchhausen, he is being taken from the pension where he was staying in Tel Aviv to a mental asylum for survivors in a development town, Arad, in Israel's Negev desert. In a dramatic metaphor, the novel's limited viewpoint explodes into an apocalyptic vision of the Holocaust. As Adam is forcibly transported from Tel Aviv to the institute in Arad, he notes the change in the scenery as he travels farther from Israel's green coastal plain and deeper into the desert: "Sand in an hourglass, that's the most precise way to describe it, thinks Adam. See how the green is devoured and disappears" (*Adam Resurrected*, New York: Harper & Row, 1978, p. 14).

This reference to sand falling through an hourglass suggests not only the passage of time or history but also the end of time, the moment when the lower half of the hourglass has filled with sand and must be turned upside down so a new cycle of time may commence. Eventually the landscape in which Adam finds himself yields entirely to desert: "yellow desert sands merg[ing] with desolate limestone"; "sky . . . the color of lemon, its sun boundless and bright"; "everything . . . desiccated, desecrated, disjointed, berserk, forever banished from everybody" (pp. 15–16). Adam's exile from culturally urbane Tel Aviv to this region of Israel where "a chain of mountains . . . divides a dead sea from a dead desert" (p. 16) imitates the Holocaust's displacement and relocation of European Jewry into Palestine. The metaphor of the hourglass implies this event marks a break in time when a new cycle in history is about to begin.

Most of the novel's action takes place in this vast stretch of sun-scorched earth. Here, Mrs. Seizling's Institute for Rehabilitation and Therapy was built with $6 million donated by a vulgar millionairess from Cleveland. While visiting Israel, Seizling had been persuaded after meeting a survivor in Tel Aviv named Schwester to build the hospital in the desert so that God would reveal Himself once again to the Jewish people. Schwester explained to her that God only speaks in the desert because that is His "palace" (p. 50) and only to the insane because they "comprehend, they are sensitive, they . . . see Him" (p. 51). In Schwester's formulation, Israel has become "the largest insane asylum on earth" because it is inhabited by those who have been condemned to live out their lives with "the knowledge . . . that they were simply raw material in the most advanced factory in Europe under a sky inhabited by a God in exile, by a Stranger," and "out of the lunatics who weep in the night . . . will emerge somebody who will enter a wadi among the rocks and be received by God in friendship and spoken to" (pp. 51–52).

In the sands of the Negev, according to Schwester, God will reveal Himself again to the Jews by speaking to a messiah, whom she comes to believe is Adam Stein, a self-centered, egotistical character made larger than life by his supernatural charm. As the novel's description of life in Mrs. Seizling's institute unfolds, it becomes clear that the survivor inmates are tormented and deranged by their need to believe—even though God has abandoned them. One of them, Arthur Fine, is there because he has become an arsonist, burning not only buildings but people as well, including his own child, so he can sanctify them as God consecrated the Jews in the crematoria. Another, Wolfovitz, composes a letter chastising God for having forgotten his daughter, who became grossly disfigured while hiding from the Nazis in the cramped quarters of a cellar in Poland that did not have enough space to allow her five-year-old body to grow.

However, Schwester scolds those survivors who question their faith. "You are laughable," she says, "like every Jew who casts stones at God for being cruel

. . . because He chose you and you chose Him, the two of you are in the same boat, and the waters of death swirl around it, until in distress, you cry out, God!" (p. 226). In their distress, the inmates turn to Adam Stein, whom they believe, along with Schwester, will reveal God's presence. However, tormented by the shame of having watched his wife and two children being led to the gas chamber as he performed as Commandant Klein's clown, he has rejected any possibility of redemption. Besides, he had become a dog when he ate from the bowl of Klein's dog. Redemption is for humans, he believes, not dogs.

After the war Adam elected to remain in Germany, having received a half million dollars as compensation for his circus, which continued to function during the war. Adam's feckless existence as a beneficiary of the German economic miracle, which he compares to living in a sarcophagus, is disrupted in 1958 after he receives news that one of his daughters has, in fact, survived and is living in Israel. However, when he visits Israel to see her, he learns from her husband that she has recently died in childbirth. Taking Adam to her grave, her husband, angry at Adam's collaboration with Klein, commands him to make her laugh as he did the victims on their way to the death chambers. Adam responds by reverting to his dog character, leading to his institutionalization.

At the institute, Adam, who has ceased to act like a dog, meets a schizophrenic child who behaves exactly as a dog, and he finds a new purpose in life, trying to teach the child to become human and stand on two legs. As Edward Alexander points out in his discussion of *Adam Resurrected*, "Even the specific metaphor here employed by Kaniuk has a literal reality in one camp in Rumania, in which arriving Jews were told: 'You have come in on two feet, and if you do not end your lives here, you will be allowed to leave on four feet only' " (Alexander, p. 113).

While he works with the dog-child, Adam eventually accepts the charge of the inmates that he become their messiah, an act that signals the beginning of recovery for him—his recognition of their pain. However, when he leads twenty of them in an escape from the institute at night into the desert so they can follow him toward God, the voice he hears is Commandant Klein's, not God's, a fact he conceals from the others. This horrifying discovery ironically allows Adam to cure himself and his dog-child patient. In the sands of the Negev that night, Adam discovers there is no sanctification for Jews, only sanctuary, and the time has come to end the Jews' several thousand-year-old dialogue with God.

In 1981 a portion of *Adam Resurrected* was dramatized in a theatrical production entitled *Adam's Purim Party*. The play was adapted from the scenes in the novel in which the inmates at Mrs. Seizling's institute stage a Purim pageant, a "purimspiel." While Purim has minor significance as a religious holiday in Judaism, since World War II the holiday's meaning has acquired a poignant resonance as a holocaust averted. It celebrates the Jewish wife of the king of Persia, Queen Esther, and her successful effort to foil Haman's plan to exterminate the Jews for refusing to bow to the king. However, the actors in the "purimspiel," who are survivors, subvert the pageant, rolling up their sleeves and showing their numbers, as they renounce their names. In this macabre theater of the absurd, Adam explains to the audience that madness is the only appropriate response to the Holocaust.

The production brought new attention to Kaniuk's work, elevating the character of Adam to the status of an icon for the figure of the survivor, which may be Kaniuk's most important legacy. As Sidra DeKoven Ezrahi has written, the play's "wide reception and the controversy it generated testify . . . to a new willingness on the part of an Israeli audience to confront the painful figure of the survivor" (Ezrahi, p. 265). Consequently critics Gilead Morahg and Yael Feldman both see *Adam Resurrected* as having made possible a renewed interest in the Holocaust in Israeli fiction during the 1980s.

The Last Jew and *Commander of the Exodus*

His longest novel and considered his most complex, *Hayehudi Ha'aharon* (*The Last Jew*, 1982) is Kaniuk's one important work of fiction that has only now been translated into English (2003). The character to whom the title refers is Ebenezer Schneursom, the first Jew to be born in a pioneer village in Judea circa 1900. He disappears from the novel but reappears forty years later as a liberated concentration camp survivor, after having become embroiled in the Holocaust while searching for his father. After the war, he tours Europe with a circus act entitled "The Last Jew." The act becomes an object of fascination for another character named Germanauthor, who goes to Israel seeking to learn more about it. While the act itself focuses largely on the history of the Jews in Spain, according to Dov Vardi, "In the background of the [novel] move cabalists and mystics of an earlier day" (Vardi, p. 682). The novel examines the legacy of Jewish culture in light of the Holocaust, treating the artifacts of that culture as survivors needing a sanctuary as well. Kaniuk has commented that the novel contains all the themes he had dealt with in his other works: "the War of Independence, the Holocaust, the absurdity of Jewish history, the dilemma of the Jewish people, the predicament of the State of Israel, the relationship between Jew and Israeli" (Fuchs, p. 74).

In writing *Commander of the* Exodus, the story of Yossi Harel, who commanded the famed ship *Exodus*, used in a failed attempt to smuggle Jewish Holocaust refugees into Palestine, Kaniuk had to confront the same code of silence that accounted in part for the initial resistance *Adam Resurrected* encountered among Israel's reading public. In an author's note, Kaniuk explains how difficult it was for him to convince Yossi Harel to open up and tell his story. "[S]oon it became clear," Kaniuk writes, "his fierce privacy owed much to the fact he had sealed his voice in tribute to his many friends who had died along the way and were buried with their secrets" (*Commander of the* Exodus, New York: Grove Press, 1999, p. viii). In the book itself, he also confronts another of the attitudes contributing to Israeli discomfort with a literature of the Holocaust: the shame Israelis associated with the Diaspora Jew's inability to resist German aggression. In recounting Yossi Harel's pivotal role in the struggle to bring Jewish survivors of the Holocaust out of Europe and into Palestine, Kaniuk describes the antipathy members of the Yishuv felt toward the victims. In one example of this resentment, he quotes David Shaltiel, the Haganah commander of Jerusalem during the War of Independence: "Those who survived, survived because they were egoists and probably looked out for themselves first. Them, it is forbidden to pity" (p. 52).

Such an attitude was prevalent among many of Palestine's Jews, who had been reared in strict adherence to the principles of Zionist ideology. However, after encountering the first groups of displaced survivors—some of whom had traveled by foot for over a year from the north of Europe to the south in Greece—longing to find a safe harbor in Palestine, Harel soon found himself identifying with the refugees aboard his ship. "[H]e not only did not disdain the mentality of the ragged refugees, but understood their misery and loved them," Kaniuk writes, "the *sabra* sixth-generation Jerusalemite . . . became a Yid, an identity that some portion of Palestine Jewry understood but could not internalize" (p. 53).

In Harel the author had found his spiritual kin, another who had managed to identify with the survivors, crossing the gulf that separated the Yishuv from the Jews of Europe. He had also found a vehicle for narrating the birth pangs of modern Israel and for telling a story that makes the Holocaust central to Israeli identity. As Kaniuk states in the prologue to his narrative, "The state of Israel was not established on May 15, 1948, when the official declaration was made. . . . It was born nearly a year earlier . . . when its gates were locked to Jews, when the British fought against survivors of the Holocaust. It came into existence when its shores were blockaded against those for whom the state was eventually designated" (p. ix).

Commander of the Exodus appears to some extent to be written as a vindication of his earlier fiction of the Holocaust. In this work Kaniuk uses the historical record to support his argument that Israel's reason for existing is as a refuge for the remnants of European Jewry decimated by Hitler's Final Solution—an argument advanced by metaphor, allusion, and symbol in *Adam Resurrected.* Whereas the Zionist pioneers who settled in Palestine viewed themselves as creating an alternative Jewish existence, Kaniuk asserts the continuity of Jewish fate in which Israel's birth is part of the cycle of destruction and rebirth in Jewish history. In his view, the state of Israel could not have come into being without the near destruction of European Jewry.

The distinction may be subtle between the attitudes of those Jews in Palestine who saw the Holocaust as a vindication of the Zionist ideological imperative that Jews divorce themselves from their passive Diaspora mentality and those who believed a Jewish state and fighting force were necessitated by the Holocaust. However, the distinction is accented dramatically when the two attitudes come into conflict in critical episodes in *Commander of the* Exodus. Born in Jerusalem in 1919 to nineteenth-century German Jewish immigrants to Palestine, Yossi Harel was reared in a Jewish community whose existence was imperiled by clashes with the Arabs that began in 1920 and culminated in the 1929 riots in which Jews in Hebron and Safed were slaughtered. At an early age, Harel learned to become a fighter, indoctrinated with the saga of Masada, the story of Jewish resistance against the Romans by Eleazar ben Yair, the leader of the Zealots, who ordered his followers to take their own lives rather than surrender. For the Jews of Palestine, two thousand years later, this legendary exploit came to represent "the sanctification of heroic death" (p. 4). Later, as the commander of three failed missions to bring shiploads of Jewish survivors to Israel, Harel rejected the ethos of Masada when he decided in each confrontation with British naval vessels to surrender for the sake of saving the lives of the Holocaust survivors he was transporting. His actions were criticized by a number of commanders in the Palmach, the elite fighting force founded by Yitzhak Sadeh, one of Harel's early mentors, because he had not ordered his refugees to resist capture at all costs. Yet, in an investigation following the surrender of the *Exodus*, he defended himself, saying, "I didn't accept the command to convert refugees into fighters, and certainly not to take wounded survivors of the Holocaust just so they could die en route" (p. 143) to Palestine. According to Kaniuk, he had come to believe that the Jews of Palestine were supposed to fight for the refugees, not the other way around.

While *Commander of the* Exodus develops themes similar to ones that appear in *Adam Resurrected*, because it is a work of nonfiction, its tone and style differ radically. Kaniuk is compelled to confront realistically the pain and sorrow of the victims of the catastrophe, absent the black humor and satire of *Adam Resurrected.* The historical record of the three voyages Harel made commanding the *Knesset Israel*, the *Exodus*, and the *Pan York* and the *Pan Crescent* is animated by Harel's poignant encounters with the survivors packed aboard his ships. He is moved profoundly by the eyes of orphans that curse God, by the distorted posture of those who stood in ways to make themselves appear taller because short inmates were more likely to be selected for death, by the story of Mitka, the boy who survived a train trip from Auschwitz to Buchenwald in the dead of winter by squeezing in between the bodies of prisoners who froze to death. What Harel saw and heard during the voyages, Kaniuk documents meticulously.

Portions of the work, however, also explain the larger geopolitical context in which the journeys took place. Kaniuk details the conspiracy of indifference in America and Great Britain to the fate of Europe's Jews before, during, and immediately following World War II, even after the enormity of the crimes committed against the Jews had become fully known. Using information from Lucy Davidowicz's *The War against the Jews* (1975) and David Wyman's *The Abandonment of the Jews* (1984) and other sources, he states that the Final Solution was the result of American and British pressure on other European countries not to allow Eichmann's Jews to cross their borders. Allied unwillingness to bomb the railroad tracks leading into Auschwitz, when they could have easily done so in 1944, was in large part a consequence of the belief that if Jews were saved, the difficulty of solving the problem of where to place them after the war would be greater.

In *Commander of the* Exodus, the absurd does not masquerade in costume as it does in *Adam Resurrected*'s "purimspiel"; instead the theater of the absurd is revealed as historical fact when the British transported the refugees they captured from the *Exodus* to Hamburg, where Holocaust survivors "again found themselves before German guards armed with rifles and clubs—humiliated and reduced to dust" (p. 148). Even after the U.N. resolution was passed in 1947 establishing a Jewish homeland in Palestine, the British continued to patrol the Mediterranean, seizing boatloads of Jews bound for their new country. Against this background, the creation of Israel became a historical imperative in Kaniuk's view, needed to rescue "the scarred refugees" of the Holocaust who "are the Jewish State" (p. 207).

Bibliography

Primary Sources

The Acrophile. Trans Zeva Shapiro. Atheneum, 1961.

Ha-yored le ma'lah. Shoken, 1963.

Himmo, King of Jerusalem. Trans. Yosef Shacter. Atheneum, 1969.

Rockinghorse. Trans. Richard Flanz. Harper, 1977

The Story of Aunt Shlomzion the Great. Trans. Zeva Shapiro. Harper, 1969.

Adam Resurrected. 1978.

Hayehudi Ha'aharon (*The Last Jew*). 1982.

Confessions of a Good Arab. Trans. Dalya Bilu and Peter Halban. Braziller, 1988.

His Daughter. Trans. Seymour Simckes. Weidenfeld & Nicholson, 1989.

Commander of the Exodus. 1999.

Secondary Sources

Abramson, Glenda. *Drama and Ideology in Modern Israel.* Cambridge: Cambridge University Press, 1998.

Alexander, Edward. *The Resonance of Dust.* Columbus: Ohio State University Press, 1979.

Ezrahi, Sidra DeKoven. "Revisioning the Past: The Changing Legacy of the Holocaust in Hebrew Literature." *Salmagundi* 68–69 (1985–1986): 245–270.

Feldman, Yael S. "Whose Story Is It, Anyway? Ideology and Psychology in the Representation of the *Shoah* in Israeli Literature." *Probing the Limits of Representation.* Edited by Saul Friedlander, 223–239. Cambridge, Mass.: Harvard University Press.

Fuchs, Esther. *Encounters with Israeli Authors.* Marblehead, Mass.: Micah Publications, 1982.

Kaganoff, Penny. "Yoram Kaniuk." *Publishers Weekly* (April 24, 2000): 70–71.

Mintz, Alan. *Hurban: Responses to Catastrophe in Hebrew Literature.* New York: Columbia University Press, 1984.

Morahg, Gilead. "Breaking Silence: Israel's Fantastic Fiction of the Holocaust." *The Boom in Contemporary Israeli Fiction.* Edited by Alan Mintz, 143–183. Hanover, N.H.: University Press of New England, 1997, pp. 143–183.

Vardi, Dov. Review of *Hayehudi Ha'aharon* by Yoram Kaniuk. *World Literature Today* 4 (1983): 682–683.

CHAIM A. KAPLAN

(1880–1942)

JOSHUA D. ZIMMERMAN

BEST KNOWN FOR his Warsaw ghetto diary, Chaim A. Kaplan was born in 1880 in Horodyszcze, in the Minsk gubernia, to a Jewish family of limited means. He attended *heder* as a boy and received a traditional Jewish secondary education, studying at yeshivas in Mir, Minsk, and Lida. In the late 1890s, Kaplan enrolled in the government-run pedagogical institute for Jewish teachers in Vilna. In 1900, Kaplan became involved in the secular Jewish school movement and moved to Warsaw, where, in 1905, he founded a pioneering secular Hebrew elementary school, which he ran for thirty-four years as he devoted himself to Jewish education. His advocacy of the study of Hebrew as a spoken language using the Sephardi pronunciation culminated in the publication of several scholarly books and modern Hebrew textbooks for children.

In 1921, Kaplan traveled to the United States, where he made contact with Jewish educators. In 1926, the Hebrew Publishing Company in New York published Kaplan's *Hebrew Grammar* and, two years later, his richly illustrated *Haggadah* with commentary (New York, 1927). The latter work included a lengthy introduction on *Pesach* (Passover) customs among Jewish communities around the world and was published also in Warsaw in Hebrew, Yiddish, and Polish and reprinted after the war in a Hebrew edition (New York, 1960). Kaplan also traveled to Palestine in 1936, intending to settle there to be with his two children, who had emigrated earlier. But he was unable to obtain a position and returned to Warsaw. The following year an anthology of Kaplan's articles on Jewish education and pedagogy was published as *Pezurai* (Warsaw, 1937). Kaplan also actively contributed to the scholarly and popular press in interwar Poland, including *Fraynd, Unzer lebn, Moment*, and *Haynt*.

Diary

When World War II broke out on 1 September 1939, Kaplan began to record the extraordinary events in a secret Hebrew-language diary. Within days of the German invasion of Poland, Kaplan commented on the historical importance of documenting the day-to-day events, as in his entry of 14 September 1939: "It is difficult to write, but I consider it an obligation and am determined to fulfill it with my last ounce of energy." Just a few months later, after Nazi Jewish policy began to make itself felt, Kaplan's commitment to the diary dramatically intensified, as revealed in the entry of 16 January 1940: "I sense within me the magnitude of this hour, and my responsibility towards it, and I have an inner awareness that I am fulfilling a national obligation, a historic obligation that I am not free to relinquish. . . . I am sure that Providence sent me to fulfill this mission."

While we now have several important Warsaw ghetto diaries, including those by Emmanuel Ringelblum, Adam Czerniakow, and Abraham Lewin, Kaplan's is distinguished by its penetrating insight into the nature of Nazi antisemitism; its frank and astute observations about the Warsaw Jewish community, the *Judenrat* and Jewish police; and the precise recording of Nazi policies, as well as observations about Polish-Jewish relations and Jewish attitudes toward Soviet Russia. From the very beginning of the Nazi occupation, Kaplan did not analyze the succession of Nazi edicts in terms of the specific consequences of each law. Rather, he sought to deduce a larger overall aim out of the haze of capricious decrees.

Kaplan sensed the disastrous implication of initial Nazi edicts even before Warsaw Jewry was subjected to the humiliation of external markings and the walled ghetto. When the Judenrat was ordered to conduct a full census of the Jewish population less than a month after the Nazi occupation of Warsaw, Kaplan commented, "For what purpose? . . . Our hearts tell us that a catastrophe for the Jewry of Poland is hidden in this demand" (16 October 1939). Five days later, following an edict barring Jews from certain sectors of the economy, Kaplan wrote of the beginning of Polish Jewry's "legal destruction" (21 October 1939). By the end of October 1939, Kaplan suspected the worst, writing, "Blatant signs prove that some terrible catastrophe, unequaled in Jewish history, is in store for Polish Jewry" (25 October 1939). The tragedy, Kaplan further commented, "is not in the humane or cruel actions of individuals, but in *the plan in general* . . ." (28 October 1939). Grasping immediately the nature of Nazi antisemitism, Kaplan maintained that "In the eyes of the conquerors we are outside the category of human beings" (28 October 1939). By the third month of occupation, Kaplan surmised that the larger Nazi aim with regard to Jews was "complete extermination and destruction" (1 December 1939).

A keen observer of international affairs, Kaplan sensed the ominous link between Nazi war aims and Nazi Jewish policy as Hitler's armies stormed across western Europe in the spring and summer of 1940. Fearing the fall of England, Kaplan wrote, "The destruction of England will mean the ultimate end for the house of Israel" (4 May 1940). As long as the Nazis remained drunk with real or imagined victories, Kaplan maintained, the Jews would enjoy some respite, while prolonged warfare and defeat would intensify Nazi aggression against Jews. As the conflict between England and Germany intensified after the fall of France, Kaplan noted in his diary "a new line of attack" by which Jewish civilians in Nazi-occupied Europe would be regarded as "combatants" who had to be "dealt with as enemy prisoners." The Nazi concept that Jews caused the war in order to bring about the destruction of the Third Reich provided, Kaplan reasoned, a kind of legal rationalization for the total destruction of European Jewry (6 July 1940).

Meanwhile, Kaplan chronicled how the Jews were being "strangled by decrees" (21 August 1940) as he records a succession of edicts barring Jews from public worship, from entering public parks, from riding in the same trolleys as Aryans, from owning horses, from treating Aryan-patients, and from purchasing German-language books, as well as the stunning decree for the creation of a walled ghetto in Warsaw, "a barbaric edict which by its weight and results is greater than all the other edicts made against us up to now" (12 October 1940).

As rumors of war between Nazi Germany and Soviet Russia appeared in spring 1941, Kaplan maintained that such a conflict would spell disaster for the Jews. "In the event of war with Russia . . . we are lost. . . . [T]he Jews will immediately become the target of revenge" (13 March 1941). As war erupted and the German army headed toward Moscow, Kaplan observed with chilling insight that a Nazi victory against Russia "means complete annihilation, morally and materially, for all the Jews of Europe" (18 October 1941). With the American entry into the war, an ecstatic Kaplan tempered his enthusiasm with the observation that henceforth, "the stupid Nazis will insist that Germany is at war with world Jewry" (12 December 1941).

Following the creation of the Warsaw ghetto, Kaplan's diary focused more on the inner life of Warsaw Jewry and in particular on the Judenrat and its Jewish police. As disease, malnutrition, and starvation gripped the ghetto community, Kaplan praised the fearless smugglers "without whom we certainly would have starved to death" (5 November 1941). By fall 1941 and the winter of 1941–1942, Kaplan chronicled the devastating impact of Nazi Jewish policy, chillingly noting that the monthly death rate had risen to 10,000, and that "our bodies have shriveled to half their normal size" (13 October 1941). He also comments on the decline in moral standards resulting from the instinct of self-preservation (4 January 1942).

Kaplan's diary is important as a record of how and when news about the Nazi Final Solution reached the ghetto. In February 1942, Kaplan recorded rumors that Hitler had decided to rid Europe of its Jews through shooting, including the mass killing of some 40,000 Jews from Vilna (2 February 1942), and that thousands of Jews had already been killed by the experimental use of poison gas (23 February 1942). When news reached Warsaw that 30,000 Jews were missing after a mass liquidation of the Lublin ghetto, and that no trace of them had been found, the question of their fate plagued Kaplan. By June 1942, Kaplan understood that they had all been transported in tightly sealed freight cars to "some secret place, unknown even to the hawk" (3 June 1942) where mass murder took place and which he would later refer to as the "kingdom of death" (22 July 1942).

The final part of Kaplan's diary chronicled the mass deportation of the Warsaw ghetto in July and August of 1942. Here, Kaplan described the terror inflicted on the Warsaw Jewish population and reserves his most scathing critique for the Judenrat and, particularly, the Jewish police who daily delivered 8,000 deportees to the Nazis as demanded. The "cruelty" of the Jewish police "is no less than that of the Nazis," Kaplan wrote on 26 July 1942, adding that "the extermination of the Jews" is being carried out not only by the Nazis but "by the Jewish slaughterers" as well. Despite imminent doom, Kaplan recorded with great detail the terror of the daily roundups and actions, proclaiming, "As long as my heart pulses, I continue my sacred task" (31 July 1942). At the height of the deportations, amid the horror of physical expulsions and brutality, Kaplan lamented the destruction of Europe's largest Jewish community:

> Jewish Warsaw is in its death throes. A whole community is going to its death! The appalling events follow one another so abundantly that it is beyond the power of a writer of impressions to collect, arrange, and classify them; particularly when he himself is caught in their vise. . . . And let it be known: From the very beginning of the world, since the time when man first had dominion over another man to do him harm, there has never been so cruel and barbaric an expulsion as this one. From hour to hour, even from minute to minute, Jewish Warsaw is being demolished and destroyed, reduced and decreased. Since the day exile was decreed [22 July 1942], ruin and destruction, exile and wandering, bereavement and widowhood have befallen us in all their fury (2 August 1942).

Kaplan's last words in his diary, written on 4 August 1942, asked, "If my life ends—what will become of my diary?"

Publication

Kaplan's diary was known in the ghetto. Emanuel Ringelblum, in his writings from late January 1943, wrote: "The Hebrew diary of the writer and teacher, Kaplan . . . numbered a thousand pages and comprised a multitude of information about daily events in Warsaw." The diary "is a faithful reflection" of the tragic experience of the average Warsaw Jew, both "his sufferings and desires for revenge." On several occasions, Ringelblum personally asked Kaplan to temporarily hand over his diary notebooks to the *Oneg Shabbat* archives for safe keeping until after the war. But Kaplan would only agree to his diary being copied, which Ringelblum was unable to do under the conditions of the ghetto (Ringelblum, pp. 490–491).

Fearing imminent deportation, Kaplan gave the diary notebooks to a Jewish friend who was working daily outside the ghetto in forced labor detachments. Chaim Kaplan perished in Treblinka sometime between late 1942 and early 1943. The precious notebooks were entrusted to Władysław Wojciek, a Pole from a village outside of Warsaw, who preserved them throughout the war and subsequently made them available to researchers. The diary first appeared in English in 1965 under the title *The Scroll of Agony*, and one year later was published in Israel in the original Hebrew. Kaplan's Warsaw diary has since been translated into German, French, Danish, and Japanese and is considered one of the most important records of the Warsaw ghetto in particular and of the Holocaust in general.

Bibliography

Primary Sources

Programah le-arba shenot ha-limudim be-vet-ha-sefer ha Ivri (A Four-Year Study Program for Hebrew School). 1913.

Hagadah shel Pesach. Yiddish translation with commentary by Chaim A. Kaplan. 1924.

Dikduk ha-lashon ve-shimushah (A Hebrew Grammar and Its Uses). 1925.

Ilustrowana Hagadah na Pecach: wydanie literacko-artystyczne (Illustrated Passover Haggadah: a Literary-Artistic Edition). Introduced and annotated by Chaim A. Kaplan. 1928.

Pezurai. 1937.

The Warsaw Diary of Chaim A. Kaplan. Translated and edited by Abraham I. Katsh. 1973.

"Extract from the Diary of Chaim A. Kaplan." In *Documents on the Holocaust.* Jerusalem, 1981, pp. 230–231.

Secondary Sources

"Chaim Kaplan." In *Encyclopaedia Judaica* CD-ROM Edition. Jerusalem: Keter Publishing House, 1997.

"Chaim Kaplan." In *Encyclopedia of the Holocaust*, vol. 2. Edited by Israel Gutman. Jerusalem: Macmillan, 1990, pp. 781–782.

Kressel, Getzel, ed. *Lehsikon ha-sifrut ha-evrit*, vol. 2. Jerusalem: Safriyat Poalim, 1967, pp. 787–788.

Leksikon fun der nayer yidisher literatur, vol. 8. New York: Congress for Jewish Culture, 1981, p. 91.

Reisen, Z., ed. *Leksikon fun der yidisher literatur, prese un filologye*, vol. 3. Vilna: B. Kletskin, 1926, pp. 495–496.

Ringelblum, Emanuel, *Kronika getta warszawskiego: wrzesień 1939—styczeń 1943.* Edited by Arthur Eisenbach. Warsaw: Czytelnik, 1988.

ILONA KARMEL
(1925–2001)

S. LILLIAN KREMER

A SURVIVOR OF the Krakow ghetto, labor camps at Plaszow and Skarzysko, and Buchenwald concentration camp, Ilona Karmel was born in Krakow, Poland in 1925 to Hirsh and Mita (née Rosenbaum). She hailed from a large, diverse Jewish family, including ultra-Orthodox Hasidim and secularists, who lived in Krakow from the seventeenth to the mid-twentieth century. Burdened by loss and bolstered by memory, Karmel speaks of her family with great sadness and love. From memories of people such as a revered uncle who distributed false identity papers for fleeing Jews and yet, remaining with his elderly mother, sacrificed his own opportunity for escape, and from memories of her own resourceful mother and sister, with whom she was incarcerated, Karmel produced fiction about "incomprehensible cruelty and . . . a human decency, . . . [unparalleled] in normal times" (Interview by S. Lillion Kremer, 24 May 1988). Karmel and her sister, Henia Karmel Wolfe, the author of two novels set in the Holocaust era, *The Baders of Jacob Street* and *Marek and Lisa*, began writing poetry in the camps. They brought their writing "like an offering" to their mother to judge, an effort Karmel later described as "a survival instinct" (Interview). A collection of the sisters' Polish poems, *Spiew za Drutamic* (*Song Behind the Wire*) was published in 1947. Following lengthy hospitalization in Sweden and numerous surgeries for injuries sustained in Buchenwald, Karmel emigrated to the United States, where she lived until her death in 2001. She studied creative writing under the guidance of Archibald MacLeish at Radcliffe and was graduated Phi Beta Kappa. Here she produced her first novel, which MacLeish recommended to his publisher. *Stephania* (1953) explores ghettoization and survivor memory. Her second novel, *An Estate of Memory* (1964), confronts the universe of labor and concentration camps. Karmel enjoyed a distinguished career as a senior lecturer at the Massachusetts Institute of Technology, where she taught creative writing. She married Francis Zucker, a physicist who had come to the United States from Germany with his parents in 1938.

Stephania

Perhaps because she wrote *Stephania* in 1953, so soon after the war's end, with Holocaust trauma still fresh, or perhaps because she was writing for the first time in an adopted language, for an American audience that she understood was not yet prepared to accept a detailed, realistic account of the concentration camps, the Holocaust enters Karmel's first novel only through memory and metaphor. The book is set in a Swedish hospital where the protagonist undergoes surgical and therapeutic treatments for a war-induced back injury, reflecting Karmel's three years of surgical rehabilitation for injuries sustained during the final death march from Buchenwald, when a tank ran over her, crushing both legs. The Krakow ghetto emerges organically through survivor recollections and conversations with hospital roommates. Stephania's anguish is born of her need to bear witness, coupled with her recognition of the difficulty of conveying Holocaust reality to auditors unexposed to such a history.

Karmel addresses the limitations of language in conveying Holocaust reality to the uninitiated in a scene where Stephania pauses to define the word "ghetto" for her Scandinavian listeners, and by implication, for readers:

> "It was the place where we had lived the first two years of the war." Strange, she thought, how you had to explain each word used then, as if a special language had been spoken in those days, a language understood only by those who had lived through them. "It was—how can I describe it to you?—just a few streets the Germans had cut off from the rest of the city. And walls around them, high walls so that you could not get out when you wanted

to. "Yes," she repeated slowly, "you could not get out when you wanted—that was it—the ghetto" (*Stephania*, Boston: Houghton Mifflin, 1953, p. 314).

Karmel's ghetto descriptions range from a realistic account of fifty thousand people crowded into a few streets, the number swelling daily with newcomers from outlying towns and villages, to the picture of a space too crammed to accept falling raindrops. Thus, she eases the reader into the virtually unknowable ghetto terrain, employing commonplace images to suggest the oppressive conditions.

A love story, defined and enacted in Holocaust terms, serves as interpretive bridge to the unfamiliar ghetto world of starvation, overcrowding, and deportations. Here a young woman is attracted to her lover by the dignity he exhibits in the midst of humiliation and by his courageous search for food. The lovers do not utter conventional terms of endearment, do not speak of plans for marriage and family. They hope to meet "in freedom," a place they characterize as "streets through which you could walk alone with no guards around you; and [a] home, not crowded with hundreds of people, but real homes where you would have your own room, which you opened with your own key" (p. 322). Love is expressed by a gift of food or by risking life by leaving the ghetto illegally to deliver a forgotten *Ausweis* (work pass) to one's lover. Just as the *Shoah* precipitates the lovers' initial meeting, it marks their separation when Jan is deported to a labor camp.

With a few notable exceptions, survivor-writers have focused on the concentrationary period, and omitted or given short shrift to survivor trauma, which has become a major element in American Holocaust fiction. *Stephania* is among the first English-language literary treatments of a protagonist whose postwar life and thought is plagued by Holocaust memory, the phenomenon that has come to be known as survivor syndrome. Guilt for outliving loved ones, among the most poignant aspects of survivor syndrome, emerges in Stephania's extended postwar memorial service for her father, and in self-rebuke. Guilt for her impatience with her father's wartime powerlessness is the catalyst for an imagined tribunal inviting the judgment of Holocaust colleagues as to whether her duty was to save herself and her mother or to compromise their opportunity by remaining with her father, whose Jewish appearance would betray the family. Despite confirmation by her imagined peers that she acted dutifully, Stephania adheres to an unrealistic higher ethical standard, one that is removed from Holocaust actuality, and protests that somehow she should have saved all three. Suspicious of her imagined peers' confirmation because "all of them who survived, had done what she did, in a less terrible way perhaps, . . . by forgiving her they forgave themselves, too" (p. 263), she then seeks the verdict of those untouched by Holocaust experience, and unexposed to its history. At first naively trusting in their capacity for objectivity, she later recognizes that they are unqualified to judge because "They had not been there. They would not understand. . . . They had lived in a different world" (p. 264). Postwar trauma is acknowledged not only in Stephania's psychological and physical pain, but also in Karmel's evocation of the Holocaust imagery of confining ghetto walls to describe the patient's tight, confining postwar body cast.

An Estate of Memory

Reaching far beyond *Stephania* in its mature style, its structural sophistication, its psychological depth, and its historic dimension, *An Estate of Memory* charts the ordeal of four women in Polish ghettos and labor camps. The sisterhood is composed of Tola Ohrenstein, outspoken daughter of a famous mercantile family; Barbara Grunbaum, so Aryan in appearance that she is known as the "big Pole"; Alinka, a fifteen-year-old orphan-waif, who has worked for the Germans since she was thirteen; and Aurelia Katz, "a professional victim" (*An Estate of Memory*. New York: Feminist Press, 1986, p. 138), whose pregnancy provides motivation for the women to nurture life in a universe of death. The novel derives its contrapuntal form from its characters' memories and their dramatically articulated wartime suffering. Its complex structural form eschews the linear chronological development and simple flashback of *Stephania*, instead plunging directly into the chaos of the camp universe, which encourages readers to navigate a bewildering new environment without conventional literary connections and thereby experience disorientation evocative of prisoner turmoil.

The traditional language of imaginative literature often proves inadequate to Holocaust delineation. As Primo Levi discovered, even Dante's description of the Inferno is mild compared to the Nazi universe. In *Survival in Auschwitz*, Levi cautioned his readers that their Holocaust comprehension can only be partial, for their sense of cold and hunger could not compare with the intensity of the camp inmate's experience because "they [cold and hunger] are free words, created and used by free men who lived in comfort and suffering in their homes" (pp. 112–113). In "Art and Culture," Elie Wiesel writes: "Language had been corrupted to the point that it had to be invented anew, and purified as well. . . . Often we told less—so as to make the truth more credible" (p. 410). Like her fellow survivors, Karmel avoids language that strains to overleap reality. She turns instead to the language of domestic reality, to caustic imagery drawn from life "in freedom," to chart Holocaust experience. A family's escape from a ghetto threatened with deportation to a ghetto safe because the deportation had just ended there is mapped by frantic movement, "to and fro, to and fro, like traveling salesmen always covering the same territory. . . . As in a spa new arrivals replace guests forced to leave, so here refugees from towns emptied of Jews replaced those deported" (p. 59). Karmel's incongruous pairing of spa guests with ghetto prisoners heightens the impression of the constraint and poverty that constitute ghetto existence. Similarly, Karmel introduces Holocaust reality through shockingly dissimilar figurative language to suggest how commonplace atrocity had become. A Polish facilitator insists on excluding a man of obvious Jewish appearance from a Jewish refugee group of Aryan appearance by arguing " 'It can't be done, . . . it just cannot,' . . . like a furniture-mover unable to transport too heavy a piece"(p. 61). Tola Ohrenstein invokes commercial imagery to describe her parents' death as "like coins slipped from a torn purse" (p. 64), and the domestic imagery of "death . . . being brought to the sick—like breakfast to bed" (p. 66) and children playing "deportation," to recount the liquidation of the ghetto hospital. Barbara Grunbaum's frantic efforts to feed fleeing refugees are represented in terms of a busy hostess preparing for a large social gathering: "Exactly twenty sat down to dinner . . . more and more were coming, as if to a long-awaited wedding" (p. 76). This analogy heightens the discrepancies of ordinary life and the new order, the discrepancy between a full and empty larder, the extraordinary demands placed on women to provide nourishment from inadequate food supplies. The grotesquery of the Nazi universe is translated in preparations for a German gas attack: "On this day, just as before a wedding, sewing began; only instead of sewing frill or lace onto the gala dress, everyone was making masks out of gauze, cotton wool and baking soda" (p. 77). Even the assault of the first bombs by the Germans is narrated in domestic terms: "From a knife placed carelessly across the bowl a drop of honey hung, elongated like a pendant. . . . And when the drop fell, this was war" (p. 78). Deliberately displacing conventional war imagery employed by male authors with unprecedented use of domestic imagery, Karmel not only heightens the traumatic impact of military aggression on a civilian population, but makes war accessible to readers fortunate enough not to have experienced it. Karmel's domestic imagery provides a bridge whereby readers cross into the author's concentrationary world and records the inconceivable that was conceived by the Third Reich and experienced by its victims.

Through integration and individuation of varied narrative strands that constitute each woman's history, Karmel introduces the characters' precamp experiences and surpasses her depiction of the Holocaust terrain introduced in *Stephania*. Illustrative is her presentation of Barbara Grunbaum's history through Proustian spontaneous recollection initiated by sight of a seemingly unrelated object. A Plaszow camp fence reminds Grunbaum of times past and of another fence—behind which her servants concealed her from the Nazis. As memory floods her consciousness, readers learn that this Jewish woman who is incarcerated in the Polish barracks was arrested as a political prisoner, that she joined the resistance because she felt guilty that she was being protected while trainloads of Jews were being transported to the killing centers. In contrast, Tola Ohrenstein's willed memories and interior monologue introduce the effort she and her mother make to escape incarceration by passing as Aryan women—on a forbidden train journey in the company of outspoken Polish antisemites, Tola and her mother cross themselves, lower their heads while passing a church, lace their conversation with an invented Christian family and devotional interests, and lard their speech with antisemitic rhetoric—certain confirmation of their assumed identity.

The primary settings of *An Estate of Memory* are two forced labor camps: Plaszow, located on the outskirts of Krakow and administered by the sadist Amon Goeth, and Skarzysko, site of infamous chemical workshops and picrine (picric acid) factories. Karmel's powerful descriptions of deleterious camp conditions and poignant representation of their physical and psychological impact on inmates are among the best in Holocaust literature. In Skarzysko, the foursome share quarters consisting of mud-splashed, ash-and-straw-littered, rotten plank floors, furnished with lice-infested bunks and slop pails surrounded by suffocating odors of chlorine and stale urine.

Compelling descriptions map the horrendous physical impact on women of the Nazi universe, where every aspect of normal life is denied, every measure calculated to debase the victims. Dehumanization of women ravaged by typhus and dysentery is fostered by insufficient access to filthy latrine facilities. Having been infected with typhus herself, Karmel effectively chronicles the delirium and the feverish pain of afflicted inmates: "Intent on the burning within themselves, they panted on their bunks, . . . the inflamed bodies pressed. . . tight . . . the same parched moans, the bedsores, shiny like patches of silk . . ." (p. 292). Complicating the health hazards of malnutrition and lice, labor in Skarzysko's infamous munitions factories induces rapid death when working with picrine, or prolonged illness when working with other chemicals. Unlike the typhus sufferers, for whom there is hope if they can get some decent food, the yellowed, shriveled picrine people (prisoners who worked with picric acid) are helpless; "their disease pursued them in the yellow dust, poisoning their breath" (p. 120). Like all Holocaust victims, Karmel's characters are preoccupied by hunger. Their lives focus on the acquisition, distribution, and supplementation of inadequate rations; their conversations and relationships reveal the scarcity of food. The women think about food, talk about it, imagine it, dream about it. They rightly measure their value to the Germans using the calculus of food distribution. Response to hunger also reveals the moral code of the prisoner population. To "organize," to steal food from the Nazis, is moral; to steal from a dead inmate before someone else claims the cache is acceptable. To steal from a fellow prisoner, however, is occasion for severe verbal and physical reprimand. A sign of the women's mutual help is their capacity for sharing food and guarding each other from eating their rations too quickly. The prisoners' moral superiority to their oppressors is frequently evidenced in their altruism, in their extraordinary efforts to obtain and share food. Upon hearing of Aurelia's narrow escape from the Radom ghetto liquidation, Barbara's reaction, delivered with characteristic hyperbole, is an invitation for Aurelia and Alinka to move to her bunk and a reprimand to Tola for her failure to bring this story to her attention earlier. Tola's reluctance to welcome others into the alliance she has forged with Barbara is premised on a realistic assessment of the additional burden of sharing hard-won but meager "organized" food among four rather than two. Characteristic as this pragmatic assessment is of Tola, so too are her paradoxical herculean efforts to secure extra food for the pregnant Aurelia and to obtain medicine and food for both Aurelia and Alinka during their bouts with typhus. Creating complex motivations, Karmel dramatizes the magnanimity as well as the lapses of the starving women.

The daily misery of hunger, hard work, illness, and prolonged roll calls is complemented by the heightened terror of punitive roll calls and selections. The twice-daily bureaucratic attendance check is calculated to demoralize the victims as the entire camp population is assembled to be counted, sometimes waiting for hours, ill-dressed, in inclement weather before the counting commences. The degradation and agony inflicted at special punishment roll calls is the subject of two pivotal scenes where the immoral women of Karmel's novel are subjected to cruel individual and collective punishments: rigorous calisthenics, flogging, prolonged standing, lengthy periods of kneeling on gravel, and death by shooting (including one of the main characters at the end) or hanging in the presence of the entire camp. The terror of punishment roll calls is matched by the dread of periodic selections. Never immediately evident whether a selection is for a work transport or for death, each such event is cause for alarm. Combining stream-of-consciousness and third-person description, Karmel faithfully captures the fear that engulfs the women as they learn of an imminent selection. Some try to find hiding places; the older rouge their pallid faces with blood; the young delude themselves that only the old, less productive workers will be taken, but finally admit that anyone is subject to selection.

Moral anxiety accompanies the terror of physical survival. In an early Plaszow selection scene, Tola must decide whether to use her own hiding place or surrender it to another—and if to another, which of several needy candidates is most deserving. A later selection focuses both on Tola's elemental fear and on the moral consequences of her defiance as she remains behind hiding in the barracks. Her terror is palpable: "Fear was like an animal; it pounced upon her, clawed, choked her breath, she pounced back, clutched at it, till she forced it back under her body and pressed and pressed" (p. 30). Terrified for herself and her coconspirators, who have first hidden with her in the middle tier of barrack bunks and then deserted their hiding places to attend the roll call, Tola strains to calm herself, to comfort her aching body with promises of future rest, water, food, and fresh air. Her anxiety is heightened when soldiers enter the barrack, throw bedding and pots to the floor, strike rifle butts against the bunks. As night turns to day and the women have not returned, Tola assumes that they have been transported to another camp, that she is the sole survivor, and that it is just a matter of time until the SS discover her rummaging for a scrap of bread. Her thoughts alternate, from the consummate power of the SS men who can dissolve ghettos and camps within hours to the comfort that no camp has yet been liquidated in reprisal for an escape, the pretext for this roll call.

Although Nazis play only peripheral roles in *An Estate of Memory*, often appearing as one-dimensional figures from the perspective of their victims, their appearance is more sustained than in most survivor fiction, and enhances Karmel's nuanced exploration of radical evil. The only historical figure Karmel presents is SS *Sturmbannführer* Amon Goeth, who appears infrequently and briefly, always in the role of sadist. True to the historic model, the fictional Goeth is dramatized as diabolically denying camp inmates even the meager rations they were allotted by German law, striding through the camp accompanied by an attack dog trained to strike in response to the word "*Jude!*," threatening to sever the finger of a woman who has difficulty removing her wedding band, and arbitrarily selecting old women to be flogged and others to be shot merely to satisfy his whim. Typically, Karmel describes the SS metonymically, as helmets and glistening boots, fists, or "the arm with the swastika band" (p. 204) designating victims for work assignments, punishment, or death. The Plaszow soldier Schneller-Schneller, nicknamed by the weary prisoners who hear only his bellowing commands to move "faster! faster!" as he marches them to work, bears the name that Karmel and others in Plaszow actually assigned one of their guards. Skarzysko's Meister Grube is distinguished by the women as kind because he abjures arbitrary beatings. In contrast to these shadowy figures, the novel's most substantial and complex German characterization is that of a naive young soldier who, moved by the youthful Alinka and his own misconception that Hitler meant to punish only the parents but spare Jewish children, shows the girl a measure of kindness. His metamorphosis into hardened soldier is dramatized in contradictory behavior—from dispensing peppermints to the scrubgirl to beating picrine-afflicted old women. That Karmel's interest in this young man is more psychologically and philosophically nuanced than her other German portraits is suggested in Tola's conviction that "He beats because he's crazed by what he sees" (p. 268), a credible conclusion given his cooperation in smuggling Aurelia's baby out of the camp, albeit his action is based on his mistaken conviction that the Führer means no harm to children.

Although militant resistance is impossible, subversion of Nazi goals is constant as the prisoners slow production and sabotage products destined for the German war effort. Karmel's secondary characters, minor functionaries and work supervisors, help the prisoners in their resistance efforts. "Standing six," guarding against the arrival of the Germans and their collaborators while others cease working to rest or to warm food, is an important form of active resistance. Organization and cooperation are foremost in standing six. The Jewish supervisor himself gives the order to stand six, directing Tola to signal when the camp commander or SS men appear. Foiling selections is another act of resistance, enacted by an OD man (functionaries who operated as police, supervising prisoners) who "spaced the children far apart, and always next to someone short, so that they would appear like adults, only undersized . . . and like a hostess before a party camouflaging the worn-out furniture, displaying those still handsome to their advantage, he now sent an old woman to a dark corner, now put a husky girl to the fore" (p. 71). Given the context, such domestic imagery is startling; it renders the horror of a selection accessible to those innocent of the *Lager*.

Acts demonstrating the victims' persistent decency, despite their immersion in a hitherto unimagined environment of corruption and radical evil, demonstrate how solidarity with the group enhances the individual's chances for survival. Scenes of attending and providing for the sick during the Skarzysko typhus epidemic are among the most poignant examples of women's bonding and subversion of camp authority. Starved and sick women, exhausted from slave labor, nurse those who are even closer to death. To help one another through dysentery, typhus, and starvation, the women engage in all manner of commercial ventures to net a piece of bread, a cup of soup, or medicine. Tola secretly sells her gold tooth to help the typhus-ravaged Aurelia, and Barbara sends instructions out of the camp for the sale of her possessions, hoping to alleviate the suffering of the neediest in her barracks. Devoted to making as many as she can more comfortable, by sharing food, assuming the work of the disabled, and taking on extra work to win an additional potato or cup of soup for a sick comrade, Barbara extends her role from manor house lady bountiful to camp savior. The women beg and peddle their belongings for one another; feed and warm each other; wash the bloody, bruised flesh of the flogged offenders; nurse each other in childbirth and in illness. They commiserate in hunger and in pain; comfort and encourage each other through depression and fear; console those who have lost friends and relatives in the punishment roll calls and selections, and share memories and plans for a better life in the future. Often Karmel juxtaposes scenes of gratuitous German violence with vignettes of Jewish women sustaining each other in a psychologically supportive alliance. Like many survivor writers, Karmel incorporates these gestures of mutual assistance to demonstrate that no matter how beleaguered the victims, they struggled to retain the very humanity the Nazis sought to deny. When the continuation of Jewish life itself is a crime, the women's cooperative efforts to acquire food, to maintain their health through illegal purchases of medicine, to assist in a birth and smuggle the child to safety, to snatch a friend from a selection, are not only feats of bonding, but defiant resistance.

Chief among Karmel's interests are the moral implications of *Lager* existence for both slaves and slavemasters. The Germans evidence no moral or ethical dilemmas about their behavior. Neither do the Ukrainian guards or Polish foremen. Only the principal

Jewish characters, fighting daily against terrible odds to survive, contend with moral and ethical dilemmas. Mistakenly applying orthodox moral standards to the Holocaust universe, they question and decry their own weaknesses and chastise each other for failing to maintain ethical ideals. Even the few who momentarily explain their transgressions by attributing them to the Nazi standard recant and repent. The ethical dilemma of the privileged block elders and work supervisors who follow German orders to garner better treatment for themselves is an object of Karmel's examination. The Jewish OD men are briefly but judiciously rendered from the perspective of the women they dominate. Although there is no doubt they harry and berate the inmates to work more efficiently, and some exploit the women sexually for "gifts" of extra food or selection exemptions, some endanger their own safety to alleviate prisoner suffering, and refuse any payment. The contradictory nature of their existence, serving the enemy while trying to help their victims, is exemplified in meeting production schedules while conspiring with the workers to slack off, endangering weak adults while safeguarding children during a selection, and punishing women for infraction of the rules while assisting in an illegal birth and the escape of a Jewish infant.

Although Karmel dramatizes the moral dilemma of privileged prisoners, the dominant voices are those of ordinary women prisoners, whose moral quandaries arise during the struggle to survive in a universe designed for their destruction. The beleaguered agonize in deciding whether to save themselves or to resist escape knowing that collective retaliation will follow; whether to protect themselves during a selection or to allow another to use one's hiding place; whether and how to control one's tongue rather than lash out against a tormentor, an informer, a denouncer; how much food to eat when everyone is starving; how to decide whose suffering should be allayed and whose should be ignored. The women's integrity is manifested in Barbara's plea to the Meister (the Commander) to allow Tola, who she claims is her sister, to accompany her when, because of her healthy appearance, she is assigned to a relatively good job. Refusing to heighten Barbara's risk by confirming the lie, Tola forgoes the opportunity to improve her own chance for survival at Barbara's expense. Conversely, when Alinka is assigned a relatively safe job, Aurelia must choose whether to hold her tongue or insist that they be allowed to stay together as "mother and daughter," thereby risking Alinka's reassignment to hazardous work. Countering Barbara's appraisal that she will jeopardize the child's safety, Aurelia asserts that their mutual support is more vital to the survival of each than is safe work for one. Never shrinking from the complexities of the *Lager* universe, Karmel portrays both extraordinary generosity and meanness of spirit, which coexist in camp relationships fraught with paradox.

Karmel reveals the moral dimensions of victims' response to deprivation and brutality most clearly in the antagonism that develops between Tola and Barbara. In search of a mission, Barbara begins the concentrationary experience with a vision of her own saintliness and a desire to be heroic; hence she leaves the relative security of the Polish prisoners to join the Jewish women. Tola, who is introduced as a highly self-conscious, defensive, rational loner, yearns to be well-regarded. Tola's story traces gradual capitulation and accommodation to the Nazi universe; Barbara's tale maps defiance.

Tola exhibits the most extreme metamorphosis, eventually veering from rebel to accommodator, succumbing to years of deprivation by abandoning her selfless pattern of communal service and taking a position as work supervisor in order to focus her energies on her own survival, justifying her reversal by asserting that corruption rules the camp universe and that she has as much right to save herself as another. When Tola privatizes her survival strategy, she embarks on a course of conduct she recognizes will alienate her from the group. Contrary to Barbara's belief that she has accepted the job to help the others, Tola confesses that her motive is self-interest: "She wanted safety and the bread that would come later at night" (p. 381). To the charge that she will be a slave driver, that she will be ordered to do something terrible, Tola replies, "Someone else will do it if I don't" (p. 343). Her compliance with the system appears when benevolent rule fails her and she adopts a tyrannical demeanor, threatening her charges with punishment. As a work supervisor, Tola leads a double life, constantly plotting how she will manipulate the women to satisfy the Germans to whom she is responsible and, yet, find ways to help the women survive. She grows hostile toward her charges, who view her as "the exploiter grown fat on their misery" (p. 378). Karmel suggests, through Tola's thoughts, how difficult it is to resist the privileged job and how burdensome it is to discharge it ethically. Not until the final days of a Skarzysko death march does Tola acknowledge that the price for her survival is too great and determine that she will try to save the women or die with them.

Although Barbara's compromised demeanor is far less devastating than Tola's self-interested ethical lapse, she too undergoes a metamorphosis from Plaszow saint to Skarzysko benevolent despot, becoming a fierce disciplinarian of infirmary patients in her charge, exchanging her sympathetic mode of nursing for a command posture. No longer tender and solicitous while nursing sixty patients, she becomes a fiend for cleanliness. The sick must air and sweep the barracks and wash, even when they feel too weak to move. Beating the women without remorse, insulting them without apology, she forces them to battle their illness. In the concentration camp, discipline had its place, and she has had to abandon her saintly image to better serve the needy. So desperate does she become to provide food for Alinka during a typhus bout, that she exploits her position as hospital orderly. Observing which patients are dealing with vendors, she begs portions of their food for Alinka and, when necessary, pressures them to share their meager supply, or have her suspend attention to their medical needs.

Karmel invites readers to ponder the elastic moral boundaries of the *Lager* universe, the replacement of moral absolutes by ambiguities born of necessity, which distinguish the thievery by Amon Goeth from that of his victims who "organize" food and medicine, or make deals for special privileges to forestall death. Barbara and Tola forfeit their lives as they strive to save the lives of other inmates. Barbara defies an order to include Alinka in a roundup of hospital patients during the Skarzysko liquidation, and is taken in her friend's place. Tola sacrifices herself when she tries to warn a girl that a guard is taking aim at her during a death march. In giving her life to save another, Tola is redeemed. As the women unlearn and relearn human possibilities, Karmel achieves her goal "to understand human beings in those events and find something redeeming in a single individual" (Interview, Kremer). The spirit of all the women, their sacrifices, their relentless struggles, their nurturing kindness in a setting designed to strip them of any semblance of humanity, lives on in the reader's memory because Karmel has imagined these women and recreated her own camp universe.

Critical Reception

Karmel's first novel, *Stephania*, received widespread enthusiastic reviews. Martin Rice was typical in his acclaim of Karmel as a "writer with serious things to say and the ability to say them movingly and with forthrightness," an author who had produced "a solid substantial novel," a young author who "writes with the sure craftsmanship of an experienced writer" (p. 21). Although hailed by Archibald MacLeish as "a tremendous achievement," *An Estate of Memory* initially attracted only modest critical attention and limited readership. The contrasting reception accorded the two books does not reflect the author's craft but the publication of *An Estate of Memory* at the height of the turbulent Vietnam era, a time when critics and lay readers were reluctant to think about the Holocaust, much less read fiction set in the European slaughterhouse. In her "Afterword" to the novel, fellow survivor and scholar Ruth Kluger Angress observed that *An Estate of Memory* "is in the tradition of the great modern prison books" in its concern for "freedom"; that it "is the best antidote" against the bifurcated simplification of seeing the camp prisoners either as "martyred saints or snarling animals whom the instinct of self preservation had driven below the threshold of humanity" (p. 445). With the passage of time and reissue of the book by the Feminist Press, *An Estate of Memory* is steadily gaining its deserved audience and scholarly attention. Heralded by preeminent Holocaust scholars, *An Estate of Memory* has been described as "a monumental story of the struggle for survival, perhaps the most moving account of the devotion, the sacrifices, and the breakdown in the fragile network of group survival in concentration camp literature" (Ezrahi, p. 70) and as "a powerful psychological portrayal of life in a concentration camp" (Horowitz, p. 155). Karmel's work is a fine example of historic truthfulness, psychological complexity, moral integrity, and literary artistry.

Bibliography

Primary Sources

Spiew za Drutami [*Song Behind the Wire*]. With Henia Karmel-Wolfe. 1947.
"Fru Holm." 1950.
Stephania. 1953.
An Estate of Memory. 1986.

Secondary Sources

Angress, Ruth K. "Afterword." *An Estate of Memory*. New York: Feminist Press, 1986, pp. 445–457.

Ezrahi, Sidra DeKoven. *By Words Alone: The Holocaust in Literature*. Chicago: University of Chicago Press, 1980, pp. 67–95.

Horowitz, Sara R. "Ilona Karmel." *Jewish American Women Writers: A Bio-Bibliographical and Critical Sourcebook*. Edited by Ann R. Shapiro. Westport, Conn.: Greenwood Press, 1994, pp. 146–157.

———. "Memory and Testimony of Women Survivors of Nazi Genocide." *Women of the Word: Jewish Women and Jewish Writing*. Edited by Judith Baskin. Detroit: Wayne State University Press, 1994, pp. 258–282.

Kremer, S. Lillian. "*An Estate of Memory*: Women in the Holocaust." *Holocaust Studies Annual* (1991). Edited by Sanford Pinsker and Jack Fischel. New York: Garland Publishing Company, 1992, pp. 99–110.

———. "Holocaust-Wrought Women: Portraits by Four American Writers." *Studies in American Jewish Literature* 11:2 (fall 1992): 150–161.

———. "Ilona Karmel." *Women's Holocaust Writing: Memory and Imagination.* Lincoln: University of Nebraska Press, 1999.

Levi, Primo. *Survival in Auschwitz: The Nazi Assault on Humanity.* New York: Collier/Macmillan, 1961.

Rice, Martin. Review of *An Estate of Memory*, by Ilona Karmel. *Saturday Review* 36 (9 May 1953): 21.

Wiesel, Elie. "Art and Culture after the Holocaust." In *Auschwitz: Beginning of a New Era? Reflections on the Holocaust.* Edited by Eva Fleischner. New York: KTAV Publishing, 1977. pp. 403–415.

Interviews

Nichols, Lewis. "Talk with Ilona Karmel." *New York Times Book Review* (29 March 1951): 2.

Unpublished Interview with S. Lillian Kremer. 24 May 1988.

ANNE KARPF

(1950–)

PHYLLIS B. LASSNER

AS EFFORTS TO gather the testimony of aging survivors intensify, the next generation confirms that the story of the Holocaust does not end with their parents' memories. Every meeting of their worldwide organizations and the proliferation of their writing demonstrate that the living history of the Holocaust will not die. In transmitting the story of the Holocaust to their children, survivors leave a crucial legacy that cannot be lost or denied because it shapes the lives not only of their children but of their grandchildren. Whether survivor parents told their stories or kept silent, their children's sense of self in some way is identified with and has internalized the anxieties and coping strategies that remained indelibly imprinted on the psyches of their survivor parents.

In her book, *The War After: Living with the Holocaust* (1996), the sociologist and journalist Anne Karpf adds testimony, political history, and psychological analysis to the story of the enmeshed relationship between the character and fate of her survivor parents and her own. Karpf offers a comprehensive diorama of the ongoing trauma of Holocaust experience. Just as survivors needed to bear witness to the Final Solution, so the testimony of their children breaks the silence surrounding the struggles of the so-called second generation. As though rescuing their own subjectivity from their parents' overwhelming experiences, the second generation is showing that the emotional tortures of the Holocaust live on not only in their parents' memories and nightmares. Even the will to live and to love beyond the Holocaust can carry forth its pain as the children of survivors inherit the psychological vestiges of their parents' suffering. But perhaps most significantly, as Karpf's book chronicles the communicative process by which survivor stories are transmitted, it validates the psychological process that makes the Holocaust the second generation's own story.

Psychological History of the Holocaust

Anne Karpf was born in London on 8 June 1950. Her mother, Natalia Weissman Karpf, was born in Krakow, Poland, and trained to become a concert pianist. She performed in Poland before the war and in England after the war. Anne's father, Joseph Karpf, was born in Galicia on the border of the Russian part of Poland. He studied law in Vienna and then also attended art school. He joined his father's many business enterprises, which, after his father's death, he ran until he was deported to Russia when the war broke out.

Karpf dramatizes her fraught relationship with her survivor parents through the book's structure, the three parts of which present her interpretation of how her life was born of her parents' stories. Part 1 of *The War After* is Karpf's memoir of growing up with and suffering the effects of her parents' Holocaust legacy, and this is juxtaposed with each parent's testimonies of their prewar, wartime, and postwar experiences. The fact that her parents' testimonies were transcribed and edited and the book was written thirteen years after Karpf first interviewed her parents in itself reveals the emotional drama of Holocaust transmission and interpretation. Karpf's book could be written only when she was ready to come to terms with the relationship between her parents' cataclysmic shifts and her own. The book confronts the shift from her parents' stable prewar lives to catastrophe and then from her anxieties to their adjustments. Karpf articulates the aftershocks of these shifts in her analysis of her intertwined relationship with her parents, an analysis that moves from direct narration to the questions that prompt, and therefore shape the focus of, her parents' narratives. In effect, these questions reflect not only her desire for information but her need to understand the nature of their emotional responses and their relationship to her own. She thus asks her mother: "Would you have liked them to have bombed the camp?" (London: Heinemann, 1996, p. 88). And her father: "Weren't you terrified?" (p. 58). "Didn't you feel a sense of incredible anger?" (p. 61). The Holocaust stories of Natalia and Josef Karpf, having shaped their daughter's life, are then brought to life through her narrative construction and interpretation.

The selfhood of the second generation is also shaped by their parents' postwar adjustment to a new life in a new land, which includes the birth and care of their children, in this case, daughters Eve and Anne. Once again, Anne asks her mother about her relationship to past and present, a question that assumes a relationship to Anne's own past and present: "Wasn't that difficult for you [that] the world outside resumed, almost as if nothing had happened?" (p. 150). Then, asking for confirmation of her own emotional experience of the Holocaust legacy: "When we were little, there must have been a lot of sadness in the house" (p. 156). This juxtaposition of her parents' personal testimony to her own experience, her direction, and her life writing represents an interpretive strategy that is designed to provide both a confrontation with the traumas with which Karpf feels infused and a process of healing and defining her own identity. Karpf thus constructs a narrative form that effects a form of therapy.

The subject of the confrontation is her irrevocable identification with and attachment to her parents, and the outcome she hopes to achieve is an individuated relationship—lovingly close but with emotionally safe boundaries. In coming to understand and therefore demystify her parents' monstrous experiences, she also discovers that her mother's "extraordinary resilience" is not a sign of superhuman heroism, nor does it represent some omnipresent threat of danger and loss that may beset them both. Karpf discovers that resilience is the necessary strategy through which her own development can negotiate and revise the portentous models of either ghoulish or triumphalist fairy-tales and fables with which her childhood imagination had been invested. Karpf prods her parents' memories for the explicit details of their entrapments and survival, and then she uses this knowledge to repair her own defensive memory lapses, and thus flesh out and develop a more reality-tested model for her life and identity. Like many Holocaust writers she feels the urgent need to countermand those who would represent survivors as embodying heroically uplifting messages that audiences find personally inspiring. Thus she objects to projects such as the Steven Spielberg–produced documentary *The Last Days*, about survivors of the Hungarian roundups in 1944, because none of the survivors suggests any problems with their postwar lives in the United States. Such representations are misleading, she maintains, because they offer no sense of a disturbing "war after."

Karpf herself, however, does not consider that the process of adjusting to the social culture of Britain or the United States may have affected their responses and outlooks. Though she ignores this cultural and psychological contingency, Karpf attempts to deromanticize and historicize the psychodynamics of post-Holocaust experience. She admonishes readers who comfort and distance themselves from both survivors' "anaesthetized parts," that is, their "necessary autism," and their degrading experiences (p. 249). She criticizes those who impose interpretations onto Holocaust testimony that make survivors sacred beings. Karpf argues that the transmission of survivors' psychic pain is a psychological reality, and that *The War After* repudiates any analyses of the problems of the second generation as determined by strictly internal drives and conflicts or fantasies. For Karpf, the traumas resulting from Holocaust experiences cannot be explained by psychoanalytic theories of a generic, internally conflicted human development. These analyses, she argues, imprison survivors once again, only now within their own damaged psyches. An alternative model of human psychology that Karpf advocates for the second generation is grounded in the specific material circumstances that formed their relationship to their parents' appropriate responses to life-threatening realities.

Karpf's commitment to this contextualized model was already apparent three years before the publication of *The War After*, in her review of a book about mother-infant bonding. With clear parallels to her relationship with her own mother, Karpf showed her concerns about decontextualized psychoanalytic theories of attachment and the transmission of psychic pain. She fully agreed with Diane Eyer's book, *Mother-Infant Bonding: A Scientific Fiction* (1992), which criticized the faulty research that led to myths valorizing mothers who "were superglued to their babies immediately after birth" ("Gum Disease," in *New Statesman and Society*, 5 February 1993, p. 47). Like Eyer, Karpf emphasizes the external psychological realities that form mother-child bonding and also validate the malleability of mother and child.

A significant feature of the psychological reality of the Holocaust is the history of the reception of the Holocaust by the psychological establishments and their theories of trauma. In part 2 of her book, Karpf connects the political contexts of British policies toward postwar Jewish refugees to the influential psychoanalytic community in Britain, influenced so powerfully by the rescue of Sigmund Freud and his daughter Anna from Nazi-ridden Vienna. Despite the fact that so many psychoanalysts were Jewish refugees, their theories and practices ignored the reality of Holocaust trauma. Karpf sees this void as the result of the psychoanalysts' own difficulties in adapting to social pressure to become "British" while coping with their own traumas, of having lost their homeland and having lost family who could not escape the Nazis.

Like the survivors in Steven Speilberg's documentary *The Last Days*, those who were trained to believe in the power of memory appear to have also repressed theirs.

The Political History of the Holocaust

Part 2 of *The War After* offers a history of British attitudes and policies toward the Jews, including literary and other cultural representations, together with an account of British Jewish responses to pressures to acculturate. This history culminates in a survey of Britain's obstructionist policies. Karpf argues that not only did the British Home and Foreign Offices reject the possibility of saving European Jews, but also, despite the relative success of the *Kindertransport*, which saved 10,000 children up to the age of sixteen, Britain's policies and practices made it complicit with the hostile indifference of other nations and with the Nazis' drive to destroy Jewish life and culture. If British officialdom represents the transformation of social antisemitism into political policy, official British Jewry, in Karpf's view, did little to assert an effective counterattack. Fearing the rise of British antisemitism, the British Board of Jewish Deputies primarily worked to forestall any acrimonious response that might threaten the stable, if always tense, relationship between British Jewry and their gentile neighbors. Rather than openly making welcome the few Jewish refugees who managed admittance, they merely counseled polite manners and morals that would help the newcomers keep a low profile.

Karpf also shows that despite, or perhaps because of, the subtlety of British antisemitism, fears of its persistence were not unfounded. As recently as the 1980s and 1990s, the rhetoric of antisemitism and an emphasis on a Christian British character informed media reporting while incidents of "extreme violence (defined as potentially life threatening)" inspired growing attention to security for Jewish buildings. Karpf examines the ways in which the ongoing, postwar rejectionist policies toward Jewish immigration affected her parents, who had a strongly expressed Jewish identity. In turn, their struggle to adjust economically and culturally is accorded the political contexts that define the nature of the world she was born into. Combining her parents' memories with the history not only of Britain's obstructionist policies but of their ideological sources in nineteenth-century antisemitism exposes a persistent British cultural politics of blaming the victim. Although her historical research is not the result of her own archival research, but a synthesis of others' work, it is clearly necessary to the process of discovering the roots of her own suffering. The book's emphasis on this contextual connection represents a critically ironic commentary. Each section, on her parents' prewar, wartime, and postwar lives, raises questions about the others, and the world of the Holocaust shows the complacent ignorance of the world outside. All together, they allow us to see how the persistence of British antisemitism is not something apart from, but is deeply implicated in, the Holocaust. Part of Karpf's purpose in part 2 of *The War After* is to show how cultural attempts to bridge this divided experience and connected politics were not only flimsy but undermined the ability of survivors' testimony to make a lasting impact. Popular-culture constructions of the Holocaust such as the expurgated edition of *The Diary of Anne Frank* and subsequent films and plays provided uplifting and hopeful political and ethical messages that elided the horrors of Holocaust experience.

Interpretive Implications of *The War After*

Part 3 of Karpf's book synthesizes her psychological and political narratives into a chronicle of her own experiences of loss, birth, and reconciliation. After years of combined physical and emotional suffering, including self-mutilation and unresolved ambivalences about her relationship with her parents and her lover, she embraces commitment to her marriage and her two children and to a negotiated peace settlement with her parents. Juxtaposed with diary entries chronicling her father's final year, she offers reflections on how her mourning of him actually altered her approach to the sense of loss she had derived from her parents' Holocaust experiences. His slow dying enables her to find new and positive ways of identifying with him while understanding how his oppressive personality masked a vulnerability. His death then offers a symbolic separation from her parents' Holocaust experiences. As a way of melding intellectual understanding with emotional catharsis, Karpf connects these changes to her experience traveling to Poland, where she establishes a material historical and political context for her self-knowledge. As she visits the landmarks of her parents' past she raises questions about the emotional effects of this odyssey on her mother and on her narrative.

In one sense, the book's juxtaposition of her parents' testimony with Karpf's own has the overall effect of giving equal weight to the experiences of Holocaust survivors and the second generation. Instead of achieving such balance, however, this structure expresses the emotional strains issuing from the effort to achieve it. While the anger with which Karpf infuses her historical summary of British policies and British Jewry lends credence to the book as personal testimony, the emotions embedded in her presentation of her parents' testimony may be problematic. The often strained metaphors of her personal meditations and her anxious questions to her parents re-create the psychological disturbance the book is meant to be resolving. This is apparent in the way her questions and reflections shape not only her book, but her parents' stories, and as a result, her book re-creates the very attachment to her parents she struggles to relieve. These narrative tensions show how the search for subjectivity in relation to her parents' history may require analysis not only of their irrevocable attachment, but of their historical separateness.

Karpf's awareness that whatever her own suffering, it cannot be compared to that of her parents, produces an overlay of new suffering—in the form of guilt for balancing her story with theirs. Nowhere is this more apparent than when she returns from Poland with cassettes of Yiddish songs. Breaking down into "terrible shocked sadness" (p. 311) and sobbing as never before, Natalia Karpf's response to the music provides her daughter with an experience that cannot be balanced with an inherited sense of loss. Moved to examine her motives for the entire project of recapturing her parents' past, Anne Karpf also recognizes a new resolve of her own—to embrace the present and the future through the experience of becoming a mother for the second time. It is this embrace that allows her to see her parents' coping strategies as a positive life force and not merely as evidence of lives submerged in the forces of terror. At the end of this compelling narrative, however, a reader may feel that a more explicit acknowledgment of the incomparable nature of the first- and second-generation experiences, and how Anne Karpf's own suffering, while tied to her parents', represents a story that is also separate from theirs, would add the measure of subjectivity for which her book expresses such powerful craving.

Bibliography

Primary Sources

"Gum Disease: Review of Diane E. Eyer, *Mother-Infant Bonding: A Scientific Fiction*." 1993.
The War After: Living With the Holocaust. 1996.
"Memories Aren't Made of This." 2001.
"Return to the Death Camps." 2001.

Secondary Sources

Cheyette, Bryan. Review of *The War After*. *New Statesman* (5 July 1996): 44–45.
Golding, Martin. Review of *The War After*. *British Journal of Psychotherapy* 14, no. 2 (1997): 237–239.
Isaacs, Esther. "Surviving the Survival." Review of *The War After*. *Jewish Book News and Reviews* 12, no. 1 (February 1997): 4–5.
Moorehead, Caroline. "In Enemy Territory." Review of *The War After*. *Times Literary Supplement*, 30 August 1996, p. 36.

JAN KARSKI

(1914–2000)

NECHAMA TEC

BORN IN 1914 in Lodz, Poland, Jan Kozielewski is known by his assumed underground name of Jan Karski. He was a devout Catholic, a World War II hero, and an emissary between the underground in Poland and the Polish government-in-exile. Among the numerous honors that were bestowed upon him was Poland's highest military decoration, the order of Virtuti Militaris, and in Jerusalem a tree bearing his name was planted on the Avenue of Righteous Gentiles among the Nations.

Karski lost his father when he was a young boy. His brother, Marian, eighteen years his senior, became a father substitute and supported Karski's educational and professional pursuits. His mother, Walentyna Kozielewska, instilled in her young son a tolerance for people who differed from him, especially Jews. With this emphasis on tolerance came an equally strong concern with social justice. Catholicism played an important role in Karski's life, but it could not compete with the high value he placed on independence.

With a university degree, as an aspiring diplomat, Karski entered the Polish foreign service. The 1939 war interrupted his career; he enlisted in the Polish army with a rank of a second lieutenant. Taken prisoner by the Soviets, Karski escaped. He reached Warsaw and joined the newly established Polish underground. As a member of the underground, later known as AK (Home Army), Karski became an international emissary and courier. David Engel thinks that Karski was chosen for this kind of work because of his apolitical background, impressive physical stamina, and photographic memory. Karski sees his life-threatening assignment as follows: "I was only a courier. My duty was to transport information. Nothing else. I was a nobody. I acted as a mailbox or a gramophone record, hurried from one side of the front to the other. Everybody had me swear that I would tell what I heard to authorized persons only" ("The Mission That Failed," p. 329).

This modest self-assessment does not reflect his wartime contributions. As a twenty-five-year-old man, in 1940 Karski left for his first mission to France. There, in addition to the information he submitted to the Polish government-in-exile, at the request of his superiors, he wrote a report about life in Poland under the German and Soviet occupations. A portion of this report dealt with the Jewish plight and how the German occupation impacted upon Jewish-Polish relations. In this document, Karski suggested the creation of a common front, an alliance through which the weaker partners—the Jews and the Poles—would cooperate in opposition to their deadly enemy, the German occupational forces. He argued that such a Jewish–Polish alliance would be morally advantageous to the Polish people. At the same time, he deplored the fact that the Polish masses did not seem to sympathize with the Jews. Insightful and concise, he described how the Germans targeted the Jews for destruction as early as 1940 (Engel, *An Early Account of Polish Jewry*, pp. 9–10).

From this mission Karski returned to Poland via Hungary and Czechoslovakia. Within a few weeks he was once more sent to France. This time the Gestapo in Slovakia arrested him. Under torture, Karski revealed no secrets. Still, he was apprehensive that eventually he might succumb under more prolonged suffering. He attempted suicide by cutting his wrists but was revived by the enemy. The brutal interrogation resumed only to be interrupted by a daring and successful rescue operation executed by a Polish commando group. After he recovered he continued to serve the Polish underground ("The Mission That Failed," p. 326).

Karski's wartime political and humanitarian preoccupation included strong opposition to the Nazi policies of Jewish annihilation. Within the context of his duties to Poland, he willingly undertook additional tasks that he thought would alleviate Jewish suffering.

Soon an opportunity presented itself to alert the leaders of the free world to the systematic murder of the Jews. In the latter part of 1942, in preparation for an underground transatlantic journey, Karski met with Jewish leaders in Poland and agreed to deliver their messages to the Allies and others whom these Jewish representatives saw as influential and with whom he could meet.

To add more credence to this undertaking, with the help of the Jewish underground leaders, Karski smuggled himself twice into the Warsaw ghetto to gain firsthand knowledge of the Jewish plight. To report on another phase of Jewish destruction, dressed as a guard, Karski was smuggled into the transit camp Izbica Lubelska from which Jews from many European nations were robbed of their possessions, humiliated, brutalized, and murdered. The survivors of these initial assaults were transferred to Belzec and gassed upon arrival (Wood and Jankowski, pp. 128–130). Not only did Karski risk his life in these illegal visits, he endangered his psychological well-being as well when he confronted the inhumane treatment of Izbica prisoners (Wood and Jankowski, p. 127).

In England and the United States, Karski met with many people, including influential world leaders such as President Roosevelt and the British foreign minister, Anthony Eden. Karski's reports about the plight of the Jewish people and the messages from the Jewish leaders who pleaded for help fell on deaf ears. For the Allies, as for other governments, the German systematic murder of the Jews was definitely not a priority. Years later, commenting on this part of his mission, Karski described it as "an obvious failure. Six million Jews died, and no one offered them effective help. Not any nation, not any government, not any church. The help they did receive, heroic help, was provided only by individuals" ("The Mission That Failed," p. 333).

In part, these frustrating 1942 contacts with high-ranking government officials convinced Karski that the Jews were abandoned by all world governments, an idea he repeated often under different circumstances. He believed that although in wartime Europe the murderers of Jews by far outnumbered those who wanted to save them, "the Jews were not totally abandoned. They were abandoned by governments, social structures, church hierarchies, but not by ordinary men and women" ("The Mission That Failed," p. 334). He was also convinced that it was counterproductive to concentrate only on the murderers of Jews and ignore the minority that was determined to save them. He argued that the historical truth must be preserved showing how thousands of Christians tried to save Jews, ready to die in the process. Some actually did. He was convinced that by overlooking those who risked their lives to save Jews we perpetuate the idea that "everybody hates the Jews." He concludes that it is both historically incorrect and psychologically unhealthy to concentrate on the idea that no one wanted to save the Jews (personal communication, 1999).

In his first written report for the Polish government-in-exile (France, 1940), he included vivid examples of Jewish helplessness and humiliation. For example, this report contains the following descriptions:

> One time I was at the Gestapo to obtain a pass of some sort. In came a Jewish woman, a member of the educated class, dressed in a fur coat, frightened. She was expecting a child. She was requesting a pass for herself or for her doctor to be on the street after 8:00 P.M. should it be necessary to begin delivery then.
>
> The female secretary, A. Volksdeutsche, responded, 'You don't need a pass. We are not going to make it easy for you to give birth to a Jew. Dogs are dying from hunger and misery, and you still want to give birth to Jews? Heraus! Heraus!' (Engel, An Early Account of Polish Jewry, pp. 7–8).

In another part of the same report, Karski wrote:

> I was in the Kercelak [a pedlar's stand in Warsaw]. A frozen Jew is the proprietor. A German soldier comes by. He takes socks, combs, soap—wants to walk off without paying. The Jew demands money. The soldier pays no attention. The old man raises his voice; his frightened neighbors hold him back and calm him; they are afraid for him. The old man shouts, or rather howls: "What will he do to me? What will he do to me? He can only kill me. Let him kill me. Let him kill me. Enough of all this. I can't go on any more."
>
> The German walked away; he didn't pay. As he was leaving, he muttered, "Verfluchte Juden. [Damned Jews]" (Engel, *An Early Account of Polish Jewry*, p. 8).

Karski was also sensitive to and identified with the dangerous and life-threatening circumstances of the hard-working, low-rank underground workers. In his book *Story of a Secret State* (1944), his comments are filled with compassion, "Pitiful were the young girls who distributed the underground press. It was a thankless job—this was a simple mechanical task—men did not want it; men insisted on playing more important roles. The death rate among these girls was very high" (*Story of a Secret State*, Houghton Mifflin, p. 283). Couriers had a slightly higher rank than those who distributed illegal literature. Most of them were also women. Keenly aware of the special dangers that the women couriers faced, he informs us that a courier's job required that many people

> knew every detail of her life—and in clandestine work that was bad. She almost invariably had compromising papers with her. Her comings and goings were calculated to avoid suspicion and she had to be present in many places. The average "life" of a female officer was no more

than a few months . . . Among the resisters [couriers] their task was the most demanding, their sacrifices the greatest and their work the least recognized. They were overloaded with work and doomed from the start (p. 266).

Late in 1943 the Polish government reassigned Karski to the Polish Embassy staff in Washington when they learned that the Germans intended to arrest him on his return to Poland from a trip to the United States for slandering the Third Reich. All along Karski was disappointed by the Allies' refusal to stand up to the systematic annihilation of the Jewish people. In part, he saw this inactivity as a reflection of indifference and hypocrisy.

The United States became Karski's permanent home. In 1944 he wrote *Story of a Secret State* to inform "the public about what was happening to the Jews in Poland" ("Alerting the Allies," p. 9) and began an active lecture series on the Holocaust. Then when the war ended, as a personal gesture of defiance, he stopped lecturing about the Holocaust. By 1952 he earned a Ph.D. at Georgetown University in Washington, D.C. He stayed on as a professor, teaching courses on East European affairs, comparative government, and international affairs. Thus, the end of the war and his academic life put a stop to Karski's public lectures on the Holocaust. In 1962 he married Pola Nirenska, a distinguished dancer and choreographer, a Polish Jew.

He revisited his personal past only at the insistent urgings of Claude Lanzmann, the creator of the film *Shoah*. Asked to comment about the world's reaction to the Holocaust, Karski explained,

> After the war, I read in the newspapers how the Western leaders—statesmen and generals, church hierarchs, civic leaders—were outraged about what had happened to the Jews. These leaders claimed that they hadn't known about the Nazis' genocidal policies while they were being carried out: the murder of six million innocents, they said, had been kept a secret. This version of events persists in many quarters, even today. This version is no more than a myth. They knew ("Alerting the Allies," p. 9).

When questioned as to reasons for this supposed lack of knowledge, Karski replied:

> Hypocrisy. Everybody who wanted to know about German crimes against the Jews could have known and not only through me. There were many other sources. But this truth could not get through. This was not only because of ill will. The Holocaust, the systematic extermination of an entire nation, happened for the first time in the history of mankind. People were not prepared for such truth. And that is why these truths were rejected, even subconsciously. The most trustworthy witnesses were rejected. There are things which minds and hearts refuse to accept ("The Mission That Failed," p. 334).

On 13 July 2000, Jan Karski's death deprived the world of a distinguished humanitarian and defender of the oppressed.

Bibliography

Primary Sources

Story of a Secret State. 1944.

"The Mission That Failed: A Polish Courier Who Tried to Help the Jews: An Interview with Jan Karski." *Dissent* 34, no. 3 (1987): 326–334.

"Alerting the Allies: An Emissary's Story." *Dimensions* 7, 2 (1985): 3–9.

The Great Powers & Poland, 1919–1945. 1985.

Tolstoy, Alexei. "A Polish Underground Worker." Thomas Man, In *Terror in Europe: The Fate of the Jews*. London: National Committee for Rescue from the Nazi Terror, n.d. [1943].

Secondary Sources

Engel, David. "An Early Account of Polish Jewry under Nazi and Soviet Occupation Presented to the Polish Government-in-Exile, February 1940." *Jewish Social Studies* 45, no. 1 (1983): 1–16.

———. "The Western Allies and the Holocaust: Jan Karski's Mission to the West, 1942–1944," *Holocaust and Genocide Studies* 5, no. 4 (1990): 363–380.

Korczak, Jerzy. *Karski*. Warsaw: Oficyna Wydawnicza Rytm, 2001.

Wood, E. Thomas, and Stanislaw M. Jankowski. *Karski: How One Man Tried to Stop the Holocaust*. New York: John Wiley & Sons, Inc., 1994.

YITZHAK KATZENELSON

(1886–1944)

ZIVA SHAVITSKY

YITZHAK KATZENELSON WAS a poet and dramatist in Hebrew and Yiddish who continues to be greatly admired for his lengthy *Song of the Murdered Jewish People* as well as the telling pages of his *Vittel Diary*. The overwhelming reception of these two works resulted in the common perception of Katzenelson as mainly a Holocaust writer. This has led to the overshadowing of Katzenelson's prolific writing before the outbreak of World War II. Nevertheless, these two monumental works warrant continued reading and recognition, albeit in light of illuminating details from the author's life before Jewish embroilment in the war.

Biographical Details

Katzenelson was born on 11 May 1886 in Karelitz, in the Minsk district of White Russia, to Benjamin Katzenelson, a Hebrew writer, and Henda Davidson, the daughter of the township's rabbi, Yehiel Davidson. Both father and son were the last of a great family tradition of rabbinical and biblical scholarship and creative writing.

Katzenelson began writing in 1904 in Yiddish for Mordechai Spektor's *Yidishe Folkstsaytung*, and I. L. Peretz's *Yidishe Bibliotek* and in Hebrew for David Frischmann's *Ha-Dor*. Many of his earlier writings were published in children's and youth magazines. He had lived mostly in Łodz, where he opened a secular Hebrew school and acted as its principal until the outbreak of World War II. He was especially talented in delivering accounts of Jewish childhood in Europe and in writing for children. Katzenelson was also a pioneer of the Hebrew theater. The theatrical company he established in Łodz staged plays by I. L. Peretz, Sholom Aleichem, Hirschbein, and others, as well as his own Hebrew plays. Katzenelson was greatly influenced by Heinrich Heine, whose poems he translated into Hebrew. In addition, many of Katzenelson's poems were put to melody and became popular folk songs. Often nicknamed the "favorite son of Hebrew poetry," Katzenelson wrote concurrently with C. N. Bialik, David Frischmann and Joseph Hayyim Brenner, Y. D. Berkovitz, and Zalman Shneur, all of whom recognized his unique and captivating style. He continued to write after the outbreak of the war and published some of his poems in the Warsaw underground press. Katzenelson's life revolved around these three axes—education, theater, and creative writing.

While in Łodz, Katzenelson regularly attended the Borochov Agricultural Training Farm and was a great supporter of Zionism. He had always hoped for continued resettlement in Palestine and was an avid supporter of his relative Berl Katzenelson, leader of the Zionist labor movement and a central figure of the second Aliyah and Palestine. During this time, Katzenelson visited Palestine several times but did not fulfill his dream of settling there. During the early years of the war he was in the Warsaw ghetto, where his wife and two of his sons were killed. It was at this time that he joined the Jewish partisan organization *Deror*, and apart from other activities, he published some of his poems in the movement's magazine, founded and managed the movement's theatrical group, and educated the younger members. In May 1943 Katzenelson, who had possession of a fake Honduran passport, was transferred to the Vittel concentration camp in France. Vittel, a small town in eastern France, had once been a holiday resort, but during the war it became an internment camp for prisoners who were British, North American, South American, and Poles. Writer Menachem Poznansky and Katzenelson corresponded during the latter's stay in Vittel. In April 1944 Katzenelson was deported to Auschwitz, where he and his surviving son perished on 3 May 1944.

Katzenelson's works are typified by lightness underscored by a deep elegiac tone. His stories, however, especially those composed for or about children, always begin with an assurance that all will end well; the tragic dimension is present but never forms the main bulk of his fiction. His greatest strength was in delivering sensory accounts of an experience, a feeling, or an event, simply transforming the facts of the matter into perfect lyrical expressions that capture the most elementary and tenuous details that make each subject unique.

Katzenelson is of the same generation as Bialik, a generation of poets with an individualistic style, each bearing his own specific trademark. Katzenelson was known for his poetry's naiveté and its childlike beauty. This innocence, it has been said, was not forced or recreated but was a quality that the young writer was innately familiar with. Not only in his children's poems do his mischief and frivolity come to poetic expression, but also in his later works produced after the onset of the war. Innocent, simple, and basic feelings were given perfect artistic expression through a free and flexible approach to rhythm and the poetic medium. Katzenelson allowed himself to deviate from the accepted norms of rhyme and meter, utilizing perhaps before all others a colloquial dialect of a Hebrew yet not thoroughly spoken in the Diaspora. At times, this colloquialism lends innocence to the delivered material; at other times, it heightens the pathos and tragic depth of his poems.

Katzenelson enchanted his readers with his long poems, but most acclaimed were his works of Hebrew drama. His home in Łodz was a center for local Jewish authors and artists, and Katzenelson was greatly admired by contemporary authors and poets—Bialik, I. L. Peretz, Frischman, Brenner, Y. D. Berkovitz, and David Shimoni. His songs, which became symbols of the Jewish spirit in the Diaspora, contain an element of the prewar existence of European Jewry that encompasses the hope, strength, and collectivism that typified his life and that of his colleagues and contemporaries.

Commonly perceived as a secular writer celebrating newfound secularism in Jewish life in the Diaspora at the turn of the century, Katzenelson is also seen by some as a firm believer. This view is further supported by the fact of his adherence to both Hebrew, the language of renewal and rebirth, and Yiddish, the language of his forefathers and their rich heritage. His bilingualism is central in his writing.

Vittel Diary

The only two texts in Katzenelson's possession in the Vittel concentration camp were a Bible and a collection of C. N. Bialik's poems. These two texts—the earliest and the latest artifacts of Hebrew literature—together with the poet's increasing sense of doom, contributed to the writing of his diary. He also composed a play while in Vittel, but his writing in the first year in the camp was fragmented and angst-ridden. From the pages of his diary emerges the unvanquished light that shines from his endless love for those who died and those who were yet to die.

The diary, although aimed at recording the daily happenings in Vittel, contains mostly exclamations of terror and anger in the face of the events the author had witnessed and experienced. The entries occur on most days, but at times there is a long break between entries. These form not a view into the inner workings of a concentration camp, but a lens through which the reader may understand the feelings of a man who saw and knew what was taking place around him, and the emotional reaction that the sights and sounds aroused within him. The words contained in the *Vittel diary* are the memoirs of a murdered nation, containing the outcry and the elegy for the victims, as well as hatred and vengefulness against their murderers. The writer of the diary clearly believes that the Jews of the Warsaw ghetto knew they were doomed, that the transports would not bring them to different labor camps; yet they wanted to believe that they were traveling to a labor camp. Katzenelson explains the refusal to believe that the Germans were systematically slaughtering the Jewish population was proof that the Jews retained their humanity. "Blessed are we," he wrote, "that could not believe it! We could not believe it because of the Image of God that is in us. Only a heart tainted with villainy could comprehend or imagine the possibility of such an abomination!" (quoted by Alexander, p. 25). Katzenelson demands justice—punishment for those who committed the atrocities he witnessed, as well as a blessing for the remains of the nation, and a prophecy for what was to take place after his death. Katzenelson voices not a muted cry, but a livid exclamation:

> No! No! It must be recorded. The whole world must know what happened. A whole nation has been murdered in broad daylight before its very eyes, yet no one has ventured to utter a word! Not a single drop of our blood must go forfeit. The whole story must be told. (*The Literature of Destruction: Jewish Responses to Catastrophe,* David Roskies ed. Philadelphia: JPS, 1989, p. 532).

Song of the Murdered Jewish People

Song of the Murdered Jewish People was written between 3 October 1943 and 18 January 1944 in the Vittel concentration camp. Despite being one of his final works, it was the first to be published, in Paris in 1945. The long Yiddish poem contains fifteen cantos, each of which is dated and has fifteen stanzas of four lines. After three and one-half months of writing, Katzenelson, aided by a fellow internee at Vittel, Mrs. M. Novitz, hid the poems in the ground, hermetically sealed in three bottles, beneath the roots of an old tree, "by the exit, on the right, beside the sixth column with a crack in the middle," relates Novitz (*Vittel Diary*, 20 ed. Israel: Ghetto Fighters' House & Hakibbutz Hameuchad House, 1972, p. 38).

The undying love for those who had perished fueled Katzenelson's poem, rekindling the flame that was quivering toward darkness. Like his diary, this poem expresses a call to make audible all the muted voices of the dead and dying. In the first canto of the poem, the poet exclaims:

> Scream from the beasts' entrails in the wood, from the fish in the river
> That devoured you. Scream from furnaces. Scream, young and old.
> I want a shriek, an outcry, a sound, I want a sound from you,
> Scream, O murdered Jewish people, scream, and scream aloud!
>
> (*The Literature of Destruction: Jewish Responses to Catastrophe*, p. 532).

Rather than focusing on chronological order, the poet focuses on moments in the genocidal process, the particular experience that epitomizes the catastrophe. Illustrative is his lament for the murdered children in Canto VI (2–4 November 1943). The canto begins with reference to the great deportations of the Warsaw ghetto, "ten thousand Jews a day. . . . Soon they took fifteen thousand." He moves on in the third strophe to characterize Warsaw as a "wasteland," "a cemetery," and then in the persona of hidden witness focuses on the lost children, individual Jewish children, terrified, weeping, comforting younger siblings:

> Almost all without father or mother, eaten by cold, hunger and vermin,
> Saintly messiahs, sanctified by pain . . .
> Flung into the big wagons like heaps of dung—
> And were carried off, killed, exterminated . . . (p. 540).

In this fusion of the lyricism of agony with the objective chronology of events, the poet mourns the loved ones and accuses a passive deity whom he indicts for deceiving the Jewish people who dutifully upheld the covenant.

The dominant response to this poem is characterized by astonishment at the writer's transformation from a "favorite son" indulging in entertaining parables and light-hearted poetry to the prophetic mourner of Jewish annihilation in the Diaspora. There is, however, a counterargument that claims that the writer's earlier works contain the seeds for the resonant poem discussed herein. From the mid-1930s, Katzenelson developed an intuitive awareness that accurately predicted the fate of European Jewry. Some have argued further that the existential anguish that emerges in some of Katzenelson's prewar works may indicate an uncanny depth of emotion and perception of Jewish life in the Diaspora, not simply an acceptance of Jewish tradition as grounded and complete but as an entity that one must continuously struggle to maintain. As embodied in the writer's pseudonym *Yitzhak Ivke* (in Hebrew "he shall laugh, he shall cry"), the dualism of these two polar attitudes toward life exists in many of his earlier works.

At the time he wrote his poem, Katzenelson already knew the magnitude of Jewish annihilation in Europe. He had lived in Warsaw and lost his wife and two of his sons. This poem, a unique composite of poetry and documentation, delivers an impressive account of his experience in a way that still maintains his romantic lyrical prowess. The tragic permutations of life in the ghettos and camps are preceded by an introduction, followed by an account of the great Warsaw ghetto deportation of 1942, an account of the events in Łodz in 1939, and the personal losses that were suffered there. This is then followed by a delivery of the beginning of the revolt and the destruction of the ghetto and a final epilogue that broadly encompasses the experience of genocide in Poland and the poet's cry for revenge. He commemorates those who had died—mentioning their names, evoking their spirits, imagining them standing en masse before him, in their millions, unable to see him. He describes the abductions, the violence with which families were separated, and the actions of the Jewish police.

In the ninth chapter, the centerpiece of the poem, Katzenelson decries

> And thus it came to pass, and this was the beginning . . . Heavens tell me, why?
> Tell me, why this, O why? What have we done to merit such disgrace?
> The earth is dumb and deaf, she closed her eyes. But you, heavens on high,
> You saw it happen and looked on, from high, and did not turn your face (p. 541).

For those who shared Katzenelson's camp experience and knew his writing, Katzenelson was perceived as the one who would "immortalize their agony and their struggle." In its link to lamentation tradition, Katzenelson's work achieved, according to Sidra Ezrahi, the status of "national elegy" (p. 107).

Bibliography

Primary Sources

Vittel Diary (22.5.43–16.9.43). 1964.

Lid funem oysge'harg'etn yidishn folk (German & Yiddish). *Dos Lied vunem ojsgehargetn jidischn volk* (*Grosser Gesang vom ausgrerotteten judischen Volk*) (*The Song of the Murdered Jewish People*). 1945.

Secondary Sources

Alexander, Edward. *The Resonance of Dust: Essays on Holocaust Literature and Jewish Fate*. Columbus: Ohio University Press, 1979.

Even-Shoshan, Shlomo. *Al Ha'Avnaim—Besod Sofrim uSefarim* (On Potter's Wheels, about Writers and Books). Tel Aviv, Israel: Hakibbutz Hameuchad Publishing House, 1979.

Ezrahi, Sidra DeKoven. *By Words Alone: The Holocaust in Literature*. Chicago: University of Chicago Press, 1980.

Helman, Yudka, ed. *Edut* (Witness) 11 (December 1994).

Roskies, David, ed. *The Literature of Destruction: Jewish Responses to Catastrophe*. Philadelphia: The Jewish Publication Society, 1988.

Sadan, Dov. *Bein Din LeHeshbon—Masot al Sofrim uSefarim* (Between Debate and Reckoning). Tel Aviv, Israel: Dvir Publication, 1963.

Weinfeld, David, ed. *HaShira HaIvrit BePolin bein shtei Milchamot HaOlam* (Hebrew Poetry in Poland between the Two World Wars). Jerusalem: Bialik Institute, 1997.

KA. TZETNIK (Yehiel Dinur)

(1909–2001)

ZIVA SHAVITSKY

IN 2001, THE anonymous author Ka. Tzetnik—Yehiel Dinur—passed away in Israel. Until this time, his life had been shrouded with mystery, despite his enormous success as a novelist. Only since his death have his readers been able to discover the true details of his life. He was also known as Yehiel Feiger, changing his name to Dinur when he came to Israel, and many believed he was born in 1971. Very little is known about his parents, siblings, and wife, all of whom died in the Holocaust. Dinur studied at the Yeshivah in Lublin, and worked in Poland as a journalist. He also wrote Hebrew poetry, some of which was published in *Darkenu* (Our Path), a periodical based in Velsen, from 1939 to 1940. With his internment in Auschwitz, this prior life dissolved into thin air, giving way to the monolithic experience of being a Holocaust survivor. Dinur's works embody the central dilemma of an author struggling to grapple with the memory of the Holocaust, simultaneously compelled to write about it and yet unable to express it.

Life and Career

Yehiel Dinur chose the name Ka. Tzetnik 135633, his concentration camp number, as a pseudonym. His was not a literary pseudonym, he claimed, because he did not believe that his writings were literary; rather, he simply wrote the testimonies of those whose right to do so themselves was brutally taken away from them. He stated this claim when giving testimony in the Adolph Eichmann trial in Israel, in June 1961, a testimony that led to his collapse before the seated listeners and before the executioner, protected in his glass booth. Dinur testified:

> I was in the planet of Auschwitz for about two years. Time there is not like it is here on earth. Every moment passes there along different wheels of time. The inhabitants of that planet had no names, they had no parents, they had no children. They didn't wear clothes as we do here. They breathed according to different laws of nature. They didn't live according to the rules of this world. They were never born, they never conceived. Their name was a number. . . . ("Eichmann Trial—The District Court Sessions." www.nizkat.org / hweb / people / e / eichmannadolf\transcripts\sessions\session–068–01).

At the trial Dinur was presented with the iconic striped uniform of the camp. It was his own, and he kept it for sixteen years. He was Ka. Tzetnik, a survivor. In the Tel Aviv courtroom, he returned to Auschwitz.

The details of Dinur's identity before he became an internee at Auschwitz were erased with the imposition of his number—135633. In effect, he was born in 1943, in Auschwitz, delivered by the *kapo* soldier who burned the numbers into his arm. The letters *Ka* and *Tze* (K and Z in German) stand for *Konzentrationslager*—concentration camp. He was reluctant to be interviewed, reluctant to speak at the trial of the man who ripped his ticket to freedom, a fake Honduran passport, into shreds and discarded it so nonchalantly some four decades earlier. Dinur was always battling to keep his two identities separate. Ka. Tzetnik and Dinur were two separate individuals, and two that the man could not reconcile. Having to state his real name in the Eichmann trial was an aberration to his mind, and this is what led to his collapse.

Dinur began writing about the Holocaust shortly after he was rescued from it, in February 1945. While staying in a British military camp in Italy, he wrote *Salamandra*, which was published in Israel before the author's arrival there in 1947. In Israel Dinur continued writing but could only do so enclosed in the basement that was his room in Tel Aviv. He would write there for weeks, without coming into contact with the outside world, submerged in a trance. Even after his marriage to Nina Asherman and the birth of their two children, he continued writing in this fashion. Two decades after his arrival in Israel, at the urging of his wife, the author left for Switzerland and underwent a series of experimental therapeutic sessions that utilized hallucinatory substances in order to recover from the posttraumatic shock he was suffering. He never completed the sessions.

Dinur also published *House of Dolls, The Clock* and *Piepel*, all semi autobiographical novels centering on the character of Harry Preleshnik in *Star Eternal*, a reflection of Dinur himself. Harry Preleshnik appears in volume 1 of *Salamandra*, and volume 2 of *House of Dolls* focuses on Harry's sister Daniella. Expressing his own sense of destiny, Dinur writes about Preleshnik: "They had left him behind on their way to the crematorium. In each one's eyes was the command: Tell it! Do not forget! He had to keep going until he had fulfilled his vow!" (pp. 118–119).

Loss of time is a central theme in Dinur's works. People no longer know their age, the seasons; the Jewish calendar loses its relevance to life. This is heightened by Dinur's shift from past to present tense in his narration. Memory too is obliterated. Whenever memory returns to life in Auschwitz, it brings pain to the characters. People are stripped of their names, as the author himself expressed so poignantly in his insistence to remain Ka. Tzetnik. People's individual identity relates solely to their number, and this is the only thing that may salvage them from death.

Salamander

A salamander is a wondrous animal, described in legend as being born in a place where fire burns for seven consecutive years. So is the main protagonist of the story at hand, who lives through the inferno of the seven years of the war; and so is the general sense one gets from Dinur's literary works—that had it not been for the survivors, the salamanders that lived through all the hellish torment of the Holocaust, the story of those who perished would not have made it through the inferno.

The novel tells the story of Harry Preleshnik, a gifted Jewish musician living in Poland. Harry falls in love with Sonia Schmidt, the daughter of an industrialist who decides to migrate to Israel but does not do so. Harry witnesses the growing Nazi threat and wishes to join Sonia and her father in Israel. But Schmidt rejects Harry's request because of the harsh living conditions in Israel at the time. What follows is the Holocaust, the life of slavery and constant fear of death in the ghetto, further suffering in the concentration camp, and final death in Auschwitz. Harry manages to survive, but his beloved Sonia does not, despite her wisdom and cunningness, despite her survival in the Warsaw rebellion. Harry, whose job is to remove gold teeth from the burnt bodies, recognizes her emaciated corpse by the black birthmark on her cheek. The novel describes the impossible situations with which people had to contend in the Holocaust, and the power of loyalty in such events.

House of Dolls

This novel, like Dinur's other works, is semidocumentary and semiautobiographical. The people and the facts of being in Auschwitz are changed, but the experiences described are as truthful and loyal to reality as can be found in a novel. This book, as well as *Piepel*, are a continuation to *Salamander*, and together they form a history of sorts of a Jewish family in the twentieth century from the perspective of the sole survivor. *House of Dolls* describes the life and death of Daniella Preleshnik, the author's own sister. She was only fourteen years old when the war began. Having completed her school year, basking in the glory of an innocent adolescent life, she goes for a trip with her friends from which she never returns. She is sent to a women's camp that serves as a brothel for German soldiers; this is the House of Dolls. Daniella's torturous experiences in this hellish world of perverse barbarism are described from the moment of her departure from her parents' home to her death by the bullet of an SS officer. Moni, her younger brother, also becomes the victim of Nazi sadism and features more prominently in Dinur's novel *Piepel*, titled after the term for a boy used by the block chiefs (barracks commanders) for sexual gratification.

Part of the experience of Auschwitz is the distortion or perversion of language by camp commanders. For example, the word "latrine" changes meaning in this parallel universe: "All the world knows what latrines are for. Doubtless, that is what they were set up for in Auschwitz, too. But here everybody knows that 'latrine' means 'stock exchange.' " The latrine becomes a metaphor for the function of Auschwitz as a whole, the place where exchange of life occurs, no longer a place in the periphery of human life.

The Clock

The Clock, published in English as *Star Eternal*, is a distillation of the Holocaust experience. It is structured as a prologue and epilogue to the event, both taking place in the narrator's town, Metropolis. This structure reinforces the fragmented experience of life before the Holocaust, and life after it. Time, represented by the city's big electric clock, seems to stand still, thus losing its meaning in life. Over the wartime years encompassed in the novel (1939–1945), nothing had changed. Dinur uses a simple form of Hebrew. He seems reluctant to seek aid from rich metaphorical descriptions of the event and its experience, but finds space in a limited, restrained, and thorough literary mode. This laconic style gives perfect expression to the author's experience and that of his characters, as though language, too, had been traumatized and dulled.

One way in which Dinur delivers the immediacy of the experience is by speaking in second person, addressing each and every reader—when you stand there, face to face with the "other planet" (Bartov, p. 54). Another way in which Dinur cuts to the heart of the Holocaust experience is by personifying Death, which becomes tangible and omnipresent in the novel. The reader is penetrated by sentences like "They moved through . . . creatures whose will had been completely drained from their veins" (*House of Dolls*, p. 85).

The events of the Holocaust are not described in a causal, logical progression. Events such as the digging of mass graves for Jewish victims by Jewish hands are presented suddenly, without background information or preparation. This technique parallels the abruptness with which these events occurred in the lives of those ensnared in the war.

Themes

In all these works, as well as the other works that make up the grand opus subtitled *The Chronicles of a Jewish Family in the Twentieth Century*, a linking thread is love—a unique kind of love that can only grow in a place like Auschwitz, a love that would cause someone to give his last crumb of bread to his friend. Harry's love for Sonia is that which keeps him alive through all the abominations. Even after her death, their love continues to save him from death, as it is this love that propels him to live. Likewise, it is Harry's younger sister Daniella's love for him that keeps her alive. Dinur writes of his love for all those people in his life whose experiences are delivered in these novels.

> He was surprised: Why did he feel no fear? But he was not surprised. He was happy with it, comfortable not feeling fear. No one could harm him now. He felt that now he had crossed the border. Once there was a border, and he crossed it. Crossed—but did not go far. He could still look back, to the place he had left, and could see everything, everything, as if he were still there.

This absence of fear is linked to the absence of tears in the camps themselves. Tears, writes the author, are the normal human expression of suffering. In the camps, no one cries, because no one can. Life here is not normal, people do not behave naturally. The only semblance of normality remains with the narrator. Having known some of the internees before the war, he comments on their changed behavior, their altered faces, dulled of life. He can comment, judge, and write about the atrocities in a macabre way, looking at them through the eyes of the Nazi guards, calling the piles of corpses "filth." Finally, the narrator too loses all humanity, is prevented from feeling sorrow, and is unable to shed a tear.

Critical Reaction

The reception of Ka. Tzetnik's works was mixed. His sextet has an unrelenting obsession with violence and perversity that made the books popular among Israeli-born youth before 1967, and yet the books were also the target of much criticism for the very elements that made the stories so gripping. Ka. Tzetnik's writing has been said to be at times mediocre, with an immature and melodramatic delivery of relationships between adults, both sexual and emotional, which is probably the reason the novels were so popular with younger audiences. However, many critics, while acknowledging these limitations, still commend Ka. Tzetnik for his ability to write about the Holocaust in an undistilled, raw, and highly disturbing fashion that transcends other banal or simplified artistic representations of the events. Ka. Tzetnik also surpasses other Holocaust fiction in the poignant realization that all those involved in the Holocaust were replaceable; moreover, he realizes that had he himself been standing in the place of the SS officer, and the latter was interned in Auschwitz, events would have unraveled no differently than the way divulged in these novels.

What is unique about Dinur's writing about the Holocaust experience is that he enhances fact. Guided by it, motivated by it, and traumatized by it, the author gives it superior permanency by giving it an expression that is lacking in a pure documentary style of writing. He lends emotion to the torment and injects every character with humanity. These are not sketches or snapshots of the people who perished, but a detailed description of their crises and inner turmoil. Dinur does not write suspenseful or sensationalistic literature, but he succeeds in recreating the anomaly that makes the Holocaust such an irreconcilable existential experience and such a rich basis for creative expression.

Nina Dinur, the author's wife and translator, wrote: "Ka. Tzetnik 135633 regards his work as 'an act of faith in humanity, faith in the Fourth Dimension.' This was born of the belief that survival was granted him by God-at-Auschwitz in exchange for the vow: 'To continue telling of this Other Planet even unto the last of my breath.' "

Bibliography

Primary Sources

Salamandra. (Sunrise Over Hell). 1946.

(Beit ha-bubot: khronikah shel mishpahah Yehudit ba-meah ha-esrim). *House of Dolls*: The chronicles of a Jewish Family in the Twentieth Century. 1953.

Ha-Shaon (Star Eternal). 1960.

Kar ∴ o Lo Piepel (They Called Him Piepel). 1961.

Ka-hol-Me-effer (Sequel to the House of Dolls). 1966.

Piepel. 1988.

Shivitti. 1988.

Ha-imut. 1989.

Ha-tsofen. 1994.

Secondary Sources

Bartov, Omer. "Kitsch and Sadism in Ka-Tzetnik's Other Planet: Israeli Youth Imagining the Holocaust" *Jewish Social Studies* 3, 2 (1997): 42–76.

Brierly, William D. "Memory in the Work of Yehiel Dinur." *Hebrew Literature in the Wake of the Holocaust*. Edited by Leon I. Yudkin. Rutherford, N.J.: Fairleigh Dickinson University Press, 1993.

Dinur, Nina, quoted in "Ka-Tzetnik 135633." *Contemporary Authors Online* 1999.

Liptzin, Solomon. *A History of Yiddish Literature*. New York: Jonathan David Publishers, 1988.

Litvin, Eran, ed. *Madrich beNose HaShoah uTekumat Israel beSifrei Ka-Tzetnik*. (*Reference Guide Anthology*, on: "*Shoah* and Israel's Revival in the Books of K. Tzetnik"). Tel Aviv: Hakibbutz Hameuchad Publishing House, 1993.

Yudkin, Leon I., ed. *Hebrew Literature in the Wake of the Holocaust*. Rutherford, N.J.: Fairleigh Dickinson University Press, 1993.

LOUISE KEHOE

(1949–)

DAVID BRAUNER

BORN LOUISE LUBETKIN in 1949 in Durham, England, the daughter of a well-known Russian avant-garde architect, Berthold Lubetkin, and Margaret Church, one of the first women to be admitted to England's most prestigious architectural school, Louise Kehoe was forty years old when she first discovered her Jewish ancestry. Having initially studied pharmacy at Nottingham University, Kehoe graduated from Bristol University Dental School in 1974 and set up her own practice, where she worked for nine years before suffering a nervous collapse brought on by anorexia nervosa. She moved, with her husband, Len, to the United States in 1984. After the death of her father in 1991, the revelation of her Jewish past, and in particular the fate of her paternal grandparents (who were murdered at Auschwitz), became the catalyst for a process of voracious self-education ("I read everything that I could lay my hands on concerning Jewish history, culture and tradition" ["What Being Jewish Means to Me," 1995]) that led to Kehoe's conversion to Judaism in 1994. In 1995 she published *In This Dark House*, an account of her journey from a deeply troubled childhood, adolescence, and early adulthood to the point of her conversion. A freelance journalist and garden designer, Kehoe lives with her husband in New Hampshire.

Work

In This Dark House is a difficult book to classify. A second-generation Holocaust memoir that barely mentions the Holocaust; a book about Jewish identity in which, for nine-tenths of the narrative, there appear to be no Jews; the history of a family whose history is fictitious; a partly fictionalized account of a life whose bare facts can hardly be imagined, *In This Dark House* focuses on the troubled relationship between the author and her father, Berthold Lubetkin. In 1939, at the height of his fame, the Russian-born avant-garde architect (perhaps best known for the Penguin Pool at London Zoo) abruptly left his thriving London practice to live and work as a farmer in the remote rural village of Upper Killington in Gloucestershire, in a house portentously named World's End. Lubetkin and his English wife, Margaret, went on to have four children (though the second child, Andrew, died tragically at the age of two after a botched tonsillectomy), the last of whom was Louise. Raising his three remaining children in "an atmosphere of . . . resolute misanthropy" (*In This Dark House*, New York: Penguin, p. 30) and "deliberately . . . igniting a savage rivalry" (p. 22) between them, Lubetkin is a psychologically and physically abusive, despotic, and at times sadistic father; the book contains many harrowing accounts not simply of Lubetkin's profound cruelty to his children, but of the legacy of this cruelty in later life. In her thirties, for example, Kehoe enters an abusive relationship and later develops a near-fatal case of anorexia nervosa as a result of the "leaden sense of worthlessness" (p. 85) engendered in her by her father. Yet Margaret Lubetkin—"Mama," as she is known by the children and by Lubetkin himself,

> insisted against all the evidence that he did indeed love us, and that if only we knew him better . . . then we would understand what made him the monster he could sometimes be, and would forgive him for it. "One day," she said, "he'll explain everything to you. Then you'll understand" (p. 52).

As it turns out, despite vowing to do so at Mama's deathbed, Lubetkin never does explain himself, and it's left to Kehoe to uncover the truth: Lubetkin is a Jew who has (perhaps) never forgiven himself for having failed (or failed even to try) to rescue his parents from Nazi-occupied Warsaw (they were eventually deported from the Warsaw ghetto to Auschwitz, where they were killed).

Because Kehoe defers this revelation until very late in the book, while at the same time planting clues in the manner of an author of detective fiction, many of the crucial episodes in *In This Dark Room* accrue a retrospective resonance, or to put it another way, are imbued with dramatic irony for the reader with foreknowledge of the narrative. These ironies and resonances extend from the apparently mundane statement that "Just about the only aspect of Dad's past about which there was no doubt . . . was that Berthold Lubetkin was not his real name" (p. 55) (in fact it is his real name) to the emotive description of one of the "savage rituals of farming life" (p. 42), the removal of the least fit cows from the herd for slaughter:

> At some point there would be a head count, and it would be determined that a sufficient number of the herd had been singled out. Then the tall-sided cattle truck, which had been parked across the driveway as an additional barricade, was maneuvered into the entry of the farmyard. The back of the truck was flung open, a ramp was let down, and the loading began . . . The men encircled the hapless animals, beating and clubbing them, forcing them forward up the ramp (p. 43).

Disturbed by the plight of these cows, the young Kehoe asks Mama what their fate is to be, and is not reassured by the explanation that they are being taken to market to be sold to other farmers.

> I had seen the once-placid brown eyes, now dilated with terror, staring accusingly out at me through the air vents in the side of the truck, and I had lain awake at night after the cows had gone, listening to the mournful lowing of the lucky ones . . . who, because they were still useful, had been allowed to stay—until the next time (p. 44).

On a first reading, this account might seem simply to be an indictment of the inhumane treatment of farm animals, but on rereading it in the light of the fate of Kehoe's grandparents (to whom her book is dedicated), or to a mind from the outset "engraved with the Holocaust" (to use Norma Rosen's suggestive phrase), it functions as an analogue for the Nazi treatment of the Jews, in particular for the daily inspection at the death camps that divided the inmates into two lines: the frailer herded into the gas chambers, the stronger granted a temporary stay of execution. The Holocaust is more directly invoked later in the book, when Kehoe describes seeing newsreel footage of "the liberation of Buchenwald and the burning of the Warsaw ghetto" and visiting the "eerie statue of an emaciated figure which stands alone on the shore of a quiet, clear-watered lake near Nantua in southwest France, a memorial to the thousands of Jews who were zealously rounded up by the Vichy regime and deported to their deaths in Auschwitz" (pp. 95, 96). This image haunts her even before she realizes that she has any connection with those victims of the Nazis, and it hints at a symbolic link between the skeletal figures of the camp inmates and her own starved body during her period of anorexia.

Indeed, in its treatment of Kehoe's anorexia and its origins, *In This Dark Room* is ostensibly very much a story of its time and place: like many autobiographical accounts of abusive childhoods published in America in the last decade, it is a story of survival, with a strong redemptive trajectory, tracing the author's emergence from a state of suicidal despair that manifests itself most clearly in the near-fatal episode of anorexia, into a sense of self-worth. Disinherited by her father, she reclaims her birthright; disconnected from her real Jewish family, she becomes "part of an enormous, venerable worldwide family" that provides her with a larger "feeling of connectedness" ("What Being Jewish Means to Me"). In the process of searching for Lubetkin she finds herself, and even apparently finds it in herself to forgive him: the book finishes with a symbolic gesture of reconciliation in which Kehoe buries a soft toy cherished by her and her father under an apple tree at World's End with the words: "You need him more than I do. I think you always did" (*In This Dark House*, p. 230).

Yet this is, finally, neither a triumphalist nor a conciliatory book. What remains with the reader is not Kehoe's compassionate attempt to understand, and even at times to extenuate her father's behavior ("I think," she speculates, in spite of all evidence to the contrary, that "Dad secretly hoped that the truth would one day come out" and that he "longed to stop running and come home" [pp. 220, 223]), but her indictment of his double betrayal of his parents: "By hiding his Jewishness and denying his identity he was in effect turning his back on his parents, abandoning them to their horrible fate, murdering them all over again" (p. 223). It is not so much the healing of the wounds as their perpetration that invest *In This Dark House* with a visceral power. Although Kehoe explains her father's abuse of her and her siblings in terms of displaced self-hatred ("He hated himself . . . for surviving . . . And . . . he let his bitter self-loathing spill over to taint his children . . . who reminded him daily of his parents and his past" [p. 215]), this is not so much a book about survivor guilt, or indeed about the Holocaust, but rather about the damage that a culture of secrecy and betrayal within a family inflicts on all its members.

Bibliography

Primary Sources

In This Dark House. 1995.

"What Being Jewish Means to Me." *New York Times*, 12 March 1995.

"The Lives of Berthold Lubetkin." Directed by David Kerr. *The Works*, BBC 2 May 1996.

Secondary Source

Brauner, David. *Post-War Jewish Fiction: Ambivalence, Self-Explanation and Transatlantic Connections*. Harmondsworth: Palgrave, 2001.

Thomas Keneally

(1935–)

SUE VICE

THOMAS KENEALLY was born in Sydney, Australia, on 7 October 1935 into a family of Irish Catholic origin. After high school at St. Patrick's College, Strathfield, Keneally trained as a priest at St. Patrick's College, Manly. He abandoned his theological studies in 1960, yet a thread of wry Catholicism persists in his writing. Keneally worked as a laborer, clerk, and schoolteacher before the publication of his first novel, *The Place at Whitton*, in 1964. He married Judith Martin in 1965; they had two daughters, Margaret and Jane, and divided their time between Sydney and Bilgola, a beach community north of the city. In 1967 Keneally won the prestigious Miles Franklin Award for *Bring Larks and Heroes*, which allowed him to work full-time as a writer.

After 1967 Keneally produced almost a book a year, covering subjects that range from Joan of Arc to aboriginal history, World War I to contemporary Sudan. His novel *Bettany's Book* (2000) concerns a present-day Australian woman's interest in her roots. Keneally has also served as a Distinguished Professor of English and Comparative Literature at the University of California, Irvine, where he taught in the university's program in writing.

Keneally's work has been nominated for the Booker Prize four times: in 1972 for *The Chant of Jimmie Blacksmith* (which also won the Royal Society of Literature Award), for *Gossip from the Forest* in 1975, and for *Confederates* in 1979. He won the prize in 1982 with *Schindler's Ark*, which also won the *Los Angeles Times* fiction prize. In Australia, Keneally has won the Miles Franklin Award (given to literary works depicting Australian life and settings) twice, for *Bring Larks and Heroes* (1967) and *Three Cheers for the Paraclete* (1968). Thomas Keneally was awarded the Order of Australia in 1983 for his services to Australian literature. He is also a fellow of the Royal Society of Literature, and a fellow of the American Academy of Arts and Sciences.

A Catholic Author

Keneally's Catholic background and eclectic interests would not necessarily lead the reader to expect the kinds of work he has produced nor a great interest in the Holocaust. Yet it was a novel about the Holocaust, *Schindler's Ark* (which in the United States has always been known as *Schindler's List*) that cemented his reputation as an internationally esteemed novelist. Keneally's novels usually show an interest in retrieving lost histories, especially those of oppressed or minority groups. His works often pit an individual against his or her social environment. For instance, *A Family Madness* (1985) is about a fading rugby professional who casts off his former life as a result of encountering Belorussian exiles living in Sydney. Other than *Schindler's Ark*, *A Family Madness* is the only Keneally work that touches on the Holocaust era, although its concern is with the perpetrators of genocide while Jews are entirely offstage. In *Schindler's List*, the pattern of individual resistance to circumstances reaches its extreme: Oskar Schindler lives among but works against the Nazi hierarchy in occupied Poland.

Schindler's List is striking as an example of Holocaust literature. As is the case for many imaginative works on the Holocaust, there has been some question about its generic status: Is it fictionalized history or a documentary novel? The question of generic classification is made harder because *Schindler's List* does not so much rely on historical documentation as a springboard for fiction (as does, for instance, D. M. Thomas's *The White Hotel*) but rather sets itself the task of bringing such documentation to the public's attention through fictional means. Keneally's novel is also unusual in treating a Holocaust rescuer; other texts tend to concentrate on survivors (Saul Bellow's *Mr. Sammler's Planet*) or perpetrators (Martin Amis's *Time's Arrow*). In this sense *Schindler's Ark* is a Holocaust text with a "happy ending," one that is not set in the camps and concerns survival rather than death. Although some critics have lamented the interest shown in the unrepresentative nature of Schindler's story, it is its very atypicality that makes it engaging. The adaptation of Keneally's book into Steven Spielberg's 1993 film *Schindler's List* sparked off great interest in Schindler and other rescuers and contributed to growing interest in the Holocaust, especially since the film's release coincided with the fiftieth anniversary of the liberation of the camps.

Keneally's concern with injustice, histories of oppression, and the role of the individual in history is surely the genesis of his interest in the story of Oskar Schindler. Schindler is credited with rescuing 1,100 people: He is one of the very few individuals who saved over a thousand Jews. This Sudeten German—an ethnic German living in Moravia, in Czechoslovakia—was an unsuccessful entrepreneur before the war. He went to Poland in December 1939 at the age of thirty-one looking for business opportunities and established an enamelware factory in Cracow that he staffed with Jewish workers. The factory was enlisted, ironically, to supply ammunition for the German war effort. Although it was not notable for its success in this endeavor, it did provide a secure haven for its workers. Schindler achieved this feat through his close professional and personal connections with the local Nazis, in particular Amon Goeth, the commandant of the slave-labor camp at Plaszów on the outskirts of Cracow. Goeth was one of many Nazis Schindler charmed and bribed in order to get his way.

Schindler's factory was transferred from Cracow to Brinnlitz, Moravia, in 1944 when the Cracow ghetto was due to be liquidated, and he insisted that all the Jews on his list of workers accompany him. Schindler managed to keep "his" Jews alive until the end of the war through a mixture of brazenness and chicanery. After the war, Schindler failed to prosper and was often helped out by the Jews he had rescued, whom he took to meeting for reunions. He died in reduced circumstances in Germany at age sixty-two and is buried in the Catholic cemetery in Jerusalem.

The occasion on which Keneally learned about Schindler has become something of an apocryphal story and was related time and again during the filming of *Schindler's List*. While on vacation in Beverly Hills, Keneally visited the luggage shop belonging to Leopold Page. He bought a briefcase but also gained the idea for a novel. Page, né Poldek Pfefferberg, was one of the 1,100 Jews rescued by Oskar Schindler during World War II, and he told Keneally his story on this and many subsequent occasions. The character based on Pfefferberg is one of the few substantial Jewish figures in Keneally's novel.

Keneally's account of this meeting reveals several significant features about the genesis of his book. First, like most of Keneally's projects, this text is historically based. Secondly, although its central focus is Schindler, the picture of him presented in the book relies on the testimony of many of the Jews he rescued as well as on Schindler's own postwar account of his actions. Third, the viewpoint that readers get in *Schindler's List* is largely that of Leopold Page and others like him who recall Schindler with great warmth and gratitude. This means that rather than trying to chart the mysterious and intriguing progress of an apparently amoral, womanizing businessman who appears accidentally to have fallen into the role of rescuer, Keneally assumes from the beginning an altruistic Schindler with a plan of rescue. Such an assumption makes the story more plot- than psychology-driven.

Keneally initially insisted that his work was factual and that *Schindler's Ark*, as it was then known in Britain, was described thus in the publisher's publicity before publication. Yet the text is not even journalistic; it is a novel, a fact that became clear to editors at Hodder and Stoughton, the British publisher, when Keneally's typescript was received and read. This realization led the publishers to recategorize the book and issue it as fiction but with an explanatory author's note by Keneally. In this note Keneally claimed to have used "the texture and devices of a novel to tell a true story" (p. 13), in other words to have been selective about the material he used, to have speculated on people's inner states and "reconstructed" conversations, and to have created a narrative out of raw material that was rather more chaotic than it now appears. To the material he gathered about Schindler, Keneally introduced chronology, pace, and patterning, including the highlighting of set-piece scenes (such as the game of cards played by Schindler and Goeth over Helen Hirsch's future) and the introduction of literary imagery, such as the opposition between the "dark brothers" Schindler and Goeth, one a rescuer, the other a murderer.

Schindler's List as a Literary Text

The narrator of *Schindler's List* is both distinctive in his own right and is constructed to suit the text's blend of fact and fiction, although the very presence of a narrator indicates that we are reading fiction. The narration shifts interestingly between a Jewish viewpoint—for instance, one that emphasizes the Poles' unsympathetic attitude to the Jews, which may have originated with Leopold Page and other survivors—and one that is external to what happens to the Jews, often identified with Schindler's own view of events. The narrator is sometimes factually omniscient, for example in giving a condensed history of the Jews in Poland, and at other times admits that he is unreliable. For example, the narrator begins the description of a party held by Schindler in 1939 by signaling the partiality of his knowledge and the fact that fiction will have to substitute for a gap in the record:

> Though it is not possible to say exactly what the members of the party talked about that night, it is possible from what Oskar said later of each of these men to make a plausible reconstruction (London: Sceptre, 1986, p. 72).

Although on a first reading *Schindler's List* appears textually straightforward and seamless, it enlists other literary devices that signal its reliance on survivor testimony and its factional status—that is, its status as a novel based on factual material. Rather than plausibly reconstructing dialogue too often, direct speech is sometimes summarized by the narrator or presented without quotation marks. It is interesting that the latter effect appears only in the British edition of *Schindler's Ark*; quotation marks have been added for clarity in the American edition to, for instance, this example from the British edition:

> Oskar called out. You can't do that here. I won't get work out of my people if you start shooting. I've got high priority war contracts (p. 234).

The absence of quotation marks signals the fact that this dialogue is only an approximation of what might have been said but at the same time gives the effect of verisimilitude. In the American edition, by contrast, it is simply as if Schindler's words are being quoted verbatim.

Many reviewers termed Keneally's book "faction," which is a partially useful term for *Schindler's List* and acknowledges Keneally's use of literary devices, such as those described above, in telling a historical story. The mixed nature of Keneally's text is consistent throughout. It does not change registers, like D. M. Thomas's *The White Hotel*, which moves abruptly from imaginative writing to citation of a documentary source. Rather, it is a mixture in the sense that factual material is always conveyed fictively. *Schindler's List* offers the reader what Peter Quartermaine calls a "ringside seat to history" (p. 68). The reader feels that he or she is transported back to the time of the events described, which are rendered in the terms of individual detail rather than being part of a wider picture. For instance, Keneally symbolizes a moral turning point in Schindler's career externally as a single moment in time, by having him watch in horror the liquidation of the Cracow ghetto from a hill overlooking it (pp. 141–143). This scene is strikingly reproduced in Spielberg's film.

Critical Reputation

As with many Holocaust novels, *Schindler's Ark* has been received with both great enthusiasm and unequivocal condemnation. Some critics, including Robert Taubman, welcomed the fictional representation of a figure like Schindler. He is remarkable as an ordinary man whose actions were extraordinary, unlike rescuers in special positions with whom a reader would be less likely to identify, such as the Swedish diplomat Raoul Wallenberg, who was killed after the war by the Russians. On the other hand, some, including Marion Glastonbury, questioned the wisdom of devoting a novel to a Nazi party member whose story suggests that readers may gain comfort from the story of a Holocaust rescuer. Others objected to Keneally's treatment of Schindler as simply enigmatic; the mystery of his motives is neither fully acknowledged nor solved. Some have protested that Schindler may have had mercenary reasons for sheltering the Jews in his workforce. This seems unlikely, given the money and energy—thoroughly documented by Keneally—that he spent in doing so. However, it is not clear that Schindler had a plan to rescue "his" Jews in quite the absolute way it looks with hindsight and in *Schindler's List*.

Literary objections included the fact that in all his novels, according to Michael Hollington, Keneally's characters are not skillfully differentiated, and despite appearances, he keeps telling the same story. His protagonists are "vital, life-affirming Irishmen (who are sometimes Aboriginal Irishmen, sometimes German industrialist Irishmen)" (p. 42). It has been claimed that the book's unmodulated portrait of Polish antisemitism makes it, in the title of Bogumil Kosciesza's review, "a novel informed by prejudice" against the Poles. More generally, critics have pointed out that because the Jewish characters are robbed of autonomy and meaningful action by Nazi policies it was clearly easier for Keneally to write a Holocaust novel featuring the staples of choice, action, and success when the central character was an Aryan. However, the great strengths of *Schindler's List* are its accessibility and readability (it is the best-selling Booker Prize winner to date), and the lasting interest in the Holocaust that it has sparked.

Bibliography

Primary Sources

The Place at Whitton. 1964.
The Fear. 1965.
Bring Larks and Heroes. 1967.
Three Cheers for the Paraclete. 1968.
The Survivor. 1969.
A Dutiful Daughter. 1971.
The Chant of Jimmie Blacksmith. 1972.
Blood Red, Sister Rose. 1974.
Gossip from the Forest. 1975.
Season in Purgatory. 1976.
A Victim of the Aurora. 1977.
Confederates. 1979.
Passenger. 1979.
The Cut-Rate Kingdom. 1980.
Schindler's Ark. 1982.
A Family Madness. 1985.
The Playmaker. 1987.
By the Line. 1989.
Towards Asmara. 1989.
Flying Hero Class. 1991.
Woman of the Inner Sea. 1993.
Jacko. 1993.
A River Town. 1995.
Bettany's Book. 2000.

Under the Pseudonym of "William Coyle"
Act of Grace. 1988.
Chief of Staff. 1991.

Drama
Halloran's Little Boat. 1968 (adaptation of *Bring Larks and Heroes*).
Childermas. 1968.
An Awful Rose. 1972.
Bullie's House. 1981.

Children's
Ned Kelly and the City of Bees. 1978.

Nonfiction
Moses the Lawgiver. 1975.
Outback. 1983.
Australia: Beyond the Dreamtime. 1987.
The Place Where Souls Are Born: A Journey to the Southwest. 1992.
Now and in Time to Be: Ireland and the Irish. 1992.
The Eureka Stockade. 1993.
Memoirs from a Young Republic. 1993.
The Utility Player: The Des Hasler Story. 1993.
Our Republic. 1995.
Homebush Boy—A Memoir. 1995.
The Great Shame. 1998.

Secondary Sources

Fensch, Thomas, ed. *Oskar Schindler and His List: The Man, the Book, the Film, the Holocaust and Its Survivors.* Forest Dale, Vt.: Paul S. Eriksson, 1995.
Glastonbury, Marion. Review in the *New Statesman*, quoted in Michael Hulse, "Virtue and the Philosophic Innocent: The British Reception of *Schindler's Ark*." *Critical Quarterly* 25, no. 4 (1983): 43–52.
Hollington, Michael. "The Ned Kelly of Cracow: Keneally's *Schindler's Ark*." *Meanjin* 42, no. 3 (March 1983): 42–46.
Hulse, Michael. "Virtue and the Philosophic Innocent: The British Reception of *Schindler's Ark*." *Critical Quarterly* 25, no. 4 (1983): 43–52.
Johnston, Richard. "The Rise of Faction." *Quadrant* (April 1985): 76–78.
Kosciesza, Bogumil. "A Novel Informed by Prejudice." *Commonweal* 10, no. 9 (May 6, 1983): 284–285.
Pierce, Peter. *Australian Melodramas: Thomas Keneally's Fiction.* St Lucia, Queensland, Australia: University of Queensland Press, 1995.
Quartermaine, Peter. *Thomas Keneally.* London: Arnold, 1991.
Rose, Gillian. "Beginnings of the Day: Fascism and Representation." In *Modernity, Culture, and "the Jew"*. Edited by Bryan Cheyette and Laura Marcus. Cambridge, Eng.: Polity, 1998.
Schwarz, Daniel R. "Keneally's and Spielberg's *Schindler's List*: Realistic Novel into Epic Film." In *Imagining the Holocaust.* New York: St. Martin's Press, 2000, pp. 209–238.
Silver, Eric. *The Book of the Just: The Silent Few Who Saved Jews from Hitler.* London: Weidenfeld and Nicolson, 1992.
Taubman, Robert. "Holocaust Art." *London Review of Books* 20 (January–February 1983): 23.
Vice, Sue. *Holocaust Fiction.* London: Routledge, 2000.
Wundheiler, Luitgard. "Oskar Schindler's Moral Development During the Holocaust." *Humboldt Journal of Social Relations* 13, nos. 1 and 2 (1985–1986): 333–356.

Inteviews and Archives

Interview by Laurie Hergenhan. "Interview with Thomas Keneally." *Australian Literary Studies* 12 (1986): 453–457.
Depositions by Oskar Schindler, Itzhak Stern, and other survivors are to be found in the archives at Yad Vashem, Israel.

IMRE KERTÉSZ

(1929–)

RITA HORVÁTH

Life

IMRE KERTÉSZ WAS born in 1929, in a nonobservant, assimilated, petty bourgeois Jewish family in Budapest, Hungary. His father, László Kertész, was a timber merchant, and his mother, Aranka Jakab, a clerk. Kertész's own family is reflected in the way the protagonist of *Kaddish for a Child Not Born* describes his family; they were, he says "city Jews, Budapest Jews, that is to say, not Jews at all, but of course not Christians either; we were the kind of non-Jewish Jews who still observe holy days, long fasts, or at least, definitely, until lunch" (*Kaddish*, Evanston, Ill.: Northwestern University Press, 1997, p. 16). His parents divorced when he was five years old. Both of his parents remarried, and they fought for custody over him. He was sent to a boarding school, and when he was eleven the court decided to place him with his father. Under the prevailing antisemitic racial laws of the pro-Nazi Hungarian government, he began high school in a separated Jewish class in 1940. His father was taken to forced labor and was killed during a march in Fertörákos. In 1944 Kertész himself was deported to Auschwitz and then to Buchenwald, and Zeitz, a camp belonging to Buchenwald. He was liberated in Buchenwald. He returned to Hungary, where he lived with his mother and finished high school.

After liberation Kertész adopted a leftist political position, and he joined the Communist Party in 1946. By 1949, however, the Communist takeover and the elimination of democracy in Hungary had left him disillusioned. He worked as a journalist until 1950, when he lost his job for political reasons. Beginning in the 1950s he coped with life under a Communist dictatorship by exiling himself to the margins of the society. He became a writer and a translator. He wrote comedies and radio plays in order to earn a living, but he does not regard these as part of his art. In the 1980s, and especially after 1989 with the fall of the Communist regime, he became a well-known and successful writer in Hungary and Europe, especially in Germany. His works were translated into many languages, and he became a central figure of Holocaust literature. This great change in his life engendered many moral, emotional, and psychological problems amounting to a crisis of identity, which Kertész forcefully tackled in *Valaki más: A változások krónikája* (Somebody Else: The Chronicle of the Changes, 1997). In 2002, Kertész was awarded the Nobel prize.

Oeuvre

Kertész, a survivor of the concentration camps, is an extremely self-conscious artist. This manifests itself first in his philosophically and poetically charged prose and in the careful construction of his novels. He also analyzes his art and its contexts in essays and interviews. Although existentialism is primarily the philosophical basis that infuses his writing, he acknowledges that his work cannot escape the influence of the entire European philosophical tradition and culture, even though, in his view, these were invalidated once and for all in Auschwitz.

Kertész's aim is to create some kind of value out of his personal experiences in the Holocaust and out of the Holocaust experience in general. Personal and impersonal goals are always present in his writing and work together to the same end. The personal motivation behind his prose is to turn the "fateless" fate that was assigned to him by the Nazi dictatorship into his own meaningful fate. In *Gályanapló* (Galleydiary), he notes: "The invaluable importance of the novel is that it is a process in which a human being recovers his/her life. . . . The only possible subject of a novel is the recovery of life, living life through, and being filled with it for one devout moment before we die" (2nd edition, Budapest, Hungary: Magveto, 1999, pp. 187–188). In the essay "A száműzött nyelv" (The Exiled Language) he argues that those who aim to be witnesses of the Holocaust have to reconstruct their selves which were lost in the extermination camps. Moreover, they have to reconstruct their selves precisely upon the basis of their horrifying camp experiences.

Kertész's public reason for creating value out of the Holocaust experience is to establish that a break occurred in Western civilization. Kertész views the Holocaust as a universal starting point, something that belongs to human nature and is always already present. He regards the Holocaust as a "trauma of the European civilization," and he wants to participate in the process of solving what he sees as the most crucial existential question of this civilization: "whether this trauma will live on in the form of culture or in the form of neurosis; in the form of creativity or destruction in the European societies" ("A száműzött nyelv," *Elet és Irodalom*, 24 November 2000, p. 4). A previously valid ethical and moral consensus disappeared altogether in the Holocaust, says Kertész: European culture, which he regards also as a survivor of Auschwitz, thus needs a new post-Holocaust language to represent this rupture. Only in this new language, which is discontinuous with the pre-Holocaust language, is it conceivable to talk about the Holocaust. Kertész feels that there is a community of artists—Jean Améry, Tadeusz Borowski, Paul Celan—who create and speak this new language, which he describes as "atonal," borrowing from the terminology of musicology. Tonality or harmony had been an unquestioned consensus in music. Therefore, atonality, the absence of a unified tone, declares the invalidity of all previous, especially moral and ethical, conventions. The ungrammatical word "fateless," which serves as the title of Kertész's first novel (*Sorstalanság*, 1975), already demonstrates the new language, which is constructed from the fragments of pre-Holocaust language. In *Fateless*, words and ideas appear in a broken, discontinuous way, devoid of the logic that held them together previously. For example, the word "honor" appears in the novel to describe unwillingness to escape from being deported: "I think I had enough time for it [escape], but still my sense of honor proved to be the stronger of the two urges," the protagonist says (Evanston, Ill.: Northwestern University Press, 1992, p. 42). "I do recall being relieved that the other boys were there around me [in the brick factory]: Rozi and Silky Boy, Leather-Worker, Smoker, Moskovics and all the others. It seemed that no one was missing: they too were honorable" (p. 45).

The problem of creating a new language is one of the reasons why it took thirteen years for Kertész to write his first novel. It records, in stages, the story of a fourteen-year-old boy who is deported from Budapest to Auschwitz, survives until the war's end, and then returns to Budapest. The narrative stages are set by the conventions of Holocaust narratives, conventions that came into existence as early as 1945–1946. We can see these conventions at work already in the protocols taken with survivors about their experiences by the National Relief Committee for Deportees in Hungary. They include a description of the home from which the person is uprooted, existence under the aegis of the yellow star, life in the ghetto or the transit camp, the journey on the train, the arrival at Auschwitz and the selection, life and the deterioration of one's body in the concentration camp, and finally survival and entering the post-Holocaust era.

The portrait of the protagonist who will not forget, who will become the "medium of Auschwitz," is the most autobiographical element in *Fateless*. At one moment as the boy lies on the floor of the station of Buchenwald, extremely close to death, he experiences

> occasional openings in the sky, an unexpected aperture here and there, and for a fleeting second a shiny hole; this was like the sudden suggestion of some depth from which a ray of light hit me from above, a quiet, inquisitive glance, an indefinitely colored eye, but doubtless made of light. It reminded me of the doctor who had once examined us in Auschwitz (p. 136).

Thus, the reader and the protagonist realize that the transcendence of this world is the reality of the doctor making the selection on the ramps of Auschwitz. In the boy's vision, the selecting doctor's eye replaces God's eye. This revelation is accompanied by another condition that is necessary to become a "medium of Auschwitz": the full immersion in the illogical logic of the camp universe. Immediately after his revelation, the boy selects himself for death by adapting the system to which he was introduced on the ramps of Auschwitz. He sees the people left on the station floor as "The remnants of the cargo—its garbage, to speak more exactly—which they had presumably deposited here for a time" (p. 136).

This moment alludes to the moments of his arrival at Auschwitz, when he figures out the rules of the activity of the selecting doctor: "And so I saw with the eyes of the doctor how many old or otherwise unusable men there were here" (p. 64). There is, however, one ethical point that the writer strictly observes, in accordance with the imperative of Judaism to remember the victims individually (*Yad vaShem*). Kertész, the author, makes a special effort, whenever the protagonist mentions somebody in the camp universe either by name or by a characteristic, to individually mention the person at least once more in the novel, and usually we learn his or her fate. This becomes apparent when we learn about the death of the Smoker, which goes unnoticed by the physically deteriorated protagonist, but the reader understands it from the given information.

Kertész thus sets his goals as an artist, yet he is painfully aware of the trap inherent in any literary project concerning the Holocaust. He asserts, for example, in a 1971 note in *Gályanapló* that someone who can write about concentration camp experiences successfully in literary terms surely cheats and lies. Then he demands that he write according to this insight. While in *Fateless* he sets out the moral and existential aims of a survivor, in *Kaddis a meg nem született gyermekért* (*Kaddish for a Child Not Born*; 1990) he portrays the disastrous personal consequences of being a survivor. In *Kaddish* he shows, drawing upon Paul Celan's "Todesfuge" ("Death Fugue") that the protagonist cannot escape from aiming to kill himself, to finish what the Nazis had started. One of the most terrifying and devastating aspects of his survival is that he cannot free himself from the self-hatred resulting from an earlier partial identification with the murderers. One of the means to finish the Nazis' job is to remain childless: by not having a child he actually implements the Nazis' racial objectives, but he perceives himself to be incapable of changing his destructive behavior. Personally, the survivor is still trapped in the concentration camps. In *Kaddish for a Child Not Born*, Kertész formulates this both directly—"Auschwitz did exist, or rather, *does* exist" (p. 28)—and indirectly—for example, when he states that he lives "in this prefab apartment building in the heart—nay, not heart, but the [anus] of Jozsefvaros [a district of Budapest]" (p. 27). The translators used the word "intestines" instead of the more accurate term, "anus"; Kertész here alludes to the fact that the Nazis referred to Auschwitz as the "Anus Mundi."

Kertész's works deal with Auschwitz and with the theoretical and practical question of how one can write about it either directly or indirectly. When he deals with it indirectly, he considers the phenomenon of dictatorship, which deprives people of the fate that would follow from their individual characteristics and forces them into prefabricated roles, or "functions" as Kertész calls them. He is especially interested in how this happens and what are, or can be, the consequences if one survives such a process. Kertész claims that the fact that he lived through different forms of Communist dictatorships helped him to understand his experiences as a child and youth. Furthermore, it enabled him to survive his survival, both by not rendering false hope of true liberation and by constantly providing a basis against which to construe Fascism and interpret the pre- and pro-Fascist semidictatorship of the 1930s in Hungary.

Although Kertész is able to comment upon dictatorship and postdictatorship eras using the perspective derived from his experience of the Holocaust, ultimately his calling is to write of the Holocaust. As he formulates it in *Gályanapló*, "nothing interests me really, only the myth of Auschwitz. . . . Whatever I am thinking about, I am always thinking about Auschwitz. If seemingly I am talking about something else, I still talk about Auschwitz. I see everything else as imbecility in comparison to it" (p. 36). Kertész's work has been driven by this calling and made him a preeminent contributor to postwar Hungarian-Jewish literature. Scholars have expressed special admiration for the Holocaust novels *Fateless, A kudarc* (Failure; 1988), and *Kaddish for a Child Not Born*—called by Zoltán András Bán "a trilogy of fatelessness"—as densely poetic and self-reflexive masterpieces that speak directly to the postmodern sensibility.

Bibliography

Primary Sources

Sorstalanság (*Fateless*). 1975.
A nyomkereső: Két regény (The Searcher of Traces: Two Novels). 1977.
A kudarc (Failure). 1988.
Kaddis a meg nem született gyermekért (*Kaddish for a Child Not Born*). 1990.
Az angol lobogó (The British Flag). 1991.
A holocaust mint kultúra: Három előadás (The Holocaust as a Culture: Three Lectures). 1993.
Gályanapló (Galleydiary). 1992.
Jegyzőkönyv (Record). 1993.
Valaki más: A változások krónikája (Somebody Else: The Chronicle of the Changes). 1997.
A gondolatnyi csend, amíg a kivégzőosztag újratölt: Monológok és dialógok (Short Silence to Think Until the Firing Squad Reloads Its Guns: Monologues and Dialogues). 1998.

Secondary Sources

Angyalosi, Gergely, et al. "Irodalmi kvartett: Kertész Imre 'Valaki más' című könyvéről beszélget Angyalosi Gergely, Bán Zoltán András, Németh Gábor, és Radnóti Sándor." *Beszélő* 6 (1997): 104–108.
Balassa, Péter. "A hang és a látvány: Miért olvassák a németek a magyarokat?" *Jelenkor* 7–8 (1995): 664–668.
Basse, Michael. "Auschwitz als Welterfahrung: Der ungarische Schriftsteller Imre Kertész." *Merkur* 6 (1999): 559–564.
Bán, Zoltán András. "A Trilogy of Fatelessness." *New Hungarian Quarterly* (winter 1991): 36–41.
Bikácsy, Gergely. "Öntagadás mint alkotás: Kertész Imre avagy a nevetés kegyelme." *Orpheus* 2–3 (1993): 162–169.
Drügh, Heinz J. "Der wilde Osten: Das politische Blick und seine litterarische Reflexion: Ein Versuch über Imre Kertész Erzählung Protokoll." *Neohelicon* 2 (1998): 257–288.

Flower, Dean. "*Fateless*." *Hudson Review* (summer 1993): 397–398.

Földes, Anna. "Regényre várva." *Magyar Hírlap* 286 (1992): 3.

Földényi, F. László. "Az erkölcsi magány terhe." *Magyar Lettre Internationale* (summer 1997): 2–3.

Gács, Anna. "Egy különös regény: Kertész Imre: Gályanapló." *Jelenkor* 10 (1992): 857–860.

György, Péter. "Egy mondat értelmezéséhez: Kertész Imréröl." *Orpheus* 4 (1991): 39–49.

Heller, Ágnes. "A Holocaust mint kultúra: Kertész Imre könyvéröl." In *Az idegen*. Budapest: Múlt és Jövö Lap- és Könyvkiadó, 1997, pp. 92–101.

Klein, Judith. " '. . . als ware ich selbst der Dichter': Übersetzen als Thema und Metapher literarischer Texte: an Beispielen von Isaak Babel, Aharon Megged, und Imre Kertesz." *Zeitschrift für Literaturwissenschaft und Linguistik* 99 (1995): 155–160.

Lányi, Dániel. "A 'Sorstalanság' kísérlete: Kertész Imre regényéröl." *Holmi* 5 (1995): 665–674.

Lengyel, Balázs. "Közvetlenül és áttételesen." In *Verseskönyvröl verseskönyvre: Líránk a hetvenes években*. Budapest: Magvetö, 1982, pp. 234–244.

Mahler-Bungers, Annegret. "Kathartisches Erinnern: Zum Werk von Imre Kertész." *Zeitschrift für Psychoanalytische Theorie und Praxis* 3 (1997): 257–274.

Molnár, Gábor Tamás. "Fikcióalkotás és történelemszemlélet: Kertész Imre: Sorstalanság." *Alföld* 8 (1996): 57–71.

Spiró, György. "Non habent sua fata: A 'Sorstalanság'—újraolvasva." *Élet és Irodalom* 30 (1983): 5.

Székely, András. *Kertész Imre: Válogatott bibliográfia, 1975–1998*. Budapest: Self-published, 1999.

Szirák, Péter. "Emlékezés és példázat Lengyel Péter, Kertész Imre, és Szilágyi István elbeszélő prózájában." *Studia Litteraria* 35 (1997): 71–93.

Turai, Tamás. "A hiten túl, a pusztulás előtt: Esszé Kertész Imréről, és az írói mítoszról." *Jelenkor* 4 (1992): 310–316.

Interviews

Interview by Imre Barna. "Lágerirodalom. Beszélgetés Balassa Péterrel, Kertész Imrével és Szilágyi Ákossal." *Kritika* 4 (1994): 21–24.

Interview by Zoltán András Bán. "Egy eléggé szűk ketrecbe zárt író." *Beszélő* 41 (1992): 38–43.

Interview by Zoltán András Bán. ". . . az embernek még otthon is gázálarccal kellett lélegeznie." *Élet és Irodalom* 39 (1995): 3.

Interview by Katalin Budai. "A művészethez elég az igazság." *Magyar Napló* 14 (1991): 14–17.

Interview by Judit Csáki. "Sors és sorstalanság." *Kritika* 3 (1992): 24–26.

Interview by Magda Ferch. "A megfogalmazás kalandja: Kertész Imre a szellemi élet hiányáról, a Nyugat vastagabb léggömbjéről és az önvizsgálat fontosságáról." *Magyar Nemzet* 29 (1996): 18.

Interview by Mihály Kornis. "Miért van ott, ahol van?" *Beszélő* 43 (1991): 39–42.

Interview by Zsuzsa Láng. " 'Én kétféle diktatúrát is átéltem': Beszélgetés Kertész Imrével." *Népszabadság* 34 (1993): 17.

Interview by Attila Schauschitz. "Auschwitz ideális kiindulópont." *Magyar Narancs* 44 (1993): 36–37.

" 'Bántani akarom az olvasóimat': A magyar Kertész Imre 'Sorstalanság' című művéről." *Élet és Irodalom* 21 (1996): 5.

Interview by Anna Szalai. "Words and Images." For the Jerusalem Literary Project. Edited by Eleonora Lev. Videotape, 8 hours.

Interview by Gábor Szántó T. "Auschwitz szól belőlem." *Szombat* 4 (1994): 35–41.

Interview by Cecília Szebényi. "Át nem lépve a szabadság kapujának küszöbét." *Beszélő* 9 (1994): 32–34.

Interview by Tamás Szőnyei. "Nem érzem magam téves helyen, amikor Németországban olvasok fel." *Magyar Narancs* 51–52 (1996): 8–9, 32.

Interview by Lajos Márton Varga. "Egy városnak életfeladat kell." *Népszabadság* 81 (1994): 8.

Interview by Monika Vig. "Az eltökélt pesszimizmus." *Magyar Narancs* 22 (1991): 10.

Interview by István Vörös. "A vizsgálódó mondat." *Élet és Irodalom* 45 (1999) 3–4.

Interview by András Willheim. " '. . . magamban szakadatlanul glosszákat írok': Beszélgetés Kertész Imrével." *Orpheus* 2–3 (1993): 149–161.

HEINAR KIPPHARDT

(1922–1982)

ANAT FEINBERG

"THE PAST WILL come to rest only once it has really become past. Currently, this is not the case. Neither in theory nor in practice. We consider our past an inexplicable malady . . . , but its causes can be accounted for, the malady can be averted, recurrence can be prevented," maintained dramatist Heinar Kipphardt (*Theater shücke*, vol. 1, Cologne, Germany: Kiepeuhewer and Witsch, 1978, p. 355).

Life

Born on 8 March 1922, Heinrich Mauritius, later Heinar Kipphardt, grew up in the small town of Heidersdorf, in Silesia, Germany. While he was still in school, in 1933, his father, a dentist well known for his social democratic affiliation, was arrested and sent to the Dürrgoy concentration camp near Breslau (present-day Wroctaw, in Poland), and later, until 1937, to Buchenwald. Following his release in 1937, the family moved to Krefeld, in the Ruhr area of western Germany, where Kipphardt finished the gymnasium (secondary school) with an abitur (exit exams) in 1940. He began studying medicine but was drafted into the German army in 1942 and served on the Soviet front until 1944. Shortly before Germany surrendered to the Allies in May 1945, he deserted. Soon after the war, he resumed his medical studies in Düsseldorf, where after obtaining a doctorate, he began working in a psychiatric clinic. Hoping to contribute to the construction of a new socialist society, he emigrated to East Germany in 1949. He worked in various clinics there and was ultimately appointed psychiatric assistant at the Charité hospital in East Berlin.

From 1950 to 1959 Kipphardt was dramatic adviser at the renowned Deutsches Theater. Along with playwright Peter Hacks, he belonged to the followers of the German poet and playwright Bertolt Brecht's politically committed Epic theater, which sought to disengage emotionally from the performance. Neither the aim nor the means of this movement were in accord with the state-decreed theory of socialist realism, and Kipphardt became a more and more irritating dissident in the German Democratic Republic (GDR). In his satire *Shakespeare dringend gesucht* (*Shakespeare Urgently Sought*), which premiered in 1952, he points to the inadequacy of traditional forms, urgently advocating an engaged drama. His voice became more biting in *Der staunenwerte Aufstieg und Fall des Alois Piontek* (*The Awe-Inspiring Rise and Fall of Alois Piontek*), 1956, a tragicomic farce, and in *Die Stühle des Herrn Szmil (The Chairs of Mr. Szmil*), 1961, a witty satire about criminal mechanisms and political intrigues in an authoritarian state. Dismissed from the Deutsches Theater in 1959, Kipphardt was one of the first artists to leave the GDR. He settled in Düsseldorf and later in Munich, where he became dramatic adviser at the Kammerspiele. Yet here, too, he turned out to be political liability, and his contract was not extended in 1971.

In the Matter of J. Robert Oppenheimer

The play that made Kipphardt famous worldwide was *In der Sache J. Robert Oppenheimer* (*In the Matter of J. Robert Oppenheimer*), one of the most accomplished examples of documentary drama, which premiered in Berlin under the director Erwin Piscator in 1964. Basing his stage text on the hearings of the Atomic Energy Investigation Commission, which had summoned the world-famous scientist in 1954, Kipphardt used tape recordings and film material, as he explored the moral dilemma of the physicist in the age of nuclear weapons. Oppenheimer, director of the Los Alamos center for nuclear research during the development of the atomic bomb (1943–1945), had been accused by the Atomic Energy Commission of having delayed the full development of the hydrogen bomb and of entertaining contacts with Communists. Kipphardt shows the schizophrenic state of the prominent scientist who develops the bomb, his moral dilemma. Upon restaging the play in 1977, Kipphardt felt that the theme of the responsibility of a scientist in modern society had not lost its relevance. "In the nuclear state dwells the state which keeps vigilant surveillance over its citizens," he wrote (program notes to the 1977 production, translated by Anat Feinberg).

Joel Brand: The Story of a Deal

The year 1965 saw the premiere of Peter Weiss's *Die Ermittlung* (*The Investigation*) and Kipphardt's *Joel Brand: Die Geschichte eines Geschäfts* (*Joel Brand: The Story of a Deal*)—two prominent examples of documentary drama reexamining Germany's past, the workings of the Nazi system, and the mass murder of European Jewry. Kipphardt had first dealt with the crimes committed during the war, with questions of guilt and responsibility, in the documentary play *Der Hund des Generals* (*The General's Dog*, 1962), making use of photo material and documents projected onto a screen in order to suggest authenticity and factual accuracy.

Joel Brand begins seventeen years after the war, as General Rampf is accused of having sent sixty soldiers to a senseless death. Kipphardt's *Zeitstück* (period play) clearly seeks to confront the past and to expose systematic unwillingness of individuals and the German people to deal with their past. *Joel Brand* deals with the plan to barter one million Hungarian Jews for 10,000 trucks and other goods. The SS Lieutenant Colonel Adolf Eichmann negotiates with leaders of Hungarian Jewry toward the end of the war, in 1944. On Eichmann's order, Joel Brand, a member of the "Relief and Rescue Committee" of Budapest, travels to Istanbul and to Syria to negotiate the deal but is arrested by the British Secret Service and brought to Cairo. The Allies doubt the intentions of the Germans and turn down the offer. The deal is ultimately thwarted by political and military considerations. Aware of the horrible fate awaiting the Jews of Budapest, Joel Brand is a victim of circumstances. The play features historical personages, such as the Relief and Rescue Committee members Rezso Kasztner and Joel Brand on the Jewish part, and Eichmann and the Nazi official Kurt Becher on the Nazi side. Kipphardt shows the futility of the negotiations, which are marked by lies, illusions, and self-delusions. Eichmann appears as the bureaucrat par excellence who adopts not only a very specific style of speech, which he himself described at his trial as "officialese" (*Amtssprache*), but even mannerisms and acquired gestures calculated to present himself as the prototype of the "administrative murderer" (*Schreibtischmörder*). As opposed to Becher, who does not disguise his antipathy for the Jews and yet is eager to exhaust the possibilities of the deal, Eichmann shows cynical matter-of-factness: he negotiates halfheartedly with the Jews even as the transports themselves are being organized.

The Eichmann one encounters in *Joel Brand* inspires fear, contempt, and repulsion in the ordinary spectator. Kipphardt wrote his docudrama in the wake of Eichmann's trial in Jerusalem (1961), in which over one hundred witnesses, the majority of whom were survivors, went on the witness stand and recounted tales of suffering and horror, while the accused was mostly silent in his glass booth, hardly ever looking at the audience. *Oberstrumbannführer* Eichmann, no heroic evildoer, no diabolical creature, but a diligent bureaucrat of evil who exemplifies the "banality of evil," according to the Jewish philosopher and political theorist Hannah Arendt, piqued Kipphardt's imagination.

Brother Eichmann

Years after the moderate success of *Joel Brand*, *Bruder Eichmann* (*Brother Eichmann*), Kipphardt's last play, premiered posthumously in Munich in 1983. It is Kipphardt's second docudrama about Eichmann and yet it offers a very different protagonist. Interestingly, the specter of Eichmann's personality, as laid bare in Jerusalem, haunts a great number of plays written in the intervening twenty years, from Martin Walser's *Der schwarze Schwan* (*The Black Swan*, 1964) to Thomas Bernhard's *Vor dem Ruhestand* (*Eve of Retirement*, 1979). Kipphardt started working on *Bruder Eichmann* (a title reminiscent of Thomas Mann's essay "Bruder Hitler") in 1965 and told a reporter he intended to present the makings of a bourgeois man of duty. Years later he elaborated that his intention was to show "how a fairly average young man from Solingen . . . becomes in a quite normal manner the monstrous figure Adolf Eichmann, the administrative authority in the genocide of European Jewry."

Kipphardt based his docudrama on the recorded interrogation that Captain Avner Less conducted with the prisoner prior to the trial itself. Kipphardt tries to reconstruct the uneventful biography of Eichmann to show how short the distance is between hell and the "good" intentions of one who has come to idolize duty. In the first part of the play spectators are presented with the facts of Eichmann's life, but the playwright takes poetic license in selecting those episodes he considers supportive of his argument, reshuffling and modifying them in line with his chosen position. The result is in a sense paradoxical. On the one hand, Eichmann dominates the stage (a prison cell), because the "story" told is his own; on the other hand, the murderer is presented as a man under heavy guard, a victim of sorts, who arouses a degree of sympathy in the spectators. The latent danger that sympathy for Eichmann may be aroused in the spectators is even more present in the second part of the play. The objective re-creation of biography gives way to an alarming melodramatization. Kipphardt neglects the typescript of the interrogation, building up the climax of the play through a number of episodes that, though authentic, actually belong to the posttrial period of Eichmann's incarceration. The episodes include a scene in which Eichmann writes a letter to his wife; a meeting between the couple; a number of meetings in which the Canadian priest Reverend Hull and his wife try to reconcile the sinner with the Deity he has denied; the execution; and, finally, an epilogue in which we hear about Eichmann's cremation. All these episodes are emotionally taut. The incipient sympathy that spectators might have felt for Eichmann in the first part of the play increases to the point that by the end they have to remind themselves that the object of that sympathy is the man who saw to it that the ovens never cooled.

Was Kipphardt's a serious dramaturgical mistake made by a skillful dramatist, or was the dramatist carried away by his moral-political argument? Both conjectures have some truth. Kipphardt chose the French man of science, philosopher, and author Blaise Pascal's dictum as an epigraph for his play: "Evil is never done so completely and so well, as when it is done with a clear conscience." Eichmann's case illustrates it, as do a number of interim, analogous scenes: Eichmann's soul mates from the contemporary scene are introduced: an American B-52 bomber pilot flying over Vietnam, a cynical Italian police investigator who interrogates a young woman suspected of terrorist activities, the former Israeli Defense Minister Ariel Sharon, who reportedly tried to evade his responsibility for the slaughter of Palestinians in two refugee camps in Lebanon, and others. All these ministers of evil are supposedly Eichmann's brethren, who have become—so the play argues—monsters, perpetrators of evil in the full flood of righteous conviction. Ironically, Kipphardt seems to have fallen victim to the epigraph he chose. Urged on by his own "clear conscience" and the desire to protest against the escalation of violence and terror in the postwar world, he plays down the scale of Eichmann's crimes and ends up viewing them as different only in degree—not in kind—to the crimes of others. Adopting a relativistic view, Kipphardt creates an Eichmann who is only one of many criminals with his hands dipped in blood.

Bibliography

Primary Sources

Stücke I (including *Shakespeare dringend gesucht; Die Stühle des Herrn Szmil; Der Hund des Generals; In der Sache J. Robert Oppenheimer*). 1973.

Stücke II (including *Joel Brand, Die Geschichte eines Geschäfts; Die Nacht in der Chef geschlachtet wurde; Die Soldaten; Sedanfeier*). 1974.

Inder Sache J. Robert Oppenheimer (*In the Matter of J. Robert Oppenheimer*). 1967.

Bruder Eichmann. 1983.

Gesammelte Werke in Einzelausgaben (Collected works in separate volumes). Edited by Uwe Naumann with the cooperation of Pia Kipphardt. Reinbeck: Rowohlt, 1986ff. Including *Bruder Eichmann. Schauspiel und Materialien*. 1986; *Traumprotokolle*. 1986; *März. Roman und Materialien*. 1987; *In der Sache J. Robert Oppenheimer. Ein Stück und seine Geschichte*. 1987; *Shakespeare dringend gesucht und andere Theaterstücke*. 1988; *Joel Brand und andere Theaterstücke*. 1988; *Schreibt die Wahrheit. Essays, Briefe, Entwürfe 1949–1964*. 1989; *Ruckediguh—Blut ist im Schu. Essays, Briefe, Entwürfe 1964–1982*. 1989; *Die Tugend der Kannibalen. Gesammelte Prosa*. 1990; *Umgang mit Paradiesen. Gesammelte Gedichte*. 1990.

Secondary Sources

Bartelheimer, Lotte, and Maximilian Nutz, eds. *Heinar Kipphardt: 'In der Sache J. Robert Oppenheimer'. Materialien*. Stuttgart: Klett, 1984.

Becker, Peter von. "Kein Bruder Eichmann!" *Theater Heute* 3 (1983): 1–3.

Cuomo, Glenn R. " 'Vergangenheitsbewältigung' through Analogy: Heinar Kipphardt's Last Play 'Bruder Eichmann'." *Germanic Review* 2 (1989): 58–66.

Feinberg, Anat. "The Appeal of the Executive: Adolf Eichmann on the Stage." *Monatshefte* 78, no. 2 (summer 1986): 203–214.

———. *Wiedergutmachung im Programm. Jüdisches Schicksal im deutschsprachigen Nachkriegsdrama*. Cologne: Prometh, 1988.

Geissler, Erhard. "Bruder Frankenstein oder Pflegefälle aus der Retorte?" *Sinn und Form* 6 (1984): 1289–1319.

Innes, Christopher. *Modern German Drama: A Study in Form*. Cambridge: Cambridge University Press, 1979.

Kowal, Michael. "Kipphardt and the Documentary Theater." *American German Review* 5 (1966–1967): 20–30.

Linzer, Martin. " 'Bruder Eichmann' von Heinar Kipphardt." *Theater der Zeit* 2 (1984): 3.

Naumann, Uwe, and Michael Töteberg. *In der Sache Heinar Kipphardt*. Mit Bibliographie von Nicolai Riedel. *Marbacher Magazin* 60 (1992).

Pikulik, Lothar. "Heinar Kipphardt: 'Bruder Eichmann' und Thomas Bernhard: 'Vor dem Ruhestand'." In *Deutsche Gegenwartsdramatik*. Edited by Lothar Pikulik, Hajo Kurzenberger, and Georg Guntermann. Vol. 1. Göttingen: Vandenhoeck and Ruprecht, 1987, pp. 141–191.

Poore, Carol. " 'Reportagen der Innenwelt': The Example of Heinar Kipphardt's März." *German Quarterly* 2 (1987): 193–204.

Rossmann, Andreas. "Genosse Eichmann? Goldoni for Peace." *Theater Heute* 1 (1984): 44–46.

Steiner, Carl. "Heinar Kipphardt, 'Robert Oppenheimer' and 'Bruder Eichmann': Two Plays in Search of a Political Answer." In *America! New Images in German Literature*. Edited by Heinz D. Osterle. New York: Lang, 1989, pp. 199–211.

Stock, Rudolf. *Heinar Kipphardt*. Reinbek, Germany: Rowohlt, 1987.

Danilo Kiš

(1935–1989)

BROOKE HORVATH

Perhaps the most celebrated Serbian writer of the twentieth century, Danilo Kiš was born on 22 February 1935 in Subotica, Yugoslavia, near the Hungarian border. Kiš's father, Eduard, was a Hungarian Jew who worked as a railway inspector; his mother, Malica (Dragićević), was an Eastern Orthodox Montenegrin Serb. Kiš grew up in Novi Sad on the banks of the Danube, where the promulgation of antisemitic legislation at the time caused his parents to have him baptized into the Orthodox faith—which, he said, helped him survive the Holocaust. Following the massacre of Jews throughout the Voyvodina region of Yugoslavia and Hungary by Hungarian fascists in January 1942, the family began what Kiš described as "repeated, sudden, incomprehensible uprootings," his father's attempts, through constant relocation, to "escape his destiny" (*Homo Poeticus*: *Essays and Interviews*, ed. Susan Sontag, New York: Farrar, Straus & Giroux, 1995, p. 24). The effort was unavailing, and after narrowly escaping death in 1942, Eduard was sent to Auschwitz in 1944, where he died.

Living out the war years in Hungary, Kiš, his mother, and sister, Danica, were repatriated to Cetinje, Montenegro, in 1947 when Kiš was thirteen. Living with his maternal grandfather, Kiš completed the gymnasium curriculum and entered the University of Belgrade in 1954, graduating in 1958 with a B.A. in comparative literature (the first student to pass through the university's newly created comparative literature department). After working part-time at the Center for the Theory of Literature and Art in Belgrade, he began to lecture on Serbo-Croatian language and literature at the universities of Strasbourg, Bordeaux, and Lille. Eventually, Kiš settled permanently in Paris, where he died of lung cancer on 29 October 1989.

Although Kiš worked slowly, his collected works fill fourteen volumes. The recipient of several awards, including the Ivan Goran Kovačić Award (Yugoslavia's Book of the Year prize, 1977), the Award Ivo Andrić (1984), and in 1990 the Bruno Schulz Prize (given to a "foreign writer underrecognized in the United States"), Kiš was active throughout his life as a poet and translator (principally of French, Hungarian, and Russian poetry), literary theorist and polemicist, playwright and essayist. It is, however, as a writer of fiction that Danilo Kiš made his reputation and in the process changed the Serbian literary landscape.

Kiš's Art of Fiction

As part of the literary generation that came of age in the early 1960s, Kiš was responsible for helping to introduce into Yugoslavian literature many of the narrative devices associated with modernism and postmodernism: fragmentation, nonlinearity, parodic playfulness, magical realism, narrative self-consciousness, a rejection of psychologism, and the use of documentary techniques. Indeed, it was Kiš's appropriation of others' texts that allowed members of the Yugoslavian literary establishment to accuse him of plagiarism as the excuse for the vicious attacks that greeted the publication of *A Tomb for Boris Davidovich* (1976) and provoked Kiš's polemical/critical masterwork, *Ćas anatomije* (The Anatomy Lesson, 1978). Influenced by modernist and postmodern writers (especially Vladimir Nabokov, Jorge Luis Borges, Ivo Andrić, Miroslav Krleźa, and Bruno Schulz, as well as the French *nouveau roman* and the Russian formalists), Kiš's cosmopolitan poetics combined with his Jewishness to make him, in the words of Tomislav Longinović, "a thorn in the sides of [the] purist guardians of the national literature" (*Borderline Culture*, p. 110).

This thorn proved especially vexing because Kiš focused so much of his work upon not only fascist but also communist totalitarianism. Although he professed to believe that "in literature there is no truth," that "people with 'something to say' should leave literature alone," and that doubt is the hallmark of "literary truth" (*Homo Poeticus*, pp. 256, 164, 169), Kiš's novels and stories invariably attempt to give voice to the voiceless and to defend the importance of the individual. He responded to Theodor Adorno's contention that "to write poetry after Auschwitz is barbaric" by observing that the problem was "not so much moral as literary . . . how to speak of such things without lapsing into banality" (p. 263). For Kiš, writing about the inhumanity of German fascism and Soviet communism—what he termed the twentieth century's "paranoid reality" (p. 54)—required neither psychological probing nor moral harangue but the gathering and binding together of "a mass of documentation and facts" to "endow them, through the imagination, with new form" (pp. 53, 271).

This aesthetic, however, developed gradually, and Kiš's early work (*Early Sorrows*, 1969; *Garden, Ashes*, 1965) is dominated by a poetic use of language that creates anything but the "cold and distant tone" critic Norbert Czarny found characterizing the later work (p. 282). Indeed, the three volumes comprising his autobiographical "family cycle" chart a movement from lyrical realism through modernism into postmodernism.

Psalam 44 and "The Family Cycle"

Although Kiš would eventually refer to his "family cycle" as his first three books, he in fact began his career as a writer of fiction with the publication of two short novels, *Mansarda* (1962) and *Psalam 44* (1962). Neither is available in English, and shortly before his death Kiš requested that the latter, set in Auschwitz-Birkenau, never be translated. Nevertheless, *Psalam 44* is included in Kiš's collected works and constitutes his initial (and most direct) depiction of the camps. Offering a realistic and unblinking look at the horrors of Nazi efforts to eradicate European Jewry (including Kiš's first description of the Novi Sad massacre, which almost claimed his father), *Psalam 44* features characters modeled on Joseph Mengele (infamous Auschwitz physician) and Miklós Nyiszli (Hungarian physician and camp inmate who published a memoir of his experiences). The plot turns on the birth of a Jewish child and the successful escape of both child and mother from what the scriptural psalm 44 terms "the place of dragons" where, for faith's sake, Jews are being "killed all the day long." Kiš's story finds in the survival of these two, according to Marianna Birnbaum, a "promise for their entire people" and a message "of resistance and of hope" (p. 354).

For English-speaking readers, however, Kiš's fiction begins with the trilogy *Early Sorrows*; *Garden, Ashes*; and *Hourglass*, (1972), the progression of which Kiš likened to an artist's progression from sketch to drawing to final painting (*Homo Poeticus*, p. 262). Based on his experiences growing up in war-torn Yugoslavia and Hungary, and increasingly dominated by his unstable and absent father, the trilogy makes clear how central to Kiš's literary imagination were what the critic Gabriel Motola has termed "the burst passions of the eternally wronged" (p. 619). Yet it is equally true that the trilogy works to individualize those Jews caught in the obscene machinery of antisemitic fascism while making plain that Jewishness was but one (sometimes important, sometimes unimportant) facet of lives such as those led by Kiš and his father.

Although published after *Garden, Ashes*, *Early Sorrows* was the first book written and is stylistically the most conventional of the trilogy. Assuming the fictional guise of Andy Sam, Kiš offers, in *Early Sorrows*, nineteen brief vignettes of his childhood that, although told retrospectively, generally retain the boy's naïveté: his first childhood flirtation, the shame of wetting the bed, autumn fields after the circus's departure, a trip to the doctor for scabies medication, memories of his dog Dingo, the day he pretended (to his father's malicious delight and his mother's dismay) to be his Jewish grandfather going door to door selling feathers.

The Holocaust hovers just out of sight and beyond the boy's comprehension in these wistfully poetic sketches: the soldiers passing through the village; Andy asking a passing stranger if, in his travels, he has seen Andy's absent father; the family's reduced circumstances that necessitate gathering pinecones for fuel and tending a neighbor's cows; the need to move in with relatives. "The Pogrom" (whose title links the Holocaust to the long history of European antisemitism) finds Andy an uncomprehending witness to a raid upon a Jewish warehouse, and "Pages from a Velvet Album" recalls the return of Andy's aunt from Auschwitz with the news that his father is dead. Hearing this, Andy cannot help imagining that his father died a fool's and a coward's death, was sent to his doom because of a refusal to work, turning to women for comfort while, "crying like a baby, [he] spread the awful stench of his traitorous intestines" (*Early Sorrows [For Children and Sensitive Readers]*, translated by Michael Henry Heim, New York: New Directions, 1998, p. 86).

Many of the same events are covered in *Garden, Ashes*: Andy's hayloft intimacies with Julia Szabo; Eduard's mysterious absences; the family's dependence upon resentful, indifferent relations. Structurally more complex than *Early Sorrows*, *Garden, Ashes* shifts its point of view from that of Andy as uncomprehending child to that of the mature author, in the process altering the reader's perspective on Eduard, who is initially deified (as sacrificial martyr, mythic mystery, intellectual rebel), then debunked (as a drunken madman who has clownishly and selfishly courted his own destruction). The language is lush, elegiac, the causes of his father's quixotic rebellion and victimized megalomania told in elliptical fragments. Irony wars with lyrical periphrasis, realism with surrealism, while the Holocaust rumbles enigmatically in the background and Andy's "muddy tale" of his father gets "woven together from one unreality after another" (*Garden, Ashes*, translated by William J. Hannaher, New York: Harcourt Brace Jovanovich, 1975. 99).

Even as Eduard tells Andy that "you can't play the role of a victim all your life without becoming one in the end" (p. 106), the narrator tells us that his father continued to "[follow] his star, which he would lose amid the sunflowers, only to find it again at the edge of the field—on his greasy black frock coat" (p. 88) before disappearing into a cattle car bound for the camps. If Eduard in his attempts to gain control over his world resorts to fantasy, role playing, alcohol, madness, and writing, his son also turns to writing, to mad, magical prose meant to mystify and mythicize his father and thereby rescue him from oblivion. But what *Garden, Ashes* suggests, finally, is that Eduard's death is in fact the result of the self-dramatizing myths he has spun about himself and his transhistorical significance—myths not all that different in motivation from those that spawned the Holocaust.

In *Hourglass*, Kiš's prose undergoes a metamorphosis, becoming "as dry and accurate and pitiless as a legal investigation," in the words of Edmund White (p. 371). Moreover, *Hourglass* achieves its effects—including the further demystification of Eduard Sam (here identified only as "E. S.")—by replacing conventional plot development with sixty-seven disconnected fragments constituting fictional "documents" of four distinct types that recur throughout the novel and, like a mosaic, tell the story of E. S.'s final months before his disappearance into Auschwitz: "Travel Scenes" with their objective snapshot glimpses of E. S.; "Notes of a Madman" with their first-person window into his tortured psyche; "Criminal Investigation," in which E. S. is interrogated (perhaps only in his head) by authorities seeking evidence against him; and "A Witness Interrogated," in which another is grilled for incriminating information about Eduard. The result is an aesthetically playful yet powerfully credible investigation into the grimmest of material, a crime story of documentary objectivity (the novel's concluding letter is, according to Kiš, an actual letter from his father, written in 1942 in the midst of the Nazi genocide), of authenticity uncolored by narrative subjectivity. The effect is to make intimately personal the inhuman scale of Nazi atrocities while simultaneously resuscitating the Holocaust as the alien, incomprehensible, disorienting event it was, thus enabling readers to confront the Holocaust afresh while rendering its historical truth dispersed, ambiguous, dicey. The novel's final lesson is that "it is better to be among the persecuted than among the persecutors" (*Hourglass*, translated by Ralph Manheim, New York: Farrar, Straus & Giroux, 1990, p. 274).

A Tomb for Boris Davidovich and *The Encyclopedia of the Dead*

Like *Hourglass*, *A Tomb for Boris Davidovich* deals, in Kiš's words, with "strong individuals plunged into the current of history at decisive moments . . . people whose only compass is doubt . . ." (*Homo Poeticus*, p. 46). Having treated the Holocaust, Kiš found it necessary to explore the equally horrific atrocities of the Soviet gulags and Stalinist antisemitism. *A Tomb for Boris Davidovich* (subtitled in the Serbian edition "seven chapters of a common story") was the result. It tells of revolutionaries variously betrayed by the Comintern as well as of Baruch David Neumann, persecuted by Christian fanatics in fourteenth-century France. This is Kiš's means of suggesting both the cyclical nature of historical suffering and the recurrence of ideologies maintained through fear and oppression. Neumann's story is in fact a translation (as Kiš acknowledges) from a French version of an account found in the fourteenth-century *Registers of the Inquisition*. Indeed, throughout *Boris Davidovich* Kiš draws facts, characters, story lines, and verbatim passages from historical documents (for example, texts by Karlo Štajner, Aleksandr Solzhenitsyn, and Roy Medvedev) to create stories that "lay bare" the book's "historicity" and "renounce arbitrary fabrication." This "documentary approach" is, he adds, "an anti-romantic, anti-poetic principle" meant to place authenticity beyond doubt (*Homo Poeticus*, pp. 43, 54–55).

If Kiš's work has dealt throughout with realities that border on the fantastic, the stories comprising *The Encyclopedia of the Dead* (1985) often treat other kinds of fantastic realities drawn from documents (newspapers, ancient texts, accounts of the Mormons' genealogical efforts): a dream trip to a library housing a reference work minutely detailing the lives of every otherwise anonymous person who ever lived; a heretical challenge to early Christianity; a young girl who foresees in her mirror the brutal murder of her father and sisters; a retelling of the legend of the seven sleepers of Ephesus. "The Book of Kings and Fools" reworks the "unbelievably fantastic" history of *The Protocols of the Elders of Zion*, imagining its creation and dissemination, its ties to the Soviet secret police and effects upon European antisemitism. Although not as tightly unified as *Boris Davidovich*, *The Encyclopedia of the Dead* manifests a preoccupation with death and mutability, with what and who make history.

Kiš and Jewishness

Kiš described himself as "a Jew insofar as others see me as one," as "Jewish more by fate than by culture" (*Homo Poeticus*, pp. 274, 266). He said that Judaism played a small part in his life and that he did not wish to be considered a Jewish writer, that being Jewish was a curse, a "family calamity" (p. 109). Of "the Jewish problem" that inhabits the heart of his work Kiš remarked, "it is the only content of my life that can be called literary. It gives me everything I need: victim, executioner," adding that invariably in his fiction "the Jew is the symbol of all the pariahs of History" and "the historical paradigm of our century" (pp. 183, 207, 216).

All that said, Kiš stands as one of the major imaginative voices of the twentieth century in large part because he found the means to render, vividly and authentically, what the Holocaust and the Soviet purges meant to those caught in these infernal machines and consequently what these events mean to the course of human history. "Literature," he once declared, "must correct History. . . . What is the meaning of 'six million dead'(!) if you don't see an individual face or body—if you don't hear an individual story?" (p. 206). In his essay "Between Hope and Hopelessness" he said of his own novels and stories that he hoped they "do not allow the reader to soothe his conscience in relation to the camps, Auschwitz and Kolyma equally, with some comforting theory of 'historical necessity' and 'a brighter future,' " adding that he hoped as well that they "have not contributed hatred" to the world's sum of woes (*Review of Contemporary Fiction* 14.1 [1994]: 133). To Holocaust literature, then, Danilo Kiš has contributed what we must always hope to find: individuals, human faces, and a human conscience.

Bibliography

Primary Sources

Mansarda / Psalam 44 (The Attic/Psalm 44). 1962.
Bašta, pepeo (*Garden, Ashes*). 1965. (1975.)
Rani jadi, za decu I osetljive (*Early Sorrows [For Children and Senstive Readers]*). 1969. (1998.)
Po-etika (Poetics/Ethics). 1972.
Peščanik (*Hourglass*). 1972. (1990.)
Po-etika: knijiga druga (Poetics/Ethics: Book Two). 1974.
Grobnica za Borisa Davidoviča (*A Tomb for Boris Davidovich*). 1976. (1978.)
Čas anatomije (The Anatomy Lesson). 1978.
Homo Poeticus (reworking of two *Po-etika* volumes). 1983.
Noc i magla (Night and Fog; a play). 1983.
Djela Danila Kiša (Works of Danilo Kiš). 1983. (Contains the first ten volumes listed under *Sabrana dela Danila Kiša.*)
Enciklopedija mrtvih (*The Encyclopedia of the Dead*). 1985. (1989.)
Život, literatura (Life, Literature). 1990.
Gorki talog iskustva (The Bitter Sediment of Experience). 1990. (Posthumous collection of interviews.)
Pesme i prepevi (Poems and Poetic Translations). 1992.
Lauta i ožiljci (The Lute and Scars). 1994. (*Lauta i ožiljci* is a section of *Skladište*; the story "The Lute and Scars" can be found in *The Prince of Fire: An Anthology of Contemporary Serbian Short Stories*. Edited by Radmila J. Gorup and Nadezda Obradovic. Pittsburgh: University of Pittsburgh Press, 1998.)
Skladište (Warehouse). 1995.
Varia (Latin in the sense of "miscellany"). 1995.
Pesme, Elektra (Poems, Electra; a play). 1995.
Homo Poeticus: Essays and Interviews. 1995. (Collection of essays and interviews from a variety of sources, including *Čas anatomije*.)
Sabrana dela Danila Kiša (Collected Works of Danilo Kiš). 1995. (14 vols.) (Includes *Mansarda*; *Psalam 44*; *Rani jadi*; *Bašta, pepeo*; *Peščanik*; *Noc i magla*; *Grobnica za Borisa Davidoviča*; *Čas anatomije*; *Homo Poeticus*; *Enciklopedija mrtvih*; *Pesme, Elektra*; *Varia*; *Skladište*; and *Život, literature*.)
Eseji: autopoetike (Essays: Autopoetics). 2000.

Selected Secondary Sources

Anders, Jaroslaw. "Games, Ashes." Review of *Garden, Ashes* by Danilo Kiš and *The Book of Blam* by Aleksander Tisma. *The New Republic* (9 August 1999): 40–45.
Birnbaum, Marianna D. "History and Human Relationships in the Fiction of Danilo Kiš." *Cross Currents* 8 (1989): 345–360.
Brodsky, Joseph. Introduction. *A Tomb for Boris Davidovich*. New York: Penguin, 1980, ix–xvii.
Bynum, David E. "Philosophical Fun and Merriment in the First Fiction of Danilo Kiš." *Serbian Studies* 2, no. 4 (1984): 3–20.
Czarny, Norbert. "Imaginary-Real Lives: On Danilo Kiš." Translated by Catherine Vincent. *Cross Currents* 3 (1984): 279–284.
Gorjup, Branko. "Danilo Kiš: From 'Enchantment' to 'Documentation.' " *Canadian Slavonic Papers* 29 (December 1987): 387–394.

Horvath, Brooke, ed. Danilo Kiš number. *Review of Contemporary Fiction* 14, no. 1 (spring 1994): 97–208.

Juraga, Dubravka, and M. Keith Booker. "Literature, Power, and Oppression in Stalinist Russia and Catholic Ireland." *South Atlantic Review* 58, no. 4 (November 1993): 39–58.

Longinović, Tomislav Z. *Borderline Culture: The Politics of Identity in Four Twentieth-Century Slavic Novels.* Fayetteville: University of Arkansas Press, 1993.

———. "Danilo Kiš." In *Dictionary of Literary Biography*, vol. 181. Edited by Vasa D. Mihailovich. Detroit: Gale Research, 1997, pp. 119–124.

Matvejević, Predrag. "Danilo Kiš: *Encyclopedia of the Dead.*" *Cross Currents* 7 (1988): 337–349.

Motola, Gabriel. "Danilo Kiš: Death and the Mirror." *Antioch Review* 51 (fall 1993): 604–621.

Oja, Matt F. "Fictional History and Historical Fiction: Solzhenitsyn and Kiš as Exemplars." *History and Theory* 27 (1988): 111–124.

Shishkoff, Serge. "Košava in a Coffee Pot or a Dissection of a Literary *Cause Célèbre.*" *Cross Currents* 6 (1987): 341–371.

White, Edmund. "Danilo Kiš: The Obligations of Form." *Southwest Review* 71 (summer 1986): 363–377.

Interviews

Lemon, Brendan. "An Interview with Danilo Kiš." *Review of Contemporary Fiction* 14, no. 1 (spring 1994): 107–114.

Sontag, Susan, ed. *Homo Poeticus: Essays and Interviews.* New York: Farrar Straus Giroux, 1995. This volume reprints nine interviews conducted between 1973 and 1989.

Alfred Kittner

(1906–1991)

AMY COLIN

Alfred Kittner was born on 24 November 1906 in Czernowitz, the capital of the Bukovina, into an assimilated German-Jewish family. His multiethnic homeland was the eastern-most crown-land of the Austro-Hungarian monarchy and produced a multifaceted culture, including a variegated Austro-German, Romanian, Ukrainian, and Yiddish literature. The first trauma in his life was the death of his mother. The second tragic event was the outbreak of World War I, which forced many Bukovinians, including Kittner's father, a well-known physician, to flee with his two sons to Vienna, where Kittner attended high school and the first years of the gymnasium. After the war, Kittner returned to Czernowitz, completed a German-speaking high school, military service, and later studied German literature at the University of Czernowitz. For financial reasons he was forced to interrupt his studies and make a living as a journalist working for the leftist liberal newspapers *Der Tag* and *Czernowitzer Tagblatt.*

At the age of sixteen Kittner wrote poems, but also felt drawn to art and illustrated stories. Among his later literary models were Joseph Eichendorff, Clemens Brentano, E. T. A. Hoffmann, Franz Kafka, Gustav Meyrink, Rainer Maria Rilke, Georg Heym, Ernst Toller, and the visionary poets Alfred Mombert and Theodor Däubler. Their world of thought, along with Franz Kafka's, Gustav Meyrink's, and Alfred Kubin's surreal poetic universe, fascinated him.

In 1932 Stefan Zweig, who had read Kittner's work, praised his talent, underlining that it manifested itself in a distinct and almost absolute way in his poems (Zweig's letter of 19 May 1932 *Schattenschrift*, Aachen: Rimbaud Verlag, 1988, p. 109). Similarly, Jakob Haringer and Felix Braun encouraged Kittner's artistic endeavors. In 1937, Kittner received a poetry award at a literary competition initiated by the journal *Wiener Tag*. A year later, Kittner published his first volume of poems (written during the years 1928 to 1938.) *Der Wolkenreiter* (1938, The Rider of Clouds) testifies to Kittner's attachment to the Austro-German culture in spite of Hitler's rise to power and the poet's isolation within a Romanian-speaking environment.

Under the first Soviet occupation of the Bukovina in 1940 and 1941, Kittner worked as a librarian and a collaborator of the journal *Internationale Literatur*. In 1941, when Romanian fascist troops conquered the Bukovina, Kittner was forced into the Czernowitz ghetto from where, in the summer of 1942, Roumanian fascists deported him and his family, along with many other victims in cattle wagons to Transnistria's death camps (eastern Ukraine). Like all other deportees, Kittner was forced to march for days through deserted land and woods. Many victims died on these marches. Others were robbed and beaten, and the survivors were placed in a deserted quarry, where they endured cold and hunger. Most deportees died of starvation, exhaustion, or typhoid fever. Like all other deportees, Kittner was forced to shovel stones and perform other excruciating tasks. Sometimes during the hard labor he whispered German verses; even in the death camp Kittner defiantly continued to write poetry in German. The beauty of the poem set against the somberness of reality gave him the strength to continue to survive against all odds.

After liberation from the death camp, Kittner returned to Czernowitz, and then, in 1945, went to Poland and Romania. In Bucharest, where Kittner settled, he worked first as a radio announcer, then as an employee of the ARLUS library (society for cultural connection with the Soviet Union), and later as a scientific director of the Library of the Institute for International Cultural Relations, and finally, since 1958, as a freelance writer. After the death of Alfred Margul-Sperber, Kittner became his successor as *Doyen* of German literature in Romania, and was highly respected by Romanian writers and artists.

There were periods when Communist authorities persecuted Kittner and forbade the publication of his work. In more liberal times, three volumes of his poetry appeared. Kittner received a poetry award from the Romanian Writers' Union, and was allowed to travel to Western Europe to give lectures and participate in international conferences. In 1980, during a visit to Germany, he decided to stay for good. In an act of revenge, the Romanian secret police confiscated the bibliophile's outstanding book collection, which included thousands of volumes and many valuable manuscripts. Some were destroyed, others scattered, and many sequestered in an inaccessible archive. In spite of this trauma, Kittner, who had settled in Düsseldorf (Germany), continued to work on his poetry as well as on translations until his death on 14 August 1991, unexpectedly, after a stroke.

Poetry

Kittner's early poetry, collected in *Der Wolkenreiter*, invokes his search for other worlds, which are at once cosmic realms and spheres of artistic creation. It is in the quest for such fictional realms distant from the somberness of political developments that the lyrical "I" comes into being, unfolding its own poetic voice. Kittner's key poem, "Der Wolkenreiter," conveys the master theme of the entire volume by vivifying a voyage that leads the lonely rider from a dreamland into cosmic coldness and isolation. Kittner, a modern troubadour who was well aware of his affinities to François Villon and Peter Hille, fused neo-romantic images with expressionist metaphors and Kafkaesque renderings in order to convey the isolation of the creative mind in a society marked by materialism and overshadowed by nationalism, fascism, and antisemitism.

Kittner's later poetry, written in the ghetto and the death camp, is scarred by his experience of the *Shoah*. His poems are testimonies documenting the crimes and sadism of perpetrators as well as the sufferings of the deportees and their will to resist. No pathos, no superfluous ornamentation embellish his poems. Their style is dense, somber, and factual. His "verse chronic of a deportee," (*Schattenschrift* p. 116) as Kittner called his poetry written between 1942 and 1945, was published in the volume *Hungermarsch und Stacheldraht: Verse von Trotz und Zuversicht (Hunger Marches and Barbed Wire: Verses of Stubbornness and Confidence*, 1956). The volume consists of four cycles. The first is "Vom Steinbruch führt kein Weg zurück" ("No Trail Leads Back from the Stone Quarry"), written in a factual, reportlike style, details the deportation, vivifying the sufferings and despair of the deportees as they were first locked in the cattle wagons transporting them to Transnistria, then forced to march through wasteland and deserted woods, and finally imprisoned in a stone quarry, where most of them died of hunger or typhoid fever. "Tagwerk des Todes" ("Daily Work of Death), the second cycle, includes Kafkaesque renderings of daily life in the death camp, but also poems invoking reminiscences of happier times. The third cycle, "Schauer des verwehten Tages" ("Shiver of the Day Gone By"), discloses the ways in which the trauma of the *Shoah* scarred the deportees' psyche, while the fourth, "Und immer leuchtet noch der Stern" ("And the Star Continues to Shine"), testifies to the poet's will to live. Alfred Margul-Sperber called Kittner's chronice of a deportee, in particular this last section, "a diary written in hell." Yet for Margul-Sperber this testimony written in a border zone between life and death documented the significance of hope and the poet's confidence in life in spite of all tragedies.

Kittner republished his *Shoah* poetry in *Flaschenpost* (*Letter in a Bottle*, 1970), which received a literary award from the Romanian Writers' Union, *Gedichte* (*Poems,* 1973), a representative selection of his work from 1925 to 1972, and *Schattenschrift* (*Shadow Writing*, 1988), a volume of poems written from the perspective of a survivor as well as texts linking memories of past sufferings with reflections about the present. In recognition of his literary achievements, Kittner received the Gryphius Award. At Edith Silbermann's insistence, Kittner recorded his memories of the death camp on tape. After his unexpected death, Edith Silbermann edited and published his memoirs in a volume entitled *Erinnerungen* (*Memoirs*, 1994).

Editor and Translator

In Romania, Kittner made a name for himself not only as a writer, but also as an editor and translator (into German) of forty different Romanian poets. In addition, Kittner published a comprehensive edition of Alfred Margul-Sperber's poems and of Oscar Cisek's work. One of Kittner's most important contributions to literary studies is the co-edited volume *Versunkene Dichtung der Bukowina: Eine Anthologie deutschsprachiger Dichtung* (*Sunken Poetry of the Bukovina*, 1994), for it is the first comprehensive collection of German poetry written by German, Austrian, Romanian, Ukrainian, and Jewish poets from the Bukovina. This selection of five hundred poems from thousands of texts Kittner had collected since the 1920s continues the work of Alfred Margul-Sperber, who, in the 1930s, failed to publish an anthology of German-speaking Jewish poets from his homeland due to Hitler's rise to power.

Critical Reception

Contemporary literary criticism does not yet include any major study of Kittner's poetry, but many reviews have been published in Romanian, German, Austrian, and Israeli newspapers and journals, articles, introductions to his edited volumes, and postfaces to his own collections of poems. When *Der Wolkenreiter*, Kittner's first volume of poetry, appeared reviews published in *Nationalzeitung* (Basel, 19 November 1939), the Czernowitz *Allgemeine Zeitung* (December 1939), and the *Czernowitzer Morgenblatt* (17 January 1940) praised Kittner's talent. Robert Flinker, a German-Jewish writer from the Bukovina, commended Kittner for his courage to search for truth and beauty at a time overshadowed by violence and war. When Kittner's volume *Hungermarsch and Stacheldraht* appeared, Alfred Margul-Sperber's preface to this volume and Oskar Walter Cisek's review (*Neue Literatur*, 18 March 1957) drew the public's attention to the political implications of Kittner's work. Petre Motzan's valuable articles on Kittner's poetic development uncover similarities to Alfred Kubin, Kafka, and Jean Paul, but also analyze the radical transformation of Kittner's style from the early neo-romantic poetry to the factual style of the later work. Motzan, along with other critics such as Bernd Kolf, Jürgen Wallmann, and Oskar Walter Cisek, read Kittner's poetry as a fusion of *Erlebnisdichtung* (poetry based on personal experience) and *Bildungsdichtung* (verses of a *poeta doctus*, a poet drawing on a broad knowledge of literature). For some scholars, Kittner's preference for traditional forms was a political act at a time when the Nazis were abusing classicism in order to propagate their ideology and to show that they were the heirs of German culture. Kittner, along with other Jewish poets, wanted to prove that the persecuted Jewish poets were the true heirs of German cultural traditions (Colin). These poets did not wish to give up their German mother tongue even in the death camp. Kittner later defiantly continued to write poems in this style, which he considered atemporal, in order to assert a poetic voice shaped by the *Shoah* in post–World War II German writing.

Bibliography

Primary Sources

Works

Der Wolkenreiter (The Rider of the Clouds). 1938.

Hungermarsch und Stacheldraht: Verse von Trotz und Zuversicht (Hunger Marches and Barbed Wire: Verses at Stubborness and Confidence). 1956.

Gedichte (Poems). 1970.

Flaschenpost (Letter in a Bottle). 1970.

Gedichte (Poems). 1973.

Schattenschrift (Shadow Writing). 1988.

Erinnerungen 1906–1991 (Memoirs). Edited by Edith Silbermann. Aachen: Rimbaud Verlag, 1996.

Correspondence

"Alfred Kittner—Alfred Margul-Sperber. Der Briefwechsel (1932–66)." In *Zeitschrift für die Germanistik Rumäniens*, no. 1 (1992): 58–71.

Translations

Bart, Jean. *Europolis*. Berlin: Verlagder Nation 1974.

Breda, Marin. *Wagemu* (Daring). Bucharest: Jugend-Verlag, 1960.

Bart, Jean. *Europolis*. Berlin: Verlagder Nation, 1974.

Stancu, Zaharia. *Wie sehr hab ich dich gelieb* (How deeply I loved you). 1970 Klausenberg: Dacia-Verlag.

Porumbacu, Veronica. *Tore* (Gates). Bucharest: Kriterion Verlag 1975.

Edited Works

Alfred Margul-Sperber: Das verzauberte Wort. Der poetische Nachlaß 1914–1965. Bucharest: Jugend-Verlag, 1969.

"Gedichte aus der Bukowina: Verhallter Stimmen Chor." *Neue Literatur* (Bucharest) 22, no. 11 (1971): 36–58 and no. 12 (1971): 44–66.

Versunkene Dichtung der Bukowina: Eine Anthologie deutschsprachiger Dichtung. Co-edited with Amy Colin. München: W. Fink Verlag, 1994.

Essays

"Nachwort" zu Oskar Walter Cisek. In *Gedichte. Eine Auswahl*. Bucharest, 1972; "Ortswechsel." In *Schattenschrift*, pp. 92.

"Alfred Sperber—Der Mensch und das Werk." In *Alfred Margul-Sperber: Geheimnis und Verzicht. Das lyrische Werk in Auswahl*. Bucharest: Kriterion, 1975, pp. 589–612.

Secondary Sources

Colin, Amy. *Paul Celan: Holograms of Darkness*. Bloomington: Indiana University Press, 1991, pp. 24–29.

Csejka, Gerhard. "Der innere Quell. Zum 70. Geburtstag Alfred Kittners. Ein Gespräch." *Neue Literatur* (Bucharest) 11, no. 11, 22 (1976): 7–15.

Kolf, Bernd. "Dauer durch die Zeit: Mit Alfred Kittner zum lyrischen Erlebnis." *Karpathenrundschau* 5, no. 3 (1971).

Konradt, Edith. " 'Fluchtgepäck Zeitenmüll'. A. Kittners Wege im Leben." *Südostdeutsche Vierteljahresblätter* (München), no. 39 (1990): 14–16.

Motzan, Peter. "Erlebnis- und Bildungslyriker: Alfred Kittner." *Neue Literatur* (Bucharest) 5, no. 27 (1978): 78–85.

———. *Die rumäniendeutsche Lyrik nach 1944: Problemaufriß und historischer Überblick*. Cluj: Dacia, 1980, pp. 117, 125–26.

———. "Nachwort." In *Schattenschrift*. Aachen: Rimbaud Verlag, 1988.

Nichifor, Hilde. "Alfred Kittner." In *Literatura romana. Ghid bibliographic*, Teil II. Bucharest, 1982, p. 514.

Wallmann, Jürgen. "Alfred Kittners rumäniendeutsche Lyrik." *Die Tat* 9, no. 4 (1976).

A. M. Klein
(1909–1972)

MICHAEL GREENSTEIN

ABRAHAM MOSES KLEIN, the founding father of Canadian-Jewish literature, was born to Kalman and Yetta Klein in Ratno in the Ukraine on 14 February 1909. The family fled the pogroms of Eastern Europe and arrived in Canada in 1910. Klein's parents thought that he would fare better in school as a native-born Canadian, so he officially claimed to have been born in Montreal. After a thorough Jewish education in Montreal from private tutors and at Talmud Torah, he attended McGill University, participating in the debating society. From 1930 to 1933 he studied law at the Université de Montréal. Indeed, his training as a lawyer enters some of his writing, as when his search for justice takes the form of satire. Klein wrote prolifically until his final years of silence from 1955 until his death in August 1972. He did not write or talk, and he remained reclusive during this final period of his life. Indeed, satire and silence are two dominant features of his poetry and prose, and his years of silence are like a response to Theodor Adorno's famous dictum "no poetry after Auschwitz" ("Engagement," *Noten Zur Literatur*, vol. 3, Frankfurt: Suhrkamp, 1963, p. 125).

In recognition of his achievements, Klein received the following awards: Edward Bland fellowship, 1947; Governor General's Award, 1948, for *The Rocking Chair* and *Other Poems*; Quebec literary prize, 1952; Kovner Memorial Award, 1952; Lorne Pierce Gold Medal, Royal Society of Canada, 1957, for outstanding contribution to Canadian literature.

Journalism

As a socialist who ran for political office in Montreal and as editor of *The Canadian Jewish Chronicle* from 1939 until 1955, Klein was fully aware of Nazi atrocities against European Jewry. As early as 8 July 1932, he sounded a note of warning against antisemitic propaganda that spread through international journalism, writing: "Its headquarters seemed to be Germany: When Hitler sneezed, they caught cold. Thus the pest of Jew-hatred, like the bubonic plague, was being brought from continent to continent, through the medium of rats" (*Beyond Sambation: Selected Essays and Editorials 1978–1955*, edited by M. W. Steinberg and Usher Caplan, Toronto: University of Toronto Press, 1982, p. 27). Klein's strategy in this passage is to combine a perspective on medieval European history with the imagery of disease and pestilence in order to attack the spread of antisemitism.

The month following this published warning, Klein demonstrated with prophetic clarity the fate of Jews in Germany:

> For although we declared that antisemitism was to the Hitlerites an extra-curricular activity, it is a well known failing of human nature that man spends more energy on his hobbies than on his vocations. The Jew now stands condemned in Germany as the eternal alien; the deluded mobs who voted for the Brown Shirts now know where to find a scapegoat on which to vent their wrath and explode their indignation. It is a scapegoat with a beard; it is a Jewish scapegoat (*Beyond Sambation*, p. 30).

Klein simultaneously criticizes assimilationist "Germans of the Mosaic persuasion" who blame East European Jews for "invading" German cities and fostering a Fascist reaction. He takes note of and hope from Jews who turn to Zionism in "Germania" (note the sickness implied in "germ" and "mania") to emigrate to Palestine ("The German Elections," *Beyond Sambation*, pp. 29–31). Klein's article ends on an apocalyptic note, but the grimness of real corpses outweighs the hope for spiritual corpses:

> The Hebrew legend has it that in the darkest hour of Israel's need the Messiah will appear, and that when he appears the bodies of the dead will roll underneath the

earth until they rise in the Holy Land. The darkest hour, it seems, is at hand; and the spiritual corpses are already crawling towards the East ("The German Elections, *Beyond Sambation*, p. 32).

This redemptive insight and foresight, a decade before the genocide, explains, in part, Klein's silence a decade after the Holocaust; the fact that his warnings fell on deaf ears may have contributed to his final breakdown.

Klein's 1938 editorial response to *Kristallnacht* (anti-Jewish riots in Germany and Austria that were organized by the Nazis), "Vandal and Victim," attacks countries for not accepting Jewish refugees from Germany. Klein pierces through Goering's propaganda about the "spontaneity" of uprisings against Jews of the Reich and calls upon all democratic governments to outlaw Germany. Again he employs the rhetoric of pestilence that deserves quarantine; he coined the puns "Hitlerics" (the hysterics of Hitler) and "Hamaniac" (a persecutor of Jews), drawing on historical precedents and applying specific Jewish suffering to crimes against humanity in general.

Klein documents the rise and fall of the Third Reich; his journalism highlights the plight of European Jewry. He mocks Mahatma Gandhi's pacifism vis-à-vis the Jews and Joseph Stalin's hypocrisy in his early alliance with Adolf Hitler. He insists on the involvement of Canadian Jewry in events affecting European Jews.

They cry to us across a continent and an ocean, to us who by an accident find ourselves here in a land of freedom, who might as easily have missed the boat and remained there! They cry to us from the darkness of the concentration camp at Dachau, from the ghetto of Prague, from the encampments of refugees! They cry to us for succor and aid from the monster who is goose-stepping upon their lives! Shall their cry remain unanswered? (*Beyond Sambation*, p. 61).

Klein could not help but be aware of the sad irony that European inmates thought Canada was a land of plenty, and the word "Kanada" in the camps always referred to a more privileged area. Klein's emphatic call to the civilized world spills over to his poetry, where his rhetoric complements his exclamatory prose.

Poetry

"Childe Harold's Pilgrimage," written in 1938, is Klein's first poem to allude openly to the Nazis. Immersing himself in archaic language, the poet assumes the persona of Zvi Hirsch; *Zvi* is Hebrew for "deer," and *Hirsch* is Yiddish for "deer." In Jewish lore the innocent deer would be a wandering Jew. Although Klein borrows his title from the nineteenth-century Romantic poet Lord Byron, the poem has little in common with Byron's poem, except that both depict wanderers. After alluding to Pharaoh (head of Egypt at the time of the Exodus), Haman (adviser to King Nebuchadnezzar), and Torquemada (adviser to King Ferdinand and Queen Isabella at the time of the Spanish Inquisition), the poet culminates his antisemitic list with:

Sieg heil!
Behold, against the sun, familiar blot:
A cross with claws!
Hearken
The mustached homily, the megaphoned hymn:
Attila's laws!
He likes me not (*Complete Poems, Part 2: Original Poems, 1937–1955*, edited by Zailig Pollock, Toronto: University of Toronto Press, 1990, p. 476).

Klein counters Hitler with a rhetorical arsenal that consists of hysterical exclamations, alliteration, linkage of swastika and eagle, and synecdoche before the final understatement.

In 1940, Klein again searched for the appropriate vehicle to combat Hitler in another historical poem, "*In Re* Solomon Warshawer." Combining poetic technique with legal document, Klein reimagines the legend of King Solomon, banished from his throne by the demon Asmodeus. In this modernized version, Hitler replaces Asmodeus, and Solomon wanders through Europe, where he is captured by the Nazis. This grim poem opens in Warsaw in 1939, and the speaker is a Nazi soldier who introduces Solomon:

On Wodin's day, sixth of December thirty-nine,
I, Friedrich Vercingetorix, attached
to the VIIth Eavesdroppers-behind-the-Line,
did cover my beat, when, suddenly, the crowd I watched
surrounded, in a cobbled lane one can't pass through,
a bearded man, in rags disguised, a Jew (*Complete Poems*, 473).

Once again, Klein resorts to historical perspective in his comparison of the old barbarian of Roman times to Hitler, the new barbarian; Wodin, a pagan god of the Anglo-Saxon world, further emphasizes the primitive barbaric quality of the contemporary scene. The satiric understatement of "Eavesdroppers-behind-the-Line," used to refer to a military regiment, adds to the grotesque mood of the poem, for the "eavesdropper" records verbatim the words of the Jewish beggar. The detached, matter-of-fact witness contrasts with the brutality of the action:

Whom have I hurt? Against whose silk have I brushed?
On which of your women looked too long?
I tell you I have done no wrong! (p. 493)

After Solomon declares his innocence, "the good folk laughed." This alternation between the italicized, impassioned words of the Jew and the calm reportage of the German constitutes a pseudo-dialogue, or a total breakdown in the possibility of dialogue, between enemies.

When asked for his papers, the Jew produces a Hebrew pamphlet and a signet ring. This wandering Jew has assumed various identities throughout his history. In the midst of this description the ominous occurs as nonchalant understatement that conceals cruelty: "It was at this point the S.S. man arrived./when he was revived,/he deposed as follows." The dramatic and traumatic gap between the victimizer's arrival and the victim's revival highlights concealed violence, for within this gap is a beating and torture. The Jew then resumes his chronicling of persecution from the Inquisition to pogroms. He reveals that his signet ring belonged to King Solomon, who has been dethroned by Asmodeus or, in modern times, by Hitler. After these declarations, his speech is interrupted once again, and his fate is sealed:

> At this point the S.S. man departed.
> The Jew was not revived. He was carried and carted,
> and to his present gaoler brought;
> awaiting higher pleasure (p. 498).

Both in his mythic and actual dimensions, Solomon personifies the fate of the entire Jewish people at the hands of the Nazis.

Klein's inventiveness recurs in "Ballad of the Nuremberg Tower Clock," with its twelve stanzas of rhyming couplets collapsing history. "Nuremberg tower-clock struck one: / The swastika clawed at the sun" (*Complete Poems*, p. 537). Repeated cacophonies and awkward rhythms imitate goose-stepping Nazis and frenzied mobs, and suggest that time is out of joint. "Ring wrong! Ring wrong! The clock struck two:/Behind a curtain trembled a Jew. With each passing hour the apocalyptic and demonic clock foreshortens history: "Gestapo music rose to heaven:/The clock, delirious, struck eleven" (p. 538). The poem ends with the clock consuming itself: "And O in that eleventh chime/ Expired, as did human time" (p. 538). Klein's gothic ballads with their medieval resonance are grim but appropriate vehicles for shrinking the distance between North America's freedom and Europe's tragedy. Personification and synecdoche bring home Klein's message all too clearly.

Klein revisits Germany in "Ballad of the Thwarted Axe" (1941), in which alternating quatrains depict the abuse of justice in a "German People's Court." Again he combines his expertise in law with his knowledge of contemporary events. Odd-numbered stanzas paint an objective picture of courtroom drama, while even-numbered, italicized refrains heighten the chilling effect beyond mere mockery of justice.

> The judges sat in their blood-red robes,
> The victim in the dock was stood,
> The clerk read a number on a writ,
> And the room smelled blood (*Complete Poems*, p. 539).

This bloody opening stanza gives way to a gruesome concluding stanza, in which justice is entirely thwarted in the death of Jewish victims.

> *Headsman, headsman,—cheated man!*
> *Whom thorough judges mock*
> *You shall have no use for your axe,*
> *A ghost stands in the dock!* (p. 540).

At the time of this poem's composition, Klein's application of medieval torture to modern times seemed like an appropriate response; years later, however, after full revelation of the concentration camps, Klein saw the extent of his underestimation, and his resultant despair, by the 1950s, led to his final silence. Even though he resorts to earlier Jewish responses to persecution and to a humanist tradition in Western civilization, he cannot ultimately find solace in either of these sources.

In contrast to his use of archaic language, Klein also experiments with neologisms and puns influenced by his study of James Joyce's *Ulysses*. In "Sennet from Gheel" his portmanteau words exhibit his multilingual traditions, as well as his reaction to a Europe gone mad:

> And these touched thunders, this delyredrum
> Outbrasting boom from shekels of cracked steel
> Arrave the whirled goon dapht, as zany in Gheel!
> Mad as a hater, come, Nick knows warfrom!
> Bedlam, Bicetre, and hundemonium . . .

This lunatic asylum of 1941 contains the pandemonium of Huns, while "zany" serves as a kind of anagram for Nazi. Each of these linguistic twists distances and objectifies experience, but a decade later the poet internalized this madness into silence.

In "The Golem" (1942) Klein uses a different tactic: he reverses the legend of a rabbi creating a golem, or a monster without a soul, to save Jews; instead "rabbi Nubal" (a reference to the British Prime Minister Neville Chamberlain) bears responsibility for the creation of the golem, who, in this poem, represents Hitler.

> This is the golem.
> He is wooden, and he is painted brown.
> In walking, he carefully lifts each foot
> As if to kick it out of muck.
> The mechanism in his throat goes cluck-cluck-cluck.
> His dexter, at the hailed word, goes up and down.

Upon his upper lip, six hairs are stuck (*Complete Poems*, p. 572).

The Hitleriad

Klein's Holocaust poetry in the early 1940s culminated in *The Hitleriad* (1942–1943)—twenty-seven sections of mock-heroic verse modeled on Alexander Pope's *The Dunciad*. The main aesthetic problem with Klein's long poem, however, is the difference between his subject matter and the eighteenth-century political and literary opponents of Pope, who were worthier of satiric treatment. Klein's satiric vehicle is not always appropriate to the tragic and catastrophic events of World War II. His opening invocation, for instance, demonstrates the problematic nature of his long poem, more suited to Dante's *Inferno* than Pope's Augustan world.

Heil heavenly muse, since also thou must be
Like my song's theme, a sieg-heil'd deity,
Be with me now, but not as once, for song:
Not odes do I indite, indicting Wrong!
Be with me, for I fall from grace to sin,
Spurning this day thy proferred hippocrene,
To taste the poison'd lager of Berlin! (*Complete Poems*, p. 581).

There is a vast difference between an ordered neoclassical world, in which literary reputations die with a stroke of the pen, and the genocidal world of the 1940s. Klein's punning is unworthy of the Holocaust: the puns on "hail" and "lager" are as far removed from concentration camps as John Milton's heavenly muse is from Europe's inferno. One despairs of Klein's wit, and of any heavenly muse or deity who is greeted with the Nazi *sieg-heil*. If one were actually to taste that poisoned lager, the poem would end at the first stanza.

Yet the poet persists with his heroic couplets that condemn Hitler, for Klein aligns himself within an ethical, prophetic tradition that would not allow him to remain silent throughout World War II in his relative Canadian comfort. In section II of *Hitleriad*, the poet anatomizes Hitler's face as a "vegetarian blob" (p. 582) and in section III, he reverses Nazi theories about racial superiority:

Judge not the man for his face
Out of Neanderthal!
'Tis true 'tis commonplace,
Mediocral,
But the evil of the race
Informs that skull! (*Complete Poems*, p. 583).

Short and dark, Hitler fails to conform to his own vision of a blond Nordic race. He was "littered" (p. 583) rather than born, to Schicklgruber, his illegitimate father. The poet then mocks *Mein Kampf*.

Section XI exposes Hitler's hatred of Jews:

Add then, the insured craft with which he chose
The chosen people for his choicest prose:
Here was a scapegoat to his measure made,
Big enough to inform his wild tirade
And too small to return its foe his due:
The strange ubiquitous Jew! (p. 589).

Klein's wit backfires occasionally in the chiasmus of these couplets about selecting the chosen, but he rebounds in the contrast between big and small.

Through a series of oxymorons, the poet catalogs contrasting antisemitic stereotypes: bearded Hebrew cosmopolitan, alien yet local, rich and poor, unsocial and ambitious, religious and atheist. After holding the Jew responsible for inflation and heat waves, taxes and frosts, he concludes:

The theorem did not matter, nor its flaws,—
Sufficient to sneer "Jew" to win applause,
Yelp "Jude," and await the frenzied jeers—
And thus assure the Reich its thousand years! (p. 590).

Rhyming couplets afford rhetorical elasticity between Jewish understatement and Nazi hyperbole, "Visiting even on the blondest Jew / The crime his great-great-great-grandmother knew!" (p. 590). *The Hitleriad* stretches line and lineage with repeated exclamation marks.

After listing various Jewish stereotypes, Klein catalogs Hitler's henchmen—the Nazi elite. Paul Joseph Goebbels is club-footed, rat-faced, and halitotic. Herr Alfred Rosenberg is "burdened with double shame: / A Baltic birth, and a Semitic name" (p. 591). Hermann Goering is an oversized arsonist. Fashionable Joachim von Ribbentrop is "double-swasticrossing Ribbentrop. / Think him not milksop, no, nor champagne-sop" (p. 592). Franzvo Von Papen is a spy and diplomat. "And Himmler, Heinrich, mild and meek, / Most studious of the human shriek" (p. 593). Having named names at great length, Klein concludes:

Let us not name the names, but let us speak
Only about munition'd dividends,
Of markets rising to an envied peak,
Of rubber's conscienceless elastic ends,
Of timely trains by fascists always mann'd,
And of umbrellas, which, alas, did leak.
Those who have memory will understand (p. 595).

By the end of the poem, Klein shifts from satire to a plan for justice and righteousness. This shift occurs in section XXV:

But not with human arrogance come I
To plead our Maker's cause, and make His cause

The mighty measure of my feeble words.
Himself, in His good time, the Lord of Hosts,
The slowness of His anger moved at last,
And His longsuffering at last forespent
Will rise, will shine, will stretch forth His right hand
And smite them down, the open impious mouth,
The tongue blaspheming, silencing, in the dust! (p. 603).

In this transition, Klein abandons the earlier couplets' rhyme scheme in favor of straightforward statement, suited to his plea for the restoration of justice and righteousness. He continues in humble tones, without the earlier rhetoric:

I come now rather as a man to men,
Seeking the justice for that voice which cries
Out of the ground, the voice of our brothers' blood!
That blood will not be still again,
Those bones unblessed will still arise,
Yes, and those living spectres, of the mind unhinged,
Will still beat at our padded memory, until
Their fate has been avenged! (pp. 603–604).

The double meaning of "still" emphasizes the permanence of Klein's eternal judgment against the temporary nature of current historic tragedy.

Section XXVI continues with the key verb "come," as the poet calls forth his fellow Jews to reunite with him in a kind of resurrection, or messianic coming:

Let them come forth, those witnesses who stand
Beyond the taunt of perjury, those ghosts
In wagons sealed in a forgotten land,
Murdered;
Let them come forth and speak, who lost their speech
Before the midnight gun-butt on the door,
The men made dumb with their last voiceless screech
In ghetto-yard, and on the Dachau floor,—
Let them accuse now, who did once in vain beseech!
(p. 604).

In legalistic and poetic terms, Klein addresses the silence of the *Shoah* as well as a personal silence that remained with him during his final years.

While *The Hitleriad* was written during the war, "Song of Innocence" (1947) deals, satirically and succinctly within ten lines, with the aftermath of the Holocaust:

About the Crematorium where the Jews
Burn, the Nations sit in their pews,
Watching the heavenly Carbonic Bands
Cast shadows over the Bibles in their hands.

It shocks their Piety, this Altar, and they look
Away, and into the good Book.
Devotion done, they lift their eyes to see
The sky clear, full of Grace again, smoke-free;
And on the smoke-stack score-board-dots:
A Six and one-two-three-four-five-six Noughts (*Complete Poems*, p. 678).

Satire directed against hypocrisy and indifference may be appropriate, but the concluding "score-board," like some sections of *The Hitleriad*, seems inappropriate for measuring the loss of millions of people, because numerical ingenuity cannot do justice to genocide.

Klein was disappointed by *The Hitleriad*'s reception both by Jewish critics in New York, who neglected it, and by non-Jewish critics in Canada, who considered it a failure. Although the poet Irving Layton generally praises Klein's wit in his review of *The Hitleriad*, he points out the pitfalls of the satiric approach to such subject matter. According to this line of criticism, Klein lacks the consistent viewpoint, objectivity, and discriminating reticence between the real and ideal, for his subject provides him with only the real. On the one hand, Klein cannot say enough; and on the other hand, he is superfluous and fails to stand apart from the object of his satire. The most positive assessment of the poem comes from Miriam Waddington, who argues that caricature and the formal stanzas themselves provide the necessary aesthetic distance.

The Second Scroll

First published by Knopf in 1951, *The Second Scroll* is Klein's most complete treatment of the Holocaust. Part fiction, part poetry, part essay, this brief "novel" covers the first half of the twentieth century, beginning with pogroms in Eastern Europe, moving to the Holocaust, and finally focusing on the newly founded State of Israel. Each of the five chapters, named after the Pentateuch, is followed by a gloss. "Genesis" opens with a domestic Montreal perspective in counterpoint to the European part of the family of Uncle Melech Davidson—a messianic figure. The nameless narrator is Melech's nephew, who goes on a quest for his uncle. From the outset, Klein focuses on names, for in this novel of namelessness and facelessness he confronts his own impending silence as well as "silence" at the heart of the *Shoah*. "For many years my father—may he dwell in a bright Eden!—refused to permit in his presence even the mention of that person's name" (*The Second Scroll*, edited by Elizabeth Popham and Zailig Pollock, Toronto: University of Toronto Press, 2000). Although brothers-in-law across the Atlantic do not speak to each other after Melech seemingly abandons his faith, the narrator observes: "reports of his Talmudic exploits kept sounding in our house and there made a legend of his name"(p. 6).

As Klein sees it in *The Second Scroll*, the Holocaust is bracketed between Ratno's pogrom and the creation of the State of Israel. "Genesis" ends with the German invasion of Poland, which traps Uncle Melech in Kamenets, not far from Ratno, "where he was enveloped by the great smoke that for the next six years kept bellowing over the Jews of Europe—their cloud by day, their pillar of fire by night" (p. 12). If Melech is a kind of Jewish Everyman representative of an entire people, the "the great smoke" is similarly a metonymy for the Holocaust—at once too large and too little to stand for genocide. Similarly, the final biblical phrasing of cloud and pillar of fire cannot console victims or survivors of the *Shoah.*

"Exodus" picks up some of this apocalyptic imagery as the narrator imagines

> a great black aftermath cloud filling the heavens across the whole length of the humped horizon. The cloud then began to scatter . . . until revealed there shone the glory of a burnished dome—Hierosolyma the golden! (p. 13).

On the one hand, Klein sees a historical continuum between the Holocaust and the creation of the State of Israel; on the other hand, *The Second Scroll*, unlike some of his poems of the 1940s, allows Klein the historical perspective to look back over the events of World War II. This retrospective appears in the form of a letter from Melech to his Montreal family, in which he describes his survival throughout the war.

> Today I write as one who having fled from out a burning building runs up and down to seek, to find, to embrace the kinsmen who were with him in the conflagration and were saved. And we were all in that burning world, even you who were separated from it by the Atlantic—that futile bucket (p. 15).

Klein telescopes history in a kind of bifocal vision: the burning building is realistic enough yet too small to encompass the enormity of crimes against humanity; vision expands to an entire burning world to include all Jews and, by extension, all of humanity. The narrator then shrinks the ocean to a bucket to implicate innocent North Americans who should have done more to save the lives of European Jews.

Klein's survivor accounts for all victims. "I bless the Heavenly One for my rescue. It is wonderful to be alive again; to know that the trouble, the astonishment, the hissing is over; to eat, not husks or calories, but food; to have a name; and be of this world" (p. 15). From his pious upbringing Melech had lapsed into Bolshevik beliefs and abandoned the faith of his fathers; a survivor of the Holocaust, he is now a *ba'al teshuvah*, or one who has returned to religion and family. From a mere number in the camps, this survivor regains his name and humanity—a name that reflects God, *Hashem*, The Name. The guilt of the survivor enters his discourse:

> At times I feel—so bewildered and burdened in my gratitude—that the numbered dead run through my veins their plasma, that I must have their unexpired six million circuits, and that my body must be the bed of each of their nightmares (p. 15).

The first stage is a total identification with all who perished, to the point of anatomical transplant and transfusion. Then, guilt enters and a reversal of mood occurs: "sensing their death wish bubbling the channels of my blood, then do I grow bitter at my false felicity—the spared one!—and would almost add to theirs my own wish for the centigrade furnace and the cyanide flood" (p. 15).

Melech's 1949 letter from a refugee camp in Bari, Italy, tries to reconstruct the events of a decade: "I try—I look about me at the Jews of this camp, the net of our accounting, and try to compose backwards from these human indices the book of our chronicles" (p. 15). He cannot make sense of individual and mass numbers:

> I scan the tattooed arms—the man before me bears the number 12165—and wonder whether it is in *gematria* ["hidden" meanings of Hebrew words according to the numerical value of their letters] that there lies the secret of their engravure (p. 16).

In puzzlement, he studies his brethren who cheated the chimney, and all he can do is explain what happened to him in Kamenets, Poland, late in 1939 when the communists capitulated. Melech is bearded, caftaned, and fringed.

> These were years obsessed by a premonition of doom continually postponed. We were ghettoized, with none coming or going without special permission. We were catalogued: blue cards, yellow cards, red cards—our oppressors changed them at their whim so that even starvation in its various penultimate hues was uncertain. With the six-pointed Star of David we were inoculated against the world. We lived from prayer to prayer (pp. 16–17).

On one Sabbath, soldiers burst into the synagogue and defile it under the command of a lieutenant who is a specialist in Semitic affairs. He shouts "*Hagba*" (lifting of Torah) as an infant is tossed in the air from a Torah Scroll until its skull is cracked. Next this specialist announces "*hakofos*" (marching around synagogue in Torah procession) as he forces women to strip and circle the room. Then he calls "*aliyoth*" (being called up to read from the Torah) as the men are called up to the pulpit and are beaten. That afternoon the Jews of Kamenets dig a pit outside of town where they are shot to death. Melech escapes because during the first volley of shots a number of bodies fall upon him; at night he finds his way to a neighboring forest. Klein condenses the remaining crucial years into one short paragraph, as if to suggest that the rest is unspeakable.

In its emphasis on redemption and the newly founded State of Israel, the rest of *The Second Scroll* attests to what Melech has undergone and escaped from 1940 until 1945. The paragraph begins with the kindness of the forest animals in contrast to the bestiality of human beings and ends with Melech's restoration at the hands of good Christians who prevent him from sinking to an animal level.

"Gloss Beth" (second Gloss) appended to the "Exodus" chapter in the form of a poem, "Elegy," focuses entirely on the Holocaust. The poem recapitulates themes and images that appear throughout *The Second Scroll*, from names and naming to quests and questions of identity and dialogue:

> Named for my father's father, cousin, whose cry
> Might have been my cry lost in that dark land—
> Where shall I seek you? On what wind shall I
> Reach out to touch the ash that was your hand? (p. 66).

Klein goes beyond mere empathy to a full embrace and identification with the victim: he begins with the synecdoche of "cousin" who represents an entire family that in turn represents the entire Jewish people. Exchanges of the poet's "cry" for his relative's "cry" and the poet's "reach" for his relative's "hand" further exemplify his strategy of synecdoche—at once too small and too overwhelming to be accomplished. Similarly, "ash" functions metonymically for the entire Holocaust, as in the poetry of Paul Celan and Nelly Sachs. These ashes are means of assessing transatlantic tragedy:

> The Atlantic gale and the turning of the sky
> Unto the cubits of my ambience
> Scatter the martyr-motes. Flotsam-of-flame!
> God's image made the iotas of God's name!
> Oh, through a powder of ghosts I walk; through dust
> Seraphical upon the dark winds borne;
> Daily I pass among the sieved white hosts,
> Through clouds of cousinry transgress,
> Maculate with the ashes that I mourn (p. 66).

Klein shrinks distances and takes measurements—the moral dimensions of a world recently gone mad. His own personal tribulations increasingly serve as synecdoche for this entire world around the middle of the twentieth century. The four corners of the world diminish to the poet's microcosm, even as God's omnipresence is reduced to iotas of a name. In this post-Holocaust world, Klein attempts to recreate identity; in a world where names have been erased, he writes names as if he were a new Adam naming the world *ex nihilo*.

At line 14, Klein repeats his earlier question, "Where shall I seek you?" (p. 66). His ubiquitous cousin is figured through the synecdoche of David's cinctured bone and Miriam's dark hair. These individuals have to be multiplied millions of times until there is total identification: "The faces are my face!" (line 29). Varieties of repetition in "Elegy" create a *mise en abyme*—an infinite reflection of the poet through millions of lives and "Death multitudinous" that results in vertigo (p. 67). After a tour of Europe, emptied of its Jews, the poet offers earlier examples of persecution throughout history, then turns to the perpetrators and beseeches God to punish them severely.

The poem ends with a prayer for redemption so that all of those lives will not have been lost in vain.

> Gather the flames up to light orient
> Over the land; and that funest eclipse,
> Diaspora-dark, revolve from off our ways!
> Towered Jerusalem and Jacob's tent
> Set up again;
> Again renew them as they were of old (p. 70).

At the center of the chapter "Leviticus," Melech finds himself in the Vatican studying Michelangelo's frescoes in the Sistine Chapel. His Hebrew letter, "On First Seeing the Ceiling of the Sistine Chapel," forms the basis of "Gloss Gimel," which was appended to his third chapter. Melech's cryptic homily, with its polyphonous evocation of Aramaic, reinterprets Michelangelo's figures in a direction away from the New Testament; Melech applies Old Testament figures to twentieth-century events, denying any Christian values. Standing beneath the figure of Ezekiel, he refers to the "Sistine lime pit of his own day" (p. 31). With midrashic ingenuity he interprets Noah's drunkenness as a parable of murder, an intoxication with blood, and *The Expulsion from Eden* as the flight of the world's refugees.

In convoluted prose Melech imitates Michelangelo's baroque paintings and implicitly condemns the Vatican for not saving Jews. The scattering of limbs on the ceiling recalls dismembered Jews in concentration camps.

> For as I regarded the flights of athletes above me the tint subcutaneous of well-being faded, the flesh dwindled, the bones showed, and I saw again the *relictae* of the camps, entire cairns of cadavers, heaped and golgotha'd: a leg growing from its owner's neck, an arm extended from another's shoulder, wrist by jawbone, ear on ankle: the human form divine crippled, jack-knifed, trussed, corded: reduced and broken down to its named bones, femur and tibia and clavicle and ulna and thorax and pelvis and cranium: the bundled ossuaries: all in their several social heapings heaped to be taken up by the mastodon bulldozer and scavengered into its sistine limepit (p. 73).

Klein creates a *pentimento* (similar to a palimpsest) as he superimposes his own vision of contemporary history over the original paintings. At the same time as he adds, however, he also subtracts the flesh and life of murdered Jews who diminish humanity by their very loss. Klein anatomizes what he might have witnessed firsthand or through numerous photographs. This graphic description of bones from Ezekiel to concentration camps continues in his interpretation of Noah's animals: "How could this scene—this cattle issued from what cattle-cars, these sheep to slaughter led . . . speak otherwise to me than of recent furnaces and holocausts?" (p. 75). In this indictment, Klein identifies Christian history as bearing responsibility for betraying its own faith. Klein spoke but was not heard and, in the end, turned silent.

Bibliography

Primary Sources

Hath Not a Jew . . . 1940.
The Hitleriad. 1944.
The Rocking Chair, and Other Poems. 1948.
Beyond Sambation: Selected Essays and Editorials 1928–1955. 1982.
Complete Poems. 1990.
The Second Scroll. 2000.

Secondary Sources

"A. M. Klein's Montreal." *Journal of Canadian Studies* 19, no. 2, 1984. Special issue.
Brenner, Rachel Feldhay. "A. M. Klein and Mordecai Richler: Canadian Responses to the Holocaust," *Journal of Canadian Studies* 24, no. 2 (summer 1989): 65–77.
Caplan, Usher. *Like One That Dreamed: A Portrait of A. M. Klein.* Toronto: McGraw-Hill Ryerson, 1982.
Fischer, G. K. *In Search of Jerusalem: Religion and Ethics in the Writings of A. M. Klein.* McGill-Queen's University Press, 1975.
Greenstein, Michael. *Third Solitudes: Tradition and Discontinuity in Canadian-Jewish Literature.* McGill-Queen's University Press, 1989.
Hyman, Roger. "Aught from Naught: A. M. Klein's *The Second Scroll.*" *English Literary Studies.* University of Victoria, 1999.
Marshall, Tom, ed. *A. M. Klein.* Toronto: Ryerson, 1970.
Mayne, Seymour, ed. *The A. M. Klein Symposium.* University of Ottawa Press, 1975.
Pollock, Zailig. *A. M. Klein: The Story of the Poet.* University of Toronto Press, 1994.
Rozmovits, Linda. "A Narrative Messiah: The Redemptive Historiography of A. M. Klein's *The Second Scroll.*" *Prooftexts* 11.1 (January 1991): 25–39.
Spiro, S. J. *Tapestry for Designs: Judaic Allusions in The Second Scroll and The Collected Poems of A. M. Klein.* Vancouver, 1984.
Waddington, Miriam. *A. M. Klein.* Toronto: Copp Clark, 1970.

Cecilie Klein

(1925–)

TOBE LEVIN

As GHOULS IN striped pajamas stripped the cattle car of baggage, Cecilie Goldenzeil Klein's brother-in-law exchanged his watch for the whispered warning, " 'Give your child to an older woman! . . . Tonight will be the gassing and burning of the very young and the old, and mothers with children!' " (*Sentenced to Live*, New York: Holocaust Library, 1988, p. 77). Klein's mother heard; her sister Mina did not. Gently removing the baby from her daughter's arms, Mrs. Goldenzeil explained that women with children would be spared hard labor. In Klein's book *Sentenced to Live* (1988), she writes, " 'You're young and . . . [can] work,' she told Mina, vowing to take good care of her grandson. 'You must promise to look after Cillie' " (p. 77). This magnificent maternal gesture preserved both sisters' lives, for the dedication of Cecilie and Mina to each other in Auschwitz—they were called "die zwei gute Geschwister"—contributed to their survival. But this selfless act also offers one powerful motive for the memoir's genesis: in nightmares, Klein's mother appears urging, "Cecilie, bear witness" (*Sentenced to Live*, p. 146).

In Jasina, Czechoslovakia, in 1925, Klein was the sixth child born into a Hasidic family. Her mother, Rosa, ran a grocery while her clothier father, David, earned a living tutoring, after antisemitic arsonists destroyed the Jewish business district. The Goldenzeils hovered in the middle class. As a teen, Klein apprenticed in a dental laboratory and was reunited at war's end with her fiancé, survivor Joe (Shiku) Klein, a dental technician. They moved to the United States where, after conquering tuberculosis, Klein raised three children, attended the State University of New York (SUNY), Old Westbury, and began lecturing on the Holocaust after publication of her memoir *Sentenced to Live* (1988; rpt. 2000) and *Poems of the Holocaust* (1985). Cancer took Joe Klein in 1987; in 2000, Cecilie moved to Monroe Township, New Jersey, with her second husband.

An SS photograph, discovered after the war and now in *Yad Vashem* (the Jerusalem Holocaust Museum), shows Mrs. Goldenzeil holding Danny, shortly before both were taken to the gas chambers. Klein, whose father died before the war, also lost her eldest sister, Fran, her brother-in-law Avraham, and her nieces and nephews Hershi, Dori, and Etie, all murdered at Auschwitz. Her beloved brother Chaim perished when Nazis torched a hospital. Though another brother and sister survived in Palestine, Klein has never recovered from these losses: "A survivor . . . [makes] large weddings, invite[s] a great many people, but the ones she wants most will never arrive" (*Poems of the Holocaust*, Jerusalem: Gefen, 1985, p. 49).

Survivor Trauma

Sentenced to Live—an ironic title—reveals "how it feels to be a concentration camp survivor" (p. 141). The book, including pre- and postwar family photos plus moving poems in German and English, chronicles not only Nazi persecution in the foothills of the Carpathian mountains near the Polish border but also the ordeal afterward in the United States. Suffering from anhedonia—emotional numbness—Klein seeks to fit in, especially for the sake of her oldest son, Peter, who asks, "why don't you smile?" (*Sentenced*, p. 133). For "Inside [Cecilie] nothing ever smiled" (*Poems*, p. 51). The singular hardship of survivors confronted by America's aberrant, dogmatic cheerfulness—its "happy mood" (*Poems*, p. 25), its view of "life [as] one great ball" (*Poems*, p. 33), developed in "Sisterhood" and "The Friend," is summed up in "Sisterhood" 's reproach: "You were born here, and don't know from pain" (*Poems*, p. 26). Remaining "shattered," as Meir Ronnen writes in the *Jerusalem Post*, the survivor can't heal: "For so many years I wondered why I had been spared, if it hurts so much to live" (*Sentenced*, p. 137). Determined to be "like all the mummies . . . in America" (*Sentenced*, p. 133), Klein nonetheless continues at ease only with other survivors, for "the world judged the victims" (*Sentenced*, p. 5).

What in fact had the Holocaust wrought? Due to Mr. Goldenzeil's Polish citizenship, the family was targeted for deportation well before the rest of Hungary's Jews when, in 1939, Jasina became part of Hungary. Fugitives without papers, Klein, Mina, and their mother, literally had to dodge the law. When the eldest sister, Fran, was imprisoned in Bachko Topolya concentration camp, a frightened Klein went alone to Budapest to try to secure her release. A row between Klein's landlady and a neighbor aroused police interest in the allegedly Polish tenant. Together with her roommates, Klein was taken into custody. The other girls' papers proved their Hungarian citizenship, and only Klein's sangfroid convinced the officers that, if given a chance, she would retrieve the "forgotten" identification. Again, she had to flee.

On 19 March 1944, when Nazis rioted in Budapest and the Nuremberg Laws were strictly applied, Klein joined Mina and Mrs. Goldenzeil in Chust, home of Mina's husband, Nathan. Here the dreaded "evacuation order to the 'Jewish Quarter' " (*Sentenced*, p. 66) overtook them in mid-May.

In Birkenau, Klein's poetic gift attracted the benevolence of Blockeldest Fela, who, during selections, hid the sisters in a storage room. However, her protection ended when all of Block 8 stood before closed gas chamber doors: "Who had bungled . . . —the Nazi dispatcher or God?" (p. 92). Because the corpses, "blood and excrement" (p. 93) had not yet been removed, the doomed were reprieved and sent to Nuremberg to slave for Siemens. That factory destroyed, Mina and Klein were then transported to Stutthof, a Sudetenland munitions plant, and were liberated from Holeichen concentration camp.

Bearing Witness

The World Gathering of Holocaust Survivors in Jerusalem enabled Klein to become "a living witness" (*Sentenced*, p. 137) but with the agony of impotence that that entails. Testimony, as urgent and obsessive as it may be, wrestles with two impediments. First, after the war, the young poet, whose facility greatly enhanced her chances of survival, would find herself hobbling in ill-fitting English, deprived of a fluent tongue, and handicapped by an education violently ended when Jews were expelled from school–Klein had been fourteen. She will survive acutely aware that she is not "what she could have been [and] will never be" (*Poems*, p. 49). Second, bearing witness would prove to be both impossible and self-destructive. "Revenge is not mine for the culprits are free/ [I have a] prison . . . locked within me" (*Poems*, p. 42). Yes, perpetrators' offspring may disrespect them: "By your children you'll be called to task./ Why did you kill them, will ask . . ." (*Poems*, p. 43). But what of survivors' daughters and sons? Should they even be told? "Why should the young ones suffer our pain?/ What good if they know?" (*Poems*, p. 48).

When her children were little, they would often find mommy crying. "Why?" they would ask. "Just a headache, my dears" (*Sentenced*, p. 5). Klein would say . . . To bear witness, I fear, is to break taboo.

Gender as Theme

Klein has said that she "wanted to have lots of children because each child . . . [she was] bringing back from Auschwitz" (Goldhagen, p. 197). Through motherhood, the survivor has gleaned all possible joy, her memoir significant for its focus on gendered experience. The seventeen-year-old dates; eats less to dress well (traveling to Auschwitz in her finest gray coat); and expresses sensitivity to "the stench of unwashed bodies" (*Sentenced*, pp. 53–54) on the soup line. As a girl, Klein is offered rescue by a Hungarian policeman and accepts only on condition that four relatives can hide, too—impossible, but key to the youth's devotion to her family and especially her mother, who "cradles" (*Sentenced*, p. 71) her all night before they board the train. Sexually harassed by her boss (*Sentenced*, p. 46), Klein highlights specific female humiliation, such as intimate body searches: "a woman with a stick poked around our private parts" in full view of "selected citizens of Chust, who had volunteered to witness the degradation of their Jewish neighbors . . . until recently . . . their friends, even their sweethearts" (p. 73). Given the shower and shaving ritual at Birkenau; cessation of menstruation; recruitment for a military brothel; gang rape of a fourteen-year-old ballerina a memory that is powerful enough to make all ballet distasteful (after Auschwitz, Klein has never attended)—the specific vulnerability of women emerges. Even after liberation, Klein and Mina worry about Nathan and Joe: "Will they still love us as we look now, as we are now?" (p. 107)—a preoccupation more easily expressed by a woman than a man. Gender made a difference in the Holocaust; women suffered a "double vulnerability," the "Nazi machine . . . fueled [not only by anti-semitism but also by] misogyny" (Cohen).

Bibliography

Primary Sources

Poems of the Holocaust. 1985.
Sentenced to Live. 1988. 2000.

Secondary Sources

Cohen, Judy. "Lessons Learned from Gentle Heroism: Women's Holocaust Memoirs." http://www.interlog.com/~mighty/essays/lessons7.htm (10 Aug. 2001).
Goldhagen, Daniel J. *Hitler's Willing Executioners.* New York: Alfred Knopf, 1993.
McGrain, Michelle. "A New World. Survivors Immigrate to America." http://www.urbana.k12.oh.us/699/DC/hsmcgrain.htm (10 Aug. 2001).
Ronnen, Meir. "Shattered." *Jerusalem Post.* 29 Sept. 1989.

Interview

Interview by Tobe Levin. 17 August 2001.

GERDA WEISSMANN KLEIN

(1924–)

MARLENE HEINEMANN

BORN 8 MAY 1924, in Bielsko, Poland, to Julius and Helene Mueckenbrunn Weissmann, Gerda Klein was deported in June 1942 to Sosnowitz, Poland, and later to the Bolkenhain, Märzdorf, Landeshut, and Grünberg labor camps in Germany. She was liberated 7 May 1945, by American soldiers in Volary, Czechoslovakia. She married Kurt Klein on 18 June 1946. They have three children: Vivian (Mrs. James Ullman), Leslie (Mrs. Roger Simon), and James Arthur.

Significance

Klein is the author of a relatively early Holocaust memoir, *All But My Life* (1957), which has been in print for over thirty years and which has won much praise from critics. Among Holocaust memoirs, the Klein memoir is written in an exceptionally life-affirming manner. With the release in 1995 of the Academy-Award-winning documentary film *One Survivor Remembers*, which she narrated, Klein has widened her audience. She is the author of several other books, including a book explaining the Holocaust to children, *Promise of a New Spring: The Holocaust and Renewal* (1981), and a collection of letters exchanged between herself and Kurt after the war, *The Hours After: Letters of Love and Longing in War's Aftermath* (2000), which includes some observations on the wartime and postwar experiences of herself and other Holocaust survivors.

All But My Life

All But My Life traces the disintegration of fifteen-year-old Klein's normal life after the German occupation of her hometown, Bielsko, Poland, in 1939. Her elder brother Arthur is deported to Russian-occupied territory and later to a camp in Poland. Her parents, who live with Klein in the basement of their home and then in the Bielsko ghetto, are eventually sent to Auschwitz. They and all other members of Klein's family perish in the Holocaust, except for an uncle, living in Turkey. Klein works on weaving looms and spinning machines in three labor camps: Bolkenhain, Landeshut, and Grünberg, all in Silesia, Germany. At Bolkenhain and Landeshut, she works for the Kramsta-Methner Frahne Company. She does other work at a fourth camp, Märzdorf.

The skill in weaving that Klein acquires in Bolkenhain saves her from being sent to a death camp and spares her from some of the miseries, such as starvation, thirst, exposure, hard labor, and selections for death, common in other camps. However, the conditions under which the weavers live are not ordinary: the work is especially hard and long (eleven to thirteen hours a day), requires constant running, and produces chronic eyestrain. The weavers and spinners are plagued by breaking threads and the threat of punishment for "mistakes," considered by the supervisors to be sabotage.

Conditions in Klein's four labor camps range from relatively less terrible (as in Bolkenhain and Landeshut) to more life threatening (as in Märzdorf and Grünberg). At Märzdorf, Klein is punished with day and night hard labor for refusing to have sex with a supervisor. She is saved by a combination of her friend Ilse's intervention and the director of Bolkenhain's timely search for trained weavers. In Grünberg, the weavers are in danger of contracting tuberculosis, a condition that results in being sent to Auschwitz. In addition, Klein, with other inmates, undergoes a severe facial beating by an SS guard.

As the end of the war approaches in the winter of 1945, Klein and her comrades endure a death march of 350 miles over a three-month period in which all but 120 of the 4,000 slave girls perish from starvation, disease, exposure, and exhaustion. Klein gives some indirect credit for saving her life to the ski boots that her father made her wear at the time of deportation.

The narrator of the memoir portrays her wartime identity with notable optimism about her ability to transcend the prevalent horrors. She is able to do this by retaining her faith in God and her ability to fantasize about her homecoming to her family at the end of the war, although she does worry that her parents may be dead. Her hope of survival allows her to endure many hardships in the camps. To help keep her and her friends' hopes alive, Klein writes skits and acts in them for her fellow prisoners in Bolkenhain, where conditions are fairly good. In Grünberg, where conditions are much worse, she describes playing make-believe games with her friend Liesel.

Her memoir provides a collective portrait of the young Jewish women who are inmates in the camps. Klein depicts the substitute family that she and her three closest friends form, which allows them to pool their resources and give each other support. While conditions are not life threatening, the support contributes to the maintenance of hope. Klein portrays herself as the most hopeful among her friends, and refers to her influence on her friend from Bielsko Ilse's moods. When conditions get worse, the friends contribute to each other's survival chances. At Grünberg, where food rations are reduced, Klein and Suse, her Viennese friend, get a better job, which pays more food, allowing them to share extra soup with Ilse and Liesel, a Czech member of the group. At Märzdorf, Ilse saves Klein from day and night hard labor by accompanying her to work and telling the supervisor that the inmate whose number has been called is Klein's instead of her own, whose number it actually is. This leads to both being restored to weaving work at Landeshut. On the death march, Klein, Ilse, Suse, and Liesel keep each other, as well as others, from falling asleep, and thus from freezing to death, when they have to spend the night outside during a snowfall. The memoir conforms to scholarship, which suggests that camp inmates, especially women, formed surrogate families for mutual assistance and support. Klein also describes other life-affirming group activities such as the celebration of birthdays and religious holidays and discussions among the inmates.

Klein uses her privileged position of survivor to bear witness to the lives and deaths of many who were less fortunate. These portraits add to the value of the memoir as a picture of Holocaust reality that transcends survivorship. Emblematic of these reports is the statement about Lotte, an acquaintance who dies on the death march, "I cannot help but want to tell her story for I might be the only one left in the world who knows it" (*All But My Life,* New York: Hill and Wang, 1995 p. 130). A prominent place is given to the story of Abek Feigenblatt, a Jewish artist who loves Klein and goes voluntarily to a concentration camp near Landeshut to be near her. He does not survive. Klein's telling of Abek Feigenblatt's story is in apparent agreement with Terrence des Pres's assessment of the survivor's will to bear witness about the concentration camp experience as intrinsic to the experience of survival (des Pres, pp. 30–38).

Klein reports, in the epilogue to the 1995 edition of her book, that she remains anchored to the past by both pleasant and unpleasant memories. She also reveals that her life's work as a volunteer for Jewish organizations allows her to give "back a small part of what I have received," part of which is inexplicable survival (*All But My Life*, pp. 261).

Critical opinion is divided as to whether Holocaust literature should celebrate the heroism of those who were touched by the *Shoah.* The view of Lawrence Langer is to reject any depiction of transcendence of the Holocaust ordeal (Langer, pp. 4, 162–143). Esther Fuchs, writing about Klein's documentary film/video *One Survivor Remembers* and other Holocaust films, criticizes the films for presenting idealized characters because this implies that the evil of the Holocaust lies in destroying superior people. These heroines "are glorified for being high-minded, innocent, optimistic, humane, kind, beautiful, and asexual" (Fuchs, pp. 98–99). Self-idealization seems to be a characteristic of many autobiographies and recent Holocaust memoirs in particular. Estelle C. Jelinek has seen a tendency toward self-idealization in men's autobiographies, while women try to convince the reader of their self worth (Jelinek, p. 15). Self-dramatizing Holocaust memoirs (which show prisoners in defiance of their Nazi persecutors) are written, especially from a distance of many years, by both men and women when they wish to convey participation in resistance activities (Heinemann, pp. 61–62, 64–74).

Several critics and reviewers have either written favorably about the heroism of characters in *All But My Life* or have tried to explain it through something intrinsic to the experience. Harold M. Foster has praised the memoir, in part, because it enhances the nobility of people. He advocates making the memoir required reading for American high school students (Foster 1997, pp. 56–59). Virgilia Peterson, an early reviewer, tries to account for the virtuousness and lack of conflict among the inmates by assuming that Klein wrote the memoir in part "as the last gift she can still bestow upon parents, brother, childhood friends, devoted suitor and companions in slavery who . . . failed to survive" (Peterson, p. 12). The tendency of survivors to write positively of the dead in Holocaust literature has been described by Elie Wiesel as an impulse to erect "an invisible tombstone to the memory of the dead unburied" (Wiesel, p. 25). The Holocaust memoir may constitute the act of mourning and memorialization that survivors were not permitted at the time of the deaths of their companions. Survivor guilt, documented by numerous survivors and others, and the charge of guilt for not resisting more, may have motivated Klein to portray herself and other inmates as uniformly noble. She expresses a suggestion of survival guilt when she wakes up in a hospital after liberation: "I remembered [Tusia] lying dead in the snow. Why am I here? I wondered. I am no better" (Klein, *All But My Life*, p. 218). It seems fair to consider the author's opinion. In a personal letter, she said that the teenaged inmates cooperated with each other out of a desire to resist their common enemy. "If and when there was any friction, it was not beyond the norm found in ordinary life." That was her experience, she says.

The near-universal praise that *All But My Life* has received from reviewers includes the assessment of its style and formal elements, but there have not been many in-depth critical studies. Praising *All But My Life* as an "extraordinarily well" written book, Foster refers to its evocative and loving language (Foster 1997, p. 59). Samuel L. Simon calls the memoir "one of the most beautifully written documents" he has ever read and "as sensitive and disturbing a story as is 'The Diary of Anne Frank.' " Marlene E. Heinemann finds resistance acts in the memoir believable because of the closely drawn relationship between risks taken and the emotional interdependence of survivor characters (Heinemann, p. 127).

The memoir resembles a novel of psychological realism with poetic elements. It is filled with details, both those of the external world and those of a more psychological nature. Small gestures and conversations portray personal character and the dynamics of family relations and the responses, of each person to new stages in the continuing disaster. The lyrical quality of the memoir gives it the quality that Alvin Rosenfeld has called "the presentation of feeling through certain brilliant images" in Holocaust literature, a technique that aids the reader's access to the vicarious experience of the *Shoah* (Rosenfeld, p. 80). Prominent images include a watch lying on the carpet of the Weissmanns' living room on the morning of the German occupation of Klein's hometown, with the watch's hands stopped at 9:10, freezing time; and Ilse giving Klein a raspberry, following Klein's brutal beating, representing the small miracle of inmate assistance in the camps.

The Hours After: Letters of Love and Longing in War's Aftermath

The Hours After, which is primarily a collection of love letters between Klein and her fiancé Kurt from May 1945 to May 1946, also contains numerous observations and recollections of the Nazi German occupation of Poland and Klein's experiences during and after the Holocaust. Some of these details are contained in her letters to Kurt, while others are included in commentary written decades later at the time of publication in 2000. Many of these observations seem more objective and less colored by survival guilt and imagination than those contained in the memoir. In the recent book Klein is sometimes better able to describe the suffering of her family, of her acquaintances, and of herself. For example, she describes her parents, at the time just before deportation, with greater realism than in the memoir: "I did not want to picture my father as he looked after his heart attack: gaunt, gray, and weak, or my mother as the emaciated, frail, worn-down, aging woman she had become by the time of our separation" (Klein, p. 44). She also refers to the difficult situation of many other young women who survived the camps and death march but could not adjust to freedom (Klein, p. 223).

In *The Hours After*, these problems are subordinated to the central theme of suffering redeemed by the love between Klein and Kurt. While their developing romance occupies the end of the memoir *All But My Life*, the theme of redemption is more central in *The Hours After*. Klein explicitly attributes to her husband and children the power to help her overcome her tragic losses.

The structure of *The Hours After*, in which the postwar correspondence of Klein and Kurt alternates with present observations, provides the perspective of both the past and the present and offers more clarity than would be possible from only a collection of letters. The language of the letters is intimate, colloquial, and often highly descriptive. Both authors are gifted writers. The original German has been translated into English, but the translator is unnamed.

All But My Life and *The Hours After* complement each other, although they can be read separately. They are highly readable, and they emphasize transcendence of the horrors and suffering.

Bibliography

Primary Sources

All But My Life. 1957.
The Blue Rose. 1974.
Promise of a New Spring: The Holocaust and Renewal. 1981.
A Passion for Sharing: The Life of Edith Rosenwald Stern. 1984.
One Survivor Remembers. 1995. Video.
All But My Life. 1997. Sound Recording.
The Hours After: Letters of Love and Longing in War's Aftermath. 2000. Written with Kurt Klein.

Secondary Sources

Baumel, Judith Tydor. *Double Jeopardy: Gender and the Holocaust*. Portland, Oregon: Vallentine Mitchell, 1998.

Contemporary Authors Online. The Gale Group, 1999.

des Pres, Terrence. *The Survivor: An Anatomy of Life in the Death Camps*. Oxford: Oxford University Press, 1976.

Foster, Harold M. "All But My Life." *English Journal* (February 1979): 50–51.

———. "Embracing *All But My Life* by Gerda Weissmann Klein." *English Journal* 86, no. 8 (December 1997): 56–59.

Fuchs, Esther, ed. "The Construction of Heroines in Holocaust Films: The Jewess as Beautiful Soul." In *Women and the Holocaust: Narrative and Representation*. Lanham, Md.: University Press of America, 1999.

Heinemann, Marlene. *Gender and Destiny: Women Writers and the Holocaust*. Westport, Conn.: Greenwood Press, 1986.

Jelinek, Estelle C. *Women's Autobiography*. Bloomington: Indiana University Press, 1980.

Kremer, S. Lillian. *Women's Holocaust Writing: Memory and Imagination*. Lincoln: University of Nebraska Press, 1999.

Langer, Lawrence. *Holocaust Testimonies: The Ruins of Memory*. New Haven, Conn.: Yale University Press, 1991.

Mitgang, Herbert. "All But Hope Was Lost." *The New York Times* (November 3, 1957): 61.

Peterson, Vergilia. "A Polish Victim Remembers." *New York Herald Tribune Book Review* (October 27, 1957): 12.

Rosenfeld, Alvin H. *A Double Dying: Reflections on Holocaust Literature*. Bloomington: Indiana University Press, 1980.

Simon, Samuel L. *Library Journal* 82 (October 15, 1957): 2532.

Wiesel, Elie. *Legends of Our Time*. New York: Avon, 1968.

VICTOR KLEMPERER
(1881–1961)

MICHAEL OSSAR

"You I will eat last"
(Polyphemus to Odysseus).

VICTOR KLEMPERER WAS born in 1881, the eighth of nine children of Rabbi Wilhelm Klemperer, in Landsberg an der Warthe (the conductor, Otto Klemperer, was a cousin). In 1890 the family moved to Berlin, where Wilhelm became the rabbi of a reform congregation. Klemperer attended the humanistic gymnasium in Berlin and then left school at the age of sixteen to begin a three-year commercial apprenticeship, after which he returned to school and took his graduation exam, the *Abitur*. In 1906 he married pianist Eva Schlemmer, a Lutheran. He studied philosophy, German and Romance language literatures at the universities of Berlin, Munich, Geneva, and Paris, earning his Ph.D. with a dissertation on the German novelist Friedrich Spielhagen and converting to Lutheranism (like his three older brothers) in 1912. After a stint as a journalist in Berlin he chose to continue his studies at the University of Munich. Under supervision of Karl Vossler he wrote a *Habilitationsschrift*, a two-volume study of Montesquieu, and in 1914 was offered a lectureship at the University of Naples.

In 1915 Klemperer enlisted in the army and fought on the front in Flanders until he was wounded and transferred to the military censorship office in Kovno and Leipzig. He was decorated and like many Jewish veterans hoped that his service at the front and his medal would protect him after Hitler came to power. After the war, in 1919, he became an assistant professor at the University of Munich and in 1920 he was offered a full professorship in Romance literature at the Technical University of Dresden, where he taught until he was relieved of his duties by the Nazis and forced to retire in 1935 because, unbeknownst to him, he had become a Jew again on 30 January 1933. The question of identity and of the nature of his "Germanness" plays a major role in the diaries of this convert from an assimilated family who eschewed jingoistic nationalism but at the same time felt himself a patriotic and grateful heir to the cultural traditions of his fatherland. At one point he remarks that if pressed he would have to admit that Germany meant very much to him and Judaism nothing, and later on he consistently rejects Zionism as just another manifestation of militant nationalism even as the noose closes around his neck.

All during the Third Reich Klemperer sought refuge in his scholarly writing, working particularly zealously on his history of eighteenth-century French literature until the ever-increasing body of restrictions made this impossible: he was prohibited from using the university library, later from borrowing books from lending libraries, still later from borrowing books from Aryans, and from having a telephone. Finally, his typewriter was confiscated. As a result, he fled still further inward, devoting himself to his diaries, since 1938 to his autobiography, and to a study of the language and propaganda of the Third Reich, which appeared in 1947 and immediately became a bestseller.

In 1940 the Klemperers were driven from their house and quartered in various so-called *Judenhäuser* (Jews' houses), large villas converted to house the Jews who had not yet been deported to the death camps because they were married to Aryans. Just prior to the infamous firebombing of Dresden on 16 February 1945, Klemperer had to deliver deportation notices to a number of members of the Jewish community. He and Eva were likely scheduled to be killed several days later, but in the chaos of the firebombing that killed so many of their tormentors and some of their comforters, they escaped separately. Freed by what Peter Gay calls one of the "tasteless ironies of history" they miraculously found each other, removed Victor's yellow star, and set out for the home of Agnes Scholze, a Wendish Catholic and opponent of the Nazis who had once worked in the Klemperers' house. Afraid that in the last days of the war they might be recognized and identified to the Gestapo, the couple sought refuge with Annemarie Köhler, a Christian surgeon who had helped them with rations and clothing and in many other ways at great danger to herself. Next, the Klemperers stayed at the house of Hans Scherner, a party member but an old friend, until they were again forced to move. Altering their papers to disguise their Jewish name, they eventually made their way to Bavaria. When the war ended they laboriously returned to Dresden and to their house.

In November 1945 Klemperer chose to join the communist party. Although he had strong doubts and at one point noted the similarity between the Soviet propaganda posters of Stalin and the Nazi posters of Goebbels, he also felt sincerely that the KPD was the party most likely to take denazification seriously. On 1 November 1945, Klemperer's professorship at the Technical University of Dresden was restored to him. In 1947 he accepted a position at the University of Greifswald, and in 1948 he moved to the University of Halle. Simultaneously he taught at the Humboldt University in Berlin from 1951 until 1954 and became a member of the Deutsche Akademie der Wissenschaften. Eva died in 1951 and he married Hadwig Kirchner the following year, who on his death in 1961, and following his wishes, deposited his diaries in the Saxon State Library in Dresden where they were rediscovered by a former student, Walter Nowojski, who edited them with Hadwig's help.

The Wartime Diaries

The eminent British historian C. V. Wedgwood once remarked that history has to be lived forward but is written in retrospect. We have any number of studies written in retrospect but we have relatively few contemporaneous diaries that record how the Third Reich appeared from the perspective of one of its victims—Peter Gay, in his review, calls this a murder mystery as seen through the eyes of the victim. Klemperer's wartime diaries, which begin with scenes of domestic life, with money worries and visits to the cinema and dinner parties and university politics and comical attempts to learn how to drive, record with absolute honesty and precision the thoughts and feelings of a man more perceptive than many statesmen. They tell the story of a man who struggles to maintain his psychological equilibrium and his naked physical existence as the circle closed tighter and tighter around him and finally reduced his world to a few rooms in a "Jews' house." We readers looking back on this period have at our disposal whole libraries that try to explain it, whole armies of researchers with names like "functionalists" (historians Martin Broszat and Hans Mommsen) and "intentionalists" (Lucy Davidowicz). So when we read, say, that Bruno Walter is returning to Germany to give a concert tour in the late thirties or that Sigmund Freud did not emigrate until 1938 and Peter Gay not until 1939, we wonder how they could have been so unperceptive. A great part of the value of these diaries is that they show us how the monumental events that we now know so well appeared to people who lived in Germany and who heard nothing but Nazi-controlled radio and read nothing but a Nazi-controlled press. In fact, the Jews in Klemperer's situation were a subset of this populace who didn't even have access to newspapers and the daily army bulletins and were reduced to interpreting rumors. As Frank Kermode remarks, the *Kristallnacht* (the day on which normal life became impossible for Klemperer, according to Martin Chalmers, editor and translator of Klemperer's diaries) was inconceivable until it happened. At one point Klemperer notes how he and his house mates concluded that when the frequency of the word "heroic" in the army bulletins increased the war was going badly. We learn how the Reichstag fire, the nonaggression pact, the Anschluss, the invasion of Poland, the Battle of Britain, the fall of Stalingrad, the North African campaign, the landing on Sicily, the Normandy invasion, and the attempt on Hitler's life looked from inside to a person who knew neither the outcome of the war nor whether he would live another day.

Unlike Anne Frank's, Klemperer's diaries are completely unsentimental (on 10 April 1933 he writes "Man is bad" [*I Will Bear Witness: The Diaries of Victor Klemperer*, Vol. 1, New York: Random House, 1998, p. 13]) and they are completely revealing; it is clear that Klemperer never expected his very private notes to be published. They show his desperate attempts to find a way to build a house for Eva as a way to help her through her fits of depression. We read of his half-hearted attempts to emigrate and his fear that he could not survive in exile, that he would be dependent on the generosity of his more successful brothers of whom he was jealous, so that when emigration finally became impossible in the summer of 1941 he seems almost relieved. We read of his doubts in his professional achievements but also his anger at not obtaining a position at a major humanistic university. We see his obvious love for Eva and we witness Eva's heroically loyal and tireless efforts to keep Victor alive with every ounce of her (limited) strength, but we also read of his pangs of conscience for exposing Eva to danger by asking her to transport his diaries to safety. We read his self-reproaches for stealing potatoes from an elderly woman who often did not eat all her rations.

We hear the story of his imprisonment by the Gestapo for failing to darken a room at night and the story of his forced labor. It is clear that the diaries were an obsession, at once a flight from a world of daily increasing peril and a means of gaining the psychological stability to fight back, the "balancing pole" of a tightrope walker as Klemperer once put it, and a heroic attempt to record what had happened to him and people like him akin to that of Emmanuel Ringelblum recording the destruction of the Warsaw ghetto.

Above all, the reader is struck by two very different but equally pervasive phenomena. On the one hand there is the ubiquitous cruelty of opportunists like nearly all of Klemperer's colleagues at the university, of strangers on the street (mostly young thugs), and the almost daily flood of ordinances restricting his life and compressing it just as the world of the narrator in Poe's story about the Inquisition, "The Pit and the Pendulum," closes in on him as the walls move ever closer. At one point Klemperer takes the trouble to list thirty-one different restrictions, the violation of any one of which would likely have meant his death (one example: his beloved cat had to be killed, presumably because it was non-Aryan). But there is a second phenomenon, equally striking to the reader, and that is the frequent instances of human decency he experiences: of tradesmen secretly giving him a few extra potatoes, of Aryan friends who would visit under cover of darkness, of strangers who would risk their lives to shake his hand or remark that the weather would change soon. Of course it must be noted that as desperate as Klemperer's situation was, he did write from outside the death camps looking in and not, like Elie Wiesel or Primo Levi, from inside looking out. His entry of 24 October 1944 records rumors that six or seven million Jews have been "shot or gassed" in the east; this is hearsay for him, not experience; the Germans Klemperer saw on the home front in Dresden and those that Daniel Goldhagen describes in parts II, IV, and V of his book, *Hitler's Willing Executioners: Ordinary Germans and the Holocaust*, were different people.

All of these incidents of cruelty and of human decency are recorded equally honestly; all are recorded with great precision and sketched with a few efficient strokes of the pen. Often Klemperer will tell of someone who was a Nazi but a decent person nonetheless, seduced by perverted nationalism; a Gestapo officer who whispers advice to an old woman ordered to report to Gestapo headquarters telling her not to go. Any reader inclined to see the German people in Manichean terms will, when confronted with such instances of individual behavior, come away from this book with a keen sense of just how complicated the world was between 1933 and 1945.

At the same time that Klemperer is recording this complexity he, as a true heir to his beloved Enlightenment, is trying to make sense of it. One of the most frequently recurring rubrics in these diaries is "vox populi," Klemperer's attempt to ascertain whether some bit of gossip he has heard or overheard is in any sense representative. Soon, as he becomes increasingly aware of the useless nature of this undertaking, the rubric changes to "voces populi." One reason the German public greeted the publication of this book in 1995 so fervently was that it appeared to provide evidence to refute Daniel Goldhagen's assertions in *Hitler's Willing Executioners*, the German translation of which appeared in 1996. These assertions grew out of a Harvard doctorate dissertation. Instead of studying Nazi elites and decision makers (like most previous studies), Goldhagen looked at the "ordinary people" who actually did the killing, and tried to figure out their motivation by conducting interviews and examining documents. He concluded that there had long been a pervasive strain of what he called "eliminationist antisemitism" in Germany. The diaries caused a sensation in Germany, selling over 160,000 hardback copies by 1998 and spawning numerous public readings, a dramatic version, and a thirteen-part television program. If even Klemperer could not discern which voices represented a consensus among his countrymen, then it seemed clear to some that Goldhagen was wrong in ascribing a pervasive "eliminationist" antisemitism to the Germans and claiming that this explained why the Holocaust had occurred in Germany and not elsewhere.

A reader outside Germany, however, might be reminded of Andrew Mellon's remark that he had no reason to go to a horse race because he already knew that one horse could run faster than another. We already knew that "ordinary Germans" other than Hitler committed the atrocities described in Goldhagen's book and we already knew (at least Hannah Arendt and Theodor Adorno knew) that there were large numbers of individual Germans who in various ways and to various degrees resisted Hitler's tyranny and antisemitism. When he arrived in New York in 1938, Thomas Mann famously said "where I am is Germany," thus echoing Klemperer's conviction, maintained until very nearly the last days of the war, that his own brand of "German-ness," derived from the Enlightenment, represented the real Germany and that the Nazis represented an irrational, Romantic perversion of it. For all his acuity, however, like a man with a supersensitive hearing aid, Klemperer was never able to sort out in his own mind which of the "voces populi" were in the majority and which were background noise. For Thomas Mann to make a grand gesture and say that where he was was Germany might be rhetorically effective but it was also quixotic and vacuous if the other "seventy-nine and a half million out of eighty million Germans" (*I Will Bear Witness: The Diaries of Victor Klemperer*. Vol. 1, p. xv) living in Germany thought otherwise, as Klemperer believed, especially after March of 1936 and during the period of the early wartime successes. In April of 1933 and even later on he viewed antisemitism as a brilliantly effective strategy, as the glue that held the Third Reich together, Hitler's most potent psychological weapon (e.g., "How deeply Hitler's attitudes are rooted in the German people" [*I Will Bear Witness: The Diaries of Victor Klemperer*, Vol. 1, p. 253]). However, in March 1942 he writes, "I think for every *one* believer . . . there are by now fifty unbelievers" (*I Will Bear Witness: The Diaries of Victor Klemperer*, Vol. 2, p. 24). If one takes into account all of Klemperer's conjectures on the voces populi, on the question of the genocidal antisemitism of the sort claimed by Goldhagen, they seem in the end to approximate Saul Friedländer's assessment:

> During the 1930s, the German population, the great majority of whom espoused traditional antisemitism, did not demand anti-Jewish measures, nor did they clamour for extreme implementation. Amongst most ordinary Germans there was acquiescence regarding the segregation and dismissal from civil service of Jews. There were some individual initiatives to benefit from their assets, and there was some glee in witnessing their degradation. But outside party ranks, there was no massive popular agitation to unleash violence against them, or to expel them from Germany. The majority accepted the steps taken by the regime, and looked the other way (Saul Friedländer, 1997; quoted by Susie Ehrmann).

Other readers both within and without Germany read the diaries to see when the isolated Klemperer first became aware of the death camps as an index of when the average German must have known: the first mention of Auschwitz occurs in March 1942, just a few months after the Wannsee conference. Marcel Reich-Ranicki, the influential literary critic, noted after reading these diaries that no German civilian could plausibly claim ignorance. However, the actual entry for 16 March leaves the reader with a somewhat more complicated impression:

> In the last few days I heard Auschwitz (or something like it) . . . mentioned as the most dreadful concentration camp. Work in a mine, death within a few days . . . Buchenwald, near Weimar, is said to be not necessarily and immediately fatal, but "worse than prison." Twelve hours of work [a day] under the SS (VK II, pp. 28–29).

Although Klemperer seems never to be under any illusions about the ultimate fate in store for the Jews as a race and for himself in particular (Thomas Powers notes in the *London Review of Books* that he was typical in every way except that he survived), still the reader realizes with horror just how much worse than he imagined, how inconceivable even to a perceptive and sophisticated mind the scope and functioning of the death camps actually were. An interesting footnote: Klemperer records the astonishment of some Christian friends when they learned of the extent and the egregiousness of the restrictions imposed on the Jews.

The Instrumentalization of the Diaries

The reaction of the German public to *I Will Bear Witness* is just one in a long series of painful communal attempts to come to terms with Germany's past: the Nuremberg trials, the Bitburg controversy, the historians' debate, the showing of the American film *Holocaust* and of Edgar Reitz's *Heimat* films on German television, the reception of *Schindler's List*, the resignation from the Bundestag of Philip Jenninger, the reaction to Goldhagen's book, the controversy about a Holocaust memorial in Berlin, the debate about "Leitkultur," the *Wehrmacht* exhibition, Martin Walser's speech on the posthumous award of the Geschwister Scholl Prize to Klemperer, "Das Prinzip Genauigkeit," and the Walser-Bubis controversy. This is not the place to consider this series of milestones in what one of the most influential German philosophers of the postwar period, Jürgen Habermas, called critical public discourse, and we have already noted how Klemperer's diaries were exploited as part of the complicated German reaction to Daniel Goldhagen's book. Significantly, the general public at the many debates between Goldhagen and professional historians was overwhelmingly on Goldhagen's side. Ultimately, the horrors his book described were beyond dispute, as Ulrich Greiner emphasized when he referred to a debate without controversy, a *Konsens-Debatte*. Members of the German historical establishment (especially moderates and leftists: Eberhard Jäckel, Hans-Ulrich Wehler, Hans Mommsen, Reinhard Kühnl) attacked Goldhagen for the lack of novelty of his thesis (seen as a resurrection of the discredited charge of collective guilt), the insufficiency of his research into governmental structures, selective quotation, and ignorance of other research. Of course these charges may all be justified without disproving his central thesis. It was for this purpose that Klemperer's diaries were appropriated.

A final example of the instrumentalization of these diaries grew out of the speech that the neoconservative novelist Martin Walser gave on the awarding of the

Geschwister Scholl Prize to Klemperer in 1995. The speech was generally seen by its critics (Habermas walked out) as a problematic attempt to use Klemperer to revive the discredited thesis of a German-Jewish symbiosis, a thesis that had been famously attacked by Gershom Scholem. Scholem was a philosopher, as well as a professor at Hebrew University in Jerusalem. An expert on Jewish mysticism, he has been the author of such works as *Major Trends in Jewish Mysticism*, *On the Kabbalah and Its Symbolism*, and *From Berlin to Jerusalem*. Stuart Taberner demonstrates how Walser accomplishes this by emphasizing Klemperer's patriotic devotion to German culture, by concentrating on his autobiographical writings prior to 1933, and by positing a putative authentic German tradition "entirely unrelated to the deviant concept of racial superiority imposed by Hitler" (Taberner, p. 715). Taberner demonstrates how Walser, by drawing his examples primarily from the diaries of the early period of relative indifference to rabid antisemitic dogma and from the later period of war-weariness, tries to place the blame for the National Socialism "discontinuity" in German history on power elites, on Hitler, on the "stab in the back" legend ("without which the second catastrophe [i.e., Hitler] wouldn't have happened"), thus exculpating the broad mass of the populace (Taberner).

Michael Brenner, professor at the University of Munich, points out how Walser, in emphasizing Klemperer's struggles to define his identity and to reclaim his German-ness from the Nazi perversion of it, is basically assenting to the common assumption of both the antisemite Heinrich von Treitschke and the liberal Theodor Mommsen in the original "antisemitism debate" in Berlin of 1879: if the Jews were to survive in the sea of German culture, it could only be at the price of divesting themselves of their Jewishness. The "problematic symbiosis," it turns out, has become no less problematic since Gershom Scholem.

Bibliography

Primary Sources

Paul Lindau. 1909.

Die Zeitromane Friedrich Spielhagens und ihre Wurzeln (The Contemporary Novels of Friedrich Spielhagen and Their Roots). 1913.

Montesquieu. 1914.

Geschichte der französischen literatur (History of French Literature). 1920.

Einführung in das Mittelfranzösische (Introduction to Middle-French). 1921.

Idealistische Neuphilologie: Festschrift für Karl Vossler zum 6. September 1922 (Idealistic Neo-Philology: Festschrift for Karl Vossler on September 6, 1922). With Eugen Lerch. 1922.

Die moderne französische Prosa (1870–1920) (Modern French Prose [1870–1920]). 1923.

Vom Geiste neuer Literaturforschung: Festschrift für Oskar Walzel (On the Spirit of Modern Literary Scholarship: Festschrift for Oskar Walzel). With Julius Wahle. 1924.

Klemperer, Victor, Helmut Anthony Hatzfeld, and Fritz Neubert. *Die romanischen Literaturen von der Renaissance bis zur französischen Revolution* (Romance Literatures from the Renaissance to the French Revolution). With Helmut Anthony Hatzfeld and Fritz Neubert. 1924.

Idealistische Philologie (Idealistic Philology). With Eugen Lerch. 1925.

Frühdrucke aus der Bücherei Victor von Klemperer (Incunabula from the Library of Victor von Klemperer). 1927.

Die moderne französische Lyrik von 1870 bis zur Gegenwart: Studie–erläuterte Texte (Modern French Lyric Poetry from 1870 to the Present: Study and Texts with Commentary). 1929.

Corneille inconnu (The Unknown Corneille). With Pierre Corneille. 1933.

LTI: Notizbuch eines Philologen (LTI: A Philologist's Notebook). 1947.

Die moderne französische Prosa. Studie und erläuterte Texte (Modern French Prose: Study and Texts with Commentary). 1948.

Delilles "Gärten": Ein Mosaikbild des 18. Jahrhunderts (Delille's 'Gardens': A Mosaic of the 18th Century). 1954.

Geschichte der französischen Literatur im 18. Jahrhundert (History of French Literature in the 18th Century). 1954.

Vor 33-nach 45: Gesammelte Aufsätze (Before 33—After 45: Collected Essays). 1956.

Geschichte der französischen Literatur im 19. und 20. Jahrhundert, 1800–1925 (History of French Literature in the 19th and 20th Centuries, 1800–1925). 1956.

Moderne französische Lyrik (Dekadenz-Symbolismus-Neuromantik): Studie und kommentierte Texte. Neuausgabe mit einem Anhang: Vom Surrealismus zur Résistance (Modern French Lyric Poetry (Decadence-Symbolism-Neo-Romanticism): Study and Texts with Commentary). 1957.

LTI: Notizbuch eines Philologen (LTI: A Philologist's Notebook). 1966.

Die unbewältigte Sprache. Aus dem Notizbuch eines Philologen LTI (Unfinished Language. LTI: From a Philologist's Notebook). 1966.

LTI. Die unbewältigte Sprache. Aus dem Notizbuch eines Philologen (LTI. The Unfinished Language. From a Philologist's Notebook). 1969.

LTI: Notizbuch eines Philologen (LTI: A Philologist's Notebook). Leipzig: Reclam, 1975.

Die Zeitromane Friedrich Spielhagens und ihre Wurzeln (The Contemporary Novels of Friedrich Spielhagen and Their Roots). Hildesheim: Gerstenberg, 1978.

Curriculum vitae: Jugend um 1900 (Curriculum Vitae: A Youth around 1900). 1989.

Zwiespältiger denn je: Dresdner Tagebuch 1945, Juni bis Dezember (More Ambivalent Than Ever: Dresden Diary 1945, June to December). 1995.

Ich will Zeugnis ablegen bis zum letzten: Tagebücher (*I Shall Bear Witness: The Diaries of Victor Klemperer*). With Walter Nowojski and Hadwig Klemperer. 1995.

Leben sammeln, nicht fragen wozu und warum (To Collect Life, to Not Ask Why). With Walter Nowojski and Christian Löser. 1996.

Und so ist alles schwankend: Tagebücher Juni bis Dezember 1945 (And So Everything Is Tottering: Diaries June to December 1945). With Günter Jäckel and Hadwig Klemperer. 1996.

An Annotated Edition of Victor Klemperer's LTI: Notizbuch eines Philologen. With Roderick H. Watt. 1997.

I Shall Bear Witness: The Diaries of Victor Klemperer. Translated and edited by Martin Chalmers. 1998.

I Will Bear Witness: The Diaries of Victor Klemperer. 1998.

Victor Klemperer: Ein Leben in Bildern (Victor Klemperer: A Life in Pictures). With Christian Borchert, Almut Giesecke, and Walter Nowojski. 1999.

So sitze ich denn zwischen allen Stühlen: Tagebücher (Thus I Sit between All Chairs). With Walter Nowojski and Christian Löser. 1999.

The Language of the Third Reich LTI, Lingua Tertii Imperii: A Philologist's Notebook. With Martin Brady. 2000.

Secondary Sources

Althaus, Hans-Peter. "Distanz und Nähe: Deutschjüdische Wissenschaftler und das Jiddische." *Zeitschrift für germanistische Linguistik* 29, no. 1 (2001): 23–39.

Aschheim, Steven E. *Scholem, Arendt, Klemperer: Intimate Chronicles in Turbulent Times.* Bloomington: Indiana University Press, 2001.

Bernstein, Richard. "How Little Things Add up to Horror: I Will Bear Witness. A Diary of the Nazi Years 1933–1941. Review." *New York Times*, 11 November 1998.

Birken, Lawrence. "Prussianism, Nazism, and Romanticism in the Thought of Victor Klemperer." *German Quarterly* 72, no. 1 (winter 1999): 33–43.

Brady, Philip. "Shoveling Snow." *Times Literary Supplement (TLS)*, 24 January 1997, p. 27.

Brenner, Michael. "Der neue alte Antisemitismusstreit." *Süddeutsche Zeitung*, 21 December 1998.

Craig, Gordon A. "Destiny in Any Case: Ich will Zeugnis ablegen bis zum letzten: Tagebücher 1933–1945. Review." *New York Review of Books*, 3 December 1998, pp. 4–6.

Dirschauer, Johannes. *Tagebuch gegen den Untergang: Zur Faszination Victor Klemperers.* Gießen: Psychosozial-Verlag, 1997.

Ehrmann, Susie. *The Diaries of Victor Klemperer.* Lecture presented at the Jewish Holocaust Museum and Research Centre, Melbourne, Australia, 18 July 1999. http://www.arts.monash.edu.au/affiliates/hlc/lectures.html.

Felluga, Dino. "Holocaust Iconoclasm and the Anti-Intellectual 'Jetztzeit' as a Response to the Postmodern Impasse." *Ariel: A Review of English Literature* 31, no. 4 (2000): 149–161.

Frankel, Max. "Life of Fear: I Will Bear Witness. A Diary of the Nazi Years 1942–1945. Review." *New York Times*, 2 April 2000.

Frommer, Friedrich Karl. "Und es ist alles so schwankend. Review." *Frankfurter Allgemeine Zeitung*, 13 July 1996.

Gay, Peter. "Inside the Third Reich: I Will Bear Witness. A Diary of the Nazi Years 1933–1941. Review." *New York Times*, 22 November 1998.

Gerstenberger, Heide. " 'Meine Prinzipien über das Deutschtum und die verschiedenen Nationalitäten sind ins Wackeln gekommen wie die Zähne eines alten Mannes': Victor Klemperer in seinem Verhältnis zu Deutschland und zu den Deutschen." In *Im Herzen der Finsternis: Victor Klemperer als Chronist der NS-Zeit.* Edited by Hannes Heer. Berlin: Aufbau, 1997, pp. 18–20.

Goldenbogen, Nora. " 'Man wird keinen von ihnen wiedersehen': Die Vernichtiung der Dresdener Juden 1938–1945." In *Im Herzen der Finsternis: Victor Klemperer als Chronist der NS-Zeit.* Edited by Hannes Heer, Berlin: Aufbau, 1997, pp. 92–109.

Goldhagen, Daniel J. *Hitler's Willing Executioners: Ordinary Germans and the Holocaust.* New York: Alfred A. Knopf, 1996. Reprinted as Vintage Book Edition, Random House, 1997.

Greiner, Bernd. " 'Zwiespältiger denn je': Victor Klemperers Tagebücher im Jahr 1945." In *Im Herzen der Finsternis: Victor Klemperer als Chronist der NS-Zeit.* Edited by Hannes Heer. Berlin: Aufbau, 1997, pp. 144–151.

Habermas, Jürgen. *Strukturwandel Der Offentlichkeit: Untersuchungen Zu Einer Kategorie Der Urgerlichen Gesellschaft.* Neuwied, Germany: Luchterhand, 1962.

Heer, Hannes. *Im Herzen der Finsternis: Victor Klemperer als Chronist der NS Zeit.* Berlin: Aufbau, 1997.

———. "Vox populi: Zur Mentalität der Volksgemeinschaft." In *Im Herzen der Finsternis: Victor Klemperer als Chronist der NS-Zeit.* Berlin, 1997.

Jacobs, Peter. *Victor Klemperer: Im Kern ein deutsches Gewächs. Eine Biographie.* Berlin: Aufbau Taschenbuch Verlag, 2000.

Kamper, Heidrun. "Sprachgeschichte-Zeitgeschichte: Die Tagebücher Victor Klemperers." *Deutsche Sprache. Zeitschrift für Theorie und Praxis* 28, no. 1 (2000): 25–41.

Kermode, Frank. "Displaced Person: Peter Gay recalls his childhood under the Nazis in Berlin and his flight with his family to America." Review of *My German Question. New York Times*, 25 October 1998.

Klinkenborg, Verlyn. "Editorial Observer: The Noble Ideal of Rationalism in Nazi Dresden." *New York Times*, 29 November 1998.

Kuhnke, Manfred. "Klemperers Tagebuch–Ein Jahrhundertbuch" *Deutschunterricht* 49, no. 1 (1997): 51–52.

Liebsch, Heike. " 'Ein Tier ist nicht rechtloser und gehetzter': Die Verfolgung der jüdischen Bevölkerung Dresdens 1933 bis 1937." In *Im Herzen der Finsternis: Victor Klemperer als Chronist der NS-Zeit.* Edited by Hannes Heer. Berlin: Aufbau, 1997, pp. 73–91.

Lifton, Robert Jay. "Spring Theater/Evoking the Holocaust: The Challenge of Reimagining the Unimaginable." *New York Times*, 25 February 2001.

Möhring, Gabriele. " 'Ich war nichts als Deutscher, und ich dankte meinem Schöpfer, Deutscher zu sein' Rückblicke eines jüdischen Bildungsbürgers." *Praxis Geschichte* 8, no. 5 (1994): 22–27.

Nerlich, Michael. "Victor Klemperer, oder ein Tagebuch aus dem Inferno." *lendemains* 21, no. 82/83 (1996): 135–144.

———. "Victor Klemperer und die unendliche deutsche Misere." *lendemains* 21, no. 82/83 (1996): 145–147.

———. "Die unendliche Misere: Zur deutschen Rezeption der Tagebücher Victor Klemperers." *Frankfurter Rundschau*, 3 January 1996.

Powers, Thomas. "The Everyday Life of Tyranny: I Shall Bear Witness. The Diaries of Victor Klemperer, 1933–41. Review." *The Guardian*, 14 September 2000. Reprinted from the *London Review of Books.*

Przyrembel, Alexandra. "Die Tagebücher Victor Klemperers und ihre Wirkung in der deutschen Öffentlichkeit." In *Geschichtswissenschaft und Öffentlichkeit: Der Streit um Daniel J. Goldhagen.* Edited by Johannes Heil. Frankfurt a.M.: Fischer Taschenbuch Verlag, 1998, pp. 312–337.

Reemstma, Jan Philipp. " 'Buchenwald wird von anderen geschildert werden: ich will mich an meine Erlebnisse halten': Stenogramme aus der Vorhölle." In *Im Herzen der Finsternis:*

Victor Klemperer als Chronist der NS-Zeit. Edited by Hannes Heer. Berlin: Aufbau Verlag, 1997, pp. 170–193.

Reiss, Hans. "Victor Klemperer (1881–1960): Reflections on His 'Third Reich' Diaries." *German Life and Letters* 51 (1998): 65–92.

Rieker, Yvonne. " 'Sich alles assimilieren können und doch seine Eigenart bewahren': Victor Klemperers Identitätskonstruktion und die deutsch-jüdische Geschichte." In *Im Herzen der Finsternis: Victor Klemperer als Chronist der NS-Zeit*. Edited by Hannes Heer. Berlin: Aufbau, 1997, pp. 21–34.

Rosenthal, Cindy. "Spring Theater/Evoking the Holocaust: Two Works That Scream 'Pay Attention.' " *New York Times*, 25 February 2001.

Rox-Helmer, Monika. "Die Tagebücher Victor Klemperers." *Geschichter lernen* 69 (1999): 23–29.

Schober, Rita. "Erinnerungen an Victor Klemperers Wirken nach 1945." *lendmains* 21, no. 82/83 (1996): 163–184.

Siehr, Karl-Heinz, ed. *Victor Klemperers Werk: Texte und Materialien für Lehrer*. Berlin: Aufbau Taschenbuch Verlag, 2001.

Taberner, Stuart. " 'Wie schön wäre Deutschland, wenn man sich noch als Deutscher fühlen und mit Stolz als Deutscher fühlen könnte': Martin Walser's Reception of Victor Klemperer's *Tagebücher 1933–1945* (How Wonderful Germany Would Be If One Could Feel Oneself a German and Do So With Pride) in *Das Prinzip Genauikgkeit und Die Verteidigung der Kindheit*." *Deutsche Vierteljahrsschrift* 73, no. 4 (1999): 710–732.

Trumpener, Katie. "Diary of a Tightrope Walker: Victor Klemperer and His Posterity." *Modernism-Modernity (MoMo)* 78, no. 3 (September 2000): 487–507.

Walser, Martin. *Das Prinzip Genauigkeit: Laudatio auf Victor Klemperer*. Frankfurt a. M.: Suhrkamp, 1996.

———. *Deutsche Sorgen*. Frankfurt a. M.: Suhrkamp, 1997.

Weber, Bruch. "Theater Review: Year by Year, a Witness to the Nazis' Affronts." *New York Times*, 13 March 2001.

Weinrich, Harald. "Der Gedächtnismann." *lendemains* 21, no. 82/83 (1996): 35–38.

Wildt, Michael. "Angst, Hoffen, Warten, Verzweifeln: Victor Klemperer und die Verfolgung der deutschen Juden 1933 bis 1941." In *Im Herzen der Finsternis: Victor Klemperer als Chronist der NS-Zeit*. Edited by Hannes Heer. Berlin: Aufbau, 1997, pp. 49–72.

Würzner, M. H. "Das Tagebuch als 'Oral History.' " *Amsterdamer Beiträge zur älteren Germanistik* 48 (1997): 169–173.

zur Nieden, Susanne. *From the Forgotten Everyday-Life of Tyranny: The Diaries of Victor Klemperer*. Translated by Vanessa Agnew. Amsterdam: Rodopi, 1999.

Irena Klepfisz

(1941–)

JOAN MICHELSON

No one quite believes I was really there. These eyes actually saw the Warsaw Ghetto. To them it's as if I'd been in a documentary, rolled myself up the sides of a mass grave and stepped off the screen. And here I am walking around just like everybody else (Klepfisz, "Bread and Candy: Songs of the Holocaust," *Bridges: A Journal of Jewish Feminists and Our Friends*, p. 14).

I do not want to live in the past. I need to move and build. I want to contribute towards a literature which is rooted in my experience (Klepfisz, "Secular Jewish Identity: *Yidishkayt* in America," *Dreams of an Insomniac: Jewish Feminist Essays, Speeches, and Diatribes*, Portland, Ore.: The Eighth Mountain Press, 1990, p. 163).

The Difficult Challenge of Holocaust Poetry

Of all the literary art forms, poetry, as an abstract genre, is the most problematic as a conveyor of politics and history. Aspiring toward music, emblematic, multi-layered, resonant, and a refuge against time itself, the poem is pressed between the opposing pulls of the aesthetic and issues of culture. It is no surprise that the poet who takes on the Holocaust faces an exceptionally difficult challenge. This is as true for the contemporary Yiddish-American poet and essayist Irena Klepfisz, who is carrying Holocaust poetry forward into the twenty-first century, as it was for the German poet Nelly Sachs, who was already fifty years old and a mature poet in the first year of the war. Separated by half a century whose upheavals outstrip imaginings, the poets share a continuous and essential search: they are looking for both a home in language and a home for language. Language itself, embracing the trials of word and sound, of alphabet and nuance, of the literal and the mystical, of the documentary and the metaphorical, shaped into poems, builds a bridge to bring together the elusive, disparate worlds of poetry and the Holocaust. The centrality of language in its more overt sense, guiding the problematic choice of which language to use, and, in its more oblique sense, wrestling with silence and the unspoken, links Klepfisz to the poets Nelly Sachs, Paul Celan, and Dan Pagis.

Like these poets, Klepfisz experienced language displacement as she was moved from one country to another. Born in Warsaw in 1941, she spoke Polish as a small child. In Sweden, for three years after the war, she learned Swedish. At the age of eight, she moved to New York, where she learned American English in the public school and Yiddish in the Bund's after-school education program. She became an English major at City College of New York, was graduated with honors, and went on to earn an M. A. and Ph. D. at the University of Chicago. Finding a home in English, informed, enhanced, and enlarged by the Yiddish she learned in a Bronx community "where a small part of Poland seemed to be alive" (*Dreams of an Insomniac* p. 147), she has come to locate her identity in language rather than geography. Given this sense of self, and as a Holocaust survivor and the daughter of a survivor, she has been "salvaging and sheltering an echo of a European era in which she never lived" (*Dreams of an Insomniac*, p. 143) and finding a path of her own as an address to issues rooted in the Holocaust.

Biographical Background

Klepfisz was born the only child of Rose Perczykow and Michal Klepfisz, members of the Jewish labor Bund. Her father, a leader in the Jewish resistance, died a hero and martyr on 22 April 1943, the third day of the Warsaw Ghetto Uprising and two days after her second birthday. After his death, she was taken from the Catholic orphanage outside the ghetto, where she had been placed for her safety, and with her mother was smuggled into the countryside, where they lived in virtual isolation, passing as Catholic Poles until the end of the war. Most of her family died in Treblinka. In 1946, Klepfisz and her mother emigrated to Sweden and, in 1949, found themselves in New York in a Jewish American working-class neighborhood.

Development as a Writer: Subject, Voice, Imagery, Form, Tone

For early poems, Klepfisz drew on models from the English tradition until, in the wake of the suicide of her friend and mentor, Elsa, a fellow child survivor, Klepfisz gave voice to the broken woman. During the 1960s, as if possessed, she wrote poems "not entirely in her control" (*Dreams of an Insomniac*, p. 168). These poems spoke of violent assault hermetically sealed within the Holocaust and within the mind and psyche of the female victim.

In a frequently anthologized poem, "Bashert" (predestined, inevitable), Klepfisz treats a recurrent theme of women's Holocaust writing, that of passing as Gentiles. Mother and daughter share a survival strategy filled with trepidation and constant fear of discovery and denunciation or inadvertent self-betrayal. The scene is Poland, 1944, narrated from the perspective of a child who has been left behind with an old peasant, willing to claim her as a grandchild because her Jewish identity is unknown. The daughter reflects on her mother's precarious fate at that time and her own terror of separation:

Walking towards an unnamed town for
some kind of permit.
She is carrying her Aryan identity papers . . .
Her terror in leaving me behind, in risking the
separation is swallowed now, like all other feelings.
But as she walks, she pictures me waving . . . imagines
herself suddenly picked up, the identity papers challenged.
And even if she were to survive that, would she
ever find me later? (*Dreams of an Insomniac*, p. 168)

Seeming wise beyond her years, the child fugitive knows that she must perfect her Christian persona: "say . . . prayers to the Holy Mother . . . just as the nuns taught"; she understands her mother's plight, "living in complete isolation, with no point of reference outside of herself. . . . Almost everyone of her world is dead . . ." (*A Few Words in the Mother Tongue: Poems Selected and New (1971–1990)*, Portland, Ore.: Eight Mountain Press, 1990, p. 187). In "Resisting and Surviving America," she writes, "As a child, I was old with terror and the brutality, the haphazardness of survival" (*Dreams of an Insomniac*, p. 61).

In the early 1970s something changed, possibly resulting from an act of self or "solid" therapy, as Klepfisz describes writing poems in the 1960s from within what she imagined to be "Elza's madness" (*Dreams of an Insomniac*, p. 168). She became less concerned with releasing pain and more with the shaping of the poem. She began to add space to the layout, to separate words, to give silence a central and functional role. Hand-in-hand with this went a reversal in pitch and tone. Voiced rage gave way to a deceptive quiet and to irony embedded in understatement, which slipped out of the sealed world of Holocaust trauma with its flames, sewers, dogs, and butcher knives, to unleash power from more civilized images: houseplants, refrigerators, windows, and books. While the Holocaust continued to color everything she wrote, it was no longer singular and tyrannical. In her play *Bread and Candy: Songs of the Holocaust*, a dramatized discussion of personal issues in relation to the Holocaust, history is brought into focus around a performance of Yiddish songs. There is another quieted and different approach in her long poem, "Searching for My Father's Body." In this poem, historical documents are incorporated into lyrical narrative, resolving an issue raised in *Bread and Candy* by bringing the text of poetry, a product of craft, meter, recurrent metaphors into the historical, cultural context. Furthermore, she has reconciled some of the issues around language by the creation of a series of bilingual (Yiddish-English) poems. It is in the bilingual nine-part poem "Di rayze aheym/The Journey Home" that she unites the personal with a collective memory, a dual obligation central to Jewish discourse:

to see what can be wrenched
from the unconscious
crowded darkness
fun ir zikorn
  of her memory.
It is there
di gantse geshikhte
fun folk
  the entire history
of the people. (*A Few Words in the Mother Tongue*, p. 217)

As Israeli poet Ronit Lentin observes, "To Klepfisz, writing, as a process of interpretation and recovery, of asking fundamental questions about the uses of history rather than simply of self-expression, is one means of survival" (Shapiro, p. 167). The physical gaps in her poems are both reflective of painful Holocaust silences and the dichotomy between language and silence, the inability to speak and the obligation to bear witness:

Zi shvaygt.

Di verter feln ir
She lacks the words
And all that she can force
is sound
unformed sound:
a
der klang
the sound
o
dos vort
the word
u
di tsung
the tongue
o
dos loshn
the language
e
di trern
the tears. (*"Ditsung*/The Tongue", *A Few Words in the Mother Tongue,* p. 223)

Poetry and Politics

In her essay "Forging a Women's Link: Some Possibilities for Jewish American Poetry," Klepfisz traces her confrontation with "feminist ideas, women's lives, lesbian love, the whole gay world" (*Dreams of an Insomniac*, p. 169). In the 1970s, she came out as a lesbian feminist and with four other lesbian writers published her first book of poetry, *Periods of Stress* (1975). Slowly and with difficulty, she progressed toward an integration: the re-rooted Bund Yiddish culture of her past and the American lesbian culture of her present. Her earlier focus on the Holocaust as a historical event led her toward issues of assimilation and the effect of the Holocaust on current and future generations. This material is included in her essays, which, collected in *Dreams of an Insomniac*, cast light on her diverse commitments, activities, experiences, and preoccupations. Among the essays is "Oyf keyver oves: Poland, 1983," a report and analysis of a visit to Warsaw that she made with her mother forty years after the ghetto uprising in which her father was killed. In this period, she writes that her "perception of Jewish content . . . has broadened . . . [to include] political work—consciousness raising on feminist, gay and Jewish issues, building Jewish awareness of yiddishkayt, teaching Yiddish, translating significant material, working towards a peaceful solution in the Middle East" ("Forging," *Dreams of an Insomniac*, p. 174).

In her poem " '67 Remembered," which takes its bearings from her graduate years in Chicago, she writes, "Time passes. Everything changes./We see things differently . . . We wake up take new positions/ to suit new visions" (*A Few Words in the Mother Tongue*, p. 233). Written more than twenty years after the Yom Kippur War and more than forty years after World War II, and addressed to a fellow survivor ("Siberia . . . the Germans at your heels," p. 232) now living in Jerusalem, she has not left the Holocaust behind but rather has broadened its reach by extending her frame. Correspondences leap out at the reader. "That war" (in Israel) is positioned in a relationship with "that other," the Holocaust, unnamed in this poem. "Power" is set against "peace" (pp. 233–234). Elsewhere, in later poems, are other links: the marginalized community of the feminists connects with the marginalized survivor community of the Yiddish-speaking Bronx Jews; the dislocation of refugees with the dislocation of immigrants; the madness that brought about her fellow child-survivor, poet-friend and mentor's suicide with the madness that destroyed the Yiddish writer Fradel Schtok.

Professional Achievements

Klepfisz is the author of *A Few Words in the Mother Tongue: Poems Selected and New (1971–1990)*, of *Dreams of an Insomniac: Jewish Feminist Essays, Speeches, and Diatribes*, and of the theater piece "Bread and Candy: Songs of the Holocaust." She is a co-editor of *The Tribe of Dina: A Jewish Woman's Anthology* and *Di Froyen: Women and Yiddish*. Her scholarly work includes articles on Eastern European Jewish women activists and Yiddish women writers. She teaches Jewish Studies at Barnard College and serves as the editorial consultant for Yiddish and Yiddish literature in the Jewish feminist magazine *Bridges*. Her poems and essays have been published individually in numerous book anthologies and magazines. A new edition of *A Few Words in the Mother Tongue* was published by the Eighth Mountain Press in 1999.

Critical Reception

Klepfisz's writing has earned the admiration of academic scholars and poets. Maeera Shreiber concludes that Klepfisz is a "startling presence. Her complex vision informs her restlessly experimental enterprise and her work is an important corrective to more exuberant theorizing of diaspora" (Shreiber, p. 284). Adrienne Rich comments on the uniqueness of Klepfisz's poem "Bashert" and hails it as "a great borderland poem . . . emerging from the consciousness of being of no one geography, time, or culture; of moving inwardly and outwardly between continents, land-masses, eras of history" (Introduction, *Selected Poems*, p. 20). Gisela Ecker, a German academic, highlights the value of Klepfisz's "hyphenated" identity and her speech on behalf of those who can no longer speak (pp. 129–130), while Evelyn Torton Beck, an American who, like Klepfisz, was a child immigrant, points to the significant portage of culture carried by Klepfisz's use of language. Miriyam Glazer views Klepfisz's poetry as "a poetry of the viscera, the heart, the mind, and the soul . . . a political poetry whose ideology is shaped by the magma of lived experience," as a poetry "rare in this country" (Glazer, p. 227).

Irena Klepfisz is a contemporary poet who is taking her place within Holocaust literature by providing new directions for this unwieldy genre. Out of her personal heritage in which the private and public are joined, through a vision inherently political, expressed through writing impeccable in craft yet daring in exploration, she offers a new poetic voice. She has developed a broad range in response to refined and redefined perspectives. In this work lie the imprint and the impact of the Holocaust.

Bibliography

Primary Sources

Periods of Stress. 1975.
Keepers of Accounts. 1982.
Different Enclosures. 1985.
Dreams of an Insomniac: Jewish Feminist Essays, Speeches, and Diatribes. 1990.
A Few Words in the Mother Tongue: Poems Selected and New (1971–1990). 1990.
"Bread and Candy: Songs of the Holocaust." 1991.

Secondary Sources

Beck, Evelyn Torton. Introduction to *Dreams of an Insomniac: Jewish Feminist Essays, Speeches and Diatribes (1976–1990)*. Portland, Ore.: Eighth Mountain Press, 1990.
Borghi, Liana. "Irena Klepfisz: Accounts of Self-Enclosure." *Rivista di Studi Anglo-Americani* 9 (1993): 167–177.
Castro, Ginette. "Irena Klepfisz, poete de la survie et de la difference juives en Amerique." *ACRAA* (1993): 139–148.
Ecker, Gisela. "Irena Klepfisz's 'Fradel Schtok' and the Language of Hyphenated Identity." *Anglistik-and-Englischunterricht* 53 (1994): 129–139.
Glazer, Miriyam. Review of *A Few Words in the Mother Tongue: Poems Selected and New (1971–1990). Studies in American Jewish Literature* 11, no. 12 (Fall 1992): 226–232.
Hedley, Jane. "Nepantilist Poetics: Narrative and Cultural Identity in the Mixed-Language Writings of Irena Klepfisz and Gloria Anzaldua." *Narrative* 4, no. 1 (Jan 1996): 36–54.
Helfgott, Esther Altshul. "Irena Klepfisz: A Life in Print. The Early Years, 1975–1992." Dissertation Abstracts International. Ann Arbor, MI (DAI) (1995) March, 55:9 Degree granting institution: University of Washington, 1994.
Keiner, Judy. "Paradox Regained? The Writings of Irena Klepfisz." *Jewish Quarterly* 39 (Fall 1992): 37–40.
Kwinter, Michelle. "Irena Klepfisz." In *Contemporary Lesbian Writers of the United States: A Bio-Bibliographical Critical Sourcebook*. Westport, Conn.: Greenwood, 1993.
Lentin, Ronit. "Irena Klepfisz." In *Jewish American Women Writers: A Bio-Bibliographical and Critical Sourcebook*. Edited by Ann R. Shapiro. Westport, CT: Greenwood Press, 1994.
———. "Surviving and Resisting America: The Use of Language as Gendered Subversion in the Work of American Jewish Poet Irena Klepfisz." *Teanga—the Irish Yearbook for Applied Linguistics* 12 (Fall 1992): 61–72.
McCorkle, James. "Contemporary Poetics and History: Pinsky, Klepfisz, and Rothenberg." *The Kenyon Review* 14, no. 1 (Winter 1992): 171–188.
———. "Forging a Women's Link in Di Goldenkeyt: Some Possibilities for Jewish American Poetry." In *Conversant Essays: Contemporary Poets on Poetry*, 370–375. Detroit: Wayne State University Press, 1990.
Milner, Jenney. "Nourishing Difference, Bridging Distances." Review of *Dreams of an Insomniac*: Jewish Feminist Essays, Speeches, and Diatribes. *Sojourner* (September 1991): 39–40.
Rich, Adrienne. Introduction to *A Few Words in the Mother Tongue: Poems Selected And New (1971–1990)*, 13–25. Portland, Ore.: Eighth Mountain Press, 1990.
Roth, Laurence. "Pedagogy and the Mother Tongue: Irena Klepfisz's 'Di rayze Aheym/The Journey Home.' " *Symposium: A Quarterly Journal in Modern Literature* 52, no. 4 (Winter 1999): 269–278.
———. "Statues of Liberty: Assimilation and Twentieth Century American Jewish Poets." Dissertation Abstracts International. Ann Arbor, MI (DAI) (1995) May, 55:11. Degree granting institution: University of California, Los Angeles, 1994.
Scamp, Jutta. "Beyond Assimilation: Difference and Reconfiguration in the Works of Irena Klepfisz." *Zeitschrift fur Anglistik und Amerikanistik: A Quarterly of Language, Literature and Culture* 47, no. 3. Issue edited by Jyl Lynn Felman and Rebecca Goldstein. (1999): 229–243.
Shreiber, Maeera Y. "The End of Exile: Jewish Identity and Its Diasporic Poetics." *PLMA* 113, no. 2 (March 1998): 273–287.

RUTH KLÜGER

(1931–)

MICHAEL OSSAR

I'm writing for Germans. . . . You don't need to identify with me—in fact, I'd prefer that you didn't. . . . But at least allow yourselves to be provoked, don't draw back, don't say right away "this doesn't concern me or it concerns me only within the narrow confines of a border carefully drawn with a ruler and compass" or that you have already subjected yourselves to the photographs of piles of bodies and thus fulfilled your responsibilities for expressing guilt and sympathy. Become passionate, seek confrontation (Ruth Klüger, *weiter leben*: *Eine Jugend*, Göttingen: Wallstein Verlag, 1992, p. 141).

FELIX ROHATYN, THE Viennese-born investment banker who guided New York City back from the brink of bankruptcy in the 1970s, recently told of his escape from Vichy France at the age of thirteen. He and his mother drove along a route they had been assured was safe, when to their horror they rounded a curve to find a German checkpoint at the border crossing. Unable to turn around and certain of their fate, they approached the crossing. After checking the papers of the car ahead of them the border guard started to light a cigarette in a gust of wind, and, unwilling to interrupt that task, he simply waved Rohatyn and his mother through. If it had not been for that gust of wind, Rohatyn told his interviewer, he would have died that day. Since then he has regarded his life as borrowed time that would have to be repaid.

weiter leben

In her critically acclaimed and best-selling book, *weiter leben* (*Still Alive*, 1992), another Viennese, Ruth Klüger, tells how she escaped death at Auschwitz. Just thirteen, the same age as Rohatyn at the time of his flight, she and her mother were being selected in May of 1944 for what was ostensibly a forced labor transport to work in a munitions plant. Her mother was chosen, Ruth was not. Even though her mother was unsure which path led to life and which to death, she urged her to sneak into another line and try again. As she approached the SS-man making the selection, his secretary, also a Jew, risked her life to whisper to Ruth to lie about her age, to say that she was fifteen. After some skillful urging by the secretary the officer sent Ruth along with her mother, to life instead of to death. Of course it is no doubt true that every escape by the few who survived a system built on arbitrariness appears from a distance as chance. But it is instructive to compare Klüger's reaction with Rohatyn's. Where Rohatyn saw his salvation as a gift from God, Klüger regarded hers as an incomprehensible and unpredictable human good deed. Indeed, in Göttingen after the war, she rejected the reproach of one of her German students against Israelis who harbored anti-Arab prejudices and thus had "learned nothing from Auschwitz." She replied that Auschwitz was a perverse abomination that taught nothing, certainly not tolerance and enlightenment. On the contrary, the theology Klüger gleans from her experience is more adequately adumbrated in the mordant joke with which she begins her essay "Dichten über die *Shoah*: Zum Problem des literarischen Umgangs mit dem Massenmord" (Writing about the *Shoah*: On the Problem of the Literary Treatment of Mass Murder in *Spuren der Verfolgung: seelische Auswirkungen des Holocaust auf die Opfer und ihre Kinder*: Edited by Gabriel Hardtmann. Gerlingen: Bleicher Verlag, 1992.

This bad joke takes place at a time when the synagogues no longer burned because they had all been burned down, sometime after Kristallnacht and somewhere in Hitler's Europe. A pious Jew in a strange city finds, to his joy, a small group of like-minded souls who are having a religious service in a cellar. A Jewish service can take place anywhere that ten adult Jewish men can assemble. There is no need for a rabbi. So he enters and is astonished to see that the prayers are spoken in a whisper. "Why,"

> he asks, "don't you talk in a normal tone? The street is empty, only Jews live in this building, what's the point of this barely comprehensible murmuring?" "Take it easy," someone replies, irritated, "if you keep on screaming like that, He will hear us, and if He finds out that we still exist, we're done for" (p. 204).

The awful and paradoxical ambiguity of the pious Jews in this anecdote is an ambiguity that characterizes *weiter leben* as well. It is a book that subjects racial stereotypes to withering scorn, but also is itself full of ambiguity and stereotypes; a book in which Klüger refers to her female readers, commenting "why should I assume I have male readers? They only read what is written by other men" (p. 81); a book in which she claims that women understand virtue better than men (p. 131); a book in which she remarks that Californians, while not unintelligent, read only newspapers; a book in which she notes at one point, "I hated Theresienstadt, a swamp, a manure pit" (p. 103) and at another, "I loved Theresienstadt in a way" (p. 102); a book in which she describes a little girl who felt that Vienna was hostile to children, especially Jewish ones, in its very core: "one stepped onto the street and immediately one was in enemy territory" (p. 14), but who also loved Vienna ("Vienna is for me the city I didn't succeed in fleeing from," p. 17).

Of course these reactions are provoked by events that permit of no rational interpretation, and it is the great merit of this book that Klüger, at every point in her experience, reveals to us her feelings with absolute and often painful honesty: her love for her father, a gentle man who had taught her to play chess, who met her after school, a doctor who was arrested and sent to Auschwitz (did this man whom she loved climb over the corpses of children like other men in the gas chamber?). Klüger tells of her memories of her grandmother, who died in Theresienstadt. She also relates details of her stormy relationship with her superstitious and paranoid mother, Alma, who on their arrival in Auschwitz invited Ruth to run with her into the electrified barbed wire. Klüger writes, "my mother and I have no common language. Hers is used for manipulation, not communication" (p. 254). (Later, in New York, Klüger's mother did attempt suicide.) She reveals her dislike of her aunt, which she refused to suppress in her book even though the aunt was later gassed. She does not conceal her contempt for her uncle, who left his wife behind when he fled to America. She tells of her scorn for the lifestyle of the American benefactors who paid the passage for her and her mother from Germany in the fall of 1947 but who had not been willing, earlier, to underwrite a visa for her father. She vents her anger at the self-serving prevarications of Gisela, the German wife of a colleague in Princeton, who informs her that Theresienstadt was not so bad after all. She tells of her friendship with "Christoph" (Martin Walser, now a famous neo-conservative German novelist), a fellow student she has a relationship with in Regensburg after the war. She tells of her friendship with three women she meets in Vermont, which lasts her whole life long. She reveals her anger at her mother's treatment of Ditha, a Viennese girl her mother had "adopted" in Theresienstadt and, later, unfairly rejected. She discusses her complicated relationship with her husband, an American paratrooper and, later, a history professor at Berkeley, from whom she is now divorced (her earlier works appear under her married name, Angress). Finally, she expresses her anger at the pychoanalyst her mother sent her to in New York, who was so insensitive and had so little sense of her fragility that he asked her to consider what made her so arrogant, prickly, and sanctimonious and why it was so hard for her to make friends.

Klüger *was* arrogant, indeed, even for the sympathetic and admiring reader, *Trotz* (defiance, obstinacy, refractoriness), her proud insistence on her individuality, her Otherness, emerge as her defining, salient characteristics. This fact contributes hugely to the value of her book. At every point, she tells us with ruthless candor her feelings: the feelings of a little girl who could still ride to a Jewish school (she attended eight in four years) on the streetcar if she wore a yellow star (which had to be bought at ten pennies each from the Nazis) but who could not sit down, who could still go to a park when she was seven but could not sit on a bench (in compensation she "was allowed to reckon herself among the 'chosen people' " [p. 17]), who had to sneak into a theater far from her home in order to see a Disney movie and was observed and berated by her neighbor's daughter, who learned to read from antisemitic signs in Vienna, who eventually could no longer attend school and could find refuge only in the little bit of green at the Jewish cemetery, who experienced three concentration camps through a child's eyes and who was not able to write these feelings down until nearly fifty years had passed. One particularly instructive example of this *Trotz*: as she is riding on the trolley through a tunnel, she feels a man touching her. At first she fears a child molester, but instead it is a man who under cover of the darkness of the tunnel gives her an orange. Klüger remarks:

> When the train emerged from the tunnel, I had already put it into my pocket and looked up gratefully to the stranger, as he looked benevolently down at me. My feelings, however, were mixed . . . I didn't like playing this role. I wanted to see myself as a resister, not a victim, and therefore did not want to be consoled. Tiny, secret demonstrations like this didn't help at all, were in no sense

commensurate with what was happening, didn't even begin to compensate for the progressive impoverishment and limitations on my life. It was a sentimental gesture, in which the benefactor saw himself revealed in his good intentions, but for me, not even as useful as the consoling words of the usherette at the Snow White film. But I would have caused him embarrassment and probably great difficulties if I had rejected the alms in the full streetcar, if I had given it back to him, perhaps with the words "You are making it pretty easy for yourself. I don't give a shit about your orange." An inconceivable reaction (*weiter leben*, p. 50).

Of course the truth of Klüger's feelings is indisputable, even impressive, but it is also true that the man in the streetcar was making a human gesture, a sign of solidarity in the only way he knew how. One wonders to what extent the rage of a life robbed of its childhood and youth—the rage engendered by returning to Germany and hearing highly regarded scholars apologizing for Konrad Adenauer's practice of appointing former Nazis to positions in his government, of dealing with hypocritical and self-serving people unwilling to look at what had happened in Germany without casting about for justifications and excuses—caused her to see, in retrospect, incidents like the one in the streetcar through the lens of the adult survivor. The East German novelist Christoph Hein was once asked about the reliability of memory in autobiography, and he replied that even if he were proved factually wrong in his memories, for him "Bohemia would still be on the seacoast" (interview by Christian Eger, "Gespräch mit Ruth Klüger: 'In meiner erinnerten Wirklichkeit liegt Böhmen nicht am Meer' " *Mitteldeutsche Zeitung*, 26 May 1999). When this was quoted to Klüger, according to an essay in the *Mitteldeutsche Zeitung*, she responded: "Autobiography is the most subjective form of history, but it is still history. From the very beginning I say: that's the way it was. I interpret it. My memory interprets it with me. But I'm talking about a reality that has actually taken place. In this reality, Bohemia doesn't lie on the seacoast" (Eger, p. 14).

Weiter leben is at once a *Bildungsroman* and an autobiography, and like all autobiographies it repesents a conscious choice, a series of decisions about which fragments of an exceptionally difficult and rich life to omit and which to include. Klüger tells us why she decided to write it. In 1988, more than forty years after the war, she visited Germany to run a program for American students in Göttingen, when she was run over by a cyclist and seriously injured. The evident concern of her students and German colleagues (to whom the book is dedicated) and this second confrontation with death recalled to her mind almost involuntarily her first confrontation: "For years I repressed the damage. I thought I had emerged spiritually and physically unscathed. Now I know that I am not well. In the beginning, I saw myself as exceptional and developed a kind of pride—I'm someone who can survive a concentration camp. Only later did I become aware of my fragility" (Interview with Sigrid Löffler. "Davongekommen: Jetzt noch über Auschwitz schreiben? Ruth Klüger ist es gelurgen, ohne Pathos und gefühlsgenau" in *Die Zeit*, 1993). What resulted from this realization was the story of her childhood in Vienna and of her first consciousness of the fact that she was "the Other," a foreign body in this city she both loved and hated (a moment the writer Jean Améry says comes in the life of every Jew). Klüger writes, "[Vienna] was home, in an uncanny way. Joyless and hostile to children. Hostile to Jewish children to its very core" (p. 67).

Klüger was only seven years old when the Nazis marched into Vienna after the Anschluss in 1938, when she asked to be called Ruth instead of Susi—the first sign of the problem of finding an identity that looms so large in this book. *Weiter leben* is the story of three concentration camps seen though the eyes of a teenager with a fine perception for details that escaped the attention of more jaded adults, details that burn themselves into the consciousness of the reader. We learn that the children in Theresienstadt who came from Poland in August 1943 are afraid to use the shower for fear of poison gas, a fear based on rumors that the less perceptive adults do not credit. We learn that when the doors of the cattle cars are opened just at the moment when the air has become impossible to breathe, instead of the expected fresh air, the child is confronted with the gruesomely sweet smell of the crematoria, equally impossible to breathe. We observe Klüger snatching an intellectual life from wherever she can get it in Theresienstadt, listening to the Berlin Rabbi Leo Baeck interpreting for the children in the camps the biblical story of creation (although Klüger is repelled to learn that he took care to pay his gas bill before being carted off to the camp). We learn how writing and reciting poetry helped her survive emotionally. Throughout her book appears the image of her totem, "der liebe Augustin," who in Viennese folklore stumbled drunken into a pit of corpses of those who had died of the plague, slept the night there, and emerged unscathed the next day: a symbol of both luck and the indomitable will to live.

But *weiter leben* is not just an autobiography, it is also a *Bildungsroman*. It describes the sense in which a basically nonreligious person became a Jew (a process Klüger has in common with a great many survivors, for example, Jean Améry) and it describes the genesis of her feminism in her abadonment by her father, in the religious ceremonies that favored men, in the male face of war, in the brutality of the male concentration camp guards (as opposed to that of the female guards), in the patronizing attitude of her husband and academic colleagues.

Biography

Klüger was born in Vienna in 1931, the daughter of a doctor, Viktor Klüger, who was imprisoned by the SS "for performing abortions," and who fled within the week and then was eventually caught after his flight to Italy and Vichy France and murdered. Her half-brother, Jiři, six years older than she, was also killed. In 1942, at the age of eleven, she was deported with her mother to Theresienstadt, and two years later she was sent to Auschwitz. She spent the last months of the war in Christianstadt/Gross-Rosen, and in the chaos of the Russian advance in February 1945 she and her mother were able to flee the forced march and make their way to Straubing, a small town in Bavaria, where her mother got a job working for the American occupation forces and then for the United Nations Refugee Relief Agency. When her mother moved to Regensburg, Ruth followed and, after graduating from the Straubing Gymnasium by dint of studying with tutors, she enrolled at the university at Regensburg. Finally, mother and daughter were able to emigrate to New York, where Klüger studied at Hunter College and worked at various jobs. When, after she had graduated, she was unable to cross the border to work in a Mexican village with the American Friends Service Committee, she traveled on to California, where she worked as a librarian and eventually decided to get her Ph.D. in German studies at Berkeley in 1962, encouraged by the émigré scholar, Heinz Politzer. She embarked on a distinguished academic career as Germanist and an expert on Gotthold Ephraim Lessing and Heinrich von Kleist. She had two sons from her marriage with an American historian. Klüger has taught at a number of the most prestigious institutions in the country: Princeton, the University of Virginia, University of Kansas, the University of Cincinnati, and the University of California at Irvine. Currently, she divides her time between Irvine and Göttingen.

Critical Reception

Since its publication by the Wallstein Verlag, a small publishing house in Göttingen, in 1992, *weiter leben* has appeared in seven editions, selling over 97,000 copies in the hardback edition and over 100,000 in the paperback edition. Within a year of its publication it was the subject of more than 130 articles and reviews. It has been translated into French, Hungarian, Italian, Spanish, Japanese, Czech, and Dutch. An English translation by the author was published in the fall of 2001.

The popular reception of *weiter leben* was overwhelmingly positive. It was reviewed by all the important German newspapers and was the subject of a discussion on the popular and influential TV literary magazine, *Das literarische Quartett*, on 14 January 1993, where Marcel Reich-Ranicki, the host of the program and critic of the *Frankfurter Allgemeine Zeitung*, called it "among the best of what has appeared in the last two, three, four years in the German language." Stephan Braese and Holger Gehle have provided an acute analysis of the critical reception, proceeding from Klüger's announced intention, expressed in the epigraph above, of provoking an honest and frank dialogue between Germans and Jews. Indeed, the book is dedicated to her "[German] friends in Göttingen" and she told Sigrid Löffler that she had written it for Martin Walser, who appears in the book as "Christoph" and for her exemplified "the German who didn't listen, but who was . . . always friendly, an intellectual [gifted] with scepticism and sensitivity" (Löffler, "Davongekommen" in *Die Zeit*, 1993).

The conversation with Christoph described in the last third of her book is just one of many encounters between Klüger and non-Jewish Germans, both in *weiter leben* itself and in the many readings and lectures she gave after its publication—a serious attempt to stimulate the dialogue she had hoped for. In the event, Braese and Gehle conclude, the critical reception only confirmed Gershom Scholem's thesis that a true German-Jewish dialogue was impossible. Instead, they see the reception of Klüger's book as evolving into an inner-German monologue. In a perhaps understandable attempt to read the book as a human document, Klüger's story is stripped by many critics of its Jewishness and redefined in transcendent terms that, with all goodwill, represent a kind of falsification.

Body of Works

Klüger has dealt with the Holocaust and its consequences not only in her autobiographical book *weiter leben*, but also in several critical essays of which "A 'Jewish Problem' in German Postwar Fiction" and "Dichten über die *Shoah*: Zum Problem des literarischen Umgangs mit dem Massenmord" ("Writing about the *Shoah*: On the Problem of the Literary Treatment of Mass Murder") are perhaps the most interesting. The former examines not the Holocaust itself but the portrayal of Jews in selected examples of German fiction and film of the period from 1955 to 1980. She considers Hans Scholz's *On the Green Banks of the Spree* (1955); Bruno Apitz's *Naked Among Wolves* (*Nackt unter Wölfen*, 1958); *Zanzibar or the Final Reason* (1957), *The Redhead* (1960), and *Efraim* (1967) by Alfred Andersch; Günter Grass's *The Tin Drum* (1959); Volker Schlöndorff's film *The Sudden Wealth of the Poor People of Kombach* (1970); Gerhard Zwerenz's *The Earth Is Uninhabitable Like the Moon* (1973); Rainer Werner Fassbinder's film (inspired by Zwerenz's book) *City, Sewage, Death* (1975); and, finally, Fassbinder's film *Lilli Marleene* (1980). Her conclusion is that in these works the relationship between Jews and Germans is presented in various distorted ways dictated by the psychological imperatives of the authors and of the readers, the postwar generation of Germans:

> Even in the best of these works, the depiction of Jewishness is marred by a failure of literary sensibility, an element of kitsch or a turn towards the pornographic, an appeal to the least desirable sentiments or the most accessible sentimentalities in the reader or viewer . . . a disturbing pattern emerges: the impetus to resurrect, not the memory of German Jewry, but the myth of Shylock, as victim and victimizer, and of his counterpart, the gallant Gentile Antonio. Does Germany have a literary culture which, even where it consciously faces the past, reveals itself in its escape fantasies and its resentful and defensive reactions to be unconsciously more than ever in full flight from an army of ghosts? ("A 'Jewish Problem' in German Postwar Fiction," *Modern Judaism* 5, no. 1 (1985), pp. 231–232).

Unlike the ghosts in Ilona Karmel's *An Estate of Memory*, for which Klüger wrote the afterword (Karmel writes: "Then, blurred by sleep, a voice would call a name of long ago, another called, then another. She listened: from the estates of blessed memory the dead were coming into the night" [New York: Feminist Press, 1986]), the ghosts of our past, of our generation are memories not of the pre-lapsarian freedom antedating the Holocaust, but of death: "the estate of memory is now the ditches and camps where we left the dead, blessed or not" (p. 456).

The essay "Dichten über die *Shoah*" ("Writing about the *Shoah*") deals specifically with books about the Holocaust, most of them by non-Germans: André Schwarz-Bart's *Der Letzte der Gerechten (The Last of the Just)*, Elie Wiesel's *Nacht (Night)*, Primo Levi's *Ist das ein Mensch? (Is That a Man?)*, Cordelia Edvardson's *Gebranntes Kind sucht das Feuer (Once Burned, Twice Fascinated)*, Aharon Appelfeld's *Badenheim 1939*, Peter Weiss's *Die Ermittlung (The Investigation)*, Rolf Hochhuth's *Der Stellvertreter (The Deputy)*, Tadeusz Borowski's *Die steinerne Welt (World of Stone)*, Jerzy Kosinski's *Der bemalte Vogel (The Painted Bird)*, *Das Tagebuch der Anne Frank (The Diary of Anne Frank)*, and two films: the American *Holocaust* TV series that caused such a sensation in the German-speaking world, and Claude Lanzmann's *Shoah*. Klüger claims that unlike the careful and exhaustive coming to terms with the Nazi period in German historiography, the portrayal of the Holocaust in works of literature and film (which she claims attract relatively little attention, although one can certainly not say this of *The Diary of Anne Frank* or of the *Holocaust* film series) has been sentimentalized and falsified. It must be the intention of Holocaust literature, she writes, "to permit the reader no emotional ossification which later develops into resentment and repression. . . . Instead of turning away from it in discomfort and disgust—a reaction that necessarily leads to misunderstandings and sentimentalities—one could participate in it by making one's own attitude into a literary theme" ("Dichten über die *Shoah*," p. 220).

Ruth Klüger has been the recipient of numerous important literary prizes, among them the Rauriser Literaturpreis (1993), the Johann-Jacob-Christoph von Grimmelshausen-Preis (1993), the Niedersachsen-Preis (1993), the Marie-Luise-Kaschnitz-Preis (1995), the Anerkennungspreis zum Andreas Gryphius-Preis (1996), the Prix Mémoire de la *Shoah* (1998), the Thomas-Mann-Preis (1990), and the Preis der Frankfurter Anthologie (1999).

Bibliography

Primary Sources

"The Generations in *Emilia Galotti*." 1968.
"Interrogation in Wolfram's *Parzival*." 1969.
"The Christian Surrealism of Elisabeth Langgässer." 1970.
"Kafka and Sacher-Masoch: A Note on *The Metamorphosis*." 1970.
"The Narrative Prose of Eugen Gottlob Winkler." 1970.
"*Weh dem, der Lügt*: Grillparzer and the Avoidance of Tragedy." 1971.
" 'Dreams that were more than dreams' in Lessing's *Nathan*." 1971.
The Early German Epigram: A Study in Baroque Poetry. 1971.
"Das Gespenst in Grillparzers *Ahnfrau*" (The Ghost in Grillparzer's *Ahnfrau*). 1972.
"Lessing's Criticism of Cronegk: Nathan in Ovo?" 1972.
German Studies: The Woman's Perspective. German Studies in the United States. 1976. With Walter F. W. Lohnes and Volters Nollendorfs.

"Kleist's Treatment of Imperialism: *Die Hermannsschlacht* and 'Die Verlobung in St. Domingo.' " 1977.

"Schnitzler's 'Frauenroman' *Therese*." 1977.

"*Der Butt*: A Feminist Perspective." 1982.

"A 'Jewish Problem' in German Postwar Fiction." 1985.

"Afterword" to Ilona Karmel's *An Estate of Memory*. 1986.

"Der eingerichtete Mensch: Innendekor bei Adalbert Stifter" (Man in His Setting: Interior Decoration in Adalbert Stifter's Works). 1986.

"Wunsch- und Angstbilder: Jüdische Gestalten aus der deutschen Literatur des neunzehnten Jahrhunderts: Akten des VII. Internationalen Germanisten Kongresses" (Images of desire and anxiety: Jewish figures from the German literature of the nineteenth century: proceedings of the Seventh International Congress of Germanists). 1986.

"Gibt es ein 'Judenproblem' in der deutschen Nachkriegsliteratur?" (Is there a 'Jewish problem' in postwar German literature?). 1986.

"Die Leiche unterm Tisch: Jüdische Gestalten aus der deutschen Literatur des neunzehnten Jahrhunderts" (The corpse under the table: Jewish figures from the German literature of the nineteenth century). 1986.

"Kleists Abkehr von der Aufklärung." 1987.

"Jewish Characters in Thomas Mann's Fiction." 1990.

"Dichten über die *Shoah*: Zum Problem des literarischen Umgangs mit dem Massenmord" (Writing about the *Shoah*: On the Problem of the Literary Treatment of Mass Murder). 1992.

weiter leben: Eine Jugend (*Still Alive: A Holocaust Girlhood Remembered*). 1992.

Lesen Frauen Anders? (Do Women Read Differently?). 1994.

Frauen lesen anders (Women Read Differently). 1996.

Von hoher und niedriger Literatur (On High and Low Literature). 1996.

Secondary Sources

Braese, Stephan, and Holger Gehle. "Von 'deutschen Freunden': Ruth Klüger's *weiter leben—Eine Jugend* in der deutschen Rezeption." *Deutschunterricht* 47, no. 6 (1995): 767–787.

Eger, Christian. "Gespräch mit Ruth Klüger: 'In meiner erinnerten Wirklichkeit liegt Böhmen nicht am Meer.' " *Mitteldeutsche Zeitung*, 26 May 1999.

Gehle, Holger. " 'weiter leben' in der deutschen Buchkritik." In *Kassiber*. Edited by Stephan Braese and Holger Gehle. Hamburg, 1994, pp. 11–24.

Hein, Helmut. "Weiter leben. Ruth Klüger bei Atlantis." *Die Woche*, 9 July 1992.

Holloway, Evelyn. "Schattenschrift: Jüdische Identität in der modernen Literatur. Zu den österreichischen Schriftstellern Franz Kafka, Ruth Klüger, Robert Schindel." *Literarität*, 39–43.

Isenschmid, Andreas. "Recht machen kann man es nicht: Die Rauriser Laudatio auf Ruth Klüger und ihr Buch 'weiter leben.' " *Basler Zeitung*, 9 July 1993.

Jerziorkowski, Klaus. "Der Tod, ein deutsches Buch: Ruth Klügers liebevoll zorniger Lebensrückblick 'weiter leben.' " *Die Zeit*, 16 October 1992.

Kammler, Clemens. "Ein Ereignis im Auschwitz-Diskurs: Ruth Klügers Autobiographie *weiter leben. Eine Jugend* im Unterricht." *Deutschunterricht* 47, no. 6 (1995): 19–30.

Kreutzer, Hans Helmut. "Die Auschwitznummer nicht verdecken." *Süddeutsche Zeitung*, 14 November 1992.

Löffler, Sigrid. "Durst und Todesangst: Der Lebensbericht der Wienerin Ruth Klüger zeigt, daß über den Holocaust noch lange nicht alles gesagt ist." *Profil*, 14 December 1992.

———. "Davongekommen: Jetzt noch über Auschwitz schreiben? Ruth Klüger ist es mit 'weiter leben. Eine Jugend' gelungen, ohne Pathos und gefühlsgenau." *Die Zeit*, 5 August 1993.

Lorenz, Dagmar C. G. "Memory and criticism: Ruth Klüger's *weiter leben*." *Women in German Yearbook* 9 (1993): 207–224.

Lühe, Irmela von der. "Das Gefängnis der Erinnerung: Erzählstrategien gegen den Konsum des Schreckens in Ruth Klügers *weiter leben*." In *Bilder des Holocaust: Literatur–Film–Bildende Kunst*. Edited by Manfred Köppen and Klaus R. Scherpe. Köln, Weimar, and Berlin: Böhlau, 1997, pp. 29–45.

Pomikalko, Ellen. "Tolle Prosa." *Brigitte*, 18 May 1993.

Reich-Ranicki, Marcel. "Von Trotz getrieben, vom Stil beglaubigt: Rede auf Ruth Klüger aus Anlaß der Verleihung des Grimmelshausen-Preises." *Frankfurter Allgemeine Zeitung*, 16 October 1993.

Rothenberg, Michael. "Between the Extreme and the Everyday: Ruth Klüger's Traumatic Realism." *Auto-Biography Studies* 14, no. 1 (Summer 1999): 93–107.

Scholem, Gershom. "Wider den Mythos vom deutsch-jüdischen Gespräch." In *Auf gespaltenem Pfad. Zum neunzigsten Geburtstag von Margarete Susman*. Edited by Manfred Schlösser. Darmstadt: Erato-Presse, 1964, pp. 229–232.

Schwarz, Egon. "Klüger, Ruth: weiter leben: Eine Jugend." *German Quarterly* (Spring 1993), 286–288.

Stein, Hannes. "Genauigkeit und Skrupel. 'weiter leben', ein Debüt: Die Lehr- und Wanderjahre der Ruth Klüger." *Frankfurter Allegemeine Zeitung*, 2 October 1992.

Taylor, Jennifer. "Ruth Klüger's *Weiter Leben. Eine Jugend*: A Jewish Woman's 'Letter to Her Mother.' " In *Out from the Shadows: Essays on Contemporary Austrian Women Writers and Filmmakers*. Edited by Margarete Lamb-Faffelberger. Riverside, Calif.: Ariadne, 1997, pp. 77–87.

Walser, Martin. "Ruth Klüger zur Begrüßung." *Das Kulturjournal: Bayrischer Rundfunk*, 27 September 1992.

SARAH KOFMAN
(1934–1994)

STEVE McCULLOUGH

SARAH KOFMAN WAS born in Paris in 1934 and committed suicide there on 15 October 1994. She was a respected philosopher and prolific writer who taught at the Sorbonne for over twenty years and wrote influential studies of Freud, Nietzsche, and Kant, among others. She identified herself with the philosophically and politically radical "post-68" generation of intellectuals and was counted, with such thinkers as Jacques Derrida, Jean-Luc Nancy, and Phillipe Lacoue-Labarthe, among the foremost French philosophers of this generation. Kofman read philosophy at the Sorbonne in the 1950s and then taught at various lycées before returning to the Sorbonne for doctoral studies. She began her dissertation research on Nietzsche under Jean Hyppolite in 1966 and continued under the supervision of Gilles Deleuze after Hyppolite's death in 1968. She is best known for her work on Nietzsche and Freud but wrote on a remarkable breadth of topics. It is from her critical engagement with Nietzsche and Freud, however, that her distinctive philosophical interests arose.

Kofman critically read the works of canonical philosophers, delving into how their ideas were shaped by unthematized presuppositions. This interest in philosophy's classically psychoanalystic sense of unconscious led her to frequently address the erasure of gender in the history of metaphysics, and several of her books explicitly bear on issues of gender and femininity in philosophical discourse. Francoise Ducroux describes Kofman's philosophical effort as "a search for how an articulated thought is intertwined with a subjective structure and history. It is men and women who make history, and it is men and women who make philosophy: not pure minds" ("How a Woman Philosophizes." *Enigmas*, pp. 134–140). Kofman thus sought to find the philosopher in the philosophy; and her own writing, in turn, tends to blur the boundary between philosophy and autobiography.

Works

Kofman was also a Holocaust survivor; she went into hiding in Paris with her mother after the deportation of her father, in the summer of 1942, and remained there for the duration of the war. Toward the end of her life, Kofman identified these experiences and losses as the root of her desire to write. She addresses the Holocaust most explicitly, however, in two late works: *Smothered Words* (1987), her study of Maurice Blanchot, and *Rue Ordener, Rue Labat* (Ordener Street, Labat Street, 1994), her memoir of survival.

Smothered Words is a complex blend of literary criticism, philosophy, and biography devoted to the problem of thinking and writing about Holocaust experiences. It is dedicated to and written about three men: Kofman's father, Holocaust survivor Robert Antelme, and philosopher/novelist Maurice Blanchot. She writes "as a Jewish woman intellectual who has survived the Holocaust to pay homage to Blanchot for the fragments on Auschwitz scattered throughout his texts" (*Smothered Words*, trans. Madeline Dobie, Evanston, Ill.: Northwestern University Press, 1998, pp. 7–8). Taking up Blanchot's writing (especially *The Infinite Conversation* and *The Writing of the Disaster*), Kofman contemplates her own father's murder and the danger inherent in any story that makes sense of the Holocaust. "About Auschwitz and after Auschwitz no story is possible, if by story one means: to tell a story of events which makes sense" (Kofman, p. 14). The danger of storytelling, in fiction or historiography, is that the story is fully itself, it "says all it has to say in saying it" (Kofman, p. 16). In contrast, traumatic events of cataclysmic suffering are never fully present, and language fails both in such situations and ever after with respect to them. She thus praises Blanchot's resistance to storytelling conventions, and she brings *The Human Race*, Antelme's memoir of internment, into the discussion as an example of tortuous writing that attests to its own impossibility of telling the story of the Holocaust and calls for writing as a response to that impossibility.

Smothered Words is also an intimate response to the death of Kofman's father, Rabbi Berek Kofman, who was reported beaten unconscious and buried alive by a *kapo* (prisoner placed in charge of other prisoners) for refusing to work on the Sabbath. This violent and proximate loss clearly had traumatic repercussions for Kofman, but this pain has simultaneously been an insistent demand for philosophical reflection; nowhere do the personal and the philosophical cross more explicitly for Kofman than in her reflections on speaking about the death of her father:

> Because he was a Jew, my father died in Auschwitz: How can it not be said? And how can it be said? How can one speak of that before which all possibility of speech ceases? Of this event, my absolute, which communicates with the absolute of history, and which is of interest only for this reason. To speak: it is necessary—*without (the) power* (pp. 9–10).

Kofman thus returns to the death of her father repeatedly and unexpectedly in *Smothered Words* and tells the story of his deportation in a variety of ways. The first is a bare recitation of data about her father and his deportation transport, followed by a reproduction of the portion of the Serge Klarsfeld Memorial (which presents an alphabetized list of deportees along with birth date and place) where Berek Kofman's name appears. This voice of "neutrality" contrasts with a later more personal, narrative recollection of the day of his deportation (Kofman, pp. 10, 34). Kofman engages in this repetition and formal experimentation in an attempt to work through some of the conflicting demands of testifying to the historical and experiential impact of the Holocaust in linguistic forms that are inevitably partial and unsatisfactory.

Kofman's attention to both Blanchot and the death of her father takes up the difficult and important work of linking Blanchot's often abstruse philosophy with material historical injustice. Kofman does this by comparing the literal smothering of her father with the difficult task of testifying to such atrocity. Kofman writes that the lot of survival is "to have to speak without being able to speak or be understood, to have to choke" (Kofman, p. 39). The title *Paroles suffoquées* (*Smothered Words*) thus arises from both the atrocious nature of her father's death and Blanchot's and Antelme's analyses of the impossible necessity of testimony to atrocity. This connection is not merely symbolic; following Blanchot, Kofman argues that her father and the Holocaust witness both occupy the untenable position of the subject called to respond to the infinite: the Jewish God on the one hand and the experience of suffering on the other. Speaking of her father, Kofman says,

> In this unnameable "place" he continued to observe Jewish monotheism, if by this, with Blanchot, we understand the revelation of the word as the place in which men maintain a relation to that which excludes all relation: the infinitely Distant, the absolutely Foreign. A relation with the infinite, which no form of power, including that of the executioners of the camps, has been able to master, other than by denying it, burying it in a pit with a shovel, without ever having encountered it (p. 35).

Kofman thus asserts that the death of her father attests to the limits of Nazi power, whose recourse to murder indicates the incapacity of such power to reverse refusal. Blanchot claims that humanity is characterized by need and that situations of utter suffering and destitution reveal the bottomless and impersonal nature of that need and the impossibility of extinguishing it. Kofman summarizes this paradoxically optimistic and despairing situation: "Man 'after Auschwitz'? The Indestructible. But this means 'that there is no limit to the destruction of man' " (p. 73).

Kofman's only foray into narrative writing (aside from a few autobiographical fragments collected and translated as "Autobiographical Writings" in *SubStance* 49 [1989]) was her penultimate book, *Rue Ordener, Rue Labat*, a sober account of her years of hiding in Paris during the German occupation. Widely reviewed and well received in the literary and popular media, *Rue Ordener, Rue Labat* has been praised for its unadorned and vivid portrayal of survival. However, it has also been criticized for being merely factual and failing to vivify any characters other than the narrator. This reading perhaps falls prey to the deceptive simplicity of this short work, which intertwines Kofman's historical reportage with her deft assessment of her childhood perceptions as well as her mature process of remembering and representing.

Kofman's narrative links memory with writing from its opening words. It begins with a description of her father's fountain pen, which is all she has left of him. Broken but patched together, no longer functional, the pen rests on her desk "and makes me write, write" (*Rue Ordener, Rue Labat*, trans. Ann Smock, Lincoln, Ne.: University of Nebraska Press, 1996, p. 3). Emblematic of the impossibility of expression that drives the need to write, this image unites writing, memory, and loss and suggests that Kofman's voluminous philosophical writings, too, have attempted to address this inarticulable past: "Maybe all of my books have been the detours required to bring me to write about 'that' " (p. 3). Indeed, a footnote links the wartime experience of being hidden in a small dark room with her writing of *Camera Obscura* (1973), and other notes draw various links between her childhood experiences and her adult reading and writing.

In contrast to some of her daring philosophical writing, Kofman's memoir is written in a laconic and unadorned style. The narrated events begin on 16 June 1942, the day of her father's arrest at their apartment on rue Ordener. Between July and February, Kofman's mother attempted to find hiding places for each of her six children. Kofman's intense attachment to her mother rendered her unhideable, as she refused to eat and often fell ill if separated from her. Looming Nazi violence is presented as less real to young Sarah than this infantile anxiety: "The real threat: separation from my mother" (p. 27). They must thus hide together and are eventually taken in by a Christian woman, whom Kofman calls Mémé, on rue Labat. The relationships between Kofman, her mother, and Mémé are the main focus of the memoir, which explores young Sara's growing estrangement from her mother and her intimacy with this new gentile mother-figure. Wider contexts and events such as the war, the Holocaust, and even Kofman's relationships with her siblings appear in the narrative only when they are relevant to this primary triangle of relationships.

Rue Ordener, Rue Labat presents an intimate portrait of the identity crises involved with survival in hiding. Kofman's initial attempts to hide were foiled by her intense attachment to her mother but also by her steadfast refusal to break the *kashrut* laws enforced by her now-absent father. Her childish insistence on eating kosher despite its danger and difficulty reflects the experience of hidden Jews who found themselves forced to break the laws defining their cultural existence as Jews in favor of brute survival. Kofman reports being easily won over to gentile food and behavior by the generous and attractive Mémé, who insists that Sarah has been poorly served by her upbringing: "Knowingly or not, Mémé had brought off a tour de force: right under my mother's nose, she'd managed to detach me from her. And also from Judaism" (p. 47).

The end of the war brings on a battle of wills between Kofman and her mother; Sarah reacts to her removal from rue Labat just as she did to her mother's attempts to hide her in the early years of the war. She has tantrums, refuses to eat, runs away, and ultimately provokes a court case to determine her custody. Mémé's beauty and proclivity for physical affection, which Kofman finds so appealing and charged with ambiguous sexual attractiveness, are seen by her mother as dangerous, and she accuses Mémé of sexual impropriety (a possibility that Kofman is careful to neither confirm nor deny). Although Mémé is awarded custody of Kofman by the French court, Kofman's mother forcibly reclaims her daughter, and so her maternal role, although Kofman is able to carry on a clandestine correspondence with her chosen surrogate.

This conflict over maternal relations is strongly implicated in larger conflicts between Jewish distinctiveness and assimilation. In Kofman's presentation of these childhood crises, her relationship with Judaism in general is inevitably understood by reference to her family relationships, primarily her relationship to her mother. She presents Judaism as no more independent of individual Jews than philosophy is independent of the work of individual philosophers. In "Damned Food," one of her autobiographical fragments, Kofman describes her familial and religious life as a tapestry of maternal and paternal imperatives: her father, the Rabbi, enforces the "you must not" of the kosher laws, whereas her mother announces a contrasting "you must," demanding that her children eat as much as possible. In the absence of her father, Kofman attributes to her mother all the coercive power of lawgiving, a role her mother ably fills, as she is parsimonious with affection and profligate with punishment. Thus, although the young Kofman returns to Judaism after the war when living at a Jewish children's camp for the children of deportees, her ongoing conflict with her mother leads to a final loss of religion shortly before she begins her university studies. *Rue Ordener, Rue Labat* narrates Kofman's story as far as her ultimate estrangement from both Mémé and her mother as she heads off to the Sorbonne, at which point her philosophical writing may perhaps be said to take up the rest of the story of her life.

In her mature attempts to express and interpret these childhood conflicts and attachments, Kofman draws on her adult experiences with art (chapter 18 of *Rue Ordener, Rue Labat* describes Freud's maternal-attachment interpretation of a painting by Leonardo da Vinci, which Kofman chose as the cover image for her first book) and film (chapter 19 of *Rue Ordener, Rue Labat* describes her reaction to Hitchcock's *The Lady Vanishes*). She thus makes explicit both the role of representational strategies in the work of memory and the ongoing interpenetration of past and present that makes any simple distinguishing between them impossible. Throughout the book, Kofman makes reference to the meager resources she has on hand to reconstruct the memory of her father. Among these are the fountain pen and an early photograph: the one is emblematic of the role of writing in reconstructing the past, and the other is an example of how even the "raw materials" of memory are themselves already mediated by representation. Kofman's recollection of the past is, despite its unadorned style, a self-conscious reflection on the construction of the past in a present that has, itself, grown out of that past. She therefore restricts her testimony to presenting and analyzing her own idiosyncratic perceptions and responses and attempts neither to generalize nor to explain her experiences.

Kofman's memoir ends with her report that at Mémé's funeral "the priest recalled how she had saved a little Jewish girl during the war" (p. 85). In these final words of the text, the irony, brevity, and inadequacy of this graveside eulogy underscores Kofman's insistence that representation is both insufficient and necessary to the work of remembering. Both her memoir and her corpus of philosophical writing thus attest to the complex textual nature of reconstructing a past scarred by irrevocable loss. For Kofman, writing arises in response to infinite demands it cannot fulfill and so demands this abyssal responsiveness in turn from readers.

Bibliography

Primary Sources

L'enfance de l'art: Une interprétation de l'esthétique freudienne (*The Childhood of Art: An Interpretation of Freud's Aesthetics*). 1970.
Nietzche et la métaphore (*Nietzsche and Metaphor*). 1971.
Camera obscura: De l'idéologie (*Camera Obscura: Of Ideology*). 1973.
Quatre romans analytiques (*Freud and Fiction*). 1974.
Autobiogriffures. 1976.
Aberrations: Le devenir-femme d'Auguste Comte. 1978.
Nietzsche et la scène philosophique. 1979.
L'enigme de la femme: La femme dans les textes de Freud (*The Enigma of Woman: Woman in Freud's Writings*). 1980.
Le respect des femmes (Kant et Rousseau). 1982.
Comment s'en sortir? 1983.
Un métier impossible: Lecture de "Constructions en analyse." 1983.
Lectures de Derrida. 1984.
Melancolie de l'art. 1985.
Pourquot rit-on? Freud et le mot d'esprit. 1986.
Paroles suffoquées (*Smothered Words*). 1987.
Conversions: Le Marchand de Venise *sous le signe de Saturne*. 1987.
Socrate(s) (Socrates: Fictions of a Philosopher). 1989.
SubStance. 1989.
Séductions: de Sartre à Heraclite (Seductions: From Sartre to Heraclitus). 1990.
Don Juan ou le refus de la dette. 1991. (co-written with Jean-Yves Masson)
"Il n'y a que le premier pas qui coute": Freud et la spéculation. 1991.
Explosion I: De l' "Ecce Homo" de Nietzsche. 1991.
Explosion II: Les enfants de Nietzsche. 1993.
Le mepris des Juifs: Nietzsche, les Juifs, l'antisemitisme. 1994.
Rue Ordener, rue Labat. 1994.
L'imposture de la beauté et autres textes. 1995.

Secondary Sources

Deutscher, Penelope, and Kelly Oliver, eds. *Enigmas: Essays on Sarah Kofman*. Cornell: Cornell University Press, 1999: 134–140.
Dobie, Madeleine. "Sarah Kofman's *Paroles suffoquées*: Autobiography, History, and Writing 'After Auschwitz.' " *French Forum* 22, no. 3 (1997): 319–341.
Hoft-March, Eilene. "Still Breathing: Sarah Kofman's Memories of Holocaust Survival." *Journal of the Midwest Modern Language Association* 33, no. 4/34, no. 1 (Fall 2000/Winter 2001): 108–121.
Scheaffer-Jones, Caroline. "Sarah Kofman's *Rue Ordener, rue Labat* and Autobiography." *Australian Journal of French Studies* 37, no. 1 (January–April 2001): 91–104.

EUGEN KOGON

(1903–1987)

WULF KOEPKE

EUGEN KOGON WAS born in Munich on 2 February 1903. After the early death of his parents, he was brought up in a Catholic family and in Catholic boarding schools, first the Benediktinerinternat Schweiklberg, a town in Bavaria, then with the Dominicans in Vechta/Oldenburg. At the University of Munich he joined the Jungmännerverband der Katholischen Jugendbewegung, Catholic youth movement, and became an ardent pacifist. University studies in business and sociology followed, first in Munich, where he received a Volkswirt-Diplom, then in Florence and Vienna, where he received a Dr. rer. pol. (a Ph.D. in the Social Sciences) in 1927. The topic of his dissertation was "Der Korporativstaat des Faschismus" (The Corporative State of Fascism). He was the editor of the Catholic weekly *Schönere Zukunft* in Vienna, from 1928 to 1932. During that time, he became an adviser to the Christian Trade Unions. From 1932 to 1934 he served as editor in chief of the paper of the Christian Unions, *Neue Zeitung*. From 1934 to 1938 he served as manager of private funds, which took him on numerous trips across Europe, helping victims of Nazism to save their fortunes and providing money for the resistance against the Nazi government, which came to power in Germany in 1933. Twice during stays in Germany, in 1936 and 1937, he was arrested by the Gestapo.

One day after the *Anschluss* (annexation of Austria by Germany), or 12 March 1938, Kogon was arrested by the Gestapo and, after lengthy interrogations in the Gestapo prison, sent to the Buchenwald concentration camp, near Weimar, in September 1939. He remained there until the camp's liberation on 11–12 April 1945, and became a leading member of the clandestine opposition of the inmates.

Following liberation, Kogon became an adviser to the Psychological Warfare Division of the Allied Headquarters near Frankfurt. In 1946, he became one of the founders of the monthly liberal Christian magazine *Frankfurter Hefte* and continued as one of the editors until 1984. He was among the founders of the Christlich-Demokratische Union (CDU), but as a Christian socialist, he later moved closer to the Sozialdemukratische Partei Deutschlands (SPD). He was a leading activist in the European movement, for some time the president of the Europa-Union in Germany. From 1951 to 1968 he was professor of political science, a newly reintroduced discipline, at the Technical University at Darmstadt. Kogon remained active as a journalist, especially as a radio and television commentator and host of political discussions. He was also the organizer and participant in numerous conferences designed to further democratic ideas and to preserve the memory of the Holocaust and the German resistance against Nazism.

Kogon was an indefatigable speaker and a prolific writer. His editors estimate that he produced around 1,700 works. These predominantly journalistic pieces, around 10,000 pages total, have been collected and published in parts since 1995. Kogon had several book projects that were not realized, his last one called *Rückblick auf den Nationalsozialismus* (National Socialism in Retrospect)—a dominant theme of his writing, looking back to the Nazi years and taking stock of what has happened since. However, he completed one enormously significant project early on, the work that made him famous, *Der SS-Staat* (*The SS-State*, 1946), and later *Die Stunde der Ingenieure* (*The Hour of the Engineers*, 1976). His collected works, without these two books, comprise nine volumes. Volume one, *Ideologie und Praxis der Unmenschlichkeit. Erfahrungen mit dem Nationalsozialismus* (*Ideology and Practice of Inhumanity. Experiences with National Socialism*), 1995, collects pieces for the projected book on National Socialism and continues the ideas contained in *Der SS-Staat*.

Der SS-Staat

Der SS-Staat, Kogon's crucial text for Holocaust studies, grew out of the report on Buchenwald concentration camp assigned to him by the American Psychological Warfare Division, soon after his liberation from the camp. Kogon, as a trained sociologist and political scientist, did not just report his and others' personal experiences but analyzed the ideology that led to the creation of these camps and the mentality of the SS that made the camps into what they became. The report contained not only invaluable firsthand documentary material but offered the potential for generalizations beyond the specific Buchenwald situation. As a consequence, its first American and German readers urged Kogon to expand it into a book, which he did in a remarkably short time, considering his still fragile state of health after years of suffering. The original report was published only in 1995, under the title *The Buchenwald Report*, and in 1996 in German as *Der Buchenwald Report*.

Kogon, as he discusses in his foreword written in December 1945, hesitated to confront his readers with horrors almost beyond the limits of comprehension, but he felt compelled to do so to tell the "naked truth" and to shock the Germans out of their arrogance and resistance to accepting the facts. He asserts in his introduction that there can be no doubt as to the authenticity and truth of the testimonies, facts, and statistics. Carefully preserving the style of the detached social scientist, he nonetheless makes clear how emotionally involved he must be. Kogon was a severe critic of the Allied policy of collective guilt of the Germans. Instead of offering the Germans the chance to realize what they had done as a people, even though they may have been ignorant of many facts individually, the overwhelming accusation of collective guilt drove the Germans into denial and stubborn defiance. Kogon never ceased to attack this denial and to spread enlightenment about the horrible crimes and the acceptance of the German guilt. Equally, he stood up for the honor of those in the German resistance against Hitler.

Der SS-Staat was first published in 1946 by the Frankfurter Hefte. In 1947, Bermann-Fischer, then in Stockholm, brought out a new edition that insured an international distribution. In 1948, Kogon added a new introductory chapter, "Der Terror als Herrschaftssystem" (Terror as a System of Government). Since then, the book has become an indispensable classic of Holocaust literature, and numerous editions and translations into eight languages have appeared. The first English translation appeared in London in 1950. By 1974, 262,000 copies had been sold.

The basic thesis of the book is that the concentration camps were not aberrations but the logical consequence of the ideas of Heinrich Himmler and his organization, the SS. The SS constructed a total system, a *Staat*, that assigned social ranks, privileges, and duties to the various populations it encompassed, from the luxurious life of the SS leaders to the extermination of so-called undesirables. Even within the inmate populations of the camps, the social order was rigidly maintained: from the political prisoners to Jews, Gypsies, criminals, homosexuals, and those persecuted for their religion. Kogon debunks the myth of the morally "clean" SS men, demonstrating the overall corruption and bribery. Above all, he describes the extremes of sadism and gratuitous cruelties in the forms of various punishments, the deprivation of everything that makes life human, the discipline and order designed to dehumanize and destroy the inmates. He never strays from the style of factual observation and documentations, and is always careful to limit his claims to stay on safe ground. The systematic narration includes a description of the procedures for new arrivals; daily routines; typical work assignments; punishments; food rations; accommodations; latrines; living conditions for the different ranks of the SS; personalities of various commanders, doctors, and guards; self-help and organizational problems of the inmates; and problems of letter writing and receiving food from family members—all of this culminating in the analysis of the structure of the "state" of the SS within the Nazi state. Kogon also includes an account of the end of the camps, specifically Buchenwald, through the Allied occupation, and he asks the inevitable questions: how much did the German people know of the real conditions in the camps, and how much did they participate? His book includes a chapter on the extermination camps as well, not from firsthand experience, of course, but on the basis of the early reports from survivors and documents made available to him by the Allies. Kogon was on the lists for transport to Auschwitz several times but always managed to avoid shipment to the East.

Taken as a whole, the book is indeed overwhelming. Its power is even stronger because of its detached tone. Kogon leaves no doubt where he stands but is careful to stay with the facts. All general statements are supported by specific examples. Beyond the horror of the facts, Kogon confronts the many moral dilemmas that life and survival in the camps caused. Even in retrospect, good and evil could not be divided without difficulties, and sometimes, for Kogon, it seems impossible to separate them altogether. Beyond the obvious message that such a system should never be used again by humans against humans, Kogon offers accumulating evidence that moral conduct in all groups of the camps, from the SS to the "criminals" among the inmates, cannot be judged in a uniform manner. He also differentiates with respect to the knowledge of the German population regarding the Holocaust and their participation.

Remembering National Socialism and the Holocaust

In the essays of the volume *Ideologie und Praxis der Unmenschlichkeit* (*Ideology and Practice of Inhumanity*), written between 1946 and 1985, Kogon picks up most of the themes and aspects of his analysis in *Der SS-Staat* from the point of view of later years and with his experiences of the Federal Republic of Germany (West Germany). He reiterates the main point that the camps were a well-thought-out, although often chaotic, system, and that the Germans need to confront the radicality of the persecutions and extermination policies. As a prominent political scientist, journalist, confessing Roman Catholic, and known antifascist, Kogon was often asked for his views. He commented on the Eichmann trial, on the Frankfurt Auschwitz trials, and especially on the exterminations themselves.

In the volume *Begegnungen* (*Encounters*, 1997), the editors collected Kogon's autobiographical articles, tracing his life and career to the very end. Some accounts recall the concentration camp experience and eulogize former friends and comrades. He stresses the "spirit of 1945," the determination of the survivors to create a humane world of peace and freedom. As in the other writings, his later articles are devoted to the goal of a unified Europe and to the memory of the past, so that it should never happen again. In the end, Kogon speaks to the generation of his grandchildren and calls on them to create a new world.

In 1983, at age eighty, Kogon was the most prominent coeditor of the documentation *Nationalsozialistische Massentötungen durch Giftgas* (*National Socialist Mass Killings by Poisonous Gas*), which summarized all the evidence for the installations and technical and chemical procedures in all the camps where such killings occurred, especially Auschwitz-Birkenau and the other extermination camps of Belzec, Sobibór, Chelmno, and Treblinka, with the best estimates of the number of the victims. Kogon's own concluding chapter, "Wie es möglich war" (How It Was Possible), stresses as its first point that the book shows, once again, that these things did indeed happen—the denial of Auschwitz is impossible. He identifies as the root cause "die nationalsozialistische Weltanschauung" (the National Socialist Worldview) (p. 289) in its authoritative formulations and proclamations by Adolf Hitler. A worldview like National Socialism must by necessity lead to such extremes.

A major concern of Kogon was the memory of the atrocities and the awareness of succeeding German generations of them and of the fact that the Germans had failed to come to grips with them after 1945. Also in 1983, he spoke on this topic to students at the University of Tübingen, a speech and essay placed last by the editors in the volume *Ideologie und Praxis der Unmenschlichkeit*.

Eugen Kogon died on 24 December 1987. He never wavered from his positions of fundamental humanism, pacifism, and Christian socialism. He fought for a united Europe and for real democracy in Germany. But more than anything else, he reminded the Germans that they had to live with the darkest period of their history, not as a myth but as a reality to be confronted in all its horrors, yet also in all its different shades of human courage and weakness.

Bibliography

Primary Sources

Der SS-Staat (*The SS State*). 1946. English translation: *Theory and Praxis of Hell in the German Concentrations Camps and the System Behind Them*. 1950.

Die Stunde der Ingenieure. Technologische Intelligenz und Politik (*The Hour of the Engineers. Technological Intelligence and Politics*). 1976.

Alter und Aktivität. Zur Ideologie vom Ruhestand (*Age and Activity. On the Ideology of Retirement*). 1976.

Eugen Kogon—ein politischer Publizist in Hessen (*Eugen Kogon—A Political Journalist in Hesse*). Selections, ed. Hubert Habicht. 1982.

Nationalsozialistische Massentötungen durch Giftgas (*National Socialist Mass Killings by Poisonous Gas*). Ed. with others. 1983.

The Buchenwald Report. 1995.

Der Buchenwald Report. 1996.

Ideologie und Praxis der Unmenschlichkeit. Erfahrungen mit dem Nationalsozialismus (*Ideology and Practice of Inhumanity. Experiences with National Socialism*). Collected essays, Vol. 1 of Kogon's collected works. 1995.

Europäische Visionen (*European Visions*). Vol. 2. 1995.

Die restaurative Republik. Zur Geschichte der Bundesrepublik Deutschland (*The Restorative Republic. On the History of the Federal Republic of Germany*). Vol. 3. 1996.

Liebe und tu, was du willst. Reflexionen eines Christen (*Love and Do What You Want. Reflections of a Christian*). Vol. 4. 1996.

Die reformierte Gesellschaft (*The Reformed Society*). Vol. 5. 1997.

Dieses merkwürdige, wichtige Leben. Begegnungen (*This Strange, Important Life. Encounters*). Vol. 6. 1997.

Bedingungen der Humanität (*Conditions of Humanity*). Vol. 7. 1998.

Konservative Anfänge (*Conservative Beginnings*). Vol. 8. 1998.

Die Idee des Christlichen Ständestaates: Frühe Schriflen 1921–1940 (*The Idea of a Christian Corporate State: Early Writings 1921–1940*). Vol. 8. 2000.

Secondary Sources

Kogon, Michael. Introductions to all the volumes of Kogon's collected works.

Mayer, Hans, and Alfred Grosser. *Die Rolle des politischen Schriftstellers: zwei Vorträge. Eugen Kogon zum 75. Geburtstag am 2. Februar 1978.* Darmstadt: Technische Hochschule, 1978.

Prümm, Karl. *Walter Dirks und Eugen Kogon als katholische Publizisten der Weimarer Republik.* Heidelberg: Carl Winter, 1984.

Stankowski, Martin. *Linkskatholizismus nach 1945—die Presse oppositioneller Katholiken in der Auseinandersetzung für eine demokratische und sozialistische Gesellschaft.* (Sammlung Junge Wissenschaft) Cologne, Germany: Pahl-Rugenstein, 1974.

There are several other survivor reports on Buchenwald, one example being *Buchenwald, ein Konzentrationslager*, Bericht von Emil Carlebach, Paul Grünewald, et al. Frankfurt: Röderberg, 1984.

Gertrud Kolmar

(1894–1943)

MONIKA SHAFI

IN A LETTER written in July 1942 in Berlin, Gertrud Kolmar declared: "Already as a child I would have liked to be a Spartan woman, later on, I wanted to become in any case a heroic woman. . . . Today . . . I can be . . . an 'original hero' (without attracting any unwelcome attention)" (*Briefe an die Schwester Hilde 1938–1943*, München: Kösel Verlag, 1970, p. 160). Kolmar sought to fulfill her longing for a heroic destiny in her literary work, where she could boldly transgress social, historical, and gender boundaries and create vast imaginary continents and geographies. The heroic persona, the self-determined, extraordinary human being able to master a difficult fate, became one of the dominant paradigms of her oeuvre. Yet, what started out as a poetic representation turned, during Nazi rule, into a blueprint for coming to terms with her own persecution. The fictional persona whom Kolmar had explored in numerous forms and disguises now served as a real-life script and empirical practice in order to resist the terror that was invading her life. The path from the Spartan to the heroic woman thus delineates not only Kolmar's conflicted literary development and poetic identity, but it also reflects how she transformed a fictional concept into a personal defense mechanism to help guard against the degradation and exclusion imposed on her (Shafi, 1995, pp. 28–30).

Biography and Literature, 1894–1933

Gertrud Käthe Chodziesner was born in Berlin on 10 December 1894, the eldest daughter of Ludwig Chodziesner, a well-known and highly respected lawyer. Ludwig Chodziesner grew up in Chodziesnen, a small town in the province of Posen that until 1918 belonged to Prussia, but he had left his lower-class, provincial origins quickly behind. In 1894, he married Elise Schönflies, who came from a wealthy Jewish family known for their businessmen and scholars. Chodziesner's rise to prosperity and prominence mirrored migration and social patterns typical of late-nineteenth century German Jews, and he appeared to represent a model of successful Jewish integration into the educated German bourgeoisie.

Gertrud grew up in the comfortable environment of the assimilated Jewish upper class, a world she shared, for example, with her cousin Walter Benjamin, whose advice on literary matters she sought a few times in later years. Yet, the shy and rather introverted child seems to have felt ill at ease with the family's active social life, and from an early age she withdrew into the world of history, animals, and nature and her rich inner life. In contrast to her three younger siblings, she also did not approve of her parents' assimilated outlook and well-to-do lifestyle. Instead, she professed an early interest in her Jewish identity and history, and these topics figure prominently in her later work, particularly in the texts written during the time of the Third Reich.

Gertrud's schooling followed the conventional course set for girls of her class, but in 1916 she was awarded a language diploma for French and English that would have entitled her to teach at middle schools and high schools. Apparently, her language abilities were phenomenal, and she later taught herself Russian and in the last years of her life added Hebrew, a language in which she even began to compose poetry. Starting in 1919 she worked for several years as a private instructor for various families. A gifted and dedicated educator, she was specially apt in dealing with disabled children.

In 1917 Gertrud's first publication, a slim volume titled *Gedichte* (Poems), appeared under the pseudonym "Kolmar," which is the German translation of her father's hometown of Chodziesnen. This publication—initiated by her father without her knowledge—followed the most decisive and devastating event of her early years, a love affair that resulted in an abortion. It appears that Kolmar was pressured by her family to terminate the pregnancy, a decision that had a monumental impact on her subsequent life and poetic work. For one, maternal images and figures abound in Kolmar's texts, and mothers most often are cast as lonely and sad characters who deplore the loss of a child and who are tormented by guilt and (self) blame. A number of poems either directly or indirectly address the traumatic event itself, allowing Kolmar also to voice her critique of Wilhelminian society's double moral standard and bias and explore how a society constructs its outsiders.

The years following this traumatic event were not a very productive period for Kolmar. In 1927, however, she traveled to France where she participated in a language course held in Dijon, completing it with high honors. This journey released a burst of creative energies. She returned to her parents' home in Finkenkrug, an almost rural suburb of Berlin, where in the next five years she wrote the cycles *Weibliches Bildnis* (Image of Woman), *Tierträume* (Animal Dreams), and *Kind* (Child). Women, children, and animals are the most prominent figures in Kolmar's oeuvre, and these three cycles can be regarded as her *magnum opus*. During the same time period, Kolmar also composed the cycles *Das preussische Wappenbuch* (The Prussian Book of Coats of Arms) and *Bild der Rose: Ein Beet Sonette* (Image of the Rose: A Flower Bed of Sonnets).

Weibliches Bildnis, Kolmar's most important lyrical creation, paradigmatically reflects major themes, images, and ideas of her work. Divided in four "Räume" (spaces), the cycle of seventy-five poems chronicles experiences and stages of womanhood and portrays a wide range of women encompassing mythical ("Leda") and biblical ("Judith," "Esther") characters as well as prostitutes, witches, or dancers. In its entirety, the cycle can be read as a generic female (auto) biography (Shafi, 1995, 84–86) that is dominated by images of women suffering from unrequited maternal or erotic love. Informed by seemingly very traditional gender codes, Kolmar portrays these women as outsiders, loners, and victims who often embrace their estrangement or are willing to sacrifice themselves. They accept rather than challenge their marginal position. Yet, many characters also forcefully assert their independence from societal norms, insisting on the validity of their different world views. In the opening lines of the poem "Die Jüdin" (The Jewish Woman), for example, the self describes both isolation and strength:

> I am a stranger.
>
> Since no one dares approach me
> I would be girded with towers
> That wear their steep and stone-gray caps
> Aloft in clouds (Smith, p. 109).

Her large literary production notwithstanding, Kolmar shunned Berlin's lively literary scene. In the late 1920s and early 1930s, she made some effort to have her poetry published, but after 1933 Nazi legislation made this increasingly difficult and eventually impossible. In 1934, Kolmar published a number of poems from the large cycle *Das preussische Wappenbuch* under the title *Preussische Wappen* (Prussian Coats of Arms). These poems focused less on the heraldry suggested by their title than on a broad critique of modernity and civilization. They contrast the alienation of contemporary society with a primeval world of untamed nature and animals, as can be seen in the last stanza of "Wappen von Allenburg" (Allenburg):

> The mighty beasts struck terror into man.
> With cunning tricks he hunted innocence,
> And wounded it, and slew it as it ran:
> In earthly childhood. That has passed long since
> (Smith, p. 171).

For Kolmar, animals are an integral part of creation, equal to human beings, and she profoundly questions the Judeo-Christian tradition that legitimatized killing these creatures. In numerous poems, Kolmar assumes the role of animals, particularly despised animals such as toads or snakes, and celebrates their beauty.

In 1938, the Jüdische Buchverlag Erwin Löwe (The Jewish Publisher Erwin Löwe) published under the title *Die Frau und die Tiere* (The Woman and the Animals) a selection from Kolmar's cycles *Weibliches Bildnis* and *Tierträume*. But following Nazi legislation after the pogrom of November 1938, Kolmar's most important publication, *Die Frau und die Tiere*, had to be destroyed before it could reach the public. From 1936, Kolmar's poems were also recited during cultural evenings organized by the Jüdischer Kulturbund (Jewish Cultural Organization) and praised, often enthusiastically, in Jewish newspapers. For the reclusive and withdrawn poet who had created almost her entire oeuvre without any audience such recognition came too late (*Briefe*, p. 14).

Response to Hitler's Rise to Power, 1930–1933

Kolmar had recognized very early on the danger the Nazi dictatorship presented to Jews and to all those opposed to its rule, and beginning in the early 1930s she addressed the issues of antisemitism and racism in a series of new and startling works. In 1930, after the death of her mother, whom Kolmar had taken care of during her long illness, she wrote her first prose piece, the short novel *Eine jüdische Mutter* (A Jewish Mother). Despite its formal and stylistic flaws, the novel captures the increasingly violent antisemitism during the last years of the Weimar Republic, and it also explores questions of Jewish identity and assimilation. Martha Wolg, née Jadassohn, the Jewish mother of the title, experiences her Jewishness primarily as a maternal and erotic quality, but Jewish identity is not connected to any sense of community. She sees herself as the quintessential Other and outsider, finding love and acceptance only with her five-year-old daughter, Ursa. When the child is brutally raped, Martha kills the traumatized girl with an overdose of medication because she has no hope for recovery. Much of the novel's subsequent plot is dedicated to Martha's fruitless search for the rapist, which allows Kolmar to canvass Berlin's cityscape and present Martha's misguided sense of justice and maternal love as well as her highly conflicted self-image that feeds on sexual-racial stereotypes. According to Dagmar Lorenz, Martha's portrait touches on the issue of Jewish self-hatred since she both resents and espouses racial views and stereotypes.

In 1933, Kolmar also composed *Das Wort der Stummen* (The Word of the Silenced), a cycle that contained several poems detailing antisemitism, hatred, persecution, torture, and death. The cycle's title refers both to the silencing of the victims and to the poet's mission to voice their ordeals. The poem "Anno Domini 1933," for example, describes how a mob verbally assaults an East-European Jew and his child, and, frenzied by Nazi rhetoric, then attacks him. "You crooked nose, Levi, Saul / Here, take the blood toll and shut your trap! / [. . .] A kick with a boot, a cudgel blow / In the third, Christian-German *Reich*" (*Gertrud Kolmar. Weibliches Bildnis. Sämtliche Gedichte*, München: Kösel, 1987, pp. 748–749).

Among this group is also a poem called "Im Lager" (In the Camp), a frightening account of the prisoners' tortured bodies and anguish. Kolmar probably knew about the existence of concentration camps because her cousin Georg Benjamin had been arrested in April 1933 and after a few months in the infamous prison Berlin-Plötzensee was sent to the concentration camp Sonnenburg. "In the Camp" describes how the prisoners—men, boys, and women—are dehumanized, losing their bodies, minds, and souls: "And their eyes stare emptily / With a crumbling, decaying look / To hours, when in a dark hole / Strangled, trampled, beaten blind / Their tortured moans, their crazed horror / An animal, crawled on hands and feet . . ." (*Gertrud Kolmar. Weibliches Bildnis. Sämtliche Gedichte*, p. 741). The poem ends with a reference to Christ, thus contrasting torture and salvation and evoking the heroic mastery of an unbearable fate.

Kolmar responded to the growing oppression and persecution of Jews also in a series of historical works that center on Robespierre, a figure who had fascinated her for a long time. An essay ("Das Bildnis Robespierres" [The Image of Robespierre]), a cycle of poems (*Robespierre*), and a short play, *Cécile Renault*, all explore different aspects of the revolutionary hero and his legacy. Kolmar's forays into French history, which were based on a detailed knowledge of the events themselves as well as their historical interpretations, can be read both as a response to Nazi dictatorship and as a general treatise on justice, ethics, and heroism. The historical setting of these texts is, however, less a camouflaged reference to contemporary politics—a strategy that numerous German (exiled) authors adopted in an array of historical works—than a medium to reflect on the qualities of the heroic individual.

Kolmar's framework for understanding Robespierre is not based primarily on political or historical standards but on moral and ethical categories. She constructs Robespierre as a completely pure, selfless, and virtuous man who was above mundane temptations and petty power struggles. She sees him as engaged in an unrelenting and uncompromising quest for justice and morality that sets him apart from his fellow human beings and that ultimately leads to his downfall. Kolmar states that she would have liked to work for Robespierre as a civil servant, and the overall adulatory mood and religious imagery of the essay suggest that she shaped Robespierre as an identificatory figure in response to Nazi persecution. Her interpretation also reveals how a heroic self-definition guided her perception and actions at a time when alternative scenarios of resistance were still available. The contours of this heroic image were drawn sharper as Nazi policies rapidly dismantled the legal and social status of the Jews before engaging in their systematic destruction.

Biography and Literary Works, 1933–1943

In the years between Hitler's takeover and the November pogrom of 1938, Jews in Germany "suffered the agonizing double bind of preserving their sanity and normalcy of their lives while assessing the mounting danger around them, helpless to stop it" (Kaplan, p. 3). Kolmar's poetic response to this process can be gleaned from her last lyrical cycle, *Welten* (Worlds), which presents a different approach to the Nazi regime than the historical work of the early 1930s. *Welten* can be considered as Kolmar's poetic testimony. The author embarks on a final yet magnificent journey through ancient landscapes, exotic topographies, and mythical realms. In *Welten*, Kolmar abandoned for the first time the traditional poetic form, using a free verse style that seems to push language to its breaking point, as can be seen from the following lines in the poem "Türme" (Towers): "A snowy oal swims soundless, sifting snowflakes, through the crystal singing silence of the night . . . And colored cow-wheat smiles upon the powerless dungeon tower, while grasses idle mournfully on buried walks" (Smith, p. 215). Overall, an elegiac mood characterizes *Welten*, whose figures and landscapes are engulfed by sadness, hopelessness, and utter isolation. The poet appears to bid farewell to the world, mournful that her voice was not heard.

Kolmar's own life in Berlin, where she lived from the late 1920s until her deportation to Auschwitz in February 1943, chronicles the different stages of Nazi persecution leading from "social death" (Kaplan, p. 5) to physical annihilation. While her brother and her two sisters managed to escape in time, Kolmar's own emigration plans never materialized. The exact reasons remain unknown, but one can speculate that Kolmar felt obliged to take care of her father who, apparently, refused to leave Germany. Because of his distinguished career as a lawyer who identified with Germany, Ludwig Chodziesner may have been unable to read the warning signs until it was too late. After the November pogrom, father and daughter were trapped. In November 1938, they were forced to sell their home and move into one of the so-called Judenhäuser (Jew Houses), where they had to endure ghettolike conditions, starvation, and complete loss of privacy. The latter was the most difficult for Kolmar to cope with, but she was still able to deal with it artistically.

In 1939, shortly after her move into the *Judenhaus*, Kolmar wrote a short play, *Möblierte Dame (mit Küchenbenutzung) gegen Haushaltshilfe* (Furnished Lady [with Use of Kitchen] for Household Help). *Möblierte Dame* is a character satire and probably the most unusual and surprising text in Kolmar's oeuvre. The brief text sharply criticizes those Jews who failed to recognize the growing danger and who tried instead to maintain an everyday normalcy—satirized in the play as the female protagonist's continuous quest for culinary pleasures—while her community is systematically destroyed. Yet, the ironic sketch of the foolish, lazy woman reveals one of the fundamental dilemmas of the Jews in Nazi Germany, namely the need to decide and prepare for a life outside Germany and the inability to perceive of a non-German identity and lifestyle.

Despite the horrible conditions Kolmar endured, including forced labor in munitions factories, she continued to write. Around 1940, she composed the novella *Susanna*, which probes themes related to *Eine jüdische Mutter* but treats them in a different setting and language. While waiting desperately for her affidavit to arrive, a Jewish governess recalls the time she spent with her pupil Susanna many years ago. The gorgeous, but "insane" Susanna is yet another variation on the theme of (Jewish) outsider and other. Narrated in hauntingly beautiful images, Kolmar evokes the world of the East-European *shtetl*, and she explores the causes that led to its destruction.

From 1938 until shortly before her deportation, Kolmar also corresponded with her youngest sister, Hilde, who had emigrated in 1938 to Switzerland. These letters were first published in 1970 as *Briefe an die Schwester Hilde 1938–1943* (Letters to the Sister Hilde 1938–1943). The extensive correspondence, the only detailed private record to survive, is a crucial document not only for understanding Kolmar but also for the history of the Holocaust. Written under tight censorship, Kolmar could only make veiled references to her situation, carefully camouflaging, for example, the father's deportation to Theresienstadt (September 1942). Unable to describe the deprivations, exhaustion, the fear and danger, she focused instead on literary matters and repeatedly reflected on what she called "amor fati: love of one's destiny" (*Briefe*, p. 196). In their entirety the letters, which have been read as "spiritual autobiography" (Langer, 1982, p. 194) or as "epistolary autobiography" (Shafi, 2000, p. 105) reveal how Kolmar tried for almost five years to resist and defy her oppressors by creating a spiritual sanctuary. This inner realm, in which only "eternal events" (*Briefe*, p. 111) mattered, allowed her to maintain a sense of selfhood and to shield herself from Nazi terror. In contrast to other Jews, whom she often sharply criticizes for their nostalgic longings, Kolmar refuses to turn back to a lost German past, looking instead toward Jewish history and a Jewish-based identity. By consciously selecting other times, spaces, and modes of self-representation, Kolmar tries to dissociate herself as much as possible from the daily horror in order to be able to endure it.

Response to the Holocaust

James Young has pointed out that although the *Shoah* affected all Jews, "each victim 'saw'—i.e. understood *and* witnessed—his predicament differently, depending on his own historical past, religious paradigms, and ideological explanations" (p. 26). Kolmar's primary mode of response to the Holocaust and the events surrounding it was that of a complex heroic (martyr) paradigm. She clearly explained this position in a letter written in December 1942:

> That's the way I want to encounter fate, be it high as a tower, be it black and looming as a cloud. Even if I don't know my fate: I have accepted it in advance; I have opened myself up to it in advance, and therefore I know that it won't crush me, that it won't consider me too small (*Briefe,* p. 187).

The development of this paradigm from a primarily *literary* self-identification to a *personal* response can be traced throughout Kolmar's writings. Many different influences, ranging from her personal experiences and Jewish heritage to her roots in German idealism and classicism and her profound critique of modernity, have contributed to this image. Kolmar's primary goal was to keep the self spiritually and morally intact. This kind of resistance privileges the inner strength and resilience of the individual who when confronted with a seemingly unbearable fate finds refuge in her own courage and endurance. Langer cautioned against Kolmar's "personal formula for spiritual survival" (1982, p. 204) since the humanistic basis of her approach was negated by the reality of Auschwitz. Yet, one can also argue that Kolmar could control only her spiritual life and that any affirmation of self, especially in the form of writing, was an act of resistance and extraordinary courage.

Importance to Holocaust Literature

Gertrud Kolmar was a witness and a victim of the Holocaust. Her life chronicles all its stages, from social death and, in her case, also literary death, to deportation and murder. The texts written between 1930 and 1943 explore different responses to the *Shoah*, reflecting Kolmar's roots in Jewish history and in eighteenth-century German literary and philosophical traditions. Within this complex and contradictory framework, Kolmar did not primarily focus on issues of representation but on depicting and understanding distinct phases of the Holocaust and building a spiritual defense against it. This specific personal and literary testimony connects Kolmar to Holocaust literature.

Critical Reception

The bulk of Kolmar's work appeared posthumously, but it failed for the most part to get the attention of critics, scholars, or the public. Her work did not fit into the dominant postwar literary trends in West or East Germany, and as a *victim* of the Holocaust she also did not allow for any exculpation. The past fifteen years, however, have seen a steady growth of scholarly investigations, driven initially by feminist critics, as well as new editions of her poetry and prose. Kolmar research now covers a broad spectrum of often overlapping positions, ranging from deconstruction, feminism, and traditional hermeneutics to studies of Kolmar's place within German-Jewish literature. Although often compared to Nelly Sachs and Else Lasker-Schüler, Kolmar still remains the less well-known poet in this triad. Her work, wedged uneasily between tradition and modernity, continues to challenge us to uncover its bold, subversive messages.

Bibliography

Primary Sources

Gedichte (Poems). 1917.
Die Frau und die Tiere (The Woman and the Animals). 1938.
Welten (Worlds). 1947.
Das lyrische Werk (The Lyric Work). 1955.
Preussische Wappen (Prussian Coats of Arms). 1958.
"Susanna" (Susanna). 1959.
Das lyrische Werk (The Lyric Work). 1960.
"Gertrud Kolmar: Das Bildnis Robespierres" (Gertrud Kolmar. The Image of Robespierre). 1965.
Die Kerze von Arras. Ausgewählte Gedichte (The Candle of Arras. Selected Poems). 1968.
Briefe an die Schwester Hilde 1938–1943 (Letters to Sister Hilde 1938–1943). 1970.
Eine Mutter (A Mother). Reprinted as *Eine jüdische Mutter* (A Jewish Mother). 1978.
Das Wort der Stummen. Nachgelassene Gedichte (The Word of the Silenced. Posthumous Poems). 1978.
Gertrud Kolmar: Weibliches Bildnis. Sämtliche Gedichte (Gertrud Kolmar: Image of Woman. Collected Poems). 1987.
Susanna. (Susanna). 1993.
"Möblierte Dame (mit Küchenbenutzung) gegen Haushaltshilfe" (Furnished Lady (with Use of Kitchen) for Household Help). 1994.

Translations

Selected Poems of Gertrud Kolmar. 1970.
Dark Soliloquy: The Selected Poems of Gertrud Kolmar. 1975.

Secondary Sources

Bormanis, John. "Gertrud Kolmar Completes Her Poetry Cycle Weibliches Bildnis and Thus Reshapes Her Identity as a Jewish Woman Poet." In *Yale Companion to Jewish Writing and*

Thought in German Culture 1096–1996, 492–498. Edited by Sander L. Gilman and Jack Zipes. New Haven, Conn.: Yale University Press, 1997.

Brandt, Marion. *Schweigen ist ein Ort der Antwort. Eine Analyse des Gedichtzyklus "Das Wort der Stummen."* Berlin: C. Hoffmann, 1993.

Kaplan, Marion. *Between Dignity and Despair: Jewish Life in Nazi Germany*. New York: Oxford University Press, 1998.

Langer, Lawrence L. "Survival Through Art: The Career of Gertrud Kolmar." Publications of the Leo Beck Institute. *Year Book* 23 (1978): 247–258.

———. "Gertrud Kolmar and Nelly Sachs: Bright Visions and Songs of Lamentations." In *Versions of Survival: The Holocaust and the Human Spirit*, 191–250. Albany: State University Press of New York, 1982.

Lorenz, Dagmar C. G. "More than Metaphors: Animals, Gender and Jewish Identity in Gertrud Kolmar." In *Transforming the Center. Eroding the Margins: Essays on Ethnic and Cultural Boundaries in German-Speaking Countries*, 21–28. Edited Dagmar C. G. Lorenz and Renate S. Posthofen. Columbia, S. C.: Camden, 1998.

———. *Keepers of the Motherland: German Texts by Jewish Women Writers*. Lincoln: University of Nebraska Press, 1997.

Natzmer Cooper, Gabriele von. "Das süßere Obst der Erkenntnis: Gnosis und Widerstand in Gertrud Kolmars 'Lied der Schlange.' " *Seminar* 4 (1993): 138–151.

Schlenstedt, Siliva. "Suche nach Halt in haltloser Lage: Die Kulturarbeit deutscher Juden nach 1933 in Deutschland und die Schrifstellerin Gertrud Kolmar." *Sinn und Form* 4 (1989): 727–742.

Shafi, Monika. "Turning the Gaze Inward: Gertrud Kolmar's *Briefe an die Schwester Hilde 1938–1943*." In *Facing Fascism and Confronting the Past: German Women Writers from Weimar to the Present*, 103–115. Edited by Elke P. Frederiksen and Martha Kaarsberg Wallach. Albany: State University Press of New York, 2000.

———. *Gertrud Kolmar: Eine Einführung in das Werk*. Munich: Iudicium, 1995.

———. "Vorbemerkung zu Gertrud Kolmars Stück *Möblierte Dame (mit Küchenbenutzung) gegen Haushaltshilfe*." In *Gertrud Kolmar: Orte*, 129–131. Edited by Marion Brandt. Berlin: Kontext, 1994.

Smith, Henry A. "Gertrud Kolmar's Life and Works." In *Dark Soliloquy: The Selected Poems of Gertrud Kolmar*, 3–52. New York: Continuum, 1975.

Stern, Guy. "Schrifsteller in extremis." In *Literatur im Exil: Gesammelte Aufsätze 1959–1989*, 74–93. Ismaning, Germany: Hueber, 1989.

Woltmann, Johanna. "Gertrud Kolmar 1894–1943." *Marbacher Magazin* 63 (1993).

Young, James. *Writing and Rewriting the Holocaust: Narrative and the Consequences of Interpretation*. Bloomington: Indiana University Press, 1988.

RACHEL KORN
(1898–1982)

GOLDIE MORGENTALER

RACHEL HÄRING KORN is one of the major poets of modern Yiddish literature. She was born in 1898 in Pokliski in East Galicia, Poland. Korn's family had owned farmland for several generations and she was raised on the family farm, the eldest of three children. This upbringing distinguished her from other Yiddish writers, whose backgrounds and sensibilities were primarily urban, and it accounts for the great lyricism and intimacy with which she writes about nature. Korn learned Polish in the village school and her first published poems and stories were written in Polish.

It was only after her marriage that she learned to read and write Yiddish under the tutelage of her husband. Deeply shocked by a series of pogroms in the independent Polish republic that had been established after World War I, Korn stopped writing in Polish and from 1919 on wrote and published only in Yiddish. She began her career as a Yiddish writer with a series of short stories, followed by an outpouring of poetry.

Korn's Place in Yiddish Literature

Once she began to publish in Yiddish, Korn was quickly recognized as one of the language's new literary talents. As Chava Rosenfarb wrote in *Yiddish Poets in Canada*:

> The young Rokhl Korn took Yiddish literature by storm. She was a revelation. It seemed as if she, the country girl, had driven her Galician country wagon straight into the hustle and bustle of Yiddish Warsaw's literary marketplace, bringing with her the smell of the soil, the aroma of freshly baked country bread, and the fragrance of feminine sensuality (p. 18).

Korn's appearance on the Yiddish literary scene coincided with the flowering of Yiddish culture and literature that followed World War I. It also coincided with the flowering of women's poetry in Yiddish. Most of the important women poets of this time were American. Korn's was the major European voice, although she resembled the other women poets in throwing off the restraints of religion and male authority and in writing openly about sexuality. The freshness and accuracy of Rachel Korn's poetry revolutionized both Yiddish nature poetry and Yiddish love poetry.

Poetry

Korn's first book of poetry, *Dorf* (Village, 1928), contains portraits of the country people among whom she had grown up. Some of the verse sketches from this volume are among Korn's best-known poems. However, even in this period before World War II, Korn's writing was permeated by a sense of foreboding. This anxiety is evident not only in her poems, but also in the collection of short stories she published in 1936 under the title *Erd* (Earth). Both the stories and the poems deal with the losses that Jewish peasants in particular suffered during the antisemitic attacks that occurred in the aftermath of World War I and the establishment of the Polish republic. By the time she published her second book of poems, *Royter mon* (Red Poppies, 1936), the theme of loss had grown even more pronounced. For instance, in "My Home," Korn describes how her mother, who had been widowed young, divided her time between caring for her fields and caring for her three children, how she had dreamed of harvests and of round red cheeks. But all the mother's worries and hopes were useless: Strangers now live in the old home. The speaker concludes ominously:

> My life is like a dark house
> without windows or doors,

open to all winds and all storms,
and my heart, like a lip,
wants to drink up the black clouds
over the factory chimneys
that hail hard drops of human sweat
and rain childish tears (*Royter mon*, Jewish PEN Club, 1936, p. 40).

When World War II broke out, Korn was in Lvov, visiting with her daughter, who was studying medicine. By the time her husband arrived to join them in 1941, Korn and her daughter had left the city, escaping to Soviet Russia on the last eastbound train. Korn's husband, mother, two brothers, and their families remained in Poland, where they all perished.

With her daughter, Korn wandered all over "the inconsolable earth," her name for the Soviet Union. In 1944 she finally arrived in Moscow where she was welcomed and assisted by the Yiddish cultural community, which included Shlomo Mikhoels, Peretz Markish, and David Bergelson. Korn's wanderings with her daughter are commemorated in the poem "To My Daughter," written in Moscow in 1944:

When I led you out, the earth spurted blood and terror
with every step we took.
The greatest good was sudden death,
and a mother's blessing—the sure mercy of a bullet for her child (*Paper Roses: Selected Poems of Rachel Korn*, Toronto: Aya Press, 1985, p. 17).

Korn lived in Moscow until 1946, when she decided to return to Communist Poland. She settled in Lodz, where she was elected to the executive of the newly reestablished Yiddish Writers' Union. The union sent her as a delegate to the PEN congress in Stockholm, where she decided to stay until she could get permission to emigrate. In 1948 Korn, her daughter, and son-in-law emigrated to Canada and settled in Montreal.

After the shock of the Holocaust and her own tragic experiences, Rachel Korn's wanderings had come to an end. In Montreal she continued to write, turning out poetry and short stories in Yiddish and securing her position as one of the great masters of Yiddish poetry. The Canadian landscape reminded her of her native Galicia, and in such poems as "Let There Be Snow" and "All the Winds" she translated the long Canadian winter into a metaphor for the desolation of uprootedness, using her Canadian present as a shortcut back to the ruins of her lost home.

Korn's work was praised by all the major critics of Yiddish literature. Elie Wiesel called her "the poet of the sufferings, wanderings and memories of the Jewish people," adding that "Yiddish literature would not be what it is—and I would not be what I am—had Rachel Korn not opened the way for us" (p. 11).

Many of Korn's most moving poems and stories deal with the Holocaust. Her most anthologized story, "The Road of No Return," is set in a Galician village on a fall day in 1942. The spare narrative tells of one family's struggle in the face of a Nazi decree that each family send out one of its members to face a certain death. Korn's story describes the self-sacrifice of the grandmother, but also suggests the dehumanizing effect that being forced to make such a decision has on the family.

Because Korn herself evaded the concentration camps, her Holocaust stories deal with this subject obliquely, through the narrator's encounters with those who did experience the camps. In "Bronia," Korn tells the story of a woman she met in a displaced persons camp in Sweden after the war, who managed to hide her own young child and that of her dead sister in the concentration camp. Bronia's inspired and successful effort to save her niece from the gas chamber results ultimately in the loss of her own child, as if every tiny victory over death in the camps must be paid for with an even greater loss.

Many of Korn's Holocaust poems deal with the sense of loss, of "letters carried to addresses now rubbed out" as Korn writes in "The Watchman." In particular, the loss of her mother is a repeated refrain in Korn's work and the subject of some of her most moving poetry, such as the following from "My Mother Often Wept." "A birch tree may be growing on the mound / heaped by a murderer's hands / in thick woods near the town of Greyding, / and only a bird goes there to honour the dead / where my mother lies in an unknown grave / a German bullet in her heart" (*Generations: Selected Poems*, Oakville, Ont.: Mosaic Press, 1982, p. 46).

In her Holocaust poetry, Korn's love of nature melds with her sorrow, as in "The Words of My Alefbayz": "The words of my alefbayz / smelled of wild poppies and periwinkle . . . but they were branded with a number at Treblinka, / charred in the smoke of Belzec and Maidanek" (*Generations*, p. 39). Unlike her male counterparts, Korn's approach to the Holocaust is completely personal and intuitive. Not for her the grand sweep of Jacob Glatshteyn's "Good-night World," or H. Leivick's "I Never Was in Treblinka." She leaves the philosophizing to others. Her sensibility is thus closer to that of Abraham Sutzkever, and one suspects that the difference between these two poets and their American contemporaries lies in the fact that both experienced the Holocaust firsthand in Europe rather than distantly in America. The voice in Korn's poems is intimate and terribly sad; it is a voice that is focused on the particular rather than the general. It achieves its power through the lucid and simple articulation of the pain of loss.

In her most famous lyric, "The Other Side of the Poem," Korn combines several of her favorite themes—the depiction of nature, the invocation of the mother, the approaching night of catastrophe, and the sheer power of creativity to reanimate the past:

On the other side of the poem amazing things may
 happen
even on this overcast day
this wounded hour
that breathes its fevered longing on the window pane.

On the other side of the poem my mother may appear
and stand in the doorway for a while lost in thought,
and then call me home as she used to long ago:
You've played long enough, Rachel. Don't you see? It
 is night (*The Penguin Book of Modern British Verses*,
 New York: Penguin 1988, p. 524).

Korn was a two-time winner of the Lamed prize for poetry and prose in 1949 and 1958. She also won the H. Leivick prize and the Itsik Manger prize of Israel, as well as the award for Yiddish poetry from the Jewish Book Council of the United States. She died in Montreal in 1982.

All translations from Korn's poems are by Seymour Levitan.

Bibliography

Primary Sources

Poetry

Dorf (Village). 1928.
Royter mon (Red Poppies). 1936.
Heym un heymlozikayt: lider (Home and Homelessness). 1948.
Bashertkayt: lider 1928–48 (Destiny: Poems 1928–1948). 1949.
Fun yener zayt lid (On the Other Side of the Poem). 1962.
Di gnod fun vort (The Grace of the Word). 1968.
Oyf der sharf fun a rege (On the Edge of an Instant). 1972.
Farbitene vor: lider (Altered Reality: Poems). 1977.

Short Fiction

Erd (Earth). 1936.
Nayn dertseylungen (Nine Stories). 1957.

Translations

Lider un erd (Poems and Earth). Hebrew translation by Shimson Meltzer. 1966.
Generations: Selected Poems. Edited by Seymour Mayne, translated by Rivka Augenfeld, et al. Oakville, Ont.: Mosaic Press / Valley Editions, 1982.
Paper Roses: Selected Poems of Rachel Korn. Translated and edited by Seymour Levitan. Toronto: Aya Press, 1985.

Anthologies That Include the Works of Rachel Korn

Antologie fun der yidisher proze in poiln, tvishn beyde velt milkhomes (1914–1939) [Anthology of Yiddish Prose and Poetry in Poland between the two world wars (1914–1939)]. Edited by Y. Y. Trunk and Aaron Zeitlin. New York: Cyco, 1949.
A Treasury of Yiddish Poetry, New York: Holt, Rinehart, Winston, 1969.
An Anthology of Modern Yiddish Literature, Mounton: The Hague, 1974.
Canadian Yiddish Writings, Montreal: Harvest House, 1976.
The Penguin Book of Women Poets, New York: Penguin, 1979.
The Poets of Canada, Edmonton: Hurtig, 1978.
Voices Within the Ark: The Modern Jewish Poets, Yonkers: Pushcart, 1980.
The Spice Box: An Anthology of Jewish Canadian Writing, Toronto: Lester, Orpen, Dennys, 1981.
The Penguin Book of Modern Yiddish Verse, New York: Penguin, 1987.
Truth and Lamentation: Stories and Poems on the Holocaust, Urbana: University of Illinois Press, 1994.
Found Treasures: Stories by Yiddish Women Writers, Toronto: Second Story Press, 1994.
The Last Lullaby: Poetry from the Holocaust. Syracuse: Syracuse University Press, 1998.
When Night Fell: An Anthology of Holocaust Short Stories. New Brunswick: Rutgers University Press, 1999.

Secondary Sources

Bikel, Shloime. *Shrayber fun mayn dor*. New York: Matones, 1965.
Glatshteyn, Yakov. *In tokh genumen; esayen 1948–1956*. New York: farlag fun yidish natsionaln arbeter farband, 1956.
Gross-Zimmerman, N. "Di shtile negideste." In *Intimer videranand: esayen*. Tel Aviv: Peretz farlag, 1964.
Korman, Ezra. "Rokhl Korn." In *Yidishe dikhterihs* (Yiddish Women Poets). Chicago: Farlag L. M. Sh'ayn, 1928.
Niger, Shmue. *Yidishe shrayber fun tsvantsikstn yorhundert*. New York: alveltlekher yidisher kultur kongres, 1973.
Ravitch, Melekh. *Mayn leksikon: yidishe dikhter, dertseyler, dramaturgn in poiln tvishn di tsvey groyse velt milkhomes*. Montreal: fun a komitet, 1947.
Reisin, Zalmen. *Leksikon fun der yidisher literatur prese un philologie*, Vol. 3. Vilna: Kletskin, 1929.
Rosenfarb, Chava. *Yiddish Poets in Canada*. Mississauga: Publications for the Jewish Studies Program at University of Toronto, 1994.
Wiesel, Elie. "In Praise of Rachel Korn." In *Generations*. Oakville: Mosaic Press, 1982.

Archives

Rokhl Korn's archives are housed at the Jewish Public Library in Montreal, which also has an extensive file on her work in its Jewish Canadiana Collection.

Jerzy Kosinski

(1933–1991)

DANIEL R. SCHWARZ

A DEFINITION OF Holocaust fiction must extend beyond camp and ghetto sites to include terrifying war narratives of the Polish zeitgeist in the war years. Jerzy Kosinski's *The Painted Bird* (1965) is such a text, but also one that exemplifies how the murkiness of the war allowed for the author's self-invention. Kosinski's *The Painted Bird* describes the life of a child abandoned at six years of age by parents who thought he might better survive the German invasion of Poland if separated from them in 1939. The boy is not identified as a Jew and his ethnicity is left ambiguous. Indeed, although the boy is sent to the country in 1939, the time period is not fully grounded by the narrator's consciousness of the period's history; thus the dark-featured boy is as much a timeless victim of Polish xenophobia as a victim of prejudice in a particular time.

The title of *The Painted Bird* is taken from the custom of peasants who painted birds and then released them to rejoin the flock, which, seeing them as aliens, killed them.

> The painted bird circled from one end of the flock to the other, vainly trying to convince its kin that it was one of them. But, dazzled by its brilliant colors, they flew around it unconvinced. The painted bird would be forced farther and farther away as it zealously tried to enter the ranks of the flock. We saw soon afterwards how one bird after another would peel off in a fierce attack. Shortly the many-hued shape lost its place in the sky and dropped to the ground (New York: Houghton Mifflin, 1965, p. 44).

Similarly, the novel's protagonist sees himself as one who has been painted by experience and cannot rejoin his flock. Moreover, the title implies that those who are "painted" as Jews or Gypsies, as communists or "other," are ostracized by the dominant group.

Not only did Kosinski create imaginary worlds in his novels, but his novels played a crucial role in creating his character and personality. Until Kosinski's presentation of his life was challenged, the story he told of his early years sounded much like the story of his fictional protagonist in *The Painted Bird*, hardly surprising because he originally claimed his story as autobiographical. Although he really was born in 1933 in Lodz, Poland, doubts about the authenticity of his claim that *The Painted Bird* was based on his life began in 1964, as soon as he submitted his manuscript. By the time Eliot Fremont-Smith and Geoffrey Stokes questioned his account of his life in their 1987 *Village Voice* article, a strong shadow of suspicion accompanied him.

Kosinski had not, in fact, been abandoned by his parents during the war and suffered the humiliations of his protagonist. His father, Mleczyslaw, was a classicist who changed his surname from Lewinkopf to Kosinski (a very common Polish name). His mother, Elizbieta, was a concert pianist. The family had moved together from Lodz to Sandomierz. Although the family moved several times during the war, they were able to maintain a semblance of normal life, primarily because Kosinski's father had sufficient funds to pay for the family's protection. Kosinski earned a B.A. from the University of Lodz in 1950 and came to the United States in 1957.

In America he passed himself off as a non-Jewish Pole. Later, even after accepting his Jewishness, he was defensive about the behavior of the Poles.

It is difficult for us to separate Kosinski's opportunism from his narrator's trauma. Although Kosinski sold *The Painted Bird* as an autobiographical account, it clearly is a work of fiction. Kosinski's ultimate fiction was himself. Thus we read *The Painted Bird* with double optics, on one hand, immersed in the world of his text, and on the other, aware that his life was often a performance, a myth he created of an omnipotent childhood.

In response to issues his novel raised, Kosinski wrote *Notes of the Author on The Painted Bird* in 1965, which was appended to the German edition and later self-published as a nineteen-page booklet. In this pamphlet he acknowledges that "to say that *The Painted Bird* is non-fiction may be convenient for classification, but it is not easily justified. . . . [I]n the attempt to recall the primitive, the symbols are sought more pertinently and immediately than through the superficial process of speech and dialogue" (quoted in Langer, p. 169). It is surprising how Kosinski's own commentary has shaped criticism of the novel. Thus for Lawrence L. Langer, a sympathetic critic, Kosinski's "pertinent exposition of fantastic intentions . . . prompted in part by the accusations of Polish critics that he was defaming the national character," is a contribution to "an aesthetic of atrocity" (p. 168).

A related question that emerged later is whether *The Painted Bird* is a work of single authorship. The issue of whether Kosinski wrote *The Painted Bird* has been alive for some time. As early as 1973, when Kosinski was a candidate for president of PEN, concerns were voiced on the degree to which he relied on others in writing the book. Kosinski had originally written the book in Polish. According to the Kosinski biographer James Park Sloan, George Reaves worked on the manuscript. Furthermore, Sloan writes: "Several editors and translators participated as 'consultants' on the English text of *The Painted Bird*" (Sloan, p. 316).

More important than Kosinski's self-invention is his fictional representation of the Holocaust memory. Kosinski relies on incorporating dual perspectives: the voice of an omniscient third-person adult narrator and the voice and perceptions of a young child. The reader may not quite believe in the naive voice of the child, perhaps hearing, at times, the artistry of the older creator behind it. *The Painted Bird* begins with an italicized third-person preface:

> *In the first weeks of World War II, in the fall of 1939, a six-year-old boy from a large city in Eastern Europe was sent by his parents, like thousands of other children, to the shelter of a distant village. . . . In sending their child away the parents believed that it was the best means of assuring his survival through the war. Because of the prewar anti-Nazi activities of the child's father, they themselves had to go into hiding to avoid forced labor in Germany or imprisonment in a concentration camp. They wanted to save the child from these dangers and hoped they would eventually be reunited* (p. 1).

At this point the young boy's voice takes over. The boy identifies himself not as a Jew, although he speaks of having dark features—he is "olive-skinned, darkhaired, and black eyed"—and he is taken for both Gypsy and Jew. The boy not only never identifies himself as a Jew, but speaks once of going to a Catholic church with his parents and presumably believing in a teleology reflecting God's loving presence. He gradually loses his cultured childhood and learns from the peasants that in a grim universe, only the fittest survive. The self dissolves into fragments, and the only continuity other than the voice is the varied assaults on his physical and psychic being; it is often a disguised version of a weird sadomasochistic narrative like Pauline Reage's novel *The Story of O.*

The presumably retrospective narrator draws upon the narrator's memories of his experience from ages six through twelve. From a retrospective point of view, Kosinski dramatizes the complexity of a child's feelings as the child tests and discards a variety of ethical perspectives, but the words and feelings cannot always be separated from the older speaker. A version of Henry James's third-person omniscient voice—or of free indirect discourse—might be more effective than Kosinski's first person because it does not pretend to speak for the young child, only to render his feelings.

One traditional theme in Holocaust fiction is the conversion experience, although at times it is a counterconversion away from faith and humanist values. In *The Painted Bird*, the boy, separated from his middle-class moorings, re-creates himself. Kosinski's text is a kind of bildungsroman manqué; it traces the boy's maturation but it is a maturation to disillusionment and, finally, if not nihilism, cynicism.

In the nine years between the *Village Voice*'s challenge of his account of himself and his suicide in 1991, Kosinski's life was in a downward spiral. Like the scholar Paul de Man, Kosinski reinvented himself when he came to the Unites States from Europe. In his last novel, *The Hermit of 69th Street*, he defends Chaim Rumkowski, the Jewish leader of the Lodz ghetto, who collaborated with the Nazis. According to Sloan:

> For Kosinski, it was essential to come to grips with Lodz, where he spent his adolescence, where his relatives died or were consigned to death camps, and where he would have certainly perished had his family not gone to Sandomierz and Dabrowa. . . .
>
> What lay behind Kosinski's tenacious defense of Rumkowski? Not a fighter himself, despite the rhetoric of his novels, he needed a model of extreme *choice* in the effort to survive. Rumkowski exemplified man caught in a web of *chance*, in a *blind date* with fate shared by *Poles and Jews*, who looked frankly and realistically at his situation, taking what was, in his terms, the only possible action. In doing so, he reconfirmed the model of behavior in that crisis with which Kosinski was most intimately aware—the actions taken by [his father] Moses Lewinkopf (Sloan, pp. 409–410).

Like Primo Levi and Tadeusz Borowski, Kosinski wrestled with feelings of emptiness and worthlessness, characteristics we see in many Holocaust authors and their characters, including Art Spiegelman's self-dramatization in *Maus*. Would not Kosinski have considered himself the ultimate painted bird, honored and decorated with awards and then, at least from his vantage point, vilified by others who wanted to ostracize him from the flock? Forced from the flock by an exposé in the *Village Voice*, he completed the transformation of himself into victim by killing himself.

Whether or not feelings of persecution have roots in Kosinski's paranoid fantasy, the novel stands as a historical allegory for victimization of the innocent. The boy has lived the terror of persecution; he is the perpetual outsider, hated for his difference and otherness. He is a naive, almost anesthetized, witness to the trains taking Holocaust victims to their death and to how the xenophobic, ignorant Polish peasants found refuge for their cruelty to Jews in the blood libel that Christ was killed by Jews.

The speaker's narrative tells of his suffering an astonishing variety of abuse and exploitation by peasants who lord it over Jews and Gypsies, even while behaving barbarously. Gradually every remnant of the human values of love, reason, sympathy, and decency disappear from his world. The boy learns the suspicion and folk culture of the peasants. Later in his wanderings he is exposed to versions of Christianity and Marxism. At times the speaker crosses over into the culture that abuses him and becomes part of it. Yet, as Sidra DeKoven Ezrahi notes:

> [I]n spite of the verisimilitude of event and situation established in the first-person narrative, the novel lacks a plausible existential center and takes on the dimensions of a folk or fairy tale. The boy is never named (the author himself, in notes to the German translation of the novel, refers to him as "the Boy"; even in a universe in which characters exchange names and forge identities so frequently, such complete anonymity is rare), and he soon relinquishes as useless whatever biography he had (University of Chicago Press, p. 153).

Had the boy suffered the physical torture he describes, he would have been long dead; nor can one quite believe in the incredible sadism of the Polish peasants when Garbos puts up hooks to hang the boy while his vicious dog Judas stands below waiting for the young boy to fall. Indeed, this book is full of acts of mindless torture and its overuse, not merely of violence, but also of perversion and sadism, at times short-circuits a sympathetic reading. Kosinski enjoys describing sexual excess beyond the need of his text, as when he depicts the Kalmuk's rape and pillage with pornographic zeal.

The cumulative atrocities climax in the boy's being thrown into human excrement and becoming mute. The phantasmagoric language—owing something to Franz Kafka and perhaps Bruno Schulz's *Street of Crocodiles*—reflects the nightmare world of the Holocaust; images of mutilated nature extend the effect of the sadistic actions performed on the boy's body or psyche. Yet, although Kosinski writes of a world in which man devolves into beast, the boy's resilience is in juxtaposition to wasteland images.

Ironically when, as the narrator recalls, he answers a telephone and speaks, he returns to himself and to civilization by means of the very technology used to destroy much of Europe and European Jewry. His words remind us that speech is crucial to our sense of self: "I opened my mouth and strained. Sounds crawled up my throat. Tense and concentrated I started to arrange them into syllables and words. I distinctly heard them jumping out of me one after another, like peas from a split pod" (p. 213).

We know Kosinski felt ties with Joseph Conrad, another Pole writing in English, but unlike Conrad he had more trouble with written English than with spoken English. Kosinski may have had in mind Marlow's *Heart of Darkness*, where a retrospective narrator descends into a world of horror, confronts experiences that challenge his humanistic beliefs, and after resisting a return to a world in which he no longer feels comfortable, finally reintegrates himself into the world he once left. When Marlow realizes that terms like "enemies" and "criminals" are applied indiscriminately to natives, he becomes disillusioned with his position as "emissary of light" assigned by European culture. Similarly, Kosinski shows European pretensions to civilization to be a sham in the face of the abuse of an innocent boy—a boy who becomes, to Polish peasants, both "enemy" and "criminal" because he is different.

Bibliography

Primary Sources

Books and Pamphlets

(Documents Concerning the Struggle of Man: Reminiscences of the Members of the Proletariat). 1954.

(The Program of the People's Revolution of Jakob Jaworski). 1954.

The Future Is Ours, Comrade: Conversations with the Russians (under pseudonym Joseph Novak). 1960.

(American Sociology: Selected Works, Editor). 1963.

No Third Path (under pseudonym Joseph Novak). 1962.

The Painted Bird. 1965. Revised 1970.

Notes of the Author on The Painted Bird. 1965.

Steps. 1968.

The Art of the Self: Essays á propos "Steps." 1968.

Being There. 1971.

The Devil Tree. 1973. Revised 1981.

Cockpit. 1975.

Blind Date. 1977.

Passion Play. 1979.

Pinball. 1982.
The Hermit of 69th Street: The Working Papers of Norbert Kosky. 1988.
Passing By: Selected Essays, 1962–1991. 1992.

Articles

"Dead Souls on Campus." *New York Times*, October 12, 1970, 45.
"The Reality Behind Words." *New York Times*, October 3, 1971, 3.
"The Lone Wolf." *American Scholar* 41 (fall 1972): 513–519.
"Packaged Passion." *American Scholar* 42 (spring 1973): 193–204.
"To Hold a Pen." *American Scholar* 42 (fall 1973): 56–66.
"Against Book Censorship." *Media and Methods* 12 (January 1976): 20–24.
" 'Seven Beauties'—A Cartoon Trying to Be a Tragedy." *New York Times*, March 7, 1976, 1, 15.
" 'The Banned Book,' as Psychological Drug: A Parody." *Media and Methods* 13 (January 1977): 18–19.
"Is Solzhenitsyn Right?" *Time* (June 26, 1978): 22.
"Our 'Predigested, Prepackaged Popular Culture.' " *U. S. News and World Report* (January 8, 1979): 52–53.
"Time to Spare." *New York Times*, May 21, 1979, A19.
"Telling Ourselves to Make It Through the Night." Review of *The White Album*, by Joan Didion. *Los Angeles Times Book Review*, May 27, 1979, 29.
"Combining Objective Data with Subjective Attitudes." *Bulletin of the American Society of Newspaper Editors* 43 (July/August 1981): 19.
"A Brave Man, This Beatty. Brave as John Reed." *Vogue* (April 1982): 316, 318, 319.
"How I Learned to Levitate in Water." *Life* 7, no. 4 (April 1984): 129–132.
"A Passion for Polo." *Polo* Official Publication of the United States Polo Association (May 1985): 115–118.
"Exegetics." *Paris Review* 97 (fall 1985): 92–95.
"Death in Cannes." *Esquire* (March 1986): 82–89.
"Restoring a Polish-Jewish Soul." *New York Times*, October 22, 1988, 1, 27.
"The Second Holocaust." Boston *Sunday Globe*, Focus, November 4, 1990, A17.

Secondary Bibliography

Aikant, Satish C. "Self and Survival: Jerzy Kosinski's *The Painted Bird*." *Indian Journal of American Studies* 28 (1998): 1–2, 85–90.
Baker, Russ W. "Painted Words." *Village Voice*, March 15, 1994, 58–59.
Ezrahi, Sidra DeKoven. *By Words Alone: The Holocaust in Literature*. Chicago: The University of Chicago Press, 1980.
Harpham, Geoffrey Galt. "Survival in and of *The Painted Bird*." *Georgia Review* 35 (1981): 142–157.
Hicks, Jack. *In the Singer's Temple: Prose Fictions of Barthelme, Gaines, Brautigan, Piercy, Kesey, and Kosinski*. Chapel Hill: University of North Carolina Press, 1981.
Janowska, Dorota. "Kosinski on Language: *The Painted Bird* and *The Hermit of 69th Street*." In *Jerzy Kosinski: Man and Work at the Crossroads of Cultures*. Edited by Agnieszka Salska and Marek Jedlinski. Lodz, Poland: Wydawnictwo Uniwersytetu Lodzkiego, 1997.
Klinkowitz, Jerome. "Two Bibliographical Questions in Kosinski's *The Painted Bird*." *Contemporary Literature* 16 (1975): 126–128.
———. "Betrayed by Jerzy Kosinski." *The Missouri Review* 6 (summer 1983): 157–171.
Lale, Meta, and John Williams. "The Narrator of *The Painted Bird*: A Case Study." *Renascence* 24 (summer 1972): 198–206.
Langer, Lawrence L. *The Holocaust and the Literary Imagination*. New Haven, Conn.: Yale University Press, 1976.
Lavers, Norman. *Jerzy Kosinski*. Boston: Twayne, 1982.
Lilly, Paul R., Jr. *Words in Search of Victims: The Achievement of Jerzy Kosinski*. Kent, Ohio and London, England: Kent State University Press, 1988.
Lupack, Barbara Tepa. "Introduction." In *Critical Essays on Jerzy Kosinski*. Edited by Barbara Tepa Lupack. New York: G. K. Hall, 1998.
Richter, David H. "The Three Denouements of Jerzy Kosinski's *The Painted Bird*." *Contemporary Literature* 15 (summer 1974): 370–385.
Sanders, Ivan. "The Gifts of Strangeness: Alienation and Creation in Kosinski's Fiction." *Polish Review* 19 (1974): 171–189.
Schwarz, Daniel R. "Beyond the Camps: Kosinski's *The Painted Bird*." In *Imagining the Holocaust*, 173–194. New York: St. Martin's Press, 1999.
Sloan, James Park. *Jerzy Kosinski*. New York: Dutton, 1996.
Spendal, R. J. "The Structure of *The Painted Bird*." *Journal of Narrative Technique* 6 (1976): 132–136.
Stokes, Geoffrey, and Eliot Fremont-Smith. "Jerzy Kosinski's Tainted Words." *Village Voice*, June 22, 1982, 1, 41–43.

ABBA KOVNER
(1918–1987)

LEON I. YUDKIN

ABBA KOVNER WAS born in Sebastapol, in the Crimea, in 1918 but was raised in the legendary city of Vilna (Vilnius), known as the Jerusalem of Lithuania, a great center of Hebrew and Yiddish learning, rabbinic studies, and the Haskalah (Enlightenment) movement as well as various Zionist organizations. Vilna had been ruled variously by Poland, Lithuania, and Russia from 1920 to June 1941. On 19 September 1939 the Red Army entered Vilna, and a few weeks later the city was returned to the Lithuanians under the terms of an mutual aid agreement with the Soviets. In July 1940, however, Lithuania (and Vilna with it) was incorporated into the Soviet Union. On 24 June 1941, two days after Germany invaded the Soviet Union, the Nazis entered Vilna. Jews were subjected to the standard brutalities under Nazi occupation. Thousands were executed by the Nazis with the collaboration of the local Lithuanians in nearby Ponary.

Kovner escaped the initial massacre, hiding in a nearby Dominican convent. In September, two ghettos were established. Kovner, together with other resisters, organized the Fareynigte Partizaner Organizatsye (FPO), the underground youth organization of the combined factions of Jewish Vilna. They worked on resistance operations from within secret headquarters in the ghetto until their smuggling of weapons and contact with partisans in the forest became a threat to the continued existence of the ghetto, and until Jacob Gens, the Jewish head of the ghetto, ended his support and protection of the FPO. After the tragic death of rebel leader Itzick Wittenberg, Kovner assumed the commander's position.

In June 1943 Himmler called for the ghettos of Lithuania to be liquidated. During the liquidation process, the FPO called on the ghetto population to disregard the order to report for deportation and to rise up in rebellion. With the final liquidation of the Vilna ghetto on 23 and 24 September, the population was dispersed to concentration camps and to the Sobibor extermination camp, while others were murdered at Ponary. During the final deportation, Kovner directed the FPO's operations and the escape of the ghetto fighters through the sewers and into the forests, where they joined the partisans to continue fighting.

After liberation, Kovner emigrated to Palestine and served as a leader of the Brihah movement, which sought to bring other Jewish immigrants there. An organizer of illegal immigration foiling the British blockade, he was imprisoned, then freed, and served as an officer in the Givati brigade in the Israeli war of independence (1948), the subject of his two-volume fictional work *Panim el Panim* (Face to Face), published between 1953 and 1956. Kovner settled on kibbutz Ein Hahoresh, where he lived until his death in 1988. He and his wife, Vitka, had two children. His life, rich in experience, powerful and traumatic, informs all his writing. This body of work constantly poses the question: How is it possible to remain human in this cruel world? A novelist, essayist, and, most notably, a poet, he received the Israel Prize for Literature.

Early Poetry

Kovner made the genre of the long poem, the "poema," a form peculiarly his own, and he is almost unique among his contemporaries, Hebrew poets who started writing within the post-1948 Israeli state, to adopt this genre and then to deploy it as the primary mode of expression. His first venture into book publication was the long poem, *'Ad lo or* (Until No Light, 1947), which constitutes an evocation of the partisan fighting. Later poems recall the subsequent war, the struggle for an independent Israel in the Middle East. But whether the scene is a forest in Byelorussia or Lithuania or the territory that was to become Israel, the poems are not primarily narrative. Had Kovner wanted to tell the story of the events, he would have adopted a different mode (as he did in his prose work *Panim el Panim*), but in these poems, there is more drama than storytelling. The long poem is not lyrical, not narrative, and not balladic, although it has elements of these other forms. Streams of modernism, expressionism, and surrealism enter the long poem. Kovner believes it necessary to adopt this very specific and relatively unusual genre in order to concentrate the total story into one emotional perception, to present something extensive but unitary.

In *'Ad lo or*, Kovner attempts to present the feeling of an embattled fighter, although as far as Europe is concerned, the fighter is engaged in an unequal struggle, challenging an enemy overwhelmingly powerful, and the odds are hopelessly uneven. (It is in the later stages of Kovner's work, in the fight for the Israeli state, that we approach the situation of some sort of "normal" war, as recorded in the sequence of poems, *Pridah mehadarom* [Separation from the South, 1949]). As Kovner says in the preface to *'Ad lo or*, everything in the poem is not written as allegory with certain plot points corresponding to something else, but as "pure symbol, the symbol of Fate." The writing is presented in the first person by a narrator thirsty for revenge. The narrator's feelings are akin to erotic lust for the destruction of the railway lines held by the hated Nazi enemy. That lust is contrasted with the utterly pervasive presence of death. It is not the separate incidents that Kovner aims to present accurately, scrupulously, and in historical and social perspective, but rather the feeling of the writing individual, expressing his authentic being and sense of the moment. The focus of Kovner's poetry is not so much that hated other, the enemy, but rather the Jewish partisan himself, the hero of the poem / story. The hero seeks his own survival, and he longs for the touch of a mother. The poem attempts to recover the sense of that struggle and persistence, although—perhaps because—the voice has been silenced, and also to present the essence of the daily lives of Jewish and Russian partisans in the Lithuanian forests.

The central figure of this collection is specifically, although anonymously, known by the single apellation, "the partisan." The tone deployed in the raising up of this figure is one of exalted pathos. The fighter bears the garland, now anointed, on his brow. The language used is religious and messianic: "a commandment," and "the primary sanctification belongs to the fighter." But the second chapter (as in many long poems, the work is sectioned into chapters) heralds a new figure, that of the (still anonymous) woman. Zvia Ginor points out that while Kovner is not a poet in the lamentation tradition, "some of the conventions and metaphors of the traditional, classic lament are employed . . . the central one being that of the city personified as woman" ("Paradise Betrayed," p. 86). She is the second-person addressee, an object of intense, erotic yearning. The passion of the writing is evenly placed at the edge of love and death, and there is a constant awareness of the proximity of separation to attachment.

Another long poem of Kovner's, *Hamafteah tsalal* (The Key Sank, 1950), did not receive much attention on first publication but was republished in a collection called *Mikol ha'ahavot* (Of All the Loves, 1965). As a statement derived from past experience, this tragic drama of an individual hero in the ghetto focuses on the tension between a reluctant community and heroic youth and constitutes a summation of attitude. It is not only a narrative but also a conclusion. The twelve sections of the poem narrate the entry of the Nazis into an East European city, the ghettoization of the Jews, the establishment of resistance units, the escape of a single partisan, and the early stages of liquidation of the city. A dialogue is conducted specifically between "mother" and "daughter" in which the latter brings up the camp following the disaster. But the only message that can be justly transmitted is one of resignation, the acceptance of defeat. The final words are: "the end of it all is / We are all defeated. / The dead and the living" (*Mikol ha'ahavot*, p. 178). Little satisfaction can be gained on any count. The language is symbolic. Ravens appear, hungry for the prey, and then, higher still, hovers the eagle. The mode is heroic, and the hero, of his nature, stands out from the crowd, "facing the thousand." Still, the mother is in the background, although his own view of the scene diverges from hers, as it does from that of the others around. What is stressed above all is the sense of the isolated one, holding his own, alone. But he is explicitly not a redeemer, and he does not come on a "white horse."

Alan Mintz attributes Kovner's ability to deal with a large number of historic events successfully to his combined appropriation of H. N. Bialik's "technique of radical metonymizing in the representation of catastrophe" and "a dramatic and imagistic minimalism that owes something to both modernist verse and the newsreel techniques of film" (p. 260). The poet expects the reader to rely on his knowledge of the Holocaust to understand the generic terms—"the thousands" are the Jews, "he" is the Nazi, and the partisan who escaped is called "the one." Animal imagery abounds; the vantage point of the Nazi invasion of the city is that of a crow circling the city and a goat perched on a rooftop. The speaker, identified as "the one" as opposed to the thousand, understands Germany's genocidal intent from the beginning. In contrast to the escaped partisan, the remaining thousands are the target of the poet's indictment for failing to resist. With the successful escape, Mintz continues, the poem "switches its poetic debt, both in theme and prosody, from Bialik to Alterman. The identity of the partisan becomes fused with the figure of the wanderer . . . in Alterman's poetry . . ." (p. 262). We now witness the metamorphosis that occurs with a shift from the environment of Eastern Europe with its anxieties and lamentation to that of the traveling resister—the fighter who is committed to return—and infiltration of the Nazi universe. Mintz reads this pattern as "the complete Zionist poem on the Holocaust" because it "encompasses the decline and destruction of the European Exile as well as the rejection of and escape from it. . . . The figure of the partisan, . . . mediates between the abject image of the victim-survivor and the proud (and evasive) image of the sabra-bystander" (p. 262).

This collection was notable in Kovner's bibliography on two counts. First, it was the first collection that included discrete lyrical short poems, rather than the long poem (poema) genre that the author had developed (although it did contain one long poem). Second, it was his first serious attempt to write love poetry. The integration of love and war thematically as well as the integration of the formal qualities of long and short poems represents an attempt at a holistic expression. The elements of violence (destruction, hatred) and love seem to be irremediably preclusive and opposite. But in order to inhabit a single universe, the poet looks for a unitary frame. The experience of the past is incorporated into the obsessions of the present in order to render a satisfactory account of life. Pictorial imagery and formal, modernist tendencies deployed here for the first time also become part of the poetic confrontation with the contemporary world.

Historically, much happened to Kovner over a relatively short period: the move from suppression and guerrilla warfare to conventional war, the change of landscape, the transformation of the Jewish minority condition of oppression to Jewish sovereignty, and the casting of Hebrew as an official and majority language of state. It seemed that a new poetics was also to be called for, yet Kovner, aware of the classic Hebrew literature of the past, tried to accommodate the contemporary idiom into the ancient *piyut* (verses). In an interview, Kovner says of the poetic forms in this phase of his work:

> These are forms taken from ancient verses (*piyut*), such as the "cone" (*gavia*) form. But this is not just an external feature. The form is involved with labour, and there is the intention [to] hold the time in which I live in these ancient forms. Such forms are adopted as it happens for the more brutal poems that express the modern era. This is an attempt to synthesize two opposite poles which are not amenable to synthesis. But this is the bridge (Luria, p. 19).

The past and the present were to become one, and he was also concerned about being a writer of current relevance and technique.

There is a long tradition of lament as a discrete genre (the *qinah*) in Hebrew poetry. It is found in the Bible in the prophetic literature and in the Book of *Lamentations*, for example. Again in late antiquity and in early medieval poetry it is a common form of expression. Kovner resurrects it in his memorial poetry, in *Mikol ha'ahavot* (Of All the Loves, 1965): "Heavens that have not stumbled, clean of smoke and of ashes. / Again they colour the floor of memory for my head—bless, O my soul, / That of all the loves—I have preserved from being trampled underfoot a flower that has fallen / Amongst the pages of the book. / Do not rebuke me" (*Mikol ha'ahavot*, Tel Aviv: Sifriyat poalim, 1965, p. 1). Then, the speaker addresses the figure from the past, that person whose coffin will never be lowered from his shoulders.

Kovner's poetry from *Mikol ha'ahavot* onward is reflective, inward looking although addressed to the female other, conversational, indeed close to prose, and idiomatic in language and tone. But the underpinning sense is tragic since the female addressee, the beloved, is never to return. The new idiom is a device for accepting the inevitable and a key to resignation. There is a residue of the former entity, but it is a shadow: "[O]nly your returning shadow / Exists. Never / Will my hands touch you. Never / Will your coffin be lowered from my shoulders" (*Mikol ha'ahavot*, p. 16). Two things emerge in parallel, also contingent on each other. One is that the past is always with us, and the second is that the original state can never be recovered. That original love is still with him, although its object is irrevocably gone. But the first person narrator, the "I," is always present, because it is this "I" that bears witness to the events and that has to record them and be their wavering testimony. Who is this first person? He is the one who "[h]ates new furniture . . . where your fingerprints show not their imprint" (p. 28). He is the one who "[l]oves beautiful / Legends, which are really legends, / Where the wise men have not obliterated from their essence the wolf / And the forest" (p. 28). And he concludes in that poem: "And believe it or not / I was also there drinking wine / Drinking and drinking without any desire / To weep" (p. 28). The narrator is part of it, he was part of it, but he will carry on in this present life.

We know very little of the narrator's proven, external existence, just of his fixation with this woman. And we know even less of her, even how much of his obsession is based on observable fact. As he writes in one poem: "Of all whom I have espoused, only you have I known, / Because it is you whom I have invented" (p. 31). Kovner treads a fine line between reality and fantasy, but there is an expressed wish to "[g]o / In a straight line / Back / To the world" (p. 43). Although the poem is addressed to the "master of dreams," it seems that hope is lacking. Why else would the narrator want to prepare himself for a visit to the grave of Rabbi Eliyahu, the famous Vilna Gaon (genius)? As he lacks for nothing materially and has a child, and his wounds have apparently healed, there seems to be nothing that he could require, except . . . hope (p. 47). There is a constant thrust of potential danger, the fire that might burn him (p. 48). His feelings toward the woman are ambivalent, both violent and nostalgic, sensing her abandonment, and longing for her return.

Prose Writing

In the early 1950s, Kovner's attention moved from poetry to prose. As with his poetry, the writing reflected the major public events that had always preoccupied him. The early poetry had related the horrors and the sensibility both of the Jewish genocide and resistance and then of the Israeli war of independence. The major prose work too, the two-volume opus, *Panim el Panim* (Face to Face, 1953, 1955), does not escape the events. For this reason the reader, including the author himself, finds it difficult to fit this work into the normal categories of generic distinction. Kovner is careful in his introductory words to make two disclaimers: the first, that this constitutes a history, and the second, that it is really a novel. What it attempts to do, he says, is "to relate something that time and place disdain. And although all the characters in the story are my own, these things really happened, here, recently, at the portal of our own times" (*Panim el Panim*, Tel Aviv: Mevhavyah Ha-Kibutz harartsi, 1955, Introduction).

The hero of this group is the specific fighting collective, at whose helm is the Palmach, the workers' activist arm of the Haganah, the defense force that was soon to be merged, with the declaration of the State of Israel, into the national army (Tsahal). The concerns here are military and exclusive, focused on the self-conscious element that would create the conditions for a new nation. In this way, a displaced exile could assume a sort of home and still be fighting for a recognizable future. The linguistic texture is rich, the sentences long, sinewy, balanced, and epigrammatic, and the doctrine of war is reflective. The scene is viewed not exclusively from the angle of one of the parties to the conflict and not only as seen by one Jew who fought in the resistance and who is now trying to establish a homeland in war. It is also observed from outside the fray, with commentary on human behavior in conflict and on the force of those events. The sense of catastrophic disaster, destruction on an enormous scale, is palpable as war fever intensifies, arms pour in, and the populations become convinced that, since total war is inevitable between the two parties, each had better seize the initiative and become stronger to assure of victory.

The events described follow the United Nations resolution of 29 November 1947 in favor of setting up two separate states in the area of Palestine, one Arab and one Jewish. Episodes of the War of Independence, which became emblems of iconic heroism in Israeli historiography and mythology, are here described in all their gory and tragic detail as lives are lost, mistakes are made, and shortfalls in personnel and equipment bemoaned. The dreadful shortage of rifles and their inadequate nature put the *yishuv* (Jewish population of Palestine) at a dreadful disadvantage in the face of an enemy considerably superior in numbers and firepower. As the defense of what is to be the new Israel proceeds, the embryonic Israeli army also finds itself fighting the British, who challenge them and impound their ammunition. Death is all around, and despair approaches. The story is told from the point of view of the Jews, and the narrator attempts not just to capture the feelings and emotions of the inexperienced young commanders, but also to enter into them, microscopically in the wake of the events described, moment by moment. But the current situation is also seen by several of the participants in the light of the European quagmire, which they have just left.

Only two to three years have elapsed between the end of the war and the establishment of Israel. Both events involved fighting desperately against a much more powerful, or at any rate more numerous, enemy, with the prospect of imminent death constantly at hand. The enthusiasm, which is described as reaching poetic proportions, arises from the new situation in the wake of the United Nations declaration. The Jewish offensive has begun, it is well organized and systematic, everyone has now been issued with a rifle, and Jews can take the initiative and take the fight into the enemy camp. Victory was sensed, and it marked the path to the setting up of a Jewish state. The political climacteric of the book is the defense of Jerusalem. The effort made to engage in the breaking of the siege of the city is symbolic as well as strategic, and it represents the struggle for the very essence and existence of the total concept of the Jewish state itself. But we also have the full horror of the war, the casual deaths, the indifference, the lack of care for the other and even for one's own fighters.

As the author moves on to the second part of his account in this heavy, semidocumentary novel, the fighting moves into a new, more decisive phase. The Jewish state is declared as an independent political entity, although this is reported indirectly to the protagonists. Swaths of territory are conquered, and, in one view, this could herald the close of war. But now another possibility looms and is voiced. Is it not the case that every "end" is always another beginning? (p. 25). For there follows the intervention of armies from fully fledged Arab states, especially the Arab Legion of "Jordan," the populous and powerful Egypt, as well as Syria, Iraq, and Saudi Arabia. The course of the war can be understood better, as the fighters see the need to clear the territory of the potential enemies, "who are still sitting on our heads" (p. 48). Jewish settlements are seen as a security ring, and Arab villages as vulnerable sites. We also see new aspects of our chief protagonists, for example, the new Israeli fighter, Katyushka, as a survivor from Poland. The past is always invading the present. These flashes of past reality intrude in the effort not only to live the present, but to build for the future, to survive, to create career prospects, and to enjoy a creative life. The narrative problem is to present the situation of the consciousness and the ongoing internal dramas of the several protagonists as well as the changing war scene. The solution is to relay the actual history and the changing fortunes of the war indirectly, as reported to the characters. Such writing is not only factual and representational, but deeply emotional too, given the enormous suffering involved, and the sufferers are not only those who fight, but also those who wait on the side, the mothers and the families, who wait to hear about what is happening on the ground. Kovner's prose language, like that of his poetry, is rich and multi-toned, testifying to a background steeped in the sources long antecedent to his emigration to Israel, and the doctrines and experience emerging from the text reveal much about the views on Zionism and Jewish destiny then prevalent. Why suffer, it is asked. And the answer comes in the form of a further question: Is there any plausible alternative to the struggle for the homeland?

Later Poetry

Obsessive themes return in Kovner's later poetry. The most haunting collection of poems, *Ahoti qtana* (My Little Sister, 1967), again addresses the beloved woman, now a heroine of the resistance. The volume takes the form of the "poema" once more, and the addressee is part solid woman and part myth. Kovner's chief translator has written: "It will be clear, at the end, that Kovner is writing one poem and that his poem (reversing the sense of Eugene O'Neill's autobiographical play) is a long night's journey into day" (Kaufman, 1973, p. xxi). Certainly, that is Kovner's aspiration. Both the course of his life and his movement (emigration and writing) shadow statements of progression and teleology. There is a movement charted from oppression to self-determination, from occupied and oppressed central Europe to Palestine, from guerrilla fighting to conventional warfare, from subjugated Jewish community to independent state. One can chart this intended direction in the poetry and prose as well. But the dead often overwhelm the living, just as the living act as the beacon for those who died. And in *My Little Sister* the dead speak too, through the pathetic voice realized in this collection. The narrator searches out the little sister, and he lends her his voice in an attempt to build a bridge between him and her over the vast chasm of time and place. The poetry of Kovner, particularly represented by this most famous of his poems, is a kind of reaching out.

My Little Sister is representative as well as special. Shirley Kaufman writes in her introduction: "[t]he central fact in Kovner's life is his confrontation with the half-dead, half-crazed girl from the mass grave at Ponary. Her face haunts every line he writes. We never see her eyes, her features—we never know her name. But we hear her voice. And the silence after the voice" (Kaufman, 1986, p. xv). He mediates the voice of the little sister, eventually silenced for the poet / narrator, through his own words. But these words are framed by ancient Hebrew poetry, specifically by the Biblical *Song of Songs* and the ancient liturgical *piyut*, with its insistent rhythms, repetitions, and resonant assonances, with their *midrashic* associations of the convenantal bond between God and the Hebrews.

The sister is compared to "[s]peaking ash" (*My Little Sister and Selected Poems 1965–1985*, Tel Aviv: Mehavyar Sifiyal poalim, 1970, p. 15), so she has a voice, but she is also the residue of what had been a fire. Thus she is saved in a convent, facing the nuns, "[l]ike faces of monuments in a foreign city" (p. 17). She is a "dove," with a "torn wing" (p. 20). The poet then goes on to use the language of ancient *piyut*, familiar from the festival prayer books: "Their palms were gathered / In supplication" (p. 28). For the sister to get into the precincts behind the walls she has to ascend the ladder. The walls constitute a formidable barrier, and the ladder acts as a bridge, just as it did for the angels in Jacob's dream (Genesis 28:12). Only then could God appear to Jacob and issue His promise and blessing. In section nine of the Kovner poem, God seems to be a more sinister, even potentially threatening presence, spying behind the sister's back while approaching. And now there is another God, with starving eyes, "[p]regnant with love" (p. 24), tempting strongly in another direction. At this point, his memory (presumably, the memory of him) is crucified and swept outside the fence, and she "plays" with another God. There is the constant presence and pressure of desire in the convent without the normal outlets of sexual release available. The sister rejects the temptation to mourn, because of what "others would say" (p. 58). The parties to an imagined projected meeting are the speaker, the sister / bride, and God. What happened to the covenant that had been supposedly cut between God and man? "My sister sits. Beside her / A small dish of honey! Such a huge crowd! / The braids of the loaf / Twisted by the father. / Our father, thank goodness, took his bread / Forty years from the same oven. He never imagined that / That a whole people would go up in the ovens / And the world, with God's help, still go on" (p. 59). The same oven for making bread and for burning people: both sanctification and destruction. What is God doing? Could there be a more fragrant breach of the covenant? The sister / bride has been brutally betrayed.

We have: "Nine Sisters drenched with pleasure" (p. 15, *ednah*, "pleasure," associated with erotic pleasure) and little prospect for them or for the sister of fulfillment through human contact. The narrator's sister has become "like a wilted tendril" (p. 62), weighed down by frustrated potential. Still the poet searches her out, as does the male protagonist his beloved in the *Song of Songs*. But it seems that she is not destined for the normal course of life, marriage, and death. Perhaps, it is suggested, she was never born, as her (our) mother mourned her who had not come into the world. The poem concludes with the invocation to "my mother." Kovner returns to the covenantal theme in "A Canopy in the Desert," a contrasting counterpart, as Eli Pfefferkorn demonstrates, in "an attempt to mend the Covenantal rupture through a poetic evocation of the past . . . in this poem, unlike 'My Little Sister,' his questioning looks toward mending the fractured covenant through a reconciliation symbolized by the renewal of the marital contract" (pp. 13, 17).

The End as the Beginning

The last poems of Kovner were published posthumously in the year of his death. They conclude on the same note as they began, in the genre of the long poem, with strong Biblical echoes, particularly from *The Song of Songs*. Although Kovner, according to many reports, rejected the apellation applied to him of "poet of the Holocaust," the primary motifs of his writing hardly changed, although they did move thematically, as they did autobiographically, along to a scale of three: Holocaust, resistance, and war. The fateful and paradigmatic life of the author returns constantly as a thread in his opus. Although his later life is set out narrationally, sometimes in considerable specificity, it is always colored by his earlier history, and the later events tend to derive their significance and resonances from the earlier, dramatic imprints.

In *Selon qetering* (Sloane Kettering, 1987), for example, the narrative of the long poem is directly autobiographical: a description of his visit to New York and his hospitalization there, followed by his return home to Israel. In this "poema," the decorative typeset is important, and it illustrates the subject of life and death, one overwhelmingly encountered in hospital. But its contemporary relevance finds its redoubled relevance in the theoretical refusal, or at least reluctance, to go once more "under the knife" (*Selon qetering*, Tel Aviv: Hakibuts hameuhad, 1987, p. 15). To refuse to go under the knife was what the Jews were invited to do in the ghettos of Nazi-occupied Europe. Once more, we encounter the credo and practice of Kovner's writing in his belief, frequently expressed, that poetry is a form of prayer. The "hero" of the poem is both the narrator and the third-person subject. But he also speaks in the first-person plural, entering his belief that: "Soon / soon we shall know / If we have learned to come to terms with stars / That are not extinguished with our death." And the conclusion is: "Whither now? / It is still not yet noon / Even. Yet a cloud has begun very slowly / To cover the sun / That he so longed for when abroad" (p. 132). The "he" is of course the narrator too.

The final collection of Kovner's poetry, *Shirat roza* (Rosa's Song, 1987), appeared posthumously. Rarely in Hebrew poetry has there been such a frank engagement on the part of the author with the search for truth through a fearless and transparent encounter with his own life history. Central to the critical interpretation of Kovner's poetic voice is, according Zvia Ginor, his consistent adoption of the traditional Hebrew persona of *sheliah tsibur* (emissary of the people) to fuse the private and collective Jewish history of the mid- and late-twentieth century (1995, pp. 241–245). This persona, Ginor argues, "enabled Kovner to reconcile his genres and compose his late great poemas of personal heroism, making the transition from voicing the historical collective to liberating the voice of an ambivalent, lyrical 'I' " (1995, p. 245). As Alan Mintz observes, "Kovner's poetry, like his biography, has bridged the moments of the Holocaust and the struggle for independence, he has spoken within Hebrew letters, as a *persona grata*, with the special authority of both a survivor and a Palmach fighter, all the more so because his identity as a survivor was that of a fighter as well" (p. 260). That Kovner conducted this enterprise primarily by means of a somewhat recondite genre of Hebrew poetry also testifies to his engagement with the historical backbone of Hebrew poetry, its ancient and medieval liturgy, as well as with forms of the Hebrew poetry of the earlier part of the twentieth century. That Kovner, as poet, and in his writing, goes beyond what might be regarded as the delimiting notion of "poet of the Holocaust" also places him in his desired and more universal framework of poet of the human fate. This fate especially marks out the Jewish fighter born into such turbulent times and making such a spirited commitment to the reinvigoration of both collective and personal life.

Bibliography

Primary Sources

Poetry

'Ad lo or (Until No Light). 1947.
Pridah mehadarom (Separation from the South). 1949.
Hamafteah tsalal (The Key Sank). 1950.
Admat hahol (The Earth of Sand). 1961.
Mikol ha'ahavot (Of All the Loves). 1965.
Ahoti qtanah (My Little Sister). 1967.
Hupa Bamidbar (A Canopy in the Desert). 1970.
Tatspiot (Observations). 1977.
Selon qetering (Sloane Kettering). 1987.
Shirat roza (Rosa's Song). 1987.

Collections of Poetry

Kol Shirey Abba Kovner [Collected Poems]. Vols. 1, 2, 3. Edited by Dan Miron. 1996–1998.

English Translations of Kovner's Poetry

Abba Kovner and Nelly Sachs: Selected Poems. Translated by Shirley Kaufman and Nurit Orchan. 1971.
A Canopy in the Desert: Selected Poems by Abba Kovner. Translated by Shirley Kaufman, with Ruth Adler and Nurit Orchan. 1973.
My Little Sister and Selected Poems 1965–1985. Translated by Shirley Kaufman. 1986.
Israeli Poetry: A Contemporary Anthology. Translated by Warren Bargad and Stanley F. Chyet. 1986.

Prose

Panim el Panim (Face to Face). 1953.
'Al hagesher hatsar: Masot be 'al pe (On the Narrow Bridge: Oral Essays). Edited by Shalom Luria. 1981.
Abba Kovner: Seventy Years. Edited by R. Kurczak and Y. Tuvin. 1988.
Megilot Ha'edut (The Scrolls of Testimony). Edited Shalom Luria. 1993.
Aba Kovner: Beyond Mourning. Edited by Muki Tzur. Tel Aviv, Israel: Am Oved, 1998.

Secondary Sources

Arad, Y. *Ghetto in Flames: The Struggle and Destruction of the Jews in Vilna in the Holocaust*. New York: Holocaust Library, 1982.
Barzel, Hillel. "A Creation from the Abyss" [Hebrew]. In *Meshorerei besora*, vol. 2, 292–368. Tel Aviv, Israel, 1983.
Ezrahi, Sidra DeKoven. "Dan Pagis Out of Line: A Poetics of Decomposition." *Prooftexts* 10 (1990): 335–363.
Feldman, Yael S. "Whose Story Is It Anyway? Ideology and Psychology in the Representation of the *Shoah* in Israeli Literature." In *Probing the Limits of Representation*. Edited Saul Friedlander. Cambridge, Mass.: Harvard University Press, 1992.
Gutman, Yisrael, and Chaim Schatzker. *The Holocaust and Its Significance*. The Zalmar Shazar Center: The Historical Society of Israel, 1984.
Ginor, Zvia Ben-Yoseph. "The *Sheliah Tsibur* as a Poetic Persona: Abba Kovner's Self-Portrait." *Prooftexts* 15 (1995): 227–248.
———. *Ad Kets Hab'daya* (Beyond the Legend: A Study of Abba Kovner's Poetry) [Hebrew]. Tel Aviv, Israel: Hakibbutz Hamuechad, 1996.
———. "Paradise Betrayed or the Betrayal of Paradise: Vilna as Memory in Abba Kovner's Poetry.' *Hebrew Studies* 37 (1996): 83–98.
———." 'Meteor-Yid': Abba Kovner's Poetic Confrontation With Jewish History." *Judaism* 189.48.1 (Winter 1999): 35–48.
Hrushovski, Binyamin. "Abba Kovner *Vehapoema Haivrit Hamodernit*." *Abba Kovner: Mivhar ma'amarey biqoret 'al yetsirato* (Abba Kovner: A Selection of Critical Essays on His Writings). Edited by Shalom Luria. Tel Aviv, Israel: Hakibuts hameuhad, 1988.
Lahat, Shlomo. *Abba Kovner: Shiv 'im shanah*. Tel Aviv: 1988.
Luria, Shalom, ed. *Abba Kovner: Mivhar ma'amarey biqoret 'al yetsirato* (Abba Kovner: A Selection of Critical Essays on His Writings). Tel Aviv: Hakibuts hameuhad, 1988.
Mintz, Alan. *Hurban: Responses to Catastrophe in Hebrew Literature*. New York: Columbia University Press, 1984.
Pfefferkorn, Eli. "Abba Kovner: The Rent Canopy and the Cleft Covenant." *Modern Language Studies* 24, no. 4 (Fall 1994): 11–24.
Roskies, David G. *Against the Apocalypse: Responses to Catastrophe in Modern Jewish Culture*. Cambridge, Mass.: Harvard University Press, 1984.
Schaffer, Carl. "Fantastic Elements in Holocaust Poetry: Abba Kovner's 'Ahoti Ktanah.' " In *The Poetic Fantastic: Studies in an Evolving Genre*, 79–87. Edited by Patrick D. Murphy and Vernon Hyles. New York: Greenwood Press, 1989.
Ya'oz, Hannah. "Ha Sho'ah ke Mitizatsiah ve Kronkretizatsia ba Shirah ha Tse'irah." *Moznayim* 56, no. 5 (1983): 25–27.

HANNA KRALL
(1937–)

MONIKA ADAMCZYK-GARBOWSKA

HANNA KRALL WAS born on 20 May 1937 in Warsaw into an acculturated Jewish family. Her parents and other relatives perished in the Majdanek concentration camp while she survived outside the camp, helped by a number of Polish people (according to her estimates, more than forty individuals contributed to saving her life). She graduated from the School of Journalism at the Warsaw University and for a number of years worked as a journalist for major Polish newspapers, including the Warsaw daily *Życie Warszawy* (1955–1966) and the relatively liberal weekly *Polityka* (1966–1981). Since 1981, after the introduction of martial law in Poland, she has worked as a freelance writer contributing periodically to the liberal Catholic weekly *Tygodnik Powszechny*, and later, after the abolishment of the Communist regime in Poland in 1989, to the major daily *Gazeta Wyborcza*. As a foreign press correspondent of *Polityka* from 1966 to 1969 she stayed in the Soviet Union; her experiences from that period resulted in three published volumes of journalism.

Interview with Marek Edelman

Krall's career was launched by her book interview with Marek Edelman, one of the leaders of the Jewish Fighting Organization in the Warsaw ghetto who decided to stay in Poland after the war, working as a cardiologist in Lodz. (In the late 1970s he got involved in the opposition movement in Communist Poland and since that time has been politically involved.) The interview was first published in the Wroclaw-based monthly *Odra* (1976) and a year later appeared in book form under the title *Zdażyć przed Panem Bogiem* (*To Outwit God*) after a difficult struggle with censorship conducted by Zbigniew Kubikowski, the editor-in-chief of *Odra* at that time. The interview focuses on the days of the liquidation of the ghetto and is shocking in its conscious deheroization of the ghetto uprising (fairly characteristic of Edelman's skeptical and restrained manner as revealed on other occasions) through the recollection of some prosaic or even shameful details, but simultaneously pays tribute to those who perished in the uprising and reveals their stamina and sacrifice.

From the compositional point of view this is neither a typical interview nor a historical account. Chronological order is not preserved; as in most later works by Krall, "yesterday" is constantly mixed with "today." The facts from 1943 and the mid-1970s are intermingled with remarks on the writer's own process of creation as well as on the possible reactions to the type of unconventional approach that she purposefully chose. The passage below illustrates the strategy adopted in the whole book:

> "We have to write about one more thing," he [Edelman] says.
>
> Why he is alive.
>
> When the first soldier of the liberating army came in, he stopped him and asked, "You are Jewish—so how come you're alive?" The question seemed laced with suspicion; perhaps he'd turned somebody in? Perhaps he'd taken somebody else's bread? So I should ask him now whether by chance he didn't survive on somebody else's account, and if not, then why he actually did survive (*To Outwit God*, Evanston, Ill.: Northwestern University Press, 1992, p. 238).

A similar pattern is employed consistently, contributing to a characteristic rhythm of the narrative: direct statements by Edelman, immediate authorial explanations, facts from Edelman's life indirectly recalled, and Krall's internal monologue regarding how she should proceed or what questions she should ask next and what should be left unsaid. Often she gives various hypothetical answers to difficult, fairly impossible questions in order to show that it is not really possible to answer them fully or directly. In the above case she offers examples of two possible answers: an SS man who was shooting in Edelman's vicinity on one particular day wore the wrong glasses or that on another occasion an acquaintance noticed him on a platform car heading for *Umschlagplatz*:

> he should have died for certain, and again some coincidence saved him. In the first case, he was saved by the SS man's astigmatism; in the second by the fact that Mietek Dab [his acquaintance] happened to be walking down the street on his way from work (p. 240).

But the reader of course knows that none of these answers explains the mystery of survival and consequently the sense of absurdity, unpredictability, and horror is reinforced.

In the preface to the first English language edition of the book (titled *Shielding the Flame: An Intimate Conversation with Dr. Marek Edelman, the Last Surviving Leader of the Warsaw Ghetto Uprising*), Timothy Garton Ash foresees that:

> The English speaking reader may at first be a little baffled by Hanna Krall's style of writing, a kind of Polish "New Journalism," leaping, sometimes breathlessly, and without explanation, from past to present and back again . . . All I can say is: please persevere, do read on. The author has good reasons. The point of this mixing will soon become clear. In the end, through all the doubt and questioning, Marek Edelman's story does itself, triumphantly, "show as an affirming flame" (p. xiii).

One does not have to agree with this somewhat upbeat conclusion but there is no doubt that the book requires some effort on the part of the reader and some prior knowledge of Edelman's life story: understanding the history of the uprising and the peculiarities of political and social life in postwar Poland might help a great deal in its absorption, especially because Krall uses plenty of references to facts and figures of its public life as well as elliptic and allusive statements. The book was also adapted for the stage and appeared in English under a still different title (*To Steal a March on God*), which shows the difficulty in finding a suitable rendering of the original one. As in the case of the book, lack of prior knowledge of the context might be an obstacle in its reception.

Journalistic Fiction

The interview with Edelman was the beginning of Krall's present phase. In her books that followed, such as *Taniec na cudzym weselu* (A Dance at Somebody Else's Wedding, 1993) or *Dowody na istnienie* (Proofs of Existence, 1995) she combines stories about the Holocaust itself with descriptions of Jewish life in Poland before the destruction, re-creating minute details of that existence. In this manner the stories of destruction become even more real and devastating. A large group of the prototypes for her characters are "children of the Holocaust," now in their late fifties and sixties, who often do not know how they survived, who their parents and grandparents were, and what happened to them. Some of them have labored for many years to learn this, others have just discovered their origin, and some prefer not to dwell in the past at all. Krall calls these people the coauthors of her stories and, as she has repeated on numerous occasions, she wishes to save them from oblivion. She is afraid, as she mentioned in a number of interviews and at public occasions, that a purely historical and statistical approach to the Holocaust focusing on mass murders, deportations, and descriptions of death camps, gas chambers, and other atrocities, might create fear and a sense of horror in modern readers, rather than evoke real compassion, possibly even having the reverse effect of causing them to avoid the topic in the future. Real empathy, according to Krall, can rather be evoked by recalling individual fates and concentrating on feelings and emotions. In her stories she writes not only about survivors, but also about their rescuers, informers, more and less indifferent witnesses, as well as perpetrators. Indirectly she raises the question of how readers would behave in similar situations, but does so in an unobtrusive, albeit sometimes provocative, way.

Krall focuses on the paradoxical vicissitudes of her characters (most of them based on real people), a number of them having been children during the Holocaust. In *Sublokatorka* (*Subtenant*), her only novel so far (first published in Paris in 1985 because of strict censorship in Poland at that time), she ironically contrasts the tragic disparity between the Polish and Jewish experience under the Nazi occupation through the symbolic "brightness" (stereotypically perceived "heroic" deaths of Polish resistance fighters) and "darkness" (the equally stereotypical "passive" fate of the Jews in the ghetto). She draws this parallel by presenting both collective and individual stories, the latter embodied in the fictitious figures of the Polish Maria and Jewish Martha, and historical figures of Krystyna Krahelska and Rywka Urman. Krahelska dies as an insurgent (in the Polish uprising of August 1944) from a bullet and is lying

> on her back, still among the sunflowers, still looking into the sun. And brightness is when you die so beautifully and brightly. (Nothing reveals darkness and confirms brightness better than death.) And the incident with Rywka's child happened in the Warsaw ghetto at 18 Krochmalna Street. Rywka was standing in the yard, her hair disheveled, her eyes mad, with the body of Berek Urman, her son, lying in front of her. Berek had died the previous day, but we shall put some dots here, because we are trying to tell what the hungry Rywka was trying

to do with the body of her son (*Subtenant,* Evanston, Ill.: Northwestern University Press, 1992, pp. 10–11).

Again, as in the Edelman story, the novel may constitute a rather difficult read for the Western reader because of numerous historical references to political events in Poland after World War II, presented through a multilayered plot. Although one is tempted to see in the title *Subtenant*—a frightened little girl in a Jewish orphanage right after the war, an opposition and Solidarity activist three and four decades later—the alter ego for the author herself, the writer has always avoided any explicit references to her own biography, carefully guarding her own privacy.

The reference to Krochmalna Street, which evokes associations with the Yiddish stories of Isaac Bashevis Singer, does not seem incidental here because from time to time in her stories Krall refers to the world of both Singer brothers as the world "before everything." In her view the most terrifying fictitious situations and characters described by the Yiddish masters pale next to the real stories of the *Shoah*. Krall emphasizes the fact that Bashevis Singer was afraid of the Holocaust: "And so were his unclean spirits, demons, dybbuks, devils and imps. They did not venture into the hell" ("The Armchair," in Polonsky, p. 320) which the people Krall brings to life in her stories knew too well. Apart from re-creating the life "before everything" and describing the horror of war experiences, she constantly refers to the landscape after the destruction marked by the erasure of the Jewish memory in Poland for many decades after the Holocaust. At the end of one of her best pieces, based on the life story of Tomasz Blatt, a survivor of Sobibor concentration camp, she describes their journey through little towns and villages in the Lublin region, the area inhabited by numerous Jews before the war. Blatt mentions people he knew:

> "A Jewess with a baby. A beautiful Jewess. Two Jewish women in Dobre, Fredek in a stable. Shmuel in the forest . . . . They are all here," he made a circle with his hand—"and no graves. Why aren't there any Jewish graves. Why is nobody sad?" We passed Izbica, Krasnystaw and Lopiennik. The sun was setting. Everything became even uglier and greyer. Perhaps because ghosts are circling around. They do not want to go away when people do not regret their absence, when they are unmourned. All this greyness comes from the unmourned ghosts. ("Portret z kula w szczêce" [A Portrait with a Bullet in the Jaw], in *Taniec na cudzym weselu,* [A Dance at Somebody Else's Wedding, 1993], War Szawa, Poland: BGW, 1994, p. 94).

Krall's style is characterized by brief, restrained narrative, with a focus on dialogues and monologues of the people she writes about, and very little authorial comment. Some of her stories were influenced by her travels and people she has met on her way, as well as the contacts she established through the network of survivors and their rescuers; others are influenced by her reading of historical works. For example, one of her works in the most recent volume *Tam juz nie ma żadnej rzeki* (There Is No River There Anymore, 1998) was influenced by Christopher Browning's well-known study *Ordinary Men: Reserve Police Battalion 101 and the Final Solution in Poland* about the infamous unit of "average" Germans who massacred tens of thousands of Jews. It was in that book that she found traces of the story of Apolonia Machczynska, the inhabitant of Kock who attempted to save more than twenty Jews in her granary and was killed together with them by "the ordinary Germans" from Hamburg, who were too old to fight on the "real front."

Reception in Poland and Abroad

Krall's work has been received quite favorably in Poland. Among many other awards (for example, the underground Solidarity prize and the prize of the Polish PEN Club), in 1998 she received the Award of the Culture Foundation given for major achievements to outstanding artists and scholars. Her books have been translated into many languages. They seem to have gained most recognition in Germany and Sweden. The reception in America was originally rather unfavorable. Among notable examples of negative response it is worth mentioning the passionate reaction by the esteemed Jewish American historian Lucy Dawidowicz who criticizes both Edelman and Krall; the former for staying in Poland after the war, the latter for what she considers the writer's confusing style, bordering on "chatter" and mixing "matters of importance" with "trivialities" (Dawidowicz, p. 66). This response shows a difficulty in reconciling two varying perspectives as well as the critic's lack of knowledge about the situation in Poland after the war. Dawidowicz blames Krall for being silent about a number of matters, such as antisemitism, and is not fully aware that at that time, in order to be published in Poland at all, Krall had to speak between the lines to get through the thick net of political censorship. Suffice it to say that Krall's next, much more outspoken book, *Subtenant*, could not be published officially in Poland until 1989.

It is hard to say whether Krall's (as well as other Polish Jewish writers') limited or lukewarm reception in the United States has been caused by the general lack of interest in Polish literature there or by a different perception of the Holocaust. Krall discussed that problem indirectly in her story "Tylko króciutko" ("Briefly Now," in Polonsky, pp. 303–311), in which she describes a group of Polish Jewish women survivors visiting New York in the 1980s and facing, among others, the question of why they are returning to the graves, that is, why they want to go back to Poland rather than stay in the United States. Their interlocutors mean Jewish graves because for them Poland is primarily a large Jewish cemetery, while in fact these women return also to their Polish graves, that is, the graves of their gentile relatives, because they survived the war as children adopted by Christian families or were assimilated through mixed marriages. (The motif of two mothers appears quite often in Krall's stories, the attachment of her protagonists to mothers who are not "real," mothers, and their desperate attempts to deal with "the Jewish void" of their birth mothers.)

On the other hand, in "Briefly Now," "Niepamiêć" ("Nonmemory," in *Dowody na istnienie* [Proofs of Existence, 1995]), and numerous other stories, Krall shows how the long silence over Jews in Poland led to the acculturation of survivors who do not even know the basic principles of Jewish tradition and custom, such as the lighting of Sabbath candles, not to mention keeping a kosher home. This is even more dramatic among those who discovered their origin as adults and only now are trying to explore their roots by browsing through archival materials, searching for long-lost relatives, and developing interest in Judaism.

Krall might be accused of repeating certain patterns and narrative strategies, as well as overusing a restrained manner of presentation with little authorial comment, but in a sense this is her consciously and carefully crafted voice selected to describe the tragedy of the Holocaust via multiple voices of survivors and witnesses. She herself compared her approach to putting together a broken jug.

Critics have noticed her growing use of the fairy tale convention, which makes some of her stories read like documentary fables. This is visible both in the creation of the setting (a wood near a shtetl, snow-covered mountains, an old abandoned building) and in the focus on the spiritual and miraculous in the lives of her characters. For instance in "The Dybbuk" a middle-aged handsome American Jewish professor develops a passionate interest in Poland and wooden synagogues. Behind a seemingly innocent story lurks one from the Warsaw ghetto where the professor's stepbrother, born a long time before his own birth, perished and the thought of whom has now entered the post-Holocaust sibling's mind. As Krall states in "Zbawienie" ("Salvation," in *Dowody na istnienie*) the reporter's work taught her that logical stories in which everything is clear are sometimes untrue while things that cannot be explained actually happen.

In her more recent stories she often searches for divine intervention and interprets some unbelievable events that befall her protagonists by the presence of the Grand Scriptwriter, as she calls him, who creates and controls human fates. The question of God's whereabouts at the time of the Holocaust permeates the narrative, but the answer obviously cannot be given. As in the conversation between the two descendants of the murdered Jews of the shtetl of Lelow the question remains unsettled:

> "You will not reach salvation if you don't get to know yourself and your errors," said a rabbi from Jerusalem, the rebbe of the Lelow chassidim. "Remember, it's never too late to return to God, may His name be blessed."
>
> "There was no salvation here, rabbi. There was no room for any God," says Chaim Środa, the son of Josef the glazier. (*Dowody na istnienie*, p. 56, translation by Monika Adamczyk-Garbowska).

Bibliography

Primary Sources

Na wschód of Arbatu (East of Arbat). 1972.
Syberia, Kraj możliwości (Siberia, a Land with Potential). With Zygmunt Szeliga and Maciej Iłowiecki. 1974.
Dojrzałość dostêpna dla wszystkich (Maturity Accessible for Everyone). 1977.
Zdążyć przed panem Bogiem (*To Outwit God*, first published in English as *Shielding the Flame*). 1977.
Sześć odcieni bieli (Six Shades of White). 1978.
Sublokatorka (*Subtenant*). 1985.
Okna (Windows). 1987.
Hipnoza (Hypnosis). 1989.
Trudności ze wstawaniem (Difficulties in Getting Up). 1990.
Taniec na cudzym weselu (A Dance at Somebody Else's Wedding). 1993.
Co siê stało z nasza bajkâ (What Happened to Our Fairy Tale). 1994.
Dowody na istnienie (Proofs of Existence). 1995.
Tam już nie ma żadnej rzeki (There Is No River There Anymore). 1998.
To tyjesteś Daniel (Thou Art Daniel). 2001.

Secondary Sources

Backer, Paul. Review of *To Steal a March on God*, by Hanna Krall. *Slavic and East European Journal* 4, (1997): 710–712.
Dawidowicz, Lucy S. "The Curious Case of Marek Edelman." *Commentary* 3 (March 1987): 66–69.
"Hanny Krall dowiadywanie siê świata." An interview with Katarzyna Janowska and Witold Bereś. *Kontrapunkt, Magazyn Kulturalny Tygodnika Powszechnego* (28 April 1996): i–iii.
Kot, Wiestaw. *Hanna Krall*. Poznan, Poland: Rebis, 2000.
Polonsky, Antony, and Monika Adamczyk-Garbowska. *Contemporary Jewish Writing in Poland: An Anthology*. Lincoln and London: University of Nebraska Press, 2001.
Wróbel, Józef. *Tematy żydowskie w prozie polskiej 1939–1987*. Kraków: Universitas, 1991.

LOTTE KRAMER

(1923–)

PETER LAWSON

LOTTE KRAMER WAS born Lotte Karoline Wertheimer in Mainz, Germany, on 22 October 1923. Her father, Ernst, a playwright when a young man, later became a vintner to support his family during the Depression. Her mother, Sofie (née Wertheimer), remained a housewife. Both Lotte's parents were deported to Piaski, near Lublin, Poland, on 20 March 1942. After the war, the Red Cross reported them missing. Lotte's education consisted of four years at an elementary state school, followed by secondary education beginning in 1934 at a newly founded Jewish school. Her schooling stopped after 9 November 1938 (*Kristallnacht*). In July 1939, Lotte traveled to England on a *Kindertransport* (children's transport). Four years later she married Frederic Kramer, a schoolfriend from Mainz. Their son, Stephen, was born in 1947. Kramer studied art and art history at evening classes, and exhibited her work at several galleries. In order to educate succeeding generations about the Holocaust, she has given regular readings of her poetry in Germany. A bilingual volume, *Heimweh-Homesick* (1999), was commissioned by Mainz University and published in Frankfurt. Kramer is "a longstanding member of the Council of Christians and Jews, and also of the local interfaith group" (*Jewish Year Book 2000*, p. 69).

Poetry

The trauma of being a Jewish child in Nazi Germany, and subsequently learning of the death of both parents, inhibited Kramer from expressing emotions about the Holocaust for many years. She started to write poetry "rather late in life, facing up to traumatic childhood experiences in Nazi Germany after 35 years" (*Contemporary Poets*, p. 601). Kramer explains: "Much of my work deals with that subject and its aftermath, with the dualism inevitably connected with it" (*Contemporary Poets*, p. 601). She returns to her observation of post-*Shoah* silence over three decades in "Stone-Setting" (in *Family Arrivals*, 1981): "For thirty years I locked your nameless graves. / I stamped on grief" (*Family Arrivals*, Hatch End, Eng.: Poet and Printer, 1981, p. 20).

Indeed, many of Kramer's poems represent reengagement with painful, long-repressed memories. To this extent, her work resembles that of Karen Gershon and Gerda Mayer, who also come to terms with personal *Kindertransport* experiences through poetry written years after emigration to Britain. In "Cocoon," for example (from *Earthquake and Other Poems*, 1994), Kramer depicts a middle-aged *Kinde* who hides behind a "willed amnesia," which the poet rejects: "She says she can't remember anything / Of people, language, town; not even school / Where we were classmates" (*Earthquake and Other Poems*, Ware, Eng.: Rockingham Press, 1994, p. 34).

The poem concludes by suggesting that courageous acceptance of a German Jewish and *Kindertransport* past, together with its "terror, exile, fear," is a prerequisite for rediscovering "love": "She is cocooned, safe as an English wife, / Never to split that shell and crawl through love" (p. 34).

Often in Kramer's verse, vignettes of life in Nazi Germany stabilize such terror and fear through anecdotal narrative and traditional forms. For example, both "Germany 1933" (from *The Shoemaker's Wife*, 1987) and "A New Subject" (from *Earthquake and Other Poems*) narrate classroom incidents through quatrains of rhyming iambic pentameter. In "Germany 1933," opposition to Nazi racism is shown to be still possible, as a Jewish child is voted class favorite before the eyes of a Nazi teacher:

> "Now choose the one to lead, to march ahead,
> To keep your trust, unfurl the swastika."
> The teacher urged a ballot on the class.
> "The one you like the most," he archly said.

The children chose and named a Jewish child (*The Shoemaker's Wife*, Sutton, Eng.: Hippopotamus Press, 1987, p. 16).

From this subversion by innocents, Kramer turns her satiric gaze to another classroom scene in "A New Subject" to debunk racial "science" as nonsense. Here, a Nazi teacher means to instruct his class on the nature of Aryan superiority:

"What is your name? Ah, Heinz, ah, very good.
Now face the class. You see in this blond boy
The perfect specimen of purest race;
His bones are powerful, his hair is fair,
His eyes are blue set in an eager face.
No shameful mixture in his blood or breed.
This is your future now, our Germany!
You grin—you laugh—you too—I'll have no cheek
From anyone! What is the matter, speak?"
"Please Sir, it makes no sense, it's true, you see
Heinz is a Jew" (*Earthquake and Other Poems*, p. 16).

When not unmasking Nazi folly, Kramer recalls the kindness of those German Gentiles who retained their sense and humanity during the Third Reich. In *The Shoemaker's Wife*, for example, she records a woman's courageous resistance to her sons' banning of Jews from a cobbler's store:

She came to us walking, at night,
Our bundle of mended shoes.
Hot secrets in her shopping bag.
By the door in the hall she stood
And cried (*The Shoemaker's wife*, p. 17).

Other poems relate Gentile betrayal. For example, in "Two Boys 1940–44" Kramer wonders how a French collaborator could continue to live with apparent equanimity after sending two children to their deaths:

How did he plough his land and reap
With children's ghosts, their splintered nails,
How did he clean his grubby skin
From their cold questions in its cracks
And shrug away his ailing sin? (*The Shoemaker's Wife*, p. 22).

Personal trauma and its aftermath are the subjects of "The Red Cross Telegram" (from *Family Arrivals*). Evoking the sadly typical experience of final parental contact for the *Kindertransport* youth, this particular telegram, bidding her "farewell, beloved child" (p. 15) is heart-wrenchingly conveyed. Here Kramer asks:

How can I ever sing
A requiem
In silent, dark despair,
Transfiguring
Your calvary of nails
And gas and graves (*Family Arrivals*, p. 15).

The reference to Jesus ("calvary of nails") suggests a parallel between the significance of the crucifixion for Christians and the Holocaust for Jews, and may signify the vehicle the Jewish poet chooses to make her poem accessible to a wider Western audience that cannot relate to Jewish suffering as it does to its own cultural icon of unmerited torment. In "Warsaw Vigil 1940s" (*Selected and New Poems 1980–1997*, 1997), the parallel becomes more explicit as "Jewish Jesus" watches over "the hidden Jews / A handful only / Outside Ghetto walls" (pp. 120–121) who are marking Yom Kippur (The Day of Atonement) in Nazi-occupied Poland.

Imagining Lost Lives

Like Karen Gershon and Gerda Mayer, Kramer is grateful to her adoptive country. She depicts Britain as "the heart's island" that calls her "to whispering benedictions" (*The Shoemaker's Wife*, p. 13). By contrast, Kramer sees continental Europe as: "Hard and calloused with bitter blood" ("At Dover Harbour," *The Shoemaker's Wife*, p. 13). Several of Kramer's poems are meditations on the fate of those trapped on the Continent during World War II, and the way their deaths interact with her life. The fate of Kramer's parents is particularly pertinent here. In "A Glass of Water," for example, the poet refuses to slake her thirst "in solidarity" with the "Hearsay world, the heat, / The stench, you could not share / In Poland's cattle-trucks" (*Selected and New Poems 1980–1997*, Ware, Eng.: Rockingham Press, 1997, p. 122).

Her attempt at affiliation with the murdered Jews of Europe may consist "of useless obsequies," but it helps Kramer to situate and record as fact the "hearsay world" of agonizing deaths in claustrophobic "cattle-trucks," where she was not present as a witness (p. 122).

Beyond the immediacy of the Holocaust universe, even the poet's secure postwar life is overshadowed by psychological consequences of the *Shoah*. Kramer's glass of water has "shadows that will stay" (*The Shoemaker's Wife*, p. 19) with the poet's everyday actions. Similarly, as Kramer closes her front door, she imagines her mother shutting hers "that last time," and thus evokes a lost German Jewish way of life:

Or maybe, you looked around
As if before
A holiday, leaving
No trace of dust,
No crumbs for pests, no moths
In cupboards, carpets;
Covered the chairs,
The settee from the glare

Of light and sun,
Turned off the water, gas . . . ("On Shutting the Door," *The Shoemaker's Wife*, p. 19).

Holocaust Imagery

Throughout Kramer's oeuvre, a variety of objects, places, and actions serve as metonymical allusions to the *Shoah*. For example, an airport in *Family Arrivals* suggests the steam and wheels of train stations which, in turn, evokes Kramer's *Kindertransport* journey and her parents' deportation. Again, in "Disused Railway Line" (*The Desecration of Trees*, 1994):

We follow this flat
Staircase, aware
Of dead journeys
To destinations
Crumbling with unuse (*The Desecration of Trees*, Frome, Eng.: Hippopotamus Press, 1994, p. 55).

A country ramble here resonates with echoes of the Holocaust and the victims' vertical "staircase" to heaven. By contrast, "Chimneys" (from *The Phantom Lane*, 2000) is relatively explicit, as English and Nazi German flues are compared:

Far off, some other chimneys
Busy belching smoke and stench
Meant death—but not in this rich earth
Where baking clay not burning flesh
Was custom for a while (*The Phantom Lane*, Ware, Eng.: Rockingham Press, 1983, p. 13).

The Holocaust exists more subtly in many of Kramer's poems as a parallel universe, almost *symboliste* in its hovering, intangible presence. For example, while "April Wind" (from *A Lifelong House*, 1983) is set on a spring day in contemporary England, it also evokes the ever-present, though long-past, *Kristallnacht*:

An augury of rough spring
Falling on hill country, one April,
Years ago, when the breaking
Of glass stunned my grandfather's
Heart, not dead, in this wind's cry (*A Lifelong House*, Sutton, Eng.: Hippopotamus Press, 1983, p. 13).

"April Wind" should be read in conjunction with an earlier poem, "Grandfather," which describes how Nazis smashed and "barricaded" this German Jew's "shop and house" (*Family Arrivals*, p. 11).

In the most innocuous scenes, Kramer depicts emotional fallout from the Holocaust. In "Transmutations" the narrator touches the "full bough" of a "hawthorn hedge," only to discover: "It spills ashes, blinding my shoes" (*A Lifelong House*, p. 17). Ashes spill again in seemingly incongruous contexts. In "Coffee Grinding," for example, the aroma of beans "clears the ashes out of sleep" (*The Desecration of Trees*, p. 14). A poem set in one of England's stately homes, "At Burghley House," recalls "a November day / Bright with dread and ashes" (*The Desecration of Trees*, p. 24). This is the luggage of the Holocaust; as Kramer says in "Homecoming" (from *Ice-Break*, 1980): "I travel with my luggage bone to bone" (*Ice-Break*, Peterborough, Eng.: Annakinn, 1980, p. 4).

There is quiet pain in these poems. In "*Kindertransport Reunion*" (*The Phantom Lane*), Kramer gathers with fellow "survivors" to ask: "Whereto now?" Despite the pain and the suffering in "circles of hell," her answer affirms the future: "Begin again in wonder at the brain's / Possibilities, stare at the lilac's candles / Renewing their perfume each spring" (p. 13).

Bibliography

Primary Sources

Scrolls. 1979.
Ice-Break. 1980.
Family Arrivals. 1981.
A Lifelong House. 1983.
The Shoemaker's Wife and Other Poems. 1987.
The Desecration of Trees. 1994.
Earthquake and Other Poems. 1994.
Selected and New Poems 1980–1997. 1997.
Heimweh-Homesick. 1999.
The Phantom Lane. 2000.
"Reflections." In *Jewish Year Book 2000*, 69–75. Edited by Stephen W. Maffil. London: Valentine Mitchell, 2000.

Secondary Sources

Allnutt, Gillian. "The Alues of Love," *Poetry Review* 88, no. 4 (winter 1998): 28–29.
Andrews, Karin. "A Lifelong House," *Agenda* 22, no. 2 (summer 1984): 65–67.
Cotton, John. "Lotte Kramer." In *Contemporary Poets*, 601–602. Edited by Tracy Chevalier. Chicago: St. James Press, 1996.
Fainlight, Ruth. "Book Review." *European Judaism* 28, no. 1 (spring 1995): 95.
Greening, John. "Psychic Reality." *PN Review* 118 (November 1997): 79–80.
Karpf, Anne. *The War After: Living with the Holocaust*. London: Heinemann, 1996.
Raine, Kathleen. "Lotte Kramer." *Agenda* 32, nos. 3–4 (autumn–winter 1994–1995): 298–301.
Smith, Sheila. "Achieved with Experience and Sweat." *The Jewish Quarterly* 161 (spring 1996): 71–73.
Storey, Edward. "The Gift of saying the Unsayable." *Common Ground* 2 (1998): 28–36.
Szirtes: George. "Book Reviews." *European Judaism* 31, no. 1 (spring 1998): 150–151.
Williams, Merryn. "Poetic Assessment: Lotte Kramer." *Acumen* 29 (September 1997): 15–17.

HENRY KREISEL
(1922–1991)

MICHAEL GREENSTEIN

HENRY KREISEL WAS born in Vienna in 1922 to Helen and David Kreisel, and received his elementary and secondary education there. Kreisel's family spoke Yiddish as well as German, and he had a traditional Cheder education. Following the *Anschluss* (annexation of Austria by Germany) of 1938 he escaped to England, where he was classified as an "enemy alien" and interned. Two months later Kreisel and his father, among fifteen hundred internees, were shipped to Canada. There, having lived in two internment camps, Kreisel was reclassified from "prisoner of war" to "refugee," and was able to attain immigrant status (Hart, p. 325). Kreisel writes in the introduction to "Diary of an Internment," his 1974 reworking of the record of those months:

> In many ways the internment camp experience is central to my own development. Suspended in a kind of no man's land for more than eighteen months, I could look back at the horrendous events of the 1930s and see them in some kind of perspective, and I could prepare myself intellectually for the tasks I wanted to undertake in the future (Neuman, p. 23).

Preparing himself intellectually for writing meant turning to English—free[ing] [him]self from the linguistic and psychological dependence on German" ("Diary of an Internment," Neuman, p. 21)—as his language of composition. Such preparation did not, however, protect Kreisel from anger as he recognized the ironies of his own experience:

> I felt a sense of outrage, because I was so completely conscious of never having done anything, and I was acutely aware of my status as "victim"—victim first of Nazi tyranny, and then, ironically, victim because by nationality I belonged to a nation with which Britain was at war, but with which I also felt myself at war. I therefore resented the appellation of "enemy alien." I had never before been so acutely aware of irony and paradox, and I think that the experience has left a lasting effect on the way I see things (from a letter to Robert Weaver, 27 March 1956, Neuman, pp. 45–46).

Kreisel later attended the University of Toronto, and in 1954 obtained his Ph.D. from the University of London. After settling in Edmonton, he became academic vice president of the University of Alberta. He has been awarded the President's Medal of the University of Western Ontario for his short story "The Traveling Nude," and in 1960 was elected a fellow of the International Institute of Arts and Letters.

The *Shoah* in Kreisel's Work

The *Shoah* plays a prominent role in both of Kreisel's novels, *The Rich Man* (1948) and *The Betrayal* (1964), as well as in some of his shorter fiction. In the short story "Homecoming: A Memory of Europe after the Holocaust," Mordecai Drimmer returns to his native Polish town, Narodnowa, immediately after the war in search of remaining members of his family. The only survivor he discovers is his uncle David Mentel, who informs him of the destruction of the Jewish ghetto and of the loss of family. "Homecoming" is thus about the impossibility of coming home after the Holocaust when no home remains for most of European Jewry. Drimmer's name suggests the trauma and the dreamlike quality of Kreisel's story, which hovers between the nightmare of the Holocaust and the dreamlike possibility of redemption and rebuilding a new life in a post-Holocaust world.

The opening sentence, "The little dirt road wound along like a moving snake" (Edmonton: NeWest Press, 1981, p. 39), prepares for the serpentine quality of Drimmer's quest to locate family and home, while the simile introduces the first of a series of demonic animal images indicative of Europe's depravity during World War II. Drimmer, who is identified only as "the young man" until midway in the story, encounters a Polish peasant who thinks that he is, in turn, a rich man, a spy, and the devil—these shifting identities underscore the peasant's ignorance, the instability of Jewish identity, and a world whose identity has been put into question by the *Shoah*. The antisemitic peasant informs Mordecai of the destruction of the Jews of Narodnowa.

The first thing Mordecai sees as he approaches the town is the church spire through a haze of misty twilight. The smoke of destruction covers the landscape. "It was as if he were walking through a dream seeing things, feeling things, but perceiving them as through a gently-swaying screen of gauze, now very clear, now hazily shimmering and never quite real" (p. 51). In his confused post-Holocaust perception, Drimmer dreams that he sees his mother, father, and sister, but the gargoyles of the church mock his vision. Although most of his family has perished, Mordecai meets another survivor, Rachel, and the story ends with the two of them planning for a new life in America.

The family name, Drimmer, reappears in another short story, "Chassidic Song," in which Arnold Weiss, grandson of Moses Drimmer, encounters Josef Shemtov, a Chassid. On a flight from Montreal to New York, the secular academic Weiss asks the Chassid if he is going to a *Farbrengen*—a gathering of Chassidim. When Shemtov asks him where he learned that word, Weiss replies that he must have heard it at his grandfather's house in Poland. Because grandfather Drimmer died in 1932, the Chassid says that he was spared "The Hitlerites. The holocaust" (p. 28), and begins to relate his own story of survival. Shemtov was not quite thirteen when the Nazis invaded his town, and he was the only member of his orthodox, but not Chassidic, family to survive. Saved by a Christian family, he runs away from them at the end of the war to a refugee camp, embittered against God: "The *Rebonoh shel Olem* deserted me" (p. 33). Carried along by fate, he finds himself in Winnipeg and finally in Montreal, where he follows a Chassid to prayer services on a Friday evening and learns the joy of prayer: "Then suddenly, the Presence entered into me, like a stream. . . . I sang" (p. 35). The story ends as the plane lands in New York; Shemtov urges Weiss to remember his grandfather, who had been a singing Chassid too. In this meeting between secular and Chassidic Jews, Kreisel explores a common heritage before and after the Holocaust.

The Rich Man

Kreisel's first novel, *The Rich Man*, is set for the most part in Vienna in 1935. The Danube River and Blue Danube Waltz form part of the novel's symbolic backdrop, where any romantic illusions are undercut by the realities of prewar Europe. A factory worker in Toronto, Jacob Grossman, decides to visit his Viennese family, who believe him to be a successful Canadian businessman in a position to assist them financially. At the German border a stormtrooper with a black swastika enters Jacob's train for inspection. "It was then that Jacob saw the strange and ominous insignia on his cap—two crossed bones and a leering death's-head" (Toronto: McClelland and Stewart, 1961, p. 43). Much of the novel involves political discussions among family members concerning 1930s Austria and Chancellor Dollfuss's announcement of the closure of Parliament in 1933. Jacob's brother-in-law, Albert, declares that Austria doesn't matter because it is an insignificant country with only six million people, reminding the reader ominously of that significant number of Jews killed during the Holocaust. Albert is fully aware of the power of Hitler's voice and wants to leave Austria for a safer country, but doesn't have the money to uproot his family. Seeing that Jacob as the rich relative from Canada, his family looks to him for salvation, but Jacob is powerless. When he leaves for Canada at the end of the novel, Jacob gives his sister seventy-six dollars, all the money he has left: "I have come to put out a big fire with one pail of water" (p. 205). Through a series of symbols and indirect references, Kreisel conveys a sense of the pre-Holocaust world of his native Vienna, and prefigures the impotence of North American Jewry to rescue Europe's Jews.

The Betrayal

Where *The Rich Man* focuses on Europe before the war, Kreisel's second novel, *The Betrayal*, deals with the consequences of the Holocaust. Although *The Betrayal* is set in Edmonton in 1952, the narrative turns to events during the war, as Theodore Stappler seeks revenge on Joseph Held, who betrayed him and his mother to the Gestapo. Earlier, through bribery, Held had arranged for the escape of some Jews out of Austria to France, but in the Stapplers' case he was unsuccessful. Other betrayals in the novel, such as Stappler's own desertion of his mother, contribute to the complex reaction to the Holocaust. In addition, Kreisel uses the doppelganger motif to identify his characters' involvement with each other and to complicate relationships between victims and victimizers during and after the Holocaust. The word "strange," which appears in the opening and closing sentences, highlights Kreisel's estrangement and defamiliarization in his fictional approach to the Holocaust.

While the narrator, Mark Lerner, teaches the history of the French Revolution, one of his students confronts him with more recent history and he is forced to reevaluate his own fate as he remembers his grandfather who came to Canada "straight out of the crowded slums of the Warsaw ghetto—the same that during the war was to be so completely, so tragically annihilated. There, but for the grace of God, might I have been" (Toronto: McClelland and Stewart, 1971, p. 9). The words of Katherine Held, his refugee student, send a shudder through him, shrinking the distance not only between student and teacher, but also between Europe and Canada, so that Lerner himself becomes a kind of survivor. "Because what might have been was more than a mere abstraction, I felt suddenly as if a somber reality, the specter of Auschwitz, had invaded my office" (p. 15). Through Katherine, the Holocaust becomes more concrete in Edmonton and the novel's symbols and characters serve to concretize any abstraction of the Holocaust.

Stappler relates a dream about his mother to Lerner in what is a sublimation of her fate during the Holocaust. A strange and familiar barren landscape, a baleful evening, massive obelisks, and black clouds like outstretched fingers of a gigantic hand fill his dream. A man stumbles from rock to rock until he sees a ghostlike woman, Stappler's mother. Unable to help her, he stands by the shore of a stagnant lake where gaseous fumes rise and poison the air. Through Stappler's nightmare, memories of the Holocaust invade innocent Edmonton. Stappler's paralysis—his inability to save his mother from deportation to the concentration camps—highlights other betrayals in the novel as well as the complexities of survival throughout the years of World War II. Joseph Held is also involved in this failed attempt to save Jews, and Stappler observes Held in Saarbrücken talking to "one of the devil's men" (p. 83) who wears the black uniform of the elite guard with the gleaming death's-head insignia on his cap.

The hotel clerk where Stappler stays in Edmonton also happens to be Jewish, and tells Lerner about his cousin's escape from Poland before the war. Many of his aunts, uncles, and cousins remained and met their fate in gas chambers and concentration camps. "One of my cousins got out alive. He came over here after the war. You know, sometimes I wonder how that guy can live with all the memories" (p. 146). Stappler also has his memories of Europe as he recalls a classmate, Kretschmar, who hit him in the face. "Kretschmar, the lover of the saints and the martyrs, forgot all about love and everything else the saints and martyrs might have taught him, and became the soldier of his lord, just as many years afterwards he became the loyal servant of his earthly Messiah, Adolf Hitler" (p. 157). Joseph Held regrets that he could not save Stappler's mother, and sums up his life as "Darker than night. Deeper than hell" (p. 181). Listening to Held's words, Lerner reacts: "I saw suddenly the tragedy of Europe in the lives of these two men" (p. 181). The novel ends with Joseph Held committing suicide and Theodore Stappler heading further north, disappearing into the Arctic wilderness, as if to erase history in Canadian emptiness. *The Betrayal* demonstrates how far the post-Holocaust world reaches—as far as northwestern Canada, so remote from Europe's concentration camps.

The Rich Man was the first Jewish novel in Canada to focus on the Holocaust. Kreisel's groundbreaking fiction combines Canadian prairie regionalism and European Jewish history from the dual perspective of an Edmonton author who managed to escape from Hitler's tyranny, unlike the majority of Canadian-Jewish writers who grew up in either Montreal or Winnipeg, and write from a more centralized Canadian perspective. Not quite mainstream, Kreisel's fiction has made a significant contribution to Canada's Holocaust literature.

Bibliography

Primary Sources

The Rich Man. 1948.
The Betrayal. 1964.
The Almost Meeting and Other Stories. 1981.

Secondary Sources

Hart, Alexander. "Writing the Diaspora." Ph.D diss. The University of British Columbia, December 1996.

Neuman, Shirley, ed. *Another Country: Writings By and About Henry Kreisel*. Edmonton: NeWest, 1985.

Anna Langfus

(1920–1966)

JUDITH KAUFFMANN
(Translated by Ruth Morris)

FOR A WRITER whose works are largely fiction, inspired by a highly personal experience of war, the problematic issue of relationships between life and literary writing, though often considered unsophisticated and out of date, is a crucial one. Anna Langfus's novels are the upshot of complex interactions between memory, creative imagination, and writing. In her works, the effect of truth—of presence and transparency—of testimony is combined with fictional devices. Such deliberate choices place a special responsibility on the shoulders of the writer-cum-witness, as we are confronting revisionist distortions of historical facts.

The Woman, Her Life

Born in Lublin in 1920 to an assimilated affluent middle-class Jewish family, Anna Langfus lived a sheltered life. In 1937 she left with her husband for Belgium where she studied science. Back in Poland in the summer of 1939, she was caught by the war: anti-Jewish measures, ghetto, Polish Resistance, arrest by the Gestapo, internment in Plock Prison, her husband shot before her eyes, her parents deported. The only member of her family to survive the Nazi persecutions, she moved to Paris in 1947. She married a survivor whom she met in Warsaw, by whom she had a daughter, Maria. She taught mathematics, wrote for Jewish magazines—*L'Arche* (the "shows" section) and *L'Information juive*—and played an active role in the cultural life of Sarcelles, a crowded popular suburb of Paris. She died suddenly in 1966.

The Writer, Her Work

Anna Langfus, precocious like Anna Frank, was just fifteen when she published her first stories in Polish magazines. Her French career includes theater—*Les Lépreux* (1952, unpublished), directed by Sacha Pitoëff in 1956—and three novels—*Le sel et le soufre* (*The Whole Land Brimstone*, 1960), which won Switzerland's Veillon Prize, *Les Bagages de sable* (*The Lost Shore*, 1962), which was awarded the Prix Goncourt, and *Saute, Barbara* (*Jump, Barbara*, 1965).

Although her books received wide coverage in newspaper literary supplements when they were published, academic research has not yet given Anna Langfus the full attention she deserves. The few important studies of her work that have been undertaken include a general analysis by Sidra DeKoven Ezrahi, Judith Klein's study of *Le sel et le soufre*, and thematic papers by Ellen S. Fine, Joë Friedemann, and me.

The War Novel

Le sel et le soufre, Langfus's first novel, tells the story of a young Polish woman in the Nazi upheaval. Inspired by the author's own life, this was the book that meant the most to her. It is also probably her most important and most accomplished work. An example of "literature of survival," *Le sel et le soufre* has a three-stage structure (Ezrahi). In the first stage, "Collapse of the 'Ancien Régime,' ": the family cocoon in which the heroine Maria has been sheltered from her surroundings is disrupted, and the catastrophe splits apart her world. The second stage describes the "Descent into the 'Anus Mundi,' " from confinement in the ghetto, abandoning her parents, joining the Resistance and going underground among Aryans, through Gestapo prison, her husband's execution, to forced labor camp. Utterly desperate, the young woman tries unsuccessfully to taunt her torturers into killing her. In the last stage, "After the Liberation," the survivor, wandering back to her devastated home through post-war Poland where the Jews are now out of place, is condemned to live. All alone.

The Postwar Novels

With her second novel, *Les Bagages de sable*, Langfus intended to write "a lightweight little story" with "a young girl, an old gentleman, the Côte d'Azur" (*La Nouvelle Critique*, 1965), but the main character of the sequel, who lives with the same ghosts as the heroine of *Le sel et le soufre*, and whose false name she still bears, forces a familiar face on her creator, making her realize that she cannot escape her past. Thus, the reader discovers that the survivor's real name has never been revealed, further testimony to her enduring Holocaust trauma.

Uprooted and unsettled—Langfus would say "disordered"—one day in a Paris square, the Polish refugee Maria meets a retired teacher, who invites her to go away on holiday with him. Beneath the Mediterranean sun they engage in a game of seduction—with undertones of sexual exploitation. Becoming involved with a group of teenagers, the young woman seeks the bright, breezy paradise—"the lost shore"—of her childhood, but when a girl of whom she has become fond takes her own life, she is terribly shaken. Tempted by the same desire to go all the way, she tries to drown herself "far from the shore, in the heart of pink darkness" (*The Lost Shore*, London: Collins, 1963, p. 205). However, like all survivors who have "contracted the war sickness" (p. 53), she has already experienced her own death: she is beyond suicide. Condemned to be eternally on the run, she cries over herself, "who was incapable of going through with anything, . . . capable only of cheating and evasion" (p. 207). And finally she surrenders to the old man, forfeiting her independence and dignity in an apparent self-destructive act. Maria settles down to vegetate, in a self-satisfied manner, until her aging lover, brought low by flu, calls his wife for help. Thrown out into the street she chooses a solitary life, leaving behind her the silence "rent by the discordant and almost painful cry of a bird" (p. 255).

Saute, Barbara opens in Berlin, 1945. A soldier in the victorious armies is wandering around amidst the ruins. He is haunted by his memories of the night that his wife and little girl were slaughtered, while he escaped out a window. A street urchin jumping rope reminds him of his little Barbara. He picks the child up and joins a convoy of refugees making their way to Paris. After a painful start on his new life—the humiliating experience of learning a manual job, and a hard time during which the Jewish survivor and the little German girl learn to get along with each other—Michael seems to be making progress. He plans to marry again (the boss's daughter) and return to architecture, but the past comes back with a vengeance, sweeping away the survivor's fragile mask of normality. Michael runs away taking the stolen child back to the Berlin street where he kidnapped her. When a passerby asks him the time, he aims his revolver at him. The man collapses. Period.

The guilty feelings of a father who survived because he shirked his responsibilities as his wife and child were being murdered, also constitute the subject matter of the play, *Les Lépreux* (The Leprous). However, anticipating public rejection of a drama with such brute violence, Langfus chose to write prose fiction because of its ability to present violence at a distance. Focusing on feelings of guilt, *Saute, Barbara* ends on an ambiguous note: does the character really perform the final, murderous gesture? Is it a hallucination or the symbolic suicide of a man who is tortured by the shame of having survived? Should we read into it the writer's imaginary revenge? Knowing that this book is Anna Langfus's last (she died shortly afterwards), one can fully appreciate the tragedy underlying the disturbing conclusion of her literary testament-to-be.

Writing: between Testimony and Fiction

Le sel et le soufre could be defined as a "novel of testimony" (Nathalie Heinich, p. 42), because it associates the realism and truth of autobiographical writing with the flexibility and freedom of fiction. This novel possesses the attributes of an autobiographical text: on a formal level, it is a story in the first person; in terms of subject matter, its content is directly inspired by the author's life, as shown by the information provided in the author's biography on the cover, and in the media (press interviews). Because this book reports on an authentic experience, on both an individual and a collective level, it involves a major investment on the part of the writer. The effect of testimony—of presence at the event—imbues the person who can declare "I was there" with a special authority: it confers to the witness-writer the right to speak and at the same time adds weight to her words.

Choosing to write a novel is, for Langfus, the upshot of internal needs. "For me, writing is a way of ridding myself of something" (WIZO, interview quoted in Fine 1993, p. 107), but she cannot confront the bare facts in their unbearable violence a second time. The transposition offered by the novel form favors the detachment necessary to observe things from the outside. The narrator relates her tale in a personal fashion, using the first person, but she never discloses her actual identity.

Even at the end of the book the reader does not know her family name or her real first name. With its Christian roots, Maria, her first name, underscores her undercover identity. This mask is also a rhetorical device that enables the writer, through a hybrid, veiled form of the third person, to produce an oblique representation of reality.

The dissociation between the author and her fictitious character reproduces the split between her "suffering self" and her "writing self": "I had the impression that the girl who had lived and suffered, and the narrator were two very different people, that one had relinquished to the other only an incomplete and rapidly distorted experience" (WIZO, quoted in Fine 1993, p. 98). The problems of reporting on horror proceed from blanks in memory and imperfections of language. As Anna Langfus puts it, words "fade in the face of the reality that they are supposed to translate" (*La Nouvelle Critique* interview, 1965). Because the public was not ready to confront reality head on, she contends that a minimalist solution is required to communicate something of this unspeakable experience: "Say much less in order to express more." Consequently, she searches for images and comparisons, "to camouflage things, . . . to cut them down to our own size" (*Saute, Barbara*, Paris: Gallimard, 1965, p. 17).

In order not to betray her authentic experience, Langfus deals solely with those aspects of the *Shoah* with which she was familiar: the ghetto and the preliminaries to deportation (raids, *Umschlagplatz*), political imprisonment, and forced labor camp.

She treats some of those common places, like the *Umschlagplatz* and the labor camp, in a very personal way, which fuses grotesque realism (digestion and excrements) with the liberating creative power of imagination. Following are two exemplary episodes. The first one describes Maria's struggle with the crowd gathered in the ghetto main square. She feels like a giant stomach has closed about her, "beginning its monstruous digestion" (*The Whole Land Brimstone*, New York: Pantheon Books, 1962, p. 56). The repulsing vision of individuals mingling into a "seething mass" (p. 55), while mirroring her own anxiety, awakens some anguish deeply rooted in all human beings.

The other event takes place in the labor camp as the female prisoners organize a clandestine party on New Year's Eve. The wild dances—tango, waltz, foxtrot, and polka, with musical accompaniment by "a comb wrapped up in paper"—end in a carnivalesque disaster. Having knocked the pail over, the women spend the rest of the night picking up the dirt, "while from the comb-and-paper band overhead came the sardonic strains of a funeral march" (p. 265). Maria and her mates have managed to turn their prison upside down into a locus where solidarity and imagination triumph—at least for a while.

Maria's Aryan disguise helped her, like her creator, to avoid the horror of the extermination camps. At the same time, this non-Jewish dimension of her life enables her to relate her personal history as an assimilated Jew, for which the identity-based definition is, one could say, basically determined by the Nazi racial criteria. It is, according to Ezrahi, the struggle to survive of an individual stripped of most organic links with the destiny of her group. Maria describes her time in prison as the drama of a person reduced to nothing but the self, in the utter solitude of an "opaque emptiness" (p. 192). What helps her to resist is her "instinct . . . swifter than will-power" (p. 191). She practices a technique that most survivors eventually adopt: she closes herself off from the intolerable suffering of her surroundings. She speaks of "cutting off contact," "switching herself off," "absenting herself," "hoodwinking herself." She falls into a state of drowsiness and lethargy, "a state of torpor common to hibernating animals." The result is metamorphosis into a "smooth, hard, insentient ball" (p. 201).

For human beings deprived of everything that defined them in the eyes of others (marital and social status, etc.), the last bulwark before total dissolution is the maintenance of physical integrity: "Honestly, conscientiously, I strove to propel this body for which I was responsible" (p. 194), says Maria, immured in her cell. By doggedly refusing to give in to external circumstances (such as cold and torture), by clinging to walking—a basic and fundamental physical activity—she preserves the dignity of the two-legged vertical human being. This down-to-earth, last-ditch resistance, which denies any heroic aspects, is probably one of the specific attributes of women's struggle for their survival. When the quintessential female experience—motherhood—is referred to, it is barely hinted at, mentioned in a slightly ironic, derisory tone: in order to nurse her mutilated hand, she "cradles" her thumb on her shoulder "like a baby" (p. 212). Battling for life is the only possibility in the extreme conditions of detention and should not be judged exclusively by its outcome. Maria's strong self-centeredness, which is often highlighted and on the whole criticized by some readers and a few critics (Fine 1993, p. 109), comes into its own. A factor contributing to her survival is her guarded independence. Sometimes selfishness is simply a synonym for being faithful to one's own self.

Survival: Death-in-Life/Life-in-Death

The description of the survivor that begins in *Le sel et le soufre* continues in *Les Bagages de sable* and

Saute, Barbara. Michael, the male narrator of the latter book, articulates the basic points about return. For those survivors who have crossed an irreversible border, returning to normality is out of the question: "I already belong to a different species. It is a long time since I made a distinction between what I imagine and what I do" (*Saute, Barbara*, p. 12). The world has become a kind of theater where everything is mere artifice, deception, facade:

> Once and for all, excluded from reality. As the director of a company of traveling comedians, I carry along with me all the sets, all the props. But the decision as to which play to stage is not mine. Improvisations occur round the clock, sets are erected at a breakneck speed, and in a flash the comedians are on stage. Capricious and anarchical, they drag me pitilessly into this incoherent play, insisting that I play opposite them, until a word, a silence, a look reveals the yawning chasm beneath my feet and throws me down into the abyss, screaming as I go (p. 210).

Speaking of the *Shoah*'s impact on her characters in an interview, Langfus explained that these creatures inhabit a "twilight country ... where nothing more happens, where above all nothing more can happen ..., can affect [them]" (*L'Arche*). The ordeal has changed the being. Perception of the fundamental dimensions of human life—time and space—has been profoundly disturbed. The past—Barbara the dead child of the murdered people—and the present—Minna the living child of the murdering people—meet in a blurred hallucination. For Michael, time has frozen at the moment disaster struck him, "and henceforth [he will] relive this night over and over again" (p. 95). Everything has been consumed: "I live in Barbara's death" (p. 208), the tortured father will say. And his world topples over the edge when an anonymous German asks him for the time!

Personal Stories, Subjective Testimony, Collective History

Les Bagages de sable and *Saute, Barbara*, stories of survival, touch on the impossible attempts of a few survivors to return to the world of normal human beings. Having escaped by some miracle, the emotionally crippled people of these narratives have survived so they can testify, every one on his or her own terms, to having been "tormented to the depths of their souls" (*Saute, Barbara*, p. 56). With its hypertrophy of the self, *Le sel et le soufre* tips the scales toward an overstated subjectivity. The extreme close-up view magnifies perceptions. It may produce a shortsighted, partial perception of events, but reporting on an extremely strong experience, it throws light on some part of the actual world. While laying no claims to be exemplary, this "novel of testimony" relates one very personal and authentic story out of a tragic chapter in the history of the evil human beings have inflicted on other human beings.

Bibliography

Primary Sources

Le sel et le soufre (*The Whole Land Brimstone*). 1960.
Les Bagages de sable (*The Lost Shore*). 1962.
Saute, Barbara (*Jump, Barbara*). 1965.

Secondary Sources

Ezrahi, Sidra DeKoven. *By Words Alone. The Holocaust in Literature*. Chicago: University of Chicago Press, 1980.
Fine, Ellen S. "L'écriture comme mémoire absente." *Les Nouveaux Cahiers*, no. 101 (summer 1990).
———. "Le témoin comme romancier: Anna Langfus et le problème de la distance." *Pardès* (1993).
———. "Anna Langfus, écrivain-témoin." *Les Nouveaux Cahiers*, no. 115 (winter 1993–1994).
Friedemann, Joë. "Comique et tragique: de l'insouciance à la brisure: le rire dans les romans d'Anna Langfus." *Cahiers Comique et Communication*, no. 3 (1985).
Heinich, Nathalie. "Le témoignage, entre biographie et roman: la place de la fiction dans les récits de déportation." In "La *Shoah*: silence ... et voix." *Mots*, no. 56 (September 1998).
Kauffmann, Judith. "Pour (re)lire Anna Langfus. Survivre/résister. Et après ..." In *Revue d'histoire de la Shoah*, Paris, (forthcoming).
Klein, Judith. *Literatur und Genozid. Darstellung des nazionalsozialistischen Massenvernichtung in der französischen Literatur*. Wien-Köln-Weimar: Böhlau Verlag, 1992.
Lappin, Adh. "From Nightmare to Fairy Tales." *The Reconstructionist* (May 1963).
Ruszniewski-Dahan, Myriam. *Romanciers de la Shoah. Si l'écho de leur voix faiblit* ... Paris: L'Harmattan, 1999.

Interviews

"Les écrivains devant le fait concentrationnaire." *L'Arche* (March 1961).
Conference at WIZO (Women's International Zionist Organization). Without title, unpublished (March 1963). Quoted by Ellen S. Fine: "Le témoin comme romancier: Anna Langfus et le problème de la distance." *Pardès* (1993).
"Anna Langfus ou le malheur vaincu." Interview by Claudine Cerf and Michel Cohen-Musnik. In *Kadimah* (31 January 1963).
La Nouvelle Critique (August 1961).
La Nouvelle Critique (June 1965).
Interview by Jeanine Delpech. In *Les Nouvelles littéraires* (22 November 1962).

Irving Layton
(1912–)

MICHAEL GREENSTEIN

Born in Romania in 1912, Irving Layton came to Montreal with his parents, Keine and Moishe Lazarovitch, at the age of one, and was educated at Baron Byng High School and Macdonald College, where he earned a B.S. in agriculture. After brief service in the Canadian army (1942–1943), he did postgraduate work in economics and political science at McGill University. In response to the post-1955 silence of his mentor, A. M. Klein, quieted by the Holocaust as well as his lack of recognition as a poet, Layton developed a vociferous persona and in the prophetic tradition railed against social, political, and religious hypocrisy in general, and the barbarism of the Holocaust in particular.

Layton's Poetry: "Ex-Nazi"

Layton's post-Holocaust poetry establishes a dialogue with the past by dramatically encountering history in the present. The four stanzas of "Ex-Nazi" frame a meeting between the poet and his neighbor, a former Nazi. The opening stanza creates a mood that is both realistic and surrealistic, beginning with the poet playing blindman's bluff among scarred bushes. In this game the poet will eventually open his eyes and his readers' to history, where scarred bushes hint at the bruised relationship between neighbors in the present and the damaged history of Jewish and German neighbors in the past. Run-on lines suggest the poet's sightless groping until he stumbles upon an "unguessed-at pole," which is not only an unfamiliar part of the landscape but also "Spooky as an overturned ambulance" (*Collected Poems*, Toronto: McClelland and Stewart, 1971, p. 54). The stanza's concluding simile furthers the accidental nature of the first simile in unmistakably Eliotian terms: "Like a sick anti-semite / The morning struggles to reveal itself." Struggle and revelation are at the heart of "Ex-Nazi."

His neighbor approaches in the second stanza, and the poet comments on the decay of nations and his neighbor's veins, which are full of pus. These white blood cells are part of the stanza's overall coloring, which not only counters the idea of racial purity but also suggests blankness and the ghostly presence of history. The brain-sick neighbor thinks he will transform and purify himself into a snowman that eventually melts into the March landscape, but that kind of escape is not readily available, for melting snowman and March landscape are "ravaged like the face of Dostoievski." Like the first stanza, the second concludes with two similes, from earlier morning to night when "the whitened streets / Lean into his dreams like a child's coffin." The poet's opening game culminates in the image of the child's coffin that haunts his Nazi neighbor.

The third stanza clears nocturnal guilt in the seasonal shift from winter and spring to summer. At noon the brain-sick neighbor meets himself (in contrast to the poet's earlier groping) in the "summer craze of the sun"—landscape and character interacting in pathetic fallacy. His neighbor appears boyish and innocent as his dog's tail flicks guilt from his conscience. Summer sun in the final stanza desiccates the wet guilt of the second stanza. Between poet and neighbor hangs a pale dust, "Like particles / Of sacrificial smoke." This final simile points directly to the Holocaust, to earlier similes in the poem, and to the scarred bushes of a landscape that is both post-Holocaust and Nazi past that will not disappear even in a new world.

Layton's Poetry: "Das Wahre Ich"

Layton repeats the pattern of "Ex-Nazi" in his later poem, "Das Wahre Ich" (p. 292), but he avoids similes in his direct confrontation with his hostess, who serves him tea and biscuits after informing him that she was a Nazi twenty years earlier. A matter-of-fact opening about the woman's past affiliations gives way to the present domestic setting where the poet praises her hospitality and the mobiles she has fashioned "in the comfortless burdensome evenings." Her face is as sad and thin as those mobiles moving in the small wind created by the poet's voice, yet a terrible stillness holds them both. The poet concludes with a rhetorical question: "At this moment, does she see my crumpled form against the wall, / blood on my still compassionate eyes and mouth?" Her mobiles (flattened forms of Jewish victims) serve as witnesses of history. The German title attests to a vicious past that lingers and hovers as indelicately as those mobiles; her mortal Jewish enemy is immortalized in "Das Wahre Ich."

If Layton rails stridently against antisemitism and fascism, he is also capable of rendering lyrically his affiliation with victims of the Holocaust. In four four-line stanzas that flow without any punctuation, "Rhine Boat Trip" (p. 389) evokes the spirit of Heine, as the poet glides along the river whose silent beauty clashes with the horrors of history. Castles on the Rhine are haunted by ghosts of Jewish mothers searching for their ghostly children. The first half of each stanza pictures the current landscape, which is undercut in the second half by crimes of the past. Clusters of grapes become myriads of blinded eyes staring at the blinding sun. The hair of Lorelei recalls the beards of murdered rabbis, and their sweet songs are silenced by the wailing rising from cattle cars moving invisibly across the land. The poet witnesses ghosts, blindness, invisibility, and silence in the historic German landscape.

Other Poems

Layton avoids punctuation in "At the Belsen Memorial" (p. 391), where abbreviated lines in a vertical column lend the appearance of a memorial gravestone. The opening line, "It would be a lie," serves as a refrain for the poem as well as a comment about poetic presence and past absence. When the poet states in the first person that it would be a lie to say that he heard screams, and concludes that he heard nothing, we could substitute a historic witness who claimed ignorance and innocence in the 1940s. Likewise the poet denies seeing bones or smelling the odor of decomposing bodies; nor does he touch ghosts of emaciated children. Having listed each of his senses, the poet is transformed into towering black stone like his columnar poem on the page, which concludes blankly: "Come: / read the inscription." The poem thus becomes its own Belsen memorial.

One of the epigrams to *The Pole-Vaulter* (Toronto; McClelland & Stewart, 1974) is taken from a Jew in Treblinka who says that inmates of the camp must live to tell what humans are capable of doing to one another. In opposition to Adorno's "no poetry after Auschwitz," Layton bears witness and explains in his foreword that his book began with a visit to the Anne Frank house in Amsterdam in July 1973. He proclaims that Anne with her courage and imagination is the prototype of all pole-vaulters and goes on to attack Soviet communism for its similarities to Nazi Germany.

"Midsummer's Dream in the Vienna Stadpark" (p. 15) begins with a waltz by Johann Strauss as background music that makes Auschwitz and Belsen belong to another planet entirely. The poet imagines Anne and her family in the park, and the Viennese applaud her because she wept when she saw Gypsy children led to the gas chamber. Layton structures his dream in six four-line stanzas with rhymes that echo the illusory quality of the surrounding music.

Layton attacks this European post-Holocaust illusion in his next poem, "The Final Solution" (p. 16), which conveys the banality of evil. The horrors of the past have all been dismissed in the music of nickelodeons playing Berliner love ballads. Amid the merriment no one can taste blood in perfect Rhenish wine. Indifference to history takes the form of such rhetorical questions as: so what if history was having one of its fits, and what is one supposed to do with a mad dog? Mundane activities of eating, drinking, or visiting art museums ignore the disappearance of poets and actors who once gave life to Vienna and Warsaw. The poet sees the children of *reingemacht* ("purefied") Europe with their knapsacks, ignorance, and indifference. He concludes with the nickelodeon that grinds on like fate: "The day is too ordinary for ghosts or grief."

"The Shadow" (p. 18) continues in a similar vein with the poet condemning indifference and amnesia to the *Shoah*. He releases his shadow like a switchblade or "cavernous grin of a ghost," for he is both victim and survivor out to avenge his lost brethren in a Viennese hofbrau. He sits at his table, leans flat against the wall, and makes sure that he doesn't spill a drop of beer or blood on the patrons' mothballed Nazi uniforms. His metamorphosis and cry to be taken off the wall recall Kafka, while cardplayers slam down their cards as if they are fists on an old Jew's skull. He revels in the surrounding mediocrity and guiltless murders as the Viennese waltz down Taborstrasse to the sounds of an orchestra directed with a baton made of a clipped mustache. The shadows of the poet and Hitler cast a pall on post-Holocaust Vienna.

In poems addressed to his sons, Layton advises them to become gunners in the Israeli army, for only in moral and physical strength does he see any kind of redemption to the crimes of the past.

Bibliography

Primary Sources

The Collected Poems of Irving Layton. 1971.
Engagements: The Prose of Irving Layton. 1972.
The Pole-Vaulter. 1974.
The Covenant. 1977.
Europe and Other Bad News. 1981.
Fortunate Exile. 1987.

Secondary Sources

Frances, Wynne. "Irving Layton." *Journal of Commonwealth Literature* 3 (July 1967): 34–48.
Greenstein, Michael. "Canadian Poetry After Auschwitz." *Canadian Poetry* 20 (spring/summer 1987): 1–16.
Mandel, Eli. *Irving Layton*. Toronto: Forum House, 1969.
Irving Layton: The Poet and His Critics. Mayne, Seymour, ed. Toronto: McGraw-Hill Ryerson, 1978.

Barbara Lebow

(1936–)

EDWARD ISSER

Barbara Lebow was born on 1 May 1936 in Brooklyn, New York, the daughter of a fur merchant, Herman (Hy) Lebow, and an interior designer, Pauline Engel. Lebow attended secondary school at the Fieldston School in Manhattan, where she studied ethical culture and developed a strong social consciousness. She earned a bachelor of arts degree at Vassar College. She began writing children's plays in 1964, when she joined the Academy Theatre Developmental Workshop in Atlanta, Georgia, and between 1965 and 1990 she was a playwright-in-residence with the Academy Theatre, which has produced more than a dozen of her works, including her first one-act play (in 1965). Lebow was also an integral part of the Academy Theatre's Human Service Project, which creates works for, and with, disenfranchised audiences—prison populations, the physically disabled, the elderly, the homeless, and the developmentally disabled. In 1991 she became the resident playwright with the Alabama Shakespeare Festival and Theatre in the Square in Marietta, Georgia.

Lebow has been the recipient of numerous fellowships and awards including the Atlanta Mayor's Fellowship in the Arts (1986), the Georgia Governor's Award in the Arts (1988), the Theatre Communications Group/Pew National Residency Grant (1994–1996), a Guggenheim Fellowship (1997); and a National Endowment for the Arts/Theatre Communications Group Residency Program for Playwrights (1998–2000). In addition, she has been a finalist four times for the Susan Smith Blackburn Prize for Playwriting (for *A Shayna Maidel* in 1985; *The Keepers* in 1995; *The Empress of Eden* in 1996; and *The Left Hand Singing* in 1998) and two of her plays (*A Shayna Maidel* and *Little Joe Monaghan*, 1981) were cited in Burns Mantle's *Best Plays.*

Attacking stereotypes and calling for social justice has been a constant theme of Lebow's work. In 1967 she coauthored an Academy Theatre production, *Night Witch*, with Frank Wittow. This play deals with antisemitism in the American South and is based on the historic Leo Frank mob lynching. Frank, a Jewish businessman, was falsely convicted of murdering a Christian girl and was murdered by an angry mob of southern antisemites. In Lebow and Wittow's play, a black employee implicates his Jewish boss in the crime, to the pleasure of the police captain whose prejudice toward the transplanted northern Jew exemplifies local fear of "outsiders" and "the other."

A Shayna Maidel

After laboring as a playwright in almost total obscurity for twenty years, Barbara Lebow achieved enormous success in the American theatrical scene in 1985 with *A Shayna Maidel.* Like the stage adaptation of *The Diary of Anne Frank, A Shayna Maidel* is a work about the Holocaust that is appealing (and perhaps nonthreatening) to a diverse audience—a Holocaust play that has achieved true popularity. *A Shayna Maidel* ran for more than a year and a half off Broadway and has been produced dozens of times across the United States and around the world. In 1991 the play was adapted and retitled *Miss Rose White* and was presented as a Hallmark Hall of Fame television production broadcast on 26 April 1992. The show won four Emmy Awards including Outstanding Movie of 1992.

A Shayna Maidel, in an indirect manner, dramatizes a chilling event from Lebow's childhood. Lebow grew up in New York City within an assimilated Jewish-American family whose members identified themselves as cultural Jews and were not particularly religious. In 1946, when Lebow was ten years old, two distant relatives arrived in her Manhattan home. These relatives—a teenage girl and her mother—were survivors of the Nazi concentration camps. The Lebow family took in the survivors temporarily until they relocated with other relatives in Canada. Lebow remembers feeling alienated and estranged from these women, who may have been related by blood but who were wholly alien to her world. Her strongest memory was one of anger because she was forced to give her bedroom to these strangers.

As Lebow grew older and came to understand the circumstances surrounding the experiences of these women, she felt shame and revulsion regarding her own petty reaction. Haunted by the guilt of survival, of having lived a comfortable childhood in New York City while girls her own age were being slaughtered, Lebow wrote *A Shayna Maidel* about the reunification of a family after the Holocaust. Lebow has said that she never intended to write a play specifically about the Holocaust, as she believed she had no right to do so since she did not experience the event herself. She does, however, explore the impact of the *Shoah* upon the American Jewish community.

A Shayna Maidel dramatizes the experience of a family sundered by the Holocaust and explores how the family slowly heals in the aftermath of the event. Mordechai, the patriarch of the family, came of age in Poland, married, had two daughters, and eventually left for America with his younger daughter, Rayzel. Mordechai's wife, however, and their elder daughter, Lusia, who was married and had a child, remained behind in Poland and were sent to concentration camps. Mordechai's wife died in a death camp, but Lusia survived, and she journeys to America after the end of the war. The action of the narrative commences with the arrival in 1946 of Lusia at her younger sister's Manhattan apartment. The play describes, in a naturalistic fashion, the vast cultural and emotional distances that now separate the two sisters from each other and from their father. Rayzel, the younger sister, has Americanized her name to Rose, speaks no Yiddish, refuses to keep kosher, and seeks total assimilation with the culture around her. Mordechai, the father, clings to his Old World customs and has difficulty adjusting to American culture. Lusia, who arrives directly from a displaced persons camp, speaks only broken English and is emotionally shattered by her experiences during the war.

Barbara Lebow uses expressionistic devices to represent the fractured psyche of Lusia, the death camp survivor. Lusia's memories of her lost mother, husband, child, and best friend torment her constantly and propel her into hallucinatory encounters with these figures from her past. The author, however, avoids the simple technique of the flashback and instead creates dreamlike sequences that never remove the action from its setting in Rose's New York apartment. Lebow employs the effective device of beginning each dream sequence by having the actors speak Yiddish for the first few lines and then shifting into fluent English. Lusia, who normally speaks broken and heavily accented English, is able to speak perfectly when she communicates in her dream world.

It is no oversight that the name of Lusia's death camp remains unknown; this is a play about lacunae and silence. Barbara Lebow takes for granted that her audience will know the terrifying facts about the roundups, the deportations, the selection process, and the conditions inside the camps. The details of Lusia's arrest and her camp experiences are barely alluded to and never enacted. Only events that occurred prior to her capture and those that transpired after her release are dramatized. The author's decision not to represent or describe life in the camps forces the audience to imagine the horror that the young survivor has undergone.

There are two discoveries that occur during the course of *A Shayna Maidel* that propel the action forward and unite the two sisters against their overbearing father. The first revelation is that Mordechai has hidden a letter from his dead wife intended for Rose. The second, much more damaging revelation, is the knowledge that Mordechai failed to save his wife and daughter when the opportunity arose. Lusia and her mother could have escaped to America had Mordechai sent the necessary funds. Lusia tells Rose that Mordechai refused to borrow money because of his male pride:

> We was supposed to come here! Was your promise. I want Rayzel should know this. Mama was all ready we should wait. So we wait. Then comes a letter from your Tanta Perla. She's asking us why Popa won't take no money. Some group in Brooklyn is giving him money so we could come and he should pay it back later. But Popa says no. He won't take from no one (*A Shayna Maidel,* p. 78).

The father's refusal to accept assistance condemns his wife and daughter to the death camp. But Mordechai shows no outward remorse for his action and learns nothing from the experience. He clings to his role as an Old World patriarch and seeks to maintain fiscal and emotional control over his family. He opposes Rose's independent way of life, her apartment, her job, her change of name, and her friends. He also denies Rose connection with her dead mother by withholding the letter sent from Poland. This shutting out of the mother is an attempt by Mordechai to maintain his emotional monopoly over his daughter.

Lusia, however, rebels against her father's domination and refuses to play the role of a submissive daughter. She stands up beside her younger sister and helps her to confront their father. Lusia wants her younger sister to know that Rose was her mother's *shayna maidel*—pretty girl—and that they never forgot about her in Poland. Lusia confronts Mordechai and demands that he give Rose the letter: "You don't want even to read to her what Mama is saying. Now you don't want even to touch something of Mama's. From shame. From shame!" (p. 79).

Mordechai finally relents and gives Lusia the letter addressed to Rose. Lusia translates the Yiddish for her younger sister and reads out loud the last communication there will ever be between mother and child. In the first line of the letter the mother admits, "I'm not a learned woman," and the rest of the document continues in a simple sentimental manner (p. 80). Rose, however, is not concerned about the contents of the letter as much as she is touched by its mere existence. The letter, and the baby spoon that accompanies it, fills the emotional gap in her life. The letter and spoon are tangible proof that she was not forsaken by her mother. Rose is healed by this knowledge and is able to gain individual autonomy.

The final scene of the play brings the narrative full circle and combines the dreamworld of Lusia with the reality of postwar America. Duvid, Lusia's husband who has been missing and presumed dead, arrives at the door of Rose's apartment. A surrealistic dream sequence follows during which the family is joined by the spirit of the dead mother. Rose is able to physically embrace her mother and then the entire family dances together in celebration. The family is reconciled to each other and to their past.

Bibliography

Selected Stage Productions

Little Joe Monoghan. 1981.
The Adventures of Homer McGundy. 1985.
A Shayna Maidel. 1985.
Cyparis. 1987.
The Keepers. 1988.
Trains. 1990.
Cossacks in the Kettle. 1994.
The Homonculus of Cordoba. 1994.
Tiny Tim Is Dead. 1994.
The Empress of Eden. 1995.
The Sunday Seat. 1995.
Cobb County Stories. 1996.
Games. 1996.
The Left Hand Singing. 1997.
Lurleen. 1999.

Secondary Sources

Isser, Edward R. "Toward a Feminist Perspective in American Holocaust Drama." *Studies in the Humanities* 17, no. 2 (1990): 139–148.
Mandl, Bette. "Alive Still, in You: Memory and Silence in *A Shayna Maidel*." In *Staging Difference*. Edited by Marc Maufort. New York: Peter Lang, 1995, pp. 260–265.
Pearce, Michele. "The Trouble with Cobb County." *American Theatre* 13, no. 7 (September 1996): 58–59.
Sterling, Eric. "Barbara Lebow." In *Contemporary Jewish-American Dramatists and Poets: A Bio-Critical Sourcebook*. Edited by Joel Shatzky and Michael Taub. Westport, Conn.: Greenwood Press, 1999, pp. 102–108.

ISABELLA LEITNER

(1922–)

MYRNA GOLDENBERG

BORN ON 28 May 1922, in Kisvarda, Hungary, into a comfortable middle-class merchant family, Isabella Katz was the second of six children, five girls and one boy. Her father, Mendel, a wine, champagne, and liquor merchant well versed in Talmud, traveled to the United States on business several times during the 1930s. Recognizing the growing German threat, he left Hungary in 1939 to find a job and lodging in the States and to arrange to bring his family to safety. Mendel Katz finally secured the necessary immigration papers and made it safely to the United States, but it was too late for his family. Leitner explains in her first book, *Fragments of Isabella*, that her mother's appointment to meet the American consul on 8 December 1941, in Budapest, was canceled because Hungary had joined Germany in a declaration of war against the United States. The memory of her mother and her promise to survive is a thread throughout *Fragments* and its sequel, *Saving the Fragments*. In a telephone conversation with Myrna Goldenberg, Leitner recalled her mother as an erstwhile poet with a strong social conscience, reinforcing the description in *Fragments* as "the poor man's Mrs. Roosevelt" (*Fragments of Isabella*, New York: Dell, 1978, p. 23).

From 1941 to March 1944, conditions were neither comfortable nor safe for Hungarian Jews, but they worsened relentlessly when Germany occupied Hungary in March. The Katz family suffered all the humiliations, isolation, and deprivations that were prelude to deportation in May 1944. For example, at the roundup of the Jews in Kisvarda, Isabella, her brother, and four sisters helplessly witnessed a young SS soldier whip her mother. Transported in cattle cars without sanitation or food, they arrived in Auschwitz in Poland, where Isabella's mother and youngest sister were gassed upon arrival. Surviving Auschwitz and the labor camp Birnbaumel, she and two sisters escaped on 23 January 1945, during a blizzard on the death march to Bergen Belsen in Germany. Her third sister's attempt to escape during the death march failed; she reached Bergen Belsen in a much weakened state and died shortly after liberation. Her brother, Philip, survived six concentration camps.

Two days after their escape, Isabella and her sisters were liberated by the Soviets and, by March 1945, transported to Odessa. They boarded the SS *Brand Whitlock* in April 1945 and landed auspiciously in Newport News, Virginia, on V-E Day, 8 May. FBI agents who joined them aboard ship debriefed the three sisters all day, 9 May. On 10 May, the SS *Brand Whitlock* anchored in Baltimore, where the Katz sisters disembarked. Hosted by a distinguished Baltimorean, Judge Simon E. Sobeloff, they were reunited with their father within days. Isabella is extremely proud to be among the first, if not the first, Holocaust survivor to arrive in the United States.

Isabella and the writer Irving A. Leitner married in 1956; they have two sons, Peter and Richard, and one grandchild, Julian. The Leitners reside in New York City and Isabella continues to speak and write about her experiences during the Holocaust.

Fragments of Isabella

Leitner's first book, *Fragments of Isabella: A Memoir of Auschwitz* (1978), written with her husband, is a dramatic first-person account of her experiences from 28 May 1944 through the end of May 1945. As the title implies, the memoir is a succession of clipped scenes of her life, abruptly presented, usually in short sentences and short chapters, all of which are connected by the thread of German and Hungarian antisemitism and the cruelty meted out by the Nazis. *Fragments* and *Saving the Fragments* are largely bursts of episodes of anguish and irony tinged with sarcasm and bitterness. These two memoirs are highly personal reactions to the pain inflicted by the Germans. Focusing almost exclusively on the inhumanity she experienced and, to a lesser extent, on the sadism she observed, she assumes the reader's familiarity with the historical events that the year May 1944 to May 1945 comprises. Uncomplicated, even though it includes millions of words of testimony, documentation, historical analysis, and reflection that have surfaced since the Eichmann trial in 1961–1962, Leitner's story is a portrayal of her anger at the victimization imposed by the Nazis. Therein lies its strength and its limitations. The casual reader is discomfited, if not seared, by Leitner's intense feelings but not informed about the larger historical narrative that is the cause of her pain and anger. However, *Fragments* is memorable and haunting in its genuine portrayal of emotion.

Leitner begins *Fragments* in freedom, in May 1945, in New York, observing young American women whose naïveté and unconcern sharply contrast with her past year under the Nazis. American girls are bedecked, "wear stockings, ride in automobiles, wear wristwatches and necklaces, and they are colorful and perfumed . . . healthy . . . living" (pp. 13–14). Without transition, we move to Auschwitz: "Our heads are shaved. We look like neither boys nor girls. We have diarrhea. No, not diarrhea—typhus" (p. 14).

Later she describes the separation from her mother, soon after their arrival at the infamous death camp:

> Mama! Turn around. I must see you before you go to wherever you are going. Mama, turn around. You've got to. We have to say good-bye. Mama! If you don't turn around I'll run after you. But they won't let me. I must stay on the "life" side.
>
> Mama! (p. 31).

Her emotional language in the preceding passage is typical of her narrative style—impressions that reflect the infusion of her post-Holocaust knowledge and her persistent bitterness into the portrayal of her experiences from 1941 on.

Some episodes are no longer than one-and-a-half pages with generous margins. One particularly powerful chapter, "The Baby," is twenty-four lines long. Addressing the baby directly, Leitner's direct and disconcerting prose is unforgettable:

> Most of us are born to live—to die, but to live first. You, dear darling, you are being born only to die. How good of you to come before roll call though, so your mother does not have to stand at attention while you are being born. Dropping out of the womb onto the ground with your mother's thighs shielding you like wings of angels is an infinitely nicer way to die than being fed into the gas chamber. . . .
>
> You belong to the gas chamber. Your mother has no rights. She only brought forth fodder for the gas chamber. She is just a dirty Jew who has soiled the Aryan landscape with another dirty Jew. How dare she think of you in human terms? (pp. 40–41).

The ironies in these passages shape a relentless anger that permeates most of the book, especially the parts relating Nazi oppression. The rest of the book focuses on her experience of rescue by the Soviets, the transport from Odessa to Newport News, Virginia, on a U.S. merchant marine ship, and short evocations of joy after coming to America. However, these passages are shaped by inescapable Auschwitz memories and her hatred of the Germans: "Bye, Auschwitz. I will never see you again. I will always see you" (p. 60). Aboard ship, she and her sisters shared a cabin with a German-American whom she observed unnoticed one evening: "She is sitting on her bed and, with her precious memorabilia spread all about, kissing the stamps with Hitler's face on them." Leitner comments, "May you suffer, wherever you are. Amen" (p. 96).

As the title implies, *Fragments* represents the impact of the Nazis on her life: her family was destroyed; her youth was cut short; her entire world was disrupted. Eventually, even the birth of her first son is celebrated against the memory of the crematorium in Auschwitz. Peter weighs "seven pounds, four and a half ounces. I weighed seven times that much when the housepainter [Hitler has often been characterized as a housepainter] painted thick, gray streaks in the sky" (p. 105). In contrast to the traditional narrative, her memoir is a record of shreds of the fabric of her experience, more of a series of discrete impressions that eventually form a recounting of painful experiences. Each shred, or short fragment, is spare and vivid; each a minimal etching that engages the imagination indelibly and uncomfortably. Thus, *Fragments* is a heartrending personal book that demands much of its readers. Indeed, her own anguish is so vividly related that the reader waivers between compassion and protective distance. For example, in Auschwitz at the end of the processing stage, Philip somehow manages to find them and cries: "Listen to me. Listen! Eat whatever they give you. Eat. If they give you shit, eat shit. Because we must survive. We have to pay them back" (p. 36). Six months later, Leitner needs to assure herself of her own and other prisoners' humanity: "We are pure and beautiful. We have nothing in common with them. They are Germans. We were both of mothers the smell of whose burning flesh permeates the air, but what were they born of? Who sired them?" (p. 58).

Leitner's tight focus on her responses, the fragments of her experiences, stand in strong relief against a dimly depicted historical background. The juxtaposition of sharp feelings against a vague backdrop of horror, though dramatic, precludes intimacy because the reader needs distance. From the first sentence, though, Leitner demands the reader's engagement. She reveals that she is a woman addressing other women: "Did you go to the movies? Did you have a date? What did he say? That he loves you?" (p. 13). The reader is made uncomfortable as the contrast continues: "yesterday, May 29, 1944, we were deported" (p. 13). The difference in appearance and attitude of American women and Hungarian Jewish women becomes starker as Leitner describes the luxury of being allowed to be beautiful, well groomed, "healthy . . . living. Incredible!" A year before, in Auschwitz, "We haven't menstruated for a long time . . . Lice are having an orgy in our armpits, their favorite spots. . . . We're hot at least under our armpits, while our bodies are shivering" (p. 14). Thus, within its first pages, *Fragments* confronts us with the threat of annihilation through amenorrhea and disease, suggesting gender-specific differences as well as the real threat of death through disease.

In these very vivid slices of experience and responses to German cruelty, Leitner introduces her readers to unimaginable horrors of the Third Reich and some of its infamous sadists. Josef Mengele and Irma Griese specifically leave Isabella scarred. Leitner relates the incident, also remembered by many other women prisoners, when Griese ordered her sister Chicha to kneel and hold two heavy rocks in her outstretched arms for hours. We meet the very young Nazi officers who prove the desperation of the Third Reich as it enlists its youthful population to fight its declared enemies, the Jews. Her pleas to them to keep her family intact suggest the importance of the family in eastern European Jewish life.

She invokes God to account for the madness she sees around herself: "Did God take leave of his senses?"(p. 16). The brutality is random. This God, in fact, is the proverbial god of the foxhole: "God! God, help us! This once. You have not shown us any mercy all these months. . . . Can't you do something? God? Don't let us die" (p. 80).

Addressing her dead mother twenty years later, Leitner promises her that she will perpetuate her mother's belief that " 'what is good in all of us' should be their religion . . . and then you will always be alive and the housepainter will always be dead. And children someday will plant flowers in Auschwitz, where the sun couldn't crack through the smoke of burning flesh. Mother, I will keep you alive" (*Fragments*, p. 103).

Quite unintentionally and devoid of feminist theoretical analysis, *Fragments* introduces the issue of gender. Leitner forcefully declares sisterhood as a strategy of survival. She and her three sisters form a community, a unit of mutual caring and love that forces them to stay alive: "If you are sisterless, you do not have the pressure, the absolute responsibility to end the day alive" (p. 44). Leitner talks about each sister, expecting the others to escape selection even at their most despairing moments—"they expected me to get back. The burden to live up to that expectation was mine, and it was awesome" (p. 45). Leitner further explains in *Fragments*:

> The responsibility of staying alive had its own inherent torture. At times, it doubled the alertness, at times I wished I were alone, not to be asked to go constantly, on a twenty-four hour basis, against the tide. After all, the business of Auschwitz was death. It is not everywhere that death is so easily to be gotten (p. 45).

The significance of this confession is profound: without someone to live for, a relative, a surrogate sister or mother or daughter, one's chances for survival, one's motivation to survive, was diminished. As if to underscore the point, Leitner discusses survival and sisterhood most directly in her chapter called "Musulmans," the term used to describe the prisoners who succumbed to the terrible conditions, stopped eating the meager soup and sawdustlike bread, took on the posture of Muslims bent in prayer, and became fodder for the crematorium. Musselmen, she implies, did not have another person to pull them from their passivity.

The vast majority of published Holocaust memoirs by women echo Leitner's depiction of one woman bearing responsibility in order to be available for a relative or surrogate relative. The absence of a feminist consciousness, as is the case in Leitner's writing, does not diminish the relationship among connectedness, feminism, and well-being. Moreover, while Leitner's voice is more feminine than feminist, we can appreciate the significance of the role of caring in the overall strategy of her survival. Although this need to connect to another person in the face of systematic deprivation, humiliation, and torture is echoed in most survivor literature, women memoirists, like Leitner, are explicit and unambiguous about the role of caring for another woman as a factor in survival. Other women survivors also speak about their dependence on a mother, a cousin, a sister, or even a daughter. Leitner was deported and imprisoned with her natural sisters; she had no need to create a surrogate family, although a fifth woman, a Gentile from Budapest, was routinely included in the Leitner sisters' grouping of five and loved by them.

Leitner's references to physical beauty, stunning clothes, menses, childbearing, and lipstick reflect her socialization. Although critical feminist interpretation that seeks gender-specific examples to inform theory may be open to challenge, Leitner's early recognition of the impact of caring relationships in the concentration camp context is both noteworthy and telling. Quite independently, she corroborates the beneficial effects of women's tendency to create caring relationships. At the same time, by graphically describing Irma Griese's sadism, she does not imbue women's nature with a caring essence. In the end, though, we are struck with the importance of relationships in survival.

Saving the Fragments

Fragments is framed by the month of May, and insofar as a headnote can frame a book, so is *Saving the Fragments*. For Leitner, May has become a "damned" month: "May should be abolished. May hurts. . . . For more than twenty years," she writes, "I have walked zombie-like toward the end of May, deeply depressed" (*Fragments*, p. 102). Six months in Auschwitz followed by three more months of imprisonment, escape, and struggle toward liberation, and three more months of recuperation and adjustment point to the significance of May for Isabella: "The world ended in May. I was born in May. I died in May." *Fragments* covers that year. *Saving the Fragments* opens with "The sun made a desperate effort to shine on the last day of May in 1944. The sun is warm in May. It heals. But even the heavens were helpless on that day" (*Saving the Fragments: From Auschwitz to New York*, New York: New American Library / Plume, 1985).

Saving the Fragments (1985), also written with her husband, documents Isabella's and her sisters' lives from January to May 1945. Liberation in January by the Soviets brings food as well as the fear of rape, although many of the liberated women prisoners, Polish in this narrative, engage openly and frequently in sex with their liberators. While the war continues to the west, Isabella and the other liberated prisoners take care of routine chores such as doing laundry, keeping house, tending cattle, and so on. This second memoir chronicles the journey back to freedom, a journey from a time when "[a] force so evil ruled heaven and earth that it altered the natural order of the universe, and the heart of my mother was floating in the smoke-filled sky of Auschwitz" (headnote).

In *Saving the Fragments*, God is not the biblical source of wisdom, reason, or principles but rather the "man in the heavens" of those Jews not caught in Hitler's war and who thus had the luxury to maintain their faith and nurture a dialogue with God. Leitner's father, "more fanatically religious than ever . . . tries to bribe us into believing in the mercy of God" and cannot fathom his daughter's anger: "My lips freeze in temple. I cannot praise the Lord. I am trying hard to live with the clutter in my head. Let me be" (*Saving the Fragments*, pp. 113–114).

Leitner is clear that the Auschwitz experience changed her profoundly. Even the headnote expresses her struggle to live normally: "I have tried to rub the smoke out of my vision for forty years now, but my eyes are still burning, Mother." Moreover, "parts of us are dead, and for moments we hurt from our inability to retrieve the heart or hurt of yesteryear. We want to cry not for the dead but for what is dead in us. Will what we were return?" (p. 14). She wonders throughout this book whether "saving the fragments [will] be an impossible task?" (p. 16). As she and her sisters continue to walk deeper and deeper into the areas liberated by the Soviets, they come face to face with a large group of captured Germans being marched westward. She wants revenge, "something must appease the deep yearning for vengeance that has festered for so long in our hearts" (p. 19). They consider throwing rocks, but they settle for tossing tiny pebbles. The next day, they resume their journey to life and note that normalcy returns slowly, "Our killer instinct subsides" (p. 21). They reach Odessa, where they meet a Yiddish-speaking British former prisoner of war who takes them to American sailors who will take them to the United States, where they will reunite with their father. Months later, Philip, too, joins them.

After these books went out of print, they were republished as one book revised only in its packaging, *Isabella: From Auschwitz to Freedom*. Eventually, a fourth book, a children's version of her story, *The Big Lie: A True Story*, was published. In 1994, *Fragments* was dramatized into a video, narrated by Gabrielle Reidy of Dublin's Abbey Theater. The video is a very dramatic reading, which, though powerful, lacks the reader engagement of the book.

There are virtually no secondary sources on Leitner's books. *Fragments* is occasionally referenced in works about survival and gender and the Holocaust. Although it lacks the depth of insight and the generosity of spirit or intellect that characterize the literary Holocaust memoirs of Elie Wiesel, Primo Levi, Ana Novak, Lucille Eichengreen, and Livia Bitton-Jackson, and the fictionalized memoirs of Ida Fink and Carl Friedman, *Fragments* is distinctive and memorable and provides strong support to the assertion that bonding contributed significantly to women's survival.

Bibliography

Fragments of Isabella: A Memoir of Auschwitz. 1978.
Saving the Fragments: From Auschwitz to New York. 1985.
Isabella: From Auschwitz to Freedom. 1994.
The Big Lie: A True Story. 1993 (children's version).

H. Leivick

(1888–1962)

EMANUEL S. GOLDSMITH

H. LEIVICK'S ABILITY TO find comfort in suffering and hope in despair helped Jews to live through the tragedies of the Russian Revolution and the Holocaust. His visions of triumph over tribulation and his affirmation of meaning despite absurdity helped many to rebuild broken lives and shattered aspirations. His championing of Yiddish in a period of traumatic decline fired the determination of lovers of the language to continue their struggle for its preservation and advancement.

Background

Leivick (pen name of Leivick Halpern) was born in 1888 and raised in Igumen, an isolated White Russian *shtetl* in which legends of the Prophet Elijah, hopes for a Messiah, and tales of the thirty-six hidden saints upon which the world rests, still flourished. He grew up in abject poverty—his mother baking bread and bagels which she sold in the marketplace and his father teaching local girls to read and write Yiddish. Even in his studies at school, young Leivick seemed to be drawn to suffering. He recalls that one of his first meditations on suffering concerned the fate of the ram trapped in the thicket by its horns and destined to be slaughtered in Isaac's stead. If Isaac's neck managed to escape the knife, did another neck have to take its place? asked Leivick. Could the altar not remain vacant?

In his first book of poems, Leivick recalled that as a child he felt he was in possession of a great secret that had to be concealed from others. Observing how people suffered in silence, he absorbed their silence and imagined that when he grew up something great and wonderful would emerge from suffering.

I will be the first to see the great and wondrous,
No longer hide it from anyone.
I will go from door to door, knock on every window pane
To announce the bright morning.
I know not who chose me from among all,
Estranging and alienating me in shame.
With head hung low, I accepted my fate,
Purifying my youth in anticipation ("Yinglvayz" [As a Child]. *Ale Verk,* vol. 2. New York, 1940, p. 9).

A brilliant yeshiva student, Leivick soon discovered Hebrew *Haskalah* literature and early Zionist writings. He was especially taken with Jewish history and, in particular, with books about the Spanish Inquisition. Expelled from the yeshiva when he was caught reading the first modern Hebrew novel—Abraham Mapu's *Love of Zion*, he eventually abandoned the piety of his father and of the yeshiva, and joined the socialist and proletarian Jewish Labor Bund of Russia and Poland so that he might contribute to the realization of the age-old dream of liberation and redemption for his people, his class and humanity. Arrested for revolutionary activity during the revolution of 1905 and refusing the assistance of a defense attorney, he was sentenced to four years of imprisonment to be followed by permanent exile in Siberia (Leivick's memoirs of his years of imprisonment and those in Siberia are contained in his *Af Tsarisher Katorge*, 1959). The words the young revolutionary spoke to his accusers are familiar to every reader of Yiddish literature. "I do not wish to defend myself. I do not want to deny anything. I am a member of the Jewish revolutionary party, the Bund. I do everything I can to overthrow the self-appointed Czarist regime of bloody hangmen together with you" (quoted in Pat, p. 147). Leivick later looked on his years in prison and Siberia as providing his fundamental training in compassion and human values. Although he was witness to frightful pain, suffering, and degradation, he also saw magnificent displays of compassion and empathy.

In America

Leivick's suffering did not cease when he escaped to America in 1913. He contracted tuberculosis and spent several years in sanatoria in Denver, Colorado, and Liberty, New York. The experience in Denver provided the basis for "The Ballad of the Denver Sanatorium," one of his most haunting longer poems.

Leivick won international acclaim when his drama, *The Golem* (1921), was produced on stages around the world and when, in Hebrew translation, it became part of the standard repertoire of the Habimah Theatre in Palestine. In *The Golem*, Leivick successfully clothed a realistic analysis of contemporary events (the Russian Revolution of 1917) in the garments of medieval Jewish legend—a formula to which he returned in several later dramas. His *Rags* (1928), a play about Jewish immigrant life in America, was also a major success when it was produced by Maurice Schwartz at the Yiddish Art Theater in New York.

In the 1920s and early 1930s, Leivick's position in the world of Yiddish letters brought him invitations to address audiences the world over. His trips to Poland, the Soviet Union, Palestine, and South America were important events in the cultural history of their Jewish communities.

Though highly critical of the Soviet regime, Leivick was sympathetic to the objectives of Communism and contributed to Yiddish communist newspapers and magazines in the United States. He sundered his ties with the Communists, however, when they supported the Arab cause during the Palestine riots of 1929. Following the signing of the Stalin-Hitler pact of 1939, he repudiated his ties with all Yiddish organizations and publications in any way sympathetic to the left. He helped establish new Yiddish cultural publications such as *Yiddish*, *Vokh*, and *Zamlbikher* and organizations such as the Yiddish Literary Society and the Congress for Jewish Culture. From 1930 on, he became a regular contributor to *Der Tog*, a pro-Zionist daily in which he published both articles and poems.

With the rise of Nazism, many of the nightmares and prophecies of horror contained in Leivick's writing through the years seemed to come true. Yiddish readers could not help but regard him as a modern-day Jeremiah who had foretold the destruction and was now bewailing it. During the Holocaust he became the seismograph of world Jewry and his reactions to what was taking place were expressed in hundreds of articles and poems. The verse in *I Was Not in Treblinka* (1945) and the plays *Miracle in the Ghetto* (1944), *The Rabbi of Rothenberg* (1945), and *The Wedding in Fernwald* (1947) are among the most important literary works to emerge from those terrible years. Leivick's experiences during a tour of the displaced persons camps on behalf of the World Jewish Congress after the war are contained in his book *With the Surviving Remnant* (1947).

In his last dramatic poem, *In the Days of Job* (1953) and in his final volumes of verse, *A Leaf on an Apple Tree* (1955) and *Songs to the Eternal* (1959), Leivick reached new heights of literary fulfillment and artistic insight. They are justly regarded as the crowning achievements of his literary career. The paralytic stroke he suffered in 1958, which rendered him mute and immobile until his death in 1962, appeared to many of his readers to be yet another uncanny fulfillment of premonitions expressed in his poems through the years.

Chains and Suffering

The rhythm of Leivick's first poems was that of the heavy dragging of clanging chains plowing through the Siberian wastelands, and of the whir of whips cutting stripes into flogged humanity (Gross-Zimerman, p. 138). Two symbols dominate these poems: white snow and chains. A connection between purity and pain was thus established in Leivick's earliest work, which is reminiscent of the biblical and Talmudic doctrine of suffering as atonement. The appreciation of beauty and the awareness of mystery, which came to the fore in Leivick's later writings, are already evident in this poem. Here, too, are the sensitivity to suffering and disappointment, to hopelessness and pain, which are at once profoundly Jewish and deeply human and universal.

Although many readers and critics were at first repelled by Leivick's obsession with suffering, which seemed to verge on the aberrational, they knew that it was very much in keeping with Jewish religious tradition. By poetically objectifying his flogged body and trampled soul, and by sublimating his guilt feelings into a symbol of human conscience, Leivick corroborated the Jewish concept of martyrdom. With its concomitant elements of conscience and asceticism, martyrdom in Judaism is an affirmative and optimistic approach to life because it encourages both a reconciliation with reality and a hope in the development of a higher, more sensitive, and more courageous type of human being (Bickel, p. 93). *Kiddush hashem* or martyrdom took on a new meaning during the persecutions of modern times that culminated in the Holocaust. Such motifs, which dominated many of Leivick's poems of the 1920s, appeared prophetic when viewed from the perspective of the 1930s and 1940s.

The Holocaust

Despite his conviction that the unspeakable terror experienced by victims during their last moments could never be told and that poets could only leave marks on unknown graves, Leivick produced a number of significant poems on the Holocaust. When Leivick proclaimed in a poem that he personally preferred the martyrdom of the Ten Rabbis of Roman times memorialized in the Yom Kippur liturgy to the Maccabees who fought for the independence of Judaea in the second century before the common era, his voice reverberated with Jewish pride and authenticity. His poems of the Holocaust, while identifying with the victims and expressing his guilt for not having shared the fate of the martyrs, also sounded notes of defiance and revenge in celebrating the Warsaw Ghetto Uprising.

They also had rifles,
These Jews of Warsaw,
And bullets, grenades,
These Jews of Warsaw.
They fired
And struck their target
These Jews of Warsaw.
And blessed be
Every Jewish bullet
That pierced
The heart of a Nazi.
But doubly blessed be—
Forever blessed be—
The placard of six short words.
To the Ten Commandments an Eleventh they add:
Arise, Jews, don't succumb to despair! ("Gvald, yidn, Zayt Zikh Nit Meyaesh" [Arise, Jews, Don't Succumb to Despair]. *In Treblinke Bin Ikh Nit Geven*, New York: Cyco Farlag, p. 126f).

Leivick's earliest poetic responses to events leading to the Holocaust may be traced to his poem about Mussolini's conquest of Abyssinia (1937) and to the poetic cycles "Hitler-Night Motifs" (1938), "Reminiscences" (1939), and "Songs about the Yellow Patch" (1940). The opening poem of "Hitler-Night Motifs" concludes as follows:

The sun hangs crucified on a swastika
The moon, a Hitler face,
Swells with racist hatred
And extinguishes the Milky Way's light ("Hitler-Nekht Motiun" ["Hitler Nights Motifs"]. *Ale Verk*, vol. 2, p. 575).

"Songs about the Yellow Patch" opens with the following:

How does the yellow patch look
With a red or black Jewish star
On the arm of a Jew in Nazi-land
Against the white backdrop of a December snow?
How would a yellow patch look
With a red or black Jewish star
On the arms of my wife and sons
And on my own arm
Against the white backdrop of a New York snow?
Indeed,
The question, like a gnat, burrows into my brain.
The question, like a worm, eats at my heart ("Lider Vegn der Celer Late" ["Songs about the Yellow Patch"]. *Ale Verk*, vol. 2, p. 639).

On one hand, Leivick's Holocaust poems depict the physical, psychological, and spiritual horror and torment of the victims. On the other, they record the poet's guilt and anguish for not having shared the suffering of the martyrs, for turning their pain into poetry, and for failing to voluntarily wear the yellow patch with the Jewish star in order

To encourage Israel in the land of the hangmen
And to praise and exalt our arm
That proudly wears this glorious ancient sign
In all the countries of the world.
Indeed—
The question, like a gnat, burrows into my brain,
The question, like a worm, eats at my heart ("Lider Vegn der Celer Late," p. 640).

Even in his earliest reactions to the tragedy, Leivick became the spokesman for defiance and resistance. His work served both to warn that the enemy was on his way and to urge and stiffen moral, psychological, and physical resistance. As literary critic Shmuel Niger correctly explained, "The more threateningly there opened before us the abyss of death, of the deepest sorrow, of the most terrible fear, the more fearlessly did Leivick's poetry gaze into this darkness, the more stubbornly did it warn us of the impending danger, the more courageously did it resist" (*H. Leivick*, p. 387). At the same time, Leivick's work reflected the frustration caused by the poet's inability to actually help save lives and fight back. The motto of his collected Holocaust poems therefore reads "Oh, who on the tracks of the march to Treblinka / Will forgive the guilt of writing songs?" (*In Treblinke Bin Ikh Nit Geven* [*I Was Not in Treblinka*], New York: Cyco Farlag, 1945, p. 3).

"I should have died together with you," he proclaims in "but I didn't have the strength." ("Badarft Hob Ikh" [I Should Have]. *In Treblinke Bin Ikh Nit Geven*, p. 12).

Now I do all I can to camouflage
The quiverings of my words and my body.
Neither sorrow nor anger can drown
In their stormy depths my guilt for living,
My guilt that the flames of Treblinka
Did not enter my limbs.
Now our words turn into masks
Hiding all our failures
To account for a slaughtered child. ("Badarft Hob Ikh," p. 12)

In the spirit of the Torah, the Psalms, and the Hasidic tradition, Leivick's protests are often directed at God as well as himself. His complaints against God sometimes reach new levels of brazenness and bitterness.

In his boots the Creator himself
Walks over mounds of bodies—
As the murderer slaughters mothers, brides
And children—to while away the time.

Then he salutes
His creature Hitler,
Kisses him in the blood
Of murdered victims at day's end ("Afn Grenets fun Blutike Zakhn" [On the Boundary of the Bloody Things]. *In Treblinke Bin Ikh Nit Geven,* p. 158).

Whether God or the victims still exist or not, the final responsibility for the Holocaust belongs with God. There is simply no one else to call to account for all the brutal tragedies of history.

A hill of ashes bears clear witness
To one wrongly bound on the altar.
From Mount Moriah to Maidanek
The distance is as short as Isaac's walk.
The sentence still belongs to you, Creator ("Der Kheshbn iz Nokh Ats Mit Dir, Bashefer" [The Accounting Is Still Yours, Creator]. *In Treblinke Bin Ikh Nit Geven,* p. 17).

After the Holocaust, the poet bade the Prophet Isaiah reappear and fulfill his vision of the end of days.

Dream your dream again, great prophet,
Appear again amid the crumbling walls,
. . . comfort the mother
Who cries and mourns her lad who lies here burned.

The mother climbs out of the bunker
With cradling arms turned to you.
Oh prophet, bring the end of days,
Restore to life the lad who lies here burned ("Un A Yingele Vet Zey Firn" [And a Little Boy Will Lead Them]. A Blat af an Eplboym [A Leaf on an Apple Tree], Buenos Aires: Kiyem Farlog, 9 1955, p. 11).

Leivick reminded his readers that the words of Maimonides, sung in the concentration camps and gas chambers, had been raised to a symbol of eternal resistance, survival, and hope:

Jews in bunkers sing *ani ma'amin,*
I believe in Messiah's coming.
Though he tarries, I believe—
He will come from there, from here.

He will come, he must come, *ani ma'amin.*
Don't ask when or where!
Jews sing *ani ma'amin.*
He is coming. He's already here ("Yidn Zingen Ani Mamin") [Jews Sing "I Believe"]. A Blat af an Eplboym, p. 48).

Influences

Leivick's poetry shows the influences of medieval Jewish ethics, mysticism, and asceticism. These concerns were very much alive in the Jewish community of the Russia of his youth. Echoes of the mystical parables of the Hasidic master, Rabbi Nahman of Bratzlav, of the ethical concerns of the Mussar or ethical movement of Rabbi Israel Salanter, and of the historical and nationalist concerns of the Yiddish poet and revolutionary Abraham Walt Lyessin (1872–1938), are very much in evidence in Leivick's work. There is also a parallel between Leivick's preoccupation with suffering and the pathos and moral seriousness of the great Russian writers of the nineteenth century. Leivick successfully linked the ambiance of the Russian writers with the Yiddish literary tradition. In his own person, "he succeeded in forging a rich Jewish artistic personality which, however influenced at first by the Slavic mood, nevertheless managed to relate that influence to the more profound dream-world of his Jewish childhood" (Glatstein, p. 85). In the United States, Leivick deepened his concern for the suffering and downtrodden, but also learned to control his pathos and exploit the power of silence in his poetry. He sought, as he stated in a poem, to "tear seven hides from words and peel their skins until the kernels deep inside were revealed in their pristine splendor" ("Vort un Zakhn" [Words and Objects]. Ale Verk, vol. 1. New York, 1940, p. 525). However, he looked askance at the attempt of some of the young rebels in Yiddish literature to totally dissociate themselves from the concerns of society and form an isolated, aesthetic island in the sea of Jewish life. Where many of the members of the literary group, *Di Yunge* (the young Rebels) were satisfied with the pursuit of art for art's sake, Leivick was concerned with morality and with the meaning and destiny of life for both the individual and society.

The existential engagement of Leivick's work repelled many of the *Yunge*, who would have none of what they regarded as Leivick's sanctimoniousness and self-righteousness. They also failed to appreciate his linguistic innovativeness. "In their attempt to find poetic terms and images for things in their familiar environment and in normal human experience, the *Yunge* failed to take note of Leivick's great achievement in finding terms for things which lacked words in Yiddish until then" (Tabachnik, p. 280).

Words and Mysticism

Leivick's relationship with words was unique in the annals of world literature. He expected words to behave morally. "He strongly demanded of the word that it 'adjust' its private life to the role it plays publicly in the poem. This conception of the word, as a living soul with consciousness and responsibility, of which moral demands could be made, is one of Leivick's infrequent concurrences with Yiddish folklore" (Bickel, p. 101). Leivick differed from the *Yunge* in the mystical bent of much of his writing. He always had a deep concern with what he termed the "other side of things." He was preoccupied with the meaning and destiny of reality and often transported himself poetically into the past or the future.

Leivick's lyrical poems are reminiscent of the so-called reflective poetry (*shirey higayon*) of the Hebrew literature of the Haskalah. They combine "emotional expression and personal impression with a reflective reaction which is sometimes exegetical and revelatory" (Bertini, "Aharit-Davar." In H. Leivicks *Al Tehomot Holekh Veshar*, Tel Aviv: Sitriyat Poalim, 1977, p. 88). The reflection, which sometimes appears tangential or insignificant, is in fact the point of the poem because Leivick was never an indifferent spectator of life, observing and satisfying himself merely with the formulation of the visible.

Messianic Redemption

Throughout his literary career, Leivick grappled with one of the great ideas of Jewish history and produced a trilogy of plays (*Chains of the Messiah*, *The Golem*, and *The Comedy of Redemption*), the poetic drama *The Wedding in Fernwald*, and a number of shorter poems on the Messianic theme. Taken together, these works comprise a major poetic history of the Messianic idea, a record of the growth of hope and the longing in the heart of the author and his contemporaries, and a framework in which the Messiah symbol might become relevant in our time.

In a forward to the Hebrew translation of the redemption trilogy, Leivick wrote that

> especially now, after years of catastrophe and destruction in our lives, events which were followed by the miracle of the birth of the State of Israel—only now does it seem to me that we stand anew before the first sensing of Messiah's existence, before the feeling that he is with us, but we still do not see his full countenance, his revealed likeness. We are in the minutes of the Beginning, and feel his existence in the tremor of the heart, as on the day in which there arose in us the legend of his birth (*Hezyoney Geulah*, Tel Aviv: Mosad Bialik, 1956, p. ix).

The dominant motif of Leivick's Messianic plays and poems is the sense of responsibility for all those who suffer. In addition, he emphasized that the redemption cannot be forced. Like the Messiah of whom Isaiah spoke, who would "act with justice for the hopeless and decide fairly for the humble" (Isa. 11:4), Leivick's Messiah is motivated by a horrifying sense of responsibility for those who suffer and those who are wronged. Leivick's message is that people must be made aware that the Messiah can be found in their own midst.

In *The Wedding in Fernwald*, Messiah refuses to resume his task in the land of the living after the horrors of the Holocaust. But when he visits the displaced persons and witnesses the zeal with which they rebuild their lives, he comes to realize that he must accept his responsibility to remain with the Jews who have survived the destruction. Like the people of Israel, Messiah too must agree to live. "Just as long ago, after he had been in Egypt, the Jew accepted the Torah, so must he now, after Dachau, accept life. For as the Torah is holy, so the life of a Jew is holy—and perhaps even holier" (New York: Cyco Farlag, 1949, p. 147).

In *The Wedding in Fernwald*, Messiah goes to the crematoria with the victims. When a sick and half-blind Jew falls to the ground, Messiah lifts him on his shoulders, carries him, and goes with him and the others to the oven in Dachau. When asked what he accomplishes if, of his own will he goes to the gas chamber, Messiah replies: "It is not I who accomplish. It is the love of Israel that accomplishes. Today I can do nothing but carry out the will to love the Jewish people which goes to the gas chamber" (p. 89). In "The Ballad of the Desert," Leivick links the generation of the Exodus with the generation of the Holocaust. Leivick, his parents, his elementary school teacher, and Moses and Aaron are the heroes of this poetic fantasy, which views Jewish history as an ever-recurring cycle in which God is forever rediscovered in the pain of the bush's flames, which burn and burn but are never extinguished.

The Eternal God

The word *eybik* (eternal) has constantly recurred in Leivick's poetry through the years. It occurs in his reminiscences of his childhood, in the title of one of his most famous poems, and again in the title of his final volume of verse: *Lider Tsum Eybikn* (Songs to the Eternal, 1959). The word links the poet to the divine presence and simultaneously conveys intimations of personal and collective immortality.

> The world grabs me with hands that pierce.
> It carries me to the pyre, to the auto-da-fé.
> I burn and burn but am not consumed
> I rise again and march away.
> I sow my poems as one sows seeds,
> They sprout and grow like stalks and weeds,
> A plow am I and turn the soil,
> I rise again and march away. ("Eybik" [Eternally]. *Ale Verk*, vol. I, p. 648).

Although Leivick's poetry is more concerned with human morality and destiny than with God, the sense of God's presence has an important place in his poems. Leivick often compared Yiddish poetry to traditional Jewish prayer. In *Eseyen un Redes* (Essays and Addresses), he writes: "It seems to me that Yiddish poetry today is undoubtedly still an emanation of our entire millennial mentality and essentially a religious experience. . . . I often feel when I write a poem as if I were praying. I feel the poem itself as a prayer." (New York: Congress for Jewish Culture, 1963, p. 47).

Leivick's work was essentially an affirmation of the sacredness of human life and the durability of the human spirit. His poetry appeals to the modern temper because it affirms meaning despite chaos and hope despite tragedy. In *In The Days of Job* (1953), he explored the cosmic dimension of human relationships and pondered the need for empathy with the sufferings of other species. He always knew how to evoke sparks of compassion and humanity in his readers. Despite his preoccupation with pain and sorrow, his quest for the meaning of suffering was aglow with assurance and hope. He universalized his own odyssey and his people's history in order to renew the prophetic vision of brotherhood and redemption for all humanity. In the valley of death he reaffirmed the transcendent dimension of suffering and the sacredness of life by "weaving God's sorrow into himself and carrying the song of God's words everywhere" ("Shtil Vi Du" ["As Quiet as You"] *In Treblinke Bin Ikh Nit Geven*, p. 162).

Bibliography

Primary Sources

Der Goylem (*The Golem*). 1921.
Shmates (*Rags*). 1928.
Ale Verk (Complete Works). vol. 1 – Lider; vol. II – Dramatishe Poemes. 1940.
In Treblinke Bin Ikh Nit Geven (*I Was Not in Treblinka*). 1945.
Maharam fun Rutenberg (*Rabbi Meyer of Rothenburg*). 1945.
Di Khasene in Fernvald (*The Wedding in Fernwald*). 1949.
In di Teg fun Iyev (*In the Days of Job*). 1953.
A Blat af an Eplboym (*A Leaf on an Apple Tree*). 1955.
Hezyoney Geulah (Visions of Redemption). 1956.
Lider Tsum Eybikn (*Songs to the Eternal*). 1959.
Af Tsarishe Katorge (In Czarist Banishment). 1959.
Eseyen un Redes (Essays and Addresses). 1963.
Oysgeklibere shriftn. 1963.
Al Tehomot Holekh Veshar. 1977.

Secondary Sources

Bickel, S. *Detaln un Sakhaklen*. New York, 1943.
Biletsky, Y. H. *Hadramaturgya Hahezyonit shel H. Leivick*. Tel Aviv: Hakibutz Hameuhad, 1979.
Glatstein, J. *Af Greyte Temes*. Tel Aviv: Farlag Y. L. Peretz, 1967.
Gross-Zimerman, M. *Intimer Videranand*. Tel Aviv, 1964.
Niger, Shmuel. *H. Leivick*. Toronto: Gershon Pomerantz Esey-Bibliotek, 1951.
———. *Yidishe Shrayber fun Tsvantsikstn Yorhundert*. New York: Congress for Jewish Culture, 1972.
Pat, Y. *Shmuesn mit Yidishe Shrayber*. New York, 1954.
Rivkin, Borekh. *H. Leivick: Zayne Lider un Dramatishe Verk*. Buenos Aires: Farlag Yidbukh, 1955.
Tabachnik, A. *Dikhter un Dikhtung*. New York, 1965.
Valdman, H., ed. *H. Leivick Zamlbukh*. Paris: Kultur-Kongres, 1963.
Waldman, M. *H. Leivick, Poète Yiddish, Hommages et Textes Choisis (de Halpern Leivick) Recueillis par M. Waldman*. Paris, 1967.
Winer, Gershon, ed. *Shtudyes in Leivick*. Ramat-Gan: Yidish-Katedre i.n. fin Rina Kosta, Bar-Ilan Universitet, 1992.
Yanasovitsh, Yitskhok. *H. Leivick: Etishe Akhrayes un Moralisher Patos*. Tel Aviv: Komitet far Yidisher Kultur in Yisroel, 1977.

Interviews and Articles

Interview by Yankev Pat in *Shmuesn mit Yidishe Shrayber* (Conversations with Yiddish writers), New York, 1954.
Relevant letters and other documents may be found in the library of the YIVO Institute for Jewish Research, which is located in the Jewish History Center in New York City.

Olga Lengyel
(1908–2001)

MYRNA GOLDENBERG

A REMARKABLE ACCOUNT of Olga Lengyel's eight months as a prisoner at Auschwitz-Birkenau, *Five Chimneys* is noteworthy because it was written and published in 1947 and is therefore among the very earliest Holocaust memoirs published in English. It remains among the most vivid. Lengyel's account is unique not only for its extreme detail, but also because it is extraordinarily analytical, nonsentimental, and comprehensive. Its closest literary counterpart is Primo Levi's *Survival in Auschwitz*, also first published in 1947, in that both are topically arranged, loosely chronological, and exceptionally clear. Levi, however, is relatively objective, quietly philosophical, and often poetic, while Lengyel is contemplative and descriptive. She laced her memoir with confessions of guilt and questions of moral judgment.

Early Life and Deportation

Born on 19 October 1908, in Cluj, Transylvania, Lengyel was the daughter of a prominent Jewish businessman and philanthropist, Dr. Ferdinand Bernat-Bernard, director of and primary stockholder in the Transylvanian Coal Mines, and Idus Legman Laszlo, who devoted herself to charity work, especially to the Transylvanian Orphanage. The family lived a privileged, assimilated life, aware of, but apparently not significantly affected by, the open antisemitism that characterized the city and, more broadly, Hungary. As the only child, Olga was educated from an early age to manage the family's assets. She studied the arts and pursued literature at the University of Cluj, and, after her marriage at age sixteen to Miklos Lengyel, a surgeon, she trained to qualify as her "husband's first surgical assistant" (*Five Chimneys*, London: Granada, 1972, p. 12).

Lengyel opens *Five Chimneys* with a confession that appropriately establishes her as a sympathetic narrator:

> *Mea culpa*, my fault, *mea maxima culpa!* I cannot acquit myself of the charge that I am, in part, responsible for the destruction of my own parents and of my two young sons. The world understands that I could not have known, but in my heart the terrible feeling persists that I could have, I might have, saved them (p. 11).

According to her memoir, a jealous colleague denounced Miklos Lengyel to the authorities on the grounds that Lengyel had boycotted the Boger Company and was therefore a traitor. Lengyel was released, but a subsequent summons led to immediate deportation. She rationalized that his reputation as a surgeon would protect him; in her naïveté, she volunteered to accompany him, along with her parents and sons. Olga had not believed the persistent and explicit British Broadcasting Corporation and Polish refugee reports from 1939 through 1943 about Germany's treatment of the Jews, and, against the protests of her family, Olga prevailed, becoming "the author of [her] parents' misfortunes and [her] children's as well" (p. 15). Her parents and children were gassed upon arrival at Birkenau, and her husband was shot a few months later when he tried to minister to a fellow prisoner.

In her 1948 *Shoah* Foundation interview, however, Olga explained that when Miklos Lengyel was arrested a second time, she had been forced to "sell" the hospital and all the family's assets to a pro-German colleague to retrieve her husband, but she was duped. Her trust in German honor was betrayed, and she, her children, and her parents were taken directly from the so-called sale to the municipal prison and the deportation point. Although her descriptions of the particular circumstances of her arrest and deportation reflect her family's relatively privileged standing in the medical community, in any event, the Lengyels and the Bernat-Bernards would have been caught in the mass deportation of Hungarian Jews in May 1944, after Hungary's capitulation to the Germans.

In the Camp

Lengyel, because of her stature as a community leader, was selected to be cocaptain of the nightmarish seven-day journey in a cattle wagon intended to transport eight horses but which instead carried ninety-six persons, primarily "people of culture and position." Lengyel's extraordinary description of their arrival at Auschwitz-Birkenau, including their confinement in the cattle wagon among the dead and dying for eight nights, leads to the unforgettable scene in which she urges her mother to accompany her sons, David and Thomas, "to the left," where she thought they would be spared forced labor. She had believed the Nazi SS officer "who had assured us that the aged would remain in charge of the children. . . . I had persuaded my mother that she should follow the children and take care of them. At her age she had a right to the treatment accorded the elderly" (p. 24), and Lengyel felt reassured that there would be someone to look after her sons. In fact, however, the group of the young and the aged were sent directly to the gas chambers. Her subsequent awareness of the impact of her well-intended choice and her repeated vulnerability to German deceit dramatically color the rest of her narrative and have a chilling effect on her readers.

The memoir continues in cinematic depictions of the shame and humiliation embodied in the processing of prisoners into the camp, the filth and crowded conditions in which they lived, her sister prisoners, the hierarchy of the barracks, the "social system" of the prisoners, the accomplishments of the camp underground, and the daily routines of survival, including the various coping mechanisms that women used:

> No spectacle was more comforting than that provided by the women when they undertook to cleanse themselves thoroughly in the evening. They passed the single scrubbing brush to one another with a firm determination to resist the dirt and lice. That was our only way of waging war against the parasites, against our jailers, and against every force that made us its victims. (p. 135)

She provides a brutally clear depiction of the system of bartering food for sex with male prisoners whose work on maintenance squads gave them access to the women's camp; women begged the male workers for food—"the coin that paid for sexual privileges" (p. 190). She also reports that the guards' sexual appetites were fed by camp brothels, to which German prostitutes and, despite the prohibition against sexual relations with the "inferior" races, "attractive internees," were assigned (p. 189). Unlike most Holocaust memoirists, she explains the role of sex in prisoners' lives and the use of sex as a weapon of the Nazi hierarchy. In an uncharacteristically insensitive yet exceptionally frank section, she expresses disgust at lesbians and women prisoners who give each other physical comfort; at the same time, however, she questions her application of pre-Auschwitz standards to the hell of the concentration camp (pp. 195–203). She goes on to describe sadistic acts, including violation by dogs on young girls and other unimaginable scenes of sexual violence either ordered or engaged in by Irma Griese, known as the "blonde beast of Belsen" or "the angel of Auschwitz" because of her angelic beauty. She repeats ironic camp slang that demonstrates the prisoners' awareness of their doomed situation, as well as their use of humor as a coping mechanism, for example in calling the crematorium "the bakery" (p. 31).

An infirmary job afforded Lengyel some relief from the horrible overcrowding in the camp, as well as a way of helping sister prisoners. As part of the infirmary staff, Lengyel helped deliver babies and then, "when [they] opened [their] mouths to breathe," was required to administer "a dose of a lethal product," making "murderers of even us" (p. 114). Most important, she was invited to join the camp underground, largely in the role of "a post office," an anonymous messenger, one link that connected one segment of the information chain to the next; in that capacity, she later understands, she probably helped prepare for the 4 October 1944 uprising that resulted in the destruction of one and one-half crematoria (p. 80). She provides no further explanation of her involvement with the underground, nor was she identified in the roundup that followed the uprising, but she emphatically credits her involvement with this network with rescuing her from serious despair, giving her purpose and resolve to live:

> I did not know much of the nature of the enterprise in which I was participating. But I knew that I was doing something useful. That was enough to give me the strength. I was no longer prey to crises of depression. I even forced myself to eat enough to be able to fight on. To eat and not let oneself become enfeebled—that, too, was a way to resist. We lived to resist and we resisted to live (pp. 170–171).

After the Camp

In January 1945, fully aware that the death march from Auschwitz to the west was indeed a march to death, she took advantage of a temporary commotion in the ranks and she and two friends fled to the forest. After a harrowing escape, she and one of her sister escapees remained in Poland for a very brief period. The immediate weeks following her escape and liberation mirror the chaos of a continent caught in the throes of retreating and advancing armies. Feeling unsafe and wanting to reunite with the remnant of her family, a maternal cousin in Paris, she traveled a circuitous route through Krakow, Warsaw, Prague, Lublin, and Odessa. To expedite her journey to Paris, she accepted a French Canadian identity, which was so transparent a lie that it caused understandable suspicion and innumerable delays. Yet, after a series of remarkable coincidences, by 4 March 1945 she reached Marseilles, where her Parisian cousin, a doctor who had resumed his profession soon after the French regained their country, supported her, installing her in an apartment in Paris.

To sustain herself, she wrote and sold articles about her experiences and, before the end of December 1945, sold her memoir under its first title, *Hitler's Ovens*. Published in 1947, *Hitler's Ovens* was written in several languages, revised into Hungarian, and then translated into French. It was very well received and became required reading in French secondary schools. The book's success was noticed in the United States, and Lengyel was invited to lecture by universities and antiwar groups. She arrived in New York in June, but she became very ill with pneumonia soon thereafter and spent her first six months in America sick, poor, and alone. However, a distant relative named Emil Lengyel, as well as a number of academics and prominent anti-German and other antiwar activists, helped her establish herself, organize the Just Peace Movement, and begin the process of getting her family's inheritance. In 1963 she was able to buy the building in which she had lived since 1946—58 East 79th Street—which she renovated and in which she established the Memorial Library and Art Collection of the Second World War in memory of her husband and father. Her unfulfilled dream was to establish a school devoted entirely to the study of World War II.

At some point, she remarried (which she sharply denied on the 1998 *Shoah* Foundation tape) and moved to Cuba, where she and her second husband established an orphanage. Again, she was forced to flee this time to Mexico, when Fidel Castro overthrew Fulgencio Bastista. Lengyel had a daughter but soon divorced her second husband, who remained in Mexico with their daughter.

Lengyel was entirely assimilated. Though she never denied that she was Jewish, she chose not to affiliate and, in response to questions about her religion, she answered, "none." She preferred to accept all religions at face value and focus on common threads among people. In her memoir, she avoided any suggestion of her Jewishness, misleading scholars, such as Harry Cargas, to believe that she was a Hungarian Christian.

Influenced by her experiences in Auschwitz, she established an organization for the purpose of educating children, primarily orphans, and named it with her Auschwitz number, 25403. She revisited Aushwitz-Birkenau twice and was a frequent lecturer about her Birkenau months as well as a devotee of Hollywood's Holocaust-related films, especially Steven Spielberg's *Schindler's List* and *The Last Days*. She was also portrayed as a key character in *Angel*, a play about Irma Griese written by Jo Davidsmeyer; Lengyel's role in the play is to illuminate Griese's character, specifically through a conversation between the two while Lengyel assists another prisoner, a doctor, perform an abortion on Griese.

Having to relive her experiences in order to write about them, particularly the guilt she felt at hastening the death of her mother and sons, caused Lengyel extreme anxiety and lifelong insomnia. A slight but sturdy woman who had been a sickly child, she had a very strong will to live and coped as best as she could in order to survive during and after the war. Lengyel closes her memoir with an affirmation of her faith in the individual, a faith based on examples of "human dignity" and moral strength: "If, even in the jungle of Birkenau, all were not necessarily inhuman to the fellow men, then there is hope indeed" (p. 229). After devoting her life to waging a campaign against hate, Lengyel died on 11 April 2001 in New York City.

Bibliography

Primary Sources

Five Chimneys: A Woman Survivor's True Story of Auschwitz. 1947. Interview by N. Fisher for Survivors of the *Shoah* Visual History Foundation, New York, New York. Timecodes 1 through 11. 28 August 1998.

Secondary Sources

Cargas, Harry James. *The Holocaust: An Annotated Bibliography*, 2nd ed. Chicago: American Library Association, 1985.

Clendinnen, Inga. *Reading the Holocaust*. Cambridge, U.K.: Cambridge University Press, 1999.

Davidsmeyer, Jo. *Angel: A Nightmare of the Holocaust*. 1994. Available from the playwright, *www.jodavidsmeyer.com*.

Goldenberg, Myrna. "Lessons Learned from Gentle Heroism: Women's Holocaust Narratives." *Annals of the American Academy of Political and Social Science* 548 (November 1996): 78–93.

———. Telephone conversations with Olga Lengyel's secretary, 18 April and 27 May 2001.

Heinemann, Marlene E. *Gender and Destiny: Women Writers and the Holocaust*. Westport, Conn.: Greenwood Press, 1986.

Kremer, S. Lillian. *Witness Through the Imagination: Jewish American Holocaust Literature*. Detroit: Wayne State University Press, 1989.

———. *Women's Holocaust Writing: Memory and Imagination*. Lincoln: University of Nebraska Press, 1999.

Padover, Saul D. ". . . And the Germans Jeered." *Saturday Review of Literature*, 2 August 1947, pp. 9–10.

Patterson, David. *Sun Turned to Darkness: Memory and Recovery in the Holocaust Memoir*. Syracuse: Syracuse University Press, 1998.

Rittner, Carol, and John K. Roth, eds. *Different Voices: Women and the Holocaust*. New York: Paragon House, 1993.

Ritvo, Roger A., and Diane M. Plotkin. *Sisters in Sorrow: Voices of Care in the Holocaust*. College Station: Texas A & M University Press, 1998.

Todorov, Tzvetan. *Facing the Extreme: Moral Life in the Concentration Camps*. New York: Henry Holt, 1996.

Uhr, Carl G. "A Woman's Account of Life in a Nazi Extermination Camp." *San Francisco Chronicle*, 3 August 1947, pp. 16–17.

Werner, Alfred. "Records of Horror." *New York Times Book Review*, 3 August 1947, p. 16.

RONIT LENTIN

(1944–)

ERIC ZAKIM

RONIT LENTIN'S WRITINGS span a number of subjects and genres, both academic and popular. While the Holocaust does not always figure as the direct focus of Lentin's attention, it is never completely absent. Indeed, Lentin's interests always intersect and overlap, from feminist activism and women's studies, to the politics of the Israeli-Palestinian conflict and the effects of the Holocaust on a second generation, children of survivors. We might be tempted to posit some sort of totalizing intellectual project to encompass all of them: feminism, perhaps, or rather a general sensitivity to what it means to be a woman in the world, but even that categorization, however broad and unessentializing, could not capture the complex interconnections and interdependencies that Lentin's work makes manifest among the myriad subjects she engages in her critical and fictional writings.

In terms of the Holocaust—another candidate as a broad organizing category for Lentin's thinking—Lentin is something of an activist, targeting the silences that have prevailed historically in Israeli public and private culture about the political and social effects of the destruction of European Jewry. That history extends for Lentin to the present day, not just in how the Holocaust, or the *Shoah* as she would insist, continues to affect political policy in the Israeli-Palestinian conflict, but also in how the *Shoah* lives on in the dark psychological recesses of a second generation, the daughters and sons of survivors. The silence Lentin strives to combat is personal and political, both at the same time and separately: Neither the personal nor the political can be reduced allegorically to symbolize the other. The story of the *Shoah* that needs to be told has deep psychological roots, and becomes a type of Freudian recuperation. Trauma will never disappear, but the debilitating effects of repression, on the person and on the state, can be cast aside through a methodology of confessional revelation of the *Shoah*'s influence on society and on individuals.

Autobiography

In much of what Lentin writes, she herself appears. In her major works of fiction, *Night Train to Mother* (1989) and *Songs on the Death of Children* (1996), the protagonists are lightly veiled autobiographical figures reflecting, through fantasy or reality, many of Lentin's own geographic and intellectual peregrinations. Born in Israel in 1944, Lentin left the country soon after receiving her B.A. in social work at the Hebrew University, and settled in Ireland in 1969. There, Lentin worked as a journalist and published fiction before studying at Trinity College, University of Dublin, for her doctorate in sociology, which she earned in 1996. Since then, Lentin has continued at Trinity College in a faculty position and is active in journalism, fiction, academic journals, and organizations committed to women's and Irish issues.

The outlines of Lentin's career do little, however, to inform about the necessity of biography in her intellectual project. Lentin does not simply draw on her own life experiences for her work. Rather, that work finds meaning as it reflects on the very concept of personal narrative, on the idea of reflection and expression of the scholar and writer. Thus, Lentin's recent book of sociology on *Shoah* silence in Israel and its effects on second-generation women, *Israel and the Daughters of the Shoah: Reoccupying the Territories of Silence* (2000), goes far beyond the usual *Shoah* trope of placing the author in the academic narrative (she is herself the daughter of *Shoah* survivors). Instead, the entire study analyzes silence in second-generation women, and their overcoming silence, all through personal narrative. This is a book both *of* and *about* nine women's narratives—ten if we count Lentin herself—all daughters of survivors, each confronting the traumas and problems of coming from survivor families, and each (Lentin is sure to tell us) reflecting her own process of understanding and confronting her own familial demons. This is not a book only about personal narrative: out of these women's stories emerges a complex political critique of how Israeli society has suppressed precisely *their* stories, *their* avenues of expression. Autobiography thus insists upon itself as both methodology and subject of this study.

Politics

The silence and silencing of Israel's population of *Shoah* survivors has become an important topic of recent Israeli scholarship and cultural representation. As well, since the late-1980s, a second-generation voice of the children of *Shoah* survivors has clearly emerged in Israel, ten years after Helen Epstein's *Children of the Holocaust* appeared in America, but now a significant presence in the Israeli cultural sphere. Lentin's work both reflects these trends and develops them further. Lentin participates in a second-generation discourse of attacking the Israeli suppression of its survivors, the way that Israel privately and publicly shunned their presence, choosing to emphasize only Jewish heroism during the war. Her political critique of this history is, however, more incisive than a simple acknowledgement of the silencing of survivors and the public refusal to recognize individuals' trauma. Beyond that, Lentin builds a gender criticism of Israel's *Shoah* remembrance policies that takes on a multiplicity of critical meanings, always remaining sensitive to how gender infects all levels of discourse involving the *Shoah*: on a personal level, revealing the differences in women's and men's experiences and memories of the event; on a social level, outlining the different roles played in survivor families by men and women (of both first and second generations); and in a political critique, developing a metacritical analysis of how Israel as a state worked to define its own masculinst identity through a feminization of the *Shoah* as a whole.

The danger of this multivalent critique is the ease with which these levels might collapse into allegory, especially an allegory of gender opposition standing in for the conflicts of the state, and thus an allegory of Israel's political stance toward the Palestinians as a national response to the *Shoah*. Lentin deftly avoids this trap even as she builds a complex argument about how the *Shoah* affects and infests recent politics in Israel. The *Shoah*, for Lentin, never can be reduced to a determinant moral category for the state, but ever remains an insistent element of personal biography. Thus, in *Songs on the Death of Children*, Lentin creates a male character attached to the *Shin Bet*, Israel's internal security force, who is also a son of Holocaust survivors. We read his sadistic and manipulative actions toward women and toward Arabs as a product of that upbringing, but not as the determined outcome of the *Shoah* experience. Rather, the personal trajectory of trauma, his growing up *within* trauma, takes a politically nefarious form, but not necessarily so.

Even as an analytical tool for criticizing Israeli policy during the first Intifada, the *Shoah* in this novel does not take on the enlarged proportions of state allegory; instead, individual politics reflect the personal psychopathologies of survivor families. Politics emerge out of a lived experience, not as a result of the semiotic grip of the *Shoah* on the state. As in *Israel and the Daughters of the Shoah*, Lentin insists in the novel on personal narrative, both in order to understand the origins and difficulties of a deteriorating political situation, and in order to understand a possible way out. The interviews conducted by Lentin's protagonist, Pat, an Irish-Jewish journalist, who seeks out both Palestinian and Jewish Israeli women, parallel Lentin's sociological work in *Israel and the Daughters of the Shoah*, and her earlier pioneering book in Hebrew, *Conversations with Palestinian Women* (1982). For Lentin, generic division is meaningless; her project comes together in a political critique of silence, and answers that silence by writing women's narratives.

Journeys

For Lentin, the negotiation of her myriad subjects—Israel, Ireland, women, silence, the *Shoah*, memory—involves a personal journey, both for the women interviewed by her or her characters, and for herself. Her work is her own journey, a traveling across time, across borders, across political and ideational boundaries. Indeed, her living in Ireland as a diasporic Israeli certainly figures as one of the distances Lentin struggles to collapse. Her first major novel, *Night Train to Mother*, begins that journey, both chronologically and geographically, by taking her protagonist from Israel to Romania in search of the voices of her foremothers from the late nineteenth century through the aftermath of the *Shoah*. We read these voices through the frame of a contemporary story, and the novel ends with the protagonist finally boarding a plane for the journey back to Israel, but that trip merely marks the beginning of something much more difficult. "Where did the journey begin?" Lentin writes near the very end of the novel, (Dublin: Attic Press, 1989, pp. 218–219) an odd question that admits that the difficult part of the confrontation with the past, with Europe, with the

Shoah, might only now be starting on the trip back, in the encounter again with Israel, and within the protagonist's own contemporary life. Lentin finishes that novel, writing "Did it begin here, on the tarmac before boarding the Tarom plane leaving Bucharest? Up until now you have been traveling one way—the journey back will take the rest of your days" (p. 219). The self-reflexive narrative—the second-person address that speaks to the self—voices the undercurrents of all Lentin's writing and outlines the various autobiographical journeys her work takes. The journey back is the journey to close that self-reflexive distance, to understand the purpose and the reason for the journey to Romania in the first place. The criticism that analyzes and fights the suppression of women's voices; the fictional characters always searching for lost family members and lost childhoods (lost in the silence that permeates survivor families); the political voice that refuses to allow the *Shoah* to justify oppression in Palestine, these are all parts of a journey of self-disclosure whose goal is always to bring that disembodied part of the self—that distanced second-person narrator of *Night Train to Mother*—back into an integrated and unified narrative.

Bibliography

Primary Sources

Fiction

"Tea with Mrs. Klein." In *Triad: Modern Irish Fiction*. With James Liddy and Tomas O Murchadh. Dublin: Wolfhound Press, 1986, pp. 5–56.

Night Train to Mother. 1989.

Songs on the Death of Children. 1996.

Nonfiction

Sihot 'im nashim palestiniyot (*Conversations with Palestinian Women*). Milfras, 1982.

"Israeli and Palestinian Women Working for Peace." In *The Women and War Reader*. Edited by Lois Ann Lorentzen and Jennifer Turpin. New York: New York University Press, 1998, pp. 337–342.

Israel and the Daughters of the Shoah: Reoccupying the Territories of Silence. New York: Berghahn Press, 2000.

"A Howl-Unheard: Women *Shoah* Survivors De-placed and Re-silenced." In *When the War Was Over: Women, War and Peace in Europe, 1940–56*. Edited by Claire Duchen and Irene Brandauer-Schoeffmann. London, New York: Leicester University Press, 2000, pp. 179–193.

Memory and Forgetting: Gendered Counter Narratives of Silence in the Relations Between Israeli Zionism and the Shoah. San Domenico di Fiesole, Italy: European University Institute, Robert Schuman Centre, 2001.

Edited Collections

Gender and Catastrophe. London and New York: Zed Books, 1997.

The Expanding Nation: Towards a Multi-Ethnic Ireland. Dublin: Ethnic and Racial Studies, Dept. of Sociology, Trinity College, 1998.

Emerging Irish Identities. Trinity College (Dublin, Ireland): Department of Sociology, National Consultative Committee on Racism and Interculturalism, 1999.

(Re)searching Women: Feminist Research and Practice in the Social Sciences in Ireland. Dublin: Institute of Public Administration, 2000.